October 26-28, 2015
Lisbon, Portugal

Association for Computing Machinery

Advancing Computing as a Science & Profession

ASSETS'15

Proceedings of the 17th International ACM SIGACCESS Conference on
Computers & Accessibility

Sponsored by:

ACM SIGACCESS

Supported by:

Google, Microsoft Research, The Paciello Group, and NSF

Association for
Computing Machinery

Advancing Computing as a Science & Profession

The Association for Computing Machinery
2 Penn Plaza, Suite 701
New York, New York 10121-0701

ISBN: 978-1-4503-3400-6 (Digital)

ISBN: 978-1-4503-4100-4 (Print)

Additional copies may be ordered prepaid from:

ACM Order Department
PO Box 30777
New York, NY 10087-0777, USA

Phone: 1-800-342-6626 (USA and Canada)
+1-212-626-0500 (Global)
Fax: +1-212-944-1318
E-mail: acmhelp@acm.org
Hours of Operation: 8:30 am – 4:30 pm ET

Printed in the USA

ASSETS 2015 Foreword

It is our great pleasure to welcome you to the *17th International ACM SIGACCESS Conference on Computers and Accessibility (ASSETS 2015).* The ASSETS conference has a long-standing tradition of exploring the design, evaluation, and use of computing and information technologies to benefit people with disabilities and older adults. This year, in its 17th edition, ASSETS 2015 is again the premier forum for presenting innovative research on mainstream and specialized assistive technologies, accessible computing, and assistive applications of computer, network, and information technologies.

The call for papers attracted submissions from Australia (1), Austria (4), Belgium (2), Brazil (11), Canada (2), China (1), France (8), Germany (4), India (2), Ireland (1), Israel (2), Italy (3), Japan (1), Netherlands (2), Portugal (8), Puerto Rico (1), Republic of Korea (1), Saudi Arabia (1), Singapore (1), Spain (4), Sweden (1), Switzerland (1), United Kingdom (12), and the United States (53). Our growing community generated more technical paper submissions than ever before at an ASSETS conference, and we had the immense pleasure to work with our technical program committee to decide which would be accepted to the conference. We received 127 submissions from which we selected 30 for inclusion in the program, for an acceptance rate of 23%. For the first time at ASSETS, decisions were made by consensus of the program committee members, who discussed the papers extensively both online and via video calls. The program committee also reviewed 81 posters submissions (49 accepted) and 18 demo submissions (15 accepted).

The program committee consisted of 42 senior members of our committee who worked with 5 advanced doctoral systems to produce a total of 381 reviews. We would like to thank them for their incredibly diligent and considered work.

The ASSETS 2015 program is organized as follows:

On Monday (Day 1), the program starts with a keynote presentation by Dr. Jon Schull who is the President of the Enable Community Foundation. Dr. Schull's keynote is titled as "Enabling the future: Crowdsourced 3D-printed prosthetics as model for open source assistive technology innovation and mutual aid" and he will tell us about the fantastic work that he and e-NABLE are doing in the area of crowdsourcing 3D-printed prosthetic hands. Following the keynote, we will have a series of technical paper sessions organized around Speech Technologies, Reading and Language, and New Perspectives on Accessibility Research. The day will end with a Reception and hands-on Demo Session with awards for the best demos!

On Tuesday (Day 2), the program will continue with sessions on Non-Visual Access to Graphics, Sign Language, 3D Interaction, Accessibility and Work, and Exercise and Physical Activity. We will also hear short talks from the finalists in the ACM Student Research Competition. The day will conclude with a special reception at a historic Lisbon Museum supported by the Paciello Group. Awards for the Best Paper and the Best Student Paper will be given at this reception.

On Wednesday (Day 3), the program will conclude with technical sessions on Making Speech Accessible and Usable, Accessibility and Cognition, Text Input, and Improving Non-Visual Access. We will then turn over the reigns to next year's chairs to tell you about ASSETS 2016.

Putting together ASSETS 2015 was a team effort. We first thank the authors for providing the content of the program. We are grateful to the program committee who worked together very hard in reviewing papers and providing feedback for authors. We also thank our Treasurer and Registration

Chair Faustina Hwang, our Posters and Demos Chairs Shaun K. Kane and Luis Carriço, our Doctoral Consortium Chairs Giorgio Brajnik and Eelke Folmer, our Student Research Competition chairs Markel Vigo and Amy Hurst, our Mentoring chair Kathleen Mccoy, our Local Arrangements Chairs Tiago Guerreiro and Hugo Nicolau, our Web chair Aitor Apaolaza, our Student Volunteers chair João Guerreiro, our Accessibility chair Raja Kushalnagar, our Publicity chairs Luz Rello and Yevgen Borodin, and our Graphics Design chair Joshua Hailpern for all their contributions to the conference and these proceedings. Finally, we would like to thank our supporters: Google, Microsoft Research, the National Science Foundation and the Paciello Group, and our sponsors ACM and SIGACCESS for their support.

We hope that you will find this remarkable program interesting and thought provoking and that the conference will provide you with a valuable opportunity to share ideas with other researchers and practitioners from institutions around the world and welcome you again to ASSETS 2015!

Yeliz Yesilada
ASSETS 2015 General Chair
METU NCC, Northern Cyprus

Jeffrey P. Bigham
ASSETS 2015 Program Chair
Carnegie Mellon University, USA

Table of Contents

ASSETS 2015 Organization xiii

ASSETS 2015 Sponsor & Supporters xv

Keynote Address
Session Chair: Jeffrey P. Bigham *(Carnegie Mellon University)*

- **Enabling the Future: Crowdsourced 3D-printed Prostheticsas a Model for Open Source Assistive Technology Innovation and Mutual Aid** 1
  Jon Schull *(Rochester Institute of Technology)*

Speech In and Out
Session Chair: Shaun Kane *(University of Colorado)*

- **Faster Text-to-Speeches: Enhancing Blind People's Information Scanning with Faster Concurrent Speech** 3
  João Guerreiro, Daniel Gonçalves *(Universidade de Lisboa & INESC-ID)*
- **Towards Large Scale Evaluation of Novel Sonification Techniques for Non Visual Shape Exploration** 13
  Andrea Gerino *(Università degli Studi di Milano)*, Lorenzo Picinali *(Imperial College London)*, Cristian Bernareggi, Nicolò Alabastro, Sergio Mascetti *(Università degli Studi di Milano)*
- **Getting Smartphones to Talkback: Understanding the Smartphone Adoption Process of Blind Users** 23
  André Rodrigues *(Universidade de Lisboa)*, Kyle Montague *(University of Dundee)*, Hugo Nicolau *(Rochester Institute of Technology)*, Tiago Guerreiro *(Universidade de Lisboa)*
- **A System for Controlling Assisted Living Environments Using Mobile Devices** 33
  Paulo A. Condado, Fernando G. Lobo *(Universidade do Algarve)*

Reading and Language
Session Chair: Tiago Guerreiro *(University of Lisboa)*

- **A Spellchecker for Dyslexia** 39
  Luz Rello, Miguel Ballesteros, Jeffrey P. Bigham *(Carnegie Mellon University)*
- **Accessible Texts for Autism: An Eye-Tracking Study** 49
  Victoria Yaneva *(University of Wolverhampton)*, Irina Temnikova *(Qatar Computing Research Institute)*, Ruslan Mitkov *(University of Wolverhampton)*

Perspectives on Accessibility Research
Session Chair: Simon Harper *(University of Manchester)*

- **Usage of Subjective Scales in Accessibility Research** 59
  Shari Trewin *(IBM T.J. Watson Research Center)*, Diogo Marques, Tiago Guerreiro *(University of Lisbon)*
- **User Participation When Users have Mental and Cognitive Disabilities** 69
  Stefan Johansson, Jan Gulliksen, Ann Lantz *(KTH Royal Institute of Technology)*
- **A Unifying Notification System to Scale Up Assistive Services** 77
  Charles Consel *(Bordeaux INP & Inria)*, Lucile Dupuy *(Inria)*, Hélène Sauzéon *(University of Bordeaux & Inria)*
- **Disability and Technology – A Critical Realist Perspective** 89
  Christopher Frauenberger *(Vienna University of Technology)*

Non-Visual Access to Graphics

Session Chair: Shiri Azenkot *(Cornell Tech)*

- **The Tactile Graphics Helper: Providing Audio Clarification for Tactile Graphics Using Machine Vision** 97
  Giovanni Fusco, Valerie S. Morash *(The Smith-Kettlewell Eye Research Institute)*
- **ChartMaster: A Tool for Interacting with Stock Market Charts using a Screen Reader** 107
  Hong Zou, Jutta Treviranus *(OCAD University)*
- **Collaborative Creation of Digital Tactile Graphics** 117
  Jens Bornschein, Denise Prescher, Gerhard Weber *(Technische Universität Dresden)*
- **Transcribing Across the Senses: Community Efforts to Create 3D Printable Accessible Tactile Pictures for Young Children with Visual Impairments** 127
  Abigale Stangl, Chia-Lo Hsu, Tom Yeh *(University of Colorado- Boulder)*

Sign Language and the Third Dimension

Session Chair: Hironobu Takagi *(IBM Research - Tokyo)*

- **Comparing Methods of Displaying Language Feedback for Student Videos of American Sign Language** 139
  Matt Huenerfauth *(Rochester Institute of Technology)*, Elaine Gale *(Hunter College, CUNY)*, Brian Penly, Mackenzie Willard, Dhananjai Hariharan *(Rochester Institute of Technology)*
- **Demographic and Experiential Factors Influencing Acceptance of Sign Language Animation by Deaf Users** 147
  Hernisa Kacorri *(The Graduate Center, CUNY)*, Matt Huenerfauth *(Rochester Institute of Technology)*, Sarah Ebling *(University of Zurich)*, Kasmira Patel, Mackenzie Willard *(Rochester Institute of Technology)*
- **How 3D Virtual Humans Built by Adolescents with ASD Affect Their 3D Interactions** 155
  Chao Mei, Lee Mason, John Quarles *(University of Texas at San Antonio)*

Accessibility and Work

Session Chair: Erin Brady *(Indiana University-Purdue University Indianapolis)*

- **The Invisible Work of Accessibility: How Blind Employees Manage Accessibility in Mixed-Ability Workplaces** 163
  Stacy M. Branham *(University of Maryland, Baltimore County)*, Shaun K. Kane *(University of Colorado Boulder)*
- **Understanding the Challenges Faced by Neurodiverse Software Engineering Employees: Towards a More Inclusive and Productive Technical Workforce** 173
  Meredith Ringel Morris, Andrew Begel *(Microsoft Research)*, Ben Wiedermann *(Harvey Mudd College)*
- **Using In-Situ Projection to Support Cognitively Impaired Workers at the Workplace** 185
  Markus Funk, Sven Mayer, Albrecht Schmidt *(University of Stuttgart)*

Exercise and Physical Activity

Session Chair: Jon Froehlich *(University of Maryland)*

- **"But I don't take steps": Examining the Inaccessibility of Fitness Trackers for Wheelchair Athletes** ....
  Patrick Carrington, Kevin Chang, Helena Mentis, Amy Hurst *(University of Maryland, Baltimore County)*
- **Exploring the Opportunities and Challenges with Exercise Technologies for People Who are Blind or Low-Vision** 203
  Kyle Rector, Lauren Milne, Richard E. Ladner, Batya Friedman, Julie A. Kientz *(University of Washington)*

Making Speech Accessible and Usable

Session Chair: Matt Huenerfauth *(Rochester Institute of Technology)*

- **Online News Videos: The UX of Subtitle Position** 215
  Michael Crabb *(Robert Gordon University)*, Rhianne Jones, Mike Armstrong, Chris J. Hughes *(BBC R&D)*

- **Tracked Speech-to-Text Display: Enhancing Accessibility and Readability of Real-Time Speech-to-Text** 223
  Raja S. Kushalnagar, Gary W. Behm, Aaron W. Kelstone, Shareef S. Ali *(Rochester Institute of Technology)*
- **Evaluating Alternatives for Better Deaf Accessibility to Selected Web-based Multimedia** 231
  Brent N. Shiver *(IBM Research – Austin)*, Rosalee Wolfe *(DePaul University)*

Non-Visual Access

Session Chair: Yu Zhong *(Google)*

- **ForeSee: A Customizable Head-Mounted Vision Enhancement System for People with Low Vision** 239
  Yuhang Zhao, Sarit Szpiro, Shiri Azenkot *(Jacobs Technion-Cornell Institute)*
- **Zebra Crossing Spotter: Automatic Population of Spatial Databases for Increased Safety of Blind Travelers** 251
  Dragan Ahmetovic *(Università degli Studi di Milano)*, Roberto Manduchi *(University of California Santa Cruz)*, James M. Coughlan *(Smith-Kettlewell Eye Research Institute)*, Sergio Mascetti *(Università degli Studi di Milano)*
- **Social Media Platforms for Low-Income Blind People in India** 259
  Aditya Vashistha *(University of Washington)*, Edward Cutrell *(Microsoft Research India)*, Nicola Dell, Richard Anderson *(University of Washington)*

Text Input

Session Chair: Yu Zhong *(Google)*

- **Typing Performance of Blind Users: An Analysis of Touch Behaviors, Learning Effect, and In-Situ Usage** 273
  Hugo Nicolau *(Rochester Institute of Technology)*, Kyle Montague *(University of Dundee)*, Tiago Guerreiro, André Rodrigues *(Universidade de Lisboa)*, Vicki L. Hanson *(Rochester Institute of Technology & University of Dundee)*

Cognitive Disabilities

Session Chair: Shari Trewin *(IBM)*

- **Inclusion and Education: 3D Printing for Integrated Classrooms** 281
  Erin Buehler, William Easley, Samantha McDonald, Niara Comrie, Amy Hurst *(University of Maryland, Baltimore County)*
- **Towards Efficacy-Centered Game Design Patterns for Brain Injury Rehabilitation: A Data-Driven Approach** 291
  Jinghui Cheng, Cynthia Putnam, Doris C. Rusch *(DePaul University)*

Poster Session 1

- **A Pilot Study about the Smartwatch as Assistive Device for Deaf People** 301
  Matthias Mielke, Rainer Brück *(University of Siegen)*
- **Using OnScreenDualScribe to Support Text Entry and Targeting among Individuals with Physical Disabilities** 303
  Sidas Saulynas, Lula Albar, Ravi Kuber *(University of Maryland, Baltimore County)*, Torsten Felzer *(Technical University of Darmstadt)*
- **Developing SAGAT Probes to Evaluate Blind Individuals' Situation Awareness when Traveling Indoor Environments** 305
  Abdulrhman A. Alkhanifer, Stephanie Ludi *(Rochester Institute of Technology (RIT))*
- **Dytective: Toward a Game to Detect Dyslexia** 307
  Luz Rello *(Carnegie Mellon University)*, Abdullah Ali *(University of Maryland, Baltimore County)*, Jeffrey P. Bigham *(Carnegie Mellon University)*
- **Design and Evaluation of a Simplified Online Banking Interface for People with Cognitive Disabilities** 309
  Mario Erazo, Gottfried Zimmermann *(Stuttgart Media University)*

- **GraCALC: An Accessible Graphing Calculator** 311
  Cagatay Goncu, Kim Marriott *(Monash University)*
- **ARCoach 2.0: Optimizing a Vocational Prompting System Based on Augmented Reality for People with Cognitive Impairments** 313
  Yao-Jen Chang, Ya-Shu Kang *(Chung Yuan Christian University)*,
  Yao-Sheng Chang *(Chung Chou University of Science and Technology)*,
  Hung-Huan Liu *(Chung Yuan Christian University)*
- **BendableSound: A Fabric-based Interactive Surface to Promote Free Play in Children with Autism** 315
  Deysi Ortega, Franceli Cibrian, Monica Tentori *(CICESE)*
- **Designing Kinect2Scratch Games to Help Therapists Train Young Adults with Cerebral Palsy in Special Education School Settings** 317
  Yao-Jen Chang, Ya-Shu Kang *(Chung Yuan Christian University)*,
  Yao-Sheng Chang *(Chung Chou University of Science and Technology)*,
  Hung-Huan Liu, Cheng-Chieh Wang, Chia Chun Kao *(Chung Yuan Christian University)*
- **Model-Based Automated Accessibility Testing** 319
  Giorgio Brajnik *(Università di Udine)*, Chiara Pighin *(Interaction Design Solutions)*,
  Sara Fabbro *(Interaction Design Solutions)*
- **Usability for Accessibility – A Consolidation of Requirements for Mobile Applications** 321
  Clauirton Siebra *(Samsung R&D Laboratory & Federal University of Paraiba)*,
  Tatiana Gouveia, Anderson Filho, Walter Correia, Marcelo Penha *(Universidade Federal de Pernambuco)*,
  Marcelo Anjos, Fabiana Florentin *(SIDI – Samsung)*,
  Fabio Q. B. Silva, Andre L. M. Santos *(Universidade Federal de Pernambuco)*
- **An Investigation into Appropriation of Portable Smart Devices by Users with Aphasia** 323
  Gennaro Imperatore, Mark D. Dunlop *(University of Strathclyde)*
- **Japanese Sentence Handwriting Learning System for Special Needs Education** 325
  Iwao Kobayashi, Nami Nemoto *(Tokyo Gakugei University)*,
  Kiwamu Sato, Kaito Watanabe, Hiroshi Nunokawa, Naohiro Ogasawara *(Iwate Prefectural University)*
- **DroneNavigator: Using Drones for Navigating Visually Impaired Persons** 327
  Mauro Avila, Markus Funk, Niels Henze *(University of Stuttgart)*
- **Calendars for Individuals with Cognitive Disabilities: A Comparison of Table View and List View** 329
  Frode Eika Sandnes, Maud Veronica Lundh *(Oslo and Akershus University College of Applied Sciences)*
- **Mobile Phone Access to a Sign Language Dictionary** 331
  Michael D. Jones *(Brigham Young University)*, Harley Hamilton *(Georgia Tech.)*,
  James Petmecky *(Brigham Young University)*
- **Teaching Accessibility, Learning Empathy** 333
  Cynthia Putnam, Maria Dahman *(DePaul University)*, Emma Rose *(University of Washington, Tacoma)*,
  Jinghui Cheng, Glenn Bradford *(DePaul University)*
- **Road Sensing: Personal Sensing and Machine Learning for Development of Large Scale Accessibility Map** 335
  Yusuke Iwasawa *(The University of Tokyo)*, Koya Nagamine *(Sophia University)*,
  Yutaka Matsuo *(The University of Tokyo)*, Ikuko Eguchi Yairi *(Sophia University)*
- **Adaptive Assistance to Support and Promote Performance-impaired People in Manual Assembly Processes** 337
  Manuel Kölz *(Schnaithmann Maschinenbau GmbH)*, Darrell Jordon *(University of Applied Sciences Reutlingen)*,
  Peter Kurtz *(University of Technology Ilmenau)*, Thomas Hörz *(University of Applied Sciences Esslingen)*
- **Issues Influencing the Uptake of Smartphone Reminder Apps for People with Acquired Brain Injury** 339
  Matthew Jamieson *(University of Glasgow)*, Marilyn McGee-Lennon *(University of Strathclyde)*,
  Breda Cullen, Stephen Brewster, Jonathan Evans *(University of Glasgow)*

- **"Read That Article": Exploring Synergies between Gaze and Speech Interaction** 341
  Diogo Vieira *(University of Aveiro & Microsoft Language Development Center)*,
  João Dinis Freitas *(Microsoft Language Development Center)*,
  Cengiz Acartürk *(Cognitive Science Middle East Technical Univ)*,
  António Teixeira *(University of Aveiro)*, Luís Sousa *(Microsoft Language Development Center)*,
  Samuel Silva *(University of Aveiro)*, Sara Candeias *(Microsoft Language Development Center)*,
  Miguel Sales Dias *(Microsoft Language Development Center & University Institute of Lisbon)*
- **Exploring the Use of Massive Open Online Courses for Teaching Students with Intellectual Disability** 343
  Rodrigo Laiola Guimarães, Andrea Britto Mattos *(IBM Research)*
- **VITHEA-Kids: A Platform for Improving Language Skills of Children with Autism Spectrum Disorder** 345
  Vânia Mendonça, Luísa Coheur, Alberto Sardinha *(INESC-ID)*
- **The Development of a Framework for Understanding the UX of Subtitles** 347
  Michael Crabb *(Robert Gordon University)*, Rhianne Jones, Mike Armstrong *(BBC R&D)*
- **An Empirical Study for Examining the Performance of Visually Impaired People in Recognizing Shapes through a Vibro-tactile Feedback** 349
  Waseem Safi, Fabrice Maurel, Jean-Marc Routoure, Gaël Dias *(University of Caen Normandie)*
- **Breaking Barriers with Assistive Macros** 351
  André Rodrigues *(University of Lisbon)*
- **Making Connections: Modular 3D Printing for Designing Assistive Attachments to Prosthetic Devices** 353
  Megan Hofmann *(Colorado State University & Carnegie Mellon University)*
- **Sensory Substitution Training for Users Who Are Blind with Dynamic Stimuli, Games and Virtual Environments** 355
  Shachar Maidenbaum *(Hebrew University of Jerusalem)*
- **SlidePacer – Improving Class Pace for Deaf and Hard-of-Hearing Students** 357
  Alessandra Brandao *(Rochester Institute of Technology)*
- **Sequential Gestural Passcodes on Google Glass** 359
  Abdullah Ali *(University of Maryland, Baltimore County)*
- **Talkabel: A Labeling Method for 3D Printed Models** 361
  Lei Shi *(Cornell Tech)*
- **Haptic Gloves Prototype for Audio-Tactile Web Browsing** 363
  Andrii Soviak *(Stony Brook University)*
- **Exploring New Paradigms for Accessible 3D Printed Graphs** 365
  Michele Hu *(City University of New York)*
- **The Effects of Automatic Speech Recognition Quality on Human Transcription Latency** 367
  Yashesh Gaur *(Carnegie Mellon University)*

Poster Session 2

- **Web Search Credibility Assessment for Individuals who are Blind** 369
  Ali Abdolrahmani, Ravi Kuber, William Easley *(University of Maryland, Baltimore County)*
- **A Voting System for AAC Symbol Acceptance** 371
  E. A. Draffan, Mike Wald, Nawar Halabi *(University of Southampton)*,
  Amatullah Kadous, Amal Idris *(Hamad Medical Corporation)*,
  Nadine Zeinoun, David Banes, Dana Lawand *(MADA)*
- **A Direct TEX-to-Braille Transcribing Method** 373
  Andreas Papasalouros, Antonis Tsolomitis *(University of the Aegean)*

- **Spoken Language, Conversational Assistive Systems for People with Cognitive Impairments? – Yes, If.** 375
  Ramin Yaghoubzadeh, Stefan Kopp *(Bielefeld University)*
- **Correction of the Fundamental Voice Frequency Using Tactile and Visual Feedback** 377
  Rodrigo Leone Alves *(Federal Institute of Rio Grande do Norte)*, Carlos M. G. S. Lima *(University of Minho)*, Raimundo C. S. Freire *(Federal University of Campina Grande)*
- **TinyBlackBox: Supporting Mobile In-the-Wild Studies** 379
  Kyle Montague *(University of Dundee)*, André Rodrigues *(Universidade de Lisboa)*, Hugo Nicolau *(Rochester Institute of Technology)*, Tiago Guerreiro *(Universidade de Lisboa)*
- **APLUS: A 3D Corpus of French Sign Language** 381
  Annelies Braffort *(LIMSI-CNRS)*, Mohamed Benchiheub *(LIMSI-CNRS & CIAMS-UPSud)*, Bastien Berret *(CIAMS-UPSud)*
- **Supporting Everyday Activities for Persons with Visual Impairments Through Computer Vision-Augmented Touch** 383
  Leah Findlater, Lee Stearns, Ruofei Du, Uran Oh *(University of Maryland)*, David Ross *(Atlanta VA R&D Center of Excellence in Vision and Neurocognitive Rehabilitation (CVNR))*, Rama Chellappa, Jon E. Froehlich *(University of Maryland)*
- **A Haptic Device to Support the Use of a Glucose Monitor by Individuals Who are Blind or Visually Impaired** 385
  Matthew Standard *(Virginia Commonwealth University)*, Jacob Park *(Aesculap, Inc.)*, Dianne T. V. Pawluk *(Virginia Commonwealth University)*
- **Exploring Interface Design for Independent Navigation by People with Visual Impairments** 387
  Erin Brady *(Carnegie Mellon University)*, Daisuke Sato *(IBM Tokyo)*, Chengxiong Ruan *(Carnegie Mellon University)*, Hironobu Takagi *(IBM Tokyo)*, Chieko Asakawa *(Carnegie Mellon University & IBM Tokyo)*
- **MoviTouch: Mobile Movement Capability Configurations** 389
  Jan David Smeddinck, Jorge Hey, Nina Runge, Marc Herrlich *(University of Bremen)*, Christine Jacobsen, Jan Wolters *(Schröder-Wolters GbR)*, Rainer Malaka *(University of Bremen)*
- **Feel the Web: Towards the Design of Haptic Screen Interfaces for Accessible Web Browsing** 391
  Andrii Soviak, Vikas Ashok, Yevgen Borodin, Yury Puzis, I.V. Ramakrishnan *(Stony Brook University)*
- **Multiomodal Application for the Perception of Spaces (MAPS)** 393
  Richard J. Adams *(Barron Associates, Inc.)*, Dianne T. V. Pawluk *(Virginia Commonwealth University)*, Margaret A. Fields *(Virginia Department for the Blind and Vision Impaired)*, Ryan Clingman *(Virginia Commonwealth University)*
- **Opportunity: Inclusive Design for Interactive Simulations** 395
  Emily B. Moore, Clayton Lewis *(University of Colorado Boulder)*
- **Development of BCI Based Softwares to Assist People with Mobility Limitations in the School Inclusion Process** 397
  Regina Heidrich, Marsal A. Branco, João B. Mossmann, Anderson Schuh, Emely Jensen *(Universidade Feevale)*
- **The Impact of Stuttering; How Can a Mobile App Help?** 399
  Iva Demarin, Ljubica Leko, Maja Škrobo *(University of Zagreb)*, Helena Germano, Patrícia Macedo, Rui Neves Madeira *(Instituto Politécnico de Setúbal)*
- **Exploring the Potential of Wearables to Support Employment for People with Mild Cognitive Impairment** 401
  Victor Dibia *(City University of Hong Kong)*, Shari Trewin, Maryam Ashoori, Thomas Erickson *(IBM T.J. Watson Research Center)*
- **Predictive Link Following for Accessible Web Browsing** 403
  Jiri Roznovjak, John Magee *(Clark University)*
- **Appliance Displays: Accessibility Challenges and Proposed Solutions** 405
  Giovanni Fusco, Ender Tekin *(Smith-Kettlewell Eye Research Institute)*, Nicholas A. Giudice *(University of Maine)*, James M. Coughlan *(Smith-Kettlewell Eye Research Institute)*

- **People with Parkinson's Disease Using Computers** 407
  Maria Hartikainen, Saila Ovaska *(University of Tampere)*
- **Mobile Integrated Assistance to Empower People Coping with Parkinson's Disease** 409
  Carla Pereira, Patrícia Macedo, Rui Neves Madeira *(Instituto Politécnico de Setúbal)*
- **SECPT Framework – A Travelling Experience Based Framework for Visually Impaired People** 411
  Jing Guan, Clifford Sze-Tsan Choy *(The Hong Kong Polytechnic University)*
- **Depicting the Keypad Mouse Interface: Exploring Pointing Behaviors of Three Input Devices** 413
  J. Eduardo Pérez, Xabier Valencia, Myriam Arrue, Julio Abascal *(University of the Basque Country UPV/EHU)*
- **A Model-based Tool to Develop an Accessible Media Player** 415
  María González-García, Lourdes Moreno, Paloma Martínez *(Universidad Carlos III de Madrid)*
- **Video Analysis for Includification Requirements** 417
  Alexander Hofmann, Helmut Hlavacs *(University of Vienna)*

Demo Session

- **Accessible Mobile Biometrics for Elderly** 419
  Ramon Blanco-Gonzalo, Raul Sanchez-Reillo *(University Carlos III of Madrid)*,
  Löic Martínez-Normand *(Universidad Politécnica de Madrid)*,
  Belen Fernandez-Saavedra, Judith Liu-Jimenez *(University Carlos III of Madrid)*
- **Can We Make Dynamic, Accessible and Fun One-Switch Video Games?** 421
  Sebastián Aced López, Fulvio Corno, Luigi De Russis *(Politecnico di Torino)*
- **ChatWoz: Chatting through a Wizard of Oz** 423
  Pedro Fialho *(Universidade de Évora)*, Luísa Coheur *(Universidade de Lisboa)*
- **Eyes-free Exploration of Shapes with Invisible Puzzle** 425
  Andrea Gerino *(Università degli Studi di Milano)*, Lorenzo Picinali *(Imperial College London)*,
  Cristian Bernareggi, Sergio Mascetti *(Università degli Studi di Milano)*
- **TactileMaps.net: A Web Interface for Generating Customized 3D-Printable Tactile Maps** 427
  Brandon Taylor, Anind Dey, Dan Siewiorek, Asim Smailagic *(Carnegie Mellon University)*
- **ARMStrokes: A Mobile App for Everyday Stroke Rehabilitation** 429
  Jin Guo, Ted Smith, David Messing, Ziying Tang, Sonia Lawson, Jinjuan Heidi Feng *(Towson University)*
- **READ: A (Research) Platform for Evaluating Non-visual Access Methods to Digital Documents** 431
  Laurent Sorin, Julie Lemarié, Mustapha Mojahid *(University of Toulouse)*
- **Using Dynamic Audio Feedback to Support Peripersonal Reaching in Visually Impaired People** 433
  Graham Wilson, Stephen A. Brewster *(University of Glasgow)*
- **An Enhanced Electrolarynx with Automatic Fundamental Frequency Control based on Statistical Prediction** 435
  Kou Tanaka, Tomoki Toda, Graham Neubig, Sakriani Sakti,
  Satoshi Nakamura *(Nara Institute of Science and Technology)*
- **Nonvisual Access to an Interactive Electric Field Simulation: Work in Progress** 437
  Clayton Lewis, Derek Riemer *(University of Colorado)*
- **Balance Assessment in Fall-Prevention Exergames** 439
  Miguel Brito, João Jacob, Rui Nóbrega *(Universidade do Porto)*, António Santos *(Fraunhofer AICOS)*
- **ASL CLeaR: STEM Education Tools for Deaf Students** 441
  Jeanne Reis *(Boston University)*, Erin T. Solovey *(Drexel University)*, Jon Henner *(College of the Holy Cross)*,
  Kathleen Johnson, Robert Hoffmeister *(Boston University)*
- **EnTable: Rewriting Web Data Sets as Accessible Tables** 443
  Steven Gardiner, Anthony Tomasic, John Zimmerman *(Carnegie Mellon University)*

- **A Game to Target the Spelling of German Children with Dyslexia** 445
  Maria Rauschenberger *(University of Applied Sciences Emden/Leer & OFFIS)*,
  Silke Fuechsel *(University of Applied Sciences Emden/Leer)*,
  Luz Rello, Clara Bayarri, Azuki Gorriz *(Cookie Cloud)*
- **The Implementation of a Vocabulary and Grammar for an Open-Source Speech-Recognition Programming Platform** 447
  Jean K. Rodríguez-Cartagena *(UPR Río Piedras)*,
  Andrea Claudio-Palacios, Natalia Pacheco-Tallaj *(University High School)*,
  Valerie Santiago-González, Patricia Ordonez-Franco *(UPR Río Piedras)*

Author Index 449

ASSETS 2015 Organization

General Chair: Yeliz Yesilada *(Middle East Technical University Northern Cyprus Campus)*

Program Chair: Jeffrey P. Bigham *(Carnegie Mellon University, USA)*

Treasurer & Registration Chair: Faustina Hwang *(University of Reading, USA)*

Posters and Demonstrations Chairs: Shaun K. Kane *(University of Colorado Boulder, USA)*
Luis Carriço *(University of Lisbon, Portugal)*

Doctoral Consortium Chairs: Giorgio Brajnik *(University of Udine, Italy)*
Eelke Folmer *(University of Nevada, Reno, USA)*

Student Research Competition Chairs: Markel Vigo *(University of Manchester, UK)*
Amy Hurst *(UMBC, USA)*

Mentoring Chair: Kathleen McCoy *(University of Delaware, USA)*

Local Arrangements Chair: Tiago Guerreiro *(University of Lisboa, Portugal)*
Hugo Nicolau *(University of Lisboa, Portgual)*

Web Chair: Aitor Apaolaza *(University of Manchester, UK)*

Publicity Chair: Luz Rello *(Carnegie Mellon University, USA)*
Yevgen Borodin *(CharmTech Labs, USA)*

Student Volunteer Chair: João Guerreiro *(Technical University of Lisbon)*

Accessibility Chair: Raja Kushalnagar *(Rochester Institute of Technology, USA)*

Graphic Design Chair: Joshua Hailpern *(HP ArcSight, USA)*

Program Committee: Amy Hurst *(University of Maryland, Baltimore County, USA)*
Andreas Stefik *(University of Nevada, Las Vegas, USA)*
Alistair Edwards *(University of York, UK)*
Anna Cavender *(Google, USA)*
Anne Marie Piper *(Northwestern University, USA)*
Christopher Power *(University of York, UK)*
Clayton Lewis *(University of Colorado, USA)*
Bolchini, Davide *(Indiana University Purdue University Indianapollis, USA)*
David Flatla *(University of Dundee, UK)*
Eelke Folmer *(University of Nevada, Reno, USA)*
Elliot Cole *(Institute for Cognitve Prosthestics, USA)*

Program Committee (continued): Erin Brady *(Indiana University Purdue University Indianapollis, USA)*
Faustina Hwang *(Reading University, UK)*
Karyn Moffatt *(McGill University, Canada)*
Gerhard Weber *(Technische Universitat Dresden, Germany)*
Giorgio Brajnik *(University of Udine, Italy)*
Hironobu Takagi *(IBM Research, Tokyo, Japan)*
Iyad Abu Doush *(Yarmouk University, Jordan)*
Joanna McGrenere *(University of British Columbia, Canada)*
Jon Froehlich *(University of Maryland, USA)*
Jonathan Lazar *(Towson University, USA)*
Joshua Hailpern *(HP Labs, USA)*
Kathy McCoy *(University of Delaware, USA)*
Kyle Montague *(University of Dundee, UK)*
Larry Goldberg *(Yahoo!, USA)*
Leah Findlater *(University of Maryland, USA)*
Leo Ferres *(University of Concepcion, Chile)*
Luz Rello *(Carnegie Mellon University, USA)*
Markel Vigo *(University of Manchester, UK)*
Matt Huenerfauth *(Rochester Institute of Technology, USA)*
Raja Kushalnagar *(National Technical Institute for the Deaf at Rochester Institute of Technology, USA)*
Richard Ladner *(University of Washington, USA)*
Roberto Manduchi *(University of California, Santa Cruz, USA)*
Scott McCrickard *(Virginia Tech, USA)*
Shaomei Wu *(Facebook, USA)*
Shaun Kane *(University of Colorado, USA)*
Shiri Azenkot *(Cornell Tech, USA)*
Tiago Guerreiro *(University of Lisbon, Portugal)*
Walter Lasecki *(University of Michigan, USA)*
Yu Zhong *(Google, USA)*
Yun Huang *(University of Syracuse, USA)*

Student Reviewers: Jens Bornschein *(TU Dresden, Germany)*
Patrick Carrington *(University of Maryland, Baltimore County, USA)*
Kotaro Hara *(University of Maryland, USA)*
Kyle Rector *(University of Washington, USA)*
Kristen Shinohara *(University of Washington, USA)*
Michelle A. Williams *(University of Maryland, Baltimore County, USA)*

ASSETS 2015 Sponsor & Supporters

Sponsor:

SIG ACCESS
Special Interest Group on Accessible Computing

Supporters:

Google™

Microsoft® Research

THEPACIELLOGROUP

NSF

Enabling the Future: Crowdsourced 3D-printed Prosthetics as a Model for Open Source Assistive Technology Innovation and Mutual Aid

Jon Schull

e-NABLE
RIT MAGIC-ACT
Jon.Schull@rit.edu

ABSTRACT

e-NABLE[1] – an online community that designs, customizes, fabricates, and disseminates 3D-printed prosthetic hands and arms, for free – extends the methods and philosophies of Open Source software to hardware, assistive technology development, and human resources. I'll tell the story of this remarkable community, and discuss emerging trends and opportunities for academic research, and trans-academic collaboration.

Categories and Subject Descriptors

H.1.2 [**Information Systems Applications**]: User/Machine Systems - Human information processing; K.4.2 [**Computers and Society**]: Social issues - Assistive technologies for persons with disabilities

General Terms

Human factors, Design

Keywords

3d-printing, crowdsourcing, assistive technology

1. BIOGRAPHY

A biological psychologist, inventor, entrepreneur, and human-computer interaction researcher, Dr. Jon Schull is President of the Enable Community Foundation, and founder of e-NABLE, an online community that designs, customizes, fabricates, and disseminates 3D-printed prosthetic hands and arms, for free. Schull, eNABLE, and its members have been featured in conferences, magazines, and news shows worldwide. Schull's Ph.D. is in Biological Psychology. He is the author of 19 patents, and is the former director of RIT's Center for Student Innovation. In his current role as Research Scientist in RIT's Center for MAGIC (Media Arts Games Interaction and Creativity), Schull coordinates the Access and Collaboration Technologies (ACT) lab.

[1]enablingthefuture.org

ASSETS'15, October 26–28, 2015, Lisbon, Portugal.
ACM. 978-1-4503-3400-6/15/10
DOI: http://dx.doi.org/10.1145/2700648.2809870.

Faster Text-to-Speeches: Enhancing Blind People's Information Scanning with Faster Concurrent Speech

João Guerreiro, Daniel Gonçalves
Instituto Superior Técnico, Universidade de Lisboa / INESC-ID
Rua Alves Redol 9, 1000-029, Lisboa, Portugal
joao.p.guerreiro@ist.utl.pt, daniel.goncalves@inesc-id.pt

ABSTRACT
Blind people rely mostly on the auditory feedback of screen readers to consume digital information. Still, how fast can information be processed remains a major problem. The use of faster speech rates is one of the main techniques to speed-up the consumption of digital information. Moreover, recent experiments have suggested the use of concurrent speech as a valid alternative when scanning for relevant information. In this paper, we present an experiment with 30 visually impaired participants, where we compare the use of faster speech rates against the use of concurrent speech. Moreover, we combine these two approaches by gradually increasing the speech rate with one, two and three voices. Results show that concurrent voices with speech rates slightly faster than the default rate, enable a significantly faster scanning for relevant content, while maintaining its comprehension. In contrast, to keep-up with concurrent speech timings, *One-Voice* requires larger speech rate increments, which cause a considerable loss in performance. Overall, results suggest that the best compromise between efficiency and the ability to understand each sentence is the use of *Two-Voices* with a rate of 1.75**default-rate* (approximately 278 WPM).

Categories and Subject Descriptors
H.5.1 [**Information Interfaces and Presentation (e.g. HCI)**]: Multimedia Information Systems – *Audio Input/Output*.

General Terms
Design, Experimentation, Human Factors.

Keywords
Concurrent Speech; Speech Rate; Screen Reader; Text-to-Speech; Blind; Visually Impaired; Scanning; Skimming; Auditory Perception; Cocktail Party Effect.

1. INTRODUCTION
Blind people rely mostly on the auditory feedback of screen readers to consume digital information. Efficiency is a problem especially in situations where relevant information must be recognized among large amounts of irrelevant one. Sighted users use *scanning* as a strategy to achieve this goal, by glancing at all content expecting to identify information of interest to be subsequently analyzed with further care. Increasing the speech rate is one of the main techniques that blind people use for this purpose and may be used either alone or combined with other strategies (e.g. navigate through heading or links) [5].

Although researchers have reported a gradual decrease in intelligibility and comprehension as the speech rate increases [27], they have also shown its ability to accelerate information consumption substantially. For instance, two distinct experiments [3] and [27] reported blind users' ability to understand at least 50% of the content using rates nearly three times faster than the default rate (500 Words per Minute – WPM).

Despite the benefit provided by faster speech rates, we have argued before that the screen readers' sequential auditory channel is impairing a quicker overview of the content, when compared to the visual presentation on screen [15]. We proposed the use of concurrent speech to accelerate the scanning for relevant content, by taking advantage of the *Cocktail Party Effect*. It describes the ability to focus the attention on a single voice among several conversations and background noise, but still be able to detect interesting content in the background [8]. Moreover, the identification and intelligibility of the concurrent voices may be enhanced with the use of different spatial locations and different gender voices (e.g. [6]).

In a previous experiment [15], we have reported that blind users are able to identify and understand one particular sentence when listening to two or three simultaneous sentences (news snippets), suggesting that current screen readers can be imposing limitations on the way auditory feedback is being provided. While these results point out concurrent speech as a proper alternative to faster speech rates, only a direct comparison can determine their relative benefits and limitations. Moreover, in that experiment users had to identify and understand one relevant sentence. However, searching for relevant content does not require users to understand the whole content, but it asks for a decision of which information items (e.g. news) are relevant and deserve further attention.

In this paper, we compare the use of faster speech rates against the use of concurrent speech when scanning for relevant digital information. We combine these two approaches by gradually increasing the speech rate with one, two and three voices. In order to guarantee a fair comparison, we assign different speech rates depending on the number of *Voices* (*One-Voice*, *Two-Voices* or *Three-Voices*), so that they take the exact same time to read the same number of sentences. We refer to it as *Information Bandwidth* condition; the higher the bandwidth, the lesser time it takes to read the sentences (independently of the number of *Voices*). We present an experiment with 30 visually impaired participants, where in each condition they had to listen to news snippets and identify all that belong to a specific subject. In particular, we aim to answer the following research questions: 1) What *Voice* condition enables the best content comprehension for

ASSETS '15, October 26 - 28, 2015, Lisbon, Portugal

ACM 978-1-4503-3400-6/15/10$15.00
DOI: http://dx.doi.org/10.1145/2700648.2809840

each *Information Bandwidth*?; 2) How does increasing the speech rate affect scanning for relevant content with one, two and three voices?; and 3) What combination of speech rate and number of voices enable the fastest scanning for relevant content, while maintaining the basic understanding of the content?

Results show that the *One-Voice* condition performs significantly worse than concurrent speech as the *Information Bandwidth* increases. Moreover, both *Two* and *Three-Voices* maintain their high performances in the first conditions. This means that smaller increments in the concurrent voices' speech rate enables faster scanning for relevant content, maintaining the comprehension of the sentences. In contrast, to keep-up with concurrent speech timings, *One-Voice* requires larger speech rate increments, which cause a considerable loss in performance. Overall, results suggest that the best compromise between *Information Bandwidth* and the ability to understand each sentence is the use of *Two-Voices* with a rate 1.75**default-rate* (~278.4 WPM).

2. RELATED WORK

The access to digital information, for instance on the web, imposes several barriers for visual impaired users, as web pages are usually designed with visual interaction in mind [13]. A great effort has been made to assure the accessibility of digital content to visually impaired people. Studies have been conducted in order to understand how visually impaired users cope with their difficulties to access digital information (e.g. [31]). Moreover, the strategies that they use to accelerate their browsing experience, such as navigating through headings or increasing the speech rate [5] help them browse more efficiently ([5] [28]). Researchers have also suggested the use of summarization in order to reduce the amount of information to read while providing only a gist of the content [1] [18].

The speed to process digital information is still a major problem for visual impaired people [5] [17], particularly when compared with sighted peers [4] [28]. In this section, we review work related with the two approaches compared in this article: the usage of faster speech rates and concurrent speech.

2.1 Using Faster Speech Rates

Mainstream screen readers such as *JAWS*, *NVDA*, *VoiceOver* or *Talkback* soon started to enable the manipulation of their voices speech rates. The need for an easy and interactive way to change the speech rate with immediate response [3], resulted in faster ways to control it, such as using keyboard shortcuts instead of navigating to the respective menu. This interactivity allows users to control the speech rate depending on the content intelligibility requirements and allows them to deal with the exhaustion caused by the use of very high speech rates [29].

Previous research has explored the intelligibility and comprehension of synthesized speech at higher speech rates, observing a gradual decrease as the speech rate increases (e.g. [27] [30]). Furthermore, other experiments have shown that visually impaired people are able to listen and understand synthesized speech at higher speech rates than sighted people (e.g. [29]). However, this ability depends on factors such as the person's age, being a native speaker and familiarity with both the synthesizer and the voice [27].

Asakawa and colleagues [3] reported that blind advanced users were able to listen to sentences in Japanese at speech rates 2.8 times faster (approximately 500 WPM) than the default rate of the screen reader and still understand at least 50% of the information. Moreover, novice users were able to listen to a screen reader 1.6 times faster than the default rate and be able to understand the entire content. Stent and colleagues tested speech rates up to 550 WPM (in English), reporting a comprehension above 50% with a 500 WPM rate for all synthesizers tested [27].

2.2 Using Concurrent Speech

The human ability to process concurrent speech is supported by the *Cocktail Party Effect* [8]. In the middle of conversations and background noise, one is capable to focus the attention on a single voice and still detect interesting content in the background and shift the attention accordingly. Literature reviews have documented several features that increase concurrent speech intelligibility. Such features include the use of dichotic speech (separate the sound sources between ears) when using two competing voices [6] [8] and the use of spatial audio with three or more voices [6]. Another example is the use of different gender voices [6] [10], due to the human brain's ability to segregate different sound frequencies. The benefits of its usage are more moderate when already using spatial audio, but it is clearly preferred to the use of the same or similar voices [15]. Some evidence supports that blind people, in particular early-blind, show enhanced sensitivity to discriminate speech sounds [20] due to the process of *neuro-plasticity* – the reorganization of unused areas of the brain for different purposes [7].

In line with experiments about the *Cocktail Party Effect* and with the increasing use of speech in the interaction with computers, researchers have tried to leverage this phenomenon to convey information more efficiently, particularly to screen reader users. *Sasayaki* [23] is a web browser that augments the standard auditory channel with a whispering voice that, among other things, may locate the screen reader position in the web page or provide important contextual information. Goose and Moller [14] also use two voices, but added spatial audio to indicate the location in the web page. *SpatialTouch* [16] is a non-visual multitouch QWERTY keyboard for tablet devices that supports two-handed input through spatial and simultaneous audio feedback. It relies on male and female voices, which spatial location depend on each character position in the keyboard.

Both *Spatial Speaker [26]* and *AudioStreamer* [25] use simultaneous speech to present different sentences in different spatial locations. The first is able to present text files read in pre-defined spatial locations, while the latter reads three audio news programs and detects head movement to select the current focus of interest. On the other hand, SpeechSkimmer [2] divides the content of the same sentence between the two ears to present it faster, by selecting the most important segments to an ear and the remaining to the other.

We have conducted an earlier experiment with visually impaired people to understand the limits of concurrent speech when scanning for relevant content [15]. Participants had to listen to two, three or four simultaneous news snippets while trying to identify the relevant one and understand its content. We found that such task is easy to perform when listening to two simultaneous voices and for most people with three. However, four voices considerably decreases both the identification and intelligibility of the relevant sentence.

The studies and projects described in this section support the use of concurrent speech to accelerate the consumption of digital

Table 1. The speech rate as the number of times it is faster than the default-rate (and mean WPM) for all IB X Voice conditions

Voices	Information Bandwidth (IB) Condition					
	2	3	3.5	4	5	6
1	2 (325.6 wpm)	3 (488.4 wpm)	3.5 (569.8 wpm)	4 (651.2 wpm)		
2	1 (159.1 wpm)	1.5 (238.7 wpm)	1.75 (278.4 wpm)	2 (318.2 wpm)	2.5 (397.8 wpm)	3 (477.3 wpm)
3		1 (161.7 wpm)	1.167 (188.7 wpm)	1.333 (215.5 wpm)	1.667 (269.6 wpm	2 (323.4 wpm)

information. Similarly to the use of faster speech rates, our former experiment [15] suggests it could be leveraged by screen reader users when scanning for relevant content.

3. EXPERIMENTAL SETTING

In this experiment, we investigate two approaches that intend to accelerate blind people's scanning for relevant digital content: 1) the use of faster speech rates; and 2) the use of concurrent speech. In addition, we combine these two approaches and compare the identification of relevant content with one, two and three voices, using different speech rates. An important concept in this investigation is that of *Information Bandwidth* (*IB*), which refers to how fast the information is transmitted in comparison to a baseline condition – one voice with the default speech rate (*default-rate*). For instance, an *IB* of 2 means the content is transmitted two times faster, which can be through the use of *Two-Voices* with the *default-rate* or *One-Voice* twice as fast. We defined 6 *IB* conditions, where we assigned different speech rates to each *Voice* condition so that they take the same time to complete. In Table 1, are depicted all *IB X Voice* conditions (detailed in *Section 3.2.2*). We aim to answer the following research questions:

1. What *Voice* condition enables the best content comprehension for each *Information Bandwidth*?
2. How does increasing the speech rate affect scanning for relevant content with one, two and three voices?
3. What combination of speech rate and number of voices enable the fastest scanning for relevant content, while maintaining the basic understanding of the content?

3.1 Auditory Feedback

Current *Text-to-Speech* (TTS) software restricts the auditory feedback to a unique, sequential auditory channel. Therefore, we relied on the *Text-to-Speeches* framework[1], the same way we did in our previous concurrent speech experiment [15]. This framework is able to position several simultaneous pre-recorded audio files in a 3D space and supports the use of digital filters (*Head Related Transfer Functions)* that simulate the acoustic cues used for spatial localization [33].

All sentences were pre-recorded to .wav files, using three different voices (two male and one female) from *DIXI* [22], a TTS developed by *INESC-ID's Spoken Language Systems Laboratory*[2] and now commercialized by *Voice Interaction*[3]. These voices had the following mean pitch and Words Per Minute (WPM) rate using the experiment dataset:

Female (*Violeta*)**.** Mean pitch of 186.2 Hz and 162.8 WPM

Male1 (*Vicente*)**.** Mean pitch of 111.3 Hz and 155.3 WPM

Male2 (*Viriato*)**.** Mean pitch of 98.0 Hz and 166.9 WPM

The voices selected were based on studies that suggest the use different gender voices to enhance speech segregation [6] [10]. We only used voices with similar pitches (*male1* and *male2*) in the condition with three voices, but in very far spatial locations (right and left ears, respectively). Moreover, the *female* voice was placed between them (in a central position), to maximize the segregation of the three voices. Such spatial and frequency differences assured the segregation of the voices, without the need to manipulate their frequencies, which would reduce their quality without guaranteed benefits on speech segregation [15].

In order to obtain the desired speech rate variations, we manipulated the audio files using the *Praat* software[4] with a linear time compression algorithm (PSOLA [21]). Small gains could be accomplished with non-linear methods that use, for instance, silence-cut, but with a significant increase in system complexity [19]. Furthermore, we measured the sound intensity levels of all sound files, obtaining a mean intensity value in decibels. Then, we used *Praat* to adjust the voice intensities so that all voices had the same mean intensity level.

3.2 Methodology

We based our decisions on the results of previous experiments, regarding both the speech rates used and the concurrent speech setting. Moreover, we performed a pilot study with 5 people, where we gradually increased the speech rate with one, two and three voices in order to determine their maximum values.

3.2.1 Concurrent Speech

Previous research about the *Cocktail Party Effect* has shown that speech intelligibility decreases as the number of voices increase (e.g. [6]). In particular, we have reported a greater decrease with four voices [15]. As a result, besides a one-voice condition, we only included two and three concurrent voices.

In order to enhance speech segregation, we used different, spatially separated voices (Figure 1). The spatial separation was inspired on experiments that use equally spaced positions in the users' frontal horizontal plane (e.g. [6] [11] [15]). In the *One-Voice* condition, we use a single channel with a *Female* voice. In *Two-Voices*, the speech sources were separated by 180º, where the *Female* and *Male1* voices talked to the users' right and left ear, respectively. With *Three-Voices*, the speech sources were separated by 90º, where the two *Male* voices talked to the users' right and left ears, with the *Female* voice in a central position.

[1] https://bitbucket.org/sound/texttospeeches (Visited in 07/2015)

2 http://www.l2f.inesc-id.pt/

3 http://www.voiceinteraction.eu/

[4] http://www.fon.hum.uva.nl/praat/ (Visited in 07/2015)

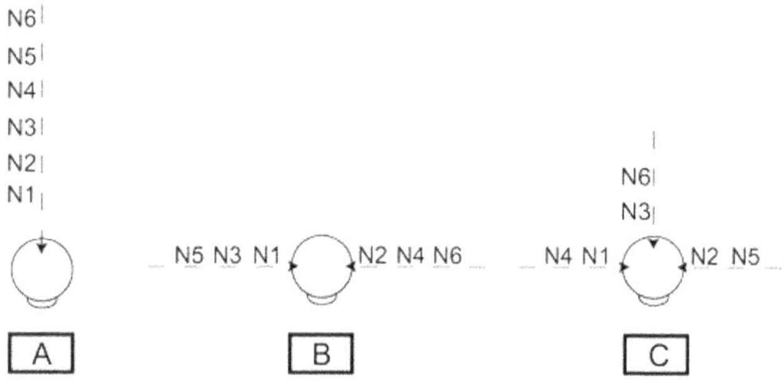

Figure 1. The voices spatial positions in the frontal horizontal plane for A) One, B) Two and C) Three voices. It shows a sequence of 6 sentences (*News*) for all conditions.

3.2.2 *Information Bandwidth (IB) Conditions: Voices and Speech Rates*

A direct comparison between the use of faster speech rates and the use of concurrent speech, can only be achieved if both approaches take the same time to read the same amount of information. Table 1 shows all the *IB X Voice* conditions and the speech rate increment comparatively to the *default-rate* (and the mean WPM rates of the voices used).

For instance, an *IB* of 2 requires the use of two concurrent voices with the *default-rate* (condition *2 X 2*) or a single voice twice as fast (*2 X 1*). Likewise, three *default-rate* voices (*3 X 3*) match the use of one voice three times faster (*3 X 1*) or two voices 1.5 times faster (*3 X 2*). These first two conditions correspond to a final time to complete reading the content of half and one third the *default-rate* reading time with one voice, respectively. In the subsequent conditions, we reduced gradually the time needed to read the entire content, which resulted in faster speech rates either with one, two or three voices. The pilot study helped us to determine the maximum speech rates for each number of voices in order to avoid to frustrate and to overwhelm the participants.

In order to enable the direct comparison among the use of one, two or three voices, we used six sentences in all conditions. This means that in the conditions with one voice, the participants received the six sentences sequentially. In contrast, with two voices they listened to three sequences of two simultaneous sentences, and two sequences of three simultaneous sentences with three voices (exemplified in Figure 1). In all conditions, a short *beep* was played between news to indicate the end of the current sentence(s) and to prepare the following.

4. DATA COLLECTION

We referred to *Relevance Scanning* as the process of assessing "*which pieces of information are relevant and deserve further attention*" [15]. In our prior experiment, we restricted the number of relevant sources to one and asked the user to understand its content. In contrast, herein we focused exclusively on the relevance assessment, but forcing the users to make such decision for all sentences instead of focusing on a single one. With this goal in mind, we were able to measure the participants' ability to obtain a basic understanding of all sentences in order to determine their relevance.

We gathered a dataset of 200 news snippets from a Portuguese news site archive, which included only raw text and had similar sizes and durations (between 11 and 14 seconds). The news were divided in three groups, so that their durations could differ the maximum of one second from each other. This is most important in the concurrent speech conditions, since larger periods with one voice would benefit them. In order to overcome that issue, we stopped all concurrent voices at the same time (when the first one ended).

4.1 Relevance Scanning Task

All news were categorized in three different topics by the researchers: "*sports*", "*politics and economy*" and "*television, arts and celebrities*". We validated this categorization by asking 4 people to categorize all news. All news that could fit different categories were excluded.

In all trials, participants were told one of these topics and had to identify which news were related to that specific topic. Such task demanded the user to try to understand the topic of all news in order to assess its relevance. The news were chosen randomly such that none was presented twice per participant. We guaranteed the existence of two to four relevant news in all trials, but participants were unaware of this fact, believing there could be zero to six (all relevant) news.

4.2 Procedure

The experiment took approximately 50 minutes per participant and was conducted in a single session in a training center for blind and visually impaired people. First, we informed the participants that the overall purpose of the experiment was to investigate two approaches to accelerate the scanning for relevant digital information: faster speech rates and concurrent speech. Then, we performed an oral questionnaire about demographic data, screen reader usage and conducted a working memory assessment using the *Digit Span* of the revised *Wechsler Adult Intelligence Scale* (WAIS-R) [32].

Afterwards, we explained the experimental setting, which included the existence of conditions with one, two and three voices and how they work; the task of identifying the relevant news among six news and how to make such identification. In all conditions, the participants were in a sit position with the hands on top of a table. To mark one sentence as relevant, participants needed to tap the table in front of them:

1. **One-Voice.** Tap any of the hands to select the current sentence as relevant;
2. **Two-Voices.** Tap with the right or left hand to select the current sentence of the right or left ear, respectively (should tap both if both are relevant, but not necessarily tap at the same time)
3. **Three-Voices**. Same as Two-Voices for lateral sources, but should tap on top of a book between the two hands (placed there for the purpose) to select the central voice.

The three possible topics were thoroughly described in order to clarify their meaning and avoid interpretation doubts. Finally, we referred that participants could always correct a selection, during (e.g. withdraw a selection after understanding the tap was incorrect) and after a trial (e.g. "*I didn't tap the first on the left, but at the end I understood that it was relevant as well*").

Participants performed three practice trials before starting the evaluation, one for each number of voices in their first available *IB* condition. They performed every *IB X Voice* condition presented in Table 1 twice, resulting in 30 trials per participant. We randomized the order of the *Voice* conditions within every *IB* to enable a fair direct comparison between conditions that take the

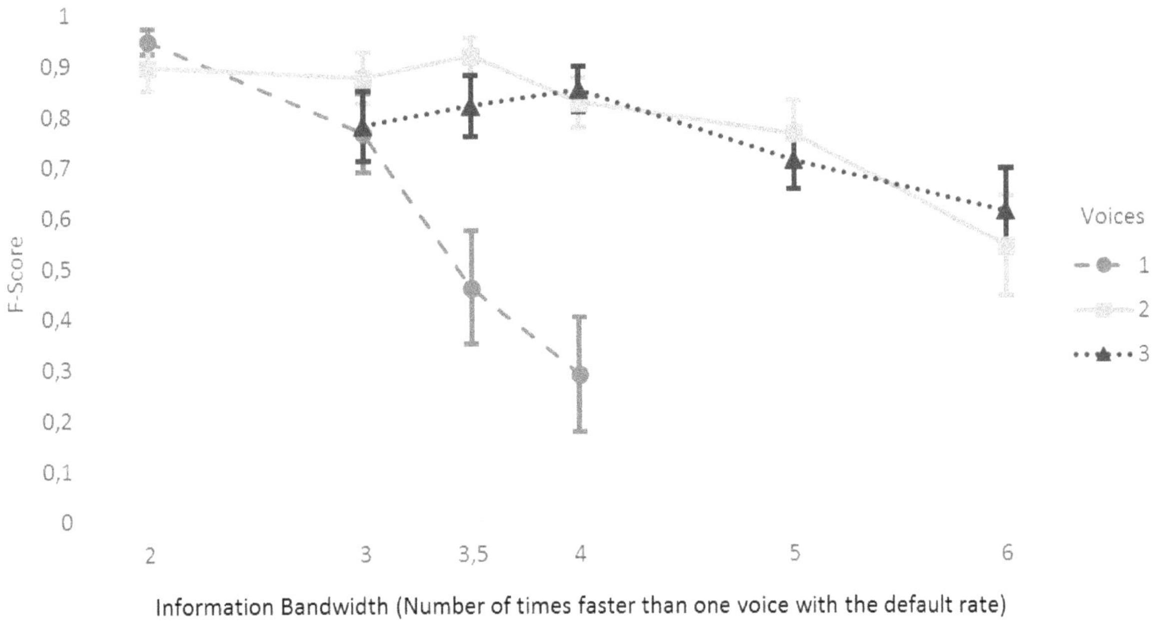

Figure 2. F-Score performance for all *Information Bandwidth X Voice* condition. Error bars denote 95% confidence intervals.

same time to complete. The *IB* conditions had a fixed ascending order, as we wanted to take advantage of the little practice of previous trials to understand the speech rate limits with one, two and three voices, rather than understanding which *IB* condition presents better results for novice users.

In each trial, we first indicated the *Voice* condition and the relevant topic that participants needed to identify (e.g. *sports*); then, we played the news and participants identified the relevant ones as they listened to them. After the consecutive two trials with the same *IB X Voice* condition, participants were asked the *Single Ease Question* [24], which required them to rate the task easiness for that condition, using a 7-point *Likert Scale* (from *Very Difficult* – 1 – to *Very Easy* – 7) .

4.3 Apparatus

The auditory feedback was provided by the aforementioned *Text-to-Speeches* framework. Participants used *AKG K540 Headphones* that were connected to the researcher laptop and were able to adjust the volume to a comfortable rate. The researcher controlled the whole experiment through a Java application and registered the participants' answers as they selected the relevant news. Both sound and video were collected during the whole session for further analysis.

4.4 Participants

We recruited for this experiment 30 visually impaired participants, 9 female and 21 male. Their ages ranged from 23 to 64 (M=43.43, SD=12.07) years old. None participant reported having neither severe nor moderate hearing impairments. There were 12 fully blind (light perception at most) and 18 low vision participants. Moreover, 28 participants used screen readers to interact with their devices on a daily basis. Nineteen (19) participants had a congenital visual impairment or acquired it before turning 18 years old.

4.5 Design and Analysis

We used a within-subjects design where participants performed each *IB X Voice* condition (in Table 1) twice, resulting in a total of 30 trials. One participant did not perform the last two conditions (*6X2* and *6X3*) due to fatigue, while another did not perform one condition (*6X2*) due to time restrictions. Overall, this experiment resulted in 894 trials.

In order to evaluate the participants' accuracy identifying the relevant news, we relied on the *F-Score* as it accounts both for *Precision* and *Recall* (their harmonic mean). *Precision* refers to the fraction of identified news that were in fact relevant, while *Recall* refers to the fraction of relevant news that were identified. This measure accounts both for erroneous identifications and missing identifications. When no news are identified, the *Precision* value is undefined and the *F-Score* equals the *Recall*, which is zero. *Shapiro-Wilkinson* tests were applied to the dependent variable *F-Score* in all *IB X Voice* conditions. As they were not normally distributed, we applied the *Friedman* test when comparing three or more groups and the *Wilcoxon Signed Rank* test to perform the *post-hocs* between pairs of samples (with *Bonferroni corrections* to deal with multiple comparisons).

5. RESULTS

Our main goal was to understand how the use of faster speech rates and concurrent speech affect the performance of a *Relevance Scanning* task. In this evaluation, participants were required to pay attention to six news and identify the ones referring to a particular topic. First, we compare the use of different voices within *Information Bandwidth* (*IB*) conditions. Furthermore, we analyze how each *Voice* condition evolves as the *IB* increases. Figure 2 shows the *F-Score* for each *IB X Voice* condition. Finally, we analyze the effect of users' characteristics on their performance and their subjective opinions and ratings to all *IB X Voice* conditions.

5.1 F-Score Within *Information Bandwidth*

The first *IB* condition – **2** – comprises only two *Voice* conditions (*One-Voice* and *Two-Voices*), because the speech rate would have been slower than the default one in the *Three-Voices* one. In this condition, a *Wilcoxon Signed Rank* test (Z=-1.940, p=.052) showed no significant differences, but a slightly superior *F-score* for the *One-Voice* condition (M=0.949, SD=0.070) than the *Two-Voices* one (M=0.897, SD=0.130).

The following three *IB* conditions – **3**, **3.5** and **4** – comprise the three *Voice* conditions. *Friedman* tests showed significant differences among *Voice* conditions, within each *IB* (p<.01 in all comparisons). *Post-hoc* analysis of *IB* **3** revealed a significant advantage for the *Two-Voices* (M=0.875, SD=0.142) condition over the *One-Voice* (M=0.766, SD=0.216) and *Three-Voices* (M=0.780, SD=0.192) (p<.01 in both comparisons). Moreover, no significant differences were found between *One* and *Three-Voices* conditions (Z= -0.157, p=.875).

IB **3.5** presented clearer differences among the *Voice* conditions (p<.001 in all post-hoc comparisons). Again, the *Two-Voices* condition presented a significantly higher *F-score* (M=0.918, SD=0.101), followed by *Three-Voices* (M=0.820, SD=0.170) and at last by *One-Voice* (M=0.461, SD=0.312).

In the *IB* **4** condition, *Two-Voices* (M=0.826, SD=0.138) and *Three-Voices* (M=0.852, SD=0.126) obtained clearly higher *F-Scores* than the *One-Voice* (M=0.289, SD=0.315) condition (p<.001 in both comparisons). However, in this case *Two-Voices* and *Three-Voices* scores presented no significant differences (Z=-1.067, p=.286). *IB* **4** was the last condition with *One-Voice*. This decision was based on literature reviews and a pilot study, but it is reinforced by these results as they showed a clear disadvantage in comparison to its alternatives.

IB **5** presented no significant differences between the use of *Two-Voices* (M=0.763, SD=0.183) and *Three-Voices* (M=0.712, SD=0.162) (Z=-1.320, p=.187). Although with lower *F-Scores*, *IB* **6** presented no significant differences (Z=-0.913, p=.361) between the two conditions as well (*Two-Voices*: M=0.542, SD=0.265; *Three-Voices*: M=0.61, SD=0.232).

5.2 F-Score Within *Voice* Conditions

In this section, we analyze the effect that the increase of *IB* (and speech rate) has on each *Voice* condition. Figure 2 depicts a clear and consistent decrease in performance in the ***One-Voice*** condition as the *IB* increases (p<.001 in all consecutive comparisons). This result is explained by the very fast speech rates that this condition reaches. To cite one example, *IB 4* results in a speech rate four times faster than the *default-rate*, which is approximately 651.2 *WPM*.

As the *IB* increases, the speech rates of both *Two-Voices* and *Three-Voices* conditions increase at a lower rate than with *One-Voice*. In particular, *Two-Voices* and *Three-Voices* speech rates are half and one-third the rate of the *One-Voice* condition, respectively. These smaller rate increments across *IB* conditions resulted in smoother differences overall.

The ***Two-Voices*** analysis revealed a very similar performance in the first three *IB* conditions (2, 3 and 3.5). In fact, the mean performance slightly increased (non-significant: Z=-1.605, p=.109) from *IB* 3 to 3.5 (from 0.875 to 0.918), probably due to the slighter increase in speech rate and a minor practice effect from previous conditions. *IB* 4 showed a significant difference in comparison to *3.5* (Z=-3.061, p<.005) and was the first to present a considerable difference when comparing with the first condition (*IB* 2) (Z=-2.328, p=.020). In this condition, the speech rate of both voices equals 2**default-rate* and even though its performance decreased, it reached a mean *F-Score* of 0.826. Furthermore, 7 participants identified correctly all news in both trials in this condition (14 in the first condition), suggesting it may also be used for *Relevance Scanning*. Although results did not show a significant difference between *IB* 4 and 5 (Z=-1.061, p=.289), they showed a difference between 5 and 6 (Z=-3.725, p<.001).

The ***Three-Voices*** condition started in the second *IB* condition (*IB* **3**) with a mean *F-Score* of 0.780. The speech rate increases very smoothly with three concurrent voices, which explains the absence of significant differences among *IB* 3, 3.5 and 4. The mean performance ended up reaching the maximum of 0.852 in *IB* 4, possibly due to the brief practice time in the previous conditions. The analysis revealed significant differences between *IB* 4 and 5 (Z=-3.328, p<.001). Finally, the comparison between *IB* 5 and 6 also suggested a small difference in F-Score performances (Z=-2.250, p=.024). In these two conditions, only 3 participants were able to answer correctly to both trials.

In all *Voice* conditions, performance was affected by *Recall* as *IB* increased. Most participants were still able to identify correctly the relevant snippets (high *Precision* values), but failed to identify other relevant snippets in higher *IB* conditions. For instance, the mean *Precision* values for both *Two-Voices* and *Three-Voices* conditions were always above 0.88 (between 0.970 and 0.882). The *One-Voice* condition reached lower, but still high values in the 3.5 and 4 *IB* conditions (0.831 and 0.758, respectively). In contrast, the mean *Recall* reached 0.413 and 0.256 in the same *IB* conditions with *One-Voice*. In particular, in the *IB 4* condition, 13 participants did not select any snippet as relevant, resulting in undefined *Precision*, zero *Recall*, and zero *F-Score*.

The mean *Recall* values for both *Two-Voices* and *Three-Voices* conditions also decreased as the *IB* increased. *Two-Voices* reached 0.771, 0.742 and 0.478 in the *IB* 4, 5 and 6 conditions, respectively, showing a greater decrease in the last one (the speech rate is 3**default-rate*). In the same *IB* conditions, *Three-Voices* reached 0.797, 0.639 and 0.532, respectively.

5.3 User Characteristics

Mann-Whitney U tests revealed no significant differences between fully blind and low vision participants for all *IB X Voice* conditions. Likewise, no differences were found between people that acquired their visual impairment early or late in life.

Medium to large negative correlations (from *rho*=-.411 to *rho*=-.591, p<.05) were found between the participants' ages and their *F-Scores* in all conditions where the speech rate is 2.5 times the *default-rate* or higher (*One-Voice* with *IB* 3, 3.5 and 4; and *Two-Voices* with *IB* 5 and 6). Such correlations are supported by previous research that demonstrated a decline in speech perception with higher speech rates as people age (e.g. [12]). Furthermore, a negative medium correlation was found between age and the *IB* 3.5 *X Two-Voice* condition (*rho*=-.445, p<.05), but we found no explanation to such correlation.

The working memory is known to affect the ability to block out distracting information in concurrent speech scenarios [9]. In line

Table 2. Results of the Single Ease Question for all Information Bandwidth X Voice conditions.

Information Bandwidth	Voices	Median	Q1	Q3	IQR
2	1	6	5	7	2
	2	5.5	4.25	6	1.75
3	1	4	2	5	3
	2	5	5	6	1
	3	5	4	6	2
3.5	1	2.5	1	4	3
	2	5	4	6	2
	3	5	4	5.75	1.75
4	1	1.5	1	3	2
	2	5	4	6	2
	3	5	4	6	2
5	2	5	3	5	2
	3	5	3.25	5	1.75
6	2	3.5	2	5	3
	3	4	2	4	2

with this relation, we found medium to high positive correlations between the participants' digit span scores and all *Three-Voices* conditions (*rho*=.390 to *rho*=.543, p<.05), but none with *One-Voice* and *Two-Voices*. This suggests that the use of *Three-Voices* may hamper the ability to scan for relevant content, for people with lower working memory. However, a long-term analysis could help to determine if they could benefit from practice and overcome such disadvantage as they become more proficient.

5.4 Subjective Feedback

Table 2 shows the *Median*, *Quartiles 1* and *3*, and *Inter-Quartile ranges (IQR)* of participants' answers to the *Single Ease Question* (1 to 7), for all *IB X Voice* conditions. *Friedman* tests revealed significant differences both within *IB* and within *Voice* conditions (p<.01 in all tests). The condition *IB* 2 was the only one where participants rated *One-Voice* as easier (Z=-2.690, p<.01). Participants commented they felt more comfortable listening to a single voice because they use it daily and do not need to divide their attention.

In the subsequent *IB* conditions (3, 3.5 and 4), *One-Voice* was rated as significantly more difficult than both *Two-Voices* and *Three-Voices* (p<.001 in all *post-hocs*), which supports the performance *F-Scores* previously presented. In contrast, when comparing the ratings given to *Two* and *Three-Voices* there seems to be a small difference in prejudice of the latter only in *IB* 3 (Z=-1.969, p=.049), and no significant differences in the others. This can be explained by the first impact when listening to *Three-Voices*. However, the very slight increase in speech rate did not increase the difficulty in the subsequent *IB* conditions (3.5 and 4). *Three-Voices* started to be considered marginally more difficult in *IB* 5 (Z=-1.964, p=.054 in comparison to *IB* 3). Yet, the difficulty increased significantly from 5 to 6 (Z=-3.214, p<.001).

Two-Voices ratings evolved very similarly, as the first marginal difference was found between *IB* 2 and 4 (Z=-1.941, p=.052), but was amplified in the next conditions (Z=-2.441, p=.015 between *IB* 4 and 5; and Z=-3.611, p<.001 between 5 and 6). On the other hand, the *One-Voice* condition was considerably more difficult as the speech rate (and *IB*) increases (p<.001 in all *post-hocs*).

Only four participants expressed their preference for *One-Voice* overall, but recognized the greater difficulty to understand the content in the last two *One-Voice* conditions (*IB* 3.5 and 4). One participant referred that: *"with such high speech rates I was only able to capture a few keywords, but was not able to get a deeper understanding of the content"*. In contrast, in the same *IB* conditions, *Two-Voices* and *Three-Voices* enabled a *"greater understanding of the content, since it is straightforward to focus on a particular voice and also to switch the attention to another"*. The breaking point was in the last *IB* conditions, where *Two* and *Three-Voices* reach faster speech rates. One participant stated that *"the problem is that with faster speech rates I do not have the time to roam through all voices, but I can understand them!"*

In general, as the *IB* increased, participants preferred the use of *Two-Voices* (until IB 3.5 or 4). However, only three participants clearly stated that the use of *Three-Voices* was excessive. In contrast with previous experiments where the central voice was found more difficult to understand, herein 21 participants (70%) noted an equal ability to understand all sound sources. This may be related to the greater contrast between the central voice and the others. One participant commented that he *"could easily focus his attention on the lateral sources due to their locations, but also in the central voice because it was so different from the others"*.

After completing all trials, four participants reported their preference for specific topics (e.g. *sports* or *politics*). They noted that it is easier to capture the topic if they are indeed interested and know more information that can help in that process. One participant stated: *"I like soccer, so if I listen a player's name I immediately relate it to sports. However, if I listen a television series or an actor's name it is more difficult as I do not know many of them"*.

6. DISCUSSION

Based on the results described in the previous section, we present the main *take-home* messages by revisiting our research questions.

It is better to use *Two-Voices* or *Three-Voices* with slightly faster speech rates than *One-Voice* with very fast speech rates. Within *Information Bandwidth* (IB) comparisons showed an explicit advantage for concurrent speech conditions, unless for the first condition where *One-Voice* has a speech rate of 2**default-rate*. In the subsequent conditions, the *One-Voice* speech rate has to increase substantially in order to keep up with *Two-Voices* and *Three-Voices* completion times. The use of speech rates faster than 3**default-rate* markedly decreased the ability to identify the relevant sentences with *One-Voice*, when compared with the alternatives within *IB* conditions. For example, with a bandwidth of 3.5, the *One-Voice F-Score* performance averaged 0.461, while Two-Voices and Three-Voices averaged 0.918 and 0.820, respectively. In this condition, 1, 12 and 8 participants identified correctly all news with *One*, *Two* and *Three-Voices*, respectively. In line with this results, *Two-Voices* was significantly better than *Three-Voices* in the first conditions (up to *IB* 3.5), but their values became very similar as the speech rate (and *IB*) increased.

Gradually increasing the speech rate motivate a major performance loss with *One-Voice*, but a smoother evolution with *Two* and *Three-Voices*. Reducing the time needed to read the six sentences implies a speech rate increment, but at different rates for *One*, *Two* and *Three-Voices* conditions. Results revealed that the larger increments with *One-Voice* lead to a consistent decrease in the ability to identify the relevant sentences (F-Score averages decreased from 0.949 to 0.766, 0.461 and 0.289). In contrast, both *Two-Voices* and *Three-Voices* maintained a very similar performance until the *IB* conditions 3.5 and 4, respectively. This means that the smaller speech rate increments in concurrent speech conditions alongside with a very brief practice from preceding trials enabled participants to maintain their performance, while reducing the time needed to complete the task.

Using *Two-Voices* with 1.75*default-rate* or 2default-rate* is the best compromise between a basic comprehension of the sentences and the speed to process them.** More often than not, participants felt uncertain about the use of concurrent speech before starting the experiment. However, in addition to a clear advantage in performance, participants also preferred the concurrent speech conditions as the *IB* increased. In particular, most participants referred to *Two-Voices* in *IB* 3.5 or 4 as the best compromise between the speed to process all the information and the comprehension of the news topics. These conditions reached a performance of 0.913 and 0.826, respectively. Similar results were also achieved by *Three-Voices* in *IB* conditions 3.5 and 4. Although these values did not show an always perfect identification of the relevant sentences, participants reported an advantage when identifying news of topics that they are genuinely interested and therefore have more knowledge. Overall, the results suggest that the best compromise between information consumption speed and comprehension is the use of *Two-Voices* with a rate 1.75**default-rate* (~278.4 WPM). However, some participants were able to maintain their performance with faster rates. Similarly to what occurs with the use of a single auditory channel, we believe that experience will enable users to gradually increase the concurrent voices rate.

7. CONCLUSIONS

Both the use of faster speech rates and concurrent speech can accelerate blind people's scanning for relevant digital information. We have presented an experiment that compares these two approaches and combines them by gradually increasing the speech rate with one, two and three voices. Results show that *Two* and *Three-Voices* with speech rates slightly faster than the *default-rate*, enable a significantly faster scanning for relevant information, while maintaining its comprehension. In contrast, to keep-up with concurrent speech completion times, *One-Voice* requires larger speech rate increments, which cause a greater loss in performance. Overall, the use of *Two-Voices* with a rate 1.75**default-rate* (~278.4 WPM) enables the most efficient *Relevance Scanning* without a loss in performance. However, several participants were also able to maintain a basic understanding of the sentences in the *IB 4* condition with both *Two-Voices* (2**default-rate*) and *Three-Voices* (1.333**default-rate*). Furthermore, when analyzing the effect of user characteristics, we found that *Age* correlates negatively with their performance when speech rates are higher than *2.5*default-rate*. Moreover, the participants' working memory correlated with their performance with *Three-Voices*, suggesting an effect on the ability to ignore distracting information. A long-term experiment may help to understand if practice can mitigate such effects.

In this experiment, we limited the news snippets durations, in order to guarantee that the concurrent speech sources ended at the same time. It would be interesting to understand how scanning for relevant content is affected by the length of the sentences. In particular, in the last conditions with *Three-Voices*, participants referred that the main problem was not having time to go through all voices, reporting no difficulties to understand their content.

Along with other experiments inspired in the *Cocktail Party Effect,* this experiment supports the use of concurrent speech to accelerate blind people's scanning for digital information. The use of faster, concurrent speech clearly outperformed the use of a single voice with very fast speech rates. While this experiment focused on the identification of relevant news snippets, it would be interesting to explore different contexts and tasks where this approach could be leveraged. Similar scenarios are the ones of websites and applications that comprise lists of items, where only part of them are relevant to the user (e.g. Social Networking Sites, search engine results, RSS feeds, e-mail). Another interesting scenario is the one of notifications that could use a secondary voice to avoid interrupting the user. In contrast, scenarios that require full attention and the comprehension of the whole text do not seem to be appropriate to the use of concurrent speech, nor very fast speech rates as supported by the greater decrease in *Recall*. In future work, we will investigate different scenarios and interaction methods to enable the consumption and exploration of digital information using simultaneous speech sources.

8. ACKNOWLEDGMENTS

The authors would like to thank Fundação Raquel e Martin Sain, Carlos Bastardo and all participants. We also thank both Voice Interaction and INESC ID's Spoken Language Systems Laboratory. This work was supported by the Portuguese Foundation for Science and Technology, under grants UID/CEC/50021/2013 and INCENTIVO/EEI/LA0021/2014.

9. REFERENCES

[1] Ahmed, F., Borodin, Y., Puzis, Y., and Ramakrishnan, I. V. 2012. Why Read if You Can Skim : Towards Enabling Faster Screen Reading. In *Proceedings of the International Cross-Disciplinary Conference on Web Accessibility (W4A).*

[2] Arons, B. 1997 SpeechSkimmer : A System for Interactively Skimming Recorded Speech. *ACM Transactions on Computer-Human Interaction (TOCHI) - Special issue on speech as data 4*, 1, 3–38.

[3] Asakawa, C., Takagi, H., Ino, S., and Ifukube, T. 2003 Maximum listening speeds for the blind. In *Proceedings of the International Community for Auditory Display (ICAD), pp. 276–279.*

[4] Bigham, J., Cavender, A., Brudvik, J., Wobbrock, J., and Ladner, R. 2007. WebinSitu: a comparative analysis of blind and sighted browsing behavior. In *Proceedings of the 9th international ACM SIGACCESS conference on Computers and accessibility (ASSETS).*

[5] Borodin, Y., and Bigham, J. 2010 More than meets the eye: a survey of screen-reader browsing strategies. In *Proceedings of the International Cross-Disciplinary Conference on Web Accessibility (W4A)*

[6] Brungart, D. S., and Simpson, B. D. 2005. Improving Multitalker Speech Communication with Advanced Audio Displays. *Air Force Research Lab Wright-Patterson AFB OH.*

[7] Burton, H. 2003. Visual cortex activity in early and late blind people. *The Journal of neuroscience : the official journal of the Society for Neuroscience 23*, 10, 4005–11.

[8] Cherry, E. 1953. Some experiments on the recognition of speech, with one and with two ears. *The Journal of the acoustical society of America.*

[9] Conway, M. 2001. Sensory-perceptual episodic memory and its context: autobiographical memory. *Philosophical transactions of the Royal Society of London. Series B, Biological sciences 356*, 1413, 1375–84.

[10] Darwin, C. J., Brungart, D. S., and Simpson, B. D. 2003 Effects of fundamental frequency and vocal-tract length changes on attention to one of two simultaneous talkers. *The Journal of the Acoustical Society of America 114*, 5, 2913.

[11] Drullman, R., and Bronkhorst, A. 2000. Multichannel speech intelligibility and talker recognition using monaural, binaural, and three-dimensional auditory presentation. *The Journal of the Acoustical Society of America 107, 4, 2224-2235.*

[12] Fostick, L., Ben-Artzi, E., and Babkoff, H. 2013 Aging and speech perception: Beyond hearing threshold and cognitive ability. *Journal of basic and clinical physiology and pharmacology 24*, 3, 175–183.

[13] Goble, C., Harper, S., and Stevens, R. 2000. The travails of visually impaired web travellers. *Proceedings of the eleventh ACM on Hypertext and hypermedia - HYPERTEXT*, 1–10.

[14] Goose, S., and Moller, C. 1999. A 3D Audio Only Interactive Web Browser : Using Spatialization to Convey Hypermedia Document Structure. *Proceedings of the seventh ACM international conference on Multimedia, pp.* 363–371.

[15] Guerreiro, J., and Gonçalves, D. 2014. Text-to-Speeches: Evaluating the Perception of Concurrent Speech by Blind People. In *Proceedings of the 16th international ACM SIGACCESS conference on Computers & accessibility*, ACM, pp. 169–176.

[16] Guerreiro, J., Rodrigues, A., Montague, K., Guerreiro, T., Nicolau, H., and Gonçalves, D. 2015. TabLETS Get Physical: Non-Visual Text Entry on Tablet Devices. In *Proceedings of the SIGCHI conference on Human factors in computing systems*, ACM, 39-42.

[17] Guerreiro, J., and Gonçalves, D. 2013 Blind People Interacting with Mobile Social Applications: Open Challenges. In *Mobile Accessibility Workshop at CHI.*

[18] Harper, S., and Patel, N. 2005 Gist Summaries for Visually Impaired Surfers. In *Proceedings of the 7th international ACM SIGACCESS conference on Computers and accessibility*, pp. 90–97.

[19] He, L., and Gupta, A. 2001. Exploring benefits of non-linear time compression. In *Proceedings of the ninth ACM international conference on Multimedia*, ACM, pp. 382–391.

[20] Hugdahl, K., Ek, M., Takio, F., Rintee, T., Tuomainen, J., Haarala, C., and Hämäläinen, H. 2004. Blind individuals show enhanced perceptual and attentional sensitivity for identification of speech sounds. *Brain research. Cognitive brain research 19*, 1, 28–32.

[21] Moulines, E., and Charpentier, F. 1990. Pitch-synchronous waveform processing techniques for text-to-speech synthesis using diphones. *Speech communication 9*, 5, 453–467.

[22] Paulo, S., Oliveira, L. C., Mendes, C., Figueira, L., Cassaca, R., Viana, C., and Moniz, H. 2008. Dixi–a generic text-to-speech system for european portuguese. *Computational Processing of the Portuguese Language*, 91–100.

[23] Sato, D., Zhu, S., Kobayashi, M., Takagi, H., and Asakawa, C. 2011. Sasayaki : Voice Augmented Web Browsing Experience. In *Proceedings of the SIGCHI Conference on Human Factors in Computing Systems*, pp. 2769–2778.

[24] Sauro, J., and Dumas, J. S. 2009. Comparison of three one-question, post-task usability questionnaires. In *Proceedings of the SIGCHI Conference on Human Factors in Computing Systems*, ACM, pp. 1599–1608.

[25] Schmandt, C., and Mullins, A. 1995. AudioStreamer: exploiting simultaneity for listening. In *Conference companion on Human factors in Computing Systems (CHI'95)*, ACM, 218–219.

[26] Sodnik, J., and Tomažic, S. 2009. Spatial Speaker : 3D Java Text-to-Speech Converter. In *Proceedings of the World Congress on Engineering and Computer Science*, vol. II.

[27] Stent, A., Syrdal, A., and Mishra, T. 2011. On the Intelligibility of Fast Synthesized Speech for Individuals with Early-Onset Blindness. . In *Proceedings of the international ACM SIGACCESS conference on Computers & accessibility*, ACM, 211–218.

[28] Takagi, H., Saito, S., Fukuda, K., and Asakawa, C. 2007 Analysis of navigability of Web applications for improving blind usability. *ACM Transactions on Computer-Human Interaction 14*, 3, 13–es.

[29] Trouvain, J. 2007. On the comprehension of extremely fast synthetic speech.

[30] Valentini-Botinhao, C., Toman, M., Pucher, M., Schabus, D., and Yamagishi, J. 2014. Intelligibility analysis of fast synthesized speech. In *Fifteenth Annual Conference of the International Speech Communication Association.*

[31] Vigo, M., and Harper, S. 2013. Coping tactics employed by visually disabled users on the web. *International Journal of Human-Computer Studies 71*, 11, 1013–1025.

[32] Wechsler, D. 1981. WAIS-R manual: Wechsler adult intelligence scale-revised. *Psychological Corporation.*

[33] Wenzel, E. M., Arruda, M., Kistler, D. J., and Wightman, F. L. 1993. Localization using nonindividualized head-related transfer functions. *The Journal of the Acoustical Society of America 94*, 1, 111–123.

Towards Large Scale Evaluation of Novel Sonification Techniques for Non Visual Shape Exploration

Andrea Gerino
Dept. of Computer Science
Università degli Studi di Milano
EveryWare Technologies
andrea.gerino@unimi.it

Lorenzo Picinali
School of Design Engineering
Imperial College London
l.picinali@imperial.ac.uk

Cristian Bernareggi
Dept. of Computer Science
Università degli Studi di Milano
EveryWare Technologies
cristian.bernareggi@unimi.it

Nicolò Alabastro
Dept. of Computer Science
Università degli Studi di Milano
nicolo.alabastro
@studenti.unimi.it

Sergio Mascetti
Dept. of Computer Science
Università degli Studi di Milano
EveryWare Technologies
sergio.mascetti@unimi.it

ABSTRACT

There are several situations in which a person with visual impairment or blindness needs to extract information from an image. Examples include everyday activities, like reading a map, as well as educational activities, like exercises to develop visuospatial skills.

In this contribution we propose a set of 6 sonification techniques to recognize simple shapes on touchscreen devices. The effectiveness of these sonification techniques is evaluated though *Invisible Puzzle*, a mobile application that makes it possible to conduct non-supervised evaluation sessions. *Invisible Puzzle* adopts a gamification approach and is a preliminary step in the development of a complete game that will make it possible to conduct a large scale evaluation with hundreds or thousands of blind users.

With *Invisible Puzzle* we conducted 131 tests with sighted subjects and 18 tests with subjects with blindness. All subjects involved in the process successfully completed the evaluation session, with high engagement, hence showing the effectiveness of the evaluation procedure. Results give interesting insights on the differences among the sonification techniques and, most importantly, show that, after a short training, subjects are able to identify many different shapes.

Categories and Subject Descriptors

H.5.2 [**INFORMATION INTERFACES AND PRESENTATION**]: User Interfaces—*Evaluation/methodology, Auditory (non-speech) feedback, User-centered design, Interaction styles*; K.4.2 [**COMPUTERS AND SOCIETY**]: Assistive technologies for persons with disabilities

ASSETS'15, October 26–28, 2015, Lisbon, Portugal.

ACM 978-1-4503-3400-6/15/10 ...$15.00.
DOI: http://dx.doi.org/10.1145/2700648.2809848.

Keywords

Accessibility; Visual impairment or blindness; Sonification; Image recognition; Gamification; Remote evaluation; Touchscreen devices

1. INTRODUCTION

Access to images is a challenge for people with visual impairment or blindness and this causes hindrances in developing visuospatial skills as well as in education, for example to study STEM subjects. People that can rely on residual sight generally use magnifiers in the form of a physical lens or an electronic device. A different approach is needed by people with blindness or people that cannot rely on residual sight[1].

To overcome these difficulties, one common approach consists in transferring the image on a physical support that can be haptically perceived. Examples include tactile drawings (either printed with special printers or hand-drawn) and the arithmetic board. These solutions have the main advantage of being of immediate use and conceptually simple but also have several drawbacks. First, in many cases these supports need to be manually created (e.g., a tactile drawing) or they need to be printed with expensive hardware. Second, physical supports are bulky and this is a limitation, for example, when they are used for educational purposes. Third, in order to be clearly readable, these physical supports cannot contain too many details, including text and other symbols.

In order to overcome these limitations, a different approach consists in conveying the image information through the acoustic channel by sonification. Several solutions adopting this approach have been proposed in the scientific literature. Some of them do not involve an interacting system or are based on an interaction mediated by a keyboard. In both cases, a blind person cannot rely on proprioception to support the image understanding process. Vice versa, other solutions are based on touchscreen devices that allow users to explore the image with their fingers, hence taking advantage from proprioception. As we show in this contribution,

[1]In this contribution we refer to "people with blindness" or "blind people" to also indicate people with low vision that cannot rely on residual sight to explore enlarged images.

these solutions, which we call *sonification modes*, can adopt different combinations of exploration paradigms, audio rendering techniques and sound generators. Given the large variety of possible solutions, a challenging task is to compare them to evaluate advantages and drawbacks.

In this contribution we propose a set of 6 sonification modes that combine elements of existing techniques with novel solutions, such as sound spatialisation (employing both interaural level and time differences) and music equalisation filtering. The proposed solutions have been designed to sonify binary images representing shapes and to be effective also with a short training.

This contribution also shows the application of a methodology to quantitatively compare these sonification modes through large scale experiments. The core idea of the methodology is that tests should be totally automated, in the sense that no intervention by the supervisor should be needed. This is achieved through *Invisible Puzzle*, an iPhone application that instructs the user on how to use one sonification mode, challenge him/her to recognize some (hidden) shapes and measures the performances. *Invisible Puzzle* adopts a gamification approach that engages test subjects and allows them to quickly get proficient with the sonification modes.

Our ultimate goal is to publish a complete and publicly accessible game that makes it possible to conduct an evaluation of sonification techniques with hundreds or thousands of subjects with visual impairments. In its current version *Invisible Puzzle* is a fully functional prototype aimed at evaluating the effectiveness of the sonification modes as well as challenges in the design and architecture. *Invisible Puzzle* presents 16 tasks to the user; In each task the user has to recognize a shape through sonification and distinguish it from other three. In order to evaluate the proposed sonification modes, as well as the scalability of the proposed methodology, we conducted fully-automated (no supervisor intervention) tests with 131 sighted people and 18 blind people. Results show that after a short training, in most cases, subjects correctly recognize a shape after only a few seconds of active exploration. Furthermore, thanks to the increasing difficulty of the presented tasks, *Invisible Puzzle* can effectively guide users through the sonification learning process, allowing them to gradually become proficient.

This paper is organized as follows. Section 2 describes the related work. The 6 proposed sonification modes are presented in Section 3, while Section 4 describes the proposed evaluation methodology as well as the user-centered design process of *Invisible Puzzle*. Section 5 presents the experimental results. Finally, Section 6 concludes the paper and identifies future work.

2. RELATED WORK

The problem of non-visual exploration of images has been widely studied in the scientific literature. The solutions proposed can be broadly divided in two groups: tactile or haptic representations and image sonification. We now focus on the latter group with particular attention to the techniques that can be adopted to recognize shapes on touchscreen devices.

Sanz et al. [10] present a survey of sonification systems used to represent visual scenes. The sonification techniques are categorized according to the sonification function (proportional or derivative [8]), the channel (monaural or binaural) and the paradigm adopted to convey visual information (psychoacustic, artificial or mixed).

Another review on image sonification methods and studies has been carried out by Sarkar et al. [11]. Several algorithms have been reviewed and categorised considering two macro-categories: *Transfer Function Generation* (image-to-sound mapping model) and *Rendering Auditory Data* (how to render the auditory data from the auditory representation of the image).

Yeo and Berger [14] created a framework for designing image sonification methods, categorising various aspects of the sonification process, such as time and spatial exploration, image analysis and sonification mapping. The authors point out the difference between two methods for organizing data for auditory display: *Scanning* and *Probing*. In the *Scanning* method, image data is scheduled to be sonified in a predefined order. Differently, in the *Probing* method, the user can inteactively change the portion of the image to be sonified.

Dallas and Erickson [2] propose a technique to convert an image into sound by mapping the vertical position of each pixel to frequency, the horizontal position to time and brightness to loudness. For example, an image can be sonified by scanning it from left to right. At each instant the sound represents the current vertical portion of the image. This technique is adopted in the vOICe project [7] that aims at enabling sight impaired persons to explore frames captured through a camera.

Yoshida [15] investigates a method for exploring images on a touchscreen device through sound. Two sonification modes are designed: local area sonification and distance-to-edge sonification. In the first mode, when the person slides the finger over an edge, a sound representing the line is played. In the second mode, a pulse train signal is used to represent the finger's distance to the closest edge.

Su et al. [12] developed TimbreMap, namely an iPhone application aimed at enabling people with sight impairments to explore maps through sonification. TimbreMap presents two sonification modes: line hinting and area hinting. The former mode produces a sound while the user is following a path segment. If the user's finger wanders away from the path segment, a stereo sound cue is played to guide the finger towards the nearest path segment. The latter mode fills with sound different areas surrounded by paths. This mode was introduced to convey global information about the map.

Taibbi et al. [13] propose *AudioFunctions*, an iPad application to support visually impaired students in exploring function graphs. *AudioFunctions* adopts three sonification techniques to convey information about a function graph. The "non-interactive" technique sonifies the whole function with an approach similar to the one proposed by Meijer. The "mono-dimensional interactive" technique is similar but allows the user to choose the vertical portion of the image to be sonified by dragging a finger along the horizontal bar that represents the x axis. Finally, the "bi-dimensional interactive" technique is similar to Yoshida's "local area sonification".

3. SONIFICATION MODES

Several sonification modes have been developed, all based on a parameter mapping approach [5]. The sonified parameter is the luminance of a specific area of the image. Each sonification mode is characterized by three main components:

- *Exploration paradigm* - defines how the image can be explored, and which portion is considered for sonification given the position of the finger on the screen. Two exploration paradigms are defined, both based on a *probing* approach as defined by Yeo and Berger [14].
- *Audio rendering technique* - transforms the selected image portion into higher level information.
- *Sound generator* - finally generates the sound signals.

In this contribution we describe a single sonification mode based on the *bi-dimensional* (2-D) exploration paradigm (Section 3.1). A larger number of sonification modes (5) were developed for the *uni-dimensional* (1-D) exploration paradigm (Section 3.2). An example of each sonification mode is available online[2].

3.1 2-D exploration

We designed the 2-D exploration paradigm to provide a benchmark paradigm likely to be intuitive for the user, as it mimics how a person with visual impairment or blindness explores drawings on swell paper. A similar solution is defined as "bi-dimensional interactive" by Taibbi et al. [13] and "local area notification" by Yoshida et al. [15]. 2-D exploration allows the user to touch the screen and to sonify the specific pixel touched in that moment[3]. The rendered sound therefore depends on both the horizontal and the vertical position of the finger on the screen, hence the name *bi-dimensional (2-D) exploration.*

Considering that the parameter to sonify is solely the luminance of a single point, no further data transformation is required for this particular exploration mode. The luminance value of the single pixel is therefore rescaled within the audio rendering stage, sent to the sound generator and associated with the frequency of a sinusoidal wave with fixed amplitude. The frequency range goes from 100 Hz for the lowest luminance value (i.e., black colour), and 1000 Hz for the highest (i.e., white colour).

3.2 1-D exploration

The 2-D exploration paradigm requires users to explore the image along two dimensions to perceive all image features. Our intuition, also confirmed by experimental results (see Section 5), is that 2D exploration is time consuming.

1-D exploration paradigm was designed to tackle this issue by allowing the user to explore the image by touching the screen and moving their finger up and down on a single dimension only. The sonified portion of the image does not correspond only to the touched pixel (as for the 2-D exploration), but to the whole horizontal line (*flush line*) at the same height of the touch point. The horizontal (left-right) position of the finger on the screen is not relevant for this particular exploration paradigm.

1-D exploration paradigm is similar to the technique proposed by Dallas [2], as it simultaneously represents all image features on the flush line. However there are two main differences: firstly, our solution is interactive as it adopts a *probing* approach, while the one by Dallas adopts a *scanning* approach. Secondly, while the solution proposed by Dallas sonifies image features along a vertical line, our approach sonifies an horizontal line. This choice was driven by the fact that we use audio spatialization (based on both interaural time and level differences) to convey additional information about the explored images. In fact, our intuition is that it is more natural for the user to associate left-right spatialized audio information to graphical features on an horzontal line.

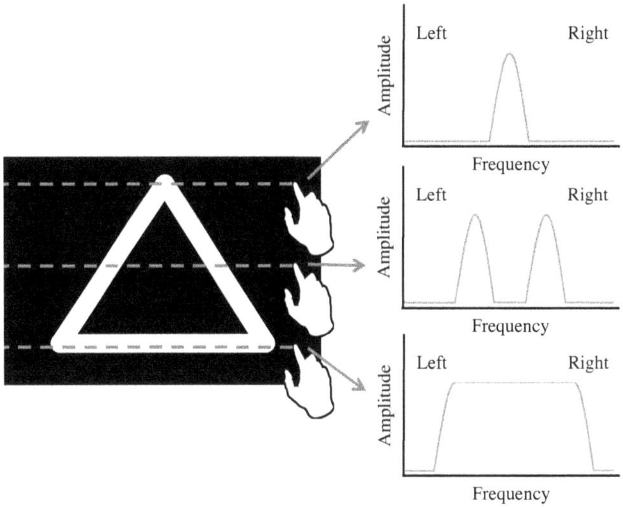

Figure 1: Schematic overview of the 1-D interaction and sonification modes.

In general terms, the luminance of the pixels on the *flush line* is rendered generating a low-frequency sound for pixels located on the left part of the screen, gradually changing to high frequency for pixels located on the right part of the screen. Furthermore, sounds generated from pixels on the left part of the screen are spatialised on the left, gradually changing to the centre and the right for pixels on other parts of the *flush line.* A schematic representation of the 1-D interaction and sonification modes can be found in Figure 1.

It is important to underline that all the sounds corresponding to a single *flush line* are reproduced at the same time, not sequentially moving on the line from left to right. In order to allow for a clear discrimination between concurrent low and high frequency sounds, the spatialisation was implemented using both Interaural Level Differences (ILD) and Interaural Time Differences (ITD). The ILD range was set to a maximum of 20 dB for left-right position, linearly scaled down to 0 dB for the centre position. Similarly, the ITD range was set to a maximum of 1 ms. These values are consistent with spatial hearing literature [9].

The high-low frequency and left-right spatialisation mapping were developed to be as intuitive as possible, taking inspiration from the keyboard of a piano, with the low frequency notes on the left and the high frequency notes on the right. The frequency ranges utilised for the sonification are consistent with the equal loudness curve, therefore with the frequency range for which the human hearing has enhanced loudness sensitivity [9].

Two different audio rendering techniques have been developed using this exploration paradigm, namely *Variable Frequency* (VF) and *Fixed Frequency* (FF).

[2]`http://webmind.di.unimi.it/assetsip15/`

[3]Clearly, the fingertip touches more than a pixel, however we rely on the mobile OS function that identifies a single pixel that intuitively represents the center of the touch.

3.2.1 1-D Variable Frequency

The 1-D Variable Frequency audio rendering technique has been designed in order to represent image features on the flush line at the highest possibile resolution (i.e. there is a continous mapping between the x coordinate of each pixel on the flush line and the generated sound's frequency and spatialisation parameters). A luminance threshold is established. Each pixel on the *flush line* with luminance above this threshold value is sonified with a sound generator, whose frequency is associated with the horizontal position of the correspondent pixel. The frequency range is scaled between 100 Hz for the first pixel on the left, and 1618 Hz for the last pixel on the right. Furthermore, low frequency sounds are spatialised on the left, gradually moving towards the right for high frequency sounds, as described previously.

With this particular audio rendering technique, a horizontal white line corresponds to a number of sounds equal to the line length in pixels (possibly a few hundreds). This could potentially create issues in terms of saturation of the output audio channel and, more importantly, it creates a redundancy of information. The ability of the human hearing system to discriminate between several sounds at different frequencies is in fact ultimately limited.

To address this problem, a minimum distance is established between sonified pixels. This is achieved as follows. Starting from the left side of the screen, when a pixel is found with luminance above the threshold, a few following pixels are not sonified regardless of their luminance. The number of these pixels is determined in order to allow for a maximum of 24 concurrent sounds. This value was established considering the maximum sensitivity of the human hearing system in terms of frequency bands detection (the Bark scale [16]).

Two sound generators are usually employed in literature for image sonification: pure tone and noise. We implemented both of them.

- **1-D VF Pure**. The sound generators produce pure sinusoidal sounds.
- **1-D VF Noise**. The sound generators produce narrow-band noise (1/3 octave band width).

3.2.2 1-D Fixed Frequency

Due to the particular features of the audio rendering process (i.e., variable frequency and fixed amplitude), both 1-D VF sonification modes allow for smooth frequency changes when exploring an image. However, several sounds with very similar frequencies might be present at the same time and at the same amplitude, creating comb filters and phasing, which are perceived as a marked *vibrato* effect. Our intuition is that this *vibrato* effect could be unpleasant for users.

To tackle this problem we designed the 1-D Fixed Frequency audio rendering technique that generates sounds at 24 predefined frequencies. The *flush line* is divided into 24 equally-sized sectors. The average luminance of each sector is directly sonified modifying the amplitude of 24 sound generators, each reproducing continuously a signal at a fixed frequency, from 100 Hz for the generator correspondent with the sector at the extreme left of the screen, to 1440 Hz for the generator correspondent with the band at the extreme right. The number of sectors is consistent with the number of concurrent sound generators described in Section 3.2.1.

For example, the amplitude of a generator correspondent with a sector in which there are only black pixels is 0, gradually scaled up to 1 (maximum) for a sector in which there are only white pixels. The sound of each generator is spatialised from the left to the right, considering the horizontal position of the associated sector.

In 1-D FF we use the two sound generators already defined for 1-D VF. However, considering the level of annoyance generated by listening for long period of times to pure tones and random-generated noise, we decided to also introduce a third solution which employs a music signal as sound generator. This option is expected to be more enjoyable.

- **1-D FF Pure**. The sound generators produce pure sinusoidal sounds.
- **1-D FF Noise**. The sound generators produce narrow-band noise (1/3 octave band width).
- **1-D FF Music**. Instead of 24 sound generators, one for each sector, a single sound generator consisting of a music track player is used. The sound is split into 24 bands, each with centre frequencies going from 100 Hz to 1440 Hz in 1/3 octave bands. The average luminance of each sector on the *flush line* is associated with the amplitude of the corresponding band (left to right, low to high frequency, left to right spatialisation). As an example, if the luminance of a sector on the right of the *flush line* is high, and for all other sectors is low, then only some high frequency components of the actual music will be audible, spatialised on the right. The track chosen for the playback is an 8-seconds extract from a pop song, continuously looped as soon as the user keeps the finger on the screen. Thanks to the presence of a drum-kit and of several tuned instruments (no voice), the frequency spectrum is rather broad (40 Hz to 20 kHz).

Due to the particular features of the audio rendering process (i.e., fixed frequency and variable amplitude), the 1-D FF Noise and 1-D FF Pure sonification modes generates stepped frequency variations without the *vibrato* effect perceivable in the VF modes. Furthermore, the variable amplitude, associated with the pixel luminance, allows for a higher compatibility with grayscale images if compared with the threshold rendering technique adopted for the VF modes. We leave the evaluation of this sonification mode with grayscale images as a future work.

4. EVALUATION METHOD

The overall goal of the experimental evaluation is to understand how effectively each sonification mode allows subjects to perceive images. To achieve this goal, we measure how precisely subjects can recognize images through sonification and how large is the effort involved in this process. We also associate these measures with users characteristics, like age, experience with games, etc.

The challenge is to design a scalable evaluation procedure that makes it possible to involve a large number of subjects with a limited management effort. Our approach is to automate the evaluation procedure in such a way that it can be administered without supervision, possibly remotely. The automated procedure first trains the subject to use the sonification. Then, it instructs him/her to complete some tasks and collects quantitative usage data. Finally, the procedure also administers a questionnaire.

In our preliminary experiments we observed a problem with the automated evaluation: in absence of a supervisor, subjects were less motivated to concentrate on the tasks and to complete the evaluation procedure. This poses an additional challenge: the evaluation procedure should engage the subjects, so that they are encouraged to devote an effort in completing it. This requires the evaluation procedure to be carefully tuned in order to avoid being boring (e.g., tasks should not be too easy) or frustrating (e.g., tasks should not be too difficult).

4.1 Invisible Puzzle

In order to conduct the experimental evaluation tackling the aforementioned objectives, we designed the *Invisible Puzzle* application. Its main functionality is to challenge the user to complete tasks, each one consisting in the recognition of a shape. The interaction works as follows: in the *exploration view* the user explores a (hidden) shape through sonification. When the user believes to have recognized the shape, he/she enters a double tap gesture. *Invisible Puzzle* then presents the answer view (see Figure 2) that contains the explored shape together with other three ones, in random order. The user has to identify the explored shape by touching it. For blind users, the four possible choices are described with a text-to-speech synthesizer.

Figure 2: An answer view.

Invisible Puzzle performs an instrumented remote evaluation [4] automatically collecting, for each task, a number of metrics that include the answer and the *exploration time* i.e., the time during which the user actually touches the screen in the exploration view.

For a given subject, *Invisible Puzzle* conducts the entire evaluation procedure using a single sonification mode. There are two motivations for this choice. Firstly, from the methodological point of view we want to exclude that the results collected for one task are biased by the fact that the user has previously experienced a different sonification mode. Secondly, from the user point of view, it is simpler to learn how to explore shapes with a single sonification mode.

Regarding subjects' training, the goal is to let the user quickly grasp the basics of the sonification mode without requiring supervisor intervention or a long explanation. At the beginning of the evaluation procedure, *Invisible Puzzle* introduces the user to the challenge (i.e., recognize hidden images) and to the basics of the interaction paradigm by playing a very short video (15 seconds) that also includes a spoken explanation. After the video, a "learning task" is presented in which the shape is visible (a textual description of the shape is also provided for blind users). Users can freely explore the image, hence getting acquainted with the sonification mode.

As we show in Section 5, after these two training steps a large portion of users (up to 50% for some sonification modes) is still unable to recognize a simple shape (i.e., a dot on the center right of the screen). In order to offer further training, *Invisible Puzzle* adopts two solutions. First, upon a wrong answer is given, *Invisible Puzzle* displays the correct answer and asks the user to repeat the task in order to precisely associate the audio feedback with the known shape. Second, following a gamification approach [3], exploration tasks are designed to gradually increase in difficulty and are organized in four groups, each one consisting of four tasks. The first three groups focus on a particular type of shape each (i.e., points, line segments and polygons, respectively). A "learning task" is presented at the beginning of each of the first three groups, but not at the beginning of the fourth. The shapes in the fourth group include elements from previous ones. This is intuitively more challenging as the user does not know what to expect (e.g., a line segment or a polygon). We recorded two videos, for 1-D and 2-D exploration paradigms, showing how users are introduced to *Invisible Puzzle*[2].

The increasing difficulty of the tasks implies that it is possible to gradually introduce new elements. For example, the first two tasks in the point group present a single point, while the last two present two points each and, in particular, the last task presents two points on the same *flush line.* Thanks to this approach it is possible to avoid that the user faces tasks that are too challenging and hence frustrating. At the same time, by finely tuning the increasing difficulty of the tasks, it is possible to presents tasks that are not too easy hence engaging the user. This is in line with the "Flow theory" from Csikszentmihalyi [1].

At the end of the evaluation procedure, *Invisible Puzzle* automatically administers a questionnaire to the user. The questionnaire is made of a first section of questions about the user (age, experience with music and video games), a second section with a 5-point Likert scale composed by 9 items and, finally, an open text section for comments. The Likert items investigate the users' experience with the application (e.g., whether they enjoyed playing). Table 1 reports the list of Likert items that we take into account in Section 5.

Q1. I enjoyed playing with *Invisible Puzzle*
Q2. I would like to play with *Invisible Puzzle* again
Q3. Playing with *Invisible Puzzle* required me a lot of concentration
Q4. I have found the sounds comforting/pleasant

Table 1: Some of the Likert items in the questionnaire.

4.2 The design of Invisible Puzzle

We designed *Invisible Puzzle* with a user centered approach through a series of iterations. The whole process benefitted from feedback from many subjects, including one of the designers who is blind and other three blind people. From the interaction design point of view, the most challenging part is to introduce the user to two basic activities:

to explore the screen and to terminate the exploration (with a double tap).

In its first version, *Invisible Puzzle* presented a textual explanation of these activities. However, we observed that most users did not understand the principle of the image exploration.

To tackle this problem in the second version we added, after the textual description, the "learning task". However we observed that many sighted users, in particular with the 2-D sonification mode, tended to tap on the visible dots rather than to slide the finger on the screen; consequently in the following task, with an hidden shape, users did not know how to interact.

To address this problem, we substituted the initial textual explanation with a video that includes a speech-based description. This description is more detailed than the purely textual one and includes the explanation of the challenge (i.e., to recognize hidden shapes). With this solution, most users were able to use the 2-D sonification mode, but still some users had problems with the sonification modes based on the 1-D exploration paradigm. The reason is that users did not understand that the image was sonified in its full width independently of the horizontal coordinate of the point being touched.

To address this problem, we changed *Invisible Puzzle* so that, when using the 1-D exploration paradigm, it forces the user to slide the finger over a small column on the right edge of the screen (all touches outside this column have no effect) and it visually represents the *flush line*. However we observed one additional problem: some users did not understand how to terminate a task and hence remained stuck on the first one. For this reason in its current version, if the user stops touching the screen for a given time, *Invisible Puzzle* shows a text (and reads it for blind users) reminding how to complete the task.

Thanks to this design process we developed the introductory part of *Invisible Puzzle* that allowed all users involved in the experiments to complete the tasks without the need of an external explanation.

5. EVALUATION RESULTS

5.1 Experimental setting

In order to get statistically significant results, *Invisible Puzzle* was tested by a considerable amount of subjects. Considering the difficulties in recruiting individuals with visual impairment, we decided to carry out the test also on individuals without visual disabilities. Results from the two groups can help obtaining statistically significant data to guide future development and experimental studies for both visually impaired and sighted subjects. Previous studies have followed a similar approach [6]. Table 2 and Table 3 report the number of sighted and blind subjects involved in the tests.

All tests were conducted on iPhone 5 and iPhone 5*S* devices (that have the same screen size) and during the tests subjects wore Apple *EarPod* headphones. Tests with sighted users were conducted both in Italy and in the UK, while tests with blind users were conducted in Italy only[4]. Tests were conducted in various environments with limited ambient noise, including students' library, laboratories and also the cafeteria.

Tests were not supervised, in the sense that subjects were asked to conduct a test and no other information was provided, excluded the expected duration of the test (i.e., approximately 15 minutes).

5.2 Results with sighted subjects

Table 2 reports mean values and standard deviations (σ) for all the measured parameters and values. We first consider the percentage of correct answers, which are displayed in the boxplot in Figure 3. This value represents the percentage of tasks in which subjects gave the correct answer in the first attempt. Its dual value is what we consider the "error rate" i.e., the number of failed tasks (this value can be easily derived from the percentage of correct answers). We can observe that the mean performance with the 2-D sonification mode is slightly better than with the 1-D. Considering that the data sets are normally distributed, a one-way ANOVA analysis was conducted. The results show that there are no statistically significant differences between the six sonification modes [$F(5, 125) = 1.005, p = 0.418$].

Interestingly, there are statistically significant differences [$F(1, 129) = 12.502, p = 0.001$] between subjects that do not play musical instruments (67% correct, $\sigma = 13.38$) and those who do (75% correct, $\sigma = 12.79$). On the other hand, no statistically significant difference can be found between individuals who play computer games (one or more hours per day and one hour per week) and individuals who don't (less than one hour per week) [$F(3, 127) = 1.117, p = 0.345$].

The performances with the various sonification modes exhibit clearer differences in terms of exploration time, as shown in Figure 4. Indeed 2-D and 1-D FF Music require a longer exploration time with respect to the other four sonification modes. One-way ANOVA analysis reveals that the differences between the six sonification modes are statistically significant [$F(5, 2090) = 88.887, p = 0.000$]. As expected, post-hoc Tukey analysis highlights that the significant differences are between 2-D and 1-VF Pure ($p = 0.000$), 1-VF Noise ($p = 0.000$), 1-FF Pure ($p = 0.000$) and 1-FF Noise ($p = 0.000$); and between 1-D FF Music and 1-VF Pure ($p = 0.000$), 1-VF Noise ($p = 0.000$), 1-FF Pure ($p = 0.000$) and 1-FF Noise ($p = 0.000$). It is important to underline that in this case the inferential analysis was carried out considering the time taken to complete every single trial, and not the average trial time for each user.

Considering again exploration time, statistically significant differences [$F(1, 2094) = 3.850, p = 0.05$] are found between subjects that do not play musical instruments (mean exploration time 15.61s per task, $\sigma = 11.42$) and those who do (mean exploration time 14.61s per task, $\sigma = 11.93$). There are also statistically significant differences [$F(3, 2092) = 13.147, p = 0.000$] between the computer games playtime groups. A post-hoc Tukey analysis reveals that the significant differences are between the individuals who play computer games more than 1 hour per day and all the other groups, therefore 1 hour per day ($p = 0.001$), 1 hour per week ($p = 0.004$), and less than 1 hour per week ($p = 0.000$).

Considering data collected through the questionnaire, other interesting aspects emerge (see Table 2 again). Firstly, higher concentration (mean 4.43, SD 0.67) is required for the 1-D FF Music sonification mode, if compared with sonification modes adopting the pure sound generators (mean 3.71, $\sigma =$

[4] *Invisible Puzzle* is localized in Italian and English.

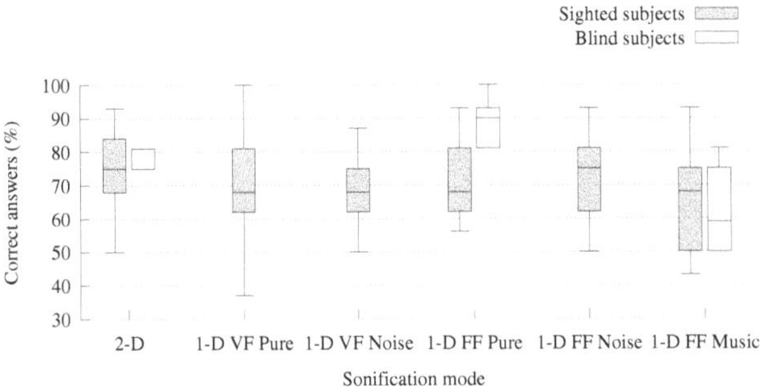

Figure 3: Correct answers for each sonification mode.

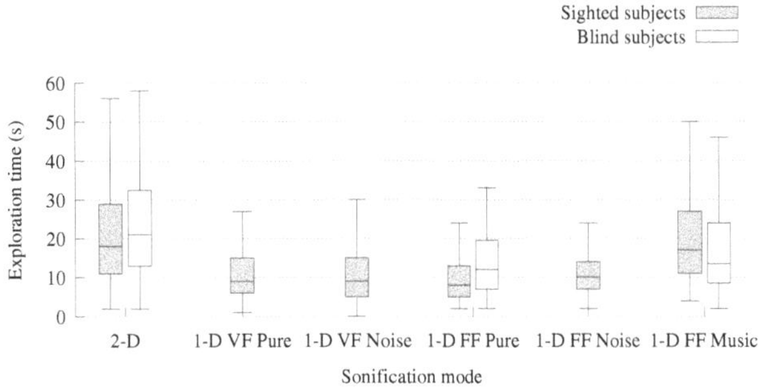

Figure 4: Mean exploration times for each sonification.

Sonification	Participants	Correct answers		Exploration time (s)		Q1 (enjoy)		Q2 (play again)		Q3 (concentration)		Q4 (pleasantness)	
		%	σ	m	σ	m	σ	m	σ	m	σ	m	σ
2-D	24	75.0	13.0	22.1	14.1	3.4	0.7	3.1	1.0	3.8	0.9	2.2	1.0
1-D VF Pure	22	69.6	15.7	11.6	7.3	3.9	0.7	3.5	0.9	3.8	1.0	2.8	1.1
1-D VF Noise	21	67.8	11.9	11.6	7.9	3.9	0.8	3.4	1.1	3.9	0.9	3.1	0.9
1-D FF Pure	22	71.3	10.8	10.6	8.3	4.4	0.6	4.1	0.5	3.4	0.9	3.7	0.9
1-D FF Noise	21	73.5	12.9	12.5	9.0	3.8	1.1	3.9	1.1	4.4	0.8	3.2	1.0
1-D FF Music	21	68.1	16.7	21.4	14.1	4.0	0.7	3.3	1.1	4.4	0.6	4.3	0.8
Total	131	70.9	13.6	15.1	11.6	3.9	0.8	3.6	1.0	3.9	0.9	3.2	1.1

Table 2: Results with sighted subjects ("m" = mean).

0.97) and the noise sound generators (mean 4.19, $\sigma = 0.89$). One-way ANOVA analysis reveals that these differences are statistically significant [$F(2, 128) = 6.776, p = 0.002$], and post-hoc Tukey analysis highlights significant differences between pure tone and noise ($p = 0.005$) and pure tone and music ($p = 0.02$).

The least enjoyable sonification mode is 2-D, while the most enjoyable is 1-D FF Pure. One-way ANOVA analysis reveals that differences are statistically significant [$F(5, 125) = 3.241, p = 0.009$], and post-hoc Tukey analysis highlights significant differences between 2-D and 1-D FF Pure ($p = 0.002$).

Similar results hold considering how subjects declare to be interested in playing again with *Invisible Puzzle*. Indeed, subjects are less interested in playing with 2-D, while 1-D FF Pure is the sonification mode that raised the highest interest.

Finally, as expected, music is the most pleasant sound generator (mean 4.38, SD .805), followed by noise (mean 3, 17, $\sigma = 0.986$) and pure (mean 2.94, $\sigma = 1, 20$). One-way ANOVA analysis reveals that differences are statistically significant [$F(2, 128) = 14.298, p = 0.000$], and post-hoc Tukey analysis highlights significant differences between music and noise ($p = 0.000$) and between music and pure ($p = 0.000$).

5.3 Results with blind subjects

In the evaluation with blind subjects we compared only three sonification modes: 2-D, 1-D FF Pure and 1-D FF Music. This is motivated by the fact that, in order to obtain statistically relevant results with the relatively small number of subjects with visual impairments, we preferred to conduct 6 tests for each of the 3 sonification modes listed above, rather than uniformly distributing the tests among the 6 sonification modes. Table 3 reports the results.

Concerning the percentage of correct answers (see boxplot in Figure 3), 1-D FF Pure yields better results than 2-D and 1-D FF Music. Since the dataset is little and not normally distributed, an independent samples Kruskal-Wallis test was conducted, showing statistically significant differences between the sonification modes ($p = 0.045$).

1-D FF Pure yields better results also considering exploration time. In this case the population is normally distributed, therefore one-way ANOVA analysis was used. The differences are statistically significant [$F(2, 285) = 13.583, p = 0.000$], and Tukey post-hoc shows significant differences between 2-D and 1-D FF Pure ($p = 0.000$) and between 2-D and 1-D FF Music ($p = 0.001$).

Considering the results of the questionnaire, it emerges that 2-D requires more concentration than the other two sonification modes. Also, unexpectedly, 1-D FF Music is the least enjoyable with a large difference with respect to 1-D FF Pure. As a consequence, subjects would be much less interested in playing again using 1-D FF Music rather than 1-D FF Pure. Finally, subjects found the sound of 1-D FF Pure as pleasant as the sound of 1-D FF Music. This was also unexpected.

5.4 High-level considerations about experimental results

This contribution focuses on two main aspects: the effectiveness of the sonification modes and the scalability of the evaluation system. For what concerns the sonification modes, we can conclude that, despite the very short training, users can successfully recognize most of the shapes after a few seconds of exploration. Consider for example the third task in the "polygon" group (see Figure 5). Using 1-D exploration paradigm, it is only possible to identify the correct answer by distinguishing two different sounds, one for the left edge (with constant frequency) and the other one for

Sonification	Participants	Correct answers		Exploration time (s)		Q1 (enjoy)		Q2 (play again)		Q3 (concentration)		Q4 (pleasantness)	
		%	σ	m	σ	m	σ	m	σ	m	σ	m	σ
2-D	6	77.0	7.5	25.8	18.5	3.6	1.2	3.8	0.9	4.6	0.5	3.6	1.0
1-D FF Pure	6	82.2	22.8	15.2	11.5	4.5	0.8	4.3	1.0	4.3	0.5	4.5	0.5
1-D FF Music	6	62.5	13.11	18.0	12.9	3.5	0.8	3.3	0.8	4.0	0.8	4.5	0.8
Total	18	73.9	17.1	19.7	15.2	3.8	1.0	3.8	0.9	4.3	0.6	4.2	0.8

Table 3: Results with blind subjects ("m" = mean).

the other two edges. We expected this to be a challenging task, after the short training allowed to the users, but we were proven wrong, as 86% of the subjects gave the correct answer with the 1-D exploration modes.

(a) Correct (b) Wrong (c) Wrong (d) Wrong

Figure 5: Answers of the third task in the "polygon" group.

In many cases, subjects have not been able to identify the exact shape, but still recognized its main characteristics. Consider the last task, which resulted to be, as expected, the toughest one (see Figure 6). Intuitively, with all proposed sonifications modes it is hard to distinguish the large circle from the pentagon and from the octagon, as they all have the same size. Vice versa, the small circle should be easily ruled out, due to its size. Indeed, only 3% of the subjects gave the small circle as the answer. This is characteristic of the fact that, with the various sonification modes, subjects can easily perceive the dimension of the shape being explored.

It is even more remarkable that, as reported by some subjects, using the FF audio rendering technique, they could perceive discrete levels in the audio frequencies (which is actually a characteristic of FF audio rendering) and hence were induced to give pentagon or octagon as the answer. Indeed, 77% of subjects gave either pentagon or octagon as the answer. While, on one hand, this result highlights a limit of the FF audio rendering technique, on the other hand we were surprised by how quickly subjects got so proficient with the sonification mode to perceive such a fine audio detail.

(a) Correct (b) Wrong (c) Wrong (d) Wrong

Figure 6: Answers of the last task.

Comparing the performance of sighted and visually impaired subjects (see Tables 2 and 3), we can observe that very similar results are obtained by the two classes of users for the 2-D exploration mode in terms of both percentage of correct answers and exploration time. Differently, with 1-D FF Pure visually impaired subjects achieve a higher percentage of correct answers, at the cost of a higher exploration time. On the contrary, with 1-D FF Music, subjects with visual impairments have a lower percentage of correct answers and a lower exploration time. Considering the answers to the Likert Items, there are similar results for blind and sighted subjects. One difference is that blind subjects apparently find that *Invisible Puzzle* is less enjoyable with 1-D FF Music (mean value 3.5) with respect to sighted subjects (mean 4.0).

Considering the scalability of the evaluation system, one challenge was to quickly introduce the user to the exploration paradigm. Thanks to the application of the user-centric approach described in Section 4.2, all subjects successfully completed the evaluation procedure without the need of any external explanation. This does not mean that the introductory explanation (i.e., the video) provides an exhaustive explanation on its own. Rather, it is the combination of the explanation with the following user experience that actually guided subjects in getting proficient with the sonification modes. To support this conclusion, consider that, with the 1-D sonification modes, only 66% of the subjects provided a correct answer in the first task. This mean that, before starting the first task, 1/3 of subjects have not really grasped how the sonification mode worked. However more than 90% of subjects that gave a wrong answer in the first task, after repeating it, gave a correct answer in the second one.

Another challenge involved in the evaluation procedure is to engage the subjects, so that they complete the procedure without distractions. Results show that *Invisible Puzzle* achieve this objective and, in particular, there are some sonification modes that help involving the subjects. We expected 1-D FF Music to be more involving. Instead, it resulted that the music being played requires higher attention and overall the sonification mode that results more enjoyable by both sighted and blind subjects is 1-D FF Pure.

6. CONCLUSIONS

This paper presents 6 sonification modes that allow people with blindness to explore shapes in images. The large number of tests, conducted with both sighted and blind subjects, give evidence that the overall technique is effective and that there are some sonification modes that allow a faster and more enjoyable detection. In particular, 1-D FF Pure has the best trade-off among percentage of correct answer, exploration time and general user satisfaction. Thanks to *Invisible Puzzle*, the evaluation process did not require the presence of a supervisor, and this made it possible to collect 149 tests in less than 2 weeks, with a limited managing effort.

As a future work, we intend to further develop *Invisible Puzzle* and to publish it as a video game in on-line stores (e.g., AppleStore). This would make it available to a much broader audience. In particular we expect that, by advertising *Invisible Puzzle* in communities of people with visual impairments, it will be possible to remotely collect a large amount of evaluation data from sighted and blind people using devices with different screen sizes (e.g., iPad).

Invisible Puzzle can be extended along a number of directions. First, it is possible to improve the technique to evaluate how clearly subjects identify the hidden shape, by asking them to draw the shape on the device. Then the drawn shape can be automatically compared to the hidden one. We believe that this solution, possibly coupled with the already adopted multiple choice question, could give more insights on the actual user's understanding of the image. Second, it is interesting to evaluate to which extent more complicated images can be perceived. This also include the use of grayscale images and, by designing new sonification modes, color images. While in theory the three solutions based on 1-D FF can be already used on real-world grayscale images, their effectiveness for this kind of application needs to be carefully evaluated. Third, with a longer training it could be possible to make several sonification modes available to the same user. This allows the user to choose the preferred one and, possibly, to switch among them while exploring a single image in order to capture different aspects of it. Fourth, it is possible to introduce additional features to make the exploration more interactive, like the possibility to zoom in and out in the image or the separation of the image into layers, each one explorable separately from the others.

7. ACKNOWLEDGMENTS

Authors would like to thank Ginevra Are Cappiello and Alice Brovelli from the organization "SIT - Social Innovation Teams" for their help in the design of *Invisible Puzzle* and all the volunteers who tested our application providing precious data and valuable feedback.

8. REFERENCES

[1] M. Csikszentmihalyi. *Flow.* Harper Perennial Modern Classics. HarperCollins, 2009.

[2] S. A. Dallas Jr and A. J. Erickson. Sound pattern generator, Mar. 29 1983. US Patent 4,378,569.

[3] S. Deterding, M. Sicart, L. Nacke, K. O'Hara, and D. Dixon. Gamification. Using game-design elements in non-gaming contexts. In *CHI'11 Extended Abstracts on Human Factors in Computing Systems.* ACM, 2011.

[4] H. R. Hartson, J. C. Castillo, J. Kelso, and W. C. Neale. Remote evaluation: the network as an extension of the usability laboratory. In *Proc. of SIGCHI.* ACM, 1996.

[5] T. Hermann and H. Ritter. Listen to your data: Model-based sonification for data analysis. *Advances in intelligent computing and multimedia systems*, 1999.

[6] B. F. Katz and L. Picinali. *Spatial audio applied to research with the blind.* INTECH Open Access Publisher, 2011.

[7] P. B. Meijer. An experimental system for auditory image representations. *Biomedical Engineering, IEEE Transactions on*, 39(2), 1992.

[8] E. Milios, B. Kapralos, A. Kopinska, and S. Stergiopoulos. Sonification of range information for 3-d space perception. *IEEE Neural Systems and Rehabilitation Engineering*, 2003.

[9] B. C. Moore. *An introduction to the psychology of hearing.* Brill, 2012.

[10] P. R. Sanz, B. R. Mezcua, J. M. S. Pena, and B. N. Walker. Scenes and images into sounds: a taxonomy of image sonification methods for mobility applications. *Journal of the Audio Engineering Society*, 62(3), 2014.

[11] R. Sarkar, S. Bakshi, and P. K. Sa. Review on image sonification: a non-visual scene representation. In *Recent Advances in Information Technology (RAIT), 2012 1st International Conference on*, pages 86–90. IEEE, 2012.

[12] J. Su, A. Rosenzweig, A. Goel, E. de Lara, and K. N. Truong. Timbremap: enabling the visually-impaired to use maps on touch-enabled devices. In *Proc. of the 12th Int. Conf. on Human computer interaction with mobile devices and services.* ACM, 2010.

[13] M. Taibbi, C. Bernareggi, A. Gerino, D. Ahmetovic, and S. Mascetti. Audiofunctions: Eyes-free exploration of mathematical functions on tablets. In *Computers Helping People with Special Needs.* Springer, 2014.

[14] W. S. Yeo and J. Berger. A framework for designing image sonification methods. In *Proceedings of International Conference on Auditory Display*, 2005.

[15] T. Yoshida, K. M. Kitani, H. Koike, S. Belongie, and K. Schlei. Edgesonic: image feature sonification for the visually impaired. In *Proc. of the 2nd Augmented Human Int. Conf.* ACM, 2011.

[16] E. Zwicker. Subdivision of the audible frequency range into critical bands (frequenzgruppen). *The Journal of the Acoustical Society of America*, 2(33), 1961.

Getting Smartphones to Talkback: Understanding the Smartphone Adoption Process of Blind Users

André Rodrigues[1], Kyle Montague[2], Hugo Nicolau[3], Tiago Guerreiro[1]
[1]LaSIGE, Faculdade de Ciências, Universidade de Lisboa,
[2]University of Dundee, [3]Rochester Institute of Technology
afrodrigues@fc.ul.pt, kmontague@dundee.ac.uk, hmnics@rit.edu, tjvg@di.fc.ul.pt

ABSTRACT
The advent of system-wide accessibility services on mainstream touch-based smartphones has been a major point of inclusion for blind and visually impaired people. Ever since, researchers aimed to improve the accessibility of specific tasks, such text-entry and gestural interaction. However, little work aimed to understand and improve the overall accessibility of these devices in real world settings. In this paper, we present an eight-week long study with five novice blind participants where we seek to understand major concerns, expectations, challenges, barriers, and experiences with smartphones. The study included pre-adoption and weekly interviews, weekly controlled task assessments, and in-the wild system-wide usage. Our results show that mastering these devices is an arduous and long task, confirming the users' initial concerns. We report on accessibility barriers experienced throughout the study, which could not be encountered in task-based laboratorial settings. Finally, we discuss how smartphones are being integrated in everyday activities and highlight the need for better adoption support tools.

Categories and Subject Descriptors
H.5.m. Information interfaces and presentation (e.g., HCI): Miscellaneous; K4.2 [Computers and Society]: Social Issues – Assistive technologies for persons with disabilities.

General Terms
Performance, Experimentation, Human Factors.

Keywords
Blind; Novice; Smartphone; Adoption; Touchscreen; Challenges.

1. INTRODUCTION
Mobile phones have evolved from single-purposed communication devices into "Swiss Army"-like tools that support a wide range of tasks, including navigating, listening to music, texting, shopping, and so forth. Smartphones enable people to access a wealth of information and services through their extensive connectivity; they have the potential to empower people in everyday tasks.

ASSETS '15, October 26-28, 2015, Lisbon, Portugal
© 2015 ACM. ISBN 978-1-4503-3400-6/15/10…$15.00
DOI: http://dx.doi.org/10.1145/2700648.2809842

Since the inclusion of screen reading software, such as *Talkback* or *VoiceOver,* modern touchscreen smartphones have become more popular amongst blind and visually impaired people. Upon the emergence of these services, research on mobile accessibility has been mostly focused on specific tasks, mainly text-entry [2, 4, 13, 14], but assuming that the device and operating system are accessible. This research has also been limited to laboratory experiments where users engage in artificially created tasks for short periods of time.

However, anecdotally, we have observed that several blind people continue to use their older feature phones and see a keyless future as a daunting one [6]. For many other users, interacting with these devices is still confusing and challenging to master. Little is known about the daily experiences of blind people with these devices, or how they are integrated into their everyday activities. Moreover, even less attention has been paid to novice smartphone users and their learning experiences, particularly during the adoption process, i.e. transition from an older phone to a touch-based smartphone.

In this paper, we investigate smartphone adoption and usage by novice users with visual impairments through a combination of longitudinal device usage, weekly interviews, and interaction observations. We focus our attention on the concerns and expectations of 5 novice blind users before owning a smartphone, the learning and usage over an 8-week period, and how they feel about their initial concerns and expectations.

Results show that users delay the adoption of a smartphone due to several reasons, including a concern of not being able to master the device as desired and failing to communicate with family and friends. The first contact with these devices is challenging as users are confronted with both a lack of support and a set of inconsistencies in how the device/accessibility services behave. At the end of the study, participants still experience their initial concerns, and lack proficiency in interacting with their devices. Nevertheless, despite their inefficiency and inefficacy in comparison to their feature phones, participants value the benefits of using current technologies, such as smartphones. Moreover, they show resilience and willingness to continue exploring and improving their ability to use these devices.

These results reveal the shortcomings of current accessibility tools for mainstream mobile devices as felt by novice blind users, shedding light on improvements needed in the support tools provided (e.g. usage tutorials) and in solving the inconsistencies users face every day.

2. RELATED WORK
Our research is informed by prior work on touchscreen accessibility for blind and visually impaired users and the real-world usage of mobile technologies.

2.1 Non-visual interaction with smartphones

Mainstream touchscreen device manufacturers have recognized that an increasingly number of blind people want to use touchscreen mobile devices. Therefore, these platforms come preloaded with a range of accessibility tools and services, some of which are designed specifically for non-visual interactions. Android's *Talkback* and iOS' *VoiceOver* enable visually impaired users to explore the interface elements by either dragging their finger around or performing a sequence of swipe and tap gestures while receiving audio feedback - similar to the techniques proposed by Kane and colleagues [8]. While these accessibility services allow blind users to interact with the technology, they can result in much slower interactions than those of sighted users [13]. One particular task that has been vastly explored is text input, where alternative gesture-based [7], multiple selection- [4] and Braille-based [3, 13, 14] methods have been devised.

Difficulties in operating a touch-based phone without visual feedback have also been acknowledged by other researchers working on haptic feedback [5] or even on how to teach touch gestures to blind people [12]. On a more general note, the number of options and novel interaction paradigms is also likely to disable users to adopt this technology. This gave space to the release and maintenance of commercial alternatives that, using a touch-based phone, support a more structured interaction, similar to the one seen on older phones (e.g., Mobile Accessibility[1]).

While non-visual operation of a touch-based smartphone seems to be a concern, there are, to our knowledge, no reports on the very first contact and daily usage of these devices by blind users. In this paper, we look at the challenges faced by novice blind participants since their first experience with an unknown smartphone. We then report a set of barriers, concerns, and experiences that enrich the knowledge base on how to improve the accessibility of such devices.

2.2 Real-world Usage and Adoption

Prior studies have investigated real-world technology adoption and usage by people with disabilities. Using interviews and participant diaries, Kane et al. [9] explored the accessibility challenges faced by people with visual and motor impairments when using mobile devices. More recently, Anthony et al. [1] analyzed YouTube videos of people with physical disabilities interacting with touchscreen devices, which were supported with online surveys on technology usage. This approach captured the unique and interesting ways in which people have augmented or crafted solutions to support their interactions with touchscreen devices. Furthermore, the study highlights real-world usage scenarios and interaction contexts from individuals with motor impairments. Similarly, Naftali et al. [11] conducted in-the-wild case studies with four people with motor impairments to explore the impact of environmental context on their mobile interactions using a combination of interviews, participant diaries, and contextual session observations.

While previous studies offer novel insights about real-world technology usage by individuals with disabilities, data is still limited to a particular time-window through reflective participant diaries. Commonly in-the-wild user studies do not allow the researchers to obtain objective performance measurements of device interactions, as previously seen within laboratory evaluations. One exception is the work by Montague et al. [10] who conducted a four-week in-the-wild user study involving participants with motor-impairments, using a custom built game to capture touchscreen interaction performance measurements. However, this approach was limited to collecting interaction data within the custom built game - overlooking the interactions that participants were making with other device applications.

In the current study, we go beyond the state of the art on understanding technology usage and adoption by resorting to a combined approach of data collection comprising qualitative weekly data, quantitative weekly controlled assessments, and in-situ device usage data. This information enables us to better understand how users learn and evolve, their usage patterns, and limitations.

3. METHODOLOGY

This paper focuses on uncovering and understanding the smartphone adoption experiences of blind users. We used a combination of coded interviews and observations, alongside with an analysis of device usage from a two-month in-the-wild user study with five participants.

3.1 Research Questions

We aim to answer the following research questions:

- What are the main concerns and expectations of novice smartphone blind users?
- How well current systems support the novice user in a first contact?
- When are these devices integrated on everyday activities?
- What are the barriers to smartphone adoption by novice blind people?
- What role did external influences play in the adoption process?
- How different is their smartphone usage from their previous device?

3.2 Participants

Five participants with visual impairments, four males and one female, took part in our user study. Participants' age ranged from 23 to 55 (M=37.2, SD=15.2) years old. They were recruited from a local social institution, and all participants were legally blind as defined within our IRB approved recruitment. None of the participants owned or used smartphone devices; however, they were all experienced desktop screenreader users Table 1 provides further information about participants, including their technology usage and experience.

Table 1 . Participant profile, where YB (Years of Blindness) UD (Use per Day)

ID	Age	Sex	YB	Old device	UD	Features
P1	55	M	52	Nokia C5	5-7	Calls, SMS
P2	34	F	11	Nokia E52/ Nokia 3230	>10	Alarm, Calls, SMS
P3	51	M	25	Nokia N70	2-4	Alarm,Calendar, Calls, SMS
P4	23	M	9	Nokia E66	>10	Alarm,Calendar, Calls, SMS
P5	23	M	5	Nokia C5 / Nokia E65	>10	Calls, SMS

[1] http://codefactoryglobal.com/app-store/mobile-accessibility/

3.3 Apparatus

Participants were each provided with *Samsung S3 mini* touchscreen smartphones running the Android 4.1 operating system. We enabled the *Talkback*[2] screenreader and pre-installed our data collection service, TinyBlackBox (TBB). The TBB service was designed to run constantly in the background, capturing the users' interactions with any and all applications within the device. User interactions are encrypted and stored locally on the device, alongside the interface DOM tree from which the interactions took place. On a daily basis the device would attempt to communicate with the Google Cloud services to securely transfer an outstanding set of log files using an available Wi-Fi network connection.

3.4 Procedure

The user study spanned for two months (8 weeks), and consisted of the following components; 1) pre-adoption interviews and background data, 2) introduction session with *Talkback* tutorial, 3) in-the-wild device usage, 4) weekly sessions with researchers 5) post-study interview.

3.4.1 Pre-adoption Interview and Background Data

We met with the participants at a local social institution for blind people. All sessions were audio recorded to maintain fluid conversation flow, and to allow for data analysis afterwards. Participants first completed a background questionnaire, provided details of their existing mobile phone, device usage, and prior experience with touchscreen interfaces. All participants owned and used feature phones, as shown in Table 1. Moreover, none had previously used a touchscreen smartphone. During the pre-adoption interview, participants were asked to discuss in more detail their current mobile device, particularly what they liked or disliked about it; how they felt about smartphones and touchscreens; what were their expectations, i.e. things they would like to do with the device, how long they thought it would take to learn how to use the device, and challenges or concerns with using smartphones; and finally, they were asked about their existing support network, i.e. friends or family that could assist them with learning to use the smartphone. To capture a quantitative baseline of mobile device usage, we collected data from the participants performing a set of basic tasks on their former phones (check the time; add a contact; call a contact; call a number; answer a call; read a new SMS; reply to an SMS (no text); create a new SMS conversation; open target app, and complete text-entry trials).

3.4.2 Talkback Tutorial and Basic Tasks

Participants were first introduced to the smartphone, including its physical buttons and features - i.e. how to turn it on and off, the volume controls, and touchscreen. We then enabled the *Talkback* accessibility service on the device and started the Android *Talkback* tutorial application. Participants were then given the device back and asked to follow the tutorial instructions and complete the *Talkback* introductory training. Whenever they had any doubts, they could ask the researcher present. The researcher would then explain verbally how the user could accomplish the given task. The *Talkback* tutorial in Android 4.1 is composed of 4 lessons each introducing at least one new gesture to users. The lessons are Explore the Screen, Scrolling through Lists, Context Menus and Reading Granularities. Afterwards, participants were guided through all basic phone tasks: lock/unlock, check battery, check time, make/receive SMS/calls, explore app menu and add a new contact. During these tasks, we asked participants to think aloud and talk about their experiences while learning to use *Talkback* and the device. The tutorial sessions were video recorded and the TBB framework captured device interactions.

3.4.3 In-the-Wild Device Usage

To capture the participants' adoption experiences, we asked each participant to replace their existing feature phone and use the provided smartphone as their primary device. We assisted the participants with installing their carrier SIM cards, and transferring their device contacts onto the new device. Participants were informed of the TBB data collection service, and provided examples of the data that would be collected. The in-the-wild usage of the adoption phase was scheduled to run for two months. While it was not expected to cover the participants' full learning experience, i.e. from novice to expert, , it allowed sufficient time to trace the adoption process and conduct additional controlled assessments of key behaviours through weekly sessions.

3.4.4 Weekly Sessions

We met with the participants for 30-60 minutes on a weekly basis to collect performance measures of the aforementioned basic tasks and conduct small interviews. We asked participants to discuss their experiences with the device on that week, describing any challenges or concerns they may have had; informing us of new installed applications or activities they tried that week with the device; and finally, we allowed them to request assistance with using the device - as they would with family or friends. We would then attempt to answer the participants' questions; where possible we would provide the participants with verbal responses only, to avoid training them on device interactions and usage.

3.4.5 Post-Study Interview

After the eight-week period, we conducted the post-study interview with the same procedure as the pre-adoption. Interviews lasted from 15-30 minutes. We asked questions related with their answers in the pre-adoption interview such as *did their concerns and expectations come to fruition? Did their personal opinions change? Would they make the transition again? What would they do differently? Would they recommend the device to others? What advice would they give to novice users?* Finally, *what are the challenges looking forward?*

3.5 Data and Analysis

A total of 50 interviews were conducted: 5 pre-adoption, 40 weekly and 5 post-study interviews. We followed an iterative coding process where two researchers independently created codebooks. Each researcher coded the same two adoption interviews and two weekly interviews, after which the codebooks were refined and merged. Using the merged codebook, the researchers proceeded to analyse five weekly and two adoption interviews which lead to further refinement of the codebook and finally a Cohen's kappa agreement of k=.85 (SD=.08) was achieved.

The results from the thematic analysis were complement with observations and log data from the weekly tasks and log data collected in the wild. We gathered a total 7175 in-the-wild

[2]https://play.google.com/store/apps/details?id=com.google.android.marvin.talkback

sessions from the five participants. A session starts with an activation of the screen and ends when the device goes to standby.

4. FINDINGS

In this section, we present our findings structured by the phases explained in the procedure: Pre-Adoption, First Contact, Weekly Evolution, and Post-Factum. Weekly Evolution comprises the data collected from the weekly session tasks, interview, and in-the-wild data.

4.1 Pre Adoption: Concerns and Desires

4.1.1 The need to adapt.

Feature phones are slowly disappearing from the marketplace - forcing blind users to, sooner or later, make the transition to smartphones. These devices are now mainstream and having one is seen as a gateway to social inclusion.

> *"I have nothing against my current phones, but I would be more inserted into society and in today's technology". (Participant 5 – P5)*

4.1.2 More than a phone.

One of the many benefits of smartphones is their ability to provide richer communication channels (e.g. email, *Whatsapp*, *Facebook*). Smartphones can also be the solution to some of the current inaccessibility problems users face every day with standard out of the box technology.

> *"[With a smartphone] I can have access to the Internet, email... and to be able to listen to music, I like my MP3 player but it is extremely hard to control I have to keep asking for help" (P2)*

4.1.3 Concerns.

While the participants were usually aware of the benefits of owning a smartphone, they were considered too expensive and viewed as a luxury item. Participants associated it with the use of Internet and therefore attribute its cost to the retail price plus the hidden costs of internet data usage.

Moreover, participants showed some concerns with using such "luxurious devices in public, stating that simply carrying them around, poses additional security risk in public transports.

Finally, how to manipulate and interact with a touch-based smartphone is still a mystery to many people. This lack of knowledge triggered several sentiments of self-doubt. Participants were afraid they would perform actions unwillingly and they would have to rely on their spatial ability.

> *"I will need to target where I know something is rather than feeling where it is" (P5)*
> *"I mean, I cannot see the keys, so how am I going to be able to select the letters? How will I be able to tell where they are?" (P2)*

The lack of tactile feedback and screen size on touchscreens are fundamental characteristics that lead blind users to feel smartphones were never intended for them. They believe smartphones were adapted to fit their needs after development and, therefore, will inherently have accessibility problems. They show conflicting views of the device, even the same participant. Expecting to have problems while enabling them to use new features such as the music player as previously stated. They are simply unaware of what to expect:

> *"I don't know how accessible touchscreen applications are" (P2)*

4.1.4 Expectations.

Doubts on the interaction method and thoughts on the inaccessibility of the device resulted in participants expecting a difficult transition that required the assistance of others. However, expectations on adoption time highly depended on individual needs. While one user expected to take months to feel comfortable with the device others believed it would take only a few days or weeks. One participant was committed to the changed and needed to make the transition in a day:

> *"I have to learn it the day I get it. People will keep messaging and calling me. If I don't answer people will start to think I am dead [smiling]. I have to at least answer my mother!" (P2)*

Most smartphones come out of the box with a screenreader available. Thus participants had higher expectations for it as opposed to their feature phones where the screenreader was an external software that had to be installed. They expected applications to be inherently more accessible.

4.2 The Daunting First Contact

Talkback tutorial revealed to be a problematic task for all users, only 1 out of 5 successfully completed all the lessons. The tutorial disables the interactive area while explaining what users need to do next. This explanation is triggered whenever users accomplish a task or take too long to finish. The latter triggers even while people are interacting with the screen interrupting the task and forcing them to listen to a long explanation again. Users felt frustrated since they weren't in control of the flow of the lesson and their learning experience.

Overall, the tutorial application was unable to recognize successful and unsuccessful tasks several times. As an example, let us consider the Explore Screen lesson; users were asked to perform a slide from left to right to navigate to the next option. While they were trying to perform the gesture, their fingers would end up touching an icon on the screen and the tutorial assumed they had performed the correct gesture when in fact they just dragged over a random option. As a result, none of the participants understood they could use the slide gesture to go to next focusable option.

Moreover most of the tasks did not have an intended target, yet they rely on affecting the interface (e.g. focus a target, scroll the list), the users are only aware that they performed the intended gesture but have little knowledge how they affected the interface. As an example the list lesson asks users to select an option, users would simply tap anywhere on the screen and went to the next

Figure 1. Samsung S3 Mini with capacitive buttons at the bottom of the device.

step of the lesson having no idea what they just did other than they taped the screen.

4.2.1 Gestures.

Lesson 3 and 4 from the *Talkback* tutorial required users to perform an L based gesture to open the special *Talkback* menus. Four out of five participants were unable to consistently open the menus even after 15 tries. They struggled with performing the gesture fast enough, in the correct area, with the correct shape, and even when they successfully did so they struggled with the following menu. As a result, these users skipped one or both of the last two lessons. When they opened these menus the interaction method changed. They now had to focus an item by dragging the finger around a circular area, which is completely different from the previous grid/list layouts, and lift their finger to select the intended option. The participants were confused as to why the interaction method suddenly changed.

4.2.2 Capacitive buttons.

The back and settings buttons have no physical cues and are activated on touch. Participants struggled with distinguishing between the bounds of the screen and capacitive buttons (Figure 1). This is especially challenging given that no audio feedback is provided for either the back or the settings buttons. This issue was exacerbated when they did not press them intentionally.

4.2.3 Physical cues.

Touchscreens lack physical cues, as such participants attempted to use whatever they could to facilitate screen exploration. P4 *noticed that the basic apps basic (i.e. shortcuts to Phone, Messages, App Drawer, etc) were located in the bottom of the home screen above the physical home button of the device.* Consistently throughout the session whenever he had to select one of these apps, he would first locate the home button to start the exploration from there. The lack of physical cues made impossible for participants to distinguish between the touchscreen and the capacitive buttons. Participants ended up inadvertently pressing the back button when using the edge of the device as a physical cue.

4.2.4 Text-Entry

Even though text-entry was one concerns exposed in the pre-adoption interview participants were able to use input text after a brief explanation of the interaction method of virtual keyboards. Analysis of the text-entry performance is outside the scope of this paper.

Table 2. Weekly task table per participant where it's represented the first week from which participants started to consistently be able to perform the task.

Task	P1	P2	P3	P4	P5
Check time	W1	W1	W1	W1	W1
Add Contact	W6	W4	-	W6	-
Call Contact	W2	W4	W3	W4	W8
Call number	W2	W3	W1	W1	W1
Answer Call	W1	W1	W1	W1	W1
Receive Text Message	W6	W1	W1	W1	W5
Send Message	W1	W1	W5	W1	W3
Send new Message	W7	W5	W6	W3	W7
Go to <App>	W1	W1	W2	W3	W3

4.2.5 Interaction Method

Participants were introduced to two different exploration methods and three different selection methods in less than two hours. The three selection methods are associated to different features. On lift is used to input text and to select options on the contexts menus of *Talkback*. Double tap is the default method to select any focused option. On press is used on the physical home button and the two capacitive buttons on each side (back and settings). During the session participants were mixing some of these methods, double tapping to input text or trying to select options using on lift. Some of them asked why would there be different selection methods between functionalities.

After the *Talkback* tutorial participants relied solely on explore by touch by dragging their fingers rather than directional gestures. Only when participants felt the need to navigate through all options on the screen and asked how they could achieve it, the researcher explained once again both methods. This illustrates how ineffective *Talkback*'s tutorial was, even in explaining essential features.

4.3 Learning and Evolution

Guided by the thematic analysis of the weekly interviews we present the following themes: Barriers, Concerns & Insecurities, Influences, Positive Experiences and Attitude. Each theme provides an insight into the adoption process supported by observations, data from weekly tasks, and in-the-wild device logs.

4.3.1 Barriers

During the study the amount of barriers referred-to never subsided, they only changed in form. Participants were constantly tackling new challenges as they overcame the previous ones.

Gestures. Difficulties with performing intended gestures directly affected participants' ability to operate the device, especially in the first week. They struggled even with simplest gestures (e.g. double tapping). The underlying causes varied from accidental touches, timing issues, and unrecognized taps. While P5 *used his fingernail to double tap*, P2 *performed it too slow and end up focusing a different target*. P1 *holding hand would inadvertently touch the screen, preventing the target to be selected*. As the weeks went by the basic gestures problems were observed in less frequency during the weekly sessions and were far less mentioned during the interviews.

Unlock. The unlock mechanism was unnecessary complex; it was composed of a double tap followed by a slide. Participants struggled with these gestures even without the time constraint required by the unlocking mechanism. Thus, during the first three weeks, we observed participants performing several attempts to unlock their devices. In most severe case, P1 was *unable to consistently unlock in the first 3 attempts* throughout the study from week one to week eight.

Interaction Method. Most participants kept the same interaction method throughout the study. Those that initially struggled with gestures ended up solely using explore by touch. While most used both methods, P5 *used almost exclusively gestures to navigate around the interface avoiding explore by touch.*

Capacitive Buttons. The capacitive buttons continued to be a problem during the firsts three weeks. Participants would inadvertently press them and struggle to recover the previous state. Confused by the different interaction methods they would sometimes double tap the buttons as if they were interface elements selecting the action twice.

Navigation Inconsistencies. Applications keep the previous state depending on how they were closed and how they were implemented to resume when reopened. These inconsistencies made it challenging for participants to learn how interface elemnts are displayed and build a mental model of the application in order to repeat previous interactions.

> *"One thing I noticed is every time I try something I always find things different and since I can't find regularities I cannot learn [how to do it]" (P1)*

Scrolling. Without recurring to *Talkback* gestures, scrolling lists becomes a challenging task. Users have to perform a two-finger slide inside the list's bounds to drag it. Participants faced several challenges on: 1) where to position their fingers, and 2) understand how finger movement affected the scrolling. For instance, some participants inadvertently opened the status bar on the top of the screen while trying to scroll through the contacts. As a result, tasks involving the contact list (e.g. call a contact and send new text message) were the most problematic as seen in Table 2. Participants tended to rely on the dial phone in the first weeks while learning to manipulate lists.

> *"I never know how much I move when I slide, I don't know if I skipped a few options or not" (P1)*

Paradigm Shift. The applications on the smartphone are quite different from the ones in feature phones. Many of the initial barriers can be attributed to the mismatch between participants' expectations (i.e. mental model) and the actual interfaces. *P1 was expecting to have the different folders of Inbox/Sent/Drafts in the SMS app rather than a conversation paradigm where all messages are grouped by contact.*

Accessibility Compliance. After the first four weeks, barriers started to shift to a more feature- or application-driven. As participants delve into new applications they started to face accessibility issues not so commonly found in the out of the box essential apps. They found many buttons without a description, forcing them to create coping strategies around it.

> *"I found that the send button is always changing number, I have to remember that it is the button next to the text box" (P2)*

Assistance of Others. Although relying on others is probably one of the most effective coping mechanisms, help may not be always available. In a similar situation the same participant stated:

> *"I still can't use Endomondo, because instead of start and end, the buttons are numbers and I don't know which is which" (P2)*

This demonstrates that some barriers are hard to surpass without the assistance of others, which can have dramatic consequences. P3 and P4 mistakenly changed the language of the device and from that point onwards were unable to recover. P3's family was not able to solve the issue; therefore he did not use the device for the remaining part of the week. Sighted people are not familiar with *Talkback* and may not be able to assist screen reader users. When this happens, users and helpers engage in collaborative tasks to tackle the issue. P1 was struggled with inserting the password on his home network and his daughter was not able to navigate the device with *Talkback*:

> *"I went into the Wi-Fi configuration screen just like I learned, and then I asked my daughter to select the network and insert the password". (P1)*

Feedback. Smartphone interactions are accompanied by specific audio feedback. During the initial weeks users had no understanding of what this audio cues meant and therefore struggled to understand interface states. P5 *In forms kept pressing the edit box over and over again to get to the keyboard and it took him a while to realize the sound he was hearing meant the keyboard was already opened in the bottom side of the screen.*

Audio feedback sometimes does not respond as users would expect and therefore break their trust in the accessibility service. The TTS sometimes would not immediately respond to user interactions due to buffering effects that led to users only receiving the audio cues from the option focus being shifted but not to what.

> *"We are searching for the buttons and we just hear poc, poc, poc, but it doesn't say anything" (P3)*

This mistrust in the system led users to not realize their gesture simply were not being recognized and instead thought the system was simply slow. The delay between interaction and feedback caused users to take action and adapt to it. P3 and P4 sped up the *Talkback* voice while P2 *simply started waiting for the feedback before interacting.*

Coping. When confronted with a barrier, users tended to have one of four approaches. First they would ask for help, if help was available. If they felt it was an interface or application they would simply reboot the device. If possible they would rely on other devices to search for a solution or simply accomplish the desired task on a secondary device.

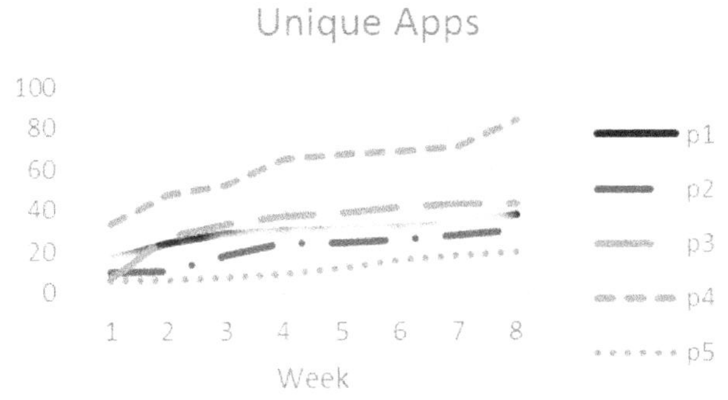

Figure 2. Cumulative number of unique applications visit during the eight weeks by each participant.

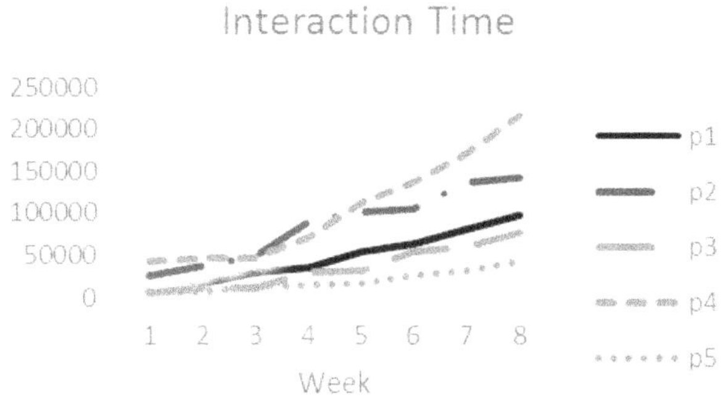

Figure 3. Cumulative interaction time during the eight weeks by each participant in seconds.

4.3.2 Concerns & Insecurities

This theme aggregates all the reports of the users concerns when using the device including their reported insecurities and privacy issues.

During the first three weeks users had difficulties controlling the screen reader and felt uncomfortable while doing so. Users stressed how insecure they felt in public transportation. This caused users to avoid using the device in public places some even after the eight-week period.

> *"What I like the least is the fact that I feel like a complete idiot looking for the options and then not being able to use them" (P2)*

Users showed some resistance with sharing information due to the lack of knowledge of how it would be shared. They were afraid that by sharing their location, or having their calendar synchronize somehow others would be able to tell their location/schedule without their permission. As newcomers to the smartphone paradigm they were not familiar with registering in apps through their Google or Facebook accounts - When they opened applications for the first time that warranted for a registration, the participants were left weary and some did not proceed with the registration before confirming with a friend that they had the correct app installed.

4.3.3 Influences

This theme gathers the collected information on how users were influenced by outside sources in their exploration and usage; and how they influenced others.

Other smartphone users can directly affected the way users interacted with their device by sharing their experiences. Most will undoubtedly help but when users are misguided it can have a negative effect on their learning process. P3 was told about a gesture he could do from a iPhone user. During the following weekly session P3 tried to do a gesture he learned to no success due to that gesture being specific to iPhone.

Sharing experiences can also be exactly what the users need to bootstrap their device usage. P4 in the first weekend with the device explored the it with a friend. P4 was by far the most adventurous explorer in the first week alone he used 33 unique applications (Figure 2). Knowing other smartphone users greatly promoted the discoverability of new applications.

Some participants were also impacting how others perceived smartphones.

> *"My mother never liked new technologies, she got used to phones really slowly. She found my device funny and enjoyed playing with it. She is even considering buying one of this for herself. Its funny how the device is gathering fans." (P2)*

4.3.4 Positive Experiences

In this theme we gathered reports of users success stories. Through them we can have a glimpse into their evolution.

Users find positive experiences wherever they can and accordingly to their proficiency with the device. Users had very different experiences as one can assess looking at the weekly tasks in Table 2. Users who struggled the most reported positive experiences associated with basic tasks or exploration. P5 was one of the users that used the device the least and struggled the most as seen in Figure 3 by the eighth week the user positive experiences were still related to basic tasks.

As more weeks went by the positive experiences shifted to being app related or more complex tasks. P1 complement his pc use with the device and now checks for emails on the phone before reading them on the pc. To P4 the smartphone was becoming much more than a phone he kept installing TV apps, games and educational applications, he was particularly happy with social apps. P3 found great joy in utilities apps such as *CamFind* which directly affected their feelings towards the device.

> *"CamFind is very useful around the house. With 2 blind people is great. I like the device more with each passing day" (P3)*

Users found joy when they accomplish something without any external help even if it was simple phone features as setting the phone on vibrate.

4.3.5 Attitude

This theme gathers the attitudes of the participants about the device usefulness and their ability to handle it during the study.

When users struggle they avoid situations where they have no control like avoiding to use the device in public. In extreme cases they go as far as warn their families about their inability to control the device in order to avoid misunderstandings if they aren't able to answer/call:

"Pretend that I don't have a phone" (P1)

Motivated by their need to adapt they pushed through their difficulties. Users felt compelled to adopt the device no matter what in order to fit in with their surroundings. When users were neglect of successful experiences they started to report frustration and self-doubt. When they finally broke through everything changed.

"After I was able to send the message I think I stopped thinking I couldn't do it" (P1)

Users believe their performance would never reach the one with their old phones due to things being inherently harder. From week four onward users started feeling more comfortable and recognized they could do more with the devices. As they started to explore the device it was becoming evident this was more than a phone to them.

During the study users clearly set self-goals. With each passing week users tried to address their previous barriers and sometimes came back with success stories.

"It's hard to handle the post navigation in Facebook" (P1 Week4)
"I can now navigate between the posts but I still can't read the full text I still have to learn" (P1 Week5)

4.4 Post-factum: Perceive Challenges and Benefits

In the post-interview we were interested in understanding how they perceived their adoption and how they would improve it. Did their concerns come to fruition? Were their expectations met? What was important and what would advise others to do? What are the next goals?

4.4.1 Concerns

The participants that expressed concerns on using the device in public continue to feel this way. Two participants (P1, P3) felt that this device was worse as a phone, it was more difficult to use and slower than their previous device. Not all users shared this consensus, P2 and P4 saw smartphones has being better even for the most common tasks:

"In my old one the only thing I'm faster is searching for contact, even writing a text I am faster here". (P4)

P5 was the user who struggle the most and in his pre-adoption interview thought he was learning a device not design for him, the experience with the device changed his view on smartphones:

"My opinion has changed. They aren't that hard, as everything else we just need to learn to use them" (P5)

4.4.2 Expectations

Most underestimated how much time it would take for them to get used to the device and how much of a challenge it would be. Some felt that they were used to the device after two weeks (P4), while others state they still are not completely comfortable (P3). P2 has met her initial expectations and was happy she able to send messages in the first week. User's ability with one of the basic tasks did not translate quickly into the other. In P2 case her prowess with the messages did result in a quick adoption of all features as seen in Table 2.

4.4.3 Looking back

Dedication can be the key to the adoption as most users felt they should have spent more time exploring the device. A gradual transition by relying in a second phone can help users keep their spirits up making the adoption smoother. However, it can also slow the process P5 felt he might benefit from a forceful transition

"I know that if I was forced to use just one I would have done things quicker" (P5)

Having someone to rely on was crucial in the early adoption stages not only as an aid, but also as an assurance that if something went wrong they had someone to go to.

Users regretted not being able to share their experiences with others or not have it done sooner. They believed cooperative exploration would have quickened the learning process.

To improve the learning process one common request was the creation of a manual with a step-by-step guide on how to accomplish the basic tasks.

Participants felt that the device is still not accessible to all blind users. While they would recommend the device, they wouldn't recommend it to everyone

4.4.4 More than a phone

To the participants their device became so much more than a communication device. The new applications and features are becoming part of their daily life and playing a role in supporting their independence:

"Just the other day I had difficulties seeing my medication, I took a photo with CamFind it told me what the medication was." (P4)

To some users the added functionalities came at a cost. Two users believe they made a trade-off between more features and easiness of use.

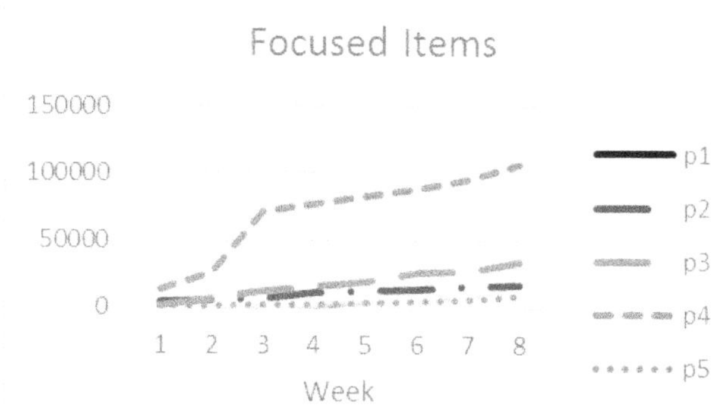

Figure 4. Cumulative number of items that were focused during exploration throughout the eight weeks per participant.

They don't believe they will ever be quicker with smartphones. Yet, they clearly see the advantages.

> *"It allows you so much more than a regular phone wont, we can use it almost as good as our old ones. I believe it's a trade off in favor of the smartphone" (P1)*

4.4.5 Looking forward

Participants were keen to continue to improve their device usage even if only motivated by the inherent need to adapt:

> *"Someday there will only be smartphones, we have to live with it" (P3)*

Most set their goals as they had been doing week by week, each had one particular application or feature within an application that they wanted to master. One user saw the smartphone as an opportunity to learn something he even struggles to do on a pc.

> *"I would like to browse the Internet, it's something I even struggle with the computer" (P5)*

One user was particularly interested in the navigation capabilities of the device; he was determined to be able to use them.

Lastly, one user felt he had reached full adoption and believed he could do whatever is possible to do with the device. This confidence is not surprising given the amount of exploration he had with the device far surpasses other participants, as shown by the total number of items focused during the weeks in Figure 4.

5. DISCUSSION

Based on our findings we are now in a position to answer our research questions.

What are the main concerns and expectations of novice smartphone blind users?

Pre-smartphone adoption blind users had two major concerns safety and fear of the unknown. They perceive having a smartphone as an additional security risk due to the unwarranted attention it brings. This insecurity was deeply felt in the initial weeks where even users that used their previous phone on a public setting did not anymore. Only when participants felt in control their attitude changed. Since they had yet to interact with the device they feared they would be unable to use it due to not having any physical cues and fearing they would have to rely on their spatial abilities. Their fears were exacerbated by thinking smartphones were inherently not designed for them, and as such they would have to adapt to an inaccessible device, an opinion they no longer share. Most expected a much faster and easier adoption, they struggled more than they anticipated. From the starting point most believed they would never perform better than with their current phone, but felt they add to adapt mainly due to the market pressure.

How well current systems support the novice user in a first contact?

The *Talkback* tutorial simply was not enough for users to even get started. They struggled with some of the gestures presented and even after eight weeks we still see no reports or data where they use complex gestures. During the tutorial they were even misguided into thinking they had performed the correct gesture when in fact they didn't. The gesture to go to the next option was not learned during the tutorial, which caused users to struggle during the tutorial and in the following weeks with the exploring of applications. Using just explore by touch is a demanding task that heavily relies on the users memory and spatial ability, to explore new applications. It is crucial to improve the tutorial session in order to reinforce how, when and which gesture is more appropriated to the task. The tutorial presents users with the basic gestures but makes no effort in providing feedback on how they affect the underlying interface. We complemented the tutorial with a guided session through the basic tasks. Although users were able to perform all the tasks, most felt they learned too much in a short space of a time. From just basic tasks users had to learn three different selection methods (lift, press and double tap) and learn where to apply each. Moreover, they had a multitude of new interfaces to learn. As such, when looking back many users had the desire for a manual that they could rely on. There is a need to provide better learning mechanism for blind users on mobile devices.

When are these devices integrated on everyday activities?

Given the opportunity users will quickly integrate smartphone in their daily activities to improve their independence or simply as a source of entertainment even if they are yet to fully control the device.

What are the barriers to smartphone adoption by novice blind people?

Throughout the weeks we saw how the different barriers evolved. In the initial weeks users mainly faced gestures related issues. The biggest hurdle was understanding the new paradigm they were in. Suddenly users couldn't find any consistency in the applications. They no longer have one single path between point A and B, but any number of ways to do the same thing. Applications now have states, depending on whether you back or home they close or go to the background and resume in different ways. This mixed in with every application behaving differently to the back button led to users struggling to learn to interfaces and repeat tasks. We need better methods to convey this new paradigm to users. From all interface elements, lists were with no doubt the harder ones to grasp, we believe this begins with a poor tutorial and gets worse when they reach the contact list. Applications had elements with no descriptions or simply not reachable through a non-visual exploration. Application developers need to start respecting basic accessibility guidelines and strive to make their application friendly to a non-visual exploration.

What role did external influences play in the adoption process?

Users felt that without someone who they could rely on to help them they would possibly have an insurmountable barrier. During the firsts weeks users relied on their friends and family to help them with configurations, app installments or simply understanding the basic interfaces. The primary coping strategy for users throughout was asking others for help. Looking back users wished they knew people that were using the device so they could share experiences and help each other.

How different is their smartphone usage from their previous device?

Most had their previous phone for more than a couple of years, it comes as no surprise that in eight short weeks most feel they are slower. The smartphone is much more than a phone. It is allowing them to be more socially active through Internet communication and social apps such as *Whatsapp*, *Facebook*. It is becoming an educational tool for them to study and learn languages. It's becoming a means towards independency and a solution to problems using utilities apps such as *CamFind* (e.g. identify medicines). At the very least for all it is a mobile entertainment device, to listen to music, play games, read a book or simply watch TV.

6. CONCLUSIONS

We conducted an eight-week study with five novice blind participants. We observed their adoption process through a combination of interviews, weekly assessments, observations and in-the-wild data. We present a detailed understanding of the adoption process of a blind user moving from a feature phone to a touchscreen smartphone. We uncovered theirs struggles, motivations and accessibility issues from the very first contact with the device and throughout the initial eight weeks of usage. The accessibility issues raised and their evolution should be taken into account. Others can play a huge role in the adoption process. They can be the propellers for application exploration or simply someone to share an experience with. Users will not always be able to resort to others for assistance. We saw that the current tools in place are not enough and can even provide the wrong stimuli to novice users. There is a need for better adoption support tools that take into account the evolving needs of participants for assistance. Given the opportunity users will quickly integrate smartphones in their daily lives, even if at first it is not a full-fledged phone. They will take advantage of its capabilities for entertainment, education, social activities and even to improve their independency through utility apps. Finally, these results were only possible due to the variety, quality and amount of usage data and opinions collected during the eight-week period. In order to uncover and improve the accessibility of these devices future research should seek to have similar in depth approaches enriching the quality of their data from multiple sources.

7. ACKNOWLEDGMENTS

We thank all the participants and the Fundação Raquel e Martin Sain in Lisbon. This work was partially supported by FCT through funding of the scholarship, ref. SFRH/BD/103935/2014, LaSIGE Research Unit, ref. UID/CEC/00408/2013 and RCUK (EP/G066019/1).

8. REFERENCES

[1] Anthony, L., Kim, Y., & Findlater, L. (2013). Analyzing user-generated youtube videos to understand touchscreen use by people with motor impairments. In Proceedings of the SIGCHI Conference on Human Factors in Computing Systems (pp. 1223-1232). ACM.

[2] Azenkot, S., Rector, K., Ladner, R., and Wobbrock, J. Passchords: secure multi-touch authentication for blind people. In Proceedings of the 14th international ACM SIGACCESS conference on Computers and accessibility, ASSETS '12, ACM (2012), 159–166

[3] Azenkot, S., Wobbrock, J. O., Prasain, S., & Ladner, R. E. (2012, May). Input finger detection for nonvisual touch screen text entry in Perkinput. In Proceedings of Graphics Interface 2012 (pp. 121-129). Canadian Information Processing Society.

[4] Bonner, M., Brudvik, J., Abowd, G. and Edwards, W.K. No-Look Notes: Accessible eyes-free multi-touch text entry. Proc. Pervasive '10, Springer (2010), 409-427.

[5] Buzzi, M. C., Buzzi, M., Leporini, B., & Paratore, M. T. (2013). Vibro-Tactile Enrichment Improves Blind User Interaction with Mobile Touchscreens. In Human-Computer Interaction–INTERACT 2013 (pp. 641-648). Springer Berlin Heidelberg.

[6] Buzzi, M. C., Buzzi, M., Leporini, B., & Trujillo, A. (2014). Designing a text entry multimodal keypad for blind users of touchscreen mobile phones. In Proceedings of the 16th international ACM SIGACCESS conference on Computers & accessibility (pp. 131-136). ACM.

[7] Guerreiro, T., H. Nicolau,, J. Jorge & D. Gonçalves, (2009). NavTap: A Long Term Study with Excluded Blind Users. In Proceedings of the 11th international ACM conference on computers and accessibility (ASSETS'09), 99–106. NewYork: ACM Press

[8] Kane, S. K., Bigham, J. P., & Wobbrock, J. O. (2008). Slide rule: making mobile touch screens accessible to blind people using multi-touch interaction techniques. In Proceedings of the 10th international ACM SIGACCESS conference on Computers and accessibility (pp. 73-80). ACM.

[9] Kane, S. K., Jayant, C., Wobbrock, J. O., & Ladner, R. E. (2009). Freedom to roam: a study of mobile device adoption and accessibility for people with visual and motor disabilities. In Proceedings of the 11th international ACM SIGACCESS conference on Computers and accessibility (pp. 115-122). ACM.

[10] Montague, K., Nicolau, H., & Hanson, V. L. (2014). Motor-impaired touchscreen interactions in the wild. In Proceedings of the 16th international ACM SIGACCESS conference on Computers & accessibility (pp. 123-130). ACM.

[11] Naftali, M., & Findlater, L. (2014). Accessibility in context: understanding the truly mobile experience of smartphone users with motor impairments. In Proceedings of the 16th international ACM SIGACCESS conference on Computers & accessibility (pp. 209-216). ACM.

[12] Oh, U., Kane, S. K., & Findlater, L. (2013). Follow that sound: using sonification and corrective verbal feedback to teach touchscreen gestures. In Proceedings of the 15th International ACM SIGACCESS Conference on Computers and Accessibility (p. 13). ACM

[13] Oliveira, J., Guerreiro, T., Nicolau, H., Jorge, J., & Gonçalves, D. (2011). Blind people and mobile touch-based text-entry: acknowledging the need for different flavors. In The proceedings of the 13th international ACM SIGACCESS conference on Computers and accessibility (pp. 179-186). ACM.

[14] Romero, M., Frey, B., Southern, C., & Abowd, G. D. (2011). BrailleTouch: designing a mobile eyes-free soft keyboard. In Proceedings of the 13th International Conference on Human Computer Interaction with Mobile Devices and Services (pp. 707-709). ACM

A System for Controlling Assisted Living Environments Using Mobile Devices

Paulo A. Condado
DEEI-FCT & CENSE
Universidade do Algarve
Campus de Gambelas, 8005-139 Faro, Portugal
pcondado@gmail.com

Fernando G. Lobo
DEEI-FCT & CENSE
Universidade do Algarve
Campus de Gambelas, 8005-139 Faro, Portugal
fernando.lobo@gmail.com

ABSTRACT

We present *EasyHouse*, a system developed to allow people with disabilities and their family members to control their home environment (e.g., turn on/off a light, turn on/off the TV) using a *smartphone*. The user interface was designed to be adjustable to the needs of each user.

The development of *EasyHouse* followed an iterative user-centered design approach. A paper-based low-fidelity prototype was built based on user requirements and from the first author's own experience as a researcher with cerebral palsy. After several design and evaluation iterations, a functional prototype has been evaluated in a real context with real users. Preliminary results indicate that the proposed system is suitable for both people with and without motor disabilities, and provides an adequate method for controlling home appliances when there is a family member with motor disabilities.

Categories and Subject Descriptors

H.5.2 [**Information Interfaces and Presentation**]: User Interfaces; J.7 [**Computers in Other Systems**]: Command and control; K.4.2 [**Social Issues**]: Assistive technologies for persons with disabilities

General Terms

Design, Human factors.

Keywords

Mobile accessibility; Intelligent environments; Home automation; Motor disabilities; Cerebral palsy

1. INTRODUCTION

Open a door, turn on a television, switch off a light, or turn off an air conditioner, are simple tasks for most people. Unfortunately, individuals with motor disabilities face difficulties when interacting with the surrounding world. For example, light switches may be located too high for someone on a wheelchair. Over the years, people with disabilities have adapted their own houses to surpass their limitations, changing rooms, electrical installations, among other things.

Domotic equipment has been used to provide suitable solutions for helping people with disabilities and the elderly at home [1, 10]. These equipments avoid extensive structural modifications at the users' homes (e.g., reinstalling light switches near the floor), allowing their utilization by other family members. Moreover, users without severe hand coordination problems are able to control every domotic device anywhere and anytime using remote controls, traditional computers or mobile devices. However, people with poor coordination are sometimes unable (or face difficulties) to use remote controls or standard domotic mobile applications because the devices are too small.

Most domotic solutions available on the market are not specifically designed to help people with disabilities. In most cases, these products are originally developed for people who have economic power for living in smart environments and their creators often forget to address interaction methods for people with disabilities and the elderly. It is important to change this way of thinking, since a good user interface must be designed to be accessible for all. The system presented in this paper is suitable for both people with disabilities and their family members, offering a mobile application with a user interface adjustable to each user's needs.

The remainder of the paper is organized as follows. The next section explains related work, describing interaction methods for mobile devices that were specifically created to facilitate the use of such equipments by people with motor impairments, domotic technologies and its utilization in assisted living, and other assistive technologies. Section 3 and 4 present the development and evaluation of the system. Section 5 summarizes the major contributions, gives directions for future work, and concludes the paper.

2. BACKGROUND

Mobile devices have enough processing power and memory to run assistive applications (e.g., text-to-speech systems or screen readers) and help people with disabilities. However, the main advantage of small computer devices is also their major disadvantage: Such equipments are too small to be easily used by people with severe motor coordination difficulties. Fortunately, researchers have been developing accessible text-entry methods to allow people with poor motor coordination to use *smartphones* or other touch-screen devices [15, 5, 14, 7].

ASSETS'15, October 26–28, 2015, Lisbon, Portugal.
© 2015 ACM. ISBN 978-1-4503-3400-6/15/10 ...$15.00.
DOI: http://dx.doi.org/10.1145/2700648.2809839.

Some researchers advocate that integrated intelligent environments can be used to assist elderly people and those with disabilities [1]. In the last decades, domotic technologies, also known as home automation systems, have been used to develop assisted living systems that are able to improve autonomy and quality of life of dependent people [10]. There are different approaches to create an easy-to-use assistive intelligent environment. Some have studied manners to create smart homes that perform tasks without human intervention, using advanced algorithms to control the environment based on users' profiles. Others have worked to implement systems that empower people with information and appropriate interfaces to do everyday tasks [9].

Different kinds of interfaces have been used to control smart environments. For example, an interaction method based on gesture recognition was developed by Bien et. al. [2], another one based on voice recognition was proposed by Yerrapragada and Fisher [16], a hybrid brain-computer interface was studied by Edlienger et. al. [4], and a mobile application for controlling intelligent environments was studied by Peixoto [12]. All these researchers have tried to create natural easy-to-use interfaces for providing a better interaction between users and their home appliances.

An important thing to note is that those environments should be designed to be secure, flexible, adaptive, non-intrusive, and easy-to-use. Any habitant should be able to control lights, media centers, doors, windows, and other devices anytime and anywhere without much effort. Researchers and developers should not only develop the product for helping people with disabilities to overcome their limitations, but also need to design the interface to comply with other residents' needs. As described by Bien et. al. [2], it is important to understand the way of interaction of each resident with the domotic devices in order to design a user-friendly interface control.

3. AN ACCESSIBLE SMART HOME CONTROLLED BY MOBILE DEVICES

Some researchers have studied technologies that are available to implement smart homes, and inhabitants' behavior, in university laboratories [9]. Indeed, such places gives them the opportunity to understand how people interact with environments and a chance to design alternative interaction methods. However, we believe that intelligent environments should be studied in real scenarios, allowing to learn more about the real interaction between inhabitants and their environment. It is also essential to understand the relations between people who have disabilities and other inhabitants. There is an important barrier to achieve that: Most testers are not available to open the doors of their houses and share private data with strangers.

To address the above issue, a prototype was built at Paulo's (the first author of this paper) own house because neither him nor his family had an issue with opening the doors of their home to potential testers. Moreover, Paulo has cerebral palsy himself, with mild motor coordination problems and speech disabilities, and deeply believed that the system could very useful for helping him in his daily activities.

It is well known that researchers and developers should not participate in the evaluation process of their own designs to avoid influencing the results due to their knowledge of the user interface. Nonetheless, Paulo indirectly participated in the evaluation process because the proposed system was built and tested at his own house and several quantitative tests were measured automatically by running scripts over the log files produced by the system in real-time usage. In addition to Paulo, we conducted informal interviews with other people for requirement elicitation as well as for usability tests. These people provided valuable information about their needs, limitations and preferences.

In order to create a novel application for mobile devices to allow both people who have motor disabilities and their family members to control home appliances, we bought some domotic equipment, namely X10 devices, credit-card sized computers, Arduino UNO boards, and sensors and actuators for developing an intelligent environment at Paulo's house.

X10 is a communication protocol that allows the control of electrical devices. Although there are more recent and more sophisticated protocols (such as ZigBee and Z-Wave) we opted to use X10 because it is still widely used and the equipment was more affordable. With X10 the communication is made between transmitters and receivers through a traditional power line installation on a house. These transmitters/receivers are incorporated in wall lamp switch modules, wall-mounted dimmers, appliance modules, and so on.

3.1 Understanding user requirements

The best way to design and implement a smart home for people with disabilities and their families, and its user interfaces, is to understand their lifestyle, social interactions, preferences, needs, limitations, and desires.

Paulo reflected about his own needs and motivation, his current life style, the way he uses different technologies to improve his quality of life and of those surrounding him, and used that in order to realize what kind of system was needed to control domotic devices. His wife, Tânia, was also asked to describe an ideal intelligent environment to help her in everyday activities. Tânia described an environment where home appliances are easily controlled by different devices (e.g. *smartphones*, *smart watches*, *tablets*, or conventional personal computers).

We started to design the proposed system based on Paulo and Tânia's observations, information gathered from the informal interviews, and the knowledge about accessible interaction methods for mobile devices. We tried to use inexpensive equipment for creating technological rich environments.

3.2 Low-fidelity prototypes and heuristic evaluations

The concept of navigating through groups and sub-groups, present in traditional scanning systems and in text-entry methods such as *EasyWrite* [7], seemed a prefect metaphor for walking through rooms and turn on/off home appliances. Inspired by that work, we implemented the concept of navigating through groups using listviews, adapting the dimensions of list items to the needs of each user. A user without hand coordination problems is able to use the application without any special configuration, those with hand motor disabilities are able to adapt the dimensions of the interface elements to their requirements.

The basic idea of the proposed mobile application is illustrated in Figure 1, based on the first low-fidelity prototype by showing a storyboard with the sequence of steps that a person must make in order to switch on or off the bedroom lights. As shown, the user navigates through listviews to

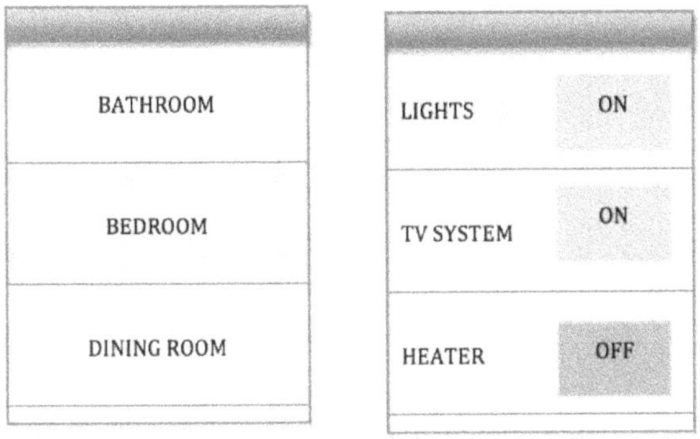

(a) (b)

Figure 1: The first low-fidelity prototype of the proposed user interface. Subfigures 1(a) and 1(b) show the sequence of steps required to control the bedroom lights. In 1(a) the user selects the bedroom. Then in 1(b) the user can see the status of various things (lights, TV system, heater) in the bedroom, and may decide to change it.

find the desired item. This idea was largely inspired by the concept behind *EasyWrite* [7] and also on traditional mobile applications for controlling intelligent environments.

We followed an iterative design approach based on several design-evaluation cycles. Heuristic evaluations were performed using ten heuristics that were designed to detect common usability problems [11]. Heuristic evaluations allowed us to redesign the user interface in order to solve some issues. We added three additional elements to the user interface (see Figure 2). The first one is placed at the top-center of the interface and provides information regarding the hierarchical level. This element allows knowing in which room the user is controlling the home appliances. The other two elements (buttons) are placed above the list items that contain the domotic devices and allow a person to (1) navigate to another room or (2) turn off all home appliances inside the room. These two buttons were originally placed on the menu, but we realized that the interface needed to be modified in order to achieve a simpler and more effective design.

Our previous experience helped to avoid designing a user interface with too many menu options, because we found that unsuitable for people with hand coordination problems. Moreover, we tried to create a minimalistic user interface to allow both people with and without disabilities to interact more naturally with the surrounding environment.

3.3 Functional prototypes

After the last paper-based low-fidelity prototype was finalized and evaluated, we developed the high-fidelity and functional prototypes for Android. The choose Android because we wanted to use an operating system that allows the development and testing of applications for free.

The mobile application was developed as a part of a larger system to allow users to add, modify and remove their own home appliances. The application connects to a local server, gets the status from the domotic devices, and controls them. The server, called *EasyHouse* server, provides the services and controls the different home appliances through the TCP gateway daemon for the X10 CM15A. A webpage was developed to allow users to control and manage their domotic devices using a common web browser. The *EasyHouse* server, web server, database management system, and all other parts of the system were installed on a Raspberry Pi, a small and inexpensive computer that is becoming quite popular.

The system was also developed to allow small source modifications in order to work with other domotic technologies (such as ZigBee, Z-Wave, or Insteon) and to be more flexible. Moreover, although the X10 standard is inexpensive and the most widely used in home automation, it provides an incomplete control over home appliances through the home's power lines [6]. There are many other protocols that guarantee new and better features. For instance, a radio frequency communication standard based on IEEE 802.15.4, called ZigBee, would be a good alternative to the X10 standard and allows using much more home appliances [3]. Z-Wave is another well known communication protocol for home automation and is also comparable to ZigBee in terms of networking [13]. Insteon is a protocol developed by SmartLabs Inc. and supports both radio frequency and power line communications [8]. Some Insteon products are manufactured to be X10-compatible. Therefore, a user with a X10 network is able to migrate to an Insteon network.

The first high-fidelity prototype was totally based on the last low-fidelity prototype. The preferences menu allows the setting of the appropriate size of the user interface elements (see Figures 2(c)). Therefore, the dimensions of list items vary according to users' needs and preferences.

The current version of the mobile application has small differences from the first functional prototype. A new component was added which allows users to control the brightness of lights, based on the evaluations to be presented in the next section.

4. EVALUATION

Both qualitative and quantitative methods were used to identify usability problems that users experienced while operating the proposed system. Two kinds of quantitative tests were performed: (1) automated tests based on data recorded on log files, and (2) usability tests on pre-defined tasks performed by Paulo's wife and two other individuals: Pedro and Susana [1]. Pedro and Susana both have mild motor hand disabilities. Tânia has no disabilities.

The automated tests were done for a continuous period of time (one month) and monitored Paulo and Tânia's usage of the system in their house in real time. These tests helped us to eliminate several usability issues. We have also conducted more traditional usability tests with three individuals other than Paulo. In these more traditional tests, we decided that Paulo shouldn't be a tester because the system was developed by him and that could bias the results.

Ideally, we would have liked to perform all tests in a real environment but we didn't have the resources (both human and financial) to install and test the system in different houses. To remediate the situation, we opted to invite the three previously mentioned individuals to test the system on pre-defined tasks. We recognize that the number of testers is too small to have statistical relevance. Nonetheless, they give an idea of the time needed by people to use the system and complement the qualitative tests also performed with the same individuals.

[1]Names are fictitious in order to protect the identity of users

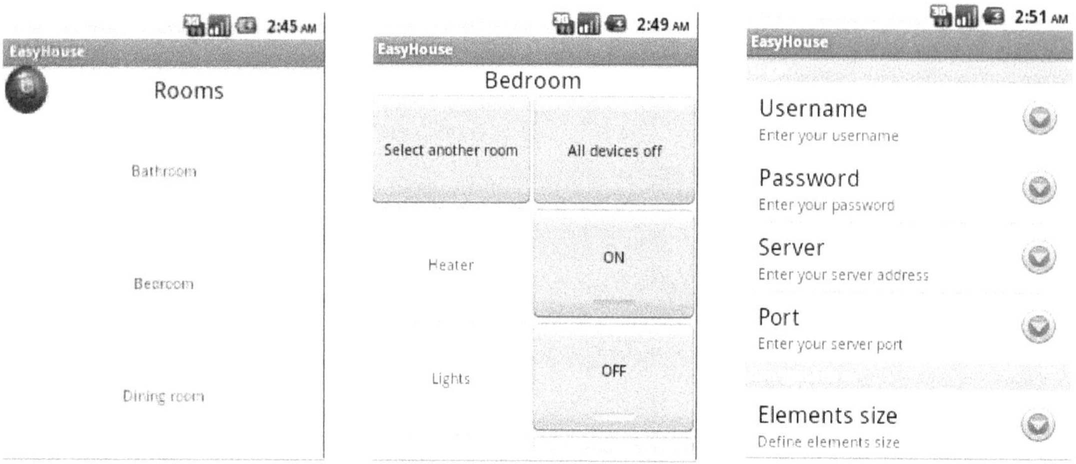

(a) (b) (c)

Figure 2: First high-fidelity prototype developed for Android.

We also gathered information and took into consideration the performance regarding the following issues: (1) successfully finding home appliances in the mobile application, (2) successfully controlling domotic devices and getting their status information, (3) learning to use the application quickly, (4) successfully recovering from errors, and (5) using the interface naturally.

User satisfaction and efficiency have been determined based on data collected from questionnaires.

We used two *smartphones* with the Android operating system to control the home appliances using the *EasyHouse* application. Both devices have 3.5-inch displays and identical characteristics. However, while Paulo preferred to define the dimensions of the user interface according with his preferences, his wife Tânia used the default settings.

4.1 Quantitative analysis

Paulo and Tânia were the subjects of automated tests, without having predefined tasks to accomplish in a limited amount of time. They simply used the system according to their own needs and the different actions were registered in log files to allow us to make a quantitative analysis and measure the errors committed while performing those actions.

An error has been considered when a specific domotic device changed its status more than once in less that 25 seconds. In other words, sometimes a user may press a wrong option by accident and usually he or she corrects it. Such actions are registered in a log file allowing us to determine possible usability issues. A script was written to process the log file and detect such errors. The results shown in Table 1 contains data collected during a one month period of usage. Both Paulo and Tânia quickly learned to use the system.

Tânia used the *EasyHouse* application 84 times, while Paulo used it 88 times over the same period, but she made a few more errors. Tânia also used the conventional remote control in order to manage the different home appliances. Tânia told us that she uses the remote control as a complement to the mobile application and likes to have a backup system. On the other hand, Paulo only used *EasyHouse* to control the domotic devices installed in his bedroom.

Table 1: Number of interactions (#I) and errors (#E) committed by Paulo and Tânia, detected automatically through inspection of log files.

	Paulo		Tânia	
Day	#I	#E	#I	#E
1	1	0	8	2
2	6	1	2	0
3	2	0	6	0
4	10	2	0	0
5	2	0	5	1
6	0	0	4	0
7	10	4	4	0
8	2	0	0	0
9	3	0	0	0
10	8	0	0	0
11	0	0	0	0
12	0	0	0	0
13	0	0	1	0
14	5	0	0	0
15	0	0	2	0
16	0	0	0	0
17	10	1	7	1
18	3	0	3	0
19	3	0	10	6
20	1	0	1	0
21	1	0	3	0
22	3	0	2	0
23	0	0	0	0
24	0	0	3	0
25	0	0	2	0
26	1	0	8	3
27	5	1	10	1
28	9	1	0	0
29	1	0	0	0
30	1	0	2	0
31	1	0	1	0
Total	88	10	84	14

Paulo prefers to use only the mobile application because (1) he always has the mobile with him, (2) He does not like to use the small remote controls, and (3) He does not like

Table 2: Performance (time in seconds) of subjects with the EasyHouse system and a remote control (RC).

	Pedro		Susana		Tânia	
Task	EasyHouse	RC	EasyHouse	RC	EasyHouse	RC
1	2.9	5.2	3.2	6.1	2.0	2.3
2	4.5	7.9	7.2	8.1	3.2	3.5
3	13.1 (8.9 + 4.2)	18.5 (12.0 + 6.5)	14.5 (7.5 + 7.0)	20.2 (13.0 + 7.2)	7.2 (4.8 + 2.4)	7.7 (5.0 + 2.7)

to waste time finding the remote control; the *EasyHouse* system is more practical for him.

Regarding the more traditional quantitative tests, three tasks of increasing complexity were idealized and subsequently tested by Pedro, Susana, and Tânia. The tasks simulate different scenarios that can occur in daily usage in a real home. All testers had a period of 20 minutes to get themselves familiarized with the system. During the 20 minute period, Pedro and Susana changed the size of the user interface components to make them bigger, and used that setting subsequently during the tests. Tânia opted to used the predefined size. Recall that Pedro and Susana have mild motor disabilities, while Tânia does not. A description of the tasks follows next.

Task 1 (simple): Turn off all domotic equipment from the smart room (Paulo's bedroom). Subtasks:

1. Select the desired room in the user interface.
2. Turn off all devices (main light, TV, and lamp) using whatever method the user finds most convenient.

Task 2 (medium): It's getting dark and you would like to relax a bit in the smart room by turning on the lamp and the TV. Subtasks:

1. Turn on the lamp.
2. Turn on the TV.

Task 3 (complex): Turn on all devices on the smart room and then dim the lamp. Two minutes later, switch off the TV and the main light. Subtasks:

1. Turn on all devices.
2. Dim the lamp.
3. Two minutes later, turn off the TV and the main light.

Table 2 shows the time needed by each tester to accomplish each task, using both the *EasyHouse* system and a card-sized remote control, KR22E, that allows users to send On, Off, Dim and Bright commands to four different X10 devices. None of the testers did errors (i.e., pressed a wrong option) during the tests. On Task 3, we measured the time separately, before and after the 2 minute pause.

The remote control KR22E was bought by us together with the X10 devices. It is the standard, off-the-shelf way of controlling lamps and other electrical appliances enabled with X10 devices. The remote control is obviously limited in terms of usability as it requires the user to remember which button correspond to which lamp/appliance. Moreover, it has a fixed number of options which is usually small. For example, the KR22E only allows the control of four lamp/appliances. *EasyHouse* was built not only to overcome such limitation but also to make it accessible for people with hand motor disabilities.

4.2 Qualitative analysis

We elaborated a questionnaire in order to help us understand users' perception of *EasyHouse*. The set of eight questions included in the questionnaire is specified below:

1. How easy/difficult was controlling home appliances with the *EasyHouse* system? *(very difficult, difficult, easy, very easy)*
2. Was it easier or more difficult than traditional methods for controlling intelligent environments? *(much more difficult, more difficult, equally difficult, easier)*
3. Did you change the default size of the interface elements? *(yes, no)*
4. How easy/difficult was it to navigate through options to find the desired item? *(very difficult, difficult, easy, very easy)*
5. How easy/difficult was it to control a domotic device? *(very difficult, difficult, easy, very easy)*
6. How fast do you think you learned to use the *EasyHouse* system? *(very slow, slow, fast, very fast)*
7. What is your level of satisfaction regarding the mobile application? *(very satisfying, moderately satisfying, barely satisfying, unsatisfying)*
8. How tiring is controlling a home appliance? *(very much, somewhat, a little bit, not at all)*

Table 3: Questionnaire results

Q.	Pedro	Susana	Tânia
1	very easy	very easy	easy
2	easier	easier	equally difficult
3	yes	yes	no
4	very easy	very easy	easy
5	very easy	very easy	easy
6	very fast	very fast	fast
7	moderately	very satisfying	moderately
8	not at all	not at all	not at all

The answers obtained from the questionnaire are shown in Table 3 and allowed us to take some interesting conclusions. All users were satisfied with the *EasyHouse* system and none found it tiring. All of them found the system easy or very easy to use. Pedro and Susana preferred using *EasyHouse* compared with a traditional remote control. Tânia, on the other hand, didn't have a preference for a particular method.

4.3 Discussion

The evaluation revealed that *EasyHouse* is useful and easy to use for both users with and without motor disabilities. People without disabilities appear to see this system as any other method for controlling home appliances. On the other hand, people with hand coordination problems are able to adapt the user interface to their own needs.

Although the number of testers is too small to obtain statistical significant conclusions, it is important to stress that *EasyHouse* has been used daily at Paulo's house, both by him and his wife Tânia, to perform everyday activities. Paulo uses it as a substitute for other systems that are commonly used to control intelligent environments, accomplishing a better interaction with the surrounding environment. Tânia uses it as a complement for the remote controls. This is a proof-of-concept that the system is useful in practice. The fact that Pedro and Susana didn't find any severe usability problems with *EasyHouse* can be perhaps explained due to their similar level of motor disability with Paulo: all have mild hand motor disability.

5. SUMMARY AND CONCLUSIONS

This paper presented *EasyHouse* and its development process. The system allows both people with hand coordination problems as well as their family members to control home appliances using a mobile device. *EasyHouse* is flexible, adjustable and is easy-to-use. It can be used in varying ways to control intelligent environments.

Preliminary tests have shown that *EasyHouse* is suitable and useful for all family members, allowing each user to adapt and use it according with his/her needs. *EasyHouse* has been evaluated both with pre-defined tasks as well as in a real context with real users in order to understand its advantages and limitations.

We plan to to perform further development and evaluation of *EasyHouse* to improve its usability and allow a better user experience. We also plan to explore alternative methods such as image recognition and/or speech recognition techniques to provide different ways for controlling home appliances. By doing so, *EasyHouse* can evolve into a more complete and adequate system to control assisted intelligent environments.

6. ACKNOWLEDGEMENTS

This work was sponsored by FCT/MEC under grant SFRH/BPD/65187/2009.

7. REFERENCES

[1] J. Abascal. Ambient intelligence for people with disabilities and elderly people. In *Proceedings of the ACM's Special Interest Group on Computer-Human Interaction (SIGCHI), Ambient Intelligence for Scientific Discovery (AISD) Workshop*, 2004.

[2] Z. Z. Bien, J.-H. Do, J.-B. Kim, D. Stefanov, and K.-H. Park. User-friendly interaction/interface control of intelligent home for movement-disabled people. In *Proceedings of the 10th International Conference on Human-Computer Interaction*, pages 304–308, 2003.

[3] J. M. Corchado, J. Bajo, D. I. Tapia, and A. Abraham. Using heterogeneous wireless sensor networks in a telemonitoring system for healthcare. *IEEE Transactions on Information Technology in Biomedicine*, 14(2):234–240, 2010.

[4] G. Edlinger, C. Holzner, and C. Guger. A hybrid brain-computer interface for smart home control. In *Proceedings of the 14th International Conference on Human-Computer Interaction. Interaction Techniques and Environments*, pages 417–426. Springer, 2011.

[5] K. A. Faraj, M. Mojahid, and N. Vigouroux. BigKey: A virtual keyboard for mobile devices. In *Proceedings of the 13th International Conference on Human-Computer Interaction. Part III: Ubiquitous and Intelligent Interaction*, volume 5612 of *Lecture Notes in Computer Science*, pages 3–10. Springer Berlin / Heidelberg, 2009.

[6] K. Gill, S.-H. Yang, F. Yao, and X. Lu. A zigbee-based home automation system. *IEEE Transactions on Consumer Electronics*, 55(2):422–430, 2009.

[7] R. Godinho, P. A. Condado, M. Zacarias, and F. G. Lobo. Improving accessibility of mobile devices with easywrite. *Behaviour & IT*, 34(2):135–150, 2015.

[8] C. Gomez and J. Paradells. Wireless home automation networks: A survey of architectures and technologies. *IEEE Communications Magazine*, 48(6):92–101, 2010.

[9] S. S. Intille. The goal: smart people, not smart homes. In *Proceedings of the International Conference on Smart Homes and Health Telematics*, pages 3–6. IOS Press, 2006.

[10] T. Kleinberger, M. Becker, E. Ras, A. Holzinger, and P. Müller. Ambient intelligence in assisted living: Enable elderly people to handle future interfaces. In *Universal Access in Human-Computer Interaction. Ambient Interaction*, volume 4555 of *Lecture Notes in Computer Science*, pages 103–112. Springer Berlin / Heidelberg, 2007.

[11] J. Nielsen. *Usability Engineering*. Morgan Kaufmann, 1994.

[12] A. M. Peixoto. B-live home-aplicação móvel para sistema de domótica habitacional. Master's thesis, Universidade de Aveiro, Portugal, 2012.

[13] T. G. Stavropoulos, K. Gottis, D. Vrakas, and I. Vlahavas. awesome: A web service middleware for ambient intelligence. *Expert Systems with Applications*, 40(11):4380–4392, 2013.

[14] K. Vertanen and P. O. Kristensson. Parakeet: a continuous speech recognition system for mobile touch-screen devices. In *Proceedings of the 14th International Conference on Intelligent User Interfaces*, IUI '09, pages 237–246, New York, NY, USA, 2009. ACM.

[15] J. O. Wobbrock, B. A. Myers, and J. A. Kembel. EdgeWrite: A stylus-based text entry method designed for high accuracy and stability of motion. In *Proceedings of the 16th annual ACM Symposium on User Interface Software and Technology*, UIST '03, pages 61–70, New York, NY, USA, 2003. ACM Press.

[16] C. Yerrapragada and P. Fisher. Voice controlled smart house. In *Proceedings of the IEEE International Conference on Consumer Electronics*, pages 154–155. IEEE, 1993.

A Spellchecker for Dyslexia

Luz Rello
HCI Institute
Carnegie Mellon University
luzrello@cs.cmu.edu

Miguel Ballesteros
LT Institute
Carnegie Mellon University
NLP Group
Universitat Pompeu Fabra
miguel.ballesteros@upf.edu

Jeffrey P. Bigham
HCI and LT Institutes
Carnegie Mellon University
jbigham@cs.cmu.edu

ABSTRACT

Poor spelling is a challenge faced by people with dyslexia throughout their lives. Spellcheckers are therefore a crucial tool for people with dyslexia, but current spellcheckers do not detect real-word errors, which are a common type of errors made by people with dyslexia. Real-word errors are spelling mistakes that result in an unintended but real word, for instance, *form* instead of *from*. Nearly 20% of the errors that people with dyslexia make are real-word errors. In this paper, we introduce a system called *Real Check* that uses a probabilistic language model, a statistical dependency parser and Google n-grams to detect real-world errors. We evaluated *Real Check* on text written by people with dyslexia, and showed that it detects more of these errors than widely used spellcheckers. In an experiment with 34 people (17 with dyslexia), people with dyslexia corrected sentences more accurately and in less time with *Real Check*.

Keywords

Dyslexia; Spellchecker; Real-Word Errors; Spelling Errors.

Categories and Subject Descriptors

K.4.2 [**Computers and Society**]: Social Issues—*Assistive technologies for persons with disabilities*; K.3 [**Computers in Education**]: Computer Uses in Education.

1. INTRODUCTION

Dyslexia is the most frequent language-based learning disability. 10% of the population has dyslexia [13], which represents from 70 to 80% of the language-based learning disabilities. Dyslexia is defined as a neurological specific reading and spelling disorder by the World Health Organization [34]. People with dyslexia have difficulty not only with reading but also with writing.

A main challenge is that people with dyslexia do not consciously detect spelling errors [26]. As a result, the text that people with dyslexia write contains more errors, even if they are trained; and adults with dyslexia keep making spelling errors without noticing [31]. Spelling errors can negatively affect how the people making those errors are perceived. For instance, it can lead to lower grades on school work, and cause people to think those making the errors are less intelligent.

Spellcheckers should help people with dyslexia make fewer errors, but they tend to miss real-word errors – a category of errors that people with dyslexia are especially likely to make. A real-word error is a correctly spelled word that is not the one the user intended to write. For instance, the sentence bellow has six spelling errors, but they are not detected by common spellcheckers because they are real words.[1]

*We *sow *quit a *big *miss *take we *maid.*
We show quite a big mistake we made.

In fact, a comparison of the most popular spellcheckers on different error types showed that real-word errors were the least flagged by the spellcheckers [23]. While grammar checkers promise to solve such problems in some cases eventually, the grammar checkers available in common software cannot detect many real-word errors now and many real-word errors are grammatical even if statistically unlikely. Moreover, real-word errors are frequent. Considering the errors written by people with dyslexia, 17% and 21% are real-word errors in English and Spanish texts, respectively [25, 28].

In this paper we present a method to detect and correct real-word errors in Spanish. To evaluate the usefulness of the method we performed three experiments. First, we evaluate the accuracy of the method using a corpus of real-world native Spanish speakers with dyslexia. Second, we compared the method with the most widely used spellcheckers. Third, we carried out an experiment with 34 people, 17 with dyslexia, to test the efficiency of the detections and the corrections using real sentences written by people with dyslexia.

The contributions of this paper are:

- a method to detect and correct real-word errors in Spanish;
- *Real Check*, a system that detects more real-word errors than the most widely use correctors;
- a study showing that *Real Check* makes people with dyslexia to correct sentences in a faster and more accurate way.

[1]For instance, Microsoft Word 2013 and LibreOffice 4.2.6.3 on Ubuntu 14.04 do not detect them.

ASSETS '15, October 26-28, 2015, Lisbon, Portugal.
Copyright 2015 ACM ISBN 978-1-4503-3400-6/15/10 ...$15.00.
http://dx.doi.org/10.1145/2700648.2809850.

2. RELATED WORK

Our work is related to *(i)* spellcheckers for dyslexia based on user modelling, and *(ii)* spellcheckers based on natural language processing (NLP) that target real-word errors.

2.1 User Modeling for Dyslexia

The first approach to apply user modeling to error correction for users with dyslexia was an adaptive corrector called *Babel* [30]. It contained new rules addressing the permutation of letters as well as a user model of the writer's spelling errors to adapt the detection and correction of typical errors to a specific user. Spooner [30] evaluated the spellchecker using text written by people with dyslexia and found out that it was more effective for some users.

Other Approaches. Li *et al.* [16] developed a model, *PoliSpell*, that aims at typical errors made by people with dyslexia, such as boundary errors and real-word errors. The authors plan to evaluate it in future work. Similarly, Gustafsson [10] developed a user model-based spellchecker for Swedish users with dyslexia, although it is yet to be evaluated.

2.2 Real-Word Error Correction

2.2.1 Semantic Information

Hirst and Budanitsky [12] developed a method using WordNet [20] together the semantic distance formula by Jiang and Conrath [15] to detect words that are potentially anomalous in context. The idea behind this approach in that words appearing together are semantically close. If the word was semantically distant from nearby words it was considered a potential error. The authors tested the method on an artificial corpus of English errors achieving from 23 to 50% recall and from 18 to 25% precision.[2]

2.2.2 Probability Information

Second, there are methods that use probability information using n-grams [14, 18, 33]. In these methods a word becomes an error candidate if the probability of the ngram within its context is lower than the one obtained by replacing one of the words with a spelling variation. The methods by Mays *et al.* [18], Wilcox-O'Hearn *et al.* [33] and Islam and Inkpen [14] used word-trigram probabilities for detecting and correcting real-word errors and they were all evaluated on the same corpus: 500 articles from the 1987-89 Wall Street Journal corpus where real-word errors were randomly inserted every 200 words. To the best of our knowlegde, the method by Islam and Inkpen [14] achieved the best results: 0.890 (R)[3] 0.445 (P) 0.593 (F1) for error detection, and 0.763 (R) 0.381 (P) 0.508 (F1) for error correction. Similarly, Verberne [32] proposed a trigram-based method where any word trigram occurring in the British National Corpus [5] is correct, and the rest are a likely error. The system was evaluation with part of the Wall Street Journal corpus, 7,100 words with 31 errors inserted every 200 words approximately. The results yield a 0.33 (R), 0.05 (P) and 0.086 (F1) for error correction.

2.2.3 Confusion Sets

Third, there are a number of approaches that rely on confusions sets. Confusion sets are pre-defined sets of commonly confounded words, such as *cruse|crews|cruise|curse* or *from|form*. Once a word belonging to confusion set appears in a context, these methods perform different types of word sense disambiguation to predict which member of that confusion sets is the most appropriate for that context. There are rule-based methods [24, 25] as well as machine learning approaches [7, 9]. Using a corpus of texts written by people with dyslexia as development dataset, Pedler [25] designed three rule-based methods: a frequency-only based system, a syntax-based (using bigram probabilities), and semantic method (using WordNet). The author evaluated the best performing method (the semantic one) using 6,000 confusions sets and two corpora written by students, containing 199 and 1,049 real-word errors, respectively. For each of the corpus results were 31.1% and 23.4% (R); 83.3% and 77.2% (P) for error detection, and 70.3% and 60.3% (P) for error correction. To the best of our knowledge the machine learning approaches achieves the highest results –but using automatic corpora [7, 9]. These methods were tested running confusion sets on Wall Street Journal corpus and results are presented for each of the confusion sets. Golding and Roth [9] method detects about 96% of context-sensitive spelling errors, in addition to ordinary non-word spelling errors. Carlson *et al.* [7] method improved the scalability of the previous method as well as its performance reaching to 99% of accuracy for some confusion sets.

Commercial tools. We found a commercial spellcheckers that aim at English real-word errors either for people with dyslexia[4] or general population.[5] We could not find any documentation about how these commercial tools were developed.

2.3 What is Missing?

The method we present in this paper differs from previous work in the following aspects: First, it is for Spanish while the previous methods are for English. Second, it advances previous NLP approaches combining the probabilistic information from Google Books Ngram Corpus –using also 4- and 5-grams– with Spanish confusion sets together with a language model and rules over dependency parse trees. Third, it is evaluated by 34 people with and without dyslexia using –not an artificial corpus– real texts written by people with dyslexia.

3. METHOD

First, we collected texts written by native Spanish speakers with dyslexia to be able to develop and evaluate our method. Second, we developed an algorithm that works in 3 steps: *(i)* confusion set extraction, *(ii)* n-gram matching, and *(iii)* two filters, a language model and a dependency parser. For the development of the system we used a small subset of 22 sentences held-out from the final evaluation (Section 4.1).

3.1 Crowdsourcing Dyslexic Errors

Since written errors by people with dyslexia differ from regular spelling errors [25, 31], we collected text written by people with dyslexia to develop and evaluate our spellchecker. To do so, we made a public call to look for volunteers via the main associations of dyslexia of a Spanish native speaking country. We recruited two groups of people, one in Madrid

[2]Definitions of precision and recall are given in Section 4.2.
[3]R stands for recall, P for precision and F1 for F-measure.

[4]Ghotit Dyslexia Software: `http://www.ghotit.com/`
[5]Ginger Software: `www.gingersoftware.com/`

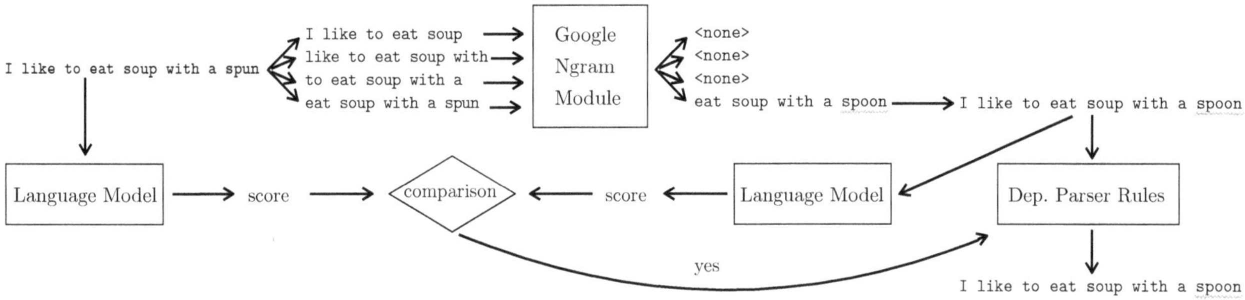

Figure 1: Workflow of the algorithm.

and one Barcelona, with whom we met to collect real-word errors. We asked them to bring with them texts written by people with diagnosed dyslexia and a laptop to introduce the errors using an on-line form. The volunteers were eight adults with diagnosed dyslexia, seven mothers and one father with children with dyslexia -four of them came with their children (eight children)-, and two secondary school teachers. We collected real-word errors with-in the sentence they appear from old notebooks, school essays, and texts written with a computer but without using spellcheckers. We gathered almost 600 sentences candidates but only keep 366; we discarded (a) the sentences which did not have real-word errors (such as typos or possible words but do not appear in the dictionary); (b) ungrammatical sentences; and (c) sentences that contained repeated errors. The selected sentences had at least one real-word error (1.12 errors per sentence) and their length ranged from 5 to 15 words.

3.2 Creating Confusion Sets

We analysed the errors linguistically [27], and found a simple set of rules would cover the great majority of real-word errors. Words that tended to be confounded differ from one to another in only one or two characters, or in the order of the characters, such as *casa ('house')* and *saca ('take out')*. Since Spanish has a shallow orthography, that is, the orthography of a word represents its pronunciation in a transparent and regular way, we could compile a list of confusion sets automatically using a Spanish dictionary[6] without requiring phonetic transcriptions. To this end, we used the Levenshtein Automaton dymamic algorithm [29].[7] We extract for each word all possible candidate words at Levenshtein distance 1 if the original word has 4 characters or less, and at Levenshtein distance 1 and 2 if it has more than 4 characters. We also calculate all possible anagrams for a word that occurs in the dictionary. As a result we had a resource of 1,250,781 different confusion sets in Spanish.

3.3 N-gram Matching

Once we have a confusion set for each word in the sentence, our system performs n-gram matching on the Google Books Ngram Corpus (2012 edition). This corpus consists of n-grams and their usage frequency over time,[8] and is derived from 8,116,746 books, over 6% of all books ever published. The corpus has 854,649 volumes and 83,967,471,303 tokens in Spanish [17].

Our algorithm works as follows (Figure1), given a sentence we generate all possible sentences in which each word has been changed for every word in its confusion set, we call them candidate sentences. The system extracts all possible 5-grams of the original sentence and all the candidate sentences. For each 5-gram the system extracts all possible 3-grams within the 5-gram and all possible 4-grams within the 5-gram. Finally, it checks for the existence of the n-grams[9] for the original sentence and for each candidate sentence. Candidate sentences that are more frequent due to 4-grams count twice as candidates found for 3-grams. In other words, if the candidate sentence is more frequent according to the n-gram corpus, we mark the candidate word to be a "suggested" correction and the original word to be a detected real-word error.

The system selects at most 7 suggestions for a single word. If there are more than 7, it filters out the less frequent ones, based on frequency in the Google Books Ngram Corpus, so it basically selects the top most frequent suggestions.

3.4 Filter-1: Language Model Filter

The third step of the algorithm is a language model,[10] we use the BerkeleyLM [22] with the pretrained Spanish n-gram model[11] trained on the WEB-1T corpus [3]. We use the language model to filter out ungrammatical suggestions.

The filter works as follows: once the system has found a candidate word, we run the language model to get the score of the candidate sentence that has the original word replaced by the candidate one. If the score is lower than the score of the original sentence, then the candidate is filtered out, otherwise it keeps going (Figure1). This filtering approach is similar to the one implemented in the grammatical error correction system by Felice *et al.* [8]. In our case only sentences in which stop words[12] have been changed are evaluated with the language model, since we found that, in

[6]We use the GNU aspell dictionaries which are freely available via `http://aspell.net/`

[7]`https://github.com/klawson88/LevenshteinAutomaton`

[8]`http://books.google.com/ngrams`

[9]Being n, either 3 or 4. We found that the 5-gram approach did not find any of the 5-grams included in the development set, so we decided to only explore 3-grams and 4-grams.

[10]A language model is a system that assigns a score to a sentence according to a probability distribution. In other words, it predicts whether a sentence belongs to a language or not, so it gives higher scores to sentences that truly belong to that particular language, in our case, Spanish.

[11]It can be found at `http://tomato.banatao.berkeley.edu:8080/berkeleylm_binaries/`

[12]We use the list of stop words that is freely available at `https://code.google.com/p/stop-words/`

preliminary experiments on the development set (see Section 4.2), the language model did not help for other kind of real-word errors.

3.5 Filter-2: Dependency Parsing

As a fourth step and another way of filtering erroneous candidates, we use the joint dependency parser, lemmatizer, part-of-speech tagger and morphological tagger of Bohnet and Nivre [2] trained on the Spanish CoNLL-2009 data [11].[13]

A dependency parser outputs a syntactic dependency tree of a sentence, and this one, in particular, provides lemmas, part-of-speech tags and more fine grained morphosyntactic tags. By using the dependency tree, the part-of-speech tags, the lemmas and the morphology, we came up with a set of rules that filters the suggestions found in the Google Ngram Corpus and that are better ranked according to the language model. The rules are the following: (1) if the suggested word is a verb and is not in participle/gerund form but it has as syntactic head a token with lemma *haber,'to have'/estar, 'to be'*, then it is filtered out; (2) if the suggested word has been tagged as singular/plural, but it is the head of a determiner which is plural/singular, then it is filtered out; and (3) if the suggested word has been tagged as singular/plural, but it is the head of a plural/singular determiner, then it is filtered out.

4. EVALUATION

We evaluated our method in three ways: (i) an evaluation of the system using dataset that consists of sentences written by people with dyslexia; (ii) an evaluation of the system in comparison with widely used spellcheckers; and (iii) a user evaluation with 34 participants.

4.1 Evaluation Datasets

We compiled 3 different datasets: *(i)* a development set consisting of 22 sentences with errors that is held-out from the rest of the experiments; *(ii)* a evaluation dataset consisting of 344 sentences used for the system evaluation and the comparison with other spellcheckers; and *(iii)* a subset of *(ii)* of 37 sentences used for the user evaluation.

4.2 System Evaluation

The development set was only used to the development of the system: to tune the language model parameters and threshold described in Section 3.4 and to come up with the rules depicted in Section 3.5. During the development of the system, we applied both filters and a 3-4-5-gram approach. We managed to achieve good results for both the correction and detection of real-word errors on the development set (Detection: F1=0.67. Correction: F1=0.83), by manually enriching the confusion sets, setting up thresholds for the language model,[14] implementing the rules over dependency trees, and by deciding to remove the string matching for 5-grams since it did not yield to any improvements.

Once we had the system tuned to perform well in the 22 sentences of the development set, we carried out the final experiment on the test set for evaluation.

[13]The results –including punctuation symbols– of the parser are 98.82 for POS accuracy, 98.02 for morphology tagging, 92.70 for lemma prediction, 88.04 LAS and 91.22 UAS [11].

[14]The best threshold ended up being 0, and this is why we did not describe it in detail in Section 3.4.

Real-word Error Detection							
Real Check	TP	TN	FP	FN	P	R	F1
3	**256**	1404	317	**105**	44.68	70.91	54.82
4	158	1623	98	203	61.72	43.77	51.22
3-4	**256**	1409	312	**105**	45.07	**70.91**	55.11
3-4-LM-DP	238	1487	234	238	50.42	65.93	**57.14**
TextEdit	17	1719	2	344	89.47	4.71	8.94
Pages	26	1719	2	335	92.86	7.20	13.37
OpenOffice	17	1719	2	344	89.47	4.71	8.95
MS Word	21	**1721**	**0**	340	**100.0**	5.82	10.99
Google Docs	135	1718	3	226	97.83	37.40	54.11
Real-word Error Correction							
Real Check	TP	TN	FP	FN	P	R	F1
3	136	1404	437	**105**	23.73	56.43	33.42
4	120	1623	136	203	46.88	37.15	41.45
3-4	**137**	1409	431	**105**	24.12	**56.61**	33.83
3-4-LM-DP	121	1487	351	123	25.64	49.59	33.80
TextEdit	10	1719	133	344	6.99	2.82	4.02
Pages	14	1719	220	335	5.98	4.01	4.80
OpenOffice	13	1719	195	344	6.25	3.64	4.60
MS Word	11	**1721**	237	340	4.44	3.13	3.67
Google Docs	127	1718	**11**	226	**92.03**	35.98	**51.73**

Table 1: Real-word error detection (above) and correction (below) results. 3 is a system that works with 3-grams. 4 works with 4-grams. 3-4 works with 3-grams and 4-grams. LM-DP means that the system has the filters implemented (dep.parser and language model). Best results are presented in bold.

In Table 1 we depict the results of each of the components of the system standing alone and in combination, showing the results of a simple 3-gram approach, a 4-gram approach, a 3-gram-4-gram approach, and the latter with the parsing and the language model filters. The table shows the number of true positives (TP), number of true negatives (TN), the number of false positives (FP), the number of false negatives (FN), precision (P) which is calculated as P=TP/TP+FP, recall (R) which is calculated as R=TP/TP+FN and the F1 score (F1) which is calculated as F1=2TP/(2TP+FP+FN). Note that, following [14], in the error correction task, if any of the suggestions given for a word is correct then it is considered as a TP.

4.3 Comparison with Spellcheckers

We compare our model with spellcheckers that are implemented in widely used word processing software: Microsoft Word,[15] Google Docs,[16] OpenOffice,[17] Pages,[18] and TextEdit.[19] We could not include commercial spellcheckers that aimed at real-word errors (Section 2) because they are only available for English.

As shown in Table 1, our system(s) achieved competitive results for both the detection and correction of real-word errors. The inclusion of a language model leads to a more precision oriented system, which can be useful depending on the task. The only spellchecker that provides competitive

[15]`https://products.office.com/en-us/word`

[16]`http://docs.google.com`

[17]`https://www.openoffice.org/`

[18]`https://www.apple.com/mac/pages/`

[19]`https://developer.apple.com/library/mac/samplecode/TextEdit`

results compared to us is the one implemented under the Google Docs on-line tool that it is better in the correction of errors. With an implementation towards a high precision and lower recall, it is capable of detecting half of the errors and it provides high precision results. However, it is worth noting that our implementation outperforms its results for error detection, and we therefore correct more errors.

4.4 User Evaluation

To evaluate the effect of the spellchecker on the correction of texts we conducted an experiment with 34 participants divided into two groups: participants with dyslexia and strong readers. Objective measures were collected using an on-line test in which each participant had to correct 37 randomly selected sentences containing real-word errors. Subjective measures were gathered via questionnaires.

4.4.1 Design

In our experimental design, *Correction Type* served as an *independent measure* with three levels: *None* denotes the condition where the text was presented without using any spellchecker method; *Error Detection Only* denotes the condition where the text was presented to the participant enabling only the option that highlights the errors detected by our spellchecker (Figure 2, up); and *Error Suggestions* denotes the condition where the text was presented to the participant enabling all the options of our system, highlighting the error candidates and showing suggestions for the correction of the error candidates (Figure 2, down).

We used a within-subject design, that is, each participant contributed to the three conditions. To cancel out order effects, the sentences and the conditions were presented to the participant shorted randomly.

For quantifying the efficiency of the participants using our corrector we defined four *dependent measures*: two objective and two subjective. We collected the objective measures from the interaction with our on-line test, while subjective measures were collected by self-report questionnaires using 5-point Likert scales. The dependent measures are:

Writing Accuracy: the correctness degree of the sentence. We measured correctness of the sentences in a scale from 1 to 100. If the sentence was left with no modifications we raked the accuracy as 0. If the sentence was perfectly correct matching the intended sentence *Writing Accuracy* equals to 100. For the cases that did not fall into these categories (140 out of 1,258 data points) we manually analysed the input of the participants to identify the following categories from the input responses:

- *Punctuation and capital letters:* where the participant changed the punctuation and capitalization of the sentences. Since the sentences were correct, they had a score of 100.

- *Semantic errors:* where the participants detect the error and wrote another word correctly but is was not the intended word. Since these sentences were correct we also gave them 100 score. *e.g. un café tostado ('a roasted coffee')*, instead of *un café cortado ('one coffee machiatto')*.

- *Accentuation:* where the participant detected the erroneous word but made an accentuation mistake when writing the intended word. *e.g. raiz* instead of *raíz ('root')*. The score of these errors were 75.

- *Typo:* where the participant detected the erroneous word but made a typo mistake when writing the intended word. These cases had a score of 25.

- *Wrong:* where the participant included more erroneous words in the sentence than in the input. These sentences had a score of 0.

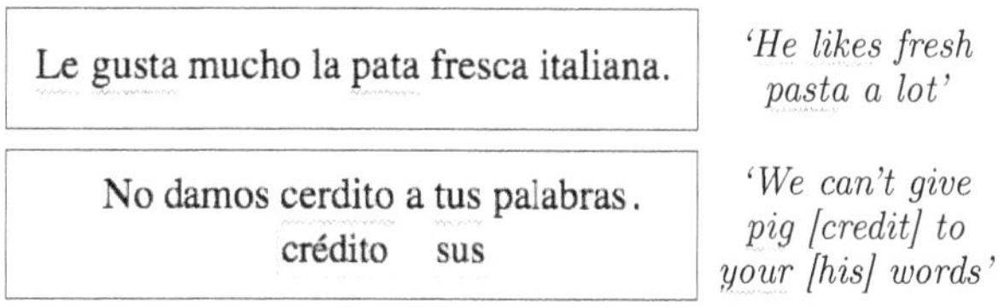

Figure 2: Screenshots of two sentences used in the experiment presented under the conditions of *Detection Only* (up) and *Suggestions* (down).

Correcting Time: Time in seconds that the participant spent correcting the sentence. It was calculated in milliseconds starting from the time that the participant is exposed to the sentence until they click submit. Once the sentence was modified by the participant, there was no indication to show whether the sentence was correctly corrected or not.

Subjective Writing Accuracy For each of the conditions the participants had to rate how accurate they found their performance correcting the sentences. For instance, *Using the word suggestions I corrected the sentences... 1* = Very bad *to 5* = Very good.

Subjective Writing Time For each of the conditions the participants had to rate how fast they found their performance correcting the sentences. The scores range from 1 = *Very slow* to 5 = *Very fast.* For instance, *Using the highlight option I corrected the sentences... [scale].*

4.4.2 Participants

We recruited 34 participants divided into two groups: 17 with dyslexia and 17 'strong readers' —people without dyslexia who were familiar with Spanish orthographic rules and able to evaluate the corrector.

The average age of the participants with dyslexia was 38.65 with a standard deviation of 11.19, and their ages ranged from 20 to 50 years old. The ages of the strong readers ranged from 25 to 58 (M= 38.29, SD = 12.92). All the participants were Spanish native speakers.

Except from one participant, all of them used spellcheckers frequently when: 3 participants used the iOS corrector installed in Pages word processor, 2 did not know because they used LaTeX and the corrector depends on the packages, 1 participant used the spellchecker from Google Docs and the rest (27 participants) used Microsoft Word spellchecker.

With the exception of two participants with dyslexia who dropped high school, 4 participants had finished high school, 2 and 4 participants had college and university degrees, respectively; and 4 had professional education. On the other hand, all the strong readers except from 2, who finished college, have finished their university degrees.

4.4.3 Materials and Procedure

Evaluation Dataset. We randomly extracted 37 sentences, that is 11% from the text set (344 of sentences written by people with dyslexia, Section 3.1) and run *Real Check* over the sentences. The corrector output served as an evaluation dataset.

Test. The evaluation dataset was integrated in an on-line test implemented using json. Each of the sentences were presented randomly within a *Correction Type* condition.

Once the participants agreed to take part in the study, we gave them specific instructions. Then, they first took the on-line test were they had to fix the sentences, and second the completed an on-line questionnaire.

4.4.4 Results

First, we use the Shapiro-Wilk test for checking if data fits a normal distribution and the Bartlett's test to check for homogeneity. For both groups, Shapiro-Wilk tests showed that the six datasets (one per condition per group) were not normally distributed for the *Correcting Time*. Similarly, Shapiro-Wilk tests showed that no datasets were normally distributed for the *Subjective Correcting Time* of both groups. Also, Bartlett's tests showed that none of the datasets had an homogeneous variance for all the measures and both groups.

As our data was not normal nor homogeneous, we include the median for all our measures in addition to the average and the standard deviation. For the same reason, to study the effects of the dependent variables we used the two-way Friedman's non-parametric test for repeated measures plus a complete pairwise Wilcoxon rank sum post-hoc comparison test with a Bonferroni correction that includes the adjustment of the significance level. We used the same procedure to show effects of the conditions within groups, dividing the data for each group. For the Likert scales we also used non-parametric tests [6].

Table 2 summarizes the main statistical measures for each of the conditions per group.

Writing Accuracy. There was a significant effect of *Correction Type* on *Writing Accuracy* ($\chi^2(2) = 10.015$, $p = 0.007$). The results of the post-hoc tests show that:

- **Between Groups:** Participants with dyslexia had significantly lower writing accuracy under all conditions ($M = 86.72, Mdn = 100.00$, $SD = 32.43$) than the stronger readers ($M = 93.48, Mdn = 100.00$, $SD = 23.72$, $p < 0.001$).
- **Participants with Dyslexia:** There was a significant effect of *Correction Type* on *Writing Accuracy* ($\chi^2(2) = 19.452$, $p < 0.001$) (Table 2).
  - *Suggestions* had the highest *Writing Accuracy* mean. Participants with dyslexia wrote more correctly text using *Suggestions* than *None* ($p < 0.001$).
  - *Detection Only* had the second highest *Writing Accuracy* mean. Participants with dyslexia wrote more correctly text using *Detection Only* than *None* ($p = 0.004$).
- **Strong Readers:** We could not find effect of *Correction Type* on *Writing Accuracy* for the strong readers group ($\chi^2(2) = 1.047$, $p = 0.596$).

Correcting Time. There was a significant effect of *Correction Type* on *Correcting Time* ($\chi^2(2) = 639.44$, $p < 0.001$). The results of the post-hoc tests show that:

- **Between Groups:** Participants with dyslexia had significantly shorter attempts to correct the sentences ($M = 12.47, Mdn = 10.23$, $SD = 12.80$) than the strong readers ($M = 12.62, Mdn = 7.96$, $SD = 16.41$, $p < 0.001$).
- **Participants with Dyslexia:** There was a significant effect of *Correction Type* on *Correcting Time* ($\chi^2(2) = 349.76$, $p < 0.001$) (Table 2).
  - *Suggestions* had the shortest correction time mean. Participants spent significantly less time using *Suggestions* than *Detection Only* ($p < 0.001$), and *None* ($p < 0.001$).
  - *Detection Only* had the second shortest correction time mean. Participants spent significantly less time using *Detection Only* than *None* ($p = 0.004$).
- **Strong Readers:** There was a significant effect of *Correction Type* on *Correcting Time* ($\chi^2(2) = 263.27$, $p < 0.001$) (Table 2).
  - Strong readers spent significantly less time correcting sentences using *Suggestions* than with *Detection Only* ($p < 0.001$) or the absence of the condition, *None* ($p = 0.002$).
  - We could not find effects between *Detection Only* and *None* conditions for the strong readers ($p = 0.722$).

Subjective Writing Accuracy. There was a significant effect of *Correction Type* on *Subjective Writing Accuracy* ($\chi^2(2) = 22.40$, $p < 0.001$). The results of the post-hoc tests show that:

- **Between Groups:** Participants with dyslexia had significantly lower subjective writing accuracy under all conditions than the stronger readers ($p = 0.046$), Table 2.
- **Participants with Dyslexia:** There was a significant effect of *Correction Type* on *Subjective Writing Accuracy* ($\chi^2(2) = 13.90$, $p = 0.001$) (Table 2).
  - Participants with dyslexia perceived that they wrote more accurate text using *Suggestions* than with the absence of the condition ($p = 0.005$).
- **Strong Readers:** There was a significant effect of *Correction Type* on *Subjective Writing Accuracy* ($\chi^2(2) = 8.86$, $p = 0.012$) (Table 2).
  - Strong readers reported that they wrote more accurate text using *Suggestions* than with the absence of the condition ($p = 0.080$).

Subjective Correcting Time. There was a significant effect of *Correction Type* on *Subjective Correcting Time* ($\chi^2(2) = 26.28$, $p < 0.001$), see Table 2. The results of the post-hoc tests show that:

- **Between Groups:** We could not find significant differences between groups on *Subjective Correcting Time* ($p = 0.073$).

Dependent Variable/Condition	*People with Dyslexia*			*Strong Readers*		
	Mdn	$M \pm SD$	%	*Mdn*	$M \pm SD$	%
Writing Accuracy						
None	100	78.05 ± 39.8	100	100	91.97 ± 25.79	100
Error Detection Only	100	89.83 ± 27.92	115	100	92.65 ± 25.08	101
Error Suggestions	100	93.01 ± 25	119	100	95.96 ± 19.51	104
Correcting Time						
None	10.26	11.97 ± 7.30	119	8.33	12.35 ± 14.06	111
Error Detection Only	11.93	15.44 ± 18.72	154	8.50	14.37 ± 19.73	129
Error Suggestions	8.375	10.03 ± 9.13	100	6.97	11.17 ± 14.96	100
Subjective Writing Accuracy						
None	4	3.76 ± 0.75	100	4	4.24 ± 0.75	100
Error Detection Only	4	4.24 ± 0.66	112	4	4.53 ± 0.80	107
Error Suggestions	5	4.65 ± 0.70	124	5	4.75 ± 0.58	112
Subjective Correcting Time						
None	3	3.41 ± 0.80	100	4	3.94 ± 0.83	100
Error Detection Only	4	4.24 ± 0.75	124	5	4.59 ± 0.62	116
Error Suggestions	5	4.59 ± 0.71	135	5	4.62 ± 0.81	117

Table 2: Median, mean and standard deviation of the dependent measures per condition and group. We include the relative percentage with respect to the smallest average value per condition.

- **Participants with Dyslexia:** There was a significant effect of *Correction Type* on *Subjective Correcting Time* ($\chi^2(2) = 19.62$, $p < 0.001$) (Table 2).
  - Participants with dyslexia perceived that they corrected the sentences significantly faster using the *Detection Only* and ($p = 0.020$) *Suggestions* ($p = 0.001$) than *None*.
- **Strong Readers:** There was a significant effect of *Correction Type* on *Subjective Correcting Time* ($\chi^2(2) = 8.14$, $p = 0.017$), see Table 2.
  - Strong readers reported that they spent significantly less time correcting sentences using *Suggestions* than with the absence of the condition ($p = 0.033$).

5. DISCUSSION

We discuss the different evaluation results as well as the limitations of our system based on the error analyses.

5.1 System Evaluation

Our system achieves competitive results compared with other similar approaches [14], nevertheless it is worth noting that they use an automatic generated test set for evaluation, while we use real world sentences written by people with dyslexia. This makes evaluation more challenging, since written errors by people with dyslexia are sometimes semantically similar [25], not only orthographically similar.

5.2 Comparison with Spellcheckers

The only spellchecker that provides competitive results compared to us is the one implemented under the Google Docs on-line tool that it is better in the correction of errors. However, the number of errors corrected by Google Docs is significantly smaller than in our system, since they provide a very precision oriented outcome. Nonetheless, since readers with dyslexia cannot consciously detect errors [26], we hypothesize that a more recall oriented system, like ours, would be useful for this target population. It is worth noting that our implementation outperforms Google Doc results for error detection, the number of true positives is higher in both tasks, and the number of false negatives is smaller in both tasks.

5.3 User Evaluation

Our evaluation with people with dyslexia and strong readers demonstrated that our spellchecker leads both populations to more efficient corrections. Using the suggestions proposed by our corrector, both populations wrote significantly more accurate text in less time. While no effects were found for strong readers in the error detection condition, the fact that the error candidates were highlighted was beneficial for participants with dyslexia, since the written accuracy improved significantly and the correction time decreases significantly. Readers with dyslexia perceived that they could write more accurately and in less time using our corrector.

5.4 Error Analyses and Limitations

Some real-word errors are difficult to detect because they are both grammatically and semantically correct. For example, *Real Check* does not detect the error **No ha gustado mucho tu propuesta ('Your proposal was not liked')* where the intended sentence was *Nos ha gustado mucho tu propuesta ('We do like your proposal')*. Future work may address this by considering document-level context, as it is done NLP tasks, such as anaphora resolution [21].

Another limitation comes from the coverage of Google n-grams. Some of the sentences that were written with dyslexia did not have a match in any of the n-grams at disposal. In order to overcome this issue we will try alternative approaches used in recent NLP tools, such as word vectors [19], word clusters [4], and synonym generation systems [1]. This would enhance the coverage of the method since it will allow to try with different string matching approaches, in spite of the exact string matching approach that it is implemented in the current version.

Real Check does not detect some special kind of real-word errors that involve word boundary errors, for instance *más cara ('more expensive')* instead of *máscara ('mask')*, a system that detects this kind of errors would need to increase the processing load of the algorithm geometrically. Tokens should be checked by pairs and, for instance, the dependency parser filter would need to deal with subtrees instead of tokens. It is worth noting that none of the systems shown in Table 1 solves this problem.

6. CONCLUSIONS

The main contribution of this paper is a method that detects real-word errors in Spanish with 50.42 precision and 65.93 recall. Our *Real Check* system offers an improvement over widely-used spell checkers in both error detection and in error correction. An evaluation with 34 people shows that both people with dyslexia and strong readers correct sentences more accurately in less time with *Real Check*.

Acknowledgements

We thank the following associations that support people with dyslexia who helped us collect written errors: *Madrid con la Dislexia ('Madrid for Dyslexia')*[20], *Associació Catalana de Dislèxia ('Catalan Association of Dyslexia')*[21], and *Avecedari Associació i Glifing('Avecedari Association and Glifing')*[22].

We especially thank those who contributed significant amount of written errors, including Cristina Villanueva with Emma and Berta; Gloria Dotor Ferreira; Queti Porras with Miquel Romero Porras and Pedro Romero Porras; Luis Darriba Fernández; Montse Segarra Calvis with Gris Ventura-Gibert Segarra; Justina Pilar Velasco Ayala with Juan; Gloriana Hernanz Plaza with Ana Sánchez Hernanz; Joan Albà with Júlia Albà Coll; Úrsula M. Cózar; Ángeles Fernández Begines; Montserrat García with Mercè Gonzalez Calderón and Silvia Roca; Sergio Herrero; Fer del Real; Ruth Rozensztejn; Luciana Salerno; and Pepi Saravia.

The contents of this paper were developed under a grant from the National Science Foundation (#IIS-1149709), a Google Research Award, and a grant from the National Institute on Disability, Independent Living, and Rehabilitation Research (NIDILRR grant number 90DP0061-01-00). MB was supported by the European Commission under the contract numbers FP7-ICT-610411 (project MULTISENSOR) and H2020-RIA-645012 (project KRISTINA).

7. REFERENCES

[1] R. Baeza-Yates, L. Rello, and J. Dembowski. A simple context aware synonym simplification method. In *Proceedings of the NAACL-HLT 2015*. Association for Computational Linguistics, 2015.

[2] B. Bohnet and J. Nivre. A transition-based system for joint part-of-speech tagging and labeled non-projective dependency parsing. In *EMNLP-CoNLL*, 2012.

[3] T. Brants and A. Franz. {Web 1T 5-gram Version 1}. 2006.

[20]`http://www.madridconladislexia.org/`

[21]`http://www.acd.cat/`

[22]`http://www.avesedari.com/ca/glifing/`

[4] P. F. Brown, P. V. Desouza, R. L. Mercer, V. J. D. Pietra, and J. C. Lai. Class-based n-gram models of natural language. *Computational linguistics*, 18(4):467–479, 1992.

[5] L. Burnard. Reference guide for the british national corpus (world edition), 2000.

[6] J. Carifio and R. Perla. Resolving the 50-year debate around using and misusing Likert scales. *Medical education*, 42(12):1150–1152, 2008.

[7] A. J. Carlson, J. Rosen, and D. Roth. Scaling up context-sensitive text correction. pages 44–50, 2001.

[8] M. Felice, Z. Yuan, Ø. E. Andersen, H. Yannakoudakis, and E. Kochmar. Grammatical error correction using hybrid systems and type filtering. In *Proc. CoNLL: Shared Task*, pages 15–24, Baltimore, Maryland, June 2014. ACL.

[9] A. R. Golding and D. Roth. A winnow-based approach to context-sensitive spelling correction. *Machine learning*, 34(1-3):107–130, 1999.

[10] M. Gustafsson. A spell checker with a user model for Swedish dyslexics. *Projektarbeten 2003*, page 69, 2003.

[11] J. Hajič, M. Ciaramita, R. Johansson, D. Kawahara, M. A. Martí, L. Màrquez, A. Meyers, J. Nivre, S. Padó, J. Štěpánek, P. Straňák, M. Surdeanu, N. Xue, and Y. Zhang. The conll-2009 shared task: Syntactic and semantic dependencies in multiple languages. pages 1–18, 2009.

[12] G. Hirst and A. Budanitsky. Correcting real-word spelling errors by restoring lexical cohesion. *Natural Language Engineering*, 11(01):87–111, 2005.

[13] International Dyslexia Association. Frequently Asked Questions About Dyslexia, 2011. `http://www.interdys.org/`.

[14] A. Islam and D. Inkpen. Real-word spelling correction using google web it 3-grams. In *Proc. EMPLN'09*, pages 1241–1249. ACL, 2009.

[15] J. J. Jiang and D. W. Conrath. Semantic similarity based on corpus statistics and lexical taxonomy. In *Proceedings of International Conference on Research in Computational Linguistics*, 1997.

[16] A. Q. Li, L. Sbattella, and R. Tedesco. Polispell: an adaptive spellchecker and predictor for people with dyslexia. In *User Modeling, Adaptation, and Personalization*, pages 302–309. Springer, Berlin, Heidelberg, 2013.

[17] Y. Lin, J.-B. Michel, E. L. Aiden, J. Orwant, W. Brockman, and S. Petrov. Syntactic annotations for the google books ngram corpus. In *Proc. ACL'12 (demonstrations)*, pages 169–174. Association for Computational Linguistics, 2012.

[18] E. Mays, F. J. Damerau, and R. L. Mercer. Context based spelling correction. *Information Processing & Management*, 27(5):517–522, 1991.

[19] T. Mikolov, K. Chen, G. Corrado, and J. Dean. Efficient estimation of word representations in vector space. *arXiv preprint arXiv:1301.3781*, 2013.

[20] G. A. Miller, R. Beckwith, C. Fellbaum, D. Gross, and K. J. Miller. Introduction to WordNet: An on-line lexical database. *International Journal of Lexicography*, 3(4):235–244, 1990.

[21] R. Mitkov. *Anaphora resolution.* Longman, London, 2002.

[22] A. Pauls and D. Klein. Faster and smaller n-gram language models. In *Proc. ACL'11*, pages 258–267. Association for Computational Linguistics, 2011.

[23] J. Pedler. Computer spellcheckers and dyslexics - a performance survey. *British Journal of Educational Technology*, 32(1):23–37, 2001.

[24] J. Pedler. Using semantic associations for the detection of real-word spelling errors. In *Proceedings from The Corpus Linguistics Conference Series*, volume 1, 2005.

[25] J. Pedler. *Computer Correction of Real-word Spelling Errors in Dyslexic Text.* PhD thesis, Birkbeck College, London University, 2007.

[26] L. Rello. *DysWebxia. A Text Accessibility Model for People with Dyslexia.* PhD thesis, Universitat Pompeu Fabra, 2014.

[27] L. Rello, R. Baeza-Yates, and J. Llisterri. A resource of errors written in Spanish by people with dyslexia and its linguistic, phonetic and visual analysis. *Language Resources and Evaluation*, to appear.

[28] L. Rello, R. Baeza-Yates, H. Saggion, and J. Pedler. A first approach to the creation of a Spanish corpus of dyslexic texts. In *LREC Workshop NLP4ITA*, pages 22–27, Istanbul, Turkey, May 2012.

[29] K. U. Schulz and S. Mihov. Fast string correction with levenshtein automata. *International Journal on Document Analysis and Recognition*, 5(1):67–85, 2002.

[30] R. Spooner. *A spelling aid for dyslexic writers.* PhD thesis, University of York, 1998.

[31] C. Sterling, M. Farmer, B. Riddick, S. Morgan, and C. Matthews. Adult dyslexic writing. *Dyslexia*, 4(1):1–15, 1998.

[32] S. Verberne. Context-sensitive spell checking based on word trigram probabilities. *Unpublished master's thesis, University of Nijmegen*, 2002.

[33] A. Wilcox-O'Hearn, G. Hirst, and A. Budanitsky. Real-word spelling correction with trigrams: A reconsideration of the mays, damerau, and mercer model. In *Computational Linguistics and Intelligent Text Processing*, pages 605–616. Springer, 2008.

[34] World Health Organization. *International statistical classification of diseases, injuries and causes of death (ICD-10).* World Health Organization, Geneva, 10th edition, 1993.

Accessible Texts for Autism: An Eye-Tracking Study

Victoria Yaneva
University of Wolverhampton
Wolverhampton, UK
V.Yaneva@wlv.ac.uk

Irina Temnikova
Qatar Computing Research Institute
Doha, Qatar
itemnikova@qf.org.qa

Ruslan Mitkov
University of Wolverhampton
Wolverhampton, UK
R.Mitkov@wlv.ac.uk

ABSTRACT

People with Autism Spectrum Disorder (ASD) are known to experience difficulties in reading comprehension, as well as to have unusual attention patterns, which makes the development of user-centred tools for this population a challenging task. This paper presents the first study to use eye-tracking technology with ASD participants in order to evaluate text documents. Its aim is two-fold. First, it evaluates the use of images in texts and provides evidence of a significant difference in the attention patterns of participants with and without autism. Sets of two types of images, photographs and symbols, are compared to establish which ones are more useful to include in simple documents. Second, the study evaluates human-produced easy-read documents, as a gold standard for accessible documents, on 20 adults with autism. The results provide an understanding of the perceived level of difficulty of easy-read documents according to this population, as well as the preferences of autistic individuals in text presentation. The results are synthesized as set of guidelines for creating accessible text for autism.

Categories and Subject Descriptors

H.5.2 [**Information Interfaces and Presentation**]: User Interfaces—*Screen design*; K.4.2 [**Computers and Society**]: Social Issues—*Assistive technologies for persons with disabilities*

Keywords

Autism, Readability, Reading Comprehension, Text Simplification, Easy-Read, Eye Tracking

1. INTRODUCTION

Autism Spectrum Disorder (ASD) is a neurodevelopmental disorder characterised by impairment in communication and social interaction and stereotyped repetitive behaviour [2]. It is a condition of high prevalence, affecting about 1 in 100 people in the UK [8], and it is considered that for every three known cases, there are two undiagnosed individuals who might need a diagnosis at some point in their lives [4]. Broadening the diagnostic criteria and raising awareness of these criteria are expected to result in an even higher number of autism diagnoses, especially among women and girls. Impairment in communication, both in terms of language comprehension and social interaction, is a central characteristic of autism. People who have ASD experience various problems in reading comprehension, such as inability to understand context, process long and complex sentences and comprehend figurative language and abstract words [19, 21, 33].

Attention also develops differently in those with autism, with a record of atypical attention patterns dating back to as early as the first mention of this condition by Leo Kanner in 1943 [26]. For instance, the autistic individual may rely on only one sensory modality, while several are relevant to a task — a phenomenon known as stimulus overselectivity [29]. In the context of a reading task, some autistic people might focus exclusively on small fragments of local information with less account for global, contextual and semantic information [22]. These reading difficulties have been pointed out as a reason for the lower educational achievements of students with ASD [9], resulting in future problems with employment; only 6% of the adults with autism in the UK are employed full-time [31].

To address this growing issue there are a number of tools designed to facilitate written communication in people with autism (Section 2.1). These tools are developed for autistic people with a wide range of abilities, starting with severely impaired individuals who could use images in Picture Exchange Communication Systems (PECS) to construct sentences. At the high end, there is text simplification software such as OpenBook [3] for relatively high-functioning individuals, who only need assistance with certain linguistic constructions, such as splitting difficult sentences, accessing a word definition, or having a concept illustrated by an image (Section 2.1). An alternative to computer-oriented solutions are human-produced easy-read documents, following a pre-defined set of guidelines for writing in Plain English [17, 40]. Regardless of the media used to make the text accessible, the output of most computer-based systems and Plain English guidelines has the following common characteristics: it is a document containing short paragraphs of simple text, accompanied by an image related to the meaning of the paragraph or to some of the words in it. However, up to the present point there have not been any studies investigating the influence of text and image combinations on the atypical attention in autistic readers, and whether

ASSETS'15, October 26–28, 2015, Lisbon, Portugal.

ACM 978-1-4503-3400-6/15/10 ...$15.00.
DOI: http://dx.doi.org/10.1145/2700648.2809852

these readers make use of the image as a comprehension cue. Even though autistic people are known to have difficulties inferring meaning from symbols and drawings as opposed to photographs (Section 2.3), currently both types of images are widely present in easy-read documents (Section 3). Furthermore, there is no information on whether or not autistic adults with no developmental delay prefer to have images inserted in the texts they read and whether they perceive the level of difficulty of Plain English texts as suitable for their comprehension skills. This paper presents the first study to use eye-tracking technology with ASD participants in order to evaluate text documents. The main contributions of the study are as follows:

- The study investigates the differences between autistic and non-autistic individuals in the proportion of time they spend looking at images and text paragraphs, with a view to improving the development of user-centred document layouts and interfaces.

- It tests the existing assumption (Section 2.3) that autistic people are more efficient in decoding images with high resemblance to their referent in reality (photographs), rather than images with low resemblance to the referent (symbols) on a group of adults with autism with no developmental delay. Confirmation that such difference exists would cast light on the most suitable set of images to be used in the development of accessible reading documents for adults with autism, as well as in other software designed for this population.

- It tests the perceived level of difficulty of Plain English texts on adults with autism, in order to establish whether they are perceived as too difficult or too easy, thus potentially leading to the participants losing interest in the reading material and having their concentration reduced.

- Finally, the study contributes to a greater awareness of the participants' own preferences on text presentation with regard to the use of images.

The next section presents related work on tools for aiding language comprehension in individuals with ASD (Section 2.1) and image processing in autism (Sections 2.2 and 2.3). Section 3 focuses on the common characteristics of human-produced easy-read documents on the web. Sections 4 and 5 describe the hypotheses and experimental methodology, the results of which are given and discussed in Sections 6 and 7. The guidelines for improving accessibility of text documents for readers with autism are presented in Section 8 and conclusions are summarised in Section 9.

2. RELATED WORK

A number of studies report that software and technologies are well-received among autistic individuals due to reasons such as the autistic need for sameness and structure, the ability of the tools to continuously repeat given actions and instructions and, last but not least, the fact that they lack the complexity of social situations [35, 7].

2.1 Language Assistance Tools for Autism

Recognising the need of autistic individuals for assistance with language tasks, there are a number of software tools developed to assist both children and adults with autism from a broad range of linguistic and intellectual abilities. Probably the most intuitive example of such software are the various types of PECS, where the person produces a sentence by combining different images or images with words on a tablet screen or a personal digital assistant (PDA) [10]. Another tool which helps with language production is the *VAST-Autism*[1] app , which combines videos with written words and auditory cues to help autistic and apraxic individuals acquire certain words, phrases or sentences, similar to the way *Mind Reading*[2] uses a library of 412 basic human emotions to teach autistic individuals to recognise facial expressions. Another IPad application which helps the expressive vocabulary of children, autistic people and people with other special needs is *Stories About Me*[3], allowing them to combine photos with text and voice recordings, in order to produce their personal story. In terms of facilitating receptive language skills, the tool *OpenBook*[4] [3] provides automatic conversion of text documents by allowing the users and their carers to perform operations such as sentence splitting, inserting word definitions, explaining the meaning of idioms, replacing a word with a synonym, customising the text and page layout, etc. A text summarisation option is also available to provide the users with short versions of the document, and image insertion is used to illustrate unknown words or to reinforce the retention of recently acquired ones. The tool is available for English, Spanish and Bulgarian and has been evaluated on both children and adults.

A common feature in all tools mentioned above is the use of images to facilitate the cognitive processing of information. Nevertheless, information on the use of images in software interfaces is scarce. Some user requirement surveys stress that no bright colours or background images should be used [34]. A survey with 120 autistic respondents and their families concludes that sensory integration and attention issues should be addressed by allowing users to set colours or sounds [35], but it did not investigate preferences on the use of images or visual cues in software. The next section discusses current research on the way people with ASD process images with high and low resemblances to their intended referents.

2.2 Photographs and Symbols

The Oxford Dictionary of English defines the word symbol as "a mark or character used as a conventional representation of an object, function, or process" [5]. The cognitive processing of symbols and photographs, as, respectively, weak and strong representations of their referred objects, requires two different levels of symbolic understanding. In the process of childhood development, children first play with real objects and learn to associate them with the activity they are used for. When they learn to match the real object with a photograph of it, they demonstrate a higher level of symbolic understanding, the next step of which is learning to

[1]https://itunes.apple.com/us/app/vast-autism-1-core/id426041133?mt=8

[2]http://www.jkp.com/mindreading

[3]https://itunes.apple.com/us/app/stories-about-me/id531603747?mt=8

[4]http://www.openbooktool.net/

[5]Oxford English Dictionary [Online] Available at: http://dictionary.oed.com]

Figure 1: Examples of a symbol and text pair (above) [32] and a photograph and text pair (below) [11]

match the object to a drawing or a symbol and which culminates in the acquisition of a word to denote this whole set of entities [12, 6]. In the case of easy-read documents, both images with a strong resemblance to their intended referent (photographs) and images with a low resemblance (drawings and symbols) have been widely used (Figure 1). Without entering the philosophical debate on the differences between symbols and signs, the current paper uses the term "symbol" in order to refer to images in adapted documents, different from photographs of real people or objects, for example.

2.3 Symbolic Understanding in Autism

Children with autism are considered to have greater difficulties decoding vague representations, compared to typically developing individuals, due to their impaired ability to generalise, grasp context, or reason about the intention of the author [23, 1]. This evidence suggests that the type of images used would have a greater impact on the perception of the autistic users than on that of the neurotypical (non-autistic) ones. In line with this assumption, some developers of language assistance software for people with autism highlight challenges such as "the issue of identification of the most appropriate set of pictures for this system" [37] and hypothesise that:

In [the] case of a child with autism, due to their difficulty with abstraction and generalization, the pictures need to have a strong resemblance to their referents. The more relevant these pictures are to the child's culture and environment, the easier it is for them to use the system. [37] (p.35)

However, until now, this assumption has not been evaluated and both images with strong and weak resemblances to their referents (photographs and symbols) have been widely used. Furthermore, there is no evidence whatsoever on whether this difference in perception continues in adulthood and whether adult users with autism take longer to process images with a low resemblance to their referent.
One way to test this is to use overt visual attention as a proxy to the cognitive load each set of images imposes on the participants. The term overt attention refers to attention which is observable (e.g. where and when the eyes are changing their position on the screen) as opposed to covert attention, which is not directly observable (e.g. the actual cognitive processing of what the eyes are (or are not) looking at). Overt attention has been used for decades to investigate the cognitive load imposed on participants in different tasks such as reading, watching videos, using website menus, etc. [39, 13, 18]. In this paper we use overt visual attention in order to establish which set of images, photographs or symbols, imposes a greater cognitive load on the participants, as well as to identify any differences in the attention patterns between the two groups in a task of reading easy-read documents.

3. EASY-READ TEXTS ON THE WEB

Easy-read documents are documents specifically produced for people with comprehension difficulties by following a set of guidelines for writing in Plain English [17, 40]. A document is considered written in Plain English when its readability level is higher than 65 according to the Flesch Reading Ease Scale [15] or at a corresponding level according to other readability formulae. In order to find out the common characteristics of easy-read documents on the web, available to people with special needs, a pool of 100 randomly selected easy-read documents was created, consisting of an overall 71,627 words and 11,522 sentences.
Table 1 summarises some of the characteristics of the sample, where Flesch Reading Ease: 0=very difficult and 100 = very easy [15]; Flesch-Kincaid Grade Level (**FKGL**): 0 = very easy and 12=very difficult [27], **SL** stands for sentence length in words, **WL** for word length in syllables, **AA** for age of acquisition of the content words and **F** for familiarity. All measures have been obtained using the Coh-Metrix 3.0 software [30].

Table 1: Characteristics of 100 easy read documents

	SL	WL	AA	F	Flesch	FKGL
Mean	6.6	1.4	314	581	78	4
Min	2.8	1.2	236	566	43	0.3
Max	15	1.9	410	596	100	10
SD	2.6	0.1	35	6.3	12	2

The documents included in the pool were obtained from various charity organisation websites (n=38), government departments (n=26) and healthcare services (n=32), as well as demos of adapted books (n=3) from the US and the UK. All documents were written in English.
While still providing valuable information about the level of difficulty of a text, readability formulae are not entirely suitable for evaluation of easy read materials due to the great number of stand-alone words, email addresses, links to websites, etc. Furthermore, the choice of appropriate pictures, the layout of the text and the appropriateness of the material for the intended audience cannot be measured by the currently existing formulae. In the present study, human-produced easy-read documents have been chosen as a gold standard for accessible documents. This was partly done in order to allow generalisation of the results across a broader range of tools and human-produced documents instead of evaluating the performance of only one of them, and partly because people with special needs have much wider access to such documents compared to their access to specialised software.

4. HYPOTHESES

The participants in the study were 20 people diagnosed with autism and 20 non-autistic control subjects, who all read 9 texts, while having their eye movements recorded by an eye tracker.

The study investigates whether there are any between-group differences in the proportion of time each group spends looking at the image in 39 text and image pairs (see Figure 1). The study also investigates which type of images, photographs or symbols, elicit longer fixation times and thus impose a heavier cognitive load on the participants. We also want to find out how the level of difficulty of easy-read documents is perceived by adults on the spectrum. Comparing the perceived level of difficulty of the 9 texts presented would also give information on whether texts considered to be written in Plain English but have different readability levels would evoke different responses from the participants. Finally, we investigate what the text presentation preferences of the two groups are, by including a survey question at the end of the experiment. These research questions are summarised in the following 4 hypotheses:

H.1: There is no difference between groups on the proportion of time spent looking at the image for each text and image pair.

H.2: For each group, there is no effect on the time spent looking at photographs and symbols.

H.3: There is no difference between groups on the perceived level of difficulty of the presented documents.

H.4: There is no difference between groups regarding the text presentation preferences.

The design and procedure of the experiment testing these hypotheses are presented in Section 5.

5. EXPERIMENTAL METHODOLOGY

5.1 Design

The study implemented both between-group and within-group comparison design, where the independent variable was the use of images in texts and had three levels: texts with photographs (20 photographs in total), texts with symbols (19 symbols in total) and plain texts (with no images). After reading each text and having their reading fixations recorded by an eye tracking device, the participants were asked one literal multiple choice question about its meaning, in order to ensure that they were reading for meaning as opposed to just skimming through the text. The questions testing the comprehension of the participants were chosen to be literal due to the simplicity of the easy-read texts, where, by default, no strong inferential or reorganisational skills are needed in order to comprehend their meaning. As an example, a text about eating habits, where various types of foods were discussed, would be followed by a literal multiple choice question with only two possible answers:

High fibre foods include: a) Meat and milk or b) Bread and beans?

Knowing that they would need to answer a question after the text is removed from sight, all participants read the documents carefully (as evidenced by the gaze pattern videos produced by the eye tracker) and were all able to answer 100% of the questions correctly. The answers to these questions are used as a control variable only and are not included in the analysis of this study. After reading each text and answering the multiple choice questions, participants would rate their subjective perception of the difficulty of the text on a Likert scale from 1 to 5, where 1 stood for "very easy" and 5 stood for "very difficult". Finally, all participants answered a question about their reading preference, where they could choose between reading texts with a) photographs, b) symbols, c) plain text (no images) or d) "It makes no difference to me". Participants were allowed to choose more than one or none of the answers and were encouraged to elaborate on their choice if they wanted to. Based on the above design, we considered 6 metrics in total. Images and text paragraphs were defined as areas of interest (AOIs) and a number of gaze-based metrics were obtained based on how many times and for how long participants looked at these areas. The metrics used in this study are:

Average Time Viewed (ATV): The average time an AOI was viewed by all participants measured in seconds. This is an average from the total dwell time, including the durations of all fixations and all revisits.

Average Number of Fixations (AF): The average number of gaze fixations from all participants in a given AOI.

Average Number of Revisits (AR): The average number of go-back gaze fixations from all participants in a given AOI. Go-back gaze fixations are fixations in the span of a given AOI elicited after the gaze path has left the AOI and has then returned to revisit it. Revisits are a valuable source of information for heavy cognitive load and the way information from different parts of the screen is integrated.

Reading time score: This measure was developed by estimating the mean reading time per text in each group and then dividing the result by the number of words in the text. This was done in order to control for the differences in length between the 9 texts. Reading time has been used as an indicator of reading difficulty, with examples of texts similar in length but differing in the time they require for reading based on their complexity level [14].

Perceived level of difficulty: This measure was obtained through 1-5 Likert items after each text where the participants would rate the level of difficulty of the text as they have perceived it. This measure was chosen instead of reading comprehension questions as it more accurately reflects the subjective impressions of the participants on text difficulty and is thus more useful for evaluating their attitudes towards the difficulty of Plain English texts.

Text presentation preference: Information was gathered through the following survey question: "In your everyday life, do you prefer reading texts with: a) photographs, illustrating the main ideas b) symbols, illustrating the main ideas, c) plain texts without any images or d) "It makes no difference to me".

5.2 Participants

20 adults (7 female, 13 male) with a confirmed diagnosis of autism (n=10 Autism Spectrum Disorder, n=9 Asperger's syndrome and n=1 semantic-pragmatic disorder) were recruited through 4 local charity organisations. Participants

in the control group were 20 non-autistic adults (11 female and 9 male). None of the 40 participants had comorbid conditions affecting reading (e.g. dyslexia, learning difficulties, aphasia etc.), but some participants were diagnosed with comorbid depression (n=4, ASD group; n=1, control group) and anxiety (n=6, ASD group). Mean age (m) for the ASD group was m=30.75, with standard deviation SD=8.23, while for the control group it was m=30.81, SD=4.8. Years spent in education, as a factor influencing reading skills, for the ASD group were m=15.31, SD=2.9, and for the control group, m=17.25, SD=2.15. None of the participants in the two groups were diagnosed with having a learning disability or a developmental delay, so no matching for mental age was required [25]. All participants were native speakers of English and had normal or corrected vision. Results from 3 participants from the ASD group were discarded due to poor calibration or data loss (too many head movements during reading), resulting in dramatic inaccuracies in more than 70% of the data collected from them. Hence, the results analysed were obtained from 17 ASD and 20 control participants.

5.3 Materials

A challenge to the design of this study was the selection of an appropriate number of texts to give sufficient statistical power to the experiment without imposing a heavy work load on the participants with ASD. The inclusion of a large number of test materials was not feasible, due to the fact that people with autism are known to experience difficulties with concentration and attention [9, 38] and sensory issues [16, 28], in addition to the longer time they take to comprehend instruction, to calibrate the eye tracker [36], and to get accustomed to new environment, such as the room where the experiment takes place [5]. The materials used in the study were easy-read documents. In order to ensure that the texts included in this study were representative of the easy-read information available to a person with special needs, they were selected from the pool of 100 easy-read documents discussed in Section 3. Out of the 100-document pool, a sample of 7 texts comprising of 39 image and text snippets was carefully chosen for the experiment, based on the following criteria: **Topic** (all documents included did not require any prior knowledge nor did they discuss sensitive topics), **Source** (the selected documents covered all sources listed above, such as charity organisations, government and healthcare departments), **Readability level** (documents (or parts of documents) were included so as to cover a diverse number of readability levels), and **Images** (both photographs (n=20) and symbols (n=19), were included, each of them accompanied by paragraphs of text as opposed to one- or two-word descriptions). As the easy-read documents contain images by default, the 2 texts in the condition "plain text without images" were selected from the WeeBit readability corpus [41]. They were also written according to Plain English requirements and their readability scores were medium compared to the 7 easy-read documents selected. Thus, the study included 9 texts overall, the information of which is summarised in Table 2. Readability scores have been obtained using the Coh-Metrix 3.0 software [30].

5.4 Apparatus

The device used for recording the gaze of the participants during task performance was a Gazepoint GP3 video-based eye tracker [20] (60Hz sampling rate), with a 19" LCD monitor. No equipment was attached to the participants. The eye tracker was calibrated individually for each participant using a 9-point calibration procedure. The use of a chin rest is not recommended due to sensory issues common within autism [38], which is why the distance between each participant and the eye tracker was controlled by using a fixed chair only, and was roughly 85 cm.

Table 2: Characteristics of the texts included in the experiment

	Type	Words	Images	FKGL	Flesch
T1	Photos	77	4	8.16	60.11
T2	Photos	96	5	6.73	67.33
T3	Symbols	74	6	2.71	92.54
T4	Photos	178	8	5.52	75.33
T5	Symbols	77	6	5.79	70.67
T6	Symbols	121	6	1.75	95.00
T7	Photos	58	4	6.63	68.16
T8	None	178	0	4.67	80.22
T9	None	163	0	4.93	79.548

5.5 Procedure

All participants performed the experiment in a quiet room with only the researcher (first author) present. Some of them (n=2) requested to have the lights diminished due to sensory issues, which was done in order to ensure their comfort during the experiment. First, each participant was given a verbal instruction on the sequential order in which the experiment was going to proceed and on the functionality of the eye tracker. Each participant was given the opportunity to ask questions and to request a break at any point if they felt tired. Recalibration was performed if the participants needed to get up during their breaks. Demographic information was collected after the instruction was given. After that the instruction was reinforced a second time and the calibration procedure started. Each of the documents was presented on screen in a randomised order and participants could take as long as they needed to read it. After each document the participant would be asked a comprehension question verbally, without having the opportunity to look at the text while answering. At the end of the experiment the survey question was asked and participants were debriefed.

6. RESULTS

The software used for the analysis of the fixation points from the eye tracker and their grouping into specific areas of interest (AOIs) such as images or text paragraphs, was the Gazepoint analysis system, specifically developed for the GP3 Gazepoint eye trackers [20]. Statistical data was analysed using IBM SPSS Statistics software, Version 20 [24].

6.1 Attention to Images

H.1: *There is no difference between groups on the proportion of time spent looking at the image for each text and image pair.*

First, we compared the overall time participants from both groups spent looking at the 39 images. A Shapiro-Wilk test showed that all the gaze-based measures datasets, namely Average Time Viewed (ATV), Average Fixations (AF) and

Average Revisits (AR), are non-normally distributed. Hence, the study used a Mann-Whitney U test to assess the null hypothesis according to all three gaze-based measures. The test significantly rejected this hypothesis confirming a difference between the groups, where the participants with autism were shown to spend significantly longer time not only looking at the images, (ATV: U=338.5, N1=17, N2=20, p=0.000, two-tailed; AF: U= 290.000, N1=17, N2=20, p=0.000,two-tailed) but also revisiting them (AR: U=331.000, N =17, N2=20, p=0.000, two-tailed). However, a significant difference between the absolute times participants spend looking at the images may result from longer overall reading times in the ASD group. To investigate this further, for each group we added up the average viewing times (ATV) for each image together with the ATV of its corresponding paragraph, so that we had AOIs containing the ATV for 39 text and image pairs. Then the ATV of each image was computed as a percentage of the time for each pair (taken as 100%) in the following way: ATV per image (%) = ATV per image and text pair — ATV per text paragraph. A Mann-Whitney U test indicated that there is a statistically significant difference between the two proportions (U=461.00, N =17, N2=20, p= 0.003, two-tailed), and thus **H.1** was rejected, with the ASD group spending a greater proportion of time on images compared to the control group, which is evidence of an atypical attention pattern in this population. The proportion of time the ASD group spent looking at the images totalled 20.32%, compared with 13.42% for the control group, leaving the ASD group with 79.68% of their time spent on reading the text and 86.58% for the control group.

6.2 Photographs vs. Symbols

H.2: *For each group, there is no effect on the time spent looking at photographs and symbols.*

A Shapiro-Wilk test showed that the data is non-normally distributed for Average Time Viewed (ATV) (Symbols: p = 0.001, Photographs: p=0.011) and Average Revisits (AR) (Symbols: p=0.000, Photographs: p=0.163) in the control group, while the Average Fixations (AF) dataset for both control and ASD group and the datasets ATV and AR for the ASD group were normally distributed (Control group: Symbols p=0.001, Photographs p=0.011; ASD group: Symbols p=0.091, Photographs p=0.332). Hence, a paired-samples t-test was used to compare the data in the "symbol" and "photograph" classes for the ASD group for all three measures and for the AF dataset from the control group. A Wilcoxon Matched Pairs test was in turn used to compare the non-normally distributed ATV and AR datasets for the control group. First a test for outliers was performed, which showed that there were no outlier values in the datasets. The paired-samples t-test showed that in the ASD group there was no significant difference between the time spent viewing images according to the ATV measure (t =-1.389, df =18, p=0.182, two-tailed), AF (t=-1.339, df =18, p=0.197, two-tailed) or AR (t=0.378, df=17, p=0.710, two-tailed). Similarly, the results from the Wilcoxon Matched Pairs test revealed that there is no significant difference between the times participants in the control group spent looking at symbols or photographs for the ATV and AR measures (ATV measure: z=-0.765, N—Ties=19, p=0.444, one-tailed; AR measure: z=-0.763, N—Ties=17, p=0.445, one-tailed), and a paired-samples t-test confirmed the same for the AF measure (t=-0.298, df=18, p=0.769).

The results failed to reject the H.2 hypothesis that there is no significant difference between the times participants from both groups look at photographs and symbols. The results indicate that photographs and symbols impose similar cognitive loads on the participants from both groups and thus both sets are equally suitable for use in easy-read documents for adults with ASD.

6.3 Level of Difficulty

H.3: *There is no difference between groups on the perceived level of difficulty of the presented documents.*

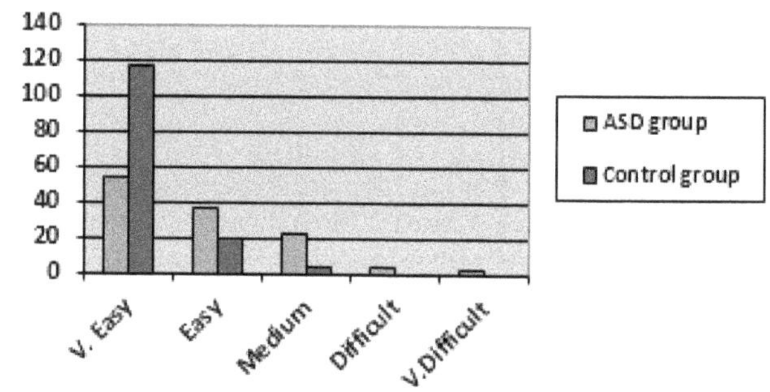

Figure 2: Frequency of text rankings for each category

A Shapiro-Wilk test showed that for the ASD group the data was not normally distributed for all texts, with the exception of Text 8, and for the control group the data was not normally distributed for all texts. Hence, to study the occurrence of any significant differences between the perceived level of difficulty in the 9 texts (Figure 2), we used a Friedman's non-parametric test for repeated measures, which showed no statistically significant difference between the perceived level of difficulty in both groups for all 9 texts (ASD group: $\chi^2(8)$ = 9.679, p=0.139, control group: $\chi^2(8)$ = 10.145, p = 0.119), indicating that documents at readability levels between 61 and 95 Flesch Reading Ease score are considered as the same class of difficulty by the ASD group.

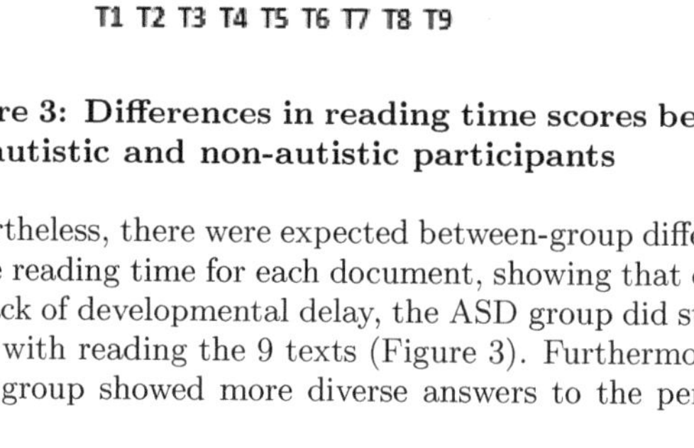

Figure 3: Differences in reading time scores between the autistic and non-autistic participants

Nevertheless, there were expected between-group differences in the reading time for each document, showing that despite the lack of developmental delay, the ASD group did struggle more with reading the 9 texts (Figure 3). Furthermore, the ASD group showed more diverse answers to the perceived level of difficulty of the texts with answers ranging between very easy (n=54), easy (n=37) and medium (n=23) to even reaching difficult (n=4) and very difficult (n=2). The control group, on the other hand, had a predominant rate of very easy (n=117) and easy (n=20) and none of the participants ranked any text as difficult or very difficult (Figure 2).

6.4 Text Presentation Preferences

H.4: *There is no difference between groups regarding the text presentation preferences.*
There was a strong preference for the inclusion of images among the ASD group (58.81%), of which 23.5% preferred reading texts with photographs and 35.3% preferred reading texts with symbols. The control group did not declare such a strong preference to images with 60% of the participants stating that it makes no difference to them and 30% voting for the inclusion of images but were undecided as to whether they preferred photographs (15%) or symbols (15%) (Figure 4).

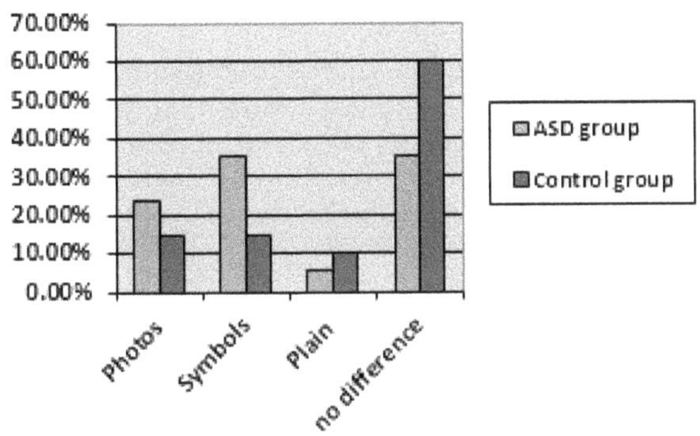

Figure 4: Preferences of the two groups on text presentation

7. DISCUSSION

The results indicate that there is a significant difference between autistic and non-autistic individuals in the proportion of time they spend looking at images and text paragraphs, with autistic participants relying on the image more than the non-autistic ones. This result may have an implication on the design of user-centred software in two ways.
First, it is evidence that visual cues take up a significant part of the attention of autistic participants and that they would make useful comprehension cues if they are closely related to the meaning of the text paragraph they accompany.
Second, it confirms that there are differences in attention between neurotypical and autistic people with regards to images and that the improper inclusion of images in text documents or software interfaces may have a negative effect by distracting the autistic users much more than the intuition of the neurotypical developers may suggest.

Both photographs and symbols have been found to elicit similar cognitive load on the participants, which means that in the case of adult autistic users without developmental delay, both sets of images are equally suitable to be included. This finding is not in conflict with previous research, as it is the only study on images so far that has included adult autistic participants instead of children. It is possible that there would be a significant difference between the two sets if the participants were children, as it may be the case that symbolic understanding in autistic individuals reaches levels equal to those of neurotypicals later in their lives. In this sense, the results of this study with regard to the types of images should not be generalised to children or to autistic individuals with learning difficulties.

The fact that texts written in plain English are perceived as ranging from very easy and easy to difficult and even very difficult by the participants with autism, while non-autistic participants rate them predominantly as very easy, is an indication that these texts are well understood by the autistic participants without being as trivial to them as they have appeared to be for the non-autistic ones. Perceived level of difficulty is not a direct measure of interest but one could hypothesise that texts which are too easy would bore the readers and thus reduce their motivation to read the document. The results suggest that even though our autistic participants were adults without a learning disability, this is not the case with them, and that Plain English texts are indeed a suitable level of difficulty for this population.
One factor which may have influenced these results is that the study did not use deception and all participants knew that it investigated reading in autism. The autistic participants might have suggested they were expected to have some sort of reading deficits and have thus tried to apply a more fine-grained classification of the difficulty of the texts compared to the non-autistic ones. Nevertheless, differences in the interpretation of Likert items are a well-known flaw in all types of studies using this measure, while in the case of this study the results from the Likert scale are in agreement with the longer reading times of the autistic participants, which support the conclusion that they indeed did not find the texts as easy as the control participants did.

The slight majority of the autistic participants preferred to have images included in the documents they read (58.81%), with 23.52% of them preferring photographs and 35.29% preferring symbols, while roughly the same proportion of the non-autistic participants were indifferent as to whether images were included in the text or not (60%). This is another difference between neurotypical and autistic individuals, which should be taken into account when creating accessible texts for this population, even when the target group is adults.

Limitations of this study are the relatively small number of documents assessed and the small number of participants. The first one is imposed by the difficulty experienced by autistic participants in concentrating for long periods of time, as discussed in Section 5, and could only be overcome if the participants come for several shorter sessions. The second limitation is typical of all areas of autism research, which makes the results from these studies difficult to generalise and is the reason for the many inconsistencies in autism study replications. The reason that the samples in ASD research tend to be small is the varying levels of ability of this population and the number of comorbid disorders, (learning difficulties, dyslexia, depression, apraxia) which are so common within autism but in many cases need to be excluded for the purposes of research.

8. IMPROVING TEXT ACCESSIBILITY FOR READERS WITH AUTISM

The results of the study presented above are synthesized in a set of recommendations regarding text accessibility for adult readers with autism. These recommendations aim to improve the development of text documents, Web content or software interfaces targeted to autistic adults, as well as text conversion and language assistance tools, such as the ones described in Section 2. The recommendations based on the results from this study are as follows:

1. Illustrate the main ideas in text paragraphs through the insertion of images relevant to the meaning of the paragraph.
2. If a relevant image is unavailable or the idea of the text is too abstract to be depicted as an image, do not put anything. A non-relevant image has the potential to affect autistic readers' comprehension and reading speed.
3. Do not insert logos, advertisements or any other visual information, which is not directly relevant to the meaning of the text.
4. Insert the image as close as possible to the sentence or groups of sentences it refers to.
5. Photographs and symbols are equally suitable, so data sets from both domains could be utilized. However, refrain from using symbols which are too abstract or their understanding requires substantial prior knowledge in a certain area.
6. Use texts written in plain English. See plain English guidelines for a more detailed information on how to write for people with disabilities [40]. A general rule of thumb is that the text should have a score higher than 65 according to the Flesch-Reading Ease formula [15].
7. Allow the readers to skip through the pages at their own pace, as reading times may be longer compared to the general population.
8. In the case of videos, allow longer times for the users to read the text or captions and to process the visual information.

It is important to note that due to the heterogeneity of autism, these recommendations should be applied with caution and should not be generalised to children with autism or adults at the lower ends of the autism spectrum where signs of a learning disability are evident.

9. CONCLUSIONS AND FUTURE WORK

The study provided evidence for the differences in attention patterns between participants with and without autism and suggested that both photographs and symbols are equally useful for including in easy-read documents and software interfaces. Documents written in Plain English are understood by all participants with autism but are not all ranked as 'very easy'. This suggest that this level of difficulty was suitable for the autistic participants to understand without being too trivial for them, even though they were adults and had no learning difficulties. Finally, the study indicates that the majority of people with autism prefer to read texts with images, unlike neurotypicals, for whom it mostly makes no difference whether there are images in the text or not. An interesting direction for future work is to analyse the types of visual cues which aid comprehension for autistic adults, as well as to analyse their gaze fixations for particular constructions in the texts.

10. ACKNOWLEDGEMENTS

The authors would like to thank all participants who took part in the study, as well as the charity organisations, which facilitated their recruitment. Special thanks to the three anonymous reviewers for their constructive criticism and to Dr. Luz Rello for her valuable help and advice.

11. REFERENCES

[1] M. L. Allen. Brief report: decoding representations: how children with autism understand drawings. *Journal of autism and developmental disorders*, 39(3):539–43, Mar. 2009.

[2] American Psychiatric Association. Diagnostic and Statistical Manual of Mental Disorders (5th ed.), 2013.

[3] E. Barbu, M. T. Mart, and L. A. Ure. Open Book : a tool for helping ASD users' semantic comprehension. In *Proceedings of the 2th Workshop of Natural Language Processing for Improving Textual Accessibility (NLP4ITA)*, number June, pages 11–19, Atlanta, Georgia, 2013. Association for Computational Linguistics.

[4] Baron-Cohen, S., Scott, F. J., Allison, C. Prevalence of autism-spectrum conditions: UK school-based population study. *British Journal of Psychiatry*, 194:500– 509, 2009.

[5] Bejerot, S., Eriksson, J. M. and Mörtberg, E. Social anxiety in adult autism spectrum disorder. *Psychiatry research*, 220((1-2)):705–7, 2014.

[6] E. Bialystok. Symbolic representation across domains in preschool children. *Journal of experimental child psychology*, 76(3):173–89, 2000.

[7] Bosseler, A and Massaro, D. W. Development and evaluation of computer-animated tutor for vocabulary and language learning in children with autism. *Journal of autism and developmental disorders*, 33(6):553–567, 2003.

[8] Brugha, T., Cooper, S. A., McManus, S., E. Estimating the Prevalence of Autism Spectrum Conditions in Adults: Extending the 2007 Adult Psychiatric Morbidity Survey. Technical report, NHS, The Health and Social Care Information Centre., London, 2012.

[9] Brugha, T., McManus, S., Meltzer, H., Smith, J., Scoth, F.J., and Purdon, S. Autism spectrum disorders in adults living in households throughout England. Report from the Adult Psychiatric Morbidity Survey 2007. Technical report, The National Health Service Information Centre for Health and Social Care, London, 2007.

[10] Charlop-Christy, Marjorie H., Carpenter, Michael, Le, Loc, LeBlanc, Linda A. and Kellet, Kristen. Using the picture exchange communication system (pecs) with

children with autism: assessment of pecs acquisition, speech, social-communicative behavior, and problem behaviour. *Journal of Applied Behavior Analysis*, 3(3):213–231, 2002.

[11] Cheshire and Wirral Partnership NHS Foundation Trust. Healthy Eating and Being Active. Information on Diet and Exercise. Easy read leaflet, 2008.

[12] J. S. DeLoache. Symbolic Functioning in Very Young Children: Understanding of Pictures and Models. *Child Development*, 62(4):736–752, 2008.

[13] V. Demberg and F. Keller. Data from Eye-tracking Corpora as Evidence for Theories of Syntactic Processing Complexity. *Cognition*, 109(2):193–210, 2008.

[14] W. H. Dubay. The Principles of Readability. 2004.

[15] R. Flesch. A New Readability Yardstick. *Journal of Applied Psychology*, 32(3):221–233, 1948.

[16] Freeman, B. J., Ritro, E .R. and Schroth, P.C. Behavior Assessment of the Syndrome of Autism: Behavior Observation System. *Journal of the American Academy of Child Psychiatry*, 23:588–94, 1984.

[17] Freyhoff, G., Hess, G., Kerr, L., Tronbacke, B. and Van Der Veken, K. Make it Simple. European Guidelines for the Production of Easy-to-Read Information for People with Learning Disability. Technical report, ILSMH European Association., 1998.

[18] S. Frisson and M. J. Pickering. Obtaining a Figurative Interpretation of a Word : Support for Underspecification. 16:149–171, 2001.

[19] Frith, Uta and Snowling, M. Reading for meaning and reading for sound in autistic and dyslexic children. *British Journal of Developmental Psychology*, 1:329–342, 1983.

[20] Gazepoint. GP3 Gazepoint Eye tracker, 2015.

[21] F. Happe. Central coherence and theory of mind in autism: Reading homographs in context. *British Journal of Developmental Psychology*, 15:1–12, 1997.

[22] Happe, F., and Frith, U. he weak coherence account: Detail focused cognitive style in autism spectrum disorder. *Journal of Autism and Developmental Disorders*, 36:5–25, 2006.

[23] C. Hartley and M. L. Allen. Intentions vs. resemblance: understanding pictures in typical development and autism. *Cognition*, 131(1):44–59, Apr. 2014.

[24] IBM Corp. IBM SPSS Statistics for Windows, Version 20.0, 2011.

[25] Jarrold, C. and Brock, J. To Match or Not To Match ? Methodological Issues in Autism Related Research. *Journal of autism and developmental disorders*, 34(1):81–86, 2004.

[26] L. Kanner. Autistic Disturbances of Affective Contact. *Nervous Child*, 2:217–250, 1943.

[27] Kincaid, J. P., Fishburne, R. P., Rogers, R. L., and Chissom, B. S. Derivation of new readability formulas (Automated Readability Index, Fog Count and Flesch Reading Ease Formula) for Navy enlisted personnel. Technical report, CNTECHTRA Research Branch Report, 1975.

[28] Liss, M., Saulnier, C., Fein, D. and Kinsbourne, M. No Title. *Autism: the international journal of research and practice*, 10(2):155–72, 2006.

[29] Lovaas, O. I. and Schreibman, L. Stimulus Overselectivity of Autistic Children in a Two Stimulus Situation. *Behavior Research and Therapy*, 9:305–310, 1971.

[30] McNamara, D. S., Graesser, A. C., McCarthy, P. M., and Cai, Z. *Automated evaluation of text and discourse with Coh-Metrix.* Cambridge University Press, Cambridge, M.A., 2014.

[31] National Autistic Society. A Place in Society: The Importance of Planning for Life for People with Autistic Spectrum Disorders. Technical report, 2004.

[32] D. Neurosciences and L. D. Directorate. Exercise Is Good For You! Easy read leaflet, 2008.

[33] O'Connor, I.M. and Klein, P.D. Exploration of Strategies for Facilitating the Reading Comprehension of High-Functioning Students with Autism Spectrum Disorders. *Journal of autism and developmental disorders*, 34(2), 2004.

[34] N. Pavlov. User Interface for People with Autism Spectrum Disorders. 2014(February):128–134, 2014.

[35] C. Putnam and L. Chong. Software and technologies designed for people with autism: What do users want? In *Proceedings of the 10th International ACM SIGACCESS Conference on Computers and Accessibility*, Assets '08, pages 3–10, New York, NY, USA, 2008. ACM.

[36] K. A. Quill. Instructional Considerations for Young Children with Autism: The Rationale for Visually Cued Instruction. *Journal of Autism and Developmental Disorders*, 27(6), 1997.

[37] Sampath, Harini, Sivaswamy, Joyanthi, Indurkhya, Bipin. Assistive Systems for Children with Dyslexia and Autism. In *SIGACCESS Newsletter*, number 96, pages 32–36, 2010.

[38] Sasson, N. J. and Elison, J. T. Eye Tracking Young Children with Autism. *Journal of Visual Experiments*, 61, 2012.

[39] J. Theeuwes, A. Belopolsky, and C. N. Olivers. Interactions between working memory, attention and eye movements. *Acta Psychologica*, 132(2):106–114, Oct. 2009.

[40] B. Tronbacke. Guidelines for Easy-to-Read Materials. Technical report, IFLA, The Hague, 1997.

[41] Vajjala, S. and Meurers, D. On improving the accuracy of readability classification using insights from second language acquisition. In *In Proceedings of the Seventh Workshop on Building Educational Applications Using NLP*, pages 163–173, Stroudsburg, PA, USA, 2012. Association for Computational Linguistics.

Usage of Subjective Scales in Accessibility Research

Shari Trewin
IBM T.J. Watson Research Ctr
Yorktown Heights, NY, USA
trewin@us.ibm.com

Diogo Marques
University of Lisbon
Lisbon, Portugal
dmarques@di.fc.ul.pt

Tiago Guerreiro
University of Lisbon
Lisbon, Portugal
tjvg@di.fc.ul.pt

ABSTRACT

Accessibility research studies often gather subjective responses to technology using Likert-type items, where participants respond to a prompt statement by selecting a position on a labeled response scale. We analyzed recent ASSETS papers, and found that participants in non-anonymous accessibility research studies gave more positive average ratings than those in typical usability studies, especially when responding to questions about a proposed innovation. We further explored potential positive response bias in an experimental study of two telephone information systems, one more usable than the other. We found that participants with visual impairment were less sensitive to usability problems than participants in a typical student sample, and that their subjective ratings didn't correlate as strongly with objective measures of performance. A deeper understanding of the mechanism behind this effect would help researchers to design better accessibility studies, and to interpret subjective ratings with more accuracy.

Categories and Subject Descriptors

H.5.2 [**Information Systems and Presentation**]: User Interfaces—*Evaluation/Methodology*; K.4.2 [**Computers and Society**]: Social Issues—*Assistive technologies for persons with disabilities*

General Terms

Measurement, Experimentation, Human Factors

Keywords

Likert, accessibility, response bias

1. INTRODUCTION

Accessibility researchers often use Likert-type items (Figure 1) to gather feedback on proposed accessibility technologies and to compare technologies. This type of measurement is a well-established tool in HCI research [13, p. 270]. However, Likert-type items can also be prone to positive response bias. Indeed, unrelated accessibility studies with different populations have reported participants giving high usability ratings for a task or system, when comments, observations or objective performance measures suggest otherwise [7, 18, 26].

This system was easy to use

strongly disagree	*disagree*	*neither agree nor disagree*	*agree*	*strongly agree*
(1)	(2)	(3)	(4)	(5)

Figure 1: A Likert item.

Positive bias in accessibility research could arise from many sources. For example, people who volunteer for accessibility research studies may have a very positive attitude, or verbal presentation of questions may make it harder to give negative opinions. If accessibility research studies are prone to positive response bias, this is a phenomenon that accessibility researchers need to be aware of, seek to avoid whenever possible, and allow for when interpreting such data.

This paper investigates positive bias in two ways: 1) by analyzing subjective responses reported in accessibility research papers, and 2) by presenting an experiment that compares subjective responses given by a group of participants with visual impairment, and a group of students with no visual impairment, when performing the same phone-based task using two different systems, one more usable than the other.

We find that Likert-type items are widely used in accessibility research, but Likert scales with balanced sets of items are not. Within-subjects designs with target users are typical, and the use of a comparison group is rare. User ratings of accessibility research technology are higher than typical user ratings in usability studies, while user ratings of existing technologies or situations are lower.

Our study found that participants with visual impairment were less sensitive to usability problems than the student group. We point to several possible explanations for this phenomenon and suggest ways that researchers could reduce the likelihood of bias in accessibility studies.

ASSETS'15, October 26–28, 2015, Lisbon, Portugal.
 ISBN 978-1-4503-3400-6/15/10 ...$15.00.
DOI: http://dx.doi.org/10.1145/2700648.2809867.

2. BACKGROUND

Likert scales [10, 14] measure attitudes by presenting a set of statements and asking the respondent to indicate their level of agreement or disagreement with each statement by selecting from a fixed scale of responses. Each statement and response is a Likert item, illustrated in Figure 1.

The underlying assumption is that peoples' opinions will vary on a continuous dimension, from strongly negative to strongly positive, and survey participants will select the response option that most closely matches their strength of opinion. Each option is assigned a numeric code, typically 1-5. In Likert's original formulation, each response also has a verbal label, but the practice of labeling only the endpoints of the scale is also widespread. In this paper, we will use the term 'Likert-type item' to include items that use partially labeled response scales, and also items that prompt with a question rather than a statement, such as "How easy to use was this system?"

Likert-type items are widely used in human-computer interaction research to measure subjective user experience [13, 11, 15]. Established usability measures such as ISO-9241-9 [9], SUS [3], QUEST [6], and NASA-TLX [8] use Likert-type items. They are appropriate for smaller sample sizes, easy to learn and quick to execute [20]. They can be presented verbally, on paper, or digitally. Sauro and Lewis [21] found strong correlations between prototypical usability metrics, including Likert-type user satisfaction ratings, task times and errors.

In an early meta-analysis of usability studies, Nielsen and Levy [15] also found that subjective preferences gathered with Likert-type items generally corresponded well to objective performance measures. In an analysis of 127 studies they found a mean subjective rating of 3.55 +- 0.12 on a 5-point response scale. Suggesting that this value could be used to calibrate scores in future studies, they noted that "users tend to be polite and give fairly high ratings unless they are really upset with an interface" [15].

As this comment implies, responses can be subject to positive bias, especially in contexts such as laboratory studies where it may seem rude to give a negative or contrary opinion. Being based on a statement rather than a question, Likert-type items are known to be subject to acquiescence bias, in which respondents tend to agree with a statement, regardless of the content. In a classic study, Schuman and Presser [22] found that two groups of individuals showed 57% and 60% agreement with opposite statements, suggesting that the effect size of acquiescence bias can be considerable. In a Likert scale containing many individual items, the impact of acquiescence bias can be reduced by balancing the items, so that the statements do not all represent the same point of view.

The desire to give a response that presents the participant in a favorable light (social desirability) is a related well-known source of bias in psychology questionnaires. Social desirability bias is influenced by the way a question is presented [23, 16]. Computer-based presentation reduces this bias, especially if users are anonymous, alone, and able to backtrack [17].

Characteristics of the experimenter or experimental setup (demand characteristics) can also introduce significant bias. Social status and cultural differences between experimenters and participants have been shown to influence participants' stated preferences to such an extent that two different experimenters performing the same comparison of two systems can find opposite results [5].

In accessibility research studies, Likert-type items are often used to gather opinions on proposed technologies. Some researchers have reported apparent contradictions between subjective ratings and observations made during a session. For example, Gerling, Mandryk and Kalyn [7] studied older adults playing wheelchair-based games. They observed:

"In contrast to the results of the NASA-TLX, items of the ISO questionnaire investigating physical fatigue report low levels of physical demand. These findings need to be interpreted along with observations that were made during the study, which contradict subjective ratings for fatigue that were made through the ISO questionnaire; many participants seemed to be challenged by the system and became increasingly tired throughout the gaming session (heavier breathing, individual comments on physical exertion)."

Trewin et al. [26] measured the time for a group of individuals with cerebral palsy to perform a set of point-and-click tasks using a mouse or trackball, and then asked for a subjective rating of how easy the task was, on a 5-point scale. Three participants who rated the task as 'Easy' or 'Very easy' had average pointing times greater than 10 seconds, and one had an average time of 52.4s.

Another study with older users testing a voice-augmented web browsing system reported that while older adults believed themselves to have completed the tasks faster with voice augmentation, in fact they took longer [18].

Similar apparent contradictions have been noted in usability testing, where 14% of users who fail a task will still give it the highest possible satisfaction rating [19]. Proposed reasons for this mismatch include users giving a value that indicates a strong positive, but intending it to be a strong negative; and users being unaware that the task was not successfully completed.

Accessibility research, by its very nature, may be more prone to this positive bias phenomenon, for a number of reasons:

- Questions are often presented verbally by the researchers themselves, often because a paper-and-pencil presentation would not be accessible. This form of presentation may not only increase demand characteristics, social desirability and acquiescence biases, but it may also result in confusion over the meaning of a numeric value on a scale, if there is no visual prompt to refer to.
- Selection of representative participants for studies is difficult [24] - participants volunteering for accessibility research studies may be individuals with a 'can-do' attitude, or a desire to encourage and support young researchers. The user pool at the University of Dundee [4] is a notable exception, offering researchers a rare opportunity to select participants based on criteria such as age, gender and cognitive abilities. However, some bias may still be present in the willingness of individuals to join a user pool in the first place.
- Accessibility barriers may make it difficult for participants to know whether they have completed a task successfully. For example, in searching for information on a web page using screen reading technology, users may be unaware of important information they have missed.

This paper investigates positive bias in accessibility research studies by examining the accessibility literature, and exploring whether the effect can be observed in a formal experimental setting.

3. REVIEW OF LIKERT-TYPE ITEMS IN ASSETS PAPERS

3.1 Goals

To provide a deeper understanding of the use of Likert-type items in accessibility research, we examined accessibility research studies presented as full papers at ASSETS within the last 5 years. Our goals were to learn:

- How frequently such items are used
- What target populations they are used with
- How they are typically administered
- What experimental designs they are used in
- Whether there is evidence of positive bias exceeding the typical bias identified in HCI literature

3.2 Method

We examined full papers published in ASSETS between 2010 and 2014, inclusive, and identified papers containing target user evaluations of new or existing technologies. We included studies where participants evaluated artifacts produced by different technologies (for example sign language avatars, or videos created with different compression techniques), and excluded studies that only surveyed opinions without presenting any artifact for evaluation, such as a web-based survey of experiences with computer game accessibility. We did not count studies targeted exclusively at non-disabled users (e.g. crowdworkers). We included studies with older adults, and studies of sign language users, although the latter often include hearing individuals who are fluent in sign language.

For each study, we identified instances of the use of Likert-type items to gather subjective judgments, and recorded details of the experimental methodology, including the meaning of the question, whether the question was drawn from an established standard measurement instrument, how it was administered, the study design, the number of participants, participant demographics, and responses to the questions. Online studies were assumed to have anonymous response, while studies conducted in person by researchers were non-anonymous.

In analyzing the wording of items, we included all items that were described, even if no results were reported. In four papers, responses to individual questions were only given in a figure. We estimated the response values for 45 items from figures.

We normalized all response values to a 5-point response scale where 1 indicates a very negative opinion and 5 a very positive opinion. This consisted of: scaling 7-point scale values (and other scales) to the equivalent 5-point value; inverting values for reverse coded questions (where a higher value meant a more negative opinion); and shifting values on scales where the neutral point was coded as 0. We used mean response values where available, falling back on median values where no mean was provided.

Table 1: Characteristics of 51 studies published at ASSETS 2010-2014 that used Likert-type items.

Population	No. of studies	Mean/ median pts.	% with anon. responses	% within subjects	% between subjects
Visual impairment	22	10/08	0	50	14
Sign language users	8	63/19	38	88	0
Deaf or hard of hearing	4	53/23	25	100	0
Physical impairment	5	12/14	0	40	0
Older adults	6	10/10	0	66	0
Other populations	6	22/13	0	50	0
All	51	23/11	6	59	4

The number of questions within a study is dependent on the number of conditions being compared, and the range of opinions sought. This means that some studies have more influence on the analysis than others. We did not combine questions within a study, because many studies ask a range of very different questions. Thus, each individual question has equal weight.

3.3 Findings

As in HCI studies, subjective Likert-type items are widely used in accessibility research: 42% of papers included the use of Likert-type items to gather subjective opinions from participants.

Of the 135 papers published between 2010 and 2014, 101 included some form of study involving people facing accessibility challenges. Of these, 51 (50%) used Likert-type items to gather subjective opinions from participants. Table 1 summarizes the characteristics of these 51 studies, organized according to the target user population. One study that included participants with visual and physical impairments is represented as a physical impairment population.

Sample sizes ranged from case studies of three individuals up to an online study with 317 respondents [12], with a median value of 12 participants (mean 23 and standard deviation 48).

Only 8% of these studies (4 studies) had anonymous submission of user ratings, and all of these were studies involving sign language users, or deaf or hard of hearing individuals. In the remainder of studies, participants are assumed to have met with researchers in person.

Many papers did not explicitly state how the questions were presented. Nine studies described paper or electronic administration, all others are assumed to be verbal or signed. In studies with visually impaired participants (almost half of the studies), verbal presentation is the most efficient and natural way to gather such feedback, since paper and pencil questionnaires are inaccessible, and online questionnaires would require a system set up with the assistive technologies that the participant is familiar with.

Most of the studies using Likert-type items (59%) are within-subjects comparative studies. In our sample, only

6 studies collected Likert-type responses from populations with and without access issues responding to the same technology. As Sears and Hanson [24] observe, when testing an intervention designed for a specific population, a comparison group may not be appropriate.

In the 51 papers that reported using Likert-type items, 417 individual items were described, 21 of which were from control group respondents. Response values were reported for 369 of these items. Response scales varied from 4-point scales up to 21 points (NASA-TLX). 66% of items used a 5-point response scale, and 16% used a 7-point scale.

Most items (94%) were custom-designed. Only 27 (6%) were part of a previously established usability measure. The validated measures used were NASA-TLX (7 items) [8], ISO-9241-9 (4 items) [9], QUEST (1 item) [6], DEEP (8 items) [27], SUS (2 items) [3], and Browsing experience (2 items) [1], though the whole measure was not always used.

It was not possible to rigorously analyze the potential for acquiescence bias, or the use of balanced sets of items (both positively and negatively worded), because many papers did not include the precise wording of their Likert-type items. Overall, 75% of the items were described with positive language (e.g. "X is easy to use"). 9% were presented with neutral language (e.g. "experience using X"), and 16% were described with negative language (e.g. "X was confusing"). One online study [25] explicitly considered the effect of valence in wording, using two groups who were asked to respond to the items "I found the video easy to comprehend" and "I found the video difficult to comprehend". Consistent with acquiescence bias, the results for the two groups did not show an inverse relationship, and were analyzed separately.

Excluding responses from control groups, the overall mean of Likert ratings normalized to a 5-point scale where 5 is the most positive response was 3.64 for studies with non-anonymous response modes, which is slightly higher than the mean value of 3.55 reported by Nielsen and Levy [15]. Anonymous responses from the four online studies are lower, at 2.61. This low average rating is unsurprising, because three of these studies (56 items) explored sign language intelligibility in video and included conditions with deliberately degraded video quality. We cannot therefore make a fair comparison between anonymous and non-anonymous responses.

Responses to questions that were about a proposed innovation were rated even more highly (Mean = 3.74), in comparison to a mean rating of 2.9 for other questions.

These findings are consistent with positive response bias for in-person studies and items relating to proposed innovations. The lack of anonymity, verbal format and use of predominantly positive language are likely to introduce positive bias in responses. However, these papers represent the best 25-30% of papers submitted to the ASSETS conference, and are very likely to describe successful solutions to access challenges. It is possible that the proposed innovations were simply very effective.

4. USER STUDY

4.1 Design

Based on the analysis of papers of the last 5 years of ASSETS proceedings, coupled with our own observations while conducting user studies, we reasoned that if there is, in fact, an inflation in positive reports, it could be revealed by an experiment. Hence, we designed a study where we asked people to evaluate two systems with subjective scales, but purposefully introduced usability problems in one of them. We recruited two convenience samples typical of accessibility research, one of 16 people with visual impairments, and another of 16 students with no visual impairments, as a control. The experiment we will describe next has, therefore, a 2x2 design, with one factor being the population from which the sample is drawn (between-subjects), and the other the system that was evaluated (within-subjects). We will henceforth refer to the levels of factor Population as VI and Student, and to the levels of factor System as Usable and Degraded, with Degraded being the one engineered to have usability problems.

The systems we created are automated call-answering services that people dial in to on the telephone and then navigate the options recited by a recorded voice using the key buttons. We chose this kind of system for two reasons. First, because it is usable by both user groups. Second, because it is something that every participant was likely to have encountered before, and yet could be understood as an innovation proposed by the researchers conducting the study - as a new and improved call-answering service. Had we tried to evaluate an innovation that was very unfamiliar to participants, other confounds could have been introduced, such as exaggerated excitement for new technologies, or, conversely, a resistance to change.

4.2 Research questions

If there is stronger positive response bias in the visually impaired group, it should be true that it rates the systems more positively when asked. It should also be true that, in this group, the ratings are less sensitive to usability problems. We hence formulate the following research questions:

RQ1 Do visually impaired participants offer higher subjective scores?

RQ2 Is the difference between the subjective scores they assign to the two systems smaller than the difference assigned by students?

RQ3 Is the relationship between the subjective scores and objective usability measures weaker for the group with visual impairment?

4.3 Participants

We recruited 16 participants with visual impairment (the VI group) from a vocational learning center for blind people. There were 9 males and 7 females, and their average age was 45.2 years old, standard deviation (henceforth SD) 11.2, and range 23-64. Thirteen participants were legally blind, and three had low vision (the criteria for inclusion being 1. usually using cane for outside mobility and 2. usually using screen readers in computing devices). Among the blind participants, the average time of onset was 27.5 years ago (8-52, SD 16.0). Six participants reported using telephone-based information systems weekly, 6 monthly, 6 rarely, and 3 never. When participants reported never having used such a system, an expanded explanation was offered.

For the control group, we recruited 16 graduate school students with no declared visual impairment from a university campus. There were 12 males and 4 females, and their average age was 27.2, SD 7.1, range 23-53. One participant

Usable

Welcome to <Museum Name>, located at <Address>.

The museum is open every day, except Thanksgiving and Christmas day, from 10am to 5:45pm.

For admission prices, parking, travel directions, wheelchair access and hall and exhibition closings, press 1.

For information about the Haydn Planetarium Space Show, press 2.

For public programs and special events, including lectures, films, performances and workshops, press 3.

For advance ticketing, press 4.

For membership services, press 5.

For volunteer information, press 6.

For a staff directory, press 7.

For lost and found, press 8.

To repeat this message, press 9.

Degraded

Welcome to <Museum Name>, preserving our architectural heritage since 1942. It is our pleasure to serve you.

Press 1 for parking, travel directions and hall and exhibition closings.

Press 2 for information about the Frank Lloyd Wright Virtual Tour.

Press 3 for opening hours.

Press 4 for public programs and special events, including lectures, films, performances and workshops.

Press 5 to hear more options.

Figure 2: Main menu of Usable and Degraded telephone systems.

reported using telephone-based information systems weekly, and 6 monthly, and 10 rarely. The lower frequency might be explained by this sample using internet services instead of calling, as was mentioned by some of the participants.

There is considerable difference in the demographic make-up of the groups. We are aware that in some studies in which the population is a factor, the control sample is matched to the sample of interest. As we have not done that, we cannot exclude the possibility that differences between population groups are explained by demographics. However, we point out that even if we matched age and gender, other personal characteristics, which we didn't collect or measure, could be the explaining variable. Indeed, if an effect exists, it follows that it is caused by something, or some things, like personality traits, which perhaps could be measured. As we were interested in first finding evidence that the effect exists, we opted for what is a typical student sample of HCI research, and we leave the question of its causes open.

4.4 Apparatus

We sought to define tasks that could be performed in the same manner by both groups, and would be equally easy for both groups, We selected a set of auditory tasks that would be familiar to both user groups: calling an automated telephone information system for specific information. Our two designs were both modeled directly on the main menu of the American Museum of Natural History's telephone information system. The Usable system closely follows the content, structure, prompt style and navigation method of the original system. User actions are always described AFTER describing the option ('For xxx, press 2'). Navigation in this system centers around a single main menu, and users are automatically returned to this main menu if they make no selection in a submenu.

The Degraded system was an edited version of the same system, with the following changes:

- Prompts were reorganized so as to provide the user action BEFORE describing the option. ("Press 2 for xxx"). This means that users must retain the number in working memory while listening to the rest of the prompt. Since some options are long (up to 17 words), this should make the system more difficult to use.
- Additional preamble was added before presenting the menu options.
- One item of useful information (opening times) was moved from the preamble into a submenu.
- Menu options were reordered.
- One option ('buy a ticket') was moved into a submenu.
- One option ('lost and found') was removed, and replaced with a generic option in a submenu ('all other enquiries')
- Navigation was hierarchical, and information about how to return to the previous menu was added at the end of the sublevel menus.

The main menu for each system is shown in English in Figure 2. For the purposes of the experiment, both systems were translated into Portuguese and local museum names were used in place of the terms Usable and Degraded.

Each system was simulated through a desktop application, with which a user could 'call' the museum, and navigate the menus using the keyboard numpad. The menus were presented as pre-recorded human speech, to reduce effects due to the blind participants being more familiar with TTS voices than the comparison group.

We used Sauro's Single Ease Question [20], shown in Figure 3, to gather subjective feedback. This question has been validated in comparative studies [20] and performed well. In contrast to many items in the literature, it is neutrally worded. Responses are given on a 7-point scale where one extreme (1) is 'very difficult' and the other (7) is 'very easy'. For verbal administration, the question was phrased "From 1 to 7, do you think this task was easy or hard to perform, where 1 is very difficult and 7 is very easy".

Overall, this task was:

very easy O O O O O O O very difficult

Figure 3: Sauro's Single Ease Question.

Table 2: Average answer to the Single Ease Question per group and per system.

	VI	Student	
Usable	6.6 (SD=1.0)	6.8 (SD=0.6)	6.7 (SD=0.8)
Degraded	6.4 (SD=0.9)	6.0 (SD=1.2)	6.2 (SD=1.1)
	6.5 (SD=0.9)	6.4 (SD=1.1)	

Table 3: Average task completion time per group and per system.

	VI	Student	
Usable	56s (SD=37)	45s (SD=17)	52s (SD=30)
Degraded	79s (SD=49)	62s (SD=28)	71s (SD=41)
	68s(SD=45)	54s (SD=24)	

4.5 Procedure

Sessions with participants with visual impairment took place in the learning center. Sessions with students took place at their university. After giving informed consent, participants provided demographic information and were then asked to complete the same four tasks with each system. The objective for each task was:

Task 1 Find out where the wheelchair access is located.

Task 2 Find out if the museum is open today.

Task 3 Get to the Lost and Found department.

Task 4 Find out the admission price for a senior.

After stating the objective, a moderator dialed the number. Participants were instructed that, from that moment on, the moderator would not intervene at all, until the participant hung up.

They were further instructed that they could try calling as many times as they wanted, with the assistance of the moderator, until quitting or achieving the stated goal, as this is a reasonable strategy on real call-answering systems. To verify that the goal was achieved, participants were instructed to, after hanging up by themselves, verbally recount the information they were tasked to retrieve. For task 3, where there was no information to retrieve, success was assessed based on participants reaching the right option. Each participant completed all four tasks, first on one system, then on the other. The order of systems was counterbalanced. The order of tasks was kept constant, as the research questions do not call for comparisons among them. The systems were referred to using the museum names, so as not to imply any ordering between them. After each task, the experimenter asked the Ease question, presented verbally. The participant's spoken responses were recorded. Participants were asked to give a numerical response to the 'Ease' question. Immediately after they responded, the corresponding meaning of the value was reflected back to them, to confirm their intention. This was to eliminate any possible confusion about the meaning of the numerical values. The moderator used form fields in the desktop application to record if the task was completed successfully and the subjective score. The application automatically recorded, for each task, the times at which calls were dialed and hung-up, and the sequence of options selected by the participant.

4.6 Results

In the following analysis, we use standard t-tests, which are paired when comparing within-subjects measurements, and unpaired otherwise. We adjust the significance level with the Bonferroni correction when comparing *Population x System* combinations.

4.6.1 *Subjective ease*

All participants ultimately completed all tasks successfully. Table 2 summarizes the responses to the 'Ease' question. From the overall ratings, and our observations during study sessions, there is a ceiling affecting the effect sizes. We had hoped that the usability problems in the Degraded system would cause more difficulties than they actually did. Overall, participants in the VI group offered only slightly higher subjective scores (6.5 vs. 6.4 on average). The effect size being small (Cohen's d=0.01, with 0.2 being considered a standard small effect), our sample size doesn't provide adequate power to detect a difference, and hence can't say that the scores are significantly higher (t=0.72, p>0.05). We can't therefore answer the first research question conclusively, as to whether VI participants offer higher subjective scores.

Still, the differences in subjective scores by system are informative as to possible differences in sensitivity to usability problems. As expected, taking the two groups of participants together, tasks on the Usable system were on average rated as being easier to perform than in the Degraded system (0.47 mean difference, t = 4.70, p<0.00001, d=0.48). As would be expected if there was a response bias, despite the fact that the Degraded system had usability problems, it wasn't rated much worse by visually-impaired participants (0.13 mean difference), and this difference is not significant (t=1.07, p>0.025, d=0.14). The students, in contrast, offered significantly lower scores to the Degraded system (0.86 mean difference, t=5.84, p<0.0001, d=0.88). Taking the difference in ratings that participants assigned to the same task in the two systems as a measurement of sensitivity to usability problems, we find that indeed the visually-impaired group was less sensitive (t=3.79, p=0.0001) and that this effect is sizable (d=0.68). We thus find support to respond positively to the second research question: the difference between the subjective scores visually-impaired participants assign to the two systems is smaller than the difference assigned by students.

4.6.2 *Relationship with objective measure*

Table 3 summarizes the task completion times. We define task completion time as the interval between the first time the phone line was opened, and the last time a call was ended, within a task. Although we are not testing differences in measured performance, we can observe that, as expected, tasks in the Degraded system took on average more time than in the Usable system. We can also observe that the VI group took on average more time than the student group, which can be at least partially explained by the added effort of seeking the right key on a keyboard using only touch. We computed the correlation between the task completion times and the subjective score for each group. We find that for the student group, the relationship between the two measures was very strong (Pearson's r (117 d.f.) = 0.70, 95% CI [-0.78,-0.59]). For the VI group, despite the relationship also being strong, it was less so, as would be predicted by the thesis of a positive bias (Pearson's r(134 d.f.) = 0.50, 95% CI [-0.62,-0.36]). The difference in correlation coefficients, despite the ceiling effect in subjective scores, leads us to answer positively to the third and final research question: the relationship between the subjective scores and objective usability measures is weaker for the group with visual impairment.

4.6.3 *Examples*

To further illustrate the positive bias in VI participants, and as a sanity check to the statistical analysis, we present some instances of mismatch between what we perceived as being users struggling with the system, and the subjective scores they assigned to the task. We represent dialing with the letter D, and hanging-up with the letter H.

- For task 1 in the Degraded system, the optimal sequence of steps was D-1-H. One VI participant executed the sequence D-4-H-D-5-5-1-H, took more than 200 seconds to complete the task, and then rated the easiness at 6 out of seven.
- For the next task, the same participant executed the sequence D-2-5-3-5-3-H, when the optimal was D-3-H. and rated easiness at 7 out of seven.
- For task 3 in the Degraded system, another participant executed the sequence D-2-5-3-5-3-9-8-H, when the optimal would be D-5-8-H, and rated easiness at 7.
- For task 4 in the Degraded system, yet another participant took 117s to complete the task, having taken two more steps than necessary, and rated easiness at 7.

4.7 Discussion

Although we couldn't establish that those in the population of interest consistently rate systems higher, because of a ceiling effect, we did find that their subjective ratings aren't as sensitive to usability problems, and do not correlate as well with objective measures of performance. Plausible explanations for this finding could include:

- The task was easier for the participants with visual impairment
- Demand characteristics, acquiescence or social desirability bias affected the two groups differently
- The experience of accessibility barriers creates a low usability baseline
- The participants with visual impairment had a generally positive outlook
- The participants with visual impairment wanted to encourage the researchers
- The difference is the result of other unmatched factors such as participant age, study location and recruitment methods.

Further work is needed to unpack these possible factors. Our experiment provides some initial insights. Although we strove to select a task that would be equally easy for the two groups, it is possible that any auditory task might be easier for a person with long-established visual impairment who is used to receiving information auditorially. However, although the VI group did report greater use of telephone information systems, they did not complete the tasks more quickly than the students. They had a lower correlation between their task performance and subjective evaluation, suggesting that this was not the case here. It is still possible that the VI group's familiarity with such systems led to their being less affected by the usability problems we introduced.

Finally, participants' conception of what is 'easy' is inevitably shaped by their daily life experiences. People living with a disability face access barriers that others do not. The tasks here were about accessing information, which can involve access barriers for people with visual impairment. Thus, the participants' prior experiences may have created very different baselines from which they estimated ease of use. Our Usable and Degraded systems both provided the information needed to complete the tasks in an accessible form. Thus, the VI group may have rated them both as 'very easy' in comparison to other tasks they have encountered. Similar arguments would apply to other accessibility groups. For example, for individuals with dexterity impairment, a selection task may be 'very easy' if the target is much larger than typical targets, even if it takes a long time to make the selection and errors are made.

When subjective user ratings seem at odds with other measures, this can be an important indicator that the priorities of individuals with a disability differ from those assumed by researchers who may not have experience of that disability. However, to properly interpret such ratings, researchers need an understanding of how the factors above can also influence responses.

5. IMPLICATIONS FOR ACCESSIBILITY RESEARCH

Our experimental study followed the design of a typical accessibility study - a within-subjects comparison of technologies conducted in person with verbal question administration and a small number of participants. We added a second factor of two different participant groups, so as to compare ratings for the VI group and the Student group.

If a tendency to provide higher usability ratings than typical HCI users were confirmed in further work, it would suggest that accessibility studies are more likely to run into ceiling effects. This would make it difficult to find significant differences between conditions (as in our experiment), especially with small numbers of participants. It would also mean that baseline values for established usability scales may not be directly transferable to accessibility technologies. For example, on the System Usability Scale (SUS), a score above 70 is considered good, based on experience from hundreds of usability studies [2]. A higher baseline value may be more appropriate for access technologies.

Accessibility researchers can take steps in their experimental designs to avoid conditions that have been shown to lead to biased responses, as discussed below.

5.1 Use validated scales

Very few of the studies in our sample used established measures such as NASA-TLX or SUS. Such measures have often undergone extensive development to select appropriate wording, balance the set of items, and confirm reliability. Accessibility researchers could benefit from this work.

5.2 Use balanced or neutrally-worded prompt statements

Few accessibility studies have enough participants to support the use of two groups responding to oppositely worded statements, as in [25]. However, researchers could use a balanced mix of positive and negative items to mitigate acquiescence bias, or use neutral wording, as in the single ease question ("Overall, this task was:").

5.3 Consider alternatives to verbal presentation

To reduce social desirability reporting, or other bias introduced by verbal presentation, consider whether questionnaires could be administered in a more private fashion, for instance through an online format.

5.4 Use response labels to avoid confusion

Where participants do give responses verbally with no visual prompt, using response labels (e.g. "strongly agree" or "difficult") would eliminate the possibility of confusion over the mapping from labels to numbers. Where numerical responses are requested, researchers could translate the number to an appropriate label and reflect it back to participants, to confirm their intended response.

5.5 Report presentation method precisely

Many papers described that they had "administered a questionnaire", but did not state how the questions were presented. Whatever the experimental design, it is good practice to report the specific verbiage used in subjective response questions, and to explicitly state the mode of presentation and response. This allows other researchers to better understand the potential for bias.

5.6 Interpret positive ratings with care

If steps are taken to protect against bias, researchers can more confidently learn from subjective ratings, and avoid a ceiling effect that masks genuine usability differences between systems. Researchers receiving strong positive ratings for novel technologies from participants with disabilities may be wise to consider potential sources of bias in interpreting the results.

6. CONCLUSIONS

Likert-type subjective ratings are commonly used in accessibility research, in formats that may introduce positive response bias. Our study of two telephone information systems, one more usable than the other, found that a group of participants with visual impairment were less sensitive to usability problems than a group of students without disabilities, and their responses had lower correlation with task completion times. Their high ratings produced a ceiling effect that masked the usability differences found by the student group. Further work is needed to establish whether positive bias is at play. Accessibility researchers may be able to reduce positive bias by using electronic administration methods and balanced sets of Likert-type items, among other techniques. Potential positive bias should be taken into account when interpreting Likert-type responses, and applying subjective measures from HCI in accessibility research.

7. ACKNOWLEDGMENTS

This research was partially funded by FCT (UID/CEC/00408/2013, SFRH/BD/98527/2013). We thank Fundação Sain and Carlos Bastardo for their patronage, Erin Brady, and the study participants.

8. REFERENCES

[1] J. S. Ahuja and J. Webster. Perceived disorientation: An examination of a new measure to assess web design effectiveness. *Interacting with Computers*, 14(1):15–29, Dec. 2001.

[2] A. Bangor, P. Kortum, and J. Miller. Determining what individual SUS scores mean: Adding an adjective rating scale. *Journal of Usability Studies*, 4(3):114–123, 2009.

[3] J. Brooke. SUS : A retrospective. *Journal of Usability Studies*, 8(2):29–40, 2013.

[4] M. Dee and V. L. Hanson. A large user pool for accessibility research with representative users. In *Proceedings of the 16th International ACM SIGACCESS Conference on Computers & Accessibility - ASSETS '14*, pages 35–42, New York, New York, USA, Oct. 2014. ACM Press.

[5] N. Dell, V. Vaidyanathan, I. Medhi, E. Cutrell, and W. Thies. "Yours is better!": participant response bias in HCI. In *Proceedings of the 2012 ACM Annual Conference on Human Factors in Computing Systems - CHI '12*, page 1321, New York, New York, USA, May 2012. ACM Press.

[6] L. Demers, R. Weiss-Lambrou, and B. Ska. Development of the Quebec User Evaluation of Satisfaction with assistive Technology (QUEST). *Assistive Technology*, 8(1):3–13, June 1996.

[7] K. M. Gerling, R. L. Mandryk, and M. R. Kalyn. Wheelchair-based game design for older adults. In *Proceedings of the 15th International ACM SIGACCESS Conference on Computers and Accessibility - ASSETS '13*, pages 1–8, New York, New York, USA, 2013. ACM Press.

[8] S. G. Hart and L. E. Staveland. Development of NASA-TLX (Task Load Index): Results of Empirical and Theoretical Research. In *Advances in Psychology*, volume 52, pages 139–183. 1988.

[9] ISO. Ergonomic requirements for office work with visual display terminals (VDTs) - Part 9: Requirements for non-keyboard input devices. In *ISO 9241*. International Organization for Standardization, 2000.

[10] R. Johns. Likert items and scales. In *Survey Question Bank: Methods Fact Sheet 1*. 2000.

[11] M. C. Kaptein, C. Nass, and P. Markopoulos. Powerful and consistent analysis of Likert-type rating scales. In *Proceedings of the 28th International Conference on Human Factors in Computing Systems - CHI '10*, page 2391, New York, New York, USA, 2010. ACM Press.

[12] M. Kipp, Q. Nguyen, A. Heloir, and S. Matthes. Assessing the deaf user perspective on sign language avatars. In *The Proceedings of the 13th International ACM SIGACCESS Conference on Computers and Accessibility - ASSETS '11*, page 107, New York, New York, USA, 2011. ACM Press.

[13] J. Lazar, J. H. Feng, and H. Hochheiser. *Research Methods in Human-Computer Interaction.* John Wiley & Sons, 2010.

[14] R. Likert. A technique for the measurement of attitudes. *Archives of Psychology*, 22 140:55, 1932.

[15] J. Nielsen and J. Levy. Measuring usability: preference vs. performance. *Communications of the ACM*, 37(4):66–75, Apr. 1994.

[16] D. L. Paulhus. Two-component models of socially desirable responding. *Journal of Personality and Social Psychology*, 46(3):598–609, 1984.

[17] W. L. Richman, S. Kiesler, S. Weisband, and F. Drasgow. A meta-analytic study of social desirability distortion in computer-administered questionnaires, traditional questionnaires, and interviews. *Journal of Applied Psychology*, 84(5):754–775, 1999.

[18] D. Sato, M. Kobayashi, H. Takagi, C. Asakawa, and J. Tanaka. How voice augmentation supports elderly web users. In *The Proceedings of the 13th International ACM SIGACCESS Conference on Computers and Accessibility - ASSETS '11*, page 155, New York, New York, USA, 2011. ACM Press.

[19] J. Sauro. Do users fail a task and still rate it as easy?, 2009. `http://www.measuringu.com/failed-sat.php` [accessed 2015-May-02].

[20] J. Sauro and J. S. Dumas. Comparison of three one-question, post-task usability questionnaires. In *Proceedings of the 27th International Conference on Human Factors in Computing Systems - CHI 09*, page 1599, New York, New York, USA, 2009. ACM Press.

[21] J. Sauro and J. R. Lewis. Correlations among prototypical usability metrics. In *Proceedings of the 27th International Conference on Human Factors in Computing Systems - CHI 09*, page 1609, New York, New York, USA, 2009. ACM Press.

[22] H. Schuman and S. Presser. The acquiescence quagmire. In *Questions and Answers in Attitude Surveys.* 1981.

[23] N. Schwarz, F. Strack, H.-J. Hippler, and G. Bishop. The impact of administration mode on response effects in survey measurement. *Applied Cognitive Psychology*, 5(3):193–212, May 1991.

[24] A. Sears and V. L. Hanson. Representing users in accessibility research. *ACM Transactions on Accessible Computing*, 4(2):1–6, Mar. 2012.

[25] J. J. Tran, J. Kim, J. Chon, E. A. Riskin, R. E. Ladner, and J. O. Wobbrock. Evaluating quality and comprehension of real-time sign language video on mobile phones. In *The Proceedings of the 13th International ACM SIGACCESS Conference on Computers and Accessibility - ASSETS '11*, page 115, New York, New York, USA, 2011. ACM Press.

[26] S. Trewin, M. Laff, V. Hanson, and A. Cavender. Exploring visual and motor accessibility in navigating a virtual world. *ACM Transactions on Accessible Computing*, 2(2):1–35, June 2009.

[27] T. Yang, J. Linder, and D. Bolchini. DEEP: Design-oriented evaluation of perceived usability. *International Journal of Human-Computer Interaction*, 28(5):308–346, May 2012.

User Participation when Users have Mental and Cognitive Disabilities

Stefan Johansson
KTH Royal Institute of Technology,
CSC – School of Computer Science and Communication
Lindstedtsvägen 3, SE-100 44
Stockholm, Sweden
+46(0)708 23 10 64
stefan.johansson@funka.com

Jan Gulliksen
KTH Royal Institute of Technology,
CSC – School of Computer Science and Communication
Lindstedtsvägen 3, SE-100 44
Stockholm, Sweden
+46(0)730-373930
gulliksen@kth.se

Ann Lantz
KTH Royal Institute of Technology,
CSC – School of Computer Science and Communication
Lindstedtsvägen 3, SE-100 44
Stockholm, Sweden
+46 8 790 68 17
alz@csc.kth.se

ABSTRACT
Persons with cognitive or mental disabilities have difficulties participating in or are excluded from IT development and assessments exercises due to the problems finding good ways to efficiently collaborate on equal terms. In this paper we describe how we worked closely together with persons that have mental and cognitive disabilities in order to test and develop methods for participation in assessments and in processes for developing, Information and Communication Technology (ICT) products and services. More than 100 persons with mental and cognitive disabilities participated in the study (people with diagnoses such as depression, anxiety disorder, bipolarity, and schizophrenia). To explore the conditions for a more equal and fair participation we have developed and elaborated a set of methods, tools and approaches. By combining scientific research methods with well-established methods for empowerment and participation we have developed methods that are cost effective and that easily can be incorporated in existing processes. We believe that our approach have taken steps to implement possibilities for persons with mental and cognitive disabilities to take part where user participation is needed in order not to discriminate or exclude but also to improve the overall quality of the end result. The results clearly show that it is possible to include persons with mental and cognitive disabilities. A mixed method – mixed tool approach can increase the possibility for participation. The results also show that the quality of the analysis phase increases if the collaborative approach is extended to also embrace the data analysis phase.

Categories and Subject Descriptors
K.4.2 [**Computers and Society**]: Social Issues – *Assistive technologies for persons with disabilities, user-centered design.*

General Terms
Human Factors

ASSETS '15, October 26 - 28, 2015, Lisbon, Portugal

ACM 978-1-4503-3400-6/15/10...$15.00
DOI: http://dx.doi.org/10.1145/2700648.2809849

Keywords: Mental disability, mental problems, cognitive disability, accessibility, user participation, inclusion

1. INTRODUCTION
Mental disabilities are often not regarded when discussing accessibility. In this study all participants had diagnoses that can be described as mental illness. The most common diagnoses in this field are depression, anxiety disorder, bipolarity, schizophrenia but it is also common that persons suffer with mental illness without a diagnose or with a mix of diagnoses. The condition for participation in the study was that you had some form of mental illness and that you have had this problem for a long period of time. The result of the study is presented on the level of "persons with mental illness" and not "persons with specific mental illness diagnoses".

1.1 User participation when the user is mentally ill
Persons with mental illness often refrain from participating in surveys or participate in research projects. Of the over 100 persons who participated in this study there are only a few who say that they regularly answer questionnaires or participate in interviews. To make an exception requires that they become convinced that it is worth taking part in a specific case.

The general problems with user participation in accessibility studies are discussed by Sears and Hanson (1). They claim "that effective accessibility research requires the inclusion of representative users" (p4).

When it comes to developing ICT-products and services it seems unusual that persons with mental illness take part in developing processes or assessments of existing products and services. No participant in this study had been involved in such activities. Most of them had been asked to participate in different surveys but not in the area of ICT.

1.2 Cognitive issues – a companion to the mental illness
Mental disabilities often lead to a variety of cognitive difficulties (2). Participants in this study describe problems with: execution abilities, memory, concentration and focus. They also describe how persistent mental problems gradually affect such as: self-confidence, self-esteem, trust and security.

The cognitive difficulties the participants describe can often be linked to the ICF, International Classification on Functioning,

Disability and Health[1] in the following areas (numbers indicate the code of the ICF system):

- Sustaining attention, b1400
- Shifting Attention, b1401
- Short-term memory, b1440
- Organization and planning, b1641
- Time management, b1642
- Problem-solving, b1646
- Experience of Time, b1802
- Undertaking a complex task, d2101
- Completing multiple tasks, d2201
- Handling stress, d2401

To give an example: depression has a direct effect on a person's ability to act and react. A secondary effect is that depressed persons often get problems with short term memory, time management or some other higher cognitive functions. As a third hand effect you can get cognitive problems caused by the medications you are prescribed to relieve your depression.

1.3 Prerequisites for participation

People with mental and cognitive disabilities can sometimes be extra sensitive to the particular implementation of a study. Small details, unexpected changes, poor treatment or inadvertency can result in nonresponses or dropouts.

When we planned the project we paid extra attention on and emphasized the importance of giving the practicalities of the project close attention and care. Through previous practical work, we have identified a number of points that require special attention. We drew from them and elaborated them during the project. Altogether, we tried to create additional favorable conditions for participation.

1.4 The values of participation – purpose and justification

If persons with mental and cognitive disabilities are disregarded in research and development processes important information about user behavior and user preferences get ignored. It is important to explore methods for participation for groups that by prejudice can be perceived as difficult to include in surveys and projects.

1.5 Research questions

Based on the background description we wanted to explore how persons with mental and cognitive disabilities can be involved in research projects. More specifically we wanted to explore

- if traditional methods from non-formal adult education could be combined with scientific methods and tools,
- how data collection and analyses can be carried out in cooperation with the target group,
- what factors was considered important for users to decide to onboard a project and then stay to the end.

1.6 About the project

In the study over 100 persons with a mental illness participated. Activities have been implemented in major cities, smaller towns and rural areas. The participants have various diagnoses such as bipolar disorder, depression, schizophrenia, panic disorder or other mental disorders. They have had their problems for a long time. In addition to different kind of mental problems most of the participants can also describe a number of different types of cognitive difficulties.

The study was conducted between October 2013 and February 2014.

Groups of 8-12 persons where formed in three major Swedish cities; Stockholm, Lund and Karlstad and each group met at least three times with at least one week in between each meeting. A meeting lasted for three hours. Every meeting was documented through minutes and important discussions and important findings were documented with illustrations, so called "Mock-Up visualizations".

In three other cities; Uppsala, Umeå and Bräcke, we arranged half-day activities as a onetime occasion. The activity lasted for 4-5 hours with 15-20 participants at each activity.

The project was carried out in close cooperation with RSMH[2]. RSMH is a member driven organization, aiming for social inclusion for persons with mental illnesses, and there are members of RSMH who participated in the study. The members have different kind of mental illness.

A presentation of the findings from the project is presented in the paper "Cognitive accessibility for mentally disabled persons" (3). A broader literature review on cognitive accessibility (4) shows that the research in this area is limited.

2. METHOD

The overall research approach follows the tradition of Action Research (5) More specifically the method is heavily influenced by the tradition of Participatory Design (PD) (6), (7) or the more Scandinavian version called Cooperative Design (8), (9). We have therefore used an adapted form of Participatory Action Research (10). We have in the past seen many problems to actually manage to work well with user participation (11) and the traditional methods for user participation are not sufficient when users have mental problems. In this project we have explored and developed methods adapted to perform better for persons with mental problems. When traditional PD often focuses on work and activities at the workplace we have shifted focus to all aspects of life, keeping the aim of mutual understanding that characterizes PD; researchers must know more about living with a mental illness and the mentally disabled person must know more about accessibility, technology and methods for empowerment. An inspirational source is the work presented in Design side by side by Jönsson et al, especially how artefacts can work as realized thoughts (12).

2.1 Study circles

For this study we have used a concept called study circles (12). Study circles have a long tradition in the Nordic countries. A study circle is a group of adults that meet and discuss a specific topic. It is done by free will and in a democratic way. There is no teacher; instead a study circle has a leader who has the responsibility to facilitate the discussions.

Study circles as well as folk high schools are a part of a concept called "Folkbildning", a combination of the word "people" and "enlightenment[3]. It is a non-formal adult education system

[1] http://www.who.int/classifications/icf/en/

[2] RSMH, Riksförbundet Social och Mental Hälsa, www.rsmh.se

[3] http://www.folkbildningsradet.se/Folkbildning/Oversattningar/English-translations/

established over 100 years ago. Each year study associations run 300 000 study circles with some 1,8 million participants in a country with a population of 9,5 million[4]. The perspective is "lifelong learning". According to the Folkbildningsrådet, Folkbildning has the following characteristics:

- It is always voluntary for an individual to participate in "folkbildning".
- The participants have considerable opportunities to influence the content of the activities.
- "Folkbildning" is characterized by an environment in which learning and social interactions go hand in hand. The circumstances and experiences of every participant are taken into account.
- "Folkbildning" contributes to strengthening civil society through close cooperation with volunteer organizations, associations and various types of networks.

In this project one of the researchers acted as the leader for the study circles.

The concept of study circles has been further developed to so called research circles as a way for researchers and practitioners to work together to produce knowledge and gain a deeper understanding (13). The practitioners formulate problems and try to solve them. The basic idea is that researchers and practitioners meet and learn about each other's knowledge and experiences. In a structured process this will lead to actions, reflection and to new knowledge.

3. RESULT

In this part we will describe how we carefully planned and executed the study.

3.1 Recruitment

Participants were recruited through RSMH. Representatives of RSMH informed about the project and recruitment can be described as a snowball sampling. Participants could be included if they were regularly attending RSM-activities but not if they were in an active psychotic period. They should have had their mental problems for more than a year. The recruitment process was mostly conducted orally by telephone or by personal meetings. The written material we produced came to be used mostly to inform the official representatives from RSMH, but when they got the grasp of the project they turned to oral information combined with some complementary e-mailing and text messaging. The main message to the potential user was that we would like to discuss accessibility issues, things that made life difficult if you have a mental disability and especially accessibility issues connected with the digital society. As researchers we kept a low profile up to the first meeting. This was a matter of trust. If a researcher, unknown to potential participants, would make contact it is likely that many would have declined an invitation to participate. RSMH were at this point the most credible actor.

Several of the participants in the study said they had difficulties with time management. The problems may involve planning time in order for you to be on time for an appointment or to be aware that the meeting time is approaching and then bring yourself to get going. Several participants also had difficulties remembering or recalling appointments.

[4] http://studieforbunden.se/in-english/

To counteract dropouts caused by issues with time management or short term memory, we worked intensely before every meeting to contact participants to remind them of the upcoming meeting. We used e-mail, telephone and SMS-messages. We soon found that it also was common that participants reminded each other in semi-spontaneous contact chains. This was not an official activity but not entirely spontaneous either. This is troublesome for so many so there is a tradition within RSMH to help each other. In some cases one participant passed by another participant's residence to pick him or her up.

We offered to send reminders by postal mail but no one wanted to use that option.

We had no dropouts. The persons who started the set of three meetings also fulfilled them. Some could miss one meeting due to appointments with a doctor or someone else, but that did not lead to a dropout.

The persons that did participate were in between 15 and 75. The participants have various diagnoses such as bipolar disorder, depression, schizophrenia, panic disorder or other mental disorders. As expected from this kind of setting the variation between persons is large when it comes to life experiences and how their mental condition is treated medically. In this project we wanted to discuss the general rather than the specific and when it comes to identifying and discussing accessibility issues the specific diagnose might not be that important.

3.2 Intermediators

Over the years RSMH has developed a method for outreach that encourages members to participate in projects and activities. Often a trusted person from the organization acts as an intermediator. This person could be someone from the staff or the board or a member since a long time. The role of the intermediator is to be both sender and receiver of information up to a point when the participants decided to participate and to trust the researcher or the project leader. From that point the intermediator shift to a reminding, supporting and encouraging role. Another important task is to act as mediators if something goes wrong during a meeting. It might happen that someone becomes very upset, sad or angry and in such a situation the intermediator's role is to prevent an escalation of the situation. An interesting observation is that almost all participants, if needed, also acted as temporary intermediators or mediators. For example participants often calmed things down if someone was acting out too much.

A similar approach is described by Dee and Hansson (13) where they use a manager to match participants from a pool of users with the requirements from a specific scientific study.

3.3 Meeting place

We tested several different meeting places. The best meeting places were the "neutral" places. We define neutral places as places not connected to either RSMH or any "authority". Ordinary meeting rooms worked well as long as they complied with certain standards. There should be a whiteboard or two, a projector and an internet connection and wall surfaces suitable to tape up sheets of paper.

Since participants might have problems connected with enhanced sensitivity to sound, light and smell it is important that the meeting place is not disturbed by noise (high and low frequency's), disturbing lights and reflexes or strong smells. For example the humming sound of a projector can be regarded as very disturbing.

3.4 Initial meal

We had our meetings in the evenings and decided to start the session with a joint meal. Participants, researchers and representatives from RSMH joined to eat together. We had both social and practical reasons for that. Socially the intention was to equalize differences in social status and get to know each other. Many participants live with low incomes so it is not sure when they had their last meal. Practically we did not want anyone to be hungry and participating on an empty stomach is not a good idea. Hunger is not a good basis for an intimate conversation. Hunger can also trigger undesirable behaviors such as aggression or irritation and participants quite simply cannot discuss and stay focused if they are hungry. We soon found that many of the most interesting discussions started during the meal.

3.5 Trust markers

Several participants describe that they are looking for specific signs when deciding if they should take part or not. The general attitude is to decline participation or drop out if something feels awkward. When the set up for a specific study or project seem okay they might do an exception.

We call these signs as "markers of trust". If the markers are absent it is more likely that a participant chose not to take part. The participants describe this as a matter of security and trust. As a researcher you have to convince the participant that the activities you want to perform and your intentions are good and that you are a good person. So, a person or an intention can be a marker of trust but also artefacts and how they are designed can.

When we discussed this in one of the groups it was clear that the final decision whether to participate or not was actually made in between the first and second meeting. What happened during the first meeting was crucial for the final decision on fulfilling the whole participation. At this point the researcher and other persons involved are under scrutiny but also the place and artifacts.

Later on a participant expressed that she immediately felt comfortable when arriving to the meeting place. And the reassuring thing was the yellow tennis balls on the bottom of the legs of the kitchen chairs (see figure 1). This is a low-tech way of reducing noise. And the woman had thought: Someone making this effort to reduce noise must be a good person. Several members in the group said that they had the same feeling.

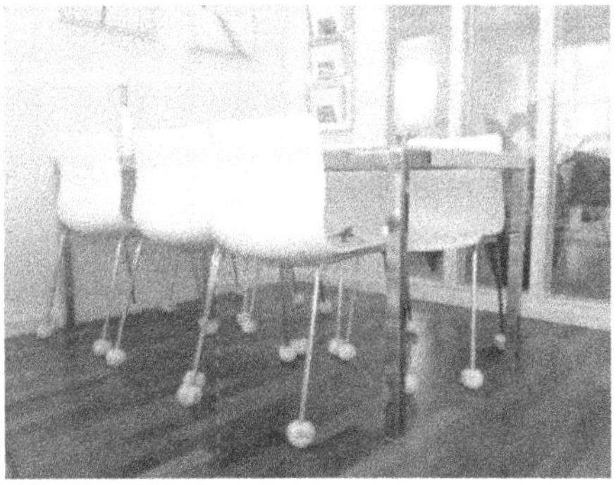

Fig. 1. The tennis balls are used as a low cost noise reduction tool. By being so visually significant they also work as a trust marker. Photo: Tommy Hagström. Used with permission.

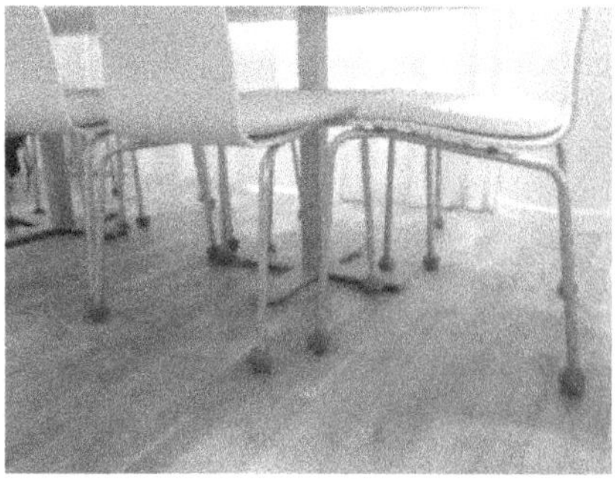

Fig. 2. In the meeting room noise reduction was carried out by expensive and almost invisible grey balls. They don't seem to work as trust markers. Though sitting on them several hours no participant mentioned them. Photo: Tommy Hagström. Used with permission.

The tennis balls acted as a trust marker, but only when really visible (se figure 2). Other trust markers were the lightning of the room and the shadows caused by the lights (rounded, soft and not edgy and frightening), the green plants in the windows and the absence of disturbing noise from ventilation.

The most important trust marker of them all was probably the initial meal.

3.6 Prioritizing exercise

In the beginning of the first session or in the beginning of a one-day activity we performed an exercise to determine what to discuss. This would set the overall frame of all discussion during the three sessions or during the day. Later on we repeated this practice again to divide a larger subject into discussable chunks. It is not the researcher who decides what to discuss. The researcher might introduce a theme but the decision is in the hands of the participants.

After some initial testing we have formalized the procedure and call it a "Prioritizing exercise". It is a moment when participants decide upon how a discussion should start or how it should proceed.

The researcher introduces the theme by asking questions. The starting question in this project was "What is it in your life that creates the biggest obstacles?" Later on questions could be

- What are the biggest obstacles with internet, computers and telephones?
- What are the biggest obstacles with local, regional and government administrations?
- What are the biggest obstacles for you as a consumer?

During 10-15 minutes the participants individually are asked to write down issues on post-it notes. The notes are collected and notes with similar issues are grouped together into clusters and each cluster is tagged with a header. This is an open process where the researcher "thinks aloud" and do the clustering in collaboration with the participants. Everyone is free to comment and question why topics are clustered or not clustered together. The researcher can ask control question such as "I put this thing together with this stuff, do you agree?"

In the next phase each participant is given five sticky notes designed as red dots. Each dot is representing a point. They are asked to use the points to prioritize what they want to discuss. They could go "all in" and place all five on one single subject or they could spread them. By using such a procedure silent participants can have as much influence on what to discuss as more talkative participants. In each group there were some participants who initially were silent and a few that remained silent almost to the end of the third session.

We went back to the list of topics during the whole process to check that prioritized issues were discussed but sometimes new topics emerged.

Fig 3: This is an example of a prioritization exercise where participants were asked to evaluate what is most important for a website to be cognitively available. The exercise was started as a discussion in this project and transformed to a stand-alone exercise that we tested with participants at the conference UD2014[5] and then at a workshop with 50 webmaster of municipal websites in Sweden. Visually, it is easy to spot the most important issues, in this case "Content must not blink and move," "simple and understandable language" and "You should not have to keep many things in mind."

3.7 To document and analyze a discussion

Each meeting was documented in detail. Two assistants had the task of documenting the discussion. They took notes and delivered minutes the day after each meeting. The researcher and the RSMH intermediator complemented the material and after that it was emailed to the participants with a call for comments. Comments could be made directly by a replying mail or in the beginning of the next meeting. But with a few exceptions no one commented by mail and few actually read the minutes and reflected on them. We had to conclude that written documentation did not really work even when produced and distributed really fast.

At the third meeting with the first group we introduced what we called mock-up visualizations. It was a test to explore if another way of summarize a previous discussion could lead to more comments and more reflection. We had noticed that when the discussion leader drew something on the whiteboard or when someone showed a picture the discussion became more vivid. To explore this reaction further we started to produce fast mock-ups where the purpose of each picture was to make some kind of statement or description that participants either could agree with or oppose to.

Many of the mock ups started with an x- and y-bar, where the x-bar often is time, to visualize how something changes over time. The y-bar could be anything that can be described on a low to high scale.

[5] http://ud2014.se/

It is important to understand that although the mock-ups might look scientific at this point they only summarize a discussion or make a statement. There is no data to back up the mock-up. If the picture works it will evoke a reaction. At later stages data can be collected if it is important to determine if the picture is true.

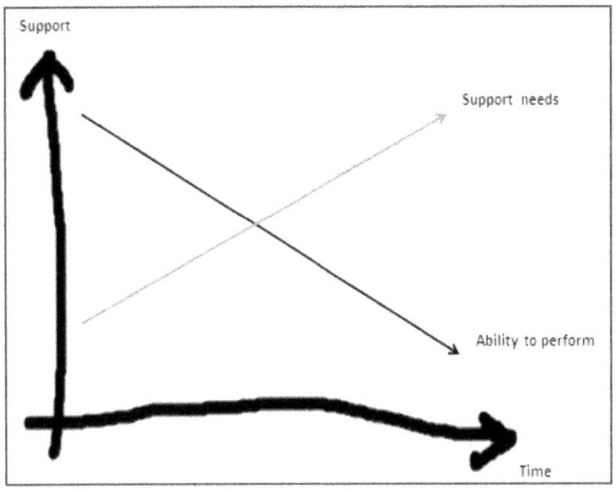

Fig 4: One of the first MockUps describes the relation between a person's ability to perform if support needs are neglected over time. We often went back and reused this picture, often as a layer in another picture.

One example (see figure 5) is composed of five layers. The starting point is a statement from the participants that there is often a relationship between costs and time (layer 1). Such a relationship was later described in terms of performance, which goes down over time if you do not get help. The longer it takes before getting help, the higher the cost (layer 2). An example of these relationships is all instances in the community who are involved in contacts with persons who have mental illness. It is represented by the boxes with text around them. One person can have between 30-50 instances to have contact with (layer 3). All those instances require that the person with mental illness should attend at meetings. Meetings are represented by dots (layer 4). The last layer is a summary description of how many believe that these meetings work. The boy with a green tongue knows exactly how his illness should be dealt with but he is often met by skepticism from those who will treat him. They often want to do their own investigations that take time and that makes the boy's performance decrease while the costs of the treatment that they finally put in will increase (layer 5).

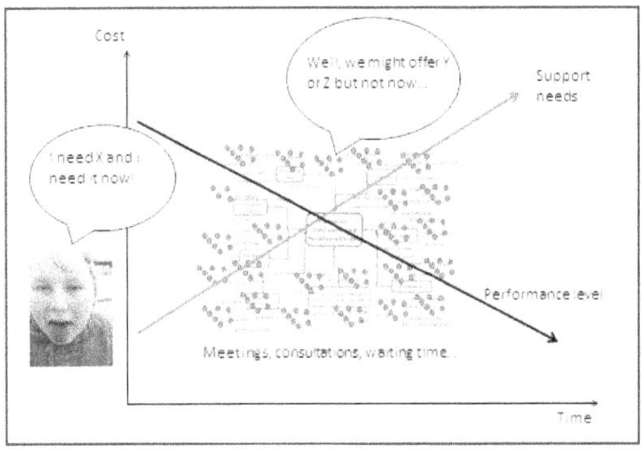

Fig. 5. Example with several layers.

After realizing the power of mock-up visualizations we used this method for the remaining part of the study and we made several visualizations together during meetings and some participants started to make their own pictures and bringing them to the next meeting.

A way of summarizing long and complex discussion is to use a comic strip technique (see figure 6).

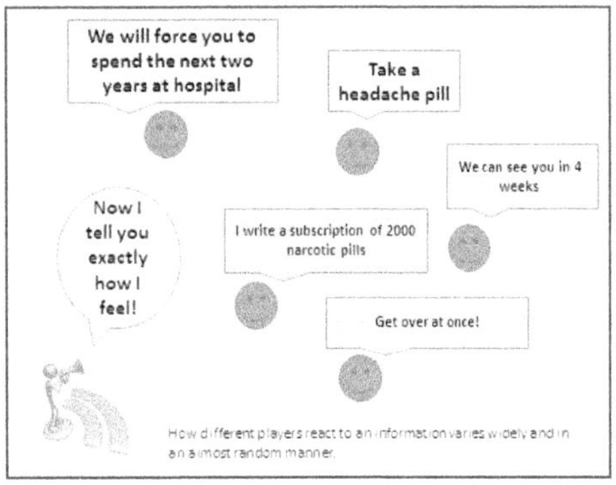

Fig. 6. When a person provides exactly the same information different instances react to this information in an almost random manner.

In another session we created a mock-up measuring tool. Someone said "the trust level is low". But how low? Maybe we could use some scale…

Fig.7. Example of a mock up scale.

The overall feeling from participants was that support systems over the last 10 years have changed in a negative way. Elements of control, punishment and mistrust have become more prominent. According to participants this is counter-productive. We used this picture to compare different systems.

3.7.1 Contact map

A basic survey which we learned was very valuable is to create a contact map (see figure 8). This began with a participant bringing a map to one of the meeting. She said that the map provides important insights about what it is like to live with mental disabilities. This turned out to be a powerful tool.

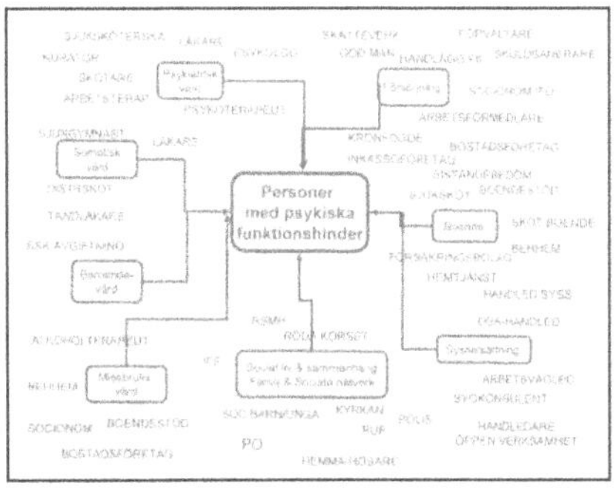

Fig. 8. One person can have up to 50 different contacts, due to the mental illness. The participants were not aware of that they at any given point can have such a large number of ongoing processes.

Fig 9. Personal contact map from a participant.

When realizing the importance of awareness around the nature of the contacts we started to produce individual contact maps (see figure 9). The map starts with the person in the middle.

In the nest step we started to discuss how you manage all those contacts. Three situations turned up as deeply troublesome; all the meetings you are supposed to attend to, the lack of coordination between all instances you have contact with and how to remember everything discussed at those meetings. It could easily be over 100 meetings a year and to manage this situation for someone with mental illness is described as overwhelming.

3.8 Universal design principles

In an exercise to discuss digital accessibility in a semi-structured way we used one of the most common descriptions of principles that constitutes if something is universally designed (16).

Fig. 10. From upper part of the circle and clockwise; Equitable Use, Flexibility in Use, Simple and Intuitive Use, Perceptible Information, Tolerance for Error, Low Physical Effort, Size and Space for Approach and Use

Participants decided to change "Low Physical Effort" to "Low Physical and Mental effort as they believed that the principles should emphasize mental efforts.

We put the name of the object in the middle of the circle and participants did first an individual exercise describing the object in relation to each principle and then we discussed our different thoughts. We invited them to imagine that they spun the circle around the current word in the middle.

3.9 Questionnaires divided to chunks

Since many participants reported unwillingness to answer to questionnaires we tried a concept of chopping them up in smaller chunks. A base for this exercise is the annual survey "The Swedes and the Internet[6], with almost 200 questions.

We identified a small number of "key questions" and used a "raise hand technique" for collecting answers. The circle leader asked and explained the questions and then did the same with answering alternatives. Participants could then raise hands when supporting a certain answering alternative. The project assistants conducted a count and we could immediately summarize the result and discuss it. The exercise can be performed in a relatively high tempo, but any participant can stop the process demanding more explanation.

By asking "Do you use a tablet", "Do you use any apps" or "Do you use Facebook" we could soon find out that the use of Facebook seemed equivalent with all Swedes but the use of tablets and apps where significantly lower.

3.10 Feedback

When discussing why you do not want to take part in surveys one repeated answer was. "It is nothing in it for me. No one reports back to me what happened. I cannot see if my participation did any difference". The participants called for feedback. They wanted to know if the effort to participate made any difference.

At the end of the last session we tried to give as much direct feedback as we could. Later on we presented the result and produced material that could be used in member activities within RSMH and in autumn 2015 a new series of study circles will start, this time led by members.

4. DISCUSSION

Reflection is often a privilege for the researcher. We need to reflect upon our data. But reflection is also a key component for the participants in this study. They needed time to think. A meeting once a week for a three week period was far better than a one day meeting, even if the total amount of hours was almost the same (see figure 11).

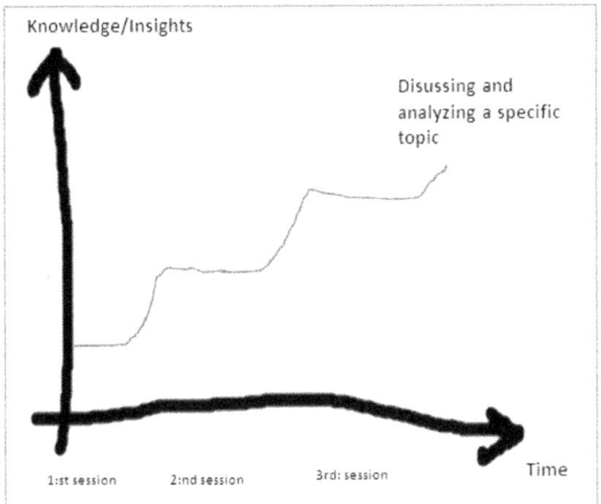

Fig 11. Visualization of how insight and knowledge benefits whit time and reflection.

The repetitiveness in a sequence of meetings is of great importance. When discussing a topic for a while the discussion fades and saturation occurs. This does not mean that participants have nothing more to say on the matter. They have nothing more to say for the moment. But the key insights might still be ahead.

[6] http://en.soi2014.se/

So by introducing the topic again, maybe fueled by Mock Up visualizations, a new vivid discussion may take place.

It is important for the circle leader to have a feeling for when a discussion is over and done with or when it has to be looped into a new session later on. When planning the next session it is important to decide whether a topic needs "another loop", if some kind of exercise is needed to get the discussions going or if it is time to let it go. Each meeting could deal with 4-6 topics. Some of them where only discussed in 5-10 minutes other up to an hour.

4.1 Data collection and analyzes intertwined

When looping discussions and giving time for reflection in between, data collection and analyzes become intertwined. Some participants did not take active part in the initial discussion of a topic. It was as if they did not have anything to say. They shifted to a more active role when the same topic returned for a second or third time. It took a while to realize that they often not participated in the "data collection" but instead contributed to the "analyze".

4.2 The visualization of discussions and thoughts

The pictures we created, the Mock Up Visualizations had a better effect than text-documentation. We did document everything on text but the participants did not use it. It was when we introduced the pictures that discussions boomed. If a picture worked it visualized an often complex discussion or even thoughts.

A really good visualization is a powerful tool. This picture has been used several times after the project (see figure 12):

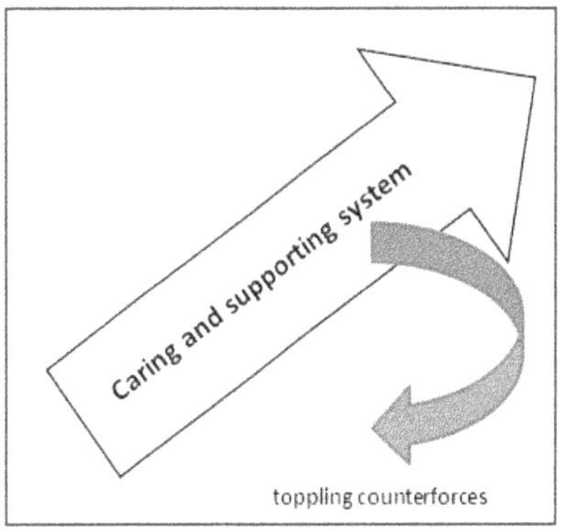

Fig 12: Toppling counterforces

It is used to identify counterproductive elements in caring or supporting activities. It has been used in workshops with government authorities and local social services. And it turns out that the staff often identifies the same toppling counterforces as the persons with mental and cognitive disabilities do.

4.3 The importance of trust

As researchers it is important to realize that the users we want to cooperate with is analyzing us and not only us. They also analyze our motives, the environment and the actual study we want them to take part in. They also have a history with them. Past experiences of participation may inflict on the present one.

4.4 Examples of outcomes

A presentation of the findings from the project is presented in the paper "Cognitive accessibility for mentally disabled persons" (3).

One example is that almost all participants had experienced losing vital information from their mobile phones when changing model or changing subscription. Since the mobile phone is described as a vital assistive device by many of the participants, losing important information can lead to severe consequences.

Another important finding is the rejection of log in and identification techniques. Many users claim that they will not use (or deeply dislike) any of the methods provided today. They find it too difficult to identify themselves and this excludes them from vital services and functions.

A third example is that almost no one had special assistive products to support their cognitive problems. The participants relay heavily on mainstream products and services and the call for those products and services to be more cognitively accessible.

5. CONCLUSIONS

We have presented how user participation can be arranged to meet the needs for accessible participation processes in itself. The way we as researchers arrange the actual participation process is of great importance if we want everyone to be able to take part. One key insight is that many users need time. They need time to understand the subject or object they are supposed to participate upon. They need time to decide if they at all want to take part and if your research project is of that importance that they should take part. And then they need time to discuss, reflect and analyze. As researchers we are eager to get immediately responses from our participants. But we believe that the quality of answers will improve if we deepen our cooperation with the users. This cooperation should go beyond data collection and into analysis. Many key insights in this project emerged over time and during the interplay between data collection and analyze of previously collected data...

Another key insight is the importance of a careful setup for the participation process. Many potential difficulties can be avoided or alleviated through planning.

A third insight is the importance of trust. If trust is not present the participation process will probably be seriously damaged.

A mixed-method approach is useful. It is the combination of methods and tools that enables a full and rich participation.

People with mental and cognitive issues are often regarded as difficult to work with or even get in touch with. Having mental and cognitive disabilities is difficult for any of us but such difficulties does not justify a de-selection of users from this large group. A universally designed and accessible society needs the voice from this large group.

6. ACKKNOWLEDGEMENS

We want to thank all participants. We also want to thank Tommy Hagström, Louise Tengstrand and Jonas Andersson for making it possible to carry out this project. We want to thank the Post and Telecom Authority (PTS) for funding this research.

7. REFERENCES

1. *Representing users in accessibility research.* **Sears, Andrew och Hanson, Vicki L.** ACM Transactions on Accessible Computing (TACCESS), 2012, 2012, Vol. Vol.4(2).
2. *Cognitive training and supported employment for persons with severe mental illness: one-year results from a randomized controlled trial.* **S. R. McGurk, K. T. Mueser, and A. Pascaris,.** 4, u.o. : Schizophr. Bull, 2005, Vol. 31.
3. *Cognitive accessibility for mentaly disabled persons.* **Johansson, Stefan. Gulliksen, Jan. Lantz Ann.** 2015.
4. *Accessibility to electronic communication for people with cognitive disabilities : a systematic search and review of empiricla evidence.* **Borg, Johan, Lantz, Ann och Gulliksen, Jan.** u.o. : Universal Access in the Information Society, 2014.
5. *Action research and minority problems. Journal of social issues.* **Lewin, Kurt.** Journal of social issues, 1946.
6. *Participatory design: Principles and practices.* **Schuler, Douglas, and Aki Namioka.** L. Erlbaum Associates Inc., 1993.
7. *Participatory design: the third space in HCI.* **Muller, Michael J.** Human-computer interac-tion: Development process, 2003.
8. *Design at work: Cooperative design of computer systems.* **Kyng, Morten and Joan Greenbaum.** u.o. : Lawrence Erlbaum Associates, Incorporated, 1991.
9. *Work-oriented design of computer artifacts.* **Ehn, Pelle.** Stockholm : Arbetslivscentrum. , 1988, Vol. 78.
10. *Participatory action research.* **Whyte, William Foote Ed.** Sage Publications, Inc. 1991.
11. *User centered design in practice-problems and possibilities.* **Gulliksen, Jan, Ann Lantz, and Inger Boivie.** Sweden: Royal Institute of Technology 315, 433. 1999.
12. *Design side by side.***Jönsson, Bodil, Anderberg, Peter Brattberg, Gunilla Breidegard, Björn. Eftring, Håkan... and Whitelock, Ingrid** Studenlitteratur, 2006.
13. *Seven aspects of democracy as related to study circles.* **Larsson, Staffan.** 2001, Journal of Lifelong Education, ss. 199-217.
14. Research Circles. *Lost in Practice - Transforming Nordic Educational Action Research.***Rönnerman, Karin, and Anette Olin.** SensePublishers, 2014.
15. *A large user pool for accessibility research with representative users.* **Dee, Marianne och Hanson, Vicki L.** ACM, 2014. Proceedings of the 16th international ACM SIGACCESS conference on Computers & accessibility. ss. 35-42.
16. *Maximizing Usability: The Principles of Universal Design.* **Story, Molly Follette. MS.** Assistive Technolgy. RESNA, 1998, Vol. 10.

A Unifying Notification System To Scale Up Assistive Services

Charles Consel
Bordeaux INP / Inria
Talence, France
charles.consel@inria.fr

Lucile Dupuy
Inria
Talence, France
lucile.dupuy@inria.fr

Hélène Sauzéon
University of Bordeaux / Inria
Talence, France
helene.sauzeon@inria.fr

ABSTRACT

Aging creates needs for assistive technology to support all activities of daily living (meal preparation, dressing, social participation, stove monitoring, *etc.*). These needs are mostly addressed by a silo-based approach that requires a new assistive service (*e.g.,* a reminder system, a pill prompter) to be acquired for every activity to be supported. In practice, these services manifest their silo-based nature in their user interactions, and more specifically, in the heterogeneity of their notification system. This heterogeneity incurs a cognitive cost that prevents scaling up assistive services and compromises adoption by older adults.

This paper presents an approach to scaling up the combination of technology-based, assistive services by proposing a unifying notification system. To do so, (1) we propose a decomposition of assistive services to expose their needs in notification; (2) we introduce a notification framework, allowing heterogeneous assistive services to homogeneously notify users; (3) we present how this notification framework is carried out in practice for an assisted living platform.

We successfully applied our approach to a range of existing and new assistive services. We used our notification framework to implement an assistive platform that combines a variety of assistive services. This platform has been deployed and used 24/7 at the home of 15 older adults for up to 6 months. This study provides empirical evidence of the effectiveness and learnability of the notification system of our platform, irrespective of the cognitive and sensory resources of the user. Additional results show that our assisted living platform achieved high user acceptance and satisfaction.

Categories and Subject Descriptors

K.4.2 [**Computers and Society**]: Social Issues—*Assistive technologies for older adults*; J.4 [**Social and Behavioral Sciences**]: Psychology

General Terms

Notification Systems, Field Study, Human Factors, Measurement, Performance

ASSETS'15, October 26–28, 2015, Lisbon, Portugal.
© 2015 ACM. ISBN 978-1-4503-3400-6/15/10 ...$15.00.
DOI: http://dx.doi.org/10.1145/2700648.2809855.

Keywords

Assisted living platform; Assistive technologies; Pervasive computing; Notification Systems; Field Study; Human Factors; Measurement; Performance

1. INTRODUCTION

Despite the many technological innovations available to assist older adults with cognitive decline in their daily life [31], their silo-based nature makes it a challenge to aggregate them as the older adult requires more services to assist an increasing number of daily activities.[1] A proliferation of technology-based services incurs an unrealistic cognitive load for the user, as documented in the literature on aging [34]. A key obstacle to scaling up technology-based assistive services is the heterogeneity of their user interfaces: because most existing services are developed using a silo-based approach, they impose their own specific interfaces. Older adults thus need to learn these interfaces, even though they often are not proficient with technology. The cognitive cost of this learning process may outweigh the potential benefits of the assistive device, preventing its adoption [22].

The range of services needed to assist older adults is so wide and diverse that attempting to unify their user interactions appears unrealistic. Yet, a close examination of existing services permits to outline a decomposition of their user interactions into two categories: *notifications* and *task-specific interactions.* In this context, notifications are issued by assistive services to provide the user with some information such as a situation and an event. As an example, consider a reminder system where notifications request the user's attention when an event has occurred, displaying the event information. These notifications can be made generic to cover, not only the reminder system, but a variety of assistive services, lowering their cognitive cost. Task-specific interactions are those mainly concerned with configuring the assistive service and feeding it with data, if necessary. For example, if the reminder system relies on a shared Web calendar, its network address needs to be defined at configuration time via task-specific interactions. As well, new events need to be entered in this service via task-specific interactions.

Reviewing existing assistive services [14] reveals that this decomposition can be applied to most of them. Furthermore, according to interviews we conducted with stakeholders, task-specific interactions are often performed by professional and family caregivers. For example, events are entered in a calendar by caregivers (doctor appointments, visit of a family member, *etc.*). In practice, our approach can accomodate existing assistive services by wrapping their notifications with a software layer, or be used as a basis to design new assistive services. In both cases, our approach provides guide-

[1] abledata.com

lines to define notifications for assistive services. For the service developer, these guidelines take the form of an API.

This paper. We present an approach towards unifying interactions between the user and assistive services. This approach consists of a decomposition method that separates user interactions into task-specification ones and notifications. Then, notifications are homogenized to facilitate the recurring usage of the assistive services. In practice, we provide an API to support notifications and to enforce their homogeneity. Besides the API, notifications are further homogenized by the use of a unique channel between the user and the assistive services. In the first implementation of our platform, this unique channel corresponds to a tablet. By enforcing the use of an API and unifying the presentation of notifications on a tablet, new assistive services can be introduced without incurring additional cognitive cost, aside from the task-specific interactions.

To validate our approach, we show how it successfully applies to a number of existing and new services that cover the three main domains of assisted living, namely, monitoring of activities of daily living (ADLs), safety and security, and social participation [27]. Specifically, our proposed API is implemented in an assisted living platform that has been deployed at the home of 15 older adults, aged 81 on average. Furthermore, we are conducting a field study, using our platform equipped with a variety of assistive services, at the home of older adults. Preliminary results show that our approach to scaling up the assistive services via a uniform notification system is effective and learnable, and achieves user acceptance and satisfaction. Finally, our field study allows us to go beyond a lab study: we put into practice our notification framework with assistive applications and test our implementation in the wild.

2. RELATED WORK

Cognitive cost of assistive services. Using assistive services incurs a cognitive cost for users. As showed by Lindenberger *et al.*, an assistive service may not be adopted, if the resources (physical and cognitive) it requires, outweigh the payoff [22]. Beyond the cost of an assistive service, Sherer *et al.* recommend that a user with cognitive decline should not be introduced to more than three assistive tools, to prevent the older adult from being confused and overwhelmed [34].

These works identify the limitations to introducing services for assisted living purposes. They call for approaches to facilitating interactions with assistive services and lifting the limit on the number of services a declining older adult can cope with.

Design principles for older adults. Designing technology for older adults have been studied extensively by the HCI community. A comprehensive account is given by Fisk *et al.* [12]; it includes the characterization of older adult users, a presentation of design principles and guidelines, and examples illustrating the approach. As promoted by the authors, user-centered design should drive the development of assistive systems, taking into account the characteristics of aged-related declines in abilities.

Fisk *et al.* concentrate on the development of assistive tools from a unitary perspective. Not only does this perspective yield silo-based technologies, but it does not address the issue of combining these technologies. As increasingly many assistive technologies are needed to address the difficulties of the aging user, a unifying approach is needed to scale up the assistance.

Notification systems. Most studies on notification systems investigate the costs, benefits and the optimal display of notifications in the context of desktop and mobile computing tasks [26]. Some works are centered on the human attention system and study the effects of notifications on ongoing computer tasks (*e.g.,* [24]). To guide the evaluation of notification systems, McCrickard *et al.* propose a design model of user goals that is based on three critical parameters: interruption, reaction, and comprehension [25]. The design of our notification system addresses each of these parameters. Other works of notification systems examine notifications in the context of users with sensory impairments and assess the disruptiveness and effectiveness of notifications using multimodal interactions [38, 39]. User acceptance of notifications has also been explored; Vastenburg *et al.* conducted a user study of acceptance of notifications in a controlled home setting [36]. They show that user acceptance depends on whether the level of intrusiveness of a notification is related to its level of urgency. We use this key finding to structure our model of notifications.

Assisted living platforms. There is a range of platforms for assisted living aimed at older adults that have been developed for more than a decade, as surveyed by Chan *et al.* [6] and Rashidi and Mihailidis [31]. Most of these platforms are used in a setting where participants come to a research apartment to perform certain tasks (*e.g.,* [31, 30, 1]). This setting makes it difficult to assess user acceptance and satisfaction of the proposed approaches because the user does not interact with the technology on a daily basis, over a period of time. Furthermore, older adults adopt routines to optimize their daily functioning at home [3]. This situation calls for field studies in a naturalistic setting to strengthen the evaluation of assisted living platforms.

Area-specific assistive services. The HCI community has proposed principles and guidelines to design assistive services that target specific needs of older adults. This includes family/peer interaction (*e.g.,* PeerCare [32] and Message Center [41]), monitoring daily activities (*e.g.,* Digital family portraits [33] and DigiSwitch [4]), and monitoring health-related activities (*e.g.,* medication taking [20, 21, 17]).

Our work explores how a notification framework can contribute to scaling up the combination of silo-based assistive services across domains of assisted living, while achieving user acceptance and satisfaction.

3. A UNIFYING FRAMEWORK FOR NOTIFICATIONS

This section presents our framework, which unifies notifications of assistive services. To do so, we first introduce how user interactions can be split into two groups: notifications and task-specific interactions. Second, we define a model for notifications that consists of two types of interactions, their interaction protocol, and their API. Third, we instantiate this model by showing how a tablet can be used to realize notifications. Last, we briefly present an assisted living platform that implements our proposed framework.

Throughout this section, we illustrate our approach with examples of assistive services taken from all domains of assisted living. Each step of our approach is instantiated with one of these examples. A selection of all the examples we have studied is presented in Figure 1.

3.1 Decomposing Interactions

Task-specific interactions mostly involve providing both configuration parameters and specific data to an assistive service. For assistive services that are networked, typical configuration parameters include network parameters, privacy requirements, and caregiver contact information. Let us examine our decomposition of interactions with respect to the main domains of assisted living. For the

Domain	Service	Description	Task-specific interactions	Notifications	Type
Safety	Activity checker	It checks whether the user gets out of bed in the morning prior to a set time	Latest time	Alert	C
	Pill prompter	It reminds the user to take medication	New prescription	Reminder & Pill info	C
Security	Night door monitoring	It alerts the user if the entry door is open at night.	Night parameters	Alert	C
	Stove monitor	It monitors the use of the stove and alerts the user when the stove is left unattended more than a set time	Max. time unattended	Alert	C
ADLs	ADL reminder	It reminds the user to perform certain ADLs	ADLs of interest and their schedules	Reminder & ADL info	NC
	Bill management	It reminds the user of recurring bills to be paid	Company name	Reminder & Billing info	NC
Social participation	email notifier	It notifies the user for new email messages	List of VIP email addresses	Notification & message excerpt	NC
	Municipal events	It announces social events for senior adults, organized by their municipality	Preferences	Notification & event name	NC

'NC' and 'C' correspond to the type of notifications that is either non-critical or critical, respectively.

Figure 1: Our approach applied to examples of assistive services and target user profiles

domain of ADLs, consider the example of a pill prompter: an assistive service that reminds the user of medication to be taken. An example of a task-specific interaction for this service is to enable the caregiver to define/update a doctor's prescription. Another example is to customize the service by defining the snooze length for alerts. Notifications include issuing a reminder to take pills and an alert when the prescription is about to expire.

For the domain of safety and security, consider the example of a door monitor; this assistive service aims to prevent the entry door of a home from being left open and unattended. Task-specific interactions for this service includes its adaption to the user's needs and preferences. For example, the service may be parameterized with respect to the time during which the door can be open unattended, and the period during which door activities are considered to be daytime. Notifications consist of alerting the user when the door is left open.

For the domain of social participation, let us take the example of an email notifier. This assistive service notifies the user when (s)he receives email messages. Task-specific interactions for this service include setting the email account, parameterizing the occurrences of notifications (w.r.t. number of messages, specific senders, *etc.*). Notifications consist of informing the user of new message(s) (possibly displaying an excerpt from message(s)).

3.2 A Model for Notifications

Now that interactions have been classified as task specific and notifications, we need to further work on the notifications by introducing a model of interactions. This model is simple but realistic in that it has been applied to a range of existing and new assistive services (see Figure 1).

3.2.1 Notification Types

Field experiments show that user acceptance of notification systems depends on the level of urgency of the messages (*e.g.,* [35]). To account for this key finding, we defined two categories of notifications: non-critical and critical. Non-critical notifications are the ones that do not need to be immediately attended to by the user; they announce a situation or an information. In contrast, critical interactions correspond to situations of assistance that may involve safety or security; the user's attention is thus requested. Determining whether a notification is non-critical or critical depends on a number of parameters, such as the nature of the assistive service, the target user, the user environment, *etc.* Not only do we introduce these types of notifications at a conceptual level, but we also provide mechanisms to ensure that this distinction is propagated throughout the development of an assistive service so as to deliver an appropriate level of intrusiveness.

A major benefit of the critical/non-critical dichotomy is that it allows to reduce the cognitive cost of both the interpretation and the decision making process relative to notifications. Such approach is highly recommended for older adults [22].

For our deployed assisted living platform, examples of non-critical notifications include an email notice, an event reminder, and a fridge door monitor. These assistive services do not depend on whether the user acknowledges their announcements. Critical interactions have been used for applications such as the entry door monitor, the stove monitor, and the activity monitor. In these examples, the absence of user input typically leads to eventually solicit a caregiver. More examples can be found in Figure 1.

3.2.2 Interaction Protocols

As reported by Vastenburg *et al.*, user acceptance of notifications in the home can be improved by adjusting the level of intrusiveness of the presentation to the message urgency [36]. As a result, non-critical and critical notifications call for different interaction protocols. The protocol for non-critical interactions is that a situation or some information is announced. We propose that after a given time, if the user has not attended to the notification, it disappears and is assumed to be accumulated with other unattended non-critical notifications.

Critical notifications require user input because, by the definition given above, they involve safety or security. Consequently, when an assistive service issues a critical notification, we propose to give it a high level of intrusiveness to match the high value of the message [36]. Specifically, the notification will be repeated until the user responds. Furthermore, after a given time, the service will take emergency actions, such as turning off the stove and, in most cases, calling a caregiver.

3.2.3 An API

Our model is mapped into an API to enforce it at development time. In doing so, the programmer of an assistive service implements the service notifications following the notification types determined by the human factor expert for a given target user profile. Each user profile takes into account the dimensions relevant to the task to be assisted: the physical status, the functional status and the cognitive status. Typically, a door alert will trigger a non-critical notification for users with very good autonomy and a critical notification for lesser autonomous users. The collaboration between the programmer and the human factor expert is essential to ensure that the level of intrusiveness of the notification corresponds to the urgency of the situation and the user profile. In practice, our platform allows for different applications to be available for a given task (*e.g.*, door monitor) thanks to an online catalog. As a result, users with different profiles will be given different assistive services. This approach contributes to achieving user acceptance. Figure 1 provides examples of notifications, whose types (rightmost column) are defined with respect to the user profiles of our user study.

Notice that our API abstracts over the way notifications are implemented. As will be discussed next, they may be carried out with a tablet. In principle, other devices could be used such as a TV or even a smart phone. We describe the main operations included in our API at a conceptual level, omitting the programming details.

A non-critical notification corresponds to an operation that takes a title, a notification content and an image. The title is used to categorize the notification in a pre-defined list (*e.g.*, caution, reminder, FYI). The notification content corresponds to the message to be delivered to the user. An image can be used when dual coding (image and text) improves user performance to respond to the notifications of the application, as suggested by Warnock *et al.* [39]. Rendering the image depends on the functionality of the device used for interactions.

Because of its nature, a critical notification prompts the user to provide information that allows the application to take a course of action. Consequently, in addition to the input parameters of the non-critical notification, the critical one also takes a list of possible responses for the user to choose from. The user selects one of them to answer the question that corresponds to the notification message parameter.

Finally, it could be argued that our API prevents existing assistive services from being reused. In most cases, reuse can be achieved by wrapping an existing service with our API. This strategy is facilitated by the fact that assistive services are commonly implemented in the form of a Web service. In this case, we implement a software layer that operates the target Web service and calls our API whenever notifications need to be sent to the user.

3.3 An Interaction Support: A Tablet

We now instantiate our model of notifications with respect to a device, namely a tablet. Older adults have been shown to adapt well to touchscreen tablets [12] and to perform better than with the desktop and mouse [11]. As well, a key advantage of this device is that it can autonomously support interactions with a user, unlike a TV that requires a remote control for user input.

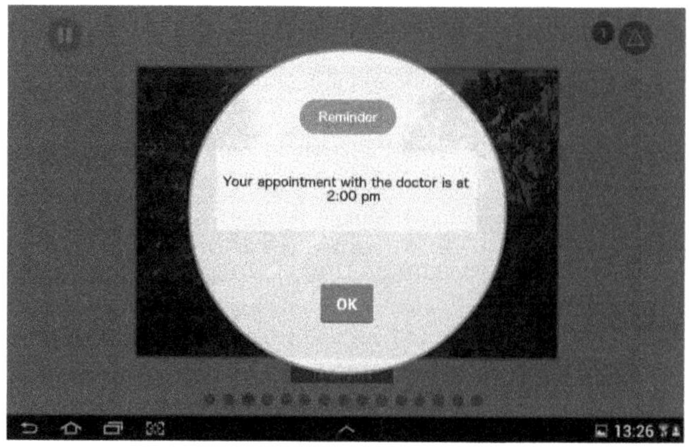

Figure 2: An example of a non-critical notification

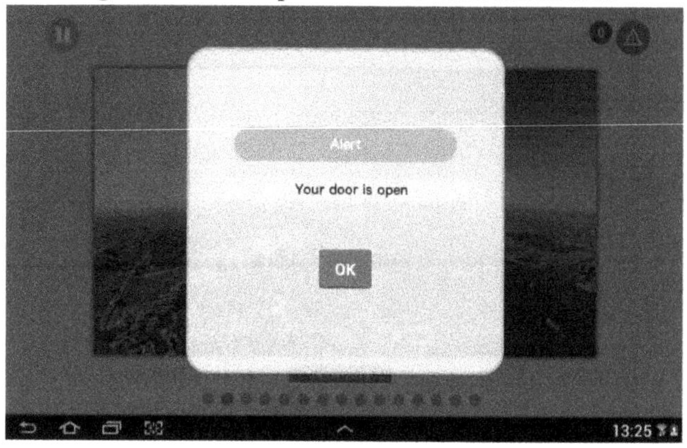

Figure 3: An example of a critical notification

To account for the capabilities of our target users, we strive to minimize the attentional resources required by assistive services. To do so, we increase multisensory integration to render notifications, making it easier to discriminate between notification types for older adults [18, 28]. In practice, we leverage the features of the tablet to implement multi-modal coding of notifications, integrating tones, shapes, colors, and text. Let us now examine how our approach is carried out in practice and what benefits are brought to the user.

To allow the user to distinguish between non-critical and critical notifications, a specific tone was chosen for each type of notifications. As a result, users can quickly make the difference and do not bother going to the tablet when they hear a non-critical notification and are busy doing something else. To reduce the level of intrusiveness for non-critical notifications, our implementation uses a softer volume and tone for these notifications than for critical ones. By reducing the intrusiveness of these interruptions, we address the first of McCrickard *et al.*'s critical parameters of notification systems [25].

In addition to using different tones, we also use two different visual frames to display non-critical and critical notifications. Examples of notifications are displayed in Figures 2 and 3. As can be noticed, notifications are surrounded by a different shape, depending on their criticality: a green circle for a non-critical notification and an orange rectangle for a critical one. This strategy further reduces attentional resources and improves the ability for the user to distinguish between the two types of notifications, lowering the cognitive cost for making a decision. As such, this strategy improves the reaction to notifications using preattentive processing, thus addressing the second of McCrickard *et al.*'s critical parameters of notification systems [25]. Note that in the current implementation, images are not used for notifications.

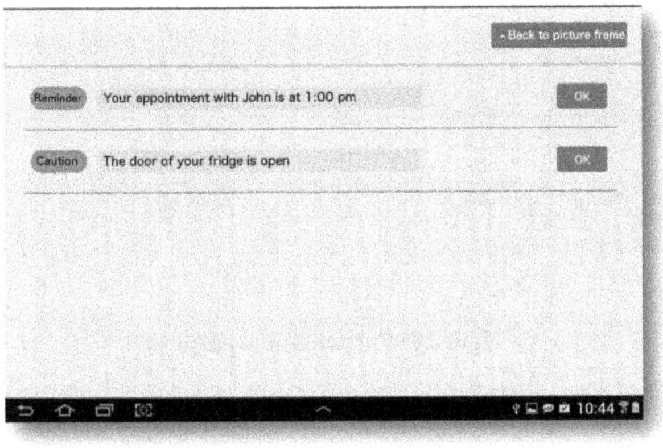

Figure 4: An example of a list of unattended notifications

Non-critical notifications can be attended at a later time by the user. In this case, they are gathered and are accessible by the user at their convenience. Unattended notifications are signaled to the user by the icon in the right corner of the tablet screen. This is illustrated in Figure 5 where the number of unattended notifications is displayed in a blue circle, at the top right corner of the screen. In Figure 4, we show a list of unattended notifications that the user can access by touching on the blue triangle. In contrast, a critical notification does not disappear from the screen and the tone is played periodically, until the notification is handled by the user.

Towards addressing the comprehension parameter of McCrickard *et al.*'s model [25], we keep messages short and located at the center of the notification window. To further explore this parameter, it needs to be considered in the context of assisted living. For critical notifications, the goal of the system is for the user to understand the message and resolve the safety-critical situation that triggered the notification. As explained earlier, the notification repeats until the message is understood and the situation resolved. For non-critical notifications, the message can be kept in the list of unattended notifications until the user decides that remembering the information is no longer necessary.

Notice that the API can be leveraged to enrich the interaction with the user. For example, a light could be used in addition the tablet to signal a notification. As is proposed by devices such as HUE by Philips,[2] we could even use a different color to indicate whether the notification is non-critical or critical. Along the same line, notifications could be played to the user via a voice synthesizer. These choices allow to tailor the presentation of notification to the user's preferences, improving their satisfaction and adoption.

Finally, introducing an API allows to factorize the expertise in designing user interactions that are adapted to older adults. In particular, the format of the notification text is defined by default according to the standards used for older adults and disabled users (ISO 22411).[3]

3.4 The Assisted Living Platform

Our proposed approach is been carried out in practice in a platform for assisted living, dedicated to older adults. This platform is based on a range of building blocks, both hardware (*e.g.*, motion detector, contact sensor, smart switch) and software (*e.g.*, calendar, photo album, address book). In addition, the user is provided with a tablet, which is stationary, plugged, and located at a central location in the user's home. Interactions between the user and the assistive services revolve around this tablet. To prevent the tablet from stigmatizing the user, when it is idle, it becomes a digital frame, as shown in Figure 5. This service streams photos from a shared album (*e.g.*, Picasa photo) that can be updated by family members and friends; it greatly contributes to the user acceptance and satisfaction of the platform.

Figure 5: Digital frame

For the sake of completeness, note that the tablet provides the user with a control mechanism (top left corner of the screen) that allows to pause the platform at anytime for different durations.

3.5 Deployed Services

The assistive services of our field study cover the three domains of assisted living. Safety and security are addressed by two assistive services that monitor the entry door. During daytime, one service prompts the user when the door is open and left unattended for a given period of time. During nighttime, another service alerts the user when the door is opened. Both services use a critical interaction and solicit a caregiver if the user does not respond to the alert.

ADLs are covered by an application that reminds the user to perform a given set of activities (*e.g.*, preparing a meal, dressing), when they have not been performed within a time window. This application leverages work on activity detection by Caroux *et al.*[5]. In this domain, another application sends reminders to the user prior to the due date of utility bills. Finally, a service monitors the fridge door to ensure it is not left open for too long.

Regarding social participation, an email notifier announces social events for older adults, organized by their municipality. Another service sends a notification when new email messages have been received by the user.

For the sake of completeness, note that other assistive services, beyond the scope of this work, are running in our participants' home. As mentioned earlier, when the tablet is idle, it turns into a digital photo frame. This service can be seen as stimulating social participation because family members and friends share their photos on this album. This digital frame does not require any interaction from the user. Another assistive service provided by our platform is a light path, to guide the user to the bathroom at night. This light path is controlled by the switch of a bed light. Here, we leverage an existing interaction to control the assistive service.

[2] `www.meethue.com`
[3] ISO/TR 22411 – 2008.

4. DESCRIPTION OF THE FIELD STUDY

In this section, we present a field study aimed to validate our approach. We first evaluate the effectiveness and learnability of our notification system for older adults. Then, we assess the user experience by measuring user acceptance and satisfaction. This evaluation is based on the interactions triggered by the assistive services of our platform, equipping the homes of our study participants. From the user's perspective, the tablet serves service notifications and materializes the assisted living platform. Indeed, the hardware infrastructure of the platform consists of unobtrusive entities, such as motion detectors, contact sensors (battery powered), and smart switches; they are wireless and placed at discreet locations. Software entities are Web services accessible via Internet and only visible through the stimuli they generate for the platform (*e.g.*, events). We provide empiral evidence that the notification system of our assisted living platform is suitable for older adults, even with cognitive and/or sensory loss.

Our assisted living platform was deployed in the house of 15 community-dwelling older adults (see below) for a 6-month period. Every six weeks, interaction data and questionnaires were collected to measure the longitudinal effect of the platform adoption. This data collection took place in the house of the participants and was performed by a research member of our group.

Note that the ecological nature of our field deployment requires a cautious approach considering that our participants are old older adults (81 years old on average). The assisted living platform manages potentially critical situations (*e.g.*, door alert) that preclude the use of an unsuited notification system. Indeed, deploying an unsuited notification system to achieve a control condition for an experimental setup could have deleterious consequences for the participants [40]. This situation would rightfully raise serious concerns from an ethical committee.

4.1 Participants

We recruited 15 community-dwelling, old older adults. This was done in collaboration with a public home care service for older adults. We selected participants that live alone in their apartment or house. This choice addressed four key issues. First, this situation simplifies the design space of most assistive services (*e.g.*, no user-sensitive context). Second, assistive services can be customized with respect to a unique user, contributing further to user acceptance and satisfaction. Third, as reported in the literature [23], having multiple occupants in a home introduces sources of errors when monitoring activities. In turn, this situation has a negative effects on assistive services that are context sensitive, such as the ADL reminder. A final argument is that older adults living in couple are most of the time assisted by their spouse, and thus are less prompt to request for assistance.

As described in Figure 6, our participants were recruited according to specific exclusion criteria: dependency syndrome; neurological or musculoskeletal disease or systemic disorders. The main inclusion criterion was cognitive integrity with an MMSE (Mini Mental State Examination) [13] score greater than 24 [2]. According to the Helsinki declaration (WMA, 2008), approval was sought and obtained from the ethics committee of the University of Bordeaux. All participants provided a written consent form prior to the participation in our study.

We assessed their functional status for some activities of daily living. First, we evaluated their performance in IADLs, using the timed-IADL assessment test [29]. A participant is asked to perform an activity with a time limit. If the activity is achieved without error and without exceeding the time limit, a score of 1 is given. A score of 3 means that the participant has major difficulties to perform the activity. We tested our participants on five different activities; this gave scores ranging from 5 (ideal performance) to 15 (major difficulties). In Figure 6, we observe that our 15 participants obtain near ideal scores (5). We conclude that our participants show no difficulties in performing IADLs and have a high level of autonomy.

Participants	*Mean (SD)*
Age	81.07 (6.19)
Gender	3 men and 12 women
Education years	9.60 (1.55)
Family status	14 widowed and 1 single
MMSE $[0-30]$	27.80 (1.37)
Timed-IADL $[5-15]$	5.40 (0.74)
Self-reported IADL $[9-45]$	23.80 (6.62)
Cognitive resources $[0-162]$	149.60 (7.90)
Sensory resources $[0-4]$	2.67 (0.95)

SD=Standard Deviation.
Interval notations are used for score ranges.

Figure 6: Participant profiles

Then, we asked them to self-assess their functional status, using the 9-item IADL scale [19]. For each item, the participant assesses their performance: 1 denotes no difficulties and 5 denotes major difficulties. This tool shows that we have a variety of participants in the way they see themselves performing ADLs; it ranges from 15 to 36, on a scale of 45. In summary, our participants perform well in their ADLs, although they perceive themselves as experiencing difficulties. From these data, our participants exhibit a normal cognitive decline, along with complaints related to their everyday functioning.

Finally, to measure participants' cognitive resources, we summed two scores of widely used scales assessing cognitive functioning: the Dementia Rating Scale - 2 (DRS-2[4]) [16] and the Frontal Assessment Battery (FAB[5]) [10]. Sensory resources were measured using 2 items with 3 modalities (from 0 - poor abilities, to 2 - no impairment) regarding vision or audition.

4.2 Timed usage scenarios

Inspired by the timed-IADL assessment [29], we designed a test tool to measure the user's performance in using the tablet with two everyday usage scenarios, involving a critical interaction and a non-critical one. The two usage scenarios used are defined in Figure 7.

These two usage scenarios were selected from the deployed services because they are easy to implement. This test ranges on a scale of 3; the score depends on the type and number of errors made by the user, and whether the task was performed within the allocated time. A score of 3 denotes a task performed without errors and within the allocated time. A score of 2 corresponds to a task performed with minor errors but within the allocated time. A score of 1 is when the user did not complete the task or made major errors.

4.3 Data Collected

As mentioned earlier, we evaluate our approach by collecting measures of effectiveness and learnability of the notifications, as well as user acceptance and satisfaction of the assisted living platform. The period covered by our study starts six weeks after the platform is installed and ends after six month of using it, with data collected every six weeks (at 1.5, 3, 4.5 and 6 months of use).

[4]The DRS-2 measures five basic cognitive domains: attention, initiation, abstraction, verbal and non-verbal memory.

[5]The FAB assesses executive functioning, including controlled inhibition, flexibility and conceptualization.

Task	Notification type	Task conditions	Notification	Instructions to the user	Expected behavior	Time limit
1	Critical	The user is in front of the tablet; the experimenter has left the entry door open; a notification appears	Alert: your door is open	"What is happening and how should you react?"	"The door is open". The user presses the "OK" button, goes to the entry door and closes it.	20s.
2	Non-critical	The user is in front of the tablet; the experimenter has scheduled an appointment; a notification appears	Reminder: Your appointment to the doctor is at 2:00pm	"What is happening and how should you react?"	"I have an appointment to my doctor at 2:00pm"; the user presses the OK button	15s.

Figure 7: Timed Usage Scenarios

Effectiveness and learnability. Our measure of effectiveness is the score given by the usage scenarios presented above. Our measure of learnability refers to the interaction duration to perform the task, measured in seconds. As mentioned earlier, we assessed effectiveness and learnability four times during our six-month study (every six weeks).

User acceptance. Our approach to measure user acceptance was inspired by an existing online tool proposed by Hassenzahl [15].[6] This measurement decomposes acceptance into five dimensions: ergonomic quality, hedonic quality, appealingness, anxiety and safety perception, and social influence. Answers to the questionnaire range over a scale of 7 points, from -3 to 3, including two antonyms (*e.g.*, nervous/relaxed). Each acceptance dimension of the questionnaire consists of 6 items. The global score (from -3 to 3) is computed by averaging the scores of the answers collected for the questionnaire. High acceptance is denoted by a high score.

Importantly, we did not use the Technology Acceptance Model (TAM) that stresses the perceived usefulness and perceived ease of use as the main attitudinal factors towards technology acceptance[8, 37]. Indeed, Chen and Chan conducted an experimental study involving 1012 seniors and demonstrated that technology acceptance is predicted by user characteristics, rather than attitudinal factors (perceived usefulness and ease of use) [7]. As a result, we decided to measure user acceptance beyond the two main attitudinal factors of TAM, including dimensions related to user experience using Hassenzahl's tool [15].

User satisfaction. We used the QUEST questionnaire [9] to measure user satisfaction. Each item of this questionnaire is evaluated on a scale ranging from 1 to 5. A value 1 corresponds to 'not satisfied at all' and a value 5 to 'very satisfied'. The questionnaire consists of 12 items and the total score is on a scale of 5. A high score denotes a high user satisfaction with the technology.

5. ANALYSIS

We now analyze the longitudinal measures of effectiveness and learnability over our 15 participants, for both critical and non-critical interactions with the tablet. Then, we analyze the measures of user acceptance and satisfaction. In addition, for each measure, we evaluate the impact of cognitive and sensory resources of the user to identify whether this system can effectively match the variability of the users in their declining abilities.

Effectiveness and learnability measures.
Thanks to two usage scenarios of the user managing critical and non-critical notifications, we assessed effectiveness and learnability of the platform. The performances of our participants are shown in Figure 8 for effectiveness and in Figure 9 for learnability. To study the evolution of these measures during the six-month period, we performed ANOVAs with the following statistical design: 2 independent factors [time of use (at 1.5, 3, 4.5 and 6 months) and notification type (critical *vs.* non-critical)], and effectiveness score or learnability time as dependent factors.

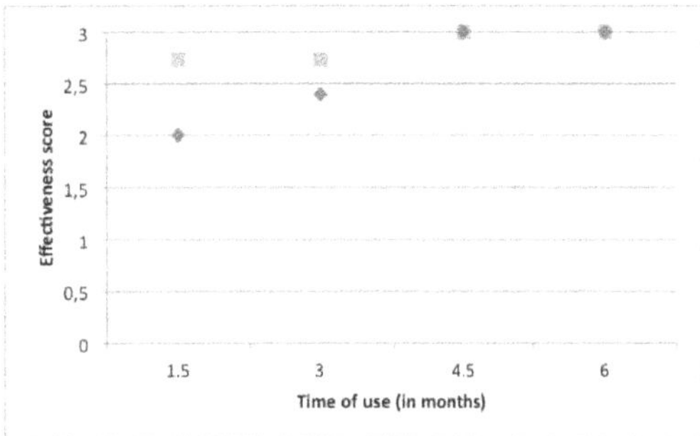

Effectiveness scores range from 0 to 3.
Diamond for critical notifications / Square for non-critical ones.

Figure 8: Evolution of effectiveness

First, we can observe a significant improvement of the effectiveness over the six-month period (effect of time: F(3.108) = 8.11; p <0.001). Moreover, the ANOVA's results indicate a significant effect of the notification type (F(3.108) = 5.74; p = 0.018), with higher values for non-critical notifications, implicating that scores are significantly higher for this notification type. No interaction between our two independent factors (*i.e.*, time × notification type) was observed (F(3.108) = 2.32; p = 0.080), which means that notification types do not evolve differently in a significant way over the period of the study.

Globally, these results indicate an improvement of effectiveness to answer both critical and non-critical notifications over the course of the study. A maximal performance is reached after 4.5 months of using our platform; this maximal performance remains over time.

Regarding learnability, we observe a significant improvement of the performance over time (effect of time: F(3.108) = 10.45; $p <$ 0.001), but no effect regarding the notification type (F(3.108) = 2.77; p = 0.100). However, the ANOVA analysis indicates a significant interaction effect between the two independent factors (*i.e.*, time × notification type) (F(3.108) = 2.65; p = 0.05), which means that the learnability of critical and non-critical notifications evolves differently over time. More precisely, at six weeks of technology use, participants take more time to answer to a critical notification than a non-critical one. However, at six months of use, users perform equally well, irrespective of notification type. These results can be explained by an effective learning of the platform over time,

[6] http://attrakdiff.de

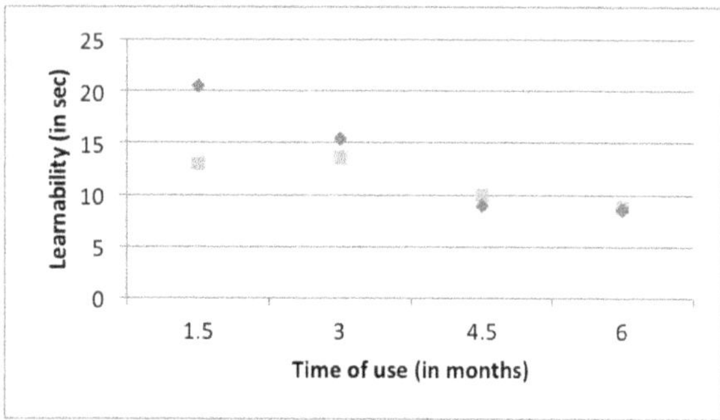

Time is measured in seconds.
Diamond for critical notifications / Square for non-critical ones.

Figure 9: Evolution of learnability

resulting in an automation of the process of answering critical notifications.

Finally, we performed two ANCOVAs with the following statistical design: time of use (at 1.5, 3, 4.5 and 6 months) and notification type (critical *vs.* non-critical) as independent factors, cognitive score (or sensory score) as continuous covariant factor, and effectiveness score or learnability time as dependent factors. Results highlight that cognitive and sensory resources have no impact on effectiveness and learnability. Thus, this platform is usable by older adults and its learnability is irrespective of cognitive or sensory loss.

Longitudinal assessment of user acceptance.
To measure user acceptance during the use of our platform, five dimensions of acceptance (ergonomic quality, hedonic quality, appealingness, anxiety and safety perception, and social influence) was assessed four times for our participants: 1) six weeks after the platform installation, 2) after 3 months of using the platform, 3) after 4.5 months, and 4) after 6 months. The longitudinal evolution of our five dimensions of acceptance was analyzed using MANOVA [5 dimensions (ergonomic quality, hedonic quality, appealingness, safety perception, and social influence) as dependent variables × 1 independent factor (time of measure)]. Figure 10 shows the acceptance scores given by our participants for theses measures, in addition to the mean score of these participants.

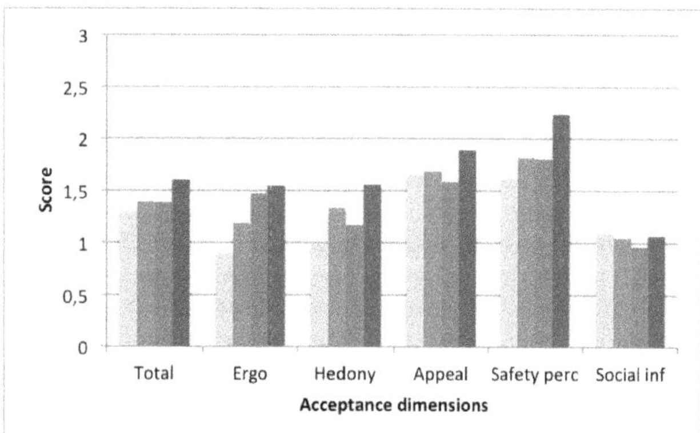

User acceptance scores from -3 to 3.
Four measures during the study (at 1.5, 3, 4.5 and 6 months) represented by the four shades of blue.

Figure 10: Evolution of user acceptance

Statistical analysis failed to be significative (all the effects with p > 0.200), but we observe that high scores are obtained over the course of the study, with an improvement for the majority of variables, mainly for the ergonomic and safety perception dimensions. The global acceptance score shows a slight increase too.

Then, in order to investigate the implication of cognitive and sensory resources on technology acceptance, we performed ANCOVAs with the following statistical design: time (at 1.5, 3, 4.5 and 6 months) as independent factor, acceptance dimensions as dependent factor, and cognitive score (or sensory score) as continuous covariant factor (Figure11). When a significant effect was found, we used inter-correlation analysis to identify the correlation (positive or negative) between the factors.

	Cognitive resources	*Sensory Resources*
Global acceptance	**F(3.53) = 4.68***	**F(3.53) = 4.04***
Ergonomy	**F(3.53) = 4.02***	ns
Hedony	**F(3.53) = 5.70***	**F(3.53) = 3.97‡**
Appealingness	**F(3.53) = 3.32 ‡**	**F(3.53) = 4.31***
Safety perception	ns	ns
Social influence	**F(3.53) = 3.24‡**	**F(3.53) = 4.68***

ANCOVAs=analysis of covariance
**p < 0.05; ‡p < 0.08; ns=non significant.*

Figure 11: ANCOVAs results controlling for cognitive or sensory scores

Results indicate a significant effect of the cognitive resources of the users on most of the acceptance dimensions (every variable except safety perception). Inter-correlations show negative relation between these factors (all the r <-0.22; all the $p < 0.07$), indicating that the more cognitive resources are deteriorated, the more technology is accepted. Regarding sensory resources, we can observe a significant relationship with some dimensions (hedony, appealingness, social influence, and the total score of acceptance), with a positive correlation (all the r >0.25; all the $p < 0.05$). This result implies that the more sensory aptitudes are diminished, the more technology acceptance is low.

Globally, these results highlight the constant improvement of user acceptance, showing that users are comfortable with the technology and confident that they can handle their interactions with it. Furthermore, we observed a better acceptance when users have poor cognitive resources and mild sensory decline, showing that the system does not require many resources to interact with it.

User satisfaction.
We administered the QUEST questionnaire to measure user satisfaction about the technology after 1.5, 3, 4.5 and 6 months of usage experience.

We observed that the satisfaction score was already high for all of our participants after 1.5 month of use (the mean score is 4.28 for a max score of 5), and did not statistically differ over time (ANOVA: F(3.53) = 0.41; p = 0.75).

By doing the same statistical design as above (*i.e.,* ANCOVAs with cognitive and sensory resources as covariant), we only observe a significant effect of cognitive resources on satisfaction score (F(3.53) = 4.68; p = 0.035), with a negative correlation (r = -0.29; p = 0.03), indicating that users with low cognitive resources are more satisfied with the technology.

Overall, participants exhibit a high satisfaction score regarding our technology, and this satisfaction remains constant over a period of six months. Moreover, this satisfaction score is further enhanced for users with poor cognitive aptitudes, and remains unchanged for user with declining sensory resources.

6. DISCUSSION

This paper presents our approach to scaling up assistive services by homogenizing notifications. We measured during a six-month study the evolution of the effectiveness, learnability, and acceptance of our platform embedded in the daily life of fifteen older adults. Moreover, we assessed the relation of such variables as users' abilities (*i.e.,* cognitive and sensory resources).

Our results indicate that unifying notifications allows the user to be fully acquainted with the interactions of our platform. This acquaintance improves over the study period, in terms of effectiveness, learnability, and acceptance.

Regarding effectiveness and learnability, we observe an effective acquaintance with the platform, irrespective of the cognitive and sensory resources of the users. This means that this platform is suitable for the interaction abilities of older adults. Interestingly, the learnability performance reveals that the time to be-performed task for critical notification condition is longer than the time for non-critical condition during the first period of technology use (1.5 months). Thus, the older participants have given more processing time for critical notifications as expected, considering the potential consequence for the participant. In other words, the critical and non-critical notifications are accurately distinguished by the participants and thus, they are processed according to their nature [22]. The increasing practice of the system allows the user to automate the process, resulting in an equivalent handling time for both notification types, after three months. This is even more evident when considering that critical notifications require more time to be handled by the participants since an action has be taken in the environment.

Furthermore, our results highlight a better acceptance for users with poor cognitive resources, particulary regarding ergonomy and hedonism. Thus, it seems that this platform effectively match older users' needs by offering services assisting cognitive decline [12] (*e.g.,* entry door monitoring or appointment reminders).

Concerning sensory abilities, we observe a lower acceptance for users with diminished sensory abilities, particulary for the dimensions of appealingness and social influence. This result could be explained by the fact that our platform use multi-modal notifications (*i.e.,* tone, text, specifc colors and shapes). This approach could discourage users with a visual and/or auditive decline from adopting the technology

To the best of our knowledge, there is no study aiming at scaling up assistive services by unifying notifications. Furthermore, there is no study measuring the effectiveness and learnability of a user interface that operates a range of assistive services in an ecological setting. Such study provides insights on how to increase the number of assistive services, without increasing their cognitive cost. More globally, our work provides some of the first empirical evidence that an assisted living platform can range over the domains of assisted living, without overwhelming older adult users [34], as shown by our results on user acceptance and satisfaction.

The design of our notification system has leveraged the literature on notifications (*e.g.,* [36, 26]) and the design principles and guidelines for technology when targeting older adults [12]. As well, we have taken into account the specificities of older adults related to their susceptibility to stimuli [40], the cognitive cost of technology [7], and a suitable model to measure their acceptance of technology [15, 7].

6.1 Limitations

Notifications are simple and may appear as lacking expressiveness. An analogy could be drawn between these notifications and text messages on a cell phone. Although this analogy oversimplifies our approach, it captures the idea that we provide a way for a variety of assistive services to deliver uniform messages to the user. This is a powerful medium to support independent living of a declining older adult without overwhelming them. Still, we are continuing the analysis of existing and new services to determine how wide a range of assistive services can be captured by our notion of notifications, and whether and how they could be enriched without incurring a cognitive cost.

Task-specific interactions are not studied. Our goal was to concentrate on the interactions that matched a common pattern, which was recurring in the usage of assistive services. Our participants accepted the way interactions of assistive services are structured as a result of our proposed decomposition. In any case, we plan to further analyze task-specific interactions using domain engineering, from software engineering, by identifying their commonalities and variabilities.

Notifications are only implemented for tablets. We have not yet explored our approach beyond tablets. In our platform, this device is stationary and always on, ready to deliver notifications. This may have been reassuring for our participants because when hearing the tone of a notification, they knew where to go to handle it. Using a TV is more difficult because it is not always one. If the platform were able to turn it on, it could be disturbing for the user.

6.2 Perspectives

Towards a methodology to design notifications for older adults. When developing assistive services, we examined existing assistive systems and the wide range of design strategies adopted by other developers regarding notifications. When notifications are recurring, this diversity gets the user confused or/and frustrated. Our approach is a step towards enabling the developer of an assistive service to use our approach as a methodology to define the notifications. The API offers a layer that abstracts over some of the implementation requirements of interacting with an older adult users (auditory, visual). We want to explore this issue further. In particular, we would like to conduct a study that consists of comparing the development of assistive services, with and without our approach.

Enriching notifications. When analyzing existing assistive services, we identified a need for a notification that would inform the user about the progression of a task being performed. This could be used in multi-step tasks, such as taking pills, personal care, and meal preparation. Typically, this information could be delivered visually as a progress bar. The application monitoring the task could use an extended API to provide the user with a feedback, whenever a notification with the environment is detected via sensors.

Leveraging the simplicity of notifications.. There is a range of users that could benefit from the simplicity and homogeneity of notifications. This includes users with intellectual deficiencies, age-related neuro-degenerative diseases (*e.g.,* Alzheimer, Parkinson) and neurological disorders (*e.g.,* traumatic brain injuries, cerebral vascular diseases). In the coming months, we are initiating a project aimed at providing an assisted living platform for adults with Down syndrome.

7. CONCLUSIONS

In this paper, we presented an approach to scaling up assistive services and address the increasingly many needs of older adults with cognitive decline. Our approach consists of decomposing the user interactions of assistive services into two categories: notifications and task specific. We observe that notifications are often the recurring interactions and they can be homogenized to lower the cognitive cost of assistive services. We propose an API to implement notifications in assistive services. We validate our approach by applying it to a range of existing and new assistive services.

Our approach is implemented in an assisted living platform. Notifications are supported by a tablet. This platform has been deployed at the home of 15 older adults. A six-month study has shown the effectiveness and learnability of the notification system of our platform, irrespective of the cognitive and sensory resources of the users. Additional results showed that our assisted living platform has achieved high user acceptance and satisfaction.

8. ACKNOWLEDGMENTS

We thank the members of the Phoenix research group at Inria for their contributions to this project. We also thank the anonymous reviewers for their thorough reviews that improved our paper significantly. Our project is funded by the following sponsors: UDCCAS, CG33, CRA, CNSA, Chambre des métiers.

9. REFERENCES

[1] Abowd, G. D., and Mynatt, E. D. Designing for the human experience in smart environments. *Smart environments: technologies, protocols, and applications* (2004), 151–174.

[2] Albert, M. S., DeKosky, S. T., Dickson, D., Dubois, B., Feldman, H. H., Fox, N. C., Gamst, A., Holtzman, D. M., Jagust, W. J., Petersen, R. C., et al. The diagnosis of mild cognitive impairment due to alzheimer's disease: Recommendations from the national institute on aging-alzheimer's association workgroups on diagnostic guidelines for alzheimer's disease. *Alzheimer's & Dementia 7*, 3 (2011), 270–279.

[3] Bouisson, J. Routinization preferences, anxiety, and depression in an elderly french sample. *Journal of Aging Studies 16*, 3 (2002), 295–302.

[4] Caine, K. E., Zimmerman, C. Y., Schall-Zimmerman, Z., Hazlewood, W. R., Sulgrove, A. C., Camp, L. J., Connelly, K. H., Huber, L. L., and Shankar, K. Digiswitch: design and evaluation of a device for older adults to preserve privacy while monitoring health at home. In *Proceedings of the 1st ACM International Health Informatics Symposium*, ACM (2010), 153–162.

[5] Caroux, L., Consel, C., Dupuy, L., and Sauzéon, H. Verification of Daily Activities of Elders: A Simple, Non-Intrusive, Low-Cost Approach. In *ASSETS - The 16th International ACM SIGACCESS Conference on Computers and Accessibility* (Rochester, NY, United States, 2014).

[6] Chan, M., Estève, D., Escriba, C., and Campo, E. A review of smart homes- present state and future challenges. *Computer methods and programs in biomedicine 91*, 1 (July 2008), 55–81.

[7] Chen, K., and Chan, A. H. S. Gerontechnology acceptance by elderly Hong Kong Chinese: a senior technology acceptance model (STAM). *Ergonomics 57*, 5 (2014), 635–652.

[8] Davis, F. D., Bagozzi, R. P., and Warshaw, P. R. User acceptance of computer technology: a comparison of two theoretical models. *Management science 35*, 8 (1989), 982–1003.

[9] Demers, L., Monette, M., Lapierre, Y., Arnold, D., and Wolfson, C. Reliability, validity, and applicability of the Quebec User Evaluation of Satisfaction with assistive Technology (QUEST 2.0) for adults with multiple sclerosis. *Disability & Rehabilitation 24*, 1-3 (2002), 21–30.

[10] Dubois, B., Slachevsky, A., Litvan, I., and Pillon, B. The FAB: A frontal assessment battery at bedside. *Neurology 55*, 11 (2000), 1621–1626.

[11] Findlater, L., Froehlich, J. E., Fattal, K., Wobbrock, J. O., and Dastyar, T. Age-related differences in performance with touchscreens compared to traditional mouse input. In *Proceedings of the SIGCHI Conference on Human Factors in Computing Systems*, ACM (2013), 343–346.

[12] Fisk, A. D., Rogers, W. A., Charness, N., Czaja, S. J., and Sharit, J. *Designing for older adults: Principles and creative human factors approaches*. CRC press, 2012.

[13] Folstein, M. F., Folstein, S. E., and McHugh, P. R. Mini-mental state: a practical method for grading the cognitive state of patients for the clinician. *Journal of psychiatric research 12*, 3 (1975), 189–198.

[14] Gillespie, A., Best, C., and O'Neill, B. Cognitive function and assistive technology for cognition: a systematic review. *Journal of the International Neuropsychological Society : JINS 18*, 1 (Jan. 2012), 1–19.

[15] Hassenzahl, M. The interplay of beauty, goodness, and usability in interactive products. *Human-Computer Interaction 19*, 4 (2004), 319–349.

[16] Jurica, P. J., Leitten, C. L., and Mattis, S. *DRS-2 dementia rating scale-2: professional manual*. Psychological Assessment Resources, 2004.

[17] Khan, D. U., Siek, K. A., Meyers, J., Haverhals, L. M., Cali, S., and Ross, S. E. Designing a personal health application for older adults to manage medications. In *Proceedings of the 1st ACM International Health Informatics Symposium*, ACM (2010), 849–858.

[18] Laurienti, P. J., Kraft, R. A., Maldjian, J. A., Burdette, J. H., and Wallace, M. T. Semantic congruence is a critical factor in multisensory behavioral performance. *Experimental brain research 158*, 4 (2004), 405–414.

[19] Lawton, M. P., Moss, M., Fulcomer, M., and Kleban, M. H. A research and service oriented multilevel assessment instrument. *Journal of Gerontology 37*, 1 (1982), 91–99.

[20] Lee, M. L., and Dey, A. K. Reflecting on pills and phone use: supporting awareness of functional abilities for older adults. In *Proceedings of the SIGCHI Conference on Human Factors in Computing Systems*, ACM (2011), 2095–2104.

[21] Lee, M. L., and Dey, A. K. Real-time feedback for improving medication taking. In *Proceedings of the 32nd annual ACM conference on Human factors in computing systems*, ACM (2014), 2259–2268.

[22] Lindenberger, U., Lövdén, M., Schellenbach, M., Li, S.-C., and Krüger, A. Psychological principles of successful aging technologies: A mini-review. *Gerontology 54*, 1 (2008), 59–68.

[23] Logan, B., Healey, J., Philipose, M., Tapia, E. M., and Intille, S. A Long-Term Evaluation of Sensing Modalities for Activity Recognition. In *Ubicomp*, Springer-Verlag, Ed. (Berlin Heidelberg, 2007).

[24] McCrickard, D. S., Catrambone, R., Chewar, C. M., and Stasko, J. T. Establishing tradeoffs that leverage attention for utility: empirically evaluating information display in notification systems. *International Journal of Human-Computer Studies 58*, 5 (2003), 547–582.

[25] McCrickard, D. S., Chewar, C. M., Somervell, J. P., and Ndiwalana, A. A model for notification systems evaluation: assessing user goals for multitasking activity. *ACM*

Transactions on Computer-Human Interaction (TOCHI) 10, 4 (2003), 312–338.

[26] McCrickard, D. S., Czerwinski, M., and Bartram, L. Introduction: design and evaluation of notification user interfaces. *International Journal of Human-Computer Studies 58*, 5 (2003), 509–514.

[27] Mokhtari, M., Aloulou, H., Tiberghien, T., Biswas, J., Racoceanu, D., and Yap, P. New trends to support independence in persons with mild dementia – a mini-review. *Gerontology 58*, 6 (2012), 554–563.

[28] Mozolic, J., Hugenschmidt, C., Peiffer, A., and Laurienti, P. Multisensory integration and aging. *CRC Press, Boca Raton (FL)* (2012).

[29] Owsley, C., Sloane, M., McGwin Jr, G., and Ball, K. Timed instrumental activities of daily living tasks: Relationship to cognitive function and everyday performance assessments in older adults. *Gerontology 48*, 4 (2002), 254–265.

[30] Rantz, M. J., Skubic, M., Koopman, R. J., Phillips, L., Alexander, G. L., Miller, S. J., and Guevara, R. D. Using sensor networks to detect urinary tract infections in older adults. In *e-Health Networking Applications and Services (Healthcom), 2011 13th IEEE International Conference on*, IEEE (2011), 142–149.

[31] Rashidi, P., and Mihailidis, A. A Survey on Ambient-Assisted Living Tools for Older Adults. *IEEE Journal of Biomedical and Health Informatics 17*, 3 (May 2013), 579–590.

[32] Riche, Y., and Mackay, W. PeerCare: Supporting Awareness of Rhythms and Routines for Better Aging in Place. *Computer Supported Cooperative Work (CSCW) 19*, 1 (Nov. 2009), 73–104.

[33] Rowan, J., and Mynatt, E. D. Digital family portrait field trial: Support for aging in place. In *Proceedings of the SIGCHI conference on Human factors in computing systems*, ACM (2005), 521–530.

[34] Scherer, M. J. *Assistive technologies and other supports for people with brain impairment.* Springer Publishing Company, 2012.

[35] Vastenburg, M. H., Keyson, D. V., and De Ridder, H. Considerate home notification systems: a field study of acceptability of notifications in the home. *Personal and Ubiquitous Computing 12*, 8 (2008), 555–566.

[36] Vastenburg, M. H., Keyson, D. V., and De Ridder, H. Considerate home notification systems: A user study of acceptability of notifications in a living-room laboratory. *International Journal of Human-Computer Studies 67*, 9 (2009), 814–826.

[37] Venkatesh, V., Morris, M. G., Davis, G. B., and Davis, F. D. User acceptance of information technology: Toward a unified view. *MIS quarterly* (2003), 425–478.

[38] Warnock, D., McGee-Lennon, M., and Brewster, S. The role of modality in notification performance. In *Human-Computer Interaction–INTERACT 2011*. Springer, 2011, 572–588.

[39] Warnock, D., McGee-Lennon, M., and Brewster, S. Multiple notification modalities and older users. In *Proceedings of the SIGCHI Conference on Human Factors in Computing Systems*, ACM (2013), 1091–1094.

[40] Wetherell, J. L., Reynolds, C. A., Gatz, M., and Pedersen, N. L. Anxiety, cognitive performance, and cognitive decline in normal aging. *The Journals of Gerontology Series B: Psychological Sciences and Social Sciences 57*, 3 (2002), P246–P255.

[41] Wiley, J., Sung, J.-Y., and Abowd, G. The Message Center : Enhancing Elder Communication. In *CHI 2006* (Montreal, Canada, 2006), 1523–1528.

Disability and Technology
A Critical Realist Perspective

Christopher Frauenberger
Institute for Design and Assessment of Technology, TU Wien
Argentinierstrasse 8
Vienna, Austria
christopher.frauenberger@tuwien.ac.at

ABSTRACT

Assistive technology (AT) as a field explores the design, use and evaluation of computing technology that aims to benefit people with disabilities. The majority of the work consequently takes the functional needs of people with disabilities as starting point and matches those with technological opportunity spaces. With this paper, we argue that the underlying philosophical position implied in this approach can be seen as reductionist as the disabled experience is arguably richer and often more complex as can be projected from the functional limitations of people. Thinkers and activists in Disability Studies have conceptualised disability in various ways and more recently, critical realism was proposed as a philosophical position through which the many different facets of the disabled experience could be incorporated. In this paper, we explore the possibility of using a critical realist perspective to guide designers in developing technology for people with disabilities and thereby aim to contribute to the philosophical underpinnings of AT. After a brief review of historical conceptualisations of disability, we introduce the critical realist argument and discuss its appeal for understanding disability and the possible roles technology can have in this context. Subsequently, we aim to translate this philosophical and moral debate into a research agenda for AT and exemplify how it can be operationalised by presenting the OutsideTheBox project as a case study.

Keywords

disability studies; philosophy of science; critical realism

Categories and Subject Descriptors

K.4.2 [**Computers and Society**]: Social issuesâĂŤAssistive technologies for persons with disabilities

1. INTRODUCTION

Our collective and individual conceptualisation of disability significantly shapes which kinds of assistive technologies are being designed. When Mankoff et al first used Disability Studies as a lens to critically reflect on work in assistive technology (AT), they demonstrated through their case studies how taking a particular stance towards disability changed the way they created and evaluated technology [12]. They state that through their exposure to the disability studies literature, they were able to develop a more nuanced understanding of the concept of "assistance" and came to critically reflect on the value of AT projects that *"may have technical merit, and may solve observable problems, but still fail to address the complex interplay of issues at work"*.

With this paper we want build on this argument and use the most recent thinking in Disability Studies to contribute to the philosophical foundation of AT and evolve its future research agenda. In particular, it is the turn to *critical realism* that we draw on. It was introduced to the discourse in Disability Studies with the promise to help dissolve the dichotomy between the medical model and social model of disability, i.e., the polarising debate whether disability is determined in the biological condition or exists purely as a social construct in the environment. What is at its core a philosophy of science, critical realism offers Disability Studies a coherent basis on which the many, often equally valid perspectives on disability could be reconciled, thus leading to a multi-facetted view of the disabled experience [21].

We argue that this approach has great appeal for the field of AT too. As we will further elaborate on below, the philosophical position towards disability designers take, implicitly or explicitly, changes the way they motivate, design and evaluate technology. Consequently, we have seen assistive technologies that focus on individual support or change the environment to make it more inclusive by removing barriers. A multi-layered and interactional conceptualisation of disability, such as the critical realist perspective offers, however would allow us to think about technologies in a different way: can technologies work across the multiple layers that all together shape the disabled experience? Can it consider the physical, the biological, the psychological, the psychosocial and emotional, the socio-economic, the cultural and the normative at the same time in meaningful ways? Can it be non-reductionist?

We argue that AT has two good reasons for wanting to ask these questions. Firstly, as Mankoff et al also highlighted, too narrowly conceived efforts to "do good" are potentially misleading in terms of the overall complexity of the disabled experience. Furthermore, as they point out *"it is important to acknowledge that there may not even be a 'right' problem to tackle "* [12]. Secondly, the increasing pervasiveness of

ASSETS'15, October 26–28, 2015, Lisbon, Portugal.

ACM 978-1-4503-3400-6/15/10 ...$15.00.
DOI: http://dx.doi.org/10.1145/2700648.2809851 .

technologies means that they play an ever greater part in experiencing and interpreting our lifeworlds. Consequently, it becomes ever more difficult to solve any problem in isolation as its solution always interacts with many other aspects of our life. The field of human-computer interaction (HCI) has responded to this challenge by recognising the need for a situated, value driven and participatory approach—what came to be termed 3rd paradigm HCI [9].

In the following we provide a brief, semi-historical account of the main approaches to conceptualise disability, including references to how those were manifested in the technologies that were created within these concepts. We then introduce the critical realist argument and discuss what this means for understanding the disabled experience. Based on this discussion, we develop a non-reductionist, future research agenda for AT and investigate its implications on methodology, evaluation, ethics and knowledge. We then briefly introduce the OutsideTheBox project to exemplify how this agenda can shape AT research. We close by recapping our argument and discussing its implications for the field of AT.

2. CONCEPTS OF DISABILITY AND ASSISTIVE TECHNOLOGIES

For the most part of the 20th century, the dominant concept society had about disability was rooted in **biological determinism** [5]. Disability was heavily medicalised and consequently inherently "a-normative", i.e., disability was conceptualised as deviation from the norm in terms of biological functions and the resulting societal responsibility is expressed in terms of "curing", "caring" or, in the best case, "supporting" disabled people to elevate their burden. This perspective firmly places the "cause" of disability in the individual and is thus providing the basis for segregation, e.g. like in traditional special needs education. We still encounter this underlying perspective on disability in much assistive technology work. Like Mankoff et al state [12], the medical model, as this view has become known in Disability Studies, has proven useful for developing assistive technology as it pragmatically provides specific requirements for design, based on the functional limitations of its users. And while many of these efforts have to be applauded as they address many real-world issues people with disabilities encounter, we also should acknowledge that designing technology in this mindset reinforces a societal concept of disability that is one-sided as it places disability solely in the individual.

The medical model has been opposed by a growing number of disability rights activists during the 1970's which culminated in the publication of the policy statement of the the Union of Physically Impaired Against Segregation (UPIAS) and the subsequent report on a meeting held with the Disability Alliance on the Fundamental Principles of Disabilities [14]. In the spirit of union activism, they verbalised the perceived oppression of people with disabilities and demanded full participation in society. They postulated *"Disability is something imposed on top of our impairments, by the way we are unnecessarily isolated and excluded from full participation in society. Disabled people are therefore an oppressed group in society."* A crucial, conceptual distinction was introduced between impairment as biological circumstance and disability as social and environmental construction—the core feature of the social model of disability. The causality of disability has been shifted from the individual into the society. The field of Disability Studies further developed the theoretical underpinnings for this approach. Oliver coined the term **social creationist** approach to signify a materialist emphasis on the construction of disability, i.e., it is factors such as physical barriers in the environment or inadequate access to the labour market and precarious income situations that disable people [15]. The materialist view has led to seeing the main task of assistive technologies in making aspects of our life accessible; barrier removal equals inclusion. Accessibility standards for the Web are a good example that embodies this philosophy.

In contrast to materialism, a **social constructionist** perspective focuses on the cultural and socio-historical context that defines disability as a category of difference. Deeply rooted in a post-modern tradition, this perspective looks closely at language and social practices to identify what makes people to be viewed as "disabled". Distinctively, this has wider implications as the social creationist approach in that it is ultimately not the economic, physical or political barriers that disable people, but ideology, social representation and the public discourse and its language that disables people. Consequently, no amount of barrier removal would lead to truly inclusive societies, because the distinction between people with disabilities and those without is inherent in the way we think and talk about them. In Disability Studies, this has led to research into terminology, imagery of disability in public discourse or media, embodiment and phenomenological perspectives; and, in a post-structuralist tradition, into the deconstruction of the category of disability. This, essentially, concerns the question "What is normal?" and the more rhetorical version "Aren't we just all different?". At this point Disability Studies found itself making very similar arguments to researchers concerning themselves with the (de)construction of gender, race and sexuality. Like post-modern feminism, the cultural disability approach seeks to destabilise categories by foregrounding the processes through which we implicitly construct them. In the design of technology, a good example of this approach being applied is the adoption of the neurodiversity stance in HCI which seeks to reframe conditions as alternative, cognitive processing styles [6]. Thus, design aims to shift its focus to the strengths of users[1] and rejects normative assumptions (see also [1]).

None of the above concepts of disabilities is without its problems when trying to describe disabled experiences. The medical model is deeply oppressive and leads to segregative societies [21]. Technology designed with this mindset is at least complicit in fostering this segregation. The social model of disability, i.e. a social creationist approach, has proven useful in activism, but is ultimately equally one-sided. There are many aspects of disabled experiences that no amount of barrier removal can extinguish and equally, no level of accessibility to technology will make disabled people fully integrated in digital societies. A post-modern approach, i.e., the cultural, social constructionist view, denies people with disabilities their individual experiences in similar ways, but for different reasons. When the disability category is dissolved, there is no room left for the sometimes

[1]While on the surface of it there are parallels to ability-based design [26], it stops well short of challenging the defining categories and therefore could not be described as a social constructionist approach.

difficult and painful experiences of an impairment. If we are all just different, why do we find it amoral to painlessly alter a baby so that they could no longer see? (Harris used similar provocative statements in his critique of post-structuralist Disability Studies [8]). Furthermore, while the knowledge of the social construction is useful, they hardly yield actionable consequences to support people with disabilities. Thus, all of these models and approaches can be seen as reductionist in one way or another.

3. THE CRITICAL REALIST PERSPECTIVE

Critical realism is a philosophy of science that was predominately shaped by the British philosopher Roy Bhaskar. He initially used the terms transcendental realism and critical naturalism to describe his ideas, but eventually those were shortened into the now widely used term "critical realism" [4]. Like any philosophy of science, critical realism is concerned about what is (ontology) and how we can know about it (epistemology). And like the variety of post-modern philosophies, it has developed as a reaction to the empiricist, more specifically the positivistic philosophy or practice of science that has so significantly shaped, and in some way still does shape, our understanding of what "doing science" means. However, while they share some features, critical realism and post-modern thought arrived at quite different standpoints.

A common point of departure for both lines of thought was to reject the (post-)positivistic idea that there is an absolute truth about things that we can find out about in an empirical way. Particularly in the social sciences, there was growing recognition that we cannot know about people in the same way that we can know about atoms. In what became known as the "linguistic turn", the post-modernist answer is that understanding social reality is much more *"akin to understanding a language than a machine"* ([11], p8), i.e., it is irreducibly complex, situated, socially constructed and interpreted. Reading Kuhn's work about scientific traditions and revolutions [10] in a post-modern way, quickly expands this argument to the natural sciences: ultimately all we accept as scientific knowledge can be seen as constructed by social agents within their respective cultures. However, continuing this line of argument further, directly leads into radical relativism in which scientific progress is reduced to an arbitrary variation of an entirely constructed reality.

Critical realism rejects this notion and starts ontologically with a quite different position: there exists a reality that is independent of our description. *"Things exist and act independently of our descriptions, but we can only know them under particular descriptions"* ([2], p250, as cited in [21]). Thus, in contrast to many post-modern traditions, it rejects that reality is a social construct itself, but acknowledges that we can only know about reality in ways that are preliminary, culturally situated and most importantly multi-facetted. Thereby, it also rejects positivism for reducing reality to what can be empirically known. Positivism infers the actual from the empirical (actualism, see [4], p7) and reduces things to observable causal events and generates knowledge by generalising invariances in these causal relationships. Critical realism argues that this is not exhaustive and that things have potentiality and mechanisms that might not have been realised ([4], p7). It focuses on the underlying structure rather than the observable surface. This also allows it to see "things" as a broader category: they maybe powers, forces or relations [2]. *"Things possess characteristics which have tendencies to interact in particular ways with other things"* ([11], p11). These tendencies are not invariant, but are better understood as properties of mechanisms of which we can know of to a certain degree. Reality, thus, exists of things that interact through mechanisms which have certain tendencies. These real things are *intransitive objects*, and humans aim to understand the nature of the real mechanisms that connect them. Their understanding of these mechanisms is fallible, interpretative and socially constructed, and hence their models and theories are *transitive objects*. Scientific progress, therefore, becomes improving one's transitive objects, and (re)building these requires more than empiricism, but human reasoning on multiple levels.

For the concept of disability, this means that it allows a non-reductionist perspective, taking into account multiple layers that make up the disabled experience (a concept that is known as stratification in critical realism). Arguing from a critical realist position, Shakespeare proposed an approach that conceptualises *"... disability as an interaction between individual and structural factors"* ([21], p74). Individual or intrinsic factors include the nature of the impairment, their own attitude towards it or their personality. Structural or extrinsic factors are for example attitudes of others, the environment, support systems or social or economic issues. It is the interplay between these factors that make up the disabled experience, or in short *"people are disabled by the society 'and' their bodies"* (ibid. p75). This holistic approach is similar to the perspective that the International Classification of Functioning, Disability and Health (ICF) published by the WHO takes [16], although critics have pointed out that the ICF seems to take the biological for granted and objective, while a critical realist approach would deny that [24].

Such an interactional approach[3] makes room for a broad range of disabled experiences, for example regarding aspects of personal attitudes, chronic illnesses, the diversity and severity of impairments or social disadvantages. But it also points very pragmatically to different ways in which the lives of people with disabilities can be improved. Integration of disabled people in the labour market, for example, can be addressed on a structural level (e.g., anti-discrimination legislation, access to healthcare) and on an individual level (e.g., training, coaching, pain management). None of these interventions is per se preferred over the other, but their impact has to be assessed through their interaction on multiple levels.

4. A CRITICAL REALIST AGENDA FOR ASSISTIVE TECHNOLOGIES

The above has reflected on the evolution of concepts that are being applied to make sense and describe the disabled experience within our society. We argue that these underlying philosophical positions fundamentally shape the tech-

[2]Exactly what things are and what their causal powers would be, is a central debate within critical realism ([11], p22 ff.)

[3]Interactional with respect to facets of the disabled experience, not in terms of interacting with technology.

nologies that are being designed for people with disabilities. Thus, the following aims to develop a future research agenda for the field of AT that is inspired by a critical realist perspective on disability.

4.1 Multi-facetted and interactional

In Disability Studies, it is the possibility to incorporate different perspectives on the central questions into one ontological and epistemological frame that makes critical realism appeal. The disabled experience is multi-facetted and Shakespeare's interactional approach allows for these very different aspects to all contribute to a holistic understanding.

To investigate what that means for AT, we must first concern ourself with the question: "What is the purpose of the technology we design?" The medical and the strong social model had pragmatic answers to this: "mitigate the functional limitation of the individual" and "remove the social barriers" respectively. But, as the disabled experience is made up from a multiplicity of mechanisms, it becomes clear that the possible roles of technologies can be equally diverse. And as Shakespeare points out, it is not only different mechanisms, but it is their interaction that determines experiences. While currently we have a great variety of technologies that serve specific purposes in the lives of people with disabilities, what we lack, is a holistic, integrative and interactional approach. To illustrate the point with an example: we might design navigation aids for the blind walking streets, but do not consider how other people are necessarily part of the experience, be it negative as the source of stigmata or positive as possible part of the solution (asking directions is very often not merely a request for help, but a natural entry point to a social encounter). Shinohara and Wobbrock make a similar point by stating *"technology use does not happen in a social vacuum"* and provide further examples from their interview study across different disabilities [23]. We also do not consider the internal, psychological state of mind. A blind person might be experienced and self-confident wit respect to how people react to his presence, or anxious and insecure about their impairment. All will effect the way they interpret the situation and the technology.

This also demonstrates the dangers of limiting the scope of design in this context. Technologies always do interfere with the system of mechanisms as a whole and interact on an individual and societal level. So if we design for the individual, the technology will also interact with the environment and vice versa. Thus, we argue for an approach that cuts across the different levels from which disabled experience is made up. We need technologies that recognise the multiple mechanisms and the way they interact. Can we design technologies that consider the physical, the biological, the psychological, the psychosocial and emotional, the socio-economic, the cultural and the normative in meaningful ways ([21], p74)? Even if the motivation for creating a technology might not be addressing all of these perspectives, it is important to be mindful of the interaction between them, to not fall into the trap of meaning good, but realising unintended consequences.

4.2 Methodology

The next question is "How can we design such technology?" Again, the reductionist models of disabilities had relatively straight forward answers as their standpoints allowed the elicitation of specific requirements for developing technology. A critical realist approach is inherently more complex. Into the many mechanisms that interact to make up the disabled experience, we seek to inject yet another one: technology. While we cannot predict by nature, with any certainty what will happen in an open system, our understanding of tendencies and mechanisms provides us with suitable targets. We cannot, however, make the mechanisms we introduce interact with a single, well-understood mechanism, but it will always effect the whole system to different degrees, i.e., technology will shift the disabled experience, on some levels in possibly unintended ways. It becomes a truly "wicked problem" [18].

Consequently, choosing an appropriate methodology has two aspects: firstly, in order to identify and understand the mechanisms that technology will interact with, a diverse mix of methods is needed to probe into the disabled experience at different levels. This can, for example involve quantitative, lab-based studies to establish medical boundaries (e.g., the mechanisms that limit the range and accuracy of physical movement for controlling an input device) and design interventions with the aim to provoke social responses when technology is introduced into a context (e.g., when groups of children with cognitive disabilities are given smart objects to create video diaries).

Secondly, the understanding gained needs to meaningfully inform design and we argue that two qualities are quintessential in this respect: participation and reflection. Critical realism cautions us about the provisionality of the understanding we can have of mechanisms in open systems. Constant reflection and short development cycles is thus key to repeatedly verify and refine that understanding. There are moral arguments to be made about participation, which we will briefly discuss below, but we argue that just from a methodological standpoint PD has much to offer as a critical realist approach. The inclusion of different stakeholders allows designers to work with experts on different levels, each interpreting our understanding of the mechanisms in different ways. People with disabilities have unique insights into the complexity of the disabled experience that are invaluable, as have carers, parents, policymakers and others. PD also effectively dissolves design-evaluation cycles and puts concepts and ideas to the test while they emerge. As such, PD becomes not only a way to catalyse knowledge to inform design, but it becomes a form of enquiry in its own right. By co-designing, we deepen our understanding of disabled experiences and their mechanisms.

4.3 Evaluation

The way we evaluate technology as it is used by people has also undergone a radical change. In the traditional paradigms, HCI conducted controlled evaluation studies that were extrapolated into the wild, or it fitted lab-based evaluation criteria onto real-world studies. The inadequacy of this approach for today's technologies goes hand in hand with the diversification of purposes technology serves, not only in the lives of people with disability. It is consequently not necessarily clear anymore what it is that should be evaluated which, in the context of this paper leads to the more fundamental question of: "What does it mean for technology to work well for people with disabilities?"

A critical realist perspective highlights the need for assessing the impact of a technology on the whole interacting system of mechanisms. So, it might be insufficient to prove that some assistive technology is delivering on what was the initial motivation (e.g., way finding, accessing information etc.) unless it becomes clear how it interacts with all other levels of the disabled experience. This, however, creates the challenge of defining a meaningful scope for evaluations. For example, we might discover that a rehabilitation device changes the social peer pressure on an older adult to do their exercises, which in evaluating the technology is more significant than any design aspect of the actual system. Evaluating assistive technologies thus, relies on including those mechanisms of the disabled experience that significantly shape it and this can be far from obvious a priori.

Another challenge is to interpret and value the change we observe, in other words, it is not always obvious what is desirable or an improvement. This also might depend on the perspective: what is positive change for policymakers might not be so positive for individuals. This is a similar issue that participatory design has grappled with in trying to define what "successful" PD work might be (compare [19, 7]).

4.4 Ethics and Morality

A conscious ethical and moral position has to be an integrative part of designing technology, even more so in the context of people with disabilities. From a critical realist perspective, it becomes clear that such a position is never achievable in advance. The complexity and multiplicity of perspectives that the critical realist conception of disability implies, requires us to constantly reflect on our position while we improve our understanding of the mechanisms that interact to make up disabled experiences in the given context of a project. Such in-action reflection has been theorised about in design to capture knowledge [20], but equally we need in-action ethics embedding the development and refinement of ethical positions deeply into our practice.

4.5 Knowledge

As a scientific field, the aim of AT is to improve our understanding about how technologies are designed, used and evaluated in the context of people with disabilities. This improved understanding is translated into a shared body of knowledge by the virtue of being re-used, re-interpreted and built upon. As control in studies of technologies "in the wild" increasingly disappears, the generation and transfer of knowledge becomes equally more challenging. Studies that are highly *relevant*, i.e. true to the given context, are often criticised for their *rigour* as they cannot generalise. Vice-versa, strictly controlled, lab-based studies are highly rigorous, but criticised for being irrelevant in real-world use – seemingly a *rigorous-or-relevant* dichotomy. Recognising this, HCI has embarked on a transformation, which is still ongoing, to redefine the way it describes and creates technologies that humans can interact with, and the way we can know about it [9].

A critical realism perspective offers to potentially resolve the *rigorous-or-relevant* dichotomy. To be *relevant*, knowledge produced has to relate to everyday life and thus acknowledge the openness and uncontrollability of the system as well as the fallibility of the process of enquiry. Equally, though, scientific outcomes have to be able to be *rigorous*, or in other words, we need to be able to objectively say that we have improved our understanding of reality by doing science. The concept of stratification in critical realism (layers of mechanisms, where lower explain higher ones) allows to enquire into the *same* reality by very different means. For example, it becomes possible to meaningfully integrate knowledge that was gai ned by understanding how the visually impaired interpret spatial auditory cues, how technology can support them to navigate unknown environments and how this new practice fits into their social patterns. Improving our understanding, i.e. generating knowledge, in this context can therefore be done either horizontally or vertically. So, either a) gaining better understanding on each level, e.g. about spatial hearing, or b) gaining better understanding how one level interacts with the another, e.g., how navigation relates to social behaviours. While the horizontal way (a) might be closer to traditional science practice, we argue that AT specifically would benefit from the vertical (b) kind of integration of knowledge.

4.6 Similarities and differences to other approaches

Recent work in AT has recognised the dangers of one-sided perspectives on the disabled experience. Shinohara and Wobbrock, for example, have studied how the use of AT is affected by social contexts and vice versa. They conclude that AT commonly provokes two misperceptions, firstly that AT is eliminating a person's disability and secondly, that this consequently makes them functionally equivalent to a person with no disability [23]. This has led Shinohara to propose a new approach for the design of AT, one that integrates designing for social acceptance [22]. While this very rightly makes the point that a strictly medical view ignores key social factors that contribute to the disabled experience in relation to technology, Design for Social Acceptance is still limited in scope, ignoring many other facets of the disabled experience, for example personal state-of-mind questions. It also carries a normative notion that rests uneasily with the proposed agenda here, in that design needs to be "accepted" by society and should be incorporated into mainstream technology to be less vulnerable to cause stigmata.

Pullin points to another important aspect, the role of æsthetics in AT, which also relates to the interaction between the medical and the social [17]. Amongst other examples, he describes the change in how we stopped regarding eyeglasses as medical aid, but a fashion accessory. It is certainly the case that AT can become a statement of choice when designed with care and intent, but the danger is that it might lead to the misunderstanding that disability can be turned into something entirely positive by choice, if only the aids are pretty enough. No matter how extravagant the glasses, one is still not able to see well without them.

Ability-based design has aimed to make a stance that focuses on what people with disabilities are good at and shift the effort of adapting for access from the user to the system [26]. The underlying ethos of the approach is laudable, but it seems to only side-step the problematic implications of the traditional philosophical stances. Focusing on functional abilities as starting points to model users for adaptable systems is equally reductionist and shifting responsibility for access from the user to the system has similar limitations as classical social creationist approaches.

Methodologically, User-Sensitive Inclusive Design [13] might be seen as the closest approach embodying a critical realist agenda. Its emphasis on participatory methods to make designers *"consider the whole person, not simply their physical characteristics"* is in the same vein of arguments made here. Being pragmatically focused on methods, however, makes Newell et al sparing out the theoretical and philosophical underpinnings of their approach.

5. OUTSIDE THE BOX

"OutsideTheBox - Rethinking Assistive Technologies with Children with Autism"[4] is a three year research project that explores new, meaningful roles of ubiquitous computing (UbiComp) technologies in the lives of children with autism. In a deep, participatory design process, we engage children 6 to 8 years old and invite them to co-design their very own smart object. The design brief is deliberately under-specified: the resulting artefacts should realise the potential of UbiComp technologies to a) afford positive experiences, and b) support children with autism in sharing those experiences in their social environment. By realising a series of case studies we demonstrate that such open participatory processes are possible and lead to designs that would have been unimaginable for adult, neuro-typical researchers. Grounded in these case studies, we populate a conceptual space with evaluated design methods that aims to provide transferable design knowledge for others to build on.

At the time of writing this project is one year old. We have engaged 4 children over a period of 7 months, meeting them approximately every second week for a one hour workshop and succeeded in co-designing a smart object with each of them. Each process involved a phase of contextual enquiry followed by concept design, crafting and prototyping. A common strategy was to take the special interests of the children as a starting point[5] and lead the child out into a creative exploration phase. More detailed results about the processes, outcomes and evaluations will be published in due time. In what follows, we want to discuss in which ways this project aims to embody aspects of the research agenda that we have laid out above.

5.1 Multi-faceted

The design brief, while deliberately open ended, speaks to two different levels of the disabled experience: firstly, the focus on positive experience, fun and meaningful engagement takes a radical first-person and outlooking perspective. It aims to construct a human-centred understanding of experience of which the disability and the technology are necessarily part of, but not as the defining features. They are part of a holistic notion of experience and play their roles as mechanisms which interact. Secondly, the goal to scaffold the sharing of these positive experiences probes into a specific feature of the condition of which we know that it is often a great challenge for children with autism. The question how we can support such sharing has a different quality as it is directed towards the child, i.e. it is ultimately an intervention that addresses a specific aspect of an impairment.

A critical realist perspective allows us to see these two angles as complementary, rather than contradictory. The vertical integration of these two goals naturally raises different kinds of design challenges, for example, how do we get from the typically narrow interests to sharable experiences? What are positive experiences and is sharing them still positive from a child perspective? As such, the design brief makes it necessary to closely investigate the interactions between intrinsic and extrinsic aspects of the disabled experience.

5.2 Methodology

The methodology in Outside The Box is radically participatory. As argued above, this enables us to do two things: firstly, we gain understanding about the lived, disabled experience. When meeting a child every second week over the course of a school year, the quality of insights into their lifeworld is very different to what could be elicited traditionally when focused on requirements. Through our interactions with the child, the parents and the teachers, an empathic understanding from different perspectives is emerging. Which leads to the second point: this understanding needs to translate into the design of technology. A critical realist perspective alerts us that this understanding is provisional, biased and maybe misjudging the mechanisms at work. The participatory approach in Outside The Box aims to respond to this by involving children in the development so that this understanding is constantly refined and adjusted in a reflective process. The boundaries between design and evaluation are blurred as the child and the researchers develop and test their ideas at the same time.

The resulting smart objects (see figure 1) are testimony to how different the directions were in which each of the design processes evolved. Their design was inspired not only by the direct input from children, but by the empathic and mindful interpretation of their lifeworlds by designers, the views of parents and teachers, and by the project's underlying values and intentions.

5.3 Evaluation

Assessing the impact of the smart objects developed on the lived experience of children is at the heart of the evaluation work being conducted in Outside The Box. We therefore take a holistic approach looking, in critical realist terms, at all the different mechanisms that interact to shape that experience. This has led us to the question of how we can conceptualise and assess experience and on which data sources we could draw on.

We are in the process of developing such a framework for experience that brings together intrinsic and extrinsic perspectives and their interaction. We therefore draw on self-reporting methods like diaries, targeted questionnaires for the family or school context, interview data from children, parents and teachers, and usage data from the smart objects. It is unclear yet, however, whether the data sources will suffice to capture all relevant interactions between mechanisms of the (disabled) experience in this context. Further work will show whether novel forms of data gathering are needed or which impact the time-frame for evaluation has on what can be captured. It will be furthermore interesting to see how the picture we draw about the experience, is interpreted by different stakeholders. For example, will parents or teachers judge the experience in similar ways as the child?

5.4 Ethics

Moral and ethical considerations in Outside The Box go beyond the concern for the physical and mental wellbeing

[4] `http://outsidethebox.at`

[5] Special interests are a hallmark feature of autism, often very narrow and pursued with compulsory passion (cf. [25]).

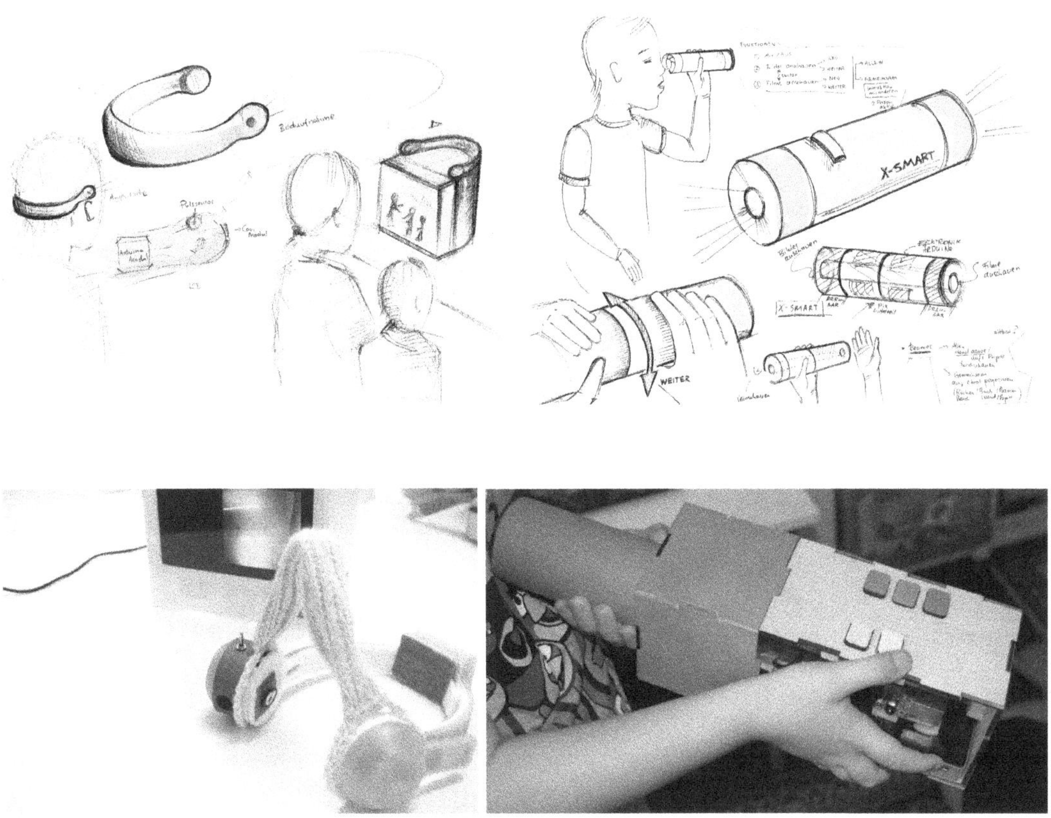

Figure 1: Initial sketches and their corresponding final prototypes of ThinkM (left, a memory machine for capturing and reflecting on difficult social situations) and XSmart (right, a story telling machine projecting cues into the hand of the child). Two examples of smart objects co-designed with children in OutsideTheBox (sketches ©Julia Makhaeva)

of our participants and thus, beyond the traditional anticipatory ethics processes formally required. By arguing for an open design process that focuses on a participant centred conception of wellbeing, the project makes a strong value statement that transparently shapes its moral standpoint. A number of technologies have been developed for children with autism, but, with very few exceptions, they match functional limitations with technological opportunity spaces, i.e., specific intervention goals drive the technological development. While, as argued throughout this paper, such perspectives have their purposes, they are also reductionist as they reduce the needs of children with autism to what they struggle with. In contrast, Outside The Box makes a point about putting wellbeing in the centre of design and starts with the often narrow interests of children with autism. Functional limitations and their effects are undoubtedly a part of this notion of wellbeing, but not their defining features.

This moral standpoint serves the project as guiding principle in planning and conducting workshops or studies in an ethically and morally responsible way. The open-ended and unpredictable nature of the work makes it necessary to constantly reflect on our decisions and whether they still embody the principle ethos of the project. We call this "in-action ethics".

5.5 Knowledge

The project generates knowledge on different levels: firstly, methodological in that new methods and techniques are developed to enable children with autism to lead on design processes. Secondly, technological know-how is generated in the way concepts and ideas are implemented as ubiquitous computing artefacts. Thirdly, knowledge in a socio-technical context is generated in terms of assessing experience in the context of the smart objects that were developed and how they support the sharing of such experience.

In Outside The Box we capture this knowledge mainly through annotated portfolios [3] which allows the construction of a synopsis across the different levels and thus is a first step towards vertically integrating knowledge.

6. CONCLUSION

With this paper we have argued that critical realism can contribute to the philosophical underpinnings of the field of AT. We have briefly discussed the various conceptualisations of disability and then introduced the critical realist perspective in Disability Studies. Inspired by the appealing features of both, the resulting multi-facetted, interactional model of disability, and the original philosophy of science, we have made the case for a critical realist perspective on designing technology for people with disabilities. The result is a proposal for an agenda for future research into AT that is non-reductionist and equally multi-facetted with respect to its motivations, methodologies, evaluation criteria, epistemology and ethics. The last section introduced OutsideTheBox as a case study to exemplify how this new agenda could be approached.

Future work will need to further investigate the implications of different philosophical positions on the practical work in AT. We believe that, in particular the vertical integration of knowledge generated on different strata is an area that will require more attention. Relatedly, Roy Bhaskar has written extensively about the centrality of experiments in scientific enquiry, albeit, his conception of experiments being rather different from empiricism. However, the contribution of this paper lies in progressing this debate and fostering a culture of critical reflection in AT.

7. ACKNOWLEDGMENTS

This work has been funded by the Austrian Science Fund [P26281-N23].

8. REFERENCES

[1] Benton, L., Vasalou, A., Khaled, R., Johnson, H., and Gooch, D. Diversity for Design: A Framework for Involving Neurodiverse Children in the Technology Design Process. In *Proceedings of the 32Nd Annual ACM Conference on Human Factors in Computing Systems*, CHI '14, ACM (New York, NY, USA, 2014), 3747–3756.

[2] Bhaskar, R. *A Realist Theory of Science.* Leeds Books, Leeds, 1975.

[3] Bowers, J. The logic of annotated portfolios: communicating the value of 'research through design'. In *Proceedings of the Designing Interactive Systems Conference*, DIS '12, ACM (Newcastle Upon Tyne, United Kingdom, 2012), 68–77.

[4] Collier, A. *Critical Realism: An Introduction to Roy Bhaskar's Philosopy.* Verso, London, UK, 1994.

[5] Corker, M., and Shakespeare, T. Mapping the Terrain. In *Disability/Postmodernity: Embodying Disability Studies*, M. Corker and T. Shakespeare, Eds. Continuum International Publishing Group, 2002.

[6] Dalton, N. S. Neurodiversity & HCI. In *CHI '13 Extended Abstracts on Human Factors in Computing Systems*, CHI EA '13, ACM (Paris, France, 2013), 2295–2304.

[7] Frauenberger, C., Good, J., Fitzpatrick, G., and Iversen, O. S. In pursuit of rigour and accountability in participatory design. *International Journal of Human-Computer Studies 74*, 0 (2015), 93 – 106.

[8] Harris, J. One principle and three fallacies of disability studies. *Journal of Medical Ethics 27*, 6 (Dec. 2001), 383–387.

[9] Harrison, S., Tatar, D., and Sengers, P. The three paradigms of HCI. In *Proceedings of alt.chi*, ACM SIGCHI (2007).

[10] Kuhn, T. S. *The Structure of Scientific Revolutions*, enlarged, 2nd edition ed. University of Chicago Press, 1970.

[11] Lopez, J., and Potter, G., Eds. *After Postmodernism: An Introduction to Critical Realism*, 1st ed. The Athlone Press, Contiuum imprint, London, UK, 2001.

[12] Mankoff, J., Hayes, G. R., and Kasnitz, D. Disability studies as a source of critical inquiry for the field of assistive technology. In *Proceedings of the 12th international ACM SIGACCESS conference on Computers and accessibility*, ASSETS '10, ACM (Orlando, Florida, USA, 2010), 3–10.

[13] Newell, A. F., Gregor, P., Morgan, M., Pullin, G., and Macaulay, C. User-Sensitive Inclusive Design. *Universal Access in the Information Society 10*, 3 (July 2010), 235–243.

[14] of the Physically Impaired Against Segregation, U. Fundamental principles of disability. Summary of a meeting, London, UK, Nov. 1976.

[15] Oliver, M. *The politics of disablement.* Palgrave Macmillan, 1990.

[16] Organization, W. H. Towards a common language for functioning, disability and health. Tech. rep., Geneva, 2002.

[17] Pullin, G. *Design Meets Disability.* The MIT Press, Cambridge, Mass, Sept. 2011.

[18] Rittel, H., and Webber, M. Dilemmas in a general theory of planning. *Policy sciences 4*, 2 (1973), 155–169.

[19] Sanders, E., and Westerlund, B. Experiencing, exploring and experimenting in and with co-design spaces. In *Proceedings of the Nordic Design Research Conference* (May 2011).

[20] Schön, D. A. *The Reflective Practitioner: How Professionals Think in Action.* Basic Books, New York, 1983.

[21] Shakespeare, T. *Disability Rights and Wrongs Revisited*, second endition ed. Routledge, Oxon UK, 2014.

[22] Shinohara, K. A new approach for the design of assistive technologies: design for social acceptance. *ACM SIGACCESS Accessibility and Computing*, 102 (2012), 45–48.

[23] Shinohara, K., and Wobbrock, J. O. In the shadow of misperception: assistive technology use and social interactions. In *Proceedings of the SIGCHI Conference on Human Factors in Computing Systems*, ACM (2011), 705–714.

[24] SÃűder, M. Tensions, perspectives and themes in disability studies. *Scandinavian Journal of Disability Research 11*, 2 (June 2009), 67–81.

[25] WHO, W. H. O. Autism Spectrum Disorders & Other Developmental Disorders – From Raising Awareness to Building Capacity, December 2013.

[26] Wobbrock, J. O., Kane, S. K., Gajos, K. Z., Harada, S., and Froehlich, J. Ability-Based Design: Concept, Principles and Examples. *ACM Trans. Access. Comput. 3*, 3 (Apr. 2011), 9:1–9:27.

The Tactile Graphics Helper: Providing Audio Clarification for Tactile Graphics Using Machine Vision

Giovanni Fusco
The Smith-Kettlewell Eye Research Institute
2318 Fillmore Street
San Francisco, California 94115
giofusco@ski.org

Valerie S. Morash
The Smith-Kettlewell Eye Research Institute
2318 Fillmore Street
San Francisco, California 94115
val@ski.org

ABSTRACT

Tactile graphics use raised lines, textures, and elevations to provide individuals with visual impairments access to graphical materials through touch. Tactile graphics are particularly important for students in science, technology, engineering, and mathematics (STEM) fields, where educational content is often conveyed using diagrams and charts. However, providing a student who has a visual impairment with a tactile graphic does not automatically provide the student access to the graphic's educational content. Instead, the student may struggle to decipher subtle differences between textures or line styles, and must deal with cramped and confusing placement of lines and braille. These format-related issues prevent students with visual impairments from accessing educational content in graphics independently, because they necessitate the students ask for sighted clarification. We propose a machine-vision based "tactile graphics helper" (TGH), which tracks a student's fingers as he/she explores a tactile graphic, and allows the student to gain clarifying audio information about the tactile graphic without sighted assistance. Using an embedded mixed-methods case study with three STEM university students with visual impairments, we confirmed that format-related issues prevent these students from accessing some graphical content independently, and established that TGH provides a promising approach for overcoming tactile-graphic format issues.

Categories and Subject Descriptors

K.4.2 [**Social Issues**]: Assistive technologies for persons with disabilities

General Terms

Design, Human Factors

Keywords

Tactile graphics; machine vision; assistive devices; finger tracking; mixed-methods; case study.

ASSETS'15, October 26–28, 2015, Lisbon, Portugal.
© 2015 ACM. ISBN 978-1-4503-3400-6/15/10 ...$15.00.
DOI: http://dx.doi.org/10.1145/2700648.2809868.

1. INTRODUCTION

Tactile graphics are adaptations of visual graphics in which lines have been raised and areas elevated or textured to make them accessible to touch. These include tactile representations of pictures, maps, diagrams, graphs, and other non-textual spatial arrangements. Tactile graphics are used for a variety of purposes, including navigation, entertainment, professional activities, and education. For students with visual impairments, tactile graphics provide critical access to educational materials, especially in science, technology, engineering, and mathematics (STEM), including the social sciences [15]. However, tactile graphics are relatively underused by students with visual impairments. For example, in a survey of academically achieving blind 9-19 year old students in the United States and Canada, only 45% reported encountering 3 or more tactile graphics per week, while 25% reported encountering 1-2 tactile graphics per week, 24% reported encountering tactile graphics only a few times per month, and 6% reported never using tactile graphics in school [35]. This is despite the inclusion of as much as 93.3% of print graphics in tactile form in braille transcriptions of secondary (9-12 grade) science and math textbooks (6.7% of graphics were found to be omitted in the braille transcriptions) [29], and feelings from surveyed students with visual impairments that tactile graphics are helpful, particularly in math and science [35].

It is extremely important that students with visual impairments have access to the content contained in tactile graphics. Many STEM concepts, such as direction, quantity, and shape, are taught in ways that rely heavily on visual reference, which poses severe access issues for students with visual impairments unless graphics are presented in tactile form [11, 18]. The ability to use graphics provides a "critical moment" in a child's mathematics and science education, which accelerates further math and science learning [24]. This is because graphics support reasoning about abstract concepts that are difficult to grasp directly, such as slope and function [14, 11]. Therefore, lack of access to tactile graphics has been singled out as one of a handful of reasons, including low teacher expectations and lack of blind peers and role models, as a cause for low interest and pursuance of careers in STEM by blind students [4].

Given their importance, why are there not more students with visual impairments using more tactile graphics? One reason for the low use of tactile graphics is that there are often confusing garphic elements, such as ambiguous symbols, which necessitate help from a sighted person and prevent students from using tactile graphics independently. The lines, symbols, textures, and spacing on tactile graphics are not standardized, unlike the specific formatting rules associated with braille and the Nemeth braille code for mathematics [29, 34]. As a result, awkward placement of labels and the low discriminability of lines, textures, and relief (elevation) may prevent a student from accessing a tactile graphic's content [2, 35]. Problematic formatting may vary between individuals due to differences in tactile sensitivity, tactile skill, cognitive abilities (e.g., memory), and experience. Additionally, some formatting issues may be unavoidable due limitations of the tactile medium, such as the larger size of braille compared to print and the greater susceptibility of tactile displays (relative to visual displays) to crowding. To deal with format-related issues in tactile graphics, students with visual impairments will often ask for clarification from a sighted teacher, paraprofessional, or peer [34, 35]. When a sighted assistant is not available, the student may be unable to use tactile graphics to complete his/her work.

In this paper, we detail problems associated with tactile-graphic formatting, as revealed by professionals who work with students who have visual impairments and also by university STEM students with visual impairments. To address tactile-graphic format issues, we propose a machine-vision system that answers questions about a tactile graphic, such as "what is on this tactile graphic?" and "what is this I'm pointing to?" This system will enable students with visual impairments to work independently with tactile graphics. The goal of this research is to confirm that tactile graphics contain format related issues that prevent students from working with tactile graphics independently, and to assess whether our machine-vision approach holds promise in addressing these issues.

2. RELATED WORK

Our system allows conventional (non-audio) tactile graphics to become audio-tactile graphics, which link sound with touch to enhance a tactile graphic with audio. Early efforts in creating audio-tactile graphics focused on tactile maps, and allowed the user to press a location on the tactile map to trigger an audio label [16]. Examples of early audio-tactile maps include NOMAD [27] and Talking Tactile Maps [5], which were made in the late 80's and 90's. More recently, Touch Graphics, Inc. has developed the Tactile Talking Tablet (TTT), which is composed of a plastic frame that holds a tactile graphic against a high-resolution touch screen [23]. The touch screen is connected to a personal computer via USB, which runs software allowing the tactile graphic to become interactive. Touching the tactile graphic can trigger audio information, or ask the computer to perform more complex computations, e.g., calculate the distance between two selected locations. The IVEO system by ViewPlus is similar to the TTT, and specifically supports Scalable Vector Graphic (SVG) images [13]. Attachment to a computer provides the TTT and IVEO considerable power and flexibility, but limits their portability.

The CamIO system [28] extends the idea of audio-tactile graphics to audio-tactile objects. CamIO uses a mounted three-dimensional (3D) camera and machine vision to watch users interacting with objects, and allows the user to trigger audio information about an object. Like the TTT, CamIO is run on a computer, limiting its portability.

A more portable solution for audio-tactile graphics is Touch Graphic's Talking Tactile Pen (TTP), which uses the Livescribe Pulse Pen [32] to provide audio information dependent on where the user touches the pen to a graphic. This is possible due to the pen's on-board microprocessor and camera, which points towards the tactile graphic. When the TTP pen is touched to a tactile graphic that is covered in a very fine, nearly invisible dot pattern, it can locate itself on the graphic and play audio to the user [22]. The pen form-factor enables the TTP to be considerably more portable than the TTT and IVEO, but still requires the specialized Livescribe Plus Pen hardware.

In contrast to the TTT, IVEO, TTP, and CamIO, which require specialized hardware and/or connection to a computer, Tactile Graphics with a Voice (TGV) runs on a smart phone and can read information from QR codes placed on tactile graphics [3]. The main motivation for TGV is to remove braille labels from tactile graphics, which often clutter the tactile graphic and can be awkwardly placed to avoid intersecting with graphic elements. Replacing the braille labels with QR codes enables the user to access the label information on demand by pointing the cell phone at the QR code. However, this requires the user to aim a camera, which can be difficult for blind users [31, 20, 37, 36], and use one of their hands to hold the camera, preventing two-handed exploration of the tactile graphic, which can be necessary for good performance [26].

3. TACTILE GRAPHICS HELPER (TGH)

The Tactile Graphics Helper (TGH) involves a mounted camera placed across the tactile graphic from the user, which views the tactile graphic and the user's hands (Fig. 1). Although our current prototype runs on a computer, like the TTT, IVEO, and CamIO, our eventual goal is to port TGH to a stand-alone tablet. The tablet could be propped upright and use a mirror to point the camera towards the workspace, using hardware similar to [1].

Figure 1: Layout of student using TGH.

Using computer vision, TGH recognizes the tactile graphic and tracks the user's fingers to allow for a natural hands-free interface between the user and TGH. This keeps the user's hands free to explore the tactile graphic. The user can verbally ask TGH for information about the tactile graphic, such as details about what the user is pointing to. Future implementations may allow TGH to accept gesture commands.

3.1 Stored Tactile Graphics Information

TGH must know some things about a tactile graphic before it can be used with that tactile graphics. The information TGH needs includes (1) a matrix map that associates every pixel in the graphic with a label ID and (2) a YAML file describing the attributes associated with each label ID. These data are created through a short manual process (approximately 10 minutes per graphic) prior to TGH use. First, TGH takes a picture of the tactile graphic and automatically crops and rectifies the image (detailed in Sec. 3.2). A human worker then loads the cropped and rectified image into a custom annotation graphical user interface (GUI), which automatically creates an empty matrix map for the image, where each cell corresponds to an image pixel laid out topographically, with the corners of the matrix to the image's corners. The pixel size of the map, which can be changed by changing the resolution of the photograph, partially determines TGH's ability to resolve locations in the tactile graphic.

Using the annotation GUI, the human worker marks regions of the tactile graphic image with colors using a Microsoft Paint type interface, Fig. 2.

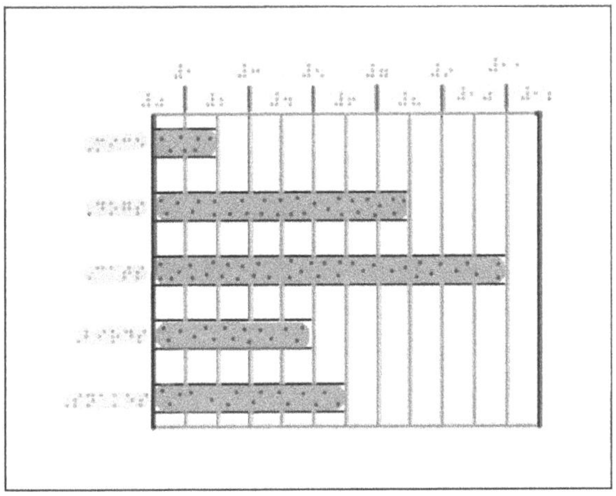

Figure 2: Tactile graphic shown in black, colors are worker-generated label IDs placed in the matrix map.

Each color corresponds to a label ID that is recorded in the corresponding pixels in the matrix map. The worker indicates for each label ID (color) the region's title, type (line, area, text, or point), characteristics (e.g., solid or dotted), function (e.g., tick mark or axis line), and quantity. The label ID information is stored in a YAML file, Fig. 3. Future implementations of TGH could generate a matrix map and YAML file as part of automatic tactile graphic creation (e.g., the systems proposed by [17, 25]).

The person annotating the tactile graphic using the annotation GUI, presumably a teacher, is shielded from the implementation details of the ID matrix map and the ID information YAML file. The GUI (Fig. 4) presents the tactile graphic (Fig. 4 left), on which the user marks each region/feature with a unique color, and a properties list (Fig. 4 right), in which the user associates each color with information about the region title, type, etc. The GUI user can

```
%YAML:1.0
Info:
    Matrix_Map_Filename: "TG_bars_matrix.txt"
    Reference_Image_Filename: "TG_bars_image.bmp"
    YAML_Filename: "TG_bars_description.yaml"
    Type: "Bar Graph"
    Title: "Animals in Pet Shop"
Features:
    F_1:
        Label ID: 1
        Title: "Data Bars"
        Type: "Area"
        Texture: "Dotted"
        Quantity: 5
  ...
```

Figure 3: Label IDs are described in YAML (excerpt).

enter information customized to the intended tactile-graphic user. For example, braille could be annotated to include the braille contents and/or the text's function (label, title, etc.). The current annotation GUI was implemented in Matlab.

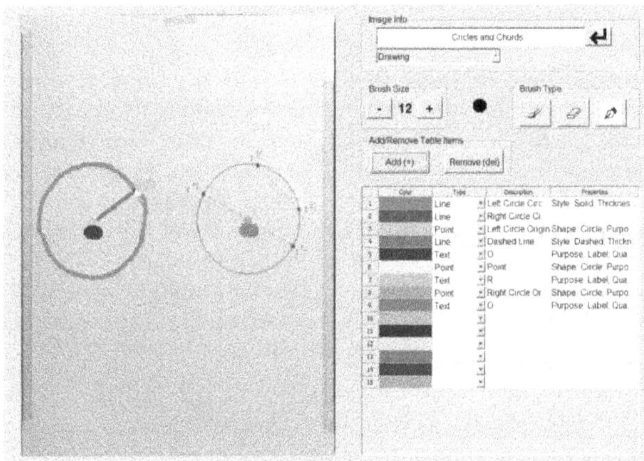

Figure 4: Annotation GUI.

Unlike previous approaches to audio-tactile graphics, with the exception of CamIO, TGH recognizes the tactile graphic and tracks the user's fingers using a mounted camera to allow for a natural hands-free interface between the user and TGH. This keeps the user's hands free to explore the tactile graphic. The user can verbally (or gesturally, in future implementations) ask TGH for information about the tactile graphic, such as details about what the user is pointing to. TGH does not require specialized hardware, and aims to allow individuals creating and annotating tactile graphics (teachers) to do so easily. One reason (provided by professionals in Sec. 4) for the low adoption of the TTP and TTT/IVEO, which are the most similar approaches to TGH, is that these technologies require specialized hardware and content is difficult (TTT/IVEO) or impossible (TTP) for teachers to author. For this reason, TGH will include not only tablet but also annotation technology, designed to allow teachers to easily author TGH tactile-graphic content.

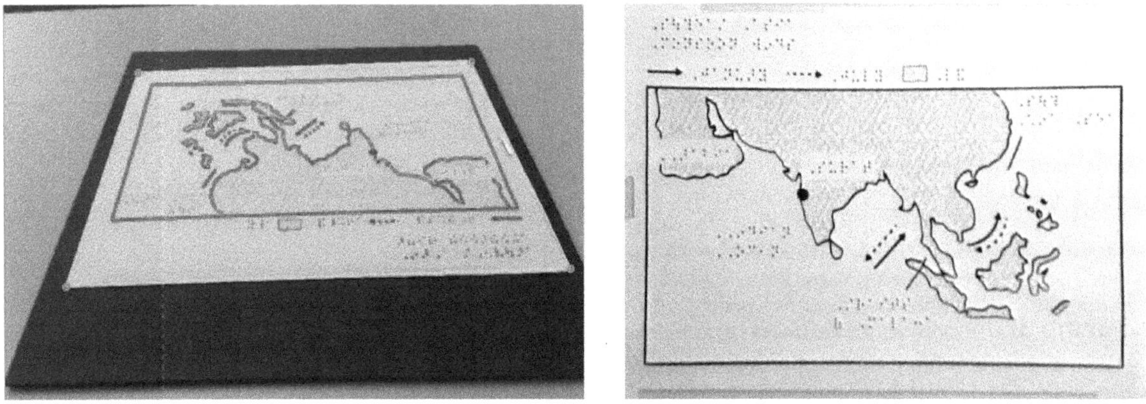

(a) TGH view, detected contour (cyan) and corners (red)

(b) Rectified graphic

Figure 5: Detection and rectification of a tactile graphic.

3.2 Locating and Rectifying a Graphic

TGH requires a brief (approximately 3 second) initialization procedure to locate and rectify (remove projective and affine distortions) a tactile graphic before the user can begin exploring the tactile graphic with his/her hands. This procedure involves placing the tactile graphic within the camera's field of view, in what will be its permanent position. TGH locates the graphic by applying an edge detector [8] to the camera input, and detecting closed convex contours that have lengths within a specified range (the approximate size of the graphic). The longest contour with a four-vertex polygonal curve approximation (i.e., a rectangle) is recognized as the graphic's outer edge. TGH uses the four vertices, which constitute the graphic's corners, to create a rectified image of the tactile graphic (Fig. 5), which it associates with a stored matrix map of label IDs.

3.3 Fingertip Tracking

Finger tracking involves segmenting the user's hands from the background tactile graphic, and then identifying fingertips on the hands. The quality of the segmentation determines the reliability of the subsequent fingertip detection algorithm. Segmentation is accomplished with the background/foreground segmentation algorithm presented in [19], using 20 gray-scale training frames (collected right before the user begins exploring the tactile graphic) to build a distribution of the background's intensity values at each pixel. During tactile graphic exploration, pixels are classified as belonging to the user's hand if the intensity differs significantly from the background mean. Drops in segmentation performance can be caused by video compression and hard shadows, and necessitates using the estimated foreground mask as initialization for a secondary hue-based hand segmentation. In practice, this produces robust segmentation results in homogeneous lighting conditions (i.e., single color light sources).

Once a blob (foreground mask) of a hand is extracted (Fig. 6(b)), TGH applies a distance transform to the binary image to extract ridges (Fig. 6(c)). Ridges are then fit with lines using Ordinary Least Squares. Lines that are too short to be fingers are discarded, while the rest are marked as candidate fingers. Fingertips are located at one of the ends of each line, the end with a ridge value smaller than a pre-chosen threshold. The tracking algorithm also discards candidate fingertips that appear for less than 5 consecutive frames, in order to minimize false detections.

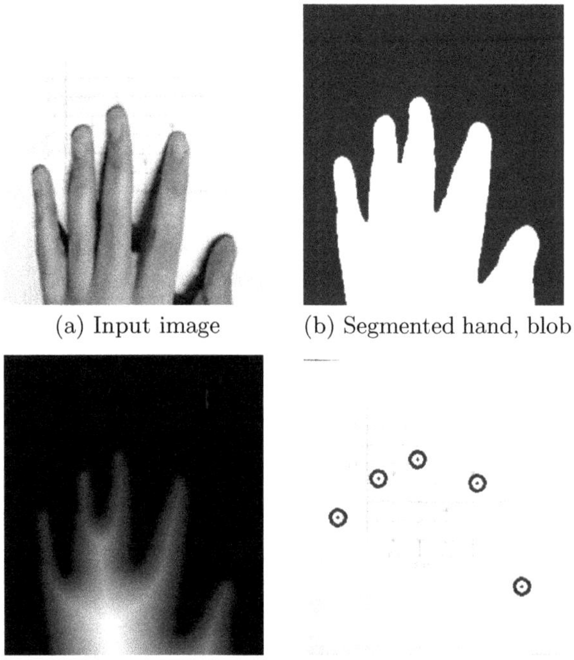

(a) Input image

(b) Segmented hand, blob

(c) Distance transformed blob

(d) Detected fingertips on input image

Figure 6: Example of fingertip detection.

3.4 Voice Commands and Response

Users can interact with TGH using voice commands for hands-free audio information about a tactile graphics. TGH performs voice recognition and speech synthesis using Voce [30]. Currently, TGH responds to the commands "what is there?" which prompts TGH to list all of the titles of features and their quantities contained within the graphic's YAML file, and "what is this?" which prompts TGH to state the title of the tactile-graphic element/feature the user is pointing to. If the user asks "what's this" while pointing with one finger, TGH places the fingertip location within the stored matrix map to retrieve the closest label ID, and then retrieves the ID's title from the YAML file. If the user has multiple fingers extended, TGH cannot resolve what the user is pointing to and says "please use one finger." If TGH cannot detect any fingertips, it states "I can't see your finger."

4. FEEDBACK FROM TACTILE GRAPHICS PROFESSIONALS

To guide our research approach, we solicited feedback from two professionals who are regarded as experts in visual-impairment accessibility, based on multiple years of experience working with students with visual impairments and engagement with professional networks by authoring newsletters and peer-reviewed publications. The first professional watched the researchers use TGH, and the second professional used TGH herself. We described our goals for TGH to these professionals and asked for feedback in an unstructured interview. Both professionals indicated that they had not worked with students who were using audio-tactile graphics.

The first professional, who worked mainly with primary and secondary school students, liked our general approach and confirmed that tactile graphics often contain formatting that prevent students from efficiently accessing educational content. He suggested that TGH should provide three distinct functions: (1) clarifying tactile graphic information (our original intention), (2) previewing tactile graphics (prompting us to add the "what is there" command), and (3) promotion of effective tactile exploration strategies. He explained that students cannot just "go" when given a tactile graphic, they need to be oriented to the graphic through a process referred to as "previewing," which involves orienting the student towards graphic elements, such as the location of axes and labels, and ensuring that the student can grasp these elements' content and function [21, 12]. Previewing is generally executed by an educational assistant or a braillist who works with the student hourly. Ultimately, students should learn to preview graphics on their own, but TGH could preview graphics for younger students, and could help older students complete school work with graphics more efficiently.

The second professional worked mainly with university students, and indicated that the ability to easily author audio information, by professionals and non-experts, was extremely important. The difficulty of authoring content prevented her and her colleagues from adopting technologies like the TTP. She felt that the time required to annotate tactile graphics (approximately 10 minutes) would not be problematic, because this was relatively short compared to how long it took to design a tactile graphic (one to several hours). Regarding the type of information provided by TGH, she suggested that personalization depending on student needs or context was very important. For example, more information could be provided for homework graphics and less on exam graphics. She felt it was unlikely that students would use TGH in a college classroom, given their limited desk space. She also suggested that the system should have the option to subvert audio input, using instead either a gesture or keyboard interface.

5. MIXED-METHODS CASE STUDIES

5.1 Methods

To investigate whether format issues prevent access to content in tactile graphics for university STEM students, and whether TGH could be helpful in these situations, we used an embedded mixed-methods case study design. Although case studies can be defined in a variety of ways by different authors, we use the definition as laid out in [10, ch. 3], which recommends that researchers should recruit/analyze no more than four or five cases (and often a single-case design is sufficient). The mixed-methods aspect of our approach allowed us to triangulate (corroborate) evidence of format issues and possible uses of TGH, using both qualitative and quantitative data [7].

This research adopted a fixed design, where the procedures of the study were planned in advance [10]. Each participant completed in order: (1) an initial semi-structured interview about the participant's general demographic information, his/her visual impairment, and experiences with tactile graphics; (2) an experiment in which the participant explored and answered questions about tactile graphics both using and not using TGH; and (3) a final semi-structured interview to gather the participant's impressions about TGH and its intended purpose. All procedures were video recorded and later transcribed.

Three participants were chosen because they were university students with STEM majors who used tactile graphics. All participants had directional light perception and could detect some form (e.g., the location of a window during the day in a dark room). The participants had no disabilities other than visual impairments. Similarities between the participants were desired to provide literal replication of results [33]. The Smith-Kettlewell Eye Research Institute approved the study's procedures, and participants provided informed consent to participate in this research.

The purpose of the intruding experiment within the context of a qualitative multi-case study was to examine whether participants' reports about format issues could be observed in practice and to document their performance with TGH. This also allowed participants to ground their final interviews in recent tactile-graphics experiences. The experiment involved one practice (scatter plot) tactile graphic using TGH, and six testing tactile graphics. All tactile graphics were adapted from available educational and assessment materials, and were therefore similar to those commonly used by students with visual impairments. These tactile graphics were chosen because TGH is designed to be used with conventional (non-audio) tactile graphics that are already available to students. Tactile graphics were produced on 8.5 x 11 in. swell paper, and annotated by the researchers using the annotation GUI (Sec. 3.1).

The six testing items consisted of two geometry graphics: (1) two side-by-side sand timers depicting types of symmetry, (2) two side-by-side circles depicting chords; two data plots: (3) a bar chart, (4) a line graph; and two maps: (5) drought in Africa, and (6) monsoon winds in Southeast Asia. (Items 1, 4, and 5 are shown in Fig. 7, item 2 can be seen in Fig. 4, item 3 can be seen in Fig. 2, and item 6 can be seen in Fig. 5.) Participants used TGH on half of the graphics, one randomly selected from each type. Geometry graphics were always first, data graphics second, and maps third, but otherwise the order was random. The participants were allowed to explore each graphic for as long as they wished before being asked 3-5 format-related questions, e.g., "what do the solid arrows represent?" and 2-3 content-related questions, e.g., "how many more snakes are there than mice?" The specific questions were pre-determined and fixed for each tactile graphic: 3 format and 2 content questions for geometry items, 3 format and 3 content questions for the graphs, and 5 format and 2 content questions for the maps. These were chosen as afforded by the individual tactile graphics.

5.1.1 *Analysis*

Theoretical thematic analysis [6] was used to identify themes in the transcriptions related to tactile graphics and TGH. Both authors examined the data and agreed on a codebook that included the themes:

1. Opinions about tactile graphics, positive or negative.
2. Opinions about TGH, positive, negative, or wanting additional functionality.
3. Errors or uncertainties with tactile graphic format, content, or exploration strategies.
4. Using TGH to get or confirm information.
5. Mishearing TGH information or forgetting commands.

The last three themes (3-5) were behaviors that could occur during the experiment, and not during interviews. Themes 1-2 could appear throughout the entire procedure.

Using the codebook with rules for coding, the authors coded 30% of the data. Excellent levels of reliability [9] were obtained ($\kappa = 0.90$, % agreement = 91%), and the second author coded the remaining data.

5.2 Participant Descriptions

P1 was a college Junior (20 years old) studying Earth Science and Statistics. His visual impairment was due to Retinitis Pigmentosa (RP), which caused gradual vision loss starting at five years old. Although he had a vision teacher since the age of five, P1 began learning braille at 15, and had taught himself contracted (grade 2) braille and Nemeth using information from the Internet. He also reported no specific lessons with tactile graphics. As part of his school work, P1 used approximately 50 tactile graphics per week. He only used graphics outside of class, because they were "not ready in time" to be used during lecture.

P2 was a college senior (23 years old) studying Psychology. Onset of vision loss was at birth due to Leber's Congenital Amaurosis (LCA). She had briefly used magnified print graphics in high school when studying AP (college-level) calculus, because "they didn't have enough resources to make [tactile graphics] in a timely fashion." However, in all other circumstances she had used tactile graphics. Despite having a vision teacher since the age of five, and having explicit lessons in Nemeth, P2 reported no specific instruction with tactile graphics. As part of her school work, P2 used approximately 20 tactile graphics per week. She rarely used tactile graphics in class because "by the time you find the tactile graphic, they're already on the fifth one." She also did not use tactile graphics for non-school purposes.

P3 was a college junior (21 years old) studying Linguistics. Onset of vision loss was at birth due to LCA. She had a vision teacher since she was three years old. However, by the time P3 reached high school, her vision teacher only provided braille materials and did not have specific time set aside for instruction. P3 indicated that she started learning braille at three years old, Nemeth at five years old, and tactile graphics at four years old. P3 was the only participant who reported receiving specific instruction with tactile graphics, beginning with simple shapes when she was four years old. However, P3 infrequently used tactile graphics. She reported that there were isolated courses that necessitated using about one tactile graphic per week in class, to study syntactic trees and the Persian alphabet. She did not use graphics more than about once per month for schoolwork outside of class. However, unlike the other participants, she reported using tactile graphics for personal use, roughly twice a month she would "look in [her] atlas."

5.3 Qualitative Results

5.3.1 *Opinions About Tactile Graphics*

Participants indicated that they all liked tactile graphics, and found them useful for their STEM courses. However, they complained that tactile graphics are slow to read and produce, and not readily available. Furthermore, all three participants indicated that they had experienced format-related difficulties with tactile graphics. For example, P1 recalled a situation with an arrow placed on top of a longer dotted line, making the two difficult to tell apart. P2 reported that it was difficult to differentiate brain structures in her anatomy diagrams, and P3 similarly felt that there was often too much detail put on graphics, which "mushed together" and made the graphics difficult to understand. In general, the participants agreed that they had experienced ongoing and past issues with lines and textures that were difficult to tell apart, elements placed too close together, and text in confusing locations. When asked how they typically overcome these format issues, all of the participants indicated that they ask for sighted assistance.

P2 and P3 were particularly concerned with 3D geometric figures in tactile graphics, such as line drawings of cylinders and pyramids. This issue was brought up repeatedly, especially by P3, who recalled that she had failed a test in elementary school due to these types of graphics. She suggested that this issue could be helped by TGH indicating surfaces as front, back, left, etc., and similarly with edges.

5.3.2 *Opinions About TGH*

All three participants thought that TGH could help with tactile-graphic format problems, including clarifying 3D figures. Participants imagined that they would use the system mostly for homework, and not in class. However P1 suggested that if the system could respond to gesture commands, he might use TGH in class to ask questions about tactile graphics without disturbing his classmates.

All of the participants disliked TGH's reliance on audio/voice input and output. The voice input created reliability problems in noisy settings. Participants wanted to have control over the voice output speed, and the ability to pause output to process information. Neither of these functions were possible with the current prototype.

The participants disagreed about what type of information they wanted TGH to provide. Both P2 and P3 liked that TGH would tell them the function of braille (e.g., "title") without reading the braille. In contrast, P1 insisted,

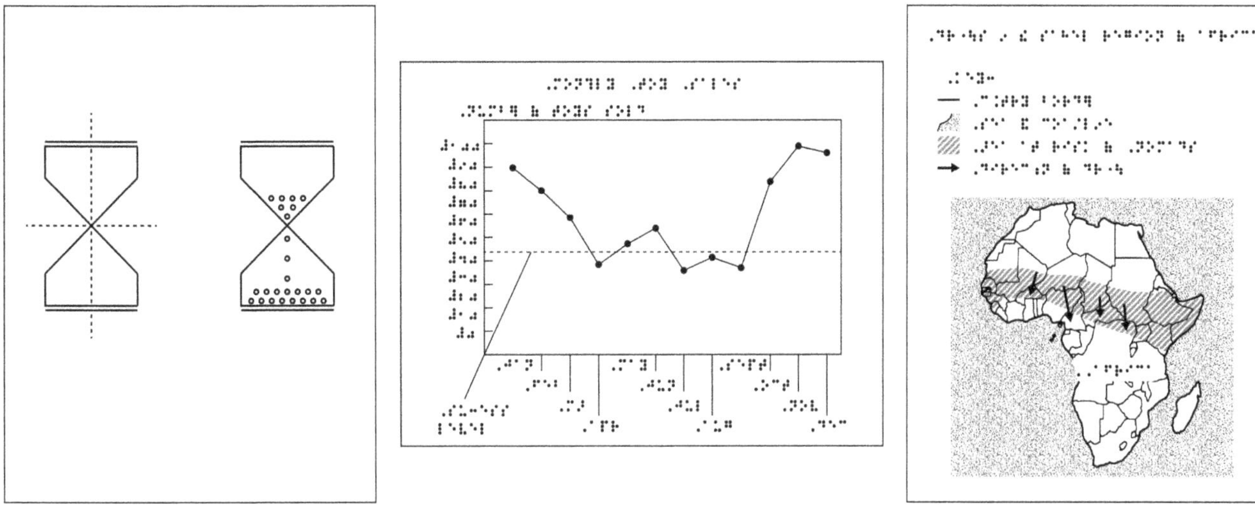

Figure 7: Three of the six test tactile graphics in the user study.

"if I point to a word, I want it to read it out. Sometimes I'm lazy." There was a similar disagreement over textures, with P3 wanting textures to be indicated as "rough" and "smooth," and P2 preferring "water" and "land." However, P3 later suggested that TGH could provide information not printed on tactile graphics, such as the name of unlabeled countries. Not only did the participants disagree about what type of information should be provided by TGH, but participants' opinions were not consistent.

5.3.3 *Tactile Graphics Errors*

A consistent error across participants occurred when we asked them to point to the city of Surat and the location of the South China Sea on the map of Southeast Asia (Fig. 5). All participants initially pointed to the braille label and not to locations marked with the relevant point symbol (dot) or label line, and only P1 corrected himself. The participants also had difficulty in locating months associated with data points in the line graph (Fig. 7), because it was difficult for participants to move in a straight line between the data points and x-tickmark labels. Finally, all participants had difficulties differentiating the lined and stippled textures on the Africa map, difficulties locating the arrows within the lined texture on the Africa map, and struggled to understand the function of the label line on the line graph. For example, when asked for the meaning of the solid line in the lower left on the line graph (a label line), P2 responded that "it looks like a slope of some sort. I don't know what it is for."

5.3.4 *Using TGH*

Participants used TGH to both confirm and get information about the tactile graphics. For example, P2 indicated that she suspected the band across Africa was the lined texture, but could not easily differentiate this from the stippled (water) texture, so she confirmed this using TGH. P1 also successfully used TGH to figure out that the solid line in the lower left of the line graph was a label line, used to label the dashed horizontal line as "success level."

The participants relied on TGH to "preview" the tactile graphic before exploring, by asking "what is there?" P1 was explicit about this, explaining to the researchers on the first graphic that he would always ask TGH for this information right away, and then systematically explore the graphic by examining the axes, then axes labels, etc. The information learned about the graphic from previewing was often repeated verbatim as answers to questions, without the participant checking the graphic to confirm the information was correct. For example, when asked how many bars there were on the bar chart, P2 said "the machine told me five. I was too lazy to count."

P3 was unique in that she asked TGH a large number of questions to see how it would respond to ambiguous situations, such as a point of intersection for multiple axes and lines, and the space between gridlines (in non-annotated empty space TGH says "nothing"). She typically embarked on this exercise after using TGH to gather more typical information about the graphic. Only P2 had issues forgetting TGH commands or mishearing TGH responses, and these occurred only once each.

5.4 Quantitative Results

The amount of time participants explored graphics before saying they were ready for questions is shown in Table 1.

Table 1: Exploration time in seconds.

	TGH	Geometry		Graphs		Maps	
P1	with	Circles:	162	Line:	176	Asia:	268
	w/o	Timers:	34	Bar:	100	Africa:	268
P2	with	Timers:	75	Bar:	118	Africa:	122
	w/o	Circles:	20	Line:	37	Asia:	60
P3	with	Timers:	237	Bar:	318	Asia:	914
	w/o	Circles:	36	Line:	159	Africa:	184

Exploration times were modeled with a linear mixed effects model, with a random effect of participant (SD = 134.71, 95% CI: 94.18, 192.66) and fixed effects of type (geometry, data, or map) and TGH (with or without). The model revealed a significant main effect of type $F(2, 15) = 3.84$, $p = 0.045$, and a significant effect of TGH $F(1, 15) = 6.82$, $p = 0.020$, $est = -82.89$ ($SE = 31.75$). Overall, participants spent more time exploring graphics when using TGH than without.

The time spent exploring graphics was likely related to the number of questions participants asked TGH (Table 2).

Table 2: Number of times participants asked TGH "what is there?" and "what is this?" separated by commas.

	Geometry		Graphs		Maps	
P1	Circles:	1, 1	Line:	1, 1	Asia:	1, 2
P2	Timers:	1, 2	Bar:	1, 3	Africa:	1, 5
P3	Timers:	1, 14	Bar:	1, 12	Asia:	1, 19

Accuracy results are shown in Table 3. With so few questions asked of each participant, the accuracy data did not reveal any significant quantitative trends. A linear mixed effects model did not reveal a significant effect of type $F(2,14) = 0.04$, $p = 0.959$, nor a significant effect of TGH $F(1,14) = 0.25$, $p = 0.62$ on accuracy.

Table 3: Accuracy (%).

	TGH	Geometry		Graphs		Maps	
P1	with	Circles:	80	Line:	50	Asia:	86
	w/o	Timers:	40	Bar:	100	Africa:	100
P2	with	Timers:	100	Bar:	100	Africa:	100
	w/o	Circles:	60	Line:	17	Asia:	71
P3	with	Timers:	100	Bar:	100	Asia:	43
	w/o	Circles:	100	Line:	100	Africa:	100

6. DISCUSSION

This research confirms that tactile-graphic format issues pose accessibility hurdles for university STEM students with visual impairments. Format issues include lines and textures that are difficult to tell apart, tactile elements that are placed too close together, and text in confusing locations. Furthermore, we confirmed that TGH can help students overcome these issues. Students reported that they often received their tactile graphics late, due to the time it takes to produce them. Therefore, TGH may be most useful for students with visual impairments when they are reviewing tactile graphics at a later time than they were covered in class. It is possible that students may find TGH particularly helpful in this situation, when they are working with tactile graphics out of context.

Previous research documenting student difficulties with tactile-graphic formatting addressed tactile graphics broadly, did not focus on STEM, and included only students in primary and secondary education, not post-secondary [2, 35]. Our finding that university STEM students continue to struggle with tactile-graphic formatting highlights the severity of this issue - if these students have problems, students who are younger and have less experience in STEM are likely to be struggling even more. Future work is needed to establish whether TGH can support younger and less advanced students. However, based on feedback from the current participants that they would have liked such a system when they were younger (e.g., for 3D figures), we are optimistic that TGH can benefit students with visual impairments from a range of educational levels.

Participants explored tactile graphics longer when using TGH than without TGH. This likely reflects more thorough examination of the tactile graphics when using TGH. When not using TGH, participants may have waited to explore a tactile graphic until they were asked questions about the graphic. Additionally, participants' exploration times may have been extended by their interest in testing TGH's capabilities (e.g., the number of times P3 asked "what's this?" shown in Table 2).

The aim of this work was to establish whether format issues in tactile graphics presented barriers to advanced STEM students with visual impairments, and if an approach such as that used with TGH has potential to prevent these problems. All participants indicated that TGH was helpful, and there were examples of each participant relying on TGH for information or clarification. Now that this has been established, future work can be done to develop a more thorough TGH technology solution and evaluation with a large number of participants.

6.1 Future Work

Based on feedback from one professional on previewing tactile graphics, TGH listed tactile graphic features when asked "what is there?". This implementation of previewing is not as comprehensive as what a teacher would do with a student, but participants found it very useful. By extending the finger tracking capabilities, TGH could provide a previewing experience more similar to what a teacher provides, e.g., asking the student to locate features on the graphic. TGH could also be used to encourage students to use effective tactile exploration skills, such as exploring the graphic systematically and using both hands.

Another area of development worth pursuing is adding gesture recognition, a keyboard interface, or virtual buttons, e.g., [20], to replace voice commands. This would allow students to use TGH without issuing voice commands, making the system usable in a noisy setting and less disruptive in a classroom.

6.2 Technology Limitations

There are several ways TGH could be improved, based on participants' opinions and errors. To be more useful, TGH needed to inform students when labels are associated with point symbols or label lines, because all students wrongly pointed to braille labels when asked to point to locations. The system should also allow greater control over the audio output. Finally, different modes of operation or personalization would allow teachers and students to decide the level of detail and type of information TGH provides, which may depend on the abilities of the student (e.g., low or high tactile acuity), the educational goal of the graphic, and context (e.g., homework versus test).

In the current implementation, customization is possible through the tactile-graphic annotation that is created by a human worker (described in Sec. 3.1). However, customization could also be implemented on the tactile-graphic user's end, perhaps by restricting or preferentially presenting certain types of information.

6.3 Conclusions

In conclusion, our findings highlight the format-related issues students encounter with tactile graphics, including line styles or textures that feel too similar to tell apart, features that are too dense to individually discriminate, and awkward placement of braille labels and label lines. These problems are commonplace in STEM graphics and cause persistent access issues for even advanced university students who rely on numerous graphics (20-50 per week) for educational content. Replacing sighted assistance with a machine-vision system to clarify tactile-graphic format issues was largely successful, although there is room for improvement. With further refinement, TGH should be able to improve students' skills and efficiency in accessing educational content contained in tactile graphics.

7. ACKNOWLEDGMENTS

We thank Dr. Huiying Shen for the approach and initial implementation of our finger detection procedure, and Anita Tung for illustrations.This work was funded by the National Institute on Disability, Independent Living, and Rehabilitation Research (NIDILRR), grant 90RE5008-01-00. The opinions expressed are those of the authors and do not represent the views of NIDILRR.

8. REFERENCES

[1] Osmo - Award-Winning Educational Games System for iPad. `http://www.playosmo.com/`.

[2] F. K. Aldrich and L. Sheppard. Tactile graphics in school education: Perspectives from pupils. *British Journal of Visual Impairment*, 19(2):69–73, 2001.

[3] C. M. Baker, L. R. Milne, J. Scofield, C. L. Bennett, and R. E. Ladner. Tactile graphics with a voice: using QR codes to access text in tactile graphics. In *Proceedings of the 16th International ACM SIGACCESS Conference on Computers and Accessibility*, ASSETS '14, pages 75–82. ACM, 2014.

[4] B. Beck-Winchatz and M. A. Riccobono. Advancing participation of blind students in science, technology, engineering, and math. *Advances in Space Research*, 42(11):1855–1858, 2008.

[5] P. Blenkhorn and D. Evans. A system for reading and producing talking tactile maps and diagrams. In *Proceedings of the 9th International Conference on Tecnology and Persons with Disabilities (CSUN)*, volume 94, pages 16–19, 1994.

[6] V. Braun and V. Clarke. Using thematic analysis in psychology. *Qualitative Research in Psychology*, 3(2):77–101, 2006.

[7] A. Bryman. Integrating quantitative and qualitative research: how is it done? *Qualitative Research*, 6(1):97–113, 2006.

[8] J. Canny. A computational approach to edge detection. *IEEE Transactions on Pattern Analysis and Machine Intelligence*, PAMI-8(6):679–698, Nov 1986.

[9] J. Cohen. A coefficient of agreement for nominal scales. *Educational and Psychological Measurement*, 20(1):37–46, 1960.

[10] J. W. Creswell and V. L. Plano Clark. *Designing and conducting mixed methods research.* Thousand Oaks, CA: SAGE Publications, 2007.

[11] T. Dick and E. Kubiak. Issues and aids for teaching mathematics to the blind. *The Mathematics Teacher*, 90(5):344–349, 1997.

[12] P. Edman. *Tactile graphics.* American Foundation for the Blind, 1992.

[13] J. A. Gardner and V. Bulatov. Scientific diagrams made easy with IVEO^{TM}. In *Computers Helping People with Special Needs*, pages 1243–1250. Springer, 2006.

[14] M. Gattis and K. J. Holyoak. Mapping conceptual to spatial relations in visual reasoning. *Journal of Experimental Psychology: Learning, Memory, and Cognition*, 22(1):231–239, 1996.

[15] H. B. Gonzalez and J. J. Kuenzi. Science, technology, engineering, and mathematics (STEM) education: A primer. Congressional Research Service, Library of Congress, 2012.

[16] R. D. Jacobson. Navigating maps with little or no sight: An audio-tactile approach. In *Proceedings of the Workshop on Content Visualization and Intermedia Representations (CVIR)*, 1998.

[17] C. Jayant, M. Renzelmann, D. Wen, S. Krisnandi, R. Ladner, and D. Comden. Automated tactile graphics translation: in the field. In *Proceedings of the 9th International ACM SIGACCESS Conference on Computers and Accessibility*, ASSETS '07, pages 75–82. ACM, 2007.

[18] M. G. Jones, J. Minogue, T. Oppewal, M. P. Cook, and B. Broadwell. Visualizing without vision at the microscale: Students with visual impairments explore cells with touch. *Journal of Science Education and Technology*, 15(5-6):345–351, 2006.

[19] C. R. Jung. Efficient background subtraction and shadow removal for monochromatic video sequences. *IEEE Transactions on Multimedia*, 11(3):571–577, April 2009.

[20] S. K. Kane, B. Frey, and J. O. Wobbrock. Access lens: a gesture-based screen reader for real-world documents. In *Proceedings of the SIGCHI Conference on Human Factors in Computing Systems*, pages 347–350. ACM, 2013.

[21] A. J. Koenig and M. C. Holbrook. *Foundations of education: Instructional strategies for teaching children and youths with visual impairments*, volume 2. American Foundation for the Blind, 2000.

[22] S. Landau, G. Bourquin, J. Miele, and A. Van Schaack. Demonstration of a universally accessible audio-haptic transit map built on a digital pen-based platform. In *Proceedings of the 3rd International Workshop on Haptic and Audio Interaction Design*, pages 23–24, 2008.

[23] S. Landau and K. Gourgey. Development of a talking tactile tablet. *Information Technology and Disabilities*, 7(2), 2001.

[24] G. Leinhardt, O. Zaslavsky, and M. K. Stein. Functions, graphs, and graphing: Tasks, learning, and teaching. *Review of Educational Research*, 60(1):1–64, 1990.

[25] K. Minatani. A proposal for an automated method to produce embossed graphics for blind persons. In C. Stephanidis and M. Antona, editors, *Universal Access in Human-Computer Interaction. Universal Access to Information and Knowledge*, volume 8514 of *Lecture Notes in Computer Science*, pages 144–153. Springer International Publishing, 2014.

[26] V. Morash, A. E. Connell Pensky, S. T. W. Tseng, and J. A. Miele. Effects of using multiple hands and

fingers on haptic performance in individuals who are blind. *Perception*, 43(7):569–588, 2013.

[27] D. Parkes. Nomad: An audio-tactile tool for the acquisition, use and management of spatially distributed information by visually impaired people. In *Proceedings of the 2nd International Symposium on Maps and Graphics for Visually Handicapped People*, 1988.

[28] H. Shen, O. Edwards, J. Miele, and J. M. Coughlan. Camio: A 3D computer vision system enabling audio/haptic interaction with physical objects by blind users. In *Proceedings of the 15th International ACM SIGACCESS Conference on Computers and Accessibility*, ASSETS '13, pages 41:1–41:2, New York, NY, USA, 2013. ACM.

[29] D. W. Smith and S. M. Smothers. The role and characteristics of tactile graphics in secondary mathematics and science textbooks in braille. *Journal of Visual Impairment & Blindness*, 106(9):543–554, 2012.

[30] T. Streeter. Voce: Open source speech interaction. `http://voce.sourceforge.net/`.

[31] S. White, H. Ji, and J. P. Bigham. Easysnap: Real-time audio feedback for blind photography. In *Adjunct Proceedings of the 23rd Annual ACM Symposium on User Interface Software and Technology*, UIST '10, pages 409–410, New York, NY, USA, 2010. ACM.

[32] M. C. Wood, J. Marggraff, M. Brown, and M. Fishbach. Interactive learning appliance, Oct. 5 2004. US Patent 6,801,751.

[33] R. K. Yin. *Case study research design and methods.* Newbury Park, CA: SAGE Publications, second edition.

[34] K. T. Zebehazy and A. P. Wilton. Scharting success: The experience of teachers of students with visual impairments in promoting student use of graphics. *Journal of Visual Impairment & Blindness*, 108(4):263–274, 2014.

[35] K. T. Zebehazy and A. P. Wilton. Straight from the source: Perceptions of students with visual impairments about graphic use. *Journal of Visual Impairment & Blindness*, 108(4):275–286, 2014.

[36] Y. Zhong, P. J. Garrigues, and J. P. Bigham. Real time object scanning using a mobile phone and cloud-based visual search engine. In *Proceedings of the 15th International ACM SIGACCESS Conference on Computers and Accessibility*, ASSETS '13, pages 20:1–20:8, New York, NY, USA, 2013. ACM.

[37] Y. Zhong, W. S. Lasecki, E. Brady, and J. P. Bigham. Regionspeak: Quick comprehensive spatial descriptions of complex images for blind users. In *Proceedings of the 33rd Annual ACM Conference on Human Factors in Computing Systems*, CHI '15, pages 2353–2362, New York, NY, USA, 2015. ACM.

ChartMaster: a Tool for Interacting with Stock Market Charts using a Screen Reader

Hong Zou
MDes (Inclusive Design)
OCAD University
205, Richmond St., Toronto, Canada
+1 416 821 9568
hz03qb@student.ocadu.ca

Jutta Treviranus
Director, Inclusive Design Research Centre
Professor, OCAD University
205, Richmond St., Toronto, Canada
+1 416 720 6430
jtreviranus@faculty.ocadu.ca

ABSTRACT

Stock market charts guide investors in making financial decisions. Online stock market charts are largely interactive, driven by real-time financial data. However, these are not easily accessible via a screen reader. To enable screen reader users to query and effectively use interactive online stock market charts, we are developing a tool called ChartMaster. In this paper, we describe an early study conducted with sixteen visually impaired persons, most of whom were financial novices, for co-designing the interaction interface for ChartMaster. An inclusive design exercise was undertaken to discover alternative interfaces using non-visual modalities to interact with stock market charts. A user-centered process of co-design using HCI methods was carried out to iteratively evaluate and refine three input solutions: audio input, text input and dropdown menu. While the users ultimately declared the dropdown menu to be the most useful of the three solutions, they wanted all possible options to choose from based on task contexts and personal preferences. User feedback confirmed that a one-size-fits-all design is not ideal for accommodating diverse user needs within the widest possible range of contexts. It was also found that the ChartMaster tool with dropdown menu interface holds potential educational value for financial novices.

Categories and Subject Descriptors

H.5.2 [User interfaces]: Evaluation/methodology, User-centered design. Theory and methods.

General Terms

Performance, Design, Human Factors.

Keywords

Stock market charts; screen reader; non-visual; multi-modal; inclusive design; usability; accessibility; visual impairment; financial literacy.

1. INTRODUCTION

The Global Economics of Disability 2014 annual report indicates that a total of 1.3 billion people with disabilities, including seniors, control $8 trillion in annual disposable income worldwide [10]. Again, between 1983 and the end of 2007, the capitalization of the world stock markets grew by 1,800% and the volume of share trading increased almost a hundred fold, from $1.22 trillion in 1983 to $111.2 trillion during 2007 [14]. However, people with disabilities, despite their financial promise, are disadvantaged in making use of online investment instruments such as stock market charts due to their low accessibility.

Over the last few decades, the stock market has seen dramatic changes, featuring a rapid growth in capitalization and trading activities, as well as increase in the number of self-directed investors worldwide. Making effective and responsible investment decisions requires research about a financial product's features and risks and the overall financial context [2]. With advances in technology, the stock market chart, one of the major tools investors use to predict the future trend of stocks, has gone through a major makeover in the past decades. Static charts have been replaced with interactive charts that enable investors to perceive, compare and analyze data points with merely a few clicks. These interactive charts are dynamic, rendered based on streaming data according to the parameters chosen by users, such as time frame, providing both real-time and historical data instantly.

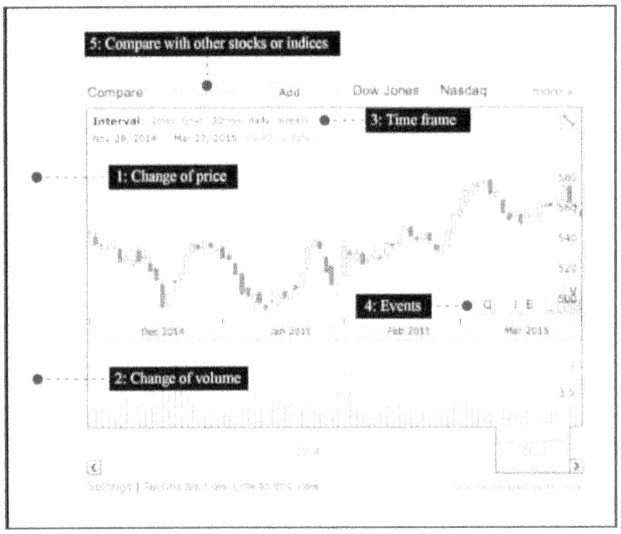

Figure 1: A typical stock market chart (Google Finance)

All interactive stock market charts are similar in structure (Figure 1) and have five components:

1. A line graph on the top of the chart presenting the change in price.

ASSETS '15, October 26-28, 2015, Lisbon, Portugal
© 2015 ACM. ISBN 978-1-4503-3400-6/15/10…$15.00
DOI: http://dx.doi.org/10.1145/2700648.2809862

2. A bar graph at the bottom presenting the change in volume.
3. Options to define the time frame through which the chart will be rendered.
4. Identifiers for events such as dividend payout, split, or quarterly financial report release.
5. Functions to enable comparison with other stocks or indices.

However, stock market charts are particularly challenging for screen reader users due to sensory, cognitive and emotional barriers. Sensory barriers are caused by the visual design of the chart. For example, some interactive charts use Flash or advanced scripting, that is not always compatible with the user's computer, browser settings, or the assistive technology installed, making it difficult for the user to perceive the charts. Cognitive barriers manifest when users attempt to evaluate, analyze, and comprehend a chart in textual format, such as in a summary or a numeric data table. Such barriers that reduce sensory and cognitive capabilities could also aggravate negative emotional reactions caused by the uncertainty and risk inherent in financial transactions.

In addition, some other features of stock market charts add to problems with accessibility. For example, when sighted users hover over the chart, specific values appear: such as day low, day high, closing, and open price. However, screen reader users can only access these data when presented in a numeric table format. The user must memorize and calculate these values based on the data stream. And, unfortunately, the way screen readers interact with numeric tables doesn't provide enough flexibility for them to get the data they are interested in. The challenge, therefore, is to make the data stream behind the charts easier to access.

This study explored ways to improve the accessibility of stock market charts for screen-reader users. While the overall goal is to develop a tool, ChartMaster, that makes it easier to access stock market charts using a screen reader, the goal of the current study is to design an optimal interface for users to query stock market charts.

This paper first presents a design challenge situated in the context noted above, and outlines the approach and methods adopted to respond to it. It then describes the different steps of the response: preliminary usability inspection, survey of related research, iterative design of alternative interaction interface solutions through four rounds of evaluative refinement, description and discussion of the findings. The contributions of this study, implications for inclusive design and human-computer interaction (HCI), and future work planned are given in the conclusion of the paper.

2. DESIGN CHALLENGE

Information and Communication Technologies (ICT) play a critical role in providing access to not only the web interfaces where transactions are made, but also the financial research tools and information needed for investment decisions. It is often that ICT acts as the only means of accessing or participating in important financial and investment functions and services [24]. In recent years, many studies have analyzed the barriers to financial literacy from cultural, social, and structural perspectives. However, little attention has been paid to the barriers individuals face from an HCI perspective. The design challenge undertaken in this study was to develop an interaction interface to improve the usability and accessibility of stock market charts, with a focus on screen reader users with visual impairments. Adopting an inclusive design approach, this study used an iterative co-design process with target users involving methods from the HCI domain.

2.1 Inclusive Design Approach

The British Standards Institute defines inclusive design as "the design of mainstream products and/or services that are accessible to, and usable by, people with the widest range of abilities within the widest range of situations without the need for special adaptation or design" [17]. This definition clearly suggests that design must accommodate the needs of a diversified user base without the implementation of separate, specialized or segregated solutions.

The Inclusive Design Research Centre (IDRC) in Toronto, Canada, provides a variant of the social approach in their reframing of disability within the design context. Rather than a personal characteristic or a binary state (disabled vs. non-disabled), IDRC frames disability as "a mismatch between the needs of the individual and the design of the product, system or service" [15]. Thus, disability is no longer considered a medical or health condition associated with the individual, but rather the result of social, physical, or political barriers that prevent or hinder an individual's ability to participate fully in society. This shift reflects a common recognition and appreciation of diversity, and in turn helps to drive the design and implementation of inclusive policies, services, and products that fit the needs of a "full range of human diversity with respect to ability, language, culture, gender, age and other forms of human difference" [15].

The IDRC recognizes three dimensions to inclusive design. First, it suggests that the optimal inclusive design should integrate personalization and flexible configurations while supporting "self-determination and self-knowledge." Second, it defines an inclusive design process as one that enables diverse designers and "extreme" users to participate in the design process through accessible and usable processes and tools. Third, it urges designers to look beyond the intended beneficiary and create a design that can trigger a "virtuous cycle of inclusion," which, in turn, will lead to both social and economic equality [15].

Guided by the above three dimensions of inclusive design, this design challenge developed multiple solutions, involved participants with visual impairments who used assistive technologies, and looked beyond screen reader users to include a consideration for novice financial tool users. Insights drawn from the inclusive design domain acted as the guiding principles throughout the research process, from the initial empathic design requirements gathering to the above co-design and evaluation process with user participation.

2.2 Human-Computer Interaction Methods

This study employed usability inspection, usability testing, think-aloud protocol, and iterative user-centered processes. The concept of usability is central to the study of HCI. According to Eason [11], a system should provide utility that is easy to use and learn, thus benefitting the user. For determining usability, the following criteria drawn from the work of noted HCI researchers [19, 23, 4] were used: usefulness (users achieve goals), effectiveness (users operate the system productively), learnability (system provides training) and likeability (users derive high subjective satisfaction).

User-centered design (UCD) is a philosophy that is based on the needs and interests of the user, with an emphasis on making products usable and understandable [19]. This study undertook an iterative UCD process through which the user requirements and design were continuously evaluated and refined. The study implemented the following user-centered design methods and techniques:

1. On-site observation: Collecting information by conducting usability testing in an environment in which the design artifact will be used.
2. Simulations (Wizard of Oz): Evaluating design concepts and gaining insights about users' needs and preferences without creating a working prototype.
3. Usability testing: Collecting user feedback using usability criteria mentioned above.

The design process consisted of three parts:

1. Manual usability inspection of 10 investment research websites using a screen reader.
2. Survey of related research on non-visual approaches to reading charts and graphs.
3. Iterative co-design of three solutions—audio input/audio output, text input/audio output, and dropdown menu—through evaluation and refinement with screen reader users.

These are described in Sections 3, 4 and 5 below, followed by discussion of the findings in Section 6 and concluding remarks.

3. MANUAL USABILITY INSPECTION USING A SCREEN READER

During June and July 2014 an analysis of the accessibility of existing stock market charts in terms of their compliance with the Web Content Accessibility Guideline (WCAG 2.0) was conducted to identify issues that need to be addressed. Manual examination was preferred over the use of automated accessibility checking tools because human judgment ensures accuracy and helps in observing the challenges from the user's perspective [27]. The objectives were:

1. To examine the compliance of current stock market charts with the four WCAG principles: perceivable, operable, understandable, and robust for screen reader users;
2. To specifically check if the stock market charts support accessibility of non-text content by providing both short and long text alternatives that "serve the same purpose and present the same information as the original non-text content." (Technique G92 of WCAG 2.0)

Ten popular investment research websites of comparable functionality (Yahoo Finance, Google Finance, Bloomberg, Wall Street Journal, Morning Star, The Street, CNBC, MSN Money, Financial Post, and The Globe and Mail) were chosen. All of these sites provide interactive charts that allow the user to acquire specific data, such as price, volume, and event in any given time frame, as well as comparison with other symbols/indices.

Usability inspection was conducted using the Jaws screen reader Version 15 from Freedom Scientific along with an HP laptop with Windows 7 operating system. The Jaws screen reader was chosen because a series of studies by WebAIM [28] reported it to be the most popularly used screen reader. The accessibility and usability issues discovered for stock market charts in terms of the four principles of WCAG 2.0—Perceivable, Operable, Understandable and Robust—are described below.

Not perceivable: All ten stock market charts exhibited difficulties in perception via the screen reader. The screen reader could only detect six out of the ten charts; this meant that the users might not even know about their existence. For the remaining four charts, the screen reader could only render the chart legend. In addition, nine out of the ten charts failed to provide a short text description. Yahoo Finance, the only website that provided alternative text for the stock market chart, merely stated, "This is an interactive chart". This terse statement is meaningless to visually impaired users.

WCAG 2.0 recommends providing chart data in a numeric table in the form of a long text description as an accessible equivalent for visual charts. Four out of the ten websites placed the numeric table on a separate page, accessible only through the navigation menu. The other six websites did not include a numeric table at all, which means visually impaired users are completely excluded from acquiring critical information about the price and volume of a stock.

Not operable: The stock market charts were not operable. Advanced scripting enables sighted users to hover the mouse over the chart and acquire specific data points. However, such mouse hovering is not possible using a screen reader. Therefore, the charts are not optimally operable using a screen reader.

Not understandable: It is common practice for a stock market chart to use abbreviations for the legends in the chart. However, when a screen reader read out abbreviations missing appropriate <abbr> attributes, they would often sound like other totally unrelated words. For example, 'Jun' was read as Jone, and 'min' as mean. In addition, where the sequence of the codes did not align with the logical order of content, information read out by the screen reader based on the order of the codes produced confusing output. For example, the following text string, which is part of the chart indicating four variations of the stock price of the Globe and Mail—"Open: 91.11, High: 91.40, Low 90.85, Close 90.92"—was read out as "90.92 close 90.85 low 91.40 high 91.11 open"; this was completely impossible to understand, especially because there were no pauses between data elements. Further, stock market charts were hard to understand even when represented through a numeric table where the information for each data point could be accessed. If each data cell in the numeric table does not include appropriate "ID" or "headers" to associate the data with the corresponding column header, the screen reader will be unable to communicate the table in a meaningful way because all one would hear is number after number without knowing what the number is meant to represent. Thus, the stock market charts were not understandable.

Not robust: Even without testing across different technologies and versions to test robustness, it was apparent from the above three results that stock market charts are not robust enough to be interpreted reliably by the screen reader.

4. SURVEY OF RELATED RESEARCH

A critical examination of literature on non-visual approaches to reading charts and graphs revealed research in the areas of natural language interfaces, haptic interfaces, sonification, and hybrid interfaces. However, these studies focus primarily on how the system can provide information to the user and not so much on enabling the users to query the system randomly to get the information they want.

4.1 Natural language interface

iGraph [12] and SIGHT [9] emerged as the two recent, most popular systems using natural language output. They use pattern recognition technology to generate a summary that enables visually impaired individuals to grasp the salient points from charts and graphs. A typical summary generated by SIGHT would be: "This bar chart titled 'Credit-card debt leaps higher' shows that there is an increase in Jan '99 in the dollar value of 6-month growth in consumer revolving credit in contrast with the decreasing trend from July '97 to July '98".

These tools provide an overview that captures the key features of static graphs (such as line graphs and bar graphs). However, they do not provide a mechanism for users to interact and access data according to their needs and interests [22]. On the other hand, they offer some useful features and analysis, such as a summary, which could be built into the ChartMaster tool.

4.2 Haptic interface

Haptic devices enable users to 'touch and feel' the simulated objects with which they interact through tactile sensations, such as the texture of surfaces, temperature and vibration [3]. For example, Ina proposed a TSR (Terminate and Stay Resident) hard-copy system that translates colour pixels on the screen into embossed dots on paper by Braille printer plotter [16]. Krufka, Barner and Aysal developed an application to automatically convert vector-based graphics into raised-line images based on a graphic's hierarchical structure [18].

While this method improves discrimination, identification, and comprehension, it might not be suitable for interacting with stock market charts for the following reasons. It requires special software and hardware, such as a Braille printer, Tactile Printer, swell-touch paper, etc., which could prove expensive for ordinary users. Further, it focuses on conveying the shape of the graph, rather than the underlying data [20] and it is constrained by the complexity of the graphs and the tactile sensitivity of individuals [20, 30]. The output is not only static and impossible to update [29] but it is also not sustainable as it could "fade" after use [20]. Finally, it is time consuming for users to perceive the graph [27].

Another method to enable haptic interfaces is by utilizing force feedback, such as through a joystick. This method is normally used in combination with audio (non-speech sonification or speech), and will be discussed in the Hybrid Interface Section.

4.3 Sonification

Sonification involves "translation" of graphical information into music or varying sound frequencies [5, 8, 13]. Although it is possible to enable users to identify trends or compare different sets within a graph, interpreting graphs through sonification generally takes more training, time and effort on the user's side. From the perspective of interactive stock market charts, sonification might not help in acquiring accurate and precise information.

4.4 Hybrid interfaces

To overcome the limitations inherent in using natural language, haptic, or sonification methods by themselves, more recent works [1, 6, 25, 28, 30] have focused on developing a multimodal visualization system to assist users in perceiving graphical information using a combination of audio, synthesized speech (both speech and non-speech sound) and haptic (forced feedback), which demonstrates that using multiple sensory modalities enables users to perform tasks such as comparing graphs or identifying the largest maximum better. Hybrid interfaces are seen to help in accomplishing tasks much faster and more accurately than using swell-paper alone. However, this approach might require additional, more expensive forced feedback devices that are not normally accessible or familiar to many users with visual impairments.

4.5 ChartMaster Design Goals

Based on the preliminary usability inspection and review of related work, the following four design goals, which influenced the form and functionality of the proposed design solutions, were adopted for ChartMaster:

1. The system should be able to have the flexibility to accurately communicate both high-level information (i.e., overall trend) and particular data points (i.e., closing price on a certain day).
2. The system should be usable by screen reader users regardless of the browser or operating system used.
3. The system should be integrated into an existing stock market research interface without the need for the end user to install any additional program.
4. The system should not require the use of any special external equipment so as to not impose extra financial burden on individuals with visual impairments.

5. ITERATIVE INTERFACE CO-DESIGN

A user-centered, iterative design process was carried out from August 2014 to February 2015 with eighteen participants. Description of the participants is given in section 5.1 and an overview of the procedure is provided in section 5.2. In addition to the interaction option of numeric data table currently recommended by WCAG 2.0 as an accessible way to present charts, three interface options–audio input/output, text input/audio output, and dropdown menu–were designed and evaluated. The dropdown menu option was tested using two methods, Wizard of Oz and working prototype, leading to a total of four iterations of interface design and user evaluation as described in sections 5.3 through 5.6. For each of the iterations, users were given the same set of tasks to complete (for example, finding the volume of a stock on a given day or finding the highest price in the past 6 months) by interacting with different alternative solutions. Users' feedback was sought in each stage and used in the design of the next iteration of the interface. Figure 2 illustrates the four sessions, showing details of the method of testing (Wizard of Oz or working prototype), and participants involved.

5.1 Participants

Ten male and eight female participants of ages ranging from the 20s to 60s were recruited. Sixteen participants had visual impairments while two did not. Of the 16 visually impaired individuals, nine used only a screen reader, six used both screen readers and screen magnifiers, and one used only a screen magnifier. Twelve of the visually impaired participants had more than 15 years of hands-on experience with the primary assistive technologies they were using, while the remaining three participants each had 10-15 years, 5-10 years, and less than three years of experience respectively.

Participants also had various levels of financial and investment experience. Of the 16 visually impaired participants, one had advanced stock market knowledge and worked as a customer service representative in an investment brokerage, while four others had moderate understanding of personal financial management and investment (e.g., they conducted currency exchange, bitcoin trading, and stock market trading either online by themselves or through an investment advisor). The remaining 11 visually impaired participants had little or no financial literacy. The two sighted participants had high financial literacy levels and trading experience as they work in an investment brokerage. Participants were mainly recruited through various mailing lists that specifically focused on visually impaired individuals. Participants were paid $15 for each session as compensation for their time and effort.

5.2 Procedure

There were a total of 18 sessions, each lasting approximately one hour. Participants were encouraged to choose a location of their preference. Fifteen chose their home, one chose a public library, one chose his office, and one chose the researcher's home. All participants used their own computer and the assistive technology they typically use to participate in testing, except the participant who did the testing in the public library. All but one participant used the Windows operating system.

The usability testing session followed a semi-structured script with spontaneous modifications based on context. Think aloud protocols were recorded where users were encouraged to speak out loud while interacting with stock market charts and graphs. Observational notes on participant behavior during the session were recorded.

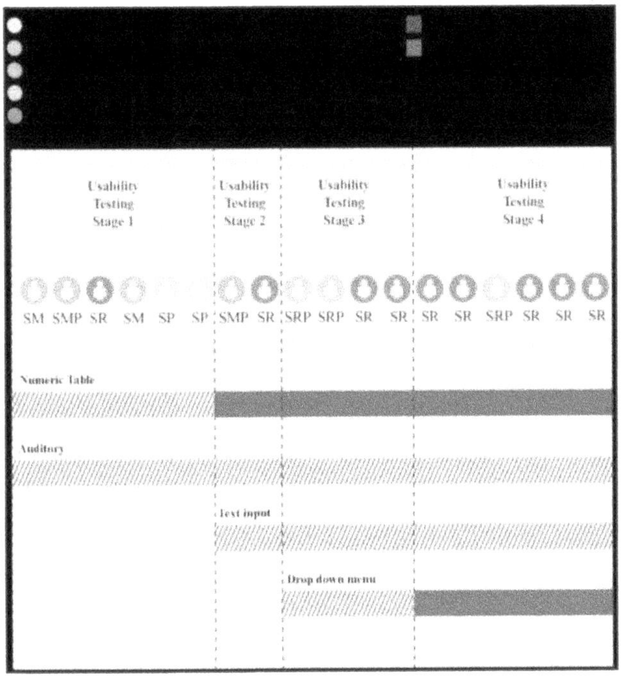

Figure 2: Usability testing: participants, materials & methods.

5.3 Iteration 1: Audio Input/Output

The first design involved audio input and audio output where the users were able to ask questions regarding information they needed from a stock market chart and the system would return an auditory answer. The interaction mechanism of this auditory solution was intended to be much like Siri used in the iPhone. However, the processing will be based on ChartMaster's own logic, which will be worked out in the next stage of development. Figure 3 shows the main process of the auditory input, inspired by Dean Rutter's diagram *How Siri works*.

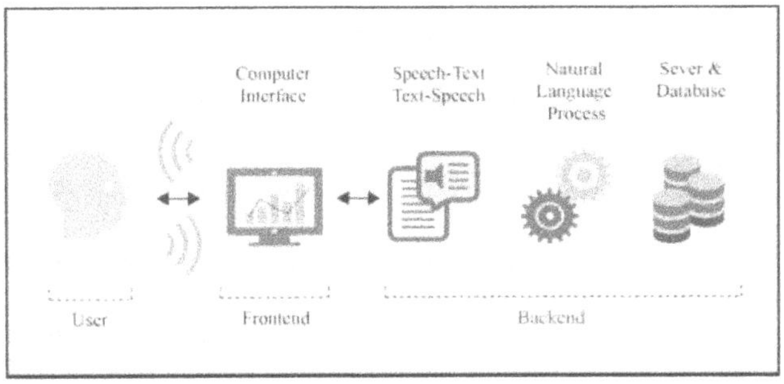

Figure 3: Main process of the auditory input.

This iteration used six participants, two of whom were sighted; three had low vision, using a screen magnifier; and one was blind, using a screen reader. A *Wizard of Oz* method was used to quickly collect feedback on the initial interface design solution (audio input/output) before commencing a full cycle of development.

This session initially evaluated the accessibility and usability issues of a numeric data table built based on a stock market chart. Screen reader users use the numeric table to learn about the chart, which they cannot perceive visually. The numeric table normally includes all of the data points used to generate the chart. The screen reader reads the table once it detects it. The participants were asked to complete a set of tasks that involved "asking" the system questions, such as "Highest price in the past 6 months?" The researcher then read out the data table as a screen reader would read it, and the participants identified the answers to the queries.

Next, in order to evaluate the audio input/output interface, the above tasks were repeated with the researcher acting like the computer and speaking out the correct answers to the participant's questions directly. For example, if the participant asked, "What is the average volume during last week?" the researcher would answer, "The average volume during last week is …"

5.4 Iteration 2: Text input/audio output

During the first iteration, several participants suggested using text input instead of voice input. "Can I type my question?" asked one participant. "I think the computer should be able to understand my typed question as well. Probably it will be more accurate." Based on this, the second iteration was designed. Instead of speaking out their query, this solution enabled users to acquire information about a chart by typing in their questions through a keyboard. The mechanism of this text input solution is very much like IBM's Watson Supercomputer, an artificial intelligence (AI) system that gained wide public attention through the popular TV quiz show Jeopardy [26]. Similar to the IBM Watson, the text input solution provides system responses as audio output. Here again, the processing logic will be considered in the next stage of development of **ChartMaster**. Figure 4 shows the main process of the text input/audio output solution.

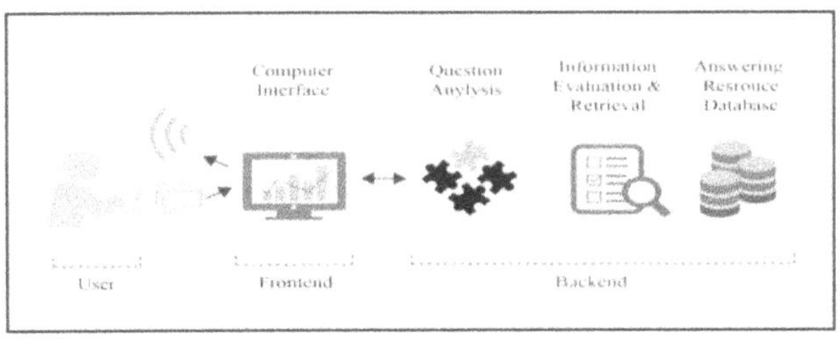

Figure 4: Main process of the text input solution.

This iteration used only two participants, both of whom used screen readers, one of whom was blind and the other with low vision. Similar to the first iteration, the researcher used the *Wizard of Oz* method to evaluate the text input/audio output design. The audio input/output design and the numeric table design were also comparatively evaluated. However, the numeric table alone used a working prototype that comprised a webpage developed with a static image of a chart and a numeric table that included all the data used to generate the chart. Appropriate visual treatment and HTML attributes were assigned to the static image chart and the numeric table to ensure they met WCAG accessibility standards.

5.5 Iteration 3: Dropdown menu/audio output

During iteration 2, both the participants suggested using a dropdown menu input to counter some drawbacks they sensed in the audio and text input methods. "Is there a filter I can use without me asking questions?" one participant asked after expressing his unwillingness to talk to a machine. The other participant asked, "How about using dropdowns? For example, I can first select 'Price,' and then start typing a symbol in the box.... It will be very fast and accurate."

A dropdown menu solution that enabled users to acquire key data points of a stock market chart, such as price, volume and events (i.e., dividend payout or stock split) for one or multiple stocks was then designed. At this stage, the focus was on simultaneous evaluation and comparison among the numeric table, auditory input, text input, and the new dropdown menu. Again, the *Wizard of Oz* method was used for all tasks as in the previous iterations except for the numeric table, where a prototype was used. Four screen reader users participated in this iteration.

5.6 Iteration 4: ChartMaster

The feedback for the dropdown menu was overwhelmingly positive. Users were thrilled after trying the prototype: "This is so cool!" "That is great! I can't believe that nobody has developed something like this before!" "I think that's it!" Participants found the drop-down menu to be an effective way to filter down and navigate through the huge quantities of data. When asked to compare between the numeric table and dropdown menu, many users simply thought these two approaches were not even comparable. In view of the above feedback, a prototype of the dropdown menu solution was designed as illustrated in Figure 5. This comprised a frontend interface generated using HTML; a backend data retrieval and calculation system controlled by JavaScript; and a Java ArrayList to store the data underlying a stock market chart.

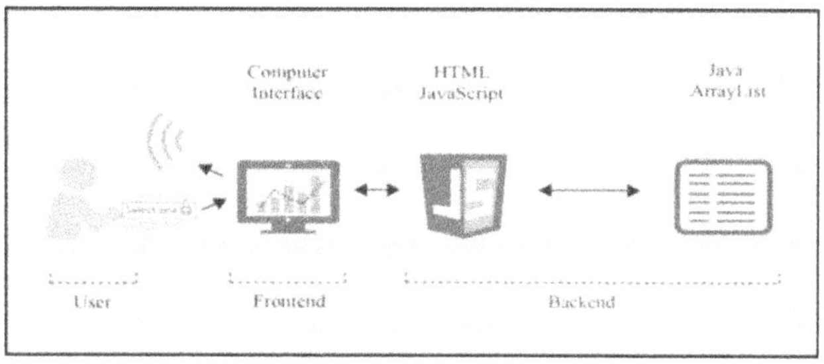

Figure 5: Main process of the dropdown menu solution

Based on the above design, an early version of the **ChartMaster** tool was developed as illustrated in Figure 6, and evaluated in the final iteration. Audio and text input solutions were also tested and compared with the dropdown menu; however, these features were tested using The *Wizard of Oz* method. The numeric table was integrated into the interface where the dropdown menu was featured, so that the users could compare both solutions using one interface. Six screen reader users evaluated the above interfaces.

The **ChartMaster tool** is designed as a link grouped with other commonly used stock market chart tools and placed at the top of a stock market chart. Once activated through the keyboard, the tool expands, pushing the chart down on the page and enabling the user to acquire information by interacting with a series of dropdown menus. When a user submits a query, the answers are displayed as a text summary at the bottom of the dropdown menu.

The dropdown menus are grouped into three categories: Information type (as shown using label "Ask for"); Time frame; and Specific data set. The information type dropdown menu is where users decide what type of information they want to acquire. The time frame dropdown menus allow users to define a time frame for the data. When combined with text input fields, these dropdown menus provide options, from which users can choose one particular day, or pick from a preset time frame, such as 5 days, 1 month, 6 months, etc., or define a random custom time frame. The specific data category provides 4 dropdown menus: Price (i.e., open, close, day high, day low), Volume (i.e., latest, highest, lowest, and average), Event (i.e., split, dividend), and Trend (i.e., overall trend, technical pattern). Currently, **ChartMaster** only allows the user to select one option from each specific data category, however, the function of selecting multiple options will be developed in future versions.

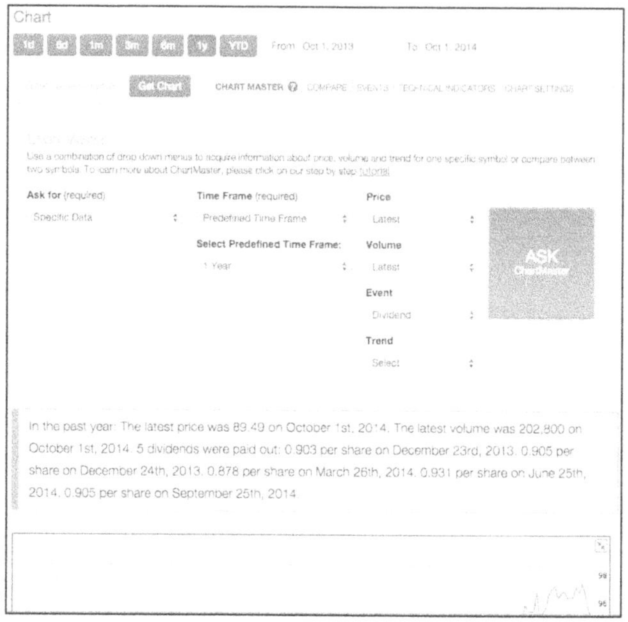

Figure 6: Expanded ChartMaster tool with dropdown menus

The **ChartMaster** includes almost all key information provided by a typical stock market chart (Figure 1), such as price, volume, events, time frame, comparison, etc. The following section demonstrates how the dropdown menu provides great flexibility for users to acquire accurate and precise information according to their needs and interests. Options within each dropdown menu are dynamic according to a hierarchy that makes sense of stock market data: the choice of information type will determine the options within the time frame, while the selection of the time frame will define the options available from the specific data set. For example, when Specific Data is selected as the information type, there are three options under time frame: Predefined Time Frame, Custom Time Frame, and Specific day;

whereas if "Compare with Current Symbol" is selected as the information type, then the options under "timeframe" will change to: Different Days and Different Months. Similarly, when "predefined time frame" or "1 year" are selected as the time frame, the options under price will then be: Latest, Highest, Lowest, Median, and Average; however, if specific day is selected, then the option under price will change to: Open, Close, Day High, Day Low.

Once the choice is made for information type, time frame, and specific data set, the user can then click on the "**ChartMaster**" button and receive a text summary of the information acquired, which will also be read out by screen reader software. Below are a few answers generated by the system demonstrating that **ChartMaster** provides great flexibility for users to acquire information according to their needs and interests.

- *One data point for one stock on a particular day*: "For May 27th, 2014: The closing price was 91.02".
- *Multiple data points for one stock on a custom defined time range*: "Between June 27th, 2014 and December 10th, 2014: The highest price was 97.61 on September 18th, 2014. The highest volume was 427,000 on August 28th, 2014".
- *Compare data points for two stock on a particular day:* "For May 27th, 2014: The closing price for ABC was 91.02. The closing price for XYZ was 100.96. The volume for ABC was 95,300. The volume for XYZ was 5,124,900. No dividends were paid out for ABC [name of the symbol]. No dividends were paid out for XYZ [name of the symbol being compared]".

These answers are composed using three key components: the data entered by the user through the dropdown menus and associated text input fields, such as "6 months" and "average price"; the data pulled or generated by the system according to the data entered by the user; and a template (including the wording and punctuation marks) which arranges and presents all of the data mentioned above in a meaningful and grammatically-correct way to the user.

The system is smart enough to give clear explanations when there is no data available according to users' request. For example, when user requires data for a day that has no trading activities, the system will inform the user, "Sorry, there was no trading activity on September 21st, 2010". And when the user asks for certain events that are not applicable to the chosen timeframe, the system will return, "In the past 6 months: No stock splits occurred."

One point worth mentioning is that the participants did not offer suggestions for designing the drop down menu options, such as the categorization of the information or the specific items in each drop down menu. It was not possible to involve the participants with visual impairments in forming the questions because as screen reader users they had not been able to interact with stock market charts and so were not having the required expertise. The first author, who is a domain expert, in consultation with two expert colleagues, designed the options and questions. While these questions are fundamental to the understanding of any stock market chart, the set of questions will be refined in a future research step with financial experts as well as novices.

6. DISCUSSION

This study aimed to design the interaction interface for the ChartMaster tool that is being developed for screen reader users to query stock market charts by making the data that is used to create the stock market charts more accessible. The tool will use a drop down menu as a structured way to query the chart to get key information from a stock market chart. A screen reader generally does not allow random access to information. It reads information, such as a chart summary, serially. The ChartMaster will allow random access to chart information.

6.1 Numeric table

W3C's Web Content Accessibility Guidelines (WCAG) recommends using numeric tables as a visual equivalent for charts. The usability testing, however, revealed that although accessing data points through a numeric table is a "fairly straightforward task," it can be "very time consuming," and take "enormous cognitive effort" especially when the task involves analyzing information based on a comparison of multiple data points. Including appropriate "ID" or "headers" for each cell as recommended by WCAG as the best practice did little to improve the usability of the numeric table. Although users could differentiate data points in the same row, it still took a huge cognitive effort to process data. Furthermore, the shortcut keys that enable quick navigation through the numeric table were seen to be too complicated and hard to master.

Users' expertise and technical constraints of the screen reader such as linear reading and the enormous amount of data in stock market chart numeric tables had a negative impact on the usability of the numeric table. Along with technical constraints, users' expertise with assistive technology, interface elements, and financial literacy were key factors impacting the usability of the numeric table. For example, participants who could use screen reader commands were able to accomplish the activity much faster and more accurately than those who did not have the same skill level. Similarly, participants who in general skip reading tables in real life were having a hard time to even figure out the structure of a table, thus failing to complete any task during the usability testing. Participants with a higher financial literacy level or with stock market experience were more comfortable in using the table than those who did not have that knowledge.

Users' language level was another important factor that impacted the efficiency of the numeric table. For example, two of the participants with 18 years of screen reader experience and advanced computer experience were able to use Jaws hot key for tables; however, it took one of the participants much less time to find the answer, because, being a native English speaker, he was able to set the screen reader speed much faster than the other user.

6.2 Audio input/output

The audio input/output approach was considered a "robust" and "more effective" approach than the traditional numeric table. Despite the initial excitement, many users, especially those with speech disabilities and those who spoke English as a second language, expressed concerns about the capability of the voice input system to recognize their voice. Many users also expressed their frustration when the system could not recognize their question. Users questioned the system's capability to provide answers as well.

The second user concern was the uncertain and unpredictable nature of the auditory solution. When the system failed to provide an answer, the users had no idea of the reasons behind it; it could be that they didn't phrase the question appropriately, or that the system was unable to interpret the question, or simply that the answer was not in the database. Users would not know how to solve the problem unless the system would detect and display the actual cause for the error.

The third concern raised by participants was that the tool might not be apparent to users. The users also implied that they would only use the tool if "it is easy to get and easy to install," and ideally the system should be able to automatically run when it detects a numeric table.

In addition, users pointed out that the machine-like synthetic speech is not "pleasant to hear," and also could cause challenges for users who speak English as a second language. Another disadvantage that was pointed out by almost all participants is that the auditory approach could potentially interfere with their privacy, especially in public places. Environmental context can also potentially hinder a user from using the tool. Finally, some users just did not feel comfortable talking to a machine.

6.3 Text input/audio output

User feedback confirmed that text input not only improved the accuracy, but also provided privacy and could be implemented in a way that users are familiar with. However, as was the same with voice input, users were still not sure if the system was able to successfully "decode" the text that was input in various formats and sometimes in grammatically incorrect form. The system's limitations in answering were also not apparent.

6.4 Dropdown menu/audio output

Iterative co-design provided a perfect platform to discover new ideas. One of the most surprising findings is that users thought the dropdown menu approach to be educational, enabling them to discover information or look at the data in ways they were not hitherto aware of. As one participant said, "This is a way to educate the user about what this tool can do, what kind of questions they can ask and what kind of answers they can get."

Secondly, dropdown menus solved three key issues that users encountered regarding the numeric table, audio input/output approach and text input/audio output approach, which are: cognitive load, accuracy, and predictability. Users don't need to manually go through each data point and try to memorize and calculate in order to acquire the information related to the stock market chart. The system will "filter" out the data based on the selection they made using the drop down menu. In addition, if users are to ask questions by speaking or using free-form text, they would not know whether or not the questions they are asking are within the scope of the system. The drop down menu avoids these problems by specifying the valid questions that the system can handle. This is good both for the user and for the system since only a subset of possible questions can be implemented.

Thirdly, users confirmed that the dropdown menu maintained the flexibility that the audio and text input approach have; this allows users to perceive and acquire information based on their needs and interests.

Finally, the concept of using dropdown menu was found to be very easy to understand. "I get it!" said another participant right after a short initial exploration of the prototype. In addition to the consistent positive feedback demonstrated above, users also provided constructive feedback to improve the accessibility and usability of the dropdown menu solution.

6.5 No single winning solution

One of the most profound discoveries in this study is that users wanted several options instead of one winning solution. During the entire course of testing, users were asked to compare numeric table, auditory approach, text input approach, and dropdown menu. They preferred the inclusion of as many options as possible to accommodate different individual preferences, learning styles and contexts of use. This finding is in conformance with previously reported research [1] where users denoted preferences in intertwining aural, speech and haptic methodologies to gain understanding of the content of charts.

7. CONCLUSION

7.1 Contributions

This study came up with an interaction interface design for the **ChartMaster** tool we are developing to enable querying of interactive stock market charts using a screen reader. Better informed investment decisions have the potential to lead to greater returns, more spending power, greater shareholder influence, more economic opportunities and better participation in design decisions, which will, in turn, improve the design of financial monitoring instruments leading to a virtuous (rather than vicious) systemic cycle of economic inclusion [23].

With **ChartMaster**, users would be able to access data points quicker and easier. And for users who don't have much investment background, this tool can guide them to look for information that they might have overlooked. Thus, the tool has educational use for both sighted as well as visually impaired investors; as well, we highlight the preference of the participants for multiple options as another curb-cut illustration. The outcomes were seen to also benefit financial novices in understanding and using stock market charts.

Compared to other related systems, **ChartMaster** has the following advanced features:

- **ChartMaster** is able to provide accurate and precise data points regardless of the complexity of the chart.
- **ChartMaster** works with underlying real data stored in a java ArrayList that is used to generate the graph instead of the graph image, allowing the system to return as many data points as possible with reduced chances for errors.
- **ChartMaster** also provides additional, yet critical, computed data points such as average, unusual value, median, highest, and lowest. These provide a benchmark for users while analyzing and comparing data.
- **ChartMaster** provides users with great flexibility to acquire information about a chart based on their needs and interests.
- **ChartMaster** could be compatible with a wide range of browsers, operating platforms, and screen reader applications as it is developed using simple and straightforward java script and commonly used interface elements (dropdown menus and text input fields).
- **ChartMaster** can be integrated into any existing interface by the stock market chart provider, without additional installation on the part of the end user.
- **ChartMaster** is easy to learn and use because it does not require extra shortcuts to operate the tool.

7.2 Implications for inclusive design

We will be adding three levels of educational materials in the form of contextual help to the design to cater to the learning needs of users at diverse knowledge levels – novice, moderate or advanced - in the form of tool tips, glossary and education centre. This enhancement echoes with the inclusive design principle that the design needs to include various options to support users' "self-determination and self-knowledge" [15].

Use of **ChartMaster** would improve the accessibility and usability of charts for visually impaired users, enabling them to participate more fully in investment activities, become financially literate and make informed financial decisions. Owing to the curb-cut effect, it could also benefit users who have speech, mobility, and learning disability, or those whose activity might be constrained by the environment, or sighted people with low financial literacy. Such curb-cut advantage results when a design is: "aware of the context and broader impact of the design and striving to effect a beneficial impact beyond the intended beneficiary of the design" [15].

The study demonstrated that users prefer a flexible configuration that provides several options enabling them to make personalized adjustments according to context. This finding confirms the importance of promoting personalization rather than finding a universally accessible, 'one-size-fits-all' solution [15]. Future designs will need to explore the possibility of integrating all four options (numeric table, auditory solution, text input solution, and dropdown menu solution) into one design. Options should be easily found and easily switched. In addition, users will be able to save their preference settings, such as search criteria that they are particularly interested in or solutions they prefer to use.

The study demonstrated the power of the inclusive design approach that derives from co-design with users. Through the iterative design process, users were getting involved during several stages of the design: they helped identify the problem, evaluated the initial concept, and provided design suggestions. One blind participant even assisted in writing the code for an accessible numeric table. Getting users involved in the design process proved extremely effective in terms of generating and refining ideas. In fact, two out of three design concepts, the text input and the dropdown menu, were directly inspired by usability testing participants' recommendations.

The experience of conducting usability testing at the users' home also had a profound impact on the design. It allowed the researcher to have a much more realistic view of how the design artifact will be used within a particular environment unique from user to user. It helped capture customer needs that otherwise could be missed in a standard testing room.

7.3 Implications for HCI

From an HCI perspective, this research clearly demonstrated the sensory, cognitive and emotional barriers that visually impaired users face while interacting with stock market charts. In her doctoral dissertation, Chandrashekar [7], states that online interaction proficiency (for screen reader users) is a composite concept closely tied to the user's 'expertise', 'experience', 'training' and 'trouble shooting skills' in using the computer, the Internet, and the screen reader. This research discovered two other aspects related to online interaction proficiency of screen reader users: 'language proficiency', or the level of English knowledge when English is not the first language, and 'domain proficiency', or the knowledge level related to the content or topic communicated through the interface.

7.4 Future work

- **ChartMaster** is now able to provide information for "historic" stock market charts, meaning a chart that represents data for past trading days; the capability could be expanded to provide information for a "live" chart with real-time data streaming in when the market is open.
- A customizable **ChartMaster** API solution will be developed that enables the creator of any chart or graph to create their own **ChartMaster** module by simply uploading a data spreadsheet to the system. This module could then be plugged into a Webpage, a PowerPoint presentation or an electronic report to allow visually impaired readers to access the charts and graphs.
- The **ChartMaster** provides textual information to visually impaired screen readers. Haptic solutions for tactile presentation of some stock market chart elements for deaf-blind users could be explored.
- Visually impaired participants, who were novice investors, emphasized the educational aspect of the ChartMaster. Given this educational potential of **ChartMaster**, sighted novice investors should be involved in future studies to expand the application of the design to a much boarder audience base. Expert investors reactions will also be sought.
- In addition, to specific data points, future versions of **ChartMaster** will communicate the visual characteristics of the chart, such as the structure of the chart, technical patterns, and the overall trend of the chart. This information requires sophisticated mathematical algorithms that have not been fully developed in the current version. However, these more difficult issues with answering the questions will be dealt with in future work.
- Two usability improvements are proposed: (1) shift the focus of the screen reader to the results when user clicks on Ask **ChartMaster** button to allow the screen reader to automatically read the answer; (2) reorganize the drop down menus so that the 'high-level summary' dropdown menu is placed before 'price', 'volume', and 'event'. This will mentally prepare the user before drilling down to detailed information.
- So far, there is little investigation of the information architecture of ChartMaster, specifically, the categorization of the different drop down menus and each data point included in each drop down menu. Future work should examine the adequacy of the current question set and modify it. It should also examine how the system could accurately and effectively answer questions.

Advances in ICT enable users to access charts and graphs today through multiple modalities: visual, textual, audio, tactile and haptic. **ChartMaster** presents an optimal inclusive design solution for most screen reader users by allowing transformation from graphical to nonvisual through a wide range of options to fit users' contextual needs. In making these charts accessible, people who use screen readers should be able to get whatever the sighted people get out of them. So, they should also be able to learn to get better at asking the questions relevant to making their investment choices. The tool might also be helpful to novice, sighted users. Inclusive design benefits everyone and provides value. As one participant remarked, "Accessibility is for everyone, not just for people with disabilities."

8. ACKNOWLEDGMENTS

Our thanks to Dr. Vera Roberts and Dr. Sambhavi Chandrashekar for their guidance and support in the project. Our special thanks are due to David Lawson for his editorial assistance.

9. REFERENCES

[1] Abu Doush, I., Pontelli, E., Son, T. C., Simon, D., & Ma, O. (2010). Multimodal presentation of two-dimensional charts: An investigation using Open Office XML and Microsoft

Excel. *ACM Transactions on Accessible Computing (TACCESS)*, *3*(2), 8.

[2] Akhtar, M. N., Hunjra, A. I., & Rehman, K. U. 2011. Determinants of Short Term Investment Decision Making. *Actual Problems of Economics, 11*, 356-363.

[3] Berkley, J. J. 2003. Haptic devices. White Paper, Mimic Technologies Inc., Seattle.

[4] Booth, P. A. 2014. *An Introduction to Human-Computer Interaction (Psychology Revivals).* New York, NY.

[5] Brown, L. M., & Brewster, S. A. 2003. Drawing by ear: Interpreting sonified line graphs. *International Conference on Auditory Display.*

[6] Carroll, D., Chakraborty, S., & Lazar, J. (2013). Designing accessible visualizations: The case of designing a weather map for blind users. In *Universal Access in Human-Computer Interaction. Design Methods, Tools, and Interaction Techniques for eInclusion* (pp. 436-445). Springer Berlin Heidelberg.

[7] Chandrashekar, S. 2010. *Is hearing believing? Perception of online information credibility by screen reader users who are blind or visually impaired* (University of Toronto).

[8] Cohen, R. F., Yu, R., Meacham, A., & Skaff, J. 2005. *PLUMB: displaying graphs to the blind using an active auditory interface.* Paper presented at the Proceedings of the 7th international ACM SIGACCESS conference on Computers and accessibility.

[9] Demir, S. (2010). Sight for visually impaired users: Summarizing information graphics textually. *Ph.D. dissertation.* University of Delaware.

[10] Donovan, R. 2015. The global economics of disability. *Return on Disability.*

[11] Eason, K. D. 1984. Towards the experimental study of usability. *Behaviour & Information Technology, 3*(2), 133-143.

[12] Ferres, L., Lindgaard, G., Sumegi, L., & Tsuji, B. 2013. Evaluating a tool for improving accessibility to charts and graphs. *ACM Transactions on Computer-Human Interaction (TOCHI), 20*(5), 28.

[13] Flowers, J. H., Buhman, D. C., & Turnage, K. D. 2005. Data sonification from the desktop: Should sound be part of standard data analysis software? *ACM Transactions on Applied Perception (TAP), 2*(4), 467-472.

[14] Grout, P. A., Megginson, W. L., & Zalewska, A. 2009. One Half-Billion Shareholders and Counting-Determinants of Individual Share Ownership Around the World.

[15] IDRC. 2013. What is Inclusive Design? Retrieved from http://idrc.ocad.ca/index.php/about-the-idrc/49-resources/online-resources/articles-and-papers/443-whatisinclusivedesign.

[16] Ina, S. 1996. Computer graphics for the blind. *ACM SIGCAPH Computers and the Physically Handicapped*(55), 16-23.

[17] Institute, B. S. 2005. British Standard 7000-6: Design management systems: *Guide to managing inclusive design.*

[18] Krufka, S. E., Barner, K. E., & Aysal, T. C. 2007. Visual to tactile conversion of vector graphics. *Neural Systems and Rehabilitation Engineering, IEEE Transactions on, 15*(2), 310-321.

[19] Nielsen, J. 1994. *Usability Engineering*. London: Academic

[20] Paneels, S., & Roberts, J. C. 2010. Review of designs for haptic data visualization. *Haptics, IEEE Transactions on, 3*(2), 119-137.

[21] Shneiderman, B.: The Eyes Have It: A Task by Data Type Taxonomy for Information Visualizations. In *Proceedings of the 1996 IEEE Symposium on Visual Languages,* pp. 336–343. IEEE Computer Society, Washington, DC (1996).

[22] Shackel, B. 2009. Usability–Context, framework, definition, design and evaluation. *Interacting with Computers, 21*(5-6), 339-346.

[23] Treviranus, J. 2014. Leveraging the Web as a Platform for Economic Inclusion. *Behavioral Sciences & the Law 32*, no. 1: 94-103.

[24] Treviranus, J., Stolarick, K., Denstedt, M., Catherine, F., & Ascunsion, J. 2010. *Leveraging Inclusion and Diversity as Canada's Digital Advantage.* Retrieved March 10, 2015: http://idrc.ocad.ca/images/stories/DraftInclusionSSHRCreportFinal)-first32.pdf.

[25] Wall, S., & Brewster, S. 2006. *Feeling what you hear: tactile feedback for navigation of audio graphs.* Paper presented at the Proceedings of the SIGCHI conference on Human Factors in computing systems.

[26] Watson. http://www.aaai.org/Magazine/Watson/watson.php.

[27] WebAIM. 2013. Accessibility Evaluation Tools. Retrieved March 28, 2015, from http://webaim.org/articles/tools/.

[28] WebAIM. 2014. Screen Reader User Survey #5 Results. Retrieved January 20, 2015, from http://webaim.org/projects/screenreadersurvey5/.

[29] White, R., & Harwin, W. 2012. *Haptics visualisation of scientific data for visually impaired users.* Paper presented at the International conference on disabilities, virtual reality and associated technologies, Laval, France, proc 9th.

[30] Yu, W., Kangas, K., & Brewster, S. 2003. *Web-based haptic applications for blind people to create virtual graphs.* Paper presented at the Haptic Interfaces for Virtual Environment and Teleoperator Systems, 2003. HAPTICS 2003

Collaborative Creation of Digital Tactile Graphics

Jens Bornschein
jens.bornschein@tu-dresden.de

Denise Prescher
denise.prescher@tu-dresden.de

Gerhard Weber
gerhard.weber@tu-dresden.de

Human-Computer Interaction Research Group
Technische Universität Dresden
Nöthnitzer Str. 46, 01187 Dresden, Germany

ABSTRACT

The Tangram Workstation is a collaborative system for creating tactile graphics. A transcriber composing a tactile graphic from a visual source is supported by a non-visual reviewer on a two-dimensional tactile pin-matrix device on which he can observe and adapt the work of his sighted team member. We present the results of an evaluation with eight teams, each consisting of a transcriber and a blind reviewer. Overall, quality of tactile graphics can be improved by a collaborative approach. In most cases blind users recommended changes on tactile graphics even when they have been prepared by professional sighted editors. The study also showed that the blind reviewer is able to do simple editing tasks independently with our workstation.

Categories and Subject Descriptors

H.5.2 [**Information Interfaces and Presentation**]: User Interfaces—*haptic I/O, input devices and strategies*; H.5.3 [**Information Interfaces and Presentation**]: Group and Organization Interfaces—*collaborative computing, synchronous interaction*; K.4.2 [**Computers and Society**]: Social Issues—*Assistive technologies for persons with disabilities*

General Terms

Design, Experimentation, Human Factors, Verification

Keywords

Tactile Graphics; Evaluation; Collaboration; Blind Users; Pin-matrix Device; Drawing-application

1. INTRODUCTION

"A picture is worth a thousand words" a well-known proverb says. Compared to text, graphical data can convey information much more compressed. Images support communication, make documents better understandable or are just visually appealing. With new powerful devices and software tools, creating and distributing pictorial content is easy. But using only visual data for conveying information excludes users who cannot attain this kind of information, such as visually impaired users.

One way to overcome this barrier is to provide an alternative verbal description of an image. This description can only stand for one interpretation, which may be insufficient, incomprehensible, incomplete or even wrong. Therefore, a tactile alternative of important images should be provided to blind people. Most blind people prefer to have a tactile graphic in addition to a textual description [20].

Tactile graphics can be produced in several ways. These methods range from simple and fast embossing on paper or foils to complex preparation of reliefs and collages [8, 13]. The different production methods vary greatly in their characteristics, such as possible resolution, the ability to display different relief levels or to simulate realistic haptic feedback.

Novel technologies allow the presentation of refreshable spatial haptic feedback on tactile displays [22, 24]. These enable non-visual users to access, for example, digital graphical or dynamic content. In this work, we apply the two-dimensional pin-based matrix display BrailleDis 7200 [19].

Production methods based on digital data, such as embossing with pin-matrix embossers or printing and fusing microcapsule paper, are very common [20]. The Tangram Workstation aims at producing tactile graphics for multiple embossing methods.

Existing tools are designed to support sighted tactile graphics transcribers only. Results often have to be redone as the required expertise is considerable. Involving the target user group in the process of creating tactile diagrams should increase the quality of the resulting product.

Therefore, we propose an approach that involves a tactile graphic consumer in early stages of production without the need of embossing the graphics physically. We assume this shall increase the readability of tactile graphics, speed up the overall production time and reduce material costs due to lack of misprints. In the following we present the Tangram Workstation which allows the collaborative creation of tactile graphics by a blind and a sighted user. A user study for evaluating the system is presented and its results are discussed in detail.

2. RELATED WORK

Common graphic editing software without special tactile graphic support functionalities is typically used [20]. Nevertheless several tools for supporting a graphic author in creating tactile graphics exist.

ASSETS'15, October 26–28, 2015, Lisbon, Portugal.

ACM 978-1-4503-3400-6/15/10 ...$15.00.
DOI: http://dx.doi.org/10.1145/2700648.2809869

Programs such as the BrlGraphEditor [3], Sparsha Chitra system [15] or QuickTac [7] and PictureBraille [17] are designed to help authors to create graphics for text-only Braille embossers. These embossers normally have a resolution of about 10 dpi. Tools offer methods to draw simple graphical objects, add Braille text or convert imported pictures into tactile representations by applying simple filters and image processing algorithms, such as thresholding, color filtering and edge detection. The converted images can be manipulated afterwards. Several line styles and fill patterns defined for the embossing matrix are supplied or can be designed.

The Tiger Designer software [23], which comes with the Tiger software suite, is designed to prepare tactile graphics for pin-matrix embossers with a higher resolution of about 20 dpi and eight different height levels for embossed dots and, in addition, for designing simultaneously generated color prints.

The TactileView software [21] not only allows the creation of graphics for Braille embossers but also to print out on microcapsule paper or pin-matrix embossers. A special feature is that the software is fully accessible for blind users using a screen reader. Interaction is possible with a digitization pen allowing for digitizing hand drawn pictures in real time. Furthermore, the software is connected to an online catalog for tactile elements which can be placed inside the current created graphic.

IVEO Creator Pro [12] is designed for creating audio-tactile images. The software creates graphics in SVG format and can add further information to graphic objects. It can also be used as viewer for audio-tactile SVG images in combination with special touch-sensitive image frame hardware.

Tools to support the transcription process with more automated mechanisms should reduce the time and, therefore, the costs for supplying accessible graphical material. One such system is the Tactile Graphics Assistant (TGA) of the Tactile Graphics Project [14]. With image processing, machine learning and optical character recognition the system can be trained to process specific types of images or text and transforms them automatically into a tactile representation.

Another example for such semi-automated systems is the Graphics to Tactile project (G2T) [6] in which image processing and color filtering is used to split the picture into color dependent layers for further processing.

Collaboration of a sighted and a blind user is a common scenario especially in educational or supporting scenarios. The screen reader Jaws, for example, allows for a remote access through the Jaws Tandem function [9]. This can be used to support as well as to train a screen reader user.

The multimodal Phantom-based McSig environment [18] is also such a cooperative training system. The system is used to train blind persons in handwriting and doing signatures. For doing this, a teacher uses a tablet PC to guide a blind student via a force feedback device.

Work on enabling collaboration in a graphic creation process exists but is based on command languages. BPLOT3 [10] enables a blind user to create a drawing on his own using a plotter control language through a command line interface or the touch input of a tablet PC while a sighted user can be supported by using a graphical user interface. A tactile feedback about what was drawn is not available until the graphic is produced as tactile hardcopy.

In the Braille transcription process it is common to use a pair of a sighted and a blind proof reader to find errors in the translated Braille text after it was semi-automatically translated. For instance, this workflow is used in the German Central Library for the Blind (DZB). The extra effort is accepted to ensure good quality Braille text products but for tactile graphical content this is not done in such an excessive way. This is one motivation for the proposed Tangram workflow which is presented in the following.

3. TANGRAM WORKSTATION

The Tangram Workstation is a collaborative workspace for transcribing and creating tactile graphics. The workstation is based on the open-source and free-to-use Libre- [1] or OpenOffice [2] Draw application that allow graphics to be produced as vector images.

The workstation includes an office suite extension called Tangram Toolbar and a separate software for non-visual interaction with the Draw application called Tangram Lector which is connected to a refreshable tactile display. In the following only the basic principles and supporting tools of the system are presented. A more comprehensive introduction of the system architecture, Tangram Lector functionalities as well as the Tangram Toolbar can be found in [4] and [5].

The basic concept of the Tangram Workstation rests on two pillars. The first is to support transcribers in creating tactile graphics more efficiently and also to train them in guidelines for good tactile graphics, such as these from the Braille Authority of North America (BANA, see [16]). The second and more innovative one is to involve a non-visual reviewer in early stages of the digital creation process for the first time. This means, the Tangram Workstation enables a blind user to give feedback about the tactile characteristics of a currently prepared graphical element and to be available as a consultant for further inquiries about readability or perspicuity. During the process of development the visual presentation is also continuously presented on a two-dimensional refreshable pin device.

3.1 Interface for the Sighted User

The transcription of tactile graphics is often done by less experienced transcribers [20]. This includes teachers, colleagues, friends or family members. To support inexperienced graphic authors in the prevention of fundamental mistakes and help professionals to be more efficient in their work, the office suite is extended with several tools for preparing tactile graphics. For example, the standard formatting settings, such as color and other properties for object fillings and outlines, are adopted. Additionally, the text settings, namely font and size, are set to values optimized for writing Braille. This enables a creator to see directly how much space a Braille label will consume inside a graphic.

Beyond adapting the basic formatting presets further useful tools are supplied. Three line styles and a palette of eleven evaluated and freely combinable tactile texturing patterns are available. Furthermore, keyboard-based access to object properties is provided, such as the objects' position and size. The editor can check graphic objects against heuristic guideline values for tactile graphics, for instance, a minimal object size.

A dockable dialog window for entering title and description to elements allows enriching an element with a title and a more detailed description to prepare graphics for an audio-haptic usage. A target medium is, for example, the IVEO audio-haptic learning system [11], which is based on

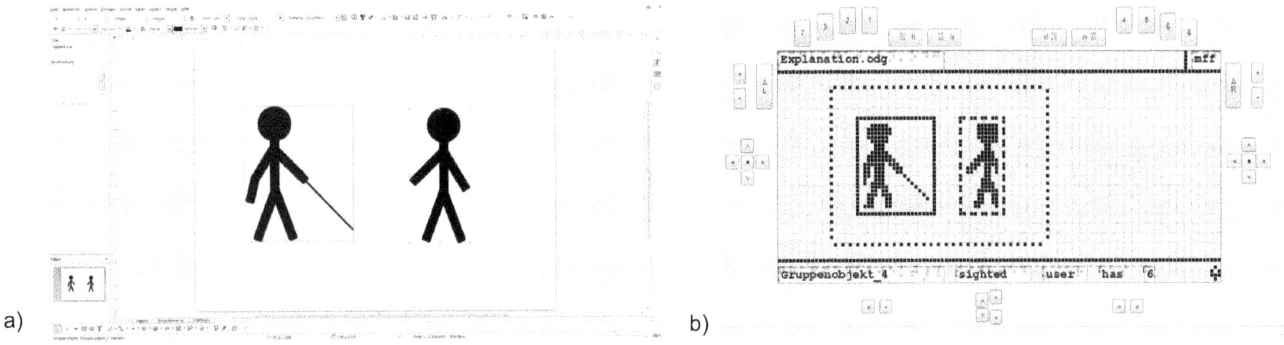

Figure 1: Example of tactile representation of the two foci (b): the Braille-focus is non-visually shown as a solid frame (left), the system focus as a dashed frame (right). The Braille-focus is marked for a short time as red blinking overlay with border in the GUI (a).

enriched SVG images. Embossed as tactile image and put on a touch-sensitive frame, the information of title and description can be achieved as auditory output by the reader by tapping or double tapping the tactile graphic element.

3.2 Interface for the Blind User

As mentioned above, a tactile pin-matrix device, namely BrailleDis 7200, is used to include blind users in the graphic production process. The drawing region of Draw‘s application window is captured and converted into a 10 dpi binary tactile image at about 10 Hz. Pixels on the screen that are darker than a defined threshold appear as raised pins, all other pixels appear as lowered pins on the BrailleDis. Inside this tactile screenshot special markings are added. The available sheet to draw on is marked as a dotted frame (see Figure 1b), for instance.

For panning operations the metaphor of a picture frame or a magnifying glass moving over the document is used. By this means, a panning operation moves the viewable section in the requested direction in contrast to moving the underlying document in this direction (which would move the viewable section in the opposite direction). To allow for adapting the level of detail of the graphical content, the workstation provides some zooming operations, too. Thereby, sections are increased or decreased with respect to their center position. The new presented section should have nearly the same center as the section presented before the zooming operation.

Graphical elements can be selected by touch gestures on the pin-matrix device. Thereby, the system distinguishes between exploration gesture, which is triggered with a button on the left side of the device, and manipulation gesture, which is triggered with a button on the right side of the device. The first only gives some audio feedback of an element. This includes the unique identifier of each object as well as title, text value, and parent or child relations. Through this the blind user can get further information about the touched element. The manipulation gesture additionally sets the focus on the element and, therefore, indicates the intention of manipulating that element.

Besides using only touch input, it is possible to go through the whole Document Object Model (DOM) tree in a deterministic way by using a key combination. Thereby, the blind user can visit document objects that are invisible, hidden or untouchable.

Beyond being a passive observer, the non-visual user can actively intervene and manipulate graphic elements by himself. He can adopt the visual parameters position, size, rotation, object filling and outline, and can enrich an element with further information by adding or changing title and description. The manipulation of elements is realized by using the buttons of the right cursor keypad of BrailleDis 7200 (for more information see [5]). In this way, the user can select one of five editing modes and make his changes while following them with one hand immediately on the tactile output of the pin device.

3.3 Focus Concepts

To allow a fully multimodal and independent working of both users, the screen user and the non-screen user have two separate foci. The first is the normal system focus that comes with Draw and is controllable through the GUI. The second is the so-called Braille-focus which only exists in the Tangram Lector software and points at an element inside the DOM of the currently loaded drawing.

Both users can be aware of the partner's currently focused element. When the blind user selects an element on the pin device, this Braille-focused object appears to the screen user as a red blinking overlay on the screen. The non-screen user can request for the current GUI focus by turning on a selection observation mode in which every focus change is reported and displayed. The system element focused in the application is marked with a blinking dashed bounding box on the pin-matrix device. The element focused by the Braille-focus is marked as a blinking solid bounding box (see Figure 1). The blinking rate is about 1.25 Hz.

The possibility to share or observe the partner's focus is a fundamental feature to enable collaboration free of conflicts. Therefor, the non-visual user can actively trigger the marking of his Braille-focus in the GUI again. A synchronization of the Braille-focus to the system focus is possible, too.

4. EVALUATION

To evaluate and improve the usability of the Tangram Workstation and its functionality we have conducted a user study. In addition, we wanted to observe the collaboration of the team of GUI and non-visual user while creating a tactile graphic. In the end, we also wanted to evaluate the quality of the resulting graphic.

Figure 2: Tangram Workstation with desktop PC and BrailleDis 7200 as non-visual interface.

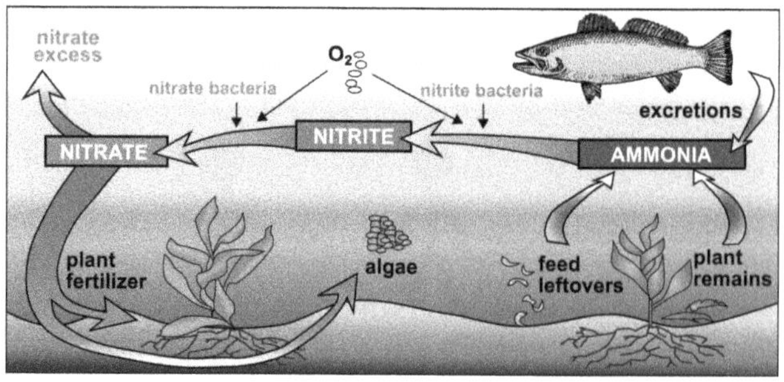

Figure 3: Picture to be transcribed into a tactile version - a nitrogen circle in underwater habitat.

4.1 Test Setting

The evaluation was conducted on a desktop PC with an Intel core i3 processor with 3.6 GHz on two physical and four logical cores having 8 GB main memory. Besides normal mouse and standard keyboard, the workstation is equipped with two 23.8" monitors having both a resolution of 1920 to 1080 pixels (see Figure 2). The operating system was Windows 8.1 and as drawing application LibreOffice Draw in the version 4.3.6.2 was used.

For the non-visual user interface a BrailleDis 7200 device by Metec AG was used [19]. This device provides a display area of 120 x 60 pins on a size of 30 x 15 cm which results in a resolution of about 10 dpi. It is connected to the PC via USB 2.0 and has a separate power supply. The device is touch-sensitive and has a touch input resolution of about 5 dpi with a frequency of 20 Hz. Surrounding the display area 19 control elements are placed including buttons which can also be used as a Braille keyboard.

During a test run the participants sat side by side on one desk. A video camera was used to document the hand movements of the non-visual user and also record the discussions, questions and problems via audio. In addition to detailed program logs by the Tangram software, containing of user interactions, program errors and audio feedback documentation, a screen-capturing tool was used to capture the GUI of the Draw application.

Two test conductors were available through the whole test run. The non-visual and the GUI user were cared for by one of the two conductors as a fixed contact for support.

4.2 Participants

We have conducted our studies with eight pairs of a sighted and a blind user. There were four female and four male sighted users which were aged between 22 and 59 (average age = 38). Four of them were tactile graphics professionals while the other four had no or minor experiences with the creation of tactile graphics. All of them had at least some experience with graphic editing software, four participants even had some experience with LibreOffice Draw. Two of the professionals use Corel Draw, one uses PowerPoint and one uses LibreOffice Draw for creating tactile graphics.

As mentioned above, tactile graphics are often produced by inexperienced persons and our workstation should also support these people. Therefore, in our studies we used both, professionals as well as laymen in this field.

The non-visual user group consisted of two female and six male legally blind users which were aged between 27 and 59 (average age = 43). Four of them were early blind and four were late blind. All of them were trained Braille readers with different experience levels in exploring and creating tactile graphics as well as in working with the BrailleDis 7200 device (see Table 1). In self-constructing tactile graphics they are mostly experienced with manual methods, such as German foil, form composition, elastic strap and pins or drawing with spur wheels. As we have found in our previous survey (see [20]), even our experienced participants rarely use digital methods. Only subjects 2, 6 and 8 having the highest experiences, are familiar with generating Braille character images and using embosser software or command languages for creating graphics.

Table 1: Experience Levels of the Blind Participants

subject	tactile graphic exploration	tactile graphic creation	pin device
#P1	high	medium	high
#P2	very high	high	very high
#P3	medium	low	very low
#P4	low	very low	very low
#P5	very high	medium	high
#P6	very high	high	medium
#P7	high	low	medium
#P8	very high	medium	high

4.3 Materials and Procedure

The image to transcribe is a diagram showing the mechanism of nitrogen transformation in an underwater habitat (see Figure 3). The image was chosen because it contains a lot of different graphical and textual objects and the topic is clear and understandable but not so common that one of the participants is an expert in this field. A short textual explanation about the context and the circumstances to the image was given as well.

Each evaluation was performed by a team consisting of a sighted graphics transcriber and a blind tactile graphic reader as non-visual lector and potential consumer.

The test run started with an introduction explaining the main goals of the project and the workstation to test. Then the two participants were separated to fill out a questionnaire about demographic data and pre-knowledge.

Afterwards the participants were separately trained in using the workstation. The sighted user got an introduction in using LibreOffice Draw, the Tangram Toolbar and a short preview on how the interaction with the non-visual user will occur. For nonprofessional transcribers the training was expanded by basic instructions about how to prepare a good alternative image description and tactile graphic. In particular this included basic guidelines, such as simplicity, avoidance of perspective, minimum size and spacing between elements as well as distinguishability of symbols, lines and textures.

The blind participants were trained on the fully functional workstation. They were introduced in basic navigation, orientation and manipulation operations as well as informed about some best practices, strategies and limitations of the system.

While professional transcribers were allowed to prepare a tactile version and an alternative textual description of the test image in advance and with a drawing tool of their choice, non-professionals should transcribe the test image into a tactile graphic with LibreOffice Draw and the Tangram tools after the training phase. Professional transcribers were allowed to make adjustments in their prepared graphic after importing it into LibreOffice.

To train communication, collaboration and the usage of the workstation a short team training phase with a sample image was conducted. After a maximum time of 30 minutes this training was aborted.

As main test the transcribed graphic was loaded into the workstation and the team was requested to explore, discuss and eventually improve it. The sighted author of the graphic gave a short description of the original picture, the context and his transcribed version. While the graphic author explained his graphic the blind reviewer was free to explore the graphic through the non-visual interface. During the non-visual exploration the partners could discuss, for instance, reading directions, recognizability of individual elements and comprehensibility of parts of the image. The non-visual reviewer could make changes on the graphic on his own or give his partner some advice for changes, which he could observe in real time. This phase ended after both team members declare that they are satisfied with the resulting graphic.

Finally the sighted and blind participants were separated again for a questionnaire to give feedback about the evaluated system and the workflow. The two graphic versions, before and after collaborative reviewing, were produced using a Tiger Pro tactile pin-matrix embosser. The participants should rate the quality of both embossed tactile versions.

4.4 Results

A complete test run including all above mentioned phases has lasted four to five hours. The average times needed for the creation of the first graphic version as well as the main phase, namely the collaborative editing, is shown in Figure 4. When comparing the expert with the laymen teams it can be seen that the experts obviously needed more time to prepare the first version. In the cooperative phase the experts needed somewhat less time compared to the laymen teams.

Altogether, creating the final graphic within the workflow of our test setting took about 131 minutes. For our special graphic we have not done a comparison with the common workflow[1]. As the participants were not experienced with the Tangram Workstation and they also were not well-rehearsed teams, a fair comparison is not possible yet. The usually needed time for producing tactile graphics is about 1 to 2 hours in most institutions [20]. It should be noted that this time is only for the initial creation, but without respect to subsequent revisions after user feedback or other kinds of extensive quality checking.

The user studies have shown that blind people can be involved in the editing process of tactile graphics by using the Tangram Workstation. Most of the functions and concepts of the non-visual interface were rated as very helpful and also as very intuitive. Especially the selection of graphic elements by tapping on it and the audio output of the corresponding information was liked very much. This kind of audio-tactile exploration is already common, for instance in the IVEO system [11]. One major advantage of this concept is that Braille labels can be reduced and a graphic can be explored easily without the need of reading the text.

The rating of some important aspects of the Tangram Workstation is shown in Figure 5. Especially the blind users gave a very positive rating not only for the provided functionalities on the pin device, but also for the cooperation with the sighted partner as well as the support of the workflow. Even the learnability was rated as good, although a lot of button commands have to be learned and a good spatial imagination is required by the pin device user.

One main aspect of the Tangram Lector evaluation was the rating of the two foci and the editing modes. Six of the eight blind users rated the focus concepts as very comprehensible, while the others rated it as medium because some experience is necessary. The editing modes for modifying graphic objects by using the right cursor keypad of the pin device were rated as very intuitive, effective, efficient and satisfying (see Figure 6). The direct feedback was also liked very much.

The drawback of reduced efficiency because of the linear changing of the editing modes (see [5]) was only criticized by two of the eight users. Two other participants proposed to add some help text for each of the editing modes to support the learnability of the system. One of these two users also would prefer to get some feedback about the current value when entering a mode. For instance, on entering the object filling mode the current selected filling pattern should be announced.

The Tangram Toolbar was rated by the eight sighted users. Most of the toolbar functions were rated as helpful and intuitive. However some functions, such as the buttons for showing/hiding the docking window and for adding some spacing between filling pattern and contour line, were not used during the test by most of the participants for which reason there are no significant results.

Besides the rating of the system, we also asked the participants which advantages and disadvantages they see compared to the conventional creation of tactile graphics. All sighted users thought that the inclusion of a blind user is an advantage as he can be asked about problems within the graphic ad hoc. Nevertheless, two of the experts criticized the low resolution of the BrailleDis 7200 as it leads to an insufficient overview for the blind user. Two other partici-

[1]The common workflow we refer to can be explained as follows: A sighted person (not necessarily a professional) creates a tactile graphic master, produces a hardcopy version, for instance with a pin-matrix embosser, and shows it to a blind user. Based on the feedback he revises the graphic master and produces a new hardcopy version which he then shows to the blind person again and so on. This procedure is done till the blind user is satisfied with the result.

pants (one expert and one laymen) are in doubt about the efficiency of the collaborative approach.

All blind users liked the possibility to play a part in the graphics production process and to directly give some feedback for enhancing the quality of the tactile graphic. The division of working tasks as well as the real-time feedback about changes was also seen as an advantage. Three blind users reported the need of a sighted partner as disadvantage. Two of the users were in doubt about the efficiency and feasibility of the workstation. One participant criticized that the workstation is not portable and needs a lot of space.

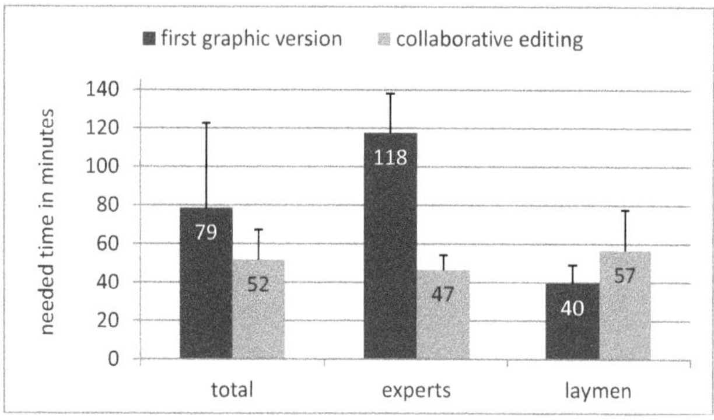

Figure 4: Time needed by the eight sighted participants for the creation of the first graphic version and the collaborative editing (means and standard deviations).

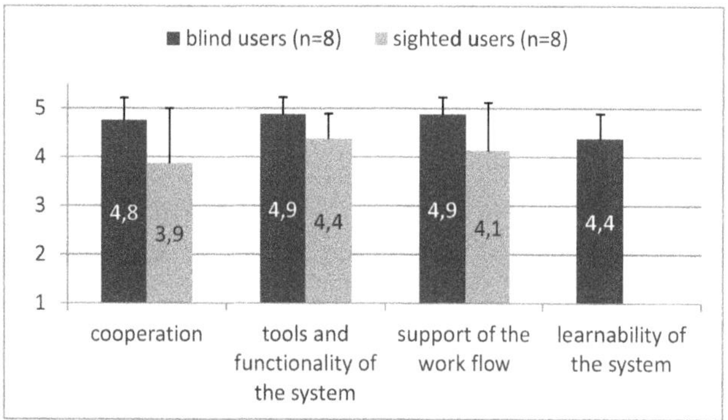

Figure 5: Rating of the main aspects of the Tangram Workstation given by the blind and sighted participants (scale: 1 = very bad to 5 = very good; means and standard deviations).

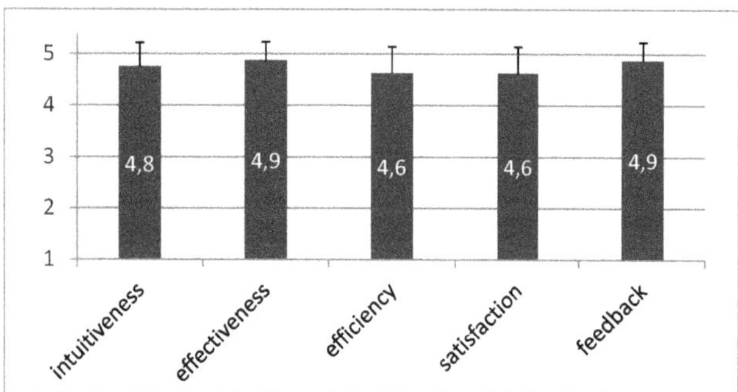

Figure 6: Rating of some aspects of the editing mode usage on the pin device given by the blind participants (scale: 1 = very bad to 5 = very good; n=8; means and standard deviations).

4.5 Observations

In the following some interesting observations on different kinds of collaboration between the team partners as well as on the non-visual interaction and the resulted tactile graphics are summarized.

4.5.1 Types of Collaboration

To find out which strategies were used during collaboration, the two test conductors being present in all tests independently set up a classification based on their own observations. Besides, an uninvolved expert on user studies made a classification, too. Thereto, he got the test protocols where the interactions and discussions between sighted and blind user were summarized textually.

All categorizations agreed that there could be observed three different kinds of blind users and their interaction on the tactile graphic:

1. Passive observer: blind user is strongly guided by the sighted user and only gives some hints when he is asked for in most cases.

2. Active consultant: blind user gives instructions to the sighted partner, but does not provide any modifications by himself.

3. Active graphics editor: blind user not only gives some instructions, but also actively provides modifications and annotates some elements with title and description while the sighted user creates or modifies other parts of the graphic.

Two of the users could be classified as type 1, one user as type 2 and three users as type 3. Two users changed their role during the test session from type 2 to type 1 and, therefore, will be classified as a mixture of type 1 and 2. The result of the classification can be explained by the fact that the two type 1 users had only minor experience with the pin device while the other users have much more training with the device. Furthermore, these two users also had the lowest experience in exploring and creating tactile graphics. However, previous experiences with the pin device seem to have more impact on the usage of the system than the user's experience level in dealing with tactile graphics.

As another result, it became clear that teams of people knowing each other were much more talkative than teams of non-related team-mates. This led to more active conversation and discussion. On the other side, the communication within the teams of the two mixed type users resulted in too much discussion for which reason the role changing in the blind users behavior can be explained.

Often the sighted graphics authors did not veto against change requests of their reviewer even when they know that the reported graphic error is caused by software problems, such as disappearing thin lines in a small zoom level (see section 5). For instance, even professionals broadened lines if they were not visible on the pin device regardless of whether they were too thin (according to some tactile graphic guideline) or not. This shows that the experiences of both users with the system are as important as their communication and knowledge of basic graphic guidelines.

The following observations could be made on the behavior of sighted experts and laymen. Non-professionals used the system more open-minded as they were more flexible in using the available tools and had more discussions with their blind partners. They also tried more different possibilities of the whole system whereas professionals more often complained about missing or not so user friendly functionalities of the Draw application. The professional participants seem to be not so flexible to use a different application to create a tactile graphic because they are used to the graphic application they are accustomed to.

Compared to non-professionals who often started a discussion about why a change intended by the blind partner is necessary, professionals seem to be more surprised about requested changes. In most cases they accepted the requests without further contradiction even if they knew that the base for the request was a misunderstanding or a presentation error due to the low display resolution.

4.5.2 Non-visual Interaction

Besides the observations on collaborative aspects of the team members the handling of the non-visual interface has to be considered, too, to allow for some explanations of occurring problems or differences in the users' interaction.

Blind reviewers with less experience in working with the pin device often tried to guess tactile figures in a small zoom level. They hesitated to ask their partner about it or to make a zoom operation to increase the object for a better recognition.

It often happened that blind users lost their context when performing zooming or panning operations. For instance, even experienced users confound the panning metaphor and chose the wrong panning direction. Major confusion was also caused if objects at the edges of the currently visible section were explored and a zooming operation clipped that element because of the center-based implementation of the zoom.

The used blinking rate for marking frames (1.25 Hz), such as for marking currently focused elements, was rated as too slow. Participants stated that they would use such frames as reference points. It would take too much time to wait for a disappeared frame to be palpable again. They also pointed out that the slow blinking frequency cannot be heard but they are used to hear mechanical sounds while blinking from their common single-line computer Braille displays which give a hint that something of special interest is presented and marked.

On the other hand, the blinking frames surrounding an object disturb the figural perception. Participants often turned the marking border off after they have found the object to get a better perception of the outlines.

All participants did not distinguish between exploration and manipulation gesture. They always used the manipulation gesture button even if they only wanted to gain information about the object, such as name, type and additional title. One blind participant proposed to enhance the audio feedback of the exploration gesture by adding the description of the element to the output. Thus it is given an additional benefit compared to the manipulation gesture.

The limited space and resolution on the pin device does not allow for giving a detailed overview about the whole graphic in DIN-A4 or Letter size in one single view without the need of navigation operations. This was criticized by two participants because they could not easily get a detailed overview of the graphic.

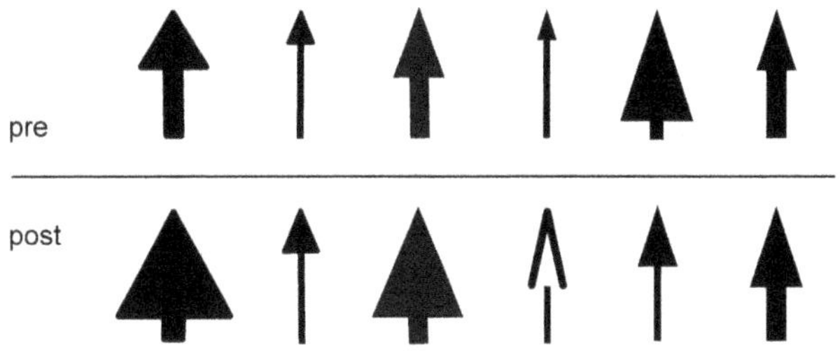

Figure 7: Comparison of tactile arrow heads before and after adaption through collaboration.

4.5.3 Produced Tactile Graphics

On average, 2.3 kinds of changes were made on the graphic during the collaborative phase (min = 1, max = 4). All in all, we have analyzed 51 discussions about possible changes throughout the entire study. These include questions of the sighted users ("Are the arrows easily recognizable?", "Should I make the lines thicker?", "Should I mirror the whole graphic that you can read it from left to right?" etc.) as well as issues of the blind participants (e.g. "The arrows should get a bigger distance from the target object.", "We should add a caption.").

In 60.8% of all cases the sighted partner has motivated the discussion. However, this only resulted to a revision of the graphic with a probability of 45.2% . In most of the cases the blind user did not agree with the modification proposal of the sighted partner. For instance, three of the sighted users asked if pictorial content (e.g. abstract fish image) should be included instead of textual labels, but all blind partners negotiate that question. On the other side, most of the comments of the blind reviewers (80%) were implemented.

Mostly, the sighted partner made the desired adaption. Only three of the blind users did some kind of autonomous annotations, such as adding a title or a description to graphical elements. One of these participants even used the editing possibilities on the pin device for showing his suggestions to the sighted partner directly in the drawing document.

By and large, the following types of modifications were made:

- changed arrows (6 of 8 teams, see Figure 7)
- widen line of boxes (3 teams, see Figure 8 left)
- add additional boxes around text labels (2 teams)
- enlarge spacing between objects (2 teams)
- add heading or other content (2 teams)
- replace pictorial by textual content (1 team)
- take text labels into legend (1 team)
- change structure of the whole graphic (1 team, see Figure 8 right)

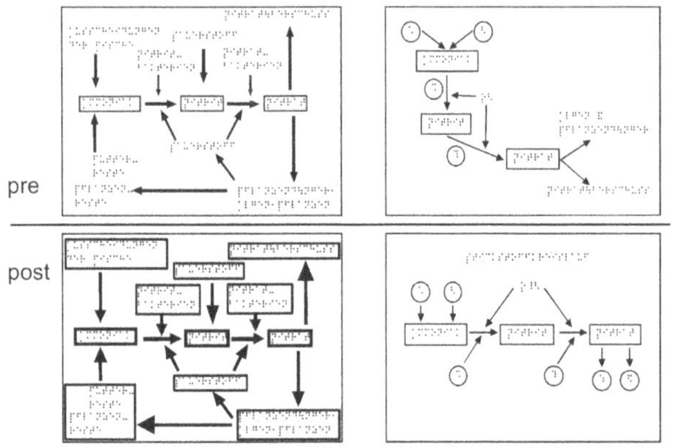

Figure 8: Examples of transcribed graphics based on the picture shown in Figure 3. The images show the tactile graphic results before and after adaption through collaboration. Text content is shown in German Braille as it was printed on the embosser.

Nearly all blind reviewers criticized the arrow heads as in most cases the transcribers used too small ones. The low resolution of the pin device deteriorates the readability even more. In the end, most final graphics were changed and produced with larger or different arrows (see Figure 7).

In some cases graphical elements will be changed to be bigger and stronger than it is needed on the final production method, for example microcapsule paper or pin-matrix embossers with resolutions up to 20 dpi. In Figure 8 such an example is shown on the left. In comparison to that the example on the right side has no changes in arrow size or line styling. Instead it shows how one of the teams has changed the complete structure of the graphic.

In the end, the resulted tactile graphics were better rated on average than the first versions which were solely created by a sighted user (see Figure 9). Especially the post versions of laymen teams seem to have great improvements. Only two expert teams gave the pre and post version the same rating because there were some improvements but also some worsenings.

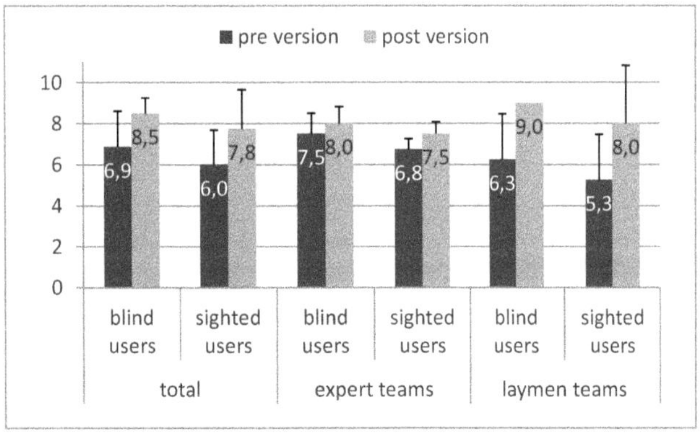

Figure 9: Rating of the produced tactile graphic versions given by the blind and sighted participants (scale: 0 = very bad to 10 = very good; means and standard deviations).

5. DISCUSSION

In the following some limits of the system that could be observed in the evaluation will be explained.

The method of taking screenshots and transforming them into downsized binary pictures leads to interpolation problems. This means lines can disappear in the tactile presentation when the image is greatly reduced in size, for example in a small zoom level (see Figure 10). This is a problem if the non-visual user is trying to get an overview over the whole image. Fine structures will not be recognizable, which can result in an incomplete or confusing impression. Moreover, it happens that lines will fall in between the interpolation raster. Thereby, a two-pin-width line occurs while other lines of the same width will stay as a one-pin-width, or even worse a line disappears because it is blurred and, therefore, it is no longer darker than the threshold determining if pins will be raised or lowered.

To solve this problem the graphical content has to be rendered with respect to the low resolution of the display. This requires the implementation of a special renderer for graphical objects. Finding a better downsizing or interpolation method for images maintaining edges in graphics could be a solution as well.

The lower resolution of the non-visual user interface will have great effect on the resulting hardcopies. Participants noticed that they would prefer a real produced tactile hardcopy for doing a final review. They also mentioned that the resulting objects will tactually differ from the impressions they got during the reviewing phase. In the end, this is mainly based on the fact that the participants did not have any experience in relating one medium to another. This means, they have problems to imagine how a low resolution element would look like on a high resolution medium. To enable such a comparison a high practical experience seems to be necessary.

To judge an object's resulting tactile gestalt it is recommended to show the real result on the target production medium - especially if fine object structures are relevant which can only be perceived in a high zoom level on the pin device. However, the overall graphic composition, structure and understandability can be soundly discussed and rated by the non-visual user. In conclusion, it should be noted that if a graphic and all its elements are rated as appropriate on a low resolution display, they are indeed readable on a high resolution medium, but without exhausting the specific possibilities of the medium.

Besides such limitations that depend on the resolution of the pin device, there are also limitations which relate to the content of the original picture, of course. Content errors caused by wrong transcription or misunderstanding cannot be identified by the non-visual reviewer because he cannot check the original graphic. Textual content is not displayed in Braille but presented as tactile ink-print on the pin device or can be achieved through auditory feedback. Therefore, no checking for correct Braille writing or typesetting is possible yet.

There are also technical limits caused by the insufficiency of the used interfaces to OpenOffice or LibreOffice. Especially the accessibility interface, which is used for touch input and focus monitoring, is very limited and needs to be improved. A mapping of a touch position on the pin device to a pixel position on the screen is computed to simulate touch interaction. The element at that screen position is requested

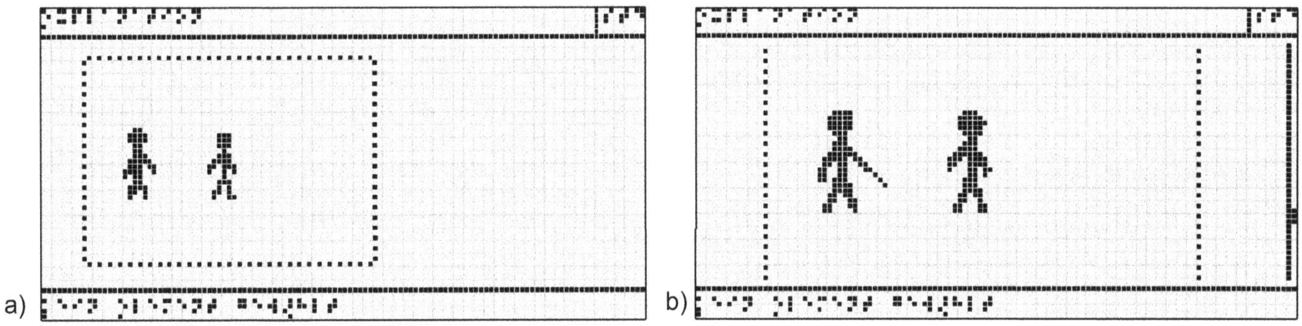

Figure 10: Example of disappearing lines by interpolation: smallest zoom-level with missing line (a), sector after zooming one step in - the line appears (b).

through the accessibility interface. The interface returns the most recently created graphic element whose bounding box is containing the requested pixel coordinates. No real collision test against opaque structures of elements is done unlike for mouse interaction. Sometimes elements cannot be used for touch interaction on the pin device because a wrong or unexpected element is returned.

A solution to overcome this problem is to implement a graphical collision test on our own or to occupy the mouse to request which object is touched. The last solution will massively disturb the work of the screen user and will lead to some kind of "mouse and focus war". A mechanism for walking through the documents' elements in a deterministic way is implemented to reduce this handicap, but this makes finding an object more costly and time consuming.

At large, the evaluation showed that the reviewing process took a lot of time, which is in contrast to our initial hypotheses. One of the most time consuming parts was the introduction phase in which the non-visual user tried to get an understanding of the graphic. However, this phase is essential to get well-grounded feedback. In a real-world scenario it does not seem to be practical to establish such a full reviewing process for every picture of a whole book.

In fact, it seems appropriate to use the system for the training of transcriber beginners and for reviewing difficult graphics or graphic parts. Nevertheless, it would be desirable to use this pair-creation process for every transcription because it is proven that blind users would add improvements even on professional transcriptions. One possible compromise could be to collaboratively design solutions for general problems and reuse these for future graphic transcriptions.

6. CONCLUSION AND OUTLOOK

In this paper we have presented a collaborative workstation for creating tactile graphics. We have shown that a non-visual reviewer is able to give feedback about the quality of a tactile graphic and, furthermore, can adapt graphics on his or her own by using the Tangram Workstation. Involved as active members into the production process, target group users did further improvements even on professionally created graphics which led to an increased final quality.

As stated in the related work chapter, previous projects only address the support of a sighted graphic producer to speed up the direct transformation of images into a more or less usable tactile representation. In contrast, our system directly focuses on the quality of the resulting tactile graphic. In no other transcription project the direct and active involvement of a non-visual user is possible. Moreover, there is no mechanism for quality management provided. A faster and semi-automated tactile image production does not guarantee a usable result.

The key to a good usable tactile graphic lies in a proper adaptation of the essence of the source image and in a well structured presentation [8, 16]. Guidelines can help to avoid beginner mistakes but knowledge about correct representation and structuring can be achieved only through practice and feedback. At this point, the Tangram Workstation has its benefits as the graphic transcriber will get direct feedback on every change that is made.

Beyond the reviewing for other users we have identified the following huge advantages:

- individualization of tactile images for one special reader
- development of a tactile representation in collaboration with a non-visual consumer
- sketching and modification of visual issues for and with a blind person in a fast and easy manner

During evaluation it became clear from user feedback that being involved into the transcription process increases the understanding of the graphic. All participants mentioned that it would take some time to get used to the system and, therefore, to use the whole potential. For instance, in their first attempts they still would produce the tactile graphic on paper several times to get a feeling for comparing the presentation on the pin device with the real tactile hardcopy.

To clarify the hypothesis if the presented system produces tactile graphics with a better quality, the resulting images have to be rated by external and, therefore, more objective reviewers.

Next steps will enable the non-visual user to become more independent in creating and deleting elements. We also will include Braille directly into the tactile presentation as this was a big wish of participants. These steps will contribute to further increasing the independence of blind users in the creation process of tactile graphics.

7. ACKNOWLEDGEMENTS

We thank all involved developers, our blind and sighted participants as well as the German Central Library for the Blind Leipzig (DZB) and the Study Centre for the Visually

Impaired Students (SZS) Karlsruhe for their support. The Tangram project is sponsored by the Federal Ministry of Labour and Social Affairs (BMAS) under the grant number R/FO125423.

8. REFERENCES

[1] LibreOffice download site. Retrieved July 23, 2015 from https://www.libreoffice.org/download.

[2] OpenOffice download site. Retrieved July 23, 2015 from https://www.openoffice.org/download.

[3] M. Batusic and F. Urban. Preparing tactile graphics for traditional braille printers with BrlGraphEditor. In K. Miesenberger, J. Klaus, and W. Zagler, editors, *Computers Helping People with Special Needs*, volume 2398 of *Lecture Notes in Computer Science*, pages 535–536. Springer Berlin Heidelberg, 2002.

[4] J. Bornschein and D. Prescher. Collaborative tactile graphic workstation for touch-sensitive pin-matrix devices. In *Proceedings of the International Workshop on Tactile/Haptic User Interfaces for Tabletops and Tablets*, pages 42–47, November 2014.

[5] J. Bornschein, D. Prescher, and G. Weber. Inclusive production of tactile graphics. In *Human-Computer Interaction – INTERACT 2015*. Accepted.

[6] D. Crombie, R. Lenoir, N. McKenzie, and G. Ioannidis. The bigger picture: Automated production tools for tactile graphics. In K. Miesenberger, J. Klaus, W. L. Zagler, and D. Burger, editors, *Computers Helping People with Special Needs*, volume 3118 of *Lecture Notes in Computer Science*, pages 713–720. Springer Berlin Heidelberg, 2004.

[7] Duxbury Systems, Inc. QuickTac 4.0 product information. Retrieved July 23, 2015 from http://www.duxburysystems.com/product2.asp?product=QuickTac.

[8] P. Edman. *Tactile graphics*. American Foundation for the Blind, 1992.

[9] Freedom Scientific, Inc. JAWS Tandem quick start guide. Retrieved July 23, 2015 from http://www.freedomscientific.com/JAWSHq/JAWSTandemQuickStart.

[10] M. Fujiyoshi, A. Fujiyoshi, A. Osawa, Y. Kuroda, and Y. Sasaki. Development of synchronized CUI and GUI for universal design tactile graphics production system BPLOT3. In K. Miesenberger, D. Fels, D. Archambault, P. Peňáz, and W. Zagler, editors, *Computers Helping People with Special Needs*, volume 8548 of *Lecture Notes in Computer Science*, pages 18–25. Springer International Publishing, 2014.

[11] J. Gardner and V. Bulatov. Scientific diagrams made easy with IVEO. In K. Miesenberger, J. Klaus, W. L. Zagler, and A. I. Karshmer, editors, *Computers Helping People with Special Needs*, volume 4061 of *Lecture Notes in Computer Science*, pages 1243–1250. Springer Berlin Heidelberg, 2006.

[12] J. Gardner, V. Bulatov, and R. Kelly. Making journals accessible to the visually impaired: the future is near. *Learned publishing: journal of the Association of Learned and Professional Society Publishers*, 22(4):314, 2009.

[13] J. A. Gardner. Tactile graphics, an overview and resource guide. *Information Technology and Disabilities*, 3(4):1996, 1996.

[14] C. Jayant, M. Renzelmann, D. Wen, S. Krisnandi, R. Ladner, and D. Comden. Automated tactile graphics translation: In the field. In *Proceedings of the 9th International ACM SIGACCESS Conference on Computers and Accessibility*, Assets '07, pages 75–82, New York, NY, USA, 2007. ACM.

[15] A. Lahiri, S. J. Chattopadhyay, and A. Basu. Sparsha: A comprehensive indian language toolset for the blind. In *Proceedings of the 7th International ACM SIGACCESS Conference on Computers and Accessibility*, Assets '05, pages 114–120, New York, NY, USA, 2005. ACM.

[16] B. A. of North America. Guidelines and standards for tactile graphics, 2010. Retrieved July 23, 2015 from http://www.brailleauthority.org/tg.

[17] Pentronics. PictureBraille product information. Retrieved July 23, 2015 from http://www.pentronics.com.au/index_files/PictureBraille.htm.

[18] B. Plimmer, A. Crossan, S. A. Brewster, and R. Blagojevic. Multimodal collaborative handwriting training for visually-impaired people. In *Proceedings of the SIGCHI Conference on Human Factors in Computing Systems*, CHI '08, pages 393–402, New York, NY, USA, 2008. ACM.

[19] D. Prescher. Redesigning input controls of a touch-sensitive pin-matrix device. In *Proceedings of the International Workshop on Tactile/Haptic User Interfaces for Tabletops and Tablets*, pages 19–24, November 2014.

[20] D. Prescher, J. Bornschein, and G. Weber. Production of accessible tactile graphics. In K. Miesenberger, D. Fels, D. Archambault, P. Peňáz, and W. Zagler, editors, *Computers Helping People with Special Needs*, volume 8548 of *Lecture Notes in Computer Science*, pages 26–33. Springer International Publishing, 2014.

[21] Thinkable. TactileView introduction. Retrieved July 23, 2015 from http://www.tactileview.com/.

[22] F. Vidal-Verdu and M. Hafez. Graphical tactile displays for visually-impaired people. *IEEE Transactions on Neural Systems and Rehabilitation Engineering*, 15(1):119–130, March 2007.

[23] ViewPlus. Tiger Software Suite. Retrieved July 23, 2015 from https://viewplus.com/product/tiger-software-suite/.

[24] T. Völkel, G. Weber, and U. Baumann. Tactile graphics revised: The novel BrailleDis 9000 pin-matrix device with multitouch input. In K. Miesenberger, J. Klaus, W. Zagler, and A. Karshmer, editors, *Computers Helping People with Special Needs*, volume 5105 of *Lecture Notes in Computer Science*, pages 835–842. Springer Berlin Heidelberg, 2008.

Transcribing Across the Senses: Community Efforts to Create 3D Printable Accessible Tactile Pictures for Young Children with Visual Impairments

Abigale Stangl
ATLAS/Sikuli Lab
University of Colorado, Boulder
Abigale.Stangl@colorado.edu

Chia-Lo Hsu
Sikuli Lab
University of Colorado, Boulder
Chialo.Hsu@colorado.edu

Tom Yeh
Sikuli Lab
University of Colorado, Boulder
Tom.Yeh@colorado.edu

ABSTRACT
The design of 3D printable accessible tactile pictures (3DP-ATPs) for young children with visual impairments has the potential to greatly increase the supply of tactile materials that can be used to support emergent literacy skill development. Many caregivers and stakeholders invested in supporting young children with visual impairments have shown interest in using 3D printing to make accessible tactile materials. Unfortunately, the task of designing and producing 3DP-ATPs is far more complex than simply learning to use personal fabrication tools. This paper presents formative research conducted to investigate how six caregiver stakeholder-groups, with diverse skillsets and domain interests, attempt to create purposeful 3DP-ATPs with amateur-focused 3D modeling programs. We expose the experiences of these stakeholder groups as they attempt to design 3DP-ATG for the first time. We discuss how the participant groups practically and conceptually approach the task and focus their design work. Each group demonstrated different combinations of skillsets. In turn, we identify the common activities required of the design task as well how different participants are well suited and motivated to preform those activities. This study suggests that the emerging community of amateur 3DP-ATP designers may benefit from an online creativity support tool to help offset the challenges of designing purposeful 3DP-ATPs that are designed to meet individual children with VI's emergent literacy needs.

Categories and Subject Descriptors
K.4.2 [Computers and Society]: Social Issues– assistive technologies for persons with disabilities.

General Terms
Design; Experimentation; Human Factors

Keywords
Visual impairment; emergent literacy; tactile pictures; tactile graphics; accessibility; 3D print; 3D model

1. INTRODUCTION
Emergent literacy is the process in which a young child constructs concepts about the function of symbols and print. It is based on experiences and meaningful language facilitated by interactions with adults. For sighted children, pictures and illustrations provide a bridge between listening and early reading behaviors. These visual stimulants play a major role in enriching the storyline and adding humor and intrigue, giving instant clues that enable the reader to reconstruct the story. Children only gradually become aware of the text over time; it is the illustrations that help a child recall the meaning and words of a story [30].

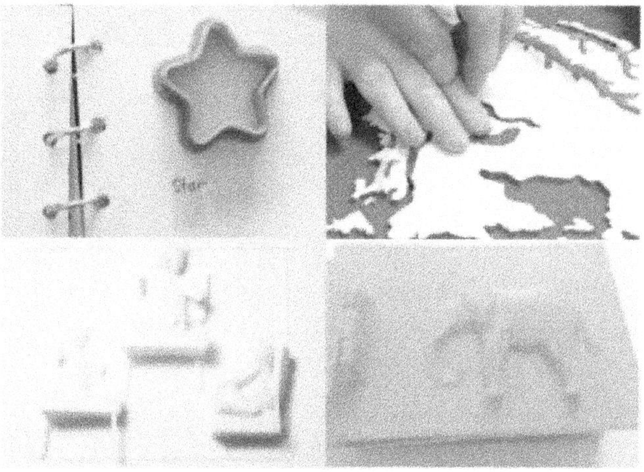

Figure 1. Top: Handcrafted 2.5D-ATP/ATG (Source: Perkins School); Bottom 3D Printed 3DP-ATP (Source: Ref. 19, 39).

Children with visual impairments (VI) often miss the opportunity to learn from illustrated children's books because their perception is limited to what can be felt by the hand, seen within a limited visual field, and heard. Children with VI often have difficulty understanding the gestalt, or whole nature of an experience [16]. Accessible tactile pictures (ATPs) consist of tactile representations that convey different kinds of messages and present information through the sense of touch to further a child's cognitive-affective and relational development [14]. Successful ATPs for young learners (kindergarten through 3rd grade) focus on representing content in a tactile manner that builds a younger child's understanding of symbolic representation and confidence to explore their environments and make associations through the sense of touch (tactile acuity). They can be used during co-reading experiences between a caregiver and a child, and help convey relationships, concepts, and story objects relevant to the child's learning. Reading and play with ATPs an important role in developing emergent literacy skills in young children with VI because they support joint attention with a child reads with caregivers [38], offer children with a means to be an active participant in the reading experience, and offer opportunities for interaction with their peers. ATPs and ATGs are most successfully used along side other verbal description of the story.

ASSETS '15, October 26-28, 2015, Lisbon, Portugal.
© 2015 ACM. ISBN 978-1-4503-3400-6/15/10...$15.00
DOI: http://dx.doi.org/10.1145/2700648.2809854

The Braille Authority of North America (BANA) indicates that solid shapes are more easily recognized than outline of shapes and objects for young readers, who are learning emergent literacy skills [10]. If designed well, ATPs can support one's learning from part to whole, and help prepare children with VI to make a stress-free transition to accessible tactile graphics (ATGs), which blind learners are likely to use as they advance in their education [14]. ATGs focus on conveying science, technology, engineering, and math (STEM) topics, which are commonly transformed representations of diagrams, charts, maps, and drawings.

The design of ATPs and other accessible materials, like the design of many assistive technologies (AT) [20], greatly benefits from the consultation and involvement of end-users and their caregivers. Of late, many caregivers and other stakeholders of children with VI have identified the opportunity of 3D printers to make low-cost, highly customized tactile forms, objects, and books containing 3D printed accessible tactile graphics (3DP-ATGs) and 3D printed accessible tactile pictures or illustrations (3DP-ATPs) [36] (Figure 1). Unlike traditional ATG and ATP production methods (embossers, thermoform, handcraft) 3D printing allows for the rapid production of solid forms and personalized ATPs. However, despite the growing popularity of 3D printers and their affordances, the complexity of the design task creates a barrier to using 3D printers for creating ATPs.

In this paper, we present formative research to identify how caregivers and stakeholders of people with VI engage in the design practice of making accessible 3DP-ATPs and how they innately approach 3D modeling, tactile graphicacy, decoding, and other skillsets to achieve the design task. Through conducting six workshops, with 67 participants in total, we observed the workshop groups' abilities, and conceptual and practical approaches to transcribing visual pictures into meaningful 3D tactile experiences.

While no one participant group fully accomplished the design task during the workshops, we noted a clear division in the groups' approaches, and thus propose how different stakeholder groups' abilities can be leveraged to accomplish the multidisciplinary design task. We expand upon the previous work on assessable tactile and sound-based materials for people with VI, and 3D printed assistive technologies (AT). This research also contributes to an ongoing effort to design and develop an online digital library and creative collaboration tool that bridges the social and design capital those committed to supporting emergent literacy.

2. BACKGROUND

ATG and ATP Production and Supply: Organizations serving blind communities have been making children's books for VI children for years. In the United States, publishers e.g., American Printing House for the Blind (APH) and National Braille Press (NBP), and tactile graphic artists have been the primary producers of ATGs and ATPs. NBP carries a catalog of 100+ children's books [32] and Seedlings, a nonprofit organization dedicated to providing low-cost Braille books for VI children, has a catalog of 1,200 titles [35]. In addition to the mass produced books, several organizations in the United States and Europe have organized ATG and ATP book competitions in order to entice artists and other stakeholders to create new material [5].

However, the supply of these books is limited due to the time and cost involved with designing and validating the content, creating the thermoform and other subtractive molds, and subsequently producing the material in bulk. Many of the books that are produced are oriented to older children, and do not contain purposeful representations for those who have not yet learned Braille or more advanced decoding skills. Furthermore, much of the material is not easily customized to meet the unique learning needs of an individual child. In turn, when purchasing traditional ATPs and books from publishers or artists, caregivers often face a tradeoff between cost, supply/selection, and appropriateness for their child's unique needs.

Need for Individualized ATPs: Many teachers of the visually impaired (TVIs) advocate that ATPs should be designed for the individual, specifically focusing on creating material that focuses on specific skill development and the knowledge needed to comprehend them [3]. The ways in which people learn tactile and haptic perception and acuity is greatly varied, and is dependent on their cognitive abilities as well as their learning environments. The caregivers (parents, TVIs, etc.) and artists who choose to take the time to manually make ATGs and ATPs for individual children have traditionally used a wide variety of textured materials, including textured fabric, paper, foam paper, and the like. These ATPs are often fragile and are not easily reproduced.

Of important note, the development of emergent literacy skills four young children with VI is not solely dependent on the use of ATPs. Students need assistance in interpreting the information being presented in ATPs [10] Best educational practices include additional activities to help individual children match pictures to sounds, letters, words, and the environment around them. A variety of touch graphic technologies providing non visual feedback, including but not limited to, The Talking Touch Tablet [27], Talking Tactile Pen [28], QR Codes to Access [9], that have been developed to embed various interfaces with auditory information that help individuals interpret information.

ATG and ATP Design Guidelines: For those who focus on designing ATP for bulk production or individual users, alike, there are resources available to guide their design work. The BANA guideline, provide ATG designers and braille transcriptionists with best practices and conventions for raised line/ 2.5D tactile representations, including: consider the cognitive obstacles to peoples' successful use of ATG and ATP; touch cannot discriminate the fine detail that sight can; extract information through a sequence of touches and then re-integrating it imposes a heavy memory load; assure that conceptual graphical representations are augmented with interpretation [10]. Like visual picture illustration, however, there is no single approach to designing ATGs and ATPs, and the guidelines will only go so far to inform one's design process. To the best of our knowledge, no formal work has been conducted to evaluate how or if caregivers and other stakeholders design ATPs according to the recently published guidelines, or whether the existing 2.5D guidelines are applicable to the design of 3DP materials.

Albeit, many TVIs, artists and other designers of ATG agree that when transcribing a graphic illustration into an ATG and ATP, graphicacy aids one's ability to create meaningful materials. Graphicacy depends on one's ability to decode graphic elements [4]. Aldrich suggests activities for teaching tactile graphicacy should include refining the scope of graphic formats being taught, strategically selecting contextual examples of graphics, presenting multiple versions of graphics representing similar concepts, prompting students to think of the merits of different formats, and providing opportunities for students to gain their own hands on experience with designing [2]. To this point, BANA states, "the best method for learning how to prepare a tactile graphic comes from hands on training, from critical feedback from other tactile producers and tactile graphics readers, and from experience [10]."

3. RELATED WORK

3D Printing ATG: Recent work has focused on the feasibility of using 3D printers to create AT and tactile materials [11, 25] however, many of these efforts only concentrate on the material feasibility of 3D printing STEM-focused tactile graphics or the interest of the community in using the technology, as opposed to issues of accessibility [39]. Discussions about the limitations of 3D printers for the production of tactile graphics and pictures due to the resolution of the prints highlight some potential limitations of the technology. However, recent advances in the technology are eliminating these concerns. Hudson shows that 3D printers are not limited to printing plastic [21].

AT Requirements: Several efforts have focused on the feasibility and requirements for using 3D printing in context of serving populations with varying ability, including individuals with cognitive, motor, and visual impairments. Buehler, et al. explored how 3D printing can address the concerns of designing AT and customized solutions for young students in special education environments [11]. They identified requirements for making 3D printers accessible to learners and caregivers in such environments, including: make accessible software, consider the learning curve, encourage sharing of existing models, and support editing existing models. McDonald, et al. discussed how digital fabrication can support the creation of educational aids for providing accessible curriculum content [31].

While these efforts provide great insight into the requirements for using 3D printers in special educational contexts, they do not discuss the range of stakeholders involved in approaching a specific AT educational design task with 3D printers. Hook et al. conducted interviews with 11 caregivers to explore the challenges that are, or might be, faced by non-professionals when making DIY-AT (generally) and the challenges of making DIY-AT for children with disabilities [20]. This research revealed the community's value of rapid prototyping technologies and the need for the creation of practical communities to help lower the barrier of entry for caregivers with little technical experience. They recommend an increase in practical services and communities that support and encourage larger numbers of non-professionals to become involved in making and adapting AT. To this point, Buehler, et al. presents a systematic evaluation of assistive technology creation and dissemination in an online community of assistive technology makers on Thingiverse [12]. They found that many of the shared DIY assistive technologies are created by people with disabilities or on behalf of friends and loved ones, and that these designers frequently have no formal training or expertise in the creation of assistive technology. Their findings did not include information related to the activities people engage in in order to design materials for children with VI, but they do call for efforts to engage people in the design of AT.

DIY AT Design Tools: A variety of efforts have been taken to design digital tools to support caregivers, stakeholders and people with disabilities designing AT [15, 22]. However, we have not found any project that supports users in creating 3D printable 3DP-ATPs for young children. In recent years, there has been a rise in the development of 3D digital fabrication tools for education and amateur users in order to lower the entry point to learning 3D modeling, in general. SketchUp [41], Tinkercad [8], and 123Design [6] have been designed to lower the threshold of learning for novice users while providing professionals a high ceiling for use. Unlike traditional 3D modeling programs (Rhino [34], SolidWorks [37], Maya [7]), amateur-focused tools tend to hide the underlying geometrical figures, algorithms, and vectors of the objects. Lastly, the CHI and IDC communities have focused on developing constructivist learning through 3D modeling with alternative inputs, including the UCube [29], KidCad [17], and FabCode [1]. Zeising et al. propose a series of criteria for a new wave of constructivist-based digital fabrication (modeling) software design, which, if applied, may continue to reduce the barriers of entry into 3D modeling [43]. All of these efforts have yet to build in support features for designing ATG/3DP-ATP.

4. RESEARCH METHOD

Our key research questions regarding the design of 3DP-ATP for children with VI are: (1) *What distinct stakeholder groups are interested and willing to contribute to developing 3DP-ATP, and how/what do they contribute;* (2) *How do these groups differ and what do they have in common in terms of motivation, design approach, and skill;* (3) *How can distinct stakeholder groups' skills be leveraged to increase the supply of 3DP-ATP?*

4.1 Stakeholder Groups

Background: Prior to this work, our team designed and 3D printed a series of 3DP-ATP prototypes. Through word-of-mouth and news media coverage, we received a large number of email requests from various people for samples. We subsequently delivered samples to meet a subset of these requests, limited to those who self-identified as parents or teachers of VI children because they were our priorities [39]. Informally, we were told by many of the recipients that, if possible, they would like to learn and be able to design and make 3DP-ATPs on their own. A majority of the requests came from parents or TVIs. However, we also received a significant number of email inquires from other sorts of people not traditionally associated with the blind community. Many expressed a strong desire to help design and make 3DP-ATPs. Prior to this work, we had not yet made a systematic attempt to understand who they were, what they might be able to contribute, and how their knowledge or skills may complement those of the parents and TVIs. We intentionally decided to exclude parents from this research due to another concurrent study focusing on how parents approach the design of ATG and other AT.

Participant Selection: First, we revisited all of the email requests we received, paying specific attention to those coming from people other than parents, TVIs, or blind people. We clustered the emails based on the job titles of the senders. In many cases, the sender would self-identify his or her job title, while in other cases, the job title could be inferred from the body of the message. We were able to identify clusters of librarians, retired-volunteers, engineers, students, artists, and reporters. This gave us a rough idea about what "other" stakeholder groups might exist. Next, we advertised to local communities such as libraries, schools, volunteer centers, art galleries and maker spaces, to offer workshops on 3D printable 3DP-ATPs at their sites. Our intent was to find a local representation of each of these other stakeholder groups in order to study them in depth.

Our outreach effort attracted six distinct local participant groups interested in running design workshops at their site, including a group of children librarians (n=6), a group of accessible media librarians, (n=6), a group of engineers with interest in supporting people with VI (n=3), a group of interaction designers interested in supporting people with VI (n=4), a group of volunteers who work at an accessible media library (n=7), and a group of TVIs and orientation and mobility (O&M) specialists (n=40).

4.2 Workshop Design and Analysis

Next, we describe the design of these workshops. The decision to conduct the workshops according to domain groups was driven by a desire to understand their perspectives deeply. We attempted to keep the basic structure of the workshop consistent across the various groups, but needed to customize some aspects of each workshop to better match a group's primary interests.

Critical Making: The goal of the workshops was not for participants to design a perfect 3DP-ATP or book; rather, it was to learn how people working with and for children with VI approach the task and apply their knowledge while using 3D modeling tools. Critical Making suggests that poignant selection of technology can empower people to fashion custom tools to accomplish specific tasks, visualize problems that are difficult to picture virtually, and to have fun by making their own toys (and learning aids). Specifically, 3D modeling and printing are tools to instigate new types of artistic and cultural expression, transformations of the notion of embodiment and materiality, renewed emphasis on the means of production, and the idea of a public good [33]. The design of our workshops was aimed at providing participants with an experience in the use of digital fabrication tools as a means for exploring, developing, and sharing their perspectives and values about the design task.

Hands-on Learning: Based on existing guidelines for teaching and learning tactile graphicacy, we took the applied arts approach of 'intelligent making' to support participant involvement. Intelligent making proposes a mix of formal knowledge, tacit knowledge, physical and mental skill, contextual awareness, innovation, and personal creative autonomy [13]. In crafting processes, the hands supply the brain with vital sensory information both inwardly from the external world and outwardly to enable the body to express the intentions of the maker. Hands are our primary interface with the world and provide the brain with rich sensory information, which is instrumental in building imagination and novel ideas [42]. Physical experience stimulates the imagination and provides anticipatory knowledge leading to performance in the creative act of making [40].

Structure: Each workshop was planned to last four hours based on the participant group leaders' recommendations. An hour and a half was allotted to introducing the design task, followed by two and a half hours of modeling/design work. The design task was scoped to focus on the transcription of existing pictures and books so that participants were not required to conceive of original drawings and narratives to support their compositions.

Each group was introduced to the topic by a sudden blindness activity, where blindfolded participants explored existing tactile graphics, pictures, and other materials through touch. In addition, examples of the tactile graphic guidelines and corresponding material were provided. Participants were then encouraged to analyze simple picture books such as *Good Night Moon* and *The Very Hungry Caterpillar* after a demonstration on how to decode such stories. Craft materials were also supplied for participants to rapidly explore their ideas in physical form. Each workshop was designed to incorporate the aforementioned elements; however, we allowed an adaptive workshop structure to suit each group's unique needs. Given the constructivist nature of the design task, we provided participants groups with opportunities to follow their own creative needs.

Technology: Prior to the workshops, our team completed a heuristic evaluation of five 3D modeling programs oriented to novice designers (Tinkercad, SketchUp, FreeCad, OpenSCAD, and 123D Design), their associated navigational and design tools, and their compatibility with producing STL files. The evaluation was conducted to inform the selection of the modeling tools to be presented and taught during the workshops. We used a five-point scale (1=intuitive, 2=easily learned, 3=moderate, 4=challenging, and 5=impossible) to evaluate the tools. We selected two tools to use during the workshops: Tinkercad (1.5) and SketchUp (2.5).

Figure 2 Workshop Activities: Discuss, Explore, and Model

Each group was provided an overview of the two selected 3D modeling environments. When participants were not familiar with the program, we guided them through the software installation process, demonstrated navigation, shape, and other tools within the interfaces, and in some cases provided follow-along instructions. We also gave a brief introduction to Thingiverse, an online STL repository and resource for finding, saving, and sharing models. Macintosh laptop computers and wireless mice were available for participants to use, and those with prior 3D modeling experience were encouraged to use their preferred software and tools.

Data Collection: During each workshop, we used discussion-motivated instruction methods to support participant inquiry and engagement in the design task. Numerous hands-on experiences were provided with existing tactile graphics and picture materials to allow participants to compare their touch-based experiences and reflect more deeply on the requirements of making tactile pictures. Field notes and video were employed to collect observations during both group discussions and talk-aloud activities during the modeling period to understand how participants were using their respective 3D modeling programs.

Analysis: Immediately after each workshop, we formalized our notes and recorded analytical memos that focused on participant concerns and considerations while approaching the design task and 3D modeling. After each workshop we used this information to improve the instruction of subsequent workshops, to identify each group's concerns and considerations while approaching the design task, which led to the finding that participant group have a unique approach to the design of 3DP-ATGs and may be able to take on different roles in a distributed design process.

Furthermore, when designing the workshops we understood that the task of designing and modeling 3DP-ATPs is complex and requires a range of skillsets to accomplish the task. We identified five skillsets: knowledge about human development (D), knowledge about emergent literacy (L), knowledge about tactile graphicacy (G), knowledge about task management (T), and modeling experience (M). After all of the workshops concluded we preformed a ranking of each participant group and their dominant skillsets among all participant based on observations of how they used the tools, related to principles of tactile graphicacy, referenced child development and literacy (1=low, 2=average, 3=high) (2). In addition to this ranking, we found clustering of skillsets, which provided deeper insight into how different participant groups can contribute to producing 3DP-ATPs.

5. FINDINGS: By Workshop Groups

5.1 Accessibility Librarians

Group Overview: Seven librarians from the Colorado Talking Book Library, where audio resources are recorded and provided to patrons with VI, participated in the workshop. The director of the library contacted us to inquire about our methods of creating 3DP-ATPs and to see if they were available for contribution. We agreed that a workshop would be a good way for the library's employees to learn more about 3D printing.

Prior Experience: The seven participants had a range of technology knowledge and skill for transcribing books into audio, but had no experience with 3D modeling, 3D printing, or transcribing books into a tactile format. Each participant was accustomed to interacting with visually impaired patrons at the library or on the phone daily.

Workshop Adaptations: Participants quickly lost focus and interest during the demonstration of 3D modeling, and asked to look at and touch some books prior to modeling.

Design Task Findings: The librarians spent an hour discussing the books (*Goodnight Moon*, *Five Little Ducks*, *Each Peach Pear Plum*, and *The Very Hungry Caterpillar*) and the constructs of a visual image and story. As a group they identified the graphical elements and discussed how to convey these elements through means other than sight. One librarian said, "*We should ignore elements of illustration that would distract from understanding the meaning of the story. We shouldn't worry about appearance as much as general shape.*" When exploring how to convey emotion, another asked, "*Is a teardrop enough? Maybe this is a story where a paired reader is with the VI child to establish context.*"

The group began to establish a set of their own guidelines to help with the task of transcribing illustrations, including: 1) observe the patterns of object/image repetition (e.g., movement, repetition, and progression); 2) take note of the social relationships established in the book's imagery and narrative; 3) observe how numeric and language literacy skills are being developed; 4) observe how emotions are conveyed in the story; and 5) recognize the historical and cultural context of the book and make representations that are relevant to a child's current context. The Talking Book librarians also reflected on the philosophical challenge in prioritizing illustration over text and the challenge to think about honoring the perspective of a person with VI.

Modeling Task Findings: In order to simplify the modeling work, we opted to demonstrate how to import models from Thingiverse into TinkerCad and subsequently how to use the tool to compose a page of tactile elements. All participants collectively elected to model one page from *Goodnight Moon* by ignoring elements of illustration that distract from understanding the meaning of story. One participant suggested that, "*We should not worry about appearance as much as general shape.*" While importing models from Thingiverse into TinkerCad and trying to place them on the "page" all participants struggled with differentiating between scaling and moving an object vertically. The use of navigation and orienting tools to improve the modeling experience was unintuitive for the participants. Some had difficulty using the zooming feature, while others were confused about saving and accessing their models on TinkerCad. Despite the fact that most of the participants struggled to get "*the program to do what I wanted it to do,*" all were satisfied with the experience at the end of the workshop. One librarian said that, "*This technology has a lot of potential for helping our community access their world.*"

5.2 Children's Librarians

Overview: The Boulder Public Library acquired a new 3D printer for their teen makerspace and reached out to our research team to learn more about the applications of the technology. Eight early-literacy librarians who were knowledgeable about reader engagement, literacy development, and children's books were keen to develop literacy-based materials and 3D print.

Prior Experience: Aside from the workshop coordinator, none of the librarians had previous 3D modeling or printing experience. All of the librarians worked with young children and their families' daily; they had infrequent visits from blind patrons.

Workshop Adaptations: Prior to the workshop, the library coordinator proactively created a plan to follow in order to maximize the use of time. She also began a conversation with her coworkers in preparation for the workshop, during which the librarians collaboratively chose three books to model: *Windblown*, *Where the Wild Things*, and *Anton Can Do Magic*. The books were selected because they represented three different reading levels and communicated the Every Child Ready to Read (ECRR) principle of "Play". Play was chosen as a central topic because of the embodied attributes of the theme and the opportunities for representing interactivity in a variety of ways. When describing their rationale for this during the introduction, one librarian explained that, "*some books are interactive. We see animals jump out of the page...books that really want the kids to come into the books and also the characters to go out.*" The participants repeatedly emphasized that the storytelling aspect of the design task was as important as representing objects in 3D.

Design Task Findings: During the entirety of the workshop, the librarians continuously brainstormed about opportunities for 3D printing in their libraries beyond tactile books, including: 1) creating open-ended toys (additive toys where evolving experiences and scenarios allow the child to be the instigator); 2) creating interactive wall installations and shadow puppetry; and 3) developing a prompt for local authors to produce original work paired with 3D model illustrations in association with National Novel Writing Month in November.

As we described and explored the tactile graphic guidelines, the librarians explained how illustrations were carefully composed to tell an important part of the story, and how original artistic choices were important to the narrative. One participant was very interested in, "*thinking about how to maintain the integrity of the original work; the pictures aren't just illustrating the story, they are telling the story.*" For example, the librarians explained that in the case of *Where the Wild Things Are*, as the main character becomes increasingly engrossed in the world of the Wild Things, the images increase in size. Another librarian pointed out how some illustrations make readers interact with the book in different ways. In some instances, book illustrations require one to turn the book's page in order to become part of the story environment. Other book illustrations focus on engaging readers in their immediate surroundings.

Throughout the modeling work, the group paused multiple times to discuss the key challenges and advantages of using 3D printing as a medium for approaching the design task. They were engaged with the materiality of the books as well as the content, deliberating on how to transcribe a detailed picture while simplifying it for printing. The librarians referred to the decoding and abstraction of the images, and discussed the advantage of graphic novels in the balance between graphical simplicity and conveying concepts. Size optimization was also taken into consideration as they considered both printer limitations and the

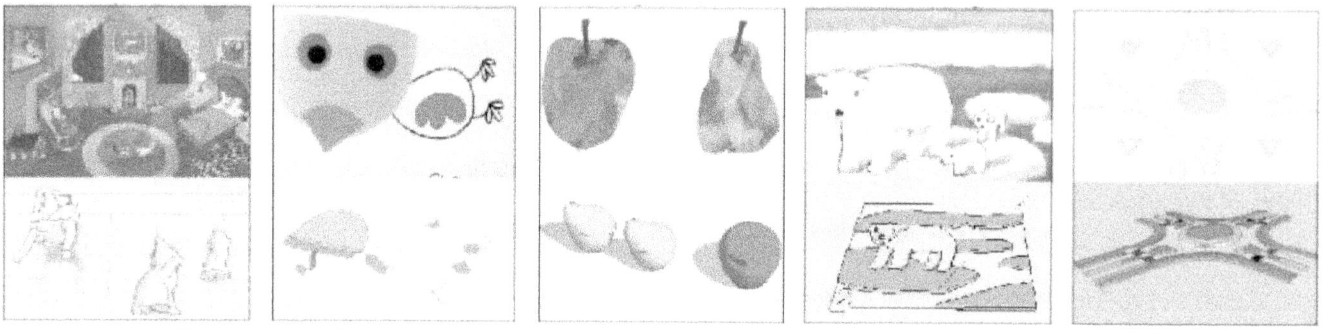

Figure 3 Examples of Workshop Groups' Models. (From left to right) Accessibility Librarians, Children's Librarians, Engineers, Interaction Designers, O&M/TVIs. (Volunteers did not produce any models).

fact that larger formats are easier for younger tactile learners. Finally, 3D printing was suggested as an activity to engage parents in storytelling. One librarian said that, *"the material act of transcribing the book would help a sighted parent think about her child's experience."*

Modeling Task Findings: Participants began modeling individually, but eventually decided to work in pairs. At the end of the workshop the group gathered to focus on modeling a "package" of models that could be used in different configurations to represent different concepts in a book. In doing so, they explored how some stories are not linear and that moving parts may provide a richer experience. While modeling in TinkerCad, participants had difficulty distinguishing between icons for rescaling objects and moving them vertically in space. They exhibited a lack of knowledge about the use of navigation tools to orient their work in space and had difficulty learning the techniques of the 3D modeling environment, such as reorienting objects from different angles. Finally, there was some confusion on the effects of grouping objects and how to select multiple objects at once. When the librarians encountered a problem with the software they verbalized the challenge, and the group often discussed solutions collectively. Most participants left with a sense of gratitude, while acknowledging that more practice would be needed with the program to achieve the design task, although they were more inclined to help with future book selection and activity creation efforts than model design.

5.3 Talking Book Library Volunteers

Overview: Seven volunteers from the Colorado Talking Book Library attended this workshop, which was organized by the director of the library (similar to 5.1). All participants were retirees, who collectively had years of experience in contributing to the library's effort to translate books into an audio format. The director of the library strategically recruited these volunteers for the workshop because of their long-term contribution to the library, and their perceived abilities and interests in technology in general.

Prior Experience: While none of the volunteers had experience with 3D printing, three had used 3D modeling programs, and several others had extensive experience with audio recording and transcription technology. All of the participants interacted with blind patrons at the library. One of the participants had a blind spouse, while another referenced his children and grandchildren's experiences using 3D printers as his motivation for attending the workshop, and the others attended to help support the library.

Workshop Adaptations: In order to focus the group conversations about transcription onto a concrete task, participants were challenged to select images from *Goodnight Moon* and find a model on Thingiverse that they thought would be accessible through touch. When working in TinkerCad, we focused on participants' efforts to navigate the screen and move forms.

Design Task Findings: The volunteers focused much of their conversation on the strategies used at the library to make content accessible. They spent little time critiquing the pre-fabricated models, but discussed how audio-transcription guidelines might be used to help with visual-to-tactile transcriptions. During the overview of the 3D modeling software, the library volunteers focused on the the applications of 3D modeling; they were most concerned with how people use different types of media, but were reluctant to go deeply into the design process and consider how to transcribe the materials.

Modeling Task Findings: In order to engage the participants in the design process we opted to spend more time walking them through the 3D modeling and printing ecosystem and helping them set up accounts on Thingiverse and TinkerCad. This process took nearly an hour. Several people were worried about setting up accounts, and one participant sent an email after the workshop saying, *"I resent having to set up an account with the CAD software...it was a great experience - just not my "cup of tea" for in depth participation."* Another repeatedly said that, *"I can't do this, I am not good with the computer."* When using TinkerCad, all participants had difficulty distinguishing between the icons for scaling and moving an object in space. One participant could not understand why objects "got bigger" as they moved across the page, and despite attempts to explain the idea of perspective within the software (closer objects appear larger), they ignored suggestions to rotate the page to a bird's-eye view for more intuitive object behavior. Compared to other groups, this group received the most guidance due to frustration with the software.

5.4 Engineers

Overview: After a local hacker/makerspace learned of our research, they offered to run a workshop for their members. Three hackers responded to the invitation, and all identified themselves as engineers. Due to the small group size we observed each participants' work as opposed to as a group.

Prior Experience: The three engineers had greatly varying familiarity and comfort with 3D modeling. The most confident modeler (Participant A) worked with SolidWorks on a daily basis as part of his job designing medical tools. Participant B was identified himself as a 3D modeling hobbyist and was most comfortable working in Sketch-Up. Participant C indicated that he had used a 3D modeling program once or twice before. All three participants were motivated to join the workshop due to previous experience living or working with people with VI or cognitive disabilities. They all expressed interest in contributing to efforts that led to equal access, though non of them had previously made ATGs or ATPs. At the beginning of the workshop each person shared their personal experiences with friends and family members who have VI.

Workshop Adaptations: The introduction and technology overview were cut short due to Participant A and B's eagerness to start using the modeling software and work independently. In turn, we spent a considerable amount of time helping Participant C become familiar with TinkerCad.

Design Task Findings: Despite the range of technical experience, all three participants' design processes and decision-making were heavily mediated through the 3D modeling tools they used. Participant A quickly chose to design pieces of fruit from the book *Each Peach Pear Plum*, and focused on creating an exact representation of the fruit. Several times through the session he discussed the challenges of modeling, as opposed to focusing on the challenge of transcribing the images. He explained that, "*the reality of it is any parent with a disabled child isn't going to have the time to sit and model, unless they do that for a living.*"

Participant B brought in a book to model from and had been practicing using SketchUp in preparation for the workshop. He had decided on a strategy for completing the design task beforehand by scanning images of the book to import into SketchUp. *The Giving Tree* was one of his favorite books. "*I want to convey the relationship between the boy (who becomes a man) and the tree. It is about love, the environment, and time.*" When describing his design process, he said that, "*the story didn't need to be told page-for-page. As long as the message gets conveyed, I feel the volume of content printed is unimportant.*" While not focusing on decoding, specifically, it was evident that he was thinking about the way content was portrayed, how to simplify difficult concepts into more basic representations.

After facing difficulty with the learning the 3D modeling programs, Participant C eventually chose to represent three bears sitting on chairs from *Goodnight Moon*. He first created a storyboard to distill the concepts of the book and chose to focus on the concept of bears sitting on chairs. Of all the participants, he focused on the particular learning purpose of the model the most.

Modeling Task Findings: During the modeling work there was very little dialogue between participants; one elected to put on headphones. However, when prompted, all were happy to help each other problem-solve while modeling. Participant A focused much of his time on identifying how to use the 3D modeling tool most efficiently to achieve the task. By using various geometric line tools alongside the extrusion tool, he was able to 3D model a pear and an extruded an apple. He focused on making sure edges were rounded due to his concern about the feeling of the plastic on a child's finger. It was evident that he was learning through trial and error, and by the end, his models of the illustrated fruit closely represented the images portrayed in the book.

Similar to Participant A, Participant B focused his modeling on how to leverage the efficiency of using SketchUp to transcribe an image. Using the rescanned images of the book, he used the freehand tool to define the shape of his model. He used the copy/paste tool to render the many leaves on the tree before extruding them all at once. Due to difficulties with downloading and loading SketchUp and creating an online account for TinkerCad, Participant C began modeling with clay. When referencing the 3D modeling program, he said, "*I thought it would be a simple thing—I'd just start a project and it'd just be flowing, and it suddenly is not...I'm feeling very frustrated.*" Despite the differing modeling styles, each participant was innovative in their solutions (whether switching media or using different modeling methods), and was proud of their final representations.

5.5 Interaction Designers

Overview: Four interaction designers with experience with education technologies and material design participated in a workshop. They learned about the research through a colleague and wanted to engage in a making task that had social implications, while learning more technical skills.

Prior Experience: Three participants had never used a 3D modeling application, while the fourth had extensive modeling experience with Maya. Of all of them, only one had used a 3D printer. The three inexperienced participants chose SketchUp because it provided an option to use the mouse to draw lines and irregular shapes, while the experienced participant chose Maya. None of the participants had experience spending time with children with VI, but two had young children and were motivated to participate to explore the use of tactile pictures in their homes.

Workshop Adaptations: After initial introduction activities, we worked more in-depth with this group to develop modeling skills. All participants had 3D modeling programs preinstalled on their computers. The Maya user was eager to start modeling and urged the others to use their experiences to inform their ideas.

Design Task Findings: Several participants brought in their favorite children's books, but the group opted to work together to complete one book, *Mommy Loves*, because they were concerned about the time it would take to complete the design task. They divided the pages up, defined a template for the page size, and collectively decided where to put text on the page. They all worked independently and remained focused on the task until the end of the workshop.

While working, the group continuously provided suggestions for how to achieve the design task, such as how to break the design task down into simpler parts by dividing up the tasks by specialty. One commented that, "*the most effective approach to designing a tactile page is not by giving the whole task to a 3D modeler initially, but to design with other materials...to identify key characteristics of the book, and then passing that off to a modeler.*" When asked whether they were interested in learning more about designing for people with VI, one responded, "*Even with professional experience with modeling animations with Maya, I realize that this field is huge and requires depth/professional efforts in it.*" Many of the group's design process and design-based decisions were focused on how to manage the task.

	A	B	C	D	E
	Group	N=#	Knowledge	Design Thinking Focus	Design Task Requirements
5.1	Accessibility Librarians	7	Media Access & Distribution	• Focused on use of existing guidelines • Focused on understand theoretical implications of transcription	• Include/honor skills of people with VI • Choose relevant (time/context) representations of information
5.2	Children's Librarians	6	Emergent Literacy	• Focused on individual learning needs • Focused on task management, community support and collaboration	• Design simple features around a concept • Consider artists' original work
5.3	Library Volunteers	7	Audio-Transcription	• Focused on novelty of the technology • Focused on how to facilitate end use	• Consider the use of audio formats to complement the 3DP-ATP
5.4	Engineers	3	Design and Engineering	• Focused on efficiency of modeling • Focused on complexity of modeling	• Have a realistic view of the work • Focus on the book's learning goals
5.5	Interaction Designers	4	Interaction Design	• Focused on management of design task • Focused on defining new design methods	• Create templates to increase efficiency • Parse the design task according to abilities
5.6	O&M/ TVIs	40	Vision Sciences	• Focused on adhering to guidelines	• Understand the child's learning context • Include VI people in the evaluation

Figure 4. Findings by Workshop Group

Modeling Task Findings: The participants using SketchUp immediately became frustrated by the unintuitive nature of the icons and the "unexpected" behavior of navigation. However they tried to work through their problems by finding alternatives. For instance, when one participant struggled to model something that looked like the illustration, they elected to take a picture of the illustration and import it into SketchUp to trace over. After this, each participant opted to work with the freehand drawing tool to transcribe a two-dimensional representation of an animal, followed by using the extrusion tool for the 3D representation. All participants found the freehand tool frustrating due to the lack of control one had using the mice as a pen or brush. Participants also found it difficult to close these free-drawn lines because the point of origin was difficult to distinguish. Participants were dissatisfied with the hard edges from using the extrusion tools.

Two of the participants lost motivation to complete the task due to the seemingly insurmountable barriers presented by the technology. *"I realized the limitations and frustrations in technology as part of the creative process...even learning the options for how to maneuver were not intuitive!"* This participant also had experience sculpting and was more accustomed to using her hands to produce work. By the end, the all four participants produced a model of a unique page in the book.

5.6 O&M Specialists and TVIs

Group Overview: Forty orientation and mobility (O&M) specialists and teachers of the visually impaired (TVIs) participated in a workshop conducted in conjunction with a Department of Education (DoE) teacher training workshop. The coordinator for the training requested the workshop after receiving requests from teachers to learn more about 3D printing.

Prior Experience: All of the participants had experience making ATGs and teaching K-12 students with VI. Only one person in the crowd had used 3D modeling software and 3D printers.

Workshop Adaptations: The DoE coordinator asked to have a demonstration on how to use 3D modeling programs to transcribe images of road intersections due to the fact that various types of intersections that can make way finding difficult for older students. While this task and modeling work focused more on the design of 3D-ATG maps than the design of 3DP-ATPs for emergent literacy, we chose to include these findings because much of the discussion-based data we collected pertained to 3DP-ATP. During the introductory activities, we created a 3D modeled tactile intersection template, and showed the participants how to construct a basic intersection based on a picture. We then presented pre-fabricated 3D printed tactile copies of Good Night Moon and prompted the participants to critique it. The group elected to break up into teams of four to model using SketchUp.

Design Task Findings: While working in the small groups, many of the participants began by sharing ideas for how to use 3D printers. One person noted that, *"tactile pictures with raised lines could be great for tactile coloring books, not for rendering concepts like background and foreground."* Another person was thrilled by the possibility of making a replacement for a special tactile book she used with a student. *"I have searched and searched for this grommet-shaped part for my book...I can't believe how much time this will save."*

While examining the pre-fabricated 3D printed tactile picture books, many people referenced known guidelines. *"Be aware of the amount of space you are putting around the objects. It's difficult to feel small objects on a flat space when you aren't aware of the story being told."* They indicated that it is important to design materials to complement the child's immediate environment/routines, with particular focus on basic experiential concepts, spatial relationships of objects on the page, and a progression of materials and activities that help develop finer tactile acuity. One person said, *"The most important thing is to keep the models simple and make sure that you work with the student to make sure they find the tactile picture makes sense to them. People learn to make sense of what is around them. Don't assume when you introduce a new tactile it will immediately make sense."* Throughout the workshop many of the O&M and TVIs advocated for involving children with VI to evaluate whether the models were accessible. *"Get more blind people involved with testing the models and graphics because they will be able to provide more useful feedback than a sighted person because they are more informed about what they need."*

Modeling Task Findings: In almost all groups, one person became the lead modeler, while others observed, discussed, and gave advice regarding their work. Those who spent the majority of their time modeling focused on learning how to make simple shapes and to navigate the modeling environment. They expressed frustrated with not knowing where to find the design tools within the menus. One modeler expressed hesitation about the technology, saying *"maybe I am interested in 3D printing for tactile graphics in a progress kind of way, but for our district it is not practical right now...it needs to become easier."* We heard this time and time again. No team produced a complete model.

Still, the majority of the O&Ms and TVIs remained positive about 3D modeling and printing technology. One person reflected that she could now create something she had been trying to find for years. Another said, *"I just can't wait to learn how to apply this technology, and visualize all the possibilities."* However, there was a generational divide between those interested in 3D modeling and related software, and those who felt that it was too complicated. One participant commented, *"I am about to retire. This technology is for the next generation to pursue."* Many teachers discussed available time being a deterrent to learning how to model, along with the lack of resources and time to participate in technology workshops.

6. FINDINGS: Across Groups

Above we summarized how each participant group approached the design task. Here we observe which aspects of the task they focused on and the associated design requirements. We note that participants approached the work according to different roles.

6.1 Designer Roles

Each group that we worked with focused on different aspects of the design task and revealed a series of requirements for creating 3DP-ATPs. Among the 67 participants, four primary ways of approaching the task surfaced. Some participants focused on developing materials to support individual needs, some focused on the creation of guidelines, while others focused on the theoretical implications. We identify these roles as:

1) End-User Advocate: During our workshops, those who work with people with VI on a regular basis (O&M specialists, TVIs, and Accessibility Librarians) strongly advocated for designing content that is both specific to individual children while adaptable to suit other children's needs. They emphasized the importance of knowing the child's cognitive ability and VI prior to modeling. These participants also designed, referenced and applied existing guidelines for ATGs/ATPs, indicating that this is standard practice within the profession. In cases that they were not aware of existing ATG guidelines, they attempted to create their own, exhibiting an understanding of how to scaffold a VI child's learning by describing specific model characteristics and identifying the appropriate levels of storytelling.

2) Content Translator: The early childhood librarians and accessibility librarians displayed an ability to apply their knowledge on emergent literacy, exhibiting a range of skills necessary for unpacking and abstracting content, and advocating for artistic intellectual property rights. They approached the task with a strong focus on how to decode visual illustrations and the meaning they convey. They emphasized how the composition of elements on a page creates a graphic narrative, and concentrated on discussing the phenomenological aspects of transcribing across the senses. These participants also placed greater value on whether or not authors' original intent and artwork are fairly represented, and made recommendations for how to look at the whole of the stories and decode certain elements, a value we did not observe in other groups. They also valued how material artifacts are used appropriately to engage children in meaningful ways, and how materials can be used to support joint attention (for emergent literacy). Most recognized that in some instances 3DP-ATPs might not convey the totality of the original author or illustrator's intent. There are trade-offs that must be considered.

3) Task Manager: The librarians also showed strong organizational skills around task management and book selection, which enabled them to quickly select and analyze the structure and components of the book, and communicate about important aspects of the transcription task. They emphasized the consideration of original artists' work and design communication (the concept, sequencing, and interactivity) efforts, in turn weighing the trade-offs between simplifying graphics and staying true to the original illustrations. They also recommended blending media to make the most appropriate representation of the information. The interaction designers exhibited a similar organizational and management ability, however they tended to look at the entire scope of the of the design task, in turn parsing out different aspects of the work to different collaborators. Their exhibited a meta-level review of the design task while modeling.

4) Modeler: The participants with previous modeling and design experience (engineers and interaction designers) showed the ability to problem-solve within the 3D modeling environments. They wanted to start by modeling with tools and discuss their approach/challenges/successes with the design task in progress, as opposed to the less technically experienced participants who spent more time analyzing the task prior to trying the programs. They tended to focus on how information was communicated through form, but not specifically on how to make the information accessible. They quickly identified the complexity of the design task and made recommendations for how to improve efficiency while modeling, and how to scope and manage the work.

6.2 Underlying Skillsets

As described in Section 4.2, after all of the workshops concluded, we ranked each participant group's dominant skillsets according to five criteria to further evaluate and summarize the strengths of each participant group: (1) Human development, (2) Emergent Literacy, (3) Tactile Graphicacy, (4) Task Management, and (5) Modeling. (Figure 5). No single group has skillsets across all five categories. Each workshop group that elected to participate in this study (except for the volunteers) showed strength in two or three skillsets, for example, the TVI's (4.6) showed strength in demonstrating and applying knowledge about human development and tactile graphicacy during their design work. Each workshop group had a different coupling of skills. These findings have implications for future work, as discussed in the next section.

	Workshop Group	D.	L.	G.	T.	M.
4.1	Accessibility Librarians	3	3	2	2	2
4.2	Children's Librarians	2	3	3	3	2
4.3	Library Volunteers	2	1	1	1	1
4.4	Engineers	1	1	2	1	3
4.5	Interaction Designers	1	2	2	3	3
4.6	O&M/TVIs	3	2	3	2	1

Figure 5. Skillsets by Workshop; D= Human Development, L= Literacy, G= Graphicacy, T= Task Management, M= Modeling

7. DISCUSSION AND FUTURE WORK

The space of designing ATGs and ATPs has existed for some time, but using 3D fabrication tools to create and design these materials is still a new field. To the best of our knowledge no other study has systematically reported on how non-professional modelers, transcriptionists, and tactile artists use the personal fabrication technology to create 3DP-ATPs. During our participant recruitment it became obvious that TVI's and O&M

specialists, librarians, interaction designers, engineers, and other volunteers, with varying skillsets, are interested in creating 3D-ATPs for children with VI. Some of the 67 participants joined the workshops due to a personal connection with somebody who is blind. Some joined as a way to increase their exposure to emerging technology, and others joined simply to contribute their skills to a meaningful cause.

We designed the workshops to introduce participants to the task and to mitigate the known barriers to designing 3DP-ATPs for the first time. Depending on their experience we provided overviews and hands-on instruction of 3D modeling programs, examples of ATGs, ATG guidelines, sudden blindness experiences, lessons in decoding and abstraction, etc. Each of the groups approached the task of creating 3DP-ATPs from a different perspective. We identified the dominant focuses in each group's design thinking, e.g. Accessibility Librarians= Focused on use of existing guidelines, and focused on understand theoretical implications of transcription (Column D, Figure 4). Each participant group's design thinking focuses and associated requirements indicate that people elect to take on a specific role in the design process: End-User Advocate, Content Translator, Task Manager, or Modeler.

Nonetheless, we noted that designing from just one of these roles or perspectives did not prove to produce a meaningful 3DP-ATP; 3DP-ATPs produced by a person with exposure to only one or two skillsets may fail to make a 3DP-ATP that tacitly communicate what is important to a child's learning. Despite our efforts to mitigate the challenges of creating 3DP-ATPs, many of the caregiver and stakeholder groups did not innately recognize the full scope of what is required by the design task or know how to apply existing ATG guidelines, and tended to stay within their domain-based comfort zones. This begs the question of whether 3D modeling and printing can be successfully leveraged by caregivers and stakeholders, who often have limited time and resources to learn new skills, for the creation of ATPs and ATGs? We believe that caregivers and stakeholders have critical knowledge to contribute to the design task, and given the right recourses will be able to create 3DP-ATPs. However, this will require making the design task more approachable to amateur makers and leveraging caregivers and stakeholders existing skillsets and motivations for creating meaningful 3DP-ATPs.

7.1 Design Activities & Associated Roles:

Participants offered valuable advice for how to make the design task more approachable. Their recommendations fall into four different categories that parse the task into activities. Each of the activities correspond to one of the four key design roles caregivers and stakeholders are prone to take on while approaching the task.

Activity A- Need Assessment and Evaluation: Understand the child's learning context at the onset of the design process and include people with VI in the evaluation of the models. → *End-User Advocates'* skills can be used to validate printable tactile pictures modeled by others for composition and tactile detail, to identify 3DP-ATP projects for specific children, and to coordinate the inclusion of end-users and caregivers in evaluation.

Activity B- Content Selection: When selecting content to translate, consider the meaning associated with the artists' original work, choose books according to the intended learning goals, and consider the use of audio formats to complement the 3DP-ATP. → *Content Translators'* skills can be used to help select books, identify the project scope with initiators, and edit content to enhance how designs are communicated across the senses.

Activity C- Representation: When designing content, choose relevant (time/context) representations of information and design simple features around a single concept. → *Task Managers'* skills can be used to help determine the sequences in which design activities should occur in the process of creating an 3DP-ATP, and to provide assistance and explicit instruction to each of the other team members—particularly the modelers.

Activity D- Production: When creating models, begin with a realistic view of the work and possibly divide the design task according to abilities, and create templates to increase efficiency. → *Modelers' Skills* can be used to develop guidelines and easily replicable samples of work, along with the task manager to engage in the design cycle with the others.

7.2 Collaborative Design Platform

The aforementioned recommendations for parsing the design task and ways using one's skill to contribute to the creation of 3DP-ATPs can be used to inform how participants interact while collaborating to create 3DP-ATPs. However, similar to the existing ATG guidelines, this information alone may not adequately prepare caregivers and stakeholders to contribute their skillsets in a collaborative fashion. In turn, we propose the design of a digital fabrication tool to unite designers from different disciplines around 3DP-ATP projects, while providing individuals to use their skills to make meaningful 3DP-ATPs.

This future research task treats the design of 3D-printed ATPs as a collaborative, transferrable process inclusive of a broad range of stakeholders including parents, teachers of the visually impaired (TVIs), librarians, and other community volunteers. Based on the findings of this study, we anticipate that an online, 3DP-ATP collaborative design platform may include features that enable people to: 1) build teams of designers; 2) propose design projects; 3) notify participants of project activities; 3) visualize progress and task allocation; 4) support communication between different team members; and 5) scaffold designers learning about ATG and ATP guidelines. We anticipate that a tool of this nature will require community management, and will look to the literature on social computing and creativity support tools to inform future designs. From findings presented in this research, we anticipate that children's librarians and TVIs would be the early adopters in order to rally other community members to help make 3DP

We plan to run additional workshops to help form multi-disciplinary teams of participants representing each of the identified roles. The aim of this research will be to identify how the team members collaboratively approach the task, whether multi-disciplinary teams disrupt the notions of the roles we present here, and what unique interface features will support their synchronous and asynchronous collaboration. To date we have not encountered teams of 3DP-ATP designers in the wild, however many caregivers identify the need for more shared resources on the design of accessible 3D material. We hope through the creation of such a tool will enable such a community to emerge.

8. CONCLUSION

In this paper, we presented insight about how six groups of stakeholders of children with VI approach the design task of 3D modeling accessible tactile pictures. Workshop participants demonstrated that the design task requires five different skillsets: disability science, literacy, graphicacy, project management, and 3D modeling. Of the 67 research participants we worked with, no one exhibited all skillsets. However, we identified that participants typically approached the design task from one of four roles: end-user advocate, content translator, task manager, or modeler. Each participant group specified requirements for approaching the design task from these associated roles, which we used to establish a framework for how caregivers and stakeholders can collaboratively design 3DP-ATPs. Future work will focus on assessing how multidisciplinary teams approach the work and how to develop creativity support tools to involve various stakeholders, and how to develop a collaborative design platform for the creation of 3DP-ATPs.

9. ACKNOWLEDGMENT

Funding for this project came from NSF IIS 1453771 for "CAREER: Adaptive Tactile Picture Books for Blind Children During Emergent Literacy", Yeh. We would also like to thank the participant groups from The Colorado Talking Book Library, The Boulder Public Library, ATLAS at CU-Boulder, Solid State Depot, and the Colorado TVIs and O&M specialists.

10. REFERENCES

[1] Agrawal, H., Jain, R., Kumar, P., & Yammiyavar, P. (2014). FabCode: visual programming environment for digital fabrication. In *Proc. of IDC'14,* 353-356.

[2] Aldrich, F. & Sheppard, S. (2000). 'Graphicacy': the fourth 'R'? *Primary Science Review, 64.* 8-11.

[3] Aldrich, F., Sheppard, L., & Hindle, Y. (2002). First steps towards a model of tactile graphicacy. *British Journal of Visual Impairment, 20*(2), 62-67.

[4] Aldrich, F. (2008). Talk to the hand: An agenda for further research on tactile graphics. In *Diagrammatic representation and inference* (pp. 344-346). Springer Berlin Heidelberg.

[5] American Printing House for the Blind. *Typhlo & Tactus Tactile Book Contest 2015,* www.aph.org/research/tactile-book-contest/, 3/3/15.

[6] Autodesk123Design, www.123dapp.com, 3/2/15.

[7] AutodeskMaya, //www.autodesk.com/products/maya, 3/2/15.

[8] Autodesk, TinkerCad https://www.tinkercad.com, 3/2/15.

[9] Baker, Catherine M., et al. "Tactile graphics with a voice: Using QR codes to access text in tactile graphics." In *Proc. of ACM SIGACCESS'14.*

[10] Braille Authority of North America, 2010. *Codebook and Guidelines*, http://www.brailleauthority.org, 2/1/15.

[11] Buehler, E., Kane, S. K., & Hurst, A. (2014). ABC and 3D: opportunities and obstacles to 3D printing in special education environments. In *Proc. of ACCESS'14,* 107-114.

[12] Buehler, E., Branham, S., Ali, A., Chang, J. J., Hofmann, M. K., Hurst, A., & Kane, S. K. (2015). Sharing is Caring: Assistive Technology Designs on Thingiverse. In *Proc. of CHI'15,*525-534.

[13] Bunnell, K. (2000). Designing through making. *The Design Journal, 3*(3), 1-3.

[14] Claudet, P. (2009). The Typhlo & Tactus Guide to Children's Book with tactile illustrations. *Les Doigts Qui Revent.*

[15] De Couvreur, L., & Goossens, R. (2011). Design for (every) one: co-creation as a bridge between universal design and rehabilitation engineering. *CoDesign, 7*(2), 107-121.

[16] Ferrell, K. A. (2000). Growth and development of young children. *Foundations of education, 1,* 111-134.

[17] Follmer, S., & Ishii, H. (2012). KidCAD: digitally remixing toys through tangible tools. In *Proc. of CHI'12,* 2401-2410.

[18] Friedman, B., Kahn Jr, P. H., Borning, A., & Huldtgren, A. (2013). Value sensitive design and information systems. In *Early engagement and new technologies,* 55-95. Springer.

[19] Hasty, L. (2006). Perkins Training Center presents: Teaching Graphicacy Skills Tactile Graphics Literacy. *Perkins School For The Blind.*

[20] Hook, J., Verbaan, S., Durrant, A., Olivier, P., & Wright, P. (2014). A study of the challenges related to DIY assistive technology in the context of children with disabilities. In *Proc. of DIS'14.* 597-606.

[21] Hudson, S. E. (2014). Printing teddy bears: a technique for 3D printing of soft interactive objects. In *Proc. of CHI'*14, 459-468.

[22] Hurst, A., & Tobias, J. (2011). Empowering individuals with do-it-yourself assistive technology. In *Proc. of ACM SIGACCESS'11,* 11-18.

[23] Hurst, A., & Kane, S. (2013). Making accessible. In *Proc. of IDC'13,* 635-638.

[24] Kim, J., Oh, H., & Yeh, T. (2015). A Study to Empower Children to Design Movable Tactile Pictures for Children with Visual Impairments. In *Proc. of TEI'15,* 703-708.

[25] Kolitsky, Michael A. "Reshaping teaching and learning with 3D printing technologies." *E-mentor* 4 (2014): 84-94.

[26] Kunz, A...& Schnelle-Walka, D. (2014). Accessibility of Brainstorming Sessions for Blind People. In *Computers Helping People with Special Needs* (pp. 237-244). Springer.

[27] Landau, S., & Wells, L. (2003). "Merging tactile sensory input and audio data by means of the Talking Tactile Tablet." *Proc. Eurohaptics'03.*

[28] Landau, S., et al. (2008). "Demonstration of a universally accessible audio-haptic transit map built on a digital pen-based platform." *Proc. 3-d Int. '08.*

[29] Leduc-Mills, B., & Eisenberg, M. (2011). The UCube: a child-friendly device for introductory three-dimensional design. In *Proc. of IDC'11,* 72-80.

[30] Lewis, S., & Tolla, J. (2003). Creating and using tactile experience books for young children with visual impairments. *Teaching Exceptional Children, 35*(3), 22-29.

[31] McDonald, S., Dutterer, J., Abdolrahmani, A., Kane, S., & Hurst, A. (2014). Tactile aids for visually impaired graphical design education. In *Proc. of ACM SIGACCESS'14,* 275.

[32] National Braille Press. *National Braille Bookstore.* www. nbp.org/ic/nbp/publications/all_books.html, 9/21/14

[33] Ratto, Matt, and Robert Ree. "Materializing information: 3D printing and social change." *First Monday* 17.7 (2012).

[34] Rhinoceros, https://www.rhino3d.com, d 3/13/15.

[35] Seedlings, http:/www.seedlings.org, 2/3/15.

[36] Siu, T. (2014) 3D Printing for Accessible Materials in Schools. *Diagram Center,* http://diagramcenter.org/3d-printing.html, 2/3/15.

[37] SolidWorks, https://www.solidworks.com, *3/5/15.*

[38] Stratton, J. M. (1996). Emergent literacy: A new perspective. *Journal of Visual Impairment and Blindness, 90,* 177-183.

[39] Stangl, A., Kim, J., & Yeh, T. (2014). 3D printed tactile picture books for children with visual impairments: a design probe. In *Proc. of IDC'14,* 321-324.

[40] Treadaway, C. P. (2009). Hand e-craft: an investigation into hand use in digital creative practice. In *Proc. ACM C&C'09,* 185-194.

[41] Trimble Sketch-Up, http://www.sketchup.com, 2/18/15.

[42] Wilson, F. R. (2010). The hand: How its use shapes the brain, language, and human culture. *Vintage.*

[43] Zeising, A., Katterfeldt, E. S., & Schelhowe, H. (2013). Considering constructionism for digital fabrication software design. In *Position Paper at Digital Fabrication in Education Workshop at IDC'*13.

Comparing Methods of Displaying Language Feedback for Student Videos of American Sign Language

Matt Huenerfauth[1], Elaine Gale[2], Brian Penly[1], Mackenzie Willard[1], Dhananjai Hariharan[1]

[1] Rochester Institute of Technology
Golisano College of Computing and Information Sciences
152 Lomb Memorial Drive, Rochester, NY 14623 USA
+1-585-475-2700
{matt.huenerfauth,bmp9681,mtw2935,dh1723}@rit.edu

[2] Hunter College, CUNY
School of Education
695 Park Ave, New York, NY 10065 USA
+1-212-772-4700
egale@hunter.cuny.edu

ABSTRACT
Deaf children benefit from early exposure to language, and higher levels of written language literacy have been measured in deaf adults who were raised in homes using American Sign Language (ASL). Prior work has established that new parents of deaf children benefit from technologies to support learning ASL. As part of a project to design a tool to automatically analyze a video of a students' signing and provide immediate feedback about fluent and non-fluent aspects of their movements, we conducted a study to compare multiple methods of conveying feedback to ASL students, using videos of their signing. Through a Wizard-of-Oz study, we compared three types of feedback in regard to users' subjective judgments of system quality and the degree students' signing improved (as judged by an ASL instructor who analyzed recordings of students' signing before and after they viewed each type of feedback). We found that displaying videos to students of their signing, augmented with feedback messages about their errors or correct ASL usage, yielded higher subjective scores and greater signing improvement. Students gave higher subjective scores to a version in which pop-up messages appeared overlaid on the student's video to indicate errors or correct ASL usage.

Categories and Subject Descriptors
H.5.2 [**Information Interfaces and Presentation**] User Interfaces – *evaluation/methodology*; K.4.2 [**Computers and Society**]: Social Issues – *assistive technologies for persons with disabilities*.

General Terms
Design, Experimentation, Human Factors, Measurement.

Keywords
American Sign Language; Education; Feedback; User Study.

1. INTRODUCTION
It is estimated that 28 million people in the U.S. are deaf or hard-of-hearing [11, 13]. During the critical years when children are acquiring their first language, they require adequate exposure to language used in context [9]. Researchers have found that even mild hearing loss creates significant challenges for children who are developing learning skills [8]. In standardized testing in the U.S., English literacy rates were lower for deaf adults: the median literacy rate of deaf high school graduates is around the fourth grade level [19] (this corresponds to U.S. students who are typically age 9). Early access to American Sign Language (ASL) has been found to benefit learning of a second language (English) [18, 24]. For instance, studies indicate that deaf children of deaf parents tend to read better than deaf children of hearing parents [17]. However, more than 80% of children who are deaf or hard-of-hearing are born to hearing parents [2, 10], and many children have difficulties in communication when parents are not fluent in ASL [4]. There are benefits when parents and caregivers rapidly learn ASL in order to support language acquisition of a deaf child, and even if parents do not become perfect signers, deaf children can learn ASL to a level of fluency consistent with native signers [16]. New parents of deaf children are busy and may benefit from technologies to support their learning of ASL [23].

In a joint project between our universities, we are investigating the design of software to automatically analyze videos of ASL students' signing and provide immediate feedback. Such a tool would allow students to practice ASL independently, whenever it is convenient for them. Typically, ASL students submit videos of themselves as homework assignments; instructors watch them and provide feedback. Such feedback is not immediate. We are investigating how to produce an automated tool to give *limited* feedback about aspects of a student's movements that are *likely* errors (see section 5.2). To be clear: our tool would not replace feedback from ASL instructors. Instead, we envision that this tool could benefit students by providing immediate feedback (with a tradeoff of being less sophisticated or less accurate). A key motivation is to produce a tool that would benefit busy students, such as new parents, but many other students may also benefit: ASL has become the third most studied language at U.S. universities; enrollments rose by 19% from 2008 to 2013 [3].

The development of the video analysis algorithms for this project is currently ongoing; however, the focus of the work presented in this paper is to determine student's subjective judgments about receiving feedback on their signing through video and to evaluate some initial concepts for the system design (which may influence the selection of features for the system). This paper presents a "Wizard of Oz" style study to explore two research questions:

Q1. Do ASL students report a subjective preference for using a tool that provides them with feedback about their signing, compared to just re-watching a video of their own signing?

ASSETS '15, October 26-28, 2015, Lisbon, Portugal
© 2015 ACM. ISBN 978-1-4503-3400-6/15/10...$15.00
DOI: http://dx.doi.org/10.1145/2700648.2809859

Q2. Are students able to understand the feedback presented by such a tool, as measured by whether they are able to produce a new ASL video in which they correct the errors?

This paper will focus on a comparison between three initial designs for how the system would present feedback for users, inspired by current technologies and practices of ASL students and instructors, surveyed in section 2. Section 3 outlines the specific hypotheses examined in this paper. Sections 4 and 5 describe the prompts, stimuli, and methodology of our study, and sections 6 and 7 present our results and conclusions.

2. RELATED WORK

As surveyed in [5], for students learning spoken languages, researchers have built technologies to automatically detect foreign accents or speech errors and provide feedback to students. These systems generally do not attempt to fully understand the message being spoken; instead, they aim to identify sounds or speech patterns that are non-fluent. Thus, they would not be able to inform a student of a semantically incorrect word choice, but they can inform the student if an unusual consonant sound was performed. Similarly, we seek to create a system that can provide limited types of feedback to students about non-fluent elements of their movements, without the system understanding the specific semantic content of the ASL sentences being performed. The limitation of this approach is that the system would not identify all types of errors in ASL signing, e.g., it could not know that a student made a error if they sign "ME ASL TEACHER" (I'm an ASL teacher) instead of "ME ASL STUDENT" (I'm an ASL student). However, the advantage is that students are not limited to performing sentences with a restricted vocabulary or sentences that follow a pre-determined script, which would be necessary to a achieve high accuracy in automatic ASL recognition software using state-of-the-art techniques, e.g. see survey in [1]. While a goal of our overall project is to develop software that could automatically analyze the signing movements of a student from a video, this paper focuses on the user-interface and usability issues of the system design. Thus, prior work on building sign-language recognition technology is not a focus of this related work section.

2.1 Automatic Analysis Education Tools

Several researchers have investigated software that can benefit ASL students that makes use of automatic video analysis technologies to recognize aspects of the sign language being performed by the student. Students in ASL courses often have difficulty "looking up" signs in an ASL-English dictionary to find translations of particular words. Wang et al. [21] implemented a system to allow users to search for words in an ASL dictionary by performing an ASL sign into a video camera; their recognition system returns a set of possible matches in the dictionary for the sign performed. As another example, Monteiro et al. [12] developed a system for automatically searching video-sharing websites to identify videos that contain sign language; such a tool could be used by students or instructors to identify linguistic material for students to practice by viewing.

The CopyCat system [6] was a game for ASL students in which they perform ASL signs or phrases (from a small predefined list) while wearing special colored gloves with accelerometers. Players of the game attempted to give commands to an onscreen character by performing ASL signs or short phrases. The system responded positively when the signs or phrases were correctly identified, thereby indicating to the student that they had performed them accurately. In this case, there was a predetermined small set of signs or phrase-templates that the system could recognize. In contrast, in our project, we are interested in a tool that would allow students to receive feedback on any ASL signs or sentences that they perform (e.g., ASL instructors at different universities may assign homework assignments on different topics). Thus, the user-interface of this prior system (controlling an onscreen character by way of issuing commands in the form of ASL) was not well-suited to our system.

In later work at Georgia Tech, Weaver et al. [23] conducted interviews with parents of deaf children to understand their needs in ASL-learning technology. Based on their findings, the researchers created software for mobile phones to display videos of signs, and students engaged in a "quiz" game in which they had to answer questions to identify the word in the video [22]. However, this software did not provide feedback to users on the accuracy of their own ASL signing.

2.2 Non-Automatic Analysis Education Tools

As a starting point for identifying candidate designs for how to provide feedback to ASL students on their signing, we examined a set of current technologies and practices that are currently used in ASL education contexts. We have arranged these options below according to the amount of scheduling flexibility that the student has in practicing and receiving feedback:

Receiving live feedback directly from an ASL instructor during a classroom interaction or private one-on-one meeting. While this method would provide the student with the highest quality feedback, it requires significant amounts of ASL instructor time per student and must be scheduled in advance. This form of feedback may occur in an ASL classroom with multiple students, but the instructor must balance their time, providing feedback to the many students in the room. The instructor would only be able to focus their attention on one student at a time during the classroom setting, as they circulate through the classroom during some type of in-class activity, e.g., students "pair up" and sign to each other while the instructor observes. Alternatively, students may schedule a private tutor for additional one-on-one live feedback, but this option may be prohibitively expensive.

Receiving feedback from an ASL instructor in a classroom setting using a recording device in the classroom. One of our co-authors teaches ASL at the university level, and students in her ASL classes currently make use of mobile devices equipped with a recording application to view and assess their signing skills during class. In order for the students to receive feedback from the instructor, she must circulate in the classroom to watch the videos on students' devices, which is challenging with at least 15 students in a classroom. The benefit of the use of the mobile devices is that the students can re-record their performance multiple times (if they notice mistakes in their own video) and then show the video to the instructor when they are ready to receive more sophisticated feedback. From a time-flexibility perspective, students must still schedule themselves to attend class, but the instructor can provide feedback to the students in the classroom asynchronously, which can be more efficient.

Students record themselves outside of a classroom setting and simply watch their own video. This method is similar to the above technique, but the student makes a self-video performing sign language (outside of a classroom setting) and watches the video to look for errors. This alternative is essentially a time-shifted version of a classic "signing into a mirror" method for practicing, which ASL students traditionally employ. While there is certainly greater time-flexibility with this self-video option, the downside is that the quality of feedback is much lower. Students may miss their own errors.

Students record themselves outside of a classroom setting and submit their video to the instructor who provides a written evaluation or grade. This is a common way that ASL students prepare and submit homework assignments for their course. The instructor assigns a topic or prompt, and students must record themselves performing ASL, which they submit to the instructor for grading. Later, the instructor provides a numerical grade and written comments. While the student has flexibility about when to record their video, the feedback received is not immediate. While the instructor is able to provide sophisticated comments, one challenge for the student is determining how the comments from the instructor relate to specific moments in time in their videos.

Students record themselves outside of a classroom and submit their video to the instructor, who uses a video-annotation tool to provide feedback that is time-synchronized to the student's video. For coaches and athletes who are perfecting a complex movement for a sport, it has become increasingly common to make use of video analysis software, e.g. Coach's Eye[1], in which an instructor/coach watches the video of the student/athlete. Such tools enable the instructor to replay the video and add annotations (e.g., arrows, lines, text boxes) that appear a specific moments of the video. In ASL courses offered at RIT, a commercially available web-based service called GoReact[2] has been used to enable students to submit videos of themselves signing and allow the instructor to watch and provide time-synchronized annotations to the student as feedback. While time-based feedback may be easier for students to "match" to elements of their performance, the downside is that time-based annotation of ASL video is a time-consuming activity, even for experts [7].

3. CONDITIONS AND HYPOTHESES

One circumstance where students may benefit from a tool that provides immediate feedback, is when preparing to submit an ASL homework assignment video. They may "rehearse" their video, with the assistance of the tool, prior to performing a final version of their video, which a human ASL instructor will "grade" to provide more sophisticated and accurate feedback to the student. In this paper, we investigate alternatives for how to best present this feedback to students. Based on the final three interfaces listed in the previous section, we have identified three design alternatives below, which we will evaluate in a study:

VIDEO: We evaluate a lower-baseline design that simply replays a student's video for them to watch.

FEEDBACK: For comparison we also present videos that provide feedback to the student on their signing, under two *sub-conditions*, listed below:

- *NOTES:* After analyzing a student's video, the system displays a written message to indicate any errors it identified in the video (or correctly performed linguistic elements that the system noticed).
- *POPUP:* After analyzing a video, the system replays it to the student with messages that appear ("pop up") on the video when linguistic phenomena or errors are detected. At the end of this video, the student is provided written messages like those in the NOTES case, to summarize the errors.

The NOTES condition is similar to VIDEO, but it is followed by text feedback about possible student errors. The POPUP condition is similar to the NOTES condition, with the addition of pop-up feedback messages during the student's video, about specific errors that may be occurring at that moment of the video.

In the context of a student viewing a feedback video in one of these conditions prior to recording themselves performing ASL (e.g., as part of a homework assignment), we hypothesized that:

H1a: Students will report a subjective preference for videos that provide feedback about their signing (FEEDBACK), as compared to just a video of themselves signing (VIDEO).

H1b: Students will report a subjective preference for videos that provide time-synchronized feedback about their signing (POPUP), as compared to non-synchronized (NOTES).

H2a: When an instructor evaluates students' ASL performances "before" and "after" they viewed a video, there will be a significantly greater improvement when the video provides feedback about their signing (FEEDBACK), as compared to just a video of themselves signing (VIDEO).

H2b: ...significantly greater improvement when the video provides time-synchronized feedback about their signing (POPUP), as compared to non-synchronized (NOTES).

Note that each of the "a" hypotheses compares the FEEDBACK condition to the VIDEO condition, and the "b" hypotheses compare the POPUP condition to the NOTES condition. Hypotheses "1" focus on subjective preferences reported on scalar response instruments; hypotheses "2" focus on the scores that an ASL instructor assigns to recordings of the students' signing.

4. DESIGN OF COLLECTION PROMPT

ASL is a natural language conveyed through movements of the hands, body, head, eyes, and face [20]. As a brief background for the reader, some relevant linguistic aspects of ASL include:

- Facial expressions are essential to conveying grammatical information, e.g., the sentence YOU LEAVE ("You are leaving") can mean "Are you leaving?" with "YN-Question" facial expression (head tilts forward with eyebrows raised to indicate a "Yes or No" question). Other linguistic facial expressions include "Negation" (in which the signer shakes their head from side-to-side), "WH-Question" (head tilts forward with eyebrows furrowed), and many others [14].
- Signers point to locations around their body in space, which are used to represent entities under discussion [20]. The signer will typically use their eye-gaze to look at these locations when they are established during signing [14].
- Fingerspelling is how ASL signers convey English words by performing a handshape for each alphabet letter. It is used for proper names, titles, or other specific uses [20], and there are specific rules for hand location and movement.

For this study, it was necessary to provide our participants (ASL students) with a prompt similar to a "homework assignment" they might encounter in an ASL course. Specifically, we needed an "expressive" assignment in which students were asked to produce a video of themselves signing ASL in response to some topic or to provide an ASL translation of some English sentences. Researchers have observed that adults learning ASL as a second language often make errors involving movement, handshape, and facial expression [15]. Therefore, for this homework assignment prompt, we wanted to encourage a wide variety of ASL linguistic features to be performed by students in a short video segment (to enable us to efficiently collect a wide variety of linguistic errors from the students).

[1] https://www.techsmith.com/coachs-eye.html
[2] https://goreact.com

We drew upon the approach to prompt-design described in [7], in which authors collected recordings of ASL, using prompts designed to encourage specific linguistic phenomena to be used by the signer. In addition, one of our co-authors is an experienced ASL instructor, who has been teaching ASL for nearly two decades. Based on prior homework assignments used in her courses (and based upon an examination of sample assignments from other university ASL programs), we designed a homework assignment at an appropriate level of difficulty for a student who had recently completed approximately 1.5 semesters of university-level courses in ASL. *Signing Naturally*[3] is a popular ASL curriculum used in U.S. universities, including at RIT, where we would be recruiting participants for this study. We therefore consulted the instructor's resource guide for the first two semesters in this curriculum when designing this prompt. The homework was structured as a translation task, in which students were presented with twelve English prompts, and the student was asked to translate each into ASL and perform it in a video:

1. My house is green; your house is blue. My house is big; your house is small.
2. Her animal isn't a brown cat. What is her pet?
3. Is your favorite animal dogs or cats (which)?
4. In high school, your favorite class was not Spanish. Now, you're an ASL student.
5. You're not her cousin. Do you know her family?
6. Chocolate, I hate. Cookies, I love. What's your favorite food?
7. Her mother is reading a book. Her father is sitting. What are you doing?
8. His children are not here. Where does your family live?
9. Now, his father likes computers. He has no books.
10. He's my sister's son. Who is your son?
11. She grew up in France. Now, her parents live in England.
12. I saw her mother in the library. She had no glasses. How does she read books?

Prior to the full study, two pilot testing sessions were conducted with this assignment to determine whether ASL students with 1.5 semesters of experience would be able to understand this assignment, whether the instructions and terminology were clear, and whether students could complete this assignment in a 70-minute experiment session (including the time needed for them to prepare and record their responses). The results from these pilot tests indicated that the assignment and our recording protocol (below) were sufficiently well-specified to begin the study.

5. OVERVIEW OF STUDY DESIGN

Because we have not yet implemented automatic video analysis methods, we conducted a Wizard-of-Oz study as follows:

1. ASL students recorded a homework-style video.
2. A human ASL expert identified errors in their video and made notes about the category of error and when it occurred.
3. A researcher consulted the expert's notes and produced a feedback video for the student (in one of the three conditions VIDEO, NOTES, or POPUP).
4. The student viewed the feedback video immediately prior to making a new video recording of themselves in response to the homework assignment.
5. Students responded to a questionnaire about their subjective impressions of the feedback video.
6. An ASL instructor evaluated each student's "before" and "after" homework videos and assigned a score to the video based on specific linguistic elements of their performance.

[3] http://www.dawnsign.com/series/signing-naturally-series/5

The study used a within-subjects design: Since the homework assignment consisted of the student making 12 short videos in response to 12 short prompts, each participant saw four prompts in each of the three conditions (VIDEO, NOTES, or POPUP) during step 3 above. Assignment of conditions to prompts (and the order in which they were presented) was counterbalanced.

5.1 Collection of Student Videos, Round 1

Recruitment advertisements for the study were posted through email messages sent to students at our university currently enrolled in their second semester of ASL (or who had recently completed that course). Of the eight participants (six female), all were students pursuing undergraduate degrees. Ranging in age from 19 to 24, five participants had taken their first ASL class within one year of participating in the study. Two participants were hard-of-hearing. None of the participants had deaf family members, and none grew up in a household that used ASL.

After completing informed consent documents and a demographic questionnaire, participants were given approximately five minutes to read through the sample homework assignment and ask clarifying questions about the instructions for the assignment. Participants were instructed to approach this assignment as if it was given to them as a homework assignment for a class that they were taking. After participants indicated that they understood the assignment, they were given twenty minutes to prepare. They were given access to the National Technical Institute for the Deaf online video dictionary[4], a student edition of the *Signing Naturally* textbook, and other hardcopy ASL dictionaries.

Immediately after the preparation phase, the participants began recording the sentences. Participants sat on a stool 1.5 meters from a video camera on a tripod at a height of 1.5 meters. The camera was connected to a Windows computer running recording software created specifically for this study. This software was controlled by the researcher and automatically saved the videos (1920x1080 resolution, 30 frames-per-second) into a designated folder. The recording process consisted of participants signing each of the 12 individual items one at a time, with short breaks in between. These breaks allowed the participants to practice and prepare themselves for recording the next utterance using the homework assignment and their notes from the preparation phase. Participants were told to begin and end the signing with their hands on their laps so that it would be obvious when the signing began and ended. They were also reminded throughout the recordings to look into the camera while signing and to keep the homework paper on a nearby stool out of the camera's view. The researcher waited until the participant indicated that they were ready to record an utterance, started the recording, and then told the participant to begin. Once the participant was done signing the utterance, the researcher stopped the recording and checked that the video file was saved properly. If the participants were not satisfied with their recording of an utterance then they were given the opportunity to rerecord the utterance as many times as needed until they were satisfied. Participants were **not** allowed to view their recordings as they were later used as a feedback condition.

When the recordings were completed, the participants were then compensated and asked if they would be willing to return at a later date. Since all first round participants indicated that they would return for the second part of the study, minimal debriefing was done at this time (to avoid revealing the purpose of the study).

[4] https://www.rit.edu/ntid/dictionary/

Table 1: Examples of error codes and correct-usage codes used for analyzing students' recordings. In this study, 17 unique error codes and 7 unique correct-usage codes were used to annotate the participants' ASL recordings.

Code	Description	Onscreen message displayed to student in FEEDBACK conditions (NOTES and POPUP)	Where the arrow should aim for POPUP stimuli
Error_topic_beginning	Did a Topic facial expression begin too far from a clause boundary?	TOPIC facial expressions must start at the beginning of the clause.	Face
Error_point_gaze	Is the signer performing a pointing sign without eye-gaze aimed at that location?	The first time you point to a location in space (to refer to someone or something), your eyes should look at the location.	Face
Error_neg_lexical	Is the signer performing a negative word without a Negation facial expression?	You performed a negative word, but there was no Negative facial expression.	Face
Error_hands_down	Is the signer putting their hands down too frequently during the signing?	You should try to sign in a fluid manner, without putting your hands down too frequently.	Torso
Error_fingerspell_loc	Is fingerspelling happening now with the hand in an inappropriate location?	During fingerspelling, your hand should be near your mouth (without blocking it) and at the height of your chin or shoulders.	Hand
Error_wh_lexical	Is the signer performing a WH question word (e.g., WHO) without performing a question facial expression?	You performed a question word, but there was no Question facial expression.	Face
Correct_contrastive	Is contrastive role shifting (torso swivel) happening now correctly?	You appeared to use good contrastive structure (torso movement) during your signing.	Torso
Correct_topic	Is a Topic facial expression being performed correctly at the beginning of a clause?	You appeared to use a Topic facial expression correctly during your signing.	Face

5.2 Analysis of Videos

In the next phase of the study, the students' videos from round 1 were analyzed by an expert (a professional ASL interpreter with over 100 hours of experience at analyzing videos of ASL to identify linguistic occurrences). This was one of the Wizard-of-Oz phases of this study; the expert was simulating the work of the future automatic video-analysis software (operating within the near state-of-the-art of ASL recognition, see [1]). For this reason, the wizard was limited to identifying specific errors (on a short list of error types that we expected our future system to identify) and for noting the timespan of the video when each occurred.

As mentioned in section 2, our proposed system would complement (not replace) high-quality feedback from a human ASL instructor, who could consider the meaning that the student intended to convey. For this reason, we expect that our system would be able to identify a specific set of linguistic errors, for example, including some of the following:

- missing or incorrectly timed facial expressions for conveying questions, topicalized phrases, negation, or time-phrases
- lack of smoothness of movement, as characterized by overly large movements, stilted or halting movements, etc.
- incorrect hand location or orientation during fingerspelling

Notably, since we do not expect the system to fully understand all of the signs performed by the student, our list of error codes does not include semantic or word-order errors. Table 1 contains a listing of some of the error codes used in this study. Given the short time duration of the videos in this study, each video was labeled with exactly two codes. In some cases (18% of videos), the expert was not able to identify two errors in the student's video that matched our set of codes. In this case, the expert labeled a correct aspect of the video, using a pre-determined set of "correct codes" (see codes with names beginning with "correct" in Table 1) so that every video was annotated with two codes total. We anticipate that our future system would also provide feedback about specific aspects of a video that were correctly performed.

Because no feedback information would be provided for recordings in the VIDEO condition, it was actually not necessary to identify specific linguistic errors in the recordings for the purpose of producing stimuli (section 5.3). However, in support of later "scoring" of videos (in section 5.5), it was necessary to identify two linguistic properties of each video that would be a focus of this later scoring process (details in section 5.3).

5.3 Preparation of Stimuli

The recordings of students in round 1 (section 5.1) and the error codes and timing (section 5.2) were used as a basis for producing the three different conditions of stimuli for the round 2 experiment (section 5.4). As mentioned previously, for each participant, their 12 short videos were partitioned into three groups (4 per group). Each group was assigned to different condition (VIDEO, NOTES, POPUP). The assignment was determined prior to participant recruitment, ensuring videos were balanced across conditions and that conditions were presented to participants in a rotated order.

To produce the stimuli for the VIDEO condition in the round 2 study, the videos collected in round 1 were used without modification. Figure 1(a) shows an image from a recording.

To produce the NOTES stimuli, some images showing text messages were concatenated to the end of the recording from round 1, shown in Figure 1(b). These notes included messages on the errors made during that particular sentence recording. It was ensured that each message was displayed for a sufficient amount of time and was in a large font size for comfortable reading. The text of this message was based on the error code (see Table 1), and it was not customized for the particular participant's video. In this way, the use of "fixed" error messages as feedback to the student was meant to simulate the type of feedback that we expect the future system to perform. In this way, the stimuli-creation work in this phase is another Wizard-of-Oz aspect of the study.

To produce the POPUP stimuli, Camtasia Studio[5] was used to add pop-up messages to the recordings from round 1, to identity errors made during signing, including an arrow pointing to part of the signer's body (e.g., face, hands, torso etc.). The location on the body where the arrow pointed was based upon the error code, as show in table 1. The text of these pop-up messages was identical to the text used in the feedback presented at the end of the NOTES stimuli. The timing of the pop-up messages was based on

[5] https://www.techsmith.com/camtasia.html

the information provided by the expert (section 5.2). To ensure that participants had sufficient time to read the messages as well as observe the respective segment under question, effects such as slow-motion and freeze-frame were employed. The font size was selected to be large enough for comfortable viewing on the display monitor used in round 2 (see section 5.4). In addition to the pop-up messages displayed during the student's recording, the videos in the POPUP condition also contained summarizing notes at the end of the video, identical to those shown in the NOTES condition. Figure 1(c) contains some images of the pop-ups shown during the video. Example stimuli from our study are available here: http://latlab.ist.rit.edu/2015assets/

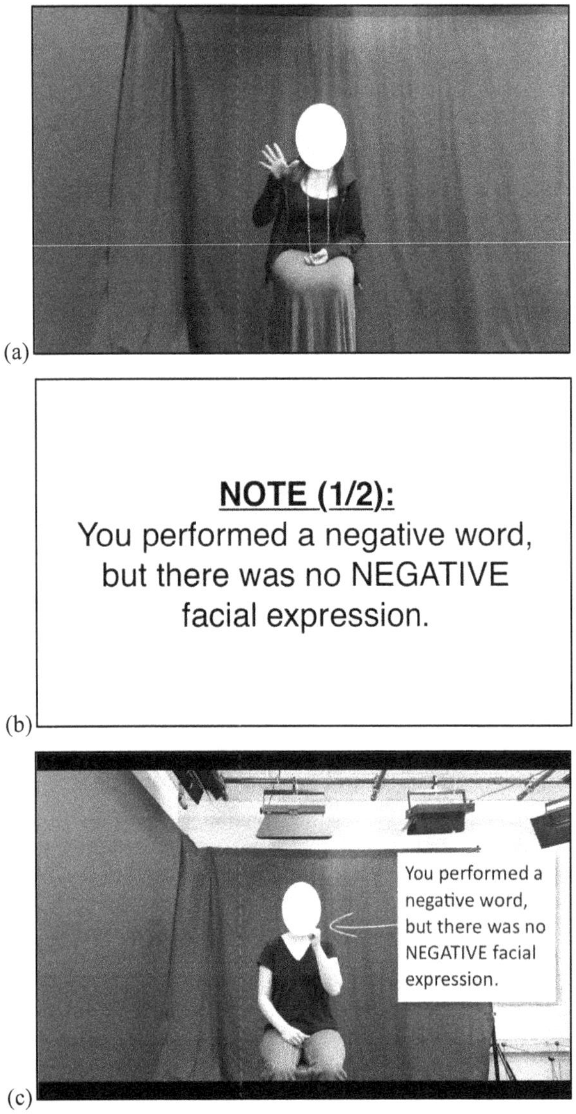

Figure 1: Images from the three stimuli conditions in the study: VIDEO stimuli displayed the student's video from round 1, as shown in (a). NOTES stimuli presented the student's video (a) followed by onscreen messages displayed after the video was finished (b). POPUP stimuli presented the students video with overlaid messages (c) followed by onscreen messages (b) containing identical text content to the pop-up messages shown during the video. The face of the participant has been obscured in these images, but it was clearly visible during the videos shown in the study.

5.4 Collection of Student Videos, Round 2

After completing a consent form, participants were given back their homework paper from the round 1 study. Many students had made notes on the homework paper during round 1 of the study while they were planning their ASL sentences, and so these sheets were retained by the researcher and given back to the participant during round 2. After briefly reviewing the homework assignment paper, the participants were ready to begin recording.

The camera setup and distance was identical to that during round 1, with one difference: a 27-inch LCD monitor was placed directly below the camera so that the participant could be shown videos immediately prior to their performing ASL sentences to be recorded. Before re-recording each of the 12 short videos for the homework assignment, the researcher showed the participant a feedback video, in one of the three conditions: VIDEO, NOTES, or POPUP. The monitor was turned on only to play the stimulus video and was shut off shortly after so that it would not distract the participants while they were making their recordings.

At the end of the study, participants answered scalar response questions about their subjective impression of the quality of each type of stimuli (VIDEO, NOTES, and POPUP) presented during the study. These questions used a 0-to-10 response scale, with 10 representing the best quality, and participants were asked to assign a score to each of the three conditions in the study.

5.5 Evaluation of Student Videos

An experienced ASL instructor (2nd author) evaluated the student recordings from round 1 and 2. This instructor is a professor and director of a Deaf and Hard of Hearing Education program at CUNY Hunter College and has been teaching university ASL courses for almost two decades. This instructor works in New York City and was not present for the recording sessions in Rochester (several hours away). Prior to sending her the videos, the RIT researchers randomly sorted and renamed the files, to hide whether each video was collected from round 1 or round 2.

The goal of this evaluation process was not to assign an overall holistic score to each video; instead, the evaluation was *targeted* to focus on linguistic properties that had been the focus of the feedback messages in the stimuli. So, for each video, the instructor was asked to assign a score for two linguistic properties; these properties were selected based on the error or correct-usage codes assigned to that video during the expert analysis (section 5.2). Across all videos in the study, the ASL instructor was asked to assign a numerical score (on a 0 to 10 scale) for these linguistic aspects of some recordings (two aspects per video): Pointing, Hands-Up-When-Signing, Size-of-Signing, Topic, Wh-Question, Negation, Yes-No-Question, Time-Transition, Contrastive-Structure, Looking-at-Camera, Smoothness, and Fingerspelling.

For example, if a video had been labeled with codes relating to the Topic facial expression (e.g., Error_topic_beginning in Table 1) and Pointing (e.g., Error_point_gaze), then the ASL instructor was asked to assign a numerical score (on a 0 to 10 scale) for the Topic and Pointing linguistic properties for that video. To evaluate the Topic property, the instructor judged whether the signer performed the topic facial expression correctly, at an appropriate time. To evaluate Pointing, the instructor judged whether the signer pointed to locations in space when signing to represent entities under discussion, whether eye-gaze was used correctly during this pointing, whether the signer was consistent in the locations that were pointed to, and whether the signer used the correct hand shape for pointing, etc.

The instructor assigned scores of 9-10 for videos with all or almost all grammatical features correctly used, 7-8 when most of the features correctly used, 5-6 when some features correctly used, and 0-5 when few to no features correctly used (or missing). The average of the two grammatical features for the video was the final score. For example, if the instructor assigned a score of 8 for Topic and 6 for Pointing, then the video received a score of 7. To evaluate the degree to which a student's performance changed from round 1 to round 2 of the study, we subtracted the score from the round 1 video from the round 2 video. For instance, if the student's round 1 video received an overall score of 7 and the round 2 video (for that same homework item) received a score of 9, then the student had a 2-point improvement in the score.

6. RESULTS AND COMPARISONS

Table 2 presents the responses from participants at the end of the study when they were asked to rate "the quality of this feedback, on a 0-to-10 scale (10=best)" for each of the three conditions in the study: VIDEO, NOTES, and POPUP.

Table 2: Subjective Evaluation Scores for Each Condition

Participant	VIDEO	FEEDBACK	
		NOTES	POPUP
"A"	10	10	10
"B"	3	7	9
"C"	6	7	7
"D"	1	5	8
"E"	5	7	9
"F"	3	9	10
"G"	3	5	10
"H"	2	7	10

Hypothesis H1a considered whether students reported a subjective preference for videos that provide feedback about their signing (FEEDBACK), compared to a video of themselves signing (VIDEO). Median response for FEEDBACK videos (union of NOTES and POPUP videos) was 8.5, and the median for VIDEO was 3. The distributions in the two groups differed significantly (Mann-Whitney U=16.5, $n_{FEEDBACK}$ =16, n_{VIDEO}=8, $p<0.05$). Thus, hypothesis H1a was supported: Videos with feedback information received higher subjective scores from ASL students.

Hypothesis H1b considered whether students reported a subjective preference for videos that provide time-synchronized feedback (POPUP), compared to non-synchronized (NOTES). Median response for POPUP was 9.5, and for NOTES, 7. The distributions in the two groups differed significantly (Mann-Whitney U=11, n_{NOTES}=8, n_{VIDEO}=8, $p<0.05$). Thus, hypothesis H1b was also supported: Students gave higher scores for POPUP.

Hypothesis H2a considered whether, when an instructor evaluates students' ASL performances "before" and "after" they viewed a video, there was a significantly greater improvement when the video provides feedback about their signing (FEEDBACK), as compared to just a video of themselves signing (VIDEO). Figure 2 displays these improvements in ASL instructor scores; the box indicates quartiles, whiskers indicate 1.5 inter-quartile ranges, and asterisks indicate outliers. Hypothesis H2a was supported: two-sample t-test, $t_{(df=71)}$=3.49, p=0.0008. The scores for students' recordings showed a greater improvement when students were shown a feedback message, as compared to simply being shown the video of their ASL signing from round 1.

Hypothesis H2b was not supported; a two-sample t-test did not reveal a significant difference in the improvement of the scores for the student videos in the NOTES vs. POPUP conditions. Notably, students gave higher subjective scores for POPUP (H1b).

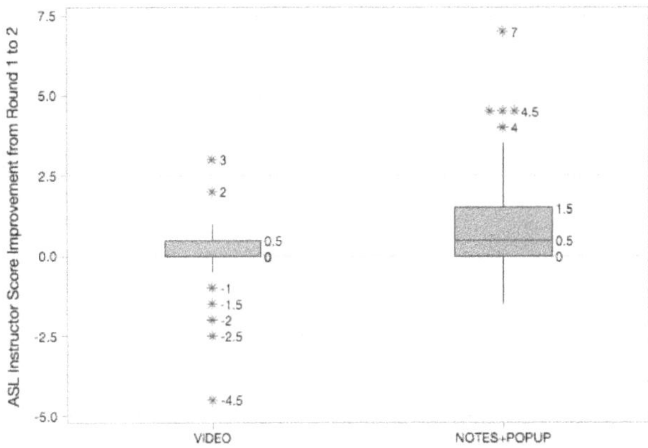

Figure 2: Boxplots of improvements in ASL instructor scores for student's recordings from round 1 to round 2 for VIDEO and for the FEEDBACK condition (NOTES+POPUP).

7. CONCLUSIONS AND FUTURE WORK

As explained in section 1, the goal of our overall project is to benefit ASL students by enabling them to review and evaluate their signing skills through automatic, immediate, outside-of-classroom feedback. Such a tool may provide students with additional time-flexibility (reducing dependence on arranging meetings), which may benefit busy students, such as new parents.

This study compared three methods of presenting feedback, inspired by current approaches used by ASL students (section 2), and we found that students gave higher subjective scores to videos with text-based feedback messages about their errors or correct-usage. As evaluated by an ASL instructor, the students who received feedback messages also showed greater improvements in their signing in round 2 videos. This finding suggests that the set of error and correct-usage codes used in this study were sufficient for providing beneficial feedback to the participants. Since these feedback "codes" were limited (they did not include errors based on the meaning of the student's video, they were not based on full-understanding of what they were signing, and they did not provide feedback messages that were specifically customized to the words of the student's video), this is a useful finding. It suggests that a future automatic video analysis system based on this type of feedback would be useful for ASL students.

Participants gave higher subjective scores to those videos that presented the text-based feedback in a time-synchronized manner with their video. This finding influences the design of automatic video analysis software for our project, suggesting that it is valuable to identify specific times in the video when errors or correct-usage occur, to support time-synchronized feedback.

While, in this study, we simulated an automated system, it was in fact human "wizards" who produced the feedback for the student. Thus, our findings may have implications for sign language educators or education researchers, suggesting how students may respond to various forms of communicating feedback information on their ASL performance, whether that feedback is produced by an automated system or by an ASL instructor. Given the increasing popularity of university courses on ASL [3], including online courses, understanding how to effectively convey feedback to ASL students electronically is increasingly important.

The limitations of this study include the risk that the Wizard-of-Oz enactment may not accurately reflect the future system. The use of a table of error-codes and uniform appearance of stimuli videos were meant to address this concern; however, a future automated system may make some errors when analyzing student's recordings (and the feedback would be more instantaneous than we were able to provide in this Wizard-of-Oz setting). In future work, we plan to explore how students respond to feedback messages from an automatic system that may be less accurate. Another limitation of this study is the relatively small number of users. While some statistically significant differences were observed (and the population size was above customary minimums for application of the statistical tests employed in the study), it would be valuable to reproduce this study with a large number of ASL students in future work. A further limitation of the study was the use of a single ASL instructor who performed the evaluation of the student videos. The use of a blind-evaluation approach, the use of well-structured linguistic feedback scores, and the significant prior experience of the ASL instructor at evaluating videos of ASL student signing were meant to partially address this concern, but in future work, we could replicate this study with additional ASL instructors independently evaluating the student videos. In future work, in addition to addressing some of these limitations outlined above, we will continue with our design and research to create an automatic feedback tool for ASL students, described in section 1.

8. ACKNOWLEDGMENTS

We are grateful to our research collaborators on this NSF-funded project, Professor Yingli Tian and her students at CUNY City College, who have provided video recording software for this study. This material is based upon work supported by the National Science Foundation under award number 1400802, 1400810, 1462280. We are grateful to Sarah Ebling, who assisted in conducting some recording sessions with ASL students.

9. REFERENCES

[1] Cooper, H., Holt, B., Bowden, R. 2011. Sign Language Recognition. *Visual Analysis of Humans,* 539-562, Springer.

[2] Gallaudet Research Institute. 2011. Regional & national summary report of data from the 2009-10 annual survey of deaf and hard of hearing children and youth.

[3] Goldberg, D., Looney, D., Lusin, N. 2015. Enrollments in languages other than English in US institutions of higher education, Fall 2013. Modern Language Association.

[4] Goldin-Meadow, S., Mayberry, R.I. 2001. How do profoundly deaf children learn to read? *Learn Disabil Res Pract* 16(4): 222-229.

[5] Hamidi, F., Baljko, M. 2013. Automatic Speech Recognition: A Shifted Role in Early Speech Intervention? In *Proceedings of the SLPAT Workshop 2013,* 55–61.

[6] Henderson, V., Lee, S., Brashear, H., Hamilton, H., Starner, T., Hamilton S. 2005. Development of an ASL game for deaf children. *Proc Interaction Design & Children*, Boulder, CO.

[7] Lu, P., Huenerfauth, M. 2014. Collecting and Evaluating the CUNY ASL Corpus for Research on American Sign Language Animation. *Computer Speech & Language.* Volume 28, Issue 3, May 2014, Pages 812–831. Elsevier. doi:10.1016/j.csl.2013.10.004

[8] Marschark, M., Sapere, P., Convertino, C. M., Mayer, C., Wauters, L., Sarchet, T. 2009. Are deaf students' reading challenges really about reading? *Am Ann Deaf* 154(4): 357-70.

[9] Mayberry, R.I., Eichen, E.B. 1991. The long-lasting advantage of learning sign language in childhood: Another look at the critical period for language acquisition. *J Memory and Language.* 30:486-498.

[10] Mitchell, R.E., Karchmer, M.A. 2004. Chasing the Mythical Ten Percent: Parental Hearing Status of Deaf and Hard of Hearing Students in the United States. *Sign Lang Studies* 4(2): 138-163.

[11] Mitchell, R., Young, T., Bachleda, B., Karchmer, M. 2006. How many people use ASL in the United States? Why estimates need updating. *Sign Lang Studies*, 6(3):306-335.

[12] Monteiro, C., Gutierrez-Osuna, R., Shipman, F. 2012. Design and evaluation of classifier for identifying sign language videos in video sharing sites. In *The Proceedings of ASSETS '12,* 191-198. DOI=10.1145/2384916.2384950

[13] Lin, F.R., Niparko, J.K., Ferrucci, L. 2011. Hearing loss prevalence in the US. *Arch Intern Med* 171(20): 1851-1852.

[14] Neidle, C., Kegl, D., MacLaughlin, D., Bahan, B., Lee, R.G. 2000. *The syntax of ASL: functional categories and hierarchical structure.* Cambridge: MIT Press.

[15] Rosen, R.S. 2004. Beginning L2 production errors in ASL lexical phonology: A cognitive phonology model. *Sign Language & Linguistics,* 7(1), 31-61.

[16] Singleton, J.L., Newport, E.L. 2004. When learners surpass their models: The acquisition of American Sign Language from inconsistent input. *Cognitive Psychology,* 49(4):370–407, Dec. 2004.

[17] Spencer, P., Lederberg, A. 1997. Different modes, different models: communication and language of young deaf children and their mothers. in M. Romski, ed., *Communication and Language: Discoveries from Atypical Development.* Harvard University Press. pp. 203-30.

[18] Strong, M., Prinz, P.M. 1997. A Study of the Relationship Between American Sign Language and English Literacy. *J Deaf Stud & Deaf Educ* 2(1): 37-46.

[19] Traxler, C. 2000. The Stanford achievement test, 9th edition: national norming and performance standards for deaf and hard-of-hearing students. *J Deaf Stud & Deaf Educ* 5(4): 337-348.

[20] Valli, C., Lucas, C., Mulrooney, K.J., Villanueva, M. 2011. *Linguistics of American Sign Language: An Introduction.* Gallaudet University Press.

[21] Wang, H., Stefan, A., Moradi, S., Athitsos, V., Neidle, C., Kamangar, F. 2010. A System for Large Vocabulary Sign Search. *Workshop on Sign, Gesture and Activity.*

[22] Weaver, K.A., Starner, T., Hamilton, H. 2010. An evaluation of video intelligibility for novice ASL learners on a mobile device. In *The Proceedings of ASSETS '10,* 107-114. DOI=10.1145/1878803.1878824

[23] Weaver, K.A., Starner, T. 2011. We need to communicate: helping hearing parents of deaf children learn American Sign Language. In *The Proceedings of ASSETS '11,* 91-98. DOI=10.1145/2049536.2049554

[24] Wilbur, R.B. 2000. The use of ASL to support the development of English and literacy. *J Deaf Stud & Deaf Educ* 5(1), 81-104.

Demographic and Experiential Factors Influencing Acceptance of Sign Language Animation by Deaf Users

Hernisa Kacorri[1], Matt Huenerfauth[2], Sarah Ebling[3], Kasmira Patel[2], Mackenzie Willard[2]

[1]The Graduate Center, CUNY
365 Fifth Avenue
New York, NY 10016 USA
+1-212-817-8190
hkacorri@gc.cuny.edu

[2]Rochester Institute of Technology
152 Lomb Memorial Drive
Rochester, NY 14623 USA
+1-585-475-2700
{matt.huenerfauth, kxp3157, mtw2935}@rit.edu

[3]University of Zurich
Binzmühlestrasse 14
8050 Zurich Switzerland
+41-44-635-71-45
ebling@cl.uzh.ch

ABSTRACT
Technology to automatically synthesize linguistically accurate and natural-looking animations of American Sign Language (ASL) from an easy-to-update script would make it easier to add ASL content to websites and media, thereby increasing information accessibility for many people who are deaf. Researchers evaluate their sign language animation systems by collecting subjective judgments and comprehension-question responses from deaf participants. Through a survey (N=62) and multiple regression analysis, we identified relationships between (a) demographic and technology experience/attitude characteristics of participants and (b) the subjective and objective scores collected from them during the evaluation of sign language animation systems. This finding suggests that it would be important for researchers to collect and report these characteristics of their participants in publications about their studies, but there is currently no consensus in the field. We present a set of questions in ASL and English that can be used by researchers to measure these participant characteristics; reporting such data would enable researchers to better interpret and compare results from studies with different participant pools.

Categories and Subject Descriptors
H.5.2 [**Information Interfaces and Presentation**] User Interfaces – *evaluation/methodology*; K.4.2 [**Computers and Society**]: Social Issues – *assistive technologies for persons with disabilities*.

General Terms
Design, Experimentation, Human Factors, Measurement.

Keywords
Accessibility Technology for People who are Deaf; American Sign Language; Animation; User Study.

1. INTRODUCTION
Access to understandable information on websites and other media is essential in many education, commerce, and social contexts, yet most online content is in the form of written language text. Many people who are deaf and hard-of-hearing experience reduced exposure to language during childhood or educational circumstances that may lead to lower written language literacy: The median literacy rate of deaf high school graduates in the U.S. is at the 4th-grade level [27]. (U.S. 4th-grade students are typically age 10.) There are over 500,000 people in the U.S. who use American Sign Language (ASL) as a primary language [22]. Given the linguistic differences between English and American Sign Language (ASL), it is possible to be fluent in one language but not the other. Thus, providing information online in ASL can make content more accessible to users with lower English literacy; furthermore, many Deaf[1] users may simply prefer to receive information content in their primary language of ASL.

While posting videos of human signers on websites may seem like a simple solution, such videos are difficult to update when information changes, and they do not enable just-in-time generation of website content from a user request. For this reason, several research groups, e.g., [9, 15, 18, 19, 29], are studying the development of software to automatically synthesize understandable animations of a virtual human performing sign language, based on an easy-to-update script as input. The key challenge is for this software to select the details of such animations so that they are linguistically accurate, understandable, and acceptable to users. Researchers generally evaluate the quality of their software by: generating animations using some current version of their software, setting up an experiment in which deaf participants view and evaluate the animations, and comparing the scores of animations produced using the software (to some baselines or to prior versions). However, the field lacks consensus about the set of demographic data that should be reported about the participants. Thus, it is difficult to compare the results across studies because some variation in comprehension or subjective evaluation scores in studies may be explained by demographic characteristics of the participants, rather than by true differences in the quality of the animations being evaluated.

The goal of this paper is to examine the use of demographic and technology-experience variables as predictors of participants' responses to (a) subjective measures of animation quality and (b) objective measures of comprehension of the content. We present a study in which ASL signers were shown ASL animations (using a variety of avatars) and were asked questions of type (a) and (b). In addition, participants were asked questions about: (i) demographic characteristics and (ii) their technology experience/attitudes. Multiple regression analysis was used to determine whether variables (i-ii) relate to participants' responses (a-b).

ASSETS '15, October 26-28, 2015, Lisbon, Portugal
© 2015 ACM. ISBN 978-1-4503-3400-6/15/10…$15.00
DOI: http://dx.doi.org/10.1145/2700648.2809860

[1] We follow the widely held convention of using the capitalized term "Deaf" to refer to people who identify as members of the Deaf Community or Deaf Culture, and we use "deaf" as a more general term.

The remainder of this paper is organized as follows: Section 2 presents related work on demographics and evaluation studies. Sections 3, 4, and 5 describe the methodology of our study, and sections 6 and 7 present the results and discussion. Finally, Section 8 summarizes our conclusions and future directions.

2. RELATED WORK

In this related work section, we examine how prior sign language animation researchers have considered demographic or attitude variables when conducting their studies. We focus on studies that have been conducted with deaf participants in the context of evaluating sign language animations (section 2.1) or to determine general acceptance of such technology (section 2.2). While some researchers have conducted studies of how various demographic or health factors affect technology use and acceptance, e.g., [1, 2, 25], this section focuses on studies with deaf participants evaluating sign language animations.

2.1 Demographics in Prior Studies

The primary focus of this paper is how demographic characteristics or technology experience of participants in a study may affect the results collected. We therefore surveyed prior sign language animation studies to identify the types of participant characteristics or technology experience/attitudes that researchers reported. Our goal was to understand the diversity of participants in prior studies and the types of data that researchers commonly collect. While there are a few examples of published results where only the number of participants and how they are self-identified is reported, e.g., [23, 30], in general the trend in the field is to include more information about the sampled population. Table 1 presents examples of representative papers, similar patterns may be found when examining larger surveys of prior evaluation studies, e.g., [3, 11, 13, 16, 19].

Common characteristics reported in studies include the age range of participants, the gender ratio of participants, and the ratio of participants identifying as deaf/Deaf or hard-of-hearing (this is indicated by the term "describe" in Table 1). Studies vary in how they measure and report the level of sign-language skill of their participants, e.g., using "signing frequency" or "self-reported sign language skills." We also see variability in whether researchers ask about participants' exposure to technology; for example, [9] included questions about "computer expertise." Researchers in [29] noted that only those participants who were unfamiliar using the Internet had negative attitudes towards their avatar; the authors stated, "*This suggests that acceptance of the avatar is greater for web-surfers and that this acceptance may increase as a person becomes more familiar with the Internet.*" There is further variation in whether researchers asked participants about their attitude towards animated avatars ("attitude to avatar") or their views about the future potential of signing animations in different real-world contexts ("animation usage"). When included, such questions provide insight into how participants may see this technology being applied, e.g. as an educational tool [9] or for giving information in public spaces [18].

Table 2 shows some values of the most commonly reported demographic characteristics from the papers in Table 1. We can see wide variation in the demographic characteristics of users in prior sign language animation studies. For example there is especially wide variation in how researchers assess the signing skills of participants to determine whether they have sufficient fluency or native-level skill to participate in the study, e.g., some described what language their participants preferred [18, 29] and others described how often they used signing [18].

Table 1: Demographic and Technology Experience Characteristics Reported in Example User Studies

Paper	*Demographic*	*Technology*	*Attitudes*
[9]	age, gender, describe, profession	computer expertise	animation usage
[18]	age, gender, describe, signing frequency, preferred language		animation usage
[29]	age, gender, preferred language		attitude to avatar
[6]	age, gender, describe, self-reported SL skills, location		attitude to avatar

Table 2: Demographic Profile of Participants in Prior Studies

Paper	*Age Range*	*Female: Male*	*Describe*	*Assessing Signing Skills*
[9]	35-50	4 : 1	Deaf	Deaf educators
[18]	16-66	"slightly less female"	"most were deaf, some were hard-of-hearing"	"all were good signers... all using signing on a daily basis"
[29]	20-53	5 : 4	deaf	Some had preference for sign language; others had no preference between signing or text.
[6]	19-56	18 : 7	17 deaf, 8 hearing	8 "good," 6 "very good," 11 "native/expert"

A key question arises from examining this table: *Do these differences in the demographic characteristics of the population of users in the study have an impact on the comprehension scores or subjective judgments of the participants?* Knowing the answer to this question would make it easier to compare the results across different studies (so that we would know whether a particular set of participants might have been pre-disposed to have positive or negative evaluations of ASL animations). Thus, the goal of our study (sections 3 to 5) is to identify demographic characteristics or technology experience/attitude factors that relate to user's scores in evaluation studies. Based on these results, we will propose a set of standard questions that could be asked of participants in a user study (and thereby reported by researchers in their publications) to facilitate comparison of results across papers.

Some studies have included anecdotal evidence of relationships between (a) certain participant characteristics and (b) the subjective judgments or comprehension scores for sign language animation: e.g., the "web-surfers" comment in [29]. However, due to the relatively small sample size of most prior studies, researchers rarely present quantitative results for sub-populations. We are not aware of any prior study that conducted an exploration of whether a large variety of participant characteristics may relate to evaluation scores for sign language animation.

2.2 Acceptance of Multiple Signing Avatars

Kipp et al. [19] carried out the most comprehensive study to date with participants evaluating multiple sign language avatars; thus, in this section, we position our new study in relation to this most-closely related prior work. In focus groups in [19], eight native signers of German Sign Language were presented with six avatars signing content in different sign languages, and they commented on their quality. While researchers in [19] showed participants animations in American Sign Language and other unfamiliar languages, in our study described in section 4, participants were shown animations in a language in which they were fluent (ASL). Further, researchers in [19] showed participants some hand-animated avatars (produced through a painstaking process of carefully posing the character). Current sign language animation research focuses on synthesized animation, in which software automatically selects aspects of the movement to allow for generation of animations from a sparse input script. Section 4 describes how our new study utilized stimuli containing human avatar animation that was synthesized (not hand-animated).

Kipp et al. [19] also conducted an online survey (N=317), in which participants rated three avatars (one was hand-animated) on a 5-point scale in regard to: comprehensibility, facial expression, naturalness, charisma, movements, mouthing, appearance, hand shapes, and clothing. The hand-animated avatar received higher scores. In our new study, we include objective comprehension questions to measure participants' understanding. Self-reports of understanding typically have low correlation to a participant's accuracy at answering comprehension questions [13].

Notably, in both the focus group and the online survey, the authors observed higher scores in response the questions "Do you think avatars are useful?" and "Do you think Deaf people would use avatars?" when asked at the end of the study (compared to the beginning). The authors speculate that additional exposure to animations influenced participants' responses. In our new study, we include a question about whether participants had previously seen computer animations of sign language (details section 3.2).

Participants in [19] also suggested use-cases for signing avatars, including: public transit, movies/entertainment, government and educational websites, and other areas. In our new study, we also asked participants to judge the usefulness of signing avatars in various contexts: information on websites, for public places (e.g. airport, train station), as a virtual interpreter in a face-to-face meeting, as a virtual interpreter for telephone relay, etc.

While [19] collected some demographics (gender, age, deaf/hard-of-hearing/hearing, and profession), they did not analyze the data to look for relationships between these factors and the survey responses. Our new study includes a regression analysis to identify demographic and/or experience factors that related to the participants' subjective responses and comprehension scores.

Given the online modality of [19], there is a possibility that participants could have been more comfortable using the Internet than the general population. In our new study (sections 3 and 4), we conduct an in-person survey in which participants evaluate sign language animations; members of our research team traveled to meet participants at convenient locations. Our goal was to encourage participation of less technology-savvy individuals and to allow for us to confirm that participants met our study criteria (and were accurately reporting their demographic data).

3. COLLECT INDEPENDENT VARIABLES

The goal of our work is to examine whether metrics relating to participants' demographics (e.g., age, gender) or technology experience/attitudes can explain some of the subjective-judgment and comprehension-question scores collected in experiments to measure the quality of sign language animation systems. This section explains the design of our questionnaire for recording these independent variables, which will be used in our multiple regression models in section 6. This section will also explain the origin of any questions that were adapted from survey instruments that were presented in prior work of other authors, e.g., [25].

While some researchers have explored the design of fully online surveys of deaf users containing both ASL and English, e.g., [26], our survey was conducted in-person, with a human signer asking questions in ASL on a laptop screen and a paper answer sheet (with questions redundantly appearing in English, to aid the participant in aligning the video and paper). Given that our study included hard-of-hearing participants, the inclusion of English was considered important, and given our aim to include older participants in the study, a "low tech" paper answer sheet was preferable. Many questions were adapted from pre-existing English surveys (section 3.2); so a professional ASL interpreter (bachelor's degree in interpreting and master's in information technology) translated items into ASL. Deaf members of the research team checked that subtleties of meaning were preserved. Several takes of each question were recorded so that we could select the best version for the questionnaire. Example videos appear on our lab website: http://latlab.ist.rit.edu/assets2015

3.1 Demographic Questions

We selected demographic questions by assembling items that were asked in prior experimental studies, e.g. [12], and questions asked in studies surveyed in section 2. Below, we list the demographic questions, preceded by the "codename" of the response variables used in our regression models in section 6.

Gender: What is your gender? (male, female, other)

Age: How old are you?

Describe: How do you describe yourself? (deaf/Deaf, hard-of-hearing, hearing, other)

WhenBecome: At what age did you become deaf or hard-of-hearing? (Note: No hearing participants were in this study.)

WhenLearn: At what age did you begin to learn ASL? (Note: all participants in this study were ASL signers.)

ParentsAre: Are your parents deaf/Deaf? (yes, no)

ParentsUse: Did your parents use ASL at home? (yes, no)

SchoolType: What type of school did you attend as a child? (residential school for deaf students, daytime school for deaf students, or a mainstream school)

SchoolASL: Did you use ASL at this school? (yes, no)

Education: Which describes your current level of education? (did not graduate high school, graduated high school, graduated college, have bachelor's degree, have graduate degree)

HomeASL: Do you use ASL at home? (yes, no)

HomeEnglish: Do you use English at home? (yes, no)

WorkASL: Do you use ASL at work? (yes, no)

WorkEnglish: Do you use English at work/school? (yes, no)

Note: After collecting data from participants (section 5), we noticed a gap in the Age range 35-42 so instead of treating Age as a continuous variable, we binned it into three groups: 18 to 24, 25 to 34, and 43 to 59, and we relabeled the variable as **AgeGroup**.

3.2 Technology Experience and Attitudes

To measure participants' frequency of technology use, we adopted the InternetSearch and MediaSharing subscales from the *Media and Technology Usage and Attitudes Scale* [25]; scoring is based on the participant's response (e.g., Never, Monthly, Weekly, Once a day, etc.) to how frequently they engaged in various activities (listed below) on computers, laptops, tablets, or mobile phones:

InternetSearch: Search the Internet for news. ...for information. ...for videos. ...for images or photos.

MediaSharing: Watch TV shows, movies, etc. Watch video clips. Download media files from other people. Share your own.

Using the same scoring, we created an ASLChat subscale:

ASLChat: Have a signing (ASL) conversation with someone using a video phone. Have a signing (ASL) conversation with someone using a computer, laptop, tablet, smartphone.

We asked participants to indicate how often they played video games (and thereby may have more experience viewing animated humans) by selecting one of three frequency ranges (below), which we coded as "advanced," "intermediate," and "beginner."

GameGroup: How often do you play games on a computer, game console, or phone? (several times a day, between once a day and once a week, less than once a week)

Next, participants were asked about their perceptions of the benefits of technology, using the PositiveAttitudes subscale of [25], in which the score is the average of responses to individual statements listed below (Strongly agree = 5, Agree = 4, Neither agree no disagree = 3, Disagree = 2, Strongly disagree = 1):

PositiveAttitudes: It is important to be able to find any information whenever I want to online. It is important to be able to access the Internet any time I want. It is important to keep up with the latest trends in technology. Technology will provide solutions to many of our problems. With technology anything is possible. I accomplish more because of technology.

Participants' impression of computer complexity was measured using two Computer Questionnaire questions from the October 2014 PRISM survey [1], using identical Likert scoring as above.

ComputerComplex: Computers are complicated. Computers make me nervous.

Finally, at the end of the questionnaire, users were asked to indicate their agreement with a series of statements (below) to evaluate their overall attitude of the usefulness of ASL animations in a variety of contexts; this novel set of Likert-type items was inspired by questions in [6, 18, 19]. Finally, users were also asked if they had previously seen computer animations of ASL:

AnimationAttitude: Computer animations of sign language could be used to give information on a website. Computer animations of sign language could be used to give information in a public place (e.g., airport, train station). Computer animations of sign language could be used as an interpreter in a face-to-face meeting. Computer animations of sign language could be used as an interpreter for a telephone relay. I would enjoy using computer animations of sign language. Other people would enjoy using computer animations of sign language.

SeenBefore: Before today, had you ever seen a computer animation of sign language? (yes, no)

4. COLLECT DEPENDENT VARIABLES

Section 2.2 described how [19] displayed animations of multiple sign languages and animations that were hand-animated; we explained why we decided to display only **synthesized** animations of **ASL** in our current study. However, there is one type of "diversity" from [19] that we did preserve in our study design: We wanted the results of this study to be applicable to a variety of ASL signing avatars, with different appearance, rendering technologies, automation capabilities, and motion synthesis. Thus, we decided to display animations of three avatars synthesized by different state-of-the-art animation platforms [15, 17, 28]. In addition, in the [19] study, each avatar performed a different message. To control for this in our study, we selected three short ASL stories from a stimuli and comprehension question collection made available to the research community in [11]. Specifically, we selected three stimuli (codenames N2, W2, and Y3) that had been rated as being the most understandable in an earlier study by [17]. Example stimuli from the current study may be viewed on our lab website here: http://latlab.ist.rit.edu/assets2015

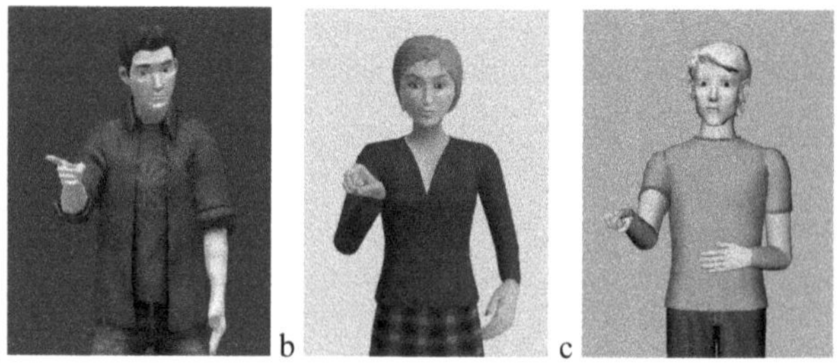

Figure 1: Screenshots from the three avatars shown in the study: (a) EMBR, (b) JASigning, (c) VCom3D.

EMBR: Animations shown in Figure 1(a) were generated using the open source EMBR platform [10] extended with ASL handshapes and detailed upper-face controls using the MPEG-4 Facial Animation standard [14]. Native ASL signers, who selected key-poses to define each sign in the lexicon, created the avatar's hand movements. Video recordings of a native signer performing the stimulus automatically drove face and head movements. To extract the facial features and head pose from video of a human signer, we used Visage Face Tracker, an automatic face tracking software that provides MPEG-4 compatible output [16], which we converted into the script language supported by the EMBR platform, as described in [14].

JASigning: Animations shown in Figure 1(b) were produced using the free Java Avatar Signing (JASigning) system [15]. All signs in the stimuli were notated in the Hamburg Notation System (HamNoSys) [24] by a deaf researcher while consulting the video recordings of an ASL native signer performing the stimulus. HamNoSys, which serves as an input for JASigning, has around 200 symbols describing the components: handshape, hand position, location, and movement. Information about the non-manual components (e.g., eyebrow movement, eye gaze, and head movement) is included in the SiGML code [8], an XML representation for HamNoSys, but time-alignment of non-manuals with the manual signs requires careful adjustment, e.g., [3].

VCOM: Animations shown in Figure 1(c) were generated using the commercially available ASL authoring tool, VCom3D Sign Smith Studio [28], which allows users to produce animated ASL sentences by arranging a timeline of animated signs from a prebuilt or user-defined vocabulary. The software includes a library of facial expressions that can be applied over a single sign or multiple manual signs. Both the hand movements and facial expressions of the avatar for the three stimuli were created by native ASL signers at a key-pose level. The VCOM and EMBR animations shared similar hand movements.

During our study, after participants answered the demographic and technology-experience questions described in section 3, they viewed a sample animation, to become familiar with the experiment setup and the questions they would be asked about each animation. (This sample animation used a different avatar than the other three animations shown in the study.) Next, after viewing each of the three main animations, an onscreen video of a native ASL signer asked participants four fact-based comprehension questions about the information conveyed in the animation. Participants responded to each question on a 7-point scale from "definitely no" to "definitely yes." As described in [11], a single "Comprehension" score for each animation can be calculated by averaging the scores of the four questions. Prior research, e.g., [12], has investigated key methodological considerations in conducting a study to measure comprehension of sign language animations with deaf users, including the use of appropriate baselines for comparison, the appropriate method for presenting comprehension questions and instructions, and other factors that we have considered in the design of this current study.

Next, the participants were asked to respond to a set of questions that measured their subjective impression of the animation, using a 1-to-10 scalar response. Each question was conveyed using ASL through an onscreen video, and the following English question text was shown on the questionnaire:

(a) Good ASL grammar? (10=Perfect, 1=Bad)
(b) Easy to understand? (10=Clear, 1=Confusing)
(c) Natural? (10=Moves like person, 1=Like robot)
(d) Was the signer friendly? (10=Friendly, 1=Not)
(e) Did you like the signer? (10=Love it, 1=Hate it)
(f) Was the signer realistic? (10=Realistic, 1=Not)

Questions (a-c) have been used in many prior experimental studies and were included in the collection of standard stimuli and questions that was released to the research community by [11]. Questions (d-f) were inspired by [19]. To calculate a single "Subjective" score for each animation, the scalar response scores for the six questions were averaged.

5. RECRUITING & DATA COLLECTION

Prior research, e.g. [13], has discussed the advantages of having deaf researchers conduct experimental studies in ASL. In this study, a deaf researcher (co-author) and two deaf undergraduate students (native ASL signers) recruited and collected data from participants, during meetings conducted in ASL. Potential participants were asked if they had grown up using ASL at home or had attended an ASL-based school as a young child. Initial advertisements were sent to local email distribution lists and Facebook groups. Our study (N=62) was completed during a four-week data collection period, a short timeframe made possible due to the many people who are deaf and hard-of-hearing associated with RIT or in Rochester, NY. It was easier for us to identify younger participants (especially college-aged students); the process of recruiting older participants took additional time and effort. The research team used personal contacts in the Deaf community to identify participants, especially older adults, who were less likely to be recruited through electronic methods. The advertisement included contact information for a deaf researcher, including an email address, videophone, and text messaging (mobile phone). Research team members also attended local Deaf community events (e.g., the Deaf Club) to advertise the study.

Researchers met participants around Rochester to conduct the 70-minute survey, using a laptop with video questions in ASL. Of the 62 participants recruited for the study, 43 participants learned ASL prior to age 5, 16 had been using ASL for over 9 years, and the remaining 3 learned ASL as adolescents, attended a university with classroom instruction in ASL, and used ASL daily to communicate with a significant other or family member. There were 39 men and 23 women of ages 18-59 (average age 25.73). For participants over age 43 (average age 53.14), there were 4 men and 2 women who learned ASL prior to age 9, 5 self-reported to be deaf/Deaf and 1 hard-of-hearing.

6. ANALYSIS AND RESULTS

The goal of our analysis was to examine how demographic factors relate to participants' responses to subjective and comprehension questions about ASL animations. In addition, we wanted to know whether variance in scores could be explained by participants' technology experience and attitudes. We therefore used multiple regression to analyze the data. Our independent variables included all of the "Demographic" and "Technology" metrics, listed in section 3. Our dependent variables included the "Comprehension" and "Subjective" scores described in section 4. Many researchers, e.g., [2], follow the recommendation of [5] that continuous-value variables be normalized by dividing the individual participant metrics by two times the group standard deviation, to facilitate easier comparison among coefficients of scalar and binary predictors. We have followed this procedure for all of the continuous independent variables in this study.

We trained two separate models for each of our dependent variables (Subjective and Comprehension): Model 1 was based upon Demographic variables only, and Model 2 was based upon both Demographic and Technology variables. The rationale for this choice is that while some prior authors have reported limited Demographic data about the participants in their studies, the set of Technology questions presented in this paper is novel. Since we had recorded many Demographic and Technology variables (section 3), it was important to explore combinations of variables in a systematic manner. We used the 'leaps' package [21] to build models of all possible subsets of features to identify the model with the highest adjusted R-squared value (indicating the total variability accounted for by the model). For Model 1, the input to 'leaps' was all Demographic variables only. For Model 2, the input to 'leaps' was all Demographic and all Technology variables. For all models, we evaluated the collinearity of the independent variables (that were selected by 'leaps') by verifying that their variance-inflation was less than 2 [4].

Table 3 summarizes the regression analysis for Comprehension.[2] In Model 1 (demographic variables only), the type of school that the participant attended had the largest coefficient (see "Estimate" column): attending a residential school for deaf students had a positive relationship with the participant's success at answering comprehension questions. Model 2 contained both demographic and technology variables, and a relationship between SchoolType and Comprehension is still present. Gender, Describe, InternetSearch, PositiveAttitudes, and GameGroup were also key components of Model 2. This suggests that when considering the results of studies that evaluate participants' comprehension of synthesized ASL animations, some variance in participants' scores can be explained by demographic and technology characteristics of each participant, e.g., their use of the Internet, positive attitude towards technology, and video game exposure. (Section 7 includes additional discussion of these factors.)

Table 4 summarizes the regression analysis for Subjective scores. In Model 1 (demographic variables only), using ASL at home had a significant and downward effect on a participant's subjective impressions. Using ASL at home was also a significant factor in Model 2, which includes both Demographic and Technology variables. Moreover, AnimationAttitude and MediaSharing were other key components of Model 2. These results suggest that when considering the results of studies that collect subjective judgments about synthesized sign language animations, researchers can expect harsher judgments from participants who use ASL at home, are comfortable with media sharing or downloading, and whose general attitude about sign language animations and their usefulness is not positive.

[2] The *Estimate* column reports the regression coefficient for the variable (how output varies per unit change in variable), *Std. Error* indicates average model error in the variable units (smaller values indicate that the observations are closer to the fitted line), and *t score* is the test statistic used to calculate the p-value for significance testing.

Table 3: Multiple Regression Model – Comprehension

Significance codes: 0 '***' 0.001 '**' 0.01 '*' 0.05 '.' 0.1 ' ' 1

	Estimate	*Std. Error*	*t score*
Model 1: Demographic	**Model 1:** Adj. R^2=0.256 (p<0.005)		
AgeGroup[25,34]	-0.344	0.195	-1.768 .
AgeGroup[35,)	-0.094	0.207	-0.452
Describehard-of-hearing	-0.242	0.149	-1.629
WhenBecome	0.204	0.126	1.624
WhenLearn	0.164	0.152	1.081
ParentsAreyes	0.252	0.166	1.516
SchoolASLyes	0.336	0.183	1.838 .
HomeASLyes	-0.177	0.147	-1.204
WorkEnglishyes	0.292	0.152	1.923 .
SchoolTypeMainstream	-0.092	0.146	-0.630
SchoolTypeResidential	0.575	0.169	3.407 **
Model 2: Demogr. & Tech.	**Model 2:** Adj. R^2=0.382 (p<0.0001)		
Gendermale	0.273	0.126	2.168 *
Describehard-of-hearing	-0.317	0.135	-2.338 *
WhenBecome	0.217	0.117	1.857 .
HomeASLyes	-0.207	0.125	-1.655
SchoolTypeMainstream	-0.029	0.140	-0.208
SchoolTypeResidential	0.662	0.151	4.380 ***
InternetSearch	-0.493	0.140	-3.513 ***
PositiveAttitudes	0.249	0.118	2.105 *
ASLChat	0.181	0.129	1.402
GameGroupBeginner	-0.307	0.129	-2.377 *
GameGroupIntermediate	-0.283	0.202	-1.399
SeenBeforeyes	0.162	0.119	1.355

Table 4: Multiple Regression Model – Subjective

Significance codes: 0 '***' 0.001 '**' 0.01 '*' 0.05 '.' 0.1 ' ' 1

	Estimate	*Std. Error*	*t score*
Model 1: Demographic	**Model 1:** Adj. R^2=0.153 (p< 0.02)		
Gendermale	-0.527	0.501	-1.05
Describehard-of-hearing	0.652	0.576	1.13
WhenLearn	-0.834	0.542	-1.54
HomeASLyes	-1.557	0.591	-2.63 *
SchoolTypeMainstream	0.659	0.584	1.13
SchoolTypeResidential	-0.538	0.643	-0.84
Model 2: Demogr. & Tech	**Model 2:** Adj. R^2=0.335 (p<0.0001)		
WhenLearn	-0.589	0.486	-1.21
HomeASLyes	-1.431	0.499	-2.87 **
SchoolTypeMainstream	0.685	0.517	1.32
SchoolTypeResidential	-0.030	0.590	-0.05
ComputerComplex	0.628	0.426	1.48
MediaSharing	-1.491	0.448	-3.33 **
AnimationAttitude	-1.373	0.448	-3.07 **

Figure 2 illustrates how Comprehension Model 2 accounts for significantly more variance than Comprehension Model 1, and the same is true for Subjective Model 2 and Subjective Model 1. An ANOVA was used to compare the models, and p-values are denoted in the graph by *** for p<0.001 or by ** for p<0.01. Model 2 represented a significant improvement in the amount of Comprehension accounted for between groups from 25.6% to 38.2%. Loosely speaking, this indicates that you can more accurately predict a signer's success at answering comprehension questions by considering both their demographic characteristics and technology experience/attitudes, rather than relying on their demographic characteristics only. Similarly, there was a significant increase in accounted variance of participants' subjective impressions of the animations from 15.3% to 33.5%.

It is not surprising that the adjusted R^2 values of the models are relatively low (<0.4), given that we predict users' comprehension and subjective scores based only on their demographic and experience/attitude characteristics. Section 2 described how prior

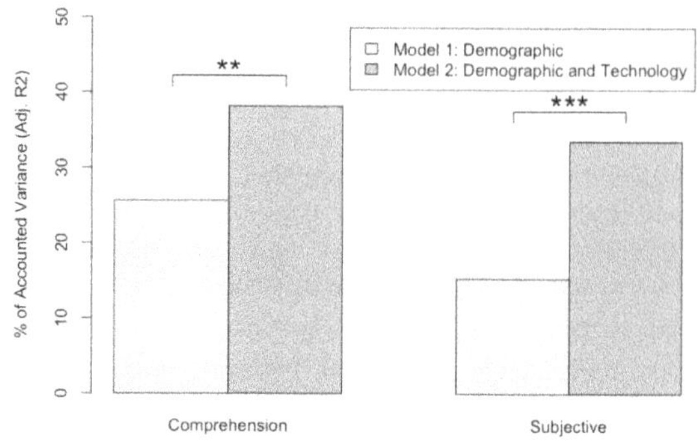

Figure 2: Regression model comparison summary. (Significance codes: 0 '*' 0.001 '**' 0.01)**

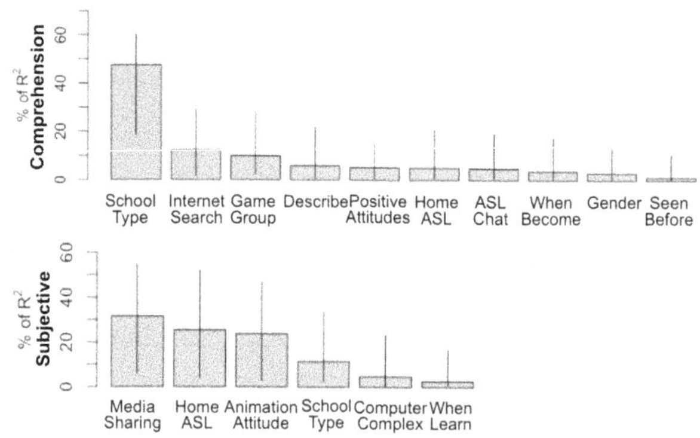

Figure 3: Relative importance (normalized to sum to 100%) of factors in Comprehension Model 2 and in Subjective Model 2, with 95% bootstrap confidence intervals.

ASL animation researchers generally assume that the value of such scores is based *upon the difference in quality or clarity of the animation stimuli that are shown to participants*. Perhaps counter-intuitively, the models in this paper do **not** include variables about the type of stimulus that was shown, e.g., the story nor the avatar, two variables that presumably relate to a participant's evaluation scores. Instead, we intentionally examined whether we could model the variance in scores based only upon demographic and experience/attitude characteristics of the participants.

7. DISCUSSION

Henceforth, our discussion will focus only on the best performing models: Comprehension Model 2 and Subjective Model 2, which contained both Demographic and Technology variables. In section 6, we considered each variable's coefficient ("Estimate" column in Tables 3 and 4) to roughly identify those with large influence. However, coefficients are sensitive to the "order" in which the variables are considered in the model. For more meaningful interpretation, we calculated the relative importance of each of the variables in Comprehension Model 2 and Subjective Model 2, using the Linderman-Merenda-Gold (LMG) metric [20], calculated using the 'relaimpo' package [7]. This analysis assigns an R-squared percent contribution to each correlated variable *obtained from all possible orderings of the variables in the regression model*. Higher bars in Figure 3 indicate variables with greater importance in the model. We employed bootstrap to estimate the variability of the obtained relative importance value, to determine 95% confidence intervals (shown as whiskers in Figure 3). Importance values may be considered significant when a bar's whiskers do not cross the zero line in the graph.

For Comprehension Model 2, which contains variables that 'leaps' selected through an exhaustive search of all subsets of Demographic and Technology variables, we observe that the variables with highest and significant relative importance are SchoolType, InternetSearch, and GameGroup. Given the much higher relative importance of SchoolType, compared to the other variables, we focus on this variable in our discussion below:

Comprehension and SchoolType. As discussed in section 6, attending a residential school seems to have a significant positive relationship with a participant's comprehension-question scores for synthesized ASL animations. We therefore encourage sign language animation researchers to include this variable in their demographic questionnaire for each study and to report this characteristic of participants in publications. When evaluating the Comprehension scores for their animations, they should consider this factor when comparing their results to those for other studies (whose participant pools may have differed in this characteristic).

Comprehension and SeenBefore. Another aspect Figure 3 that may be of interest to sign language animation researchers is the low importance of the SeenBefore variable in this model. Prior exposure of a participant to signing avatars did not explain much variance in participants' Comprehension scores. For researchers who conduct user studies with deaf participants to frequently evaluate the progress of their animation software, this finding suggests that participants who have seen prior versions of their animation system may be re-recruited for future studies (with the caveat, of course, that the new study is showing different stimuli). Since there may be a relatively small local Deaf community nearby to some research groups, this is a useful finding. We note that in this study, we had a well-balanced sample of participants for the SeenBefore variable (yes=29, no=33).

For Subjective Model 2, containing variables that 'leaps' selected through an exhaustive search of all subsets of Demographic and Technology variables, we observe that the variables with the highest and significant relative importance are: MediaSharing, HomeASL, AnimationAttitude, and SchoolType. While the height of its bar in Figure 3 indicates each variable's importance, the direction of the relationship (positive/negative) is indicated by the sign of the coefficient in the "Estimate" column of Table 4.

Subjective and AnimationAttitude. A positive relationship exists between these two variables, which is not a surprising result: If a participant has an overall negative view of the usefulness or likeability of sign language animations *in general* (as measured by the AnimationAttitude scale, section 3.2), then it is intuitive why they might have lower subjective scores *for a specific animation.*

Subjective and MediaSharing. Intuitively, we had expected that users with greater technology experience might have higher subjective scores due to their possible enthusiasm for technology. On the contrary: MediaSharing had a negative relationship to participants' subjective scores for animations. We can speculate that users with higher technology experience might have "higher standards" for the acceptable level of quality in an animation.

Subjective and HomeASL. A participant using ASL at home was also a factor with a negative relationship to their subjective score. We speculate that this might also be a case of "higher standards"; frequent ASL users may be harsher critics of animation quality.

Subjective and SchoolType. While SchoolType was important in both Comprehension Model 2 and in Subjective Model 2, the *direction of the relationship is reversed.* Attending a residential school had a positive relationship with Comprehension scores, but it had a negative relationship with Subjective scores. We note that it is reasonable that an independent variable may have opposite relationship with each of our dependent variables: Prior research has found low correlation between a participant's subjective score for an animation and his/her comprehension score for it [13].

8. CONCLUSIONS AND FUTURE WORK

The long-term goal of our research is to improve the state of the art of software for automatically synthesizing animations of sign language from a simple script of the desired message, technology that would make it easier to maintain and update information online in the form of sign language. We are also interested in understanding how to best conduct studies to evaluate the quality of such software, and the findings of this current study will affect the set of demographic and technology experience/attitude questions we ask participants in future work. Thus, a contribution of this work is a deeper understanding of the relationship between participant characteristics and evaluation scores in this field. Specifically, we found that the following variables were most important in explaining variance in comprehension and subjective scores of sign language animations:

- **SchoolType:** Assessed with a single multiple-choice question.
- **HomeASL:** Assessed with a yes/no question.
- **MediaSharing:** Assessed with four scalar response items indicating frequency of different activities, from [25].
- **AnimationAttitude:** Assessed with six Likert agreement items.

While other variables were present in models presented in section 6, the above four items correspond to the most important factors in section 7, and this abbreviated set may be useful for researchers interested in minimizing the amount of study time spent collecting demographic and technology experience/attitude data. Of course, we anticipate researchers will continue reporting other basic demographic data, e.g., age or gender, but our survey of prior work in 2.1 suggests that few current sign language animation researchers regularly collect and report these four items above.

We have previously released stimuli and evaluation questions to the research community, to promote replicability and comparison of results across studies [11]. We hope to further contribute by sharing the survey questions and ASL videos used in the study reported in this paper: http://latlab.ist.rit.edu/assets2015

Through collection and publishing of these characteristics of study participants, we anticipate easier comparisons of research results across publications. We also believe that these factors would be useful for researchers to consider if they are balancing or matching participants across treatment conditions in a study.

Compared to prior non-online studies evaluating sign language animation, this study was relatively large (N=62). However, when conducting a regression analysis of factors, there is always an advantage in having even larger and more diverse participant sets. In this case, it would be useful to recruit more participants from the Deaf community in another geographic area, to ensure that the relationships observed in the current study are preserved.

In future work, we are also interested in further exploring the variable of Age. This variable was not selected by the exhaustive all-subsets model comparison in this study, but only 10% of our 62 participants were over age 43 (none ages 35-43). In future work, we would like to conduct additional targeted recruitment of older participants. As we have learned in this study, such participants were the most time-consuming to recruit; so, this must be factored into the data-collection timeline in future work.

9. ACKNOWLEDGMENTS

This material is based upon work supported by the National Science Foundation under award number 1065009 and 1506786, and by the Swiss Science Foundation, under award 155263. We are grateful to Sandra Sidler-Miserez, who helped produce ASL animations, and to Kellie Menzies and Evans Seraphin, who assisted in the recruitment of participants and in data collection.

10. REFERENCES

[1] Center for Research and Education on Aging and Technology Enhancement. 2015. Resources. http://create-center.gatech.edu/resources.php (Retrieved May 6, 2015)

[2] Crabb, M., Hanson, V.L. 2014. Age, technology usage, and cognitive characteristics in relation to perceived disorientation and reported website ease of use. In *Proceedings of the 16th international ACM SIGACCESS conference on Computers & accessibility* (ASSETS '14). ACM, New York, NY, USA, 193-200. DOI=10.1145/2661334.2661356

[3] Ebling, S., Glauert, J. 2015. Building a Swiss German Sign Language avatar with JASigning and evaluating it among the Deaf community. *Univ Access Inf Soc.*

[4] Fox, J. and Monette, G. (1992) Generalized collinearity diagnostics. *JASA* 87:178-183.

[5] Gelman, A. (2008). Scaling regression inputs by dividing by two standard deviations. *Stat Med* 27(15), 2865-2873.

[6] Gibet, S., Courty, N., Duarte, K., & Naour, T. L. 2011. The SignCom system for data-driven animation of interactive virtual signers : Methodology and Evaluation. *ACM Trans. Interact. Intell. Syst.* 1(1): Article 6 (October 2011), 23 pages. DOI=10.1145/2030365.2030371

[7] Grömping, U. (2006). Relative importance for linear regression in R: the package relaimpo. *Journal of statistical software* 17(1): 1-27.

[8] Hanke, T. 2001. *ViSiCAST Deliverable D5-1: Interface Definitions.* Technical Report. ViSiCAST project. http://www.visicast.co.uk/members/milestones/D5-1rev1.pdf

[9] Hayward, K., Adamo-Villani, N., Lestina, J. 2010. A computer animation system for creating deaf-accessible math and science curriculum materials. In *Eurographics'10.*

[10] Heloir. A, Nguyen, Q., Kipp, M. 2011. Signing avatars: a feasibility study. In *2nd Int'l Workshop on Sign Language Translation and Avatar Technology,* Dundee, Scotland.

[11] Huenerfauth, M., Kacorri, H. 2014. Release of experimental stimuli and questions for evaluating facial expressions in animations of American Sign Language. *Workshop on the Representation & Processing of Sign Languages, LREC'14.*

[12] Huenerfauth, M., Kacorri, H. 2015. Best practices for conducting evaluations of sign language animation. *Proceedings of the 30th Annual International Technology and Persons with Disabilities Conference (CSUN'15), Scientific/Research Track,* San Diego, California, USA.

[13] Huenerfauth, M., Zhao, L., Gu, E., Allbeck, J. 2008. Evaluation of American sign language generation by native ASL signers. *ACM Trans. Access. Comput.* 1, 1, Article 3 (May 2008), 27 pages. DOI=10.1145/1361203.1361206

[14] International Standards Organization. 2004. ISO/IEC 14496-2:2004: Information technology – Coding of audio-visual objects – Part 2: Visual.

[15] Jennings, V., Elliott, R., Kennaway, R., Glauert, J. 2010. Requirements For A Signing Avatar. *Workshop on the Representation & Processing of Sign Languages, LREC'10.*

[16] Kacorri, H., Huenerfauth, M. 2014. Implementation and evaluation of animation controls sufficient for conveying ASL facial expressions. In *Proceedings of the 16th international ACM SIGACCESS conference on Computers & accessibility (ASSETS '14).* ACM, New York, NY, USA, 261-262. DOI=10.1145/2661334.2661387

[17] Kacorri, H., Huenerfauth, M. 2015. Comparison of Finite-Repertoire and Data-Driven Facial Expressions for Sign Language Avatars. *In Proceedings of HCII2015.*

[18] Kennaway, J. R., Glauert, J. R., & Zwitserlood, I. 2007. Providing signed content on the Internet by synthesized animation. *ACM Trans Comput-Human Interact* 14(3): Article 15 (Sept 2007). DOI=10.1145/1279700.1279705

[19] Kipp, M., Nguyen, Q., Heloir, A., Matthes, S. 2011. Assessing the Deaf user perspective on sign language avatars. In *Proceedings of the 13th International ACM SIGACCESS Conference on Computers and Accessibility (ASSETS '11).* ACM, New York, NY, USA, 107-114. DOI=10.1145/2049536.2049557

[20] Lindeman, R.H., Merenda, P.F., Gold, R.Z. 1980. *Introduction to bivariate & multivariate analysis.* Scott Foresman, Glenview, IL.

[21] Lumley, T. 2009. *leaps: regression subset selection. R package version 2.9.*

[22] Mitchell, R., Young, T., Bachleda, B., and Karchmer, M. 2006. How many people use ASL in the United States? Why estimates need updating. *Sign Lang Studies* 6(3):306-335.

[23] Moemedi, K.A. 2010. Rendering an avatar from sign writing notation for sign language animation. Doctoral dissertation, University of the Western Cape.

[24] Prillwitz, S., Leven, R., Zienert, H., Hanke, T, Henning, J. 1989. *HamNoSys: v2.0: Hamburg Notation System for Sign Languages: an introductory guide.* Signum, Hamburg.

[25] Rosen, L.D., Whaling, K., Carrier, L.M., Cheever, N.A., Rokkum, J. 2013. The media and technology usage and attributes scale: An empirical investigation. *Comput Human Behav* 29(6): 2501-2511.

[26] Tran, J.J., Johnson, T.W., Kim, J., Rodriguez, R., Yin, S., Riskin, E.A., Ladner, R.E., Wobbrock, J.O. 2010. A web-based user survey for evaluating power saving strategies for deaf users of mobileASL. In *Proceedings of the 12th international ACM SIGACCESS conference on Computers and accessibility (ASSETS '10).* ACM, New York, 115-122. DOI=10.1145/1878803.1878825

[27] Traxler, C. 2000. The Stanford achievement test, 9th ed: national norming and performance standards for deaf & hard-of-hearing students. *J Deaf Stud & Deaf Educ* 5(4): 337-348.

[28] VCom3D. 2015. Homepage. http://www.vcom3d.com

[29] Verlinden, M., Tijsseling, C., Frowein, H. 2001. Sign language on the WWW. In *Proceedings of 18th Int. Symposium on Human Factors in Telecommunication.*

[30] Yang, O., Morimoto, K., Kuwahara, N. 2014. Evaluation of Chinese Sign Language animation for mammography inspection of hearing-impaired people. In *Advanced Applied Informatics, IIAI'14,* 831-836. IEEE.

How 3D Virtual Humans Built by Adolescents with ASD Affect Their 3D Interactions

Chao Mei
Department of Computer Science
University of Texas at San Antonio
One UTSA Circle
San Antonio, TX, USA 78249-0667 +1 (210) 872-8618
meichaomc@gmail.com

Lee Mason
Interdisciplinary Learning & Teaching
University of Texas at San Antonio
One UTSA Circle
San Antonio, TX, USA 78249-0667
+1 (210) 458-4524
Lee.Mason@utsa.edu

John Quarles
Department of Computer Science
University of Texas at San Antonio
One UTSA Circle
San Antonio, TX, USA 78249-0667
+1 (210) 458-7433
jpq@cs.utsa.edu

ABSTRACT

Training games have many potential benefits for autism spectrum disorder (ASD) intervention, such as increasing motivation and improving the abilities of performing daily living activities, due to their ability to simulate real world scenarios. A more motivating game may stimulate users to play the game more, and it may also result in users performing better in the game. Incorporating users' interests into the game could be a good way to build a motivating game, especially for users with ASD.

We propose a Customizable Virtual Human (CVH) which enables users with ASD to easily customize a virtual human and then interact with the CVH in a 3D interaction task. Previous work has shown that users with ASD may have less efficient hand-eye coordination in performing 3D interaction tasks than users without ASD. We developed a hand-eye coordination training game - Imagination Soccer - and presented a user study on adolescents with high functioning ASD to investigate the effects of CVHs. We compare the differences of participants' 3D interaction performances, game performances and user experiences (i.e. presence, involvement, and flow) under CVH and Non-customizable Virtual Human (with randomly generated appearances) conditions. As expected, the results indicated that for users with ASD, CVHs could effectively motivate them to play the game more, and offer a better user experience. Surprisingly, results also showed that the CVHs improved performance in the hand-eye-coordination task – users had higher success rate and blocked more soccer balls with the CVH than with a non-customizable virtual human.

Categories and Subject Descriptors

H.5.2 [Information Interfaces and Presentation]: User Interfaces – Evaluation/methodology.

General Terms: Experimentation, Human Factors.

Keywords: customizable virtual human, autism spectrum disorder, 3D interactions.

ASSETS '15, October 26-28, 2015, Lisbon, Portugal
© 2015 ACM. ISBN 978-1-4503-3400-6/15/10...$15.00
DOI: http://dx.doi.org/10.1145/2700648.2809863.

1. INTRODUCTION

For persons with ASD, 3D training games may have potential benefits, such as improving the abilities to perform daily living activities (e.g., crossing the street in a 3D virtual city [1]). Bekele et al. suggest that the main benefits of virtual reality games in ASD therapy are: the games have the ability to simulate real world scenarios in a carefully controlled and safe environment, as well as controlled stimuli presentation, objectivity and consistency, and gaming elements motivate task completion [2]. Games with 3D User Interfaces (3DUIs) could potentially expand the set of effective training tasks and thus, further enhance such benefits.

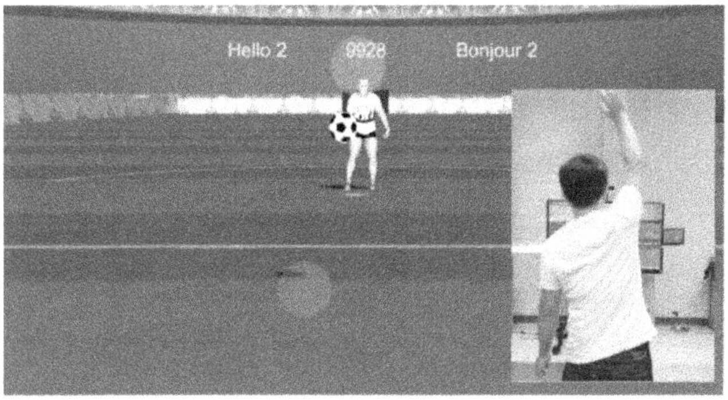

Figure 1. A user is trying to block the soccer ball kicked out by a user customized virtual human.

However, as indicated by Mei. et al [10], users with ASD showed less efficient hand-eye coordination in performing 3D interaction tasks. This could limit the benefits of 3D training games for ASD. A game that trains the hand-eye coordination in 3DUI may help users with ASD improve their 3D interaction performance.

A more motivating training game may stimulate users to try harder in the game. It may also result in users playing the game more, which could potentially improve daily lives for people living with ASD. Including users' interests in the game could be a good way to build a more motivating game. Existing 3D training games seldom take into consideration the fact that there is a wide variety of interests within ASD population. As indicated by Robert et al., everyone diagnosed with ASD is remarkably different [3]. Individuals with ASD often have very specific interests, some of which are uncommon, such as a certain alphabetical letter, washing machines, etc. Moreover, their interests are often restricted; topics outside of their specific interests often do not effectively capture their attention. The wide variety of individuals on the ASD spectrum makes it almost impossible to include all interests in 3D training games. Allowing customization and personalized content importation in the 3D training games could help address this issue and increase the game motivation and performances. Previous studies suggested that virtual humans with different appearances could evoke different reactions from general users [4-7]. However, it is not known how virtual human appearance customization would affect persons with ASD, or what effect it has on 3D interaction.

Therefore, our main research question is: how does a customizable appearance of the Virtual Human (VH) affect 3D interaction task performance and user experience for users with ASD? To investigate this question, we developed a Customizable Virtual Human (CVH) and a 3D hand-eye coordination training game - Imagination Soccer. To determine the training effects of the CVH and the game, we present a user study including adolescents who have a high ASD severity score, but were still considered as high functioning (IQ of 80 or above, and be able to speak, read and write). Specifically, we investigated: 1) if/how the CVH increases the 3D interaction performance for users with ASD, and if the CVH motivates them to play more rounds in the game, and 2)if the CVH improves the subjective user experience (i.e. presence, involvement, and flow) in the 3D training game with respect to users with ASD.

2. RELATED WORK

Our hypotheses about the potential benefits of CVH for persons with ASD were influenced by previous research in related areas: virtual humans, accessibility needs of the ASD population, customizable virtual humans/self-avatars, and the use of customization in existing ASD therapies.

2.1 Appearances of Virtual Humans

Many researchers have demonstrated that virtual humans with different appearances could evoke different reactions from users. For example, Vugt et al. reported that users respond more positively when they were exposed to virtual humans that had similar facial features to the users' faces, instead of dissimilar ones [5]. The concordance between the users' and VHs' appearances were also studied by Rivera-Gutierrez et al. [7]. They explored the effects of dynamic virtual humans on user perceptions of their interaction. The dynamic virtual humans selected their appearances according to user information such as weight, height and gender. Their results indicated that the concordance between the users' and the virtual humans' appearances positively affected the male users' perception of VH knowledge through the interaction but had negative effects on female users' perception of VH knowledge. Zanbaka et al. also reported the influence of the gender on virtual humans [4], they found that users were more persuaded by virtual humans of opposite sex. Moreover, Dan et al. conducted a study in which participants rated ergonomic posture of virtual humans [6]. The ratings were higher among the virtual humans with more realistic appearances, even though the appearances were not typically considered as a factor influencing ergonomic posture ratings. Various aspects of the VH's appearances have been shown to effectively influence users' responses. However, it is not known how virtual human appearances affect persons with ASD.

2.2 Special Accessibility Needs of ASD Population

The number of children diagnosed with Autism Spectrum Disorder (ASD) is increasing at an alarming rate. According to the Centers for Disease Control and Prevention (CDC), the prevalence of ASD in the United States has grown from 1 case per 150 children to 1 case per 68 children from the year 2000 to 2010. ASD is marked by impaired social communication and social interaction, accompanied by atypical patterns of behavior and interest [8].

Children with ASD have shown inefficient hand-eye coordination in the real world [9] and 3D interactions [10]. Hand-eye-coordination refers to the ability of the vision system to coordinate the information received through the eyes to control, guide, and direct the hands in the accomplishment of a given task, such as handwriting or catching a ball. Research has demonstrated a strong correlation between hand-eye coordination, learning abilities, and social communication skills [11]. Thus, ASD therapies have widely adopted hand-eye coordination training as a part of their curricula [12]. Practicing such abilities in a game could potentially assist with ASD therapies.

It has been well known that people with ASD have disabilities in identifying others' emotion. These disabilities have been found both for facial and bodily expressions in the real world. Such disabilities were also found in a Virtual Environment (VE). For example, Bekele et al. investigated how people with ASD responded to facial expressions in a VE [2]. The results suggested that people with ASD had facial emotion recognition deficiencies in VEs as well. Rather than the facial emotion recognition, a system is needed to evaluate and help improving the bodily emotion recognition ability, which, to our knowledge, has not been investigated in VE for people with ASD.

2.3 Customizable Virtual Humans

There are several research papers that have focused on customizing actions of VHs. These works presented several benefits of customization in VR applications. For example, Reategui et al.[13] demonstrated a virtual human that was able to present customized content in an online learning system. It was shown to have a positive impact in the users' acceptance of the system. SitePal [14] is an online application, it allows users to customize the interaction content with a speaking VH for their own websites. In a case study of SitePal, a college level course was designed with a virtual instructor built from this tool, and it resulted in higher grades of the students. However, they did not explore the effects of customizable appearances of VH.

There is minimal previous research regarding the benefits of appearance customization of virtual humans. However, we did find a paper that presented a drawback of it. Okita et al. [15] evaluated the learning process with virtual peers and showed that allowing students to customize their virtual peers led to lower performance on a test than non-customized peers. The reason could be that the customized appearance resulted in distraction. However, this result is not necessarily generalizable to the ASD population due to their different cognitive processes than the typically developed (TD) population.

2.4 Customizable Self-Avatars

Most of the research that explored virtual human appearance customization was focused on self-avatars – the representation of the user's own body in virtual reality. Customizable self-avatars are often found with interesting psychological effects and training benefits. Yee et al. found that self-avatar customizations changed users' preferences in games [16]. Bailey et al. conducted a study that demonstrated how avatar customization elicited the feeling of presence during game play. Bessiere et al.[17] explored the self-avatar identity presented in an online multiplayer game. In that game, players interacted with other online players through customized self-avatars. Results showed that players built their self-avatars more similarly to their ideal body rather than their actual bodies in real life. This correlation was stronger among those with lower psychological well-being. Ducheneaut et al.[18] compared different customization tools and suggested several factors that are important for a self-avatar customizing system, such as hair styles and colors.

These works inspired us in the design of our CVH, such as the variables that should be customizable (e.g., hair). However, self-avatars and virtual peers perform different roles in VEs. They could have a different impact on user experiences and it is unknown how this will impact ASD users' experiences.

2.5 Customization in ASD Therapy Software

Although we could not find research on virtual human appearance customizations for the ASD population, there is some research that investigated the customization of other aspects. For example, Robert et al. presented an algorithm that enabled the users with ASD to put images based on their interests into flash games. They suggested that users with ASD enjoyed customized games more than the non-customized version, but the effects of customization on ASD therapy have not been formally evaluated. Tartaro et al.[19] introduced a virtual peer who has an authorable storytelling process. It was able to support the development of communication and reciprocal social interaction skills of ASD children. These results further suggested that customizable virtual humans could potentially benefit ASD therapy.

3. OUR PROPOSED CONTRIBUTIONS

The effects of CVH in 3D training games with respect to ASD users are unknown. The main goal of our research is to find out the effects of CVH on 3D interaction performances and the effects on the motivation in 3D training games for ASD users. Specifically, this research provides novel insights into:

- How CVHs affect the performance of adolescent users with ASD in a 3D hand-eye coordination training game.
- The user experiences (i.e. presence, involvement, and flow) effects of CVH in a in a 3D training game for adolescent users with ASD.
- Generalizable guidelines for enabling future CVHs in 3D games for adolescents with ASD.

4. SYSTEM DESIGN

We developed a Customizable Virtual Human (CVH) and "Imagination Soccer" - a 3DUI-based game in which users play as a goalie in a soccer game with a CVH plays as a kicker. The ball catching task is adopted by many clinics as part of the therapy that helps improving hand-eye coordination for ASD patients. The game is designed to motivate training, improve hand-eye coordination in 3D interaction task, and increase bodily emotion recognition ability for ASD individuals.

4.1 Imagination Soccer Physical Set Up

Imagination Soccer is a VR game set up in an environment as shown in Figure 3. The system was equipped with one LED TV, one Microsoft Kinect sensor and a tablet. A laptop was used at the back end for controlling the system and rendering the graphics. The specifications of each piece of the system is listed as below:

The 55" LED TV is positioned at 1.2 meters above the ground, which makes view of the screen comfortable for most adolescents. We did not evaluate the 3DUI with immersive displays(e.g., a head mounted display), because they are not as easy to accesses as flat TVs. Moreover, we did not use a stereoscopic display since they are also not a widely available and require users to wear additional glasses, which could be distracting for some children with ASD. In addition, 2D displays can still present 3D content with very good 3D depth cues, and moreover, most of the 3D games of entertaining and training are still using the 2D displays. Therefore, for the 3D interactions in training games, we think it would be more reasonable to start doing the evaluation with an accessible setting rather than uncommon ones. We plan to investigate stereoscopic displays in future work.

The Microsoft Kinect is placed on top of the TV to track the users' motions. The tablet placed at the right side of the TV screen is used both as an input and output device. In the game, it displays a soccer ball on its screen. Users swipe the soccer ball off the touch screen in order to pass the ball to the virtual human on the screen, as shown in Figure.3(c). The position of the tablet is aligned with the virtual soccer ball on TV screen in order to provide the illusion of really sending the ball from the tablet back onto the TV screen. More details on the game process will be discussed in section. 4.3. A TOSHIBA Qosmio laptop was connected with the TV, Kinect and tablet through a HDMI cable, USB cable and local wireless network respectively.

4.2 Customizable Virtual Human

The CVH is designed to enable the users to implement an imaginary play companion, based on their individual interests. Users customize the CVH with a simple interface that is easy to learn (Figure 2.) and includes many variables that can be customized.

4.2.1 *Customizable Variables*

Users customize the CVH by modifying 9 variables. These 9 variables were partially inspired by a previous survey made by Ducheneaut et al.[18]. They made comparisons between different customization variables in games and the effect on user experiences. They suggested several factors that are important for a self-avatar customization system. We picked several popular ones that are related to the appearances of virtual humans (i.e. hair style and color, fat level, muscular level, height, skin color, and gender). Previous results were based on virtual self-avatars not a play companion, we also added some variables that could be relevant to a play companion (i.e. name, t-shirt pattern and age). The details of these variables are listed below:

- *Hair style and color* is selected from 23 different predefined hair models (i.e., 10 for male CVH, 13 for female CVH). Each hair model is in a different style or color.
- *Fat level, muscle level and height* are each set by any value from 0 (minimum level) to 100 (maximum level). They are continuous variables that morph the shape of the CVH's whole body.

- *Skin color* is selected from 2 options - light skin and dark skin.
- *Gender* is selected from 2 options - male and female.
- *Name* is set by typing any string, which appears during the game next to the score.
- *T-shirt patterns* can be customized in two ways: 1) Users search online for interesting images. The CVH automatically adjusts the image size and inserts it into a white t-shirt texture on the chest. 2) Additionally, users can select from 7 predefined t-shirt textures.
- *Age* is selected from 3 different age groups - little kids, teenagers and adults. In each age group, there are two initial models - male and female. Each initial model has different ranges for fat level, muscle level and height, according to the age and gender.

4.2.2 User Interface for CVH

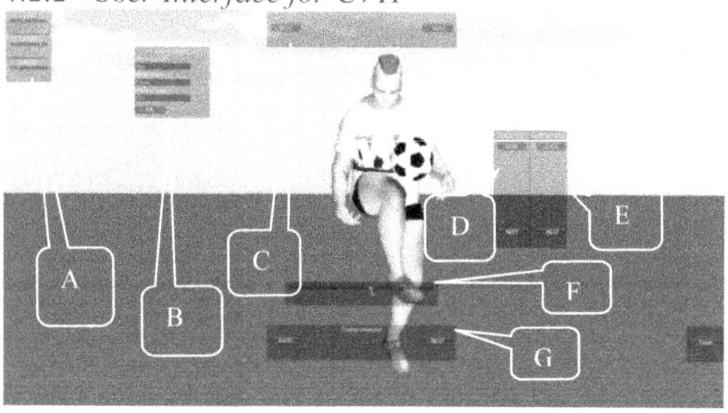

Figure 2. User Interface of CVH.

Each variable is set through a simple user interface that is easy to learn as shown in Figure 2. A VH stands in the middle and plays with a soccer ball. Users interact with three slider bars with mouse (Label A) to control the three continuous variables - fat level, muscle level and height. Age and gender (Label G), hair models (Label C), skin color (Label D) and t-shirt pattern (Label E) control were all composed from the combination of a "Last" and "Next" buttons to switch between each predefined whole body models, parts models, textures, and real-time generated textures. Users input their own name and the name of the VH through two textboxes (Label B). We positioned the control panels close to the VH's parts that they controlled (e.g. the hair control panel is placed on top of the virtual human's head). The user could observe the VH with 360 degree view using a slider bar (Label G).

4.3 Game Process

After the user finishes the customization of a virtual friend, the main game interface is presented on the TV screen (shown in Figure 1). The game trains the 3D hand-eye coordination by simulating a ball-catch scenario. It takes place in a soccer stadium. The virtual friend stands in front of the penalty kick mark with idle animation of breathing. The scoreboard is shown above the virtual friend with the names and scores of the friend and the user on it. The middle of the scoreboard shows the remaining time of the current round. The two blue discs are the representations of user's hands in the game. The user initially does a 'T' position to set the calibration before the start of the game. The initial distance of the two blue discs are mapped to the distance between the user's hands in the real world during the initial calibration. Thus, the user's arm length does not affect the difficultly level or playability of the game. The tablet is attached at the right side of the TV screen and it displays a 3D model of a soccer ball.

Figure 3. (a) Waving. (b) Jumping Jack. (c) Passing ball to VH.

Users stand approximately 2.5 meters in front of the TV screen as shown in Figure 3(a). The game can identify three kinds of motion input from users and touch input from the tablet. First, the game takes inputs from left and right hands' positions to control the two blue discs on the screen. Users position the discs by positioning their real hands. However, moving hands forward or backward does not affect the disc position in order to limit the difficulties brought by depth perception. The other two motion inputs are waving as shown in Figure 3(a) and jumping jacks, shown in Figure 3(b).

At the beginning of the game, the user does jumping jacks as a warm up activity. Jumping jacks are adopted by many clinics as part of the therapy that helps improving body coordination for ASD patients. Users' jumping jacks motions are captured and evaluated. If the user correctly performs a jumping jack, the virtual human does a jumping jack as well.

Users start the game by waving at the virtual friend, in order to indicate the user is ready to play. Next, the virtual friend waves back to the user and then kicks the ball. The target of each kick is selected from a set of equally divided 3x3 points on the TV screen. After the ball is kicked and flies for 2 sec., it hits a target location and disappears. The 2 sec. was decided through pilot studies in order to keep the game challenging, but still provide users enough time to react. The user takes these 2 seconds to judge the target through the trajectory of the ball, and then moves the discs to the target location to block the ball as shown in Figure 1. If the ball is blocked successfully, the user gets 1 point and the disc(s) that blocked the ball will flash red, otherwise the virtual friend gets 1 point. In response to a blocked ball or a missed ball, the virtual human plays various animations, showing either sad or happy emotions, respectively. The sound effects of cheering from the audience accompanies the sad animations. The sound effect of cheering from the virtual friend accompanies the happy animations. After each kick, the ball appears on the tablet, and the user needs to go to the tablet and swipe the ball in order to pass the ball back to the VH (Figure 3(c)). At the end of each round, the VH rewards the user by doing push-ups or dancing. For each point the user got, the virtual friend does a push-up. For every 5 points the user got, the virtual friend does a dance.

5. USER STUDY

We conducted user study with participants who were diagnosed with high functioning autism. In a randomized and counterbalanced within-subjects design (i.e. participants were their own controls), the participants interacted with both the CVH and a randomly assigned non-customizable VH (NCVH). The NCVH has same set of customizable variables as the CVH, however the value of the variables is randomly generated by computer and cannot be adjusted by users.

5.1 Hypotheses

Previous work suggested that including personalized content in a game may enable users with ASD to enjoy the game more than without personalized content[3]. Although this result was not formally evaluated, the authors suggest that this personalization could lead to more motivation in training. Moreover, other works have shown that ASD users are interested in defining behaviors of and interacting with virtual companions[19]. Thus, based on the literature, allowing customization of a virtual human in 3D training games may improve ASD users' overall user experience with the game and ultimately increase their motivation to continue rehabilitation.

The hypotheses are related to 3D interaction task performance and user experiences. Specifically our hypotheses are:

Hypothesis 1: Playing with CVHs will help participants to perform better and play more rounds in a 3D hand-eye coordination training game.

Hypothesis 2: CVHs will give the users a better user experience - specifically with respect to presence, involvement, and flow in the game.

Before the study, we were very confident that the CVHs would provide better user experiences for users, but less confident to say it would result in better game performance. The evidence in previous research lead us to the Hypothesis 2, but they did not clearly indicate Hypothesis 1. Due to a lack of previous work in performance effects, we designed this study to investigate a CVH's impact on both user experience and performance.

5.2 Participants

10 participants were recruited with the help of local support groups, research institutes and non-profit ASD support organizations from (removed for review), with ages ranging from 9 to 18 years. We recruited participants at adolescent ages because adolescence is an important time to develop many useful skills such as communication abilities and exercise abilities that can be potentially trained with 3D training games. Participants had been diagnosed with high functioning ASD. To eliminate the gender influence as a variable and the great gender disparity incidence rate of autism between male and female, in this current study, we did not recruit any female participants with ASD. All participants reported some prior experience and familiarity playing video games.

To be included in the study, participants with ASD had to score greater than 71 in the Gilliam Autism Rating Scale-3 (GARS-3) test. The GARS-3 questionnaire is used in identifying and estimating the severity of autism in participants. 71 is a threshold that indicates a severe autism. From their reports and our observation, these participants did not have any other disability that would limit understanding and performing the study tasks.

5.3 Study Processes

The study was conducted in an indoor lab. Only the experimenter, the participant, and the participant's guardian were allowed to present. The total duration of the study was about one and a half hours per participant, including training, customizing, performing tasks and resting. Each participant was paid 50 dollars.

5.3.1 Setup and Training

To initially setup the CVH, we first asked the users to find 3 images that they were interested in using. We used Google Image Search to find the images and save them in the game folder. The CVH automatically identified these images and generated new t-shirt textures with them. The online images were resized to fit on the chest part of the t-shirt. The new textures later appeared as customization options, when participants customized the t-shirt pattern of CVH.

We conducted a training session after the participant finished the image selection. The experimenter first showed a demo of how to perform a calibration 'T' pose with the hands, to block a ball, and to use the tablet to send the ball back. The participant then played for 3 kicks as training. The training was conducted without any virtual human so as to not bias the training.

5.3.2 Study Part 1: Time Limited Play

In the study part 1, users played with both CVH and NCVH for same amount of time. We mainly investigated how CVHs influence game performance (i.e. the 3D interaction performance) in this part. It included two sessions. Each session had time limit of 60 seconds. This time limit was determined from pilot studies - it was a time that would not make a participant feel too tired after a session. In these two sessions, the participants played one session with a CVH customized by themselves, and one session with a randomly assigned NCVH. The initial values of the customizable variables for the CVH and NCVH were all randomly set, however the variables of CVH could be adjusted by the participants and the initial variables for NCVH remained the same during the whole study. The order of the sessions was randomized for each participant. The two sessions were repeated twice. However the first two sessions were considered as warm up sessions and are not included in the study results. Between each session, users were required to have sufficient rest and finish the questionnaire regarding the user experiences in that session. If the coming session had a CVH, the participant was given the option to customize the CVH, before the session started.

In each session, the participant first stood on a playing line 2.5 meters away from the screen and did jumping jacks to warm up. The CVH/NCVH did a jumping jack reacting to each one the participant performed successfully. Participants could stop doing jumping jacks and start the game when they decided they were ready. In the game, participants first went to the tablet and swiped the ball to pass it to the CVH/NCVH. Then the participant went to back the playing line and waved their hand to tell the CVH/NCVH to start kicking. After the user blocked or missed the ball, the CVH/NCVH displayed happy or sad emotions accordingly with body animations and sound effects. Then the ball was displayed again on the tablet. The participant needed to go back to the tablet and repeat the above actions to finish another round. A scoreboard showed the scores of the participant and CVH/NCVH, the names of participant and CVH/NCVH, and remaining time. A blocked ball was counted as one point for the participant, while a missed ball was counted as one point for the CVH/NCVH.

After 60 seconds of playing time in a session, the CVH/NCVH rewarded the participant for the scores they earned. For each point the participant got, CVH/NCVH did a push up. For each 5 points the participant got, CVH/NCVH would do a dance. Therefore, participants were instructed to play as many rounds as possible within a session and were rewarded for playing more rounds. They were able to control the pace of the game by adjusting their walking/running speed when the game made them go back and forth between the tablet and the playing line.

5.3.3 Study Part 2: Free Play

In study part one, participants were given time limits to interact with CVH/NCVH to eliminate time and ordering as confounds in the study. However, we also wanted to investigate our research questions in a more realistic scenario that allowed participants to freely choose to play with the CVH or NCVH with no time limits, so that we could investigate how CVH affects the users' motivation to play the games. Thus, in part 2, participants had the freedom to play any number of sessions without any time limit on each single session. In each session, they also were free to select from NCVH or CVH and they had the freedom to customize/re-customize the CVH before each session played with it. The only mandatory rule in study part 2 was that the participant was required to play at least one kick-block under both conditions - NCVH and CVH. We expected the participants to feel more relaxed to play with these rules compared with the rules in part one.

The other settings were similar to study 1, except that instead of answering questionnaires between each session, participants answered questionnaires only when they switched between NCVH and CVH. We made this change in part 2 because too many questionnaires could have influenced the number of sessions they wanted to play. We also removed the requirement of doing jumping jacks before each session to maintain the participant's energy.

5.4 Metrics

The metrics include the participants' performances in the game, their subjective feedback, and pre/post study tests scores.

5.4.1 Game Performance

Success Rate: in each session, the Success Rate was calculated by Number of Blocks/ Number of Kicks (i.e., the percent of kicks that were blocked).

Number of Kicks and *Number of Blocks*: how many rounds were played during each session and in how many rounds did the participant successfully block the ball during each session.

5.4.2 Subjective Feedback

PIFF2 [20]: The Presence, Involvement, and Flow Framework 2 (PIFF2) is a validated questionnaire that measures many aspects of user experience specifically for video games. It is a set of 15 questions each answer was a ranking with a score range from 1 -7. The PIFF2 was answered after each session in study part 1: time limited play and when the participant switched between VH and CVH in study part 2: free play.

5.4.3 Pre/post Study Tests

Emotion Identification Score: Because the game included content showing the emotion of a VH, we investigated how effectively users could recognize emotion. Therefore, before part 1 and after part 2, we played three clips of animations in which a VH was expressing some emotion with its body. These animations came from the set of animations when the VH showed happy or sad emotions in reaction to user blocked or missed a ball. The participants were required to identify these emotions. We counted each correctly identified emotion as one point. The results remained unknown to the participants during the study.

6. RESULTS

We performed Paired t tests on normally distributed data (numerical data, such as *Success Rate*) or Wilcoxon signed rank tests where data did not have a normal distribution (ordinal data, such as the *PIFF2* questionnaire) to compare the differences of the measurements under different conditions, using Bonferroni correction where appropriate. The results are reported in this section with their related hypotheses.

6.1 Performance and Training

6.1.1 Study Part 1: Time Limited Play Performance

The first hypothesis is: Playing with CVHs will help participants to perform better and play more rounds in a 3D hand-eye coordination training game. We were less confident about this hypothesis. But surprisingly we found our study results support this hypothesis. *Success Rate*s was compared between the CVH and NCVH conditions to verify this hypothesis, since it is directly related to the 3D interaction performance. The order of CVH and NCVH was randomized in study part 1, so that *Success Rates* would not be confounded by the order.

In study part 1: time limited play, the *Success Rate*s were compared with paired t tests. We found that the *Success Rate* was significantly higher under the condition of CVH ($M = 0.93$, $SD = 0.11$) than NCVH ($M = 0.86$, $SD = 0.22$) condition; $t(9) = 1.950$, $p = 0.041$(one tailed). Figure. 4 shows the distributions of the *Success Rate* over the two conditions.

6.1.2 Study Part 2: Free Play Performance

We did not compare the *Success Rate* in study part 2 (free play), since 1) part 1 and part 2 had different timing rules, 2) the initial *Success Rate* in part 2 could be potentially affected by the training effects from study part 1, and 3) some participants only played a single kick with NCVH in order to meet the study requirement in study part 2. In this study part, participants were free to switch back and forth to any VH and played without a time limit. Thus, the number of rounds with CVH and NCVH were not necessarily equal, it could depend on how they were motivated to play with the VH. Therefore, instead of *Success Rate*s, we compared - *Number of Kicks* under CVH and NVCH conditions. We found participants played significant more rounds during the sessions played with CVH ($M = 22.2$, $SD = 12.9$) than NCVH ($M = 10$, $SD = 9.5$); $t(9) = 2.110$, $p = 0.032$(one tailed). We also compared the *Number of Blocks* which could indicate their training progress in the game and be related to how many rewards (i.e. dancing, pushups) they can get from the VH. The results showed that *Number of Blocks* is significant higher under the condition of CVH ($M = 17.7$, $SD = 9.5$) than NCVH ($M = 7.9$, $SD = 7.4$) condition; $t(9) = 2.188$, $p = 0.028$(one tailed).

6.1.3 Emotion Recognition Training

Because the game included content showing the emotion of a VH, the emotion recognition could be another training benefit of the game. Therefore, we investigated the emotion recognition training effects as well. Instead of comparing results under the conditions of CVH and NCVH, we compared the *Emotion Identification Scores* prior to and post the whole study to investigate the training effects of emotion recognition in the game. The *Emotion Identification Scores* were tested with Wilcoxon test. We found significant increases on the *Emotion Identification Scores* in tests prior to and post the study (Z = 2.460, p = 0.007).

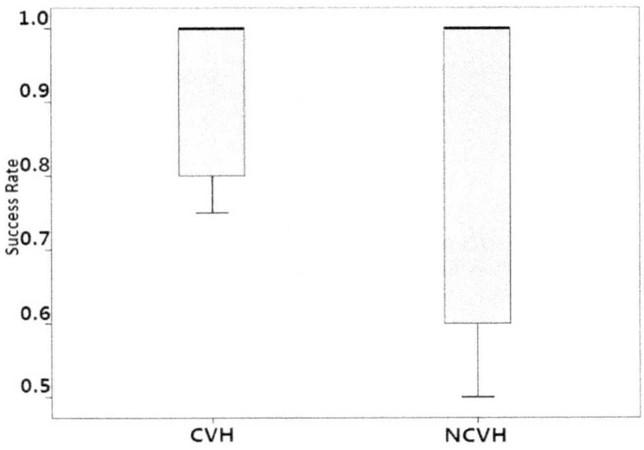

Figure 4. The box plots of the *Success Rate* over CVH and NCVH conditions in study part 1 (boxes are the range of quartiles, whiskers represent the min/max value outside the quartiles).

6.2 User Experience

The second hypothesis is: "CVHs will give the users a better user experience - specifically with respect to presence, involvement, and flow in the game". We performed Wilcoxon test on *PIFF2* questionnaire under the condition of playing with CVH/NCVH. We tested the *PIFF2* during the resting time after participants played with CVH and NCVH. In the study part 2 (free play), playing with CVH and NCVH for at least one round each was a mandatory in order to make sure this test was performed under both CVH and NCVH conditions.

In the comparison of Study Part 1 (time limited play), we found a significant difference on *PIFF2* questionnaire No.1: "I felt that I was one of the characters in the story of the game." - Role Engagement. Sense of role engagement was significantly increased (Z = -2.121 p = 0.017) under the condition of playing with CVH; a higher score for CVH condition on the item No.7: "I felt I could meet the demands of the playing situation." - Competence (Z = -1.897 p = 0.029); No. 12: "I was astonished and surprised at the game world" - Impressiveness (Z = -1.725 p = 0.042). In study part 2 (free play), we found a significant higher score for CVH on the item No.11: "I would recommend it to my friends" - Enjoyment (Z = -1.732 p = 0.041).

6.3 Post-interview

At the end of the study, we performed a short interview regarding CVH/NCVH. On interview question 1, "Which friend do you prefer to play with? Why?", 2 participants preferred NCVH, 8 preferred CVH. The 2 participants who preferred NCVH pointed out the same reason: they thought the NCVH was a better player. The main reason why participants preferred the CVH was that they liked the design. Two mentioned that they designed it to look like one of their real friends. The second question was regarding the importance of the customizable variables. The rank of customizable variables from more important to less important was: age, t-shirt pattern, body shape, hair style, height, gender and skin color. On the third interview question, "How difficult or easy was it to customize your friend (on a scale of very easy 1-7 very difficult)?". Most participants said it was very easy (1).The fourth interview question asked the participants to list a few more customization variables they would like to see in a future version of the game. Most of the answers were related to more detailed customization, such as shoes and accessories.

7. DISCUSSION

The main research question for this work is: how does a customizable appearance of the VH affect 3D interaction task performance and user experience for users with ASD? We proposed two hypotheses to investigate this question.

7.1 Performance and Training

The first hypothesis is: Playing with CVHs will help participants to perform better and play more rounds in a 3D hand-eye coordination training game. We used the *Success Rate* to reflect the hand-eye coordination ability in 3D interaction tasks. We found a significant increase on this measurement when users played with CVH in study part 1. This could mean that the CVH helped participants further improve training of hand-eye coordination and/or that participants tried harder with the CVH in study. Moreover, in study part 2, the significantly increased *Number of Kicks* in the CVH condition suggests that participants played more rounds with CVH. The *Number of Blocks* is significant higher under the condition of CVH. This measurement is based on the training goal progress they made in the game – i.e., performance of hand-eye coordination in 3DUI. During the study, we observed that most of the participants felt excited when they saw the VH dancing. As one parent said: "I never see him so excited in a game!". It is possible that participants enjoyed watching the CVH dancing, which motivated them to play more rounds and try harder with the CVH. These results support hypothesis 1.

In addition, significant higher *Emotion Identification Scores* were found in the post study test. Although they were evaluated on only a small set of bodily emotion expressions related to the game content, it sheds some light onto the potential of 3D training games.

As a limitation of the study, it is not clear if the bodily emotion recognition effects were related to CVH or NCVH, since all the participants had played under both conditions in the study.

7.2 User Experience

The second hypothesis is: "CVHs will give the users a better user experience - specifically with respect to presence, involvement, and flow in the game." We found in study part 1 (time limited play), that participants had significantly more feelings of role engagement, competence and impressiveness during the sessions played with CVH. In study part 2 (free play), participants had significant more feelings of enjoyment. Thus, these support hypothesis 2: the CVH will give the users with ASD a better user experience.

Although the results showed a better user experience brought by CVHs, it is possible that the different rules in time limited play and free play also contributed to user experiences. How the game rules influence on the user experiences could be another interesting future research question.

8. CONCLUSION

We developed a CVH that is easy for adolescents with ASD to customize a 3D Virtual Human, and a 3D hand-eye coordination training game - Imagination Soccer. In our study, we found that including customizable elements in a 3D hand-eye coordination training game could increase 3D interaction performance during the game and potentially help ASD participants to play more rounds in the a 3D training game. In addition, the CVH improved the user experience (i.e., presence, involvement, and flow) of ASD participants in the game. These results further motivate the usefulness of 3D training games for persons with ASD and highlight the need for more customization and personalization options for the ASD population.

Our findings suggest that for users with ASD, providing customizable content may result in increased motivation and/or effort, which may lead to improved performance of 3D interaction tasks.

In the future, we plan to enable more customization options for CVHs, such as customization of facial features and integrate CVHs into more 3D training games. The ultimate goal is to determine the most effective approaches to motivate the users in training games.

9. ACKNOWLEDGMENTS

We would like to thank the participants of our study and the local support groups that allowed us to recruit the participants.

10. REFERENCES

[1] AHRQ, 2013. Autism Spectrum Disorder—An Update.

[2] T. R. Goldsmith, 2008. Using Virtual Reality Enhanced Behavioral Skills Training to Teach Street-crossing Skills to Children and Adolescents with Autism Sectrum Disorders, *Doctoral dissertation, Western Michigan University*.

[3] E. Bekele, Z. Zheng, A. Swanson, J. Crittendon, Z. Warren, and N. Sarkar, 2013. Understanding How Adolescents with Autism Respond to Facial Expressions in Virtual Reality Environments, *IEEE Transactions on Visualization and Computer Graphics*, 19, 4, 711-720.

[4] R. Morris, C. Kirschbaum, and R. Picard, 2010. Broadening Accessibility Through Special Interests: A New Approach for Software Customization, *Proceedings of the 12th international ACM SIGACCESS conference on Computers and accessibility*.

[5] C. Zanbaka, P. Goolkasian, and L. Hodges, 2006. Can a virtual cat persuadeyou?: the role of gender and realism in speaker persuasiveness, in *Proceedings of the SIGCHI Conference on Human Factors in Computing Systems*.

[6] H. C. V. Vugt, J. N. Bailenson, J. F. Hoorn, and E. A. Konijn, 2010. Effects of facial similarity on user responses to embodied agents, *ACM Transactions on Computer-Human Interaction*, 17, 2.

[7] D. Lämkull, L. Hanson, and R. Örtengren, 2007. The influence of virtual human model appearance on visual ergonomics posture evaluation, *Applied Ergonomics*, 38, 6, 713-722.

[8] D. Rivera-Gutierrez, R. Ferdig, J. Li, and B. Lok, 2014. Getting the Point Across: Exploring the Effects of Dynamic Virtual Humans in an Interactive Museum Exhibit on User Perceptions, *IEEE TRANSACTIONS ON VISUALIZATION AND COMPUTER GRAPHICS*, 20, 4.

[9] A. Crippa, S. Forti, P. Perego, and M. Molteni, 2013. Eye-Hand Coordination in Children with High Functioning Autism and Asperger's Disorder Using a Gap-Overlap Paradigm, *Journal of Autism and Developmental Disorders*, 43, 4, 841-850.

[10] C. Mei, L. Mason, and J. Quarles, 2014. Usability Issues with 3D User Interfaces for Adolescents with High Functioning Autism, in *Proceedings of the 16th international ACM SIGACCESS conference on Computers and accessibility*.

[11] C. Yu and L. B. Smith, 2013. Joint Attention without Gaze Following: Human Infants and Their Parents Coordinate Visual Attention to Objects through Eye-Hand Coordination, *PLoS One*, 8, 1.

[12] N. S. P. Therapy, 2014. *Eye Hand Coordination*.

[13] E. Reategui, E. Boff, and J. A. C. b, 2008. Personalization in an interactive learning environment through a virtual character, *Computers & Education*, 51, 2, 530-544.

[14] O. Inc, 2014. "Sitepal,". DOI=*http://www.sitepal.com/*.

[15] S. Y. Okita, S. Turkay, M. Kim, and Y. Murai, 2013. Learning by teaching with virtual peers and the effects of technological design choices on learning, *Computers & Education*, 63, 176-196.

[16] N. Yee and J. Bailenson, 2007. The Proteus effect: the effect of transformed self-representation on behavior, *Health Communication Research*, 33, 3, 271–290.

[17] K. BESSIÈRE, F. SEAY, and S. KIESLER, 2007. The Ideal Elf: Identity Exploration in World of Warcraft, *CYBERPSYCHOLOGY & BEHAVIOR*, 10, 4, 530-535.

[18] N. Ducheneaut, M.-H. Wen, N. Yee, and G. Wadley, 2009. Body and Mind: A Study of Avatar Personalization in Three Virtual Worlds, in *Proceedings of the SIGCHI Conference on Human Factors in Computing Systems*.

[19] A. Tartaro and J. Cassell, 2006. Authorable Virtual Peers for Autism Spectrum Disorders, in *Proceedings of the Combined workshop on Language-Enabled Educational Technology and Development and Evaluation for Robust Spoken Dialogue Systems at the 17th European Conference on Artificial Intellegence*.

[20] J. Takatalo, J. Häkkinen, J. Kaistinen, and G. Nyman, 2010. Presence, involvement, and flow in digital games, in *Evaluating user experience in games* ed: Springer. 23-46.

The Invisible Work of Accessibility: How Blind Employees Manage Accessibility in Mixed-Ability Workplaces

Stacy M. Branham
UMBC
Baltimore, MD
sbranham@umbc.edu

Shaun K. Kane
University of Colorado Boulder
Boulder, CO
shaun.kane@colorado.edu

ABSTRACT
Over the past century, people who are blind and their allies have developed successful public policies and technologies in support of creating more accessible workplaces. However, simply creating accessible technologies does not guarantee that these will be available or adopted. Because much work occurs within shared workspaces, decisions about assistive technology use may be mediated by social interactions with, and expectations of, sighted coworkers. We present findings from a qualitative field study of five workplaces from the perspective of blind employees. Although all participants were effective employees, they expressed that working in a predominantly sighted office environment produces impediments to a blind person's independence and to their integration as an equal coworker. We describe strategies employed by our participants to create and maintain an accessible workplace and present suggestions for future technology that better supports blind workers as equal peers in the workplace.

Categories and Subject Descriptors
K.4.2 [**Social Issues**]: Assistive technologies for persons with disabilities

General Terms
Design, Human Factors.

Keywords
Assistive Technology, Blindness, Collaborative Accessibility, Vision Impairment, Workplace.

1. INTRODUCTION
Access to employment is essential to providing independence for people of all abilities. In order to maintain a fair and equal society, individuals with disabilities must be able to find employment and to acquire reasonable accommodations for performing and maintaining their job.

ASSETS '15, October 26–28, 2015, Lisbon, Portugal
 ISBN 978-1-4503-3400-6/15/10...$15.00
DOI: http://dx.doi.org/10.1145/2700648.2809864

Figure 1. Our blind office worker participants addressed accessibility challenges through a combination of assistive technology and collaboration with sighted users. Here, a participant shows a paper form with the signature line marked by a sticky note placed by her sighted colleague.

In the past several decades, efforts to increase the rate of employment by people with disabilities have proceeded along two fronts. First, public policy efforts such as the Americans with Disabilities Act have provided improved support for requesting and receiving workplace accommodations. At the same time, advances in assistive technology (AT) have made work tasks more accessible [8].

Despite advances in both disability policy and accessible technology, the percentage of workers with disabilities in the US has declined in recent years [10]. There may be several reasons for this discrepancy. For example, even when existing policies support reasonable accommodations for workers with disabilities, workers may hesitate to request accommodations because they may believe that the request will not be honored, or because they do not wish to request too much help [1]. Additionally, while assistive technologies may be available to address particular accessibility barriers, users often choose not to adopt or to discard them because they lack the appropriate functionality [12] or may draw negative social attention [9, 17].

Addressing these challenges to equal employment for people with disabilities requires an approach that considers technical and social concerns simultaneously, because these concerns together shape if, when, and how assistive devices are used in the wild. For example, a blind person who encounters an inaccessible document in her workplace may need to decide whether to seek a technical solution to make the document accessible or to ask a coworker to read the document for her.

We present findings from a qualitative field study in which five blind employees who work in a mixed-ability workplace discuss accessibility challenges they encounter. Our paper documents the "invisible work" [19] that our participants perform to identify accessibility challenges and solutions, with special consideration to how the mixed-ability social context of most office settings affects access. We conclude with suggestions for extending accessible technology design to support more accessible workplaces and to enable collaboration between people with mixed abilities.

2. RELATED WORK

This paper explores the accessibility challenges encountered by blind office workers in shared workspaces. We briefly summarize prior work on assistive technology for blind office workers as well as research on the social and collaborative aspects of using assistive technologies.

2.1 Visual Accessibility in Office Work

Our present study focuses primarily on blind office workers. While assistive technology solutions may vary greatly across work domains, many of our participants used accessible computer technology, including screen readers, to perform their everyday tasks. Summaries of commonly used desktop and mobile accessibility tools for blind and visually impaired users are provided by Jacko et al. [8] and Kane et al. [9], respectively.

2.2 Use and Non-Use of Assistive Technology

Despite the availability of assistive technologies to address a variety of accessibility issues, many individuals choose not to adopt assistive technologies. Often, assistive technologies are not adopted or are abandoned because they provide inadequate functionality or are too costly [12]. Recent work from Kane et al. [9] and Shinohara and Wobbrock [17] have explored social reasons for choosing to use assistive technologies and found that individuals often avoided using technologies that drew unwanted attention to their disability. This paper extends this prior work by exploring the use or non-use of assistive technologies and accommodations in the workplace.

2.3 Accessibility as Collaborative Work

Much assistive technology research focuses on the relationship between an individual user and a technical system (e.g., [8, 18, 21]). However, a number of recent studies have explored how assistive technology use may be affected by social interactions.

Branham and Kane [4] used the term *collaborative accessibility* to refer to how blind people and their sighted companions worked together to create an accessible shared home environment. Branham and Kane found that many of the accessible resources in the home were created and managed through discussion, planning, and compromise. The present study also considers the collaborative work of accessibility, but in the context of office workplaces. We consider how achieving collaborative accessibility in an office setting may constitute "invisible" work [19] for the person with a disability. In other words, the visually impaired worker necessarily conducts additional work to create an accessible space, even though this work may not be openly discussed or considered part of regular work responsibilities.

Assistive technology researchers have also explored how interactions between individuals with and without disabilities can inform the design of better assistive technology. Williams et al. [20] studied how blind individuals interacted with sighted companions when navigating in order to design better automated navigation aids. Burton et al. [5] also explored how crowdsourcing could provide personalized and subjective feedback on fashion decisions for blind users of the VizWiz mobile application. Brady et al. [3] investigated how friends in a blind person's social network could answer visual questions using crowdsourcing techniques. The present study explores how blind workers leverage both technology and human connections to solve accessibility problems, with the goal of gaining additional insights into designing effective assistive technologies.

Recognizing that individuals with disabilities often use assistive technologies in the presence of others, researchers have reported on the design of systems that enable users with varying abilities to work together. Savidis and Stephanidis [16] and Plimmer et al. [15], among others, have studied multimodal user interfaces that enable blind and sighted collaborators to use a shared user interface. Piper and her colleagues have studied user interfaces that enable communication between people with disabilities and clinicians [13, 14]. Hailpern et al. [7] and Flatla and Gutwin [6] developed tools that simulate the experience of a person with a disability to help partners with different abilities better understand their experience. While we do not introduce new technology in this paper, our exploration of how coworkers with mixed abilities work together in office contexts may inform the design of new technologies to support mutual understanding and collaboration across abilities.

3. FIELD STUDY

3.1 Participants

We recruited five participants who were blind office workers. Participants were recruited from previous study contact lists as well as through snowball sampling. Four of five participants were government or state employees, owing to the proximity of participants to Washington, DC and the government's proactive approach to hiring people with disabilities. However, each participant worked for a different organization. In addition, four of the five participants worked in positions that were related to serving people with disabilities. All participants used screen readers. Two participants used service animals, while all others used white canes. We interviewed each participant (Table 1) across three sessions. During the second session, we were sometimes able to interview our participants' sighted colleagues (six total, all sighted) about their views of accessibility in the office. Sighted colleagues were identified by blind participants as the people with whom they worked most closely. Participants were compensated for their time.

3.2 Procedure

Three sessions were held with each participant, for a total of 15 sessions. The first and third sessions were held at a location convenient to the participant (e.g., their home), while the second session, which included a workplace tour, was held in the participant's place of work. The first session consisted of a semi-structured interview that covered topics such as the participant's occupation, their work environment, past and present accessibility challenges in the workplace, and how they met these challenges.

During the second session, the participant took the researcher on a walkthrough of their workplace and identified accessibility concerns. This provided background for findings in Interview 1 and helped the participants remember additional examples. To determine whether coworkers were also aware of accessibility concerns, participants asked one or more of their colleagues to take the researcher on a workplace walkthrough, as well. Walkthroughs were arranged so that participants and their coworkers could not hear each other's responses.

Between the second and third sessions, participants and their colleagues were asked to independently complete an online survey to see whether the blind and sighted coworkers identified similar accessibility challenges. The survey presented a list all accessibility issues identified by both the blind participant and their sighted colleague(s) during prior interviews. For each issue, participants were asked to identify which issues were previously unknown to them, and the blind participant was given an opportunity to flag items that were not, in fact, issues for them. One participant, Daryll, identified a coworker who was unwilling to participate in the walkthrough and survey, and so Daryll was not able to complete this survey. Another participant found three willing colleagues, for a total of 10 completed surveys (four blind participants and six sighted colleagues).

We report survey results related to the types of challenges participants and colleagues identified. Survey results were discussed with participants during the third and final session. In the third, semi-structured interview, participants reflected on their colleagues' contributions, identified any additional issues that may have come up recently at work, and suggested possible solutions to accessibility issues.

3.3 Analysis

All three sessions were documented with audio recordings and handwritten notes. Pictures and short video clips were taken during walkthroughs, with participants' permission. Notes taken during interviews were expanded following the completion of each interview and were thematically coded (e.g., "finding one's own accommodations"). Accessibility issues that were confirmed by blind participants in surveys were classified into categories (e.g., "inaccessible computer software"). Themes and categories were discussed between authors. Each audio interview, including pictures and videos, was reviewed in full, leading to additional themes and targeted transcription of representative examples.

4. Findings

Our findings are organized into four sections. We begin by describing the types of accessibility issues that participants encountered. Next, we show that the degree to which a device or activity is accessible changes based on particular features of the office environment. We then describe how participants creatively addressed access problems. We finish with a demonstration of how communication breakdowns between blind and sighted colleagues can create a less accessible work environment.

4.1 Visual Accessibility in Office Work

In this section, we summarize the types of accessibility problems identified by participants and their coworkers via the surveys. Participants and their coworkers identified a total of 105 issues. We note which accessibility concerns were shared across multiple blind participants (e.g., three participants indicated similar concerns about using the JAWS screen reader when engaged in conversations with coworkers). Because Daryll's coworker was unable to complete a survey, this section documents responses from the other four participants only.

Accessibility challenges were sorted into four high-level categories defined and discussed below (Figure 2). All four blind participants who completed the survey experienced at least one accessibility challenge from each of these categories.

4.1.1 Inaccessible Environmental Features

We found that many of the "ambient" features of the environment were inaccessible to blind participants (23 issues). These items included resources such as work tools, safety equipment, furniture, decorations, and even entire rooms.

Table 1. Blind office workers who participated in our study. Participants provided their own pseudonyms.

Participant	Age	Occupation	Total Years Working	Years at Current Company	Office Environment	Visual Ability
Molly	25	Research Assistant	2.5	0.25	Works with 3 immediate colleagues, all sighted, in an office with over 100 people; job is related to research for people with disabilities; company has internal division for accommodations.	Blind since birth, no usable vision
Mary	29	Attorney	2.5	1	Works with 4 immediate colleagues, all sighted, in an organization of about 50 people; job is related to disability rights.	Blind since birth, no usable vision
Daryll	39	Customer Service Specialist	12	9	Works with 2 immediate colleagues, all sighted, in an office of over 100 people; company has internal division for accommodations.	Gradual vision loss since age 3, has used screen reader and white cane for past 9 years
Wallace	48	Executive Director	17	1	Works with 6 immediate colleagues, one of whom is blind, in an organization of about 100 people; job is related to accommodating people with disabilities.	Blind since birth, no usable vision
Catherine	54	Program Analyst	26	7	Works with 3 immediate colleagues, in an office of over 100 people; job is related to funding grants for people with disabilities; company has internal division for accommodations.	Gradual vision loss since birth, legally blind since age 16, no usable vision since 23

Multiple participants noted that awareness of safety equipment and spaces was not accessible. For example, Daryll was not aware of the existence of Designated Safe Area rooms, which were to be used in case of an emergency lock-down (Figure 2a). Even if the hall signs that identified them were made accessible with Braille, Daryll would not have known to feel for them. Mary learned for the first time during our walkthrough that the kitchen contained a fire extinguisher, a first aid kit, a recycling bin, a bulletin board, and some free snacks. Following our interview, Mary returned to the first aid kit to get some rubbing alcohol, but was unable to find it independently, and needed to ask the secretary to help her locate it. In another event between interviews, Mary's office had a tornado safety drill. She realized during the drill that she had forgotten the emergency evacuation route. Again, she was unable to make use of the visual exit signs or maps like her colleagues. Mary felt that these were serious, high-risk accessibility problems.

Several participants were unaware of the location and features of colleagues' offices. Catherine found navigating to cubicles difficult because there were no walls to guide her. Prior to our walkthrough, Mary did not know several of her colleagues had decorations in their workspaces (Figure 2b). When Mary learned that her adjacent coworker's desk was decorated with toy ducks, she decided she should decorate her own desk with butterflies.

This lack of awareness became particularly frustrating when a worker knew a resource existed and used to know where to find it, but could no longer access it because a colleague had moved it. For example, Molly's team shared equipment for running studies, and the team would regularly pack the equipment into a suitcase to transport it between different work sites. When the equipment was unloaded by colleagues, neither the equipment nor the suitcase was stored in a predictable location. Molly had to waste time looking for the strewn equipment and sometimes tripped over the suitcase when it was left in the middle of the floor:

> *"What I hate—and I think a lot of blind people hate this—is other people moving your crap all over the place." –Molly*

4.1.2 *Inaccessible Print Materials*

Print materials were a common source of inaccessibility (19 issues). This category included accessibility problems related to paper mail, faxes, files, handwritten signs (e.g., "sink out of order"), sticky notes, and whiteboard content that could not be independently or readily accessed.

Public displays were a common form of inaccessible print material. For example, Mary's office hallways were lined with numerous photographs and accompanying signs describing famous civil rights cases (Figure 2c). However, Mary could not access them. Similarly, Molly's office hallways were lined with research posters summarizing the work of colleagues (Figure 2d), which were likewise inaccessible. Mary said that she wished she could read the posters to stay in tune with related research.

4.1.3 *Inaccessible Hardware and Electronics*

Our participants' offices were filled with hardware and electronic devices that lacked appropriate feedback to be accessible to participants (16 issues). These devices often used touch screen input and visual-only output. Printers, scanners, fax machines, phones, microwaves, vending machines (Figure 2e, reported by Catherine), thermostats, and more fell under this category.

Inaccessible office telephones were the most prevalent problem in this category, accounting for nearly 50% of all reported hardware and electronics problems. Participants reported that they were usually able to access their phone's basic features, such as dialing a phone number. However, because many phones looked like Daryll's (Figure 2f), with a mix of physical buttons and visual-only displays, accessing functions such as mute, hold, and call transfer was difficult if not impossible. Additionally, caller ID, missed calls, and new voicemail notifications were almost universally inaccessible. Inaccessible phones can lead sighted outsiders to perceive the blind worker as inattentive or unresponsive. Wallace explained the social implications of this inaccessibility:

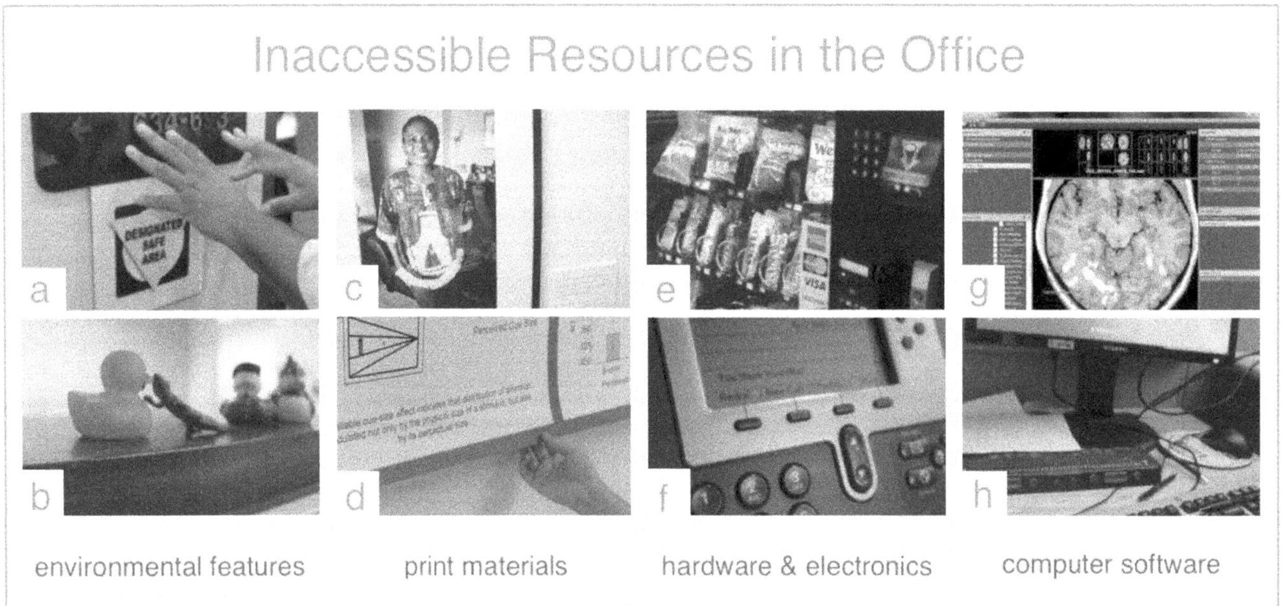

Figure 2. Examples of the types of inaccessible resources participants identified through workplace walkthroughs and accessibility surveys. We explored four categories of inaccessible resources: environmental features (e.g., a refuge room, office decorations); print materials (e.g., photographs, posters); hardware and electronics (e.g., vending machine, desk phone); computer software (e.g., MRI scan viewer, screen reader without headphones).

"If you called me and [my sighted colleague] on Monday, and we're out, and you left us both a message, [my colleague] comes in Tuesday morning and she sees the flashing light. I don't see anything. I can call my inbox and see if I have messages, but there's no prompt... [My colleague] gets a prompt and I don't. But your perception from the outside is [Wallace's colleague] returns my calls, and I don't." -Wallace

So, in addition to making more work for a visually impaired user who wants to know if he has new voicemail, inaccessible phones have negative social implications; they can lead sighted outsiders to perceive the blind worker as inattentive or unresponsive.

4.1.4 Inaccessible Computer Software

The most commonly reported accessibility challenges were related to computer software (47 issues, 42.6%). These reports included inaccessible web sites needed for work (e.g., for booking business travel), in-house software (e.g., timesheet reporting software), inaccessible features in office software (e.g., Microsoft Word's track changes feature), and documents in inaccessible formats (e.g., some PDF files, MRI brain scans).

We found that highly specialized software—either of a homegrown or highly technical nature, was often the least accessible and required significant intervention. For example, Molly's job required the use of computer programming tools like MATLAB. However, Molly ran into compatibility issues between MATLAB, the custom hardware needed for her research, and her screen reader. Molly also wanted to use special MRI exploration software, like BrainVoyager, just like her colleagues (Figure 2g). However, BrainVoyager software was completely inaccessible, excluding Molly from contributing to MRI analysis in her research team.

Other reported problems often involved JAWS or similar screen reader software (Figure 2h, reported by Catherine). In surveys alone, participants reported 11 distinct problems arising from the fact that screen readers could cause disruption, especially when used during activities requiring a clear audio channel. Participants noted that using JAWS without headphones distracted other office workers, but that using JAWS with headphones could block out important peripheral noise, make the blind worker look cut off from their coworkers, discourage impromptu conversations, and make note-taking during meetings difficult. Use of JAWS during collaboration can also cause coordination difficulties:

"One thing I learned when I was working with sighted people is they would talk while I was still listening [to my screen reader]... I can't listen to two streams at the same time. So, I'll hold my hand up like this ("stop"). I have to teach them." -Catherine

4.2 Accessibility in (Social) Context

Before we explore the ways blind workers problem-solved inaccessible work environments, we briefly introduce findings that challenge and expand traditional ways of talking about accessibility in the office. At the core of these findings is the notion that accessibility is not an essential quality of a particular device. Instead, accessibility is affected by sociomaterial aspects of the context. In other words, a device that is accessible in one setting may be rendered inaccessible in another due to social and organizational factors.

In this section, we explore how accessible technologies fail in mixed-ability settings. Accommodations that were appropriate for use by a blind *individual* sometimes caused friction in a sighted, *collaborative* office setting. For example, using a screen reader (JAWS) during *synchronous* collaboration with sighted colleagues was sometimes disruptive to all parties:

"The hardest thing for me is when we are in meetings with a client. [Sighted attendees] can go back to a paragraph in the complaint and refer to it. But I can't as easily. I didn't have a laptop at that time, and it's hard to listen to JAWS and other people at the same time." -Mary

To address this problem, some participants used a Braille-based note taker to take notes during meetings without audio interference from a screen reader. However, these special purpose devices could present their own usability problems and sometimes violated workplace security policies.

In addition to reducing the blind worker's attention, use of a screen reader could also distract sighted coworkers:

"I think it's interruptive [to sighted people] to keep the VoiceOver [screen reader] on while the admin was fixing my computer for me because the keystrokes are different. So, I'll turn it off. So, at that point, I am, as it were, blind to what they are doing, but that's what I have to do because it's just better for all [other] parties involved." -Daryll

A third challenge occurred due to the fact that sighted coworkers could not easily follow what the blind worker was doing when using a screen reader. Often the sighted and blind workers saw the same content differently, leading to confusion. Catherine explained one scenario in which she was sharing an MS Word document with a sighted colleague, but only she could see the document content:

"She said 'there's nothing on that document.' 'Yes there is, I can hear it.' Well, somehow the document had changed to white text on a white background, so it took us a while to figure that out." -Catherine

Other challenges occurred when sighted coworkers preferred software that was less accessible to more accessible alternatives. For example, Molly (who is blind) preferred to edit spreadsheets using Microsoft Excel and the JAWS screen reader, while her sighted colleagues preferred to use Apple's Numbers program. Because Molly used different spreadsheet software than her teammates, sharing files became more difficult than it would have been if everyone had used the same software.

In some cases, participants owned relevant accessible software, but had difficulty using it during collaborative activities because it could not be installed on shared devices. For example, due to budget constraints, Molly's workplace provided only a free trial version of the JAWS screen reader on her group's shared computer. This trial version timed out every 40 minutes, after which the computer needed to be restarted. Because the computer was shared, other problems arose when Molly's coworkers forgot to activate the screen reader or to reset the timer, leaving the computer in an ambiguous and potentially unusable state:

"I really get annoyed, it is just something that inherently annoys me when a bunch of people are using the same stuff as me, because I can customize things the way I want. So when people f--- around with the settings—which is totally how I feel about it!" -Molly

4.3 The Invisible Work of Accessibility

In general, our participants expressed that they were able to access the tools needed to perform their jobs. However, participants often described additional work that was required on their part in order to create an accessible workspace. This work was "invisible" [19] in that it was additional to their required job functions and largely unnoticed by coworkers and supervisors.

In surveys, we found that blind and sighted participants had different understandings of the accessibility problems around the office. That is, there was little alignment between the accessibility problems perceived by blind participants and the sighted colleagues with whom they worked most closely.

First, on average[1] 47% of accessibility issues identified by blind participants were completely new to the sighted colleagues. Second, on average 27% of the accessibility issues identified by sighted colleagues were not deemed to be problems by blind participants. In other words, sighted colleagues have limited understanding of what is and is not an accessibility problem in the office. Finally, on average fewer than 9% of problems were the same between blind and sighted colleagues' lists. Lack of substantial overlap suggests that the most significant accessibility problems from the perspective of blind participants are not as visible or salient to sighted colleagues. This interpretation was indicated verbally by most blind participants during interviews:

> *"I am surprised at how much [my sighted colleague] didn't realize. [Sighted people] take [access] for granted and they don't realize I can't tell those things." -Mary*

Consequently, most participants felt a need to actively communicate accessibility setbacks to colleagues so that delays could be better understood:

> *"I think it is easy for [sighted] people to take for granted something will just work.... If it takes me longer to get things working it is not because I am incompetent or because I am lazy. It is just because there is an extra process, and if you guys just bear with me I will make it work. It is just something that I have had to learn, that communicate, communicate."-Molly*

When encountering an accessibility problem, participants were faced with the decision of whether to try and solve the problem themselves or to seek help. Below, we share examples of each approach.

4.3.1 Finding One's Own Accommodations

Participants described a number of examples in which they investigated and solved their own accessibility problems in the workplace. Often, participants had to invent new strategies for overcoming accessibility problems:

> *"People who are using adaptive technology interfaces have to be a little smarter and a little better at problem solving than their colleagues, or they would not be able to function in a work environment." –Wallace*

Some accessibility issues arose out of malfunctioning assistive technology or compatibility issues with other software or hardware. In part, participants solved access problems on their own because they had more experience than their coworkers in debugging assistive technology. For example, Molly experienced a confusing error that none of her coworkers had encountered, so she had to troubleshoot it herself:

> *"I am pretty good at figuring out obscure solutions for problems. For example, ...I had written this code and... it was working fine and... every time a participant came in it would crash... So, just through trial and error... I finally figured out I am going to leave the same pair of headphones in and mute VoiceOver and now it doesn't crash at all." –Molly*

Another participant, Wallace, invented a solution to the problem of monitoring multiple devices at once. Because he could not use multiple displays, he instead wore multiple pairs of headphones to monitor audio from multiple devices at once (Figure 3).

Daryll, whose job relies heavily on his office phone, took it upon himself to research and negotiate the adoption of an accessible "soft phone" for his workplace that supports all the functionality of his desk phone on his computer using JAWS:

> *"The phone, at one time, was truly an inaccessible option... The accessibility issue was resolved because I had an opportunity to observe a new startup that was developing a new technology to make phone services accessible... Then, I worked on the pilot project to test run it in our system. ... We have a 508 [accessibility compliance] department, who deals with technology assessments. They didn't take as much as a direct role as I expected... I took more of a lead on that project." –Daryll*

In all of these examples, we see how the blind coworker has encountered accessibility problems and creatively identified and implemented workarounds, notably absent of institutional support.

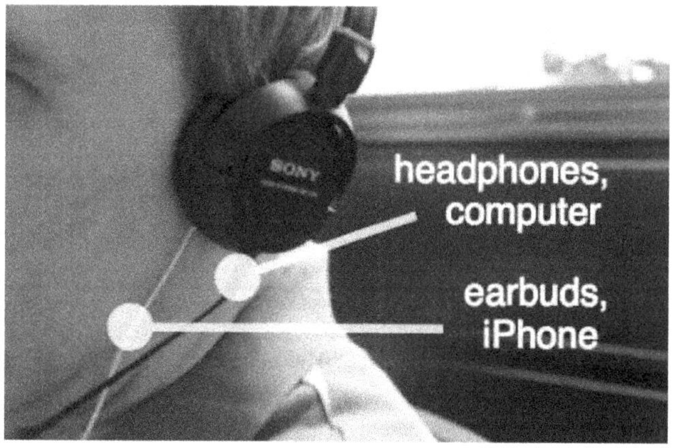

Figure 3. Wallace has developed a creative solution for the need to simultaneously monitor multiple displays, a problem long addressed by HCI researchers for sighted users. He simply layers over-ear headphones atop his earbuds to receive updates from his computer and iPhone, respectively.

Wallace, an accommodations expert, offered some insight into this sort of self-accommodation, which can be interpreted as both a burden and an opportunity for self-advocacy. The ADA almost requires self-accommodation, he explained, because it says that no one needs to be accommodated if they do not disclose a disability. Without this stipulation, employers might push unwanted technology onto an employee that effectively segregates them. On the other hand, this places the burden of identifying assistive technology needs on the individual with a disability, requiring that person to become an expert at finding their own accommodations:

> *"[As an employee], you don't want to be an AT specialist, you just want to do your job... [But, the non-expert] ends up at a disadvantage." –Wallace*

---

[1] Averages were calculated across totals for each workplace. Responses from Catherine's three sighted colleagues were combined. Daryll's workplace was omitted because he and his colleague did not complete the survey.

Wallace proceeded to give an example of how he once placed trust in a supposed specialist who advised him to buy a very expensive and—unbeknownst to him—very outdated piece of assistive technology. Thus, even when companies provide accessibility specialists, actual assistive technology users may need to route around those specialists to find the best solutions for their own needs.

Wallace further explained that someone who cannot find one's own accommodations might be overlooked for opportunities to contribute to their team at work:

> *"I think what sometimes happens is 'Oh, well, you can't do this task or use this software, so you don't have to.' And everybody else does it... No one can figure out how—including me. It's actually kind of benevolent. 'We'll just take you off of that task,' maybe they'll give you another task." –Wallace*

We call this phenomenon the *double-edged sword of self-accommodation*; finding one's own accommodations empowers one to find the best solution, but also requires work beyond official job duties. Self-accommodation was only one approach used by blind participants to gain access. Another approach was to solicit support from sighted colleagues. Involving others in the problem-solving process made access issues more visible to particular colleagues:

> *"Several of the things [my sighted coworker] said [in the survey] are things that I ask her to help me with or that we collaborate on." –Catherine*

We describe this type of collaborative accessibility below.

4.3.2 Seeking Support

When participants encountered accessibility problems that needed immediate resolution, or when they did not have an obvious or convenient technical workaround, they often sought help from colleagues and friends.

Participants offered various reasons for choosing to seek help. Catherine, a program analyst and a relatively senior employee in her organization, worked extensively with a reader assistant, and often delegated tasks to him. She explained that delegating these tasks increased her efficiency, but that she also enjoyed the opportunity to work with another person:

> *"I am more interested in efficiency than absolute independence. So, with [my reader], we'll do [inaccessible tasks] together." -Catherine*

As mentioned in the previous section, sighted coworkers often could not help solve accessibility problems, as they lacked experience with accessible technology. In these situations, participants sought help from other blind workers at different companies who were part of their social network. For example, Mary worked at a law firm that used the LexisNexis search engine for legal cases. Because her employer had a contract with LexisNexis, they were unable to provide her with WestLaw, alternative software that is widely known among blind law students and practitioners to be more accessible. So, Mary reached out to one of her blind friends to borrow a license.

Wallace similarly acknowledged that there is a culture of sharing accessibility workarounds through social networking:

> *"Social networking offers one kind of answer to [sharing accessibility tips and tricks]. I know people who... make a point of saying 'I figured out how to use this and here's tips and tricks' and they'll put something on Twitter." -Wallace*

In some cases, technology in the office was simply inaccessible to the blind worker without sighted assistance. When Wallace needed to know more about the state of his telephone, he relied on sighted colleagues:

> *"If I put my phone in a state that I don't understand, [my sighted colleague] comes over to help. Everybody in the office is probably used to being solutions to these [accessibility problems]. " –Wallace*

Sometimes the blind worker asked for help but was able to offer something in "trade" in order to feel like less of a burden. For example, Catherine worked closely with a sighted wheelchair user to complete a number of tasks that neither could complete independently, but that they could complete together:

> *"[My sighted colleague] and I often do collaborative disability assistance. I'll do stuff for her because she's mobility impaired, and she'll do stuff for me." -Catherine*

> *"We developed a collaborative cafeteria plan. We'd go downstairs and scare the [expletive] out of people because I'd push her wheelchair or get food for her and carry stuff back for her, because she can't... I'll say '[Coworker], do I have schmutz on my pants?' It takes a lot of time and friendship to get to that arrangement." -Catherine*

Problems arose when a participant needed help with tasks that were personally important to them, but not critical to their official work functions. In these situations, participants were hesitant to disrupt colleagues from work and risk being seen as needy or complaining:

> *"Things like pictures on the wall, I don't really know how to talk about that. I don't know of anything exists to fix that... because I don't want to be too difficult and seem like I'm complaining.... 'Can you explain every picture on the wall?' [It would] take a lot of time and it's not really important to work." -Mary*

Asking for assistance at the office was further complicated by the nature of professional relationships and a large community setting. Participants expressed that it was more difficult for them to collaboratively manage accessibility with colleagues at work than with family members at home:

> *"There's too many people at work, you can't make a deal with 20 people [to keep the dishwasher door closed]... you can't expect people to remember all the time. I'm not as close to them [as I am with my roommate]... the office is less accessible than home, because at home I can label my own things, I can put them in a certain spot without them being moved, I know what my own dishes feel like. There's things I can do at home that I can't do at work." -Mary*

5. DISCUSSION

While our study included a small number of participants, we uncovered a large number of accessibility issues in the workplace, including many issues in disability-friendly workplaces. Rather than being static, these accessibility problems changed over time and were continually being renegotiated by employees. This finding supports our prior work that has shown that maintaining the accessibility of a shared space involves ongoing collaborative accessibility work from those who use that space [4].

Furthermore, we have found it useful to consider accessibility problem solving as "invisible work" [19], because it was usually not recognized as part of any employee's core responsibilities. As a result, many accessibility challenges became the responsibility of the employee herself. When a blind worker requested help from a coworker, this activity was often considered to be a favor rather than the responsibility of any specific employee. As noted by Petrick [11], "[p]rior to any legislation providing civil rights for people with disabilities, the responsibility to fit into a sighted workplace fell solely on the blind person." Our study suggests that blind workers must still bear the burden of their own accommodations. Moreover, addressing this issue may be complicated by the fact that self-accommodation is also a right, one that, if removed, could diminish their own sense of freedom and independence.

As reported in our prior work studying collaborative accessibility in the home [4], we found that managing the accessibility of the shared workplace was a task that was shared by the inhabitants of that space. However, because the office settings are generally shared by a large number of colleagues that have professional rather than personal relationships, many participants found that activities that were accessible at home were not accessible at work. The decision of whether to ask colleagues for support was always carefully weighed in terms of necessity, practicality, and the depth of the relationship. Fear of being seen as needy or as a complainer was ever-present and also discouraged participants from seeking out collaborative solutions. Comparing collaborative accessibility practices at home and at work presents an exciting opportunity for future research.

5.1 Opportunities for Design

Although we did not directly address technology design in our interviews and observations, our findings illustrate a number of persistent accessibility challenges that can inform design.

First, our participants frequently stated that they preferred not to ask coworkers for help with accessibility problems. This echoes prior work that showed that blind individuals often preferred asking unknown crowd workers for help over their own friends and family [3]. Also, our participants often felt that they could not ask their coworkers for help with assistive technology problems, as their coworkers lacked expertise in that area. Thus, there may be opportunities to provide blind workers with remote help with using assistive technology via crowdsourced question answering [2]. This may require pairing blind users with crowd workers who have expertise in accessibility as well as the appropriate professional domain.

Second, blind participants often lacked awareness of resources in the environment. This lack of awareness included both necessary resources, such as emergency signage, but also elements that contribute to office culture, such as personal decorations and shared snacks. While these items might be identified using visual question answering, the user must know that there is something to look for. This suggests opportunities for designing tools to support ambient awareness of the items in the environment such as talking signs or other "discoverable" resources.

Finally, many technologies that were technically accessible raised significant social challenges for participants. Subtle issues like a voicemail system that requires noticing a blinking indicator light might lead to unfair assumptions about a blind worker's responsiveness or efficiency. The same can be said of a tricky bug arising from incompatibilities with accessibility software; sighted coworkers might attribute productivity delays to the blind worker being incompetent or lazy. There may be opportunities to develop technologies that enhance communication between blind and sighted workers that may lessen the blind workers' concerns about being seen as complaining. We also found that assistive technology can be isolating. This was particularly true of screen readers, which demanded the users' listening attention and interfered with conversations with coworkers. Screen readers and related technologies might be redesigned to be more socially aware, providing feedback to sighted coworkers about when the blind worker's attention is elsewhere.

6. CONCLUSION

Equal access to employment has benefited both from advances in accessible technology and disability rights policy. Our study illustrates that, despite the relative availability of accommodations, workers with disabilities still encounter numerous accessibility challenges in the office setting. Our participants showed resourcefulness as they developed their own accommodations and sought support from colleagues. This additional work needed to create an accessible space is unfortunately rarely seen by coworkers and supervisors, potentially leading to negative and misguided interpretations of the productivity of blind workers. Perhaps the most daunting challenge to designers identified by our study is that an accessibility solution that works in one social setting may not work in another. Our study motivates continued research surrounding how technology functions in various in-the-wild settings, particularly in mixed-ability social situations.

7. ACKNOWLEDGMENTS

We thank our participants and anonymous reviewers for their time and insights. This research was supported in part by the National Science Foundation under grant IIS-1353312. Any opinions, findings, conclusions, or recommendations expressed in this work are those of the authors and do not necessarily reflect those of the National Science Foundation.

8. REFERENCES

[1] Baldridge, D. C., & Veiga, J. F. (2001). Toward a greater understanding of the willingness to request an accommodation: Can requesters' beliefs disable the Americans with Disabilities Act?. *Academy of Management Review*, *26*(1), 85-99.

[2] Bigham, J.P., Jayant, C., Ji, H., Little, G., Miller, A., Miller, R.C., Miller, R., Tatarowicz, A., White, B., White, S., and Yeh, T. VizWiz: nearly real-time answers to visual questions. *Proc. UIST '10,* 333-342.

[3] Brady, E. L., Zhong, Y., Morris, M. R., & Bigham, J. P. (2013). Investigating the appropriateness of social network question asking as a resource for blind users. *Proc. CSCW '13,* 1225-1236.

[4] Branham, S.M. and Kane, S.K. (2015). Collaborative Accessibility: How blind and sighted companions co-create accessible home spaces. Proc. CHI '15, 2373-2382.

[5] Burton, M. A., Brady, E., Brewer, R., Neylan, C., Bigham, J. P., and Hurst, A. (2012). Crowdsourcing subjective fashion advice using VizWiz: challenges and opportunities. *Proc. ASSETS '12,* 135-142.

[6] Flatla, D.R. and Gutwin, C. (2012). "So that's what you see": Building understanding with personalized simulations of colour vision deficiency. *Proc. ASSETS '12,* 167-174.

[7] Hailpern, J., Danilevsky, M., Harris, A., Karahalios, K., Dell, G., and Hengst, J. (2011). ACES: Promoting empathy towards aphasia through language distortion emulation software. *Proc. CHI '11,* 609-618.

[8] Jacko, J.A., Leonard, V.K., and Scott, I.U. (2008). Perceptual impairments: New advancements promoting technological

access. In *The Human Computer Interaction Handbook.* New York: Taylor and Francis.

[9] Kane, S.K., Jayant, C., Wobbrock, J.O., and Ladner, R.E. (2009). Freedom to roam: A study of mobile device adoption and accessibility for people with visual and motor disabilities. *Proc. ASSETS '09,* 115-122.

[10] Nazarov, Z, Lee, C. G. (2012). Disability statistics from the Current Population Survey (CPS). Ithaca, NY: Cornell University Rehabilitation Research and Training Center on Disability Demographics and Statistics (StatsRRTC). Retrieved May 7, 2015 from www.disabilitystatistics.org.

[11] Petrick, E. R. (2015). Making Computers Accessible: Disability Rights and Digital Technology. Baltimore, MD: JHU Press.

[12] Phillips, B., and Zhao, H. (1993). Predictors of assistive technology abandonment. *Assistive Technology* 5(1), 36-45.

[13] Piper, A.M., Hollan, J. (2008). Supporting medical conversations between deaf and hearing individuals with tabletop displays. *Proc. CSCW '08,* 147-156.

[14] Piper, A.M., Weibel, N., and Hollan, J. (2014). Designing audio-enhanced paper photos for older adult emotional wellbeing in communication therapy. *IJHCS* 72(8-9), 629-639.

[15] Plimmer, B., Crossan, A., Brewster, S.A., and Blagojevic, R. (2008). Multimodal collaborative handwriting training for visually-impaired people. *Proc. CHI '08,* 393-402.

[16] Savidis, A. and Stephanidis, C. (2005). Developing dual user interfaces for integrating blind and sighted users: The HOMER UIMS. *Proc. CHI '95,* 106-113.

[17] Shinohara, K., and Wobbrock, J.O. (2011). In the shadow of misperception: Assistive technology use and social interactions. *Proc. CHI '11,* 705-714.

[18] Shneiderman, B. (2000). Universal usability. *CACM* 43(5), 84-91.

[19] Suchman, L. (1995). Making work visible. *CACM, 38*(9), 56-64.

[20] Williams, M.A., Galbraith, C., Kane, S.K., and Hurst, A. (2014). "Just let the cane hit it": How the blind and sighted see navigation differently. *Proc. ASSETS '14,* 217-224.

[21] Wobbrock, J.O., Kane, S.K., Gajos, K.Z., Harada, S., and Froehlich, J. (2011). Ability-Based Design: Concept, principles and examples. *TACCESS* 3(3), Article 9, 27 pages.

Understanding the Challenges Faced by Neurodiverse Software Engineering Employees: Towards a More Inclusive and Productive Technical Workforce

Meredith Ringel Morris, Andrew Begel
Microsoft Research
Redmond, WA, USA
{merrie, abegel}@microsoft.com

Ben Wiedermann
Harvey Mudd College
Claremont, CA, USA
benw@cs.hmc.edu

ABSTRACT
Technology workers are often stereotyped as being socially awkward or having difficulty communicating, often with humorous intent; however, for many technology workers with atypical cognitive profiles, such issues are no laughing matter. In this paper, we explore the hidden lives of neurodiverse technology workers, e.g., those with autism spectrum disorder (ASD), attention deficit hyperactivity disorder (ADHD), and/or other learning disabilities, such as dyslexia. We present findings from interviews with 10 neurodiverse technology workers, identifying the challenges that impede these employees from fully realizing their potential in the workplace. Based on the interview findings, we developed a survey that was taken by 846 engineers at a large software company. In this paper, we reflect on the differences between the neurotypical (N = 781) and neurodiverse (N = 59) respondents. Technology companies struggle to attract, develop, and retain talented software developers; our findings offer insight into how employers can better support the needs of this important worker constituency.

Author Keywords
Software development; neurodiversity; autism spectrum disorder; attention deficit hyperactivity disorder

INTRODUCTION
Autism Spectrum Disorders (ASDs) are an increasingly prevalent societal issue. Recent reports from the U.S. CDC indicate that as many as 1 in 68 children aged 8 and under are on the autism spectrum [9]. The autism spectrum covers a broad variety of symptoms and abilities; some people may be non-verbal and entirely reliant upon their caretakers even in adulthood, while others face milder (though still substantial) challenges, such as difficulty in forming social bonds with others, difficulty interpreting or conveying emotions, difficulty making eye contact, and/or difficulties maintaining mental focus on certain tasks, among others [1].

For adults with milder forms of ASD (such as Asperger's Syndrome), finding appropriate employment may be a challenge; many people with ASD are unemployed or underemployed [5], or face discrimination within their workplace [4]. Matching people with autism to jobs appropriate for their skills, interests, and personalities is an increasingly important societal issue; a good match can result in benefit not only for the autistic individual and his family, but also for employers who may value some individuals' unique skills, such as attention to small details [10].

Many people with autism have an interest in and affinity for technology [23]. Famed autism advocate Temple Grandin (who is herself autistic) specifically suggests that parents of children with autism consider preparing them for careers in computer programming [12]. Popular culture suggests that many members of the technology industry already may be "closeted" or undiagnosed autistics [31], though no numbers exist to confirm or deny such rumors. Recently, several companies, such as SAP and Microsoft, have publicly announced intentions to hire computer professionals with ASD, both as a matter of social justice and to take advantage of affinities between the profile of some individuals with ASD and the job requirements of the technology industry [13, 30, 33]. Advocacy groups such as AccessComputing provide bridge programs, advice, and other resources to make computing careers more accessible for people with disabilities, including people with ASD [7, 8].

In this paper, we present the first study of neurodiverse software developers, via interview and survey data. Understanding the perspectives and experiences of technology workers with ASD and other cognitive differences is important – if, as popular cultural suggests, the ranks of Silicon Valley contain many people with undisclosed cases of Asperger's Syndrome, or if more companies wish to follow the lead of SAP and Microsoft and actively recruit people known to have ASD into their workforce, it is important to understand whether such employees face unique challenges in achieving success in

ASSETS '15, October 26 - 28, 2015, Lisbon, Portugal.

ACM 978-1-4503-3400-6/15/10...$15.00
DOI: http://dx.doi.org/10.1145/2700648.2809841

computing careers. After describing the methodology and findings of our interviews and surveys, we reflect on how these findings might translate into changes in software development workplace and workflow practices that can better support the success of technologists with ASD and more effectively leverage the unique skills and perspectives that they may bring to their jobs.

RELATED WORK

Much autism research focuses on children (such as developing technologies for children with ASD, their parents, or their caregivers, e.g., [15, 18, 26]). This emphasis on youth is understandable in light of the evidence that appropriate interventions at a young age are particularly valuable in the treatment of ASD [24]. In this paper, however, we focus on adults with autism, and particularly on the experiences of those adults in the technology workforce. Two relatively recent reviews of the literature on adults and ASD begin by describing how little research there is on the topic, compared to the amount of research on children with ASD [2, 16]. Hendricks' meta-analysis estimates the unemployment rate among adults with ASD as 50-70% [16].

Given the comparatively little published work there is on adults with ASD and the high rate of unemployment among this population, little attention has been paid to the workplace experiences of adults with ASD. Even less attention has been given to adults on the "high-functioning" end of the spectrum [2, 28], and less still to those who work in technical fields. In fact, the only study we know of that describes the experiences of a number of tech workers with ASD is Rebholz's dissertation, *Life in the Uncanny Valley: Workplace Issues for Knowledge Workers on the Autism Spectrum* [27]. In it, Rebholz describes and analyzes interviews with nine employees, seven of whom hold "computer-related jobs."

The goals of Rebholz's study were different than ours. Rebholz sought to describe the "issues encountered by high-functioning people on the autism spectrum who are in the top quartile of American wage earners" [27, p.1]; that study's inclusion of tech workers was not an explicit goal, but a virtue of the fact that it pulled its participants from the Seattle area. By contrast, our study focuses explicitly on tech workers. As a result, the two studies are complementary: Rebholz's covers a more general range of work experience than ours and asks questions about employment law and family background; ours covers a more general range of cognitive function.

Our findings echo and bolster many of the experiences of Rebholz's participants, including the benefits of employing someone with high-functioning autism, the ability to visualize problems, the importance of explicit communication from co-workers and managers, receiving a diagnosis as an adult, the personal nature of disclosing a diagnosis and the reluctance to do so, the negative effects of corporate restructuring, distracting and open work environments, and experience with accommodations. Furthermore, our participants place many of issues in the context of technical work, specifically of writing and testing code or managing people who do. Our study also compares the experience of neurodiverse tech workers with those of neurotypical tech workers, an area that Rebholz identified as important future work.

Much of the other literature about adults on the spectrum concentrate on pre-vocational interventions [3, 21] or environmental factors [20] that influenced the employment experiences or quality of life for adults on the spectrum. Many studies (e.g., [14]) report on adults' continued struggle to maintain full-time employment.

Two studies are tangentially related: a study by Parr, et al. on leadership and ASD [25] and a study by Hurlbutt and Chalmers on Asperger's and employment [19]. The Parr et al. study investigates how a particular leadership theory affects employees with ASD [25]. In particular, how does adherence to a particular leadership style affect an employee's anxiety, and how does the employee's anxiety affect their commitment to their organization and their perception of their job performance? The researchers interviewed 52 employees (27 women; 25 men) with ASD, employed as "human service workers, research support staff, or cleaning and support staff." Employees rated their anxiety, commitment to their organization, and perception of their own performance, according to standard scales. The results showed that some leadership theories increase anxiety and negatively affect employees with ASD, even though studies have found the opposite effects in neurotypical employees.

Hurlbutt and Chalmers interviewed six adults with Asperger Syndrome and asked them questions about employment [19]. The goal of the study was to illuminate issues related to Asperger's and employment, in general, rather than the issues of people with Asperger's in a particular field. Participants were recruited at an autism conference or via social networks. Most participants had not worked in the areas in which they obtained their degrees and none were software engineers (although one participant was trained and worked as a library/information scientist). The researchers interviewed participants and asked many questions that were similar to ours, including how their diagnosis has affected them and their jobs, whether the participant had disclosed their diagnosis, and what accommodations, if any, they had received. The researchers coded the results and uncovered general employment themes that we also saw in our study: a reluctance to disclose diagnosis and the difficulties presented by social skills, environmental, and sensory factors.

INTERVIEWS: METHODOLOGY

We advertised our study via email to a distribution list within Microsoft comprised of employees who have autism themselves or who have family members with autism who have decided on their own to join that email discussion

ID	Age	Approximate Age at Diagnosis	Gender	Country	Most Recent Job Role	Diagnosis
P1	43	Late thirties	Male	USA	Software developer	ASD
P2	51	Early forties	Male	U.K.	Technology consultant	Asperger's*
P3	23	21	Male	USA	Software developer	ASD
P4	45	Early forties	Male	USA	Website architect	PDD-NOS
P5	30	30	Male	USA	Software tester	ADHD
P6	46	Early thirties	Male	U.K.	Technology consultant	Asperger's
P7	46	Thirties or early forties	Male	U.K.	Technology consultant	Asperger's*
P8	49	Thirties or early forties	Female	USA	Software developer	Asperger's*
P9	34	3	Male	USA	Software tester	ASD
P10	52	49	Male	USA	Database administration	ASD

Table 1. Demographic details of interview participants. A * in the "Diagnosis" column indicates a self-diagnosis rather than a professional diagnosis. Participants P8, P9, and P10 worked in the software industry, but were not

community (the names of members of the email list, and even the total number of members, were not available to us, as part of Microsoft's effort to preserve employee privacy). Although the list targets employees who are concerned about those on the autism spectrum, sometimes people with other diagnoses join the list. For example, one of the participants who responded to our call had ADHD, but did not identify as having ASD. While the majority of Microsoft's employees are based in the USA, a substantial number are also located in other countries (3 of our study participants were based in the U.K.).

Our email advertisement described our research team's interest in understanding the perspectives of neurodiverse software developers in order to help make software careers more inclusive. We offered a payment of $50 (or a donation of $50 to an autism-related charity such as Autism Speaks) for a one hour interview. Our call made it clear that all interviews would be confidential (no data would be reported to the participant's manager or anyone else in their organization), held outside the employee's regular workspace, and contained a calendar appointment whose title only let on that it was a meeting about software engineering. We also informed the participants that any data appearing in reports such as this would be anonymized.

Our email also indicated that recipients were welcome to share the study information with colleagues employed in the software industry at other companies; at least one reader apparently did this. We were contacted by a few software professionals who either worked for other companies or were otherwise employed, and included them in our sample (3 of our participants, P8, P9, and P10, did not currently work for Microsoft).

Interviews lasted between 45 minutes and 1 hour, and were conducted in-person for the six participants working near the researchers and via Skype for the four remote participants. We employed a semi-structured interview approach, starting with a set of core questions, but sometimes adding or removing questions based on a particular interviewee's background, interests, and responses. Interviewees were also welcome to decline to answer any questions they found uncomfortable. All interviews were audio recorded with participants' permission and the interviewers also took detailed notes. Table 1 summarizes key details about the ten interviewees.

INTERVIEWS: FINDINGS

After the ten interviews were complete, three researchers used open coding techniques to iteratively identify common themes that emerged across the interviews. We discuss those themes in the following sub-sections.

Diagnosis

A preponderance of articles on autism focus on diagnosis rates in children [2] and emphasize the importance of early diagnosis and early intervention [24]; consequently, we were surprised that with only one exception (P9), our participants did not learn that they were not neurotypical until adulthood.

Seven participants received formal diagnoses from medical professionals, while three (P2, P7, P8) diagnosed themselves. It may be the case that participants who self-diagnosed, rather than receiving a professional evaluation, may be incorrect in their labeling of their condition; however, we believe our role as researchers is to convey the experiences and perceptions of our participants, not to pass judgment on whether their diagnosis is "official" – our self-diagnosed participants had extensive knowledge of ASD (typically with other family members having formal diagnoses), and described experiences and issues highly similar to those of the participants with formal diagnoses.

Having one's children receive a formal diagnosis of ASD was a common prompt for adulthood diagnosis (or self-diagnosis), as parents recognized in themselves many of their children's traits. P2, P4, P7, and P8 noted that an autism diagnosis in one or more of their children prompted the realization that they were also on the spectrum. P9, our only participant who had himself been diagnosed in childhood (and received specialized education and therapies), also mentioned having children who were diagnosed as autistic.

Receiving a poor performance review at work was another prompt for diagnosis, i.e., if serious conflicts with a manager or other co-workers resulted in a need to consult with a mental health professional. P5, who differed from the other interviewees in having a diagnosis of ADHD rather than ASD, learned of his diagnosis by seeking professional help after receiving a bad performance review from his manager.

Interviewees found diagnosis beneficial, as it provided them with the basis for creating a plan of behavioral and sometimes medical strategies for addressing issues that interfered with their workplace success. P8 noted that having a diagnosis was a relief because, "it explains so much that I didn't understand."

There are many possible reasons for the prevalence of adulthood diagnoses in this group, including that adults from earlier generations grew up in a time when autism awareness and diagnosis was less common, that some interviewees were born overseas in countries or cultures where autism awareness and diagnosis are less common, or that many milder cases of these conditions may be less noticeable or confused with other issues.

Disclosure

We asked participants whether they had disclosed their diagnosis to either their manager or a human resources representative in their workplace. Half of the participants (P1, P4, P6, P7, P8) had chosen not to disclose (we do not know if the participants' managers suspect that their employees have ASD or ADHD). The primary motivators for non-disclosure were concerns about being judged negatively by colleagues and of possible workplace discrimination. For example, P6 said that he was "wary of outing myself," and noted that being neurodiverse is "where race, sex, and sexuality were [a few decades ago, as a civil rights issue]... autistic spectrum conditions are maybe similar, I think to that... years ago, gay people didn't feel comfortable coming out... people on the autistic spectrum are not yet comfortable about coming out." P7 explained his choice of non-disclosure by saying, "I don't think our business [computing] is mature enough around its understanding of autistic spectrum conditions at the moment." P8 noted, "I think I have a lot of skills, and I would like to be judged on my skills and not have to worry about a diagnosis." Such concerns seem well-founded; P2, who decided to disclose to his manager, revealed that his manager told him that perhaps he should consider leaving his current role, and noted that, "people could and often [do] jump to conclusions."

For the participants who did choose to disclose their diagnosis to management, a personal connection was often the prompt. For example, P3 decided to disclose his condition after hearing his manager describe how his own children had been diagnosed with ASD. P9 felt a close social/friendship relationship existed with his manager, and disclosed his own diagnosis to him as part of a larger discussion of his children's medical situation.

Software Development Challenges

Participants described a variety of challenges they faced as neurodiverse people working in the field of software development.

P1 and P6 reflected that they were often quite rigid in their interpretation of rules or in their desire for structure, i.e., becoming upset if colleagues' code didn't adhere strictly to style guidelines or if an Agile development meeting didn't follow all of the official rules described by the Agile programming movement (P1 noted, "Structure is good. That's why I like [Agile method]...").

P3, P4, and P7 discussed how they had difficulty committing to or focusing on tasks that they perceived as mundane, though they felt they excelled and displayed unusual levels of focus for tasks they found particularly compelling. P10 specifically found the task of testing code (to make sure it is bug free) problematic, as the idea that end users would use the code in the "wrong way" and that he would need to anticipate this was extremely frustrating to him. P7 noted, "one of the things I hate is being bored... if I get bored I can disengage really quickly."

P2, P8, and P10 identified that they sometimes expressed inappropriate emotions at work (and that they often were not aware of having done so unless a coworker informed them). P7 noted that code reviews, in which co-workers examine his code before committing it to the shared code repository, "can be quite confrontational," though he did not identify this reaction as being inappropriate, per se. P2 mentioned that he would "blow up" at people who critiqued his code, and didn't realize that this reaction was considered unprofessional until a colleague explained it to him.

Interpersonal and Workplace Challenges

Half of the interviewees (P1, P6, P7, P8, P10) volunteered that they knew they had poor interpersonal communication skills. This led to many workplace challenges, including difficulty interpreting nuance in the meaning of coworkers' statements, difficulty interpreting coworkers' emotions, difficulty dealing with office politics, and difficulty handling conflicts with co-workers. Team meetings were cited as being a particular cause of stress, as was the process of interviewing to get a job; for instance, P10 reflected that he had done poorly on several job interviews because he did not make eye contact with the interviewers, which he concluded resulted in their viewing him as untrustworthy. P8 suspected that she was fired from a position because of her challenges with the social aspects of her job, "I think I can block it out [the social stuff] and focus on the stuff that needs to get done... that might be part of why I was let go... I don't know... I think I didn't have the social skills for people to want me to be on." She went on to note, "It would be nice to be with a company where the social structure wasn't so complicated."

Participants also described challenges with various types of communications, including face-to-face conversations, phone calls, and even e-mail (particularly interpreting emotion or nuance in e-mail). P8 said, "sometimes in an IM they [colleagues] would say, it would look like they were in agreement, but then I'd find out later that they were not, which was very confusing… I preferred to ask people what they could do for me in person, because there were more clues as to what they really meant." P10, in contrast, preferred electronic correspondence such as email because he "can do it more slowly, [and he] can think about what [he's] saying." Selecting which medium would be most appropriate for communicating with colleagues was also a source of confusion for participants.

Some participants had opportunities to try a management role at some point in their career, and management of other people often proved challenging – P1, P4, P7, and P8 reflected on these difficulties. P8 described that she felt she had been a good manager to other employees, and expressed confusion that the employees who reported to her didn't seem to feel the same way, noting, "two of the people that I had working under me won't talk to me anymore, I don't understand why they won't talk to me anymore… they both dumped me on Facebook… I don't understand." P1 noted that people with strong technical skills who were not well-suited to management had difficulty advancing within Microsoft, where promotions were often tied to moving into a managerial role. Note, however, that some interviewees had more positive experiences in management roles, and P6 mentioned aspiring to try out management in the future.

Environmental distractions, such as noisy work spaces or software-based distractions (e.g., notifications of incoming messages from email or other programs), were particularly problematic for participants. P1, P2, P3, P8, and P10 raised this as an issue. P1 noted that open plan offices, which are quite popular in technology companies [17], were a particularly distracting environment. P3 mentioned that he wore headphones and listened to music while working to help mitigate environmental distractions. Time management and task prioritization were difficult for P1, P5, and P10.

Frequent changes in organizational structure within Microsoft were called out as problematic by P1 and P7, who found having to adapt to new sets of managers and teammates particularly stressful and anxiety-inducing.

Accommodations

We asked interviewees to describe any accommodations they had requested in the workplace (if they had chosen to disclose their status), or what accommodations they might want to ask for if they were to feel comfortable disclosing or asking.

P2 and P6 both identified business travel as an area in which employees with ASD might require accommodations. Although Microsoft's policy mandated hotel-room sharing among team members travelling to conferences to defray costs, P2 requested a private hotel room. He justified his request, explaining that after a long day of having to interact with other people at the conference, he felt that he couldn't handle the need for additional social interactions at the hotel. He needed time to "chill out and just be on my own… and get my social battery filled up." He also often requests to skip work-related social functions (such as team dinners), explaining that "it's either fun or work, I can't do both at the same time." P6, who had not disclosed his diagnosis to management, wanted to request dispensation against Microsoft's policy that employees fly in economy class during business trips, because the stress of having so many people so close to him during travel was amplified by his ASD.

P5, who had disclosed his ADHD, made several accommodations requests at the suggestion of his therapist. He requested that his manager allow him to audio record team meetings to help him remember work items assigned to him. He found that taking notes while paying attention to verbal conversations at the same time was quite difficult. He also requested that key expectations and instructions be sent to him in written form so that he could re-read the information multiple times if needed. P7 also mentioned that he would find it helpful if he could request that key expectations from his manager be conveyed in written form, though he did not disclose his diagnosis and therefore did not make this request.

P5 requested an additional private weekly meeting with his manager in order to correct any potential misunderstandings in what he was working on and make sure his work stayed on track. He also requested that his manager be more attentive to providing more detail in any conversations and emails with him, as he found any ambiguities to be very difficult to interpret and resolve.

P3, who achieved "hyperfocus" on projects of interest to him but had difficulty working on projects he found mundane, was able to reach an agreement with his manager to have greater autonomy in selecting what aspects of the system he would code. P3 was also considering requesting a treadmill desk, as he felt that exercise might alleviate anxiety that he felt during the workday.

P8 and P10 both desired the flexibility to work from home and attend fewer meetings so that they could spend their time focusing on their strengths (writing code) and have less time (and stress) devoted to interpersonal interactions. P1 and P8 noted that a private office, perhaps even soundproofed, would help mitigate the distracting and stressful effects of working in open plan offices for people with ASD.

Greater awareness and sensitivity from colleagues to the needs of neurodiverse co-workers was something all participants hoped for, though this was difficult for people to balance with the perceived risks of disclosure. P8, who had not disclosed her ASD status to colleagues, noted that one potential benefit of disclosure may simply be greater empathy from colleagues, "if people didn't get whatever social stuff they need from me, maybe they would be more understanding and explain what they need [more clearly]."

Finally, P10, who was among the half of our interviewees whose children also had ASD, observed that better health insurance coverage for caring for children with ASD would likely be valued by many employees on the spectrum, since their children were more likely than the children of neurotypical employees to have ASD.

Strengths

Despite the many challenges associated with ASD, ADHD, and related conditions, nearly all participants felt that being neurodiverse also provided them with advantages in their chosen careers relating to software development. P6 specifically emphasized that he preferred the term "Autistic Spectrum Condition" to "Autistic Spectrum Disorder," because he felt that the disorder terminology implied that there were no positive aspects involved in being neurodiverse, an assertion with which he disagreed.

Six participants (P2, P3, P6, P7, P8, P10) perceived that they were particularly gifted in noticing patterns in information and mentally visualizing information. P6 mentioned an ability to "execute the code in my head" in order to anticipate bugs. P2 described an ability to spot bugs in code by recognizing patterns in the formatting (indentation of lines, etc.). P8 said that "finding the patterns" was her favorite aspect of programming, noting, "I can't help myself, I look for patterns, that's clearly an obsession of mine, patterns, and programming is really just a huge pattern."

Several interviewees (P2, P3, P6, P7, P8, P9) noted that they were skilled at achieving a very high state of focus on authoring a piece of code or completing a specific project. P6 noted, "Aspies are very good at things like software testing… they're very good at thinking things through and excluding other thoughts from their work." P7 said, "I tend to be quite focused… I'll find something of interest to me, I'll be incredibly focused on that for a period of time, until I reach a point where I feel I personally understand it… and then I can very quickly lose interest in it." P8 explained that her ability for intense focus was "such a benefit" for her job in programming: "I love it when I can just work and not have anything else, just being focused… is very satisfying." P3 described enjoying experiencing a state of "hyperfocus" when working on certain programming projects.

P2, P6, and P9 noted that the code they authored was particularly clean and orderly, exemplifying strict adherence to rules of coding style, when compared to that of their colleagues. For example, P6 noted that colleagues who wrote "untidy code" irritated him, and attributed bugs to "nonautistic people developing the code and not thinking about boundary conditions… tidy code doesn't have those sort of problems." P2 noted that even before the advent of software development environments that would automatically indent code and support other aspects of coding style, "I would write my code in such a way that it would have that [nice formatting]."

P5 and P7 described strengths in tangential thinking – developing out-of-the-box solutions or making intuitive leaps that were valuable in their line of work. For instance, P7 noted, "I can be very insightful…I can make leaps that… quite often other people don't."

SURVEY: METHODOLOGY

To explore whether the themes that emerged from the interviews were distinct to software developers with cognitive differences or were also issues that resonated with neurotypical employees, we designed a survey to reach a larger audience.

We created an online survey using the SurveyGizmo service. The survey contained 32 questions, though some of these questions were shown only conditionally depending on prior answers (e.g., if respondents indicated they were neurotypical, they were not shown the subset of questions relating to their experiences as a neurodiverse software developer). In consideration of the sensitive nature of the survey topic, all questions were optional so that respondents uncomfortable with a particular question were free to leave it unanswered. Time-tracking software embedded in the survey indicates that participants spent a median of 6.4 minutes to complete the survey.

We sent the survey to 2,600 U.S.-based employees of Microsoft whose title indicated they were a software developer or software tester; specific employees meeting these criteria were chosen at random from the employee database to receive an email invitation to the online survey. The survey was administered during the last two weeks of October 2014. Survey participation was optional and anonymous; participants were told we would contribute $1 to the Autism Speaks charitable organization for each completed survey we received (our team donated $846 on November 3, 2014, an amount that was also matched by Microsoft's matching charitable gifts policy).

The email invitation told participants that our survey was about "Software Developer Perspectives," and explained, "Our goal is to broaden participation in software careers by people with varied cognitive profiles, including, but not limited to ASD (autism spectrum disorder), ADHD (attention deficit hyperactivity disorder), and dyslexia. Your response is important to us, even if you do not identify with any of these cognitive profiles." We decided to broaden the survey call to include ADHD and other cognitive differences since our initial interviews indicated that some people with ADHD (like P5) identified informally with employees on the autism spectrum because they felt many of their challenges were similar, and because a large proportion of our other interviewees had co-occurring challenges such as ADHD.

SURVEY: FINDINGS

Demographics

846 people completed our survey (a 32.5% response rate). 718 (84.9%) of respondents identified as male, 107 (12.6%) as female, and the remaining 2.5% chose not to specify a gender. This preponderance of male respondents is roughly in line with the demographics at software companies (for instance, Microsoft and Google each recently reported that 17% of their technical employees are female [11, 22]). 91.8% of respondents reported their age; these respondents' ages ranged from 21 to 71 years old, with a median age of 32. Although respondents all worked in the U.S., they came from diverse backgrounds, with the majority having been born abroad. 34.8% were born in the U.S., 21.2% in India, and 10.2% in China. The remainder hailed from a variety of countries, particularly locations in Europe and Asia.

50.2% reported having a Bachelor's degree in computer science, and 25.7% reported having a bachelor's degree in another field related to computing (math, electrical engineering, information science, etc.). 3.5% reported having a graduate degree (Master's or Ph.D.) in computer science, and 11.2% reported having a graduate degree in a field related to computing. 6.5% of respondents indicated that they did not hold any undergraduate or graduate degrees in a computing-related field.

Respondents reported having worked in the field of software development for a median of 9 years (min 1 year, max 40 years), and having worked at Microsoft for a median of 5 years (min 1 year, max 25 years). 73.4% reported having a software engineering role, 23.4% reported having a software testing role, with the others reporting related roles such as "Data Architect," "Electrical Engineering," "Data Center Management," etc. Respondents reported being in their current role for a median of 3 years. 9.5% reported that they currently directly managed one or more employees (including interns and/or contractors), and 42.9% reported having directly managed one or more employees at some point in the past (either at Microsoft or at a prior job).

Neurodiversity

11 respondents (1.3%) identified as having an autism spectrum disorder (including Asperger Syndrome or PDD-NOS). 38 (4.5%) identified as having attention deficit disorder (including ADD, ADHD, and ADHD-PI). 16 (1.9%) identified as having dyslexia or another learning disability. Note that 7 of these respondents identified as having more than one of these conditions (e.g., ADD and ADHD); in total, 59 of the respondents (7.0% identified as having at least one of the aforementioned conditions, while 91.6% of respondents indicated that they did not identify as having any of the conditions (additionally, 6 respondents chose not to answer the question about their cognitive profile). The 59 respondents who identified with one or more of the cognitive differences were asked to respond to a set of survey questions specific to their experiences with that condition; the following sub-sections describe these participants' responses.

Diagnosis

42.4% of the 59 neurodiverse respondents reported being self-diagnosed, while 66.1% reported receiving a formal diagnosis of their condition by a professional (one person chose not to answer the question about diagnosis type). The age of diagnosis ranged from 4 to 50 years old, with a median of 23 (mean 22.5).

Responding to a multiple choice question asking whether any of several situations prompted the respondents' diagnosis, 15.3% indicated that they were diagnosed after one of their biological children had been diagnosed with a similar condition, 20.3% were diagnosed after one or more family members (other than their children) were diagnosed with a similar condition, 15.3% were diagnosed after a challenging situation at work (e.g., conflict with another employee, poor performance review), and 6.8% were diagnosed at the suggestion of a co-worker.

When asked whether they had changed aspects of their work after receiving their diagnosis, few respondents indicated they had, with two reporting having changed companies, two having changed roles, one having changed projects, and two having changed other aspects of their work situation such as their "day to day work style."

Disclosure

We asked what categories of people respondents had disclosed their condition to. Relatively few had disclosed their condition to co-workers: 20.3% had disclosed to their manager, 3.4% (2 respondents) had disclosed to a skip-level or higher manager, 1.7% (1 respondent) had disclosed to direct reports, 22.0% to co-workers on their team (peers in the company hierarchy), and none had disclosed to HR. In contrast, 32.2% reported having disclosed their condition to friends at Microsoft who were not members of their work team, and 76.3% reported having disclosed their condition to friends or family outside of Microsoft. 16.9% had not disclosed their condition to any of these groups of people.

Discrimination

We also asked these 59 respondents whether they had ever experienced workplace discrimination related to their condition, either at Microsoft or previous employers. 58 chose to answer this question, and the majority (52, 89.7%) reported that they had not experienced discrimination. The 6 who answered affirmatively were asked to briefly describe the discriminatory incidents; not all chose to provide descriptions. One, having attention deficit disorder, noted, "There is often intolerance and sometimes outright antagonism by smart people at [Microsoft] towards people that approach tasks and work situations differently compared to their natural viewpoint." Another, also having attention deficit disorder, said, "I often receive feedback that I'm 'odd,' and that it's limiting my career advancement." Another, with dyslexia, wrote, "It takes me longer to read things, so I get left behind and have to catch up."

Accommodations

Of the 17 employees who had disclosed their condition to management or HR, we asked whether they had requested or received any workplace accommodations; 94.1% said they had not. The one employee who had requested accommodations, a developer with attention deficit disorder, had requested a "good seat in [the] team room."

We also asked all 59 neurodiverse respondents whether there were any workplace accommodations they were not currently receiving that they thought might be beneficial, such as changes to policies or practices, to equipment or software, or to their working environment. 58 chose to answer this question; 15.5% indicated they would find some accommodations helpful. Suggestions included changes to the performance evaluation process ("Despite excellent technical performance, I'm often given average reviews for reasons directly related to my ADD symptoms.") and hiring processes ("The interview process here is not geared toward people with disabilities. I also have Tourettes [sic] so I can get nervous and lock up. I will pass 40% of interviews and fail 60%."). The most common suggestion was to change workplace arrangements: "I work in a cube environment where bright lighting and noise is common. I would much rather work in an office for parts of the day where I need to be focused." (from an employee with ASD); "A more quiet environment" (from an employee with attention deficit disorder); "Private office space." (from an employee with attention deficit disorder); "Not being forced into a [sic] open floor-plan 'shared space'" (from an employee with ASD).

On-the-job Experiences

We asked all 846 respondents to describe their level of skill at various activities related to their jobs. In the following analyses, we exclude the 6 participants who did not respond to the question about their cognitive profile, since it is unclear whether they would fall into the neurotypical or neurodiverse group.

Respondents used a five-point scale (1 = significantly below average, 5 = significantly above average) to rate their level of skill at a list of several software development activities (Figure 1). Participants whose jobs did not require these activities could choose N/A or leave an item blank. We compared responses from neurotypical employees to those identifying as having ASD, ADHD, or dyslexia using Mann-Whitney *U* tests, and found no significant difference in self-rated skill for "finding bugs" (p = .30) or "visualizing the solution to a problem" (p = .10). There was a marginally significant difference in perceived skill at "employing good coding style" (neurotypical = 4.0, **others** = 4.1, p =.06). Neurodiverse employees rated themselves as

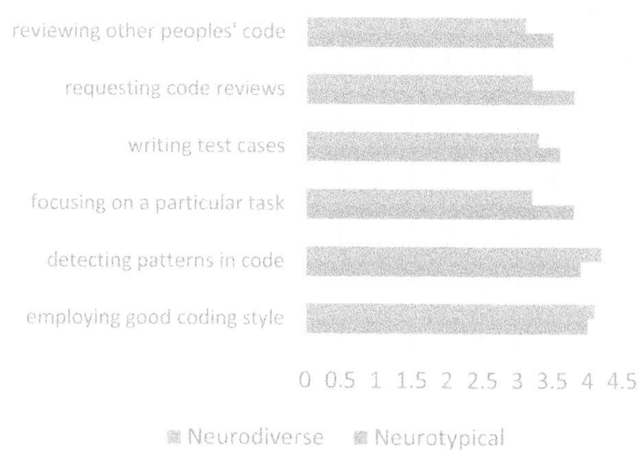

Figure 1. Software developers' self-rated skill at software development activities (ratings use a five-point scale, with five representing the highest level of skill). Only items for which neurodiverse and neurotypical employees had statistically significant differences in their ratings are shown in this chart.

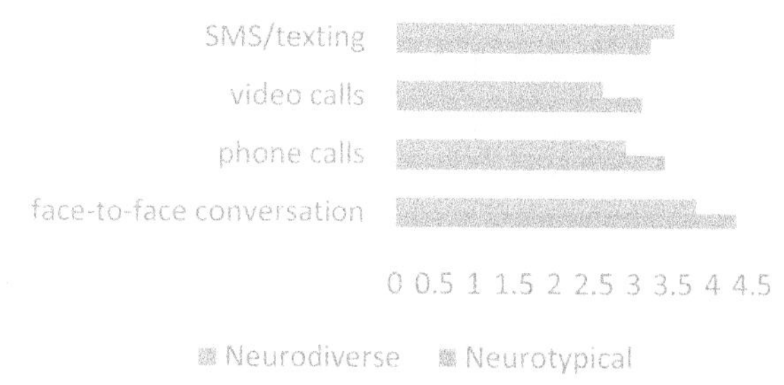

Figure 2. Software developers' self-rated comfort with various forms of communication with colleagues (ratings use a five-point scale, with five representing the highest level of comfort). Only items for which neurodiverse and neurotypical employees had statistically significant differences in their ratings are shown in this chart.

significantly more skilled at "detecting patterns in code" (neurotypical = 3.9, **others = 4.2**, $p < .01$), while they rated themselves as significantly less skilled at "focusing on a particular task" (**neurotypical = 3.8**, others = 3.2, $p < .001$), "writing test cases" (**neurotypical = 3.6**, others = 3.3, p = .04), "requesting code reviews for your own code" (**neurotypical = 3.8**, others = 3.2, $p < .001$), and "reviewing other peoples' code" (**neurotypical = 3.5**, others = 3.1, $p < .01$).

Respondents also used a five-point scale (1 = very uncomfortable, 5 = very comfortable) to indicate their level of comfort at communicating with colleagues using several types of media (Figure 2). There was no significant difference in comfort level for e-mail (p =.17), with social media (e.g., Yammer) (p = .36), with instant messaging (p = .10), or with the use of communications mechanisms within software development tools such as source control systems

Figure 3. Software developers' self-rated level of challenge for various workplace situations (ratings use a five-point scale, with five representing the highest level of challenge). Only items for which neurodiverse and neurotypical employees had statistically significant differences in their ratings are shown in this chart.

(p = .45). Neurodiverse employees rated themselves as significantly less comfortable communicating with co-workers via face-to-face conversations (**neurotypical = 4.3**, other = 3.8, $p < .01$), phone calls (**neurotypical = 3.4**, other = 2.9, $p < .01$), and video calls (e.g., Skype) (**neurotypical = 3.1**, other = 2.6, $p < .01$). Neurodiverse employees rated themselves at significantly more comfortable communicating via SMS/text messaging (neurotypical = 3.2, **other = 3.5**, $p = .03$).

Next, respondents were asked to use a five-point scale to rate how challenging they find each of several work-related situations (1 = very easy to handle, 5 = very challenging) (Figure 3). There was no significant difference in perceived level of challenge in having 1:1 meetings with one's manager (p = .47), handling reorganizations (p = .35), following written directions (p = .12), or resolving ambiguity in an assignment (p = .16). There was a marginally significant difference in level of challenge with expressing appropriate emotions at work (neurotypical = 2.4, **other = 2.7**, p = .08) and in interpreting colleagues' emotions (neurotypical = 2.4, **other = 2.8**, p = .06), with neurodiverse employees reporting both of these as larger areas of challenge than neurotypicals. Neurodiverse employees reported significantly higher perceived levels of challenge at handling changes in routines or policies (neurotypical = 2.7, **other = 3.0**, p = .04), working in a shared office (neurotypical = 3.1, **other = 3.7**, $p < .001$), working in a noisy setting (neurotypical = 3.7, **other = 4.2**, p = .001), following verbal directions (neurotypical = 2.1, **other = 2.7**, $p < .001$), determining when to seek help on a work-related task (neurotypical = 2.3, **other = 2.9**, $p < .001$), attending team meetings (neurotypical = 2.0, **other = 2.4**, $p < .01$), resolving conflicts with colleagues (neurotypical = 2.6, **other = 2.9**, p = .04), and dealing with office politics (neurotypical = 3.3, **other = 3.6**, p = .03.

Respondents used a five point scale (1 = strongly disagree, 5 = strongly agree) to rate their level of agreement with statements about their working style. There was no difference in responses to the statements "I enjoy working on projects as part of a team" (p = .48) or "I prefer to work from my own home" (p = .42). However, there was a difference in level of agreement with the statement "I enjoy working on solo projects," with neurodiverse employees preferring this type of work more strongly than neurotypicals (neurotypical = 3.8, **other = 4.1**, p = .02).

Respondents used a five point scale (1 = strongly disagree, 5 = strongly agree) to rate their level of agreement with statements about their relationships with their co-workers. The only significant difference was in reactions to the statement "I enjoy(ed) having a management role" (which was only shown to those who indicated having ever been a manager in an earlier survey question), with neurotypicals more likely to agree (**neurotypical = 3.7**, other = 3.1, p = .02). There were, however, no significant differences in response to other statements related to management, "My personality and/or skills are well-suited for a management role" (p = .95) and "I am (was) successful in my management role(s)" (p = .83).

DISCUSSION

Our survey findings lend confidence that most of the challenges reported by our interviewees are indeed more salient issues for neurodiverse employees than for neurotypical ones. As with our ten interviewees, the fifty-nine neurodiverse respondents tended to be diagnosed in adulthood, and the majority did not disclose this diagnosis to management or their human resources (HR) department. Our survey findings also reinforce the suggestion of our interviewees that neurodiverse software developers perceive themselves as more skillful at focusing intensely on tasks and noticing patterns in code than neurotypical employees. Our survey also reinforces the interviewees' opinions that working in shared or open plan offices and dealing with the people skills aspects of software development were more problematic for neurodiverse employees.

In addition to validating trends from our interviews, the survey also highlighted some additional differences between neurotypical and neurodiverse software development employees, such as the finding that neurodiverse employees reported significantly less comfort with synchronous forms of communication than their neurotypical peers; we hypothesize this may be because asynchronous tools allow them more time to review and reflect on messages and prepare considered responses; further study to investigate this issue is warranted.

Implications for Employers

Our findings suggest that a not-insubstantial minority of software development employees at Microsoft have neurodiverse cognitive profiles. Companies like Microsoft may underestimate the pervasiveness of these issues because most impacted individuals are unlikely to disclose their status to HR or management for fear of judgment or discrimination. Further, many affected employees may not even realize the nature of their condition until many years after joining a company, as adulthood diagnosis was quite common.

Creating an environment that educates all employees about conditions such as ASD and ADHD may be beneficial, both for helping affected-yet-undiagnosed individuals achieve insight into their mental state that may enable them to receive needed assistance and in creating a climate of understanding and empathy within the workplace that may increase workers' comfort in revealing their neurodiverse status. As P8 noted, "I wouldn't feel comfortable telling managers or HR… but that might have helped [me]."

Open plan offices have become particularly prevalent at tech companies [17], but our findings indicate this working arrangement may negatively impact this sub-group of employees; the most commonly requested accommodation from our respondents was to rethink this trend, or make alternative work arrangements available for employees who need it.

Limitations

Both our interviews and survey rely on self-report data, whose drawbacks include the possibility of participants intentionally or unintentionally misrepresenting their experiences. Surveys may be problematic for neurodiverse participants to complete accurately, since it is not possible to request clarification of a question's intent [25]. Additionally, there may be sampling biases – for example, the people who chose to respond to our requests for interviews may have chosen to do so because they have experiences that are much more positive or much more negative than is typical. We attempted to mitigate this by randomly sampling from Microsoft's employee list for our survey invitations, but there may be self-selection in who ultimately completed the survey as well. We combined interviews with surveys as one way to mitigate the limitations of each individual technique.

Our interviews and survey include neurodiverse respondents with a range of diagnoses, covering varying points on the autism spectrum, as well as conditions such as attention-deficit disorder and learning challenges; some participants had multiple of these diagnoses, which may not be surprising given that characteristics of ASD and ADHD co-occur in a significant portion of the affected population [29]. Our sample size did not allow us the statistical power to tease apart nuances in the differential challenges that people with different diagnoses may experience – in addition to sample size, the co-occurrence of diagnoses within a single participant and/or the variability in the specifics or severity of a diagnosis across participants makes such analyses quite challenging, though they certainly have import and merit, and are a recommended avenue for further work.

All of the survey participants and all but three interview participants were employees of Microsoft; it may be that their experiences are not generalizable to the tech industry more broadly, but may be specific artifacts of the culture at Microsoft. However, we found that the experiences of the three employees who worked at other companies were quite similar to the others', suggesting that some amount of generalization is probable.

We also acknowledge that, while our findings indicate that there is hidden neurodiversity within the technology industry, the range of neurodiversity present in our study does not represent the range of neurodiversity in society. We recognize that a substantial number of people with ASD and other conditions may not be able to live independently in adulthood and that they and their caregivers may be concerned with a very different set of employment-related issues than the issues impacting the participants in this study.

Future Work

While this research is the first to shed light on issues related to neurodiversity among technology employees, it should not be the final word on the matter. Our survey results begin to give a sense of the extent to which software developers may represent various cognitive profiles, but more systematic sampling extending beyond a single company may be important for allowing the technology industry to better understand the need to take steps to support neurodiverse employees by providing data on the pervasiveness of these issues within and beyond Microsoft; such data may also help reduce the stigma associated with being neurodiverse by illustrating the extent to which it is a common phenomenon, as well as providing initial metrics against which further progress in diverse recruiting, hiring, and retention practices can be measured.

Interviews with managers and/or co-workers of neurodiverse employees would also add valuable information and perspective to this work. In this particular case, interviewing managers and co-workers was not possible, due to the confidential nature of the interviews and the fact that most of the employees had not officially disclosed their neurodiversity. However, the growth of formal hiring initiatives for employees with ASD at companies such as Microsoft may make manager and peer interviews possible in the future for employees whose status has already been disclosed through such programs.

The knowledge that many technology employees may have profiles such as ASD also merits related research on improving software development tools and practices to better support and leverage these employees. From a software engineering research or HCI perspective, pertinent research questions may include whether there are benefits to pairing up neurotypical and neurodiverse employees for pair programming tasks, or having them review each other's' code, since each may notice different types of bugs. Perhaps there are there changes that should be made to scrum or other types of software development processes to better support participation by neurodiverse employees. It also seems important to investigate whether communications tools such as email or IM can be adapted to better support neurodiverse employees by providing assistance at interpreting affect or nuance within messages or by encouraging neurotypicals authoring messages to clarify points identified as potentially problematic. We look forward to addressing these topics in future work.

CONCLUSION

Although the media often speculates that the technology industry includes many people with autism spectrum disorders [31], and although some autism experts suggest that individuals on the spectrum consider technology as a career choice [12], and although some technology companies have announced goals of recruiting neurodiverse employees [33], there is almost no research that explores the experiences of neurodiverse tech workers and no research that we know of that compares their experiences to those of neurotypical tech workers. In this paper, we presented the findings of interviews with ten neurodiverse individuals in careers related to software development, as well as survey results describing the experiences and opinions of 846 software developers and testers, 59 of whom identified as being neurodiverse.

Our findings revealed that many technology workers receive their diagnosis in adulthood, often as a result of life events such as a child's diagnosis or poor job performance. Most do not disclose their diagnosis to HR or management, despite the fact that a variety of accommodations, such as changes in workplace layout or modes of communication, may be desired and beneficial. Neurodiverse employees also reported different cognitive styles, such as sensitivity to details and patterns, which may be an asset to their career if nurtured and recognized by employers. We hope that these findings help inspire employers and employees to effect workplace changes that help all employees better reach their potential.

ACKNOWLEDGEMENTS

We would like to thank all of our survey and interview participants; we appreciate that neurodiversity is a sensitive issue, and are grateful that participants felt comfortable disclosing their experiences to our research team.

REFERENCES

1. American Psychiatric Association. (2013). Neurodevelopmental Disorders. In *Diagnostic and statistical manual of mental disorders* (5th ed.).
2. Barnhill, G.P. Outcomes in adults with Asperger syndrome. *Focus on Autism and Other Developmental Disabilities*, 22(2):116:126, 2007.
3. Bennett, K.D. The effects of covert audio coaching on the job performance of supported employees. Ph.D. thesis, Florida Atlantic University, 2009.
4. Booth, J. Autism in the Workplace. *Trades Union Congress*, 2014. http://www.tuc.org.uk/sites/default/files/Autism.pdf
5. Bornstein, D. Building a More Inclusive Work Force. *The New York Times*. July 5, 2011.
6. Buchen, L. Scientists and autism: When geeks meet. *Nature* **479**, 25-27, November 2 2011.
7. Burgstahler, S. and Ladner, R. An alliance to increase the participation of individuals with disabilities in computing careers. *Access Computing*, 85, 3-9, June 2006.
8. Burgstahler, S. and Ladner, R. Increasing the Participation of People with Disabilities in Computing Fields. *Computer*, 40(5), 94-97, May 2007.
9. Centers for Disease Control and Prevention. "Autism Spectrum Disorder (ASD): Data & Statistics." http://www.cdc.gov/ncbddd/autism/data.html
10. Cook, G. "The Autism Advantage." *The New York Times*, November 29, 2012.

11. Google Diversity website. Retrieved Jan. 27, 2015. http://www.google.com/diversity/at-google.html#tab=tech

12. Grandin, T. "Choosing the Right Job." *Autism Research Institute Blog*, November 1999. http://www.autism.com/advocacy_grandin_job

13. Grant, T. Working wisdom: How workers with disabilities give companies an edge. *The Globe and Mail*. Feb. 27, 2015.

14. Griffith, G.M., Totsika, V., Nash, S., and Hastings, R.P. I just don't fit anywhere: support experiences and future support needs of individuals with Asperger syndrome in middle adulthood. *Autism*, 16(5):532-546, 2012.

15. Hayes, G., Kientz, J., Truong, K., White, D., Abowd, G., and Pering, T. Designing Capture Applications to Support the Education of Children with Autism. *Proceedings of Ubicomp 2004*.

16. Hendricks, D. Employment and adults with autism spectrum disorders: Challenges and strategies for success. *Journal of Vocational Rehabilitation*. 32(2):125-134, 2010.

17. Hoare, R. "Do open plan offices lead to better work or closed minds?" *CNN*, October 4th, 2012. http://edition.cnn.com/2012/10/04/business/global-office-open-plan/

18. Hourcade, J.P., Williams, S.R., Miller, E.A., Huebner, K.E., and Liang, L.J. Evaluation of tablet apps to encourage social interaction in children with autism spectrum disorders. *Proceedings of CHI 2013*.

19. Hurlbutt, K. and Chalmers, L. Employment and adults with Asperger syndrome. *Focus on Autism and Other Developmental Disabilities*, 19(4):215-222, 2004.

20. Krieger, B., Kinbanian, A., Prodinger, B., and Heigl, F. Becoming a member of the work force: Perceptions of adults with Asperger Syndrome. *Work: A Journal of Prevention, Assessment, and Rehabilitation*. 43(2), 141-157, 2012.

21. Lawer, L., Brusilovskiy, E., Salzer, M., and Mandell, D. Use of vocational rehabilitative services among adults with autism. *Journal of Autism and Developmental Disorders*, 39(3): 487-494, 2009.

22. Lowensohn, J. "Microsoft says 29 percent of its employees are female." *The Verge*, October 3, 2014.

23. Mazurek, M.O., Shattuck, P.T., Wagner, M., and Cooper, B.P. Prevalence and Correlates of Screen-Based Media Use Among Youths with Autism Spectrum Disorders. *Journal of Autism and Developmental Disorders*, 42(8), 1757-1767, August 2012.

24. Orinstein, A.J., Helt, M., Troyb, E., Tyson, K.E., Barton, M.L., Eigsti, I-M., Naigles, L., and Fein, D.A. Intervention for optimal outcome in children and adolescents with a history of autism. *Journal of developmental and behavioral pediatrics*, 35(4): 247-256, May 2014.

25. Parr, A.D., Hunger, S.T., and Ligon, G.S. Questioning universal applicability of transformational leadership: Examining employees with autism spectrum disorder. *The Leadership Quarterly*, 24(4):608—622, 2013.

26. Piper, A.M., O'Brien, E., Morris, M.R., and Winograd, T. SIDES: A Cooperative Tabletop Computer Game for Social Skills Development. *Proceedings of CSCW 2006*.

27. Rebholz, C.H. Life in the Uncanny Valley: Workplace Issues for Knowledge Workers on the Autism Spectrum. PhD. Thesis, Antioch University, 2012.

28. Renty, J.O. and Roeyers, H. Quality of life in high-functioning adults with autism spectrum disorder: The predictive value of disability and support characteristics. *Autism*, 10(5):511-524, 2006.

29. Reiersen, A.M. and Todd, R.D. Co-occurrence of ADHD and autism spectrum disorders: phenomenology and treatment. *Expert Review of Neurotherapeutics*, 8(4), 657-669, April 2008.

30. Smith, M.E. Microsoft announces pilot program to hire people with autism. *Microsoft on the Issues Blog*, April 3, 2015. http://blogs.microsoft.com/on-the-issues/2015/04/03/microsoft-announces-pilot-program-to-hire-people-with-autism/

31. *Time*. "Diagnosing Bill Gates." January 24, 1994.

32. Tugend, A. Deciding Whether to Disclose Mental Disorders to the Boss. *The New York Times*, November 15, 2014.

33. Wang, S. How Autism Can Help You Land a Job. *The Wall Street Journal*, March 27, 2014.

34. Zyskowski, K., Morris, M.R., Bigham, J.P., Gray, M.L., and Kane, S. Accessible Crowdwork? Understanding the Value in and Challenge of Microtask Employment for People with Disabilities. *Proceedings of CSCW 2015*.

Using In-Situ Projection to Support Cognitively Impaired Workers at the Workplace

Markus Funk
University of Stuttgart
Pfaffenwaldring 5a
70569 Stuttgart
markus.funk@vis.uni-stuttgart.de

Sven Mayer
University of Stuttgart
Pfaffenwaldring 5a
70569 Stuttgart
sven.mayer@vis.uni-stuttgart.de

Albrecht Schmidt
University of Stuttgart
Pfaffenwaldring 5a
70569 Stuttgart
albrecht.schmidt@vis.uni-stuttgart.de

ABSTRACT
Today's working society tries to integrate more and more impaired workers into everyday working processes. One major scenario for integrating impaired workers is in the assembly of products. However, the tasks that are being assigned to cognitively impaired workers are easy tasks that consist of only a small number of assembly steps. For tasks with a higher number of steps, cognitively impaired workers need instructions to help them with assembly. Although supervisors provide general support and assist new workers while learning new assembly steps, sheltered work organizations often provide additional printed pictorial instructions that actively guide the workers. To further improve continuous instructions, we built a system that uses in-situ projection and a depth camera to provide context-sensitive instructions. To explore the effects of in-situ instructions, we compared them to state-of-the-art pictorial instructions in a user study with 15 cognitively impaired workers at a sheltered work organization. The results show that using in-situ instructions, cognitively impaired workers can assemble more complex products up to 3 times faster and with up to 50% less errors. Further, the workers liked the in-situ instructions provided by our assistive system and would use it for everyday assembly.

Author Keywords
Augmented Reality; Assistance for Impaired Workers; Assistive System; In-Situ Projection

ACM Classification Keywords
H.5.m. Information Interfaces and Presentation (e.g. HCI): Miscellaneous

INTRODUCTION
Projectors are becoming more common and are widely available. One of the reasons for this is the operational flexibility because they can displaying content on nearly any surface. Projected content can even be automatically adjusted to the projection surface by combining the projector with a camera [13] rendering the projection distortion free. This technology can also be applied to provide instructions at the workplace where the instructions can be projected directly onto the workers field of view [7] (see Figure 1). These so-called in-situ instructions do not require the worker to focus on an external screen or on a printed manual anymore and can keep the focus on the task while viewing instructions. The technique of using in-situ projection for instructing workers is already used in some commercial approaches. For example Light Guide Systems[1] use a top-mounted projector to display the next working step. Another commercial system such as the WERKLICHT from Extend3D[2] is using a laser projector to highlight important points for assembly.

Figure 1. A participant is assembling Duplo bricks using in-situ projected instructions provided by our assistive system.

Such assistive systems offering in-situ instructions at the working place can substantially increase the inclusion of impaired workers into the working life [1]. Moreover, these assistive systems open a variety of ways to employ impaired workers, as impaired workers are enabled to work on increasingly complex products when continuously receiving instructions [17]. This additionally fosters the inclusion of impaired workers

[1]Light Guide Systems - `http://www.ops-solutions.com` (last access 05-07-2015)

[2]WERKLICHT - `http://www.extend3d.de/en/products/wl_pro/` (last access 05-07-2015)

ASSETS'15, October 26–28, 2015, Lisbon, Portugal.

DOI: http://dx.doi.org/10.1145/2700648.2809853

into company's daily business and increases the productivity in sheltered work organizations.

New research in assistive systems for impaired workers focuses on adding gamification approaches to motivate cognitively impaired workers through in-situ instructions [10, 9]. However, an in-depth analysis of the effects of in-situ instructions on impaired workers has not been conducted yet. This paper aims to close this gap with the following three main contributions: (1) we introduce an assistive system that can automatically detect a worker's actions at the workplace (2) Through a comprehensive study with impaired workers, we compare the effects of our in-situ projection-based prototype against state-of-the art pictorial instructions (3) We discuss implications in-situ instructions for planning sheltered work assembly workplaces and better integrating impaired workers into the working life.

Figure 2. A state-of-the-art assembly workplace that is used in the analyzed sheltered work organization. Pictorial instructions above the boxes which hold the parts to assemble show how the assembly has to be performed. Workers can compare their assembled product with the depicted instruction.

ANALYZING THE STATE OF THE ART

To analyze the state-of-the-art of assembling products in a sheltered work organization, we analyzed a factory of our associate sheltered work organization with 72 impaired employees and 14 supervisors that are supporting the impaired employees. The supervisors consist of one social education supervisor and 13 technical supervisors. The impaired employees are workers with either cognitive disabilities (e.g. workers with down syndrome) or workers with mental disabilities (e.g. workers with tourette syndrome or burnout syndrome). The analyzed factory is producing cutting products (e.g. scissors, pliers, or pincers) and further has a carpentry for producing tables and benches.

The analyzed factory offers 93 assembly workplaces. The number of assembly steps that needed to be preformed at each workplace were counted. This counting included steps like picking up and placing of a part as well as a tools usage as a working step. According to this method, the workplaces analyzed consist of 1 to 25 working steps per product. Our analysis revealed an average amount of 5.25 $(SD = 4.05)$ working steps per workplace.

To support workers during their working tasks, the sheltered work organization offers pictorial instructions that are mounted directly over the boxes which hold the parts to be assembled (see Figure 2). The instructions show the assembled product in the intermediate state after the part in the box is assembled. The workers can control their assembled product using the picture, e.g. if the last part was assembled correctly or where to assemble the next part. In case the workers do not understand the pictorial instructions, there is always a supervisor around who can provide help with assembling the next part.

Overall, the factory is designed to split each product into small sub tasks, which the impaired workers can perform only with the help of the pictorial instructions. This segmentation of working tasks leads to a higher level of satisfaction of the workers because they can complete a whole task without help. Just in case they need help, they can still consult the supervisors.

RELATED WORK

Augmenting reality with information goes back to Sutherland [18]. In his prototype, he overlayed the view of participants with objects that are close and objects that appear to be far away. However, the idea of augmenting working processes with visual information has been around about only two decades. In 1993, Caudell et al. [3] suggested using head-mounted displays for displaying drilling spots and instructions. Over the years, research has defined sub-categories of Augmented Reality according to the different use cases and the ways of presenting information. For example, we refer to Spatial Augmented Reality (SAR) [14] when an object is being displayed directly onto the physical space around the user. An example for SAR is the Everywhere Displays Projector [13], where information is projected directly into the physical world with respect to the physical properties. Another sub-category is Industrial Augmented Reality (IAR), which refers to using Augmented Reality for industrial use cases. Navab [11] and Fite-Georgel [5] categorize IAR according to the different use cases: product design, commissioning, training, manufacturing, inspection and maintenance, and decommissioning.

A central aspect of IAR is presenting context aware instructions at the assembly workplace. These three competing technologies currently available for this are projected feedback, using augmented tools, and using head-mounted displays. Bannat et al. [2] used a top-mounted projector to provide in-situ feedback. Further they used an RGB-camera to detect which box the worker is picking the next part from. Their system can provide context sensitive help at the workplace according to which assembly part was picked by equipping the worker with a grasping sensor. This grasping sensor ensures that the worker actually picked up an item from the box and that the sensor did not just register the placement of his or her hand above the box. Rüther et al. [15] use projection for displaying information in sterile environments. In their study they found that using projected instructions for cleaning medical instruments is well received and leads to less errors than using paper-based instructions. In 2012, Korn et al. [9] suggested using motion and voice input for sensing and triggering events at an augmented workplace using in-situ projection. They further suggested using gamification elements in conjunction with the measured interaction to motivate workers during their work tasks. Zhou et al. [21] use in-situ projection for displaying welding spots in manual welding tasks for quality control and during a welding task. They are use a stationary projector to display the feedback to the worker. On the other hand, Echtler et al. [4] suggest a hand-held approach for displaying welding spots. Considering head-mounted displays, Zheng et al. [20] compared the position of feedback that is shown on a head-mounted display during an assembly task with non-impaired workers. They conclude that the worker's task was performed faster with a display that directly overlays reality than a peripheral display.

Pictorial instructions are used to teach persons with impairments in various situations [12]. A positive effect of pictorial instructions is that they are language independent and can be easily understood. In a study with 81 impaired workers, Korn et al. [10] compared in-situ pictorial instructions to "state of the art instructions" for assembling Lego cars. They found that pictorial in-situ instructions lead to a faster assembly, but workers were making more errors compared to the control condition. Recently, Funk et al. [6] found that contour-based in-situ instructions lead to a lower task completion time and less errors compared to in-situ video and in-situ pictorial instructions for cognitively impaired workers. In their study, they also found that more complex tasks have a negative effect on cognitively impaired workers. An overview about assistive technology for persons with cognitive disabilities is provided by Sauer et al. [17]. They conclude that through continuously offering instructions, cognitively impaired workers can work on more complex products.

Overall, previous work explored how to use IAR for workplaces and found that in-situ projected instructions are having a positive effect on cognitively impaired workers. However, it is not quantitatively explored yet to which extend in-situ projected instructions are better than state-of-the-art pictorial instructions. Therefore, we designed a system which is able to provide context sensitive in-situ instructions and is easily able to change workflows.

SYSTEM

We built an assistive system for the workplace that consists of a top-mounted Kinect depth camera for sensing interaction with the system and a top-mounted projector to provide in-situ feedback according to the working steps. The system consists of a Microsoft Kinect_v2 and an Acer K330 projector. We used a tower PC with a GeForce GT740 graphics card and an i7 quad-core processor. We firmly mounted the Kinect and the projector using aluminum profiles just as they are used in the industry. The projector and the Kinect are mounted 1.4m above the working area (see Figure 4 A)). Behind the working area there are boxes containing the spare parts (see Figure 4 B)). Further, we firmly mounted a Lego Duplo plate at the table, which defines the working area (see Figure 4 C)).

Using the Kinect-depth image, the system is able to detect two types of working steps. In the first step, the system can detect which box the worker is picking a part from (see Figure 3). The system accomplishes this by continuously checking the depth data within the previously defined areas that are placed over the boxes. The covered area is in the front of the box and is 50mm high. By considering the height of the boxes, the system can distinguish between boxes that are placed above each other. Picking up an assembly part from the box is detected when 40% of the depth data within the surveyed area changes. In the second step, the system is able to detect the correct assembly of the of the picked part when placed in the working area based on depth data. When creating the work instructions, the system saves the depth data of the correctly assembled part. The system is then able to detect correct assembly by comparing the depth data in the predefined working area to the previously stored data of a correct assembly. To eliminate

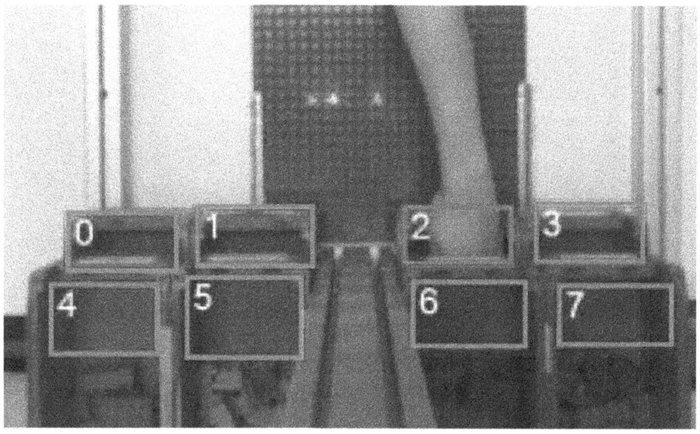

Figure 3. The pick detection of the boxes can be defined according to the workplace using the image of the top-mounted Kinect. The system can detect from which box the participant is picking a Duplo brick. Green indicates that a pick was detected, red indicates that no pick was detected.

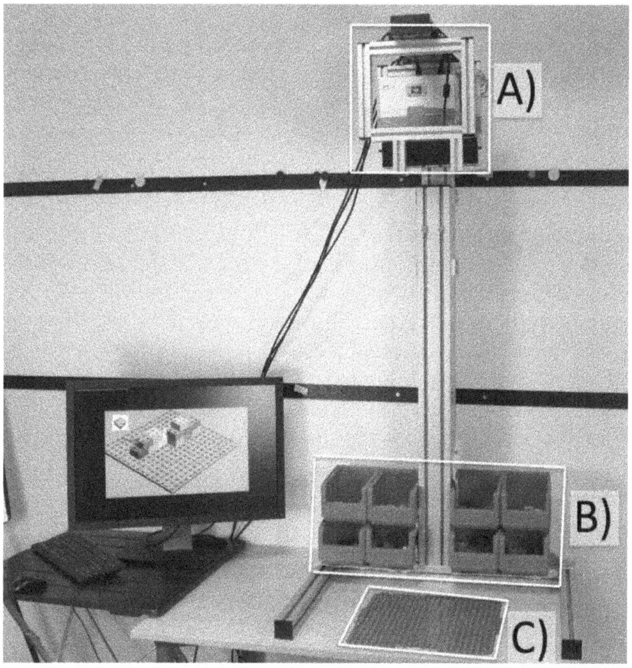

Figure 4. Our prototypical system for an assitive system providing visual in-situ instructions at the workplace. A) the top-mounted Kinect and the projector B) the boxes containing the spare parts C) the working area which is checked for correct assembly

Figure 6. The system shows the worker from which box the next part has to be picked using a green light.

sensor noise, we smooth the depth image over 15 frames and calculate a mean depth value. We defined a part to be correctly assembled when 85% of the pixels in the smoothed image match the depth data of the correct state.

For indicating which box to pick parts from, the system highlights the correct box using a green light (see Figure 6). Informed by previous research [6, 7], we designed the instructions to display the contour of the parts at the position they should be placed using a green light (see Figure 1). The system advances to the next instruction when the working step was correctly preformed (i.e. when placing the hand into a box or when assembling the previously picked part correctly). Thereby, the system implements continuous context-aware feedback according to the current working step and provides an implicit quality control based on the depth data of the assembly.

Considering setting up the system, we implemented a four point calibration to unify the depth image and the projector similar to Hardy et al. [8]. Using this approach, calibration can be done in a few seconds. For teaching a workflow, the system implements a teaching by example functionality where the correct assembly of each work step has to be demonstrated once. After a work step was performed, the user has to press a button which triggers the system to save the depth data of the correctly assembled work-piece. Based on the depth-data, it can detect where the work-piece has changed and automatically calculate the shape and position of the feedback that is projected at the assembly position. Using this functionality, the time it takes to setup a workflow is approximately three times as much as just assembling the work-piece.

EVALUATION

We conducted a user study to assess the effects of in-situ instructions provided by our assistive system and compared it to state-of-the-art pictorial instructions at a workplace with impaired workers. Informed by previous work [19, 16], we chose a Lego Duplo task as an abstract assembly task that can be easily scaled up to use more working steps without introducing a different product. Furthermore, such a pick-and-place task is a good abstraction of tasks that are usually performed in sheltered work organizations, as those tasks also require picking parts and placing them at defined assembly positions. However, using a tool on the placed assembly parts is not included in this abstract assembly task.

Method

For evaluating the system, we considered a repeated measures design with two independent variables; The used instruction, and the number of bricks in the assembled construction. We measured the task completion time (TCT) and the error rate (ER) as dependent variables. To normalize the data, we divided the TCT and the ER by the number of bricks that the construction consists of to get the time per brick (TPB) and the errors per brick (EPB).

Apparatus

We considered 5 different difficulty levels with constructions consisting of a different number of bricks (see Figure 5): 3, 6, 12, 24, and 48 bricks. As placing one brick results in two working steps, i.e. picking the brick and placing it at the correct position, the levels result in 6, 12, 24, 48, and 96 working steps. The Lego Duplo constructions in their final state are depicted in Figure 5 (a)-(e).

For the in-situ instruction condition, we used the previously described system, which highlights the box to pick from and displays the contour of the picked brick at the correct assembly position. As the assembly detection requires the participant to remove his or her hand from the assembled brick, the researcher was able to advance the feedback manually using a wireless presenter in case the participant is occluding the assembled part by leaving the hand above the assembled brick.

As a state-of-the-art control condition, we used pictorial instructions to show the next part and assembly position to the worker. We used a 28" screen next to the assembly area see Figure 4. The pictorial instructions provide three main types of information. First, the type of brick to pick, depicted by a icon in the upper left corner (also see Figures 5 (a)-(e)). Second, a picture showing the work-piece in the correct state after the current brick was assembled at the correct position. Third, a red arrow directly highlighting the position of the last placed brick. This type of information enables the participant to see the placement position of the current brick immediately. This is useful because finding the correct position of the brick could be cumbersome, especially with an increasing number of bricks. The instructions were created using the Lego Digital Designer[3]. The pictorial instructions were proceeded by the researcher using a wireless controller after the participant placed the brick at a position. This enabled the participant to fully focus on the assembly task.

Procedure

After explaining the purpose of the study, we asked the participant to sit down in front of the work station. Depending on the condition to be conducted, we either explained how a pictorial instruction is understood or how the in-situ projection shows the part to pick and where to assemble it. We

[3]Lego Digital Designer - **http://ldd.lego.com/en-us** (last access 05-07-2015)

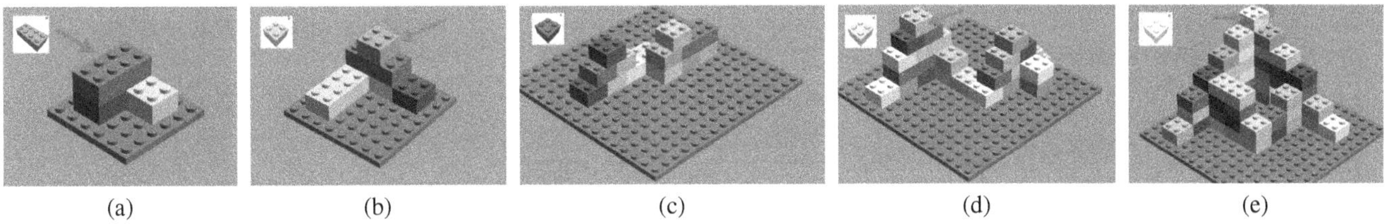

Figure 5. The constructions used in the study. We considered five different complexity levels: (a) 3 bricks, (b) 6 bricks, (c) 12 bricks, (d) 24 bricks, and (e) 48 bricks. The images depict the final step of the pictorial instructions.

instructed the participants to primarily focus on assembling the constructions correctly and only secondarily focus on the assembly time. During the experiment, the TCT was taken and the number of errors was counted independently by two researchers. The researchers started the measuring of the TCT upon showing the first instruction and stopped the measuring when the construction was finished. In case of inconsistency between the two counted error numbers, the assembled building was analyzed for errors. The researchers distinguished between picking errors and placement errors. A picking error is counted when the participant was picking a brick from a wrong box, and a placement error is counted when a brick is placed at a wrong position in the assembly area considering the relative position to the other bricks. In case a placement error effected the possibility to finish the construction correctly and not to influence further working steps, the researchers paused the experiment and the measuring of the TCT to get the assembly back into a correct state. In the pictorial instruction condition, the absolute position on the plate was not checked for correctness. The researchers instructed the participants to begin with the first brick in the middle of the plate and not determine the exact position of the brick on the plate in the pictorial instruction. This procedure was repeated for all 5 constructions for both the pictorial and in-situ conditions respectively. After each condition, subjective feedback from the participant was collected by asking for their opinion about the feedback of the respective conditions. The order of the constructions and the conditions were counterbalanced according to the Balanced Latin Square over the 15 participants. We ensured that each Performance Index group had the same 5 orders of the constructions.

Participants

Our partnering sheltered work organization uses a Performance Index to assess the performance of their workers and to be able to assign them to tasks that they are capable of conducting. The Performance Index (PI) is measured in percentages and indicates to what extent an impaired worker is capable of performing a task compared to a worker without disabilities. The PI is determined subjectively by the supervisor of the impaired worker who works with the impaired worker every day. We considered three PI groups: PI of $5\% - 10\%$, PI of $15\% - 35\%$, and a PI over 40%. We chose the participants for the study in a way that 5 participants belonging to each PI group took part in the study, which results in a total number of 15 participants.

Accordingly, we recruited 15 participants (4 female, 11 male) for the study. The participants were aged from 20 to 55 years ($M = 40.1$, $SD = 10.33$). All participants were employees of a sheltered work organization and were workers with a cognitive disability. None of the participants were familiar with the Duplo constructions that were assembled in the study. However, all participants had experiences playing with Duplo bricks before. For each participant, the study took approximately 60 minutes.

Results

We statistically compared the TPB and the EPB between the in-situ instructions and the pictorial instructions using a one-way repeated measures ANOVA. The assumption of homogeneity of variance had not been violated ($p > .05$) for the TPB and the EPB.

Considering the TPB for the task consisting of 3 bricks, the in-situ instructions were faster ($M = 6.74$ sec, $SD = 1.72$ sec) than the pictorial instructions ($M = 9.98$ sec, $SD = 3.26$ sec). The analysis revealed a significant difference between the instructions ($F(1, 14) = 18.088, p < .001$). The effect size estimate shows a large effect ($\eta^2 = .564$). For the task consisting of 6 bricks, the in-situ instructions were faster ($M = 7.18$ sec, $SD = 2.95$ sec) than the pictorial instructions ($M = 9.49$ sec, $SD = 4.41$ sec). The ANOVA revealed a significant difference between the instructions ($F(1, 14) = 5.698$, $p = .032$). The effect size estimate shows a large effect ($\eta^2 = .289$). When analyzing the 12-brick task, again the in-situ instructions were faster ($M = 7.20$ sec, $SD = 2.93$ sec) than the pictorial instructions ($M = 11.61$ sec, $SD = 5.01$ sec). The statistical comparison revealed a significant difference between the instructions ($F(1, 14) = 22.567$, $p < .001$). The effect size estimate shows a large effect ($\eta^2 = .617$). For the task consisting of 24 bricks, the in-situ instructions were faster ($M = 8.03$ sec, $SD = 3.09$ sec) than the pictorial instructions ($M = 11.53$ sec, $SD = 5.05$ sec). The ANOVA revealed a significant difference between the instructions ($F(1, 14) = 12.981, p = .003$). The effect size estimate shows a large effect ($\eta^2 = .481$). Finally, when analyzing the task consisting of 48 bricks, the in-situ projected instructions were faster ($M = 7.40$ sec, $SD = 2.00$ sec) than the pictorial instructions ($M = 14.21$ sec, $SD = 5.04$ sec). The ANOVA revealed a significant difference between the instructions ($F(1, 14) = 50.027, p < .001$). The effect size estimate shows a large effect ($\eta^2 = .781$). Figure 7 shows an overview of the results.

Considering the EPB for the task consisting of 3 bricks, the in-situ instructions were leading to less errors ($M = 0.02$, $SD = 0.08$) than the pictorial instructions ($M = .08$, $SD = .23$).

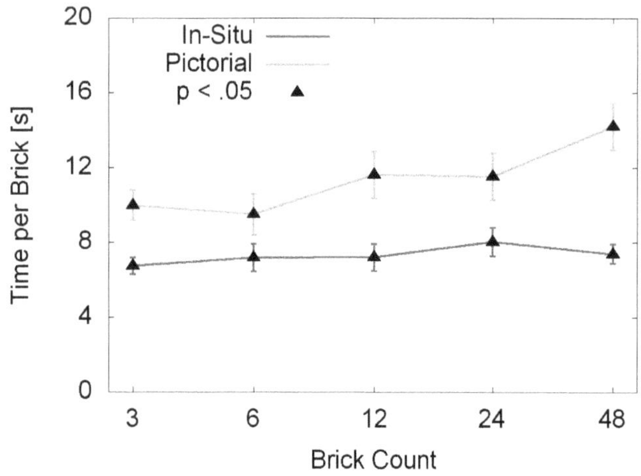

Figure 7. Overview showing the time needed to pick and assemble a brick dependent on the complexity of the product to assemble. Error bars depict the standard error. A triangle indicates a significant difference between the conditions.

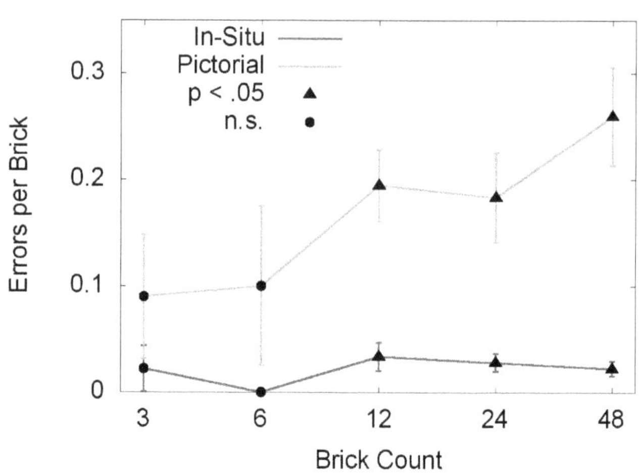

Figure 8. Overview showing the errors made dependent on the complexity of the product to assemble. Error bars depict the standard error. A triangle indicates a significant difference between the conditions.

The analysis did not reveal a significant difference between the instructions ($F(1, 14) = 1.014$, $p = n.s.$). For the task consisting of 6 bricks, the in-situ instructions did not lead to any error. The pictorial instructions lead to a few errors ($M = 0.10$, $SD = 0.30$). The ANOVA did not reveal a significant difference between the instructions ($F(1, 14) = 1.669$, $p = n.s.$). When statistically analyzing the EPB of the 12-brick task, the in-situ instructions ($M = 0.03$, $SD = 0.05$) lead to less errors than the pictorial instructions ($M = 0.19$, $SD = 0.13$). The statistical comparison revealed a significant difference between the instructions ($F(1, 14) = 27.605$, $p < .001$). The effect size estimate shows a large effect ($\eta^2 = .664$). For the task consisting of 24 bricks, the EPB of the in-situ instructions were lower ($M = .02$, $SD = .03$) than the EPB of the pictorial instructions ($M = 0.18$ sec, $SD = .16$). The ANOVA revealed a significant difference between the instructions ($F(1, 14) = 15.321$, $p = .002$). The effect size estimate shows a large effect ($\eta^2 = .523$). Finally, when analyzing the task consisting of 48 bricks, the projected instructions lead to less errors ($M = .02$, $SD = .02$) than the pictorial instructions ($M = .26$ sec, $SD = .18$ sec). The ANOVA revealed a significant difference between the instructions ($F(1, 14) = 30.455$, $p < .001$). The effect size estimate shows a large effect ($\eta^2 = .685$). Figure 8 shows a graphical representation of the results.

We further analyzed the effect of number of working steps on TPB and EPB for both pictorial and in-situ instructions using a repeated measures ANOVA. Mauchly's test showed that the sphericity assumption was not violated for TPB and EPB.

Regarding the pictorial instructions, the analysis revealed a significant difference in TPB between the different step sizes ($F(4, 56) = 7.144$, $p < .001$). Pairwise comparisons revealed that the difference in TPB between the 48 brick and 12 brick task, 48 brick and 6 brick task, and 48 brick and 3 brick task are significantly different (all $p < .05$). Considering the EPB, between the different step sizes using pictorial instructions, the analysis did not reveal a significant difference ($F(4, 56) = 2.291$, $p = n.s.$). Considering the in-situ instructions, the analysis did not reveal a significant difference in TPB between the different step sizes ($F(4, 56) = 1.264$, $p = n.s.$). Also for the EPB, the ANOVA could not show a significant difference between the step sizes ($F(4, 56) = 1.012$, $p = n.s.$).

During the study, the participants commented on the different types of instructions. Regarding the in-situ instruction, participants liked that *"the system is showing the next box"* (P7, P11) and that *"[it] exactly shows where to put the next brick"* (P3, P7, P14). A participant referred to the system as *"magic light that helps performing the task"* (P2). Considering the pictorial instructions, the participants liked that *"the instructions are shown on a computer rather than on a printout"* (P7). However, a participant stated that he was *"having problems to find the correct positions as other bricks in the image are confusing"* (P6).

The supervisors of the sheltered work organization reported that in the days after the study, the participants were asking them if they can work at the *"workplace with the lights again"* and that it was fun for them and they enjoyed working with our system. They even asked when they will be able to perform their regular tasks with the help of *"the lights."*

DISCUSSION

The results of the user study suggest that in-situ instructions have several advantages over the state-of-the-art pictorial instructions. First, the time per brick is up to 1.6 times lower using the in-situ instructions. The difference between the in-situ and pictorial instructions is statistically significant for all used complexity levels that were used in the study. Second, the errors per brick is up to 3 times lower using the in-situ instructions compared to pictorial instructions. This difference is statistically significant for the constructions consisting of 12, 24, and 48 bricks. When considering the TPB and EPB, the values across the different complexity levels are rather constant for the in-situ instructions. For the pictorial instructions, the difference between the complexity levels regarding the TPB is even significantly different. The qualitative feedback also indicates that the participants preferred the in-situ instructions over the pictorial instructions as the in-situ instructions were always showing the position. Considering the pictorial instructions, the participants found that with increasing complexity it becomes harder to find the correct assembly position albeit there was a red arrow indicating the position. We believe that this is because a more complex structure requires more cognitive processing and that the assembly position is only highlighted in the instruction and not in the assembly position itself.

Implications

The aforementioned user study revealed two implications considering the design of assembly tasks for cognitively impaired workers in sheltered work organizations. First, in-situ projected instructions should be used to instruct workers rather than pictorial instructions. When using in-situ instructions instead of pictorial instructions, impaired workers could assemble faster and with fewer errors. Second, impaired workers could be used to assemble more complex products with a steady error rate and a steady assembly time, even with increasing complexity of the working task. This could further integrate impaired workers into the working life and could lead to a higher satisfaction.

Limitations

It should be mentioned that the proposed system has certain limitations. Some of the impaired workers in the user study were leaving their hand in the working area covering the previously assembled brick which caused the system not to trigger automatically. Therefore we were using a wireless presenter to advance the feedback manually in case the workers occluded the assembled part and retained covering the bricks. We also discovered that the Kinect_v2 sensor needs to run warm first before it can accurately detect correct assembly. When teaching the reference values with a Kinect that was recently started, the data became invalid after 20 minutes. Our observations suggest starting the Kinect 45 minutes before using it for assembly detection.

Public Exhibition

To show our assistive system to a broader audience, we exhibited our system at the trade fair for vocational rehabilitation and exhibition of workshops for persons with disabilities[4] in Nürnberg, Germany. During the four days of the fair, over 400 impaired persons were able to try our assistance system. We mounted our prototype on a height-adjustable table, to enable persons using a wheelchair to use our system, too. As a demo scenario, we considered assembling a Lego Duplo wall consisting of 9 different bricks resulting in 18 working steps. We received a positive feedback throughout the demo from both impaired persons trying our system as well as supervisors working for sheltered work organizations. Visitors stated that the system was *"easy to learn and use"*. Another visitor liked that he *"just needs to focus on one thing to have a positive achievement."*

[4] `https://www.werkstaettenmesse.de` (last access 05-07-2015)

CONCLUSION

In this paper, we presented the implementation and design of an assistive system for the manual workplace that provides in-situ instructions for performing assembly tasks. Through a user study with 15 cognitively impaired workers, we found that in-situ instructions lead to faster assembly times and to less errors compared to state-of-the-art pictorial instructions. This effect is statistically significant for tasks consisting of 3, 6, 12, 24 and 48 assembled parts when considering the assembly time and for tasks consisting of 12, 24, and 48 assembled parts when considering the number of errors. These results might have a great impact on how tasks are divided into workplaces at sheltered work organizations. Especially as using an assistive system with in-situ projection could empower cognitively impaired workers to work on more complex tasks and thereby fostering inclusion. We believe that systems similar to the proposed prototype will become very relevant in sheltered work organizations soon, as cost, availability, and quality of the used components will improve.

In future research, we want to explore the effects of an assistive system offering in-situ instructions to cognitively impaired workers in a long-term study with a runtime of several months. We are particularly interested if the positive effects of in-situ instructions can be retained over a longer period of time or if the measured effect decreases over time. Further we want to assess potential effects on the cognitive load of the workers and explore potential effects on other areas of the worker's life, for example assisted living.

ACKNOWLEDGMENTS

This work is funded by the German Federal Ministry for Economic Affairs and Energy in the project motionEAP, grant no. 01MT12021E. We thank the Gemeinnützige Werkstätten und Wohnstätten GmbH for supporting us. We especially would like to thank Frank Raschhofer for perfectly organizing the study. Further, we thank Thomas Kosch and Michael Matheis for helping with the implementation and Chloe Eghtebas for proof reading our paper.

REFERENCES

1. United nations: United nations convention on the rights of persons with disabilities. `http://www.un.org/disabilities/convention/conventionfull.shtml`, 2008. [Online; accessed 02-May-2015].
2. Bannat, A., Wallhoff, F., Rigoll, G., Friesdorf, F., Bubb, H., Stork, S., Müller, H., Schubö, A., Wiesbeck, M., and Zäh, M. Towards optimal worker assistance: a framework for adaptive selection and presentation of assembly instructions. In *Proceedings of the 1st international workshop on cognition for technical systems, Cotesys* (2008).
3. Caudell, T. P., and Mizell, D. W. Augmented reality: An application of heads-up display technology to manual manufacturing processes. In *System Sciences, 1992. Proceedings of the Twenty-Fifth Hawaii International Conference on*, vol. 2, IEEE (1992), 659–669.

4. Echtler, F., Sturm, F., Kindermann, K., Klinker, G., Stilla, J., Trilk, J., and Najafi, H. The intelligent welding gun: Augmented reality for experimental vehicle construction. In *Virtual and augmented reality applications in manufacturing*. Springer, 2004, 333–360.
5. Fite-Georgel, P. Is there a reality in industrial augmented reality? In *Mixed and Augmented Reality (ISMAR), 2011 10th IEEE International Symposium on*, IEEE (2011), 201–210.
6. Funk, M., Bächler, A., Bächler, L., Korn, O., Krieger, C., Heidenreich, T., and Schmidt, A. Comparing projected in-situ feedback at the manual assembly workplace with impaired workers. In *Proceedings of the 8th International Conference on PErvasive Technologies Related to Assistive Environments*, ACM (2015).
7. Funk, M., and Schmidt, A. Cognitive assistance in the workplace. *Pervasive Computing, IEEE 14*, 3 (2015), 53–55.
8. Hardy, J., and Alexander, J. Toolkit support for interactive projected displays. In *Proceedings of the 11th International Conference on Mobile and Ubiquitous Multimedia*, ACM (2012), 42.
9. Korn, O., Schmidt, A., and Hörz, T. Assistive systems in production environments: exploring motion recognition and gamification. In *Proceedings of the 5th International Conference on PErvasive Technologies Related to Assistive Environments*, ACM (2012).
10. Korn, O., Schmidt, A., and Hörz, T. The potentials of in-situ-projection for augmented workplaces in production: a study with impaired persons. In *CHI'13 Extended Abstracts on Human Factors in Computing Systems*, ACM (2013), 979–984.
11. Navab, N. Developing killer apps for industrial augmented reality. *Computer Graphics and Applications, IEEE 24*, 3 (2004), 16–20.
12. Pierce, K. L., and Schreibman, L. Teaching daily living skills to children with autism in unsupervised settings through pictorial self-management. *Journal of applied behavior analysis 27*, 3 (1994), 471–481.
13. Pinhanez, C. The everywhere displays projector: A device to create ubiquitous graphical interfaces. In *Ubicomp 2001: Ubiquitous Computing*, Springer (2001), 315–331.
14. Raskar, R., Welch, G., and Fuchs, H. Spatially augmented reality. In *First IEEE Workshop on Augmented Reality (IWAR'98)*, Citeseer (1998), 11–20.
15. Rüther, S., Hermann, T., Mracek, M., Kopp, S., and Steil, J. An assistance system for guiding workers in central sterilization supply departments. In *Proceedings of the 6th International Conference on PErvasive Technologies Related to Assistive Environments*, ACM (2013), 3.
16. Sakata, N., Kurata, T., and Kuzuoka, H. Visual assist with a laser pointer and wearable display for remote collaboration. In *Proceedings of 2nd international conference on Collaboration Technologies* (2006).
17. Sauer, A. L., Parks, A., and Heyn, P. C. Assistive technology effects on the employment outcomes for people with cognitive disabilities: a systematic review. *Disability & Rehabilitation: Assistive Technology 5*, 6 (2010), 377–391.
18. Sutherland, I. E. A head-mounted three dimensional display. In *Proceedings of the December 9-11, 1968, fall joint computer conference, part I*, ACM (1968), 757–764.
19. Tang, A., Owen, C., Biocca, F., and Mou, W. Comparative effectiveness of augmented reality in object assembly. In *Proceedings of the SIGCHI conference on Human factors in computing systems*, ACM (2003), 73–80.
20. Zheng, X. S., Foucault, C., Matos da Silva, P., Dasari, S., Yang, T., and Goose, S. Eye-wearable technology for machine maintenance: Effects of display position and hands-free operation. In *Proceedings of the 33rd Annual ACM Conference on Human Factors in Computing Systems*, ACM (2015), 2125–2134.
21. Zhou, J., Lee, I., Thomas, B., Menassa, R., Farrant, A., and Sansome, A. Applying spatial augmented reality to facilitate in-situ support for automotive spot welding inspection. In *Proceedings of the 10th International Conference on Virtual Reality Continuum and Its Applications in Industry*, ACM (2011), 195–200.

"But, I don't take steps": Examining the Inaccessibility of Fitness Trackers for Wheelchair Athletes

Patrick Carrington, Kevin Chang, Helena Mentis, Amy Hurst
Department of Information Systems
University of Maryland, Baltimore County
Baltimore MD, 21250 USA
{carpat1, kevicha1, mentis, amyhurst}@umbc.edu

ABSTRACT

Wearable fitness devices have demonstrated the capacity to improve overall physical activity, which can lead to physical and mental health improvements as well as quality of life gains. Although wheelchair athletes who participate in adaptive sports are interested in using wearable fitness trackers to capture their activity, we have observed low adoption of wearable fitness trackers among wheelchair athletes. We interviewed five wheelchair athletes and three physical and occupational therapists to explore fitness activities, experience with wearable technology, and potential uses for wearable fitness devices. None of the wheelchair athletes we interviewed had previously used any wearable fitness devices, however four out of five were interested in tracking their physical activity. We present five thematic areas helpful for thinking about wearable computing systems and accessibility challenges that arise based on incorrect assumptions about the athletic community. We highlight opportunities for improving the impact and accessibility of fitness tracking technologies for wheelchair athletes. These opportunities include improving the analysis of data from existing sensors, instrumenting the custom equipment used by adaptive sport athletes, and revising the language used in the presentation of fitness data to create a more inclusive community of users.

Categories and Subject Descriptors

K.4.2 [**Social Issues**]: Assistive technologies for persons with disabilities

General Terms

Design, Human Factors

Keywords

Wheelchair Athletes, Wearable, Fitness, Adaptive Sports

1. INTRODUCTION

Smart watches, low-cost accelerometer-based movement trackers, and mobile phone applications are becoming increasingly popular in consumer markets to monitor and prescribe an individual's level of physical activity. The goal of these devices is to support the user in achieving their physical activity or fitness goals by allowing passive and active tracking of their activities. A large proportion of the wearable devices currently available are dedicated to fitness applications using on-body sensing, such as the Fitbit Charge band and Polar Heart Rate strap. The heart rate strap measures electrical activity generated when the heart beats. The Fitbit uses an accelerometer to capture motion data and calculate the number of steps a user takes. Those wearable devices that track fitness information have been shown to improve participation in physical activities [3][9]. Given the importance of physical activity for healthy living [25], wearable fitness trackers can assist users in achieving health related goals. Therefore, we could consider a wearable fitness tracker as an assistive technology.

Even though wearable devices offer many exciting opportunities and applications, they have not been widely adopted. According to Patel et al.[17], only 1% to 2% of individuals in the United States have used a wearable device, despite a projected $50 billion increase in sales by 2018. Patel argues that a significant challenge to widespread adoption is that wearable devices are not appealing to the groups of people who could benefit most from their use [17]. Recently, the Baltimore Business Journal published an article discussing a major fitness organization's own shareholders' concerns of its inability to appeal to the older adult demographic due to certain design choices of their fitness apparel [15]. This critique comes at a time when this same organization has endeavored to enter into the fitness apps marketplace with recent acquisitions of $555 million. This demonstrates the importance of understanding the needs of diverse user populations and the timeliness of our research in this area.

Wheelchair athletes are one group of users who could greatly benefit from wearable fitness trackers, yet are unable to use the devices as they are intended. Participation in regular physical activity and adaptive sports has been shown to improve quality of life outcomes for people with spinal cord injury and others who use wheelchairs [22] [24]. Many of those injured turn to organized fitness groups or teams such as adaptive sports. Adaptive sports include multiple sports that have been modified or specially created to accommodate people with a broader range of abilities. Although a fitness tracker would serve as an important motivator and assist a wheelchair athlete in achieving one's health related goals, these technologies have not been designed with this user group in mind. What happens to a step counter when the user does not take steps?

This paper investigates the inaccessibility of fitness trackers for wheelchair users who participate in adaptive sports. We suspect that several accessibility challenges, associated with the design of wearable systems for fitness, contribute to our observed low adoption of wearable devices among adaptive sport athletes. We

ASSETS '15, October 26 - 28, 2015, Lisbon, Portugal

ACM 978-1-4503-3400-6/15/10…$15.00
DOI: http://dx.doi.org/10.1145/2700648.2809845

also believe that understanding the needs and preferences of this active population will inform the design of wearable fitness devices for individuals with limited physical ability who would like to be more physically active. First, we examine the accessibility challenges disrupting adoption of wearable technology by adaptive sport athletes. Then, we identify five thematic areas to describe challenges associated with wearable systems: 1) Aesthetics, 2) Sensing Hardware, 3) Analysis, 4) Fit and 5) Feedback. Finally, we offer suggestions to address prominent accessibility challenges including improved analysis algorithms, instrumenting the wheelchair, and developing a more inclusive vocabulary for presenting fitness data to users.

2. WEARABLE SENSING AND FITNESS

Wearable computing refers to interactive technology that can be worn on the body. Wearable systems have been created for many applications gaming, fitness, entertainment, and productivity. In the following sections, we describe existing wearable devices that use on-body sensing, wearable fitness technology, and related applications of fitness data.

2.1 On-Body Sensing and Input

There is significant past work in developing and evaluating wearable computing systems that use sensors to detect a variety of motions and interactions. For example, Brewster et al. [4] used sound and gestures to interact with a belt-worn computer. They used both head and hand gestures to interact with the system. ShoeSense [2] captures hand gestures using a depth camera on the user's shoe. Ashbrook et al. [1] demonstrated the importance of the location of wearable devices by showing that it takes less time to access a wearable device on the wrist compared to one attached to the hip or in a pocket.

Other wearable systems utilize direct on-body sensing. For example, Saponas et al. [20] used EMG to capture muscle activity related to different grip styles. Harrison et al. designed Skinput [11], a technology that allows the user's skin to be used as an interaction surface via finger taps. Tongue interfaces [21] use sensors placed in the mouth to detect input and to enable interactions with computing devices. The LilyPad Arduino can be sewn into clothing and other soft accessories to create wearable sensors and interactive objects [5]. These examples show how on-body sensing can be used to improve interactive capabilities by capturing motion in different ways.

2.2 Wearable Fitness Technology

There is a wide range of wearable devices that are being used to track fitness. One of the most common examples is a wearable pedometer. Pedometers are used to record a step count and have been used to improve participation in physical activities [3][9]. Wearable fitness devices often capture this information and more. Many of the commercially available wearable fitness devices such as the Fitbit Flex[1] and Nike+ Fuelband[2], are able to track information such as step count, calorie expenditure, and overall physical activity by tracking motion.

These devices are well suited to activities such as running and walking. However, other types of exercises have been tracked using wearable systems. The Recofit system, created by Morris et al [16], uses an armband capture the repetitive motions inherent to strength training. This makes it possible to count repetitions when lifting weights or doing stretches.

[1] http://www.fitbit.com/flex

[2] https://secure-nikeplus.nike.com/plus/products/fuelband/

Figure 1. This figure highlights the accessibility challenges in three wearable fitness trackers currently on the market. The Fitbit charge (left) is used as a step counter, which is not a useful measurement for wheelchair users who don't walk. The clasp used on the Nike+ GPS Watch (right) can be difficult for users with limited hand dexterity to use independently.

Fitbit Photo by Global Panorama (CC BY-SA 2.0) - https://flic.kr/p/pAJdJd

Nike+ GPS Watch Photo by slgckgc (CC BY 2.0) - https://flic.kr/p/a8bBWL

Many types of fitness-related information can be captured either using a single device or through multiple devices. The Microsoft Band[3] is able to measure many details such as distance, calories burned, motion activity, sleep activity, heart rate, steps taken, and skin temperature from a single device. In contrast, people also may use multiple devices to track these features. In Section 3, we examine current trends in wearable fitness technology to show the landscape of available sensing and applications.

2.3 Reflecting on Fitness with Quantified Self

Inherent to self-tracking, there is also the need to view or report the data that is being collected. Reports of this data can be used for multiple purposes including understanding one's habits and influencing behavior change. The Quantified Self (QS) describes the technology movement focused around using tracked physical activity and data about one's habits to enhance an understanding of one's own habits. The notion is that, through reflection on this data, a person can improve their habits and health. [17]

Participation in self-tracking and monitoring activities can have several motivations. Some of the most common reasons for self-tracking and monitoring are for behavior change, curiosity, and self-discovery. MacLeod et al. [13] discussed motivations and opportunities for personal informatics to be used by people with chronic illnesses. They described potential disparities between the presumed motivation of behavior change and the actual motivation of users to self-track. In this instance, an understanding and control over their health data motivated users to use self-tracking devices. People wanted to understand the

[3] http://www.microsoft.com/microsoft-band/

effectiveness of their treatments. Whooley et al. [26] described the integration of multiple data sources to identify correlations between actions such as sleep and cognitive performance. This reflective reintegration of information from multiple sources enables the data to be used in many ways. Rooksby et al. [19] illustrate this point by describing how people use tracking data from different sources. They stress that people interweave multiple data streams and that a single tracker may not give a full representation of a person's activity. Another important point to note is that the process of tracking is not only just to measure activity, but there are also emotional [6] and social implications [12] for measuring physical activity. Reviewing and sharing data with others can create new connections and provide a platform for sharing experiences [19].

3. EXAMINING CURRENT TRENDS IN WEARABLE FITNESS DEVICES

Wearable fitness devices are often described as the dominant and most successful type of wearable computing technology[4]. We examined the landscape of currently available consumer wearable fitness-tracking technology to assess the assumptions these make about their user's ability and identify the resulting accessibility challenges. Specifically, we analyzed the Vandrico Database[5], which was created to support organizations with interests in the wearable technology marketplace. This database contains 298 wearable devices separated into seven categories: entertainment, fitness, gaming, industrial, lifestyle, medical, and pets. Of these devices, they classified 131 as fitness devices. Vandrico defines fitness applications as "providing sports-related and/or non-medical health-related benefits to the user." From this point in the paper, we will reference this definition when discussing fitness applications for wearable technologies. We describe below the landscape of wearable devices with regard to the types and interactive features of devices. Our snapshot was derived from an analysis of the 131 fitness devices included in the Vandrico Wearable database in April 2015. A summary of our analysis is shown in Table 1.

3.1 Body Location and Form Factors

We found that the most common location for wearable fitness devices was the wrist area, with a total count of 73 (55% of devices) wrist-based devices. Generally, these devices took the form of bands or straps that wrap around a user's wrist like a watch. While many of the wrist-based wearable fitness devices bear a strong resemblance to conventional timepieces, some wrist-based devices were much more minimalist in design. They had more similarities to wristbands or bracelets. The second most common wearable fitness device location that we discovered was the torso area. Devices for the torso accounted for 17% of devices in the database. This area was not nearly as common as the wrist. These devices were generally characterized by a flexible sensor that was either to be attached to the user's skin or embedded within clothing.

According to the database, the least common body locations were on the ears and ankles, each with just three devices. Wearable fitness devices designed for ears took the form of ear buds and could be operated wirelessly, reducing the chance of entangling wires. Ankle-based wearable fitness devices were generally very similar to wrist-based devices in that they had bands or straps. In fact, most of them could also be wrist worn.

3.2 Sensing Technology

According to the database, the accelerometer was the most common sensor present in 56% of devices. An accelerometer records motion data in three axes. This information can then be processed to measure key fitness metrics such as number of steps taken, exercise intensity, duration of exercise activity, etc. While, accelerometers in wearable devices are most commonly used for fitness tracking, they can also potentially be used for creating gesture-based inputs for interacting with the wearable device. The second most common sensor type, at 39%, was the heart rate sensor. Representative of its namesake, the heart rate sensor measures the user's heart rate over time. This data can be aggregated to create data visualizations for the effectiveness of various fitness activities. The third most common feature was a clock, present in 35% of devices. A fitness tracking wearable that can also function as a time tracker reduces the amount of clutter in a user's life. It eliminates the need to wear a watch or carry a smartphone during fitness activities. While the clock may not technically qualify as a sensor, it does add the sense of time to other tracking data without the need for another device. Another common sensor, prevalent in many wearable devices, was the GPS sensor, at 21%. The purpose of including a GPS sensor on a wearable fitness device is to allow the user to track his/her own movements over distances during physical activity. This type of sensor is especially useful for activities where exercise is performed over a long distance, such as running or jogging.

The least common sensor types included: a camera, hygrometer, and ultraviolet light sensor, each with one occurrence in the database. While having a camera is a generally useful feature, there are many other devices that can take pictures/videos with much better results. Therefore, it is very uncommon to see a camera on wrist-based devices, with the only notable exception being the Samsung Galaxy Gear 2. The hygrometer was also a very rare feature seen on wearables. The purpose of a hygrometer is to measure moisture and humidity in the atmosphere. This functionality is potentially useful in determining the type of exercise based on the state of weather. An ultraviolet (UV) light sensor measures the amount of ultraviolet light and is particularly useful in discerning sunlight intensity and UV danger levels on sunny days.

3.3 Interface and I/O

LCD or LED displays were available on 34% of the wearable fitness devices that we looked at. Often these displays were equipped with touchscreens; however, some only had buttons as a method of interfacing. Having a display of any kind provides users with a very interactive and information-rich method of visualizing fitness metrics. The presence of a touchscreen, or even any display screen, has almost become an expectation for any device. However, having a screen versus not having one is a tradeoff between interactivity and battery life and sometimes companies choose the latter. By sacrificing the ability to display and visualize information, some companies opt for using LED indicators and clever notification methods to convey fitness information. By doing so, battery life is often extended far past the battery life of similar solutions with screens. Devices with screens were also often equipped with speakers and/or microphones. With the addition of these two features, it is possible to integrate voice commands, audio feedback and tethered phone calling. Another common interface feature on wearable fitness devices was the vibrator or buzzer. This provides

[4] http://www.juniperresearch.com/press/press-releases/fitness-devices-to-dominate-the-wearables-market-u

[5] www.vandrico.com/wearables (accessed 4/1/2015)

Table 1. Summary of Wearable Device Features. We searched the wearable database for features of sensing technology, interface options, and body locations for wearable devices. Count is the number of devices that include the feature.

Sensing Technology	Count
Accelerometer	74
Heart Rate Monitor	51
Clock	47
GPS	28
Ultraviolet Light Sensor	1
Hygrometer	1
Camera	1

Interface Technology	Count
Display	45
Button	35
Touch Interface	25
Vibrating Motor	23
Speaker	13
LED Indicator	7
Voice Interface	1

On-Body Location	Count
Wrist	73
Torso	23
Head	14
Feet	7
Arm	5
Ears	3
Ankle	3

a means of haptic feedback for the user and allows a simple and intuitive way of notifying them of updates. Vibration motors were present for 19% of devices in the database.

4. Identifying Accessibility Challenges for Wheelchair Users

Patel et al. describe an important multi-step process of selecting and using a wearable device: 1) motivation to purchase a device, 2) the user must remember to wear it, 3) the device must accurately track the target behavior, and 4) the data must be presented to the user appropriately. Throughout this paper, we discuss accessibility challenges and opportunities during different stages of this process – in particular stages one, three, and four.

Many factors, including device design, functionality, cost, and marketing, can influence a user's motivation to purchase a wearable device. There may also be social issues that factor into motivation to purchase or use a device.

A large proportion of wearable fitness devices measure physical activity as "steps". There are many issues that stem from this dominant unit of measurement for fitness wearable technology. The first being that step count is a measurement that is not inclusive to people who are not ambulatory; i.e. those who do not take steps. This leads to a misperception that the technology is not capable of measuring relevant activities and can lead to non-use.

Certain sensor types and body location combinations may not be feasible for this population (Figure 1). For instance, a movement tracker that attaches to a foot may not accurately track a wheelchair user's movements given that it was designed for someone who can walk. Another example involves the use of galvanic skin response or other measurement techniques that rely on perspiration. People with spinal cord injury may not sweat below the level of their injury [10]. This makes chemical measurement such as the sweat analysis used by the Electrozyme[6] ineffective. The information being sensed may not inherently be inaccessible however, the design of the sensors themselves create challenges for use.

5. Expert Opinions and Experiences

We collected data from interviews with wheelchair users who participate in adaptive sports and physical and occupational therapists. We also draw from our own experience with wearable technology and wheelchair users. We report on accessibility issues and potential solutions for wearable fitness technology within the domain of adaptive sports.

[6] http://www.psfk.com/2014/11/electrozyme-wearable-fitness-sweat-sensor.html

We conducted eight semi-structured interviews to gather opinions of wearable technology and identify barriers to adoption for fitness purposes. Our aim for this study was to answer the following research questions:

1) How are wearable fitness devices providing benefits for adaptive sport athletes?
2) How are current technology/design assumptions creating barriers to wearable fitness device use?
3) What is the potential for wearable technology to improve sport/activity participation?

During these interviews we discussed general fitness activities, participation in sporting events and activities, and participants' opinions and experiences using wearable technologies.

5.1 Interview Methodology

5.1.1 Participants

We interviewed five wheelchair athletes and three physical and occupational therapists. Five participants were power or manual wheelchair users who participated in adaptive sports such as cycling, basketball, and rugby. Participants were recruited through mailing lists and snowball sampling. Participant profiles are described in Tables 2 and 3. The remaining three participants were physical and occupational therapists recruited from a local spinal cord injury rehabilitation center. Physical activity is often a component of rehabilitation activities. We included therapists in our study to gain a perspective on the role and impact of wearable technology from professionals who work with many wheelchair users.

5.1.2 Procedure

The majority of the interviews were conducted over the phone. Two interviews with therapists and one wheelchair user were conducted face to face. Participants were greeted and given a brief introduction to the purpose of the interview, the format of questions, and the duration of the study. Each interview lasted approximately 30-45 minutes. The interview consisted of four discussion areas: demographics and background, fitness routines, special equipment used for fitness, and experience with wearable technology. For the background, participants were asked demographic information as well as details about the equipment required for them to participate in their chosen sports. Next, we discussed activities related to participants' general fitness and day-to-day exercise. Finally, we discussed features of wearable devices and potential uses for wearable technology to integrate into participants' general fitness and sport-related activities.

5.1.3 Analysis

We used the features of wearable devices identified during our analysis of the wearable database to derive our original three

Table 2. Participant profiles for Wheelchair users

P#	Age/ Sex	Time using Wheelchair	Sports	Time in Primary Sport
P1	40/F	6 years	HC	2+ years
P2*	28/M	24+ years	R	<1 year
P3	57/M	37 years	B, R	35 years
P4	24/M	24 years	B, T	9 years
P5	20/M	5 years	HC	3 years

HC – Hand Cycle, R – Rugby, B –Basketball, T – Tennis

*-Power Wheelchair User

Table 3. Participant profiles for therapists

P#	Sex	Focus
T1	F	Physical Therapy
T2	F	Occupational Therapy
T3	F	Physical Therapy

themes. We performed thematic analysis using the field notes [14] from the interviews to identify strengths and weaknesses across different types of devices. We combined the results of these interviews with our analysis of the wearable database to develop the additional themes that we will discuss in section 6. Three of the authors participated in this process. The remainder of this section describes the results from the interviews followed by a discussion of challenges and opportunities for wearable devices.

5.2 Fitness Routines

Generally, participants' fitness routines consisted of their normal daily activities with the addition of sport specific practices or events one to two times per week.

P1 is very active and trains for multiple marathons with her hand cycle. She is a teacher and also moves a lot with her students.

P2 uses a power wheelchair and is physically active primarily during rugby practices once a week and stretching for therapy. He said, *"The only time I am able to push around in a chair is at rugby practice...other than that I have been in physical therapy"*

P3 is involved in several sports throughout the year but participates primarily in basketball and is currently working out with a rugby team.

P4 is a university student who lives on campus so he moves around a lot to get to and from class. Also, when the weather is nice, he will go outside and do a few laps around the block. As for basketball, he plays once a week with a recreational team.

P5 works at the spinal cord injury clinic and is an avid hand cyclist who participants in many races. He trains multiple times a week.

5.3 Equipment Used for Fitness Activities

The primary equipment used by each of our participants were specialized wheelchairs for their primary sport. Two participants used hand bikes to participate in cycling. For both wheelchair basketball and rugby, there are specialized wheelchairs used for participating in the sport. These wheelchairs often have special purposes within the sport. For instance, in rugby, there are different chairs for offensive and defensive players. The wheelchair is designed to make it easier to perform the motions necessary to play the game. Thus, the effort required to move a certain way in one wheelchair might be different from another. Figure 2 shows the two main types of wheelchairs used for rugby. Figure 3 shows a basketball wheelchair and an adaptive hand bike. These different types of wheelchairs should be taken into consideration when choosing an appropriate fitness tracker since the actions will be different from sport to sport.

5.4 Experience with Wearable Technology

5.4.1 Limited Experience with Fitness Trackers

We asked participants whether they had previously owned or used a wearable fitness device. None of the wheelchair users we interviewed had experience using wearable devices. The reasons that were given as to why they had not used one were prohibitive cost, uncertainty of capabilities, misperception of capabilities, and general non-interest.

P1 has several family members who own and use Fitbit devices. She was not sure what the device would be able to track for her or whether it would be able to capture her activities accurately.

"I've always wondered if [the Fitbit] would work. My therapists they didn't think it would work. They thought it wouldn't accurately count the propulsions. I don't know...like I'm all over the high school, that's got to count!" –P1

P5 was also unsure of whether a wearable fitness device would be able to accurately track his activity. P4 stated that he had not tried a wearable device because it cost too much. He has seen people wearing Fitbit[7] devices and would like to try it out but has not had the money to buy one yet.

P2 and P3 had not tried fitness devices due to a combination of non-interest and misperception of what capabilities the devices had. P2 felt that available fitness devices would not be useful to him because they are tailored for certain activities, which he does not do. Specifically, he stated that he wasn't interested in a fitness tracker because "they track steps and [he does] not take steps". P3 was just not interested in a wearable device for himself because he "knows [his] body pretty well".

5.4.2 Interest in Tracking Physical Activity

Four of our wheelchair users were interested in tracking their personal physical activity. P1 wanted to track her activity throughout the day for self-interest and self-reflection, and compare her activity with her family and friends who owned Fitbit devices. As a teacher, she is very active everyday with her students. In addition, she goes hiking and competes in marathons with her hand-cycle. She was interested in being able to compare data from those hikes, her daily activities, and her cycling.

[7] http://www.fitbit.com

Figure 2. Rugby players may choose a chair that is specially suited to the different positions and duties they fulfill during the game. Defensive chairs (a) have an attachment on the front designed to hook other players and keep them from moving. While offensive chairs (b) are more streamlined with skirts to guard against defensive hooks. Both are shown above.
USA Bench Photo by Brian Mouridsen (CC BY-SA 2.0) - https://flic.kr/p/onp6vm

"I'm sitting, yes, but I'm constantly rolling a round…I'm always interested to know, not steps but how much I'm actually moving around." I've got three kids…I'm never sitting around…I'm never immobile so I would love to know how much I'm burning so I could…weight that against my intake." –P1

P4 was interested in tracking information such as his heart rate, breathing, and pushing. He would use the information to learn more about how he is moving and breathing while playing basketball and tennis. Then he might be able to identify areas or activities where he can improve.

P2 was interested in using a wearable fitness tracker primarily to augment the nutrition tracking he already does for his health. He currently uses MyFitnessPal[8] to track calorie intake from the different foods that he is eating. While working with a nutritionist, he discovered that he needs to think about more than just the food he is eating.

Figure 3. Specialized and often custom equipment is used by adaptive sport athletes to improve the safety and accessibility of each sport. (Left) Adaptive Hand bike (Right) Basketball Wheelchair.

DoD News Photo by EJ Hersom (CC BY 2.0) - https://flic.kr/p/u3yfq7

Photo by 2010 World Wheelchair Basketball Championship (CC BY 2.0) - https://flic.kr/p/8jgu6P

"Miles, calories burned, heart rate would be interesting. I would use it for my own personal benefit. I could pass it on to my doctors. I've been consulting with a nutritionist…even prior to rugby. Now it's getting harder and harder to lose weight. I might be gaining muscle and losing weight but we're not sure." –P2

P3 was not interested in tracking his own physical activity or using a wearable device for himself. However, he did mention potential benefits for some rugby players.

"Some of them have problems with low-blood pressure when they work out. We've had to stop games because their blood pressure dropped. Something like that [wearable] might be good for them so they don't pass out." –P3

5.4.3 Therapist Interest in Tracking

All three therapists were interested in having their patients use a wearable device in order to track their rehab activities. This could allow the therapists to track their patients' progress toward rehabilitation goals. The following quote summarizes the theme of the therapists' interest in their patients using wearable trackers:

"What would be really cool for wearable (fitness trackers) in the rehab setting would be a way to track patients' activity. At the moment, we can suggest or prescribe that the person be active or perform different exercises but we really have no way of knowing whether they did it besides their word.

It might not be feasible to get at all of the different motions or exercises but even being able to track the major things like therapy, walking, propelling, sleeping, etc. would probably be very beneficial." –T1

[8] http://www.myfitnesspal.com

Only two of our participants (P2 and P5) mentioned therapy as a routine activity. Giving therapists tracking abilities could improve physical rehabilitation outcomes by facilitating contact when athletes are not regularly seeing a therapist.

6. Challenges of Wearable System Design

We use the data from these interviews combined with our experience with wearable technology design into consideration to identify challenges and opportunities for wearable fitness devices. In the following sections, we present challenges associated with the design of wearable systems and opportunities for improving wearable fitness devices for adaptive sport athletes.

We identified five (5) dimensions to compare across devices to highlight the strengths and weaknesses of wearable fitness devices described below:

1) Aesthetics and Device Visibility (V) – The physical appearance of the device and its' visual appeal. This also includes aspects that make the device visible or recognizable from afar.
2) Sensor Hardware (S) – The sensors used in wearable devices to capture information about the user. Combinations of these sensors can be used to produce more detailed information about the user.
3) Analysis of Sensor Data (A) – The method in which raw data is converted into useful information. This refers to how sensor data is actually processed as well as how users think data is processed.
4) Fit and Ergonomics (E) – The intended location and fit on the body for the wearable device. Some systems are more flexible than others with their location. Others are restricted to a certain location either by the form factor or the sensor.
5) Presentation and Feedback (F) – The way in which sensor data is presented and how the user receives and utilizes feedback from the system regarding their activities. This can be in the form of raw numbers, relative charts or graphs, coaching feedback, etc.

With each of the 5 components there may be particular limitations or restrictions that may lead to misperceptions and uncertainty of the technologies' capabilities. The following sections describe comments associated with each of these categories.

Overall, we propose the following relationship between these 5 factors to describe the impact design choices have on the perception of a particular wearable device. A wearable device can be described using the relationship between these 5 themes (Figure 4). We believe Feedback is strongly influenced by the analysis of data, which is closely tied to the type of sensing and the ergonomics associated with each design.

6.1 Aesthetics and Device Visibility

Our participants have different preferences when it comes to the visual aspects of wearable devices. Some people prefer devices that look more high-tech, while others are more fashion oriented. Also the overall visibility, whether you can see the device at all, is an important feature. Our participants were generally indifferent regarding specific visual features for wearable fitness devices. Three of the four participants described a preference for devices that were low-profile or inconspicuous. It would be important for the devices to blend and not "stick out" too much, so that it would not get in the way or be dangerous during a game.

Our participants did not desire a particular aesthetic, however there were some general considerations that were very important.

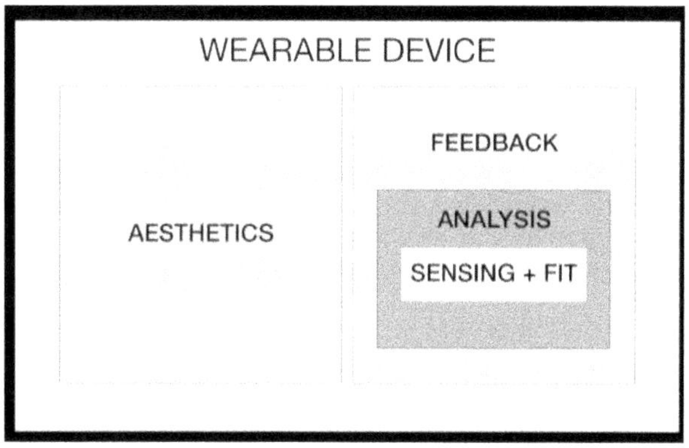

Figure 4. This diagram represents the relationship of the five thematic areas we identified that influence wearable system design choices.

The primary consideration is that the device should blend well with the person and their wheelchair. This is especially true for devices worn during competitions. P2 and P4 stated that wearing a device would be possible during practice because the rules governing accessories are not enforced as strictly.

6.2 Sensing Hardware

Based on the feedback we received about activity tracking using wearable devices, it is clear that the conceptual model employed by end-users differs from our approach as designers. The first thing to point out regarding this data is the close relationship between sensing and analysis. Especially when considering the accelerometer and gyroscope sensors, this relationship becomes apparent. Our participants were not concerned with the raw data from the sensors (position, speed, orientation) but rather they were interested in the activity-specific feedback generated post-sensing, once the data is processed. The sensing hardware seems to be appropriate to the needs of users. In the following section, we discuss sensing hardware as it pertains to the analysis required for understanding.

6.3 Analysis of Sensor Data

P1 described a desire to use a Fitbit to compare data with her family members who also use Fitbit devices. She was concerned about whether the Fitbit would be able to track her motion the same way as her family since she would be doing different activities. After further discussion, she came to the conclusion that she could create her own ratio to compare her activity with her family's data. For example, she could go for a walk with her mother or a bike ride with her daughter and compare the two-step counts knowing that they went for the same distances.

Ultimately, the analysis of the data creates an abstraction of the actual raw data, which was originally in a similar format. One person's steps compared with another person pushing a wheelchair will both yield motion data in a certain intensity and duration. In this regard, the universal unit of activity has been chosen as steps. This metaphor for motion is not appropriate when the user is not actually taking steps. While it is not clear from our participants' understanding of the devices, we posit that as activity recognition becomes more specialized and devices become better at recognizing "steps", it may become more and more challenging to give accurate credit for activities performed via other means (e.g. pushing a wheelchair). The measurement and recording of heart rate has been used as an alternative to step count for measuring physical activity, but unfortunately it is better suited for recognizing the intensity of activity rather than identifying particular actions.

6.4 Fit and Ergonomics

The most common body location for wearable devices is the wrist. This was also the most common location selected by participants as possible location for their wearable device. For P1, this was the best location because of her need to transfer between different equipment for cycling from everyday activities. For P2 and P4, the wrist was the preferred location because they felt it would be the most comfortable place to wear the device. P3 described using a headband as a possible wearable device because it would be out of the way and might give access to certain health or vital information different from a wristband. He stated that while he himself did not feel a need to track vitals, other players especially rugby players might benefit from tracking respiration, core temperature, and blood pressure while active. These were common health factors that caused stoppage during games.

The fit and ergonomics of each device can also be affected by assumptions made by the device. Certain devices are designed to be worn on a leg or ankle to track motion and steps. In this case, such a device would miss the majority of motions as they are performed using the user's upper body. Also in some situations, such as with amputees, it is physically impossible to attach the device to the intended body location. Finally, as discussed previously the device needs to fit the user well and not fall off.

6.5 Presentation and Feedback

The presentation of data is important for reflection and use of the data. If data is not presented in a meaningful way that is easy to understand then, the user might be less likely to use the device. From our interviews, we found that while participants were not currently using fitness trackers, they thought that having data presented visually with charts and graphs would be most useful to them. The majority of participants were interested in comparing data from multiple sessions and, as such, described how data could be presented for comparisons. Bar graphs were commonly described as the preferred type of chart.

7. Opportunities for Wearable Device Access

In the following section, we use identify opportunities to improve the accessibility of wearable devices to improve the benefits they can provide for adaptive sport athletes.

7.1 Update Recognition Algorithms

While existing wearable devices may not cater directly to wheelchair athletes, the abundance of available sensing-technologies and machine learning techniques should be capable of meeting the needs of this group of users. There are opportunities to improve the analysis and algorithms to accommodate users. The wrist-worn form factor would be appropriate and the combination of accelerometer and gyroscope, common to wearable fitness devices, can meet the motion tracking needs of users. The algorithms and analyses used to convert motion into activity units need to be adjusted to be more widely accessible.

The algorithms need to be trained to distinguish between everyday and sport activity. This could be achieved by collecting new training data using the existing fitness devices. It would be necessary to collect information while athletes are using the sport chairs (**Figure 2**) specifically, since the force required and type of pushing performed differs from an all-purpose wheelchair.

7.2 Instrument the Wheelchair

Related work has shown that it is possible to capture accurate motion information and sport specific metrics using a wheelchair mounted data logger [18]. Wearable fitness devices are essentially personal data loggers for consumers. Most adaptive sports use specialized equipment or wheelchairs designed to accentuate the movements needed to perform the actions necessary for the sport.

To capture the motions associated with the sport, the wheelchair could be instrumented at the wheel to capture number and speed of rotations. Sporner et al. [6] and Postma et al. [18] showed that it was possible to calculate propulsion and distance travelled by instrumenting the wheelchair with a data logger. This also may be very important to capturing information for athletes during competition especially for sports like basketball and rugby. During games, players must remove jewelry and other accessories that may get caught on another wheelchair or harm another person if contacted. In this situation, using a wrist-worn wearable would not be allowed however instrumentation of the users' wheelchair may be possible as long as the shape of the wheelchair remains the same. Carrington et al. [7] showed that people were accepting of this concept with regard to interactive systems for wheelchairs.

7.3 Support Universal Accessibility

The current vast majority of wearable fitness devices present data and offer feedback for very abled-activities. Many refer to motion data as "steps"; activities like walking and running dominate the landscape. For wheelchair users, the major motor activity is "pushing" the wheelchair. This includes pushing the wheelchair to get around or pushing for precise movements and speed during a game. Applications associated with fitness activities use terminology that is non-inclusive.

More inclusive language is needed to communicate physical activity information to a more diverse audience of users. This becomes especially important when comparing data between wheelchair users and able-bodied individuals. One of the occupational therapists we interviewed emphasized the importance of being able to share data with other people with the same level of ability, performing similar actions. This is important for both wheelchair users and able-bodied athletes.

While not specifically the focus of this paper, presentation of data can also be an issue when considering other types of sensory impairments including vision and tactile sensation. Our analysis of the interface components available on wearable devices showed that 34% have displays, 17% have a vibration motor, 10% have a speaker, and 5% have LED indicators. It would be safe to assume that based on the existing hardware, only 5% of devices may offer appropriate alternative outputs for people with other sensory impairments. For example, someone with a vision impairment might prefer audio or tactile output where someone with limited tactile sensation might prefer visual output using a screen or LEDs. Making sure these devices are universally accessible is an important issue that merits future work.

8. Conclusions and Future Work

This research highlights important accessibility challenges for wearable fitness devices. We demonstrate that currently available consumer wearable devices do not meet the needs of this diverse population of wheelchair athletes. None of the wheelchair users we interviewed had experience using wearable fitness devices, however four out of five were interested in tracking information such as activity from pushing their wheelchairs, calories burned, and distance travelled. Many were concerned that since the technology was designed for someone who walks it would not be accurate. We present opportunities to improve existing consumer-oriented wearable systems or to create custom solutions for wheelchair athletes that take advantage of the specialized equipment required for participation in adaptive sports.

We intend to expand this study to include more athletes from specific adaptive sports. Further research is needed to understand the specific roles that wearable fitness trackers can play in adaptive sports and for individual adaptive sport athletes. Better understanding of these activities may lead to innovation in wearable technologies and will be an important step toward a more inclusive fitness community.

9. ACKNOWLEDGMENTS

We thank our participants, the International Center for Spinal Cord Injury at the Kennedy Krieger Institute, Catherine Hornback, Jeremy Chang, and the UMBC Prototyping and Design Lab. This work was partially funded by Microsoft and Nokia.

10. REFERENCES

[1] Ashbrook, D. L., Clawson, J. R., Lyons, K., Starner, T. E., & Patel, N. (2008). Quickdraw: the impact of mobility and on-body placement on device access time. Proc. CHI 2008, ACM Press (2008) pp. 219-222.

[2] Bailly, G., Müller, J., Rohs, M., Wigdor, D., & Kratz, S. ShoeSense: a new perspective on gestural interaction and wearable applications. Proc. CHI 2012, ACM Press (2012) pp. 1239-1248.

[3] Bravata et al. (2007) Using Pedometers to increase physical activity. J Amer Med Assoc.

[4] Brewster, S., Lumsden, J., Bell, M., Hall, M., & Tasker, S. Multimodal 'eyes-free' interaction techniques for wearable devices. Proc. CHI 2003, ACM Press (2003) pp. 473-480.

[5] Buechley, L., & Hill, B. M. LilyPad in the wild: how hardware's long tail is supporting new engineering and design communities. Proc. DIS'2010, ACM Press (2010) pp. 199-207.

[6] Calvo, R.A. and Peters, D. 2013. The irony and re-interpretation of our quantified self. (New York, New York, USA, Nov. 2013), 367–370.

[7] Carrington, P., Hurst, A., and Kane, S.K. 2014. Wearables and chairables: inclusive design of mobile input and output techniques for power wheelchair users. In Proceedings of the SIGCHI Conference on Human Factors in Computing Systems (CHI '14) (pp.3103-3112). ACM

[8] Cervantes, C. M., & Porretta, D. L. (2010). Physical activity measurement among individuals with disabilities: A literature review. *Adapted Physical Activity Quarterly*, *27*(3), 173-190.

[9] Chan, C. B., Ryan, D. A., & Tudor-Locke, C. (2004). Health benefits of a pedometer-based physical activity intervention in sedentary workers. Preventive medicine, 39(6), 1215-1222.

[10] Cheshire, W. P., & Freeman, R. (2003, December). Disorders of sweating. In *Seminars in neurology* (Vol. 23, No. 4, p. 399).

[11] Harrison, C., Tan, D., & Morris, D. Skinput: appropriating the body as an input surface. Proc. CHI'2010, ACM Press (2010) pp. 453-462.

[12] Lupton, D. (2014, December). Self-tracking cultures: towards a sociology of personal informatics. In *Proceedings of the 26th Australian Computer-Human Interaction Conference on Designing Futures: the Future of Design* (pp. 77-86). ACM.

[13] MacLeod, H., Tang, A., & Carpendale, S. (2013, May). Personal informatics in chronic illness management. In *Proceedings of Graphics Interface 2013* (pp. 149-156). Canadian Information Processing Society.

[14] Merriam, S. B. (2014). *Qualitative research: A guide to design and implementation*. John Wiley & Sons.

[15] Meehan, S. (2015) Senior Citizens want to know why Under Armour isn't making anything for them. *Baltimore Business Journal* (March 4, 2015) accessed May 5 2015. http://www.bizjournals.com/baltimore/news/2015/05/04/senior-citizens-want-to-know-why-under-armour-isnt.html

[16] Morris, D., Saponas, T.S., Guillory, A. and Kelner, I. 2014. RecoFit: using a wearable sensor to find, recognize, and count repetitive exercises. (New York, New York, USA, Apr. 2014), 3225–3234.

[17] Patel, M. S., Asch, D. A., & Volpp, K. G. (2015). Wearable devices as facilitators, not drivers, of health behavior change. *Jama*, *313*(5), 459-460.

[18] Postma, K., Berg-Emons van den, H.J.G., Bussmann, J.B.J., Sluis, T.A.R., Bergen, M.P. and Stam, H.J. 2005. Validity of the detection of wheelchair propulsion as measured with an Activity Monitor in patients with spinal cord injury. Spinal Cord. 43, 9 (Apr. 2005), 550–557.

[19] Rooksby, J., Rost, M., Morrison, A. and Chalmers, M.C. 2014. Personal tracking as lived informatics. (New York, New York, USA, Apr. 2014), 1163–1172.

[20] Saponas, T. S., Tan, D. S., Morris, D., Balakrishnan, R., Turner, J., & Landay, J. A. Enabling always-available input with muscle-computer interfaces. Proc. UIST 2009, ACM Press (2009) pp. 167-176.

[21] Saponas, T. S., Kelly, D., Parviz, B. A., & Tan, D. S. Optically sensing tongue gestures for computer input. Proc. UIST 2009, ACM Press (2009) pp. 177-180.

[22] Sporner, M.L., Fitzgerald, S.G., Dicianno, B.E., Collins, D., Teodorski, E., Pasquina, P.F. and Cooper, R.A. 2009. Psychosocial impact of participation in the National Veterans Wheelchair Games and Winter Sports Clinic.

[23] Sporner, M.L., Grindle, G.G., Kelleher, A., Teodorski, E.E., Cooper, R. and Cooper, R.A. 2009. Quantification of Activity During Wheelchair Basketball and Rugby at the National Veterans Wheelchair Games: A Pilot Study. Prosthetics and Orthotics International. 33, 3 (Sep. 2009), 210–217.

[24] Tawashy, A.E., Eng, J.J., Lin, K.H., Tang, P.F. and Hung, C. 2008. Physical activity is related to lower levels of pain, fatigue and depression in individuals with spinal-cord injury: a correlational study. Spinal Cord. 47, 4 (Oct. 2008), 301–306.

[25] United States Department of Health and Human Services 1996. Physical Activity and Health. (1996).

[26] Whooley, M., Ploderer, B. and Gray, K. 2014. On the Integration of Self-tracking Data amongst Quantified Self Members. (Sep. 2014).

Exploring the Opportunities and Challenges with Exercise Technologies for People who are Blind or Low-Vision

Kyle Rector[1], Lauren Milne[1], Richard E. Ladner[1], Batya Friedman[2], Julie A. Kientz[3]
[1]Computer Science & Engineering, [2]The Information School & [3]Human-Centered Design & Engineering, DUB Group | University of Washington
Seattle, WA, USA 98195
{rectorky, milnel2, ladner}@cs.washington.edu, {batya, jkientz}@uw.edu

ABSTRACT

People who are blind or low-vision may have a harder time participating in exercise due to inaccessibility or lack of experience. We employed Value Sensitive Design (VSD) to explore the potential of technology to enhance exercise for people who are blind or low-vision. We conducted 20 semi-structured interviews about exercise and technology with 10 people who are blind or low-vision and 10 people who facilitate fitness for people who are blind or low-vision. We also conducted a survey with 76 people to learn about outsider perceptions of hypothetical exercise with people who are blind or low-vision. Based on our interviews and survey, we found opportunities for technology development in four areas: 1) mainstream exercise classes, 2) exercise with sighted guides, 3) rigorous outdoors activity, and 4) navigation of exercise spaces. Design considerations should include when and how to deliver auditory or haptic information based on exercise and context, and whether it is acceptable to develop less mainstream technologies if they enhance mainstream exercise. The findings of this work seek to inform the design of accessible exercise technologies.

Author Keywords

Accessibility; exercise; exergames; visual impairments; eyes-free; audio feedback; health; value sensitive design

ACM Classification Keywords

K.4.2 [Computers and Security]: Social Issues – Assistive technologies for persons with disabilities; H.5.2 [Information Interfaces and Presentation]: User Interfaces.

INTRODUCTION

People who are blind or low-vision can have a harder time participating in exercise than people who are sighted. They are also more likely to be obese [9, 42] and to maintain inadequate fitness levels starting in their youth [9]. People with more severe visual impairments are less likely to believe that exercise is important and are more likely to have parents who do not encourage them to exercise [42], and thus they exercise less [36]. They may also miss out on the social aspects of exercise, such as exercise classes that are taught by instructors who do not know how to adapt to people who are blind or low-vision [35].

ASSETS '15, October 26-28, 2015, Lisbon, Portugal
© 2015 ACM. ISBN 978-1-4503-3400-6/15/10$15.00
DOI: http://dx.doi.org/10.1145/2700648.2809846

Exercise technologies, such as exergames and fitness trackers, encourage physical activity for many users. These technologies may provide motivation, workouts, and act as a gateway to more advanced exercises [37]. However, most exergames [27] and health tracking technologies [25] have accessibility issues for people who are blind or low-vision because many of the necessary cues are visual (see Figure 1). While research efforts for exergames for people who are blind or low-vision are on-going [27, 28, 29, 34], typically these are limited to exergames that involve only upper body exercise and do not provide as much energy expenditure as full body exercise [4]. Opportunities exist to research and develop other types of exercise technologies outside of a game setting, specifically for different contexts (e.g. gym, outdoors) and with different groups of people (e.g. alone, with a sighted guide, with friends). Better access to exercise technologies has the potential to provide more independent exercise opportunities for people who are blind or low-vision. That said, blind of low-vision users could put themselves at an increased safety risk because they lack of awareness of situational factors. Because accessible exercise technologies are related to health and may provide benefits *or harms*, it is important to consider the tradeoffs.

To understand the opportunities and challenges of technology playing a role in accessible exercise, we turn to Value Sensitive Design (VSD) [5, 16], an approach that requires designers to interact with both direct and indirect stake-

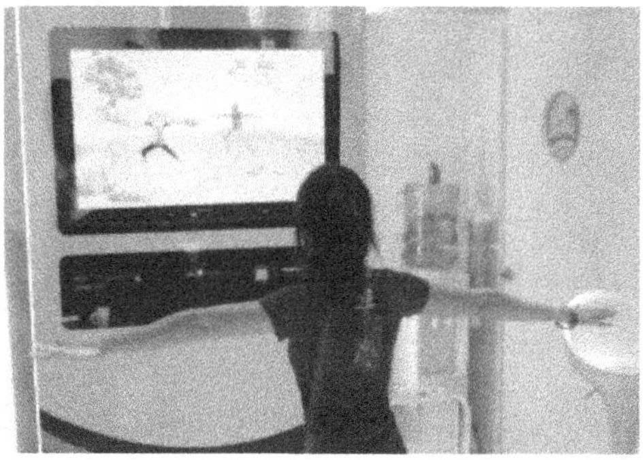

Figure 1. An exergame player is required to see the avatars on screen and text rules in the upper right hand corner to play. Image: CC BY 2.0 popculturegeek on Flickr.

holders as well as to elicit values and value tensions:

1. We interviewed 10 people who are blind or low-vision, as direct stakeholders, to learn about their current exercise habits, benefits and challenges of exercise, and how they use or do not use technology with exercise.
2. We interviewed 10 people who coach, instruct, direct, or volunteer for exercise activities with people who are blind or low-vision, as indirect stakeholders. We inquired about their experience with people who are blind or low-vision, along with how they or direct stakeholders that they work with use or do not use technology with exercise.
3. We conducted a survey with 76 people from the general population, another group of indirect stakeholders. We asked about their sentiments toward hypothetical scenarios where people who are blind or low-vision join public or semi-public exercise activities while using technology.
4. Two researchers coded the interviews and employed cross-case analysis [18] to determine the values participants felt an exercise technology should embody. We present a list of existing technologies that the participants use and discuss how those technologies do or do not address the reported values and features. We also present innovative technology mock-ups mentioned by our participants.

We have three main contributions: (1) the identification of the patterns, challenges, and technology use in exercise with people who are blind or low-vision, (2) an understanding of outsider perceptions of hypothetical exercise scenarios where people who are blind or low-vision use technology, and (3) a set of design opportunities and considerations that we hope will inform future accessible exercise technologies.

BACKGROUND AND RELATED WORK

Below, we discuss VSD in more detail and how it informs our methodology. We also present current Eyes-Free Exercise Technology in both research and practice.

Value Sensitive Design

In our study, we used value sensitive design's [5, 16] tripartite methodology to account for values from various stakeholders. VSD may start from a value, technology, or context of use [16]. Because we wanted to determine technology opportunities and considerations organically, we chose to start from a context of use: exercise for people who are blind or low-vision. Yetim provides a nice summary of the evolution of VSD [46]. The three parts consist of a Conceptual, Empirical, and Technical Investigation:

Conceptual Investigation – This first investigation involves the consideration of the stakeholders (direct and indirect) affected by a context of use. *Direct Stakeholders* are those who are directly immersed in the context of use and engage directly with the technology. In our case, our direct stakeholders are people who are blind or low-vision with varying ranges in sight and physical fitness. *Indirect Stakeholders* are people who are affected by the context, but do not directly interact with the technology. Those people include coaches, instructors, sighted guides, volunteers, or others who help facilitate fitness for people who are blind or low-vision. This may include friends, family, or bystanders who observe exercisers who are blind or low-vision.

After a preliminary identification of stakeholders, conceptual investigations typically follow by brainstorming possible benefits and harms for each stakeholder group, and a set of corresponding values and value tensions. For example, in our research direct stakeholders may experience a value tension between *independence* and *safety*, while indirect stakeholders may experience a value tension between *service* and *respect*. Indirect stakeholders could have a hard time deciding whether or not to provide *service* by helping someone who is blind or low-vision while in an exercise setting, because they might be unsure if the blind or low-vision persons might that offer to help as *disrespectful*.

Empirical Investigation – With an initial set of stakeholders and values, the empirical investigation strives to learn more about stakeholder values centered on a context of use. We conducted semi-structured interviews with both direct and indirect stakeholders about exercise habits, currently used technologies, and possible new technologies. With the corresponding data and analysis, the empirical investigation may confirm values from the conceptual investigation as well as uncover new values that were previously missed.

Technical Investigation – The technical investigation focuses on how existing technologies either support or hinder important values, in addition to having stakeholders brainstorm new and innovative technologies. Here, we assessed the reported and proposed technologies from the empirical investigation and discuss how those technologies do or do not address these important stakeholder values.

Eyes-Free Exercise Opportunities

Although there is a need for more accessible exercise opportunities, there are several organizations and sports that support accessible exercise. For example, national organizations such as the United States Association of Blind Athletes (USABA) [43] and the Canadian Blind Sports Association (CBSA) [8] facilitate sports for athletes who are blind or low-vision. Sports specifically invented for this population include Goalball and Beep Baseball, as well as adapted mainstream sports such as ice hockey (Courage Canada Hockey for the Blind [12]), skiing (Ski for Light [38]), and cricket (Cricket Association for the Blind in India [7]). These types of accessible sports are important because they provide the opportunity to participate in open sports (with changing variables such as a moving ball or players [45]), which people who are blind prefer [23] over predictable closed sports (e.g. running on a treadmill) [45]. However, they may only reach a subset of people based on location, athletic ability, or interest. Therefore, ubiquitous technology solutions have the potential to complement these organizations to reach a wider audience.

Eyes-Free Exercise Technology

With the recent popularity of exercise tracking technologies, such as Fitbit [15] and the Nike fuel band [31], there have been several research efforts investigating how to leverage these technologies and the data they collect to increase fitness. For instance, to encourage useful exercise habits for adults (e.g. [10, 15]) and for older adults who may face significant barriers to exercise [1, 14]. Although useful, these health tracking applications are often not accessible to people who are blind or low vision [25].

Accessible exergaming has been recognized as a research problem across many disciplines [26]. One option is to make an existing exergame accessible to people who are blind or low-vision. For example, with VI-Bowling [28] and VI-Tennis [27] Morelli et al. analyzed the visual cues used in Wii Sports Bowling and Tennis and converted them to audio feedback from the speakers or tactile feedback from the Wii Remote; for a track running game on the Kinect, Morelli et al. [30] developed a solution using video capture to find visual cues and communicated the information using audio and tactile feedback with a Wii Remote.

Researchers have also developed original exergames that are accessible to people who are blind or low-vision. For example, in Pet-N-Punch the player has to hit rodents and pet cats at a farm using a Wii Remote and nunchuck; participants were able to achieve light to moderate upper body exercise [29]. Eyes-Free Yoga is an original exergame that coaches yoga to people who are blind or low-vision by giving personalized feedback on yoga postures [34].

Beyond exergames, there are opportunities for innovative technologies to be developed for different contexts (e.g. gym, outdoors) and with different groups of people (e.g. alone, with a sighted guide, with friends). The design and development of accessible exercise technologies may provide an impact in both research and practice. Therefore, we hope our work will uncover important values behind accessible exercise and the opportunities for technology design.

RESEARCHER STANCE

The research team is comprised of people with backgrounds in Computer Science, Human-Computer Interaction, and Accessibility. We were able to recruit participants for our study because of prior volunteer experience at a school for the blind, prior volunteer experience at an organization that facilitates recreation for people of all abilities, and previous research experience. All of the authors are sighted, so it is possible that the interview and survey materials may have a bias toward a sighted perspective.

CONCEPTUAL INVESTIGATION

Stakeholders. We began our conceptual investigation by brainstorming direct and indirect stakeholders. Because we are studying eyes-free exercise opportunities, the direct stakeholders are people who are blind or low-vision. Indirect stakeholders include those who are involved in fitness for people who are blind or low-vision (e.g., coaches, directors, instructors, and volunteers who enable exercise) and the general public who also participate in exercise because they may impact the decision of a person who is blind or low-vision on (e.g., in fitness classes or bystanders). We did not include some indirect stakeholders in our research. In particular, we did not work with friends or family of people who are blind or low-vision. While this group is more directly involved on a personal level, they may have less expertise in an exercise setting. It is possible that a family member or friend may also be teacher, coach, volunteer, or a survey respondent so we did not let that affect our recruitment.

Harms and Benefits. Our research team also brainstormed the potential benefits and harms of different types of exercise and exercise technology and the underlying values that stakeholders attach to the space. We determined that two explicitly supported project values [5] for eyes-free exercise should be *accessibility* (people of any visual ability should be able to use the technology) and *fitness* (supports any exercise activity).

Values. The goal of this research is to uncover values related to eyes-free exercise. To identify preliminary values to help focus our interviews, we read related work about values and eyes-free technologies. The authors uncovered possible stakeholder values that include but are not limited to *independence* [2, 16, 22, 39], *safety* [22, 40], *being mainstream* [39, 40], and *confidence* [2, 16] (see Table 3 for a complete list). People should have the ability to exercise independently, whether that is with or without a friend, chaperone, or technology. In addition, they should be able to maintain a sense of safety throughout the exercise, whether that involves multiple sources of information, a viable back up plan, or exercising caution when planning a workout. When they are exercising, they should not feel like they stand out in the crowd in a negative manner, and they should feel confident during exercise. The authors hypothesized that they would uncover additional values, and the list of values would change throughout the empirical and technical investigations.

EMPIRICAL INVESTIGATION METHODS

We conducted semi-structured interviews and a survey to elicit values from direct and indirect stakeholders:

1. Group 1 (Direct Stakeholders): We conducted semi-structured interviews with people who are blind or low-vision (Table 1).
2. Group 2 (Indirect Stakeholders): We conducted semi-structured interviews with people who facilitate exercise for people who are blind or low-vision (Table 2).
3. Group 3 (Indirect Stakeholders): We conducted a survey of the general population.

Attribute	Counts
Gender	Female (6), Male (4)
Age	Range: 21-68, Median: 36
Vision	Totally blind (2), Legally blind (2), Degenerative condition (3), Light perception only (2), Peripheral vision in one eye (1)
Duration	Since birth (6), Later in life (4)
Physical Activity	Sedentary (4), Active walker (3), Active (1), Very active and travel to compete (2).

Table 1. Demographic information about Group 1 participants (Direct stakeholders – blind or low-vision).

Attribute	Counts
Gender	Female (5), Male (5)
Age	Range: 25-67, Median: 45
Vision	Sighted (4), Visually impaired (1), Degenerative condition (2), Totally blind (1) Not reported (2)
Role	Coach (2), Program manager (2), Director (1), Sighted guide (2), Pilot (2), Yoga instructor (1), Spin instructor (1)
Sports Facilitated	Swimming (1), Biking (7), Running (4), Triathlon (3), Skiing/Snowboarding (3), Kayaking (3), Rock climbing (2), Goalball (1), Beep Baseball (1), Yoga (2)
Role Duration	Range: 1.5-15 years, Median: 4 years

Table 2. Demographic information about Group 2 participants (Indirect Stakeholders – facilitate fitness)

In the interviews for Group 1, we inquired about the benefits and challenges of exercise as well as participants' exercise technology background in different contexts. First, we asked about exercise history and about whether they exercise alone, with others, or in a gym setting. We asked about technologies or accessibility solutions used during exercise. We provided hypothetical exercise scenarios with technology, offered two balanced reasons for why a certain technology may or may not be preferred, and asked for their feedback. For example:

Joe takes a mainstream yoga class. He uses a special mat (which looks like a regular yoga mat) that detects his weight distribution and gives some feedback about how to adjust his pose via one headphone so Joe can still listen to the instructor.

Idea 1: Some people say it's OK to wear headphones in a class because you will receive extra information.

Idea 2: Some people find it concerning to wear headphones because they will appear different and could possibly fall behind in the class or not hear the instructor.

Do you tend to agree with Idea 1 or Idea 2? Why?

We finished by asking about previous stories while exercising where they experienced some form of difficulty (e.g., felt unsafe, felt not confident, etc.) and about possible innovative technologies that could help in these situations.

In the Group 2 indirect stakeholder interviews, we inquired about experiences facilitating exercise with people who are blind or low-vision and, if applicable, how it differed from people who are sighted. We asked for supporting stories to obtain additional contexts and details about their experiences. We asked about technology use and asked the same use case scenarios as Group 1.

Finally, the survey for Group 3 presented three scenarios in which a person who is blind or low-vision is using an accessible technology to facilitate exercise and inquired about the thoughts of survey respondents. For example: *You are currently attending an exercise class at the gym, and a participant who is blind joins the class. Please check off the feelings that apply most to you.* Answers include: *excited, neutral, stressed, unsure of how much space to give them, and unsure of whether or not to help them.*

For all three groups, we were careful to order the questions so as not to intentionally prime the interview toward a specific value (e.g., How do you feel about safety?).

For interviews, we recruited 10 direct stakeholders who were blind or low-vision (Group 1: D1-D10, Table 1) and 10 indirect stakeholders (Group 2: I1-I10, Table 2). For the survey, 76 members of the general population were respondents to our Group 3 survey (S1-S76, 51 female, 25 male; ages 18-76; median age 34.5). We recruited survey respondents via email. We were conducting a qualitative analysis, and thus recruited until we reached data saturation, which was after 10 interviews for Group 1 and Group 2 (which is consistent with findings that that data saturation usually occurs before reaching 12 interviews in a given population [19]). All of the interviews were conducted over the phone and lasted from 30 minutes to two hours.

We audio-recorded and transcribed the interviews. For the interview transcripts and survey text responses, we employed cross-case analysis [18] where two researchers independently read the transcripts and identified themes and values. Then the two researchers met and synthesized a master set of themes and values. Next the two researchers used these themes and values to re-code the entire set of interviews. After semi-randomly selecting and coding the same five interviews, the researchers reviewed each other's work and made revisions as necessary. The researchers then independently coded the rest of the interviews. Throughout this process, the researchers met regularly to iterate on the code set.

RESULTS

First, we discuss the emergent themes, values and value tensions mentioned by all three groups followed by survey results from Group 3. These are summarized in Table 3.

Stakeholder Themes, Values, and Value Tensions

Opportunity: Knowledge transfer while exercising in a class

Knowledge is an important value for technology design in general, but there are unique opportunities in the domain of accessible exercise. **Mainstream exercise classes** are one opportunity where technology may enhance the experience for someone who is blind or low-vision, because most classes are not accessible [35]. In our interviews, no direct stakeholders reported having a positive experience in a *mainstream* exercise class. D9 reported that she took a class on martial arts, and there was a lack of *respect*: "*I did that for about a few weeks and they came and told me they would like me to have special lessons by myself. ... I was so offended and I never went back.*" Direct stakeholders reported positive experiences when the class was made accessible: "*She was very, very descriptive and really used language that was very not visual per se, but in terms of positions 'to the door' 'to the window'*" (D3). Descriptive verbal instructions may provide benefit when learning an exercise, like with Eyes-Free Yoga [34]. Because of positive social benefits from attending an exercise class (e.g., *community*), technology that communicates *knowledge* in this setting may provide multiple benefits.

When blind and low-vision participants were posed with the idea of using one headphone to hear extra feedback while in a *mainstream* yoga class, they responded positively because the technology could provide them with *knowledge* when the instructor was not available: "*the instructor cannot take time to come around to each person*" (D2) and still allow them the benefit of *community*: "*it is more preferable ... because clearly you get to work out with other people*" (D10). Survey respondents also felt that the system may provide utility to them; they "*wonder what the feedback sounds like*" (S63) and also "*want feedback about how I am doing*" (S7).

That said, some of the exercise instructors and survey respondents expressed concerns about integrating this type of technology in a class: "*Hopefully they [instructors] would be encouraging and on board with him using that adaptive piece of equipment and help him calm him a little bit if he does fall behind*" (I2). In addition, "*if the person wasn't familiar with the moves being called out by the instructor, and people got distracted trying to help, it could be embarrassing for the participant*" (S30). There is a value tension that with extra *knowledge*, the instructor, class, or participant may become distracted and no longer experience *mindfulness*. Not all instructors may be on board with such a design, especially those who specialize in instructing people who are blind or low-vision. I9, an eyes-free yoga class instructor, thought that the technology would only be useful if a teacher was not present: "*I don't think it's so good. I think if he was on his own [and] if the teacher wasn't there, it's great*" (I9).

Opportunity or Consideration	Values (V) or Value Tensions (T)
Knowledge transfer while exercising in a class	**V:** knowledge, mainstream, respect, community **T:** knowledge vs. mindfulness
Knowledge transfer while exercising with a sighted guide	**V:** accessibility, knowledge **T:** communication vs. knowledge
Rigorous outdoor exercise	**V:** mindfulness, outdoors/green exercise, safety **T:** independence vs. safety
Navigating exercise spaces	**V:** accessibility, safety **T:** accessibility vs. fitness
Audio channel design	**V:** knowledge, awareness, safety, mindfulness **T:** knowledge vs. awareness, knowledge vs. safety, knowledge vs. mindfulness
Less mainstream solutions	**V:** mainstream, community, knowledge, safety, confidence **T:** mainstream vs. knowledge, mainstream vs. community, mainstream vs. confidence

Table 3. Opportunities and considerations for design, and the corresponding values and value tensions (order mentioned).

Opportunity: Knowledge transfer while exercising with a sighted guide

Another opportunity to integrate *knowledge* in technology design is when **exercising with a sighted guide**. Sighted guides are not very *accessible* to recruit and exercise with regularly "*So my partner only being 30 miles away - I don't think there is anyone else who has a pilot who lives that close in tandem racing*" (D10), and perhaps: "*why they don't guide is because there is that pressure. You can't let them down. You can't be the slowest ever during the day*" (I5). According to the United States Association for Blind Athletes (USABA): "*Often runners are hesitant to serve as guide runners fearing they will do something or not do something that could result in injury or a poor performance for the blind athlete*" [41].

Because the purpose of a sighted guide is "*to be their eyes*" (I3) and "*our time keepers*" (I3), innovative lightweight technologies may offset the amount of *communication* needed while exercising. For example, technology could provide *knowledge* "*about the environment*" (D3) or something that would use a *"transponder to give an audible sort of – Let's say there's five racers numbered 1 2 3 4 5. It maybe could give the splits '... And number 2 is in the lead number 3 is 2 minutes behind her' ... There are the verbal cues that I do give throughout the race, all the better that it could be technology because here again that's one of the pressures on the guide is to not only run as fast as the athlete but also talk at the higher level"* (I5). Presenting *knowledge* while running in groups is feasible; Mauriello et al. developed a system that displays runner information on the back of shirts [24], which could be made accessible.

Opportunity: Rigorous outdoor exercise

Previous work has found that exercising outdoors in a rural or urban setting (termed "green exercise") lends itself to improving physical and health outcomes [33]. This was reflected as a value for many participants in our study. Participants identified *mindfulness* as a benefit to exercising *outdoors* including being *"more connected to earth"* (I7), *"out in the fresh air"* (D2), and *"away from the noise of the city"* (D4). Brisk walking with a cane, sighted guide, or guide dog is feasible, but when the pace of exercise is increased, *"trying to find somebody who is amenable who is willing to run as a guide"* (D6) is a barrier as mentioned previously. Stationary rigorous activity, considered closed exercises in adapted exercise physiology [45], may become monotonous and feel less productive: *"I know it's kind of ridiculous to expend all of that effort and not even move an inch"* (D6). While there are possible *safety* concerns, participants have a desire to engage in more open exercises [45], including **rigorous physical activity outdoors**: *"If I had more of a chance to get outdoors on a tandem outside, so that would be more exciting"* (D10).

When we presented the following hypothetical technology to both direct and indirect stakeholders: *James decides to walk around the track. With a mounted camera and headphones, he is able to hear whether or not he is staying in his lane and about nearby obstacles*, we noticed a value tension between the values of *independence* and *safety*. Several participants (D1-D4, D6-D7, I1, I3-I6, and I8-I9) were interested in using the technology and felt that *"we can't be afraid of goofing up"* (D4) and *"wouldn't be too terribly concerned if the technology failed because somehow the person got themselves to the track"* (I1). In addition, *"you can't wrap yourself up as they say in cotton wool. Just get out there and try it"* (I5) and they *"would favor it even if there is some risk involved"* (I8). Survey respondents were also positive: *"It's really cool that technology was helping the blind person in this way"* (S23).

However, two participants (D10, I10) and some survey respondents were concerned about the technology due to *safety*: *"Find someone to do it with or switch to an indoor equivalent where a sighted person isn't necessary. And if the treadmill fails you, so what? You don't hurt anybody else"* (I10). In addition, bystanders would be *"concerned that the gear will [not] work correctly and navigate around barriers"* (S68) and *"be afraid of going too close and causing the system to alert the person unnecessarily"* (S18). In addition to system errors, the technology and situation may make a person more *"susceptible to attack"* (S53) as it may call attention to one's disability [40]. Also, the technology may not warn a person in time about unexpected obstacles: *"Someone's football might fly right in their path before the camera can pick it up and warn them"* (S47).

Participants also identified strategies to mitigate these issues, for example, by becoming acquainted with the technology first (D5, D8, and I7): *"I would want to make sure that the feedback is detailed enough"* (D8). D9 and I2 were willing to try out the system as long as they had a backup plan: *"He needs to develop other skills to so that if the technology fails he would not be totally lost"* (D9). While *safety* is a valid concern, nonetheless, there is an opportunity to enable **rigorous outdoor exercise** with technology. If *safety* is accounted for in the design – with piloting, training, and proper fail cases – this line of research has the potential to generate impact.

Opportunity: Navigating exercise spaces

While *accessible* solutions such as a cane or guide dog work well in most contexts, there is a value tension with *fitness*. For instance, D1 was unable to go on a hike with their guide dog: *"I started out trying to use my guide dog but quickly disc3overed that it was very narrow and very rocky, and it was just not something that my dog was really accustomed to trying to navigate and guide me."* While it is possible to use a guide dog for running [13], D4 reported that their guide dog can get in the way of a brisk exercise walk: *"...one of those mediums being a thinking brain, and when that thinking brain which is attached to a nose tends to get a little bit too curious for its own good, which of course gets me in trouble."*

Another example of a beneficial *accessible* tool hindering a workout is using a cane at the gym. D10 resorts to only having a sighted guide instead: *"I don't carry my cane with me because I have to keep putting it down, picking it up, putting it down, picking it up ... I don't want to run into anybody"* (D10). Further exacerbating the problem is that *"gyms are not laid out in a real structured format"* (D10).

An opportunity for technology development may involve developing tools that allow people to **navigate spaces catered to exercise**. One suggestion by D9 is having *"a 3D printout of the gym"* that may help people navigate between machines. A high tech option with real time feedback may involve using a haptic laser [20] that has a smaller form factor. While hiking, D1 and D3 suggested mapping out the trail with GPS and satellite, having your phone inform you if you are walking off of the trail, and give you directions if you are led astray. This is similar to Navi'Rando, a recent accessible technology that warns hikers of bends and turns [32]. These technologies will not replace a guide dog or a cane, but may help remove some of the barriers.

Another option may be to augment current accessibility tools, as opposed to developing separate systems. Such augmentations may have both performance and safety benefits. For example, research has explored how to augment service dogs to increase the amount and type of tasks they can complete [6, 21]. The Facilitating Interactions for Dogs with Occupations (FIDO) project produced a wearable technology for service dogs so they could increase communication with their owners [21] by providing interfaces the dogs could activate with their nose, by biting, or by tugging. In addition, Bozkurt et al. introduced Cyber-Enhanced Working Dogs (CEWDs), search and rescue dogs that wear sensors and actuators to enable real time monitoring [6]. These projects demonstrate the potential to augment a guide dog and reduce the need for a harness in certain situations, which could be a *safety* risk: "*There are a number of people specifically have retired use of a guide dog because of various physical ailments they develop ... The scapula and the thorax that can really be pulled out of whack*" (D4).

Consideration: Audio channel design

As mentioned above, there are opportunities for auditory technologies to provide *knowledge* during exercise in different contexts (e.g. exercise class, exercise with a sighted guide). However, **caution must be exercised** when determining how to present audio information; it is important for someone to have an *awareness* of his or her environment even with headphones [3]. If someone was hearing constant auditory feedback while wearing two headphones outside, this could pose a serious *safety* risk: "*It's a big world outside, and it can be everything from being accosted by somebody to traffic ... You still need your hearing whenever you're in the public*" (D9). In addition, survey respondents noted that headphones "*may impair their hearing*" (S67) and they "*may miss obstacles that come up from the side or behind*" (S46).

In a more controlled setting, such as an exercise class, wearing headphones may reduce *mindfulness*: *I would not wear headphones if it would distract me from hearing the instructor. I would only want to hear the instructor*" (D4). In addition, a distracting audio interface may cancel out a working strategy, for example: "*Like the treadmills, you can pretty easily tell if the people are on them, because they thump, thump, thump really loud*" (D7).

As noted above, the audio channel can be an attractive opportunity to distribute *knowledge*, but there are value tensions with *awareness*, *safety*, and *mindfulness*. For instance, referring to the scenario where James was walking on the track with a mounted camera and headphones, participants were interested in refining *when* and *how* audio feedback was delivered: "*I would not want something that speaks when you are out of your lane, but does not give enough information for how to get back into the lane*" (D8). In other words, if the system only provided *knowledge* that there was a mistake, and not how to fix the mistake, the person may lose their orientation or become discouraged, impinging on *mindfulness* or *safety*.

This value tension between *knowledge* and that of *awareness, mindfulness, and safety* demonstrates that an important design consideration is **how to deliver audio information** (e.g. speakers, headphones, one ear bud, and bone conduction headphones). On the one hand, in a public or exercise class setting where others are present, using headphones may be advantageous: "*It is not like the feedback is bothering me because they hear it via their own headphones*" (S29). Using one ear bud may be advantageous, because "*if they just have one headphone in they can still hear the instructor*" (I4). Bone conduction headphones may also be suitable: "*It doesn't go in your ear so you can hear what's going on around you*" (I8). On the other hand, in surroundings where hearing is already difficult, technology occupying both ears may be advantageous (e.g. skiing): "*There are two way radio sets which I [would] love to get ... If they are going fast enough, the wind, the sound of the snow becomes really hard to hear your instructor just down the hill from you*" (I2).

To explore this tension and develop appropriate technologies, designers will have to consider how to **design the audio channel** by assessing the exercise and context to determine the appropriate type (e.g. auditory, tactile, verbal) and the frequency (e.g. constant, only when a correction is necessary, time based) of feedback. In addition, if the person who is blind or low-vision will need to wear headphones to receive information, appropriate headphones should be selected: "*It may be beneficial to use wireless headphones to preserve the integrity of the movements involved in the exercise*" (S13).

Consideration: Less mainstream solutions

Developing *mainstream* technology solutions may be important for an aesthetic appearance [40]. However, participants suggested that they do not mind appearing different by using a less familiar technology (e.g., mounted camera) or in a less familiar context (e.g., exercise class) to appear *less* different while exercising. While the technology might make them look "different," the outcome is that they may be able to perform the exercise and workout in a *community*: "*It's good for everyone to get to participate and if some extra equipment is necessary that's fine*" (S46). In other words, **it is okay to develop a less mainstream technology, because it will help a person who is blind or low-vision exercise in more mainstream settings.**

There are a few reasons why during exercise less *mainstream* solutions may have utility: 1) "*You're getting that extra feedback that you need to make sure you are doing it right so you don't have to rely on someone else or the instructor to give you that feedback, but you are still participating in the class*" (D5, *knowledge*), 2) "*Anything that integrates a visually impaired [person] into the normal activities of daily life that the rest of us don't even think about*" (I6, *community*), and 3) "*I think just me as a blind *person I adapt pretty quickly and then my other thing is that I am different <laughs>"* (D6, *confidence*). Developing exercise technologies that may make a person appear slightly different will give them the *knowledge* to help them join in activities and have a positive experience with others.

Participants suggested that it is okay to appear different, especially when *safety* is on the line: "*One of my times skiing ... The reason of wearing the bib that says blind on it is so other people are aware so you do stick out ... and they can be conscientious of you staying out of your way.*" That being said, it is likely still a good design goal to create assistive technologies that are minimally noticeable and give people the opportunity to identify themselves as blind if they choose.

It is worth noting that we only interviewed adults, who might have gained *confidence*: "*It's always you don't feel independent. I feel that as an adult ... I don't care*" (D3). However, this is not necessarily the case when growing up: "*I was growing up as a child, I felt very, very apart and not part of this group, because if you are different you are very self-conscious*" (D3). Mainstream sports can be discouraging: "*You only get three strikes in baseball, yea well I got 5, 7 <laughs> until I hit the ball, and when you hear the PE coach calling the catcher talking to the pitcher 'Just underhand it to him'*" (D4). In addition, people may not be understanding of an assistive technology and may: "*talk about the device this blind person is using making them feel alienated*" (S21). Thus, another important and underexplored research direction may include developing technologies to make exercise accessible and enjoyable for children who are blind or low-vision, along with technologies that facilitate play between children of all visual acuities.

General Population Response to Exercise Scenarios

76 survey respondents from the general population about their feelings and rationale toward three scenarios as follows:

1. You are currently jogging around a running track. A person who is blind walks on the track. With a mounted camera and headphones, they are able to hear whether or not they are staying in their lane and about the obstacles in front of them.
2. You are currently attending an aerobics class at the gym, and a participant who is blind joins the class. With a special mat, which looks like a regular yoga mat, it can detect their weight distribution, and they can hear feedback about how they are doing via one headphone.
3. You are currently at home using a camera and audio-based yoga program using a video game system with a friend who is blind. You are exercising next to each other simultaneously.

Scenario (1: track, 2: class, 3: home)	1	2	3
I am excited for them to participate.	84.2	89.5	86.8
I am neutral.	15.8	15.8	7.9
I am stressed out.	2.6	0.0	5.3
I would feel uneasy about the camera.	5.3	n/a	5.3
I am unsure how much space I should give them.	50.0	15.8	22.4
I am unsure of when I should try to help them.	34.2	10.5	25.0

Table 4. Percentage of participants from Group 3 who held that sentiment. Note that people could choose more than one answer. Scenario 2 did not contain a camera (N=76).

Scenario 1 occurred in an outdoor, unstructured, public space (running track). Scenario 2 occurred in an indoor, structured, public space (exercise class). Scenario 3 occurred in an indoor, structured, private space (home). Table 4 shows the sentiments of survey participants for the different scenarios. One caveat regarding Scenario 3: Participants may not have a friend who is blind or low-vision, making this scenario even more hypothetical; however, we thought the scenario would be more realistic than if it were a stranger who is blind or low-vision. This decision may have affected participants' responses for this scenario.

While participants had similar views across all three scenarios with regard to feeling excited, neutral, stressed, or uneasy about the camera, there are interesting differences that emerge with respect to space and help. With Scenario 1 (walking around the track), 50% of participants "*wouldn't necessarily know how much space to give them*" (S38). This is in stark contrast to the exercise class setting (15.8%) and home setting (22.4%), where differences were found to be statistically significant (Wilcoxon rank sum test - Scenario 1 vs. Scenario 2: $W=3876$, $p < 0.0001$, Scenario 1 vs. Scenario 3: $W=3686$, $p = 0.001$). This may reflect that when the exercise space is unstructured, more people do not understand how to give enough space while exercising near someone who is blind or low-vision.

In addition, there were differences among the three scenarios in the percentage of participants who felt unsure as to whether or not they should help. While in a class setting, only 10.5% of participants were not sure about whether or not to help: "*They already have instructions*" (S12). This may be the case because the other class members are reliant on the instructor to provide assistance. The other two settings have a larger number of participants who report being unsure about whether or not to help: at home (25%) and on the running track (34.2%), and these differences are statistically significant (Wilcoxon rank sum test – Scenario 1 vs. Scenario 2: $W=3572$, $p < 0.001$, Scenario 2 vs. Scenario 3: $W=2470$, $p = 0.02$). It is possible that with proper education about etiquette while in the home or with signs in a public space, people will know how to act appropriately when exercising around someone who is blind or low-vision.

TECHNICAL INVESTIGATION

With the emerging opportunities for eyes-free exercise technologies, we followed our empirical investigation with an investigation of current technologies and technologies brainstormed by the participants. One purpose of technical investigations in VSD is to examine how current technologies fit or omit the emergent values or issues which surfaced during the empirical investigation, and to offer stakeholders an opportunity to brainstorm new technologies that address their concerns [16]. This is important to VSD because it allows researchers to primarily reflect on the state of technology, as opposed to the stakeholders like in the Empirical Investigation. It also allows for researchers and stakeholders to brainstorm concrete ideas for this design space. Group 1 participants (D1-D10) reported technologies they currently use, and Group 2 participants (I1-I10) reported technologies that are used by people they work with or that they use themselves (because for some participants, they were also a direct stakeholder). The complete set of reported technologies is shown in Table 5. Below, we also report novel technology ideas presented by the researchers in the interviews and survey and brainstormed by participants for each emerging opportunity.

While there is an opportunity for technology to communicate **knowledge in an exercise class**, the only two reported technologies were an inaccessible heart rate monitor for PE fitness testing and a partially accessible spin bike. The heart rate monitor output was read aloud by a sighted person and does not provide any instructions as to how to complete an exercise. The spin bikes were for a spin class in which the instructor is blind (I10). Instead of relying on the inaccessible output of the spin bikes, the instructor uses "*music to indicate what you should try to be doing*" and feeling to drive the class: "*We are all working 90%. Perhaps my feet are going faster or slower. Perhaps I have more or less resistance. It is still 90% no matter what.*" In addition to the researchers proposed technology of using a special mat and headphone in an exercise class for yoga, D2 suggested using a similar technology idea for jazzercise.

Currently reported technologies also do not fill in the knowledge gap when **exercising with a sighted guide**. Despite several technologies being reported while exercising with a sighted guide or bicycle pilot: bike computer, talking heart rate monitor, heart rate monitor, RunKeeper, and Strava, only one is accessible and was used during the workout. The inaccessible bike computer was read aloud by the pilot (I5), which places more work on the guide. In contrast, I3 is a coach to athletes who use a talking heart rate monitor, reducing the load on the sighted guide. The inaccessible heart rate monitor (I6), RunKeeper (I3), and Strava (I2, I6, I8) allowed for participants to record information about their workouts and analyze it at a later time. Ideally, more technologies would be developed to allow athletes to receive real-time information about their workouts, thereby reducing the load on a sighted guide or bicycle pilot. Participants brainstormed technologies to help fill this gap:

Technology	Participant	Place	Accessible?
Stationary Machines			
Stationary Bike	D9, I3	Indoors	Yes
Bike trainer	D6, D10, I5	Indoors	Yes
Nordic ski machine	D6	Indoors	Partially
Treadmill (Running)	D8, I3, I5	Indoors	Partially
Treadmill (Walking)	D1, D2, D7	Gym	Partially
Elliptical	D7	Gym	Yes
Spin bike	I10	Class	Partially
Health Tracking			
Talking bike computer	D6, D10	Indoors	Partially
Bike computer	I1	Indoors	Yes
Bike computer (bike pilot)	I5	Outdoors	No
Talking heart rate monitor (biking)	D6, D10	Indoors	Yes
Talking heart rate monitor (running with guide)	I3	Outdoors	Yes
Hear rate monitor (biking)	D10	Indoors	Partially
Heart rate monitor (PE fitness testing)	D7	Class	No
Heart rate monitor (bike pilot)	I6	Outdoors	Partially
Pedometer (walking)	D1	Outdoors	Partially
Phone Health Tracking			
Talking stopwatch (walking on treadmill)	D9	Indoors	Yes
Wahoo fitness (biking)	D6, D10	Indoors	Partially
Pedometer apps (walking)	D6	Outdoors	Partially
RunKeeper (running with guide)	I3	Outdoors	Yes
Strava (bike pilot)	I2, I6, I8	Outdoors	Partially
Accessibility features			
Magnification on iPhone or iPad (treadmill)	D1, D4, I8	Indoors	Yes
iPhone Camera w/ digital zoom and flash (walking)	D4	Outdoors	Yes
Navigation			
Sendero look around (walking)	D9	Outdoors	Yes
GPS on BrailleNote (walking)	D9	Outdoors	Yes
Adaptive Sports Tools			
Beeper baseball	I4	Outdoors	Yes
Radios in helmet (skiing)	I1, I4, I7	Outdoors	Yes

Table 5. Technology use reported by Groups 1&2.

whether it would be an alarm to go off if the athlete is approaching the wall or another player (I4) or the transponder technology to notify of other competitors (I5) mentioned in the empirical investigation.

With respect to **independent rigorous exercise outdoors,** only one of the reported technologies fills the void: Beep baseball, which is an already open exercise [45] specifically designed for people who are blind or low-vision. In terms of the eleven other technologies, six are used while running, biking, or skiing with a sighted guide, and five are used while walking outdoors. There are interesting potential research efforts that try to close the gap between *independent exercise* while walking (e.g. more closed exercise [45]) and guided exercise while completing *rigorous activity* (e.g. more open exercise [45]). In addition to the researchers suggesting a head mounted camera and headphones to guide someone around the track, D4 also suggested developing a controlled setting for tennis, where a machine would serve audible tennis balls with both a consistent location and time frame (D4).

Navigation of exercise spaces is also not well represented by the reported technologies. D4 reported using the iPhone camera with zoom and flash to help navigate while walking, however this technology is not designed for this purpose and requires time and overhead. Secondly, D9 reported using two technologies related to navigation (Sendero look around and GPS), but they were only related to walking outdoors. There is an opportunity for technology to be developed to help people navigate new exercise spaces, such as a gym, running track, or hiking trail. D1 and D3 proposed a technology to help navigate hiking trails as mentioned in the empirical investigation. Additionally, D3 proposed giving auditory feedback to properly navigate a swimming lane, and D7 suggested wearing a camera so they could be notified as to whether or not a person is using exercise equipment.

LIMITATIONS AND FUTURE WORK

While we carefully chose our study design, there were limitations to our approach. Our recruitment entailed contacting email lists and snowball recruitment. As a result, it is possible that we may have received less of a representative sample. In addition, the authors were not able to recruit people who are blind or low-vision and are also part of a sports team such as Goalball or Beep Baseball. Finally, we were unable to have participants work with physical prototypes as described in the interviews; they were not within a close geographic distance and some of the technologies may not yet exist. For these reasons, our study and analysis of the interviews is qualitative. In addition, there were hypothetical technologies posed in the survey and in some of the interviews. The responses may be different than if the technology existed and was regularly used.

For future work, we hope to design and develop technologies that fit the four opportunities identified by this work. Ideally, designers would involve both direct and indirect stakeholders while designing, prototyping, and testing technology.

CONCLUSION

We presented opportunities and design considerations for eyes-free exercise technologies by employing value sensitive design. Specifically, we conducted interviews with 10 people who are blind or low-vision and with 10 people who facilitate fitness for people who are blind or low-vision, as well as a survey with 76 people from the general population who acted as outsiders to blind exercisers. We found four opportunities for design (Table 3): knowledge transfer while in an exercise class, knowledge transfer while exercising with a sighted guide, rigorous outdoor exercise, and navigating exercise spaces. In addition, we identified two further considerations (Table 3): how to properly design the audio channel and how to allow for less mainstream technologies to be viable options when enhancing exercise in a mainstream setting. We hope that researchers and designers can build from this work and inform future technologies that help make exercise more accessible for people who are blind or low-vision.

ACKNOWLEDGEMENTS

We thank Alan Borning for his guidance and assistance to make our project a success. Our research was funded with the National Science Foundation Graduate Research Fellowship Program for two of the authors. The University of Washington Human Subjects ethics board approved this research.

REFERENCES

1. Iñaki M. Albaina, Thomas Visser, Charles A.P.G. van der Mast, Martijn H. Vastenburg. 2009. Flowie: A persuasive virtual coach to motivate elderly individuals to walk. In *Pervasive Computing Technologies for Healthcare. 3rd International Conference on PervasiveHealth* (PervasiveHealth '09), 1-7. http://dx.doi.org/10.4108/icst.pervasivehealth2009.5949
2. Shiri Azenkot, Sanjana Prasain, Alan Borning, Emily Fortuna, Richard E. Ladner, and Jacob O. Wobbrock. 2011. Enhancing independence and safety for blind and deaf-blind public transit riders. In *Proceedings of the SIGCHI Conference on Human Factors in Computing Systems* (CHI '11), 3247-3256. DOI= http://doi.acm.org/10.1145/1978942.1979424
3. Shiri Azenkot, Kyle Rector, Richard Ladner, and Jacob Wobbrock. 2012. PassChords: secure multi-touch authentication for blind people. In *Proceedings of the 14th international ACM SIGACCESS conference on Computers and accessibility* (ASSETS '12). ACM, New York, NY, USA, 159-166. DOI= http://doi.acm.org/10.1145/2384916.2384945
4. Elaine Biddiss and Jennifer Irwin. 2010. Active video games to promote physical activity in children and youth: a systematic review. *Archives of pediatrics & adolescent medicine* 164, 7: 664-672. DOI= http://dx.doi.org/10.1001/archpediatrics.2010.104
5. Alan Borning, Batya Friedman, Janet Davis, and Peyina Lin. 2005. Informing public deliberation: Value sensi-

tive design of indicators for a large-scale urban simulation. In *Proceedings of the 2005 Ninth European Conference on Computer-Supported Cooperative Work* (ECSCW '05), 449-468. DOI= http://dx.doi.org/10.1007/1-4020-4023-7_23

6. Alper Bozkurt, David L. Roberts, Barbara L. Sherman, Rita Brugarolas, Sean Mealin, John Majikes, Pu Yang, and Robert Loftin. 2014. Toward Cyber-Enhanced Working Dogs for Search and Rescue. *IEEE Intelligent Systems* 29, 6: 32-37. DOI= http://dx.doi.org/10.1109/mis.2014.77
7. CABI. 2012. Welcome to the Cricket Association for the Blind in India (CABI) | Cricket Association for the Blind in India. Retrieved May 4, 2015 from http://www.blindcricket.in/
8. Canadian Blind Sports Association. 2012. Canadian Blind Sports. Retrieved May 4, 2015 from http://canadianblindsports.ca/
9. Michele Capella-McDonnall. 2007. The need for health promotion for adults who are visually impaired. *Journal of Visual Impairment and Blindness* 101, 3: 133-145.
10. Robert Cercos and Florian 'Floyd' Mueller. 2013. Watch your steps: designing a semi-public display to promote physical activity. In *Proceedings of The 9th Australasian Conference on Interactive Entertainment: Matters of Life and Death* (IE '13), Article 2, 6 pages. DOI= http://doi.acm.org/10.1145/2513002.2513016
11. Sunny Consolvo, David W. McDonald, and James A. Landay. 2009. Theory-driven design strategies for technologies that support behavior change in everyday life. In *Proceedings of the SIGCHI Conference on Human Factors in Computing Systems* (CHI '09), 405-414. DOI= http://doi.acm.org/10.1145/1518701.1518766
12. Courage Canada. 2015. Courage Canada Hockey for the Blind. Retrieved May 4, 2015 from http://www.couragecanada.ca/
13. Brad Crawford. 2015. A Blind Runner and His Amazing Guide Dog. Retrieved July 7, 2015 from http://thebark.com/content/blind-runner-and-his-amazing-guide-dog
14. Chloe Fan, Jodi Forlizzi, and Anind Dey. 2012. Considerations for technology that support physical activity by older adults. In *Proceedings of the 14th international ACM SIGACCESS conference on Computers and accessibility* (ASSETS '12), 33-40. DOI= http://doi.acm.org/10.1145/2384916.2384923
15. Fitbit. 2015. Fitbit Official Site for Activity Trackers & More. Retrieved May 4, 2015 from http://www.fitbit.com/
16. Batya Friedman, Peter H. Kahn Jr., and Alan Borning. 2013. Value Sensitive Design and information systems. In Ping Zhang and Dennis Galletta (eds.), Human-computer interaction in management information systems: Foundations, Springer Netherlands, 55-95. DOI= http://dx.doi.org/10.1007/978-94-007-7844-3_4
17. Nicholas A. Giudice and Gordon E. Legge. 2008. Blind Navigation and the Role of Technology. In A. Helal, M. Mokhtari & B. Abdulrazak (eds.), Engineering handbook of smart technology for aging, disability, and independence, John Wiley & Sons, 479-500. DOI= http://dx.doi.org/10.1002/9780470379424.ch25
18. Barney G. Glaser, and Anselm L. Strauss. 1967. *The discovery of grounded theory: Strategies for qualitative research.* New York: Aldine Transaction.
19. Greg Guest, Arwen Bunce, and Laura Johnson. 2006. How many interviews are enough? An experiment with data saturation and variability. *Field methods* 18, 1: 59-82. DOI= http://dx.doi.org/10.1177/1525822x05279903
20. Francis Iannacci, Erik Turnquist, Daniel Avrahami, and Shwetak N. Patel. 2011. The haptic laser: multi-sensation tactile feedback for at-a-distance physical space perception and interaction. In *Proceedings of the SIGCHI Conference on Human Factors in Computing Systems* (CHI '11), 2047-2050. DOI= http://doi.acm.org/10.1145/1978942.1979239
21. Melody Moore Jackson, Clint Zeagler, Giancarlo Valentin, Alex Martin, Vincent Martin, Adil Delawalla, Wendy Blount, Sarah Eiring, Ryan Hollis, Yash Kshirsagar, and Thad Starner. 2013. FIDO - facilitating interactions for dogs with occupations: wearable dog-activated interfaces. In *Proceedings of the 2013 International Symposium on Wearable Computers* (ISWC '13), 81-88. DOI= http://doi.acm.org/10.1145/2493988.2494334
22. Shaun K. Kane, Chandrika Jayant, Jacob O. Wobbrock, and Richard E. Ladner. 2009. Freedom to roam: a study of mobile device adoption and accessibility for people with visual and motor disabilities. In *Proceedings of the 11th international ACM SIGACCESS conference on Computers and accessibility* (Assets '09), 115-122. DOI= http://doi.acm.org/10.1145/1639642.163966
23. Lauren J. Lieberman, Barbara L. Robinson, and Heidi Rollheiser. 2006. Youth with visual impairments: Experiences in general physical education. *Re: view* 38, 1: 35-48. DOI= http://dx.doi.org/10.3200/revu.38.1.35-48
24. Matthew Mauriello, Michael Gubbels, and Jon E. Froehlich. 2014. Social fabric fitness: the design and evaluation of wearable E-textile displays to support group running. In *Proceedings of the SIGCHI Conference on Human Factors in Computing Systems* (CHI '14), 2833-2842. DOI= http://doi.acm.org/10.1145/2556288.2557299
25. Lauren R. Milne, Cynthia L. Bennett, and Richard E. Ladner. 2014. The Accessibility of Mobile Health Sensors for Blind Users. In *29th Annual International & Persons with Disabilities Conference* (CSUN '14).

26. Anthony Morelli. 2010. Haptic/audio based exergaming for visually impaired individuals. SIGACCESS Access. Comput. 96 (January 2010), 50-53. DOI= http://doi.acm.org/10.1145/1731849.1731859

27. Tony Morelli, John Foley, Luis Columna, Lauren Lieberman, and Eelke Folmer. 2010. VI-Tennis: a vibrotactile/audio exergame for players who are visually impaired. In *Proceedings of the Fifth International Conference on the Foundations of Digital Games* (FDG '10), 147-154. DOI= http://doi.acm.org/10.1145/1822348.1822368

28. Tony Morelli, John Foley, and Eelke Folmer. 2010. Vi-bowling: a tactile spatial exergame for individuals with visual impairments. In *Proceedings of the 12th international ACM SIGACCESS conference on Computers and accessibility* (ASSETS '10), 179-186. DOI= http://doi.acm.org/10.1145/1878803.1878836

29. Tony Morelli, John Foley, Lauren Lieberman, and Eelke Folmer. 2011. Pet-N-Punch: upper body tactile/audio exergame to engage children with visual impairments into physical activity. In *Proceedings of Graphics Interface 2011* (GI '11), 223-230.

30. Tony Morelli, and Eelke Folmer. 2014. Real-time sensory substitution to enable players who are blind to play video games using whole body gestures. *Entertainment Computing* 5, 1: 83-90. DOI= http://dx.doi.org/10.1016/j.entcom.2013.08.003

31. Nike, Inc. 2015. Choose Your Nike+ App. Nike.com. Retrieved May 4, 2015 from http://www.nike.com/us/en_us/c/nikeplus-fuel

32. Phys.org. 2015. Blind French hikers cross mountains with special GPS. Retrieved July 8, 2015 from http://phys.org/news/2015-07-french-hikers-mountains-special-gps.html

33. Jules Pretty, Jo Peacock, Martin Sellens, and Murray Griffin. 2005. The mental and physical health outcomes of green exercise. *International Journal of Environmental Health Research,* 15, 5: 319-337. DOI= http://dx.doi.org/10.1080/09603120500155963

34. Kyle Rector, Cynthia L. Bennett, and Julie A. Kientz. 2013. Eyes-free yoga: an exergame using depth cameras for blind & low vision exercise. In *Proceedings of the 15th International ACM SIGACCESS Conference on Computers and Accessibility* (ASSETS '13), Article 12, 8 pages. DOI= http://doi.acm.org/10.1145/2513383.2513392

35. James H. Rimmer. 2006. Building Inclusive Activity Communities for People with Vision Loss. *Journal of Visual Impairment & Blindness*, 100, suppl, 863-865.

36. Barbara L. Robinson, and Lauren J. Lieberman. 2004. Effects of visual impairment, gender, and age on self-determination. *Journal of Visual Impairment & Blindness*, 98, 6: 351-366.

37. Victoria Schwanda, Steven Ibara, Lindsay Reynolds, and Dan Cosley. 2011. Side effects and "gateway" tools: advocating a broader look at evaluating persuasive systems. In *Proceedings of the SIGCHI Conference on Human Factors in Computing Systems* (CHI '11), 345-348. DOI= http://doi.acm.org/10.1145/1978942.1978991

38. Ski for Light. 2015. Ski for Light, Inc.® Retrieved May 4, 2015 from http://sfl.org/

39. Kristen Shinohara and Josh Tenenberg. 2007. Observing Sara: a case study of a blind person's interactions with technology. In *Proceedings of the 9th international ACM SIGACCESS conference on Computers and accessibility* (Assets '07), 171-178. DOI= http://doi.acm.org/10.1145/1296843.1296873

40. Kristen Shinohara and Jacob O. Wobbrock. 2011. In the shadow of misperception: assistive technology use and social interactions. In *Proceedings of the SIGCHI Conference on Human Factors in Computing Systems* (CHI '11). ACM, New York, NY, USA, 705-714. DOI= http://doi.acm.org/10.1145/1978942.1979044

41. The United States Association of Blind Athletes. 2015. Sports Adaptations. Retrieved May 4, 2015 from http://usaba.org/index.php/sports/sports-adaptations/

42. Moira E. Stuart, Lauren Lieberman, and Karen E. Hand. 2006. Beliefs about physical activity among children who are visually impaired and their parents. *Journal of Visual Impairment & Blindness*, 100, 4: 223-234.

43. The United States Association of Blind Athletes. 2015. The United States Association of Blind Athletes. Retrieved May 4, 2015 from http://usaba.org/

44. Evette Weil, Melissa Wachterman, Ellen P. McCarthy, Roger B. Davis, Bonnie O'Day, Lisa I. Iezzoni, and Christina C. Wee. 2002. Obesity among adults with disabling conditions. *Journal of the American Medical Association*, 288, 10: 1265-1268. DOI= http://dx.doi.org/10.1001/jama.288.10.1265

45. Joseph P. Winnick. 2011. *Adapted physical education and sport.* Human Kinectics.

46. Fahri Yetim. 2011. Bringing discourse ethics to value sensitive design: pathways toward a deliberative future. *AIS Transactions on Human-Computer Interaction*, 3, 2: 133-155.

Online News Videos: The UX of Subtitle Position

Michael Crabb
Robert Gordon University
Aberdeen
Scotland
michaelcrabb@acm.org

Rhianne Jones
BBC R&D
Salford, Manchester
England
rhia.jones@bbc.co.uk

Mike Armstrong
BBC R&D
Salford, Manchester
England
mike.armstrong@bbc.co.uk

Chris J. Hughes
BBC R&D
Salford, Manchester
England
chris.hughes@rd.bbc.co.uk

ABSTRACT

Millions of people rely on subtitles when watching video content. The current change in media viewing behaviour involving computers has resulted in a large proportion of people turning to online sources as opposed to regular television for news information. This work analyses the user experience of viewing subtitled news videos presented as part of a web page. A lab-based user experiment was carried out with frequent subtitle users, focusing on determining whether changes in video dimension and subtitle location could affect the user experience attached to viewing subtitled content.

A significant improvement in user experience was seen when changing the subtitle location from the standard position of within a video at the bottom to below the video clip. Additionally, participants responded positively when given the ability to change the position of subtitles in real time, allowing for a more personalised viewing experience. This recommendation for an alternative subtitle positioning that can be controlled by the user is unlike current subtitling practice. It provides evidence that further user-based research examining subtitle usage outside of the traditional television interface is required.

Categories and Subject Descriptors

• **Human-centered computing ~ Empirical studies in accessibility** • *Human-centered computing ~ User studies.*

General Terms

Design, Experimentation, Human Factors.

Keywords

Subtitles; user experience; laboratory experiment; experiment methodology.

1. Introduction

Subtitles are a method in which the audio content from a video is shown to the viewer as text to accompany the broadcast when it is not part of the original video image itself. Recent Ofcom statistics show that over 8 million people in the UK have watched subtitled video content on at least one occasion [23]. Subtitles aid users in interpreting and understanding content that they may be otherwise excluded from. However, the positioning of subtitles on top of a video has the potential to block content that is important. This, in turn, can have a detrimental effect on the experience that subtitle users have when consuming media. This problem is amplified when viewing media in an online browser as video dimensions can decrease while text remains at a size that is still legible for the user. Therefore, while subtitles are important in contributing to the understanding of content provided through video, they can also act as a barrier to understanding this information. The presence, accuracy, and intelligibility of subtitles and the surrounding content are key in providing services that are accessible to all.

The purpose of this work is to investigate the positioning of subtitles inside a web browser window. Guidelines for subtitles have recommended a preference for subtitles at the bottom of the screen but note that the movement of subtitles so as to not obscure information is important [2]. This work investigates the positioning of these subtitles within and outside of the video being shown. It is carried out with a focus placed on small videos that are embedded within the BBC News website[1]. On average 256 million people a week visit this site [1] and subtitled content would have a positive impact for a significant proportion of these visitors. Examining the positioning of subtitles in order to explore the user experience that is attached to this service provides an opportunity to have a clear benefit in overall content accessibility.

2. Previous Work

Displaying subtitles in alternative positions to that of a traditional television experience is not a new concept [8]. Within a cinema setting, an alternative 'secondary' screen can be placed underneath the main display to view subtitles only when needed [24]. A developing area of research regarding subtitle position focuses on the dynamic positioning of subtitle blocks so as to not obscure any of the images on the screen, thus placing subtitles as a more integral part of the content [4, 13, 14]. This method, currently optimised for large television screens, shows promise in developing a new subtitle format that may be suitable for television use. However, there is a growing number of users turning to online media [22] and surprisingly little research investigating the presentation and practical improvements to the presentation of subtitles on smaller videos.

An approach that may be suitable for use with small online videos is to drop the subtitles underneath the primary content being displayed. Shahraray et al. [24] present an implementation of this where pictorial transcripts of programmes are created where a video-still is displayed with transcripts placed underneath. This method, created primarily for use in printed media, can be adapted for use within a video context. Additionally, it may be possible for the television user to decide the positioning of the subtitles to either within or outside of the main display, with this placing the choice in the hands of the user instead of the broadcaster [12]. However, little user-based research exists which examine either of these solutions. In turn, it is not known to what degree this repositioning of subtitles would affect the overall user experience

ASSETS '15, October 26 - 28, 2015, Lisbon, Portugal

ACM 978-1-4503-3400-6/15/10…$15.00
DOI: http://dx.doi.org/10.1145/2700648.2809866

[1] http://www.bbc.co.uk/news

of subtitled content, and whether this would have a positive or negative effect for the end user.

Research examining subtitle usage provides valuable information; however the results produced may only measure a small number of aspects associated with user experience. For example, user enjoyment has been examined in relation to subtitle usage with Hu [14] and Hong [13] both exploring the 'enjoyment' of subtitle usage with a single Likert-scored question in their work. Additionally, Lee et. al [19] has shown how a 7x7 grid of selections can be used to assess the mood and energy attached to subtitles in a user task. Jensema [16] has measured the readability of subtitles through a 5-point Likert scale, with participants asked to comment if subtitles were Too Fast, Fast, OK, Slow, or Too Slow. These examples show the willingness of research to accept that aspects of UX play an important part in viewing subtitled video content. However, a problem exists in determining a suitable process that can be used which encompasses a wider range of factors important in analysing the UX of subtitled video content.

Brown et. al [5] have recently used a framework specifically designed to look at the UX of subtitled video content. This was created in an attempt to consider factors that are both meaningful and reliable in examining the UX of subtitled video content; factors that are a necessity in UX work [18]. These factors, based on uncovering the benefits that a user may derive from a product [17], provide an insight to aid in understanding the experience of viewing subtitled video content.

2.1 A Framework for Data Capture

This work applied a working UX framework (see Brown et. al [5]) to measure the UX of subtitled video content in relation to variable subtitle position. This measures seven key components, all of which are important in understanding the concepts that are part of creating a positive user experience associated with subtitled video content.

Aesthetics is a measure of the visual appeal of the subtitled video content. High aesthetic appeal indicates that the content is visually pleasing. Low aesthetic levels indicate that the subtitles are displayed in a manner that is not visually pleasing to users.

Attention is a measure of the awareness that users have in relation to what is going on in subtitled video content. High levels of attention indicate that users are very focused on the video content. Low levels of attention indicate that it is difficult to focus on the subtitled video content and users may become distracted by other elements.

Involvement is used as a measure of how engaged users are with the subtitled video content. While *attention* attempts to understand a focus on the content, *involvement* is about the depth of engagement. Users reporting high levels of involvement would be 'drawn into' the subtitled. Users reporting low levels of involvement would feel less involved in the subtitled content.

Familiarity is a measure of how users feel the subtitled content is recognisable as to what they would expect subtitled content to look like; its naturalness. High levels of familiarity indicate coherence in the relationship between the subtitles and the video content. Low levels of familiarity would indicate disconnect in what is perceived as routine subtitle practice.

Perceived usefulness measures how useful the display of the subtitled content is. High levels of usefulness is categorised by users who see high levels of value in the subtitle display. Users with low levels of perceived usefulness will see low levels of value in the subtitle display.

Perceived usability is a measure of the challenge that is faced while engaging with the subtitled video content. Users that report high levels of perceived usability are likely to have found the subtitled content easy to understand, while users with low levels of perceived usability are likely to have found viewing the subtitled content more demanding.

Endurability is defined as a user's willingness to view subtitled video content using a similar method of subtitle display in the future. Users with high levels of endurability are likely to wish to use this method again, while users with low levels of endurability would be less likely to want to use this method again in the future. It is worth noting that *endurability*, while an important factor, is very difficult to analyse in lab-based research such as this.

3. Methodology

This work investigates the user experience attached to viewing subtitled news content displayed inside a web browser. The position of subtitle text within and below a video clip is investigated. This is examined to determine if it is possible to take advantage of the screen estate surrounding a video being displayed, and if this can improve the user experience associated with viewing subtitles. In this context, viewing clips inside a web browser allows extra screen space to be used for subtitle blocks – an affordance that is not possible when a video is 'full screen'.

Specifically, this work intends to determine firstly; if overall user experience can be improved by changing the position of subtitles from within a video clip to below the video clip being presented and secondly; to discover if participants perceive there to be value in a control to change subtitle position in order to suit their own individual needs.

3.1 Participants

There are many reasons as to why an individual would wish to use subtitles. This can include users who regularly use subtitles as an access service, those who use subtitles as a translation from a foreign language [26], and those who occasionally use subtitles when they are situationally impaired [20]. In this work, we are investigating the use of subtitles with users who regularly use them as an access service.

26 participants were recruited for this study (age range 22-67; M = 47.2, SD = 13.6; 7 male, 19 female). Recruitment was carried out by an external user recruitment agency. Participants were required to fit the following criteria:

- All must regularly use the Internet to consume news and current affair information
- All must use subtitles at home to watch TV with the sound on
- All must use subtitles on a regular basis (i.e. daily)
- All must not have taken part in any research in the last six months

A mix of gender, socio-cultural/economic backgrounds was also used with a mix of males and females being recruited.

3.2 Experiment Design

A 2 x 2 within participant experiment design was used. The position of subtitles (within or below the video clip) and the physical dimensions (½ or ⅔ of the overall page width) were used as independent variables. These video dimensions are included

Figure 1 - Experiment Changes in Video Size and Subtitle Positioning

based on guidance from [3]. Participant user experience (measured through a Likert scored questionnaire) was used as a dependant variable. The positioning of subtitles above a video, and the control of these subtitles by participants is visited using a qualitative methodology later in this paper.

3.3 Materials and Equipment

3.3.1 Video Clips

Four video clips were selected for participants to view based on criteria similar to that used by Burnham et. al. [6]. Videos adhered to the following guidelines:

1. The clip must be a news broadcast, selected from outside of the local region, in an attempt to ensure that topics would be unfamiliar to participants
2. No offensive, disturbing, or controversial material should be included in the clip
3. The selection of clips that should include talking head and narration clips,
4. Clip excerpts should be longer than 1 minute but shorter than 2 minutes,
5. A range of activity and engagement should be present across clip excerpts.

The clips selected fit within all of the above guidelines. The duration of clips was between 94 and 101 seconds (M = 97.5s, SD = 2.88s). A description of the 4 clips is given below:

Clip A[2] – *Woman falls 30ft from Wells Cathedral Tower.* A woman has been winched to safety by helicopter, after falling and becoming trapped at Wells Cathedral in Somerset.

Clip B[3] – *New 'Banksy' work appears near* GCHQ. "Guerrilla artist" Banksy is believed to be behind a piece of street art depicting three shadowy figures eavesdropping.

Clip C[4] – *Solar cycle path opens in* Netherlands. A public solar cycle lane has opened in the Netherlands as part of a pilot scheme.

Clip D[5] – *New UK Great Western Main line trains unveiled in Japan.* The high-speed train, which will be used on the Great Western Main Line through the Thames Valley, has been unveiled in Japan.

3.3.2 Subtitle Control System

The selection of appropriate subtitle font, colour, and background vary greatly dependant on country, broadcaster, and even device. As such, no standardised method of subtitle display exists that can be used in this work. We chose to display subtitles in a semi-transparent box that spanned the width of the video being displayed, with text being a white colour (providing adequate contrast to the background), the Helvetica font being used, and text position being centre justified (seen in Figure 1).

A system was created that allowed for the manipulation of subtitle position and the video size independent of the clip being shown. When the subtitle box was placed below or above the video, the position of surrounding web content was adjusted so that it was not obscured. Subtitles could be positioned within or below the clip being played. Video size could be set as ½ of the page width or as ⅔ of the page width (Figure 1). These sizes were chosen to fit with BBC Global Experience Language (GEL) Guidelines [25]. All videos shown were in a 16:9 ratio. The ½ width video measured 480px across, and the ⅔ measured 640px across. The full size of the window frame was 976px. The system to control these adaptions used aspects developed by Hughes et. al [15].

3.3.3 Subtitle User Experience Questionnaire

A 14 question 5-point Likert scored (Strongly Agree, Agree, Neither Agree or Disagree, Disagree, Strongly Disagree) questionnaire was used to measure the user experience of viewing subtitled content. The questionnaire used the UX concepts outlined previously by Brown et al. [5]. Questions were a mix of positive (e.g. "*This feels like a familiar way to view subtitled video content*") and negative (e.g. "*I am not used to seeing*

[2] http://www.bbc.co.uk/news/uk-27213646

[3] http://www.bbc.co.uk/news/entertainment-arts-27029515

[4] http://www.bbc.co.uk/news/technology-30024881

[5] http://www.bbc.co.uk/news/uk-30042801

subtitles viewed in this way") statements. Once completed, negative question scores were inverted and mean responses computed. This created a score for each of the 7 UX factors as well as a combined overall UX scoring.

3.3.4 *Conversation Prompts*

Conversation prompts, consisting of screenshots of different interface options, were created to stimulate conversation with participants in order to further discuss their thoughts on subtitle positioning. These were based on positioning that subtitles were viewed in during the experiment

3.3.5 *Semi-Structured Interview Script*

A semi-structured interview script was constructed to explore participants' preference on subtitle position for videos displayed on a web page. A series of questions were constructed to probe deeper into the relationship between subtitle positioning and user experience. The script was created to encourage participants to discuss the advantages and disadvantages of the different subtitle positions. It was also used as an aid to help participants discuss any preferences that existed for alternative subtitle positions. Participants were encouraged to discuss any additional factors they deemed important in shaping their preferences. This was used to further understand the user experience in relation to the positional display of subtitles. Probes relating to the concepts discussed by Brown et al. [5] were included in this script. These, and accompanying participant comments, are shown in the discussion below.

3.4 Procedure

Participants were introduced to the study, being informed that the purpose of the work was to examine their experiences of subtitled content and whether this would change based on the positioning of the subtitles and the physical size of the video they are watching. An initial conversation then occurred where participants were prompted to discuss their current experiences with subtitles.

Participants were then introduced to the *subtitle control system* and were shown the series of 4 *video clips*. Counterbalancing occurred on the order in which clips were shown, the positioning of the subtitles, and the dimensions of the video. This was accomplished using a repeated orthogonal Latin squared design [9]. Participants were asked to complete the user experience survey after viewing each video. The order in which questions were asked in the user experience survey was randomised both within and between participants.

Participants were then shown the conversation prompts representing the different subtitle conditions that they had previously encountered. Participants were asked to rate the cards and then prompted to explain their choices. These questions focused on subtitle user experience and how this related to the position of the subtitles and the dimension of the videos shown.

The semi-structured interview was then used to explore participants' views and individual preferences towards the positioning of subtitles, and how this might relate to the size of video being presented. Participants were encouraged to discuss the advantages and disadvantages of variable subtitle positions and any other key factors or issues relating to subtitle position and the overall user experience.

3.5 Analysis

A mixed-method approach was performed in analysis, a technique suggested by O'Brien and Lebow [21]. This results in a combination of quantitative and qualitative data gathered to examine the subjective user experience properties associated with subtitle usage. In quantitative (as well as qualitative) analysis, the purpose was to examine any differences that were present between different subtitle positioning techniques, with subtitle position and video size being used as Independent Variables. This resulted in a 2x2 repeated-measures ANOVA being used for analysis. Bonferroni correction was used on all testing and all data was standardised using Gelman's [11] method. Descriptive information is shown in Table 1.

In this work, an increase in scoring for each of the seven factors outlined by Brown et al. [5] indicates an improvement in user experience. However, this may not always be the case for other types of broadcast clip. Additional factors such as genre (e.g. horror) may strive to create lower levels of UX factors (e.g. aesthetics or even endurability) to improve the overall experience. The combined mean of these values are used in analysis to represent overall user experience.[6]

4. Results

A dependant measures ANOVA was used to examine if participants user experience would change based on the combination of subtitle position (below or within) and the video size (small or large). Kolmogorov-Smirnov's test of normality revealed normal distribution of the data, allowing for analysis to continue. However, no significant effect was found between these groups; $F(1,25) = .035$, $p = .853$. This indicates that no interaction effect was present between the position of the subtitles and the video size.

Table 1 - User Experience and Subtitle Positioning: Descriptive Information

	Mean	SD	SE	K-S
Below/Small	3.51	.640	.125	p > .05
Below/Large	3.61	.553	.108	p > .05
Within/Small	3.29	.716	.140	p > .05
Within/Large	3.42	.685	.134	p > .05
Total	3.46	.653	.064	p > .05

Analysis of subtitle position and video size as separate factors was then used to determine the individual effect of these two independent measures, with these being Bonferroni adjusted. A significant difference was found between subtitles positioned below ($M = 3.56$, $SD = .499$) or within ($M = 3.35$, $SD = .551$) the video clip; $t(25) = -2.38$, $p = .025$, $r = .194$. No significant difference was found between small ($M = 3.40$, $SD = .566$) and large ($M = 3.52$, $SD = .499$) video clips; $t(25) = 1.25$, $p = .224$, $d = .45$.

No effect was observed to suggest that the change in the size of a video clip positioned inside a web page would have an influence on the user experience attached to viewing subtitles on that page. However, the positioning of the subtitles either below or within the video clip does have a significant (medium [7]) effect on the user experience. In this instance, positioning subtitles below the video content instead of the traditional placement of within the video, showed to significantly increase the overall user experience that was attached to viewing subtitles.

[6] Due to the ethically sensitive nature of the research, no participants were asked to consent to their data being shared beyond the research group and as such supporting data cannot be made openly available.

	Aesthetics	Involvement	Attention	Familiarity	Usefulness	Usability	Endurability
Within	0.002	-0.045	-0.067	-0.203	0.005	0.013	0.002
Below	0.013	0.047	0.016	-0.1	0.091	0.088	0.094
Small	0.024	0.05	-0.017	-0.173	0.027	0.05	0.05
Large	-0.009	-0.048	-0.034	-0.131	0.069	0.052	0.088

Figure 2 – Radar Plots and Experiment Data comparing subtitle Within/Below the video and small/large video size

4.1 UX Framework – Dimensional Factors

Figure 2 shows radar plots comparing the overall subtitle user experience. This is used to compare between subtitles within and below the video clip being shown.

The previous analysis compared subtitle blocks within the video clip and subtitle blocks below the video clip. The results from this suggested that having the subtitle block below the video clip significantly increased the user experience that was reported by participants. The largest increases occurred in the Involvement, Endurability, and Familiarity reported by users. Participants also reported slight increases in the Attention, Perceived Usefulness and Perceived Usability that was attached to placing subtitles below the video clip being viewed. Analysis of the qualitative data provided explanation of participant's preferences for subtitle position.

4.1.1 Involvement

Did the subtitles feel connected to the visual content? Did the position have any impact on how involved or immersed you were in the content?

Responses to these questions were mostly positive. Participants stated that felt they were more involved with the subtitled videos due to content not being obscured by the placement of subtitles. For example, P.10 stated that they *much prefer having the subtitles below the screen because you're not missing anything.* Comments suggest that obscuring video content was one of the key benefits to placing subtitles below the video.

However, some participants commented that they felt more involved when subtitles were placed within the video at the bottom, with P19 stating that it was *easier on the eye*, when subtitles were positioned in this way. P.9 also preferred subtitles being displayed within the video at the bottom, adding that *they are almost integrated and you are paying attention to both things [subtitles and video content] at once.*

4.1.2 Endurability

Would you be able to watch subtitles like this for an extended period of time?

Due to the nature of the research, only subjective perceptions of the long-term endurability of positional display could be explored. Estimating the long-term endurability of a system when the only experience that a participant would have was in a lab environment does not, therefore, provide meaningful results. Participants echoed this reasoning in their own comments with P. 0 stating that it was difficult to know which would be easier and that *I'd know better if I was to spend a week watching and trying this out.*

4.1.3 Familiarity

Did this subtitle display feel familiar/strange? Was the display in line with your expectations?

Interestingly, participant questionnaire scorings indicated that subtitles placed below the video clip felt more familiar than subtitles within the video clip, even though this is something that participants had not viewed before.

> *I'm used to it like A (within) but I prefer it like B (below).* (P.2)

A possible reason for this is given by P. 15, who explains that *it felt a bit more natural. It was still weird seeing it not hovering like it normally is with the white writing over the picture.* However, despite this tendency in participants to favour this new method for displaying subtitles, some participants still showed a preference for subtitles being displayed in a comparable fashion to their previous usage. For example, P. 9 stated that they *would pick the subtitles being overlaid...because this is a familiar way of watching.*

4.1.4 Attention

Were you able to focus comfortable on the video content and the subtitles? Did the position of the subtitles have any effect on where your attention was focused during the clip?

The focus that users reported on having regarding the subtitled content was slightly higher when subtitles were placed below the video. A possible reason for this could be that subtitles positioned underneath the video are outside of a viewer's normal viewing pattern and therefore more likely to be noticed and are drawn to their attention; P.6 describes this as being *disjointed.* A second potential reason could be down to the transparency used in the subtitle background, with this creating shifting content when placed on top of the video and consequently being more difficult for users to focus on. This is noted by P.0, who also comments that the placement below the video also puts the subtitles outside of his normal vision.

> *I think that below is more apparent, but it doesn't show off to my eyes as much.* (P.0)

4.1.5 *Perceived Usefulness*

How useful do you find the subtitle display? Are there any advantages or disadvantages to placing the subtitles in this position?

Participants' comments revealed little difference in their perception of the perceived usefulness of the different subtitle positions, with this potentially due to the subtitles still being useful in both conditions (illustrated by both conditions scoring highly in the questionnaire). However, participants commented that there could be difficulties in subtitles being placed within the video:

> *When things are moving around in the background behind the subtitles it can be difficult, it's hard to use. I prefer the subtitles being underneath. You don't feel like you are at a disadvantage*

Of note here, is P.20's feeling that when problems occur with subtitle display they feel *disadvantaged.* This feeling of isolation highlights the importance of subtitles to users that rely on them. However, it is common for users to accept subtitle appearance and placement without any criticism. For example, when asked for any advantages or disadvantages that may exist between different subtitling methods, P.9 responded that *I don't want to seem really picky because subtitles are subtitles.*

4.1.6 *Perceived Usability*

Did the subtitle display have any impact on how comfortably you were able to follow the subtitled content?

The ease at which content can be understood, or its usability, is an important aspect in understanding the user experience attached to subtitle usage. A common theme arising from participants surrounding this was that it was simple to see both the video content and the subtitles. For example, P.11 expressed that *the great advantage is that you can see more of the image, so you can see what is happening.* This ability to see (and separate) the video content from the subtitles made the overall subtitled content more usable for participants. P.5 even went as far to say that subtitles being placed within the video at the bottom *are really annoying to me now.* However, one participant raised concern as to how positioning subtitles underneath the video would work with a decline in vision:

> *As you get older your peripheral vision shrinks, and for that reason having it compact is better. Having subtitles underneath I have to move around a lot more* (P. 19)

Additionally, P.6 described mixed feelings towards the usability associated with subtitles being placed below the video, stating that it was an advantage that '*you get to see the whole video [and] you don't lose any information*' however, they also note the disadvantage attached to this positioning in that '*it feels a bit disjointed and you feel like you have to jump between the two*'.

4.1.7 *Aesthetics*

How aesthetically appealing did you find the subtitled content? Did the subtitles look 'right' in the context of the webpage?

Several participants commented on improvements in the overall aesthetics of viewing subtitles when they were below the video. For example P.8 stated, *I prefer having the subtitles underneath the footage. It's not super imposed on the image it seems more like part of the image.* Another common reason for this preference was due to the improved contrast between foreground and background.

> *There's a better contrast between the subtitles and the background (*P.10)

This increased contrast was due the semi-transparent background used behind the subtitles resulting in a static background when it was not overlaying the moving images. However, this was not an opinion that was shared by all participants. For example, P. 6 stated that they preferred subtitle being overlaid on the video as when subtitles were below the video they were *jumping between the two* and not able to follow the news item as easily. This idea of separation between subtitles and content was mirrored by P. 11 who stated that *aesthetically I like the subtitles over the video better, because it's not blocked off.*

It is also worth noting that the visual difference between subtitles within the video clip and below the video clip was very small. Some participants failed to notice the difference until after they had seen a side-by-side comparison as part of the conversational prompt.

> *I wasn't conscious of this I will admit, but I prefer the dropped box, I feel like I'm getting more of the visuals.* (P.14)

The interview data explained why users preferred the subtitles below the video clip. However, it also showed variation in preference, and reasons for preference, which illustrates the limitations of a one-size-fits-all approach to subtitle position.

4.2 Alternative Positions and Giving Participants Control

After completing the original study procedure, participants were shown two further subtitle positions in order to gather feedback on their thoughts of these as alternative positioning for subtitled content. While not a primary research question in this work, these positions were used to explore alternative options that may be beneficial for users. Participants were first shown two additional *conversation prompt cards*, which provided examples of the new subtitle positions – overlaid at the top of the video and above the video. They were then asked for their thoughts and reflections on these. Following this, participants were shown a subtitled video clip and given the opportunity to adjust the position of the subtitles to any of the four positions (the original *below clip* and *bottom of clip,* and the new *top of clip* and *above clip*) in real time through an arrow control at the right hand side of the subtitles. Participants were encouraged to try all of the positions and comment on each. An analysis of further structured conversational data and observational data of participants using a control for subtitle position focused on further understanding participations preferences for subtitle position.

4.2.1 *Alternative Subtitle Positions*

Participants had mixed opinions about the two new subtitle positions - overlaid at the top, and above the video. Whilst most participants preferred subtitles to be placed at the bottom of the video or below the video, it is worth noting that some participants commented that they would prefer subtitles at the top of the video. Several unexpected reasons were given for this, from personal reading preference to situational dynamics, one participant noted that if felt natural to read the subtitles at the top of the screen and then dropping their eyes down to view the visual content. A further participant commented on the practicality of having them at the top of the screen in an environment with young children.

> *I'm used to reading it along the bottom but I'd prefer it [at the top]. If the kids are in the way I don't need to get them to move I can just look at the top.*
> (P.2)

Corrective lenses also played a decisive factor in a preference for position. Participants wearing bi-focals tended to report preferring the subtitles below the video and participants wearing vari-focals tended to report preferring it above. Whilst tentative, these examples illustrate the additional personal, social and contextual factors that effect subtitle users preferences for subtitle position.

Overall, findings from the qualitative data revealed that most participants preferred subtitles to be positioned at the bottom of the screen, either within the video clip or below the video clip. P 10 commented that *it feels uncomfortable to be reading it at the top* and that *you can get a better idea of what's going on with the text at the bottom*. This falls in line with guidelines that are used in creating usable subtitles [2], yet it is important to note that these guidelines do not work for all participants. The research illustrated that preference for a position is contingent on a number of interrelated factors. Thus highlighting the limitations of a one size fits all approach in terms of the accessibility of subtitle display.

4.2.2 Control of Subtitles

It is interesting to note that some participants were very open to experimenting with the position of subtitles and that they would try a variety of positions before deciding on the one that they preferred. P10 talked of a conflict between their preference and what they would consider a 'better' position. *I think that my preference is still having it underneath the video. Having it transparent at the top actually works better so I think that would be my second choice but I think personally I would want to be able to choose.*

On being asked to discuss the use of a control for changing the position of subtitles, participants valued being given the option to alter the position to suit their needs or requirements. However, options were divided as to whether this would take the form of a UI setting as shown to participants in the study, or a general setting. Ideally, participants noted that there was value in the *option* of having a UI control for flexibility, but they would also like to be able to set it in a position and then leave it. P.1 referred to this as a *set and forget* method of customisation. Overall, participants valued the ability to control the position of subtitles and saw worth having a feature such as this made available. For example, P15 stated that h*aving the control is good. If that was a feature I'd appreciate it. I'd use it.*

An additional theme that appeared when discussing this control was that that the position of subtitles may change based on the content that is being watched. For example, P. 21 commented that it *makes me realise that I might not have went for the option that I originally thought…it just depends on certain things.* This idea complements the concept that no single interface adaption can address the needs of all users [10] and that adaptions to accessibility service, even at a level as simple as adjusting the position of subtitles, can benefit the end user. This was echoed by P.0, who commented that *I'd like to change it [the subtitles] according to what I'm watching. Potentially I could repair the subtitles to solve the problems that I'm having with them, it would be really helpful.* Overall, participants expressed a need and a desire for feature to allow them to alter the position of subtitles to suits their personal, contextual and content related needs.

5. DISCUSSION

This research shows a significant improvement in user experience when changing the subtitle location from the standard position of within a video at the bottom to below the video clip. Additionally, participants responded positively when given the ability to change the position of subtitles in real time, allowing for a more personalised viewing experience.

An important theme that emerged in discussions about subtitle position and user experience was that user needs are not always being met. For example, fixed subtitle positions can obscure programme information, which can cause immense frustration to the viewer. Furthermore, people's preferences for subtitle position remain dependent on personal and situational needs.

This can have significant consequences on individuals' thoughts towards subtitled services at a very basic level. In the first instance, the absence of adequate subtitles can create a feeling of solitude in viewers with this resulting in a sense of segregation from other members of the audience. *It's not necessarily crucial, but it makes you feel a bit more isolated from the information* (P.20). In the second instance, people feel that their needs are not always being met by the current one-size fits all model.

A secondary theme that emerged among a small subset of users was a discourse of gratitude that subtitles existed at all, subjugated expectations of the subtitled viewing experience that ran counter to conversations of how the service can be improve. This was articulated well by P. 18 who said that *when you're deaf and you're used to being deaf, just having any subtitles at all is a big improvement so I'm not too fussy.* Whilst options to personalise the position, or the ability to control the position were recognised by this group as offering an enhancement to the service, these users didn't want to come across as being seen as being to demanding. This view of the UX of subtitles reveals the problem of lower expectations among some subtitle users with regard to their entitlement to a quality user experience that is equivalent value to non-subtitle users.

The research presented in this work was completed with participants that used subtitles due to a variety of different hearing impairments and that all viewed subtitles in their native (English) language. Additionally, participants viewed only news clips placed within an Internet browser. Keeping the scope of this study focused in this manner aids in determining outcomes for this specific situation but a number of limitations need to be considered when interpreting this work. Firstly, additional research is needed to understand if the results presented in this paper would hold true for a full screen display (either on a computer screen on standard television set). Secondly, further work is needed to understand if these results would benefit individuals that use subtitles for needs other than as accessibility services (e.g. foreign language subtitles). Finally, an understanding is needed into the effect that a change in genre would have on the positioning of subtitles as discussed in this paper, different on-screen situations may present interesting challenges in the personalisation of subtitle position. For example, an increase in speakers on screen at one time may show that an alternative subtitle display is preferable. Furthermore, this work was conducted as a lab based experiment and therefore results may be different than those experienced by individuals in their own homes and with their own computer equipment.

6. CONCLUSIONS

This work set out to determine firstly, if overall user experience can be improved by changing the position of subtitles from within a video clip to below the video clip being presented and secondly; to discover if participants perceive there to be value in a control to change subtitle position in order to suit their own individual needs. This work reported on a lab-based user study where 26 participants with hearing difficulties took part in an experiment investigating the position of subtitles within, below, and above a video clip placed in a web page. Analysis initially focused on developing an understanding of the user experience that surrounds subtitles placed within or below a video clip. This then moved on to discuss subtitles placed above a video clip and also participant reaction to being given the ability to control subtitle position.

Positioning subtitles below a video clip in a web browser, rather than within the video, leads to an increase in user experience. During this work, participants viewed 4 video clips that altered the size of the video (small and large) and also the position of the subtitles in relation to the clip (within the video or below the video). Participants answered a short questionnaire following viewing each video clip. The results from this questionnaire suggested that there is a significant improvement in user experience when subtitles are placed below the video clip being viewed, rather than within the clip. This was mirrored in conversations with participants; however a more mixed opinion on subtitle position was present indicating limitations to the current one size fits all approach that is used.

Personalisation of subtitle position was viewed positively by participants. Participants were given the opportunity to change the position of subtitles to below, within, and above a news clip. This was met with approval by a large number of participants. Some participants wishing to set it once (e.g. P1 commenting on a *set and forget* method*)*, others wished to change the position based on their surrounding (e.g. P2 commenting on *if kids are in the way*) and some commented on changing the position based on what they were watching at the time. The current one size fits all approach to positioning subtitles has clear limitations.

The UX of Subtitled Video Content can only be measured when users believe that adequate access to subtitles exists. Participants in this work highlighted concerns over feelings of exclusion when subtitles are not present, with one participant commenting that *having any subtitles at all is a big improvement, so I'm not too fussy*. This feeling of segregation that exists when subtitles are not present is important to consider in future research in this area. Providing access to clear, accurate, and reliable subtitles must occur before a larger understanding of the user experience of subtitled content can be achieved.

Combined, these results should encourage others to continue examining the use of subtitles in relation to online media. It should also allow others to further question the conventions that exist around standard subtitle practice and user experience.

7. ACKNOWLEDGMENTS

This work has been undertaken at BBC R&D with support from Gareth Ford-Williams. Thanks also go to James Sandford for all of the support he has given throughout this research. For part of this work Author 1 was supported by RCUK Digital Economy Research Hub EP/G066019/1.

8. REFERENCES

[1] A quarter of a billion people tuning in - BBC News: 2013. *http://www.bbc.co.uk/news/blogs-the-editors-23032145.*

[2] Baker, Robert G., Andrew D. Lambourne, and Guy Rowston. *Handbook for Television Subtitlers.* Independent Broadcasting Authority, 1982.

[3] BBC - GEL : *http://www.bbc.co.uk/gel.*

[4] Brooks, M. 2014. Enhancing Subtitles. *The ACM Conference on television Experience* (2014), 27–28.

[5] Brown, A. et al. 2015. Dynamic Subtitles: The User Experience. *ACM Conference on Television Experience* (2015).

[6] Burnham, Denis, et al. "Parameters in television captioning for deaf and hard-of-hearing adults: Effects of caption rate versus text reduction on comprehension." *Journal of deaf studies and deaf education* 13.3 (2008): 391-404.

[7] Cohen, Jacob. *Statistical power analysis for the behavioral sciences.* Academic press, 2013.

[8] Ellcessor, Elizabeth. "Captions on, off, on TV, online accessibility and search engine optimization in online closed captioning." *Television & New Media* 13.4 (2012): 329-352.

[9] Euler, Reinhardt, Rainer E. Burkard, and R. Grommes. "On Latin squares and the facial structure of related polytopes." *Discrete mathematics* 62.2 (1986): 155-181.

[10] Gajos, Krzysztof Z., Amy Hurst, and Leah Findlater. "Personalized dynamic accessibility." *Interactions* 19.2 (2012).

[11] Gelman, Andrew. "Scaling regression inputs by dividing by two standard deviations." *Statistics in medicine* (2008).

[12] Guarin, Sandra, et al. "Viewer selection of subtitle position on tv screen." U.S. Patent Application 12/045,152.

[13] Hong, Richang, et al. Video accessibility enhancement for hearing-impaired users. *ACM Transactions on Multimedia Computing, Communications, and Applications* (2011).

[14] Hu, Y., Kautz, J., Yu, Y., & Wang, W. (2015). Speaker-Following Video Subtitles. *ACM Transactions on Multimedia Computing, Communications, and Applications (TOMM)*, *11*(2).

[15] Hughes, C.J. et al. 2015. Responsive Design for Personalised Subtitles. *The 12th Web for All Conference* (2015) In Press.

[16] Jensema, C. (1998). Viewer reaction to different television captioning speeds.*American annals of the deaf*, *143*(4), 318-324.

[17] Law, E. L. C., Roto, V., Hassenzahl, M., Vermeeren, A. P., & Kort, J. (2009, April). Understanding, scoping and defining user experience: a survey approach. In *Proceedings of the SIGCHI Conference 2009* (pp. 719-728).

[18] Law, E. L. C., & van Schaik, P. (2010). Modelling user experience–An agenda for research and practice. *Interacting with computers*, *22*(5), 313-322.

[19] Lee, J., Jun, S., Forlizzi, J., & Hudson, S. E. (2006). Using kinetic typography to convey emotion in text-based interpersonal communication. *The 6th ACM DIS Conference*

[20] Lucas, D., Nicolau, H., Guerreiro, T., & Jorge, J. (2011). Investigating the Effectiveness of Assistive Technologies on Situationally Impaired Users. *INTERACT 2011 Workshop on Mobile Accessibility. Lisboa, Portugal.*

[21] O'Brien, H.L. and Lebow, M. 2013. Mixed-methods approach to measuring user experience in online news interactions. *Journal of the American Society for Information Science and Technology* (2013), 1543–1556.

[22] Ofcom 2013. Adults' media use and attitudes report. (2013).

[23] OfCom 2006. *Guidelines on the Provision of Television Access Services.*

[24] Shahraray, B., & Gibbon, D. C. (1995, March). Automatic generation of pictorial transcripts of video programs. In *IS&T/SPIE's Symposium on Electronic Imaging: Science & Technology* (pp. 512-518). International Society for Optics.

[25] Styleguide, G.E.L.T. Global Experience Language Tablet Styleguide for the BBC.

[26] Zanón, N. T. (2006). Using subtitles to enhance foreign language learning.*Porta Linguarum: revista internacional de didáctica de las lenguas extranjeras.*

Tracked Speech-To-Text Display: Enhancing Accessibility and Readability of Speech-To-Text

Raja S. Kushalnagar, Gary W. Behm, Aaron W. Kelstone, and Shareef S. Ali
National Technical Institute for the Deaf
Rochester Institute of Technology
Rochester, NY 14623 USA
{rskics, gwbnts, awbnpa, sxa9640}@rit.edu

ABSTRACT

Deaf and Hard of Hearing (DHH) students are under-served and under-represented in education in part because they miss spoken classroom information, even with aural-to-visual accommodations, such as a real-time speech to text Display (SD). Most SD systems utilize a trained typist to transcribe the speech into text (speech-to-text) onto a display. Still, these students encounter significant but subtle barriers in following speech-to-text displays, especially when detailed visuals are used or when the speaker is fast or uses uncommon words. Hearing students can simultaneously watch the visuals and listen to the spoken explanation, while DHH students constantly look away from the SD to search and observe details in the classroom visuals. As a result, they spend less time watching the visuals and gain less information than their hearing peers. They can also fall behind in reading the speech-text.

We discuss the implementation and evaluation of a real-time Tracked Speech-To-Text Display (TSD), that addresses these subtle barriers presented by SD systems. The TSD system minimizes the student's viewing distance between the Speech-to-Text Display and the speaker. This is done through tracking the presenter and displaying the speech-text at a fixed distance above the presenter. Our evaluation showed that students significantly preferred TSD over SD and reported that it was easier to follow the lecture. They liked being able to see both the teacher and speech-to-text, and being able to set the number of displayed lines.

Categories and Subject Descriptors

H.5.1 [**Information Interfaces and Presentation**]: Multimedia Information Systems; K.4.2 [**Social Issues**]: Assistive technologies for persons with disabilities

General Terms

Design, Experimentation; Human Factors

Keywords

Accessible Technology; Deaf and Hard of Hearing Users

ASSETS '15, October 26-28, 2015, Lisbon, Portugal.
 ISBN 978-1-4503-3400-6/15/10... $15.00
DOI: http://dx.doi.org/10.1145/2700648.2809843.

1. INTRODUCTION

Real-time speech-to-text systems transform aural speech to visual text in near real-time, within a few seconds [6] for Deaf and Hard of Hearing (DHH) students who cannot hear or understand aural speech. This aural-to-visual accommodation is usually preferred by people who have lost their hearing as adults, or DHH individuals who do not know sign language. DHH students are under-represented and under-served in education for several reasons. One of these important reasons for their under-representation is due to the fact that they miss out on lecture information, which impacts their academic success.

The introduction of accessibility laws in the 1970s and 1990s required educational institutions to provide visual-to-aural accommodations for DHH students, which resulted in substantial progress in DHH inclusion and graduation rates. There are over 31,000 DHH students enrolled in college, up 15,000 over the past 10 years in USA [16] due to the fact that entering DHH freshmen are the first cohort to have aural-to-visual access from the time they start school.

DHH students continue to be under-represented compared to their hearing peers: the graduation rate is 16% for DHH students as compared to 30% for hearing students [1]. Worldwide, the graduation and retention rates of DHH is likely worse than hearing students, because many countries' educational systems do not provide visual-to-aural accommodations for their DHH students.

People often falsely assume that current speech-to-text systems, such as Communication Access Real-Time Translation (CART) also referred to as stenography, C-Print, LegionScribe, or re-speaking [17, 12] provide full access to lecture information for DHH people. This is not the case: the live transcription of the speaker (speech-text) is neither speech nor text, and is not integrated with lecture visuals. The assumption of full access to lecture information is detrimental because it minimizes the impact of visual dispersion, time on visuals, and speech-text readability.

2. BACKGROUND AND RELATED WORK

Prior research has shown that the cognitive process of reading speech-to-text is different from reading static text or print. Speech-to-text is not formatted and constantly changes, while print is formatted and does not change [21].

Unlike speech, speech-to-text is delayed by several seconds [10], does not accurately convey the speaker's prosody such as pace or stress [4]. Unlike print, constantly changing speech-text takes a longer time to read [7].

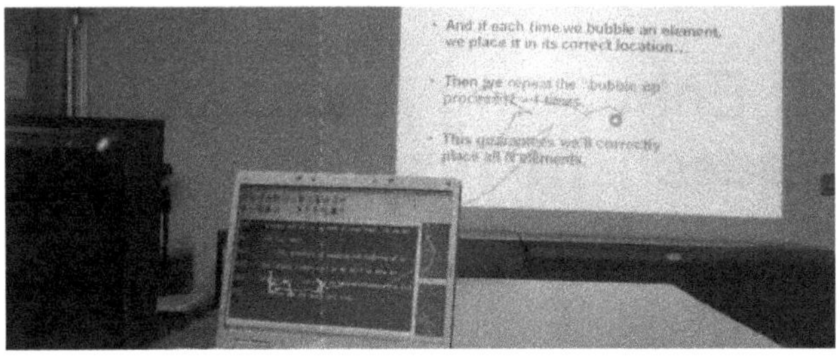

Figure 1: A trace of a student's gaze path shifting between the speech-to-text display and lecture visual (slides).

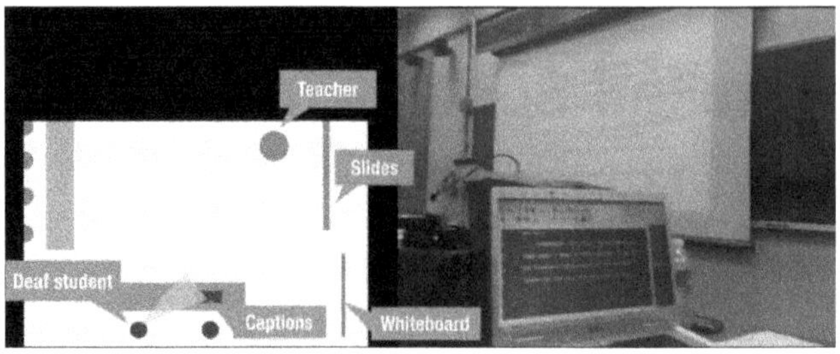

Figure 2: The visual dispersion of information sources (captions, whiteboard, slides, teacher) in a classroom.

2.1 Visual Dispersion

Visual dispersion is defined as the juggling of multiple concurrent visuals as shown in Figure 1, and is often cited as a major reason why deaf and hard of hearing students get less out of classroom lectures than their hearing peers [3, 13]. Previous research has shown that hearing students benefit from combined visual and auditory materials [18]. Hearing students are able to look at the visuals (e.g., slides) and simultaneously listen to the spoken explanation effortlessly.

Speech-to-text systems add an extra visual: the speech-text display. DHH students have to constantly look away from the speech-text display to search and observe details in the lecture visual as shown in Figure 2. They risk losing information, which can slow down or even derail learning. As a result, they spend far less time watching lecture visuals and comprehend less information than their hearing peers [9]. DHH students find it even harder to juggle the multiple visuals when the slides or demonstration has a lot of text or if the speech is fast or dense [12].

2.2 Time on Visuals

The addition of visual translation of audio in a Speech-to-Text Display (SD) essentially transforms the simultaneous viewing and listening experience of watching a lecture into a sequential reading and viewing experience. In other words, the student's cognitive task could be regarded as reading an visually enhanced narrative presented through automatic scrolling of text, supported with both video and audio supplementary material.

Unlike hearing students' integrated learning by simultaneously watching visuals and listening to speech, DHH students spend most of their time reading captions and miss understanding lecture visuals [16, 3]. Additionally, DHH students, on average, are less fluent in English than their hearing peers and read captions more slowly [8].

Moreover, both the speaker and speech-to-text system can make mistakes, and without access to the audio signal, DHH students are far more likely not to catch these errors. Humans infer meaning from context, influencing their prior probability toward those words that make sense in context. Since DHH spend far less time on the slides compared to hearing peers, they are also less likely to identify and repair these errors.

Like print, real-time speech-to-text is normally shown on a screen that has many lines of text. Television subtitles on the other hand, can be shown as on overlay on video and have far fewer lines, because it is far less likely to block video information, and also because it can be synchronized more precisely than real-time text. For static text (print), the average college student reads between 280 to 300 words per minute (wpm) [20, 2]. By contrast the average subtitling (speech-to-text representation on screen) rate for TV programs is 141 wpm and the most comfortable subtitling reading rate for DHH viewers is around 145 wpm [8].

Unlike print, the variable speed of speech-to-text force readers to read at a variable pace; and the readers cannot control or predict that pace. The viewers also need time to read the speech-to-text display, and integrate the information conveyed by the captions and visuals to follow the lecturer's intended message. Speech-to-text may also be hard to read by viewers with physical or situational visual impairments, for example in cloudy or dim environments [21].

The advantage of displaying speech-to-text on a page is that if the student misses something or is a slow reader, then the student can go back and review several seconds of dialog and then skip forward. The disadvantage is that when the student looks away to read the teacher's notes or slides, and returns to the speech-text display, the student is forced to spend a lot of time searching for the speech-text position where he or she left off [11].

2.3 Speech-to-Text Systems

There are several speech-to-text systems, such as professional shorthand typists (stenographers) using a Communication Access Real-Time System (CART) [12], crowd captioning such as LegionScribe [14], C-Print [5], Automatic Speech Recognition (ASR), or re-speaking with Automatic Speech Recognition. Each of these systems vary dramatically in terms of cost, accuracy and availability [10, 14, 15]. Regardless of how the speech-to-text was generated, all of these systems usually send the speech-text to a web server, and the student connects to the web server and views the speech-to-text either on his/her personal display or on a projected screen.

We use the C-Print[1] system, due to the fact that it is a low cost and widely available system, which was developed at the National Technical Institute for the Deaf at the Rochester Institute of Technology.

The C-Print system has been adopted at many universities and has greatly improved accessibility to classroom and lecture information for DHH students nationwide [4]. It also benefits individuals with other disabilities, such as those with a visual impairment or a learning disability.

[1]https://www.rit.edu/ntid/cprint/

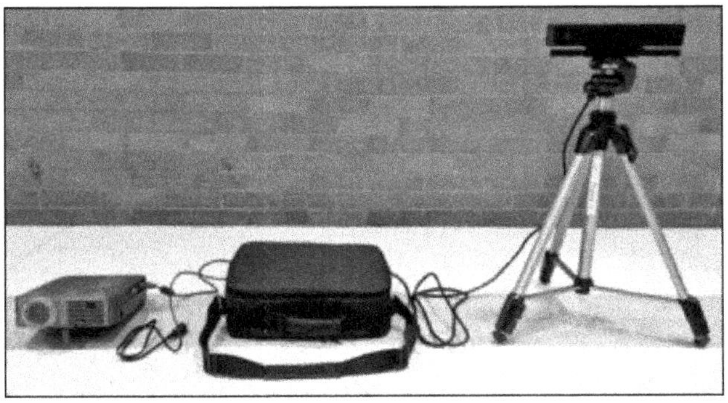

Figure 3: Tracked Speech-to-Text Display (TSD) System: Projector, laptop in a over-the-shoulder bag, and Kinect 2.

Figure 4: A snapshot of the Tracked Speech-to-Text Display (TSD) in a class. This TSD system is set to display 3 lines at a time.

The system consists of a trained typist, a laptop with C-Print software, and a web server to collect and display the transcribed text. The trained typist, called a C-Print captionist, type abbreviations and the C-Print software expands the abbreviation into a full word.

For example, when a C-Print typist hears 'coffee', they will type 'kfe', which is automatically expanded to 'coffee', and the average expansion factor is around two. The main disadvantage of C-Print as compared with CART is that a C-Print typist cannot type as fast as the natural speaking rate, especially during speaking bursts [12]. The generated output is sent to a web server. The student connects to the web server to display it on his/her computer. Alternatively, the teacher or support staff can connect to the web server and project it on the screen.

The main advantage of the C-Print system as compared with professional stenographers output is cost and availability. In terms of cost, C-Print typists need far less training and time as compared with stenographers who and are cheaper than professional stenographers, who type on a specialized keyboard using short-hand notation [10]. Although stenographers are more accurate, studies have shown that C-Print typists' accuracy is high enough that studies have not found any significant difference between C-Print and sign language interpreters in terms of student learning in the classroom [19, 4]. The main disadvantage of C-Print, like CART, is that the "flow" of text is not smooth or consistent, unlike LegionScribe [10].

3. TRACKED SPEECH-TO-TEXT DISPLAY

The Tracked Speech-To-Text Display (TSD) addresses the challenges described in the previous section: visual dispersion, time on visuals and reading speed. The goal of the TSD design is to minimize visual dispersion. The TSD system is designed to be portable and has three components: C-Print, Kinect 2, and the TSD unit as shown in Figure 3. The system can be easily set up and turned on within a few minutes by the captionist or student.

3.1 Design Criteria

Based on prior work as well our own observations and experiences, we have developed the following design criteria for designing the real-time speech-to-text system for deaf and hard of hearing students:

1. The distance between the speech-to-text display and the speaker should be minimized, so that the DHH student can see both the display and speaker within their peripheral vision.
2. The speech-to-text display should be able to display a variable number of lines that adapt to the reader's abilities and preferences. This will allow the DHH student to balance the competing demands of having enough speech-text lines to be able to review, but also not too many lines that it becomes difficult to search for the current word to resume reading.
3. Setting and starting up the system should be quick and easy so that the DHH student or captioner does not have to spend extra time to come in early.
4. The hardware should be portable and low cost, so that the DHH student or institution can afford it.

As an example, consider Jane, a fourth year deaf student enrolled in a upper level creative arts course, and Joe, a first-year deaf student enrolled in an introductory electronics design course. Both Jane and Joe prefer to watch speech-to-text accommodations that includes a low-cost, easy to set up display that they can customize and use with their accommodation provider. Their needs and preferences for the speech-to-text display settings will usually differ.

Jane is a fluent and fast reader, like other DHH students who have the ability and opportunity to access English through constant exposure to speech-to-text (closed captions) on television and class. She prefers to balance her time between reading the speech-to-text display and the teacher's interactive demonstration of creative art through the slides. She prefers fewer lines of speech-text display so that she can rapidly locate where she stopped and resume reading, when she looks back at the speech-to-text display as shown in Figure 4.

Joe, like many deaf students who do not , is not a fluent or fast reader, and prefers to spend most of his time reading the speech-text display, and then looking at the teacher's demonstration in front of the slides. As he reads slowly, he prefers to have more lines of speech-text and is willing to spend a little extra time to search and locate where he left off reading and use have extra time to skim the previous lines and catch important information to keep up with the speaker and class.

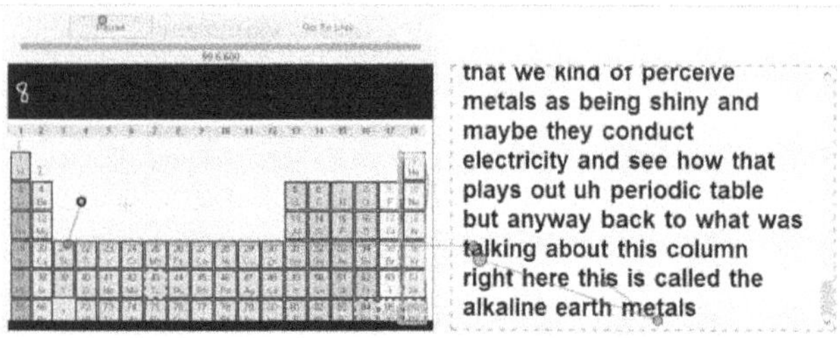

Figure 5: Eye tracking scan path (red lines) from a DHH reader following simultaneous visuals. The reader looks away from the speech-text when the instructor says "right here" to look at the visual information on the periodic table that is being referred to. Then when the reader returns to the text, the reader under-shoots their previous reading position (looking where the content *used* to be when they looked away. The reader next looks at the newest content as the speech-to-text display updates. When the reader realizes this is not the correct location, they finally scan and jump back to the correct location (the next word they had not yet read before looking away). This multi-step search process often results in missing even more information as the reader tries to recover.

3.2 Projector

Many classrooms have a projector and the TSD system can connect directly to the classroom projector. If the classroom does not have a projector, the included portable projector can be used.

3.3 Tracked Speech-To-Text Display Unit

The TSD unit consists of a laptop (Surface Pro) with an SSD that runs a Windows application written in C#, that was developed by the authors. It uses a Kinect 2 device to track the speaker's location and position, and uses that information to display the generated speech-to-text at a fixed location relative to the speaker through the projector.

3.3.1 Minimizing visual dispersion

The system then projects the captions at a fixed distance from the presenter's location, usually over their head. This enables the viewer to easily see both the transcript and presenter's information simultaneously. They can detect changes, easily follow and read the real-time transcript without missing the presenter's information.

If the display is in a fixed location next to the presenter's slides or demonstration, then students will often face a view of the speech-to-text display this is blocked whenever the presenter moves in front of the real-time transcript. Moreover, whenever the presenter moves far away from the display, it will be difficult to see both the presenter and display simultaneously.

By setting the location of the TSD display above the presenter, there is no blocked view, and the viewer will always be able to see both simultaneously as shown in Figure 4.

3.3.2 Display size

Conventional C-Print displays typically show around 10 lines of text, which corresponds to about 10 seconds of speech at the average rate of one line per minute. On the other hand, the display of several lines of text makes it harder for a viewer to identify where they stopped reading after they looked away to the teacher's writing or to the slides, as shown in Figure 5. In that example, the eye gaze trace path shows how the reader's juggling and searching between visuals interferes with their learning. This figure shows the reader's eye gaze when returning from the table to the speech-to-text.

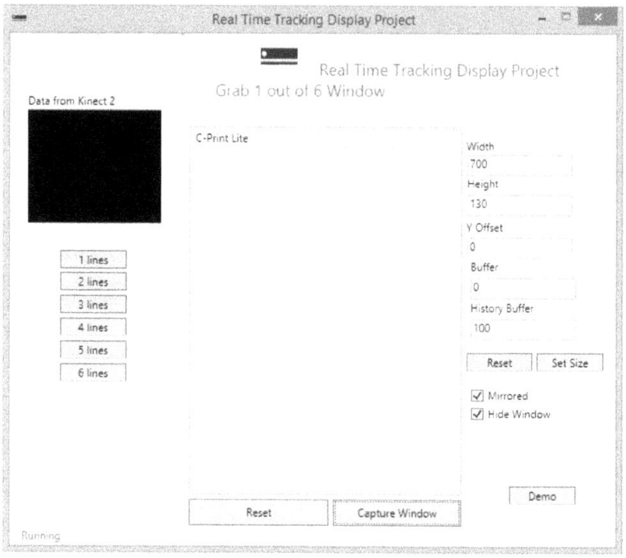

Figure 6: A snapshot of the application interface that can adjust the display location and size.

The SpeechText display can show 1, 3 or 6 lines of text, corresponding to about 1, 3 and 6 seconds of speech. Some students prefer to follow fewer lines of SpeechText, while others would prefer to follow more lines of SpeechText. The application has options to display between one to six lines of text, depending on the reader's preferences, as shown in Figure 6.

3.4 Kinect for Windows

A Kinect for Windows device, developed by Microsoft, is a physical sensor device that has the ability to obtain the depth and posture of people in front of it. It has a built-in High Definition color camera, an infrared (IR) emitter, and a microphone array, enabling it to sense the location and movement of people as well as their voices. It weighs 100 grams, is less than 120 cm wide, and costs $200. It also has an instantaneous startup. The depth sensor consists of an infrared laser projector combined with a monochrome CMOS sensor, which captures video data in 3D under any ambient light conditions. The sensing range of the depth sensor is adjustable.

The Kinect for Windows Software Development Kit enables developers to create applications that support gesture and voice recognition, through an application on a Windows computer[2]. The Kinect 2 is normally placed just beyond the front row of student desks so that it can track the movement of the instructor.

[2]http://www.microsoft.com/en-us/kinectforwindows/

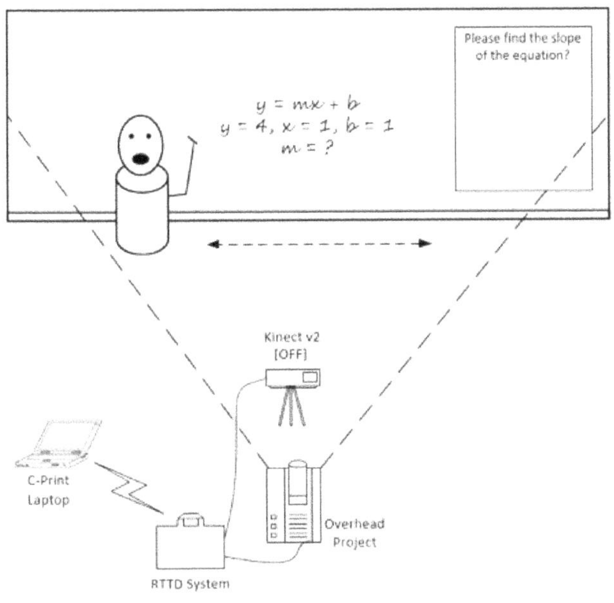

Figure 7: Static SpeechText Display: An illustration of the variable distance between between the fixed speech-to-text display on the right side of the board, and a teacher moving around, either writing or demonstrating in front of the board.

3.5 Startup time

The startup time is less than a minute, and mostly dominated by the process of unpacking the devices from the bag and plugging them into an outlet. The time to start up the software is minimal on both the Kinect and Surface Pro, and is about 15-20 seconds for the projector, whether the classroom projector or the portable projector.

3.6 Cost

The cost of the system currently varies from about $700 to $1000: $500 for the Surface Pro, $200 for the Kinect 2 at the low end, and would include about $300 for an optional portable projector to cover the situation where the classroom does not have a mounted projector.

4. EVALUATION

We ran a study in which we asked DHH students to compare the first iteration of the Tracked Speech-To-Text Display in Figure 8 against the C-Print Display in Figure 7. Based on the feedback from this study, we added an option to change the number of displayed speech-text lines. We then ran a second study in which we asked DHH students to compare the second iteration of the Tracked Speech-To-Text Display with 3 displayed lines against 6 displayed lines.

4.1 Evaluation of SD versus TSD

We evaluated the speech-to-text display (SD) and tracked speech-to-text display (TSD) using a balanced and repeated measures design in a 50 minute long Creative Arts course that had two sections.

All enrolled students in attendance had experience with C-Print, having watched it in the class lectures prior to the evaluation period.

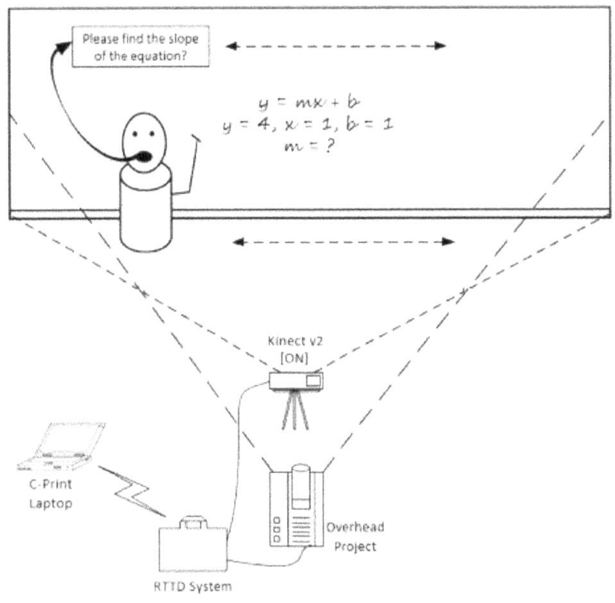

Figure 8: Tracked SpeechText Display: An illustration of the constant distance between the teacher moving around in front of the board and writing or demonstrating, and the speech-text display displayed above the teacher.

4.1.1 Procedure

For the first section on the first day, the captionist connected to a projector to display the speech-text at a fixed location (SD) as shown in Figure 7. At the next class, the captionist connected to the tracked speech-to-text display (TSD), to display the speech-text at a fixed distance from the speaker as shown in Figure 8. We reversed the order of presentation for the second section on the second day. At the start of each class, we announced the purpose of the study and that we would distribute a survey about the speech-to-text display at the end of class, and that it would take about a minute to complete. Every student completed and returned the survey. The survey had one demographic question, four Likert questions and two open-ended questions.

- D1: 'Are you deaf or hearing?'
- Q1: 'How easy is it to follow [SD/TSD]?', with a Likert scale that ranged from 1 through 5, with 1 being 'Not at all easy' to 5 being 'very easy'
- Q2: 'How easy was it to see the teacher, teacher's writing and [SD/TSD]?', with the same Likert scale response as before.
- Q3: 'How helpful is it to see the teacher, teacher's writing and [SD/TSD]?', with a Likert scale that ranged from 1 through 5, with 1 being 'Not at all helpful' to 5 being 'very helpful'
- Q4: 'Would you recommend [SD/TSD] to others?', with a Likert scale that ranged from 1 through 5, with 1 being 'Not at all recommend' to 5 being 'very much recommend'.
- O1: 'What are the strengths of [SD/TSD]?'
- O2: 'What are the weaknesses of [SD/TSD]?'

4.1.2 *Participant Comments*

The students were excited about the tracked speech-to-text display, and many wrote down comments and offered feedback about its helpfulness and on how to improve it.

Several common themes emerged on analyzing the feedback. First, they reported that while using TSD, it was far easier to see the teacher, whiteboard and the captions. They also noted that they could see the teacher's expressions and body language more clearly, and felt more 'connected' with the teacher. On the other hand, many felt that the movement of the speech-to-text display was not smooth and moved unpredictably in rhythm with the teacher's movements. Many also felt that displaying two lines of speech-to-text was not enough.

Deaf respondents who may have been slower readers reported that they could not read fast enough to keep up with two lines. Hearing respondents reported that it was very distracting to deal with the delay between speech and speech-text. That is they found it distracting to listen to the speech and to read the speech-text that was around four to five seconds delayed. Both groups wanted to see more speech-text lines for different reasons.

4.1.3 *Results*

Since the Likert scores were skewed and not normal, we analyzed the responses using the non-parametric Wilcoxon Signed-Rank test to evaluate whether there was a statistically significant difference between showing the captions in a fixed location versus showing the captions above the presenter.

A total of 44 hearing students and 18 deaf students from two sections participated in the study. First, we compared the ease of readability under SD versus TSD.

The Q1 responses to the question "How easy is it to read SD/TSD?" did not show a statistically significant difference for hearing ($Z = 3.945$, $p = 0.129$) or deaf ($Z = 4.072$, $p = 0.113$).

The Q2 responses to the question "How easy was it to see the teacher, teacher's writing and the speech-to-text/tracked speech-to-text display?" was statistically significant in favor of TSD for hearing ($Z = 1.173$, $p < 0.01$), and deaf ($Z = 1.258$, $p < 0.01$).

The Q3 responses to the question "How helpful is it to see the teacher, teacher's writing and the speech-text/tracked speech-to-text?" was statistically significant in favor of TSD for hearing ($Z = 1.093$, $p < 0.01$) and deaf ($Z = 1.287$, $p < 0.01$).

The Q4 responses to the question on "Would you recommend speech-text/tracked speech-to-text to others?" was statistically significant in favor of TSD for hearing ($Z = 1.152$, $p < 0.01$) or deaf ($Z = 1.188$, $p < 0.01$).

In other words, the students did not report statistically significant difference in ease of reading between the static speech-text display and tracked speech-to-text display.

Participant feedback analysis suggested that while the students could ignore the unpredictable movements of the teacher, they were far more sensitive to the movements of the speech-to-text display and felt that the unpredictable movements of the display was far more noticeable and disconcerting.

Overall, the responses suggested that students who wanted smoother text movement should have a choice of display views so that they can adapt to varying amounts of simultaneous visual narration text and video visuals, or to the varying amount of vocabulary complexity. On the other hand, the relatively unpredictable movements of the speech-text display did not impact the ease of watching both displays simultaneously, nor did it impact the helpfulness in seeing the displays simultaneously.

There was statistical significance in favor of recommending tracked speech-to-text displays to other DHH students.

4.2 Evaluation of TSD-3 versus TSD-6

During the original evaluation of TSD, participants commented that the movement of the speech-to-text display bothered them, while the movement of the presenter did not. They also wanted more lines, either to read earlier lines that match what they hear, or to have more time to read when they look back again on the speech-to-text display.

We revised the TSD system to address the requirement that the speech-text display movement be smooth and regular and yet follow the speaker, by adding a sliding window buffer. This buffer allowed us to slightly decouple the movement synchronization between the speaker and the speech-to-text display by allowing the distance to vary. Through lab testing with DHH volunteers, we found that the optimal size for the buffer was around 0.3 seconds. Next, we added a algorithm to smoothen the movement by limiting the acceleration (velocity rate of change and direction), while also striving to preserve a constant distance from the speaker.

To address the requirement for more lines of speech-to-text, we added functionality to display a specified number of lines between one and six, inclusive. Based on the observation that the delay between speech and speech-text was around 3-5 seconds, we opted to evaluate using a speech-text display size of 3 and 6 lines.

We evaluated this revised iteration of the speech-to-text tracked display with 3 lines shown at a time (TSD-3) and with 6 lines shown at a time (TSD-6) using a repeated measures design in a third section of a 50 minute long Creative Arts course.

All enrolled students in attendance had experience with C-Print, having watched it in the class lectures prior to the evaluation period.

4.2.1 *Procedure*

For the first section on the first day in class, the captionist connected to the TSD system, and selected the option to show 3 lines through the interface as shown in Figure 6 on the tracked speech-to-text display for 20 minutes. Then at the half-way mark, the captionist selected the option to show 6 lines through the tracked speech-to-text display.

Then at the second section on the second day in class, the process was repeated, with the order reversed: the captioner showed 6 lines for 20 minutes, and then 3 lines for the remaining 20 minutes. At the start of each class, we announced that we were evaluating speech-to-text accommodations, and that we would distribute a survey about the speech-to-text display at the end of class, and that it would take about a minute to complete. Every student completed and returned the surveys after class.

The survey had one demographic question, four Likert questions and two open-ended questions.

- D1: 'Are you deaf or hearing?'
- Q1: 'How easy is it to follow [TSD-3/TSD-6]?', with a Likert scale that ranged from 1 through 5, with 1 being 'Not at all easy' to 5 being 'very easy'
- Q2: 'How easy was it to see the teacher, teacher's writing and [TSD-3/TSD-6]?', with the same Likert scale response as before.
- Q3: 'How helpful is it to see the teacher, teacher's writing and [TSD-3/TSD-6]?', with a Likert scale that ranged from 1 through 5, with 1 being 'Not at all helpful' to 5 being 'very helpful'
- Q4: 'Would you recommend [TSD-3/TSD-6] to others?', with a Likert scale that ranged from 1 through 5, with 1 being 'Not at all recommend' to 5 being 'very much recommend'.
- O1: 'What are the strengths of [TSD-3/TSD-6]?'
- O2: 'What are the weaknesses of [TSD-3/TSD-6]?'

4.2.2 Participant Comments

The students in this section were also excited by the possibilities offered by the tracked speech-to-text display. Many students wrote down comments and feedback about its helpfulness and on how to improve it. Several common themes emerged during the open feedback period. All participants reported that they feel more 'connected' with the teacher using either TSD-3 or TSD-6, as compared to the standard C-Print display.

There was a distinct split in responses between hearing and deaf students depending on whether 3 or 6 lines were shown. Deaf students tended to prefer 3 lines, and liked the fact that fewer displayed lines reduced their search time whenever they changed gaze back on the display. They reported that too many displayed lines also increased the amount of lines and words that had to be searched to find where to pick up the reading process when interrupted. By contrast, most hearing students clearly liked 6 lines more than 3 lines. The reason for this was that the speech-to-text delay was about 4-5 seconds, which allows the readers to read from the top of a TSD-6 system and not have to deal with unsynchronized speech-to-text. By contrast, if they used a TSD-3 system, then they could not synchronize what they heard with what they read, and they felt disconcerted.

4.2.3 Results

Since the Likert scores were skewed and not normal, we analyzed the responses using the non-parametric Wilcoxon Signed-Rank test to evaluate whether there was a statistically significant difference between showing the captions above the presenter with three lines versus showing the captions above the presenter with six lines.

A total of 21 hearing students and 11 deaf students from the section participated in the study. First, we compared the ease of readability for TSD-3 versus TSD-6.

The Q1 responses for the question *"How easy is it to read [TSD-3/TSD-6]?"* showed a statistically significant difference in favor of 6 lines for the hearing group ($Z = 1.241$, $p < 0.01$), and a difference in favor of 3 lines over 6 lines for the deaf group ($Z = 1.317$, $p < 0.01$).

The Q2 responses for the question *"How easy was it to see the teacher, teacher's writing and [TSD-3/TSD-6]?"* showed no statistically significant difference for hearing ($Z = 3.837$, $p = 0.386$) or for deaf ($Z = 3.544$, $p = 0.327$).

The Q3 responses for the question *"How helpful is it to see the teacher, teacher's writing and [TSD-3/TSD-6]?"* also showed no statistically significant difference for deaf ($Z = 3.724$, $p = 0.374$), or for hearing ($Z = 3.842$, $p = 0.391$).

The Q4 responses for the question *"Would you recommend [TSD-3/TSD-6] to others?"* showed a statistically significant difference in favor of 6 lines for the hearing group ($Z = 1.243$, $p < 0.01$) and a statistically significant difference in favor of 3 lines over 6 lines for the deaf group ($Z = 1.346$, $p < 0.01$).

DHH students and hearing students appeared to utilize the speech-text in different ways, which influences their preference for number of lines.

DHH students reported that speech-text was their only access to spoken information, so the preference for 3 lines can be interpreted to mean that they wanted to read immediately and do less searching.

Hearing students preferred 6 lines, and also commented that they used the speech-text as backup, and used it to review information if they misheard or did not understand a specific word or sentence. So the preference for 6 lines can be interpreted to mean that they wanted enough lines to review missed information merely by looking at the top one to two lines of the display. Overall, the responses suggested that students use speech-text in different ways, and that it is important to offer variable lines. All participants, hearing and deaf, liked the more predictable movements of the speech-text display.

5. CONCLUSIONS

For the first TSD iteration, the participants did not significantly differ with regard to the ease of reading the captions whether presented with the traditional SD or when it tracked the presenter with TSD. The participants reported that TSD was significantly more helpful than SD and this, in turn, explains why they are significantly more likely to recommend TSD over SD.

Some comments stated that two lines are not enough. The most likely explanation is that they are not able to read fast enough, as they may not have had strong English comprehension. This suggests that the number of caption lines displayed should be adjustable in order to better serve the needs of students. Our results show that providing additional speech-text history may be worth the attention switching overhead for looking away and resuming reading. The additional history enables viewers to review words that stay on screen longer.

For the second TSD iteration, all students liked the more predictable tracking, as indicated by their comments. The students also liked the ability to review multiple lines of speech-to-text, but the deaf and hearing students appeared to use the speech-text in different ways. DHH students preferred 3 lines, while hearing students preferred 6 lines.

DHH students reported that speech-text was their only access to spoken information, so the 4-5 second delay between the speech and speech-text was not an issue. On the other hand, hearing students reported using the speech-text as backup, for example, to review information if they misheard or did not understand a specific word or sentence. Overall, the responses suggested that students use speech-text in different ways, which influences their preferences for number of lines. As such it is important to let students select preferences that best fit their learning style.

Both hearing and deaf students also liked to view the display of speech-to-text and to recommend it to others. Though open subtitles or captions are not popular in other settings such as movie theaters, this finding shows that there may be greater acceptance of speech-to-text captions in academic settings, where information retention is important.

6. FUTURE WORK

We will extend the focus of tracked speech-to-text displays from educational settings to other settings, such as panel presentations, conference settings and theatre productions.

We will explore using alternate speech-to-text systems to minimize the distraction caused by delay or by flow. For example to minimize delay, we can use CART with the system. Similarly, to smoothen speech-to-text flow, we can use LegionScribe with the system.

We will also explore using private viewing devices so that individuals can adjust the display to their own preferences, even when multiple users are in the same room. These devices will enable personalized adjustment of number of lines, font size, caption placement, and other parameters while allowing other classroom participants the choice of viewing or not viewing the text.

7. ACKNOWLEDGMENTS

This work is supported by the National Science Foundation Awards IIS-1218056 and IIS-1460894.

8. REFERENCES

[1] S. Aud, W. Hussar, G. Kena, K. Bianco, L. Frohlich, J. Kemp, and K. Tahan. The Condition of Education 2011. NCES 2011-033., 2011.

[2] R. Carver. Silent reading rates in grade equivalents. *Journal of Literacy Research*, 21(2):155–166, 1989.

[3] A. C. Cavender, J. P. Bigham, and R. E. Ladner. ClassInFocus: Enabling improved visual attention strategies for deaf and hard of hearing students. In *Proceedings of the 11th International ACM SIGACCESS Conference on Computers and Accessibility - ASSETS '09*, pages 67–74, New York, New York, USA, 2009. ACM Press.

[4] L. B. Elliot, M. S. Stinson, D. Easton, and J. Bourgeois. College Students Learning With C-Print's Education Software and Automatic Speech Recognition. In *American Educational Research Association Annual Meeting*, New York, NY, 2008. AERA.

[5] L. B. Elliot, M. S. Stinson, B. G. McKee, V. S. Everhart, and P. J. Francis. College Students' Perceptions of the C-Print Speech-to-Text Transcription System. *Journal of deaf studies and deaf education*, 6(4):285–98, Jan. 2001.

[6] G. Howell. The quality of live subtitling – improving the viewer experience, 2013.

[7] C. Jensema. Closed-captioned television presentation speed and vocabulary. *American Annals of the Deaf*, 141(4):284–292, 1996.

[8] C. Jensema. Viewer reaction to different television captioning speeds. *American annals of the deaf*, 143(4):318–24, Oct. 1998.

[9] C. J. Jensema, R. S. Danturthi, and R. Burch. Time spent viewing captions on television programs. *American annals of the deaf*, 145(5):464–8, Dec. 2000.

[10] R. S. Kushalnagar, W. S. Lasecki, and J. P. Bigham. A readability evaluation of real-time crowd captions in the classroom. In *Proceedings of the 14th international ACM SIGACCESS Conference on Computers and Accessibility - ASSETS '12*, pages 71–78, New York, New York, USA, Oct. 2012. ACM Press.

[11] R. S. Kushalnagar, W. S. Lasecki, and J. P. Bigham. Captions Versus Transcripts for Online Video Content. In ACM, editor, *10th International Cross-Disclipinary Conference on Web Accessibility (W4A)*, 32, pages 1–4, Rio De Janerio, Brazil, May 2013. ACM Press.

[12] R. S. Kushalnagar, W. S. Lasecki, and J. P. Bigham. Accessibility Evaluation of Classroom Captions. *ACM Transactions on Accessible Computing*, 5(3):1–24, Jan. 2014.

[13] H. G. Lang. Higher education for deaf students: Research priorities in the new millennium. *Journal of Deaf Studies and Deaf Education*, 7(4):267–280, Jan. 2002.

[14] W. Lasecki, C. Miller, A. Sadilek, A. Abumoussa, D. Borrello, R. S. Kushalnagar, and J. Bigham. Real-time captioning by groups of non-experts. In *Proceedings of the 25th annual ACM symposium on User interface software and technology - UIST '12*, pages 23–34, New York, New York, USA, Oct. 2012. ACM Press.

[15] W. S. Lasecki and J. P. Bigham. Online quality control for real-time crowd captioning. In *Proceedings of the 14th international ACM SIGACCESS conference on Computers and accessibility - ASSETS '12*, ASSETS '12, pages 143–150, New York, New York, USA, 2012. ACM Press.

[16] M. Marschark, J. B. Pelz, C. Convertino, P. Sapere, M. E. Arndt, and R. Seewagen. Classroom Interpreting and Visual Information Processing in Mainstream Education for Deaf Students: Live or Memorex(R)? *American Educational Research Journal*, 42(4):727–761, Jan. 2005.

[17] M. Marschark, P. Sapere, C. Convertino, and R. Seewagen. Access to postsecondary education through sign language interpreting. *Journal of Deaf Studies and Deaf Education*, 10(1):38–50, Jan. 2005.

[18] R. E. Mayer and R. Moreno. A split-attention effect in multimedia learning: Evidence for dual processing systems in working memory. *Journal of Educational Psychology*, 90(2):312–320, 1998.

[19] M. S. Stinson, L. B. Elliot, and R. R. Kelly. Deaf and Hard-of-Hearing Students' Memory of Lectures with Speech-to-Text and Interpreting/Note Taking Services. *The Journal of Special Education*, 43(1):52–64, May 2008.

[20] S. E. Taylor. Eye Movements in Reading: Facts and Fallacies. *American Educational Research Journal*, 2(4):187, Nov. 1965.

[21] F. Thorn and S. Thorn. Television captions for hearing-impaired people: a study of key factors that affect reading performance. *Human factors*, 38(3):452–63, Sept. 1996.

Evaluating Alternatives for Better Deaf Accessibility to Selected Web-Based Multimedia

Brent Shiver
IBM Accessibility
IBM Research - Austin
Austin, Texas, USA
bnshiver@us.ibm.com

Rosalee Wolfe
College of Computing and Digital Media
DePaul University
Chicago, Illinois, USA
wolfe@cs.depaul.edu

ABSTRACT

The proliferation of video and audio media on the Internet has created a distinct disadvantage for deaf Internet users. Despite technological and legislative milestones in recent decades in making television and movies more accessible, there has been less progress with online access. A major obstacle to providing captions for Internet media is the high cost of captioning and transcribing services.

This paper reports on two studies that focused on multimedia accessibility for Internet users who were born deaf or became deaf at an early age. An initial study attempted to identify priorities for deaf accessibility improvement. A total of 20 deaf and hard-of-hearing participants were interviewed via videophone about their Internet usage and the issues that were the most frustrating. The most common theme was concern over a lack of accessibility for online news. In the second study, a total of 95 deaf and hard-of-hearing participants evaluated different caption styles, some of which were generated through automatic speech recognition.

Results from the second study confirm that captioning online videos makes the Internet more accessible to the deaf users, even when the captions are automatically generated. However color-coded captions used to highlight confidence levels were found neither to be beneficial nor detrimental; yet when asked directly about the benefit of color-coding, participants strongly favored the concept.

Categories and Subject Descriptors

K.4.2 **[Computers and Society]**: Social Issues – *Assistive technologies for persons with disabilities.*

General Terms

Design, Experimentation, Human Factors, Economics.

Keywords

Multimedia accessibility, web accessibility, captioning, deaf, automatic speech recognition, speech-to-text.

ASSETS'15, October 26–28, 2015, Lisbon, Portugal.
© 2015 ACM. ISBN 978-1-4503-3400-6/15/10…$15.00.
DOI: http://dx.doi.org/10.1145/2700648.2809857

1. INTRODUCTION

In recent years, researchers have investigated the accessibility of online resources to support deaf students [1] [2] including Web-based materials [3] [4] and social communities [5]. However, less discussion has occurred about the accessibility of the Internet to deaf adults who were born deaf or became deaf at an early age. This population typically differs in its language preference from those who became deaf later in life. In the United States, they use American Sign Language as their preferred language and view English as a second language.

According to a recent survey [6], adults commonly use the Internet for reading email, searching for information, finding answers to health questions, and reading the news. In recent years, these activities increasingly involve more than the printed word -- they involve multimedia [7]. Videos often accompany written text, or even replace it. These make the Internet increasingly less accessible to the deaf community.

To address this issue, the W3C Web Accessibility Initiative developed the Web Content Accessibility Guidelines (WCAG) for accessibility solutions [8]. Further, Section 508 of the Rehabilitation Act requires that U.S. Federal agencies' electronic and information technology be accessible to people with disabilities [9]. A recent study reconfirms that these guidelines and regulations are well warranted. Researchers [10] found that the barrier of "multimedia content without text alternative" to be the most critical for users who are deaf and hard-of-hearing.

The year 2014 witnessed modest gains in addressing this issue. The FCC recently finalized new quality standards for closed captioning of broadcast television [11] and now requires that any program televised after January 1, 2016 with captions must retain its captions when shown online [12]. However the new regulations do not address any media that was previously broadcast, nor does it cover videos that were published directly to the Web. Thus the majority of multimedia on the Internet remains inaccessible to those who are deaf or hard-of-hearing.

Even with assistance from legislative statute, it is virtually impossible to manually caption every single video or audio clip on the Internet due to the staggering cost. Captioning a video manually costs approximately $9 - $30 per minute [13] [14]. The costs cover skilled captionists who not only transcribe the audio content, but also keep video's text and audio in sync.

A transcription simply contains the text corresponding to the spoken words in a video. Transcriptions have several advantages over captions. When people begin reading a transcript, they have immediate access to the entire transcript and are limited only by the speed of their reading. In contrast, captioned text is synchronized with the video and the text is only revealed as the person in the video speaks. Viewers have to divide their attention between the captions and the visual activity in the video [15]. Captioned text is limited by the speed of produced speech (180-220 words per minute), which on average is slower than the speed of reading (250-300 word per minute) [16] [17]. Transcripts cost less than captioning, but they remain expensive, usually costing $1.50 - $3.00 per minute [18]. A lower-cost alternative is automatic speech recognition (ASR) [19] [20] [21], but it does not afford the accuracy of a trained captionist or transcriptionist [22].

There is a need to develop a rationale for leveraging scarce resources to do the most good. High-quality, manual captioning is prohibitively expensive. Transcripts offer a potential advantage due to their lower cost. Captioning by ASR is cheap, but inaccurate. In order to properly inform decisions about allocating resources, we asked two groups of related questions:

1. What aspects of using the Internet prove most difficult? For multimedia content, would transcripts be an acceptable alternative to captions? What is the current user experience with automatic captioning?
2. If there were no possibility of hiring a skilled captionist or transcriptionist, would lower-quality text, generated by ASR, be better than nothing? Would a visualization of the text's quality be useful?

Addressing these questions required two studies. The first study assessed the patterns of Internet usage among the adult deaf population to understand if these patterns were similar to those in the general population. It also investigated which types of multimedia content posed the most critical barriers, and gathered preference opinion on the viability of using transcripts instead of captioning. The results from this study could potentially lend insight into how to set priorities for accessibility efforts.

In addition, the results from the first study shaped the context for the second study. This was a follow up effort that considered the user experience when viewing text that was generated by ASR as contrasted with viewing text that was created manually.

2. EXPLORATORY STUDY

One of the goals of the first study was to identify multimedia content that was considered a high priority in the deaf community that would then serve as a case study for applying and evaluating speech visualization technology. Since the current literature did not provide a clear indication of a compelling choice, this exploratory study was necessary. The study proposal was evaluated and approved by DePaul Institutional Review Board (IRB) as noted by DePaul IRB #JR052311NUR.

2.1 Participants

A total of 20 deaf and hard-of-hearing adults from various parts of the United States participated in the study. They were recruited primarily through email invitation and some others were contacted through social media outlets such as Facebook. Nineteen of 20 participants were profoundly deaf, and one participant was hard-of-hearing. Fourteen participants stated that they were born deaf while five reported becoming deaf younger than five years old. Just three became deaf at the age of five years or older. Eleven of them were aged 30-39, while nine were 40 years or older. Thirteen were identified as male and seven female.

2.2 Procedure

All interviews were conducted by a deaf facilitator via video phone. The first step of the interview was to gain informed consent from the participants. The facility provided them with an information sheet explaining the study and notifying the participant that the interview would be recorded. The participants had an opportunity to ask questions or raise concerns prior to the interview. Each participant answered several basic demographic questions and a set of questions about Internet usage. Each then responded to 13 open-ended questions regarding their experience in using multimedia over the Internet.

2.3 Interview Results

Table 1 summarizes the Internet activities selected by the participants, rank ordered by frequency of use. Email was the most frequent activity, followed by getting the news, and accessing social media sites such as Facebook or Twitter. Watching YouTube videos occurred less frequently, as did shopping online. Online auctions and education/training were the least-frequently occurring activities.

Table 1: Patterns of Internet usage by study participants

Activity	Many times a day	Once a day	Once a week	Rarely	Never
Email	19	1			
News	10	6	3	1	
Social media sites	8	7	3	2	
YouTube	2	6	7	5	
Online shopping			10	10	
Online auctions			3	14	4
Education / training			2	16	2

Responses from the 13 open-ended questions were transcribed from sign language to English. A card sort analysis [23] was conducted on the responses to each individual question to identify patterns of commonality in the responses. The following is a listing of each question and a summary of the responses, based on the card-sorting results.

1. *When you read news articles on the Internet, do you ever watch the videos? Why or why not?*

When asked whether they watch news-related videos on the Internet, all twenty participants agreed that news videos are not useful without captions. Some of them pointed out that they tend to read news articles as opposed to videos online. One participant emphasized that if there are no captions, it isn't worth watching. Another said, "It's not worth my time."

2. *Have you watched YouTube?*

All 20 users have visited YouTube at least once when using the Internet to watch videos. Out of 20, 15 watch it "sometimes." Five pointed out that videos are often not captioned. Six users preferred watching Deaf-oriented or ASL-signed videos and two mentioned teaching ASL using YouTube.

3. *Have you ever found yourself needing the information on a video?*

Everyone responded at least "sometimes" but 16 of them pointed to lack of captions. Five complained of being stuck because videos lacked captions or were not accessible. Four users mentioned resorting to searching via Google or other search engine for texts related to the video.

4. *Can you describe the type of video it was?*

Fourteen respondents reported that the video they wanted was news-related and five mentioned CNN specifically. Knowledge about what is going on in the world was emphasized by four participants. Finally, four users mentioned interest in using training videos to increase knowledge and skills and keep up with current trends. Five users complained of being referred to a page with video, but after clicking on the link they realized that it was a video without captions and thus the information was inaccessible.

5. *What do you do to obtain the information or contents from videos?*

All participants would resort to reading related text or articles when available. Half of them would use Google or search online for related text, articles, and/or posts such as Facebook to learn more about contents from videos. Three users would attempt to contact the source or author to request transcripts of the video. Three participants would resort to asking an interpreter or hearing person to help translate selected videos.

6. *How often are you frustrated about inaccessibility when you use the Web?*

Sixteen users experienced frustration while four have either developed a tolerance or have given up altogether. Eight reported frustration every day and seven reported being frustrated sometimes. A participant succinctly compared the unavailability of captions to the stirred-up feelings of frustration that occur when the Internet is down.

7. *Describe the top three frustrations that you've experienced. What happened?*

The top frustration was lack of captions on new video clips. Seventeen participants mentioned this. Five users pointed out non-captioned self-tutorials and e-learning videos as a problem. Five viewers complained about lack of captions on YouTube. Finally, three users expressed disgust when clicking on a link only to be redirected to a video without captions

8. *Are you familiar with Google automatic captions? If yes, please tell me about your experience.*

Seventeen respondents had some experience while the other three didn't have any. Twelve pointed out that the captions had accuracy issues or too many errors, and four thought they were useless or too hard to follow. However, three users felt it was a good start and a step in right direction. In addition, two said it was better than no captions at all. Two participants thought it might be useful for hearing people who spoke another language.

9. *Have you used any other automatic speech recognition technology? If so, what was it? How did it work for you?*

Fourteen respondents stated they have not used ASR technology, five have used it, and one did not respond. Three users mentioned either Dragon Naturally Speaking [24] or iPhone's Siri feature [25] but they did not elaborate on how they used it.

10. *Now I need to review a couple of items of terminology with you. Captioning is the process of displaying text on a television, video screen or other visual display. Captions typically show a transcription of the audio portion of a program as it occurs. A transcript is a document containing a complete written or printed version of content originally presented as a video or recording. Which approach do you prefer? What are the advantages and disadvantages of each?*

Captions were preferred by 19 participants because the captions were usually better than transcripts. However one participant said it is fine either way. Nine described reading transcripts as being harder to use and requiring too much effort. Eleven pointed out that captions made "logical sense" because they're always in sync with the video.

11. *Are there any situations where you prefer captions over transcripts and vice versa?*

Seven participants favored captions in all situations while five preferred captions and mentioned that transcripts were only acceptable as a backup. Four pointed out that transcripts could be useful for reference, information verification, and research. Six would rather have captions because they are in sync with videos and are easier to follow.

12. *We are currently investigating technologies that may improve accessibility. Which situations that you mentioned earlier do you feel this would benefit the most?*

News-related videos were mentioned 15 times while four participants demanded all videos to be captioned. Four believed that all television shows should be accessible and three felt that investment or financial clips should be covered. Three emphasized any television shows or movies that are already captioned should also be captioned online.

13. *Do you have any advice or suggestions in regards to improving accessibility on the Internet?*

Five participants suggested additional government involvement such as legislation, lawsuits, and FCC, and three recommended educating people about the need because there may be a lack of awareness. Four demanded everything to be captioned. Three people suggested that any videos that have already been captioned should also be captioned online. Lastly, three thought speech recognition might be useful.

2.4 Analysis

This study addressed the first group of questions mentioned in the introduction, which were:

1. What aspects of using the Internet prove most difficult?
2. For multimedia content, would transcripts be an acceptable alternative to captions?
3. What is the user experience with automatic captioning?

In regards to the question, "What aspects of using the Internet prove most difficult?" the most common theme was the lack of accessibility to news online videos. All of the participants mentioned that they have used the Internet to access the news and most of them (16/20) did so at least once a day. Some participants were especially disappointed with well-known news outlets because they made little effort to make their videos accessible.

In regards to the second question about the acceptability of transcripts as an alternative to captions, the responses indicated strongly that captions were preferable to transcripts for news videos. Of the 20 participants, 19 indicated a preference for captions, and the remaining participant said that either format was equally preferable. Further, nine of the participants described reading transcripts as being harder than reading captions and required too much effort. More than half of the participants pointed out that captions made "logical sense" because they're always in sync with the video.

Further, when asked if there were any circumstances where transcripts would be preferable to transcripts, 16 of the 20 participants responded in the negative. Five participants mentioned that the only use for transcripts were as a backup to captions.

The consensus is that captions are designed to be synchronous with the videos which make them easier to follow. There was also consensus that it takes extra work to go back-and-forth between viewing the video and reading a separate transcript. Captions shown on the video itself were perceived as easier to follow.

In regards to the final question, "What is the user experience with automatic captioning?" participant responses were mixed. Of the 17 participants who had tried automatic captioning, 12 found that the results had too many errors to be useful. However, three of the participants thought that the technology was promising and two of them stated that automatic captions were better than no captions at all.

From this first study we understood that making Internet news videos more accessible was a high priority for members of the deaf community. Further, the data indicated that captions were preferable to transcripts for the news videos, so we decided to focus our efforts on captioning. Even though transcripts are more economical to produce, the test participants strongly indicated that captioning was preferable.

Based on this information, we focused our second study on evaluating access to Internet news using captions generated through ASR. We hoped that having the opportunity to explore different styles of automatic captioning might encourage interest in utilizing this technology.

3. VISUALIZATION STUDY

This study investigated the second set of questions (listed in the introduction) that concern the acceptability of automatically-generated captions. The study addressed these questions in the context of accessing news videos. We chose news videos because they were the type of video mentioned most often in the first study. The second study also considered the utility of indicating possible errors in the captions through a visualization of the word confidence level. The study was reviewed and approved by the DePaul University Institutional Review Board (BS031313CDM).

3.1 Participants

Participants were volunteers recruited through Deaf mailing lists. Additional participants were discovered through forwarding of the solicitation email. All were 18 years or older, were deaf or hard-of-hearing and had at least some college education and had watched captioned videos. A total of 95 people participated in the study.

3.2 Stimuli

The stimuli were four videos simulating news stories, each captioned in a different style:

1. Captions created through ASR. Words recognized at a higher confidence level were displayed in a more prominent color.
2. Captions created through ASR but without the visualization technique.
3. No captions.
4. Manually-created captions.

The role of stimuli 3 (no captions) and 4 (manually-created captions) were to act as a worst case and a best case respectively. Stimulus three would simulate the barriers described in [10] and stimulus four would simulate the use of a trained captionist.

There is no perfect solution for creating stimuli for this type of test. For full control, each stimulus would have to present the same news article. However, this would create a large transfer-of-learning bias since the same story would be repeated with each treatment, and the participants would be answering the exact same questions about content on four separate occasions. Thus it was necessary to identify four different news stories.

Using actual news stories as test stimuli posed an additional problem because viewers may have seen the story previously and have prior knowledge of its content. The question became, "Where can we find stories that are not actual news stories, and how do we control for the level of difficulty of stories and the content questions?"

To control for this possibility, this study utilized four simulated news stories by selecting material from standardized 8th-grade reading tests. The material needed to be believable as a news story, but also be from a reading test that had been previously validated for level of difficulty. Four reading passages chosen from the standardized tests were produced as news stories. [26] [27]. The questions from the original standardized reading tests served as the basis for the performance metrics in this study.

Videos were created from the stories by recording a single speaker who read the stories from a software teleprompter in an environment consisting of a neutral background, a table and a chair. To control for nonverbal cues, the news reader kept his arms on the table and used a neutral tone and facial expression through the reading. We created custom software utilizing the Microsoft Speech SDK to perform the recognition and to produce the timing and color-coding for captions in the SubStation Alpha format, which we then combined with the video via Virtual Dub. We then verified that the captions were temporally aligned to the audio track of the original video before stripping the sound from the final form of the video. To emphasize, the choice of speech recognition tool is not the point of the study – at present no speech recognition tool performs perfectly. What we wanted to evaluate was whether ASR-generated captions are a viable alternative when there are no manually-created captions available.

This resulted in simulated news videos that were controlled for speaker, speaker environment, nonverbal communication as well as reading difficulty. When reformatted as Internet media, stimuli 1, 2 and 4 received captions, and stimulus 3 received no captions. The manually-captioned stimulus had no errors, and the WER did not apply to the video since it did not have captions. Because the stories were different, the performance of the speech recognizer differed as well - giving a WER of 20% in the first instance and 12% in the second. However, according to [28] the word error rates for the first two stimuli were sufficiently low that the captions retained their utility.

Figure 1 is a screen shot from stimulus one. The videos captioned through ASR also carried an icon in the upper left corner that showed a voice bubble emanating from a computer. The intent of the icon was to indicate that the captions were generated through software that might not produce results that were as accurate as those created by professional captionists.

Figure 1: Simulated news video with automatic captions visualized for word confidence level

A fully factorialized design using the four conditions was not possible due to the small number of available participants. Since we anticipated that the condition with a WER of zero would produce the best performance results, we presented this stimulus last for all of the participants. It was already anticipated that this stimulus would serve as the upper bound for participant performance and preference; placing it last would take advantage of any transfer of learning that did occur in the test and would only serve to enhance the upper bound. The remaining three stimuli were fully randomized.

3.3 Procedure

The tests were performed online. Participants read the informed consent and filled out a qualifying questionnaire to confirm their eligibility for the study. They then viewed the four simulated news videos, ranging from 2:19 to 4:12 minutes long. The first three videos were presented in randomized order to minimize order bias, while the one with perfect captions was presented last. At the end of each video, the participant answered questions that were extracted from the standardized reading tests about the video's content. While answering the questions, the participant could replay the video as often as desired. After answering the content-related questions, they rated their viewing experience. After the four videos, participants answered a post-test questionnaire, which asked the participant to rate and compare all four captioning styles. An honorarium of a $15 gift card was emailed to the participants at the conclusion of the test.

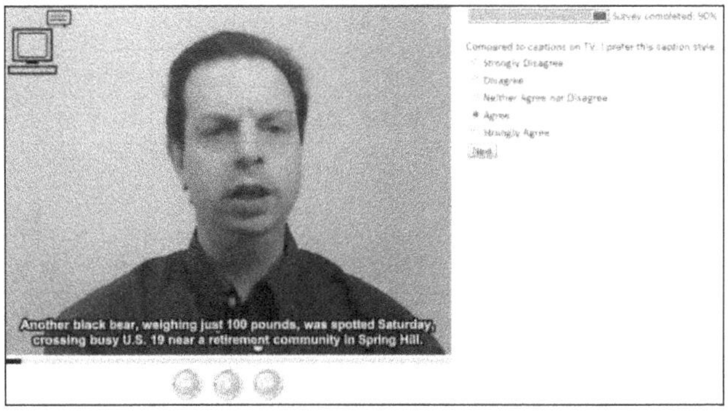

Figure 2: Screen shot of the test instrument from the user preference portion of the evaluation.

3.4 Results and Analysis

Table 2 lists performance metrics as the mean number of correctly answered questions for each captioning style. A single-factor analysis executed on the means showed that higher scores for the captions generated by ASR were significant. A post hoc analysis employing Tukey simultaneous comparison t-values showed that there were only two pairs the reflected significant differences. These were visualized ASR captions compared to no captions and ASR captions compared to no captions. The rest of the pairs fell below the critical value of 3.18 ($p = 0.01$), including comparisons with the perfectly-captioned video.

The study asked two sets of preference questions. The first set measured the participant initial reactions with the captioning style. Participants were asked to rate several aspects of the captioning style on a 5-point Likert scale (0 = strongly disagree, 4 = strongly agree). A Kruskal-Wallis analysis converted the responses into rankings. See Table 4.

For the question "The captions were easy to read," a Mann-Whitney calculation with Bonferroni adjustment identified all pairs except for Caption Style 1 (ASR captions with visualization) compared to Caption Style 4 (manual captions) as being statistically significant. For question two, "The captioning made it easy to understand the story," each of three captioned styles compared to the non-captioned style were statistically significant, but there were no differences among the three styles with captioning. The analysis of responses to question three, "I have confidence in the accuracy of the captioning," yielded a similar result. The analysis of the rankings for question four, "I like this style of captioning," produced results that were similar to the results for question 1.

Table 2: Correctly-answered content questions as a function of caption style

Caption Style	Mean	n	Std. Dev.
1. ASR captions, visualized	0.7105	95	0.26376
2. ASR captions	0.6877	95	0.23349
3. No captions	0.5579	95	0.28818
4. Perfect captions	0.6158	95	0.21481

Table 3: Pairs with significant differences

Pair	Score
Caption Style 1 vs. Caption Style 3 (no captions)	3.56
Caption Style 2 vs. Caption Style 3 (no captions)	4.18

Table 4: Participants' initial reactions to captioning styles

	Score (scale: SD D N A SA)
1. The captioning was easy to read.	
Caption Style 1	2.50
Caption Style 2	3.0
Caption Style 3	0.0
Caption Style 4	2.0
2. The captioning made it easy to understand the story.	
Caption Style 1	3.0
Caption Style 2	3.0
Caption Style 3	0.0
Caption Style 4	2.0
3. I have confidence in the accuracy of the captioning.	
Caption Style 1	2.0
Caption Style 2	2.0
Caption Style 3	0.0
Caption Style 4	2.0
4. I like this style of captioning.	
Caption Style 1	1.0
Caption Style 2	3.0
Caption Style 3	0.0
Caption Style 4	1.0

There was one additional response gathered for Caption Style 1, which used highlighting to convey the word confidence levels. Over two thirds (68 of 95) of the participants disagreed or strongly disagreed with the statement, "The color coding was helpful for understanding the story."

After viewing all of the videos, the participants responded to a second set of questions. These measures were taken after the participant had viewed all four captioning styles. This gave participants the opportunity to reflect on the various styles and compare all of them. When asked which was the hardest to understand, most the participants (80 of 95) chose Caption Style 3, which had no captions. When asked which was the easiest to understand, the selections were Caption Style 2 (44), Caption Style 4 (32) and Caption Style 1 (19).

When asked "If you had a video with automatic captions containing errors, would you want color coding to indicate possible errors?" 73 of 95 responded, "Yes." When asked, "Did you see any indication on the screen that indicated that the captions were generated through automatic speech recognition?" 51 of the 95 participants responded "Yes." When asked, "Is there a better way to indicate that captions are created with automatic speech recognition?" 33 of 95 responded "Yes."

When asked, "If you had a choice of watching a video with no captions or watching a video with captions created through automatic speech recognition, which would you choose?" the majority (85 of 95) chose the latter.

3.5 Discussion

The increasing use of inaccessible multimedia on the Internet is obviously detrimental for the deaf community. Manual captioning, providing transcripts and using ASR to generate captions are some of the possible remedies, but each has its advantages and disadvantages.

Both performance and preference results of this study lend credence to the hypothesis, "If there were no possibility of hiring a skilled captionist to create high-quality captions, would low-quality captions, generated by ASR, be better than nothing?" However, the second hypothesis, "Would visualization of the caption's quality be useful?" was not strongly supported. While it seemed like a given that ASR-generated captions would be better than nothing, we were surprised that the visual indication of this type of captions was not strongly supported at the outset of the investigation.

In the performance portion of the test, participants scored significantly higher on the videos having captions generated by ASR, both with and without visualizations of the word confidence level. When rating the captioning styles, participants found that the captions generated by ASR where easier to read and made it easier to understand the story. Further, the style most often rated as easiest to read was captioning generated through ASR. When asked the direct question, "If you had a choice of watching a video with no captions or watching a video with captions created through automatic speech recognition, which would you choose?" the overwhelming majority (85 of 95) responded in the affirmative. We believe these results would be valuable to broadcast to decision makers who are choosing whether or not to caption Internet multimedia.

The icon indicating that the captions were generated via ASR had mixed success. A little over half (53%) of the participants noticed its appearance on the news videos, and a third of the participants felt that the icon did not do an effective job of communicating its intent.

The data collected to evaluate the second hypothesis yielded mixed results. When comparing captioning styles head-to-head, participants preferred the captioning style without visualizations. However, when asked the question whether they would want a visualization to show that the captions were created via ASR instead of being manually transcribed, over 75% of the participants indicated that they wanted visualization. More research appears to be necessary in order to determine the viability of the indicator icon. One interesting avenue to explore regarding this visualization is whether, after most videos are captioned with varying degrees of quality, people would be more likely to want the icon so they would know what quality level to expect.

4. RELATED WORK

These results reinforce the results of previous studies [10] that found the multimedia content without text alternative is a critical barrier for users who are deaf and hard-of-hearing. Using ASR to generate captions results in word error rates that are consistent with other strategies for producing captions at low cost [29] [30]. The results also suggest that closed captions generated by ASR [20], [21] may be viewed as a viable alternative by deaf users when it is not possible to hire a trained captionist.

The desirability of visualizations of word confidence levels remains an open question. Consistent with the hearing participants in a study by [31], participant preference ratings in this study showed no significant difference between the captions with and without visualizations. However, over three quarters of the participants stated that they wanted the visualizations, consistent with the findings in [32].

5. LIMITATIONS

The performance metrics showed that even when there were no captions available, participants answered more than 50% of the content questions correctly. On reexamination of the content questions, it may have been that several of the questions could have been answered using previous knowledge. Also, the performance on the perfectly-captioned video was lower than that on the two videos captioned through ASR. One might reason that having no errors in the captions would lead to a higher score in answering the content questions. One possible explanation might be the order of presentation. The goal of placing the manually-captioned video last in the presentation order was to give it the benefit of any transfer of learning that may have occurred. However, participants may have become fatigued from the lengthy study.

6. FUTURE WORK

The future work will involve exploring and identifying visualization techniques that help make ASR-generated captions more useful. Creating a better visual indicator that the captions are actually generated by the speech recognition engine may help serve as a reminder that they are not perfect and will include errors. This may foster wider acceptance of ASR-based captions as a possible alternative to non-captioned videos. Additional studies are necessary to develop appropriate color-coding options to help identify words having lower confidence levels. User preferences could be utilized to allow users to customize how the colors should be presented. For example, the user can tweak how transparency, colors, and styles (underline, strikethrough, or other patterns) appear when the words fall under certain confidence levels.

It should be pointed out that the captions created by a speech recognition engine still are not of the same quality as those created by a skilled captionist. Much work needs to be done before this cost-effective alternative could become a reality. It is possible that the alternative could become a "backup" solution when a deaf or hard of hearing person comes across a non-captioned video. However, deaf advocacy groups could be concerned that organizations may attempt to substitute automatic captions in order to meet legal obligations.

Alternative strategies involving crowdsourcing might help improve the quality of automatic captions through low-cost means [29]. When ASR software has access to a speaker's voice profile, the resulting recognized text has higher accuracy. One possibility would be to maintain voice profiles for speakers online. When users desiring automatic captions submit a video, they could supply the identity of the speaker. The result would be more accurate captions. Another intriguing alternative would be to explore the application of gaming techniques similar to the crowdsourcing for soliciting volunteers for manual captioning in [30].

The benefits of utilizing speech recognition to improve Internet accessibility for deaf users are endless. It would help narrow the accessibility gap that deaf Internet users experience daily and lead to leveling of the playing field. No one should be denied access to the abundance of information that the Internet has to offer. "Knowledge is power," is a well-known quote coined by Francis Bacon in 1597 in the *Meditationes Sacrae* [33] and it resonates well with the motivation behind this work.

7. ACKNOWLEDGEMENTS

This work was performed while Brent Shiver was a student at DePaul University. A special appreciation goes to John McDonald who graciously volunteered to serve as the news anchor for the news clips. We also thank the American Sign Language Synthesizer Project team at DePaul University for taking the time to review and share feedback on the clips and online survey. Finally, we wanted to recognize the deaf participants of both experiments for contributing their time and valuable input.

8. REFERENCES

[1] Bain, K., Basson, S., and Kanevsky, D. Accessibility, transcription, and access everywhere. *IBM Systems Journal* (2005), 589-603.

[2] Sheng, L. and Xu, J. Using social software to improve learning performance of deaf university learners. In *The 2nd IEEE International Conference on Information Management and Engineering (ICIME)* (Chengdu, China 2010), IEEE, 703-706.

[3] Sloan, D., Stratford, J., and Gregor, P. Using multimedia to enhance the accessibility of the learning environment for disabled students: reflections from the Skills for Access project. *ALT-J, Research in Learning Technology* (Mar 2006), 39-54.

[4] Freire, A. P., de Bettio, R. W., Frade, E. G., Ferrari, F. B, Monserrat Neto, J., and Libardi, H. Accessibility of web and multimedia content: techniques and examples from the educational context. In *Proceedings of the 19th Brazilian symposium on Multimedia and the web* (Salvador, Brazil December 2013), ACM, 7-8.

[5] Kožuh, I., Hintermair, M., Ivanišin, M., and Debevc, M. The concept of examining the experiences of deaf and hard of hearing online users. *Procedia Computer Science*, 27 (2014), 148-157.

[6] Zickuhr, Kathryn. 2010. Online Activities. Pew Research Internet Project. Retrieved January 12, 2015 from http://www.pewinternet.org/2010/12/16/online-activities/.

[7] Cheung, A. and Slavin, R. How features of educational technology applications affect student reading outcomes: A meta-analysis. *Educational Research Review* (2012), 198-215.

[8] Caldwell, B., Cooper, M., Reid, L., and Vanderheiden, G. 2008. Web Content Accessibility Guidelines (WCAG) 2.0. W3C. Retrieved January 12, 2015 from http://www.w3.org/TR/WCAG20/.

[9] GSA IT Accessibility and Workforce. 2015. Opening Doors to IT. Section 508.gov. Retrieved January 12, 2015 from http://www.section508.gov/.

[10] Pascual, A., Ribera, M., and Granollers, T. Impact of web accessibility barriers on users with hearing impairment. In *Proceedings of the XV International Conference on Human Computer Interaction.* (Puerto de la Cruz, Spain 2014), ACM, 8.

[11] Phillips, A. 2014. FCC Issues New Rules to Improve Captioning Quality. National Association of the Deaf. Retrieved January 12, 2015 from http://nad.org/news/2014/3/fcc-issues-new-rules-improve-captioning-quality.

[12] National Association of the Deaf. 2014. FCC Requires Closed Captioning of Online Video Clips. National Association of the Deaf. Retrieved July 2, 2014 from http://nad.org/news/2014/7/fcc-requires-closed-captioning-online-video-clips.

[13] Automatic Sync Technologies, LLC. 2014. Closed Captioning Cost and Pricing. Caption Sync. Retrieved January 22, 2015 from http://www.automaticsync.com/captionsync/closed-captioning-cost/.

[14] CPC Computer Prompting & Captioning Co. 2015. CPC Closed Captioning Blog. CPC: Home of e-Captioning. Retrieved January 12, 2015 from http://cpcweb.com/blog/2012/09/the-top-5-closed-captioning-concerns-answered/.

[15] Lasecki, W. S., Kushalnagar, R., and Bigham, J. P. Helping students keep up with real-time captions by pausing and highlighting. In *Proceedings of the 11th Web for All Conference* (Seoul 2014), ACM, 39.

[16] Human Factors International. 2000. Human Interaction Speeds. Human Factors International. Retrieved January 12, 2015 from http://www.humanfactors.com/newsletters/human_interaction_speeds.asp.

[17] Smith, S. M. and Shaffer, D. R. Speed of speech and persuasion: Evidence for multiple effects. *Personality and Social Psychology Bulletin*, 21, 10 (1995), 1051-1060.

[18] CGBiz LLC. 2012. The Pre-Payment Requirement. Scribie: Audio Transcription, Perfected. Retrieved September 7, 2012 from https://scribie.com/blog/2012/09/the-pre-payment-requirement/.

[19] Wactlar, H. D., Kanade, T., Smith, M., and Stevens, S. M. Intelligent access to digital video: Informedia project. *Computer* (1996), 46-52.

[20] Jutla, D. N. and Kanevsky, D. wisePad services for vision-hearing-and speech-impaired users. *Communications of the ACM* (2009), 64-69.

[21] Google. 2009. Automatic captions in YouTube. Official Blog. Retrieved November 19, 2009 from http://googleblog.blogspot.com/2009/11/automatic-captions-in-youtube.html.

[22] National Institute of Standards and Technology. 2012. Speaker Recognition Evaluation. Information Technology Laboratory. Retrieved March 2, 2012 from http://nist.gov/itl/iad/mig/sre12.cfm.

[23] Fincher, S. and Tenenberg, J. Making sense of card sorting data. *Expert Systems*, 22, 3 (2005), 89-93.

[24] Nuance Communications, Inc. 2015. Dragon Speech Recognition Software. Dragon NaturallySpeaking. Retrieved January 17, 2015 from http://www.nuance.com/dragon/index.htm.

[25] Apple Inc. 2015. Siri: Your wish is its command. iOS 8. Retrieved January 17, 2015 from http://www.apple.com/ios/siri/.

[26] Public Schools of North Carolina. 2013. North Carolina End-of-Grade Tests -- Grade 8. Department of Public Instruction. Retrieved June 30, 2013 from http://www.ncpublicschools.org/docs/accountability/testing/releasedforms/grade8readingreleased.pdf.

[27] University of South Florida. 2013. FCAT Express Eighth Grade Reading. Florida Comprehensive Assessment Test. Retrieved June 30, 2013 from http://fcit.usf.edu/fcat8r/default.htm.

[28] Munteanu, C., Baecker, R., Penn, G., Thoms, E., and James, D. The Effect of Speech Recognition Accuracy Rates on the Usefulness and Usability of Webcast Archives. In *CHI Proceedings: Visualization and Search* (Montréal 2006), ACM, 493-502.

[29] Wald, M. Crowdsourcing correction of speech recognition. In *Proceedings of the 8th International Cross-Disciplinary Conference on Web Accessibility* (Hyderabad, India 2011), ACM, 22.

[30] Kacorri, H., Shinkawa, K., and Saito, S. Introducing game elements in crowsourced video captioning by non-experts. In *Proceedings of the 11th Web for All Conference* (Seoul 2014), 2014, 29.

[31] Vermuri, S., DeCamp, P., Bender, W., and Schmandt, C. Improving speech playback using time-compression and speech recognition. In *Proceedings of the SIGCHI conference on human factors in computing* (Vienna 2004), ACM, 295-302.

[32] Vertanen, K. and Kristensson, P. O. On the benefits of confidence visualization in speech recognition. In *Proceedings of the SIGCHI conference on human factors in computing systems* (Florence 2008), ACM, 1497-1500.

[33] Bartlett, J. 1919. Familiar Quotations, 10th ed. Bartleby.com. Retrieved August 20, 2013 from http://www.bartleby.com/100/139.39.html.

ForeSee: A Customizable Head-Mounted Vision Enhancement System for People with Low Vision

Yuhang Zhao
Jacobs Technion-Cornell Institute
Information Science, Cornell University
yz769@cornell.edu

Sarit Szpiro
Jacobs Technion-Cornell Institute
Cornell Tech
sarit.szpiro@cornell.edu

Shiri Azenkot
Jacobs Technion-Cornell Institute
Cornell Tech
shiri.azenkot@cornell.edu

ABSTRACT

Most low vision people have functional vision and would likely prefer to use their vision to access information. Recently, there have been advances in head-mounted displays, cameras, and image processing technology that create opportunities to improve the visual experience for low vision people. In this paper, we present *ForeSee*, a head-mounted vision enhancement system with five enhancement methods: Magnification, Contrast Enhancement, Edge Enhancement, Black/White Reversal, and Text Extraction; in two display modes: Full and Window. ForeSee enables users to customize their visual experience by selecting, adjusting, and combining different enhancement methods and display modes in real time. We evaluated ForeSee by conducting a study with 19 low vision participants who performed near- and far-distance viewing tasks. We found that participants had different preferences for enhancement methods and display modes when performing different tasks. The Magnification Enhancement Method and the Window Display Mode were popular choices, but most participants felt that combining several methods produced the best results. The ability to customize the system was key to enabling people with a variety of different vision abilities to improve their visual experience.

Categories and Subject Descriptors

H.5.1 [**Information Interfaces and Presentations**]: Multimedia Information Systems – *artificial, augmented, and virtual realities*; K.4.2 [**Computers and Society**]: Social Issues – *Assistive technologies for persons with disabilities*

Keywords

Accessibility, Visual Impairment, Augmented Reality Glasses, Vision Customization

1. INTRODUCTION

There are roughly 19 million people in the United States who have difficulty seeing when performing daily activities, even with corrective contact lenses or glasses [9]. Meanwhile, the National Federation of the Blind reports that there are only about 1.3 million legally blind people in the US [30]. This means that there are millions of people who have functional vision and would probably like to leverage their vision for performing daily activities more efficiently and comfortably. There has been a wealth of research on people with vision disabilities in the technology and disabilities community. However, most of this research ignores the residual vision that many people have and focuses on solutions with audio or vibrotactile interaction (*e.g.*, [11,23,54]). More research is needed to understand low vision people's abilities and preferences and innovate methods that will enhance people's visual experience [22].

We seek to seize an opportunity to improve accessibility for people with low vision using head-mounted display systems, an emerging mainstream technology. In the last few years, a variety of companies have developed head-mounted display systems for augmented reality [13,18,28] and virtual reality [33,44] applications, and simply as a way of having an always-available digital display [18,47]. These systems often include embedded cameras and other sensors. They have received attention from the press [53], consumers, industry, and researchers and will likely continue to develop and become widely adopted and more socially acceptable. As with mass-market technology, they will be relatively affordable and available to consumers, unlike specialized assistive technology [24,42,43]. As such, we believe head-mounted display systems can become effective, versatile, and practical accessibility tools, on which we can design dynamic customizable systems that directly enhance people's vision.

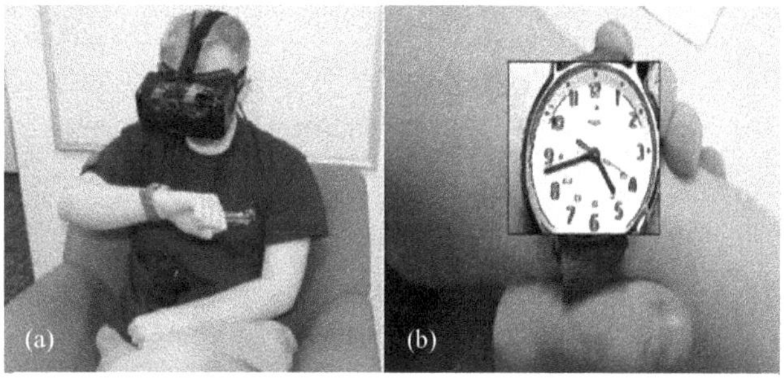

Figure 1. (a) A low vision person using ForeSee to check the time. (b) He sees an enhanced version of the watch using magnification, contrast enhancement, and edge enhancement in ForeSee's Window Display Mode.

We present *ForeSee*, a head-mounted vision enhancement system that enables people to customize their visual experience to better access information in their environment. ForeSee (Figure 1) is a video see-through augmented reality system that consists of an embedded processor, a camera, and a display that rests over the user's eyes. The camera captures the user's view, the processor enhances the captured video feed, and the display presents the enhanced video feed to the user. ForeSee has five enhancement methods: *Magnification*, *Contrast Enhancement*, *Edge Enhancement*, *Black/White Reversal*, and *Text Extraction*; and two display modes: *Full Display Mode* and *Window Display Mode*, which apply the enhancement to the full field of view or only to a region within the view. The user can customize their experience with ForeSee by selecting combinations of enhancement methods in either display mode and adjusting parameters of enhancement methods and display modes. Unlike prior work [36,52], ForeSee is designed to work with commodity hardware and enable users to

ASSETS '15, October 26-28, 2015, Lisbon, Portugal

DOI: http://dx.doi.org/10.1145/2700648.2809865

create a customizable viewing experience that is best suited to their eye conditions and a given environment or task.

We conducted a user study with 19 participants with a variety of visual abilities to evaluate ForeSee's effectiveness. Participants used ForeSee to complete two visual tasks: reading a page of printed text and reading and describing textual signs that were hung above eye-level at a distance of about three meters. We chose these tasks because they represent important daily living challenges for low vision people [10]. Participants tried all of the enhancement methods and display modes during each task.

Our key findings include: (1) ForeSee's customization function had a major improvement on the users' visual experience, (2) different users preferred different combinations of enhancement methods and display modes in different viewing tasks, and (3) Window Display Mode was beneficial to most users, helping them concentrate, multitask, and understand the context of their visual target.

In summary, this paper has two main contributions:

1. *ForeSee*, a customizable head-mounted vision enhancement system for people with low vision.
2. An extensive evaluation of ForeSee, which sheds light on the effectiveness of different enhancement methods and display modes for people with different visual abilities performing near- and far-distance viewing tasks.

2. RELATED WORK

Even though the vast majority of people with visual impairments have functional vision, there has been little research studying the challenges low vision people face and innovating vision enhancement tools. Jacko and Sears [22] advocated for the importance of research on designing systems for low vision people in 1998 emphasizing the lack of innovation in the area. However, common low vision tools such as CCTV's [25], optical magnifiers, and screen magnification software [1,3,4,5,17,29] remain largely the same as they were over 17 years ago.

The development of cameras, head-mounted displays, and image processing technology has created opportunities for low vision research. There has been some prior research on head-mounted systems for low vision people. Researchers have focused on correcting specific low vision conditions. Optometry researchers have contributed several projects [26,37,38,39,40,45,52] on different head-mounted systems and algorithms to enhance the vision of people with different eye conditions. For example, Peli [37] presented a head-mounted system with a one-dimensional analog video processing algorithm for people with reduced contrast sensitivity to provide them more detailed real-time gray scale video with lower cost, weight, and power consumption. This system was evaluated by Peli and Woods [40] with 19 participants with central field loss who were tasked with recognizing celebrity faces. Forty-two percent of the participants showed significant improvement with this system. Their lab also developed a method [52] for optical see-through displays that aims to expand people's field of view by overlaying the contours of a minified view of a wide field over the center of the user's original vision. They evaluated their method with (only) two participants with Retinitis Pigmentosa who completed visual field tests with this enhancement method on head-mounted displays. They found that the participants' field of view was effectively expanded.

Instead of developing custom hardware platforms, some researchers have recently created enhancement tools for Google Glass [18]. For example, Tanuwidjaja *at el.* developed Chroma [50], a system that projects a filtered image in the Google Glass display that highlights or changes certain colors to make them discernable to a user with color blindness. They evaluated this system with 23 colorblind participants who performed color identification tasks in different contexts. In over half the tasks, Chroma improved participants' performance. Hwang and Peli [21] implemented two edge enhancement algorithms based on positive and negative Laplacian filters on Google Glass to increase contrast for people with age-related macular degeneration (AMD). They conducted a preliminary study with three sighted participants by measuring their contrast sensitivity, finding that their contrast sensitivity improved when using this system.

Besides different eye conditions, researchers have also aimed to address challenges for low vision people in specific scenarios. For example, some researchers focused on mobility. Everingham *et al.* [15] developed a neural-network classification algorithm for a head-mounted device that segmented scenes rendered in front of users' eyes and recolored objects to make obstacles more visible. Hicks *et al.* [20] built a real-time head-mounted LED display with a depth camera to aid navigation by detecting the distance to nearby objects and changing the brightness of objects to indicate their distances. In addition to mobility, some research systems and products have been developed to assist low vision people with reading. Merino-Gracia *et al.* [27] proposed a real-time text recognition algorithm for a head-mounted device with audio feedback that aims to help blind people read. However, they only measured the performance of the detection algorithm on a particular image dataset, and did not conduct a user study to evaluate its effect on blind people. A similar product on the market called OrCam [34] is a portable device with a camera but no display that is mounted on the frame of a user's eyeglasses. OrCam recognizes text and products and provides audio feedback with a bone-conducting earpiece.

Even though different head-mounted systems and enhancement methods were developed, they were mostly designed for specific low vision conditions or scenarios. Our work aims to enhance people's vision directly, with a head-mounted system that is customizable in real-time to improve accessibility for people with different visual conditions in a variety of daily tasks. One commercial product called eSight [14] includes some similar features to ForeSee. eSight is a custom head-mounted video see-through display that costs $15,000. It supports magnification, contrast enhancement and color adjustment of a real-time video-feed. But unlike ForeSee, it only provides three basic enhancement methods and does not support combinations of enhancement modes or different Display Modes. To our knowledge, eSight has not been formally evaluated with low vision users.

In addition to the novel design of ForeSee, we also present a qualitative user evaluation to gain a deep understanding of the use of different enhancement methods on a head-mounted system. We found that most evaluations of previous head-mounted vision enhancement systems involved quantitative studies like measuring speed and accuracy in search tasks (*e.g.*, [15,26]). There has been little focus on the visual experience and user behavior with different enhancement methods and under different scenarios. Researchers have repeatedly shown that involving consumers in low vision assessments could reduce device abandonment [12,42,46], so researchers should involve participants in the evaluation of their systems as well, understanding their preferences and experiences. In this paper, we describe a study with different low vision people based on ForeSee to collect more comprehensive data, and summarize the users' preferences and use patterns of different enhancement methods. This work helps us understand how different enhancement methods serve different low vision conditions in different scenarios, thereby providing insights for the future design and evaluation methods of head-mounted vision enhancement systems.

3. THE DESIGN OF FORESEE

3.1 Design Guidelines

In our design exploration stage, we formulated the following guidelines to direct our design.

DG1. Enhance Vision Directly

We wanted to develop a system that enables people with low vision to use their residual vision for performing daily tasks. Meanwhile, we sought to seize an opportunity to use computer vision technology, which is able to perform various real-time transformations to video feeds, to enhance people's vision directly in all their daily living activities, without being highly task specific [19].

DG2. Use Standard Enhancement Techniques

As a starting point, we wanted to use standard enhancement methods that were already widely used and accepted by low vision people. It would be easier for users to adjust to such familiar techniques on a new platform.

DG3. Enable Customization according to Users' Preferences

We wanted our system to be customizable to suit users' needs and preferences. We believe this is especially critical for a technology that targets low vision people, since there are many different kinds and degrees of vision impairments [2]. Moreover, people's visual abilities frequently change over time and in different settings [30] (*e.g.*, a sunny sidewalk or a dimly-lit restaurant).

DG4. Enable Fast and Natural Interaction

As mentioned in DG3, people's visual abilities vary in different environments so they may need to adjust the system often. Moreover, people may need different settings for different tasks, such as reading a newspaper and looking for a friend in a crowd of people. As such it is not only imperative for the system to be customizable, but the user must be able to efficiently interact with the system in different situations to customize it.

3.2 System Description

ForeSee is a video see-through [6] augmented reality head-mounted device that is designed to work with commodity hardware. It consists of a display, a camera, and a processor. ForeSee captures a video feed of the user's surroundings from the user's point of view, sends the feed to the processor, and then displays the processed feed on the display. There is only one camera, so the user sees the world in two dimensions (in the future we may experiment with using two cameras to achieve a stereo 3D effect). The processor enhances the image in various ways, as described in Section 4.3. Unlike Google Glass, the display covers the user's entire field of view. This allows us to enhance the user's field of view directly, following DG1.

ForeSee enhances the user's vision by applying some combination of *enhancement methods* in different *display modes*. An enhancement method is a kind of transformation that is applied to the captured video feed. A display mode is a way of incorporating the transformed content into the original captured video. In its current state, ForeSee includes five enhancement methods and two display modes. Following DG2, we developed the enhancement methods and the display modes by examining commonly-used low vision aids and techniques for improving the visibility of printed and digital materials for people with low vision, as discussed in Section 2.

Currently, we created two display modes (Figure 2): ***Full Display*** and ***Window Display***. The Full Display Mode simply applies enhancement methods to the user's entire field of view. The Window Display Mode applies enhancement methods to a rectangular area within the user's field of view, shown in the bottom left corner of Figure 2. The user can change the width, height, and position of the rectangle. We modeled the Window Display Mode after a handheld magnifier. It also resembles the "lens" mode in many screen magnifiers where a rectangular area around the cursor is magnified [1,29].

We created five enhancement methods (Figure 2):

Magnification. Since magnification seems to be the most common vision enhancement method on both optical and digital devices, we created a Magnification Enhancement Method where the user can adjust the level of magnification. The magnification

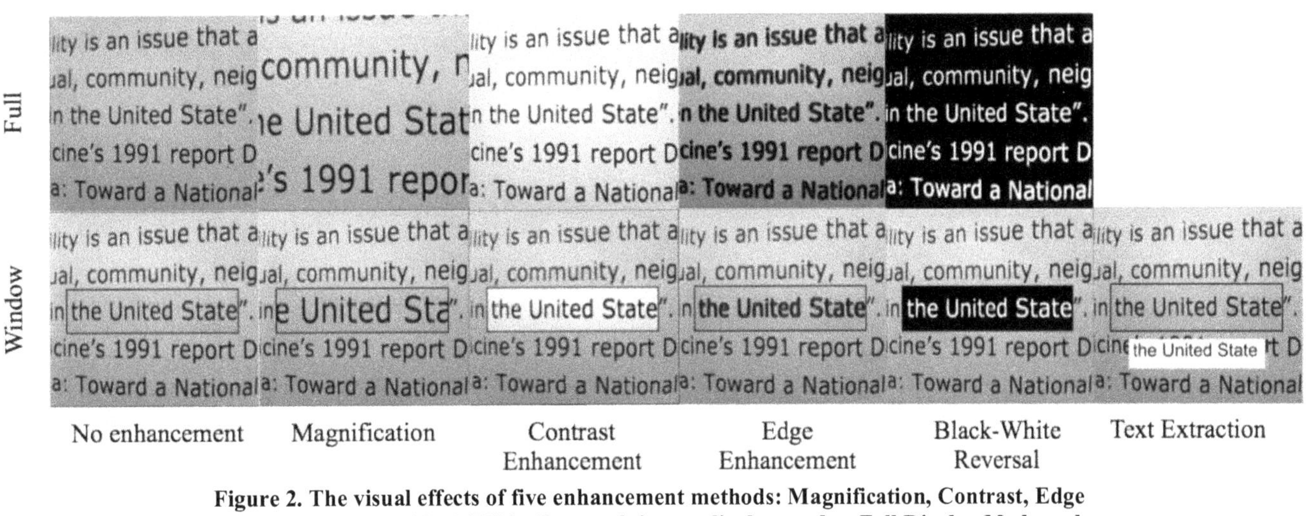

Figure 2. The visual effects of five enhancement methods: Magnification, Contrast, Edge Enhancement, and Black/White Reversal; in two display modes: Full Display Mode and Window Display Mode

Table 1. Demographic Information of the 19 Participants

ID	Age/Sex	Diagnose Result	Visua Field	Acuity	Colo Vision	Tool Used
P1	23/M	Nystagmus	Full	20/120	Good	Bifocal, telescope, software magnifier, zoom-in (magnification) on computer
P2	29/F	Optic Atrophy	Full	20/400	Could distinguish primary colors	Cane, black/white reversal on computer
P3	45/F	Pituitary gland optic nerve tumor	Limited	Unknown, but good	Good	ZoomText, CCTV, magnifier for brief reading tasks
P4	53/M	Stargardt's Disease	Full	Left: 20/800 Right: 20/600	Have color vision but not good at subtle colors	CCTV, handheld magnifiers, handheld telescopes
P5	21/F	Leber's Congenital Amaurosis	Very limited	20/600	Have color vision but not good at subtle colors	Braille notetaker, Jaws, iPhone with VoiceOver, zoom-in (magnification) to see images
P6	34/F	Retinitis Pigmentosa	Limited; 30 degrees in each eye	Unknown, but good	Good	ZoomText, cane at night
P7	34/F	Pathological Myopia; Detached retina in left eye; has cataract	Full	20/200	Have color vision but not good at subtle colors	Screen magnifiers for phone and tablet, speech input and Siri, ZoomText, color reversal
P8	56/M	Bilateral optic atrophy; Nystagmus	Full	20/220	Have color vision but not good at subtle colors	Screen magnifier, black/white reverse
P9	57/F	Usher's syndrome, Retinitis Pigmentosa	Very limited, < 5 degrees	Left: < 20/170 Right: no vision	Need high contrast to see colors	CCTV, color reversal
P10	34/F	Retinitis Pigmentosa	Limited	20/60	Color blind	Magnifier, flash light at night
P11	40/F	Detached retina	Full	Right: blind Left: 20/60	Have color vision but not good at subtle colors	Reading glasses, cane, iPhone with VoiceOver, Laptop with Zoom, CCTV
P12	65/M	Central areolar choroidal sclerosis	Unknown	Unknown	Need high contrast to see colors	CCTV, ZoomText (magnification and speech)
P13	58/F	Retinopathy of prematurity	Full	Left: 20/400 Right: 20/300	Need high contrast to see colors	Handheld monocular, CCTV, handheld magnifier, ZoomText (magnification and speech), large print
P14	51/F	Cytomegalovirus Retinitis	Very limited	Right: blind Left: unknown	Color blind	Jaws, ZoomText
P15	64/F	Retrolental Fibroplasia	Very limited	Right: unknown Left: blind	Have color vision but not good at subtle colors	Cane, screen readers (used to use magnification)
P16	55/F	Steven Johnson Syndrome	Very limited	Right: 20/200 Left 20/150	Good	Magnifier, CCTV
P17	23/M	Stargardt's Disease	Full	Limited, but unknown	More issues with contrast	Screen magnifier, color reversal
P18	36/M	Reversal class of Retinitis Pigmentosa	Full	20/300	Cannot distinguish colors of low contrast	Screen magnifiers, screen readers, color reversal
P19	68/F	Retinal myopathy, glaucoma (possibly other conditions)	Left: limited Right: almost none	Left: unknown (but limited) Right: only light perception	Cannot distinguish colors of low contrast	ZoomText, CCTV, color reversal, handheld magnifiers, iPhone with Zoom and Siri

ranges from 1 (no magnification) to 35 times the original image size in 17 increments.

Contrast Enhancement. In this method we increase the contrast of the video feed but maintain the color hues. We used a standard contrast enhancement algorithm that can be found in Szeliski [49] on page 103. We increased both the luminance contrast and color contrast by setting the RGB values of each pixel with a multiplication of 2 and an addition of -100. We then clamped the values to the standard range of [0-255].

Edge Enhancement. This method darkens and thickens the edges (or contours) in the color video stream. We used Canny's edge detection algorithm [8] to detect the edges in an image and then darkened the pixels on and surrounding the edges in the original image by setting those pixels to black. The thickness of the edge is 5 pixels.

Black/White Reversal (BWR). In this enhancement method, we used Otsu's Thresholding Method [36] to convert the video to binary (only black and white) with the threshold of 100, and then reversed the colors. People often use this type of effect (white text on a black background) when reading with CCTVs [25].

Text Extraction. This method is only available in the Window Display Mode. It detects the position of the text with the Scene Text Detection [32] in the OpenCV library [34], recognizes the text in the window using the Tesseract-OCR engine [51], and displays a digital version in Arial, size 30, with high contrast (black text on a white background) in a separate region below the window.

In accordance with DG4, we plan to incorporate an input method into ForeSee. In this study, as we only focused on understanding possible output formats on the head-mounted display, we used Wizard of Oz (WOZ) to allow users to interact with ForeSee with natural speech commands. Based on the study of different output effects, we will determine what kind of input actions ForeSee should support in the future to provide users more natural and flexible experience.

3.3 Prototype

We describe the current implementation of ForeSee. To create a video see-through system, we combined an Oculus Rift and a webcam. We used a WideCam F100 to capture the surrounding environment and an Oculus Rift DK2 with Lens B as the display on which we rendered both the captured environment as the background and different enhanced effects to enable users to get more visual information. The Oculus had a display with a resolution of 960x1080 for each eye. The webcam supported a resolution of 1920x1080 pixels with a 120 Degree ultra wide angle lens and allows manual focus. The webcam and Oculus Rift were connected to a laptop that is used as the processor of the vision enhancement system. The whole system was built with Unity and we used OpenCV to process video frames in real-time. The webcam was attached to the front of the Oculus Rift at the center between the user's eyes. The Oculus's two screens rendered the same images of the enhanced environment to simulate the effect of binocular vision.

Users interacted with ForeSee with natural speech commands, which we implemented with Wizard of Oz (WOZ). The researcher, acting as the wizard, responded to the commands and adjusted the system parameters accordingly. For example, the user could say, "move the window down," to adjust the window position in the Window Display Mode, or "make it larger," to adjust the magnification level in the Magnification Enhancement Method.

4. EVALUATION

We evaluated ForeSee by conducting a user study with 19 low vision participants. Our high-level goal was to determine whether ForeSee was a promising tool for people with low vision. Moreover, we sought to answer the following questions:

1. How did ForeSee affect people's visual experience in different scenarios?
2. How effective were each of the enhancement methods and display modes?
3. How did people customize ForeSee?

4.1 Method

4.1.1 Participants

We recruited 19 people with low vision to participate in our study (13 females, 6 males). Their mean age was 46 (age range: 21 – 68). In our recruiting materials, we called for volunteers who had "low vision" When volunteers contacted us, we conducted a brief interview over the phone to determine whether they were appropriate. If a volunteer said they used tools that enhanced their vision such as handheld magnifiers, screen magnifiers, or CCTVs, we deemed them appropriate. Participants had a variety of vision conditions (see Table 1). They all knew their diagnosed eye condition, but many did not know their precise visual acuity or visual field.

We had conducted studies with 20 participants, but one participant, P20, was unable to complete the tasks so we do not include this participant in our report. P20 arrived late and did not understand the study instructions.

Participants were compensated $20 per hour and were reimbursed for travel expenses up to $60.

4.1.2 Procedure and Materials

The study consisted of one session that lasted two to four hours (about 2.5 hours on average). Participants sat on a chair inside a well-lit office throughout the study. We offered them water and coffee and allowed them to take frequent breaks for as long as they needed to reduce the impact of exhaustion and possible fatigue on our study. We began each session by conducting a short interview where we asked participants for their age, gender, and vision condition. We then introduced ForeSee, explaining its functionality and the goals of the study.

We then asked participants to perform a set of tasks. In this paper, we focus on two of those tasks, which took about 1.5 hours on average. The tasks included reading text from (1) a handheld printed page and (2) four printed signs hung about three meters

Figure 3. Experiment Materials: (a) four printed signs of numbers or writings hung on the wall (b) a handheld printed page

away. We chose these tasks because they were representative of important and challenging daily activities. The printed page had three paragraphs in Verdana, size 20, as shown in Figure 3(b). The letters were dark on the white page. The signs included several letters or numbers each, printed in a decorative font in different colors, as shown in Figure 3(a).

For each task, the participants were asked to think aloud about their visual experience under different conditions. Specifically, we asked them to describe what they saw, their comfort level (*i.e.*, whether they experienced any eyestrain), and read the text if possible. In total, we evaluated 12 conditions for each task:

1. Completing the task without using ForeSee.
2. Using ForeSee but without any enhancement methods.
3. Using ForeSee in the Full Display Mode, with all enhancement methods, except for Text Extraction, which can only be used in the Window Display Mode (conditions 3a – 3d).
4. Using ForeSee in the Window Display Mode, with each of the five enhancement methods (conditions 4a – 4e).
5. Using ForeSee with whatever enhancement methods (It is allowed to chose multiple enhancements at the same time and combine them.) and display mode works best. The user is able to take his or her time and customize the system to maximize their visual experience.

To avoid order effects, we counterbalanced the order of some conditions and randomized the order of others. We counterbalanced the order of the tasks (near-distance and far-distance) and the order of conditions 1 and 2. We presented the enhancement methods in a random order (condition 3a – 3d and 4a – 4e), since there were too many enhancement methods to properly counterbalance them. We always presented condition 5 at the end since participants had to be familiar with all the enhancement methods and both display modes to experience it effectively.

We connected ForeSee to the researcher's laptop, mirroring the display of the Oculus on the laptop. The researcher could thus ensure that the targets were in the user's field of view.

4.1.3 Analysis

We video-recorded and took notes during each session. After the study, we transcribed the videos using a professional service and analyzed the transcripts following the general method in [7], organizing them by tasks and conditions. Two researchers discussed the themes and categories of the data together, while one of them was mainly in charge of the coding process.

4.2 Results

In this section, we report user preferences and use patterns on different enhancement methods and display modes. Among our 19 participants, P5 and P15 did not have enough vision to benefit from ForeSee on either task, so they were not able to comment on the enhancement methods of display modes.

4.2.1 Video See-Through View (No Enhancements)

In Condition 2, participants completed a task by looking at the 2D video captured by the webcam. Considering the limited focal range of the webcam and the low resolutions of the Oculus display, we expected the unenhanced view to be blurry and distorted. However, some participants preferred the video see-through display to their original vision.

In the near-distance task, 9 participants indicated that using ForeSee without enhancement improved their visual experience. Some of them (*e.g.*, P12, P14) who could not read the materials with their original vision were able to read with ForeSee. "I can't read standard printed material without magnification. With the [ForeSee], I can see an individual word" (P14). Other participants (*e.g.*, P11, P16) said ForeSee increased the distance at which they could comfortably hold the page. "The difference is that I really have to look very close [without ForeSee], so if I had [ForeSee] I wouldn't have to look this close" (P16).

In the far-distance task, most participants preferred their original vision because of the limited resolution. However, there were still three participants (P2, P14, and P16) who believed that the visual experience with ForeSee was better.

4.2.2 Magnification

Full Display Mode: Most participants felt magnification was effective: 14 participants in the near-distance task and 15 in the far-distance task. Many remarked that magnification enabled them to see more colors and details. "I certainly see more detail than before. Now the color [of the top left sign] is green or blue, like a light green or blue" (P18). Even though the magnified video has a lower resolution than the original video, participants felt they perceived more information and were better able to distinguish details and read. "It's not so clear, but clear enough to maybe read it" (P4), and "But now that it's bigger, it's blurry but I can see more" (P2).

While providing more detailed information, magnification had some disadvantages. It reduced users' visual field and made it difficult for them to identify targets. It also reduced the speed at which they perceived what they saw, especially for the near-distance task:

So much of reading is recognizing general forms and not necessarily seeing every letter. Instead of actually looking at every single letter or every single syllable. I'm doing a lot from context. (P11)

The loss in visual field negatively impacted people with tunnel vision. Two participants (P3 and P9) insisted that magnification did not improve their vision in either task: "Everything that I look at cuts in half, so although they are becoming clearer, they're cut in half for me" (P3).

Window Display Mode: In the near-distance task, fewer participants liked magnification in the Window mode than in the Full mode. One reason is that the size of the window was limited, which reduced the users' field of view and also made it difficult to track the target. "Because I'm looking inside the box, it's fine, but I just stay focused inside the box. I don't like to go outside the box. It's too much. You could miss a sentence, you could skip over a line" (P10). While in the far-distance task, targets appeared smaller, which reduced the "cut-off" and "lose tracking" phenomena, which resulted in 13 participants finding magnification useful.

Participants tended to modify the size of the window as they adjusted the magnification level, increasing the window to keep the target in the magnified view. Some suggested that the window display should automatically increase as the magnification level increases to keep the target in the window. As P8 suggested, "Actually the magnification is helping but you need the border to magnify together with it. If you don't, then what you see inside the border decreases."

4.2.3 Contrast Enhancement

Full Display Mode: Like magnification, many participants (13 out of 19) felt that contrast enhancement was beneficial. They noted that the contrast enhancement emphasized the color and increased the sharpness: "It's brighter. It's sharper. That makes it easier to recognize what it is right away" (P16).

However, contrast enhancement also had a negative effect on some participants' visual experience, especially those who were sensitive to light such as P2 and P10. They felt that the brightness hurt their eyes and distracted them from their ability to focus on the target. "It's too bright. The color bothers me, I don't know how to explain it " (P10).

Window Display Mode: Contrast enhancement was effective for more participants in the Window mode than in the Full mode. Participants no longer reported negative side effects. Moreover, we found that the window actually increased the effect of the contrast enhancement. P13 explained, "I realized something: when you add the borders [in the Window Display Mode], it increases the light in the area. The reading area seems brighter when you add the borders" (P13). The high contrast in the window, which was described as a flashlight by P12, highlighted the target and helped users locate and concentrate on the content they wanted to see: "It does highlight it. If you wanted me to focus on the 'Z,' it would help find it. It's easier to focus" (P12).

4.2.4 Edge Enhancement

Participants had strong and differing opinions about edge enhancement.

In the near-distance task, all participants except for P5 and P15 agreed that the font appeared bolder. For example, P10 explained, "It's bold. Let's say with low vision, you always have a problem with differentiating 'e' and 'a'. It [edge enhancement] gives you a clear definition to the letter. It defines the letter." However, six participants did not like this enhancement method in the near-distance task. Because the contours of each letter was thickened, it created a *crowding effect* [41] that made it difficult to read. "They're a little bit even bolder and a little bit closer together. It's a little bit harder to distinguish them" (P11).

In the far-distance task, most of the participants (14 out of 19), especially those who had more functional vision (*e.g.*, P1, P12), felt edge enhancement was distracting because it added "unfamiliar" information to the objects. The edges darkened the scene and occluded colors and details in the original objects. As P13 commented, "I can't see the color distinction as clearly. It's blurrier and the images to me seemed thicker. They don't seem natural. They seem thicker." Meanwhile, some participants (*e.g.*, P12 P17) did feel that edge enhancement helped to discover objects in their view and locate them quickly. "With the edge definition, the objects are more obviously there, because they're dark" (P12).

4.2.5 Black/White Reversal

As black/white reversal was modeled after a common effect people use when reading with CCTVs, it largely distorted the color and detail information of the objects in one's environment. Unsurprisingly, most participants (15 out of 19) did not like this enhancement method in the far-distance task.

In the near-distance task, participants had differing opinions. Ten participants preferred the black/white reversal to the original black-on-white text. It was easier for them to perceive light against the dark background than to perceive dark letters on a light background. They said there was too much glare on the original white background, which they found distracting. As P13 mentioned, "I like [black/white reversal] because there's less glare from the paper, the page. I find it's easy to see every individual letter. I like that the words are enhanced better."

On the other hand, there were seven participants who thought black-on-white was better than the reverse. They felt that the white letters were too bright, which hurt their eyes and caused fatigue. "It would be more tiring over a longer period of time because I would be getting too much glare from the letters" (P4).

4.2.6 Text Extraction

Participants had different opinions on text extraction due to different tasks. In the far-distance task, 11 participants felt that they benefited from the text extraction because it was much clearer than the original one. "I feel like if it was used for like a street sign, then that would be great. I really like the text detection. I pretty much can't see the numbers without the text detection" (P2). While in the near-distance task, fewer participants (six out of 19) preferred text extraction. Seven participants concerned about the efficiency and practicability to extract only a few words at a time when reading long paragraphs. As P17 indicated, "It's great if you're looking at distance because usually a sign or something is not going to be more than a few words, but to read like that would take you a very long time. I don't think it's practical, maybe somehow superimposing it over." Some of them (*e.g.*, P4, P11) suggested using eye-movement tracking and automatic text extraction to increase the reading efficiency.

We also discussed the presentation of the extracted text and the ability to control parameters in this task with participants to get insights about its design.

Participants wanted to be able to customize the position and style of the extracted text. Some participants felt the current location of the text (at the bottom of the display) was best because the text did not cover the center of their view (*e.g.*, P7, P10), and looking down felt natural for reading (P6). Seven participants (not counting P5 and P15), especially those with tunnel vision, had difficulty seeing the extracted text at the bottom of the display. The style of the digital text, including font size, color, and weight needed to be adjustable as well. P12 said the text extraction did not help because the text was too small for him to see. P18 suggested reversing the color of the text to white-on-black and using a bold font.

Switching their gaze between the original text in the window and the extracted digital text at the bottom of the display was challenging for some participants (*e.g.*, P6, P11). As P6 said, "I won't see the two images at the same time. I have to look at the image and then I have to look down. I have to change my position of my gaze." Some participants (P6, P10) suggested that the extracted text could replace or be located next to the original text to avoid the gaze switching.

4.2.7 Window Display Mode

We summarize general user opinions and use patterns when using the Window Display Mode. Overall, six participants preferred using the Window in the near-distance task and 12 participants in the far-distance task.

Window placement: As we expected, most participants (13 out of 19) put the selection area at the location where their sight was best (usually in the center; for P3, it's the left side because she only had vision on the left side of her right eye) and adjusted its size to fit the target object. However, P16 had a different approach. She also put the window in the center of her visual field and adjusted its size according to her target. However, she did this to compensate for a weak angle in her view. "I think to keep it center for me will always be good because that's, as I said, that's where my problem vision is, my central vision."

***Benefits**:* Participants reported several benefits from using the Window. Some (*e.g.*, P3, P18) said the window helped them concentrate on the target. Three participants (P7, P17, and P18) used the window to support multitasking. It was difficult for participants to switch from one task to another when using enhancements like magnification and black/white reversal in the Full Display Mode. For example, P17 felt disoriented when using black/white reversal: "Because, yeah, as long as you don't take your eyes off the page you're good. The second you look up, you're very disoriented." In the Window Display Mode, some participants felt the window enabled them to conduct different tasks at the same time. P7 explained:

I'm trying to think of a situation where I was reading something at my desk and if I wanted to be able to keep track of the things going on around me, then I would use the enhancement box set to a thin line so I could get the text.

Finally, some participants (*e.g.*, P1, P17) mentioned that the Window Display Mode gave people context (*i.e.*, information about the original image), especially in the far-distance task.

It gives me a point of comparison, because I can be not looking at it. I see now that I need help to zoom in, so now I see contextually. As opposed to when it's full blown, maybe the issue I had before was I don't know where I am in a world that large. I think just contextually this [can help me see]. (P17)

Weaknesses: There are also some weaknesses of the Window Display Mode mentioned by the participants.

Participants with a better peripheral vision (*e.g.*, P1, P4, P17) felt the inconsistency between inside and outside of the window distracted them because they would see the surrounding of the window peripherally. For example, P17 commented on the magnification in Window Display Mode: "There are too many text sizes going on at once. Because I'm still seeing the text changing size as I'm reading it peripherally and it's a little distracting" (P17).

Some participants (*e.g.*, P2, P12) found it difficult to find the window in their visual field. "It was probably worse because then you have to find the specific spot" (P2). What's more, most participants prefer to set the window at a fixed position and then look around to move the target in. Some of them (*e.g.*, P16, P19) felt that it required too much effort to put the particular object into the small window, especially for the crowded text in the near-distance reading task, "It's hard to put the specific line into this area. It's frustrating" (P16).

4.2.8 Combining Enhancement Methods

Most participants (15 out of 19 in the near-distance task and 14 out of 19 in the far-distance task) felt that they were able to improve their visual experience by combining enhancement methods. Figure 4 shows which methods participants chose to achieve the best visual experience.

We found that participants' preferences differed in the two tasks. All the participants changed their preferred combination according to the viewing tasks. For example, more participants (10 out of 17 participants, not including P5 and P15) chose the Full Display Mode than the Window Mode in near-distance tasks.

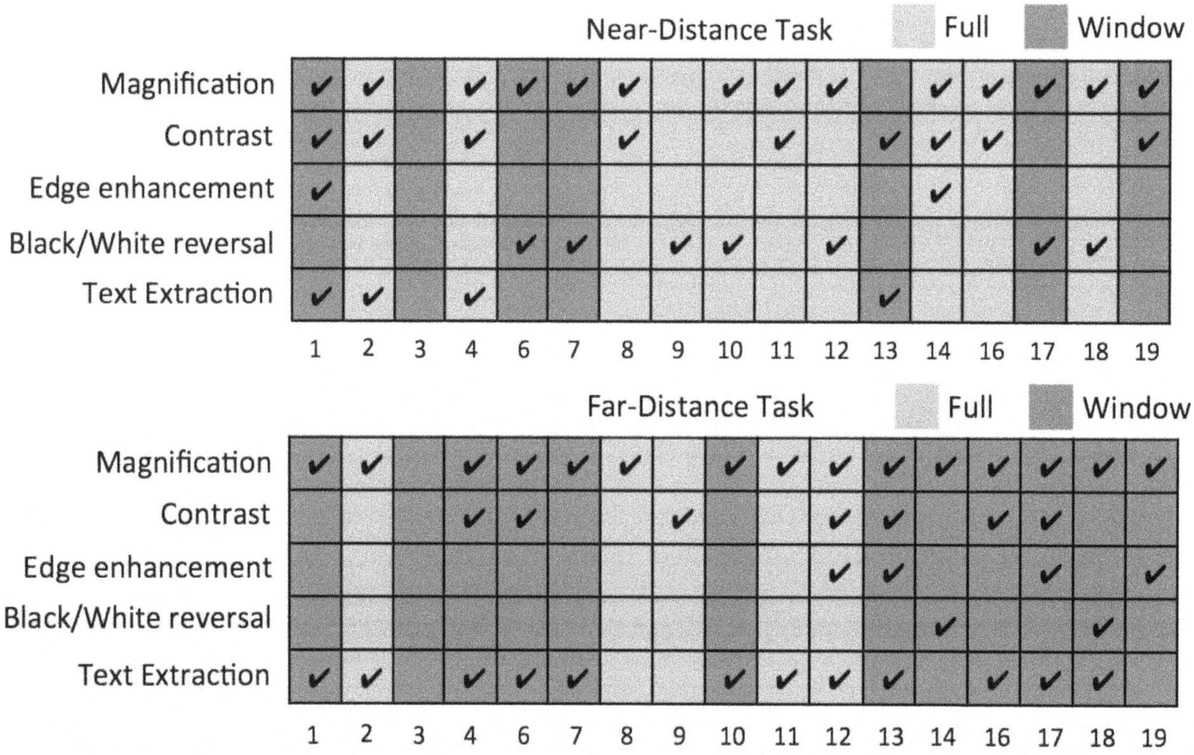

Figure 4. Enhancement method combinations preferred by each participant in the near- and far-distance tasks: The columns represent the participants (P5 and P15 are not shown because they could not conduct the combination), and the rows present the enhancement methods. We use red and blue to represent Full and Window Display Modes, respectively. In each row, we use a check mark "✔" to show the particular enhancements each participant chose in the combination. P3 has no check marks because she preferred the Window Display Mode without any enhancement in both tasks.

But most of them preferred the Window Display Mode in far-distance tasks (12 out of 17 participants) because the target is much smaller in this scenario and the window could help them focus. More participants preferred text extraction in the far-distance task (12 out of 17) than in the near-distance task (4 out of 17) because extracting all the words one by one in a large amount of text, such as the printed page that the participants used in the near-distance task, is time-consuming and not practicle.

Participants with different visual conditions chose different combinations in the same task. For example, participants with tunnel vision (*e.g.*, P3, P9) rarely chose magnification because they felt the objects were cut off too much. Participants who have more issues with colors, especially low-contrast colors (*e.g.*, P12, P17), were more likely to choose edge enhancement in the their preferred combination because it could enhance the contrast and emphasize the shape of the target.

Additionally, we found that most participants (14 out of 19 in the near-distance task and 15 out of 19 in the far-distance task) used magnification. Especially in the far-distance task, we found that other enhancement methods would only work with magnification. P12, for example, didn't feel that edge enhancement alone was beneficial in the far-distance task. However, when combing it with magnification, he said:

The edge enhancement probably helped. Plus you've got magnification going too, right? Now I could see the contour of the inside part. The edging really helped me distinguish the number.

5. DISCUSSION

Overall, we found that ForeSee was a promising vision enhancement tool for people with a wide range of vision abilities. In this section, we discuss the high-level findings, limitations, and challenges of the system and the study.

ForeSee was useful for a wide variety of visual conditions, but it would not be appropriate for people with too little functional vision (like P5 and P15), and people with too much vision. As we had expected, people who could not benefit from existing vision enhancement tools like CCTV's were also not able to benefit from ForeSee. We had designed our screening question accordingly, but we misunderstood P5's and P15's responses. During the study we found that they weren't able to perceive the difference among enhancement methods so ForeSee had no impact on their vision. On the other end of the spectrum, ForeSee is not appropriate for people with too much functional vision, such as P1, because either the 2D display or the reduced resolution would hinder their ability to see certain details. We believe that in the future, as video see-through technology advances, the resolution of the camera and the display will increase, and even fully sighted people will not perceive less information. ForeSee will then be able to enhance the vision of people with corrected and mildly low vision.

A key finding from the study was that customization (or "adaptability" [16,48]) was extremely useful. Participants improved their visual experience by combining enhancement methods and changing parameters of the enhancement methods and display modes. This was proved by our study, in which no participants chose the same combination for both tasks, shown in Figure 4. In fact, participants wanted even more ways to customize the system. When using Text Extraction, for example, they wanted to be able to modify the properties of the extracted digital text. Prior work on low vision has tended to focus on specific vision abilities [50,52] or tasks [15,20]. In contrast, we have shown how a single vision enhancement system can support a wide variety of vision abilities and tasks through rich customization. There was as much diversity of preferences among people with similar vision conditions as there was among people with different vision conditions.

The vast array of customization options can only improve the system if (1) users discover these options and (2) they can quickly adjust them. As we found in our study, people's preferences differed by task. In a real life setting, users would need to adjust the system quickly as they performed different daily activities. It is necessary to design suitable input methods to enable users to flexibly customize their visual effect on the go. Eyes-free input gestures and natural dialog systems are potential options that we are considering to help users optimize their experience or discover different settings. Additionally, we could use machine learning to learn the user's preferences and sense information in the environment (lighting condition, distance to target object, *etc.*) to automatically adjust the enhancement methods and display modes. This opens diverse and important opportunities for future work.

Another key finding from our study was that the Window Display Mode was effective for most participants, especially in the far-distance task. They explained that it helped them concentrate on the target, understand its context, and switch their gaze between tasks. However, some participants found it hard to use the window because of the inconsistency between inside and outside of the window and the difficulty to locate the window. Participants also raised an interesting direction for improving the window by automatically adjusting its size to the magnification level to keep their target in its view. Moreover, it would be interesting to adapt the *shape* of the window as well to match the target object. Exploring the properties of Window Display Mode is thus an important contribution of our work, which also differentiates our system from existing head-mounted displays (*e.g.*, eSight) and prior research.

Despite the overall positive results, the current ForeSee prototype and our study also had some limitations.

The social acceptability of the system is an important concern. Some participants (*e.g.*, P2, P11) complained about the bulkiness and intrusiveness of the current form factor. However, ForeSee is a preliminary prototype that we created to demonstrate the concept of a customizable head-mounted system and we did not expect that users would wear the current prototype in their daily life. We aimed to use this system as a first step to explore peoples' responses to different enhancement methods and modes, and get insights for future system designs.

There were also some limitations with the system implementation. As we mentioned, the resolutions of both the web camera and the Oculus display was relatively low. Moreover, processing the video feed also caused a slight delay. These factors negatively impacted the participants' attitudes towards ForeSee, but on the other hand, we gained a better understanding of the limitations of current hardware and software from the study with this prototype. This could direct researchers to develop smaller, lighter, and more suitable hardware, and more efficient algorithms for the future head-mounted system. We hope that a smaller head-mounted display with a higher resolution could be adopted to create a more acceptable system, allowing people to wear it everywhere as usual glasses. We may also use GPU computing in the future to speed up the system and provide more natural experience for the low vision users.

We faced several challenges when conducting the user study. Visual perception is complex and it was challenging to determine the effect of the different enhancement methods. During the study, participants sometimes had difficulty describing what they saw and how the enhancement methods affected their visual experience. We had to repeat and explain our questions several times and verify our understanding of the participants' description to ensure that we understood their experience. Although this process was difficult, we got interesting results as well as a deeper understanding about the benefits and weaknesses of different enhancements, which we would never get from a quantitative study.

6. CONCLUSION & FUTURE WORK

In this paper, we have presented ForeSee, a video see-through augmented reality system that improves the visual experience for people with low vision by directly enhancing what they see. ForeSee runs on commodity hardware. It captures a live video feed of the user's environment, applies some combination of enhancement methods (*e.g.*, magnification, contrast enhancement, and edge enhancement), and presents the modified video to users in real time. Through an extensive study with 19 low vision participants, we found that ForeSee's powerful customization abilities enabled people with different visual abilities to better see objects in different viewing tasks.

Our work has raised interesting directions for the future, including:

1. **Make ForeSee more practical.** We will explore ways of using lighter commodity software with higher resolution and more processing power (*e.g.*, a GPU) to reduce ForeSee's bulkiness and delay.
2. **Design efficient and natural interaction techniques**. We will explore a suitable input modality for users to customize ForeSee. Different modalities, such as speech commands, 3D gestures (*e.g.*, pointing, waving), eyes-free gestures on a smartwatch or wristband, eyes-free gestures on a smartphone or similar handheld device, or gestures on the head-mounted device itself (*e.g.*, the touchpad on Google Glass), will all be taken into consideration.
3. **Make ForeSee adaptive** [16]. Given the difficulties that low vision people may have in controlling the system, we will explore ways of using machine learning and sensors to learn the user's preferences in different environmental conditions. We will then develop algorithms to automatically adapt the enhancement methods and display modes to suit the user's needs in different contexts. We will also design suitable interactions to make sure the users could control the system manually when the system makes a mistake in the adaption.

As augmented and virtual reality technologies continue to advance, we believe ForeSee will become a powerful vision enhancement tool for people with low and even standard vision.

7. ACKNOWLEDGMENTS

We thank Chancey Fleet, Lei Shi and all the participants for their time and helpful feedback.

REFERENCES

1. AI Squared, ZoomText, http://www.aisquared.com/zoomtext.
2. American Optometric Association. What Causes Low Vision. http://www.aoa.org/patients-and-public/caring-for-your-vision/low-vision/what-causes-low-vision?sso=y. Accessed May 4, 2015.
3. Android Accessibility Help: Magnification Gestures, https://support.google.com/accessibility/android/answer/6006949?hl=en. Accessed May 3, 2015.
4. Apple, iOS Accessibility, https://www.apple.com/accessibility/ios/
5. Apple, OSX Accessibility, https://www.apple.com/accessibility/osx/
6. Azuma, R. T. (1997). A survey of augmented reality. *Presence*, *6*(4), 355-385.
7. Burnard, P. (1991). A method of analysing interview transcripts in qualitative research. *Nurse education today*, *11*(6), 461-466.
8. Canny, J. (1986). A computational approach to edge detection. *Pattern Analysis and Machine Intelligence, IEEE Transactions on*, (6), 679-698.
9. Center for Disease Control (CDC), Summary Health Statistics for the U.S. Population: National Health Interview Survey, 2004. http://www.cdc.gov/nchs/data/series/sr_10/sr10_229.pdf. Accessed May 3, 2015.
10. Cimarolli, V. R., Boerner, K., Brennan-Ing, M., Reinhardt, J. P., & Horowitz, A. (2012). Challenges faced by older adults with vision loss: a qualitative study with implications for rehabilitation. *Clinical rehabilitation*, *26*(8), 748-757.
11. Dakopoulos, D., & Bourbakis, N. G. (2010). Wearable obstacle avoidance electronic travel aids for blind: a survey. *Systems, Man, and Cybernetics, Part C: Applications and Reviews, IEEE Transactions on*, *40*(1), 25-35.
12. Dougherty, B. E., Kehler, K. B., Jamara, R., Patterson, N., Valenti, D., & Vera-Diaz, F. A. (2011). Abandonment of low vision devices in an outpatient population. *Optometry and vision science: official publication of the American Academy of Optometry*, *88*(11), 1283.
13. Epson Moverio Smart Glasses, http://www.epson.com/cgi-bin/Store/jsp/Landing/moverio-bt-200-smart-glasses.do?ref=van_moverio_2014
14. eSight, http://www.orcam.com/
15. Everingham, M. R., Thomas, B. T., and Troscianko, T. (1999). Head-mounted mobility aid for low vision using scene classification techniques. *The International Journal of Virtual Reality*, 3(4), 3.
16. Findlater, L., & McGrenere, J. (2004, April). A comparison of static, adaptive, and adaptable menus. In *Proceedings of the SIGCHI conference on Human factors in computing systems* (pp. 89-96). ACM.
17. Freedom Scientific: MAGic Screen Magnification Software, http://www.freedomscientific.com/Products/LowVision/MAGic
18. Google Glass, https://support.google.com/glass#topic=4363345
19. Harper, R., Culham, L., & Dickinson, C. (1999). Head mounted video magnification devices for low vision rehabilitation: a comparison with existing technology. *British journal of ophthalmology*, *83*(4), 495-500.
20. Hicks, S. L., Wilson, I., Muhammed, L., Worsfold, J., Downes, S. M., & Kennard, C. (2013). A depth-based head-mounted visual display to aid navigation in partially sighted individuals. *PloS one*, *8*(7), e67695.

21. Hwang, A. D., & Peli, E. (2014). An augmented-reality edge enhancement application for Google Glass. *Optometry & Vision Science*, *91*(8), 1021-1030.

22. Jacko, J. A., & Sears, A. (1998, January). Designing interfaces for an overlooked user group: considering the visual profiles of partially sighted users. In *Proceedings of the third international ACM conference on Assistive technologies* (pp. 75-77). ACM.

23. Kane, S. K., Bigham, J. P., & Wobbrock, J. O. (2008, October). Slide rule: making mobile touch screens accessible to blind people using multi-touch interaction techniques. In *Proceedings of the 10th international ACM SIGACCESS conference on Computers and accessibility* (pp. 73-80). ACM.

24. Kane, S. K., Jayant, C., Wobbrock, J. O., & Ladner, R. E. (2009, October). Freedom to roam: a study of mobile device adoption and accessibility for people with visual and motor disabilities. In *Proceedings of the 11th international ACM SIGACCESS conference on Computers and accessibility* (pp. 115-122). ACM.

25. Low Vision Center: Closed Circuit Television, http://www.lowvisioninfo.org/hightech.htm

26. Luo, G., & Peli, E. (2006). Use of an augmented-vision device for visual search by patients with tunnel vision. *Investigative ophthalmology & visual science*,*47*(9), 4152-4159.

27. Merino-Gracia, C., Lenc, K., & Mirmehdi, M. (2012). A head-mounted device for recognizing text in natural scenes. In *Camera-Based Document Analysis and Recognition* (pp. 29-41). Springer Berlin Heidelberg.

28. Microsoft HoloLens, https://www.microsoft.com/microsoft-hololens/en-us

29. Microsoft, Make Items on the Screen Appear Bigger (Magnifier), http://windows.microsoft.com/enus/windows/make-screen-items-bigger-magnifier#1TC=windows-7

30. Moore, J. E., & LeJeune, B. J. (2008). Low vision. International Encyclopedia of Rehabilitation. Retrieved from http://cirrie.buffalo.edu/encyclopedia/article

31. National Federation of the Blind: Blindness and Low Vision, https://nfb.org/fact-sheet-blindness-and-low-vision

32. Neumann, L., & Matas, J. (2012, June). Real-time scene text localization and recognition. In *Computer Vision and Pattern Recognition (CVPR), 2012 IEEE Conference on* (pp. 3538-3545). IEEE.

33. Oculus VR, https://www.oculus.com/

34. OpenCV, http://opencv.org/

35. OrCam, http://www.orcam.com/

36. Otsu, N. (1979). A threshold selection method from gray-level histogram. IEEE Trans. Systems Man Cybernet, 9(1979), pp. 62-66.

37. Peli, E. (1999). Simple 1-D image enhancement for head-mounted low vision aid. *Visual Impairment Research, 1*(1), 3-10.

38. Peli, E., Luo, G., Bowers, A., & Rensing, N. (2007). Applications of augmented-vision head-mounted systems in vision rehabilitation. *Journal of the Society for Information Display, 15*(12), 1037-1045.

39. Peli, E., Luo, G., Bowers, A., & Rensing, N. (2009). Development and evaluation of vision multiplexing devices for vision impairments. *International Journal on Artificial Intelligence Tools, 18*(03), 365-378.

40. Peli, E., & Woods, R. L. (2009). Image enhancement for impaired vision: the challenge of evaluation. *International Journal on Artificial Intelligence Tools,18*(03), 415-438.

41. Pelli, D. G. (2008). Crowding: A cortical constraint on object recognition. *Current opinion in neurobiology, 18*(4), 445-451.

42. Phillips, B. and Zhao, H. (1993). Predictors of assistive technology abandonment. Assistive Technology 5 (1), 36-45.

43. Riemer-Reiss, M.L. and Wacker, R.R. (2000). Factors associated with assistive technology discontinuance among individuals with disabilities. Journal of Rehabilitation 66 (3), 44-50.

44. Samsung Gear VR, http://www.samsung.com/global/microsite/gearvr/

45. Satgunam, P., Woods, R. L., Luo, G., Bronstad, P. M., Reynolds, Z., Ramachandra, C., ... & Peli, E. (2012). Effects of contour enhancement on low-vision preference and visual search. *Optometry and vision science: official publication of the American Academy of Optometry, 89*(9), E1364.

46. Scherer, M. J. (1996). Outcomes of assistive technology use on quality of life.*Disability & Rehabilitation, 18*(9), 439-448.

47. Sony Wearable HDTV, http://store.sony.com/wearable-hdtv-2d-3d-virtual-7.1-surround-sound-zid27-HMZT3W/cat-27-catid-3D-Personal-Viewer

48. Stephanidis, C., Akoumianakis, D., & Savidis, A. (1995). Design representations and development support for user interface adaptation. *Institute of Computer Science Foundation for Research and Technology.*

49. Szeliski, R. (2010). *Computer vision: algorithms and applications.* Springer Science & Business Media.

50. Tanuwidjaja, E., Huynh, D., Koa, K., Nguyen, C., Shao, C., Torbett, P., ... & Weibel, N. (2014, September). Chroma: A wearable augmented-reality solution for color blindness. In *Proceedings of the 2014 ACM International Joint Conference on Pervasive and Ubiquitous Computing* (pp. 799-810). ACM.

51. Tesseract-OCR, https://code.google.com/p/tesseract-ocr/

52. Vargas-Martin, F., & Peli, E. (2002). Augmented-view for restricted visual field: multiple device implementations. *Optometry & Vision Science*, 79(11), 715-723

53. Wood, M. (2015). Video Feature: Signs That Virtual Reality Is on the Verge of Taking Off. *New York Time.* http://www.nytimes.com/2015/01/29/technology/personaltech/video-feature-signs-that-virtual-reality-is-on-the-verge-of-taking-off.html Accessed on Jan, 28, 2015

54. Yu, W., Kangas, K., & Brewster, S. (2003, March). Web-based haptic applications for blind people to create virtual graphs. In *Haptic Interfaces for Virtual Environment and Teleoperator Systems, 2003. HAPTICS 2003. Proceedings. 11th Symposium on* (pp. 318-325). IEEE.

Zebra Crossing Spotter: Automatic Population of Spatial Databases for Increased Safety of Blind Travelers

Dragan Ahmetovic
Università degli Studi di Milano
dragan.ahmetovic@unimi.it

James M. Coughlan
Smith-Kettlewell Eye Research Institute
coughlan@ski.org

Roberto Manduchi
University of California Santa Cruz
manduchi@soe.ucsc.edu

Sergio Mascetti
Università degli Studi di Milano
sergio.mascetti@unimi.it

ABSTRACT

In this paper we propose a computer vision-based technique that mines existing spatial image databases for discovery of *zebra crosswalks* in urban settings. Knowing the location of crosswalks is critical for a blind person planning a trip that includes street crossing. By augmenting existing spatial databases (such as Google Maps or OpenStreetMap) with this information, a blind traveler may make more informed routing decisions, resulting in greater safety during independent travel.

Our algorithm first searches for zebra crosswalks in satellite images; all candidates thus found are validated against spatially registered Google Street View images. This cascaded approach enables fast and reliable discovery and localization of zebra crosswalks in large image datasets. While fully automatic, our algorithm could also be complemented by a final crowdsourcing validation stage for increased accuracy.

Categories and Subject Descriptors

H.2.8 [**DATABASE MANAGEMENT**]: Database Applications—*Spatial databases and GIS*; I.4.8 [**IMAGE PROCESSING AND COMPUTER VISION**]: Scene Analysis—*Object recognition*; K.4.2 [**COMPUTERS AND SOCIETY**]: Social Issues—*Assistive technologies for persons with disabilities*

General Terms

Algorithms, Human Factors

Keywords

Orientation and Mobility, Autonomous navigation, Visual impairments and blindness, Satellite and street-level imagery, Crowdsourcing

ASSETS'15, October 26–28, 2015, Lisbon, Portugal.

ACM 978-1-4503-3400-6/15/10 ...$15.00.
DOI: http://dx.doi.org/10.1145/2700648.2809847 .

1. INTRODUCTION

Independent travel can be extremely challenging without sight. Many blind persons learn (typically with the help of an Orientation and Mobility, or O&M, professional) the routes that they will traverse routinely [20], for example to go to work, school or church. Far fewer attempt independent trips to new locations: for example to visit a new friend or meet a date at a restaurant. To reach an unfamiliar location, a blind person needs to learn the best route to the destination (which may require taking public transportation); needs to follow the route safely while being aware of his or her location at all times; and needs to adapt to contingencies, for example if a sidewalk is undergoing repair and is not accessible. Each one of these tasks has challenges of its own. In particular, the lack of visual access to landmarks (for example, the location and layout of a bus stop or the presence of a pedestrian traffic light at an intersection) complicates the wayfinding process. Thus, a straightforward walk for a sighted person could become a complex, disorienting, and potentially hazardous endeavor for a blind traveler.

Technological solutions for the support of blind wayfinding exist. Outdoors, where GPS can be relied upon for approximate self-localization, a blind person can use accessible navigation apps. While these apps cannot substitute proper O&M training, they provide the traveler with relevant information on-the-go, or can be used to preview a route to be taken. A navigation tool, though, is only as good as the map it draws information from. Existing geographical information systems (GIS) lack many features that, while accessible by sight, are not available to a blind person. For example, Hara et al. found that knowing the detailed layout of a bus stop (e.g., the presence of features such as a bench or nearby trees) can be extremely useful for a blind person for figuring out where to wait for the bus [8]. Other relevant information lacking in GIS may include the presence of curb ramps (curb cuts) near intersections, or the location of an accessible pedestrian signal controlled by a push button.

We propose a novel technique to detect zebra crossings on satellite and street level images. Knowing the location of marked crosswalks is important for any traveler. A pedestrian, crossing a street outside of a marked crosswalk, has to yield the right-of-way to all vehicles[1], a difficult task for pedestrians with visual impairments. Conversely, a marked crosswalk is clearly visible by drivers, grants right-of-way to pedestrians, and is highly preferable as a location for street

[1] `http://mutcd.fhwa.dot.gov`

crossing in terms of safety. Pedestrians who are blind or visually impaired are taught sophisticated O&M strategies for orienting themselves to intersections and deciding when to cross, using audio and tactile cues and any remaining vision [3]. However, there may be no non-visual cues available to indicate the presence and location of crosswalk markings.

Blind travelers may benefit from information about the location of marked crosswalks in two main ways. First, ensuring that a route includes street crossing only on clearly marked crosswalks would increase safety during a trip. Second, this information can be used jointly with other technology that supports safe street crossing. For example, recent research [4, 1] shows that computer vision-based smartphone apps can assist visually impaired pedestrians in finding and aligning properly to crosswalks. This approach would be greatly enhanced by the ability to ask a GIS whether a crosswalk is present, even before arriving at the intersection. If a crosswalk is present, the geometric information contained in the GIS can then be used to help the user aim the camera towards the crosswalk, align to it and find other features of interest (e.g., walk lights and walk light push buttons).

2. RELATED WORK

Satellite and street-level imagery of urban areas in modern GIS are vast data sources. Computer vision methods can be used to extract geo-localized information about elements captured in these images (e.g., landmarks, vehicles, buildings). Satellite images have been used to detect urban areas and buildings [19], roads [14] and vehicles [13]. Senlet and Elgammal [18] propose sidewalk detection that corrects occlusion errors by interpolating available visual data. In street level images, Xiao and Quan [21] propose detection of buildings, persons and vehicles, while Zamir and Shah [22] tackle the issue of localizing user captured photographs.

There has been an increasing interest in adding specific spatial information to existing GIS through crowdsourcing. The impact of this phenomenon, called volunteered geographic information (VGI), is stressed by Goodchild [6]. Wheelmap[2] allows accessibility issues to be marked on OpenStreetMap, the largest entirely crowdsourced GIS. Hochmair et al. [11] assess bicycle trails quality in OpenStreetMap while Kubásek et al. [12] propose a platform for reporting illegal dump sites.

Safe and autonomous urban navigation is difficult for people with visual impairments. Smartphone apps that address this issue have been proposed. iMove[3] informs the user about the current address and nearby points of interest. Crosswatch [4] and ZebraLocalizer [1] allow pedestrians with visual impairments to detect crosswalks with smartphone camera.

Crowdsourcing is also used to assist users with visual impairments during navigation. BlindSquare[4] is a navigation app that relies on Foursquare social network for points of interest data and OpenStreetMap for street info. VizWiz[5] allows one to ask help of a remote assistant and attach a picture to the request. BeMyEyes[6] extends this approach to allow assistance through video feed. Rice et al. [17] gather information on temporary road accessibility issues (e.g., roadworks, potholes). StopFinder [16] helps people with visual impairments to locate bus stops by gathering data about non-visual landmarks near bus stops. Hara et al. [8] improve on this approach by performing crowdsourcing on street-level imagery, without the need to explore an area of interest in person. Guy and Truong [7] propose an app to gather information on the structure and position of nearby crossings through crowdsourcing of street-level images and to assist users with visual impairments in crossing streets.

Computer vision techniques use satellite and street-level images to assist persons with visual impairments. Hara et al. [10] propose the detection of inaccessible sidewalks in Google Street View images. Murali and Coughlan [15] match 360° panoramas captured by smartphone to satellite images of the surroundings for estimating the user's position in the intersection more precisely than with GPS.

Hybrid approaches using automated computer vision techniques for menial work and human "Turkers" for more complex tasks have also been proposed. Hara et al. [9] extend their previous work to combine crowdsourcing and computer vision detection of street accessibility problems, such as obstacles or damaged roads.

To the best of our knowledge, our technique is the first to use satellite and street-level imagery for automated detection of zebra crossings. The detection can be extended with crowdsourcing for a final validation step, for adding missed crosswalks and for gathering other information on the surroundings of the detected crossings that can be of use to visually impaired pedestrians in finding and aligning to the crossings. Detected crosswalks can be added to a crowdsourced GIS and used by travelers with visual impairments during navigation planning. Solutions that detect crosswalks using the smartphone video camera [1, 4] can benefit from this information to assist the user in finding crossings at long distances that cannot be captured by the camera.

3. ZEBRA CROSSING IDENTIFICATION

Multiple types of road surface markings are used across the world to define pedestrian crossings. In the United States, at least two different types of pedestrian crossing markings are available[1]. The *transverse marking* consists of two white lines, perpendicular to the road direction, with width between 6in (15cm) and 24in (60cm). The separation between the two lines is at least 6ft (180cm). *Zebra crossings*, known as "continental crossings" in USA, can be visually detected at larger distances than other crosswalk markings in the same illumination [5]. Thus, zebra crossings are common when the crossing visibility is paramount for the pedestrians' safety, for example near schools and hospitals. As such, they also inform drivers to pay more attention to the crosswalk, which is desirable for pedestrians with visual impairments who cannot rely on sight for noticing incoming vehicles.

While in this contribution we focus on U.S. zebra crossings, the parameters of the detection can be tuned for other types of zebra crossings with different geometric characteristics. Other pedestrian crossing types, such as transverse markings, can be detected with the same approach but they require significant changes to the detection algorithm and therefore they will be considered as future work.

[2]http://wheelmap.org
[3]http://www.everywaretechnologies.com/apps/imove
[4]http://blindsquare.com/
[5]http://vizwiz.org
[6]http://www.bemyeyes.org

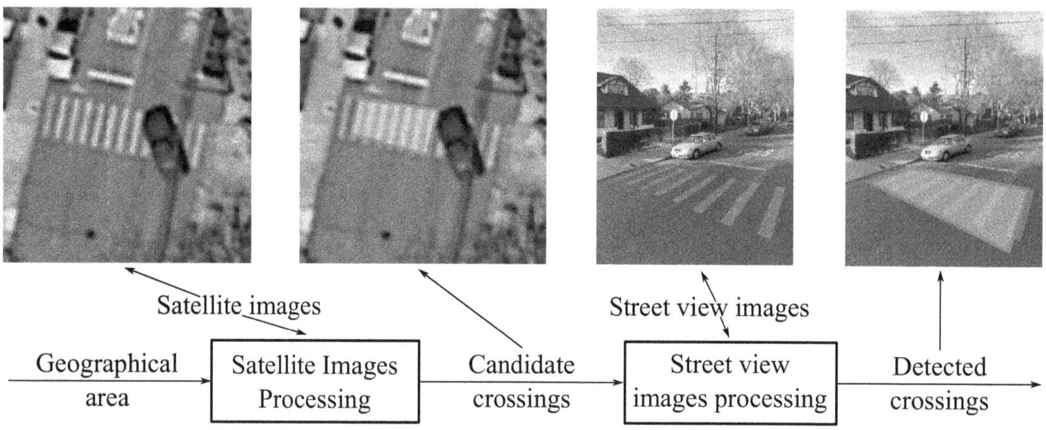

Figure 1: Technique overview

A zebra crossing is a set of parallel, uniformly painted, white stripes on a dark background. The gaps separating the white stripes are "dark stripes". Each stripe is a rectangle or, in case of diagonal crossings, a parallelogram. United States regulation dictates that zebra crossings be at least 6ft (180cm) wide, with white stripes 6in (15cm) to 24in (60cm) thick. The thickness of the dark stripes is not regulated.

3.1 Technique Overview

The proposed cascade classifier is composed of two main steps, as shown in Figure 1. The overall idea is to extract candidate zebra crossings from satellite images and then to validate them through street view images. The input of the procedure is an area A in which to detect the zebra crossings.

In the first step (see Section 3.2), the satellite images covering the input area A are downloaded from an online GIS and candidate zebra crossings are extracted from them through a computer vision technique. While the technique proposed in our solution can be applied to images from different providers, the system we developed gathers images from Google Maps.

The second step (see Section 3.3) acquires, for each candidate zebra crossing, nearby street view panoramas (if available) that might contain the zebra crossing. Zebra crossings are detected in street view panoramas and matched with the candidate crossings extracted from satellite images. In case of a match, the validated zebra crossing is returned and the result can be cached for future use.

It is also possible to extract candidate zebra crossings from all street view panoramas in the input area A and then validate them with satellite images. However, this approach would require downloading all panoramas in A, which is time consuming given the Google download limits[7] and the large amount of data. In our experiments, for an input area of 1.6km^2, starting first with satellite images required downloading $\approx$ 23MB, followed by 16MB for the street view panoramas validation. Conversely, starting from street view panoramas would have required downloading 637MB, followed by less than 1MB for the subsequent validation through satellite images. Overall, the cost (in terms of data transfer) of starting with satellite images is only about 6% of the reverse procedure that begins with street view images.

[7]`https://developers.google.com/maps/licensing`

3.2 Satellite Image Processing

Algorithm 1 describes the procedure to acquire the satellite images[8] and to process them. To acquire satellite images, we rely on the *Google Static Maps API*[9] that allows satellite images to be downloaded through HTTP calls. Each call specifies the GPS coordinates of the image center, the zoom factor and the image resolution. The maximum image resolution is constrained so, for large input areas, several HTTP requests must be sent.

We reconstruct the area A by downloading the images whose union yields A. Indeed, given a zoom factor and the maximum image resolution, it is straightforward to compute the size (in meters) of the region covered by each image. Thus, A can be partitioned in sub-regions with this maximum size (Line 2). Figure 2(a) shows an example of the partitioning step.

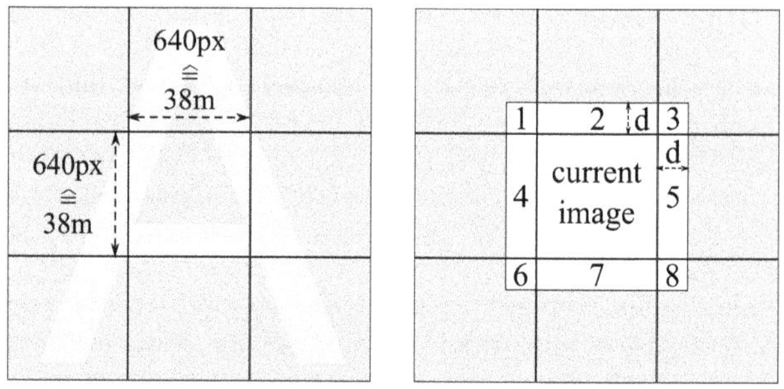

(a) Area A partitioned (b) Extended image

Figure 2: Area partitioning and extended image

Since there is a maximum daily number of requests that can be submitted to Google Maps, we only download images that do not contain roads. This can be achieved through the *Google Maps Javascript API*[10]. These APIs expose a method to compute, given an input coordinates, the closest position on a road. Before downloading an image centered at a point p, we compute the distance from p to the closest

[8]Satellite and street view imagery courtesy of Google ©

[9]`https://developers.google.com/maps/documentation/staticmaps/`

[10]`https://developers.google.com/maps/documentation/javascript/`

Algorithm 1 Satellite images acquisition and processing

Input: Rectangular geographical area A.
Output: a set Z of zebra crossings, each one represented by its position and direction.
Method:

1: $Z \leftarrow \emptyset$ {algorithm result}
2: partition A in a set R of sub-regions
3: **for all** (sub-region $r \in R$) **do**
4:   **if** (r does not contain a road) **then continue**
5:   download satellite image i of area r
6:   generate extended image i'
7:   $L \leftarrow$ detect line segments in i'
8:   $S \leftarrow$ group line segments in L in candidate crossings
9:   **for all** (candidate crossing $s \in S$) **do**
10:     **if** (s is not a valid crossing) **then continue**
11:     $z \leftarrow$ position and direction of zebra crossing s
12:     merge and add z to Z
13:   **end for**
14: **end for**
15: **return** Z

road. If this distance is larger than half the diagonal length of the image, we can infer that the image does not include any road, and hence we can avoid downloading it (Line 4). Note that this approach has a secondary advantage: it limits the number of false positives, i.e., patterns that are similar to zebra crossings that are erroneously recognized as such.

Dividing A in subregions implies that a zebra crossing spanning multiple adjacent images may be recognized in some of them or may not be recognized in any. Consider the example in Figure 3, where the white dashed line is the boundary between two adjacent images. To tackle this problem, we construct an *extended image* by merging a downloaded image with the borders of the 8 surrounding images, as shown in Figure 2(b) (see Algorithm 1, Line 6). The width of each border is chosen to guarantee the recognition of a zebra crossing, even if it is on the border between adjacent images. Still, this approach can result in a crossing being recognized in more than one image. We show in the following how to merge candidate zebra crossings that correspond to the same crossing and appear in different images.

Figure 3: Zebra crossing on two adjacent images

The detection technique extracts the line segments corresponding to the long edges of stripes from the image (see Figure 4(a)) using a customized version of the EDLines algorithm [2] (Line 7). The line segments are grouped into sets of stripes based on horizontal distance, vertical distance and parallelism criteria (Line 8). The resulting candidate crossings (see Figure 4(b)) are validated based on the stripes number and color intensity and the candidate crossings that are not validated are discarded (Line 10).

Our technique is adapted from the ZebraLocalizer algorithm for zebra crossing recognition on smartphones [1]. Differently from ZebraLocalizer, our approach does not require reconstructing the ground plane since satellite images are not subject to perspective distortion, being acquired from above the ground plane.

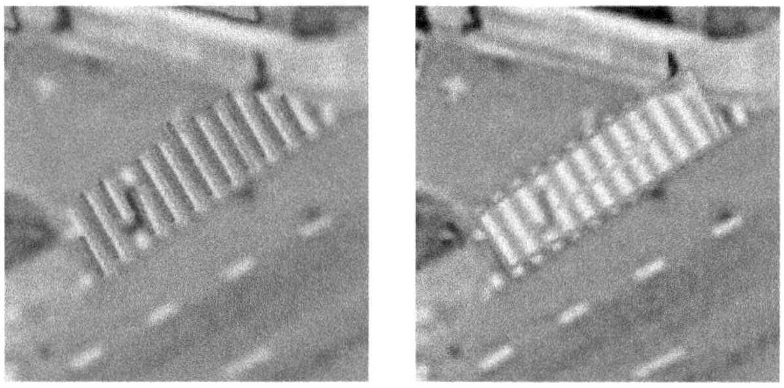

(a) Line segments   (b) Crossing

Figure 4: Satellite detection steps

If a set of stripes is not discarded, it is assumed to be a zebra crossing and it is characterized by its direction and position. Its direction is easily derived as the angle of the line perpendicular to the stripes, which should all share nearly the same angle, due to the parallelism criterion (Line 8). The zebra crossing's position is represented as the quadrilateral bounding the detected set of stripes, as depicted in Figure 4(b).

Finally, the detected zebra crossing is added to the set of results Z. As mentioned above, the same zebra crossing may be recognized in two or more different images. Hence, when inserting z in Z (Line 12), we first check if Z already contains a zebra crossing with approximately the same position and direction as z. If a similar crossing is found, the two crossings are merged.

3.3 Street View Image Processing

Algorithm 2 describes the procedure to validate a single zebra crossing through the acquisition and processing of street view panoramas. The procedure is iterated for all zebra crossings detected during satellite image processing. In *Google Maps*, street view panoramas are spherical images (i.e., they span 360° horizontally and 180° vertically) positioned at discrete coordinates distributed non-uniformly in space and they are structured in a graph that closely follows the road graph. Through the *Google Maps Javascript API* it is possible to request the panorama closest to a point in space and to retrieve the coordinates of panoramas directly linked to a given one.

For an input zebra crossing z the algorithm first identifies the coordinates c_0 of the panorama closest to it. The panorama centered in c_0 in some cases does not contain z due to occlusion by the car used to take the pictures, or by other objects and vehicles. Thus, our algorithm processes c_0 as well as other nearby panoramas until the crossing has been validated or all nearby panoramas have been processed. The set of coordinates of panoramas still to be processed is represented by C, initially containing only c_0.

Algorithm 2 Street view images acquisition and processing

Input: candidate zebra crossing $z \in Z$ represented by its position and direction.

Output: a validated zebra crossing z' represented by its position and direction or **null** if not validated.

Method:

```
1: c_0 ← get the coordinates of panorama closest to z
2: C ← {c_0} {Set of panoramas to be processed}
3: while (C ≠ ∅) do
4:   c ← pop element from C
5:   α ← direction angle from c to z
6:   i ← image at coordinates c with direction alpha
7:   L ← detect line segments in i
8:   L' ← rectify line segments in L
9:   S ← group line segments in L' in candidate crossings
10:  for all (s ∈ S) do
11:    if (s is a valid crossing) then
12:      z' ← position and direction of zebra crossing s
13:      if (z matches z') then return z'
14:    end if
15:  end for
16:  push in C coordinates of panoramas directly linked to
     c and close to z
17: end while
18: return null
```

For each panorama centered in coordinates $c \in C$, the algorithm identifies a small portion of the spherical image that actually needs to be acquired. On the vertical axis, we use a fixed pitch $(-30°)$ and vertical field of view $(60°)$ in order to exclude the portion of the panorama occluded by the car taking the picture and the portion of the panorama above the horizon, which clearly does not contain crossings. For capturing the correct horizontal portion of the panorama we first compute the direction angle α that, starting from coordinates c, points towards the center of z (see Line 5). This angle represents the center, along the horizontal axis, of the acquired image. A horizontal field of view of $60°$, given the pitch, vertical field of view, and a camera height of $2.5m$, guarantees to include, at minimum distance, a span of $3.5m$. Considering the United States regulation, this is sufficient to include from 5 to 23 stripes of a crossing, sufficient for a correct detection. See Figures 5(a) and 5(b).

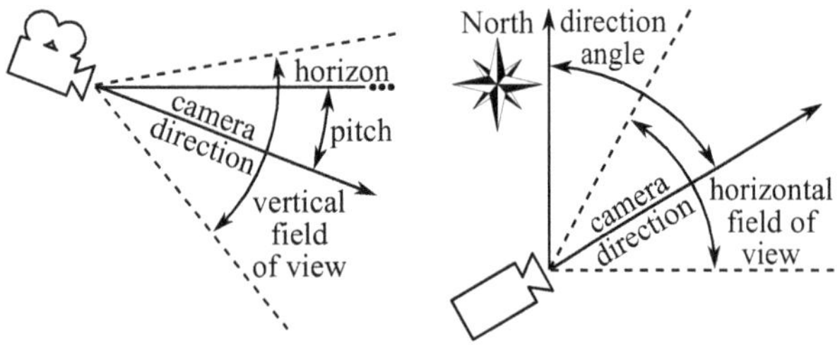

(a) Vertical field of view (b) Horizontal field of view

Figure 5: Horizontal and vertical field of view

The usage of fixed parameters simplifies a number of formulae, including those for image rectification (see below). As future work these parameters could be derived from the relative position of c and z. For example smaller pitch values can be used if z is closer to c.

The image i containing a portion of the panorama at coordinates c and with direction α is acquired and then processed with an adapted version of ZebraLocalizer [1] algorithm to reconstruct the coordinates of line segments on the ground plane (Lines 7 to 11). The difference with ZebraLocalizer is that, since camera height and pitch are fixed, we can precompute the homography to reconstruct the ground plane in all acquired images. Figures 6(b) and 6(c) show an example of ground plane reconstruction. Rectified line segments are then grouped and validated based on the same criteria described in Section 3.2.

If the set S of identified stripes represents a valid crossing z', its position and orientation are compared with those of z. Clearly, even if z' actually represents the same crossing as z, the bounding quadrilaterals of the two crossings rarely have exactly the same coordinates, due to a number of approximations introduced in the computation, including GPS imprecision and the fact that not all stripes of a zebra crossing are always identified. For example, the same crossing detected in a satellite image (Figure 6(a)) and detected in a street view panorama (Figure 6(b)) has different GPS coordinates, as shown in Figure 6(d). Similarly, the orientation of z and z' can differ.

Thus, there is a tolerance in the comparison of z with z' and a system parameter defines the maximum distance such that z and z' are considered the same crossing. Analogously, a system parameter defines the maximum angular distance between the orientation of z and z'. If z and z' represent the same crossing, then z' is returned as a valid crossing.

If the set of stripes S does not represent a valid crossing or if z' does not represent the same crossing as z, the algorithm populates C with the coordinates of other panoramas close to c (if any). The algorithm adds to C the coordinates of panoramas directly linked to c that have not already been processed during the validation of z and that are close to z (the maximum distance is bounded by a system parameter). Eventually either z is validated or all nearby street view panoramas are processed (i.e.: $C = \emptyset$); in this case **null** is returned.

4. EXPERIMENTAL EVALUATION

This section reports the results of the experiments conducted to evaluate our technique over a dense urban region of San Francisco. These results are quantified in terms of precision (the fraction of detected zebra crossings that are true detections) and recall (the fraction of true zebra crossings that are correctly detected). We demonstrate that our cascade classifier is powerful enough to identify nearly all zebra crossings, with only a small number of false positive candidates that need to be eliminated in a subsequent stage of crowdsourcing-based image inspection.

4.1 Experimental setting

To evaluate the proposed technique we considered a rectangular urban area A in San Francisco, with sides of length 1529m and 1025m and an area of 1.6km^2. The area coordinates[11], along with detected crossing portions, true positives (green pins) and false positives (red pins) have been published[12].

[11] `http://webmind.di.unimi.it/satzebra/satzebra.kml`

[12] `http://webmind.di.unimi.it/satzebra`

(a) Satellite detection (b) Street view detection (c) Reconstructed street view (d) imprecision in detection

Figure 6: Imprecision in GPS coordinates between satellite and street view detected crossings

A total of 141 zebra crossings and 152 transverse pedestrian crossings have been detected in the satellite and street view images of the area by a human operator. In the following, a zebra crossing is considered to be detected correctly if at least 4 consecutive stripes of the crossing have been detected correctly.

Concerning satellite images, with the maximum zoom level available in *Google maps* for the considered area, each image with maximum resolution of 640×640 pixels covers $38m \times 38$m. Thus, a total of 1149 satellite images are required to cover A. Since the size of each image is approximately 46KB, the size of all images covering A is 52MB. The total number of street view panoramas available in A is 1425. As we show in the following, we acquired only a small portion of these panoramas, each having a resolution of 640×640 pixels and, on average, a size of 51KB.

The tests were conducted on a laptop computer with *Intel core i7 4500u* 1.8GHz CPU and 8GB RAM.

4.2 Satellite image processing evaluation

As reported in Algorithm 1, only images containing streets are actually considered. With this approach a total of 791 images actually need to be acquired with a total size of 35MB. This means that, in A, our technique avoids downloading about one third of the images that would be otherwise required. In areas where the density of the road network is lower (like in suburban or rural areas), we can expect that an even higher percentage of images can be omitted.

The recognition process described in Algorithm 1 (Lines 7-8) detects a total of 773 zebra crossing portions. Often a single zebra crossing is detected as two or more zebra crossing portions. For example this can happen when a vehicle is visible in the middle of the crossing, causing a partial occlusion. By merging these crossing portions (Algorithm 1, Line 12) our technique identifies 199 candidate crossings.

Out of 199 detected candidate crossings, 137 correspond to actual zebra crossings. Since the number of actual zebra crossings in A is 141, recall is 0.97. A few zebra crossings are not detected due to discolored or faded paint (see Figure 7(a)) while others are almost totally covered by trees, shadows or vehicles (see Figure 7(b)). The process also yields 62 false positives, hence the precision is 0.69. In many cases, false positives correspond to rooftops (Figure 7(c)) or other parts of buildings (Figure 7(d)).

These recall and precision scores refer to parameter settings tuned for the highest possible recall so that almost no crosswalks are missed by the algorithm. Naturally, perfect recall is difficult to reach and comes at the expense of a greater number of false positives, i.e., a smaller precision. However, considering that a final crowdsourcing validation step is possible, it is much easier for crowdworkers to rule out false positives than it is to find false negatives, which requires scrutinizing the entire area of interest to identify crosswalks that have not been detected by the algorithm. Parameters can be tuned for different trade-off levels between precision and recall. The Pareto frontier shown in Figure 8 lists the best precision and recall trade-offs obtained during the tuning of the parameters.

Regarding computation time, we consider the CPU-bound process only and we ignore the time to acquire images, which mainly depends on the quality of the network connection. The CPU-bound computation required for the extraction of candidate crossings in a single image is 180ms. Running the algorithm sequentially on the 791 images acquired for A requires a total of 142s. However, note that the process can be easily parallelized and thus it would be straightforward to further reduce computation time.

4.3 Street view image processing evaluation

For each candidate crossing in Z (the set of candidate crossings computed with satellite images), there are on average 5.7 nearby street view panoramas. By considering true positives only (i.e., candidate crossings that represent actual crossings), the average number of nearby street view panoramas increases to 7.3 and only 2 candidate crossings that represent actual crossings have no street view panoramas in their vicinity (less than 1.5%). Conversely, false positive candidate crossings have a much lower number of nearby street view panoramas (on average 2.6). Indeed, 19 false positives (30% of the total) do not have any nearby street view panorama and 46 false positives have 3 or fewer surrounding panoramas (74%). This is caused by the fact that, as observed previously, many false positives are located on rooftops or other areas that are not in the immediate vicinity of streets.

As reported in Algorithm 2, our solution acquires nearby panoramas iteratively, until the candidate crossing is validated. On average, considering true positives, 1.8 street view panoramas are acquired for each candidate crossing. In 76% of the cases a true positive crossing is validated with at most two panoramas, and up to 56% are validated by processing a single street view panorama (see Figure 9). Conversely, filtering out false positives requires processing all available nearby street view panoramas. Overall, the tech-

(a) FN - discoloration (b) FN - hidden by trees (c) FP - roof pattern (d) FP - stairs pattern

Figure 7: False negatives (FN) and false positives (FP) in satellite detection and street view validation

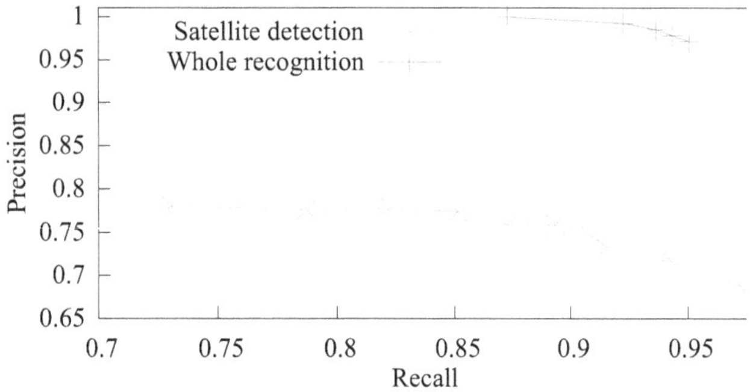

Figure 8: Pareto frontier of the detection procedure

nique requires acquiring and processing a total of 406 street view panoramas for A ($\approx$ 2 for each candidate crossing). The total size of these images is 20.3MB.

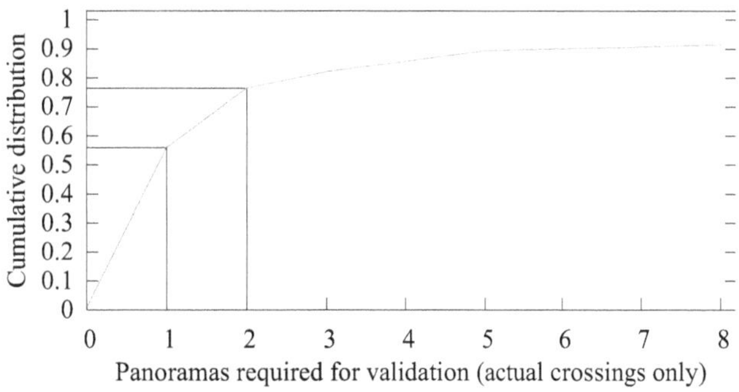

Figure 9: Used panoramas cumulative distribution

The street view-based validation (tuned for the best recall score) filters out 58 out of 62 false positives identified in the previous step, yielding a precision score of 0.97. The few false positives still present are caused by patterns very similar to zebra crossings, like the stairs in Figure 7(d). Of 137 true positives in Z, 134 are validated, resulting in a recall score of 0.98. Overall, the recall score of the whole procedure (including both satellite and street view detection) is 0.95.

As with the satellite detection, different parameter settings yield different precision and recall scores during the validation. Figure 8 shows the settings that yield the best precision and recall trade-offs during the validation.

Regarding computation time, each street view image can be processed in 46ms and hence the total computation time is 18.5s. Overall, considering the two detection steps (from satellite images and street view panoramas), the total CPU-bound computation time to process A is 161s.

5. DISCUSSION AND FUTURE WORK

While the accuracy of the detection is high, since no computer vision algorithm is perfectly accurate, we envision a subsequent stage of processing based on online crowdsourcing (as in [10]) to rule out false positives and identify false negatives. A web service will be offered to allow users to submit crossings that have been missed (possibly also integrated in a future navigation software). For pruning false positives, instead, we intend to leverage crowdsourcing services such as Amazon Mechanical Turk[13] and propose that zebra crossings detected by our computer vision algorithm be referred to crowdworkers, who will decide whether zebra crossings are indeed present in the images. The crossings database could also be augmented with auxiliary information such as the presence and location of important features such as walk lights (which could be monitored in real time by the app) and walk push buttons. These could be also added by users or automatically by a visual detection app.

The resulting crosswalk database could be accessed by visually impaired pedestrians through the use of a GPS navigation smartphone app. The app could identify the user's current coordinates and look up information about nearby zebras, such as their number, placement and orientation. Existing apps such as Intersection Explorer and Nearby Explorer (for Android) and Sendero GPS LookAround and Intersection (for iPhone) could be modified to incorporate information from the crosswalk database. Computer vision-based detection apps on smartphones, such as Zebralocalizer [1] and Crosswatch [4], could additionally use the database to help users to approach and align properly to crosswalks even when they are not yet detected by the app.

Another important way in which the crosswalk database could be used by blind and visually impaired pedestrians is for help with offline route planning, which could be conducted by a traveler on his/her smartphone or computer from home, work or other indoor location before embarking on a trip. For example, a route-planning algorithm may weigh several criteria in determining an optimal route, including the number of non-zebra crossings encountered on the route (which are less desirable to traverse than zebra crossings) as well as standard criteria such as total distance traversed. The crosswalk database could also be augmented with additional information, including temporary hazards or barriers due to road construction, etc.

[13] `https://www.mturk.com`

6. CONCLUSIONS

Our contribution presents a technique that uses computer vision algorithms to detect and localize zebra crosswalks with high accuracy in existing spatial images databases such as Google satellite and Street View. To the best of our knowledge, these features are not already marked in existing GIS services and we argue that knowing the position of existing crosswalks could be useful to travelers with visual impairments for planning the navigation, finding pedestrian crosswalks and crossing roads.

For the detection we propose a cascade classifier derived from the algorithm we previously proposed for zebra crossing recognition on smartphones [1]. The proposed solution identifies potential crossings in street areas in satellite images and validates potential crossings with nearby Street View panoramic images.

We evaluated the proposed solution on a 1.6km^2 area in San Francisco in which the pedestrian crossings were previously manually labeled. The dataset contained of 791 satellite images limited to street areas and 406 portions of Street View images referring to potential crossings. The technique achieved a precision of 0.97 and a recall of 0.95 with a computation time of $161s$ for the whole area.

The proposed approach is also complementary to existing solutions [1, 4] that leverage computer vision techniques for detecting pedestrian crossings using video cameras on mobile devices. A technique leveraging both data sources would be a helpful tool for assisting people with visual impairments to align to and safely and independently to cross roads.

7. ACKNOWLEDGMENTS

James M. Coughlan acknowledges support by the National Institutes of Health from grant No. 2 R01EY018345-06 and by the Administration for Community Living's National Institute on Disability, Independent Living and Rehabilitation Research, grant No. 90RE5008-01-00.

8. REFERENCES

[1] D. Ahmetovic, C. Bernareggi, A. Gerino, and S. Mascetti. Zebrarecognizer: Efficient and precise localization of pedestrian crossings. In *Int. Conf. on Pattern Recognition*. IEEE, 2014.

[2] C. Akinlar and C. Topal. Edlines: A real-time line segment detector with a false detection control. *Pattern Recognition Letters*, 2011.

[3] J. Barlow, B. Bentzen, D. Sauerburger, and L. Franck. Teaching travel at complex intersections. *Foundations of Orientation and Mobility*, 2010.

[4] J. Coughlan and H. Shen. Crosswatch: a system for providing guidance to visually impaired travelers at traffic intersection. *Jour. of Assistive Technologies*, 2013.

[5] K. Fitzpatrick, S. T. Chrysler, V. Iragavarapu, and E. S. Park. Crosswalk marking field visibility study. Technical report, 2010.

[6] M. F. Goodchild. Citizens as sensors: the world of volunteered geography. *GeoJournal*, 2007.

[7] R. Guy and K. Truong. Crossingguard: exploring information content in navigation aids for visually impaired pedestrians. In *Conf. on Human Factors in Computing Systems*. ACM, 2012.

[8] K. Hara, S. Azenkot, M. Campbell, C. L. Bennett, V. Le, S. Pannella, R. Moore, K. Minckler, R. H. Ng, and J. E. Froehlich. Improving public transit accessibility for blind riders by crowdsourcing bus stop landmark locations with google street view. In *Int. Conf. on Computers and Accessibility*. ACM, 2013.

[9] K. Hara, V. Le, and J. Froehlich. Combining crowdsourcing and google street view to identify street-level accessibility problems. In *Conf. on Human Factors in Computing Systems*. ACM, 2013.

[10] K. Hara, V. Le, J. Sun, D. Jacobs, and J. Froehlich. Exploring early solutions for automatically identifying inaccessible sidewalks in the physical world using google street view. *HCI Consortium*, 2013.

[11] H. H. Hochmair, D. Zielstra, and P. Neis. Assessing the completeness of bicycle trails and designated lane features in openstreetmap for the united states and europe. In *Transportation Research Board Annual Meeting*, 2013.

[12] M. Kubásek, J. Hřebíček, et al. Crowdsource approach for mapping of illegal dumps in the czech republic. *Int. Jour. of Spatial Data Infrastructures Research*, 2013.

[13] J. Leitloff, S. Hinz, and U. Stilla. Vehicle detection in very high resolution satellite images of city areas. *Trans. on Geoscience and Remote Sensing*, 2010.

[14] M. Mokhtarzade and M. V. Zoej. Road detection from high-resolution satellite images using artificial neural networks. *Int. jour. of applied earth observation and geoinformation*, 2007.

[15] V. Murali and J. M. Coughlan. Smartphone-based crosswalk detection and localization for visually impaired pedestrians. In *Int. Conf. on Multimedia and Expo (workshop)*. IEEE, 2013.

[16] S. Prasain. Stopfinder: improving the experience of blind public transit riders with crowdsourcing. In *Int. Conf. on Computers and Accessibility*. ACM, 2011.

[17] M. T. Rice, A. O. Aburizaiza, R. D. Jacobson, B. M. Shore, and F. I. Paez. Supporting accessibility for blind and vision-impaired people with a localized gazetteer and open source geotechnology. *Transactions in GIS*, 2012.

[18] T. Senlet and A. Elgammal. Segmentation of occluded sidewalks in satellite images. In *Int. Conf. on Pattern Recognition*. IEEE, 2012.

[19] B. Sirmacek and C. Unsalan. Urban-area and building detection using sift keypoints and graph theory. *Trans. on Geoscience and Remote Sensing*, 2009.

[20] W. R. Wiener, R. L. Welsh, and B. B. Blasch. *Foundations of orientation and mobility*. American Foundation for the Blind, 2010.

[21] J. Xiao and L. Quan. Multiple view semantic segmentation for street view images. In *Int. Conf. on Computer Vision*. IEEE, 2009.

[22] A. R. Zamir and M. Shah. Accurate image localization based on google maps street view. In *Oroc. of. European Conf. on Computer Vision*. Springer, 2010.

Social Media Platforms for Low-Income Blind People in India

Aditya Vashistha[†] Edward Cutrell* Nicola Dell[†] Richard Anderson[†]

[†]University of Washington
{adityav, nixdell, anderson}@cs.washington.edu

*Microsoft Research India
cutrell@microsoft.com

ABSTRACT

We present the first analysis of the use and non-use of social media platforms by low-income blind users in rural and peri-urban India. Using a mixed-methods approach of semi-structured interviews and observations, we examine the benefits received by low-income blind people from Facebook, Twitter and WhatsApp and investigate constraints that impede their social media participation. We also present a detailed analysis of how low-income blind people used a voice-based social media platform deployed in India that received significant traction from low-income people in rural and peri-urban areas. In eleven-weeks of deployment, fifty-three blind participants in our sample collectively placed 4784 voice calls, contributed 1312 voice messages, cast 33,909 votes and listened to the messages 46,090 times. Using a mixed-methods analysis of call logs, qualitative interviews, and phone surveys, we evaluate the strengths and weaknesses of the platform and benefits it offered to low-income blind people.

Keywords

Blind; Social Media; Interactive Voice Response System; ICT4D; HCI4D

ACM Classification Keywords

H.5.m. Information interfaces and presentation (e.g., HCI): Miscellaneous.

1. INTRODUCTION

About 90% of the world's 285 million visually impaired people live in low-income settings [37]. India has the largest blind population, with more than 63 million visually impaired people [21]. The majority of visually impaired people in India have limited access to computing devices, Internet services, and digital assistive technologies like screen reader software in local languages. These barriers in accessing information severely impede their education opportunities [32], job prospects [19], social status, and potential to overcome poverty.

In the last decade, social media platforms have revolutionized the way information is reported, consumed and shared and have deeply impacted the lives of billions of people around the world. In addition to providing entertainment, information, and abundant user-generated content, they are seen as an instrument of social change. Many people believe the social media revolution to be the biggest societal shift since the industrial revolution [27,42]. Social media platforms are also playing a pivotal role in supporting academic collaborations [11], managing crisis response [28], political campaigning [17,38], and organizing civil society movements like the Arab Spring [26,29]. Even during the devastating 2015 Nepal earthquake, the BBC used the public chat feature of Viber to share information and safety tips with affected people [43].

Several researchers have studied the use of social media platforms by people with disabilities in the developed world [4,5,7,31,39]. A few researchers have also analyzed the use and non-use of social media platforms by low-income people in the developing world, including studying the role of Facebook in providing employment opportunities to young adults living in urban slums in Nairobi [40], improving communication, technology and English language skills of young adults living in urban slums in South India [24], and empowering marginalized people living in urban slums in Brazil [16]. Wyche et al. studied Facebook use and non-use by low-income rural Kenyans and found that the constrained access of devices, Internet, and electricity impede online participation [41]. However, the use of social media platforms by blind people in the developing world has received no attention as yet.

There is a need to study the use (and non-use) of existing social media platforms by blind people in low-income settings, identify benefits received by them, understand the challenges encountered by them, and assess the need for designing a new accessible social media platform. The findings will inform the design of social media platforms for the 256 million visually impaired people who are living in low-income settings.

As a primary contribution, we present the **first analysis** of the use and non-use of social media platforms by low-income blind people living in rural and peri-urban India. We found that low-income blind people in India use social media platforms to expand their connections, receive instrumental benefits, uplift their social standing, and access informative and entertaining content. However, the cost of smartphones and internet access, difficulties in understanding the language of the audio output of screen reader software, inaccessible features of existing social media platforms and lack of training has resulted in many blind people either not exploring these platforms or abandoning their use. These financial constraints, socioeconomic barriers, issues with English language proficiency, and infrastructural limitations accentuate the need for designing a new social media

ASSETS '15, October 26-28, 2015, Lisbon, Portugal
© 2015 ACM. ISBN 978-1-4503-3400-6/15/10...$15.00
DOI: http://dx.doi.org/10.1145/2700648.2809858

platform that is cognizant of the constraints of blind people living in low-income settings.

In prior work, we designed and deployed *Sangeet Swara*, a new social media voice forum in the Hindi language [33]. The platform was built using Interactive Voice Response (IVR) technology and was accessible using any phone. It enabled callers to record voice messages, listen to messages recorded by others, vote on them, and share them without needing Internet access. The platform was deployed to engage low-income people and understand whether community moderation can be used for managing content on IVR systems. The platform saw significant adoption by low-income communities, receiving over 25,000 calls and 5000 voice messages from more than 1500 people in an eleven-week deployment. The details of the system design, deployment in India, results on community moderation and engagement by low-income communities are available in [33]. However, to our surprise, *Sangeet Swara* also received broad and impassioned usage by low-income blind people in rural and peri-urban India. In fact, more than 26% users of the platform were blind.

In this paper, we re-examine the usage of *Sangeet Swara* as part of the broader landscape of social media use by blind people. As a **secondary contribution**, we present new findings about how blind people from low-income settings used *Sangeet Swara*. In particular, we present detailed analysis of the content generated by blind participants, demographics, reasons for the high adoption of the platform, strengths and weaknesses of the platform, benefits and challenges offered to blind participants, and design implications for future systems.

Our analysis revealed that blind participants deeply valued their interactions with other participants on the platform. The analysis of call logs of fifty-three blind participants revealed that although they made up just 3.5% of all users, they contributed 25% of the number of recorded voice messages, 24% of the number of playbacks, 19% of the number of calls, and 25% of the number of votes cast by users. Our qualitative interviews and phone surveys also received emphatic responses from blind participants. Finally, we found that blind participants received several instrumental benefits, shared entertaining content, and built social capital using our platform.

2. RELATED WORK

The use of social media platforms by people in developed countries is a well-studied phenomenon [6,11,30]. In addition, a few researchers have studied the use of social media platforms by people with visual impairment in the developed world. For example, Fuglerud et al. studied the usability and accessibility challenges faced by visually impaired Norwegian people using social media platforms [7]. Wentz and Lazar presented a usability evaluation of the Facebook desktop and mobile interfaces, finding the mobile interface to be more accessible than the desktop interface [36]. Wu and Adamic conducted a large-scale empirical study of how blind people use Facebook and found that most of the content they produce relates to vision impairment [39]. They also concluded that blind people receive more feedback on their content, though their Facebook activities are similar to that of the general population. Brady et al. have investigated how social networking platforms can be used for asking visual questions posed by blind users [4]. Though findings from these studies are immensely insightful, it is difficult to generalize them to blind people in developing countries due to huge differences in infrastructure, economic resources, education, language, and other contextual differences.

Research on social media usage by low-income, low-literate users in developing countries has also been well studied. Prior work has demonstrated that people in low-income settings derive instrumental benefits, earn social capital, and access entertainment through social media platforms. Young adults from an urban slum in Nairobi have used Facebook to support income generation activities, search employment opportunities, and seek remittances from friends and family abroad [40]. Their counterparts in South India have used Facebook to expand their social connections, learn English language skills, and transform self-perception [24]. People from urban slums in Brazil have used Facebook to access entertainment, organize and plan protests, and communicate with friends and families [16]. Mäkinen and Kuria analyzed the role of social media platforms as an alternative medium for participatory journalism during a post-election crisis in Kenya [12]. Bosch studied the use of Facebook by South African students and lecturers for teaching and learning [3]. Bosch also explored the role of social media platforms in enabling young women in South Africa to express and experience their sexual identity [2]. Wyche et al. studied Facebook use and non-use by low-income rural Kenyans and found that limited access to computers and smartphones, expensive Internet access, and unreliable electricity impede online participation [41]. Medhi-Thies et al. deployed an audio-visual social networking smartphone application for low-literate farmers in rural India and found that farmers authored posts related to agricultural information, families, local grievances and aspirational content [14].

Several other researchers have used IVR technology to design voice forums for enabling low-income, low-literate people to record and share voice messages. Some notable examples are *Avaaj Otalo* that provides an agriculture discussion forum for farmers in India [22], *CGNet Swara* that provides a citizen journalism platform for tribal people in Central India [15], *Ila Dhageyso* that provides a civic engagement portal for tribal people in Somaliland [9], *Polly* that shares job opportunities in Pakistan [25], a content creation and dissemination portal for people in rural India [1], and others [8,10].

A few researchers in the Information and Communication Technologies and Development (ICTD) community have also conducted research on understanding the role of technology for blind people living in urban India. They provided general recommendations for low-cost assistive technology [20], explored the usage of screen reader software [13,18], and analyzed workforce participation and underemployment [19]. Pal and Lakshmanan have noted that "*access to assistive technology is beginning to create an important and vocal population of people with vision impairments who interact independently on social media*" [19]. However, the participants in their research were generally from middle or upper class urban backgrounds and not representative of blind people in rural and peri-urban India.

Research that studies the design and use of technology by low-income blind people from rural areas in developing countries is severely limited. One exception is a study that examines the challenges faced by low-income blind people in accessing educational content and their coping mechanisms [32]. The study found that acute shortages of Braille content, high quality audio books, and inexpensive text-to-speech for local languages have motivated low-income blind people to create, consume, and curate peer-produced audio content. One of the primary reasons for the scarcity of work targeting low-income blind people are the challenges experienced by researchers in making meaningful contact with them and gaining their trust.

Although researchers have studied technology use by blind people in India, few researchers have studied their social media usage. In prior work, we presented cursory findings on social media use by low-income blind people [33]. In this study, an IVR-based social media platform, *Sangeet Swara*, was designed and deployed to investigate whether community moderation can be used for managing the content generated on IVR platforms. In addition to low-income people who used the platform, the platform also received traction from low-income blind people. However, the analyses presented in [33] focus on all users of the platform rather than specifically analyzing call logs of blind participants, content generated by them, their demographic details, and the impact of the social media platform on their lives. To the best of our knowledge, ours is the first study that provides insights on how low-income blind people use social media platforms.

3. SOCIAL MEDIA USE AND NON-USE

To gain access to low-income blind people from rural and peri-urban areas, we contacted a non-profit organization, *Rajasthan Netraheen Kalyan Sangh,* in Rajasthan, India that conducts free computer training for blind people. The training lasts six months and each training batch has around eight participants. During the training, students learn to use Talking Typer, screen reader software like JAWS and NVDA, Microsoft Office, the Internet, and social media platforms. Students take an external examination at the end of six months and, after passing the examination, students receive a government-issued certificate that enables them to apply for several government jobs in Rajasthan and other states.

3.1 Methodology

We recruited current and past students of the training program and their social contacts in order to investigate social media use and non-use by low-income blind people. We used purposive sampling and snowball sampling to select participants who satisfied either of the following inclusion criteria:

- Must be a blind from low-income family
- Must be an instructor or facilitator of the training program

In order to understand the broad spectrum of social media use and non-use, we separated participants into four categories based on their social media use: recent adopters, disenchanted users, consistent users and non-users. Recent adopters were participants who joined a social media platform in the last six months, disenchanted users were participants who either stopped using social media platforms or used them rarely, consistent users were participants who used social media platforms at least once a week for more than six months, and non-users were those who never used a social media platform. We also interviewed instructors and facilitators of the training program for triangulation, and to understand the opportunities and challenges technology offers to blind students in the program.

Figure 1. Blind participants using social media platforms in the computer lab.

We focused our attention on the three most popular online social media platforms in India: Facebook, WhatsApp and Twitter.

We used a mixed-methods approach spanning several qualitative and quantitative analyses. Our primary tool of analysis was twenty-two in-depth semi-structured qualitative interviews. We conducted observations on how computers, phones, and social media platforms were used by participants. We also analyzed activities on participants' social media accounts. We interviewed eighteen social media users and non-users, two instructors and two facilitators. Each interview began with demographic questions, followed by general questions about participants' experiences with mobile phones, computers, and the Internet. We then asked several questions to understand social media practices of blind users, strengths and weaknesses of the platforms, benefits and challenges offered, and constraints that impede social media participation. The interview with facilitators and instructors focused broadly on various social, technical, societal, and economic barriers faced by low-income blind students that impede their access to social media platforms.

Out of the eighteen social media users, eight were recent adopters, two were disenchanted users, five were consistent users, and three were non-users. Twelve interviews were conducted face-to-face on the premises of the non-profit organization while ten were phone interviews. The interviews were conducted by the first author (male, 28 years) in Hindi. Each interview lasted around forty-five minutes. We digitally recorded each interview and took detailed notes on paper. We reviewed and analyzed data immediately after conducting each interview. The insights obtained from the data analysis added more questions for the next interview. We continued to recruit participants until no new observation emerged. We spent ten hours observing participants using computers and social media platforms to understand their challenges and usage patterns (see Figure 1). We also analyzed the social media accounts of five participants to understand their usage and corroborate what they reported in the interviews.

3.2 Participants Demographic Information

3.2.1 Social Media Users and Non-users

Out of the eighteen participants, eleven were completely blind and seven were partially sighted. Out of the seven partially sighted participants, one had 5% visibility, four had 20% visibility, and two had 40% visibility. Six participants were blind since birth while others lost vision at the average age of 9.75 years (min=2 years, max= 26 years, S.D.=7.28 years). Only one participant used a computer before losing vision. Fourteen participants were skilled in reading and writing Braille content. Four participants reported themselves as slow while using Braille content: three of these were partially sighted and one was a late blind.

Our sample had sixteen male participants and two female participants. The average age of participants was 24.2 years (min=17 years, max=34 years, S.D.=4.18 years). Fourteen participants were students, three were unemployed, and one person ran a Photostat and stationery shop earning a monthly income of 200 USD[1]. One participant was a middle school student, two were high school students, nine were pursuing a bachelor's degree, and two were pursuing a master's degree. Two participants had finished a master's degree, and two participants stopped studying after completing high school. The participants were from five states in India. The majority of them were from villages (N=10) and small towns (N=2). Five participants were from second-tier cities and one participant was from a first-tier city. Most of the participants were from low-income households. The median monthly household income was 166 USD (min=0 USD, max=1667 USD, S.D.=473 USD). The average number of members in a household were seven (min=4, max=13). By normalizing the monthly income by family size, we found that half of the participants lived on 0.88 USD per day and two-thirds on less than 2 USD per day. The average annual income of participants was 387 USD, roughly a quarter of the per capita income of 1610 USD in India [44]. Two participants had no family income and were living on a monthly stipend of 8 USD provided by the government. The majority of the participants were from families of daily wage laborers (N=4), farmers (N=3), small shop-owners (N=2), carpenters (N=1) and household help (N=1).

All participants owned a mobile phone. 40% reported sharing their phone with family members. Nine participants used a basic phone, seven had a feature phone and two owned a smartphone. All participants used phones primarily for sending and receiving voice calls and only one participant used it for sending SMS. Five participants used screen reader software on their phone, specifically Talkback, Talks, and eSpeak. Six participants reported using the Internet on their phone for accessing social media websites (N=5), email (N=4), news (N=3), and downloading applications and songs (N=1). All but one participant reported using a computer at least once in their lifetime. However, only ten participants reported using a computer at least once in the last three months. Fourteen participants had used a computer in a shared setting while three had computers at home. All computer users used screen reader software and five participants used magnification software. Both JAWS and NVDA screen reader software were equally popular among participants. Eleven participants reported using the Internet regularly on a computer, primarily for accessing social media websites (N=8) and email (N=7), downloading books and songs (N=3), and online shopping (N=2). Three participants used the Internet rarely on a computer while four never used the Internet on a computer.

3.2.2 *Instructors and Facilitators*

Our sample had two facilitators (both male) and two instructors (one male and one female). The average age of instructors was 27.5 years whereas the average age of facilitators was 37 years.

[1] *In this paper, we use an exchange rate of 1 USD = 60 INR*

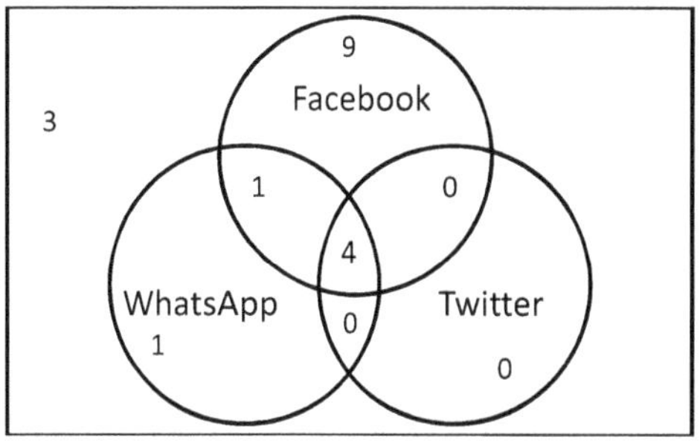

Figure 2. Venn diagram describing the distribution of social media users and non-users among 18 participants.

Both the instructors were sighted whereas both the facilitators were completely blind. The average monthly income of instructors was 200 USD whereas the average monthly income of facilitators was 780 USD. All of them had at least a Bachelor's degree. Only one facilitator owned a smartphone, while the other three used a feature phone. The participants reported using the Internet on a computer (N=4) or a phone (N=2) and had an account on at least one social media platform.

3.3 Analysis

We translated and transcribed each interview in English. We used open coding and axial coding to analyze the data obtained from qualitative interviews and observations. Our observations and interviews with eighteen social media users and non-users formed the basis for understanding the reasons for use and non-use of social media platforms. We did not analyze the social media use of the instructors and facilitators, and used the interviews with the instructors and facilitators for triangulation. We present the results of our analysis in the following sub-sections.

3.3.1 *Social Media Use*

The distribution of participants across Facebook, Twitter, and WhatsApp is depicted in Figure 2. All but three participants had used at least one of the three social media platforms. Despite this unexpectedly high adoption, seven participants were unable to answer our question: *what are social media platforms?* Many of them had never heard the term *social media* or *social networking*. In fact, one participant explained social media as "*the organizations that perform social work.*" Participants heard about Facebook, Twitter, and WhatsApp from multiple sources: friends, the training institute, and mainstream media. Nine participants learned about the platforms from their family members and acquaintances, mostly when they overheard the name of these platforms during a group conversation. Seven participants learned about the platforms during the training, while two participants heard about them while listening to a program on television that encouraged viewers to ask questions on Twitter or Facebook. Fourteen participants had an account on Facebook, six had an account on WhatsApp and four were Twitter users. Nine participants had an account only on Facebook while the number of such users for WhatsApp was only one. One participant had an account on both WhatsApp and Facebook. Four participants had an account on all the platforms. On the basis of the numbers alone, Facebook was the most preferred platform while Twitter had the least adoption.

Two of the fourteen accounts on Facebook were locked or perceived inactive by the users either because participants forgot their password or they abandoned the use of Facebook. Sixteen users were able to describe to our satisfaction the features and usage of Facebook. Two participants had never heard of Facebook. Our sample contained a wide variety of users in terms of the time since they created a Facebook account (min=7 days, max=4 years, average=12 months). The distribution of the number of Facebook friends of participants was skewed by outliers (min=4, max=700). The median number of Facebook friends was eleven while the average was 122. We found an order of magnitude difference between the median number of Facebook friends for participants in our sample and the numbers reported for blind people in developed countries [4,39]. We observed that recent adopters had fewer friends than consistent users and disenchanted users. Wu and Adamic also reported a similar finding and concluded that the difference in network size is dependent on the length of time users have been on Facebook [39]. Many participants used Facebook to broaden their social circle. On average, 75% of participants' Facebook friends were people they knew in an offline setting while 25% of their connections were people they met only online. In addition to strengthening existing connections with the blind community, some participants used Facebook to have more interactions with sighted Facebook users. This was more evident for consistent users: 69% of their Facebook friends were sighted while this number was only 17% for recent adopters. Participants used Facebook for an average of one hour each day. Two participants reported using Facebook for more than 2.5 hours each day.

Participants reported broad usage of Facebook. They used it for widening their social circle, accessing and sharing news, songs and other informational content, sending photos, and chatting. To our surprise, five participants described Facebook as an e-commerce platform. They perceived it as a platform to contact a person who runs a business on Facebook and to market your own business. One of the participants explained his Facebook experience as follows: "*Facebook is for making friends and developing your business. If anyone like to buy something, they can buy it. When I will start a business, I will give a presentation to my friends, market it, and put advertisements on Facebook.*"

Participants' Facebook experience was dominated by advertisements. Though Facebook serves advertisements to all its users, sighted users often learn to ignore these advertisements. On further investigation, we found that screen reader software divides the Facebook website into four panes. The last pane mostly consists of sponsored content. Because participants had limited experience switching between the panes using JAWS commands, these advertisements became central to their overall Facebook experience. The instructor noted that the advertisements were quite irritating to some students: "*Once the cursor moved to the last pane, many students were just lost. They got frustrated. They need much more practice to operate Facebook properly.*"

The most popular feature on Facebook was chatting with friends. This was corroborated through analysis of participants' Facebook activities. Some participants considered online chatting as "*opening doors to a new world full of opportunities.*" A majority of the participants (N=9) reported that their Facebook friends primarily use Facebook for chatting. The participants enjoyed interacting with both Facebook friends and Facebook strangers (Facebook users who are not their friends on Facebook). Facebook chatting also enabled them to have an asynchronous communication similar to SMS where they could send a reply at a time of their convenience without spending any money on telephone calls or SMS.

WhatsApp was the second-most popular social media platform among the participants. Ten people explained the usage of WhatsApp to our satisfaction. Out of those ten people, six had an account on WhatsApp. The participants considered WhatsApp primarily as a social media platform for mobile phones. We found broad usage of WhatsApp including group chatting, individual chatting, and sharing songs, videos, voice-messages and even location. Three participants considered it as a platform for strengthening existing connections rather than facilitating expansion of their social network. This is because a WhatsApp user can share information only with people on the contact list of his phone. The users in our sample enthusiastically appreciated the feature of sending voice messages to other users:

> *"I like sending voice messages on WhatsApp. It is simple to use. We hear the messages recorded in the voice of our friends. It is also cheaper than a phone call. Phone calls are good only for having long conversations. The only downside of voice messages is it requires a faster connection."*
> P1 (Male, Bachelor's Student, 23 years, Rajasthan)

The majority of participants perceived Twitter as a social media platform to connect with celebrities and experts, and have "*intelligent conversations with friends*". Though ten people knew the purpose of Twitter, only four people had an account. One account was locked. Even those who had an account, reported using it only for an average of five-minutes per day. Six users reported that either they do not have time to learn a new platform or they find it less engaging than Facebook and WhatsApp. This thought was echoed by the instructors: "*Only a few students used Twitter, mainly because none of their friends are active Twitter users*". Two participants in our sample also reported using LinkedIn and Google Plus.

Out of the five participants who were both WhatsApp and Facebook users, three stated Facebook was their favored social media platform while two preferred WhatsApp. Participants preferred Facebook because it enabled them to expand their social network. WhatsApp was preferred primarily because it enabled them to exchange voice messages. WhatsApp also instilled a sense of faith in some participants: They were more convinced that they are not talking to imposters:

> *"I trust people on WhatsApp more than the people on Facebook. Facebook has many people with fake profiles because it is easy to create a fake email ID and thus, a fake Facebook account. While creating a WhatsApp account, you have to use your own phone number."*
> P2 (Male, Bachelor's Student, 23 years, Rajasthan)

3.3.2 Benefits

Participants derived significant benefits by using social media platforms. Nine participants used these platforms as an efficient instrument to increase their social circle. Eleven participants used these platforms for chatting mainly to strengthen their existing links.

All participants deeply valued their existing offline social networks of friends, colleagues, and teachers and reported receiving valuable information about scholarships, educational material, health schemes, and employment opportunities through them. This assertion is also supported by one of the instructors who believed the network of blind students to be very cohesive: "*They know most of the blind people in the state. They will even tell you how many people in Rajasthan are blind. They rely on each other to share information.*" Fourteen participants reported that they meet their closest friends only twice in a year. Despite having access to mobile phones, they were able to interact with their friends only once or twice in a month because they could not afford voice calls[2]. These constraints are even more prominent when their friends are from different states as out-of-state voice calls incur higher call charges. One of the participants whose monthly family income is 23 USD expressed: "*I only call my friends when I have a question related to a career opportunity or to wish them on festivals. Everytime I call, I have to speak for 4-5 minutes and that is expensive.*" Though many of their friends still do not use these social media platforms, online chatting has empowered these users to have longer and more frequent conversations with friends who are using these platforms. Despite being separated by geographical distance, they reported feeling connected to their friends. These interactions not only supplement their need to access instrumental information, but also provide avenues for fun and entertainment:

> *"Now I get in touch with my friends using Facebook chat. Some of my friends live in other states as well. Now, three of my friends are in touch with me using Facebook. We can share information on business opportunities and competitive exams with each other. We also share songs."*
> P3 (Male, Unemployed, 30 years, Rajasthan)

Six participants considered social media platforms as an avenue to get information on interesting topics and current news. Five participants used these platforms for sharing photos, videos, jokes, and even documents with others.

We also found aspirational use of social media platforms. Participants used them to attain a higher social status and get respect from sighted people. Five participants reported that often they were treated in a condescending manner by society. They believed that their friends, colleagues, and sometimes even family members had an inferior outlook towards them:

> *"People think that even if we study, we will not get a job. When we go to mobile shops for recharging the Internet, they think that we are joking. They have a perception that even if I use Facebook who is going to be friends with me?"*
> P4 (Male, Bachelor's Student, 25 years, Delhi)

Despite this, participants had a strong desire to show the world that they can operate computers and are no less confident and knowledgeable than sighted users. They use social media platforms for demonstrating their use of computers and familiarity with technology:

> *"When I say to people that I use a computer, then no one believes me. They think I am blind and when they cannot operate a computer properly how I will be able to. But when I send a request on Facebook, they know it is me who has sent that request. People in my locality now know that I use the computer."*
> P4 (Male, Bachelor's Student, 25 years, Delhi)

3.3.3 Challenges

Participants experienced several challenges while using social media platforms. Most participants studied in a Hindi-medium school and had poor English language proficiency. Eleven participants complained about the language of audio output used in the screen reader software. They were unable to understand English words and the American accent output by the screen reader software and coped with it by reducing the playback speed. Three participants reported taking a few months to get used to the accent. The limited understanding of English also lowered the self-confidence and self-prestige of many participants. They felt disadvantaged and considered "*using the Internet a dream*" for people with limited skills in English and JAWS:

> *"I have to keep the speed of the talking software very slow and this hampers my productivity. Though our intellect is comparable to sighted people, we are unable to compete with them because of the lack of English skills. I feel disadvantaged."*
> P2 (Male, Bachelor's Student, 23 years, Rajasthan)

The instructors also considered the language of screen reader software to be one of the major limitations that impedes students' use of social media platforms and the Internet. According to them, 90% of the students who came to the training program in the last two years were unable to write their name in English. Their training was significantly impacted because of limited English language proficiency. The instructors coped with it by translating many portions of the course content to Hindi.

Although chatting was the favorite and most frequently used feature, many participants were unable to use this feature because of screen reader difficulties in interpreting abbreviations common in texting and code-mixing (e.g., so-called "Hinglish" a mix of Hindi and English). Many people preferred WhatsApp because they could send voice messages to chat:

> *"Nothing is better than sending messages in our voice. It helps in having a clear conversation. Many people use abbreviations for words. The screen reader software cannot read such content. It is very easy for a sighted user to read it, but blind people struggle a lot while chatting."*
> P1 (Male, Bachelor's Student, 23 years, Rajasthan)

Eight participants reported that listening to messages in the voice of senders would be the best functionality Facebook could offer. One participant even reported that this feature would be like "*lighting a candle in darkness.*" Though Facebook messenger has voice chatting functionality, none of the participants knew about it. The participants referred to the voice of screen reader software as robotic and devoid of any emotions. It impacted the user experience significantly:

> *"If I could hear the voice of my friend rather than JAWS reading his message, it would be so much better. JAWS is like a robot. I cannot get the feelings and emotions when JAWS read out messages sent by my friends. It diminishes the impact of chatting."*
> P5 (Male, Unemployed, 24 years, Madhya Pradesh)

Six participants complained about accessibility features and navigational challenges. In WhatsApp, when a user press the

[2] *The cost of voice calls in India is around 1 cent per minute.*

icon for sending a voice message, the output from screen reader software overlaps with the voice message sent by participants. This diminished the user experience of two WhatsApp users in our sample. Four participants reported that the screen reader software randomly stopped working, possibly because of an unsupported font or script. Eight participants found it challenging to navigate across panes and to remember the commands of screen reader software. Many features also do not have associated commands. For example, several participants complained about the lack of commands for Facebook chatting. Rediffmail, a popular email service in India with 93 million subscribers, was also unsupported by JAWS. Three participants found it difficult to send friend requests on Facebook. Often they do not know the email address of a friend and when they search the name on Facebook, they find hundreds of profiles with the same name. Because they are unable to distinguish among profiles by looking at the profile picture, they have to go through an "*arduous and irritating*" process of reading profile descriptions. Three participants complained about the lack of captions on photos posted by their friends. Three other participants expressed strong sentiments for the limited adoption of audio captcha on many websites: "*Can you imagine that the website of Indian Railways does not have an audio captcha? What is the point of learning a computer if I cannot even book my train tickets?*"

Many of the features and terminology are not localized to geographical regions. Four participants found it difficult to learn and understand features of social media platforms. The participants found the concepts of *wall*, *tweet*, and *follow* difficult to grasp. Both participants and instructors noted the importance of training and continued usage of the platforms to overcome these semantic barriers.

3.3.4 Social Media Non-Use

We asked the eight recent adopters whether they would be able to use social media platforms after completion of the training. Though all of them stated that social media platforms play a pivotal role in their life and they would very much like to continue using the platform, half of them reported that they would not be able to use them at all while two of them reported that they would be able to use them only rarely. This means that 75% of the recent adopters expected to become a disenchanted user or a non-user in the near future.

The major reason for social media non-use by disenchanted users, potential abandonment by recent adopters, and the inability of non-users to explore these platforms is the same: **the cost of devices and the Internet**. This finding is also supported by prior research on the use of social media platforms by users in low-income settings [3,41]. Eleven participants attributed the cost of devices and the Internet as the primary reason for their non-use of social media platforms. Many participants were living in severe poverty and owning a smartphone or a computer was seen as a luxury rather than a necessity. Many participants reported belonging to sections of society "*where no one has seen a computer or smartphone before.*" All but one participant were dependent on others for supporting their expenses. Many participants asserted that the first thing they would buy after becoming independent is a computer or a smartphone for learning more information:

> *"I rarely shave and get a haircut because I am unemployed. My financial situation is terrible and I have no family support. If there is no income, there will be no phone, no Internet, and no Facebook. When I will have enough money, I will buy a computer and make an account on Facebook."*
> P6 (Male, Unemployed, 34 years, Rajasthan)

Some recent adopters were worried that they will forget what they have learnt by the time they buy a computer because of the lack of practice. Though some organizations distribute low-cost computers and smartphones to blind people, participants reported that it would be challenging for them to pay even for the Internet: "*Paying for Internet recharge would be tough. A smartphone without the Internet is like a dumb phone.*"

Participants also expressed difficulties in visiting Internet cafés for accessing social media platforms. The facilitator of the training program reported that approximately 50% of incoming students have not taken a mobility training. All participants but three reported not stepping outside their home and training institute alone. Even if they visit an Internet café, the accessibility features are often not activated on the computers:

> *"Going to a café is a laborious task. The computers there do not have screen reader software. I have requested the owner to install them, but he is not interested because few blind people go to his café."*
> P7 (Female, Unemployed, 27 years, West Bengal)

Two recent adopters had a strategy to overcome this challenge. They planned to download NVDA in a portable flash drive and run the software from the drive itself. NVDA provides the ability to run it from a portable USB drive without needing administrative privileges on a computer.

3.3.5 Desire to Use New Media Technologies

Several participants expressed a strong desire for accessing information and entertainment using new accessible technologies designed specifically for them. The success of voice messages on WhatsApp, participants' desire to hear messages in the voice of sender, problems with the language of screen reader software, lack of access to computing devices, and severe financial constraints prompted us to seek alternative low-cost technologies that can be appropriated for them.

In recent years, various researchers and practitioners have designed *voice forums* for enabling low-income, low-literate marginalized people in the developing world to report, access and share information [1,9,15,22]. These voice forums are built using IVR technology that enables users to record voice messages and listen to the messages recorded by others using basic voice telephony. This facilitates asynchronous communication among users which is similar to chatting. The successful deployments of voice forums in the ICTD community prompted us to investigate the adoption and usage patterns of IVR technology among participants.

All participants had used an IVR system at least once in the last three months. Nine of them used it for finding out the balance on their pre-paid phones, six of them used it for speaking to a customer service center, and the rest used it to access a conference calling system. Sixteen participants found IVR technology easy to use. Only two participants found IVR systems difficult to operate and time consuming, and believed that many blind people would not even know how to use such systems. One participant avoided using IVR technology out of the fear that "*the excessive use of voice calls will damage ears because of radiation emanating from the phone.*"

In a group session, we showed a demonstration of a Hindi-language based voice forum to eight participants and two instructors where they could call a number and press 1 to record a voice message and press 2 to listen to recorded messages. This voice forum can be visualized as a single voicemail system shared by all the users. Though voicemail features are very popular in North America, they are rarely used in India. We received an enthusiastic response from the participants: everyone found the voice forum easy to use. Many participants were excited about the potential of the voice forum for voice chatting. Three participants also recorded a voice message during the demo session (one of them is shown in Figure 3). Participants liked the fact that they did not have to listen to the "*robotic voice of screen reader*" and the messages sounded natural. Six participants believed that all of their blind friends would be able to use this system. They reported the voice forum to be much better than the IVR systems they had used for accessing customer services.

Figure 3. A blind participant accessing the demo of a voice forum.

4. Voice-based Social Media Platform

In our prior work, we designed, built, and deployed *Sangeet Swara*, a social media voice forum for low-income, low-literate people in India to understand whether the participants would be able to moderate the user-generated content on the voice forum without any outside support. The deployment saw significant adoption by low-income people in rural and peri-urban India. In an eleven-week deployment, we received 25,381 calls by 1521 callers, 5376 voice messages recorded by 516 people, around 200,000 playbacks of these messages, 40,590 upvotes, 99,150 downvotes and 773 share events. Though we did not promote the platform on any of the channels accessible to blind community, to our surprise, we found that *Sangeet Swara* was extremely popular among low-income blind users in India. The detailed discussion on the design of the platform, deployment, adoption by low-income users, success of community moderation in managing content on the platform and improving the quality of user-generated content, the challenges in financial sustainability is presented in our prior publication [33].

In this paper, we focus our attention specifically on the use of *Sangeet Swara* by low-income blind people in rural and peri-urban India. In particular, we empirically evaluate:

- Content produced, consumed and shared by blind participants.
- Usability experience of blind participants.
- Impact of the social media voice forum on blind participants.

In the next sub-sections, we briefly discuss the design of *Sangeet Swara* for the sake of providing a complete picture. Thereafter, we present a detailed analysis of how low-income blind people used the voice forum, what content they produced, strengths and weaknesses of the voice forum, and the benefits and challenges offered to blind participants.

4.1 Design

Sangeet Swara enabled low-income people in rural and peri-urban India to record and listen to user-generated entertaining content like songs, jokes, poems, and anything that participants wanted to share. Similar to the *like* feature in Facebook, our system also requested callers to cast votes while listening to messages on the voice forum. Similar to the Facebook *wall*, each caller was played voice messages sequentially. The votes cast by callers were instrumental in deciding the quality of the messages and the order in which the messages were presented to callers. Similar to the *share* feature on Facebook, participants could also share a voice message with others. An account was automatically created the first time participants called our system. The username for each account was the phone number used for placing the voice call.

To access the system, participants placed a call on a toll-free number. Once the call was connected, participants were requested to select one of the four options by pressing the relevant key on their phone keypad:

1. **Access analytics on your messages.** Callers could press 1 to access the latest rank for each message recorded by them and the number of participants that heard them.
2. **Record a new message.** Callers could press 2 to record a new message. The callers were encouraged to introduce themselves in the beginning of the message. The maximum permissible length of messages was seventy seconds. After recording a message, the callers received an SMS containing a five digit numeric code corresponding to the message they recorded.
3. **Listen, rate and share messages.** Callers could press 3 to listen to the messages in the voice forum. Each message was played sequentially. At the end of each message, the callers were required to either give an upvote to the message by pressing 1 or downvote it by pressing 2. They could listen to the message again by pressing 3. They could share the message by pressing 4. On selecting the option to share content, we forwarded the caller an SMS containing the numeric code for the shared message. In the SMS, callers were encouraged to forward the SMS to their friends to share the numeric code for the message they wanted to share.
4. **Access a message directly.** Callers could press 4 to enter the numeric code for accessing a message directly. This feature alleviated the need to wait for a particular message to show up in the playback list.

Callers could barge in at any time for any prompt to indicate their selection. All the prompts were recorded in a slow and clear diction by a native Hindi speaker (male, 28 years). We developed the system by using IVR Junction [34] and Voxeo Prophecy [45].

4.2 Methodology

We used a mixed-methods approach to analyze the usage by blind participants. We conducted a structured phone survey that asked one pre-recorded question to callers every time they called the voice forum. The survey consisted of fifteen subjective questions recorded in Hindi. The questions were asked to understand the background of participants, collect demographic data, evaluate the user experience and efficacy of community moderation, and investigate the impact of the voice forum on them. The survey was completed by a total of 204 participants. Although we did not specifically ask them, while giving information on their background, 26% of the survey respondents (N=53) voluntarily identified themselves as blind [33]. **For the analyses presented in this paper, we only consider data contributed from those fifty-three respondents who voluntarily disclosed that they were blind.**

For our user analysis, we studied survey responses contributed by the fifty-three blind participants. We translated and transcribed their responses in English and analyzed them using open coding. The average length of the response was 38 words. We also studied the call logs of the fifty-three blind participants to understand usage patterns.

For content analysis, we randomly sampled a hundred messages from the voice messages recorded by blind participants and inspected them on several criteria like gender, content type, location of callers, the quality of the recording, etc.

We also conducted thirteen semi-structured qualitative interviews with blind participants to investigate the user engagement, and measure the strengths and weaknesses of *Sangeet Swara*. The interviews were conducted in Hindi by the first author. We reviewed and analyzed data immediately after conducting each interview. The insights obtained from the data analysis added more questions for the next interview. The interviews were translated and transcribed in English, and were analyzed using open coding.

4.3 Analyzing Call Logs of Blind Participants

On quantitatively analyzing call logs of the fifty-three blind survey respondents, we were surprised to see their disproportionate usage of the system. The fifty-three participants were only 3.5% of all participants on the platform. However, they were responsible for recording approximately 25% of all contributions. The median number of messages recorded by these blind participants was 13 (max=170 messages). Seven of them recorded more than fifty messages each. They placed 4784 voice calls (19% of total calls received), cast 7350 upvotes (18% of all upvotes) and 26,559 downvotes (27% of all downvotes), shared 57 messages (8% of all shared events) and listened to messages 46,090 times (24% of all playback events).

Forty-three participants answered all questions on the survey while ten participants answered the survey partially. Although a few blind participants did not record any voice messages, they were heavy listeners of the content contributed by others. Two such blind listeners called the voice forum 23 times and 123 times respectively. These listeners also recorded emphatic and verbose responses (with an average length of fifty-words) to the questions asked in the phone survey. The number of messages recorded by blind contributors, votes cast by them, messages listened by them, and the average length of responses given by blind listeners in our survey is strong evidence that blind contributors and listeners valued *Sangeet Swara*.

4.4 User Analysis of Blind Participants

The blind participants in our sample were from thirteen states in India. Two-thirds of them were from rural regions. 93% of the respondents were male, and 7% were female. The average age of the blind participants was 24.6 years (min=15 years, max=42 years, S.D.=8.1 years). They came from a broad range of educational backgrounds: 17% held or were pursuing a Master's degree, 19% held or were pursuing a Bachelor's degree, 21% were in high school, 10% were in middle school, 2% only completed primary school, 2% were uneducated and 10% were trained in music. 19% of the participants did not share information on their educational background. 24% of the blind participants were employed and earned an average monthly income of 107 USD (min= 5 USD, max=334 USD, S.D.=110 USD). 45% of the blind participants were students, 14% were teachers, 12% were unemployed, 9% worked either as a telephone operator or a singer. We did not have employment information for 20% of the participants.

All blind participants owned a mobile phone. 26% of them reported using SMS, another 26% of them reported not using SMS, and 48% of them did not share this information. Only one blind participant had an email account and three participants had a Facebook account. Many participants had never even heard of Facebook and often responded: "*We do not have a Facebook account, but we have an account in Bank of India.*" They associated the word *account* with banking services rather than Internet services.

4.5 Content Generated by Blind Participants

All one hundred messages in the random sample that we analyzed were recorded by male participants. In sixty-eight messages participants reported their location, in seventy-seven messages they shared their name and in twenty-five messages they shared their phone number publicly with all participants on the voice forum. The participants were from nine states in India. All messages but one were high-quality recordings. The average length of voice messages was 47 seconds (min= 5s, max=70s, S.D.=22.2s).

Thirty-nine messages were similar to the messages that people generally share on Facebook, WhatsApp, and Twitter. This category comprised discussion on topics trending in the platform, generic informative messages, messages intended for specific people, discussion on topics of national and regional interest, messages requesting feedback from other participants, messages requesting or sharing phone number, etc. We found seven flirtatious messages where participants showered special attention and adulation to female contributors. One person also recorded a message reprimanding those who were recording flirtatious messages for women participants. We found four messages where participants spoke about visual impairment. Twenty-four messages were poems. Most of them were written to express feelings on love, separation, motherhood, visual impairment, environment, women empowerment, success, and persistence. Twenty-one messages were songs, including folk songs (n=10), Bollywood songs (n=8), and even recordings from a playback device (n=3). To our surprise, we saw nine messages where people shared general knowledge information with each other by asking questions or recording answers to the questions asked previously. One example of a question asked on the forum is, "*When is the World Environment Day celebrated?*" Two messages were jokes. We also found two messages containing abusive language and one message where a participant recorded sexually explicit content. We have made available twenty-five randomly selected messages recorded by blind participants at https://soundcloud.com/socialmediavoiceforum/sets/random25.

4.6 Usage by Blind Participants

4.6.1 Adoption

Sangeet Swara received a huge response from blind people (see Figure 4 for a photograph of one of our users). Although 26% of the survey respondents self-reported themselves as a blind, we believe this number is a conservative estimate of the actual percentage of blind participants who used the voice forum. The representation of blind people on our platform is significantly higher than their representation on Facebook, Twitter, WhatsApp or even among the population of India. In addition, the participants were spread out all across India. They recorded several positive sentiments about the platform and shared impactful stories on how the platform was playing an influential role in transforming their lives. For example, several participants shared that the platform connected them with blind participants in other states and far-off locations. The voice forum was the first introduction to a social media platform for 99% of participants in our sample. They valued the interactions with other blind participants and derived several benefits by using the platform:

> "*Using this platform is a great experience. I listen to people from all over India, made many new friends, and heard many creative talents of other blind people. In this fast life, no one has time to listen to jokes, songs, and one-liners. Those who have time, do not have resources. Those who have resources, they do not have time. Now a days, literate, illiterate, poor, rich everyone has a mobile phone. The platform has enabled those who do not have resources to consume entertaining content anywhere, anytime, and in any quantity.*"
> U1 (Male, Telephone operator, 31 years, Maharashtra)

Many participants perceived the forum to be exclusively designed for and used by low-income blind people, primarily because of the sheer number of blind users and abundance of songs, poems and discussions central to visual impairment. For example, we found three songs on the importance of Braille and a discussion on Louis Braille during the content analysis. Blind people used the platform to meet new people and earn social capital. Many participants also exchanged their phone numbers by recording a message on the platform for having longer offline conversations with other users on the platform:

> "*The platform is a boon for blind people. It gives us the opportunity to show and improve our talent. Blind people who use the platform are very competitive and they continue to improve their messages. We also reach out to people in far-off towns and get to know them better. We get a lot of knowledge. I also get inspiration from listening to other blind people. Blind people who want to learn and make progress share informative messages with us.*"
> U2 (Male, High school student, Uttar Pradesh)

We were curious to understand how blind participants heard about the voice forum. Eleven participants reported that they

Figure 4. A blind participant accessing *Sangeet Swara*, a social media voice forum

were told about the platform either by a friend or a teacher. Five participants reported spreading information about the platform by calling their friends. During the qualitative interview, one participant reported receiving a phone call from a friend to convey the gratitude for introducing him to the platform: "*You have given me a new life. The platform is very good.*"

4.6.2 Benefits

The participants were excited that their messages were heard by people distributed all across India. When asked who (according to them) listened to the messages on the platform, many participants responded that "*literate, knowledgeable and inquisitive folks,*" and people of all generations listen to it: "*Mothers, sisters, kids, old, government workers, officers, students, farmers, everyone listens.*" The participants shared personal stories and accounts of life on the forum. We also found several messages where blind people recorded a song or poem sung by their children.

The participants regarded the platform as an avenue to access entertainment, share information, and learn skills. Many participants perceived it as a platform to show, judge and share feedback on musical talent. Five people believed that the platform was developed by *The National Academy of Music, Dance and Drama* and the Government of India to provide opportunities for low-income blind musicians. Several participants also learnt about and discussed current national and regional news. For example, five participants recorded performances and news on the 2013 North India floods:

> "*Whatever I say about this platform will not be enough. We hear good jokes, songs, poems and even useful knowledge. We listen to the important news of India and world. We also got to know the latest situation of North India floods on the platform.*"
> U3 (Male, High school student, 18 years, Gujarat)

Many participants also felt comfortable recording their career goals, aspirations and vision. They used the voice forum for motivating people to fight corruption and violence, and serve the underserved communities:

> "*I want to become a good man and fight corruption in India. Some people are using violence against women, killing the innocents, depriving the poor of the dignity. When will this end? It will end when we decide to become righteous and law-abiding citizens. We are the future, we have to make our country successful.*"
> U4 (Male, Student, 15 years, Jharkhand)

Many blind participants derived instrumental benefits from *Sangeet Swara*. Five participants reported learning social skills by using the platform. An eighteen-year old student from a small city in Madhya Pradesh reported that he "*learnt how to speak properly, how to behave, and how to respect others*" by observing the interactions of other participants. Three participants reported that the platform has improved presentation of their thoughts, refined their grammar and accent, and helped them learn new vocabulary. They attributed an increase in their self-confidence to platform:

> *"The platform has provided me a lot of self-confidence. I can learn anything from the platform. I learn a lot from general knowledge questions asked on the platform. It is a great way to learn and understand principles of life. No matter how much I praise, it will never be enough. We get entertainment and knowledge. We also learn how to record better messages. The platform gives me a lot of pleasure and knowledge."*
>
> U5 (Male, High school student, Orissa)

Sangeet Swara provided more accessible venues for women and young girls for accessing information and entertainment. A fifteen-year old female student from a small town in Uttar Pradesh found the platform better than Facebook and Twitter. She found the content on the platform informative and suggested that the platform provided her a gateway to create new friends without the need to go to a cybercafé: "*It is a great knowledge tool. We get to know more people and more people get to know me. It is much better than Internet, Facebook and Twitter because we can use it without spending money. We can chat, listen to messages, understand them and learn from them.*"

The platform was successful because it could be accessed using any phone without the need of an Internet connection. It provided several useful features like voice chatting, voting, and content sharing. As voice is a natural and accessible medium, the forum was usable by blind people with limited technology exposure. The language of the system was in Hindi and it alleviated the challenges blind people face with the language and accent of screen reader software. Because the voice forum was a toll-free line, even the poorest of the poor could also use it. It enabled several uneducated and unemployed blind people to create their own India-wide social network: "*I come from a village where it is very difficult to get educated. I want to thank you sincerely because you enabled all blind people in India to get to know each other.*"

4.6.3 Room for Improvement

Among all recorded messages, we found twenty-two messages containing abusive content. Many participants reprimanded those who recorded abusive content. Twelve blind participants complained about the abusive content during the phone survey: "*Abusive messages should not be played. It causes pain in our heart. Please note the phone number of people who record abusive content and warn those who are misusing the service. It is a true adage that one bad fish can spoil the whole pond.*" In the next iteration, we propose to include a feature to flag the messages for abusive and derogatory content.

Only a fraction of all events (*playback, vote, share, record*) were *share* events, primarily because the sharing of content required participants to read and send SMS. In our formative study, we observed that various participants either remembered the phone numbers of their friends or wrote it on a Braille paper. In the next iteration of the social media voice forum, we propose to provide a functionality where a user enters the phone number of a friend to share the message rather than forwarding an SMS. Once a valid phone number is entered, the friend will receive a call and the voice message will be played. It is also worth exploring the use of acoustic quick response codes for sharing the call position in an IVR tree with other participants [23]. The technique uses remote generation and recognition of audio codes and requires setting-up additional servers for running it.

The participants also shared suggestions for improving the design of the platform for future deployments. Six participants requested a feature to send personal messages to other participants. Two participants also requested a discussion forum where they could record replies to the messages while listening to them. We plan to include these functionalities in the next iteration.

5. DISCUSSION AND CONCLUSION

In this paper, we have presented a detailed analysis of social media use and non-use by low-income blind people living in rural and peri-urban India. We have explored strengths and weaknesses of Facebook, Twitter, and WhatsApp for blind people. Though participants derive several instrumental benefits and gain social acceptance and entertainment by using these platforms, several socioeconomic barriers, limited English language proficiency and constrained access to computing devices impede the widespread adoption. We also presented the detailed analysis of how low-income blind people in India adopted a social media voice forum that was not originally designed for them. The platform spread rapidly among them without any marketing effort and enabled them to make new connections, showcase their talent and learn information.

Though we demonstrated the strong potential of the social media voice forum for low-income blind people, financial sustainability of such voice forums is still a concern. A limitation of our work is that we provided the service for free. Future work is needed to figure out how to make such systems financially sustainable. Many participants in the formative study expressed concerns over higher unemployment rate and were desperate to get a job because of severe financial constraints. Previous studies have also indicated several challenges and discriminations blind people face before and after getting employed [19]. We are presently researching the potential of using crowdsourcing on basic phones for providing additional earning opportunities to blind participants and to subsidize the cost of participation on the social media voice forum through crowd work.

We observed that a majority of the contributors were male blind participants. The user analysis also revealed that only 7% of the participants were female. The low participation from women in low-income families was not unexpected. A majority of them do not own a phone themselves and use the phone of a male family member. Moreover, social and cultural norms discourage young and married women to share their voice and interact with strangers. Some of the female participants were highly engaged with the system. One female participant, a teacher by profession, recorded fourteen songs, poems and contributed messages to several discussions. Many male blind participants offered special attention to female participants and asked for their phone numbers for having offline conversations. Though there were several discussions on the voice forum for discouraging people to embarrass female contributors, there is a need to make both offline and online social media platforms more inclusive of low-income blind women. In the next deployment, it will be fruitful to also measure the effect of flirtatious messages, abusive messages and supporting messages targeted at female members on their participation.

One of the participants in our formative study suggested merging offline voice-based social media platform with the online social media platform like Facebook and Twitter: "*Could you design a system where we can press 1 to access Facebook, press 2 for Twitter. Can we leave a message in a voice that can be uploaded on Facebook and get translated into text?*" Though his requirements are partly supported by existing tools like IVR Junction [35], there is a need to better integrate these platforms for providing a global reach to voice forum users and facilitate seamless interactions with the global population.

One of the instructors expressed concern on the longevity of social media voice forum. He believed that such platforms will become obsolete when smartphones and Internet becomes pervasive. He argued that blind people who have access to smartphones, use the audio output of a screen reader software to check phone balance rather than using the IVR feature. However, we believe that our work has longevity. Even when people have smartphones, they will continue to use voice as a dominant communication medium. For example, voice features of smartphone applications like WhatsApp, Viber, and Skype are very popular among the present Internet population.

It is worth mentioning that many low-income blind participants either did not know about piracy or they did not care about digital rights infringement. A majority of the participants in the formative study did not know about the cost of screen reader software. For them, both NVDA and JAWS were freely accessible. Only one user bought a screen reader software for 50 USD from a non-profit organization. Many recent adopters planned to either download it or ask a copy from friends and instructors. The pervasive piracy of screen reader software in India is also reported by other researchers [13]. Even in our voice-based social media platform, we received many messages where participants recorded songs from other playback devices without caring about copyright issues.

The instructors, facilitators and many participants were enthusiastic about the promise of new media technologies in providing them information and strengthening their social connections. Many participants stated that they are living in a technological era and the road to success is difficult without learning information technology. Not everyone was excited about technology though, one participant expressed concern about the overuse of technology: "*We survive because of our other senses. We should be less dependent on technology and more on our senses.*" Participants exhorted the research community to improve existing technologies for blind people and design new media technologies that are more cognizant of their economic, social and infrastructural constraints.

6. ACKNOWLEDGMENTS

We are grateful to Jitendra Bhargav, Bhim Singh Thakur and staff of *Rajasthan Netraheen Kalyan Sangh* for their assistance with the study. We are thankful to Gaetano Borriello, Richard Ladner, Bill Thies and the anonymous reviewers for their helpful suggestions. This work was funded in part by the Noe Professorship at the University of Washington, USAID grant award AID-OAA-G-14-00014, as well as the Catalyst Center for Sustainable Development at Microsoft Research India.

7. REFERENCES

1. Sheetal K Agarwal, Arun Kumar, Amit Anil Nanavati, and Nitendra Rajput. 2010. User-Generated Content Creation and Dissemination in Rural Areas. *Information Technologies and International Development* 6, 2, 21–37.
2. Tanja Bosch. 2011. Young women and "technologies of the self": Social networking and sexualities. *Agenda* 25, 4, 75–86. http://doi.org/10.1080/10130950.2011.630579
3. Tanja E. Bosch. 2009. Using online social networking for teaching and learning: Facebook use at the University of Cape Town. *Communication* 35, 2, 185–200. http://doi.org/10.1080/02500160903250648
4. Erin L. Brady, Yu Zhong, Meredith Ringel Morris, and Jeffrey P. Bigham. 2013. Investigating the Appropriateness of Social Network Question Asking As a Resource for Blind Users. *Proceedings of the 2013 Conference on Computer Supported Cooperative Work*, ACM, 1225–1236. http://doi.org/10.1145/2441776.2441915
5. Moira Burke, Robert Kraut, and Diane Williams. 2010. Social Use of Computer-mediated Communication by Adults on the Autism Spectrum. *Proceedings of the 2010 ACM Conference on Computer Supported Cooperative Work*, ACM, 425–434. http://doi.org/10.1145/1718918.1718991
6. Nicole B. Ellison, Charles Steinfield, and Cliff Lampe. 2011. Connection Strategies: Social Capital Implications of Facebook-enabled Communication Practices. *New Media & Society*, 1461444810385389. http://doi.org/10.1177/1461444810385389
7. Kristin Skeide Fuglerud, Ingvar Tjøstheim, Birkir Rúnar Gunnarsson, and Morten Tollefsen. 2012. Use of Social Media by People with Visual Impairments: Usage Levels, Attitudes and Barriers. *Proceedings of the 13th International Conference on Computers Helping People with Special Needs - Volume Part I*, Springer-Verlag, 565–572. http://doi.org/10.1007/978-3-642-31522-0_85
8. AS Grover and K Calteaux. 2012. A voice service for user feedback on school meals. *ACM DEV*. Retrieved from http://dl.acm.org/citation.cfm?id=2160619
9. Mohamed Gulaid and Aditya Vashistha. 2013. Ila Dhageyso : An Interactive Voice Forum to Foster Transparent Governance in Somaliland. *Proceedings of the Sixth International Conference on Information and Communications Technologies and Development*, 13–16.
10. Zahir Koradia, Piyush Aggarwal, Aaditeshwar Seth, and Gaurav Luthra. 2013. Gurgaon Idol: A Singing Competition over Community Radio and IVRS. *Proceedings of the 3rd ACM Symposium on Computing for Development*, ACM, 6:1–6:10. http://doi.org/10.1145/2442882.2442890
11. Cliff Lampe, Donghee Yvette Wohn, Jessica Vitak, Nicole B. Ellison, and Rick Wash. 2011. Student use of Facebook for organizing collaborative classroom activities. *International Journal of Computer-Supported Collaborative Learning* 6, 3, 329–347. http://doi.org/10.1007/s11412-011-9115-y

12. Maarit Mäkinen and Mary Wangu Kuira. 2008. Social Media and Post-election Crisis in Kenya. *The International Journal of Press/Politics* 13, 3, 328–335. http://doi.org/10.1177/1940161208319409
13. Ted McCarthy, Joyojeet Pal, Tanvi Marballi, and Edward Cutrell. 2012. An Analysis of Screen Reader Use in India. *Proceedings of the Fifth International Conference on Information and Communication Technologies and Development*, ACM, 149–158. http://doi.org/10.1145/2160673.2160694
14. Indrani Medhi-Thies, Pedro Ferreira, Nakull Gupta, Jacki O'Neill, and Edward Cutrell. 2015. KrishiPustak: A Social Networking System for Low-Literate Farmers. *Proceedings of the 18th ACM Conference on Computer Supported Cooperative Work & Social Computing*, ACM, 1670–1681. http://doi.org/10.1145/2675133.2675224
15. Preeti Mudliar, Jonathan Donner, and William Thies. 2012. Emergent Practices Around CGNet Swara, Voice Forum for Citizen Journalism in Rural India. *Proceedings of the Fifth International Conference on Information and Communication Technologies and Development*, ACM, 159–168. http://doi.org/10.1145/2160673.2160695
16. David Nemer. 2015. Online Favela: The Use of Social Media by the Marginalized in Brazil. *Information Technology for Development* 0, 0, 1–16. http://doi.org/10.1080/02681102.2015.1011598
17. Joyojeet Pal. 2015. Banalities Turned Viral Narendra Modi and the Political Tweet. *Television & New Media* 16, 4, 378–387. http://doi.org/10.1177/1527476415573956
18. Joyojeet Pal, Yeswanth Gogineni, Kunjan Sanghavi, et al. 2012. Local-language Digital Information in India: Challenges and Opportunities for Screen Readers. *Proceedings of the Fifth International Conference on Information and Communication Technologies and Development*, ACM, 318–325. http://doi.org/10.1145/2160673.2160712
19. Joyojeet Pal and Meera Lakshmanan. 2012. Assistive Technology and the Employment of People with Vision Impairments in India. *Proceedings of the Fifth International Conference on Information and Communication Technologies and Development*, ACM, 307–317. http://doi.org/10.1145/2160673.2160711
20. Joyojeet Pal, Manas Pradhan, Mihir Shah, and Rakesh Babu. 2011. Assistive Technology for Vision-impairments: An agenda for the ICTD Community. *Proceedings of the 20th International Conference Companion on World Wide Web*, ACM, 513–522. http://doi.org/10.1145/1963192.1963365
21. D. Pascolini and S. P. Mariotti. 2012. Global estimates of visual impairment: 2010. *British Journal of Ophthalmology* 96, 5, 614–618. http://doi.org/10.1136/bjophthalmol-2011-300539
22. Neil Patel, Deepti Chittamuru, Anupam Jain, Paresh Dave, and Tapan S. Parikh. 2010. Avaaj Otalo: A Field Study of an Interactive Voice Forum for Small Farmers in Rural India. *Proceedings of the SIGCHI Conference on Human Factors in Computing Systems*, ACM, 733–742. http://doi.org/10.1145/1753326.1753434
23. Jennifer Pearson, Simon Robinson, Matt Jones, Amit Nanavati, and Nitendra Rajput. 2013. ACQR: Acoustic Quick Response Codes for Content Sharing on Low End Phones with No Internet Connectivity. *Proceedings of the 15th International Conference on Human-computer Interaction with Mobile Devices and Services*, ACM, 308–317. http://doi.org/10.1145/2493190.2493195
24. Nimmi Rangaswamy and Edward Cutrell. 2013. Local Pocket Internet and Global Social Media: Facebook and Youth Sub-Stratum in Urban India. *IFIP 9th International Conference on Social Implications of Computers in Developing Countries*.
25. Agha Ali Raza, Farhan Ul Haq, Zain Tariq, et al. 2013. Job Opportunities Through Entertainment: Virally Spread Speech-based Services for Low-literate Users. *Proceedings of the SIGCHI Conference on Human Factors in Computing Systems*, ACM, 2803–2812. http://doi.org/10.1145/2470654.2481389
26. Clay Shirky. 2011. The Political Power of Social Media: Technology, the Public Sphere, and Political Change. *Foreign Affairs* 90, 1, 28–41.
27. Brian Solis. The Social Revolution is Our Industrial Revolution. Retrieved from http://www.briansolis.com/2008/07/social-revolution-is-our-industrial/
28. Kate Starbird and Leysia Palen. 2011. "Voluntweeters": Self-organizing by Digital Volunteers in Times of Crisis. *Proceedings of the SIGCHI Conference on Human Factors in Computing Systems*, ACM, 1071–1080. http://doi.org/10.1145/1978942.1979102
29. Kate Starbird and Leysia Palen. 2012. (How) Will the Revolution Be Retweeted?: Information Diffusion and the 2011 Egyptian Uprising. *Proceedings of the ACM 2012 Conference on Computer Supported Cooperative Work*, ACM, 7–16. http://doi.org/10.1145/2145204.2145212
30. Michael A. Stefanone, Kyounghee Hazel Kwon, and Derek Lackaff. 2012. Exploring the relationship between perceptions of social capital and enacted support online. *Journal of Computer-Mediated Communication* 17, 4, 451–466. http://doi.org/10.1111/j.1083-6101.2012.01585.x
31. Theodore Tsaousides, Yuka Matsuzawa, and Matthew Lebowitz. 2011. Familiarity and prevalence of Facebook use for social networking among individuals with traumatic brain injury. *Brain Injury* 25, 12, 1155–1162. http://doi.org/10.3109/02699052.2011.613086
32. Aditya Vashistha, Erin Brady, William Thies, and Edward Cutrell. 2014. Educational Content Creation and Sharing by Low-Income Visually Impaired People in India. *Proceedings of the Fifth ACM Symposium on Computing for Development*, ACM, 63–72. http://doi.org/10.1145/2674377.2674385
33. Aditya Vashistha, Edward Cutrell, Gaetano Borriello, and William Thies. 2015. Sangeet Swara: A Community-Moderated Voice Forum in Rural India. *Proceedings of the 33rd Annual ACM Conference on Human Factors in Computing Systems*, ACM, 417–426. http://doi.org/10.1145/2702123.2702191

34. Aditya Vashistha and William Thies. *IVR Junction: Building Scalable and Distributed Voice Forums in the Developing World.*
35. Aditya Vashistha and William Thies. IVR Junction. Retrieved from www.ivrjunction.org
36. Brian Wentz and Jonathan Lazar. 2011. Are Separate Interfaces Inherently Unequal?: An Evaluation with Blind Users of the Usability of Two Interfaces for a Social Networking Platform. *Proceedings of the 2011 iConference*, ACM, 91–97. http://doi.org/10.1145/1940761.1940774
37. WHO. 2013. *Factsheet on Visual impairment and blindness*. Retrieved from http://www.who.int/mediacentre/factsheets/fs282/en/
38. Derek Willis. 2014. Narendra Modi, the Social Media Politician. *The New York Times*. Retrieved May 5, 2015 from http://www.nytimes.com/2014/09/26/upshot/narendra-modi-the-social-media-politician.html
39. Shaomei Wu and Lada A. Adamic. 2014. Visually Impaired Users on an Online Social Network. *Proceedings of the SIGCHI Conference on Human Factors in Computing Systems*, ACM, 3133–3142. http://doi.org/10.1145/2556288.2557415
40. Susan P. Wyche, Andrea Forte, and Sarita Yardi Schoenebeck. 2013. Hustling Online: Understanding Consolidated Facebook Use in an Informal Settlement in Nairobi. *Proceedings of the SIGCHI Conference on Human Factors in Computing Systems*, ACM, 2823–2832. http://doi.org/10.1145/2470654.2481391
41. Susan P. Wyche, Sarita Yardi Schoenebeck, and Andrea Forte. 2013. "Facebook is a Luxury": An Exploratory Study of Social Media Use in Rural Kenya. *Proceedings of the 2013 Conference on Computer Supported Cooperative Work*, ACM, 33–44. http://doi.org/10.1145/2441776.2441783
42. Social Media: The Biggest Shift Since The Industrial Revolution. *Social Factor*. Retrieved May 5, 2015 from http://socialfactor.com/social-media-the-biggest-shift-since-the-industrial-revolution/
43. BBC Nepali earthquake lifeline public chat channel launches on Viber. Retrieved from http://www.bbc.co.uk/mediacentre/latestnews/2015/bbc-nepali-viber-launch
44. GDP per capita (current US$) | Data | Table. *The World Bank*. Retrieved from http://data.worldbank.org/indicator/NY.GDP.PCAP.CD
45. Voxeo Prophecy Platform. Retrieved from http://voxeo.com/prophecy/

Typing Performance of Blind Users: An Analysis of Touch Behaviors, Learning Effect, and In-Situ Usage

Hugo Nicolau[1], Kyle Montague[2], Tiago Guerreiro[3], André Rodrigues[3], Vicki L. Hanson[1,2]
[1]Rochester Institute of Technology, [2]University of Dundee,
[3]LaSIGE, Faculdade de Ciências, Universidade de Lisboa
hmnics@rit.edu, kmontague@dundee.ac.uk, {tjguerreiro, afrodrigues}@fc.ul.pt, vlhics@rit.edu

ABSTRACT
Non-visual text-entry for people with visual impairments has focused mostly on the comparison of input techniques reporting on performance measures, such as accuracy and speed. While researchers have been able to establish that non-visual input is slow and error prone, there is little understanding on how to improve it. To develop a richer characterization of typing performance, we conducted a longitudinal study with five novice blind users. For eight weeks, we collected *in-situ* usage data and conducted weekly laboratory assessment sessions. This paper presents a thorough analysis of typing performance that goes beyond traditional aggregated measures of text-entry and reports on character-level errors and touch measures. Our findings show that users improve over time, even though it is at a slow rate (0.3 WPM per week). Substitutions are the most common type of error and have a significant impact on entry rates. In addition to text input data, we analyzed touch behaviors, looking at touch contact points, exploration movements, and lift positions. We provide insights on *why* and *how* performance improvements and errors occur. Finally, we derive some implications that should inform the design of future virtual keyboards for non-visual input.

Categories and Subject Descriptors
H.5.2 [**Information Interfaces and Presentation**]: User Interfaces - *Input devices and strategies*. K4.2 [**Computers and Society**]: Social Issues – *Assistive technologies for persons with disabilities*.

General Terms
Measurement, Experimentation, Human Factors.

Keywords
Blind, Novice, Text-Entry, Input, Touch, Behavior, Performance.

1. INTRODUCTION
Over the last decade, touchscreen devices began to dominate the smartphone market. In contrast to feature phones, current devices are operated by touching the screen directly, without requiring a physical keyboard; users resort to virtual keyboards to enter text on their devices. Although text-entry is an inherently visually demanding task, particularly when using touchscreen devices, accessibility services have been devised to enable blind users to perform this task. These services rely on an *Explore by Touch* paradigm where users move their fingers on the screen and the interface reads aloud the element in focus. While *Explore by Touch* can be useful, the fundamental task of text input remains slow and error prone, especially for novice users [1, 3, 19].

ASSETS'15, October 26-28, 2015, Lisbon, Portugal
© 2015 ACM. ISBN 978-1-4503-3400-6/15/10 $15.00
DOI: http://dx.doi.org/10.1145/2700648.2809861

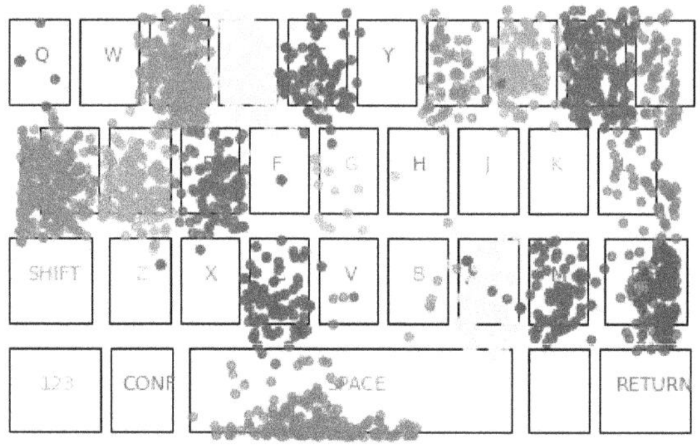

Figure 1. Lift points for all participants in week eight.

Although touch interaction and non-visual text-entry have been studied for years, research has been mainly limited to performance comparisons of input techniques [1, 3, 19, 22, 28]. In these studies, performance is often measured in terms of words per minute and errors. While these measures can establish *that* differences exist, they provide little justification for *why* and *how* they exist. In order to improve current input techniques, an understanding of touch typing behaviors is essential. However, because there is little or no knowledge on how blind users type on standard virtual keyboards it is unclear how to improve them.

This paper presents a longitudinal study that aims to understand the characteristics of novice blind users typing performance, touch behaviors (e.g. exploration gestures - Figure 1), character-level errors, and learning experience. Our goal is to inform future designs of touchscreen keyboards, with the ultimate aim of supporting fast and accurate input that can be easily used by novice blind users. We recruited five blind participants and gave them new mobile touchscreen devices. A service that ran in the background of the devices collected system-wide input usage, which enabled us to account for practice. We then collected typing data through controlled laboratory assessments over an eight-week period. To develop a detailed characterization of how blind users explore and type on virtual keyboards, we propose extending text-entry measures to include movement measures, as in pointing-related research [9, 10, 12], such as distance traveled, target re-entries, and movement profile. These measures can provide more insights on how blind people use a continuous interaction paradigm such as *Explore by Touch*. We were interested in answering three main research questions: 1) What are the most common types of errors? 2) How does typing performance evolve over time? 3) *Why* do errors exist?

Our findings have implications for the design of touchscreen keyboards and input techniques for blind and visually impaired users. Based on typing data, our results show that substitutions are the most common error type throughout the study. Participants' performance significantly improved over time, both in terms of errors and speed. We also show why improvements occur by examining hit positions, movement time, movement paths, and pausing behaviors. Correction strategies were consistent among users, but required a significant amount of time.

The main contribution of this paper is a thorough understanding of unconstrained text-entry performance, typing behaviors, and an empirical body of knowledge for future development of virtual keyboards. We provide an analysis of touch exploration measures in text-entry tasks and report on the learning experience of novice blind users, particularly on how input performance and behaviors change over an eight-week period. The findings herein presented should be of interest to mobile keyboard designers and accessibility researchers looking to gain from quantitative insights into blind users' text-entry performance with touch devices.

2. TEXT INPUT FOR BLIND USERS

Today's mainstream touchscreen devices support non-visual text input via the built-in screen readers e.g. VoiceOver and Talkback. They enable users to explore the keyboard with their finger and have the keys are read aloud as they touch them. While the visual layout of the QWERTY keyboard is identical to that presented to sighted users, the text-entry rates are much slower for visually impaired users [19]. To address this problem a number of works have proposed novel interfaces for non-visual text-entry on mobile touchscreen devices; including new keyboard layouts [3, 8] and alternative methods of inputting text [1, 16, 19, 22, 23].

What is common amongst these works is that they focus on the overall input performance metrics such as words per minute (WPM) and minimum string distance (MSD) error rates [21] to compare input methods. However, in doing so these works neglect to justify *how* and *why differences* exist between interfaces; for instance, in character-level errors [13, 27]. Similarly, the aforementioned studies use constrained text-entry tasks – where the participants are not provided with feedback on their input actions, or given the ability to correct errors. In contrast, Wobbrock and Myers [27] presented the input stream taxonomy to support unconstrained text-entry evaluations. This approach allows participants to make corrections to their typing and capture both uncorrected and corrected error rates. Using this analysis, it is possible to not only capture character-level errors, but also identify corrective behaviors.

3. MEASURES OF TOUCH BEHAVIORS

Findlater et al. [5] evaluated the typing performances of expert sighted typists on large touch surfaces. Through an analysis of touchscreen measures, they identified individual differences in key centroids and hit point deviations (i.e. x and y offsets of touch gestures with regards to individual keys). Later, they proposed personalized keyboards that could adapt to individual typing patterns and improve entry rates [6]. Guerreiro et al. [7] applied similar touch measures to investigate tablet text-entry behaviors of blind users with one- and two-handed input. While the text input performance metrics revealed no statistical difference between conditions, using the x, y offsets of the initial touch down positions, the authors uncovered that users landed closer to intended keys with two-handed input. Furthermore, when measuring movement distances of non-visual exploration, participants using two hands performed more efficient paths through the keyboard. The authors leveraged the fact that non-visual touchscreen interactions result in gestures with periods of continuous movement and traces through the interface, opposed to the discrete point interactions of sighted users.

While using movement measures is uncommon when analyzing text input, they are well established within cursor movement research. MacKenzie et al. [12], proposed seven accuracy measurements to understand users' behaviors with pointing devices. Included in these were path analysis measurements, such as target re-entries, task axis crossing, movement direction and orthogonal direction change. The authors also proposed continuous measures such as movement variability, errors and offsets. Hwang et al. [9] believed analysis of submovements within pointing device selections could reveal new insights into the challenges faced by motor-impaired users. To understand individual differences between motor-impaired users' cursor movements Hwang et al. proposed analyzing the number and duration of pauses, verification times, submovements within the intended target, target slips, and velocity profile of movements.

In this paper, we extend on existing text-input analysis techniques and propose the inclusion of discrete and continuous touch movement measurements to better understand touchscreen text input behaviors of blind users.

4. LONGITUDINAL USER STUDY

Prior research investigating non-visual text-entry on mobile devices has merely reported on the overall text input performance measurements, failing to examine the underlying characteristics of users' typing behaviors. We believe that a detailed analysis of text-input, using the proposed touch measurements, are key to expose the challenges faced by novice blind users. Our ultimate goal is to identify new opportunities to reduce the learning overhead and support better non-visual input on mobile touchscreen devices. In order to achieve these goals, we conducted a longitudinal study with blind novice smartphone users. Participants were each provided with a mobile device preloaded with our data collection tool and asked to use the device as their primary phone for eight weeks. Due to the ethically sensitive nature of the research, no participants were asked to consent to their data being shared beyond the research group and as such supporting data cannot be made openly available.

4.1 Participants

We recruited five participants with visual impairments, four males and one female, from a local training institution for blind people. Participants' age ranged from 23 to 55 (M=37.2, SD=15.2) years old, and all participants were legally blind as defined within our IRB approved recruitment criteria. They were experienced desktop screen reader users. However, none owned a smartphone or had prior experience with touchscreen screen readers.

4.2 Procedure

Our study was designed to capture the progression of typing performance of novice users. Prior laboratory studies of longitudinal text-entry evaluations report using seven sessions with noticeable improvements [1]. Thus, we decided that eight weeks (weekly sessions) would be sufficient to observe comparable progression. The user study consisted of two components: in-situ usage and weekly laboratory assessments.

4.2.1 In-Situ Device Usage

Our goal was to collect everyday text-entry usage by novice blind users. Participants received basic training on how to use a virtual keyboard. We did not define, incentivize or force usage protocols.

Instead, we developed a data collection framework that ran as a background service on their smartphones and collected usage measures, i.e. *time spent using applications* and *number of keystrokes entered*. Previously, Evans and Wobbrock [4] demonstrated that it is possible to obtain text-entry performance measurements (speed and errors) from everyday computer usage. However, analysis of everyday mobile typing performance is out with the scope of this paper – in-situ data will be used to give context of the device usage for individual participants and support the analysis of our weekly laboratory text-entry evaluations.

4.2.2 Weekly Lab Text-Entry Evaluations

Participants met with the researchers weekly, for eight weeks, and performed 20 minutes of text-entry trials. Each trial contained one sentence comprised of five words, with an average size of 5 characters, and a minimum correlation with language of 0.97. We developed an experimental application that would select the trial sentences from a written language corpus. The application randomly selected the sentences for the session to avoid order effects and captured transcribed sentences and completion times. The experimental application started the trial by reading the target sentence aloud via the device's TTS (Text-to-Speech engine). Upon finishing each sentence, participants pressed the return key twice to advance to the next trial. They were encouraged to type as accurately and quickly as possible. We used an unconstrained text-entry protocol [27], where participants were free to correct any errors they encountered. To ensure that participants would not practice the trials outside the laboratory evaluations, the application was installed on the participants' device at the beginning of each session, and uninstalled at the end. Automatic correction and cursor movement operations were not used during the trials.

Our study was carried out in Portuguese, as such there are a number of letters that are uncommon in the written language, and therefore do not appear within our trial sentences (e.g. W and Y). Subsequently, these keys will contain no examples of intended interactions within our evaluation.

4.3 Apparatus

Participants were each provided with a *Samsung S3 Mini* touchscreen smartphone, running Android 4.1 operating system. We enabled the *Talkback* screen reader and pre-installed our data collection service, TinyBlackBox (TBB). TBB was designed to constantly run in the background, capturing users' interactions with the device. This approach enabled us to capture text-entry usage data throughout the eight-week period.

The S3 Mini default input method was Samsung's own Android QWERTY keyboard. Although visually the keys have both horizontal and vertical spacing, when *Talkback* is enabled and the participants touch the screen, they receive feedback for the nearest key to their touch point. However, when moving from one key to another, the key with current focus occupies the spacing. This means that target boundaries can grow and shrink based on the exploration paths. S3 Mini's default keyboard was used throughout our study, both in laboratory evaluations and in-situ.

4.4 Dependent Measures

Text-entry performance was measured by analyzing trials' input stream [27]. We report on words per minute (WPM), total error rates, uncorrected error rates, and corrected error rates. Moreover, we investigate character-level errors and types of errors (substitutions – incorrect characters, insertions – added characters, and omissions – omitted characters). Touch exploration behaviors were measured using x, y positions and variability [5] (hit point deviations), movement time, movement distances, Path Length to Task Axis length ratio (PL/TA), count and duration of pauses within the movements [9, 10, 12], and visited keys.

4.5 Design and Analysis

We performed Shapiro-Wilk tests on all dependent measures. For normally distributed values we used a mixed-effects model analysis of variance [15]. Mixed-effects models extend repeated measures models, such as ANOVAs, to allow unequal number of repetitions; that is, unbalance data such as ours, where we have different numbers of trials per week for each participant. We modeled *Week* as a fixed effect and *Trial* was included as a nested factor within *Week*. In addition, *Participant* and the interaction between *Participant* and *In-Situ Usage Time* were modeled as random effects to account for correlated measurements within subjects over time [24].

For the measures that were not normally distributed, we applied $\log_e$ or $\log_{10}$ transforms [2], which resulted in normally distributed measures [Shapiro-Wilk $p>.05$]. We then used the mixed-effects model terms previously described for further analysis.

5. RESULTS

Our goal is to characterize novice blind users' text-entry performance and learning when using *Explore by Touch*. We describe participants' in-situ usage and relate it with text-entry performance. We analyze input speed, accuracy, and character-level errors over an eight-week period. Finally, we characterize users' touch exploration behaviors and provide insights on *how* and *why* input performance changes over time.

5.1 In-Situ Usage

Table 1 and Table 2 summarize the number of characters entered and time spent typing, respectively.

Table 1. Characters entered in-situ. Columns represent weeks.

	1	2	3	4	5	6	7	8
P1	245	405	555	678	799	133	732	1292
P2	1283	648	1548	5396	1248	411	2120	208
P3	75	697	579	1115	310	1205	1	447
P4	1002	1022	566	601	2435	603	2578	1099
P5	32	45	22	21	12	24	189	383

Table 2. Time spent typing in-situ (minutes).

	1	2	3	4	5	6	7	8
P1	66.2	62	46.6	54.6	101	26.7	46.5	85.9
P2	180	53.6	98.7	383	92.8	29.8	149	12.3
P3	1.78	85.8	99.1	170	40.7	131	0	57.7
P4	160	196	43	36.5	127	36.5	201	91
P5	5.25	3.7	7.4	1.5	0.45	1.17	15.2	65.3

Participants entered a total of 32,764 characters over eight weeks. They spent a total of 51 hours actively entering text. Generally, the number of characters entered is directly related with time spent. However, there is a high variance in usage results both between participants and weeks. For instance, while P2 and P3 were particularly active in the fourth week, others such as P4 were more active in the last two weeks. P5 was the least active with an average usage of 12.5 minutes (SD=20) per week. On the other hand P2 and P4 spent on average 125 (SD=110) and 111 (SD=65) minutes typing per week. Although analysis of in-situ performance measures is out of the scope of this paper, we will leverage usage data to control for performance improvements in all statistical analysis.

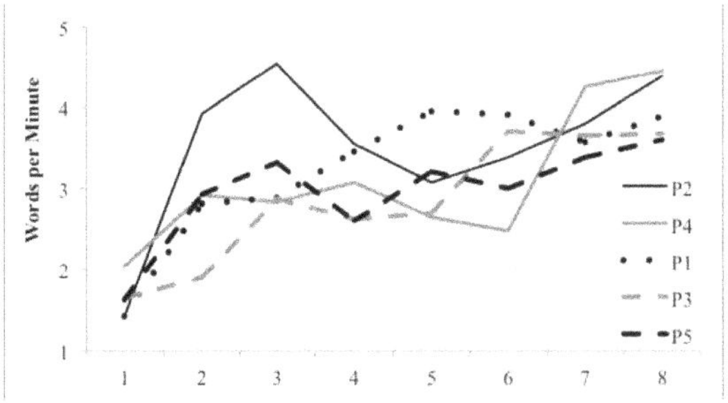

Figure 2. Words per minute over 8 weeks.

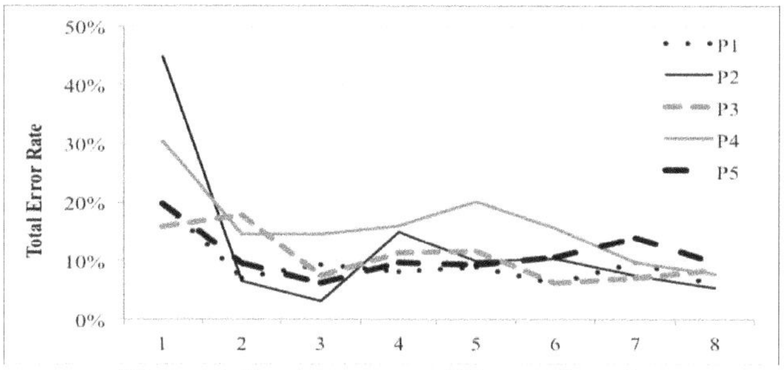

Figure 3. Total error rate (%) over 8 weeks.

5.2 Text-Entry Performance

In total, participants produced 11,560 characters from which 1,323 were backspaces, resulting in 10,237 transcribed characters. In this section we thoroughly analyze input performance regarding speed and accuracy over an eight-week period.

5.2.1 Input Speed

To assess input speed, we used the words per minute (WPM) measure calculated as (length of transcribed text – 1) * (60 seconds / trial time in seconds) / (5 characters per word).

Slow learning rate. Participants improved on average 2.4 wpm (SD=.36) from week one with 1.6 wpm (SD=.23) to 4 wpm (SD=.35) after eight weeks. We found a significant effect of *Week* on *WPM* [$F_{1,7}$=12.329, $p<.001$] as all participants improved over time. Nevertheless, considering that participants were familiar with QWERTY keyboards, learning rates are still low with an average improvement of 0.3 wpm per week.

Still improving after eight weeks. Figure 2 shows WPM graphed over eight weeks. We can see that participants are still improving input speeds at the end of the user study. Fitting power laws [25] to entry rates and extrapolating to twice the weeks gives an average entry speed of 5 wpm in week 16th.

External factors can negatively influence performance. We can also notice that P2 and P4 have atypical changes in performance in week four and seven, respectively. When debriefing P2 about this sudden drop in performance, she mentioned perceiving the speech feedback being slower while typing after installing a 3rd party app, *WhatsApp*. In fact, this is a known issue with this particular application. Although we are not able to confirm that speech feedback changed, we can show that both number of pauses and duration of pauses during movement, increased from week 3 to week 5, while movement speed and distance traveled decreased in the same time period (see Section 5.4). This suggests that external factors had an influence in this participant's typing behavior (e.g., other apps or emotional issues).

In-situ usage improves performance. Regarding P4, the abrupt increase in input speed is most likely related with the increase of usage in week seven (see Tables Table 1 and Table 2). After debriefing P4 in that week, he mentioned that he was finally using his phone to the fullest, particularly sending and receiving text messages. He stated "*... the phone is finally fully accessible to me, I can send SMS, I can send text messages via Skype, I can send all the messages that I want*". Therefore, we believe the sudden increase in input speed is due to his increase in usage of messaging applications. In fact, we found a significant medium size effect between *Input Speed* and *In-Situ Usage time* [Pearson's $r_{(290)}$=.353, $p<.001$].

5.2.2 Input Accuracy

In order to analyze input accuracy, we calculated: 1) uncorrected - erroneous characters in the final transcribed sentence, 2) corrected - erased characters that were erroneous, and 3) total error rates - erroneous characters that were entered (even those that were corrected) [27].

Total error rates tend to 7.4%. P2 achieved the highest total error rate of 45% on week 1 and finished the user study with the lowest rate of 5.4% by week 8. Overall participants started with an average total error rate of 26% (SD=11.7%) and finished with 7.4% (SD=1.7%) [$F_{1,7}$=4.176, $p<.001$]. Moreover, Figure 3 shows that error rates start to stabilize around that value.

Errors are usually corrected. Table 3 shows the uncorrected error rates for each participants and week. Overall, when given the chance, users tend to correct most errors, resulting in high quality transcribed sentences. This goes in line with previous findings for sighted users [21]. For instance, P1 and P2 had the lowest uncorrected error rates with 0% and 0.3% by week 8. On average, participants left only 1.6% (SD=1.4%) errors in the transcribed sentences by week 8, which resulted in a significant effect of *Week* [$F_{1,7}$=2.306, $p<.05$].

Table 3. Unc. error rates (%). Columns represent weeks.

	1	2	3	4	5	6	7	8
P1	4	0.4	1.9	1.4	2.3	0.3	2.6	0
P2	1	1	0.3	0	0	0	1.5	0.3
P3	7.6	8.5	3.4	4.1	0.5	2.8	1.9	2.5
P4	20	4.7	5.2	6.3	7.8	3.2	3.2	1.9
P5	11	5.6	4.3	5.3	5.3	2.3	5.1	3.3

Table 4. Corrected error rate (%). Higher is better.

	1	2	3	4	5	6	7	8
P1	74	77	63	89	81	81	77	91
P2	87	55	73	89	84	91	85	68
P3	62	50	41	72	50	46	71	57
P4	69	81	69	68	71	56	62	60
P5	86	100	60	50	92	86	89	88

23-39% of deletions were inefficient. Corrected error rates illustrates the amount of effective *"fixing"* and allows to answer the question "of the erased characters, what percentage were erroneous?" High rate means that most of erased characters were errors and should have been corrected. Participants achieved average corrected error rates between 61% (SD=12%, week 3) and 77% (SD=11%, week 7), which means that 23% to 39% of deleted characters had been correctly entered. This occurs because errors are not immediately recognized. For instance, when phonetically similar characters are entered (e.g. N→M), users only notice that mistake when the word is read aloud. To fix the error, several characters, including correct characters, are usually deleted. A detailed inspection of logs files shows that editing operations, such as cursor movement, were never used. Average corrected error rate per week is 73%, which remains fairly constant throughout the eight weeks [$F_{1,7}$=.98, p=.447].

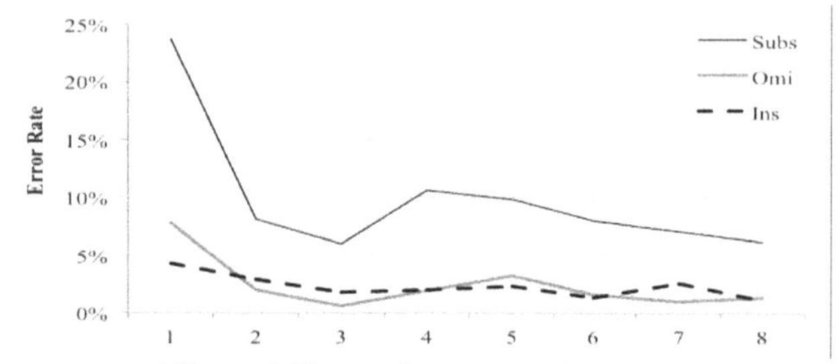

Figure 4. Types of error over 8 weeks.

13% of time is spent correcting errors. The time spent correcting errors is subsumed by input speed (see Section 5.2.1); however, such analysis does not provide insights on the cost of such corrections. Examining correcting actions shows that participants spent on average 32% (SD=17%, MIN=19% [P5], MAX=65% [P2]) of their time correcting text in the first week. Performance significantly improved over time and by week eight only 13% (SD=1.8%) of time was spent in this task [$F_{1,7}$=4.806, p<.001].

5.3 Character-Level Errors

In this section, we present a fine grained analysis by categorizing types of input errors: insertions, substitutions, and omissions [14]. We report aggregate measures, which represent the method's accuracy over all entered characters, but also at the level of individual letters [27]. These findings can help designers in addressing specific types of errors and characters.

Substitutions are the most common type of error. Figure 4 illustrates the types of errors over the eight-week period. Substitution errors were consistently higher than insertions and omissions. Although there was a significant decrease in substitution error rates over time, from 24% (SD=12%) to 6% (SD=1%) [$F_{1,7}$=3.518, p<.005], they still remain significantly higher than the remaining types of errors [$F_{2,8}$=125.321, p<.001]. In fact, substitution error rate is higher than omissions and insertions combined. This result holds true for all participants.

Similar substitution rates across keys. Overall, participants had similar error rates across all intended keys. No row, column, or side patterns emerged from weekly data. Moreover, keys near edges had similar accuracy rates to those in the center (Figure 5).

No clear substitution pattern. To analyze the most common substitution errors, we created confusion matrices. In week eight, some of the most common substitutions were Q→E (33%), B→H (17%), P→O (9%), P→L (4%), R→T (4%). Unlike sighted users that experience substitution patterns towards a predominant direction [5, 17], blind users' patterns are less clear. This is most likely related with the differences between visual and auditory feedback when acquiring keys. Further discussion on this topic is available in Section 5.4.

Adjacent phonetically similar characters promote substitutions. Since feedback is solely auditory, phonetically similar characters have the potential to be confused when blind users are exploring the keyboard. In the Portuguese language, particularly when using Android's Text-to-Speech engine, there are three cases prone to confusions: I-E, O-U, and M-N. For I-E substitution error rates are constantly low over time (0-1%) and inexistent from week five. Regarding O-U substitutions, error rates are slightly higher with 8.5% in week one and decreasing to 0.5% in week eight. Finally, concerning M-N substitutions, error rates remain between 3% (week one-three) and 6.5% (week five) across the eight-week time period. Indeed, in week eight, error rates are still 4.5%. No other adjacent pair of letters obtained such a consistently high (and symmetrical) error rate over time. These results suggest that phonetically similar letters that are close together have higher probability of being substituted.

68% of omission errors are left uncorrected. Omission error rates decreased 6.5% from week one (M=8% SD=6%) to week eight (M=1% SD=0.7%) [$F_{1,7}$=3.858, p<.005]. Unlike substitutions, the majority of omission errors are not corrected. On average 68% (SD=14%) of errors are left uncorrected. These errors are usually described as cognitive errors [11]. A common explanation is misspellings or users forgetting to type certain letters. However, leaving errors uncorrected may also be related with (lack of) feedback after an attempt to enter a character, confirming that an input action had a consequence. This option seems less likely since users received feedback after each character entry. Although omissions only account for 2.4% of errors (see Figure 4), they are the least likely to be corrected.

5.4 Touch Exploration Behaviors

In this section we provide new insights on participants' touch exploration behaviors. We examine the three stages that compose a key selection: touching the screen, moving the finger to find the intended key, and lifting the finger. For this analysis, we removed outlying points where the entered key (on lift) was more than one key distance away from the intended key in either x or y direction to account for transposition or misspelling errors.

5.4.1 Hit Point Analysis

Hit points correspond to landing positions. It is noteworthy that at this point, users do not have any feedback about the key they will land on. Unlike input from sighted users, which aims towards visual stimuli, blind users solely resort to their spatial model of the keyboard and some physical affordances (e.g. device size).

Users land on intended keys nearly half the times. By week eight, 48% (SD=12%) of key presses landed within the boundaries of intended targets. This number may seem low, but it is not unexpected given that participants did not receive any auditory feedback until this point. Nevertheless, performance significant increased from week one (M=27%, SD=15) to week eight [$F_{7,28}$=5.222, p<.01], showing that users gain a better spatial model of the keyboard. We found that at week eight, 91% (SD=5%) of the times, participants land either inside the intended key or an adjacent key. Also, landing on the correct row (M=78%, SD=7%) is easier than landing on the correct column (M=59%, SD=11%) [$F_{1,4}$=27.611, p<.01], which is not surprising given that rows make larger targets than columns.

Keys near physical edges are easier hit. Throughout the eight-week period, keys that were positioned on physical edges were easier to land on. For instance, in week eight, participants correctly landed on characters A and Q in 75% and 71% of times, respectively. On the other hand, characters such as B or M were only correctly hit 14% and 16%, respectively. The space bar consistently outperformed the remaining keys (week eight M=99%), most likely due to a combination of its positioning (on the bottom edge) and width (five times larger).

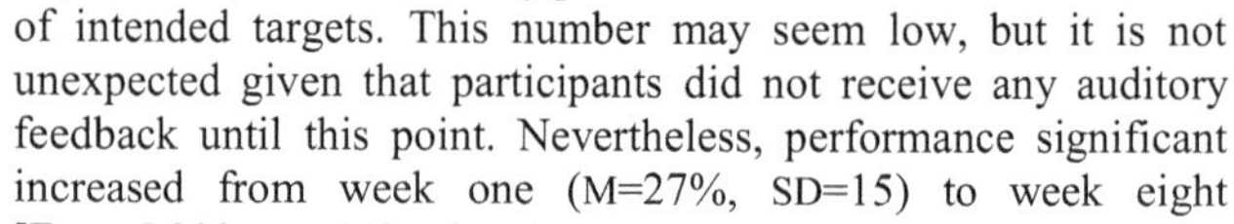

Figure 5. Substitution error rates per key. Gray keys were not used in the trials. Darker colors indicate higher error rates. Left - week 2, Right - week 8.

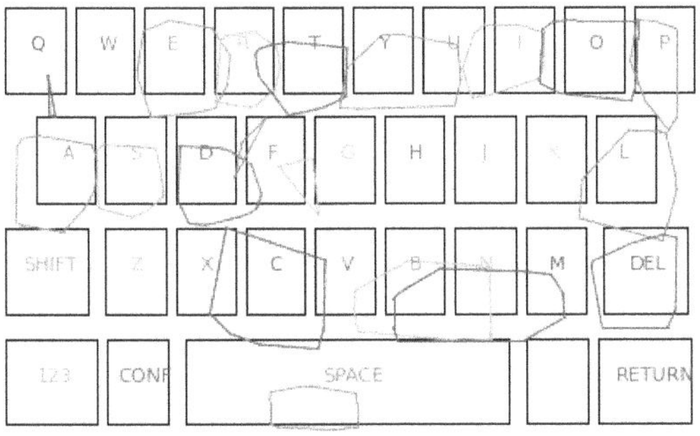

Figure 6. Polygons encompass hit points within a standard deviation of key centroid.

Emergent keyboard is shifted towards the bottom and most key overlaps are horizontal. We examined the emerging key shapes and sizes using hit points. Figure 6 illustrates the emergent keyboard for week eight; that is, the keyboard layout that results from participants' touches. In week one, the key sizes are larger and shifted towards the center of the screen, where users started their exploration, which resulted in larger overlaps between keys. By week eight, participants are able to land nearer to keys; however, there are still significant overlaps, mostly horizontally. Characters M and N are particularly interesting, since they present the largest overlap (Figure 6). Also, we can see that hit points tend to occur below the center of the intended target.

5.4.2 Movement Analysis

Previous research has investigated text-entry performance by blind users. However, analyses tend to focus on performance measures, such as time and errors. In this section, we aim to establish *why* performance improvements occur by conducting a thorough analysis of touch exploration behaviors.

Users visit on average one extra key. In the first week, the average number of visited keys per keystroke was 4.9 (SD=1.9). Participants significantly improved their performance achieving an average of 2 visited keys (SD=0.3) by week eight [$F_{7,28}$=5.133, p<.001]. Similarly, the number of target re-entries (entering the same target for the second time) also improved from 6.6 (SD=3.2) to 0.8 (SD=0.3) [$F_{7,28}$=7.498, p<.001]. This corresponds to an average of 49 traveled pixels (SD=11), where 60% of movement is done in the x-axis, which is consistent with previous results where users are more likely to land on the intended row and then perform horizontal movements.

Users learn how to perform more efficient explorations. In order to understand exploration efficiency, we calculated the Path Length (movement distance) to Task Axis length (Euclidean distance between hit point and center of target) ratio. Participants significantly improved over time from 3.6 (SD=1.3) to 0.95 (SD=0.15) [$F_{7,28}$=6.033, p<.001]. Notice that we obtained an average ratio below 1 because the Task Axis length is the distance to the center of the target. Users only require traveling to the edge of the target in order to select the key.

Keystroke time is on average 1.9 seconds. In line with previous

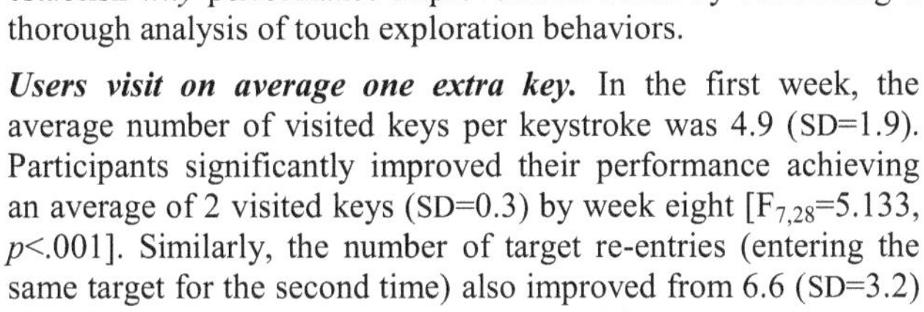

Figure 7. A circle indicates a pause; size represents its duration. Left - week 1 for P1, Right - week 8 for P1.

touch measures, movement times also improved from 4.1 seconds (SD=1.4) to 1.9 seconds (SD=0.3) [$F_{7,28}$=5.424, p<.001]. This value may seem high, but it is expected since users need to wait for auditory feedback to confirm which letter they are touching. As a consequence, entry times are directly related to speech rate and delay. Figure 7 illustrates P1's dwell times in week one and eight. Longer pauses are clearly visible in the first week. Also, because feedback is received when entering keys, pauses often occur near their edges.

Keys near physical edges require less time to press but do not result in lower error rates. We found significant differences between keys located near the device's edge, such as Q, A, P, and L, and all other keys regarding movement time [week eight, Z=2.032, p<.05]. Nevertheless, this difference does not result in accuracy improvements. In fact, border keys have a slightly higher substitution rate (week eight, 7% vs. 5.4%, n.s.).

Insertion errors have smaller movement times and distances. Insertion errors are related to unintentionally and accidentally entered characters. Knowing how to filter these keystrokes can result in performance improvements. When analyzing movement times and distances, we found significant differences between correct entries and insertion errors [$F_{1,4}$=23.287, p<.01; $F_{1,4}$=24.119, p<.01] throughout the eight-week period. These results suggest that touch data can be used to classify insertions.

5.4.3 Lift Point Analysis

Where hit point and movement analysis examined where users land on the screen and how they explore the keyboard, respectively, an examination of lift point allows us to understand the final step of selecting a key. It is particularly relevant to understand in what conditions substitution errors occur.

Lift points are spread-out over keys' boundaries. Figure 1 illustrates all lift points for week eight. Data shows that points are spread over intended keys and particularly close to their edges. Unlike sighted users [5, 17, 18], there is not a clear touch offset direction, which can have significant implications when building touch models for this user group. Moreover, hit point deviations (standard deviations) remain unchanged across time with 25.6px in week one and 24.3px in week eight, which is approximately half the size of a key. This suggests that users may be prone to slip errors; that is, slipping to a nearby key just before selecting it.

There is more to substitution errors than slips. We classified as finger slips all entries where the last visited key was the intended target. Although we are not applying a time threshold, this measure gives us all entries that need to be considered as slip errors. Overall, in week one 37.5% (SD=17%) of substitution errors were slips. In week eight we obtained a similar value of 38.4% (SD=12%) [$F_{1,7}$=2.095, p>.05]. Notice that slip errors account for less than 50% of substitution errors by week eight. Taking into account that users should receive speech feedback before selecting the intended key, we analyzed whether participants' finger paths crossed it at some point during movement. In week eight, for 64% (SD=9.8%) of substitution errors, participants were inside the boundaries of the target at some point in their touch paths; however, failed to select it in a timely manner. After identifying some of the instances where these errors occurred, we conducted a manual examination of the recorded videos. We noticed that most of the cases were related to a significant delay between speech feedback, which resulted in a mismatch between the key being heard and touched at that moment. Participants tried to compensate for this delay by performing corrective movements, but often resulted in entering the incorrect key. Further research should explore this issue by investigating the effect of auditory delay on input accuracy.

For some substitutions, intended keys are not even visited. According to the results described above, in week eight there are still 36% of substitutions where participants do not even visited the key they were aiming for. This means that they performed a selection without hearing the intended key. From visual inspection of individual keystrokes' movements, we derived several reasons for this behavior: *1) Accidental touches* – similarly to insertion errors, participants unintentionally touch the keyboard close to the intended character. These keystrokes are short in distance and time. *2) Phonetically similar keys* – this happens when users cross a key that sounds similar to the intended character (e.g. while aiming for M, the user lands on B, moves to the right, enters N, and lifts the finger), resulting in a substitution error. *3) Overconfidence on spatial model* – in some substitution instances it seems that participants overly rely on their spatial understanding of the keyboard by performing a gesture and selecting a key without waiting for feedback. Lastly, *4) Feeling lost and giving up* – some exploration paths show fine-grain movements near the intended key, going back and forth; however, participants never hit the intended character.

6. DISCUSSION

In this section we describe major results, implications for future design of virtual keyboards, and limitations of our work.

Summary of Major Results

Participants achieve an *average typing speed* of 4 WPM and 4.7% total error rate after eight weeks of usage. Although performance was still improving in the last week, *learning rate was slow* (0.3 WPM per week). Previous research has shown similar results when analyzing overall typing performance [1]. An open question until now was: why and how did users improved typing performance? Overall participants seem to gain a better spatial model of the keyboard by *landing closer to targets*, performing more *time- and movement-efficient paths* towards intended targets, and *less target re-entries*, which resulted in lower number of pauses to hear auditory feedback.

Character-level analysis revealed that most erroneous characters are *substitutions*. However, in contrast with sighted typing patterns, results do not show a clear offset pattern. Instead, touch *points are scattered over intended keys* and particularly near edges. Substitution errors can have different causes and *slip errors* only account for about 38% of these cases. One would assume that participants would only lift their fingers once they hear the intended key; however, by week eight, this is not the case for 36% of substitutions errors.

Finally, participants naturally correct the overwhelming majority of errors (98.4%), which corresponds to about *13% of their typing time*. Moreover, one third of corrections are *counterproductive* as users delete correct characters.

Implications for Design

Easier, effective, and efficient correction. Corrections are still time consuming and inefficient. None of our participants used cursor-positioning operations throughout the study. It seems that these actions are only expected to be used by expert typists, preventing novice users to do fine-grain corrections. Also, participants did not use auto-correct or auto-complete solutions, although these have great potential to be used in non-visual text-entry to correct missed errors (such as omissions) and improve typing speeds.

Synchronize speech output with touch input. Results suggest that 64% of substitution errors can be due to a mismatch between speech output and touch information. Future non-visual keyboards should prioritize synchronization between input and output modalities.

Filter unintentionally added characters. Accidental touches originate substitution and insertion errors, which in turn take time to correct. However, most of these errors can be filtered out by monitoring movement's time and distance, since they are significantly shorter than correct entries.

Use language-based solutions. The majority of omission errors (68%) go by undetected and therefore uncorrected. Language-based solutions such as spellcheckers seem to be the only plausible solution. Nevertheless, mainstream auto-correct approaches should also be able to deal with some substitution errors. Current algorithms usually weight word corrections by keyboard distance. Although blind users do not show a predominant touch offset direction, most substitution errors were adjacent keys.

Leverage land-on and movement information. Non-visual typing comprises much more than just lift positions. Movement data can provide evidence of what particular key users are trying to select. Future key recognizers should leverage this information and try to predict the most probable targets (see [20, 26] for pointing prediction). This information could be used with language models to narrow the search space of word-corrections or provide character suggestions when users delete a letter.

Touch models need to adapt to expertise. Leveraging movement data is particularly relevant on early stages of learning when users perform longer exploration paths. While expert users may land on the intended target most of the times, novice users still need to search for the intended key and wait for auditory feedback. Therefore, touch models need to be able to adapt to different typing behaviors (i.e. abilities) and learning rates.

Limitations

Our participants only included five novice blind users. Although this is a small number of participants they represent a crucial user group when the goal is to designing easy-to-use solutions and identify challenges with current virtual keyboards. Although typing performance and touch behaviors can be significantly different for expert users, the derived implications may still apply. For instance, using more efficient correction strategies or language-based solutions can further improve experts' typing performance. Further research should replicate the analysis reported in the paper with more experienced blind typists in order to examine character-level errors and touch movement behaviors.

Finally, in this user study participants were allowed to use their device in-the-wild. Although we were able to control for device usage in our analysis, our weekly laboratory assessments may have influenced learning results. Thus, it is likely that reported weekly performance may not represent a truly natural learning experience; however, it surely represents the challenges users face while learning to type on virtual keyboards.

7. CONCLUSION AND FUTURE WORK

We have investigated the unconstrained typing performance and touch exploration behaviors of 5 novice blind users over the course of an eight-week period. Results show that users improve both entry speed and accuracy, although at slow rate. Improvements are mostly due to a combination of factors, such as landing closer to intended keys, performing more efficient keyboard explorations, lower number of target re-entries, and lower movement times. By week eight, users land inside the intended key or adjacent keys 91% of the time. The most common error type is a substitution. Regarding correction strategies, users correct most of typing errors, which consumes on average 13% of input time. Overall, we provide a thorough examination on how blind users type using a virtual keyboard. Future work should apply the design implications that emerged from our results and develop new solutions to improve typing performance.

8. ACKNOWLEDGMENTS

We thank all participants from Fundação Raquel e Martin Sain in Lisbon. This work was partially supported by: RIT's Center for Accessibility and Inclusion Research, RCUK (EP/G066019/1), and FCT (SFRH/BD/103935/2014, UID/CEC/00408/2013).

9. REFERENCES

[1] Azenkot S. et al. 2012. Input Finger Detection for nonvisual touch screen text entry in Perkinput. *Proceedings of Graphics Interface (GI '12)* (2012).

[2] Berry, D.A. 1987. Logarithmic transformations in ANOVA. *Biometrics*. (1987), 439–456.

[3] Bonner, M. et al. 2010. No-Look Notes: Accessible eyes-free multi-touch text entry. *Pervasive Computing*. (2010), 409–426.

[4] Evans, A. and Wobbrock, J. 2012. Taming wild behavior: the input observer for obtaining text entry and mouse pointing measures from everyday computer use. *Proceedings of the SIGCHI conference on human factors in computing systems* (2012), 1947–1956.

[5] Findlater, L. et al. 2011. Typing on flat glass: examining ten-finger expert typing patterns on touch surfaces. *Proceedings of the 2011 annual conference on Human factors in computing systems* (2011), 2453–2462.

[6] Findlater, L. and Wobbrock, J.O. 2012. Personalized Input: Improving Ten-Finger Touchscreen Typing through Automatic Adaptation. *Proceedings of the 2012 annual conference on human factors in computing systems (CHI'12)*. (2012).

[7] Guerreiro, J. et al. 2015. TabLETS Get Physical: Non-Visual Text Entry on Tablet Devices. *Proceedings of the SIGCHI Conference on Human Factors in Computing Systems* (2015).

[8] Guerreiro, T. et al. 2008. From tapping to touching: Making touch screens accessible to blind users. *IEEE MultiMedia*. (2008), 48–50.

[9] Hwang, F. et al. 2004. Mouse movements of motion-impaired users: a submovement analysis. *Proceedings of the 6th international ACM SIGACCESS conference on Computers and accessibility* (New York, NY, USA, 2004), 102–109.

[10] Keates, S. and Trewin, S. 2005. Effect of age and Parkinson's disease on cursor positioning using a mouse. *Proceedings of the 7th international ACM SIGACCESS conference on Computers and accessibility* (2005), 68–75.

[11] Kristensson, P.O. 2009. Five challenges for intelligent text entry methods. *AI Magazine*. 30, 4 (2009), 85.

[12] MacKenzie, I.S. et al. 2001. Accuracy measures for evaluating computer pointing devices. *Proceedings of the SIGCHI conference on Human factors in computing systems* (2001), 9–16.

[13] MacKenzie, I.S. and Soukoreff, R.W. 2002. A character-level error analysis technique for evaluating text entry methods. *Proceedings of the second Nordic conference on Human-computer interaction* (2002), 243–246.

[14] MacKenzie, I.S. and Soukoreff, R.W. 2002. Text entry for mobile computing: Models and methods, theory and practice. *Human--Computer Interaction*. 17, 2 (2002), 147–198.

[15] McCulloch, C.E. and Neuhaus, J.M. 2001. *Generalized linear mixed models*. Wiley Online Library.

[16] Nicolau, H. et al. 2014. B#: Chord-based Correction for Multitouch Braille Input. *Proceedings of the SIGCHI Conference on Human Factors in Computing Systems* (New York, NY, USA, 2014), 1705–1708.

[17] Nicolau, H. and Jorge, J. 2012. Elderly Text-Entry Performance on Touchscreens. *Proceedings of the 14th international ACM SIGACCESS conference on Computers and accessibility* (2012).

[18] Nicolau, H. and Jorge, J. 2012. Touch typing using thumbs: understanding the effect of mobility and hand posture. *Proceedings of the 2012 ACM annual conference on Human Factors in Computing Systems*, 2683–2686.

[19] Oliveira, J. et al. 2011. Blind people and mobile touch-based text-entry: acknowledging the need for different flavors. *The proceedings of the 13th international ACM SIGACCESS conference on Computers and accessibility* (2011), 179–186.

[20] Pasqual, P.T. and Wobbrock, J.O. 2014. Mouse pointing endpoint prediction using kinematic template matching. *Proceedings of the 32nd annual ACM conference on Human factors in computing systems* (2014), 743–752.

[21] Soukoreff, R.W. and MacKenzie, I.S. 2003. Metrics for text entry research: an evaluation of MSD and KSPC, and a new unified error metric. *Proceedings of the SIGCHI conference on Human factors in computing systems* (2003), 113–120.

[22] Southern, C. et al. 2012. An Evaluation of BrailleTouch: Mobile Touchscreen Text Entry for the Visually Impaired. *Proceedings of the 14th International Conference on Human-computer Interaction with Mobile Devices and Services* (New York, NY, USA, 2012), 317–326.

[23] Tinwala, H. and MacKenzie, I.S. 2010. Eyes-free text entry with error correction on touchscreen mobile devices. *Proceedings of the 6th Nordi CHI* (2010), 511–520.

[24] Verbeke, G. and Molenberghs, G. 2009. *Linear mixed models for longitudinal data*. Springer Science & Business Media.

[25] Wobbrock, J.O. 2007. Text Entry Systems: Mobility, Accessibility, Universality. I.S. MacKenzie and K. Tanaka-Ishii, eds. San Francisco: Morgan Kaufmann. 47–74.

[26] Wobbrock, J.O. et al. 2009. The angle mouse: target-agnostic dynamic gain adjustment based on angular deviation. *Proceedings of the SIGCHI Conference on Human Factors in Computing Systems* (2009), 1401–1410.

[27] Wobbrock, J.O. and Myers, B.A. 2006. Analyzing the input stream for character- level errors in unconstrained text entry evaluations. *ACM TOCHI,* 13, 4 (2006), 458–489.

[28] Yfantidis, G. and Evreinov, G. 2006. Adaptive blind interaction technique for touchscreens. *Universal Access in the Information Society*. 4, 4 (2006), 328–337.

Inclusion and Education: 3D Printing for Integrated Classrooms

Erin Buehler William Easley Samantha McDonald Niara Comrie Amy Hurst
University of Maryland, Baltimore County
Information Systems Department
{eri4, easley1, sam30, cniara1, amyhurst}@umbc.edu

ABSTRACT
Over 60% of adults with intellectual disabilities (ID) in the U.S. are unemployed; this is more than twice the unemployment rate of the general population [19]. Of the adults with ID who are employed, only half receive competitive wages alongside co-workers without disabilities. While the enactment of IDEA [20] has helped to promote access to education for people with ID and other disabilities, there are still obstacles to employment. Misconceptions about ability and lack of opportunities to learn and practice employability skills contribute to this problem.

Our research explores employability and integration through the lens of 3D printing, an innovative technology touted as a means to self-employment. We successfully taught young adults with intellectual disabilities many technical skills required for 3D printing through an integrated, post-secondary course on 3D printing for entrepreneurship. In this paper we report on our methods for designing this course and discuss the benefits, challenges, and strategies for teaching 3D printing to an integrated cohort of students. We offer recommendations for educators and describe technology obstacles unique to this user demographic, and the impact of integrated, postsecondary courses on employment outcomes for students with ID.

Categories and Subject Descriptors
K.4.2 [**Computers and Society**]: Social Issues – *Assistive technologies for persons with disabilities.*

General Terms

Design, Human Factors.

Keywords
3D Modeling, 3D Printing, Cognitive Impairment, Disability, Education, Intellectual Disability, Special Education.

1. INTRODUCTION
In the U.S., intellectual disability (ID) affects 1% of the population (3,000,000+). As defined by the American Association on Intellectual and Developmental Disabilities, ID is characterized by "... significant limitations in both intellectual functioning and in adaptive behavior..." onset before the age of 18 [1]. People with ID generally have an IQ below 70 and struggle with conceptual, social, and practical skills. Similar to persons with other forms of cognitive impairment, these individuals can learn and apply new skills with appropriate support and training. Despite this fact, approximately two-thirds of adults with ID are unemployed. Legislation such as the IDEA and ADA are intended to combat prejudices and promote access to education and employment, but full compliance with these acts has been a slow, laborious process. Our research explores the social, educational, and technological features of this issue via a case study set in a college classroom hosting students with and without ID.

ASSETS '15, October 26-28, 2015, Lisbon, Portugal
© 2015 ACM. ISBN 978-1-4503-3400-6/15/10 $15.00
DOI: http://dx.doi.org/10.1145/2700648.2809844.

Figure 1. Students work in pairs drawing concepts for 3D models. Class is held in a laboratory set up for collaboration between students that has workbenches, computers, and 3D printers.

Technology literacy is a popular issue, but a discussion of how best to deliver these skills to young adults with ID is conspicuously absent from the literature. Current technology research focuses on the design of assistive technologies (AT) for and with people with disabilities, often in support of activities of daily living. There has also been significant work in special education research on ID in terms of instruction and learning support for general curricula. This missing piece, designing for people with ID in the context of technology literacy learning, may be a result of limited access to educational opportunities, particularly at the post-secondary level. At the time of this writing, only 240 post-secondary programs for individuals with intellectual disabilities have been documented in the U.S. and Canada [13]. The 240 figure includes 4-year, 2-year, and vocational institutes; for comparison, there are over 3,000 4-year institutions in the U.S. alone offering degree and certificate programs to the general public [21]. Access to education, accessible interfaces, and individual perceptions are potential obstacles to these young adults acquiring valuable technical skills in an increasingly digital world. We have implemented an integrated, postsecondary technology course for young adults with ID in order to gain a deeper understanding of these issues.

In this paper we present findings from a series of interviews with mainstream 3D print educators (Section 3), a one-on-one instructional case study (Section 4), and a semester-long course on 3D printing (Figure 1, Section 5) with a mixed cohort of undergraduate students (UG) and young adults with intellectual disabilities (ID). We chose 3D printing due to its recent popularity and praise as an innovative technology, as well as its perceived complexity and historic affiliation with advanced engineering education. In Section 5, we give details on the course implementation and design outcomes. Via the case study and course, we were able to take a close look at the dynamics between students with and without disabilities. We provide both examples and strategies related to these dynamics in Section 6.1 and we also report on technology impacts (Section 6.2) and challenges (Section 6.3) specific to students with ID. Our conclusions and future work tie these discussion points to the potential for these types of courses and how they positively effect education, perception, and employability for young adults with ID.

2. RELATED LITERATURE

We frame our research with contemporary literature regarding intellectual disabilities. This includes research related to ID and assistive technology, approaches to education for persons with ID, and related work on persons with disabilities and their interactions with 3D printing technology.

2.1 Intellectual Disability and Assistive Technology

Assistive technology (AT) can improve the independence of young adults with ID in both educational and career settings [2]. It can support students as they practice important skills related to employment such as money management and travel independence [15]. Research in this area often looks at supporting activities of daily living (ADLs) and task completion as a skill toward employability. Bauchet, *et al* built a system called "Archipel" intended to track task completion for ADLs and tested it with individuals with ID [3]. Their system could use direct input, such as interaction with prompts on a touch screen, or it could leverage input from sensors. Chang, *et al* completed two studies exploring prompting systems for persons with cognitive impairments. In one study, they leverage sensor networks, Bluetooth connectivity, and a PDA to identify task completion in a vocational setting via engagement prompts [7]. In their later work, they build a similar system, Kinempt, based on the Microsoft Kinect [8].

There are a few examples of research that look at the use and/or the learning of technology with respect to ID. Feng and colleagues have conducted two studies with a focus on technology use by people with ID. In their 2010 article, they present findings from surveys distributed to families of children with ID and they identify key challenges to computer usage for these children from the perspective of their parents [12]. In a follow on study, they conducted ethnographic observations of adults with ID in the workplace [16]. From their data, they provide descriptions of expert use of office software, communication applications, and security tools like CAPCHA for this population.

In the realm of special education, Dunn, *et al* listed six barriers that block individuals with ID from opportunities to learn about technology and related subjects [10]: Lack of STEM role models, parent-teacher misconceptions, lack of appropriate information and counseling, educators' lack of knowledge and skills to include ID students, technical barriers, and lower participation rates in both structured and unstructured STEM related activities [11]. Low expectations of the capability of students with disabilities lead to these barriers and limit the student opportunity to explore areas of STEM.

Our research extends the exploratory work looking at technology use by people with ID and we contribute new perspective on teaching a novel technology to young adults with ID.

2.2 Intellectual Disability and Education

It is a common societal belief that post-secondary education provides more job opportunities with the potential for higher salaries. In a study of students with ID, 58% of all students who attended higher levels of education were employed after completion of their education. This is compared to the 32% of students with IDs who did not receive a postsecondary education [17]. For many of these students, a lack of understanding of the decision making process and a lack of self-determination can cause poor career related choices [9]. An increased skill set in postsecondary education allows students with ID more time and practice making career related decisions that can increase their confidence and decrease negative emotions impeding the decision making process.

Our contribution supports previous literature regarding ID and special education. We explore the educational process in the specific context of 3D printing, a developing technology traditionally considered to be complex/engineering heavy and probably "beyond" the level of our students.

2.3 3D Printing and Special Populations

The physical affordances of 3D printed objects have made this technology a popular medium for tactile learning aids. Current research has explored applications of 3D printed graphics for students with visual impairments. Brown and Hurst [5] presented VizTouch, an automated tool for generating 3D printable line graphs in the context of math education. More recently, Braier, *et al* [4] wrote about the potential to provide inclusive education with 3D printed graphics and presented their own implementation of software to automate the creation of 3D printable tactile aids. Similarly, Kane and Bigham [14] wrote about the use of 3D printed information as a tool for computer science education and STEM encouragement for youth with visual impairments. These works focus largely on generating 3D prints on behalf of populations with disabilities.

The direct use of 3D printers by people with disabilities is also a growing area of interest. Buehler, *et al* described the uses and pitfalls of 3D printers in special education schools [6]. In a more general exploration of fabrication techniques for Do-It-Yourself assistive technology, Hook, *et al* presented challenges for youth with disabilities in creating 3D printed AT devices. Also exploring 3D printable AT, Buehler, *et al* uncovered that a minority population of designers with disabilities sharing their DIY-AT on the website Thingiverse[1].

Working directly with students with ID, we are able to gain further insights into how people with disabilities can learn and leverage 3D printing technology in their education and daily lives. In addition to its popularity as both a novel and novelty technology, 3D printing can also be a means to self-employment.

[1] https://www.thingiverse.com/

Some of the processes involved in 3D printing are translatable to similar manufacturing processes that require abilities like inventory stocking and tracking, receiving and processing customer orders, and following step-by-step instructions. Employability is a major goal and we believe that these peripheral benefits of 3D printing make it an appropriate technology for our participants to learn.

3. MAINSTREAM EDUCATION INTERVIEWS

We interviewed seven mainstream educators with experience teaching 3D modeling and printing to gather teaching strategies and technical recommendations for implementing a 3D printing classroom. The majority of the educators had learned 3D printing and modeling techniques from a local technology center that provides digital literacy programs to youth community members. A few of these educators were self-taught or already had industry experience and training in 3D modeling. We analyzed their stories to prepare us for challenges related to software and hardware troubleshooting, as well as common obstacles for new students learning this technology. We describe these findings below and discuss how they informed our classroom design.

3.1 Tools and Technology

In order to create an object to be manufactured on a 3D printer, one needs a 3D model. Depending on the situation, an individual may find a pre-existing 3D model that someone else designed through popular online repositories, or create their own using 3D modeling software. There is a wide variety of 3D modeling software created for novices (individuals with little to no formal training), and experts (individuals who commonly have engineering or animation training). Two popular design tools for novices include Tinkercad[2] and Sketchup[3]. Both tools are direct manipulation WYSIWYG (What You See Is What You Get) interfaces that output a standard format, and are free. They are appealing for many novices because they offer uncluttered interfaces and objects are built by combining primitive shapes (such as cubes, triangles, and spheres). While these tools can create simple standard shapes quickly it can be tedious to use them to create organic or complex shapes. Additionally, some novices have difficulty manipulating the 3D camera, and they can unintentionally create designs that are unprintable.

The educators we spoke with used Tinkercad as their primary 3D modeling tool and the Printrbot Simple Metal[4] for their 3D printing. These were the tools used and taught by the technology center, so it follows that these educators continued with the modeling and printing tools they were exposed to during training. They relied heavily on curriculum materials provided to them through the technology center combined with Tinkercad tutorials and video walk-throughs found on Youtube.com. While a few instructors supplemented the lessons with other materials, such as books published on teaching or learning 3D printing, the majority of instructors seemed satisfied with the provided information and only sought out additional resources if their students needed special support. In this case, special support usually meant a modeling technique needed for a specific creative element in a design. Based on their feedback, we decided that Tinkercad would be an acceptable introduction to 3D printing, and we integrated the existing Tinkercad tutorials into our early lessons.

3.2 The Value and Cost of Print Time

Time was the most important factor affecting the educators' ability to teach 3D modeling and printing. The educators we spoke to only had one 3D printer that was shared between 4 to 25 students. Despite modest fundraising efforts, these educators could not afford a second printer. Most instructors offered 3D printing as part of an extra-curricular club or activity and were unable to make time in their regular school curriculum for 3D printing. The restriction of a single printer and limited meeting time outside of school sessions meant educators were forced to make difficult decisions prioritizing prints. Objects can take minutes to hours or even a full day to print depending on their size and complexity.

We were able to fund the purchase of one printer for every two students enrolled in our course. We also offered extended lab hours for students and provided lab support for longer prints. Both of these steps were taken in an attempt to mitigate the issues of print time and access identified during the interviews.

3.3 3D Modeling Teaching Strategies

We identified several strategies used by educators while teaching 3D printing, including easy start-up projects for a positive introduction to design and providing detailed instructions for more complex projects. The educators also noted differences in how youth engaged in design depending on whether they were required to complete specific design projects or allowed to engage in free-form object design.

The educators reported that the most important technique for teaching 3D printing to youth was setting up success right from the start. Participants described a need to protect youth from failure especially during the early stages of learning. They also suggested that step-by-step instructions could create obstacles and induce frustration. Educators who let their students engage in more open-ended design assignments also made more references to perceived student excitement. We were warned, however, that open-ended lessons may be more engaging, but can be difficult to manage with added students and requirements.

Based on these experiences, we created a mix of open-ended and structured lessons. While our students were frequently charged with the creative design aspects, we also provided structure in terms of planning exercises and requirements for each project.

3.4 Value and Impact of 3D Printing in Education

All of the educators were quick to offer benefits to education and to youth provided by 3D printing. Several described 3D printing as a means of supporting problem solving and abstract thinking, helping students to identify and solve real-world problems. The educators also pointed out that there are benefits related to digital literacy in learning about 3D printing. Their shared sentiment was that learning about modeling and printing was a confidence booster and a necessity in the future of education. Two of these participants indicated that by teaching 3D printing, they were also incorporating lessons from other arenas of education including history, contemporary culture, and art.

For our course, we focused primarily on 3D printing and did not include additional elements beyond entrepreneurship. This afforded us teaching scenarios that incorporated problem solving and creative endeavors, particularly during the design of a project.

[2] http://www.tinkercad.com/

[3] http://www.sketchup.com

[4] http://www.printrbot.com/

In support of employment, we also added elements of finance and customer service.

4. CASE STUDY: ONE-ON-ONE TRAINING

Our preliminary interviews gave us a basis for the technical tools necessary to implement our 3D printing course. In order to test these tools and our assumptions, we conducted a pilot in a one-on-one case study of teaching and learning 3D printing with a student with ID. We wanted to identify techniques and strategies from both 3D printing and special education to incorporate into our integrated classroom environment. It was important to conduct a small-scale pilot of our curriculum because future student participants would be taking our 3D printing course for academic credit. We wanted to mitigate potential negative impacts on their experiences and grades related to untested lesson plans. The pilot was limited to one student with ID due to time constraints and participant availability.

4.1 Background

For 11 weeks during an academic semester, a lab intern with ID and short-term memory loss worked with one of the researchers to learn how to independently design and print 3D models. They met twice a week for three-hour sessions. Prior to this study, neither individual had any experience with this technology. During the beginning of the semester, they learned about general fundamentals of 3D printing and computer aided design (CAD) as well as the different available technologies. This initial training was kept generic and was not specific to an existing brand of 3D printer. After seven weeks, when the intern was comfortable with the fundamentals of 3D printing, they began training on a Printrbot Simple Metal and Tinkercad for creating 3D models.

4.2 Strategies to Support Learning

Four major strategies to instruction were used during the course of this pilot study: 1) journaling, 2) teaching for recognition through the use of instructional and memory aids, 3) using video instructions to help explain multi-step tasks, and 4) planning for problems in advance through preparation.

Our strategy to support memory through repetition was adapted from previous work, which explored participatory design for individuals with amnesia and found that reviewing can serve as a memory aid to prepare, sustain, and summarize content [22]. The decision to incorporate video instruction was influenced by previous work that explored the effectiveness of computer-based video instructions in assisting individuals with moderate intellectual disabilities to perform complex tasks [11]. We included preparation for unforeseen problems and technical failures based on previous work that found young adults with intellectual disabilities can become "stuck" if a familiar routine is unexpectedly altered [18].

4.2.1 Journaling Experiences

Both the lab intern and the researcher kept journals during the semester. Journal entries were written during the final 30 minutes of each session and consisted of a brief summary of what was learned during the day. Both journals were used to track progress and inform future lesson plans. Journal entries did not provide a firm indication of what content the intern would be able to remember from session to session, but the information captured did suggest that some days of instruction were more effective than others and this helped the researcher identify what information should be reviewed at the beginning of the next session.

4.2.2 Teaching for Recognition and Not Recall

The intern and the researcher created instructional and memory aids, including short written directions and slide shows with vocabulary guides (Figure 2). The medium of slide shows was selected to accommodate the learning preferences of the intern who preferred limited reading. Instructions were created as numbered lists with pictures depicting steps as needed. Each slide typically contained a vocabulary term on the top of the page and an illustration. By looking at the image, the intern was able to remember information about the associated vocabulary term. The intern had a hand in creating all of his instructional aids.

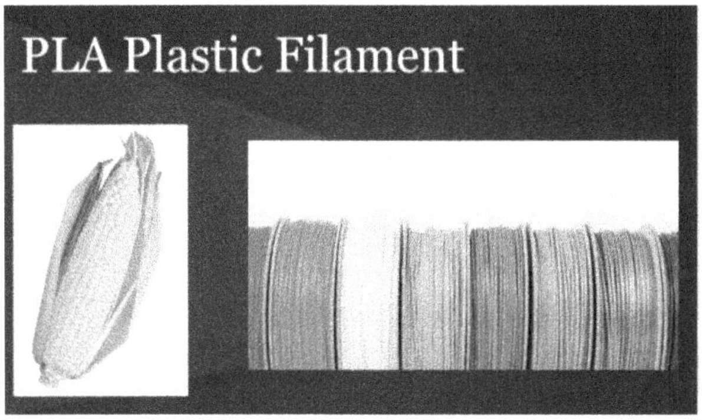

Figure 2. Learning aid designed by the intern to remember information about filament. The corn, on left, served as a reminder that PLA filament is a byproduct of biodegradable materials such as cornstarch, while the filament on the right is a reminder that PLA is available in many colors and comes wrapped on spools.

All of the slide content was either handpicked or created by the intern. The researcher assisted primarily with spelling and formatting content. These materials were reviewed once in the beginning of each session and again at the end of the session. In the event that the intern had difficultly remembering a term or concept, they would pause to review the related slides.

4.2.3 Videos as Instructions

To help break up the three-hour sessions, the intern and researcher occasionally watched videos on YouTube. These videos helped keep the intern engaged and they also helped to reinforce the steps to complex task, such as printer calibration. The videos were a successful way for the intern to gain familiarity with the steps involved in these tasks before attempting them himself. We found the videos made by Printrbot to be exceptionally helpful because they were sufficiently detailed, but still brief and they covered important topics including setup, calibration, and extrusion.

4.2.4 Planning for Problems in Advance

While 3D printing technology is advancing rapidly, the printers are not always reliable and often require troubleshooting. An example of a common printer problem is build plate adhesion—this is problem with the 3D object lifting away from the printer surface before it is complete. Printer failures such as this one can delay the printing process and cause frustration. We identified a need to plan ahead for these types of technical failures. This was addressed in two ways: 1) the inclusion of instructions that could be followed if a failure condition was met; and 2) via repetition that reinforced troubleshooting behaviors. Both techniques helped the intern decide how to react in negative situations rather than getting stuck, and these techniques helped to facilitate problem-solving skills that could be applied to other scenarios.

Figure 3. Example output from the integrated class. A) Artifacts created by students including key chains, statues, and cookie cutters. B) 3D model of a basketball court made by ID1. C) Output from the class fulfilling a job for a client (Braille rings).

4.3 Lessons Learned from Case Study

From our case study, we identified five takeaways that we incorporated into our curriculum planning for the integrated classroom: 1) building relationships, 2) creating equal partners, 3) individualized instructions, 4) strategies to mitigate technical failure, and 5) promoting engagement.

4.3.1 Building Relationships

We found that the relationship between the student and the researcher was intrinsic to the success of our case study. At the beginning of the semester, the student was quiet and reluctant to engage or contribute without prompting. As the researcher built a rapport with the student, it seemed to create a safe atmosphere and help boost the self-confidence of the student. This relationship became especially important on "off days" where the student was tired or agitated due to outside factors. The relationship provided support, a positive environment, and helped keep the student on task or refocus when they were getting off-task.

For the integrated course, we incorporated this concept by creating two-person teams, consisting of one UG student and one student with ID. During the first few class sessions, we conducted icebreaker games to get everyone talking and more comfortable. Based on common interests uncovered during these games, we then paired students together.

4.3.2 Creating Equal Partners

In addition to building a relationship, we found that it is important to emphasize the equality of the partnership. This process required both individuals to have the mutual understanding that they were working together as equals in a team and to bring positive attitudes to each session. This was not always easy to accomplish during the pilot, as the researcher was often perceived as an authority figure. Without the sense of equality, the student often hesitated with answers or deferred to the researcher when prompted to give their opinion on a task or design.

We tried to bring this element to the classroom by creating both individual and team assignments, all of which were graded with the same rubric regardless of any single student's particular ability level. This meant that everyone had the perception of equal expectations when completing individual work and teammates were mutually invested in creating quality group work.

4.3.3 Individualized Instructions

Involving the intern in the design of their instructional materials was extremely helpful to the learning process. It allowed him to have ownership of his work and to learn in a way that was comfortable for him, playing to his strengths. The process of designing instructional material was highly individualized and materials designed during this pilot study would not necessarily be generalizable for all students with ID.

In the integrated classroom, we asked the students to create instructional materials for their future reference. We gave them the option to create their materials in whatever medium best suited their learning style, whether it be written, illustration, audio, or video. We also offered resources and assistance in creating these materials if they did not already have these skills. These materials were called "instruction manuals" and we required a specific number of tasks be documented so that the students could refer to their own instructions if they got stuck. The other requirement was that the manual must have enough information, in any format, to support both teammates' learning styles.

4.3.4 Strategies to Mitigate Technical Failure

During the pilot study we experienced our share of technical failure. Strides are being made in the reliability of 3D printers, but they can still be finicky in terms of calibration and environmental factors such as air temperature affecting print outcomes. Additionally, using a cloud-based design platforms do not always go as planned. During our case study, the Tinkercad service was often unavailable during weekly sessions, and so the intern and researcher would revert to printing designs that were already created like those found on the open design community Thingiverse.com. These problems, printer failures and browser-based tool availability, were reiterations of the war stories shared with us by the 3D print educators we interviewed.

Having multiple printers available was one technique we used to head off printer failures. With all of the teams working at slightly different paces based on ability, we felt we could safely substitute one malfunctioning printer for the neighboring team's printer without any negative impact. We also created alternative modeling and design activities in the event of a software or Internet failure. We were able to incorporate concepts from other elements of the class like entrepreneurship or design theory into these "emergency" lessons.

4.3.5 Promoting Engagement

Having a contingency plan in the event of unexpected "off days" or technical failures was essential. In our case study, there were sessions in which the intern would show up two hours late for work and he would be highly unfocused. Having a plan for getting the lesson back on track was needed in order to make good use of the remaining time. The intern was offered the opportunity to leave ten minutes early in exchange for getting back on track and staying engaged. These "off days" and other issues were common enough occurrences that the schedule needed to be flexible in order to allow the intern time to complete all of his work.

Allowing time for tasks to be completed later was viewed as a better alternative to abandoning them entirely.

Based on this need for both engagement and flexibility, we incorporated strategies into the curriculum for keeping students motivated and also offered loose assignment deadlines to prevent any single student from falling too far behind after a less-than-productive session. This is discussed further in Section 6.1.3.

5. INTEGRATED CLASSROOM EVALUATION

Based on the insights gained from our earlier endeavors (Sections 3 & 4), we designed and implemented a semester-long integrated course intended to teach 3D modeling and printing skills in the context of entrepreneurship. The class included 12 students, 6 undergraduates (UG 1-6) and 6 young adults with intellectual disabilities (ID 1-6) between the ages of 18 and 27 (Table 2). The participants with ID were students enrolled in a campus-based, integrated program explicitly for adults with intellectual disabilities and were in pursuit of a certification but not a bachelor's degree. Two of the authors took turns teaching the class. When not teaching, the second instructor along with two other researchers, acted as observers or assistants to the students in class (e.g., to replace an absent team member).

Table 2. Participants in the integrated 3D printing course. Intellectual Disability (ID) and Undergraduate (UD).

*** Participant ID6 did not complete a consent form, thus only observations and no demographics were recorded.**

Part. #	Age	Gender	Part. #	Age	Gender
ID1	24	Female	UG1	20	Female
ID2	25	Female	UG2	20	Female
ID3	26	Female	UG3	27	Male
ID4	27	Female	UG4	21	Male
ID5	26	Female	UG5	22	Male
ID6	*	Male	UG6	18	Male

5.1 Classroom Setup

The class met three times per week for two 50-minute sessions followed by a 2-hour lab at the end of the week. Students met in a lab with all of the resources necessary to design and print objects. Based on the experiences described to us by the 3D print educators we interviewed and the success of our case study, we chose Tinkercad for the design software and we purchased six Printrbot Simple Metal printers. Students were encouraged to use the lab computers, but several installed modeling and printing software on their personal laptops. Course information was disseminated through an outward facing website which students could easily access from home.

5.2 Course Design

The goal for the first three sessions was to encourage students to get to know each other and form teams. To this end, the instructors paired off undergraduate students with young adults with ID based on common interests that the students mentioned during icebreaking exercises. The purpose of these small teams was to replicate the one-on-one advantages identified in our pilot case study, including building a rapport and familiarity between the students. Weekly lessons covered a brief history of 3D printing, the parts and maintenance of Printrbot Simple Metal printers, tutorials on the Tinkercad modeling software, product design, development, and marketing. Each topic was introduced for a full class period (50-minutes) followed by brief instructions and assignments in subsequent lessons. Students completed in-class tutorials, took part in discussion, and completed daily journals. In addition to daily journal entries, students completed four assignments and two projects during the semester. Journal entries provided students with an opportunity to reflect on what they learned and to work on their writing skills on a regular basis. Assignments were narrow in scope and typically focused on only developing one or two skills, but projects required students to use everything that they had learn during the semester.

Figure 4. Based on objects from Thingiverse picked by students, the class worked together to create an affinity diagram of marketable product types. Students identified several categories, including useful household items, assistive devices, electronic accessories, fashion accessories, collectables, and toys.

Assignment 1 required students to write a short autobiographical sketch. This was an extension of the icebreaker activities and also served as a means for the instructors to evaluate each student's comfort level using a computer and cloud-based file storage.

Assignment 2 required students to compile a list of items from Thingiverse that they would like to print for themselves or for someone they knew. This allowed the students to familiarize themselves with the existing 3D models and served as an introduction to Creative Commons Licensing[5], which dictates how created works can be used. Understanding Creative Commons is both a digital literacy concept and important for the entrepreneurial portion of the course. Additionally, the designs students selected were later used in an affinity diagramming (Figure 4) session to help students consider what types of objects might be marketable in preparation for their next assignment.

Assignment 3 required students to sketch out a product design, create the 3D model in Tinkercad (Figure 3B), and then write an accompanying product description. This exercise targeted skills related to creativity, design, and marketing.

[5] http://www.creativecommons.org/

Assignment 4 asked students to create an invoice form that could be used to collect customer information and order details from potential clients. With this assignment, students worked on skills related to finance, customer service, and planning by taking into account production costs, client needs and specifications, and the time necessary to design and manufacture a 3D-printed product.

Project 1 required the creation of an instruction manual with explanations of how to log in to Tinkercad, use Cura to print 3D models, and how to calibrate a Printrbot. Only one set of instructions was created per group and the completion of this assignment required both communication and writing skills.

Project 2 tasked students with the creation of their own line of products that could be sold to potential customers. This project was a cumulative assignment, and it required students to use the skills that they developed throughout the semester to create three design concepts, of which they had to select two to implement as 3D models. Of the two models, one was printed (Figure 3A) and used in a class presentation to pitch their product line.

Toward the self-employment and entrepreneurial concepts in the course, the class also worked together to fulfill a request to print 100 Braille rings (Figure 3C) as a promotional material for the department. This was a time sensitive task with a one-week deadline. To fill the order in time, students had to optimize their printing schedules and coordinate with each other to track their progress toward the total quantity requested.

5.3 Observations, Artifacts, and Analysis

Students were notified that the class would be observed and that they had the option to participate in this research. Students interested in participating provided informed consent giving us permission to document and analyze individual assignments and course progress. Students understood that participation was voluntary and had no impact on their grades. All but one student completed their consent form to formally participate in this research. ID6 gave verbal consent, however, we requested a parental review of the consent form. The form was never returned so only observations are shared about this student.

We recognize that because the students were working so closely with researchers as instructors that this may have introduced bias into their feedback. We have attempted to mitigate this by triangulating their input with our observations and the documentation of their coursework.

For each class, one to three researchers acted as observers and documented the session with written notes. The observations and artifacts from the class were collaboratively reviewed and open coded by two of the researchers to identify emergent themes.

6. FINDINGS AND DISCUSSION

Our analysis revealed five concepts: 1) relationships between students and technology, 2) integrated classroom dynamics, 3 & 4) software and hardware support, and 5) suggestions for educators. We describe each concept below and provide a brief discussion framing these ideas in the larger context of accessible technology education and societal inclusion of persons with intellectual disabilities in school and work environments.

6.1 Integrated Classroom Dynamics

By leveraging an integrated environment, both sets of students received educational benefits. We did identify some snags in the collaborative process, but overall ID students working as peers with their UG student counterparts promoted learning, confidence, and mutual understanding. We discuss some of the highlights in the subsections that follow.

6.1.1 Establishing Working Relationships

Due to the short class time, it took several weeks for students to establish comfortable working relationships with their partners. Over the course of the semester, students became more comfortable helping and communicating with their partners as they became more familiar with them. The working relationship between UG1 and ID3 led to positive social exchanges in which UG1 could correct mistakes without causing any tension. To contrast this with another group, ID1 would regularly ask for assistance from an instructor rather than their partner (UG4), who was frequently disengaged from the class.

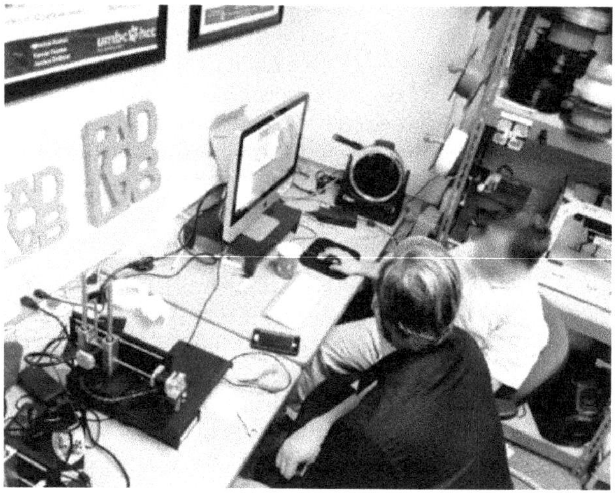

Figure 5. A student with ID prepares to print a 3D model while his UG teammate observes and offers support.

6.1.2 Turn Taking

We observed that the UG student in a group would take control of the computer and do the "driving" during the learning experience while the ID student watched but did not participate. We suspect this behavior was a mix of misconceptions about ID student abilities and a desire to complete steps quickly and efficiently. This behavior ultimately disempowers the students with ID and reduces the impact of their class time. As instructors, we addressed this behavior with a mix of gentle corrections and suggestions, such as, *"How about letting [ID2] do that? She has used [Google Drive] before."* We continued to emphasize this turn-taking concept (Figure 5) throughout the semester and found that by mid-semester both UG and ID students were getting equivalent time controlling the lab machine. In some instances, the student with ID had control longer so they could complete assignments at their own pace.

Turn taking behavior was also promoted through assigning every student the same in-class assignments and homework. While students were encouraged to work with their partners during the class period, every student was responsible for submitting an individual assignment. An additional benefit of assigning work this way was that less independent students in the class were able to work their way through complex tasks and assignments with a partner who was able to support them.

6.1.3 Motivation, Outside Factors, and Attendance

Both UG students and students with ID occasionally came to class disengaged as a result of events outside of the classroom.

While UG students would grudgingly get on board for classwork, it was more difficult to motivate the students with ID and sometimes this could not be accomplished at all inside the 50-minute class period. Sources of disengagement that we observed within the classroom included completing repetitive tasks, struggles with printer failure, and issues of personal pacing. UG4 would occasionally lose interest and start playing with his phone or browsing the Internet while his partner completed tasks. There was one instance where UG6 became noticeably upset because two prints had failed during one class period. Absenteeism was another big issue. Many of our students with ID travel significant distances to arrive on campus and a harsh winter causing school closures and dependence on family members for rides during inclement weather colluded in severely limited attendance. UG students missed class less frequently, but their absences caused more disruption. Without the UG students, students with ID who counted on their partners for reminders or support during assignments would sometimes shut down. We, as instructors, were available to help these students, but we did not have the close bonds with these students that they had with student peers and so our guidance was not always received with enthusiasm.

We tried to mitigate issues of motivation by offering short, medium, and long-term rewards both inside and outside of class time. A short-term reward might be allowing a student to pick the music in the lab if they progress through two or three steps in an assignment. This method was frequently used with ID6 who often came to class disengaged. An example of a medium-term reward was allowing the student to choose a 3D model that could be printed during class time and giving it to them as a reward for meeting their goals by the end of the session. A long-term reward that was more popular with the UG students than the ID students was the option to come into the lab for free time where they could use the printers for extended prints and projects outside the scope of the course. UG4 in particular was interested in gaining access to other types of 3D printers and would occasionally stay after class to learn additional information. We found that these strategies helped to keep students motivated.

6.1.4 Collaborative Problem-Solving

A benefit of the structure of integrated classroom setting was that ID and UG students alike had access to multiple resources to aid them when working through a problem. This included partners, peers in other groups, as well as the course instructors. Students regularly consulted with their partners and with other students in the course before asking for help from the instructors. These student explanations in combination with instructional materials supported universal design for learning by providing multiple mediums and multiple explanations of concepts. For students helping to answer questions, this also provided the opportunity to develop their communication skills.

6.2 Impacts of Technology on Students

We identified both positive and negative issues related to technology interactions in the classroom. While some are specific to the tools we used, others are more generalizable.

6.2.1 Technology as a Confidence Builder

At the beginning of the semester, only one or two students with ID were willing to experiment or show unguarded interest in exploring the software. This could be attributed to being in a new setting, feeling pressure or intimidation while working with another student, or the common tendency of some novice users to exercise restraint in technology because they fearing causing harm or making a mistake. We noted that after learning to set up a 3D printer, start a print independently, or create a 3D model, students appeared more confident in their technical skills. This was observed through students performing technical tasks on their own while asking fewer questions. A team that showed a significant shift in dynamic was a pairing between ID1 and UG4. At the beginning of the semester, ID1 was eager but reserved and frequently tried to confirm steps with their partner and with the instructors. By the end of the semester, ID1 would still approach the instructors, but would declare scenarios rather than ask questions. Instead of *"I think I'm ready for the next step?"* she would take the action on her own and only approach us for complex problems, *"The printer is broken again."*

6.2.2 Skill-Building Toward Employability

While we do not expect all of our participants to become 3D printing experts, the students did practice and gain skills toward employability. They learned specialized skills related to the process of creating and printing a 3D object, which may have some application in the field of engineering or manufacturing. More importantly and more generalizable were skills related to employment. Examples include: computer literacy, such as navigating through a file system; problem-solving by way of practiced troubleshooting; collaboration and communication skills improved through group work; and customer service skills practiced by offering print services to campus students and staff.

The majority of the students demonstrated a keen interest in making money, which was a theme woven into the curriculum of entrepreneurship. The students expressed interest in selling their designs on campus and one student, ID3, inquired about opportunities as a paid lab intern working as a 3D printing assistant in a future semester.

6.3 Technology Challenges

The 3D modeling and printing community is already well aware of the many challenges and growing pains with contemporary tools. Rather than reiterate this list, we have selected a few issues that we feel are specific to the population of new designers who have intellectual disabilities. The challenges we describe are specific to the tools we used, but we hope that by explaining these struggles in context it might contribute toward more accessible modeling and printing in future. We also offer recommendations for educators to help overcome these challenges.

6.3.1 Sign-in Issues

As part of the course structure, students were required to turn in written assignments via Google Drive and to complete their 3D modeling in Tinkercad. Students experienced many issues logging into these systems causing frustration and delays.

We tasked students with creating and keeping track of their own user login and password, but this proved too troublesome. We encouraged the students with ID to document this information themselves both to protect their privacy and to support their independence, however, several students struggled to remember their credentials or locate the documentation for those credentials. If a student repeatedly failed to provide correct credentials, the site triggered a 30 minute account lockout. In the constraints of a 50-minute class, this was detrimental to productivity. In these cases, students would have to try to recreate their work from a previous class on by designing on their partner's account.

Using Google Drive was less difficult than Tinkercad, as access to this service was through students' university login information. The students with ID were more likely to have this password documented somewhere and it proved easier to reset in the event of a complete loss. Alternatively, students could create a starting document in their partner's Drive and copy it to the appropriate location at a future date when the password issue was resolved, thus reducing delays related to replicating existing work.

6.3.1.1 Recommendations for Educators
We suggest creating a system to store student login credentials locally to avoid lockouts and lost time. There are, of course, privacy concerns related to storing user names and passwords. Creating new email accounts and generated passwords explicitly for use in the course that can then be turned over to the students for their own control at the end of the semester might be a temporary solution to this issue.

6.3.2 Speed and Reliability of Technology
Generally speaking, current 3D printers are relatively slow with large prints taking longer to produce. The class printers were set to extrude plastic at approximately 70mm per second. To print the three objects depicted in Figure 3B with 15% infill would require approximately 18.53 meters of plastic and approximately 4 hours and 16 minutes to print. Due to the brief class periods (50 minutes), students were often unable to see the finished product of their work until they returned to class several days later. This may have contributed to a delay in students fully grasping relationships between model design and print process. The duration of the class was a foreseeable problem, but our scheduling was based around the availability of our students with ID and could not be extended beyond the 50-minute window.

Another challenge was the reliability of the 3D printers. Even though the brand of printers was suggested to us based on positive experiences shared by other educators, they were still susceptible to mechanical failures—a common pitfall of contemporary 3D printing technology. Both UG and ID students were frustrated with failed prints, regardless of what caused the failure. Students with ID were more expressive with their disappointment. After a simple 2.5D model failed to print for the third consecutive time, one ID student exclaimed, *"What—again?! It's* never *gonna work!"* (ID1) while their partner merely frowned (UG4).

6.3.2.1 Recommendations for Educators
The technology behind 3D printing is improving every day, but we do not expect a plug-and-play, high quality, and inexpensive 3D printer to arrive anytime soon. While having multiple printers can help, this is not always a viable financial solution. We recommend planning longer class sessions approaching two hours. Students may need a break or extra motivators for the extended time period, but the extra minutes buy back the precious troubleshooting time that can lead to successful prints.

6.3.3 Improvements for Tinkercad and Slicing
After the students had some experience using Tinkercad, we asked them to provide us feedback on the interface. Students echoed requests for more shapes and free-style drawing modes that had also been described to us by the educators we interviewed. These are logical requests for novice designers beginning to outstrip introductory tools. One specific idea the students shared was the incorporation of the slicing process into Tinkercad to reduce the number of programs they have to interact with to start a print.

6.3.3.1 Recommendations for Educators
We identified two options to help alleviate some of the complexity of transferring design files from Tinkercad to local slicer software. The easiest, but least empowering way to do this, is for the educator to step in at the completion of the model and then carry out the slicer and printer set up instead of the student. Ultimately, this reduces the student's control over their design, robs the student of practical and conceptual skills built by interacting with the printer, and may reduce the student's understanding of the relationships between their digital model and their physical printed object. Instead, we suggest implementing clear file download destinations and easy to find icons. By adjusting settings on the browser, the educator can force all files to save to a desktop folder with a clear label. Placing an icon shortcut to the slicer software can provide the student with a drag-and-drop interaction to start the program with the target file.

7. CONCLUSIONS AND FUTURE WORK
In this paper, we presented a series of research endeavors on the implications of teaching 3D printing to students with intellectual disabilities in an inclusive context. We shared insights gained from interviews with mainstream 3D printing educators and a one-on-one instructional case study, both of which were applied toward the design of a semester-long integrated course on 3D printing for six students with intellectual disabilities and six undergraduate students without. Our findings identified the student relationships and teaching strategies unique to this mixed cohort, as well as technical challenges related to the tools used in the classroom. We consider the class to have been a success, as all students involved were able to create and design objects, and the majority of students could complete the design-to-print process independently by the end of the semester. The size of the class and the ratio of instructors-to-students may have contributed to this success.

In the greater context of education and employability for persons with intellectual disability, it is our assertion that this course and courses like it could bring about positive change. The students with ID in our course developed and practiced skills relevant in the workforce. These students also built up confidence associated with these abilities. It is especially heartening to note that by creating an integrated environment, students with and without disabilities were able to interact socially and constructively. The working relationships and classroom camaraderie helped to break down barriers, creating a comfortable atmosphere for the students with ID and dispelling misperceptions for students without. Designing accessible technology courses and promoting inclusive postsecondary opportunities for young adults with ID both provides digital literacy skills and has the potential to reduce stigmas about these individuals at a community level.

A second iteration of our integrated classroom model is already planned for the next academic year. In a subsequent course, we will further test and refine the strategies we have shared here and explore alternative tools and technologies. Our future work will continue to identify the accessibility issues related to design tools and how best to support designers of all types of ability.

8. ACKNOWLEDGMENTS
We would like to thank all of our participants. This material is based on work supported by the National Science Foundation under Grant No. IIS-1451661. Any opinions, findings, and conclusions or recommendations expressed in this material are those of the authors and do not necessarily reflect the views of the National Science Foundation.

9. REFERENCES

[1] AAIDD.American Association on Intellectual and Developmental Disabilities. 2012. http://www.aaidd.org.

[2] Alnahdi, G.Assistive Technology in Special Education and the Universal Design for Learning. *Turkish Online Journal of Educational Technology 13*, 2 (2014), 18 – 23.

[3] Bauchet, J., Pigot, H., Giroux, S., Lussier-Desrochers, D., Lachapelle, Y., and Mokhtari, M.Designing Judicious Interactions for Cognitive Assistance. *Proceeding of the eleventh international ACM SIGACCESS conference on Computers and accessibility - ASSETS '09*, ACM Press (2009), 11.

[4] Braier, J., Lattenkamp, K., Räthel, B., Schering, S., Wojatzki, M., and Weyers, B.Haptic 3D Surface Representation of Table-Based Data for People With Visual Impairments. *ACM Transactions on Accessible Computing 6*, 1 (2014), 1–35.

[5] Brown, C. and Hurst, A.VizTouch: Automatically Generated Tactile Visualizations of Coordinate Spaces. *TEI '12: Proceedings of the Sixth International Conference on Tangible, Embedded and Embodied Interaction*, ACM Press (2012), 131–138.

[6] Buehler, E., Kane, S.K., and Hurst, A.ABC and 3D: Opportunities and Obstacles to 3D Printing in Special Education Environments. *ASSETS '14 Proceedings of the 16th International ACM SIGACCESS Conference on Computers and Accessibility*, (2014).

[7] Chang, W.C.CATPro : Context-aware Task Prompting System with Multiple Modalities for Individuals with Cognitive Impairments. *Assets '08: Proceedings of the 10th international ACM SIGACCESS conference on Computers and accessibility*, (2008), 301–302.

[8] Chang, Y.-J., Chou, L.-D., Wang, F.T.-Y., and Chen, S.-F.A Kinect-Based Vocational Task Prompting System for Individuals with Cognitive Impairments. *Personal and Ubiquitous Computing 17*, 2 (2011), 351–358.

[9] Dipeolu, A.O., Hargrave, S., Sniatecki, J.L., and Donaldson, J.Improving Prediction of Significant Career-Related Constructs for High School Students With Learning Disabilities. *The Career Development Quarterly 60*, (2012), 207 – 220.

[10] Dunn, C., Rabren, K.S., Taylor, S.L., and Dotson, C.K.Assisting Students with High-Incidence Disabilities to Pursue Careers in Science, Technology, Engineering, and Mathematics. *Intervention in School and Clinic 48*, 1 (2012), 47 – 54.

[11] Dunn, C., Rabren, K.S., Taylor, S.L., and Dotson, C.K.Assisting Students With High-Incidence Disabilities to Pursue Careers in Science, Technology, Engineering, and Mathematics. *Intervention in School and Clinic 48*, 1 (2012), 47–54.

[12] Feng, J., Lazar, J., Kumin, L., and Ozok, A.Computer Usage by Children with Down Syndrome : Challenges and Future Research. *ACM Transactions on Accessible Computing 2*, 3 (2010).

[13] Institute for Community Inclusion at the University of Massachusetts Boston.ThinkCollege! http://www.thinkcollege.net.

[14] Kane, S.K. and Bigham, J.P.Tracking @ stemxcomet: Teaching Programming to Blind Students via 3D Printing, Crisis Management, and Twitter. *SIGCSE '14*, (2014), 247–252.

[15] Lanyi, C.S. and Brown, D.J.Design of Serious Games for Students with Intellectual Disability. *IHCI'10 Proceedings of the 2010 international conference on Interaction Design & International Development*, (2010), 44–54.

[16] Lazar, J., Kumin, L., and Feng, J.H.Understanding the Computer Skills of Adult Expert Users with Down Syndrome : An Exploratory Study. (2011), 51–58.

[17] Migliore, A., Butterworth, J., and Hart, D.Postsecondary education and employment outcomes for youth with intellectual disabilities. *Think College Fast Facts*, 2011.

[18] Ortega-Hurndon, F. and Mechling, L.C.Computer-Based Video Instruction to Teach Young Adults with Moderate Intellectual Disabilities to Perform Multiple Step, Job Tasks in a Generalized Setting. *Education and Training in Developmental Disabilities 42*, 1 (2007), 24 – 37.

[19] Siperstein, G.N., Parker, R.C., and Drascher, M.National Snapshot of Adults with Intellectual Disabilities in the Labor Force. *Journal of Vocational Rehabilitation 39*, 3 (2013), 157 – 165.

[20] U.S. Department of Education.IDEA - Building the Legacy of IDEA 2004. http://idea.ed.gov/.

[21] U.S. Department of Education.Digest of Education Statistics, 2013. *Digest of Education Statistics*, 2013. http://nces.ed.gov/programs/digest/d13/tables/dt13_317.10.asp.

[22] Wu, M., Richards, B., and Baecker, R.Participatory Design with Individuals Who Have Amnesia. *Proceedings of the eighth conference on Participatory design Artful integration: interweaving media, materials and practices - PDC 04*, ACM Press (2004), 214.

Towards Efficacy-Centered Game Design Patterns For Brain Injury Rehabilitation: A Data-Driven Approach

Jinghui Cheng, Cynthia Putnam, Doris C. Rusch
College of Computing and Digital Media, DePaul University
243 S. Wabash, Chicago, IL, 60604
{jcheng13, cputnam, drusch1}@cdm.depaul.edu

ABSTRACT

Games are often used in brain injury (BI) therapy sessions to help motivate patients to engage in rehabilitation activities. In this paper, we explore game design patterns as a mechanism to help game designers understand needs in BI therapy. Design patterns, originating from the work of Christopher Alexander, aim to provide a common language to support the creative work of designers by documenting solutions that have successful addressed recurring design problems. Through analyzing data we gathered on the use of commercial games in BI therapy, we generated a list of 14 'efficacy-centered game design patterns' that focused on game design considerations when addressing therapeutic goals in BI rehabilitation. We argue that our patterns can serve as a common language to support the design of BI rehabilitation games; additionally, our data-driven approach sets up a paradigm for generating game design patterns in related areas.

Categories and Subject Descriptors

K.4.2 [**Computers and Society**]: Social Issues – *handicapped persons/special needs*; K.8.0 [**Personal Computing**]: General – *games*

General Terms

Documentation, Design, Human Factors.

Keywords

Brain injury; gaming therapy; game design; game design patterns.

1. INTRODUCTION

The aim of this work is to support the creation of therapy-centered games for brain injury rehabilitation by empowering game designers. Brain injury (BI) is a leading cause of long-term disability in many societies [32]. Approximately 6.4 million children and adults in the US live with a lifelong disability as a result of a BI [35]. BIs originate from diverse causes, including external traumatic events such as car accidents and firearms, loss of oxygen to the brain, and cerebral vascular accidents (i.e. stroke) [1, 38]. People who have sustained a BI can exhibit a wide range of impairments affecting both gross and fine motor coordination; BIs can also affect cognitive abilities including problem solving, memory, learning, and speech [16, 38]. Due to the diverse causes and effects associated with BIs, rehabilitation treatments also vary widely and need to be customized by therapists; many treatments involve repetitive activities to reinforce learning. Clinical experience and cases cited in the literature have identified that it can be challenging to motivate patients to engage in repetitive activities needed for BI rehabilitation [5, 15]. As a result, many therapists use video games and gameful activities in their therapy sessions to help engage their patients.

ASSETS '15, October 26 - 28, 2015, Lisbon, Portugal

ACM 978-1-4503-3400-6/15/10…$15.00
DOI: http://dx.doi.org/10.1145/2700648.2809856.

Therapists use varied combinations of commercial off-the-shelf (COTS) games designed for the general public and games that are specifically designed for BI therapy [4]; choices of game use are influenced by budget and availability. While some COTS games were identified as both motivating for patients to engage in rehabilitation activities and effective at addressing therapeutic goals [31, 41], research has indicated that COTS games are often too fast-paced and too challenging for BI patients [36]. Further, some games provide negative feedback that could be inappropriate for people who have had a BI [25]. To mitigate the limitations of COTS games, researchers and practitioners have created games that are designed specifically for BI rehabilitation [9, 11]; these have included games run on specialized platforms (e.g. virtual reality systems [37]) and games that leverage commercially available hardware (e.g. Kinect sensors [14, 24], and Wii remotes [2]).

Efforts to create games for BI rehabilitation supports that therapy-centered game design is an important area for the future of BI therapies. However, most of the current games/systems are either experimental or if commercial (e.g. Jintronix [21] and MIRA [30]) have not reached a high level of diffusion. A common critique of games designed to address BI rehabilitation was that they are not engaging [8]; one important reason cited for a lack of engagement was the oft-limited communication and mutual understanding among game designers and subjective matter experts (e.g., therapists) when creating these games [8, 40]. Design patterns, originating from the work of Christopher Alexander, aim to provide a common language to support the creative work of designers by documenting successful solutions that have addressed recurring design problems [3]. In the field of serious games (i.e. games designed to support an external purpose [8]), game design patterns were advocated as a communication tool that supports the collaboration among team members who have diverse backgrounds [17, 23, 28].

Much of the previous work that has explored patterns in serious game design focused on educational games (see section 1.1.3 for details); however in our literature review we found that only a few researchers have investigated design patterns for rehabilitation games [17] and we were unable to find work specifically focusing on patterns that address efficacy issues for BI therapy-centered games. We argue that investigating patterns in games for rehabilitation is beneficial for researchers and designers who are interested in rehabilitation games for several reasons. First, game design patterns have the capacity to capture the qualitative (and usually heterogeneous) information about BI rehabilitation needs in a fixed structure to facilitate expansion of game design knowledge. Second, patterns have the ability to distill abstract game design knowledge from a large amount of data about how well existing games worked in therapy into a set of coherent and tangible exemplars. Finally, patterns as a common language can serve as a valuable tool to facilitate effective communication and mutual understanding among game designers and therapists. As such, game design patterns can play an important role in capturing design knowledge in games used in therapies and further inform and promote therapy-centered game design.

In this paper, we address a gap in literature by investigating patterns that focus on game design considerations when addressing therapeutic goals in BI rehabilitation; we call them 'efficacy-centered game design patterns'. In particular, we introduce a data-driven approach of pattern generation; i.e. we focus on generating design patterns via analysis of the data we gathered about the efficacy of COTS games used in BI therapy.

1.1 Related Work

This study builds upon several areas of related work, including: (1) the use of commercial off-the-shelf (COTS) games for BI rehabilitation, (2) investigation of games that are specifically designed for BI therapy, and (3) game design patterns.

1.1.1 COTS Games for BI Rehabilitation

Work that has examined COTS games presumed that these games were designed to be engaging and, if proved effective in addressing BI rehabilitation goals, they would serve as a promising candidate to achieve a balance between player engagement and rehabilitation efficacy. Researchers have investigated COTS games for BI rehabilitation on several gaming platforms, including Nintendo Wii [10, 29], Sony Play Station [41], Microsoft Xbox [31], and web-based games [42]. For example, Paavola et al. (2013) conducted a case study using Kinect Adventures on Xbox 360 for ten sessions over a month with a 29-year-old patient sustained a BI. Over the intervention, the participant showed improvements in movement performance and physical clinical outcomes including balance and gait [31]. Zickefoose et al. (2013) investigated the efficacy of Lumosity (a web-based brain training program, also available on tablets [18]) for cognitive improvement in four participants who have had a BI. They found that while participants made significant improvements through the intervention, there was limited evidence showing that cognitive skills gained were generalizable to tasks outside of the game [42]. While not focusing directly on game design, the lessons learned in the use of COTS games can greatly inform games created specifically for BI rehabilitation.

While having obvious advantages such as low cost and scalability, COTS games have several limitations for use in BI rehabilitation. For example, COTS games are usually not feasible for low functioning patients [36] and some games provide negative feedback that could be inappropriate for people who have had a BI [25]. As a result, therapists use COTS games only with a small portion of their patients; i.e., those who demonstrate higher physical and cognitive abilities [34]. In addition, research has supported the need to include adjustable features in rehabilitation games in order to accommodate the wide-ranging causes, effects and recovery paths associated with BIs [2]; COTS games usually do not include such adjustable features.

1.1.2 Creating Games for BI Rehabilitation

To mitigate the limitations of COTS games, researchers and practitioners have created games that are designed specifically for BI rehabilitation. Much of the early work focused on games that ran on specialized platforms (e.g. virtual reality systems [37]) that were usually costly and thus suffered from limited scalability to general therapeutic practices. Along with the development of motion capture technologies and the availability of motion-based game consoles (e.g. Nintendo Wii and Xbox Kinect) and portable devices (e.g. iPad), research in this area has more recently shifted towards methods that create customized games leveraging commercially available hardware; many focused on games with adjustable parameters (e.g. [2]). Examples leveraging commercial hardware to create custom games include methods using low-cost webcams [9], Kinect sensors [14, 24], and Wii remotes [2]. For example, Burke et al. (2009) developed a series of webcam-based motion-games for stroke rehabilitation; their evaluation indicated that these games had the potential to support in-home therapy [9].

Researchers have also generated design guidelines for BI rehabilitation games aimed at binding fun factors and the effectiveness of the games. For example, Flores et al. (2008) generated a list of design criteria for stroke rehabilitation games that also focused on entertaining elderly people [12]. In addition, many researchers in this area have argued that a successful collaboration between subject matter experts and game creatives is crucial for creating successful games that are both engaging and contain the appropriate therapeutic contents [8, 12].

1.1.3 Game Design Patterns

Based on the work of Christopher Alexander, design patterns are a collection of solutions that solve recurring problems in corresponding contexts [3]. After its introduction in architecture, the concept of design patterns has been adopted in many fields, including software engineering [13] and interaction design [7].

Björk and Holopainen (2004) completed the most comprehensive work applying the concept of design pattern in the field of game design [6]. Through an examination of common game mechanics, existing games, and game design methods, they generated a set of over 200 game design patterns organized in 11 broad categories. Each of their patterns included (1) a name, (2) a core definition, (3) a description of how it is used in current games, (4) a specification of designers' choices applying the pattern, (5) the resulting gameplay of the pattern, and (6) its connections to other patterns [6]. As such, their patterns constituted a very comprehensive common language of game design that could arguably be used to analyze and design games.

However, Björk and Holopainen's pattern language has been criticized for not being able to capture some of the important game design factors, such as contextual issues [22] and the expected player experience [26] and behavior [19]. Further, their patterns were not intended to cover design considerations of certain game components (e.g. level design [19]) and game types (e.g. serious games [28]). Recent research has examined game design patterns in the context of shooter games [19], role-playing games (RPG) [39], online social games [27], and mobile casual games [22]. Researchers have also explored how player experiences such as flow [26] and player motivation [27] can be addressed using game design patterns.

In addition, researchers have explored patterns in serious game design; many focused on educational games [20, 23, 28]. We identified two common themes in the literature of this area. First, researchers have used game design patterns to address a common goal/challenge in serious game design: to balance player experience (e.g. engagement) in games and the subject matter that the game addresses. For example, Huynh-Kim-Bang et al. (2010) investigated how game design patterns can help combine fun and learning elements in educational games and developed two sets of design patterns focusing respectively on fun and learning aspects of games [20]. The second theme is that game design patterns were unanimously advocated as a communication tool that supports the collaboration of stakeholders in a game development team. For example, Marne et al. (2012) investigated educational game design patterns as a collaboration space to facilitate communication and mutual understanding among teachers and game designers of educational games [28].

Only a few studies investigated design patterns for rehabilitation games [17]. Goude et al. (2007) mapped game design patterns established by Björk and Holopainen with a taxonomy of common stroke rehabilitation tasks; based on this mapping, they developed a stroke rehabilitation system that includes 20 therapeutic mini-games [17]. While closely related to our work, this work has several limitations: (1) the patterns they used were not specifically addressing therapy-centered game design issues and (2) the mapping they created was based on subjective speculations. In the literature review, we were unable to find work specifically addressing therapy-centered game design patterns. We bridge this gap by creating a common vocabulary that will help game designers focus on the needs of BI rehabilitation. In addition, our creation of this common vocabulary will be driven by data we gathered about game use in BI therapy sessions.

2. METHODS

Our efficacy-centered game design patterns were generated based on the creation and analysis of a dataset that contains game therapy "cases." In this section, we discuss (1) our definition of a game therapy case, (2) methods we used to construct the dataset of the cases, and (3) our data analysis procedure through which we generated the efficacy-centered game design patterns.

2.1 Structure of a Game Therapy Case

A game therapy case in our study describes a particular situation in which a game is used with a patient to address certain therapeutic goals. Each case contains information about (1) variables concerning patient abilities and play preferences, (2) therapy session goals, (3) information about the game used in the therapy session (e.g. mechanics and requirements), and (4) session outcomes (e.g. the game's effectiveness on the therapeutic goals and the level of player enjoyment); see Figure 1.

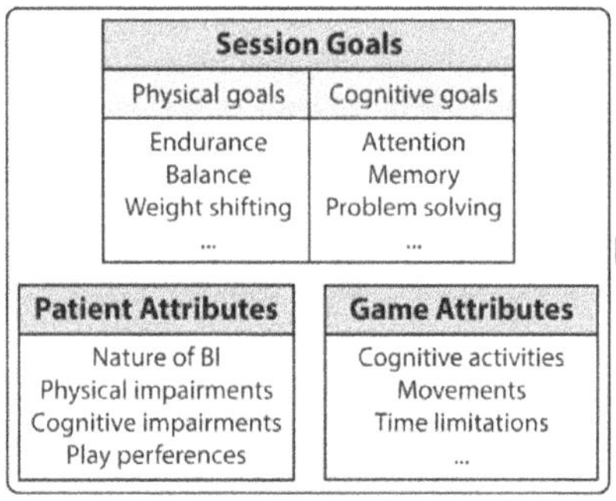

Figure 1. Summary attributes of a case

2.2 Case Collection

To construct a dataset of game therapy cases, we have been working with therapists at Schwab Rehabilitation Hospital in Chicago and Marianjoy Rehabilitation Hospital in Wheaton, Illinois to explore the use of COTS games in BI therapies. We first conducted paper-based diary studies with therapists working with patients who have had a BI to collect initial game therapy cases. We then expanded the case collection methods by including digital diary forms in user feedback questionnaires during beta test sessions of a game recommendation tool that we developed to help therapists choose appropriate COTS games for their patients.

2.2.1 Paper-based Diary Studies

In the paper-based diary studies, therapists were given a notebook containing two-page paper diary forms and were asked to record details about game therapy sessions over two-week periods. We piloted and iterated the diary forms in October 2012 at Schwab; see Figure 2 for the final version of the diary form.

On the first diary page, therapists were asked to record (1) date/time of the session; (2) session details (e.g., if a group session, the number of patients involved); (3) non-identifiable patient details (e.g., age, gender, rehabilitation measures, nature of the BI, assistive devices used, standing endurance, range of motion, fine motor control, command following and sequencing abilities); and (4) the game selections (console, game/mini-game).

On the second diary page, therapists: (1) identified the therapeutic goals (check-marked) for playing each game (the goals that were listed were derived directly from our previous work that included interviews and observations with therapists [33] and the pilot diary study in which therapists were asked to manually write down the goals; we also made small modifications on the goals based on therapist input during the diary studies); (2) provided subjective measures of the effectiveness (on a five-point scale) of the game at meeting each goal; (3) rated the level (0-4) of cognitive and physical help needed to play the game; (4) rated patient enjoyment (0-4); (5) assessed appropriate challenge (range from boredom to frustration); and (6) were invited to enter additional comments about the session.

We conducted seven periods of two-week diary studies (three at Schwab and four at Marianjoy) from December 2012 to June 2014. In total, 16 therapists participated in the paper-based diary studies, including nine physical therapists, three occupational therapists, two speech-language pathologists, and two recreational therapists. Therapists recorded data for 89 individual patients, ages ranging from 19-95 (M = 53.5); about half (N = 49, 55%) were male. Through the paper-based diary periods, we collected 244 game therapy cases.

2.2.2 Digital Diary Forms

With the initial cases gathered in paper-based diary studies, we created a game recommendation tool to help therapists choose games for their patients. Using this tool, the therapists were able to input patient attributes and session goals and then get a list of games recommended for the input situation based on the cases we collected (see [33] for how we gathered requirements for the tool).

We then conducted beta testing of the prototype system with 29 therapists. During the beta test periods, therapists were asked to make at least three queries per four weeks. After each query, we sent a questionnaire to the therapist who made the query to ask about the therapy session and their experience using the tool. As part of the questionnaire, therapists were asked to complete a digital version of the diary form to record details about game use. The digital diary form also allowed therapists to (a) add information about new games if they used a game or activity that

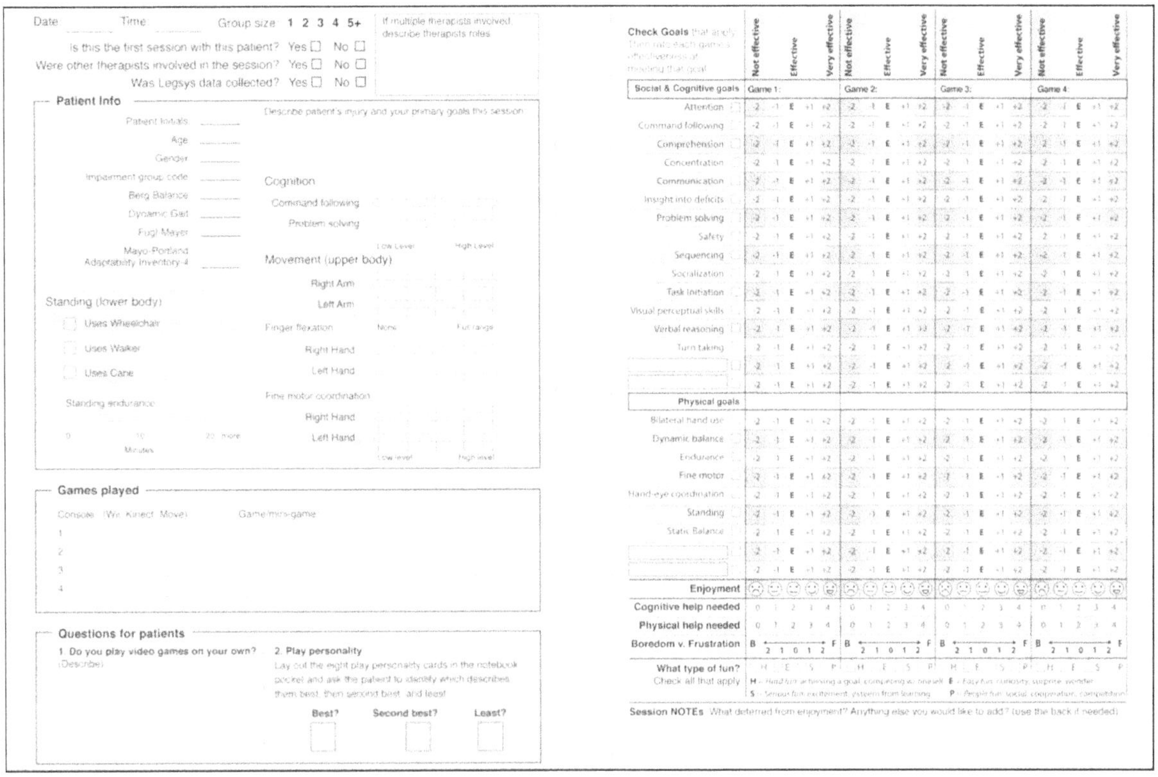

Figure 2. Final version of the diary form

was not on the recommendation list (which we then added to the case dataset) and (b) state that they did not use any games at all.

As of this writing, we have conducted two periods of four-week beta tests of the prototype between August and November in 2014; a third round is ongoing (initiated on March 2, 2015) and will last for 16 weeks. The 29 participating therapists have made queries that generated 322 new cases via the digital diary forms. In this paper, we focus on the data gathered from both the paper-based and digital diaries.

2.3 Data Analysis and Pattern Generation

Through the case collection methods (paper-based and digital diaries), to date we have created a dataset that contains 566 game therapy cases. We followed five steps to generate the efficacy-centered game design patterns based on these cases; in our approach, we focused on how well the games addressed the intended therapeutic goals.

Step 1: We calculated pairwise Pearson correlation coefficients among the effectiveness of physical and cognitive goals to explore associations among the therapeutic goals. This analysis of association among goals allowed us to identify patterns that address multiple goals and analyze the potential interactions among patterns in later steps.

Step 2: For each goal, we gathered cases addressing the goal and created a list of games that were most frequently used in those cases (i.e. we grouped the games according to the therapeutic goals they address and identified the most frequently used games for each goal). We included games that were used in more than ten cases addressing the goal. If there were less than five games in the list, we also included games used in more than eight cases.

Step 3: For each list of games (i.e. most frequently used games for each goal), we conducted a Kruskal-Wallis test to evaluate differences among the game's average effectiveness score for the particular goal; recall the scores were subjective ratings assessed by therapists. When there was a significant difference, we conducted pairwise Mann-Whitney U tests (with Bonferroni p-value adjustments) to identify the most effective and ineffective games for the goal. We identified a game as effective at addressing a goal if its average effectiveness score on the goal was higher than four (on a scale of 1-5). We labeled a game as ineffective at addressing a goal if the average effectiveness score was statistically significantly different from the score for at least one effective game. These games and their relationships to the goals formed the basis of our pattern generation.

Step 4: One author extracted the common game mechanics and rules in the most effective games (generated from Step 3) for each therapeutic goal and generated the initial list of patterns. All authors then discussed and iterated to an agreement on the pattern list and writing. In particular, we focused on extracting game design elements that contributed to their effectiveness at addressing the targeting goals. When appropriate, we compared the effective and ineffective games for a certain goal to identify important differences. When available, we also incorporated the therapists' comments explaining why they gave the effectiveness score to a game.

Step 5: We finally organized the patterns into categories and analyzed the potential interactions and relationships among the patterns.

3. DATA ANALYSIS RESULTS

Among the 566 cases we gathered, most (N = 528, 93.3%) focused on more than one goal. The most frequently chosen goals were dynamic balance (N = 350), attention/concentration (N =

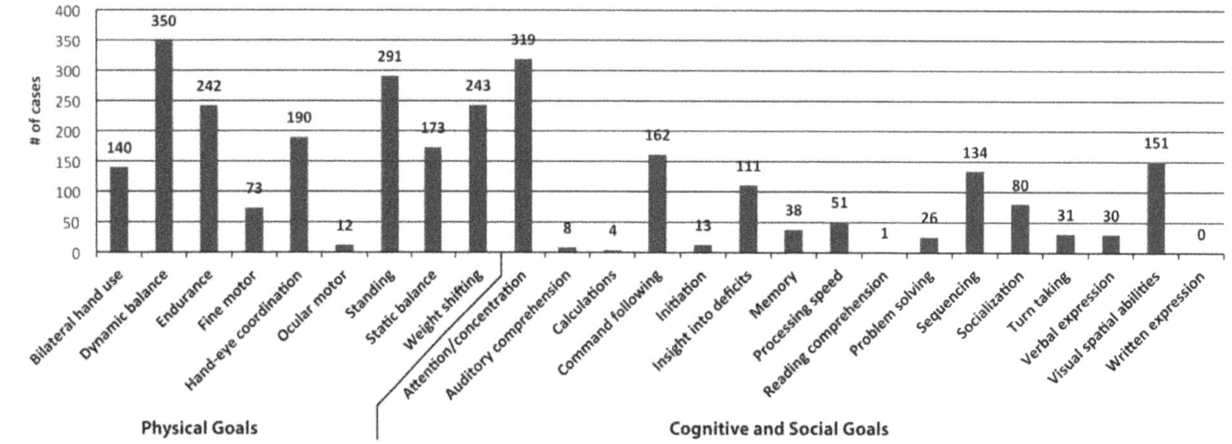

Figure 3. Goal selection frequency

319), and standing (N = 291); see Figure 3. Pairwise correlation analysis of the effectiveness of goals revealed four groups of session goals that are usually selected together and have similar effectiveness when addressed using the same games:

- Group 1: dynamic balance, endurance, standing
- Group 2: dynamic balance, standing, weight shifting
- Group 3: turn taking, socialization
- Group 4: turn taking, verbal expression

The correlation coefficient matrices among those goals are shown in Table 1; all correlations were statistically significant ($p < 0.05$).

Table 1. Correlation coefficient matrix for selected goals
(Only shows goals with moderate or stronger correlation)

	Physical goals		
	Dynamic bal.	Endurance	Standing
Endurance	0.4558*	--	--
Standing	0.4870*	0.4198*	--
Weight shifting	0.5309*	0.2701	0.5662*
	Cognitive and social goals		
	Socialization		Turn taking
Turn taking	0.4235*		--
Verbal expression	0.3316		0.4068*

* shows moderate correlation ($r > 0.4$)

In total, 112 games and mini-games were used in the 566 cases. However, game use was skewed towards a small set of games; the top ten most frequently used games appeared in about half of the cases (N = 278, 49%); see Figure 4.

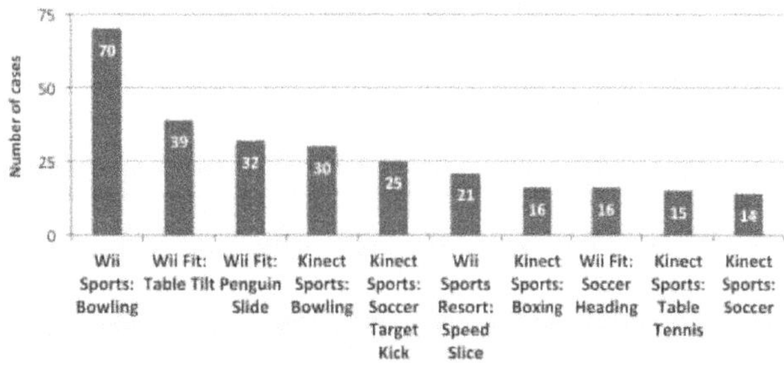

Figure 4. Top ten most frequently used games

Thirteen goals contained enough cases for us to conduct statistical analysis outlined in section 2.3 Step 3. We identified the top effective and ineffective games for those goals; see Table 2 (several goals were combined because they were addressed by the same games).

Table 2. Effective and ineffective games addressing top goals

Goal	Top effective games*	Ineffective games**
Bilateral hand use	Kinect Sports *Table Tennis* *Bowling*	Kinect Sports *Soccer Target Kick*
Dynamic balance	Wii Fit *Penguin Slide* *Table Tilt* Kinect Sports *Soccer Target Kick*	Wii Sports Resort *Speed Slice*
Standing & Endurance	Wii Fit *Table Tilt* *Penguin Slide* Kinect Sports *Table Tennis*	
Weight shifting & Static balance	Wii Fit *Table Tilt* *Penguin Slide*	Kinect Sports & Wii Sports *Bowling*
Attention/ Concentration	Wii Fit *Table Tilt* *Soccer Heading* Wii Sports Resort *Speed Slice*	Wii Sports *Bowling*
Hand-eye coordination	Wii Sports Resort *Speed Slice* Kinect Sports *Table Tennis* *Boxing*	Kinect Sports *Bowling* Wii Fit *Penguin Slide*
Insights into deficits	Wii Fit *Table Tilt*	Kinect Sports *Soccer Target Kick* Wii Sports *Bowling*
Sequencing	Wii Sports *Bowling*	
Socialization & Turn taking	Wii Sports *Bowling* Family Feud	
Visual spatial abilities	Wii Fit *Table Tilt* *Soccer Heading* Kinect Sports *Soccer Target Kick*	

* Top games whose average effectiveness score was higher than four (on a scale of 1-5).

** Games whose average effectiveness score was statistically significantly different to at least one effective game ($p < 0.05$)

4. PATTERNS

Through the data analysis, we created a pattern library that contained 14 efficacy-centered game design patterns for BI therapy. In this section, we describe our patterns, explore their relationships, and discuss how the patterns can be used in BI therapy-centered game design.

4.1 Overview of Patterns

We grouped the 14 game design patterns into four categories based on the gaming aspects they address; categories included (1) patterns related to body movements and/or the physical mechanics of the game, (2) patterns addressing issues about game rules, (3) patterns concerning perception issues, and (4) patterns concerning socialization issues. Each pattern was associated with one or more therapeutic goals denoting the aspects of BI therapy the pattern was intended to address. Table 3 summarized the patterns we identified and their main associated therapeutic goals.

Table 3. Summary of efficacy-centered game design patterns

Category	Pattern name	Main goals
Physical mechanics	Change Hands	Bilateral hand use
	Integrated Standing Duration	Standing
	Moving Different Body Parts	Insight into deficits
	Self-paced Weight Shifting	Dynamic balance; Weight shifting
	Weight Shifting to the Extremes	Weight shifting
Game rules	Fine Control	Weight shifting Balance
	Minimalist Task	Attention/ concentration
	Optimal/adjustable Pace	Processing Speed
	Randomized Events	Hand-eye coordination
	Step by Step	Sequencing; Command following
Perception	Focus and Distraction	Standing; Endurance
	Three-dimensional Space	Visual spatial abilities
Social	Collocated Multiplayer	Socialization
	Turn-based Multiplayer	Turn taking

4.2 Examples of Patterns

Each pattern in our pattern library contains (1) a name, (2) a category, (3) a set of associated therapeutic goals, (4) a problem statement describing conflicts in design, (5) a solution describing how the pattern can be used to resolve the problem, (6) examples of games that demonstrated this pattern, and (7) a list of related patterns (see section 4.3 for details). In this section, we provide one pattern example from each category.

4.2.1 Self-paced Weight Shifting

"Self-paced Weight Shifting" is a *physical mechanics* pattern addressing the *dynamic balance* and *weight shifting* goals.

Problem: Practicing dynamic balance often includes activities involving weight shifting (side-to-side and/or front-to-back). Games that require weight shifting at a fixed pace (e.g. Soccer heading on Wii Fit which requires players to weight shift to hit soccer balls kicked in at a fixed pace) were not rated as effective at addressing dynamic balance by therapists. Patients with dynamic balance issues often have limited reaction times that affect their reaction to fix-paced events.

Solution: Allow players to adjust the timing of weight shifting according to their own abilities. Do not impose fix-paced actions.

Example games:

- Wii Fit - *Table Tilt*: Player weight-shifts on a balance board in all directions to tilt a table and guide marbles through holes. There are no fix-paced events and players can perform weight shifting at their pace.
- Wii Fit - *Penguin Slide*: Player weight-shifts from side to side to control a penguin that slides on an iceberg to catch fish jumping out from the water. While the fish jump out in a fixed pace, players do not have to follow that pace to catch them.
- Kinect Sports - *Soccer Target Kick*: Player kicks soccer balls to hit the targets in a self-paced manner. Note that kicking involves weight shifting, especially when alternating legs.

Related patterns:

- Sometimes combined with *Weight Shifting to the Extremes* to further support practice of weight shifting.
- Can be combined with *Moving Different Body Parts* to support weight shifting in all directions.
- This pattern facilitates a sense of autonomy and thus can encourage player motivation. As such, it can be used to promote *Focus and Distraction*.
- *Optimal/adjustable Pace* mainly concerns the pace of events happening in the game, while this pattern concerns the pace of player actions.

4.2.2 Randomized Events

"Randomized Events" is a *game rules* pattern addressing the *hand-eye coordination* goal.

Problem: Practicing hand-eye coordination abilities usually involves perception and reaction to events. A game with periodical/predicable events can limit its effectiveness on rehabilitation of hand-eye coordination abilities.

Solution: Make events appear in a randomized manner to introduce uncertainty in the game. A fairly fast pace is often desired but the speed needs to match patient abilities. A human opponent with a matching skill or an adjustable AI opponent can usually provide unpredictable events in an optimized pace.

Example games:

- Wii Sports Resort - *Speed Slice*: Player swings the Wii remote in the direction specified on an object when it appears. The direction is randomized and the player needs to react on the specified direction within a time limit. However, the speed of this game is not adjustable; so it can only be used for high-level patients.
- Kinect Sports - *Table Tennis*: Player plays table tennis with an AI or another player. Player needs to react on the direction and speed of the ball and swing their arm

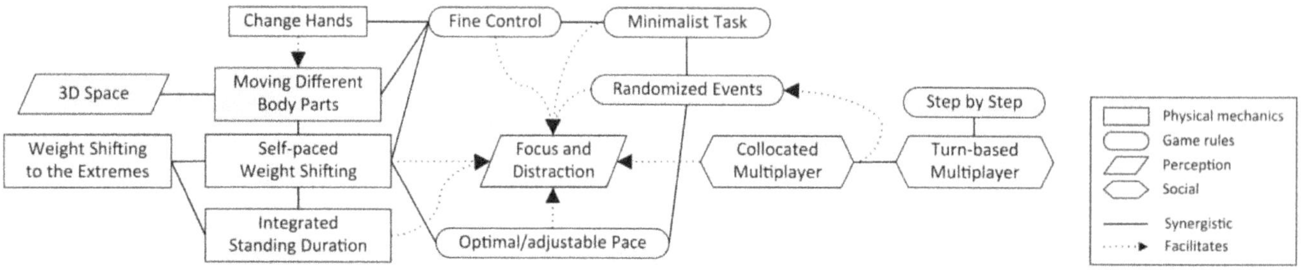

Figure 5. Relationships among efficacy-centered game design patterns

accordingly. There are several levels of AI that player can choose to match their abilities.

Related Patterns:

- Usually used with *Optimal/adjustable Pace* to make sure the *Randomized Events* happens in a pace that matches player abilities.
- *Randomized Events* can promote *Focus and Distraction.*
- Supporting real-time (i.e. not turn-based) *Collocated Multiplayer* can be a way to create *Randomized Events*.

4.2.3 *Focus and Distraction*

"Focus and Distraction" is a *perception* pattern addressing the goals of *standing* and *endurance*.

Problem: Therapists may use games to promote patients' endurance (e.g. standing endurance). However, for patients who have had a BI standing and moving usually require a considerable amount of effort. A less engaging gaming experience will discourage the efforts to practice for an extended time.

Solution: Provide intriguing gaming elements and/or activities that promote concentration for players to be fully focused on the game and be "distracted" from the fact that they are standing/moving.

Example games:

- Wii Fit - *Table Tilt*: The game has a very clear goal and a straightforward task – to guide the marble to drop through the hole. The game features detailed control to support concentration and focus.
- Wii Fit - *Penguin Slide*: The theme and music of the game provides good distraction for suitable patients. Keeping the penguin on the iceberg is a straightforward task with appropriate challenge that promotes focus.

Related Patterns:

- Can be facilitated by many patterns such as *Integrated Standing Duration*, *Self-paced Weight Shifting*, *Fine Control*, *Minimalist Task*, *Optimal/adjustable Pace*, *Randomized Events*, and *Collocated Multiplayer*.

4.2.4 *Collocated Multiplayer*

"Collocated Multiplayer" is a *social* pattern addressing the *socialization* goal.

Problem: Patients who have had a BI need to be connected with their friends and family, their community, and the rest of the world. Some patients have difficulty socializing with other people due to their disabilities caused by BI.

Solution: Games can create a "safe" socialization space. Include collocated multiplayer features to encourage in-person social interaction. Preferably, include real-life activities players are already familiar with (e.g. golfing) to facilitate socialization.

Example games:

- Wii Sports or Kinect Sports - *Bowling*: Bowling alleys are usually social spaces in real life. A video game of bowling naturally supports collocated social interaction and attracts players who used to bowl prior to BI.

Related Patterns:

- Can be used to create *Randomized Events* and facilitate *Focus and Distraction.*
- Can be used with *Turn-based Multiplayer* to support in-person socialization and turn taking.

4.3 Relationships among Patterns

Design patterns can interact with each other in various ways. We identified two major types of relationships among patterns in our library (see Figure 5 for a summary of prominent relationships):

(1) Certain patterns can be used together to provide synergistic effects targeting on multiple therapeutic goals (i.e. synergistic relationship). For example, *Self-paced Weight Shifting* can be used with *Weight Shifting to the Extremes* and *Moving Different Body Parts* to address a combination of therapeutic goals such as weight shifting, dynamic balance, and insights into deficits.

(2) Using some patterns can promote or facilitate other patterns (i.e. facilitative relationship). For example, *Focus and Distraction* can be facilitated using patterns such as *Randomized Events* and *Collocated Multiplayer*.

4.4 Using the Patterns

Björk and Holopainen (2004) suggested that game design patterns can be used to support game designers in (1) brainstorming game design ideas, (2) expanding and refining conceptual design, (3) generating solutions to game design considerations, and (4) communicating and documenting game design [6]. While our patterns support those uses, we argue that the efficacy-centered patterns are best used to generate game design ideas when the designers need information about the intended therapeutic goals and the target players who have had a BI. In other words, our patterns help game designers understand needs in BI therapy by providing information about abstract activities that are effective in addressing certain BI therapy goals; some patterns also include information about considerations in BI therapy-centered game design (e.g. player abilities).

For example, if a game designer aims to design games that focus on improving balance and supporting weight-shifting exercises, he or she may consider instantiating patterns such as *Self-paced*

Weight Shifting and *Fine Control* to generate the main game mechanics. If their goal is also to help the patients overcome neglect on one side of the body, they may also consider involving *Moving Different Body Parts*. By checking the related patterns of *Self-paced Weight Shifting*, they may become aware of the pattern *Optimal/adjustable Pace*, which they may use to accommodate a wider range of player abilities.

5. DISCUSSION

Our efficacy-centered game design patterns can serve as a common language for designing BI rehabilitation games and facilitate mutual understanding among game designers and therapists who focus on BI. Our pattern library is obviously not a comprehensive pattern language for BI therapy-centered game design (see section 5.1). However, we argue that our patterns cover the most common goals in BI therapy and included the most prominent game design elements that are effective at addressing these goals. Further, adopting the concept of design patterns allowed us to capture information about the most effective games for BI rehabilitation in a structure that can facilitate expansion of this body of design knowledge. While we plan to continue working towards building a more comprehensive pattern library for BI rehabilitation games, we also invite researchers and practitioners in this area to contribute to this effort.

In addition, design patterns helped us distill multiple variables from the large volumes of data we gathered about COTS game use in real-world therapy settings; in other words, patterns facilitated sense-making of our data for designers who are interested in creating games for BI rehabilitation. Further, our data-driven approach facilitated pattern extraction from successful COTS games. This approach strengthened the validity of our patterns and will be used in future work to expand our pattern library. We speculate that it can also be applied to related areas such as design patterns for accessible games in general.

It is worth noting that, as all kinds of design patterns, our efficacy-centered patterns should not be considered as guidelines that designers "should" follow. Instead, designers are advised to treat our patterns as a toolkit that help them generate creative game design ideas [6]. For this reason, we strived to describe our patterns in a higher level of abstraction. In addition, rehabilitation games are more than mere efficacy. They need to create an engaging experience to motivate patients engaged in the game [8]. As such, designers need to examine other game design considerations such as preference and abilities of their target players in order to create successful games for BI rehabilitation.

5.1 Limitations and Future Work

In this work, we only focused on the creation of efficacy-centered patterns. In future work, we plan to generate patterns that focus on other aspects of BI therapy games such as player experience and accessibility. Additionally, we will evaluate the effectiveness of these patterns with game designers and therapists. Further, the game therapy cases we have gathered so far were skewed towards physical goals and the most popular games; this limited the coverage of our pattern library. We are currently expanding our case gathering process to include a more diverse set of games; we are also trying to gather more cases focused on cognitive and social goals. In addition, we also plan to create an online library of therapy-centered game design patterns and create tools to help game designers who are interested in designing games for BI therapy to browse and choose appropriate patterns for their target players.

6. ACKNOWLEDGMENTS

Our thanks to the participating therapists from Schwab and Marianjoy Rehabilitation Hospitals. This work was funded by grants from DePaul's research council and a joint grant program with DePaul and Rosalind Franklin Universities. Thanks to the reviewers for their valuable comments and suggestions to improve the paper.

7. REFERENCES

[1] About Brain Injury: *http://www.biausa.org/about-brain-injury.htm*. Accessed: 2015-03-24.

[2] Alankus, G., Lazar, A., May, M. and Kelleher, C. 2010. Towards customizable games for stroke rehabilitation. *Proceedings of the 28th international conference on Human factors in computing systems CHI '10* (New York, NY, USA, 2010), 2113–2122.

[3] Alexander, C., Ishikawa, S. and Silverstein, M. 1977. *A Pattern Language: Towns, Buildings, Construction.*

[4] Annema, J.-H., Verstraete, M., Vanden Abeele, V., Desmet, S. and Geerts, D. 2010. Videogames in therapy: a therapist's perspective. *Proceedings of the 3rd International Conference on Fun and Games - Fun and Games '10* (New York, NY, USA, 2010), 94–98.

[5] Betker, A.L., Desai, A., Nett, C., Kapadia, N. and Szturm, T. 2007. Game-based exercises for dynamic short-sitting balance rehabilitation of people with chronic spinal cord and traumatic brain injuries. *Physical therapy*. 87, 10 (2007), 1389–1398.

[6] Björk, S. and Holopainen, J. 2004. *Patterns in game design*. Charles River Media.

[7] Borchers, J.O. 2001. A pattern approach to interaction design. *AI & Society*. 15, (2001), 359–376.

[8] Buday, R., Baranowski, T. and Thompson, D. 2012. Fun and Games and Boredom. *Games for Health Journal*. 1, 4 (2012), 257–261.

[9] Burke, J.W., McNeill, M.D.J., Charles, D.K., Morrow, P.J., Crosbie, J.H. and McDonough, S.M. 2009. Optimising engagement for stroke rehabilitation using serious games. *The Visual Computer*. 25, 12 (2009), 1085–1099.

[10] Deutsch, J.E., Brettler, A., Smith, C., Welsh, J., John, R., Guarrera-Bowlby, P. and Kafri, M. 2012. Nintendo Wii Sports and Wii Fit Game Analysis, Validation, and Application to Stroke Rehabilitation. *Topics in Stroke Rehabilitation*. 18, 6 (2012), 701–719.

[11] Elaklouk, A.M. and Zin, N.A.M. 2012. Requirements for Game Based Cognitive Intervention System for Acquired Brain Injury. *GSTF Journal on Computing*. 2, 3 (2012), 25–31.

[12] Flores, E., Tobon, G., Cavallaro, E., Cavallaro, F.I., Perry, J.C. and Keller, T. 2008. Improving patient motivation in game development for motor deficit rehabilitation. *Proceedings of the 2008 International Conference in Advances in Computer Entertainment Technology - ACE '08* (New York, New York, USA, 2008), 381–384.

[13] Gamma, E., Helm, R., Johnson, R.E. and Vlissides, J. 1995. *Design patterns: elements of reusable object-oriented software*.

[14] Garrido, J. and Marset, I. 2013. Balance disorder rehabilitation through movement interaction.

PervasiveHealth '13 Proceedings of the 7th International Conference on Pervasive Computing Technologies for Healthcare (2013), 319–322.

[15] Gil-Gómez, J.-A., Lloréns, R., Alcañiz, M. and Colomer, C. 2011. Effectiveness of a Wii balance board-based system (eBaViR) for balance rehabilitation: a pilot randomized clinical trial in patients with acquired brain injury. *Journal of neuroengineering and rehabilitation*. 8, 30 (Jan. 2011), 1–9.

[16] Gillen, G. 2010. *Stroke Rehabilitation: A Function-Based Approach*. Mosby.

[17] Goude, D., Björk, S. and Rydmark, M. 2007. Game design in virtual reality systems for stroke rehabilitation. *Studies in Health Technology and Informatics*. 125, (2007), 146–148.

[18] Hardy, J. and Scanlon, M. 2009. The Science Behind Lumosity (Commercial web page). *Lumos Labs*.

[19] Hullett, K. and Whitehead, J. 2010. Design patterns in FPS levels. *Proceedings of the Fifth International Conference on the Foundations of Digital Games - FDG '10* (New York, New York, USA, 2010), 78–85.

[20] Huynh-Kim-Bang, B., Wisdom, J. and Labat, J.-M. 2010. Design Patterns in Serious Games: A Blue Print for Combining Fun and Learning. *Project SE-SG*.

[21] Jintronix: 2010. *http://www.jintronix.com*.

[22] Kam, M. and Rudraraju, V. 2007. Mobile gaming with children in rural India: Contextual factors in the use of game design patterns. *Situated Play, Proceedings of DiGRA 2007 Conference* (2007).

[23] Kelle, S., Klemke, R. and Specht, M. 2011. Design patterns for learning games. *International Journal of Technology Enhanced Learning*. 3, 6 (2011), 555–569.

[24] Lange, B., Chang, C.-Y., Suma, E., Newman, B., Rizzo, A.S. and Bolas, M. 2011. Development and evaluation of low cost game-based balance rehabilitation tool using the Microsoft Kinect sensor. *Annual International Conference of the IEEE Engineering in Medicine and Biology Society* (Jan. 2011), 1831–1834.

[25] Lange, B., Flynn, S. and Rizzo, A. 2009. Initial usability assessment of off-the-shelf video game consoles for clinical game-based motor rehabilitation. *Physical Therapy Reviews*. 14, 5 (Oct. 2009), 355–363.

[26] Lemay, P. 2007. Developing a pattern language for flow experiences in video games. *DiGRA '07 - Proceedings of the 2007 DiGRA International Conference: Situated Play* (2007), 449–455.

[27] Lewis, C., Wardrip-Fruin, N. and Whitehead, J. 2012. Motivational game design patterns of 'ville games. *Proceedings of the International Conference on the Foundations of Digital Games - FDG '12* (New York, New York, USA, 2012), 172–179.

[28] Marne, B., Wisdom, J., Huynh-kim-bang, B., Paris, J. and Labat, J. 2012. A Design Pattern Library for Mutual Understanding and Cooperation in Serious Game Design. *Intelligent Tutoring Systems*. Springer. 135–140.

[29] McClanachan, N.J., Gesch, J., Wuthapanich, N., Fleming, J. and Kuys, S.S. 2013. Feasibility of gaming console exercise and its effect on endurance, gait and balance in people with an acquired brain injury. *Brain injury*. 27, 12 (Jan. 2013), 1402–8.

[30] MIRA: 2012. *http://www.mirarehab.com*.

[31] Paavola, J.M., Oliver, K.E. and Ustinova, K.I. 2013. Use of X-box Kinect Gaming Console for Rehabilitation of an Individual with Traumatic Brain Injury: A Case Report. *Journal of Novel Physiotherapies*. 03, 01 (2013), 1–6.

[32] Projections of mortality and burden of disease, 2004-2030: 2004. *http://www.who.int/entity/healthinfo/global_burden_disease/projections2004/*. Accessed: 2015-03-17.

[33] Putnam, C. and Cheng, J. 2014. Therapist-centered requirements: A multi-method approach of requirement gathering to support rehabilitation gaming. *Proceedings of the IEEE 22nd International Requirements Engineering Conference (RE 2014)* (2014), 13–22.

[34] Putnam, C., Cheng, J. and Seymour, G. 2014. Therapist Perspectives: Wii Active Videogames Use in Inpatient Settings with People Who Have Had a Brain Injury. *Games for Health Journal*. 3, 6 (Dec. 2014), 366–370.

[35] Quick Facts About Brain Injury: *http://www.biausa.org/bia-media-center.htm*. Accessed: 2015-03-17.

[36] Rand, D., Kizony, R. and Weiss, P.L. 2004. Virtual reality rehabilitation for all : Vivid GX versus Sony PlayStation II EyeToy. *Proceedings of the 5th International Conference Series On Disability, Virtual Reality and Associated Technologies (ICDVRAT)* (2004), 87–94.

[37] Rose, F.D., Brooks, B.M. and Rizzo, A. a 2005. Virtual reality in brain damage rehabilitation: review. *Cyberpsychology & behavior : the impact of the Internet, multimedia and virtual reality on behavior and society*. 8, 3 (Jun. 2005), 241–62.

[38] Silver, J.M., McAllister, T.W. and Yudofsky, S.C. 2011. *Textbook of traumatic brain injury*. American Psychiatric Publishing, Inc.

[39] Smith, G., Anderson, R., Kopleck, B., Lindblad, Z., Scott, L., Wardell, A., Whitehead, J. and Mateas, M. 2011. Situating Quests: Design Patterns for Quest and Level Design in Role-Playing Games. *Proceedings of the 4th international conference on Interactive Digital Storytelling (ICIDS'11)* (2011), 326–329.

[40] Thompson, D., Baranowski, T., Buday, R., Baranowski, J., Thompson, V., Jago, R. and Griffith, M.J. 2010. Serious Video Games for Health: How Behavioral Science Guided the Development of a Serious Video Game. *Simulation & gaming*. 41, 4 (Aug. 2010), 587–606.

[41] Yavuzer, G., Senel, a., Atay, M.B. and Stam, H.J. 2008. "Playstation eyetoy games" improve upper extremity-related motor functioning in subacute stroke: A randomized controlled clinical trial. *European Journal of Physical and Rehabilitation Medicine*. 44, 3 (2008), 237–244.

[42] Zickefoose, S., Hux, K., Brown, J. and Wulf, K. 2013. Let the games begin: a preliminary study using attention process training-3 and Lumosity™ brain games to remediate attention deficits following traumatic brain injury. *Brain injury : [BI]*. 27, 6 (2013), 707–16.

A Pilot Study about the Smartwatch as Assistive Device for Deaf People

Matthias Mielke
University of Siegen
Hoelderlinstrasse 3
57076 Siegen, Germany
matthias.mielke@uni-siegen.de

Rainer Brück
University of Siegen
Hoelderlinstrasse 3
57076 Siegen, Germany
rainer.brueck@uni-siegen.de

ABSTRACT

In the last years the smartphone became an important tool for deaf and hard of hearing people. It's no wonder that many different smartphone based assistive tools were introduced recently, among them tools for environmental sound awareness. Even though smartphones seem to be a good way to implement such tools, with the smartwatch a new class of mobile computing devices became available. In this paper results from interviews with six deaf people about the use of a smartwatch as environmental sound alert are presented. The interviews showed that a smartwatch based environmental sound alert is promising as the participants were highly interested in using such a device.

Categories and Subject Descriptors

K.4.2 [**Computers and Society**]: Social Issues—*Assistive technologies for persons with disabilities*

Keywords

deaf, hard of hearing, smartwatch, assistive technology

1. INTRODUCTION

Using the smartphone as assistive device for people experiencing disabilities became a popular approach in assistive technology research. Different applications were presented for deaf people (i.e. deaf, deafened, and hard of hearing), like hearing aids [5], communication support [4], tools to translate sounds to text [6] and for sound awareness [3]. With the commercial availability of the smartwatch, a new platform for implementing assistive applications emerged. Like a smartphone, it is equipped with sensors, a screen, and state-of-the-art CPU. Based on findings in [1] we conducted a study in which we wanted to find out, 1.) how deaf people like the idea of using a smartwatch as environmental sound alert, 2.) how the interface should look and behave, and 3.) which sounds the watch should detect. The most significant findings are summarised in the following section.

ASSETS'15, October 26–28, 2015, Lisbon, Portugal.
ACM 978-1-4503-3400-6/15/10.
DOI: http://dx.doi.org/10.1145/2700648.2811347 .

Figure 1: Full screen notification a). Notification using Android Wear's Card b).

2. INTERVIEWS

To find out about the users' needs and expectations six deaf people were interviewed (personal details in Table 1). The participants were recruited with help of a local hearing aid acoustician and a local advice centre for hearing impaired people. The study was designed as a qualitative semi-structured interview to obtain a profound understanding of the topic. A Wizard of Oz experiment was implemented to simulate the environmental sound alert application. Whenever the wizard heard one of four sounds (doorbell, knock, siren, person entering the room) he triggered the application at the watch using a Bluetooth connected smartphone. Then the watch showed the notification associated with the sound (Figure 1). The interview started after informed consent was obtained and the participants were asked to put on the smartwatch (LG G Watch) for the interview. An introduction serves the purpose to familiarise the participants with the smartwatch and the application. During the introduction the participants were encouraged to freely experiment with the watch and application, however all participants focused on the application. Participants could knock, open and close the rooms door or use videos of a siren and doorbell to trigger the application. The questioning started after the participant finished experimentation. It consisted of 12 questions addressing the design of watch, and application, sounds it should detect, reliability and privacy as well as personal information. Probe questions were prepared to encourage more detailed answers if necessary. The interviews with the deaf participants were supported by a sign language interpreter. Audio records of the interviews were produced, transcribed, and analysed using qualitative content analysis with inductively developed categories [2].

Overall Impression. All participants mentioned that their overall impression of the smartwatch is positive and that such a device would be a valuable aid in their daily life. P3 stressed the easy integration in the daily routine: "You stand up, put on the watch. So then it would be done". The use of the watch was rated as easy by the participants, but P2 and P3 stated that elderly could need support to use it.

Table 1: Participants.

Participant	Age	Sex	Hearing Level	Phone
P1	38	m	deafened	mobile
P2	63	m	deafened	smart
P3	55	f	hard of hearing	mobile
P4	47	f	deaf	smart
P5	45	m	deaf	smart
P6	40	m	deaf	smart

Use in social settings. All participants affirmed that they would use the smartwatch with the application in public. The advantage of the watch is that it is an everyday object used by most people. So it would not stand out and is not recognisable as an assistive device. Even if it attracts attention, it wouldn't concern the participants, some would explain it to people who noticed it.

Self-confidence. Two participants commented that the use of the smartwatch application could influence the confidence positively. P3 stated – based on her experiences in support group – "that all remain [...] in their home and not go out. Perhaps only coming to support group". She added that people using the watch "then perhaps [...] would go again to the streets". Likewise, P5 expressed that using the smartwatch application "would bring a lot accessibility with it." P3 assumed that getting information about sounds could encourage people to leave the safe home more often.

Privacy. Privacy related issues were only mentioned by P2. He expressed that it must not be possible for others to listen in and that information about the location must not be transmitted. It would only be acceptable to send information about the location in case of an emergency. Most participants wouldn't mind that the application analyses the acoustic environment. P5 had no opinion yet.

Design. All participants liked the design of the watch, even though P3 stated that she would prefer a round watch, which she assumed would most women. Diverse opinions were mentioned about the size of the watch. While P3 stated that the watch is rather big and "needs getting used to", P2 found the size appropriate and P6 favoured a bigger watch with a larger display to improve legibility. P5 said that the size "is dependent on the needs of the people and wishes."

User interface. The smartwatch application provides visual and tactile modality. Vibration is used to notify the user that a sound was detected and the type of the sound is shown on the display. Thus, vibration is a very important aspect of the design of the notification. This is reflected in the answers of the participants, who wanted to choose the pattern, strength, and duration according to their personal needs. P2 and P5 stated that the vibration should reflect the importance of a sound and the urgency to react to it, e.g. short vibrations for sounds with low importance and long vibration patterns for sounds with high importance. To make sure that the user notices the vibration, P1 and P6 favoured that the vibration carries on until it is acknowledged by the user. The vibration of the watch was regarded as too weak and a stronger vibration was demanded by four participants. Showing the type of sound was reported earlier to be preferred by deaf people [1]. So both types of notification use icon and text to show the type of the sound: the icon is emphasized in the full screen notification (Figure 1 a)) and the text in the Card notification (Figure 1 b)). Except for P1, who prefers a textual notification, all other participants favoured the full screen icon. With the exception of P2, font sizes were generally considered as too small, especially but not only for elderly. P2, P3, and P6 emphasized that an icon needs to be clear and expressive to facilitate the recognition of it. Due to individual preferences about the design of the icons, it should be possible to change them. P2 and P3 stressed that different sets of icons must be available to suit the visual needs (e.g. contrast, detail) of people experiencing a visual impairment. P3 expressed that icons are better recognizable than text, which is especially good for people with vision impairments.

Table 2: Sounds most often mentioned.

Sound	#	Sound	#
Smoke/Fire alarm	5	Doorbell	3
Telephone	4	Door knock	2
Siren	3	Washing machine	2
Bicycle bell	3	Baby crying	2

Sounds to recognize. A broad range of sounds that the application should recognize were mentioned by the participants. The most often mentioned sounds are listed in Table 2. The wish to use the watch in different contexts makes it necessary to implement management functionality to set sounds to detect, because not all sounds occur or are of interest in every environment. As P1 phrased it "If [...] I'm in road traffic, [...] then I would rather deactivate the recognition for the home". It should also be possible to add new sounds easily to further personalize the device. E.g. P5 wished to add the sound of the kitchen hood, since he repeatedly forgot to turn it off.

3. CONCLUSION AND FUTURE WORK

The use of a smartwatch as an environmental sound alert was appreciated by all participants of the interview, even though several participants stressed that it is only a first impression and that they would like to test it for a longer duration. Implementing an application and conducting a field experiment are the steps planned for the near future. The interviews were carried out following the principles outlined in the Helsinki Declaration of 1975 (revision 2013).

4. REFERENCES

[1] T. Matthews, J. Fong, and J. Mankoff. Visualizing non-speech sounds for the deaf. In *ASSETS'05*, 2005. ACM.

[2] P. Mayring. Qualitative content analysis. *Forum: Qualitative Social Research*, 1(2), 2000.

[3] M. Mielke, and R. Brück. Design and Evaluation of a Smartphone Application for Non-Speech Sound Awareness for People with Hearing Loss. In *EMBC'15*, 2015. IEEE.

[4] T. Pereira, B. Fonseca, H. Paredes, and M. Cabo. Exploring iconographic interface in emergency for deaf. In *ASSETS'11*, 2011. ACM.

[5] W. Wang, Z. Chen, B. Xing, X. Huang, S. Han, and E. Agu. A smartphone-based digital hearing aid to mitigate hearing loss at specific frequencies. In *MMA'14*, 2014. ACM.

[6] S. White. Audiowiz: Nearly real-time audio transcriptions. In *ASSETS'10*, 2010. ACM.

Using OnScreenDualScribe to Support Text Entry and Targeting among Individuals with Physical Disabilities

Sidas Saulynas
UMBC
1000 Hilltop Circle
Baltimore MD 21250 USA
saulyn1@umbc.edu

Lula Albar
UMBC
1000 Hilltop Circle
Baltimore MD 21250 USA
albar1@umbc.edu

Ravi Kuber
UMBC
1000 Hilltop Circle
Baltimore MD 21250 USA
rkuber@umbc.edu

Torsten Felzer
Technical University of Darmstadt
felzer@ims.tu-darmstadt.de

ABSTRACT

This paper describes a study examining the usability of OnScreenDualScribe (OSDS), a tool to support individuals with physical disabilities with text entry and cursor movement. A portable numeric keypad is used to interact with the OSDS, which can either be held by the user, or can be affixed to a surface for interaction. A study to determine the feasibility of the system was conducted with three individuals with physical disabilities. While it was noted that the time taken was higher to complete a task compared to their existing methods of computer-based input, findings also indicate that the system offers potential for tasks involving a combination of text entry and cursor movement (e.g., completing online forms). Furthermore, as the keypad is smaller in size compared with a traditional keyboard, participants suggested that it offered potential to reduce effort spent in the fatiguing process of traversal.

Categories and Subject Descriptors

H.5.m. Miscellaneous

General Terms

Performance, Design, Human Factors

Keywords

Assistive Technology, Cerebral Palsy, Input Devices, Muscular Dystrophy

1. INTRODUCTION

Estimates suggest that in the US, up to 35.2 million adults with physical disabilities face limitations in their daily life activities [5]. For individuals with limited movement (e.g., Cerebral Palsy or Muscular Dystrophy), interacting with a traditional keyboard or mouse can be challenging. The lack of usability, or the complete absence of locus of control of one's ability to perform tasks using a computer can lead to stress, frustration, and anger [6]. By providing individuals with physical disabilities with practical and reliable tools to use standard personal computers (PCs) in order to access information and services, quality of life can be improved.

This paper examines the OnScreenDualScribe (OSDS) system designed to replace conventional input devices, such as the keyboard and mouse, with a small numerical keypad that offers the same functionality [2]. The OSDS system uses an inexpensive numeric keypad and accompanying software to provide users with a compact space to perform both text input, as well as all operations that can be performed using a mouse. The compact nature of the device offers potential benefits for users of limited mobility as they would be able to perform all standard interface operations without having to traverse the normal distances which traditional keyboard users would ordinarily perform. The keypad can be held in both hands for stability, or can be affixed to a surface (e.g. lap tray, wheelchair arm). User tests were conducted to examine the challenges faced by individuals with physical disabilities when performing input based tasks and determine the efficacy and merits of the OSDS tool.

ASSETS '15, October 26-28, 2015, Lisbon, Portugal
ACM 978-1-4503-3400-6/15/10.
http://dx.doi.org/10.1145/2700648.2811348

2. RELATED WORK

A range of assistive technologies have been developed to support individuals with physical disabilities. Individuals with limited hand movement can benefit from using speech-based input solutions (e.g., Dragon Dictate). For those unable to rely on speech, other novel approaches have been proposed enabling users to utilize the functionality available to them. Examples include eye-gaze tracking [1], tongue-based interaction [4] and head-based control of the mouse [3,7]. While these solutions offer considerable promise, they are often expensive to purchase, time-consuming to set-up, and may not be targeted to the user's specific needs.

3. OSDS SYSTEM DESCRIPTION

The OSDS (Figure 1) has been designed to provide an alternative to traditional modalities so that a user with a limited level of mobility can have a more positive user experience when entering text, while also supporting cursor movement.

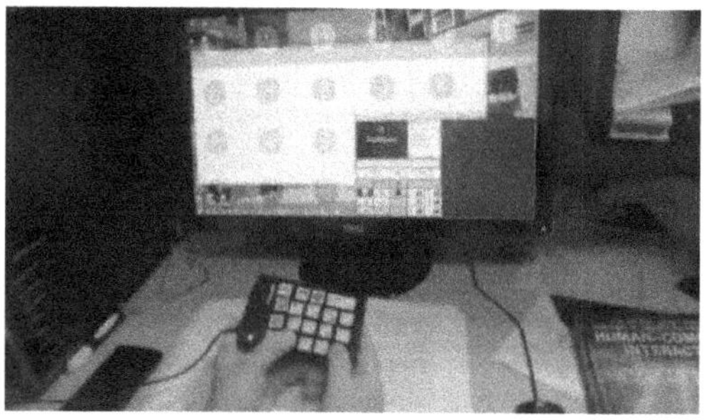

Figure 1: OSDS keypad and "DualMouse mode" screen

The numeric keypad used in conjunction with OSDS has the advantage of being both inexpensive and convenient to handle. Software intercepts keystrokes and sends input events to the active window enabling the user to enter data into a document or web-based form. OSDS operates in nine modes, each dedicated to a different task [2]. In this study, we focused on using two of the most commonly used modes, (1) basic text entry mode, and (2) mouse mode, as these would be most commonly used by target users when interacting with computing technologies.

4. PARTICIPANTS

Three individuals (two female) with physical disabilities (identified here with aliases) participated in the study.

Participant #1: Kyle is a 23 year old male who has had spastic cerebral palsy since birth. He stated that he lacks fine motor skills, does not have very good hand-eye coordination, and has limited use of all 10 fingers. He tends to type using only a few fingers at a time. When interacting with his tablet device for about an hour, spasms occur. He also feels stiffness in his fingers. This can be a frustrating experience if he is required to complete a work deliverable within a short time period, as a period of rest is needed.

Participant #2: Rachael is a 39 year old female with carpal tunnel syndrome and muscular skeletal issues. She has limited wrist movement and experiences intense cramping. Repetitive motion leads to forearm pain and requires frequent breaks when using a computer for either typing or pointing operations. After about 2 to 3 hours of continuous use, she states that the pain is so bad that it makes her "want to stop using the computer".

Participant #3: Magda is a 31 year old female with Spinal Muscular Atrophy. She requires assistance for all activities of daily living. Her movement is limited, and she is only able to interact with a few fingers in one hand. She prefers a trackball for pointing as it affords more control compared with a mouse, and she requires assistance from her caregiver on placing her hand on the device and for repositioning when her hand slips. After about 1-2 hours using a virtual keyboard, she fatigues, and often feels "stiffness in her fingers". This requires asking her caregiver to submerge her hand in warm water for relief of the symptoms.

5. METHODOLOGY

Participants were presented with four tasks which were known to be challenging among some individuals with physical disabilities, due to the fine motor skills needed. These were: (1) Type a phrase with all 26 Roman characters; (2) Perform a web search for a term and select a result; (3) Fill out a web-based form; and (4) Navigate a menu with a deep hierarchy and sub-menus. All tasks were selected, as they were thought to be commonly conducted tasks which their peers without disabilities took for granted.

After the initial interview, the participants were asked to perform the tasks listed above using their own current assistive technologies, to establish a baseline. The participants were then given a five minute overview on how to use the OSDS system. The same four tasks were then repeated using OSDS. Each task was timed and the number of errors that occurred was recorded.

6. RESULTS AND DISCUSSION

Only two participants were able to complete the trials. Although P3 thought that it would be easier for her to interact with a physical keypad compared with a traditional keyboard, she was unable to exert pressure on the keypad buttons. P1 and P2 spent on average four minutes longer using OSDS to perform interaction tasks, compared with their existing methods of input and cursor movement. The results were in part attributed to the short period of training time, combined with the positioning of the device. Both participants favored laying the device flat on a table, rather than holding it in both hands for added stability. While participants highlighted that the time taken to interact with the device was slower than expected, they valued the ability to control the cursor and input using a smaller, portable device which could easily be used with either one or two hands. It would also help them perform tasks which could be more complex to undertake (i.e. moving through hierarchical menus without worries about slipping off and having to restart the task). Participants suggested that additional rehearsal time with the system would lead to less time being spent conducting tasks. It would also help to increase levels of confidence when using the system independently. It was suggested that the system would be beneficial for tiring tasks involving a combination of cursor movement and text entry (i.e. filling out long online forms).

Suggestions were made to improve the surface layer of the graphical interface by providing more informative icons, enabling users to target buttons more quickly (i.e. adding an indicator for the TAB key or having clear numeric characters to indicate the keys for character row selection). Providing additional auditory cues could help provide informative feedback to the user about system state, and whether data was ready to be entered.

7. CONCLUSIONS AND FUTURE WORK

This paper has described an approach to meet the needs of individuals with physical disabilities with text entry and cursor movement. An exploratory study has been undertaken to evaluate the feasibility of the solution. Based on the feedback of the study, we aim to refine the application to expedite the time taken to input data. The design of the interface would be simplified, to enable users to locate commands more easily, and more detailed on-screen help would be provided to support users during the learning process. A longitudinal study would then be undertaken with a larger sample of representative participants to determine whether the refined solution can help users in their day-to-day computing tasks.

8. ACKNOWLEDGEMENTS

This work is partially supported by DFG grant FE 936/6-2.

9. REFERENCES

[1] Al-Rahayfeh, A. and Faezipour, M., 2013. Eye tracking and head movement detection: a state-of-art survey. *IEEE J. Transl. Eng. Health Med.*, 1 (2013), 11-22.

[2] Felzer, T. and Rinderknecht, S., 2013. How someone with a neuromuscular disease experiences operating a PC (and how to successfully counteract that). In *Proceedings of ACM ASSETS*, ACM, New York, NY, Article No. 29.

[3] Lau, C. and O'Leary, S., 1993. Comparison of computer interface devices for persons with severe physical disabilities. *Am J Occup Ther,* 47 11 (1993), 1022-1030.

[4] Salem, C. and Zhai, S., 1997. An isometric tongue pointing device. In *Proceedings of ACM CHI*, ACM, New York, NY, 538-539.

[5] Schiller, J.S., Lucas, J.W., Ward, B.W., and Peregoy, J.A., 2012. Summary health statistics for US adults: National Health Interview Survey - 2010, *Vital and Health Statistics,* 252, 1-207.

[6] Shneiderman, B. and Plaisant, C., 2010. *Designing the User Interface: Strategies for Effective Human-Computer Interaction* (5th ed). Addison-Wesley, Boston, MA.

[7] Wheeler, M., Wolf, F., and Kuber, R., 2013. Supporting augmented and alternative communication using a low-cost gestural device. In *Proceedings of ACM ASSETS*, ACM, New York, NY, Article No: 67.

Developing SAGAT Probes to Evaluate Blind Individuals' Situation Awareness when Traveling Indoor Environments

Abdulrhman A. Alkhanifer
Computing and Information Science Program
Rochester Institute of Technology (RIT)
Rochester, NY, USA.
akhnaifer@mail.rit.edu

Stephanie Ludi
Software Engineering Department
Rochester Institute of Technology (RIT)
Rochester, NY, USA.
salvse@rit.edu

ABSTRACT
Assessing a user's situation awareness can provide a great way to learn about the user's mental model when performing related tasks. Situation Awareness Global Assessment Technique (SAGAT) is one widely accepted measure to objectively capture a user's SA. In this work, we present our developed SAGAT probes to assess the situation awareness of blind individuals during indoor travel tasks. This work is part of our ongoing work to develop an objective method to facilitate blind travelers' situation awareness when traveling unfamiliar indoor environments. We present examples of our probes that were derived from our previously developed situation awareness requirements. Also, we briefly illustrate pilot study results with blindfolded participants.

Categories and Subject Descriptors
H.5.2 **[User Interfaces]**: *User-centered design.* H.1.2 **[User/Machine Systems]**: *Human factors*; K.4.2 **[Computers and Society]** *Social issues – Assistive technologies for persons with disabilities.*

Keywords
Situation Awareness, Situation Awareness Global Assessment Technique (SAGAT), visual impairment, Orientation Assistive Technology, and indoor navigation.

1. INTRODUCTION
Situation Awareness (SA) can be explained as the individual's understanding of the environment including the ability to predict future outcomes [2]. Orientation Assistive Technology (OAT) supports blind individuals when traveling unfamiliar indoor environments by supporting travelers' mental map about landmarks around them. Our previous paper [1] discusses our elicited and modeled SA requirements that blind individual's need when traveling unfamiliar indoor environments. Using the elicited requirements and the developed goal modeling that was based on Endsley's Goal-Directed Task Analysis (GDTA) [5], we developed Situation Awareness Global Assessment Technique (SAGAT) probes.

Endsley's SA framework [5] divides user's SA under three levels: perception, comprehension, and projection. Perception is the basic level that means that an individual has received the information about the environmental elements. Comprehension is the second level that means that an individual has used the first level information to build a cohesive understanding of his/her environment. The projection level is the ability to predict future outcomes. Most orientation assistive technologies (OATs) support users on the first two levels. This work will focus on the first two levels.

The SAGAT technique is a widely accepted objective method to capture user's SA [3]. This technique requires the pause of user's task for multiple times. During each stop, the system display is blanked. Then, the user is presented with a set of probes that assess his/her SA. Having multiple stops can help in eliminating the short-term memory loss, especially in the complex tasks. Also, it allows presenting more probes that provide a good SA coverage. Probes are developed based on a special goal requirements analysis: GDTA [5]. Answers can be compared with the current state of the user's task.

In this work, we have developed SAGAT probes to examine the SA of blind individuals when using OAT in unfamiliar indoor environments. Using our previous SA requirements analysis [1], we developed a set of SAGAT probes. The goal of this work is to design an objective method to facilitate blind individuals' SA when traveling unfamiliar indoor environments. The contribution of this paper is the development of SAGAT probes to examine the SA of blind individuals when traveling unfamiliar indoor environments.

2. Literature Review
The SAGAT method has been used in many domains such as: air fighter and civic flight simulations, car simulators, and military chain-of-command [5]. Typically, the domains that adapted the SAGAT method were in a simulator setup. While a user is performing a task, the simulator freezes at random, the screen blanked, and a set of SA probes is presented to the user. Once the user responds to the questions, the simulator resumes for the user to carry his/her task.

Using SAGAT to measure blind individual's SA during indoor travel is a novel application. To the best of our knowledge no other work has evaluated blind travelers' SA using SAGAT probes during indoor travel.

3. SAGAT Probes
Depending on the scope of the system prompts, we developed a set of probes to examine blind individual's SA. Our system is based on Drishti's orientation information [6] and Polacek, *et al.* navigational commands [7]. Our prototype is assumed to support blind individual's SA for perceiving the important environmental information as well as understanding their context (SA levels 1 and 2).

Our developed probes examine the user's understanding of his/her relative location and distance as well as the knowledge of the

ASSETS '15, October 26–28, 2015, Lisbon, Portugal.
ACM 978-1-4503-3400-6/15/10
http://dx.doi.org/10.1145/2700648.2811350

current state of nearby landmarks. In our SAGAT probes, we examine different dimensions that cover the aforementioned factors. Table 1 illustrates the probes' dimensions while explaining each.

Table 1. SA probes' dimensions

No.	Dimension	Meaning
1	Existence	The knowledge of the existence of a landmark nearby the user.
2	State	The knowledge of the state of a landmark around the user.
3	Location	The relative location of a landmark from user's current position.
4	Distance	The relative distance of a landmark from user's current position.

4. Pilot Study

To examine the feasibility and appropriateness of our developed probes, we piloted a test where we examined three blindfolded participants (2 females). Each participant performed four indoor travel scenarios in four equally controlled environments. In two randomly selected scenarios, participants traveled using a cane and our OAT system, while in the other two scenarios, participants used only their canes. In each scenario, we asked the participants to pause and respond to the probes twice. During each stop, participants were asked to respond to probes that relates to the nearby landmarks (see Table 2). Probes were presented verbally and answers were recorded for later analysis. Each landmark had four probe points. Each correct answer gets a 1, otherwise a zero.

Table 2. Examples of our developed SAGAT probes that cover SA levels 1 and 2

SA Level	Probe	Scoring Technique
1	Name all the landmarks that were around you in your path.	Each correct name gets 1
	State the aforementioned landmarks' availability status.	Each correct landmark's status gets 1
2	Using clock-based system, point out all nearby landmarks.	+/- 2 clock hours error margin
	In feet, indicate how far do you think the aforementioned landmarks are.	+/- 20% error margin

Table 3 illustrates the average SA levels that were resulted from our pilot test. SA scores were normalized. The results suggested an SA difference between participants who travel using their canes and our OAT system as opposed to the participants who only use their canes.

5. Limitations

The work presented in this paper was performed on blindfolded participants. We acknowledge that the presented results are preliminary and cannot be used to draw conclusions. We will experiment our work with totally blind individuals. Also, the use of SAGAT requires certain stops in the travel tasks. This might affect participants' chain of thoughts of the environment.

Table 3. SA average scores for the pilot test

	Use OAT	SA1	SA2	Total SA
T1	Yes	0.519	0.190	0.354
	No	0.317	0.041	0.179
T2	Yes	0.851	0.541	0.696
	No	0.230	0.041	0.136
T3	Yes	0.798	0.666	0.732
	No	0.472	0.250	0.361

6. CONCLUSION AND FUTURE WORK

In this work, we presented the development of SAGAT probes to examine blind individual's SA levels. These probes were used in a pilot test with blindfolded participants. Pilot results suggested that SAGAT probes could be beneficial to facilitate blind travelers SA in the domain of OAT systems. Our next step is to use our developed SAGAT probes with blind individuals.

7. ACKNOWLEDGMENTS

We thank all the participants who dedicated their time to contribute to this research. Also, we thank Hanan Alhussaini for her help in preparing and implementing the experimental work. Additionally, the first author would like to thank King Saud University in Riyadh, Saudi Arabia for their provided scholarship.

8. REFERENCES

[1] Alkhanifer, A. and Ludi, S. 2014. Towards a Situation Awareness Design to Improve Visually Impaired Orientation in Unfamiliar Buildings: Requirements Elicitation Study. *Requirements Engineering Conference (RE), 2014 22st IEEE International* (Karlskrona, Sweden, 2014), 21–30.

[2] Dominguez, C. 1994. Can SA be defined? *Situation Awareness: Papers and Annotated Bibliography. Interim Report No. AL/CF-TR-1994-0085*. M. Vidulich, C. Dominguez, E. Vogel, and G. Mcmillan, eds. 5–15.

[3] Endsley, M. R. Situation awareness global assessment technique (SAGAT). *Aerospace and Electronics Conference, 1988. NAECON 1988., Proceedings of the IEEE 1988 National*, 789–795 vol.3.

[4] Endsley, M. R., Bolstad C. A., Jones D. G. and Riley J. M. 2003. Situation Awareness Oriented Design: From User's Cognitive Requirements to Creating Effective Supporting Technologies. *Proceedings of the Human Factors and Ergonomics Society Annual Meeting October* 47, 268–272.

[5] Endsley, M. R. 2011. *Designing for Situation Awareness: An Approach to User-Centered Design*. CRC Press, Inc., Boca Raton, FL, USA.

[6] Ran, L. Helal, S. and Moore, S. Drishti: an integrated indoor/outdoor blind navigation system and service. *Pervasive Computing and Communications, 2004. PerCom 2004. Proceedings of the Second IEEE Annual Conference on*, 23–30.

[7] Poláček, O., Grill, T. and Tscheligi, M. 2012. Towards a navigation system for blind people: a Wizard of Oz study. *SIGACCESS Access. Comput.*, 104, 12–29.

Dytective: Toward a Game to Detect Dyslexia

Luz Rello
HCI Institute
Carnegie Mellon University
luzrello@cs.cmu.edu

Abdullah Ali
University of Maryland
Baltimore County
aali6@umbc.edu

Jeffrey P. Bigham
HCI and LT Institutes
Carnegie Mellon University
jbigham@cmu.edu

ABSTRACT

Detecting dyslexia is crucial so that people who have dyslexia can receive training to avoid associated high rates of academic failure. In this paper we present *Dytective*, a game designed to detect dyslexia. The results of a within-subjects experiment with 40 children (20 with dyslexia) show significant differences between groups who played *Dytective*. These differences suggest that *Dytective* could be used to help identify those likely to have dyslexia.

Keywords

Dyslexia; Serious Games; Detection; Screening

Categories and Subject Descriptors

K.3 [**Computers in Education**]: Computer Uses in Education—*Computer-assisted instruction*.

1. INTRODUCTION

Dyslexia is the most common neurological learning disability. Even though 10% of the worldwide population are dyslexic, few are diagnosed. Diagnosing dyslexia is non-trivial; it is expensive and generally requires an expert. In the UK, only 5% of people with dyslexia are diagnosed, and the cost of this is low literacy (over 85% of illiterate adults have dyslexia) [1]. In fact, dyslexia is called a *hidden* disability due to the difficulty of its diagnosis. A tool to screen *undiagnosed* children with dyslexia without requiring a specialist could have a crucial impact in the education system preventing school failure, which is associated with dyslexia, even if dyslexia is not related to overall intelligence [3].

To meet this need we developed *Dytective*, which, to the best of our knowledge, is the first game to screen dyslexia in Spanish.[1]

[1]This work is protected by a provisional patent application titled "Method to Detect Individuals with or at Risk of Neurodevelopmental Specific Learning Disorders using Human Computer Interaction" filed on March 20, 2015.

ASSETS'15, October 26–28, 2015, Lisbon, Portugal.
ACM 978-1-4503-3400-6/15/10.
DOI: http://dx.doi.org/10.1145/2700648.2811351 .

Figure 1: The first level of *Dytective*. Players hear the character that they should click and then click it quickly within the time limit (shown in the green circle).

2. RELATED WORK

Lyytinen *et al.* [4] created the computer game *Literate*,to identify children at risk of having dyslexia before school age in Finland. Its exercises are aimed towards the connection of graphemes (letters) and phonemes (sounds). They conducted two user studies with 12 and 41 children between 6 and 7 years old with very promising results. Later, Gaggi *et al.* [2] developed and evaluated a game with 24 pre-schoolers in Italy, that aimed at eye-hand coordination, visual spatial attention, rapid speech-sound identification and discrimination as well as visual-to-speechsound. Van den Audenaeren *et al.* [7] performed a user study with 20 pre-schoolers in Flanders and are currently developing the game *DYSL-X* for early risk detection of dyslexia, which includes letter and end-phoneme recognition as well as psycho-acoustical tests.

To the best of our knowledge *Dytective* is the first game that aim at screening dyslexia in Spanish using human computer interaction measures.

3. DYTECTIVE GAME

Running Dytective. The player's goal is to accumulate points by hitting the target letter/syllable as many times as possible in a 15 second window. The player hears the target letter/syllable and then a board is shown containing also distractors; counters with the score and with the remaining seconds were place at the top (Figure 1). After each game iteration the player go up a level.

Content Design. The game aims at three skills children with dyslexia have difficulties with: (i) letter recognition, (ii) syllable recognition, and (iii) phoneme to grapheme (sound to letter) mapping, that is, phonological awareness.

Dependent Variable	*Children with Dyslexia*			*Children without Dyslexia*			Significance	%
	M	SD	Mdn	M	SD	Mdn		
Clicks	4.63	3.10	4	6.08	2.66	6	$W = 6121.5,\ p < 0.001$	131.32
Hits	3.81	2.67	4	5.84	2.72	6	$W = 5344,\ p < 0.001$	153.28
Score	17.84	10.35	17	28.74	14.75	27	$W = 5502,\ p < 0.001$	161.10
Accuracy	0.80	0.30	1	0.95	0.14	1	$W = 7181.5,\ p < 0.001$	118.75
Speed	0.25	0.18	0.27	0.39	0.18	0.4	$W = 0.9447,\ p < 0.001$	156.00

Table 1: Results for the comparisons between groups: Means, medians, standard deviations, significance and relative percentage difference with respect to the smallest average value.

We established seven levels based on the number of cells in the grid starting with a 3x3 grid up to 7x7. To gradually increase their difficulty we defined a set of linguistic criteria based on how language is acquired and the specific difficulties of dyslexia, extracted from the analyses of the errors that people with dyslexia make [5].

- **Level 1** targets vowels; distractors (vowels only) are randomly selected.
- **Level 2** targets consonants, distractors are randomly selected among all consonants.
- **Level 3** targets similar looking letters. These are letters that have mirror *i.e. 'u' and 'n'* and rotation features *i.e. 'p' and 'd'*. For this level distractors are randomly selected among a group that shares the features of the target letter(s)/syllable(s) [5].
- **Level 4** targets consonants that share phonetic and visual rotation features (*'b','d','p','q'*) [5].
- **Level 5** targets syllables with the following structures CV *i.e. 'ca'* and VC *i.e. 'on'*.[2]
- **Level 6** is for checked syllables with CCV structure, *i.e. 'pla'*.
- **Level 7** aims at checked syllables with CCVC structure, *i.e. 'glis'*.

4. USER STUDY

We recruited 40 **participants**, 20 of them with dyslexia[3] ($M = 8.60, SD = 0.82$ years old) and 20 without dyslexia serving as a control group ($M = 8.60, SD = 0.94$). They were all were native speakers of Spanish, their ages ranged from 7 to 10 years and they were all attending school (second to fifth grade). We used a within-subjects design to compared the performance of both groups. Each participant had to play on-line to one game of each level (seven games in total),[4] being supervised by a parent or psychologist.

As **dependent variables** we measured the (i) the total number of *Clicks* per game (each participant played 7 games, one per level); (ii) total number of *Hits*, *i.e.* number correct answers per game; (iii) the final *Score i.e.* sum of correct answers or all game; (iv) *Accuracy* defined as the number of *Clicks* divided by the number of *Hits* per game; and (v) the *Speed*, calculated as the number of *Clicks* divided by the time spend (15 seconds), *i.e.* number correct answers per second.

[2]C refers to consonant and V refers to vowel.

[3]They all had diagnoses except of 3 participants which were under observation by professionals, the previous step before having an official diagnosis.

[4]`http://xyleques.com/CMU/game/`

5. RESULTS

A Shapiro-Wilk test showed that none of the data sets were normally distributed hence we used dependent 2-group Wilcoxon Signed Rank test for non-parametric data to test differences between groups. In Table 1, we show the results for the comparisons between groups. Significant differences among groups were found for all the dependent measures.

6. CONCLUSIONS AND FUTURE WORK

We have presented the first prototype of a screener for dyslexia in Spanish, *Dytective*. An experiment with 40 participants has shown very promising results suggesting that this tool could be used to screen dyslexia. Currently, we are carrying out a large scale study with *Dytective* to be able apply machine learning techniques [6] that were already found to be useful to predict dyslexia. Since estimations of dyslexia are much higher than the actual diagnosed population we believe this has a great potential impact.

Acknowledgements

We thank all the participants and their families as well as Daniela Alarcón Sánchez for supervising part of the participants at Américo Vespucio school; and Nikki García for recording her voice for the game. This paper was developed under a grant from the Department of Education, NIDRR grant number H133A130057.

7. REFERENCES

[1] Dyslexia Research Institute. Dyslexia, identification, January 2015. `www.dyslexia-add.org`.

[2] O. Gaggi, G. Galiazzo, C. Palazzi, A. Facoetti, and S. Franceschini. A serious game for predicting the risk of developmental dyslexia in pre-readers children. In *Proc. ICCCN'12*, pages 1–5. IEEE, 2012.

[3] International Dyslexia Association. Frequently Asked Questions About Dyslexia, 2011. `www.interdys.org`.

[4] H. Lyytinen, M. Ronimus, A. Alanko, A.-M. Poikkeus, and M. Taanila. Early identification of dyslexia and the use of computer game-based practice to support reading acquisition. *Nordic Psychology*, 59(2):109, 2007.

[5] L. Rello, R. Baeza-Yates, and J. Llisterri. DysList: An annotated resource of dyslexic errors. In *Proc. LREC 2014*, pages 1289–1296, Reykjavik, Iceland, May 2014.

[6] L. Rello and M. Ballesteros. Detecting readers with dyslexia using machine learning with eye tracking measures. In *Proc. W4A '15*, Florence, Italy, 2015.

[7] Van den Audenaeren et al. DYSL-X: Design of a tablet game for early risk detection of dyslexia in preschoolers. In *Games for Health*, pages 257–266. Springer, 2013.

Design and Evaluation of a Simplified Online Banking Interface for People with Cognitive Disabilities

Mario Erazo
Stuttgart Media University
Nobelstraße 10
70569 Stuttgart, Germany
me083@hdm-stuttgart.de

Gottfried Zimmermann
Stuttgart Media University
Nobelstraße 10
70569 Stuttgart, Germany
gzimmermann@acm.org

ABSTRACT

This paper is intended to inform readers about the development and evaluation of a simplified online banking interface for people with cognitive disabilities; this includes a description of the development process as well as the evaluation of the interface with users. Moreover, thoughts and experiences that went into the development will be discussed.

Categories and Subject Descriptors

H.5.2 [**Information Interfaces and Presentation**]: User Interfaces – *screen design, evaluation.*

General Terms

Design, Human Factors

Keywords

Online Banking; Interface Design; Accessibility; Cognitive Disabilities

1. INTRODUCTION

The Web is the most used channel for people to stay connected and access services; thus providing independence and convenience. The ability to access content on the Web helps individuals to maintain their independence. However, when talking about Web accessibility, there is a tendency to concentrate on people with visual and motor impairments, often overlooking users with cognitive impairments and learning difficulties [3].

Cognitive disabilities give rise to problems that completely differ from those with visual, auditory, or motor impairments. Problems with language and numbers, auditory input, and spatial orientation [4]; problems with memory, perception, conceptualization [1] and difficulties remembering sequences, deciphering text, understanding social cues or following complex processes [5]; make using current web interfaces a complex task.

Related work in the field of disabilities and banking services has taken a text only approach [2]. In Germany, some banks offer accessible online banking systems, which coexist with the traditional systems.

ASSETS '15, October 26-28, 2015, Lisbon, Portugal.
ACM 978-1-4503-3400-6/15/10.
http://dx.doi.org/10.1145/2700648.2811352

However, these systems are mostly text based variants with large fonts, simplified language and reduced functionality.

2. INTERFACE DEVELOPMENT

The development of the interface started with the research of the users, their conditions, problems and limitations with current online services. Furthermore, as part of a user centered design approach, the development of the interface emphasized the involvement of users and their caretakers in the development process. This included the use of focus groups with caretakers and user tests with individuals with some kind of cognitive limitation.

In general, the development process consisted of many stages, which go from finding and categorizing design guidelines to the evaluation of the interface with users. Overall, the development process was not linear but rather iterative; based on feedback from users and caretakers.

The interface design for the system was characterized by: (a) The representation of money amounts through images of bills and coins (see fig. 1). (b) The use of focused tasks i.e. the screen just contains a single task at a time. An example would be that a money transfer is divided into single steps. (c) Language used is as simple as possible, with short sentences and max. 70 characters pro line. (d) Avoid requiring non-numeric text-input. (e) The ability to pause a transaction and let a third person (caretaker / family) approve the transaction. (f) The interface uses as few elements as possible and employs visual cues to help users with navigation through the system.

Figure 1 shows interface designed for the online banking applications.

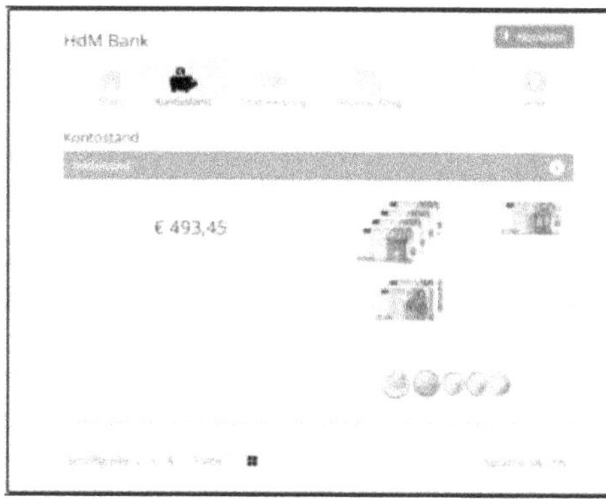

Figure 1. Simplified Online Banking Interface Screenshot

Overall, the goal of the system was to reflect a feeling of simplicity. The interface was developed to fulfill as many usability guidelines - aimed at people with cognitive disabilities - as possible, and at the same time to deliver an enjoyable experience through the use of clean visual elements and vivid colors.

During the development most of the problems found were related to users having problems with text - long sentences in most cases, or not being able to find certain element e.g. a specific button.

3. EVALUATION

The evaluation of the interface assured the interface's usability for users. Testing it with real users was a very important part of the development process. With the help of the Bruderhaus Diakonie in Reutlingen, Germany - an institution providing assistance and support for people with disabilities - we were able to get a representative group of 11 participants.

Each participant had some kind of cognitive impairment. They all had experience with banking services, and while seven participants had some experience with Internet services just two of them had used an online banking system before.

The evaluation consisted of an introduction, a description about the study and an account of the goals of the evaluation. Afterwards, the introductory questionnaire and an interview served to get more information about the participants and their limitations. Subsequently, every participant received an assignment. The assignment consisted of 3 tasks: (1) sign into the online banking service, (2) check the account balance, and (3) pay the phone bill. After concluding the assignment, an interview aided to get the participants opinion about the interface; and to know if they would use a similar kind of online banking service interface in the future.

All participants were able to complete the assignment, two users required some help in the process, mainly because of their inexperience with graphical interfaces and computers in general. The time that took users to complete the task was very variant, and was directly related to their experience with electronic devices.

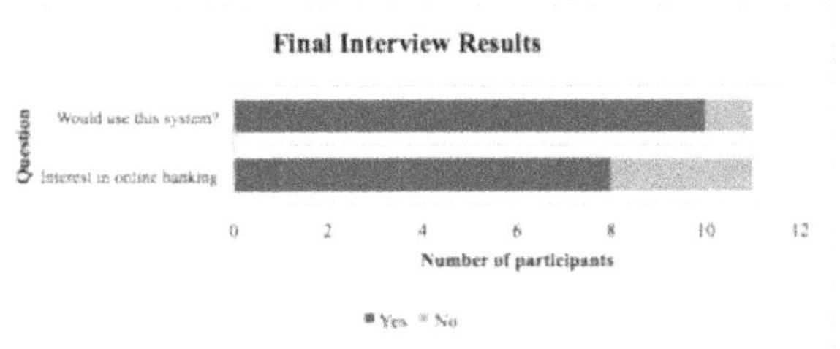

Figure 2. Final Interview Results

Figure 2 shows the results of the final interview, here one can notice that the system had a really high acceptance level among the participants.

In general, the interface had great success with the participants. It accomplished its intended goal of providing a simple way for users to use online banking. At the end, 10 out of 11 participants stated that they would use this system, although two from them were not interested in online banking at all (see fig. 2).

The interview brought some important issues into discussion, such as printed confirmations of transactions, Internet security and input. For most users (9 participants) was important to have a printed confirmation of a transaction for their records; users with some computer knowledge and Internet experience were concerned about Internet security (4 participants), they described bad experiences from relatives or acquaintances, making it the main reason why they used the Internet but not online banking. On the other hand, some users mentioned that the main impediment to use this interface were financial issues; some could not afford to buy a PC or were not interested in paying for Internet service (4 participants). Last, some users (2 participants) had no computer experience at all, which made the task of using a mouse and keyboard something new.

For many the testing process and the use of a new interface were interesting, mainly because of the new experience. Nevertheless, all participants agreed that the experience of going to a bank and getting one-to-one attention could not be replaced. In relation to participants with none-to-little computer knowledge, they had issues with the mouse and keyboard as input devices, and some complained that one "needs to learn too much" in order to use the system.

4. CONCLUSION

To conclude, research is needed to identify the problems experienced by people with cognitive disabilities and user interfaces. It can be difficult to develop for impairments that few have heard of and no one can see. But, as shown by this paper, the development of accessible interfaces for this user group is possible; it just requires a more thoughtful analysis of the users and their needs.

5. REFERENCES

[1] Hudson, R., Weakley, R., & Firminger, P. (2004). WebBoy.net. Retrieved October 29, 2014 from CSS to aid readability and clickability: http://webboy.net/presentation/ozewai2004/02.html

[2] Seeman, L. (2002, January 1). *Inclusion Of Cognitive Disabilities in the Web Accessibility Movement*. Retrieved December 20, 2014, from The Eleventh International World Wide Web Conference: http://www2002.org/CDROM/alternate/689

[3] Small, J., Schallau, P., Brown, K., & Appleyard, R. (2005). *Web accessibility for people with cognitive disabilities*. Association for Computing Machinery, 1-4.

[4] Weakley, R. (2005). *Developing sites for users with Cognitive disabilities and learning difficulties.* Retrieved October 29, 2014, from JuicyStudio.com: http://juicystudio.com/article/cognitive-impairment.php

[5] WebAIM. (2013). *Cognitive Disabilities Part 1.* Retrieved October 27, 27, from WebAIM: http://webaim.org/articles/cognitive/cognitive_too_little/

GraCALC: An Accessible Graphing Calculator

Cagatay Goncu
Faculty of IT
Monash University, Australia
cagatay.goncu@monash.edu

Kim Marriott
Faculty of IT
Monash University, Australia
Kim.Marriott@monash.edu

ABSTRACT

We present a new approach for providing mathematical and statistical graphics to people who are blind or have severe vision impairment and describe the implementation and initial evaluation of an accessible graphing calculator, GraCALC. GraCALC automatically creates a graphic from a specification of the function or a tabular data using a web based service. The graphic is then presented on a touch device, and a mixture of speech, non-speech audio and optional tactile feedback are provided to allow the users explore the screen. An overview containing a sonification of the graphic and a description similar to that created by a human transcriber is also automatically generated so as to help the user in their initial navigation.

Keywords

graphics, accessibility, vision impairment, authoring, multi-modal, audio, tactile, haptic, interaction, annotation

Categories and Subject Descriptors

H.5.2. [**Information Interfaces and Presentation**]: User Interfaces; K.4.2. [**Computers and Society**]: Social issues–assistive technologies for persons with disabilities.

1. INTRODUCTION

Limited access to information graphics remains a severely disabling consequence of blindness [1]. In particular, it restricts educational and employment choices and opportunities because of reduced access to the many kinds of mathematical and statistical graphics used in STEM (Science, Technology, Engineering and Mathematics), social sciences and business and economics.

In Australia, as in most other other developed countries, blind school students are provided with accessible versions of mathematical and statistical graphics by specialist transcribers who will produce either a textual description or a tactile graphic. Unfortunately, tactile graphics are not the best technology for providing accessible versions of graphics, because they are relatively expensive to print, and users need to wait weeks to get them despite some tools (not commonly used) which automatically generate a tactile graphic from a table or from an equation, e.g. PictureBraille[2] and Tactile Chart Tool [7].

[1]For brevity we use the term blind people to refer to people whose level of vision does not allow them to easily read printed text or graphics even when magnified.

ASSETS'15, October 26-28, 2015, Lisbon, Portugal
ACM 978-1-4503-3400-6/15/10.
DOI: http://dx.doi.org/10.1145/2700648.2811353

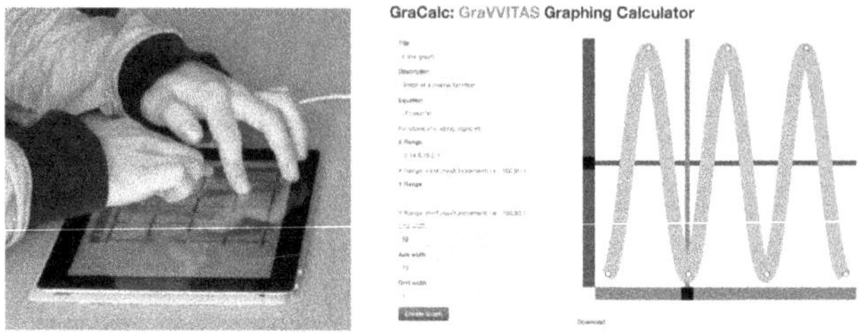

(a) (b)

Figure 1: GraCALC: (a) Usage on the iPad. (b) GraCALC web interface for constructing a graphic.

A number of accessible graphing calculators and applications have been developed that do not need expensive tactile graphics and instead provide speech or non-speech audio descriptions: Audio Graphing Calculator (AGC) [4], MathTrax[3], Maxima[4], vOICe[5], GTCalc[6], and Orion TI-84 Plus[7].

However, tactile graphics are still preferred by most students to descriptions or sonification provided by the above calculators as they prefer to be able to build up a mental model of the graph using "active" touch and to have a representation similar to that of sighted students [3]. Furthermore, extending tactile graphics by using audio is shown to be more effective, particularly in maps [1]. Recently, multi-modal (speech and/or non-speech audio and tactile) interfaces are also used successfully for presenting accessible graphics on touchscreen devices [6, 5].

This paper extends GraVVITAS [6] which uses a multi-modal interaction model to give the best experience from creating to using mathematical and statistical graphics. It does not require a tactile material, allows touch-based interaction and provides sonification, a detailed overview, optional annotation and automatic creation of graphics using a web service.

GraCALC, shown in Figure 1, and the underlying model were developed in cooperation with Vision Australia and Statewide Vision Resource Centre using a user-centered participatory design including blind secondary and university students.

[2]http://www.pentronics.com.au
[3]http://prime.jsc.nasa.gov/mathtrax
[4]http://www.ma.utexas.edu/maxima/
[5]http://www.seeingwithsound.com/winmath.htm
[6]http://www.quantumrlv.com.au
[7]http://www.aph.org/

Our model for accessible presentation of mathematical and statistical graphics is based on five key ideas of which the last four are interesting interface innovations: (i) there is no need for manual transcription as the accessible graphic is generated from a semantic specification of the function, (ii) an audio overview of the graphic similar to that created by human transcribers is generated automatically, (iii) the basic presentation of the graph is multimodal, using a mixture of tactile and audio feedback, so that the reader explores the touch screen surface with fingers from both hands to build up a mental model of the graph's spatial layout, (iv) the direct touch screen presentation is augmented with user controlled sonification, (v) support both text and recorded audio annotation of the graphic.

2. GRACALC

GraCALC works as a web service which uses R, Shiny[8], and ggplot2 [9]. It is used from two different interfaces: (i) inside the GraVVITAS app running on the iPad—see Figure 1 (a), (ii) a web page used by teachers or sighted friends—see Figure 1 (b). Both of these interfaces allow their users to specify graph function as mathematical expressions such as $x^2, sin(x), log(x)$ etc., or from tabular data. Furthermore, various parameters controlling the domain and range of the graphs as well as the gird lines and line sizes can also be specified. Once all the parameters are specified GraCALC automatically generates the graphics and the overview text. The generated graphics can then be downloaded and imported into the GraVVITAS app.

User Interface: The user interface has been designed to use VoiceOver and the standard system wide iOS gestures so far as possible to reduce the initial learning time and to provide a consistent user experience.

Menus are controlled using the standard iOS VoiceOver gestures: magic tap and rotor gestures which do not require location accuracy and limit time-based actions [8].

Basic Interaction Model: The accessible graphic is displayed in a graphic canvas on the iPad's screen. As the user explores the canvas the system determines the graphic objects under the touch points and provides a combination of speech (information about the object), non-speech (an audio boundary) audio and tactile (through vibration motors attached to the fingers) feedback. Currently the system is designed to be used with the two index fingers, typically one finger is used as a reference point while the other finger explores the graphic.

Overview and navigation: It is much more difficult to navigate or build an overview of a graphic when using only fingers to explore a graphic since this is inherently sequential and there is no analogue of peripheral vision [2]. For this reason tactile graphics often come with a braille overview. We provide similar functionality in our approach.

When the graphic is first opened VoiceOver is used to provide a description of the graphic similar to that created by human transcribers. It includes a description of the important visual features of the graph such as intercepts and turning points. It also plays a sonification of the entire line graph and, audio indicating the position of annotations.

Querying: The app allows the user to find out more detailed information about the line graph when touching it, using a triple tap gesture: (i) with one finger, it provides the coordinates of the point by speech, and (ii) with two fingers it will provide the "trend" of the line segment by sonification.

Annotations: The app also allows users to annotate a graphic. The annotations (audio / text) can be either associated with the entire graphic or with a particular location on the graphic. Annotations are indicated by a small circle on the screen and behave in much the same way as other graphical objects.

[8] http://www.rstudio.com/shiny/

3. EVALUATION

We have collaborated with 9 school students who have both severe vision impairment and a basic mathematical graph knowledge as well as with sighted teachers and transcribers at SVRC, meeting them regularly. In addition a blind university student enrolled in a computer science degree has provided feedback.

Students could understand the graph with and without tactile feedback. Students appeared to be faster when provided with tactile feedback (though we need to verify this with a user study) and most students preferred to have tactile feedback. We were surprised that 8 of the 10 students indicated that they preferred GraCALC to a tactile graphic. The main reason given was that GraCALC could create a graph instantly and could let them interact with the graphic. Furthermore, they said that the iPad was smaller and easier to transport than a tactile graphic.

4. CONCLUSION

We have presented a new model for presenting mathematical charts, plots and graphs to blind people that utilises tactile, speech and non-speech feedback. We plan to extend GraCALC to provide a wider range of mathematical and statistical charts, plots and graphs. This is relatively straightforward because it is built on top of R, one of the most powerful statistical applications.

5. ACKNOWLEDGMENTS

We acknowledge the support of ARC through LP110200469 and of our project partners the Statewide Vision Resource Center, Vision Australia, jTribe and the Catholic Education Office (Melbourne). Disclosure: Cagatay Goncu is co-founder of RaisedPixels, a company which is commercialising GraVVITAS.

6. REFERENCES

[1] A. M. Brock, P. Truillet, B. Oriola, D. Picard, and C. Jouffrais. Interactivity improves usability of geographic maps for visually impaired people. *Human Computer Interaction*, 30(2), 2015.

[2] B. Challis. Design principles for non-visual interaction. In *Proc. CHI EA'00*. ACM.

[3] M. Espinosa, S. Ungar, E. Ochaita, M. Blades, and C. Spencer. Comparing methods for introducing blind and visually impaired people to unfamiliar urban environments. *Environmental Psychology*, 18(3), 1998.

[4] J. A. Gardner. Access by blind students and professionals to mainstream math and science. In *Proc. ICCHP'02*. Springer.

[5] N. A. Giudice, H. P. Palani, E. Brenner, and K. M. Kramer. Learning non-visual graphical information using a touch-based vibro-audio interface. In *Proc. ASSETS'12*. ACM.

[6] C. Goncu and K. Marriott. GraVVITAS: generic multi-touch presentation of accessible graphics. In *Proc. INTERACT'11*. Springer.

[7] C. Goncu and K. Marriott. Tactile chart generation tool. In *Proc. ASSETS'08*. ACM.

[8] S. K. Kane, J. O. Wobbrock, and R. E. Ladner. Usable gestures for blind people: understanding preference and performance. In *Proc. CHI'11*. ACM.

[9] H. Wickham. *ggplot2: elegant graphics for data analysis.* Springer, 2009.

ARCoach 2.0: Optimizing a Vocational Prompting System Based on Augmented Reality for People with Cognitive Impairments

Yao-Jen Chang[1], Ya-Shu Kang[2], Yao-Sheng Chang[3], Hung-Huan Liu[1]
[1]Department of Electronic Engineering, Chung Yuan Christian University, Taiwan
[2]Department of Special Education, Chung Yuan Christian University, Taiwan
[3]Department of Tourism and Leisure Management, Chung Chou University of Science and Technology, Taiwan
{yjchang, yashu, hhliu}@cycu.edu.tw; yschang@dragon.ccut.edu.tw

Abstract

This study improved the ARCoach system that provided vocational training for individuals with cognitive impairments using an Augmented Reality (AR) based task prompting technology. Using cyclic codes to enhance AR tag recognition rates, the proposed system not only provided picture cues but also identified incorrect task steps on the fly and helped make corrections. Experimental data showed that the participant considerably increased the target response, thus improving vocational job skills during the intervention phases. In addition to assistive technology, our approach can apply to other AR applications where tag recognition rates need to be improved.

Categories and Subject Descriptors

K.4.2 [**Computers and Society**]: Social Issues—*Assistive technologies for persons with disabilities*

Keywords

Task prompting, Cognitive impairments, Community-based rehabilitation, Augmented reality.

Problem & Motivation

Teaching vocational job skills is a particularly important area of intervention for individuals with cognitive impairments in order to help these people develop independent living and community involvement. The present study is aimed to be a contribution to the evidence-base of effective intervention procedures to teach such vocational job skills. Further, the use of using new technologies for prompting systems is an important area of research as it is one way for individuals with cognitive impairments to gain some autonomy and control over their environment.

ASSETS'15, October 26–28, 2015, Lisbon, Portugal.
ACM 978-1-4503-3400-6/15/10.
DOI: http://dx.doi.org/10.1145/2700648.2811354

Chang et al. [1, 2] proposed a system, called ARCoach, for vocational task prompting based on augmented reality (AR). AR is a technology for a live direct or an indirect view of a physical, real-world environment whose elements are augmented by computer-generated sensory input, such as sound or graphics. The technology functions by enhancing one's current perception of reality. By contrast, virtual reality (VR) replaces the real world with a simulated one. ARCoach leveraged the capabilities of AR using a web camera to add information and meaning to a real object for task prompting in rehabilitation settings. Using AR means that the users need not be bothered with matching picture cues with realities, a prompting strategy employed by a wide array of studies. By using the system to recognize tags, the information about the surrounding real world of the user becomes assistive picture cues. Artificial information about the environment was overlaid on the real world. The information can be in text, sound, picture or a combination of the above. Use of this technology can free a job coach or trainer from the burden of having to constantly stay with users for pre-service vocational training. The importance of the study lies in utilizing new technology in the use of an AR prompting system to provide a simple, time efficient, and effective intervention. Although the ARCoach system showed satisfactory performance in the field study, the AR recognition rate was below 90%. Therefore, we proposed ARCoach 2.0 that enhanced AR recognition.

The ARCoach 2.0 system

A personal computer was employed with an external web camera running an in-house developed AR task prompting software. Open-source AR toolkits were used to identify AR tags deployed in community-based rehabilitation environments. The ARCoach 2.0 system was deployed in a university cafeteria that spared non-business hours for the short order food preparation training of adults with cognitive impairments. As shown in Fig. 1, the system consisted of an Intel Core i7 personal computer (PC), a 42-inch LCD computer monitor, an autofocus web camera (LogicTech C920), and in-house developed software. Participants prepared "food items" with the web camera 30 to 34 inches above the top of a table (50" by 25"). The food items were represented by movable AR tags on the table, each tag corresponding to a food item. An AR tag is a paper print-out of machine readable code (See Figure 2.). The ARCoach 2.0 system rendered movable AR tags on the computer monitor as food pictures they corresponded to individually. The software was coded in Microsoft C# using Visual Studio as the integrated development platform. In addition, ARToolKit, an open source tool developed by University of Washington, was employed for processing AR tags.

To prompt participants to prepare a meal, picture cues of food items for the meal were displayed on the computer screen. To teach participants to acquire the target response, the prompts were presented in a combination of sound and picture cues. By recognizing AR tags that represented food items, the system was able to alert sound cues if food items were incorrect or misplaced. Using the alerts, it was possible for participants to correct their choices on the fly.

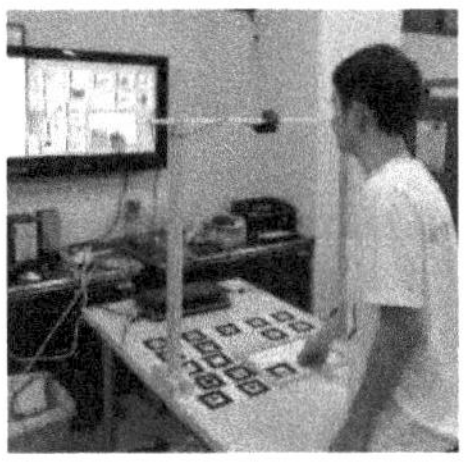

Figure 1: ARCoach 2.0

Like other AR applications, the ARCoach system [1, 2] randomly created tags with pixel size 320*320, each pixel black or white in 1:1 ratio. However, we found that tags were sometimes incorrectly recognized and a fruit item might be displayed as a beverage item on the screen. The performance was marginally satisfactory because this level of errors could cause user confusion and frustration. ARCoach 2.0 improved the precision and recall by constructing new tags such that difference between every two tags was maximized. To do so, we treated each 2-dimensional AR code as a 1-deminsional codeword string. We divided an AR code into 16 blocks with each block the size of 3*3 (See Figure 2.). Let each block be ether all black pixels or all white pixels. A black block was represented by 0 whereas a white block was represented by 1. Therefore, an AR tag was transformed into a codeword of 16 bits. Using the Cyclic Code theory [3] for error control coding, we were able to generate a codeword set of size 16 such that the Hamming distance of every two codewords was maximized.

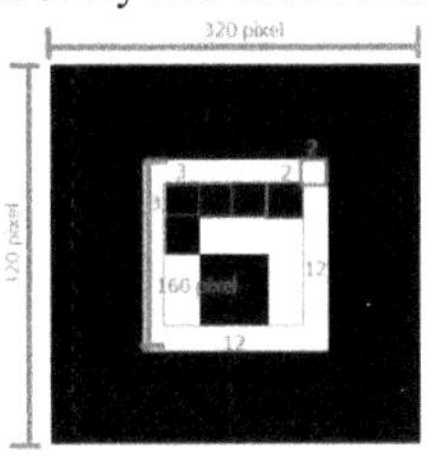

Figure 2: Designing optimal AR tags to improve recall and precision.

Experiments

Alice, Bill, and Charlie were identified for inclusion in the study. Alice, aged 21 years, had limited oral communication abilities and lived in residential provision. She had difficulties in memorizing routine procedures in her workplace. A psychologist estimated her ID to fall between the severe and profound levels. However, no formal testing or IQ scores were available because test materials were inapplicable to her. In addition to ID, she also had a diagnosis of major depressive disorder. Bill, aged 20 years, was diagnosed with a moderate ID (IQ of 51, Kaufman Assessment Battery for Children: Kaufman & Kaufman, 1983). He was unable to work under the supported employment program in the local district. Charlie, aged 25 years, had mild epilepsy and moderate ID (Adaptive Behavior Composite Score 66, Vineland Adaptive Behavior Scales: Sparrow, Balla, & Cicchetti, 1984). He underwent excellent rehabilitation and has remained employed in a paid part-time job as a recycle worker. Charlie sought a more demanding job with higher pay, such as kitchen assistance, but has been unable to secure such employment. None of the participants had previous experience with computer-based training. The names of participants have been changed in this report to protect their privacy.

Task steps were performed by the participant. A session consisted of a process of preparing five combo meals, each meal with four task steps. The experiment used 16 food items in total. A combo meal was composed of four food items. Orders included noodle meals, burger meals, sandwich meals, dumpling meals, and salad meals. For example, a noodle meal was composed of noodle, iced black tea, salad, and fruit whereas a burger meal was composed of burger, cappuccino, salad, and brownie. The sequence of five combo meals was random for participants in each trial. The participant used the ARCoach 2.0 system to prepare the meal orders one food item at a time. The food items for each kind of meals had to be strictly observed according to the standard community-based training procedure.

Results

Three participants were invited to test the AR recognition ability of ARCoach and ARCoach 2.0. Each participant worked with 40 AR tags before tag patterns were optimized and then tried again after tags were optimized. Performance was measured in precision and recall. The results were shown in Table 1.

Table 1: Comparing ARCoach and ARCoach 2.0

Participants	No optimization (random tags), ARCoach		Optimized (double cyclic code), ARCoach 2.0	
	Precision	Recall	Precision	Recall
Alice	90 %	90%	100 %	100 %
Bill	85 %	81%	100 %	100 %
Charlie	85 %	85%	100 %	100 %

Reference

[1] Yao-Jen Chang, Ya-Shu Kang, Po-Chiao Huang, An Augmented Reality (AR)-based vocational task prompting system for people with cognitive impairments, *Research in Developmental Disabilities*, Vol. 34, Iss. 10, Oct. 2013, pp. 3049–3056.

[2] Yao-Jen Chang, Ya-Shu Kang, Fang-Lin Liu, A computer-based interactive game to train persons with cognitive impairments to perform recycling tasks independently, *Research in Developmental Disabilities*, Volume 35, Issue 12, December 2014, Pages 3672–3677

[3] R. E. Blahut. Theory and Practice of Error Control Codes. Addison-Wesley, 1983.

BendableSound: A Fabric-based Interactive Surface to Promote Free Play in Children with Autism

Deysi Ortega, Franceli L. Cibrian, Monica Tentori
Department of Computer Science, CICESE
dortega@cicese.edu.mx, franceli@cicese.edu.mx, mtentori@cicese.mx

Figure 1. The BendableSound prototype. A screenshot of the first activity available in BendableSound demanding a user to tap and touch on top of the fabric to erase the black smog covering the space nebula (left). A user interacting with the space nebula seeking and moving hidden space digital elements to make sounds (center) A screenshot of the third activity demanding a user to play a song by following the notes specified by the astronaut (right).

ABSTRACT
Children with autism found free play difficult. Free play is important for children with autism to help them develop social, communication, and expression skills. Interactive surfaces (IS) offer a casual and natural collaborative and engaging experience adequate to promote free play for children with autism. In this poster, we present the design and development of BendableSound, a fabric-based IS that allows children play music when tapping and touching on digital elements appearing on top of the fabric. To design BendableSound, we followed a user-centered design process involving interviewing, observation, and design sessions with caregivers. We close discussing directions for future work.

Categories and Subject Descriptors
K.4.2 [Computers and Society]: Social Issues – Assistive technologies for persons with disabilities; K.8.0 [Personal Computing]: General – Games.

Keywords
Bendable interactive surface; free play; autism; young children

1. INTRODUCTION
Free play represents an opportunity to teach children with autism social skills, creativity, and expression [4]; but, their limited social functioning and lack of predisposition to spontaneously play prevents them from participating during free play activities. Free play is voluntary, spontaneous, engaging, pleasurable, open-ended, and sometimes involves collaboration and physical movements. These characteristics teach children with autism how to set goals and define rules when interacting with others. Music-based activities are often used during free play to promote social interactions for children with autism [3].

ASSETS '15, October 26-28, 2015, Lisbon, Portugal
ACM 978-1-4503-3400-6/15/10.
http://dx.doi.org/10.1145/2700648.2811355

It has been proved that interactive surfaces (IS) are appropriate to support typical children during free-play, because they promote creativity [2], support open-ended interactions [6], and provide visual and auditory feedback to maintain their engagement [5], specially during music-based activities [2]. Although almost all IS follow an open-ended interaction model, little has been said about what open-ended mechanisms are appropriate to support children with autism during free play: How can IS enable open-ended interactions while at the same time providing a fun experience to children with autism during free play? This work contributes with a design case study showing a novel fabric-based IS prototype (Figure 1) that enables children with autism improvise music and rhythmical sounds in an open-ended manner during free play.

2. RELATED WORK
Research has explored how to design IS to assist neurotypical children during music-based activities, mainly for learning music, and fostering creativity (*e.g.,* Vuzic [2]). However, these IS have not been evaluated with children with special needs. Other musical IS have explored how to support individuals with disabilities to assist music therapy sessions (*e.g.,* Movement-to-Music [1]), but IS supporting children with autism is still scarce. Most of the research in IS to support children with autism mimic the structure of a therapy session (*e.g.,* SensoryPaint [6], Mediate [5]); but, has not yet explore the design space of open-ended mechanisms to support children with autism during free play.

3. DESIGN METHODS
For 4 months, we conducted a contextual study in a school-clinic of children with autism. During this time, we conducted 20 semi-structured interviews and observed 4 classrooms of children with autism during free play activities, to observe the problems children with autism face during free-play and understand the everyday practices of children with autism during free-play open-ended instruction. All interviews and observations were transcribed and analyzed with techniques to derive grounded theory and affinity diagramming. We conducted 5 design sessions

to iteratively design low-fidelity prototypes of IS supporting children with autism during free play, define the interaction gestures, and discuss animation and sounds arrangement.

4. BENDABLESOUND DESIGN

We designed BendableSound (Figure 1), a novel fabric-based IS that allows children with autism to make music when tapping and touching on digital elements appearing on top of the fabric. The fabric is a digital matrix arranging the pitch of musical notes in a descending scale on the vertical axis; and the musical tempo in the horizontal axis. BendableSound uses a dodecaphonic technique of 12 musical notes arranged on a chromatic scale. This technique has a dual function; first, a dodecaphonic technique allows controlling a finite and small numbers of notes to help children with autism gradually accept different sounds; second, with the dodecaphonic technique we can build different harmonic compositions and sounds arrangements even if users have limited music knowledge. Every time a child taps, grasps, or touches an element it will play a sound according to its location pitch.

4.1 Activities

BendableSound supports two open-ended activities, and one activity combining step-by-step guidance with an open-ended interaction modality. In the first activity (Figure 1, left), children must erase a huge layer of "black smog" by tapping, touching, ripping or grasping the fabric canvas to discover sounds and a background animation of space nebula. In the second activity (Figure 1, center), children must seek hidden musical space-based elements, like spaceships or stars, that will reproduce sounds when touched or moved. During the third activity, an astronaut appears to give children guidance on how to play a song by touching on an appearing and blinking star. The star appears according to music tempo, but children are not penalized when missing a beat. Song lists that children could play with the fabric include nursery rhymes like "twinkle twinkle little star". The background animation and the digital elements change according to the theme being used. The design supports three themes: space, snow, and sea; but only the space-theme is currently available.

4.2 Gestural Interactions

The design of BendableSound ideally might have four interactions gestures available when playing with BendableSound; but only two are fully available. These interaction themes take advantage of the affordances provided by the fabric (Table 1). A user's gesture will determine the displayed animation and the sounds of the musical instrument. For example, when tapping, BendableSound will sound like a piano or a drum and the element will bounce; in contrast with pinching that will sound like a guitar or a harp and the element will swing.

Table 1. Affordances provided by BendableSound and its possible effect.

Gesture	Instrument	Example
Tap	Piano/Drum	The element will **bounce**
Drag	Piano/Drum	The element will **move**
Rip	Harp/Guitar	The element will **swing**
Pinch	Harp /Guitar	The element will **appear or disapper**

5. THE BENDABLESOUND PROTOTYPE

BendableSound uses the Kinect sensor and the TSPS[1] library to detect when users' tap or touch the fabric (Figure 2 left). The rest of the gestural interactions are still under development but are available in the fabric through wizard of oz. In the current version also only, the guitar and the piano sounds are available. BendableSound's multimedia interfaces were developed with QML and JavaScript and are projected in the fabric by an ultrashort-throw projector (Figure 2 right). The Kinect sensor and the projector are behind the fabric surface. In case some children do not tolerate the sounds of some musical instruments, due hypersensitivity issues, teachers can manually configure from BendableSound the sounds children may tolerate, the instruments available, and the interaction time (Figure 2 left). Teachers could also adjust the duration time on each activity.

[1] http://tsps.cc/

6. CONCLUSIONS AND FUTURE WORK

In this work, we showed the design and partial development of a novel fabric-based IS to promote free play by enabling open-ended musical activities for children with autism. The main contribution of this poster is the BendableSound prototype. We plan to implement the other gestural interactions available in the design of BendableSound (Table 1) and conduct a deployment study with children with autism to investigate the impact of BendableSound in supporting free play activities.

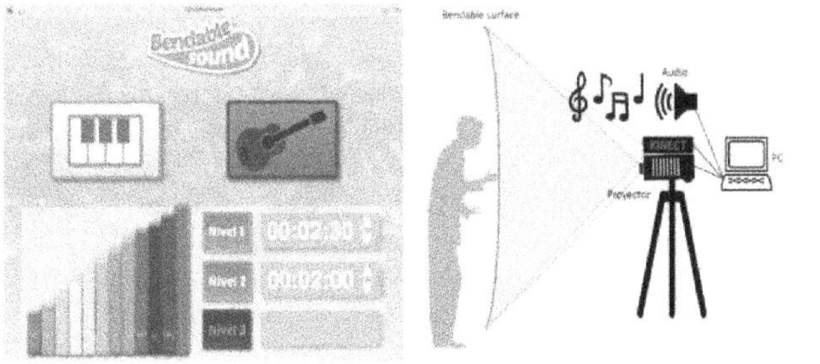

Figure 2. Setting up BendableSound. A screenshot of the settings interface where colors represent notes and icons represent available musical instruments (left). A mockup representation showing the hardware installation of the BendableSound prototype (right).

7. REFERENCES

[1] Hobbs, D. et al. 2008. The Efficacy of Combining Augmented Reality and Music Therapy with Traditional Teaching–Preliminary Results. *iCREATe'08*, 241–244.

[2] Ichino, J. et al. 2014. Vuzik: the effect of large gesture interaction on children's creative musical expression. *OzCHI'14*, 240–249.

[3] Kern, P. and Aldridge, D. 2006. Using embedded music therapy interventions to support outdoor play of young children with autism in an inclusive community-based child care program. *J. of music therapy*. 43, 4, 270–294.

[4] Lang, R. et al. 2011. Use of school recess time in the education and treatment of children with autism spectrum disorders: A systematic review. *Res Autism Spect Dis*. 5, 4, 1296–1305.

[5] Parés, N. et al. 2005. Promotion of creative activity in children with severe autism through visuals in an interactive multisensory environment. *IDC '05*. (2005), 110–116.

[6] Ringland, K.E. et al. 2014. SensoryPaint: a multimodal sensory intervention for children with neurodevelopmental disorders. *UbiComp'14*, 873–884.

Designing Kinect2Scratch Games to Help Therapists Train Young Adults with Cerebral Palsy in Special Education School Settings

Yao-Jen Chang[1], Ya-Shu Kang[2], Yao-Sheng Chang[3], Hung-Huan Liu[1], Cheng-Chieh Wang[1], Chia Chun Kao[1]

[1]Department of Electronic Engineering, Chung Yuan Christian University, Taiwan

[2]Department of Special Education, Chung Yuan Christian University, Taiwan

[3]Department of Tourism and Leisure Management, Chung Chou University of Science and Technology, Taiwan

{yjchang, yashu, hhliu}@cycu.edu.tw; yschang@dragon.ccut.edu.tw

Abstract

Children with cerebral palsy (CP) may need to undergo long-term physical rehabilitation to enhance neural development. Currently, commercial rehabilitation products cannot be customized easily and are expensive; consequently, public special-education schools generally cannot afford purchasing these products. This study employs the Microsoft Kinect technology and image recognition technology to create a rehabilitation system which may be applicable for people with CP. To motivate people with CP to engage in exercise training, we gamified the movement training of self-feeding and self-dressing for young adults with CP in special education school settings. By leveraging the Scratch language and Kinect2Scratch tool, the physical therapists (PTs) who will use the system may be able to do the customization without technical support. Preliminary results of 5 healthy college students testing the exercise games are presented. The precision and reliability of the Kinect2Scratch Games are 100% and 97.5%.

Categories and Subject Descriptors

K.4.2 [**Computers and Society**]: Social Issues—*Assistive technologies for persons with disabilities*

Keywords

exercise games; gamification; Kinect; Scratch; Kinect2Scratch; upper limb training.

Introduction

Cerebral palsy (CP) is a group of disorders that primarily involves motor impairment and is caused by damage to cells in a developing brain. Abnormal movements caused by motor impairments commonly occurs in people with CP. Activities of daily living (ADLs) are the key to whether a person can live independently. However, people with CP may have difficulty in performing (ADLs) such as dressing, bathing, and grooming.

In [1] a Kinect-based system was used to assist young adults with motor impairments in rehabilitation. By using videos in which physical therapists demonstrated rehabilitation exercises and the action-recognition function in Kinect, the young adults were able to independently perform rehabilitation without teacher presence. Although using Kinect allowed the participants to perform customized movements, the disadvantage of this approach is that customized movements can only be identified based on displacement, which limits movements during rehabilitation activities. Chang et al. [2] made their design more robust by using angles instead of displacements of joints. In this study, we gamified the previous work to motivate the upper limb training and enabled physical therapists who are usually non professional programmers to customize diversified movements based on the needs of children and achieve the goal of individualized rehabilitation exercises.

Game Design

This study primarily employed the Microsoft Kinect sensory device to establish an upper limb rehabilitation system for people with CP. This system enables physical therapists to develop series of poses for rehabilitation based on the level of motor impairment for each child. Moreover, this Kinect-based system detects joint points and subsequently calculates various angles (i.e., shoulder flexion, shoulder extension, shoulder external abduction, shoulder external rotation, shoulder internal rotation, and elbow flexion) for the mentioned poses to determine whether the movements of each student corresponded to therapist's expectations.

In specific, Kinect and its SDK automatically detect the student's joint position, and uses the data to determine whether the students' movements have reached the rehabilitation standard (for example, raise both hands four inches above the shoulders) and the number of exercises in a therapy session is sufficient. The system also includes an interactive interface with audio and video feedback to enhance students' motivation, interest, and perseverance to engage in physical rehabilitation.

Based on student ability and Individualized Education Program (IEP), a physical therapist in a special-education school

ASSETS'15, October 26–28, 2015, Lisbon, Portugal.
ACM 978-1-4503-3400-6/15/10
DOI: http://dx.doi.org/10.1145/2700648.2811356

developed various movements (hand to head and hand to mouth for example) for rehabilitation and established initial and final poses for each movement during physical education hours. To motivate the students to engage in physical exercises, a game approach was adopted. The games were implemented using the Kinect2Scratch tool, Kinect API for the Scratch programming language in addition to Kinect SDK running on Windows 7. Scratch has been widely used by non programming professionals, including the therapist we worked with, to write games for education and entertainment. Using Scratch means that the therapist can easily customizes the games we developed with less technical support after delivery. As shown in Figure 1, two games were delivered: (a) Eating and (b) Wearing the wizard hat.

For the eating game, only one food item appears on the table and the player is asked to reach the food and bring it to the mouth. The food item can appear in one of the three positions on the table. The position of the food is selected in a random fashion. The therapist uses this game to train self feeding. For the eating game, a movement is considered correct if the player reaches the only food item among the three choices and then brings it to the mouth. Either the left hand or the right hand can be trained. The player will be prompted to maintain a straight arm (i.e. holding the arm out straight with the elbow locked) during the reach process. After reaching the food, the hand must bring it to a position in the proximity of the mouth.

For the hat wearing game, the player is asked to pick the wizard hat and wear it. The hat can appear in one of the three positions on the table. The position of the hat is selected in a random fashion. The therapist uses this game to train students to dress themselves. For the hat wearing game, a movement is considered correct if the player reaches the hat among the three choices and then wears it. Either the left hand or the right hand can be trained. The player will be prompted to maintain a straight arm (i.e. holding the arm out straight with the elbow locked) during the reach process. After reaching the hat, the hand must bring it to a position in the proximity of the head.

Both games train muscle strength and overcome spasticity as the games require the player to move upper limbs to score. Kinect was used to detect the improper movements of players during rehabilitation activities and determine whether the movements corresponded to the requirements of therapists. In addition, picture- and voice-based feedback was used to enrich the rehabilitation process and increase player motivation to engage in exercise training.

(a)

(b)

Figure 1: Upper limb rehabilitation games: (a) eating (b) wearing a wizard hat

Experiments and Results

Before the games were introduced to young adults with CP, the PT invited five healthy college students to test the games. The college students were all females and their ages were between 21 and 24. The physical therapist instructed the 5 players to play the games 20 times each. Each game play took 2 min. The players were requested to rest for 5 min before proceeding with the next game. This process was performed until the two games were completed repeatedly 20 times.

Because it is a work in progress, we only focused on the accuracy of the game to test feasibility. Feasibility of the gaming system was measured in terms of the extent of exactness and completeness. A measure of exactness or fidelity is precision, whereas a measure of completeness is recall. Four possible scenarios were analyzed. Our system identifies correct movements and incorrect movements. A true positive is a movement correctly executed by the human and captured as correct by the machine. A true negative is a movement incorrectly executed by the human and captured as incorrect by the machine. A false negative is a movement incorrectly executed by the human but captured as correct by the machine. A false positive or false alarm is a movement correctly executed by the human but captured as incorrect by the machine. Based on the definitions of the four scenarios, recall = (True Positives +True Negatives)/(True Positives + True Negatives + False Negatives) and precision= (True Positives + True Negatives)/(True Positives + True Negatives + False Positives). The results are summarized in Table 1. For the eating game, Kinect sometimes has difficulty identifying the elbow and wrist positions of the moving arm when the hand is in front of the mouth. Therefore, the recall is between 92.5% and 100%.

The preliminary results show the Kinect2Scratch games have the potential to motivate exercise training for people with CP with workable precision and recall. The PT was happy with the feasibility study and prepared to introduce the system to the students by including the game-based exercise training in the IEP.

Table 1: Measuring the precision and reliability of the Kinect2Scratch Games

Participant ID	1	2	3	4	5
True Positive	19	20	17	19	20
True Negative	20	20	20	20	20
False Positive	0	0	0	0	0
False Negative	1	0	3	1	0
Precision	100%	100%	100%	100%	100%
Recall	97.5%	100%	92.5%	97.5%	100%

References

[1] Chang Y. J., Chen, S. F., Huang, J. D. A Kinect-based system for physical rehabilitation: A pilot study for young adults with motor disabilities, *Research in Developmental Disabilities*, 2011(32):6, 2566–2570

[2] Chang Y. J., Han, W. Y., Tsai, Y. C., A Kinect-based upper limb rehabilitation system to assist people with cerebral palsy, *Research in Developmental Disabilities*, Vol. 34, Iss. 11, Nov. 2013, pp. 3654–3659

Model-Based Automated Accessibility Testing

Giorgio Brajnik
Dip. Matematica e Informatica
Università di Udine,Italy
+39 0432 558445
brajnik@uniud.it

Chiara Pighin
Interaction Design Solutions
Udine, Italy
+39 0432 558445
chiara.pighin@designcoaching.net

Sara Fabbro
Interaction Design Solutions
Udine, Italy
+39 0432 558445
sara.fabbro@designcoaching.net

Categories and Subject Descriptors
D.2.2 [**Design Tools and Techniques**]: User Interfaces, State Diagrams

General Terms
Human Factors

1. INTRODUCTION
Automatic testing of website accessibility has always struggled to make progress. This is due to fundamental limitations, such as having to deal with how users interpret and make sense of information; technical problems, such as variety of guideline success criteria combined with the variety of technologies to consider; and process-oriented issues, such as accessibility testing being seldom included a part of quality-assurance within the website life cycle.

For web applications these problems are even more cogent. In fact, when using traditional tools such as The Wave or Accessibility Checker other problems appear. It is impossible to automatically scan and analyze the source code of each screen, therefore requiring cumbersome intermediate manual steps (such as pasting HTML fragments by hand into a testing tool). Another problem is the difficulty to formalize accessibility problems in terms of required source code. Finally, results are plagued by false positives and negatives, by missed manual steps, and by missed DOM fragments. Even more recent tools, such as Deque's aXe or Tenon.io, which offer powerful APIs to invoke test procedures, provide only limited means to tackle these problems. They offer a range of predefined accessibility tests that are not ad hoc for the application under test (AUT), they do not support tests that are based on navigating through screens, and sometimes they require changes to the AUT in order to invoke the testing API. The consequence is that accessibility testing is not systematically performed.

2. OUR VISION
Our vision is that automated accessibility testing should be performed within continuous integration practices, so that several requirements are tested repeatedly, and early feedback is automatically sent to developers. Of course, to achieve this, accessibility requirements need to be specifiable so that appropriate automated test cases can be defined, even when the user interface (UI) of the AUT is not completed yet.

ASSETS '15/, October 26-28, 2015, Lisbon, Portugal
ACM 978-1-4503-3400-6/15/10.
DOI: http://dx.doi.org/10.1145/2700648.2811357

The solution we envision should bring the following benefits. First, accessibility test cases should be complete, in terms of their ability to analyze each screen of the application, including those where UI components are temporarily displayed. Second, test cases should cover also specification of arbitrary action sequences (*i.e.*, when using the keyboard as an alternative modality to interact, a test case could specify that after 3 tabs the focus should be on a particular text field). Third, a tester should be able to specify test cases in terms of what needs to happen or not happen, rather than being forced to specify what the source code has to be (*i.e.*, being able to specify that after 3 tabs a certain menu is opened, rather than having to specify that there should be certain tabindexes and certain event handlers). We call this "*focus on symptoms rather than causes*". Fourth, test cases should be characterized by high levels of effectiveness (*i.e.*, leading to few false positives and negatives. Fifth, accessibility testing should be based on realistic user scenarios, similar to functional tests, based on sequences of steps needed to achieve use cases. And finally, sustainability of accessibility testing is needed: automated test cases should have a low maintenance cost, being robust against changes in the structure of the UI.

3. MODEL-BASED TESTING
Model-based testing techniques can address several of these requirements. In particular, the tool we developed (GEnerator of Test Harness for Accessibility, GETH-4A) uses models that represent the data manipulated by the UI and the behavior of the UI. Test cases refer to the models and involve oracles, *i.e.* specific procedures that analyze the DOM to check if certain properties hold. GETH-4A reads these models, integrates model annotations providing details about UI implementation, and produces Java/jUnit source code of a test harness. The generated test harness hides details about the DOM, about the particular test driver that is used to drive the AUT, and about the oracle implementations. The test engineer writes high level code for jUnit test cases, which can then be run on the desired platforms, using Selenium as a driver. The *data model* is defined using UML class diagrams that specify data entities and relationships displayed by the UI. The *behavior model* is defined using UML state diagrams, where states represent specific screen configurations. Transitions between states represent user actions (*e.g.*, clicking on a button or editing a text field). More details on these techniques are available in [1, 2]. Fig. 1 shows the GETH-4A compilation process.

Model annotations are used to encapsulate low-level and frequently changing details that would make the test harness fragile. In particular we provide annotations for user actions, so that each transition in the model can be associated to code that searches the DOM for the required web element that supports the action (for example, a button element with text="Today", upon which a "TAB" action can be performed). Models can specify multi-modal interaction, and in particular with keyboard and mouse. In this way, when using the mouse any of the available transitions can be triggered at any given time. On the other hand, when using the keyboard alone, a sequential order of activation is imposed (with the tab key as a trigger) and additional keystrokes are needed to navigate through other options (such as down-arrow).

Similarly, oracle annotations can be provided to specify what needs to be checked on the AUT. They include properties dealing with accessibility features (such as presence of an appropriate DIV with ARIA attributes; in particular any desired combination of ARIA mark-up can be used), with specific content (such as text and images) or with specific interactors (such as a given button being enabled).

4. CASE STUDY

We explored the benefits of GETH-4A in a case study applied to the webmail application Horde (www.horde.org). Due to space limitations we provide only a brief description. The test case fragment shown in Fig. 1 exercises the AUT in the sign-in screen. Instruction 1 refers to transition "enterMail" specified in the behavior model, which is implemented using details specified in the annotation shown also in Fig. 1. Instruction 2 launches predefined oracles that implement generic accessibility checks, such as images having ALT attributes, input elements having labels, etc.

Although not shown here, another test case specifies the sequence `"tab; tab; arrow-down; arrow-down; enter"` to be entered from the main screen. After that, it verifies that the "compose" page is open (by checking its URL). However, the AUT fails to open such a page: this identifies an accessibility problem due to the fact that the entries of the "Mail menu" are not reachable through the keyboard. This example illustrates the focus on symptoms of the accessibility problem rather than its causes. In addition, if a screen reader is enabled on the system where the AUT is running, the test engineer could listen to the spoken utterances and find out if there is anything unexpected.

The following benefits should emerge from adoption of GETH-4A. Because models, oracles and test cases are defined specifically for the AUT, a very small number of false positives/negatives can be expected, increasing confidence in tool results. Furthermore, because some of the oracles are generic, they can be easily reused between different projects. The test harness produced by compiling models yields a high level domain specific language that is tailored to the particular AUT, simplifying definition of test cases. Furthermore, the abstractions used in the model protect test cases from fragilities due to changes in the structure of the UI.

The tool automatically generates test run reports that are integrated within common software project management and continuous integration tools (such as Jira and Jenkins). Reports provide statistics based on states and transitions that were covered by tests and requirements that were compromised by failed tests. These can be used to better understand if the AUT is sufficiently well tested.

One limit of the current prototype is its inability to *automatically* infer the correct model when adopting a keyboard interaction modality. One source of complexity deals with situations where some control may dynamically be disabled or re-enabled, which disrupt the tabbing sequence and need to be handled specifically. Furthermore, at the moment only some of the WCAG 2.0 success criteria are covered by oracles.

REFERENCES

[1] G. Brajnik, A. Baruzzo, and S. Fabbro. Model-based continuous integration testing of responsiveness of web applications. In F. Wotawa, editor, *ICST 2015*, Graz, Austria, April 2015. IEEE.

[2] G. Brajnik and S. Harper. Detaching control from data models in model-based generation of user interfaces. In F. Frasincar, editor, *Proc. of Int. Conf. on Web Engineering*, Rotterdam, Netherlands, June 2015. IEEE.

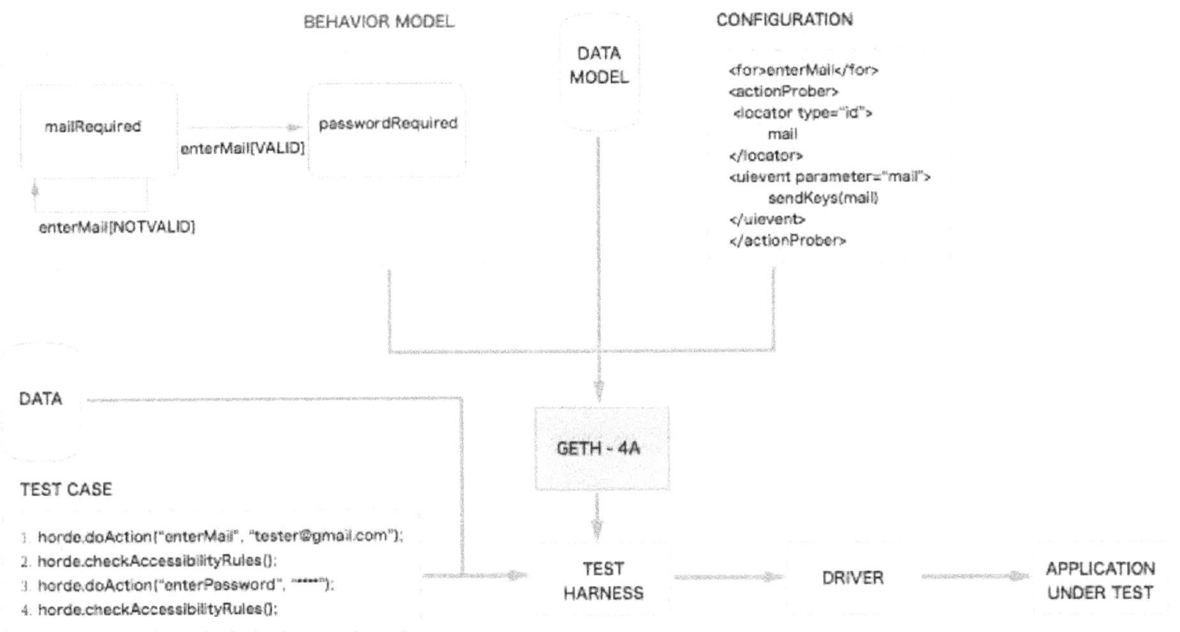

Figure 1: The GETH-4A compilation process.

Usability for Accessibility – A Consolidation of Requirements for Mobile Applications

[1,3]Clauirton Siebra, [1]Tatiana Gouveia, [1]Anderson Filho, [5]Walter Correia, [5]Marcelo Penha, [2]Marcelo Anjos, [2]Fabiana Florentin, [4]Fabio QB Silva, [4]Andre LM Santos
[1]CIn/Samsung R&D Laboratory, Recife – PE - Brazil
[2]SIDI – Samsung, Campinas – Sao Paulo Brazil
[3]Informatics Center – Federal University of Paraiba
[4]CIn – Universidade Federal de Pernambuco – Recife – PE - Brazil
[5]Design Department – Universidade Federal de Pernambuco - Brazil
{cas, tbg2,jasnf,fabio,alms}@cin.ufpe.br; {marcelo.e,f.florentin}@samsung.com; ergonomia@me

ABSTRACT
Differently of the Web Accessibility Guidelines, which are already consolidated as a reference, the initiatives to develop guidelines for accessible mobile applications are recent and several approaches present only suggestions rather than a concrete list of functional requirements. This work analyzed 247 scientific articles to identify requirements that are being considered to different types of impairments. The collected information was consolidated and classified according to groups of impairments. As result, this paper presents the main points of a checklist proposal for functional requirements, which should be considered by mobile applications to ensure accessibility with usability.

Categories and Subject Descriptors
H.5.2 [**Information Interfaces and Representation**]: User Interfaces – *input devices and strategies, interaction styles.*

Keywords
Usability; accessibility; functional requirements; mobile platform

1. INTRODUCTION
As any non-functional requirement, usability must be mapped into a set of functional requirements that tend to be associated with several modules of the application. Traditional applications already have a default pattern of requirements for usability. However, this pattern must be reviewed if applications intend to offer support for accessibility. Some efforts in this direction can already be found in the current literature [1]. However, such efforts are sparse and they still far away to present a concrete standard for mobile platform as we have for Web accessibility [2].

To create a more concrete and broader checklist, this work analyzed 247 scientific articles to identify requirements for types of impairments. The final checklist contains 36 mandatory and 18 desirable requirements, which were classified according to the impairment that they intend to support. Examples of requirements are discussed along the next sections to stress important aspects of this classification.

2. RESEARCH METHOD
A survey was applied as research method. Next schema (Figure 1) summarizes its activities.

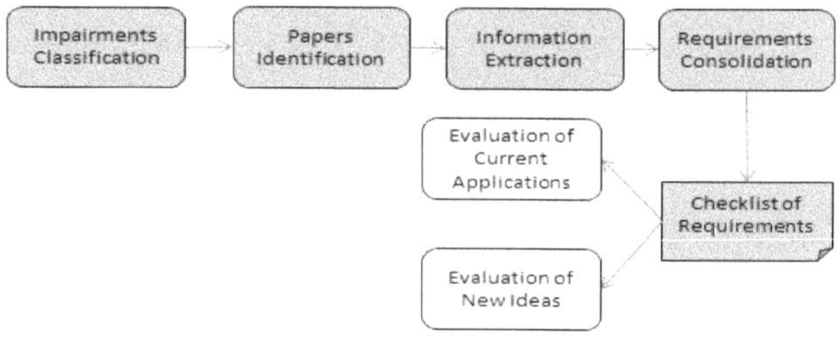

Figure 1. Steps of the research method.

This paper, in particular, discusses the four first activities illustrated in this schema. The *Impairments Classification* defined impairment categories so that requirements could be identified and analyzed in a contextualized way, once different types of impairments require different types of requirements. The categories are: General Impairment (C_0), Vision (C_1), Blindness ($C_{1.1}$), Low/Limited Vision ($C_{1.2}$), Hearing (C_2), Total Deaf ($C_{2.1}$), Partial Deaf ($C_{2.2}$), Motor (C_3), No Control on Hands ($C_{3.1}$), No Ability to Grab/Hold ($C_{3.2}$) and Limited Control on Hands ($C_{3.3}$). These categories were organized in a hierarchy (Figure 2). When a requirement is defined to one of the classes, all subclasses of this class inherit this requirement. For example, if an application intends to provide support to "Partial deaf" ($C_{2.2}$), such application should implement all requirements from "Partial deaf" to the root class ("General Impairment – C_0").

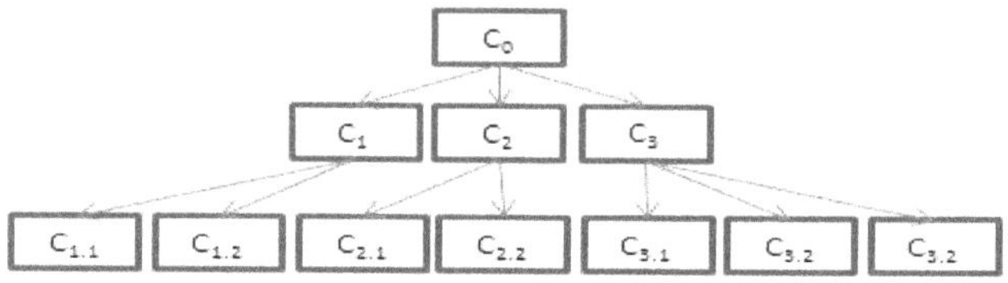

Figure 2. Classification hierarchy.

The *Paper Identification* activity carried out a web search considering both academic engines (IEEE Xplore, Scopus, Web of Science, SciELO, Medline, LILACS, BDTD and Redalycm) and commercial sites via Google. At the end we analyzed 274 scientific and technological articles. The *Information Extraction* accounted for extracting the requirements from the articles and listing them inside one of the categories C_i. Finally, the *Requirements Consolidation* analyzed the importance of the requirements, divided them into mandatory or desirable.

3. RESULTS
Our analysis identified 36 mandatory requirements (R_1 to R_{36}), which were classified into categories according to Table 1. Next paragraphs give a brief vision about some of these requirements.

ASSETS'15, October 26–28, 2015, Lisbon, Portugal.
ACM 978-1-4503-3400-6/15/10.
DOI: http://dx.doi.org/10.1145/2700648.2811358

Table 1. Number of mandatory requirements for each category

C_0	C_1	$C_{1.1}$	$C_{1.2}$	C_2	$C_{2.1}$	$C_{2.2}$	C_3	$C_{3.1}$	$C_{3.2}$	$C_{3.3}$
10	1	6	6	7	0	0	4	2	0	0

$C_{1.1}$ Requirements. A first set of requirements is associated with the generation of hearing output to compensate the lack of visual sense. For example: "*R_1 - The name of a character that is being entered must be heard*". This same kind of sound signal could be used as input. For example, the use of voice commands and ever the use of voice to text input. However, the literature for mobile devices still presents a lack in discussions about the use of these approaches for blind users and real initiatives of the marked only present very simple solutions. The use of tactile information is also important, mainly as a resource to create a "save point" command, which leads the navigation to a known place. Thus we have: "*R_5 - The system must provide a discernible tactile home that ensure that there is one key that can be easily and quickly identified on any tactile control pad, to allow users to orientate themselves within the interface*". This is useful, for example, when users found themselves lost along navigations.

$C_{1.2}$ Requirements. This category considers the adaptation of the visual information delivery, so that users could still employ computational applications in the traditional way. For example: "*R_8 - The system must ensure that the perception of text and figures can be also comprehended without the use of colors*".

C_1 Requirements. Important alerts of the system must be recognized by users and, in some cases, they must confirm the perception of these alerts to liberate the use of the system. An example of requirement is: "*R_{13} - The system must provide information alerts by other communication channels beyond visual*". In fact, this requirement is already implemented in most of the systems, where sounds and text messages are delivered in case of alerts. However, it is important to stress the mandatory feature of this requirement in the accessibility context.

$C_{3.1}$ Requirements. Applications that intend to support users in this category must necessarily provide some sort of interface to external motor impairment accessibility device. For example: "*R_{21} - The system must provide alternative ways to interaction with external interfaces such as eye tracking-ball*" and "*R_{22} - The system must offer voice recognition so that users can carry out simple voice commands to operate applications*". These requirements could be optionally considered to C_3 category. However they are mandatory to $C_{3.1}$. Furthermore, if users from $C_{3.2}$ and $C_{3.3}$ are able to interact to computational devices via keyboard and mouse, ever in a more limited form, they should do that at most of the time. Otherwise, there is a considerable chance that they loss this ability due to the lack of continuous practice.

C_3 Requirements. The requirements of this category intend to decrease both difficulty of performing actions and amount of necessary movements and actions along the normal use of systems. For example: "*R_{23} - The system must avoid time limits to use functions*" and "*R_{26} - The system must place functions, which are more frequently used, in the first level of navigation, avoiding that users need to perform several steps to reach them*".

C_0 Requirements. Independently of the category of impairment, there is a set of requirements that should be provided to any kind of accessible mobile application that aims at improving its level of usability. Examples are: "*R_{29} - Guide and provide feedbacks to users about what is going on (state of the system)*" and "*R_{35} - Avoid limits of time control to users' reading or interaction*".

The mandatory list of requirements also tries to avoid items that require the use of external accessibility devices. In fact, the use of applications should not force that their users have additional devices. However, our overall analysis concluded that some of these devices are essential to enable that applications obtain an appropriate level of usability. Our research also identified 18 desirable requirements. Examples are: "*Rd_{10} - Detect sign language and convert it to speech*" and "*Rd_{13} – Provide sonorous location of the cursor in the screen*". Most of these desirable requirements could be considered as mandatory. However, they still in an "in definition" stage of maturity so that more studies and experimentations must be carried out to evaluate their real impact on the usability of applications.

4. DISCUSSION

Several researches on mobile devices have focused on specific accessibility applications rather than trying to establish a general guideline for accessible design. Kane et al [3] proposed an accessibility guideline, however it is only focused on a particular scenario associated with the elicitation of gestures for visual impairment. Mi et al [4] proposed a more general heuristic checklist for accessible smartphone interface design, but they did not apply a classification to better contextualize their requirements. There are also contributions from outside of academy, such as the Android's Accessibility Developer Checklist [5], which lists only five requirements as mandatory to ensure a minimum level of accessibility. Another example is the W3C effort [6] to describe how the Web Content Accessibility Guidelines (WCAG) 2.0 and its principles could be applied to mobile web content. Future works intend to use the set of requirements as a form to analyze current accessibility applications and potential proposals for new products (see Figure 1). However, we first need to evaluate the own requirements to better understand the impact that they have on the usability of mobile applications. To that end, real users will be employed to support this qualitative analysis. The operationalization of this process and the definition of weights/priorities for each requirement is also part of our future investigations.

5. REFERENCES

[1] Khan, S., Tahir, M., and Raza, A. 2013. Usability Issues for Smartphone Users with Special Needs–Autism. Proc. Int. Conf. on Open Source Systems and Technologies, p.107-113.

[2] W3C. 2014. Web Accessibility Initiative (WAI), Available in [http://www.w3.org/WAI]

[3] Kane, S., Wobbrock, J., and Ladner, R. 2011. Usable gestures for blind people: understanding preference and performance. Proc. of the Annual Conf. on Human Factors in Comp. Systems, pp. 413-422

[4] Mi, N. et al. 2014. A heuristic checklist for an accessible smartphone interface design. Univ Access Inf Soc,13:351-365

[5] Android Dev. 2015. Accessibility Developer Checklist. Available in [http://developer.android.com/guide/topics/ui/accessibility]

[6] W3C. 2015. Mobile Accessibility: How WCAG 2.0 and Other W3C/WAI Guidelines Apply to Mobile. Available in [http://www.w3.org/TR/mobile-accessibility-mapping]

An Investigation into Appropriation of Portable Smart Devices by Users with Aphasia

Gennaro Imperatore
University of Strathclyde
Computer & Information Sciences
Richmond St., Glasgow G1 1XH, Scotland, UK
gennaro.imperatore@strath.ac.uk

Mark D. Dunlop
University of Strathclyde
Computer & Information Sciences
Richmond St., Glasgow G1 1XH, Scotland, UK
mark.dunlop@strath.ac.uk

ABSTRACT
As part of ongoing research we analysed user experience of a group of people with aphasia by applying the Technology Appropriation Model. Appropriation is defined as the way in which users adapt the functionality of technology to suit their needs, often in ways the designers would not have predicted. Currently over 250,000 people in the UK and 1,000,000 people in the US have aphasia. We discovered that Appropriation analysis can be a useful tool for requirements analysis of software, especially in cases where the user has trouble communicating about abstract or imagined scenarios, as is the case for many with Aphasia. We also discovered that Appropriation often stems from the user not knowing the full capabilities of the device or what applications are already available.

Categories and Subject Descriptors
D.2.1 [**Requirements/Specification**]: Elicitation Methods

General Terms
Design, Human Factors

Keywords
AAC; TApM; Aphasia

1. BACKGROUND
Aphasia is often erroneously considered as being only an impediment in speech, but it brings a variety of other symptoms such as difficulty with writing and reading and an inability to cope with numbers [4]. Many people with Aphasia are discovering the assistive potential of smart devices. The work by Brandenburg et al [1] analyses mobile technology and aphasia to identify two categories of app development: Augmented and Alternative Communication (AAC) and Therapeutic Apps. Our research focusses on developing advanced mobile AAC applications.

2. METHODS
The data analysed in this work were collected during User Centred Design sessions with 10 users with aphasia, conducted with the help of two Aphasia Help Groups: Speakability Edinburgh and the Dundee health authority research group at the University of Dundee. Our meetings were held in a roundtable fashion with each participant asked to share his or her experience with smart devices. Participants had varying degrees of communication difficulties, ranging from the very severe to those who had nearly regained their full ability to speak. Our meetings with users in both cities lasted for 2 hours divided among the number of users present. Users were asked to share their personal experiences with mobile devices and to discuss ways in which smart devices helped them in their daily lives.

After the discussions with users we applied the Technology Appropriation Model (TApM) to analyse their appropriation requirements to gather requirements for an AAC application we are developing as part of ongoing research.

ASSETS '15, October 26-28, 2015, Lisbon, Portugal
ACM 978-1-4503-3400-6/15/10.
http://dx.doi.org/10.1145/2700648.2811360

3. TECHNOLOGY APPROPRIATION MODEL
The Technology Appropriation Model was introduced by Carroll et al. in 2001 [2]. We will abbreviate to TApM, not to confuse with Davis's Technology Acceptance Modal (TAM). Salovaara [5] highlights that TApM models are primarily used in sociological contexts and little work has been done in other areas such as software/hardware accessibility. To bridge the gap this work will apply TaPM to an HCI context. As shown in Figure 1, TApM has three levels and a filtering phase as follows:

- *Level 1*: the user is unfamiliar with the technology and has his/her first contact with it.
- *Filtering*: the user decides if the technology interests him/her.
- *Level 2*: Appropriation process: the user acquires a deeper understanding of the technology through frequent use.
- *Level 3*: long term use: use of a technology over time.

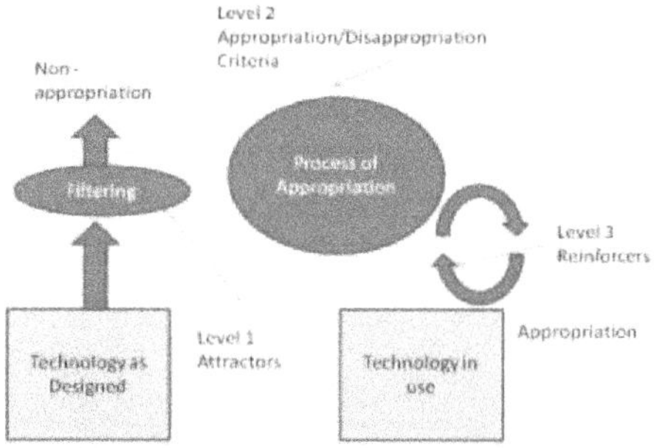

Figure 1: Technology Appropriation Model

4. ANALYSIS OF LEVEL 2 BEHAVIOUR
In level 2 of the model users start to customize their devices by installing additional apps and inventing additional uses for the apps already present on the device. To study this level the researcher must identify user motives for Appropriation to begin; these motives are called Appropriation Criteria. For example, Carroll [2] uses word coding to identify Appropriation Criteria. We, however, cannot comfortably use word coding because our data were conversational in nature. Instead we will use questions phrased in the first person from the perspective of a person with

aphasia. Analysing our meeting notes we identified four main questions that drive the appropriation filtering decisions (in addition to some less common issues):

A. Will it help me talk about myself with others?
B. Will it help me remember words?
C. Will it help me understand written documents?
D. Will it help me when I'm writing to friends and family?
E. Other

5. ANALYSIS OF LEVEL 3 BEHAVIOUR

In level 3 TApM looks at how Appropriation caters for the needs of everyday life. We identified six examples of how our users Appropriated their portable devices for everyday life:

Use of notes: All participants made use of notes either as a reminder or to store snippets of text as an aid when composing text. Notes were also used to share life experiences and personal information

Combination of Text to Speech and Speech to Text: In some cases participants combined functionality to obtain desired functionality. For instance transferring a physical document to their device via OCR and having it read back to them via Text to Speech.

Picture based Communication: Participants who had difficulty with writing saved images of favourite topics to their device and pasted them inside correspondence to convey a message to the recipient.

Dictation: Participants with a good level of speech but with problems in recalling word spelling resorted to dictation to compose emails or to store difficult words on the device.

Supported Independence: One participant and his wife appropriated iTunes. The participant's wife uses the *Find my iPhone* app to periodically check where her husband is while he is jogging.

A special use of YouTube: One participant used YouTube to re-learn lyrics to his favouite songs that he had forgotten after his stroke.

These apps are used by those who have difficulties communicating as a way to integrate or replace their communicative abilities. During the meetings participants asked questions like "Can I use my notes?", "Can I dictate to it?" In general users wanted to find all of the functions they had created via Appropriation collected into the AAC app. As such, by looking at level 3 behaviour we, see a way of identifying requirements for our AAC application based on their discussion of appropriation of current apps rather than focussing on the abstract "what features would you wish or need?". Table 1 couples questions proposed in level 2 analysis with Appropriation behaviours listed in level 3 analysis.

	Notes	Combi	Pict. B. Com.	Dict.	iTunes	Youtube
QA						
QB						
QC						
QD						
QE						

Table 1 User Appropriation Coupled with Proposed Questions

We found that users that appropriate portable devices can be classified in the following types:

1. Users who Appropriated Notes
2. Users who Appropriated Dictation
3. Users who Appropriated Text-To Speech / Speech to Text
4. Users who Appropriated Picture Based Communication

By applying TApM we gathered the following requirements:

- Use text contained in user notes to produce sentences for users to introduce themselves.
- Use text contained in user notes to collect sentences for different everyday situations.
- Include dictation for cases where user wants to store a word in the app and remembers how to pronounce it but not how it's spelt.
- Include pictures to integrate description of places, pets, and members of family

6. DISCUSSION

By examining Appropriation of a particular piece of software or hardware by a special needs community we showed that the requirements capturing process can be facilitated in cases where the target user has difficulty expressing his/her needs because of inherent difficulties that come with his condition, especially the difficulty of imagining abstract situations such as imagining himself using the application in the future. The use of TApM counters this by letting developers discuss potential requirements with users by focusing only on current use.

We discovered that Appropriation is often a result of the users not knowing that apps are available on the market for the uses he has appropriated his device

Current works in Appropriation focus on adapting design to make software or technology more appropriable by users; for example the work by Dix [3] where he proposes guidelines for software designers so that software lends itself to Appropriation. Dix uses two use-cases to prove the validity of his guidelines. It is our opinion that the reverse is also true. Appropriation should be examined to improve subsequent versions of software.

7. REFERENCES

[1] Brandenburg, C., Worrall, L., Rodriguez, A.D., and Copland, D. Mob. comp. tech. and aphasia: An integrated review of accessibility and potential uses. *Aphasiology 27*, 4 (2013), 444–461.

[2] Carroll, J., Howard, S., Vetere, F., Peck, J., and Murphy, J. Identity, Power And Fragmentation in Cyberspace: Technology Appropriation by Young People. *ACIS 2001 Proc.* (2001).

[3] Dix, A. Designing for Appropriation. *Proc. of the 21st Brit. HCI Group Annual Conf. on People and Comp.: HCI...But Not As We Know It - Vol. 2*, BCS (2007), 27–30.

[4] Galliers, J., Wilson, S., Roper, A., et al. Words Are Not Enough: Empowering People with Aphasia in the Design Process. *Proc. 12th Partic. Des. Conf.: Res. Pap. - Vol. 1*, ACM (2012), 51–60.

[5] Salovaara, A. and Tamminen, S. Acceptance or Appropriation? A Design-Oriented Critique of Tech. Acceptance Models. In H. Isomäki and P. Saariluoma, eds., *Future Interaction Design II.* Springer London, 2009, 157–173.

Japanese Sentence Handwriting Learning System for Special Needs Education

Iwao Kobayashi, Nami Nemoto
Tokyo Gakugei University
4-1-1 Nukuikita-machi, Koganei
Tokyo 184-8501 Japan
+81-42-329-7682
iwan@u-gakugei.ac.jp

Kiwamu Sato, Kaito Watanabe,
Hiroshi Nunokawa, Naohito Ogasawara
Iwate Prefectural University
152-52 Sugo, Takizawa, Iwate 020-0693 Japan
+81-19-694-2526
nunokawa@nunokawa.jp

ABSTRACT
We examined a learning system to study handwriting of Japanese sentences in special needs education. A prototype was constructed with a tablet PC. Evaluation of the system was conducted by expert reviewers and by a student who has handwriting difficulties.

Categories and Subject Descriptors
K.3.1 [**Computers and Education**]: Computer Uses in Education

General Terms
Human Factors

Keywords
Handwriting, Learning system, Special needs education, Japanese

1. INTRODUCTION
Handwriting is a key challenge for students who receive special needs education (SNE). The use of information and communication technology (ICT) in education has become a hot topic worldwide recently. Particularly, tablet PCs have garnered much attention. Therefore, handwriting-related applications and software have been examined and used for such students [1]. Nevertheless, existing applications have several shortcomings: 1) They are designed for learning to write characters and words, not sentences, which are prominent in school curriculum guidelines in Japan. 2) Writing is mainly done with fingers. Few products use writing implements. 3) Most existing applications are self-instructional. Few or no studies have examined applications for individualized instruction, which is applied many times in SNE.

This study assessed a Japanese handwriting system 1) for learning to write sentences, 2) for writing with a pen, and 3) for use with individualized instruction.

2. SYSTEM DESIGN and CONSTRUCTION
For handwriting learning tools, the following practices were targeted for students with handwriting difficulties, especially those students receiving special needs education in regular classes. Writing practice of each character of a sentence 1) within appropriately sized character boxes for learners, 2) within variously sized character boxes, and 3) while controlling size without a character box.

A prototype system was constructed based on an Android tablet PC (Excite Write; Toshiba Corp.) including an electromagnetic-guidance digitizer. A system application [2] consists of a menu, sample area, and a writing area. Learners see a sentence in the sample area and write it in the character box of the writing area, in which the traced character can be presented. In the menu, the following settings are available. 1) User Interface (UI): Presence and absence of a character box, auxiliary line, tracing character, box size, hand dominance, contrast, and line width can be changed. 2) Operation mode: in learner mode, a learner can write a sentence with a black line; in educator mode, an educator can write advice in red as a comment or an evaluation. 3) Operation menu: UI can be changed via the menu. Furthermore, pushing a "back" button, cancellation of writing can be done for each stroke. 4) Setting of practice: Before practice, educators can set some practice sentences as a prepared learning program. Additionally, they can add sentences while learning with the system. 5) Recording: The application can record written sentences and words line-by-line. After writing sentences, educators and learners can play back the sentences on a real-time basis.

3. SYSTEM EVALUATION
3.1 Expert Review
3.1.1 Methods
Five SNE teachers served as expert reviewers. All expert reviewers were 30–59-year-old men. All had sufficient experience using ICTs for SNE.

Four questions were used to assess 10 items. Question 1 included five items related to the participant himself. Question 2 included two items about system purposes from learner and educator perspectives. Question 3 involved two items for system functions. Question 4 addressed other opinions. Questions 1, 2, and 3 were five-grade evaluations; Question 4 elicited a written response.

Initially, the interviewer explained an outline of the expert review to teachers. The interviewer showed a system explanation and demonstrated it. Then sufficient time was given to teachers to use the system freely. During that period, the interviewer answered system-related questions. After using it, the interviewer gave teachers a questionnaire sheet and asked them to fill it out.

Data were analyzed using a spreadsheet. For items with five-grade evaluation, we scored answers of "insufficient" as one point, "somewhat insufficient" as two points, "neutral" as three points "somewhat sufficient" as four points, and "sufficient" as five

ASSETS '15, October 26-28, 2015, Lisbon, Portugal.
ACM 978-1-4503-3400-6/15/10.
DOI: http://dx.doi.org/10.1145/2700648.2811361

points. Mean scores of five teachers were calculated for each item. We classified the answer contents in the description item (Qu. 4).

3.1.2 Results
Table 1 presents mean scores of the five teachers on system purposes (Qu. 2). Table 2 shows those of system functions (Qu. 3).

Results of Qu. 4 showed positive opinions especially for the educational potential of voice input, reviewing what was learned, and personal learning. System function development requests were related to detailed settings of tracing and system costs.

Table 1. Mean scores of five educators on system purposes

Item	Learner	Educator
1. For learning to write sentences	4.2	4.2
2. For writing by pen	4.6	4.2
3. For use in individualized instruction	4.2	4.4
4. Total evaluation	4.4	4.6

Table 2. Mean scores of five educators on system function

Item	Score
1. User interface	4.4
2. Operation mode	4.4
3. Operation menu	4.2
4. Setting of practice	4.6
5. Recording	3.6

3.2 Educational Use

3.2.1 Methods
A 13-year-old boy diagnosed as having attention deficit hyperactivity disorder (ADHD) attended the educational use trials of the system. He has difficulty with handwriting and does very little note-taking in school; he can write characters and words at a slow pace for him. At a fast pace or when writing sentences, it is difficult for him to continue writing characters of equal size.

His personal educational supporter used the system in his learning for two months. During use, the system recorded his handwriting. During 11 sessions, 76 handwriting trials were recorded. Thereafter, recorded data were analyzed for correctness and time of writing.

3.2.2 Results
Figure 1 shows the percentage of characters, which were written out of the character box in Kanji (Chinese characters), Hiragana, and Katakana, which constitute Japanese sentences, and all three characters. Comparing results of a pre-session (before the system use, with learning based on paper materials) and the first two sessions, lower percentages were found for later sessions, especially for Kanji (Chinese characters).

For the time of writing, we calculated the mean times of writing per character in each session. Except for two sessions, times were 1–5 s. No clear tendency was found for the writing time.

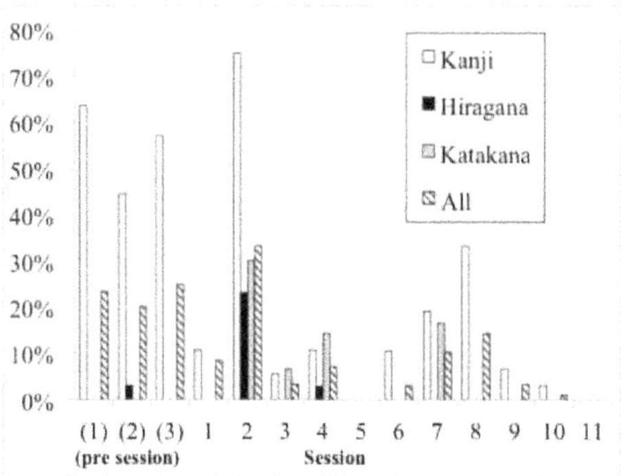

Figure 1. Results of correctness of writing.

However, for data analyzed based on the presence or absence of a character box in writing, no change was found in the absence condition, but the time was increased with sessions in the presence condition.

4. DISCUSSION
The expert reviewers' mean scores of eight of nine items were higher than 4.0., with positive opinions especially for the possibility of voice input. These results imply the system evaluation points. The recording function was regarded as particularly low. Negative opinions were given especially for tracing. Such low evaluations were given partly because these system functions were simple. Their improvement must be pursued.

Regarding educational use of the system, the boy became able to write short sentences with consistent character size, and became able to concentrate on writing sentences for a long time. These results suggest the educational effects of the system. However, his educational supporter pointed out that further system functions are necessary, e.g., much higher functions of recording and setting of difficulty level of practice sentences. Such functions might lead to development of more convenient handwriting learning tools.

5. CONCLUSION
This study examined the construction and evaluation of a learning system to study handwriting of Japanese sentences in special needs education. Expert reviewers (five SNE teachers) and a student evaluated a prototype tablet-computer-based system during use. Results revealed educational effects and possibilities, but additional system functions are expected to be necessary.

6. REFERENCES
[1] Okazaki, Y., Inoue, T., Nakamura, R., Watanabe, K., and Sonoda, T. 2015. Development and evaluation of a handwriting Kanji learning support tool adapted for dysgraphia children's learning properties. *Trans. IEICE*. J98-D, 1, 42-51. (in Japanese)

[2] Watanabe, K., Sato, K., Nemoto, N., Kobayashi, I., Nunokawa, H., and Ogasawara, N. 2015. The handwriting learning support application for special needs education. *Proc. 77th National Convention of IPSJ*. 4, 829-830. (in Japanese)

DroneNavigator: Using Drones for Navigating Visually Impaired Persons

Mauro Avila
University of Stuttgart
Pfaffenwaldring 5a
70569 Stuttgart
mauro.avila@vis.uni-stuttgart.de

Markus Funk
University of Stuttgart
Pfaffenwaldring 5a
70569 Stuttgart
markus.funk@vis.uni-stuttgart.de

Niels Henze
University of Stuttgart
Pfaffenwaldring 5a
70569 Stuttgart
niels.henze@vis.uni-stuttgart.de

ABSTRACT

Even after decades of research about navigation support for visually impaired people, moving independently still remains a major challenge. Previous work in HCI explored a large number of navigation aids, including auditory and tactile guidance systems. In this poster we propose a novel approach to guide visually impaired people. We use small lightweight drones that can be perceived through the distinct sound and the airflow they naturally produce. We describe the interaction concept we envision, first insights from proof-of-concept tests with a visually impaired participant, and provide an overview of potential application scenarios.

Keywords

navigation aid; visual impairments; drones;

Categories and Subject Descriptors

H.5.2. [**Information Interfaces and Presentation (e.g. HCI)**]: User Interfaces

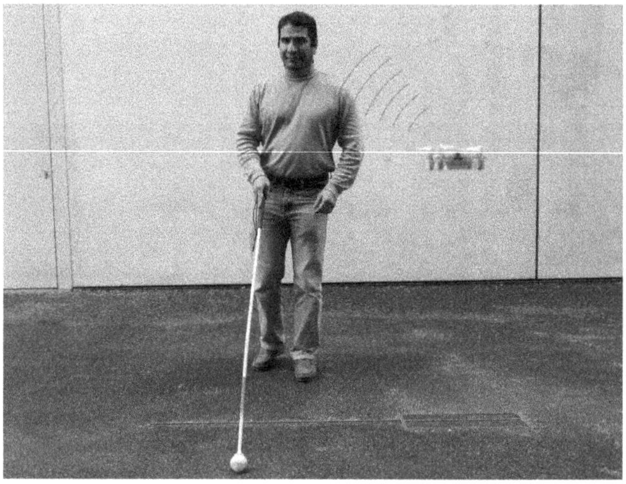

Figure 1: A user is perceiving navigation instructions by following the sound of a small drone.

1. INTRODUCTION & BACKGROUND

Assisted guidance for visually impaired persons inside unknown and known places is an important factor which increase traveling efficiency and traveler's confidence [6]. A large number of approaches have been investigated to support visually impaired users. Previous research focused on audio augmented reality [1] , tactile navigation systems [4], and smartcanes [5]. While previous work made substantial progress to support blind people, recent advances in technology enable novel wayfinding systems.

In this paper, we propose using small lightweight drones to help visually impaired persons to find their way and to locate objects. Our work is mainly inspired by work on the use of drones as companions for sports [3]. Blind users can set a destination using voice control. A small lightweight drone guides the way to the entered target. The user can easily perceive the position of the drone as it's motors emit a distinct sound. Having the drone equipped with a camera also enables to identify and locate items which are hard to spot without eyesight.

ASSETS'15, October 26–28, 2015, Lisbon, Portugal.
ACM 978-1-4503-3400-6/15/10.
http://dx.doi.org/10.1145/2700648.2811362

2. CONCEPT

In this work, we propose using small drones to navigate visually impaired persons in everyday situations. Therefore, we propose a small wearable prototype. The visually impaired person is wearing a bracelet that is carried around the wrist. A small drone is mounted on top of the bracelet. Using a voice command, the user can issue verbal commands e.g. *"navigate me to the office"*. Once the system recognized the command and calculated the shortest route, the drone starts flying and the visually impaired user can start following the drone. By tracking the distance between bracelet and drone using Bluetooth signal strength the drone always remains at a distance of 1-2 meters from the user and adjusts to the user's speed. Once the drone is at the target position, it hovers above the target coordinates. Finally, the user can issue a return to home command to attach the drone to the user's bracelet again.

While we believe that this approach has great potential for everyday situations, we envision two major scenarios for using drones as a navigation aid for visually impaired persons.

2.1 Using drones to navigate to an address or room

The first scenario is using the drone for navigating to a defined address or room. Both indoors and outdoors, a drone could follow a previously recorded path that a sighted person pre-records. Indoors the system can use a positioning system that uses the strength of WiFi-signals to navigate to a destination on a room-level accuracy. To not crash against walls or other persons drones can be equipped with distance sensors. Some drones already come with built-in distance sensors (e.g. the DJI Matrice 100[1]. Outdoors the system can use GPS to navigate the user to a previously defined address. The drone tries to stay on paths by using a built-in camera.

2.2 Using drones to find misplaced objects

More and more drones are equipped with a camera. While most drones use their camera to record videos or take pictures from a distance, a drone-carried camera can also be used to identify misplaced objects using computer vision [2]. We envision a second use-case, where a drone visually searches an environment by flying through it and comparing a reference image to a sought object. In case the object was found, the drone can guide the visually impaired person to the location of the misplaced object.

3. INITIAL INSIGHTS

As a proof of concept, we conducted two initial tests with one blind participant (male, age 37) to evaluate the feasibility of our approach. The participant had no remaining vision. For the study, we used a Cheerson CX-10 nano quadcopter, which is $4,2$ cm $\times 4,2$ cm wide, 2 cm high, and has a weight of 29 g. We chose a lightweight drone to not risk hurting the user or passers-by. We used a wizard of oz approach for flying the drone. The experimenter was controlling the drone and kept the drone in a distance of approximately 1-2 meters in front of the participant. When the target was reached, the experimenter landed the drone at the target position. As targets we used persons, furniture, and target points inside a hallway.

3.1 A lab study

To evaluate the general idea, we conducted a first lab experiment which consists of a simple navigation task i.e. walking down a corridor to a defined position. In 5 test walks, the participant had to walk to a target position and stop when the drone landed. The paths that were chosen for the test walks included straight lines and turns. One of the 5 paths included a 180° turn. Each path had an approximate length of 20 meters.

3.2 Testing external validity

Second, we conducted an experiment to verify the external validity of our approach. Thereby, the participant was guided through a crowded room with approximately 30 persons. The distance from the starting point to the target location was 20 meters.

The participant was able to follow the drone and was reaching the targets. Further, the participant did not hit any walls or other persons with the cane. The participant stated that the drone was easy to spot by its distinct sound even though the environment was noisy or reverberant. He said that *"[I] can perceive its position, beside, behind or ahead me, even when it moves around"*. Another advantage of the approach is that the participant did not need to carry additional technology. He could use his cane and follow the drone in a way he would normally walk. The three-dimensional position of the target can be perceived in a very fine-grained way. E.g. the participant was able to find an empty spot on a sofa that was 50 cm wide.

[1]`http://store.dji.com/product/matrice-100` last access 06-24-2015

4. CONCLUSION & FUTURE WORK

In this poster, we present a novel approach for navigating visually impaired persons by using small drones. In a proof-of-concept study, we found that our approach is feasible and could be used to accurately guide a visually impaired person. Further, in an everyday scenario, we show that our approach even works in noisy environments, e.g. navigating through a crowded room. Our participant liked that the drone was easy to spot and and to follow as it produces a distinct sound.

In future work, we want to conduct a user study with more participants and look into multi-user scenarios using different sound patterns for the drones. Further we want to investigate the potential of the drone's airflow as another modality to guide visually impaired users, and explore the social implications of drone-navigation for both users and passers-by.

5. ACKNOWLEDGEMENTS

This work is funded by the DAAD SENACYT Cooperation program and the German Research Foundation within the SimTech Cluster of Excellence (EXC 310/2).

6. REFERENCES

[1] Blum, J. R., Bouchard, M., and Cooperstock, J. R. WhatâĂŹs around me? spatialized audio augmented reality for blind users with a smartphone. In *Mobile and Ubiquitous Systems: Computing, Networking, and Services*. Springer, 2012, 49–62.

[2] Chincha, R., and Tian, Y. Finding objects for blind people based on surf features. In *Bioinformatics and Biomedicine Workshops (BIBMW), 2011 IEEE International Conference on*, IEEE (2011), 526–527.

[3] Graether, E., and Mueller, F. Joggobot: a flying robot as jogging companion. In *CHI'12 EA* (2012), 1063–1066.

[4] Henze, N., Heuten, W., and Boll, S. Non-intrusive somatosensory navigation support for blind pedestrians. *Proc. Eurohaptics* (2006).

[5] Martin, W., Dancer, K., Rock, K., Zeleny, C., and Yelamarthi, K. The smart cane: an electrical engineering design project. In *ASEE North Central Section Conference* (2009).

[6] Williams, M. A., Galbraith, C., Kane, S. K., and Hurst, A. just let the cane hit it: how the blind and sighted see navigation differently. In *Proc. ASSETS'14*, ACM (2014), 217–224.

Calendars for Individuals with Cognitive Disabilities: A Comparison of Table View and List View

Frode Eika Sandnes
Faculty of Technology, Art and Design
Oslo and Akershus University College of Applied Sciences
P.O. Box 4 St. Olavs plass, 0130 Oslo
Frode-Eika.Sandnes@hioa.no

Maud Veronica Lundh
Faculty of Technology, Art and Design
Oslo and Akershus University College of Applied Sciences
P.O. Box 4 St. Olavs plass, 0130 Oslo
Maud.Gine.Lundh@gmail.com

ABSTRACT
Calendars can be important memory aids for individuals with cognitive disabilities. This study compared the effect of the popular two-dimensional table calendar view and the simpler list view. A controlled experiment was conducted involving 10 individuals with cognitive disabilities and 10 controls. The results show that the list view gave significantly fewer errors and shorter searching times, while editing took longer with the list view.

Categories and Subject Descriptors
H.1.2 [**User/Machine Systems**]: Software psychology.

General Terms
Design, Human Factors.

Keywords
Calendar, cognitive disability, universal design.

1. INTRODUCTION
Cognitive disabilities include dyslexia, ADHD/ADD, learning disorders, etc. Common traits include limited memory, difficulty in orientating and limited concentration. Individuals diagnosed with a cognitive learning disability are sometimes taught to use memory aids. Both paper based and electronic calendars [1, 2] and to-do lists can be important tools for organizing ones daily activities allowing individuals with cognitive disabilities to meet the expectations of their environment and thus successfully complete higher education and participate fully in work life.

Although electronic calendars are common the research literature on general calendars is limited to a handful of studies [3]. Two popular calendar types include the table view and the event list view. The two dimensional table based calendar organize events along representative time axes such as the hours of the day along the vertical axis and the days of the week along the horizontal axis. Clearly, the two dimensional layout means that such calendars require a lot of display real-estate as open slots in the calendar are blank. Microsoft Outlook is one example of a calendar that uses the table presentation as a default view.

ASSETS '15, October 26-28, 2015, Lisbon, Portugal
ACM 978-1-4503-3400-6/15/10.
http://dx.doi.org/10.1145/2700648.2811363

An example of event list calendar includes the ANYDO smartphone application where events are listed vertically. Hence, the event list calendars are one-dimensional and it makes effective use of the display real estate. However, the viewer does not get an intuitive view of the event durations and time between events. The effective use of display real estate makes event list calendars suitable for mobile devices with small displays giving cognitively disabled users better access to the memory aids.

This study compared the effectiveness of these two calendar types for individuals with cognitive difficulties. The hypothesis was that users with cognitive disabilities would perform calendar tasks more quickly and with fewer errors using the event list based calendars compared to table based calendars, because it was assumed that the two dimensional view is cognitively more challenging to process compared to the simple event lists.

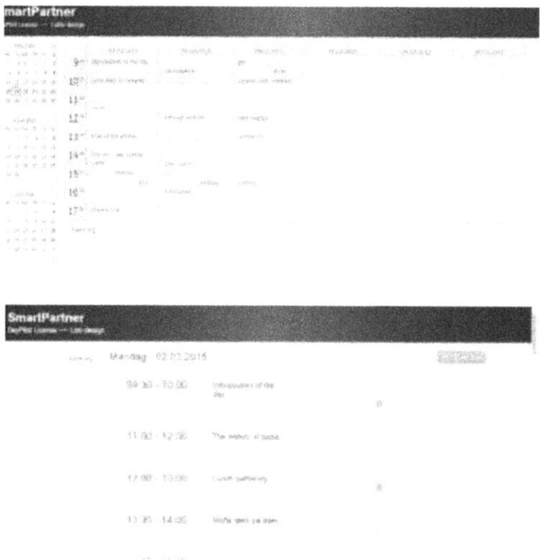

Figure 1. Screenshots of table (top) and list (bottom) views

2. METHOD
2.1 Participants
The participants were recruited by the assistance of the special interest organization ADHD Norway. A total of 10 individuals with an ADHD/ADD diagnosis participated in the experiment and 10 controls. Of the 10 ADHD/ADD participants, 3 were male and 7 female ranging from 19 to 59 years of age (mean age 31). Of the controls 4 were female and 6 male ranging from 23 to 51 years of age (mean age 28).

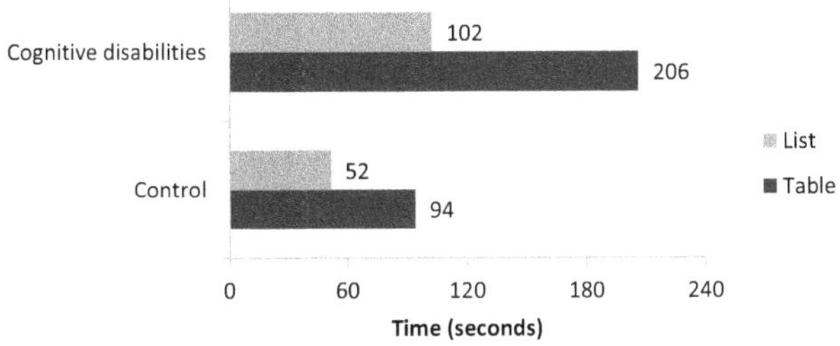

Figure 2. Total search time (task 1)

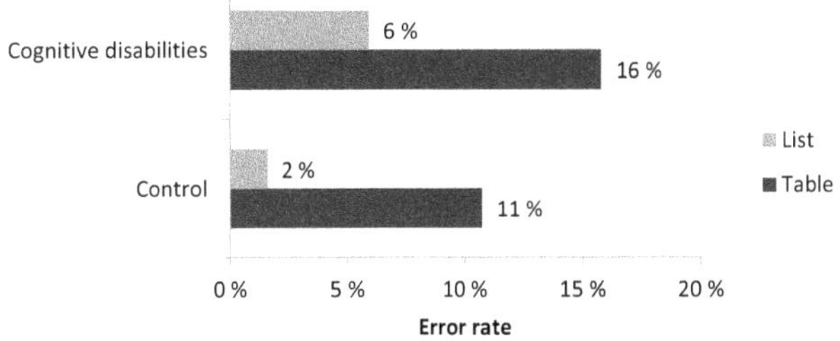

Figure 4. Total error rate searching (task 1).

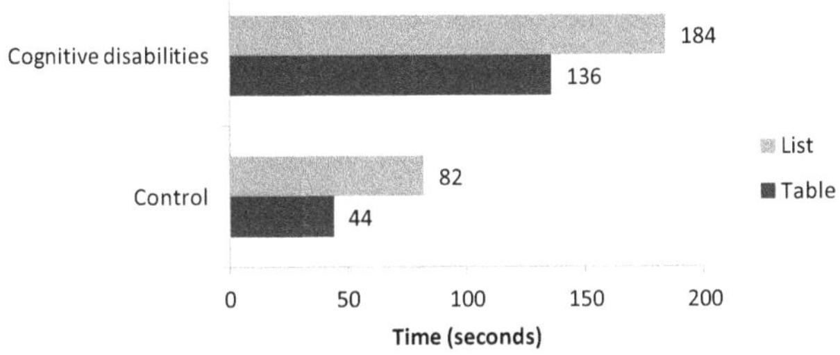

Figure 3. Total time editing (task 2)

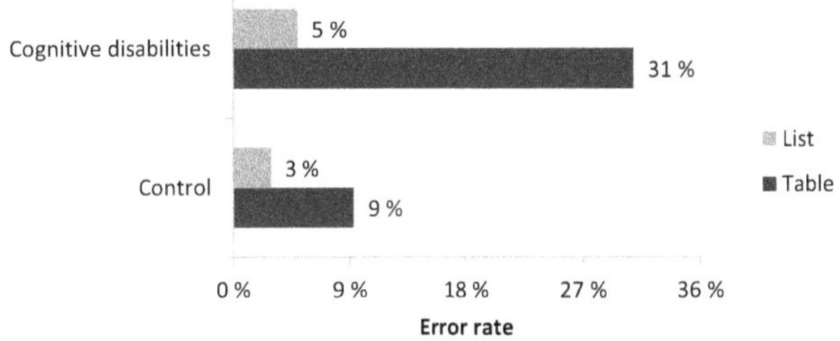

Figure 5. Total error rate editing (task 2)

2.2 Equipment

A test framework comprising a table based calendar and an event list calendar was implemented in PHP. The users accessed the calendars using a Google Chrome web browser. All the events were logged with timestamps.

2.3 Procedure

The participants were asked to perform two tasks. The first tasks involved locating and marking 15 randomly ordered events in a set schedule for a three-day food festival.

The second task was designed to probe the calendars effectiveness in supporting adding, editing and removing events. The participants were asked to add six new events, either by creating new events or altering events already in the schedule. The tasks were performed in random order to minimize learning effects.

3. RESULTS

Figure 2 shows that both groups used shorter time to complete all the searching tasks using the list view compared to the table view, but an ANOVA test showed that this difference was not significant ($F(1, 36) = 0.56$; $p>.06$). A significant difference was found between the two groups, with the control group completing the task in half the time as the other group ($F(1, 36) = 6.24$;$p<.03$).

Most participants (five controls and five with cognitive disabilities) reported that they had the impression of using less time in the table view compared to the list view. Only two controls and three participants with cognitive disabilities favored the list view. The others expressed no preference.

Figure 3 shows both groups used more time on editing operations in the list design, although the difference is not significant ($F(1, 36) = 0.17$; $p>.1$). The diagram also shows that the control group uses less time in both designs compared to the other group, although the difference is not significant ($F(1, 36) = 0.17$; $p>.1$).

Figure 4 shows that the list view resulted in significantly fewer errors for searching tasks ($F(1, 36)=19.51$; $p<.001$) while no significant difference could be detected across the two groups ($F(1, 36) = 1.86$; $p>.06$). Lists also gave significantly fewer errors for editing tasks as illustrated in Figure 5 ($F(1, 36) = 9.16$; $p<.05$).

4. CONCLUSIONS

These preliminary results show that list based calendars result in significantly fewer errors for both searching and editing tasks and significantly faster searching. Therefore, since referencing is a more common operation and individuals with high reliance on calendars have lower tolerance for errors the results points in favor of the list based calendar. The results also show that list based calendars also benefit users without cognitive disabilities.

5. REFERENCES

[1] Baecker, R. M., Richards, B. & Wu, M. (2010, October). Field evaluation of a collaborative memory aid for persons with amnesia and their family members. In Proceedings of the 12th international ACM SIGACCESS conference on Computers and accessibility (pp. 51-58). ACM.

[2] Wu, M., Birnholtz, J., Richards, B., Baecker, R., & Massimi, M. (2008, April). Collaborating to re-member: a distributed cognition account of families coping with memory impairments. In Proceedings of the SIGCHI Conference on Human Factors in Computing Systems (pp. 825-834). ACM.

[3] Neustaedter, C., Brush, A. J., & Greenberg, S. (2009). The calendar is crucial: Coordination and awareness through the family calendar. ACM Transactions on Computer-Human Interaction (TOCHI), 16(1), 6.

Mobile Phone Access to a Sign Language Dictionary

Michael D. Jones
BYU Computer Science
3328 TMCB
Provo, UT 84602
+1 801 422 2217
mike.jones@byu.edu

Harley Hamilton
Georgia Tech. College of Computing
GVU Center M/C 0760
Atlanta, GA 30302
hhamilton@gatech.edu

James Petmecky
BYU Computer Science
3328 TMCB
Provo, UT 84602
james.petmecky@byu.edu

ABSTRACT
We have built a functional prototype of a mobile phone app that allows children who are deaf to look up American Sign Language (ASL) definitions of printed English words using the camera on the mobile phone. In the United States, 90% of children who are deaf are born to parents who are not deaf and who do not know sign language [3]. In many cases, this means that the child will not be exposed to fluent sign language in the home and this can delay the child's acquisition of both their first signed language and a secondary written language [1]. Another consequence is that outside of school the child may not have easy access to people or services that can translate written English words into ASL signs. We have developed a prototype phone app that allows children who are deaf and their parents to look up ASL definitions of English words in printed books. The user aims the phone camera at the printed text, takes a picture and then clicks on a word to access the ASL definition. Our next steps are to explore the idea with children who are deaf and their parents, develop design guidelines for sign language dictionary apps, build the app using those guidelines and then to test the app with children who are deaf and their hearing parents.

Categories and Subject Descriptors
K.4.2 [Computing Milieux] Social Issues: *Assistive technologies for persons with disabilities.*

General Terms
Human Factors

Keywords
Deaf education; mobile apps

1. INTRODUCTION
Reading English is a difficult task for many students who are deaf. In 30 years of standardized testing, half of deaf high school students have been found to read at the 4th grade level or below [4].A major factor affecting their reading ability is vocabulary knowledge [2] and hence the accessibility of text.

Accessing sign language definitions for printed English words is difficult for children who are deaf and who communicate primarily in sign language. This is particularly true at home in a family setting. In the United States, more than 90% of children who are deaf are born to parents who are not deaf [3] and do not know sign language. This means that a child learning to read at home most often can not ask a parent to define a new word encountered in a book.

This problem is important to deaf children who communicate primarily in sign language and their parents. It is important to children because it creates barriers to acquiring ASL vocabulary for English words. It is important to parents because a parent might use the dictionary to build their own sign language skills in addition to using it to teach their child in the home.

Current solutions to defining English words in ASL include web pages[1] and mobile phone apps[2]. In both cases using the dictionary involves selecting the word from a list of all words in the dictionary or typing a word into a textbox. We seek to eliminate both selecting the word from the dictionary list and typing in order to minimize interruptions to reading flow.

We have constructed a functional prototype of an Android phone app that allows children who are deaf to access ASL definitions of printed English words without selecting the word from a list or typing the word into the app. The app is a front end to our SmartSign Dictionary which is freely available on the Internet[3]. To use the prototype, a user points the cell phone camera at a page of text, takes a picture and then clicks on a word to access the definition. The definition is displayed as a video streamed from YouTube.

Our next steps are to engage with children who are deaf and their parents in order to establish design and usage guidelines for sign language dictionary cell phone apps. We will then use those guidelines to finalize the app design. These guidelines may also inform the design of other related apps.

2. GOALS
We have four goals for the design of the application.

Eliminate typing. We seek to avoid requiring users to spell unfamiliar words when looking for definitions of those words.

Maintain reading flow. The app should allow the user to look up a word with minimal effort and then to return to the reading at hand.

ASSETS'15, October 26-28, 2015, Lisbon, Portugal.
ACM 978-1-4503-3400-6/15/10
http://dx.doi.org/10.1145/2700648.2811364

[1] Such as the dictionaries http://www.lifeprint.com/dictionary.htm or http://www.handspeak.com/word/

[2] Such as "ASL Dictionary" by Software Studios LLC or "ASL Dictionary from NTID" by Rochester Institute of Technology.

[3] At http://smartsign.imtc.gatech.edu/

No machine translation. Using the dictionary should not require natural language translation technology that does not yet exist. More difficult problem of automatically translating English phrases or words to ASL is left to others.

Increase dictionary use. The app should measurably increase use of the dictionary.

3. SMARTSIGN DICTIONARY PROTOYPE PHONE APP

The phone app prototype consists of two parts: the dictionary and the app itself. The dictionary is a collection of videos hosted on YouTube. At present there are 17,593 videos in the dictionary which represent a total of 65,670 words or phrases. We are actively expanding the dictionary to a target goal of 20,000 videos. The dictionary can be accessed by sending a keyword as a parameter in a URL. The server returns a JSON string which contains a list of ASL definitions for one or more meanings of that word. For each meaning of the word, the JSON contains a list of keywords, a thumbnail image and a YouTube video ID. The video can be accessed using with YouTube ID. The definitions were produced in collaboration with the Institute for Disabilities Research and Training.

The app prototype consists of three parts: taking a picture of text, picking a word and watching the definition. Taking a picture of the text is done using the cell phone camera. OCR on images with 1040x728 pixels is sufficient for this application for images taken 8-12 cm from printed text written in a 12 point font. We use the Abbyy FineReader mobile phone OCR package. When the camera plane is parallel OCR correctly identifies about 85% of the printed words (depending on lighting and other factors).

After taking a picture, the user clicks on a word in the picture to access a definition of that word. Pinch-to-zoom and swipe-to-pan allow the user to find the right word. Colored highlights overlaid on words in the image indicate words with definitions in the dictionary. For example, the image of the word "cat" in a picture is highlighted if the OCR engine recognized "cat" and the word "cat" is in the dictionary.

Clicking on a highlighted word in the image either brings up the ASL definition or brings up a disambiguation page. The disambiguation page lists ASL definitions for different meanings of the word. For example, clicking on the word "house" brings up two definitions: one for "house" as a noun and one for "house" as a verb. Each possibility includes a list of keywords in English as well as a thumbnail image. Clicking on one of the definitions on the disambiguation page brings up the ASL definition video. The user selects the word from a list but this list is includes only meanings for that word and not all words in the dictionary.

The video is streamed from YouTube and displayed in a standard video player. After the video is complete, the app returns to the image of the English text where the user can select another word.

It is significant that the dictionary is not stored locally on the phone and that the video is streamed to the phone. This means that the dictionary can evolve over time and that the app does not need to store all of the 17,593 videos. But it does mean that the app only works when connected to the internet.

4. ESTABLISHING DESIGN GUIDELINES

Our next step is to measure preferences that will be used to establish design guidelines for this and other ASL dictionary apps on mobile phones. We have decomposed the design problem into three dimensions given below and plan to measure preferences for both children and parents along those dimensions.

Input. How should the user input the word to look up to the dictionary? We have assumed that eliminating typing is a good design goal. However children who are deaf may prefer to type the word in or select the word from a list of all words in the dictionary rather than use the camera.

Selection. Assuming the phone camera is used to generate input, how should the user select the word in the picture to define? Selection methods vary based on the number of clicks required to select a word. In the prototype we implemented a two-click process in which the user clicks to take a picture and clicks a word. We have identified other selection methods that require one or zero clicks. In the one-click method, the user aims the phone camera at a block of English then clicks on the word in the camera preview to access a definition. In the zero-click method, the user aims the camera at the block of text. Once the camera stabilizes the word at the center of the camera image is defined.

Viewing. How should the ASL video definition be viewed? Should other information be presented when viewing the video or should the video be presented in isolation? We can overlay video with the English word being defined or with the entire phrase containing the word being defined. Or we can show the word at the end of the video.

5. SUMMARY

A functional prototype of the app is complete but additional work is needed to establish design guidelines. These guidelines will inform the completion of this app and perhaps guide the development of other similar apps for children who are deaf and their parents. Future work will measure whether or not the app results in increased dictionary use by children who are deaf.

6. ACKNOWLEDGMENTS

This work was supported by the Sorenson Impact Foundation, a Google Faculty Research Award and NSF IIS-1124548.

7. REFERENCES

[1] Goldin-Meadow, S. and Mayberry, R. I. 2001. How Do Profoundly Deaf Children Learn to Read? *Learning Disabilities Research & Practice* 16, 4. 222-229.

[2] Luckner, J. & Cooke, C. 2010. A summary of the vocabulary research with students who are deaf or hard of hearing. *American Annals of the Deaf*, 155(1), 38-67.

[3] Mitchell, R. and Karchmer, M. A. 2004. Chasing the mythical ten percent: Parental hearing status of deaf and hard of hearing students in the United States. *Sign Language Studies*. 4, 2. 138-163.

[4] Traxler, C. B.. 2000. The Stanford Achievement Test, 9th Edition: National norming and performance standards for deaf and hard-of-hearing students. *J. Deaf Studies and Deaf Education*. 5,4. 337-348.

Teaching Accessibility, Learning Empathy

Cynthia Putnam[§], Maria Dahman[§], Emma Rose[†], Jinghui Cheng[§], Glenn Bradford[§]

[§] College of Computing and Digital Media, DePaul University, 243 S. Wabash, Chicago, IL, 60604

[†] Interdisciplinary Arts and Sciences, University of Washington, 1900 Commerce St, Tacoma, WA 98402

cputnam@cdm.depaul.edu, maria.dahman@gmail.com, ejrose@u.washington.edu, jcheng13@cdm.depaul.edu; glenn.bradford@gmail.com

ABSTRACT
As information and communication technologies (ICTs) become more diffuse, the diversity of users that designers need to consider is growing; this includes people with disabilities and aging populations. As a result, computing education must provide students the means and inspiration to learn about inclusive design. This poster presents top-level findings from 18 interviews with professors from some of the top universities in the US. Our analysis yielded four categories of findings: (1) important student learning outcomes (the most common was for students to embrace diversity); (2) exercises and teaching materials (almost all focused on inclusion of people with disabilities in discovery and evaluation of ICTs); (3) frustrations and challenges (largely focused on how to engage students in accessibility topics); and (4) the importance of instructor initiative to include the topic of accessibility in their teaching. The unifying theme was the high importance of cultivating empathy with end users.

Categories and Subject Descriptors
K.3.2 [**Computers and Education**]: Computer and Information Science Education—*computer science education.*

Keywords
Accessibility, pedagogy

1. INTRODUCTION
As information and communication technologies (ICTs) become more diffuse, the diversity of users that developers and designers need to consider has expanded to include more people with disabilities. As a result, computing education needs to respond by providing students opportunities to learn about accessibility and designing for inclusion. This extended abstract summarizes results of a qualitative research study of practices in teaching accessibility in university-level programs in the US; specifically, we summarize findings from 18 interviews with professors from some of the top universities in the US who discussed their experiences teaching courses related to accessible computing.

While there is a clear need to include principles of accessibility and convey the importance of designing for people with disability in computing education, there is a lack of resources for instructors with little or no background in the area to know how to incorporate these topics into their curricula. While other articles have provided small-scale surveys or first person reflections about teaching accessibility [e.g, 1-3], this project fills a gap in the literature by providing results of a study across a larger number of instructors, courses, practices, materials and programs. We present a set of themes detailing best practices and challenges in teaching accessibility.

ASSETS '15, October 26-28, 2015, Lisbon, Portugal.
ACM 978-1-4503-3400-6/15/10.
DOI: http://dx.doi.org/10.1145/2700648.2811365

2. Methods
To identify instructors who teach accessibility, we started with the top 160 US universities listed in the US News and World Report. We then identified courses related to ICT accessibility and, when possible, contacted the last or current instructor. In addition to searching the top 160 US universities, we also identified other leads through the literature review and during interviews we asked our participants to refer us to other instructors who taught accessibility. In total, we contacted 236 people, which resulted in 18 completed interviews. All interviews were conducted in April-May 2014. See Table 1 for the list of participants.

Table 1: Interview Participants

Participant (A-Z)	Title (5/2014)	Institution (5/2014)
Dan Cosley	Assoc. Professor	Cornell Univ
Katherine Diebel	Instructor	Univ of Washington
Jinjuan Heidi Feng	Assoc. Professor	Towson Univ
Krzysztof Gajos	Assoc. Professor	Harvard Univ
Juan Gilbert	Professor	Clemson Univ.
Derek Hansen	Assoc. Professor	Brigham Young Univ.
Amy Hurst	Assist. Professor	Univ. of Maryland, BC
Julie Kientz	Assist. Professor	Univ. of Washington
Sri Kurniawan	Assoc. Professor	Univ of California, SC
Richard Ladner	Professor	Univ. of Washington
Clayton Lewis	Professor	Univ. of Colorado
Benjamin Lok	Professor	Northeastern Univ.
Bilge Mutlu	Assist. Professor	Univ. of Wisconsin
Steven Reiss	Professor	Brown Univ.
Seth Teller	Professor (Deceased)	MIT
Gregg Vanderheiden	Professor	Univ. of Wisconsin
Confidential	Confidential	Carnegie Mellon Univ.
Confidential	Confidential	Fordham University

In the interviews, we asked about (a) details about the course(s) they have taught that included accessibly, e.g., number of students; (b) activities and/or assignments that had been particularly successful, and to explain why; (c) a memorable experience; and (d) if they were to run into a former student what would they like to have had the student recall about the course.

3. Top Level Findings

We grouped our findings into four categories: (1) important student learning outcomes; (2) exercises and teaching materials; (3) frustrations and challenges; and (4) the importance of instructor initiative. In all four categories, the unifying theme was to teach with the goal of cultivating empathy with end users.

(1) The most common desired **student learning outcome** (expressed by 12 interviewees) was the importance of students embracing diversity in order to keep accessibility in mind as they design technologies. For example, Sri Kurniawan told us:

"The one thing that I wanted [students] to take away is to really understand that number one, they are not designing for themselves, they are designing for people with a wide range of abilities and needs and preferences."

(2) Examples of **exercises and teaching materials** fell into two subcategories: (a) approaches and (b) assignments. By far, the most common approach, mentioned by 7 of 18 instructors, was to facilitate direct interaction with people with disabilities. Clayton Lewis summarized the impetus for this activity well:

"I believe it's really critical for people to get some first hand exposure, [some] interaction with people with disabilities. I think it is a subject that is difficult to appreciate from a sort of a book-learning point of view. And not just it can be hard to understand, it's easy to misunderstand."

Derek Hansen discussed direct interaction in the context of the challenge of helping students building 'true empathy':

"I think if it's just a lecture alone on the topic I think sometimes it's hard to really help them gain empathy and understanding."

Another common approach was to simulate disabilities (mentioned by five interviewees) to help students build empathy. The most extensive model of simulating disabilities came from Gregg Vanderheiden in his description of the experience lab that he has built at the University of Wisconsin:

"...we have a series of approximately 30 experience stations (15 pairs of stations) that everybody in the class has to complete. At each of the station-pairs we give the student a different limitation (they wear a blindfold, or must use only a headstick, or use special limiting gloves to simulate arthritis, or vision limiting goggles) and two different products. One product is designed poorly (and it is very hard or impossible to use) and one that has been designed well (and it is no problem to use)."

The most commonly discussed assignments also emphasized involvement with people who have disabilities and focused on group projects to either build something using a user-centered approach or evaluate an existing application. At the University of Washington, Richard Ladner focused some computer science capstone courses on designing for diverse users and emphasized including people with disabilities not only in the discovery phases, but also in the evaluation. That way, projects "*...get critiqued, and not just by me, or by the teacher but by people with disabilities to give them feedback.*"

(3) There were several common **frustrations and related challenges** that interviewees discussed. Three of our interviewees discussed frustrations surrounding the lack of awareness about the importance of accessibility-related topics and how few students are exposed to accessibility in their programs. For example, Seth Teller explained that at MIT accessibility was covered in-depth in one elective course, but commented that the course did not reach very many students:

"*...the class only reaches twenty to thirty students a term, and our department has more than a thousand students, so I'd say the exposure by our department to students broadly is pretty limited. I'd say most of the thousand students at any given year in the program will go through the year without hearing or thinking about accessibility.*"

When we asked interviewees about activities they had tried that had been unsuccessful, they commonly mentioned how difficult it was to engage students when discussing legal and technical topics related to accessibility. For example, Krzysztof Gajos said:

"I've found that if I teach students the rules and the laws for accessibility that they fall asleep and still do a terrible job on their project, so I have shifted towards trying to build empathy."

(4) A recurring theme in the interviews is the **importance of an instructor initiative**. Because the topic of accessibility is rarely embedded in programs and courses, individual instructors often have to take the initiative to include them in their teaching. Among out 18 interviewees, 13 had a research project or agenda related to accessibility. For example, Katherine Diebel told us:

"When I was teaching, I was generally introducing accessibility topics because I'm interested in them and I view them as important rather than they were already mentioned in the existing course."

To conclude, the unifying theme throughout our top-level findings was the high importance of cultivating empathy with end users. Strategies for building empathy included (a) simulating disabilities so students get an embodied experience of using inaccessible technologies, and (b) including perspectives of people with disabilities in the classroom through testimonials, direct interaction, or other materials (e.g. movies) that attempt to present the world with an accessibility perspective.

4. ACKNOWLEDGMENTS

We would like to dedicate this project (and poster) to the memory of Seth Teller. We would also like to thank all of the interviewees for their time and thoughtful responses.

5. REFERENCES

[1] Bohman, P.R. 2012. Teaching Accessibility and Design-For-All in the Information and Communication Technology Curriculum: Three Case Studies of Universities in the United States, England, and Austria. Ph.D. Dissertation. Utah State University, Logan, UT. UMI Order Number: AAT 3546296.

[2] Keith, S., Whitney, G., and Petz, A. 2009. Design for All as Focus in European ICT Teaching and Training Activities. In *Proceedings of INCLUDE*, 1-6.

[3] Waller, A., Hanson, V.L., and David Sloan. 2009. Including accessibility within and beyond undergraduate computing courses. In *Proceedings of the 11th international ACM SIGACCESS conference on Computers and accessibility* (Assets '09). ACM, New York, NY, USA, 155-162.

Road Sensing: Personal Sensing and Machine Learning for Development of Large Scale Accessibility Map

Yusuke Iwasawa[1], Koya Nagamine[2], Yutaka Matsuo[1], and Ikuko Eguchi Yairi[2]
[1]Dept. of Engineering, The University of Tokyo, Bunkyo-ku, Tokyo, Japan
[2]Dept. of Science and Engineering, Sophia University, Chiyoda-ku, Tokyo, Japan
iwasawa@weblab.t.u-tokyo.ac.jp, nagamine@yairilab.net,
matsuo@weblab.t.u-tokyo.ac.jp, i.e.yairi@sophia.ac.jp

ABSTRACT

This paper proposes a methodology for developing large scale accessibility map with personal sensing by using smart phone and machine learning technologies. The strength of the proposed method is its low cost data collection, which is a key to break through stagnations of accessibility map that currently applied to limited areas. This paper developed and evaluated a prototype system that estimates types of ground surfaces by applying supervised learning techniques to activity sensing data of wheelchair users recorded by a three-axis accelerometer, focusing on knowledge extraction and visualization. As a result of evaluation using nine wheelchair users' data with Support Vector Machine, three ground surface types, curb, tactile indicator, and slope, were detected with f-score (and accuracy) of 0.63 (0.92), 0.65 (0.85), and 0.54 (0.97) respectively.

Categories and Subject Descriptors

H.4 [**Information Systems Applications**]: Miscellaneous; K.4.2 [**Social Issues**]: Handicapped persons/special needs

General Terms

Experimentation

Keywords

Personal Sensing, Machine Learning, Accessibility Map

1. INTRODUCTION

Current road accessibility information collecting, such as official review and crowdsourcing [4, 7], needs manpower that requires monetary assistance for professional accessibility advisers or non-professional workers. The paper proposes a methodology for low-cost accessibility information collecting benefiting by a emerging personal sensing technology with smart phone [3, 5] and a machine learning based pattern recognition [6]. The methodology consists of following three technology components: (1) a platform system that is a basic physical component and consists of sensors, networks and databases with high security and privacy, (2) machine learning algorithms for knowledge extraction that are core software components as intelligence of the system, and (3) accessibility visualization on web maps using the extracted knowledge as end-user applications for the people with special-needs. This paper reports concepts and recent evaluation of a prototype system.

ASSETS'15, October 26–28, 2015, Lisbon, Portugal.
ACM 978-1-4503-3400-6/15/10.
DOI: http://dx.doi.org/10.1145/2700648.2811366 .

2. ESTIMATION OF ACCESSIBILITY DATA WITH PERSONAL SENSING

Figure 1 shows the overview of the methodology for accessibility map developing with personal sensing and machine learning. The proposed method digitizes accessibility of roads where wheelchair drove on by sensing behavior of wheelchair users and estimating the accessibility information from the sensed data. If machine learning algorithms estimate accessibility information from the sensor data recorded by smart phone, large scale accessibility map will be established, which is difficult by traditional accessibility data collection methods that rely on manpower. These estimated results from human sensing data of wheelchair users who are moving walkway, such as climbing curbs and falling, might be regarded as less accurate than those which are collected by manpower. Accumulation of these results for long periods helps to increase accuracy of the estimation. This paper developed and evaluated a prototype system with sensing wheelchair moving with a three-axis accelerometer mounted on iPod touch, and applying supervised learning for ground surface estimation.

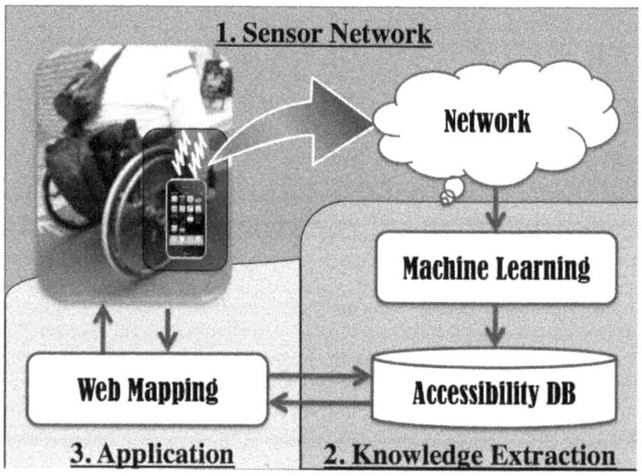

Figure 1: An overview of estimating accessibility data with human activity sensing and knowledge extraction using machine learning

3. GROUND SURFACE ESTIMATION

Our prototype system estimates types of ground surfaces with a hand-made feature extractor (FEX) and a machine-made estimation model, as shown in Figure 2. The proposed method consists of following two parts: 1) modeling phase: learning correspondent relations between sensor data and types of ground surfaces with supervised learning, and 2) utilizing phase: applying learned rule to new data for estimating ground surfaces. On utilizing phase, our system automatically estimates ground surfaces by inputting fixed size sensor data. In this paper, referring activity recognition research [1] and our pre-experiments' result, FEX were designed to calculate mean, standard deviation, max, and min of following six channels: x, y, z of the three-axis accelerometer and difference sequences of x, y, z.

We evaluated our method with outdoor activity data of nine wheelchair users, seven male and two female, six manual wheelchair users and three powered wheelchair users, aged between 20's-60's. Nine wheelchair users drove on a designated route three times for approximately 60 minutes attaching one iPod touch below a his/her own wheelchair sheet. As the result of evaluation with Support Vector Machine, one of the most famous machine learning techniques, three ground surface types, curb, tactile indicator, and slope, were detected with f-score (and accuracy) of 0.63 (0.92), 0.65 (0.85), and 0.54 (0.97) respectively. To improve the accuracy, designing optimal FEX or learning FEX itself using deep learning [5], a novel machine learning technique, are in progress.

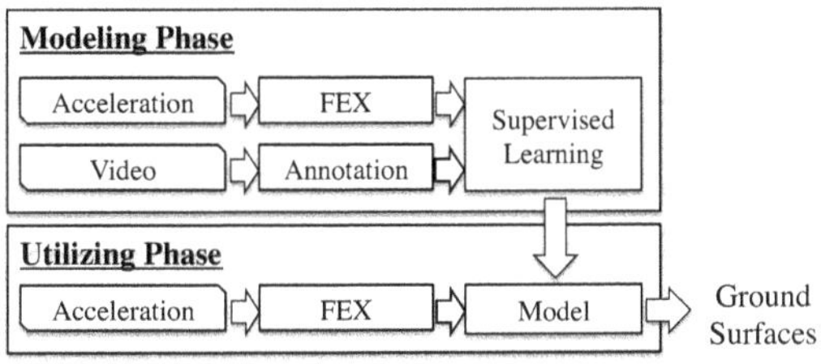

Figure 2: Ground surface estimation with a hand-made feature extractor and a machine-made model

4. WEB MAPPING ESTIMATION RESULT

Figure 3 shows web mapping of estimated curbs (red), tactile indicators (yellow), and slopes (green). As the result of visualization, although tactile indicators were regarded as less accurate, rough tendency of roads were captured. The visualization were done simply by mapping all 1414 estimated results of 27 laps data, thus there is a great potential to improve visualization by using long-period data and statistical methods considering multi time estimations. Also, there is extensibility to consider unknown and unsafe event by combining anomaly detection and human activity modeling [2]. Future work is needed to address these issues.

5. CONCLUSION

This paper proposes and evaluates prototype system with human behavior sensing technology of wheelchair users and supervised machine learning for estimation of ground surfaces. The next step would be as follows: 1) improving accuracy by using large scale data and developing sophisticated machine learning algorithms, 2) extending the estimation target by using anomaly detection technologies.

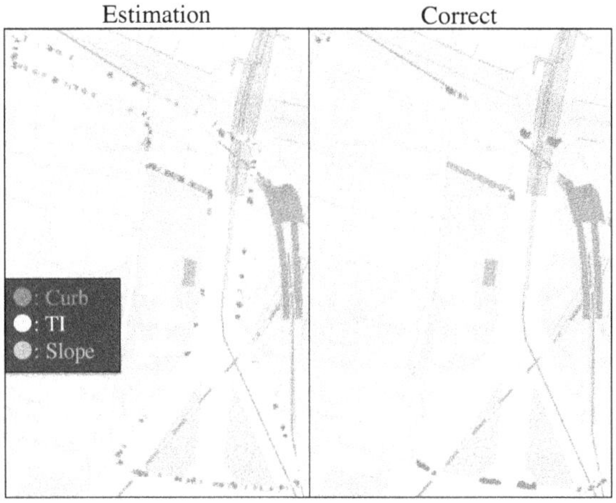

Figure 3: Visualization of estimated results of 27 laps. Ground surfaces were mapped as red (curb), yellow (Tactile Indicator, TI), and green (slope).

Acknowledgement

We are deeply grateful to all participants of experiments, Dr. Fukushima, Mr. H. Uematsu, and Mr. Y. Uematsu. This study was supported by Grant-in-Aid for JSPS Fellows.

6. REFERENCES

[1] A. Bulling, U. Blanke, and B. Schiele. A tutorial on human activity recognition using body-worn inertial sensors. *ACM Computing Surveys (CSUR)*, 46(3):33, 2014.

[2] J. L. C. Candás, V. Peláez, G. López, M. Á. Fernández, E. Álvarez, and G. Díaz. An automatic data mining method to detect abnormal human behaviour using physical activity measurements. *Pervasive and Mobile Computing*, 15:228–241, 2014.

[3] Y. Fukushima, H. Uematsu, R. Mitsuhashi, H. Suzuki, and I. E. Yairi. Sensing human movement of mobility and visually impaired people. In *The proceedings of the 13th international ACM SIGACCESS conference on Computers and accessibility*, pages 279–280. ACM, 2011.

[4] K. Hara, V. Le, and J. Froehlich. Combining crowdsourcing and google street view to identify street-level accessibility problems. In *Proceedings of the SIGCHI Conference on Human Factors in Computing Systems*, pages 631–640. ACM, 2013.

[5] D. W. Kang, J. S. Choi, J. W. Lee, S. C. Chung, S. J. Park, and G. R. Tack. Real-time elderly activity monitoring system based on a tri-axial accelerometer. *Disability & Rehabilitation: Assistive Technology*, 5(4):247–253, 2010.

[6] R. S. Michalski, J. G. Carbonell, and T. M. Mitchell. *Machine learning: An artificial intelligence approach.* Springer Science & Business Media, 2013.

[7] T. Miura, K.-i. Yabu, M. Sakajiri, M. Ueda, J. Suzuki, A. Hiyama, M. Hirose, and T. Ifukube. Social platform for sharing accessibility information among people with disabilities: evaluation of a field assessment. In *Proceedings of the 15th International ACM SIGACCESS Conference on Computers and Accessibility*, page 65. ACM, 2013.

Adaptive Assistance to Support and Promote Performance-impaired People in Manual Assembly Processes

Manuel Kölz
Schnaithmann Maschinenbau GmbH
Fellbacher Straße 49
D-73630 Remshalden
+49 (0) 7151 9732 - 139
koelz@schnaithmann.de

Darrell Jordon
University of Applied Sciences Reutlingen
Alteburgstraße 150
D-72762 Reutlingen
+49 (0) 176 55185003
darrell.jordon@student.reutlingen-university.de

Peter Kurtz
University of Technology Ilmenau
Postbox 10 05 65
D-98684 Ilmenau
+49 (0) 3677 69 - 2458
peter.kurtz@tu-ilmenau.de

Thomas Hörz
University of Applied Sciences Esslingen
Kanalstraße 33
D-73728 Esslingen
+49 (0) 0711 397 – 3269
thomas.hoerz@hs-esslingen.de

Categories and Subject Descriptors
H.1.2 [User/Machine Systems]: Human factors; Human information processing. H.5.2 [User Interfaces]: User-centered design. H5.m [Miscellaneous]: HCI. K.4.2 [Social Issues]: Assistive Technologies For Persons With Disabilities.

Keywords
Assistive technology; Human-Computer interaction; Human Machine interaction; User-centered design; Natural interaction; Adaptive Assistance; Worker-guidance; Training systems; manual assembly systems

1. INTRODUCTION
Current trends show, that industrial markets are more and more driven by the purchasing power of the buyers. In course of these circumstances the provider market is developing into a buyer market. Due to an increasing demand of individualized product, requirements concerning the production and assembly processes are changing. Mass production is increasingly being replaced by small series productions with quantities up to lot sizes of one piece with an ever-increasing number of variants. Especially in Germany the manual assembly will gain more importance due to its high flexibility. The high wage and non-wage labor costs in Germany as well as the demographic change [1] and the social responsibility for the integration of performance-impaired people, are particular challenges with high potential [2].

Motivating even higher qualified assembly operators will be more difficult in the future, because of the simplistic and short cyclically repeating work activities. The requirement will be an appropriate work task with appropriate identification character and appreciation of the work force, like the spirit of One Piece Flow.

In the future, however, it is essential to concentrate on the necessities of the work force in terms of designing the work content and workplace. Doing so provides the possibility of using their skills more efficiently and allows it to support them with technical systems. The current state of the art focuses primarily on assistive systems, which support the user within the process execution [3]. The consideration focuses less on assistive systems, which promote and develop the skills of a worker.

Therefore, the work presented here concerns mainly the development, with respect to the REFA six step method [4], of adaptive assistance systems, to optimize manual assembly by creating the conditions for self-motivation.

ASSETS'15, October 26–28, 2015, Lisbon, Portugal.
ACM 978-1-4503-3400-6/15/10.
DOI: http://dx.doi.org/10.1145/2700648.2811367

2. CONCEPT DESCRIPTION
2.1 Communication elements
In course of developing an Assembly-Instruction, different static and dynamic Instruction-Elements were created. The Instruction-Elements, containing of coloured patterns and shapes, signs as well as pictures and videos of the assembly process, are visualized on to the work place using a LED-Beamer.

2.2 Level set up
In case of developing the adaptive Assistance System it was considered reasonable to provide three Information-Levels. The higher the experience of an assembly operator, the less information content is provided by the adaptive System.

2.3 Classification scheme
The adaptive Assistance System uses the assembly time and the assembly mistakes as criteria to classify an assembly operator's performance and experience. Therefore every Information-Level has its own defined time interval [5]. The time intervals are defined in the following way and are based on methods-time-measurement (MTM) [6]:

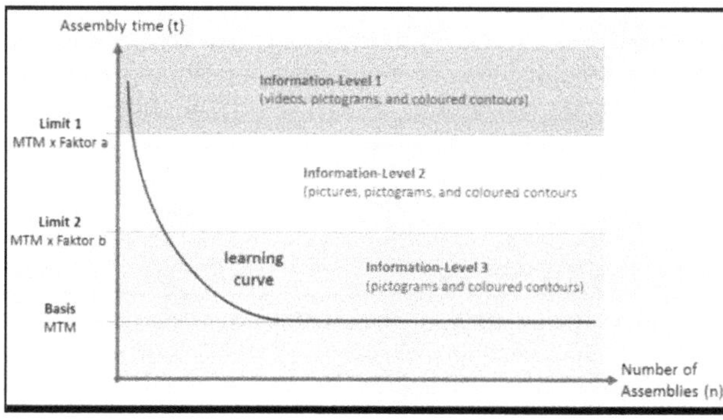

Figure 1. Sheme of an ideal learning curve including the information-levels 1-3

Generally there are four different possibilities, which can initiate a classification of the assembly operator. Two of these possibilities describe a "Level-Up", the other two a "Level-Down".

Level-Up:

(a) The assembly time conforms a higher Instruction-Level.
(b) The last five assembly times have a low variance.

Level-Down:

(a) Two consecutive assembly processes include time mistakes. A time mistake occurs when the assembly time is above of a predefined range of variation or corresponds to a time interval of a lower Instruction-Level.
(b) Two consecutive assembly processes include assembly mistakes. An assembly mistake occurs, if the assembly operator performs a false withdrawal or a false assembly of a part. The first mistake, occurring within an assembly, labels the assembly process as false.

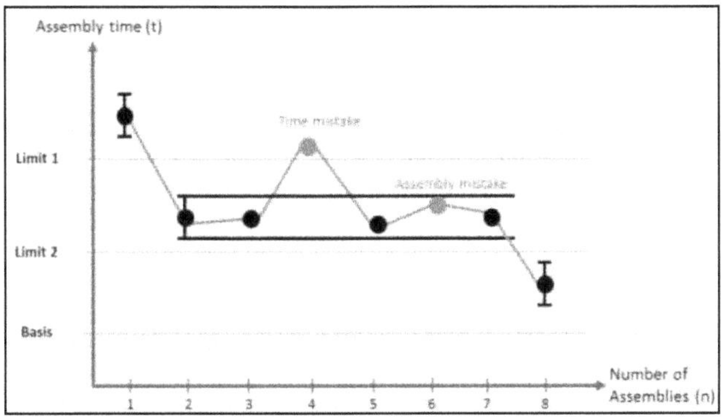

Figure 2. Example of a learning curve showing a time and assembly mistake

3. STUDY

3.1 Participant selection

- **Number of Participants:** 20
- **Age:** 25 – 63 years
- **Gender:** 35% female; 65% male
- **Mental disability:** ICD-10 F70, F71, F72

3.2 Experimental set up

The basis of the experimental set-up includes a manual assembly workplace from Schnaithmann Maschinenbau GmbH in combination with their Assistance System cubu:S. The System consists of a control unit, sensor and LED-Beamer. It was used to visualize the Instruction-Elements on to the work place of the assembly operator.

3.3 Experimental procedure

Survey of the participants with a modified form of the NASA TLX. Questions of the NASA TLX where altered in cooperation with psychologists, to provide suitable questions for impaired people. Main goal was to enquire the mood of the participants before starting the assembly process.

Assembly of two products provided by Schnaithmann Maschinenbau GmbH. The participants assembled 20 products with static Assembly-Instructions and 20 products with adaptive Assembly-Instructions. The assemblies therefore where performed with two different products. Both products included similar types of assembly processes.

Following the assemblies, another **survey** was performed. Main goal was to enquire statements about usability as well as mood changes.

4. RESULTS

The results and knowledge gained from the study, confirm the positive effects of the developed approach for adaptive assistance for performance-impaired people.

The learning curves, derived from the collected cycle times per work through, tend to have a shorter learning phase using the adaptive assistance compared to the static assistance. With respect to the generation of action routines, the observations led to results and findings that are more obvious. The majority of the 20 participants were only capable of an independent and conscious action in the execution of the work task using the tested adaptive assistance concept. According to the feedback of the participants as well as in fact of the own observations, the adaptive assistance concept is perceived as promoting optimal. The developed systematic for a targeted reduction of information content up to providing only the pick by light information encouraged the participants who were generally focused on the instructions at an early stage to independent thinking. A strongly declining error rate in the process execution after only a few work passages confirmed this. The majority of participants did not perceived this individually iterative process as overstraining or sub challenging. These gradual changes of the information content were partially not explicitly recognized. The joy and motivation of the ability to perform the entire process independently and without any assistance was therefore very large. The participants themselves as well as the observations confirmed the increasing motivation by using the assistance system.

5. REFERENCES

[1] Statistisches Bundesamt 2009: *Bevölkerung Deutschlands bis 2060.* In: *Begleitheft zur Pressekonferenz am 18. November 2009*

[2] Bächler L.; Bächler A.; Kölz M.; Hörz T.; Heidenreich T. 2014: *Über die Entwicklung eines prozedural- interaktiven Assitenzsystems für leistungsgeminderte und –gewandelte Mitarbeiter in der manuellen Montage.* In: *Proceedings Soeffke Uni Magdeburg (Hrsg) Tagung Mensch Maschine* Magdeburg, Germany

[3] Hörz T.; Kölz M.; Sieber V. 2013: *Assistenzsysteme in der manuellen Montage.* In: *Proceedings of the international forum of Mechatronics.* Winterthur, Schweiz

[4] REFA Verband für Arbeitsstudien und Betriebsorganisation e. V. 1984: *REFA-Methodenlehre der Betriebsorganisation. Grundlagen der Arbeitsgestaltung.* München, Germany

[5] Kölz M.; Bächler A.; Kurtz P.; Hörz T. 2015: *Entwicklung eines interaktiv, adaptiven Montageassistenzsystems.* In: *Proceedings of the 61. Arbeitswissenschaftlichen Kongresses. VerANTWORTung für die Arbeit der Zukunft.* Dortmund, Germany

[6] Maynard, H. B.; Stegemerten, G. J.;Schwab, J. L. 1948:: *Methods-time-measurement.* New York, US

Issues Influencing the Uptake of Smartphone Reminder Apps for People with Acquired Brain Injury

Matthew Jamieson
University of Glasgow
Institute of Health and Wellbeing
m.jamieson.1@research.gla.ac.uk

Marilyn McGee-Lennon
University of Strathclyde
Human Computing Interaction
marilyn.lennon@strath.ac.uk

Breda Cullen
University of Glasgow
Institute of Health and Wellbeing
Breda.Cullen@glasgow.ac.uk

Stephen Brewster
University of Glasgow
School of Computing Science
Stephen.Brewster@glasgow.ac.uk

Jonathan Evans
University of Glasgow
Institute of Health and Wellbeing
Jonathan.Evans@glasgow.ac.uk

ABSTRACT
Smartphone reminder applications (apps) have the potential to help people with memory impairment after acquired brain injury (ABI) to perform everyday tasks. Issues impacting the uptake of reminder apps for this group are still poorly understood. To address this, three focus groups were held with people with memory impairments after ABI and ABI caregivers (N=12). These involved a discussion about perceptions of, and attitudes towards, reminder apps combined with usability reflections during a user-centred design session (Keep Lose Change) after a walkthrough of an existing reminder app – Google Calendar. Framework analysis revealed six key themes that impact uptake of reminder apps; *Perceived Need, Social Acceptability, Experience/Expectation, Desired Content and Functions, Cognitive Accessibility* and *Sensory/Motor Accessibility*. Analysis of themes revealed issues that should be considered by designers and researchers when developing and testing reminding software for people with memory impairment following ABI.

1. INTRODUCTION
Acquired brain injury (ABI) includes trauma to the brain arising from a head injury (e.g. road traffic accidents and falls), cardiovascular events (e.g. stroke), illnesses or diseases (e.g. brain tumour or encephalitis). Individuals who have suffered ABI have a high prevalence of memory impairments. These impairments make it difficult for people with ABI to perform everyday tasks such as shopping, personal care or cooking, or healthcare tasks such as remembering appointments, treatment plans and medication. Smartphones are ubiquitous and relatively low cost devices for which reminding applications, which support prospective memory, are readily available. Smartphone reminding software has been shown to be effective in helping people to compensate for prospective memory difficulties [6]. Despite the evidence for its efficacy, the actual uptake of assistive technology by people with ABI is generally very low [2]. One reason for this could be poor perceived utility, usability and acceptability. In the context of cognitive and physical impairments after ABI, many issues including the appropriateness of the functions and interface designs of current reminding apps made for general use, perceived usability issues and attitudes towards technology can prevent uptake of this potentially useful memory intervention. Previous studies have investigated perceived usability issues prior to uptake of any type of assistive technology [1] and the usability issues which arise when actually using reminding technology on a PC [3] for this group.

The current study used qualitative methods to give a detailed picture of the issues which impact uptake of reminder apps for people with ABI. To do this we involved people with ABI (n=9) and carers of people with ABI (n=3) in a focus group session which included an example of a calendar based reminder app (Google Calendar) and a co-design session (*Keep Lose Change*).

ASSETS'17, October 26–28, 2015, Lisbon, Portugal.
ACM 978-1-4503-3400-6/15/10.
DOI: http://dx.doi.org/10.1145/2700648.2811368

2. METHOD
2.1 Participants
Two focus groups (n = 5, 2 female & n=4, 3 female) involved people with a mild or moderate ABI and self-reported memory difficulties and one focus group (n=3, 3 female) involved two family caregivers of people with mild or moderate ABI with self-reported memory difficulties and a clinical psychologist who works in a community treatment centre for brain injury. Participants were all over 18 (mean age = 47, range 36 – 68) and spoke fluent English. Only people able to provide informed consent without severe physical or sensory disability were included. All participants with ABI were adults between 38 and 60 and none described themselves as experts with technology.

2.2 Focus Groups
Focus group methodology was used because we wanted to build up a rich qualitative dataset that involved 1) a discussion of experiences and perceptions of assistive technology and 2) a demonstration of an existing solution (Google Calendar app (GC)) followed by a user-centred design session called *keep, lose, change* (KLC) [4]. A4 print-outs of each screenshot of GC were presented (Figure 1) and participants were asked 'what design features, functions and content would you keep, which would you lose and which would you change if you were redesigning this app?' They wrote feedback on green (for *keep* comments), red (*lose* comments) and orange (*change*) sticky notes and attached them to screenshots. Data from both sessions was transcribed and organized into comments, quotes,

observations or written feedback. This data was grouped into themes following the the framework approach for focus groups outlined by Rabiee [5]. While other apps may have been designed more specifically for people with cognitive impairments, GC was chosen as it is in widespread use by the general population and because previous studies have investigated the usability and efficacy of similar software [3,6].

Figure 1. Materials for the *keep lose change* session

3. RESULTS AND DISCUSSION

3.1 Themes

Six themes were established by coding the focus group data; *Social Acceptability*, *Perceived Need*, *Cognitive Accessibility*, *Sensory/Motor Accessibility*, *Desired Content and Functions* and *Experience and Expectation*.

3.2 Perceived Need

Before they will use Smartphone reminders or any other type of assistive technology for memory, people with ABI must understand the need for them and be motivated to use them. Sub-themes for this theme were *insight into memory difficulties* and *motivation to use technology*. For example one participant said, "I also forget I don't remember. And then I remember that I forget. It's a really complicated thing to deal with". This lady loses insight into her difficulties from time to time, and so forgets to set reminders that she will need. Another related issue is motivation, which can depend on the mood of the user. For example, when asked about introducing a Google Calendar to a family member with ABI, one caregiver said, "Sometimes it depends on what mood they're in. You have to pick your time".

3.3 Social Acceptability

Sub-themes of social acceptability were *social comparison* – the influence of the user comparing themselves to their peer group and *social relationships*. This theme highlights the importance of family caregivers setting an example by using reminders – one caregiver stated when asked about her use of the Google Calendar reminder, "I think it would introduce again that curiosity you see where he'd eventually ask – how did you do that? I'd like to do that myself".

3.4 Desired Content and Functions

As well as suggestions about the design and layout of the app, the focus group participants talked about the content and functionality that they would like from smartphone reminder software. An example suggestion is the inclusion of a notes section which links into a reminder notification, to store relevant information which might otherwise fade from memory (e.g. what you wanted to say to a Doctor during an appointment).

3.5 Cognitive & Sensory/Motor Accessibility

Many of the participant's comments were about the *cognitive* and *sensory / motor* difficulties that impact the use of a mobile app. In particular, difficulties with vision, especially when looking at a detailed display on a small screen were mentioned by many. Many of the keep lose change comments fed into this theme as participants wanted to 'lose' the calendar view screen or 'change' it to make larger or have a clearer colour contrast. .

3.6 Experience / Expectation

This was the largest theme comprising of the sub-themes: *experience* of the user and familiarity with the technology, and *guidance* - the extent to which the app itself guides the user. These themes overlap because inexperienced users will require more guidance from the system. While this is an uptake issue for any user group, the participants' feedback suggested that it is particularly important for people with ABI. An app with a steep learning curve may not be appropriate for this group especially in the context of learning and memory difficulties, and low tolerance for frustration.

4. CONCLUSIONS

There were several 'lose' and 'change' comments during the KLC session with Google Calendar indicating that there are several aspects of this calendar based reminder app which could be altered to make them more appropriate for people with ABI. An awareness of the issues which impact uptake can inform future design of mobile applications which can help memory and also be acceptable and usable for this group.

5. REFERENCES

1. Baldwin, V. N., Powell, T., & Lorenc, L. (2011). Factors influencing the uptake of memory compensations: A qualitative analysis. *Neuropsychological rehabilitation*, 21(4), 484-501.
2. Evans, J. J., Wilson, B. A, Needham, P., & Brentnall, S. (2003). Who makes good use of memory aids? Results of a survey of people with acquired brain injury. *Journal of the International Neuropsychological Society : JINS, 9(6),* 925–35.
3. de Joode, E. A., Van Heugten, C. M., Verhey, F. R. J., & Van Boxtel, M. P. J. (2013). Effectiveness of an electronic cognitive aid in patients with acquired brain injury: A multicentre randomised parallel-group study. *Neuropsychological rehabilitation*, *23*(1), 133-156.
4. McGee-Lennon, M., Smeaton, A., & Brewster, S. (2012). Designing Home Care Reminder Systems: Lessons Learned Through Co-Design with Older Users. *Proceedings of the 6th International Conference on Pervasive Computing Technologies for Healthcare*, 49–56.
5. Rabiee, F. (2004). Focus-group interview and data analysis. *Proceedings of the nutrition society*, *63*(04), 655-660.
6. Svoboda, E., Richards, B., Leach, L., & Mertens, V. (2012). PDA and smartphone use by individuals with moderate-to-severe memory impairment: Application of a theory-driven training programme. *Neuropsychological rehabilitation*, *22*(3), 408-427.

"Read That Article": Exploring Synergies between Gaze and Speech Interaction

Diogo Vieira[1,2], João Dinis Freitas[2], Cengiz Acartürk[3], António Teixeira[1], Luis Sousa[2], Samuel Silva[1], Sara Candeias[2], Miguel Sales Dias[2,4]

DETI / IEETA
University of Aveiro
Campus Univ. de Santiago
Aveiro - Portugal
{diogo.vieira, ajst, sss}@ua.pt

Microsoft Language Development Center
Lisboa, Portugal
{t-joaof, t-luisno, midias, t-sacand}@microsoft.com

Cognitive Science
Middle East Technical Univ
Ankara, Turkey
acarturk@metu.edu.tr

ISCTE-IUL
ISCTE - University Institute of Lisbon
miguel.dias@iscte.pt

ABSTRACT
Gaze information has the potential to benefit Human-Computer Interaction (HCI) tasks, particularly when combined with speech. Gaze can improve our understanding of the user intention, as a secondary input modality, or it can be used as the main input modality by users with some level of permanent or temporary impairments. In this paper we describe a multimodal HCI system prototype which supports speech, gaze and the combination of both. The system has been developed for Active Assisted Living scenarios.

Categories and Subject Descriptors
H.5.2 [**Information Interfaces and Presentation**]: User Interfaces – *Input devices and strategies, Natural language, Voice I/O*; K.4.2 [**Computers And Society**]: Social Issues - *Assistive technologies for persons with disabilities;*

Keywords
Multimodal; Gaze; Speech; Fusion

1. INTRODUCTION
A major goal of Human-Computer Interaction (HCI) research, is to achieve natural forms of interaction, similarly to the way humans interact. Speech is, in that sense, a dominant modality since it is usually the preferred way for humans to communicate.

Nevertheless, speech communication is inherently a multimodal process where different senses are used for interpreting spoken messages. Previous studies, notably the one that discovered the McGurk effect [5], revealed that humans employ both hearing and visual senses in speech perception. Humans also use contextual information such as head and body movements, gestures, facial expressions, characteristics of the speech signal like prosody and gaze in human-human communication [3,6,7].

In this context, we propose that the integration of user's gaze information (for instance, the fixation of one or both eyes on the computer screen), has the potential to improve the determination of the intention of the user, during a natural interaction task. Gaze information can help to predict the user purpose and, when used with speech in command and control scenarios, to decrease the confusion of the issued commands, thus improving the accuracy rates of the speech recognition systems [4, 8]. A recent review can be found in Acartürk et al. [1]. Given the potential benefit of processing user's gaze location, we decided to add this modality to an existing system designed for elderly users in the context of several Ambient Assisted Living (AAL) initiatives [2].

ASSETS '15, October 26-28, 2015, Lisbon, Portugal.
ACM 978-1-4503-3400-6/15/10.
http://dx.doi.org/10.1145/2700648.2811369

2. GAZE MODALITY
A new modality was developed and added to the existing W3C based multimodal framework developed by the authors, for projects such as the Portuguese QREN AAL4ALL and European AAL PaeLife [2, 9]. In this architecture the creation and integration of new modules is simplified, since it supports the requirements of a multimodal framework, such as extensibility, flexibility and the use of multiple input or output modalities. Some of these, already built for the framework, are touch, speech or gesture as input modalities, and text to speech synthesis as output modality. In our framework, every user interaction results in a message that is sent to an interaction manager responsible for handling all the communication and fusion across all the modalities.

This new system component provides not only the possibility for the user to interact directly with an application using only gaze, but also use it in combination with the other input modalities, such as speech. Thus, also regarding the targeted user base, two problems were simultaneously tackled: using gaze as a single modality brings the possibility for the group of users with certain permanent or temporary disabilities to interact and use the application; when simultaneously used with another input modality, fusing both interactions allows us to obtain a multimodal user experience were we are capable of deriving the intention of the user, in a less ambiguous way and with more confidence. Gaze as a modality uses an eye tracker device to obtain the user's gaze input data in real time, by means of fixations and saccade events. In parallel, the application keeps updating the modality context with the current list of 2D graphical objects painted on the application screen, which correspond to application actions that can be triggered by gaze fixations. When our modality component detects a gaze fixation over a given graphical object, as a consequence of the user staring at such object on the screen, the modality sends the matching unimodal or multimodal input command associated with that object to the interaction manager.

3. FUSION WITH SPEECH
The system currently supports speech interaction in European Portuguese, English, French, Hungarian and Polish. Spanish and Turkish will be available soon. Although several languages are supported, using speech as the only input interaction modality may suffer from some limitations including, for example, the low

level of confidence of the utterance of the user obtained from the recognizer, either due to word mispronunciation, co-articulation errors, ambient noise or precision limitations of the ASR.

To improve the recognition of the intention of the user when communicating with the system using speech, one possibility is to use information regarding the application context, narrowing the set of expected user input commands. The use of gaze can provide us with that needed context. The fusion of gaze and speech brings us the possibility of using the gaze information to disambiguate through the list of recognized words and phrases and their likelihood, obtained from the ASR process of the speech modality. This fusion process might follow two different paths: both inputs modalities result on the same output, or they don't. In the first case, the user looks at an object on the screen, and at the same time pronounces the voice command to trigger the action assigned to such object. When producing these actions, two equal commands are sent from different input modalities processors, to the same interaction manager. Since there are no differences in both commands, the fusion only calculates a new confidence score, issuing a single command to the application, which corresponds to our best guess of the intention of the user. In the second case, the fusion process interprets each input command for completeness and confidence score calculation and takes in consideration the differences in such interpretation, with the objective of merging their information together to achieve a more complete multimodal input command. That is possible by taking the incomplete unimodal command (for example, speech) and adding information obtained from the other complete unimodal command (for instance, gaze).

4. EXAMPLES OF USE

In this paper, we've added the support to gaze, as well as to speech+gaze acting as single input multimodality. With our technique, when the user's fixation is directed to a button on the PLA interface with some time persistence, it will issue a command from the gaze modality processor that triggers the same event as if the button was clicked, e.g., after 5 seconds (configurable parameter) of a user fixation on the news reader button, the application will open that option. A list of news will be then presented on the application screen and each one can also be opened using only gaze fixation, much like in the prior example. Additionally, any news article can be open if the user pronounces its title name or the first words in the news. We have further improved this user experience, with our novel multimodal approach. Eliciting his/her intention by using gaze and speech simultaneously, the user may simply utter 'read that article' while at the same time looking at the desired news title he/she wants to read, in the app screen. And although the speech command does not explicitly specify the wanted news title, our gaze modality can provide the missing information on the object the user was looking at.

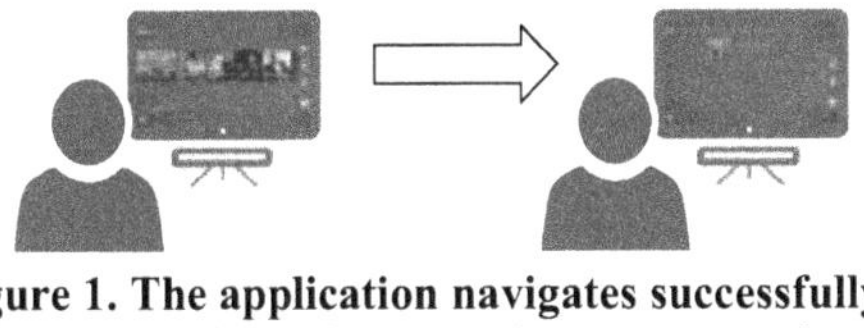

Figure 1. The application navigates successfully when the user's gaze is used to complement a speech command

5. CONCLUSIONS AND FUTURE WORK

Exploring how speech and gaze can be used together in the context of a multimodal user experience with an app such as the PaeLife PLA, is an important first step towards a more natural user experience. This work describes several use scenarios and is the first to our knowledge to combine, within a multimodal framework, speech recognition in European Portuguese with gaze, serving as a ground for further research. The adoption of gaze as a new modality creates multiple possible ways to interact with applications, developed within our multimodal framework. Also, the use of speech and gaze input modalities for tasks which are inherently performed with the eyes, e.g., visualization in Virtual or Augmented Reality, and for which speech can be used to perform tasks such as zooming or picking, with gaze providing the place-of-interest, is an interesting route to further explore in the near future. This aspect was already captured by the pioneering work of Richard Bolt from the MIT, back in 1980, in his case, by fusing speech and gesture in a visualization task in a media room. By taking advantage on our modular multimodal framework, and adding other modalities in the fusion process, the possible multimodal ways for interacting with future applications are large. Given the current state-of-the-art in the combined use of speech and gaze for HCI, there are still several challenges ahead, (e.g. eye-tracking calibration, environmental noise, etc.), particularly if we consider the development of mission critical applications. Our aim for future work is to develop a stochastic-based fusion model based on the probability density functions modelled for both gaze and speech. To achieve this goal we need not only to be able to model the user intent (for a given task), but also to tackle deeply issues such as signal synchronization and delays between input events of different modalities.

6. ACKNOWLEDGMENTS

This work was fully funded by Marie Curie IRIS (ref. 610986, FP7-PEOPLE-2013-IAPP) http://www.iris-interaction.eu/

7. REFERENCES

[1] Acartürk, C., et al. Elderly speech-gaze interaction: State of the art and challenges for interaction design. *Proc. HCII 2015*, (2015), (to appear).

[2] Almeida, N. and Teixeira, A. Enhanced interaction for the Elderly supported by the W3C Multimodal Architecture. *Proc. Conf. Nacional sobre Interacção*, (2013).

[3] Hakkani-Tür, D., et al. Eye Gaze for Spoken Language Understanding in Multi-modal Conversational Interactions. *Conf. on Multimodal Interaction*, ACM (2014), 263–266.

[4] Heck, L.P., et al. Multi-Modal Conversational Search and Browse. *SLAM@ INTERSPEECH*, (2013), 96–101.

[5] McGurk, H. and MacDonald, J.Hearing lips and seeing voices. *Nature 264*, (1976), 746–748.

[6] Oviatt, S.Ten myths of multimodal interaction. *Commun. ACM 42*, 11 (1999), 74–81.

[7] Quek, F., et al.Multimodal human discourse: gesture and speech. *ACM Trans. on Comp.-Human Interaction (TOCHI) 9*, 3 (2002), 171–193.

[8] Slaney, M., et al.Gaze-enhanced speech recognition. *Proc. ICASSP*, (2014), 3236–3240.

[9] Teixeira, A., et al. Speech-centric Multimodal Interaction for Easy-to-access Online Services-A Personal Life Assistant for the Elderly. *Procedia Computer Science 27*, (2014), 389–397.

[10] Bolt,. Richard, "Put-that-there, Voice and Gesture at the Graphics Interface", *ACM Proceedings SIGGRAH* (1980)

Exploring the Use of Massive Open Online Courses for Teaching Students with Intellectual Disability

Rodrigo Laiola Guimarães and Andrea Britto Mattos
IBM Research
Rua Tutória 1157
04007900 São Paulo, Brazil
{rlaiola, abritto}@br.ibm.com

ABSTRACT

In this paper, we report on a qualitative study that investigates the impact of using a popular Massive Open Online Course (MOOC) to complement the vocational training of students with intellectual disability (ID). We have been investigating this problem for several months in partnership with a Brazilian NGO (Non-Governmental Organization) for people with ID. Our methodology integrates different aspects of human-computer interaction (*i.e.*, requirement gathering sessions and observation of real subjects). Potential users were involved since the beginning of this research, starting with focus groups and interviews with experts, followed by the observation of a traditional vocational training session, and then the assessment of a popular MOOC in the classroom. In this paper, we discuss the process and present our preliminary results, providing some indications on how MOOCs could better support instructors and students with ID.

Categories and Subject Descriptors

K.3.1 [**Computers and Education**]: Computer Uses in Education – *Computer-assisted instruction (CAI).*

General Terms

Design, Experimentation, Human Factors.

Keywords

Educational technology; MOOC; Vocational training.

1. INTRODUCTION

In many ways, the popularization of MOOCs – sometimes described as the "tsunami in education" [3] – has made learning accessible *anywhere* and *anytime* (*i.e.*, today using just a Web browser, mobile app or even TV, interested learners can take free lessons in a variety of subjects at their convenience). While it is indisputable that MOOCs are making learning more accessible than at any time in the past, we wonder if the advances they bring can favor *everybody* (and not just the masses). In this context, the research question that we address is:

Can learning materials available on MOOCs be used for teaching students with ID?

This work is part of a long-term project that aims to understand the impact that technology can have in supporting vocational training for people with disabilities (PwD). In this paper in particular, we report on initial findings from the assessment of a MOOC as a way to complement the training of people with ID. A local NGO has actively collaborated with this research. Starting in February 2014, we invited professionals from APAE DE SÃO PAULO (Association of Parents and Friends of People with IDs: http://www.apaesp.org.br) to a number of discussions about qualification and inclusion of PwD in the labor market. In May, we observed a two-hour session of their Supported Employment (SE) program [1]. This initiative assists people with ID in obtaining and maintaining paid employment. The educational objectives of the session involved early math operations and reading time on analog clocks. The primary goal of vocational training is not to improve literacy skills, but rather help people with ID to perform tasks in their work environments. First, students did a set of exercises in paper notebook, and then, they had, one by one, to solve these exercises in front (and with help) of the others in a whiteboard. In the next sections, we provide more background information about the instructor and students.

In the subsequent months, we have systematically investigated mechanisms and technologies that can improve the learning experience of people with ID. Before considering an exploratory study with a target group of students, we first assessed a number of MOOCs available on the Web. Among them, Khan Academy (https://www.khanacademy.org) stood out because (i) its user interface is available in Brazilian Portuguese and (ii) it had exercises of interest (quizzes in early math and time) to the aforementioned group of students from the SE program. Months later, we interviewed two instructors, who had large experience in teaching people with ID (about six years each). We asked them to try Khan Academy on a tablet and use the *think-aloud* protocol to report aspects that could be of interest (or not) when teaching people with ID. One of the interviewed instructors agreed to participate of a pilot using the referred platform, and we then structured the study we discuss next.

ASSETS '15, October 26-28, 2015, Lisbon, Portugal.
ACM 978-1-4503-3400-6/15/10.
http://dx.doi.org/10.1145/2700648.2811370

2. EXPLORATORY STUDY

We performed a study to observe students' response to Khan Academy using tablets. We did not assess learning outcomes.

2.1 Participants

Five people from the SE program participated in this qualitative study: an instructor (male) and four students with ID (three female and one male). With the instructor's help, we recruited the same group of students involved in the training session observed months earlier. Their age ranged from 18-40 years old. According to the instructor, all students have moderate degree of ID, although such label tells very little about who they are or the kinds of support they may require. He also mentioned that his contact with the male student raised the suspicions of autism, which could not be further investigated due to lack of professionals. By the time of the study, the students were employed in restaurants of a large fast-food chain. Before this technology intervention in the classroom, students had about 16 hours of training with the same instructor. We had consent from them (or their representatives) for participating in the study. The research team had five facilitators.

2.2 Setting and Equipment

The study took place at APAE DE SÃO PAULO, more specifically, in a classroom where the students have had previous training sessions. A video camera on a tripod was placed in the front, facing the students, and recorded the whole activity. A ten inches tablet (there were two iPads, one Samsung and one Motorola) was assigned to each participant (including the instructor). Each tablet had a Web browser with Internet access.

2.3 Procedure

The session started with the instructor justifying the presence of the researchers in the classroom. Then, with an iPad connected to the data projector, he gave a brief explanation about the device. He was not a heavy user, but had no problems to conduct the technology-mediated session. Two students have had previous contact with tablets, whereas the other two had never interacted with one before. The instructor showed basic gestures (*e.g.*, select and swipe) and asked students to perform actions on his device (*e.g.*, start an application). Then, each student received a tablet, with which they freely interacted for some minutes. Interests included music, videos and games. This phase took 40 minutes.

The second part consisted of a 15-minute review of the topics that were being explored in the SE program. This session also involved early math operations and reading the time on analog clocks. As aforementioned, Khan Academy offers pre-existing modules on these topics. Before going to the digital exercises, the instructor required the students to put their tablets aside. He used the concrete-pictorial-abstract (CPA) approach to ensure that the students would have a thorough understanding of the concepts they were learning [2]. He said that an initial development of a concrete understanding enables students with ID to more likely learn that skill, and later grasp concepts at an abstract level. For that, he used golden beaden material and a big paper clock.

Then, with his device still connected to the data projector, he demonstrated step by step how to launch Khan Academy on the tablets (all devices had been configured with individual accounts). While doing that, he would go to the next step only after all students reached the same point. After that, students were instructed to do the exercises of early math and time individually, and at their own pace. The number and order of the quizzes varied from one student to the other (we did not have control over the Khan Academy's recommendation mechanism). Whenever needed, students could ask questions to the instructor or/and facilitator sit behind. This phase lasted for 50 minutes, and it was followed by individual interviews of participants with two members of the research team, each of which took 5-15 minutes.

2.4 Observations

Facilitators observed students individually. The instructor mediated post-activity interviews, but students had difficulties to express themselves. Conversely, the instructor's interview was more insightful. Considering the session in classroom and interviews, there are around 2 hours and 45 minutes of audiovisual recordings. Based on the analysis of the collected material, we present a summary of the results and key findings.

3. RESULTS AND DISCUSSION

All participants considered the experience very positive. With little training, students could interact with the tablet (even those who had no previous experience). They demonstrated a lot of interest and during the interviews, mentioned that they wished to have more experiences like that. Our observations and discussion with the instructor also suggest that technology played a key role empowering students, and it can potentially help developing self-esteem, autonomy, and work towards digital inclusion. Although this discussion suggests MOOCs could be of use, it is important to highlight that there are still several limitations, as discussed next.

3.1 Key Observations

Tablets did not represent a barrier. Independently of the background, degree of ID and familiarity with tablets, with some training and support, all students performed well the activity. However, the main issues were related to usability and navigation within Khan Academy (*e.g.*, students would not know where to click because they were overwhelmed by information).

Instructor could not create his own exercises. Khan Academy offers modules created and curated by its own educational team. If on the one hand this assures quality, on the other it puts limit on what the instructor can do. In order to be more effective in this context, MOOCs need to take advantage of the knowledge that instructors have about students' profiles and supports they require.

Support helped, but it requires prudence. Some students became dependent of hints provided on Khan Academy (and even of the support offered by the facilitators). Educational platforms for people with ID should consider reinforcing learning objects and guide students in such a way that they can develop autonomy.

Positive feedback helped keeping students motivated. The assurance of success provided on Khan Academy (*e.g.*, sound alert and smiley face) seemed to be a major stimulus for students, keeping confidence high when answering the subsequent questions. An interesting case was the student with suspicious of autism, who celebrated out loud after answering correctly.

Self-paced vs. mediated learning. In certain moments, students had difficulty to keep focus due to the insertion of digital technology, demanding extra effort from the instructor. This can be the case even in traditional training, but our data suggests that the balance of technology-mediated strategies for developing autonomy of people with ID (via self-paced learning) and for keeping class coordination and avoiding disruptive behavior (via mediated learning) is powerful and should be further explored.

4. FINAL REMARKS

In this paper we discuss our ongoing efforts to better understand the intersection between accessible vocational training and educational technology. Our preliminary results suggest that, although MOOCs have features of interest for teaching students with ID, there is a long way ahead in order to make them really effective. These indications directly address our research question. Our ultimate goal is that these initial insights can stimulate others, as they will be considered further on our own work. Our next steps involve experiments with our own vocational training platform targeted to PwD. This will enable us to assess the students' response and compare it with our initial results.

5. ACKNOWLEDGMENTS

This work has been partially funded by the Brazilian Ministry of Science and Technology under contract no. FINEP 03.11.0371.00. Special thanks to K. Shigeno, F. Antonioli and participants from APAE DE SÃO PAULO, who have collaborated with this work.

6. REFERENCES

[1] Bellamy, G.T., Rhodes, L. and Albin, J.M. 1986. *Supported employment*. Pathways to Employment for Developmentally Disabled Adults. PH Brookes Pub Co. ISBN 9780933716575

[2] Bruner, J. 1976. *The Process of Education*. Harvard University Press, 97 pages. ISBN 978-0674710016

[3] Bull, D. 2012. *From ripple to tsunami: The possible impact of MOOCs on higher education.* DE Quarterly, 10-11.

VITHEA-Kids: A Platform for Improving Language Skills of Children with Autism Spectrum Disorder

Vânia Mendonça, Luísa Coheur, Alberto Sardinha
Instituto Superior Técnico, INESC-ID
Av. Prof. Doutor Aníbal Cavaco Silva
Porto Salvo, Portugal
{vania.mendonca, luisa.coheur, jose.alberto.sardinha}@tecnico.ulisboa.pt

ABSTRACT
In this work, we present a platform designed for children with Autism Spectrum Disorder to develop language and generalization skills, in response to the lack of applications tailored for the unique abilities, symptoms, and challenges of the autistic children. This platform allows caregivers to build customized multiple choice exercises while taking into account specific needs/characteristics of each child. We also propose a module for the automatic generation of exercises, aiming to ease the task of exercise creation for caregivers.

Categories and Subject Descriptors
K.3.1 [**Computer Uses in Education**]: Computer-assisted instruction (CAI); K.3.1 [**Computer Uses in Education**]: Computer-managed instruction (CMI); K.4.2 [**Social Issues**]: Assistive technologies for persons with disabilities.

General Terms
Human Factors

Keywords
Autism Spectrum Disorder, language skills development

1. INTRODUCTION
Autism Spectrum Disorder (ASD) is characterized by impairments in social communication and interaction, sometimes coupled with difficulties in the acquisition of language. Research indicates an interest from autistic children towards computers, leading to the development of several applications aiming to teach academic skills [3]. However, such applications are often paid, are not available in Portuguese (our target language), do not have in mind the individual needs nor the progress of each child, and/or do not allow for caregivers to control the exercises' content. To tackle these issues, we present a platform that allows caregivers to develop customized exercises for their children to solve. In this paper, we describe its features, as well as our current focus: the automatic generation of exercises.

ASSETS '15, October 26-28, 2015, Lisbon, Portugal.
ACM 978-1-4503-3400-6/15/10.
http://dx.doi.org/10.1145/2700648.2811371

2. VITHEA-KIDS
Our solution, VITHEA-Kids, is an extension of Virtual Therapist for Aphasia Treatment (VITHEA)[1] [1], an internationally awarded platform, designed for aphasia patients and therapists, which comprises two modules. The first, the patient module, contains a set of exercises, in which the patient needs to orally reply to a certain stimulus (e.g. name the object in an image or describe an action in a video); the answer is then recorded and matched to a set of one or more correct answers. An animated talking character utters the exercises and the feedback to the patient's answer (which is limited to "very good" or "try again"). If the patient fails the exercise, the correct answer is not provided. The second, the administration module, allows therapists to create and manage exercises, users and the multimedia resources to be used in the exercises, as well as to check each patient's information and exercise statistics.

Although VITHEA-Kids is based on the infrastructure of VITHEA, it makes use of a different type of exercises: multiple choice exercises, which target vocabulary acquisition and/or the improvement of generalization skills, and are often used in applications for children with ASD. These exercises are composed by a question, a stimulus (picture or text) and a set of possible answers (textual or pictures, respectively), in which only one of the answers is correct (see Table 1). Each exercise can contain from zero to four distractors, easing the task of creating several exercises with small variations in content and difficulty.

Table 1. Multiple choice exercise

Fields	Values		
Question	Which image corresponds to this word?		
Stimulus	Fork		
Correct answer			
Distractors			

VITHEA-Kids' caregiver module allows to manage the exercises described above, as well as to upload and manage image files, and create and manage users. Unlike VITHEA, it allows for the

[1] https://vithea.l2f.inesc-id.pt/

caregiver to customize several interaction aspects, such as the utterances performed by the animated character featured in VITHEA. On the child's side, each exercise is presented by the animated character, which now also provides feedback using the utterances defined by the caregiver. However, the exercise area is now filled with the stimulus and the possible answers in a random order, and instead of orally naming the stimulus, the child should click/touch over the correct answer. Another difference is that our application provides clues: when solving an exercise, if the child picks one of the distractors, it will disappear as a way to prompt the child to pick the correct answer. The interface for solving exercises is shown in Figure 1.

Figure 1 VITHEA-Kids: child's module

The manual creation of exercises and the possibility of customization are critical features for ensuring that the application suits the characteristics of each child. However, since creating several exercises can be time-consuming for caregivers, we are currently implementing a module that allows the automatic generation of exercise content (e.g, the question, the stimulus, the correct answer and distractors). Figure 2 depicts the process of exercise generation.

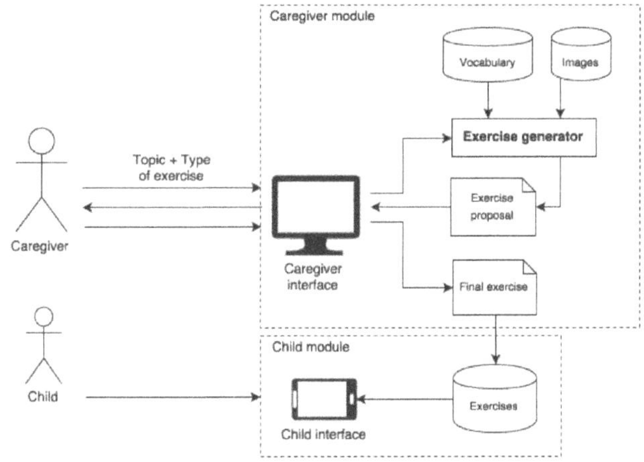

Figure 2 Automatic generation of exercises

The exercise generator takes as input the type of exercise, the topic and/or question templates and it generates content selected from external vocabulary databases in Portuguese that include word relations such as part-whole, hyperonymy or hyponymy (e.g., MultiWordNet[2], ONTO.PT [2]), and image databases that relate words to pictures (e.g., ImageNet[3]). For instance, if the caregiver asks for a multiple choice exercise, about the topic "Objects", in which a word has to be illustrated with the correct picture, the exercise generator should return the question, the stimulus and the set of possible answers (see Table 1). The resulting exercise should be presented to the caregiver, who can choose to accept it as it is, discard it, or change it. The final exercise is then saved to the database and becomes available for the child to solve it in the child application. Automatic generation of exercises has the potential for several challenges regarding Natural Language Processing (NLP), such as word sense disambiguation or gender and number agreement, and might require intermediate steps such as machine translation.

[2] http://mwnpt.di.fc.ul.pt

[3] http://image-net.org

3. PRELIMINARY RESULTS

In a preliminary evaluation to the caregiver's module, we asked a small set of caregivers to perform three different tasks: 1) create a new exercise; 2) edit an existing image file; 3) edit child's preferences regarding the animated character's utterances. They were also asked to fill a questionnaire in order to: a) measure their experience while performing the requested tasks, as well as their overall user experience, in a scale of 1 to 5 (all caregivers fully agreed that they were able to easily and quickly perform the tasks without errors, and the majority of them reported to be very satisfied with their overall experience); b) assess their interest in the possibility of automatically generating exercises (caregivers were interested or very interested in this feature) and to collect further suggestions.

4. CONCLUSIONS AND FUTURE WORK

In this document, we presented a customizable platform that allows caregivers to create and manage multiple choice exercises aimed at children with ASD. We are currently working in a module of automatic generation of exercise content using NLP techniques. At long term, this platform can be extended with many other features, including, but not restricted to: a) Allowing other types of exercise; b) Turning the animated character into an intelligent/user-tuned agent; c) Increasing the customization options (e.g., interface modification, configuration of the animated character's look); d) Automatic adjustment of the difficulty level to the child's progress.

5. ACKNOWLEDGMENTS

This work was supported by national funds through Fundação para a Ciência e a Tecnologia (FCT) with reference UID/CEC/50021/2013, and under project CMUP-ERI/HCI/0051/2013. We would also like to thank to Anna Maria Pompili for her help regarding VITHEA.

6. REFERENCES

[1] A. Abad, A. Pompili, A. Costa, I. Trancoso, J. Fonseca, G. Leal, L. Farrajota, and I. P. Martins. Automatic word naming recognition for an on-line aphasia treatment system. *Computer Speech & Language*, 27(6):1235{1248, Sept. 2013.

[2] H. Gonçalo Oliveira and P. Gomes. ECO and Onto.PT: A flexible approach for creating a Portuguese wordnet automatically. *Language Resources and Evaluation Journal*, 48(2):373{393, 2014.

[3] S. Ramdoss, A. Mulloy, R. Lang, M. O'Reilly, J. Sigafoos, G. Lancioni, R. Didden, and F. El Zein. Use of computer-based interventions to improve literacy skills in students with autism spectrum disorders: A systematic review. *Research in Autism Spectrum Disorders*, 5(4):1306{1318, Oct. 2011.

The Development of a Framework for Understanding the UX of Subtitles

Michael Crabb
Robert Gordon University
Aberdeen
michaelcrabb@acm.org

Rhianne Jones
BBC R&D
Salford
rhia.jones@bbc.co.uk

Mike Armstrong
BBC R&D
Salford
mike.armstrong@bbc.co.uk

ABSTRACT
Approximately 10% of the television audience use subtitles (captioning) to support their viewing experience. Subtitles enable viewers to participate in an experience that is often taken for granted by the general audience. However, when reviewing subtitle literature, it is uncommon to find work that examines the user experience of subtitle users.

This paper presents work on the development of a framework analysing the user experience of watching subtitled content. The framework is introduced, its usage discussed, and the overall framework is then reflected on.

Categories and Subject Descriptors
H.1.2 [**Models and Principles**]: User/Machine Systems—*human factors*

Keywords
Human-centered computing; Accessibility design; evaluation methods

1. INTRODUCTION
The framework presented in this paper encourages research that can improve the overall viewing experience associated with subtitle viewing. This requires a shift in defining what is meant by the quality of subtitles; from the quality of subtitle displays as defined principally by standard efficiency measures - to the quality of the overall viewing experience. Subtitle quality is not reducible to the subtitle display per se; it is a systematic and measured outcome of the quality of the overall viewing experience, capturing the relationship between the person, the subtitles, the content, device, and context.

User experience is a highly subjective field, focusing on the benefits that a user may derive from a product. Existing measures for evaluating subtitle quality include subjective measures such as 'enjoyment' [3], typically administered using a Likert scale. This may indicate to what extent a person has enjoyed the subtitled content but it is insufficient in identifying the reasons as to why; it describes a state, rather than seeking to understand and explain.

The implementation of frameworks measuring UX is commonplace. Yet, a literature review failed to identify a UX framework suitable for the analysis of subtitles. However, the sustained interest in systematically measuring subtitled content suggests this area is ripe for further development. This paper presents our initial work in creating a UX framework for subtitles.

ASSETS '15, October 26-28, 2015, Lisbon, Portugal.
ACM 978-1-4503-3400-6/15/10.
http://dx.doi.org/10.1145/2700648.2811372

Successful UX frameworks can take years before reaching maturity [5], and as such, this framework is very much a work in progress. This work aims to develop a systematic tool for collecting and analysing data to better understand how people experience subtitled content. It offers a method to evaluate how changes in display affect the overall UX. This is a conscious effort to promote the importance of continued research efforts to ensure equivalence of experience in TV viewing between those viewing with and without subtitles.

2. FRAMEWORK CONCEPTS
The framework for measuring the user experience of subtitles is split into seven key components, all of which are important in understanding the concepts that are part of creating a positive user experience. These concepts, combined, can provide a rich amount of detail, drawing on aspects that have not before been examined in relation to subtitle usage. The 7 concepts that make up this framework are adapted from existing literature and UX frameworks. It was important the concepts used in this framework should be both grounded in academic literature, and also appropriate for the evaluation of subtitles.

Attention is defined as awareness to what is going on in relation to the subtitled video content. Users reporting high levels of attention would be focused heavily on the video content, being able to focus clearly on the subtitled video.

Perceived usability is a measure of the challenge that is faced while engaging with the subtitled video content. Users that report high levels of perceived usability are likely to have found the subtitled content easy to understand.

Perceived usefulness is a measure of how useful the display of the subtitled content is. Users who perceive high levels of usefulness will see high levels of value in the subtitle display.

Aesthetics is a measure of the visual appeal of subtitled content. Users reporting high levels of aesthetics indicate that the content is visually pleasing. Low aesthetic levels indicate that the subtitles are displayed in a manner that is not visually appealing to users.

Endurability is defined as a user's willingness to view subtitled video content using a similar method of subtitle display in the future. Users with high levels of endurability are likely to wish to use this method again.

Familiarity is defined as a measure of how much users feel the current subtitle display is recognisable as what they would expect subtitled content to look like and in line with their expectations.

Involvement is used as a measure of how engaged users are with the subtitled content. Users reporting high levels of involvement would be 'drawn into' the subtitled content and would find this to be an engaging and enjoyable experience.

3. CURRENT USES

While the purpose of this paper is to introduce our framework, it is important to highlight its current position within academic literature. This section outlines our usage of this framework to date, however our future work in this area will also implement the use of this framework.

The positioning of **Subtitles in News Broadcast** within an Internet browser is important due to the current shift in media viewing behaviour. In this work, participants were given a short quantitative questionnaire that was based on the Subtitle UX Framework followed by an unstructured interview, with aspects of the framework being drawn out during analysis[2].

Responsive Subtitles are a concept where the text size of the subtitles behaves similar to that of responsive web design. This concept, in introduced in [4], is now being analysed using our framework in order to aid in establishing research themes.

Dynamic Subtitles are a concept where subtitles are placed in dynamic positions in the screen rather than at the bottom of the display. Participants were shown a clip from the popular television show Sherlock, with dynamic subtitles being used. This was followed by a semi-structured interview where participants were asked questions focusing on framework concepts [1].

4. REFLECTIONS ON THE FRAMEWORK

The framework cannot be used as a predictive tool for user experience: The factors identified in the framework are highly interrelated. Results generated provide indications of user experience for future work but it is very difficult to use the framework form as a predictor of UX.

The framework can be used explicitly during studies or as a tool during analysis. The framework was explicitly applied during experimental sessions and implicitly during analysis. Both methods of application generated insights. It was defined and successfully implemented as a data gathering tool and it was also proven to work as also as a qualitative analysis tool.

The framework shows value in using a mixed method approach to research. There are limited multi-method frameworks available for the analysis of UX. We hope this framework provides a dialogue for cross communication. The framework provides the ability to both rate and explain UX. In using the framework so far, we have found that a key benefit is that quantitative results have been complemented by qualitative analysis.

4.1 Reflections on Framework Concepts

The value of each concept is variable: In experiments, participants placed different values on the concepts that were most important to them. This generates insights into subtitle use on an individual basis for each participant. Furthermore, the value of the concepts also varies according to the viewing situation. For example, aesthetics was more of a priority when viewing drama with *dynamic subtitles* then viewing news with subtitles positioned at the bottom of the screen. The display, the content being viewed, and the context of use all have an effect on the UX and therefore on their view of the concepts. This reinforced the idea that one size doesn't fit all for subtitle presentation and usage.

Our understanding of the framework is evolving: We are aware of the close relationships between elements of the framework i.e. usability and usefulness, and attention and involvement. Both of these relationships need to be understood in more detail in the future. Additionally, investigation also needs to be taken to understand the role of some individual factors. For example; attention was initially used to ascertain what a person was able to focus on while watching the content. However, it generated insights into comprehension as measured by the perception of whether an individual could follow both the subtitles and the visuals.

The framework measures small aspects of properties within an experimental setting. Endurability was difficult to measure in a lab session. It is useful as an indicator of the sustainability of subtitles in the context of long-term use but it cannot accurately determine the reliability of this within short-term lab experiments. However, endurability as a category remains important and may provide more value outside of the lab.

The framework provided a communication bridge: During all of the experiment sessions, participants mirrored the language that was used in the framework. This aided in creating meaningful conversations between researcher and participant. This in turn was useful in focusing discussion onto relevant points while allowing participants to have the freedom to discuss subtitles using a (now) common language.

5. CONCLUSIONS

This paper presented a reflection into the creation of a framework to aid in helping to understand the UX that is attached to viewing subtitled content. Again, it is important to note that this framework is very much a work in progress and through its continued usage we will understand more about the concepts that are important in understanding the UX attached to subtitled content. More importantly, this framework addresses a gap that currently exists when analysing the UX of television content, no other frameworks or tools exist that focus on subtitle UX in this way. This framework is a positive move forward in the way that we think about, research, and develop accessible services. It provides a method to go beyond thinking of subtitles as only an access service and towards creating systems that can improve the overall experience of watching subtitled video content.

6. ACKNOWLEDGMENTS

This work has been undertaken with support from Gareth Ford-Williams, Head of Accessibility for BBC Future Media.

7. REFERENCES

[1] Brown, A. et al. 2015. Dynamic Subtitles: The User Experience. *Proceedings of the 2nd ACM Conference on Television Experience* (2015).

[2] Crabb, M. et al. 2015. Online News Videos : The UX of Subtitle Position. *Proceedings of the 17th international ACM SIGACCESS conference on Computers & accessibility* (2015).

[3] Hong, R. et al. 2011. Video accessibility enhancement for hearing-impaired users. *ACM Transactions on Multimedia Computing, Communications, and Applications*. (2011).

[4] Hughes, C.J. et al. 2015. Responsive Design for Personalised Subtitles. *Proceedings of The 12th Web for All Conference* (2015).

[5] Rodden, K. et al. 2010. Measuring the User Experience on a Large Scale : User-Centered Metrics for Web Applications. *Proceedings of the SIGCHI Conference on Human Factors in Computing Systems*. (2010).

An Empirical Study for Examining the Performance of Visually Impaired People in Recognizing Shapes through a Vibro-tactile Feedback

Waseem Safi Fabrice Maurel Jean-Marc Routoure Pierre Beust Gaël Dias
University of Caen Normandie – UNICAEN
14032 Caen- France
{waseem.safi, fabrice.maurel, jean-marc.routoure, pierre.beust, gael.dias}@unicaen.fr

ABSTRACT
In this paper, we present results of an empirical study for examining the performance of blind individuals in recognizing shapes through a vibro-tactile feedback. The suggested vibro-tactile system maps different shades of grey to one pattern low-frequencies tactical vibrations. Performance data is reported, including number of errors, and qualitative understanding of the displayed shapes.

Categories and Subject Descriptors
[H.5.2] [**User Interfaces**] Graphical user interfaces (GUI), Haptic I/O, User-centered design, User interface management systems

General Terms
Algorithms, Design, Human Factors, Languages

Keywords
Visually impaired people, vibro-tactile feedback, low-frequencies tactical vibrations

1. INTRODUCTION
An important accessibility drawback of current screen readers is the failure of individuals who are blind or visually-impaired to quickly get an overall sense of a webpage in terms of overall semantics, main message, structure, and interaction affordances [1]. Our work focuses on developing and evaluating a sensory substitution system based on a vibrotactile solution, cheap and efficient in noisy and public environments.

2. RELATED WORKS
Related works reviewed in this section are two-fold: first, we view previous researches on vibrotactile feedback technologies; second, we review some works leveraging the perception of layout and logical structures.

2.1. Vibrotactile Output
Many authors have proposed the attachment of vibrotactile actuators on users' body for working as mnemonic information [2]. Opticon is one of oldest systems that proposed a vibrotactile feedback [3]. Opticon translates the written word into a scanned display on the fingertips. Another interesting prototype designed for interactive tabletops has been proposed by [4], the prototype is represented by a device incorporates interactive haptics into tabletop interaction. A 2D tactile prototype has been suggested by [5] to train blind people for their independent mobility. The prototype is associated to a 2D tactile array (vibration array) which consists of 16 vibrating elements arranged in a 4×4 manner. UbiBraille is a vibrotactile reading device has been designed [6] that leverages the users' braille knowledge to read textual information. Another tactile prototype was suggested by [10]. As the user interacts with a graphics tablet, a tactile feedback is provided via a tactile matrix on a mouse. The main drawback of many proposed systems is that they need specific devices which cannot be integrated easily to handled devices.

2.2. Perception Of Document Layout And Logical Structures
Perceiving the 2D structure of web pages greatly improves navigation efficiency and memorization as it allows high level reading strategies [1]. A tactile web browser for hypertext documents has been proposed by [7]. This browser renders texts and graphics for visually impaired people on a tactile graphics display and supports also a vocal feedback. Tactos is a perceptual interaction system [8], which consists of a tactile simulator, a graphics tablet with a stylus and a computer. A structured participatory-based approach has been proposed by [9], this approach aims to develop targeted haptic sensations for purposes of web page exploration. All these mentioned approaches aim to give visually impaired people the ability for perceiving logical structures. In this paper, we contribute a vibrotactile framework, which features (1) on hardware level: cheap, little intrusive, plugged-in easily with handled devices, modular for adding easily and synchronically many tactile electronic components - piezoelectric vibrators, solenoids matrices, peltiers- in order to get a large, rich and useful tactile semantics; and (2) on software level: a graphical user interface, controlling wirelessly many parameters -vibration, amplitude, duration, rhythm, and repetition-, integrated easily with handled devices.

3. VIBROTACTILE FRAMEWORK
Our system "TactiNET" (Figure 1) provides one pattern vibrotactile feedback when the blind user touches the tablet. To achieve the desired system, we have designed an electronic circuit, which controls many micro-vibrators placed anywhere on the body. A Bluetooth connection with an android tablet allows controlling the actuators. An Android dedicated program on the tablet views an image on the screen and detects information about the user touches (X, Y, Time, and Pressure). The intensity of the light emitted by the tablet at touched points is then transmitted to the embedded device in order to control the tactile stimuli.

ASSETS'15, October 26-28, 2015, Lisbon, Portugal
ACM978-1-4503-3400-6/15/10.
http://dx.doi.org/10.1145/2700648.2811373

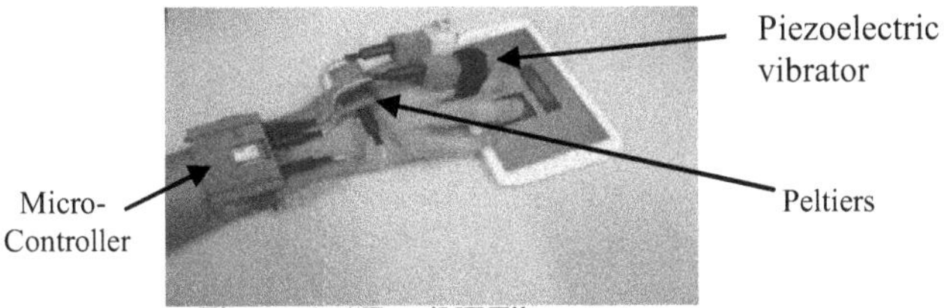

Figure 1: "TactiNET" prototype.

To validate our prototype and concepts of vibrotactile access to visual structures of web pages, we wanted first pretest our hypothesis: visually impaired people can explore and redraw simple grayscale shapes by using vibration motors.

4. PRE-TESTS PROTOCOL

We made experiments with 5 blind persons, each experiment consisted of: personal and technical questions, explanations of the test objective, a training task, and finally an evaluation task. The tested images (viewed on the tablet) contain some examples of expected results of web pages layout extraction, so success of distinguishing these shapes by blind users could be an indicator of their ability to distinguish web pages layouts. Figure 2 presents some images of evaluation phases.

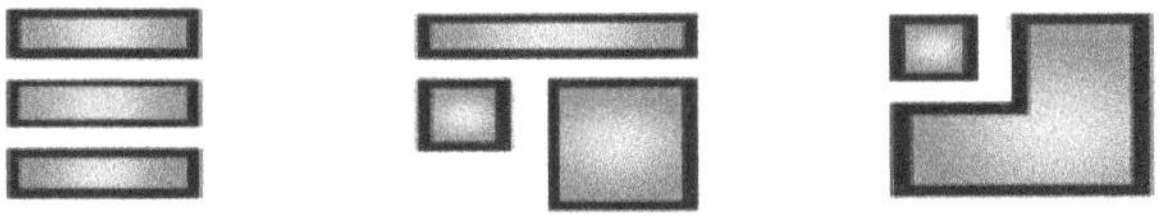

Figure 2: Images IDP1, IDP2, IDP3 (Evaluation Task).

Image IDP1 contains 3 rectangles with matched sizes and with vertical order, and the image IDP2 contains 3 rectangles with different sizes and many relations of directions, so testing these two images could indicate the ability of distinguishing sizes, and distinguishing relations of directions. Image IDP3 contains different shapes, so it could test the ability to distinguish different shapes in the same image. We created different transitions of gray scale for each shape to analyze the reaction through a continuous decreasing/increasing intensity generated by the micro-motor.
For each image in the evaluation task, we asked users to explore it and to answer for some questions (cf. in table 1, symbol ✓ represents a correct answer and the symbol X an incorrect one).

Table 1. Answers of questions for images IDP1, IDP2, IDP3

User-ID	ID0			ID1			ID2			ID3			ID4		
IDP	1	2	3	1	2	3	1	2	3	1	2	3	1	2	3
Number shapes	✓	✓	X	✓	X	X	✓	X	✓	X	✓	✓	✓	✓	✓
sizes of shapes	X	X	X	X	X	X	✓	X	X	X	✓	✓	✓	✓	✓

At the end of the test, we asked each user to draw the recognized graphical patterns founded in each touched image (we used another tablet for redrawing). Some users could redraw forms nearly identical to original evaluation images. Figure 3 views the redrawing results of the user who answered successfully to all questions.

Figure 3. Results of redrawing images IDP1, IDP2, IDP3

5. ANALYSIS OF RESULTS

We notice from data in table 1 that the best performance is for the user with ID4, and this may be because this user is the youngest between others, and it could be because she was the only one who has already used touched devices (an iPhone, in her case working with VoiceOver), and this could be an indication that more training users more getting better results. Redrawing comparison with touched images can conclude: 1- ability of distinguishing sizes of shapes, because the degree of scaling between redrawn shapes is nearly equal to the degree of scaling between real shapes. 2- ability of distinguishing relations of directions (vertical order, left to, right to…), because relations of directions between redrawn shapes are nearly identical to relations of directions between real shapes.

6. CONCLUSION AND PERSPECTIVES

We have presented an embedded device dedicated for visually impaired people to explore simple grayscale shapes using vibrations. First results are promising: after a short training period, tested persons were able recognizing basic patterns. Many enhancements to be achieved such as increasing the number and quality of micro-vibrators, and more controlling frequencies and amplitudes.

7. REFERENCES

[1] Maurel, F., Dias, G., Routoure, J-M., Vautier, M., Beust, P., Molina, M., Sann, C. "Haptic Perception of Document Structure for Visually Impaired People on Handled Devices", Procedia Computer Science, Volume 14, Pages 319-329, 2012.

[2] Kammoun, S., Jouffrais, C., Guerreiro, T., Nicolau, H., Jorge, J., "Guiding Blind People with Haptic Feedback". In Pervasive Workshop on Frontiers in Accessibility for Pervasive Computing, New Castle, UK, 2012.

[3] Bliss, J., Katcher M., Rogers C., Shepard R., "Optical-to-Tactile Image Conversion for the Blind", Published in: Man-Machine Systems, IEEE Transactions, Volume:11, Issue:1, March; pages: 58 – 65, 1970.

[4] Marquardt, N., Nacenta, M., Young, J., Carpendale, S., Greenberg, S., Sharlin, E., "The Haptic Tabletop Puck: tactile feedback for interactive tabletops." Proceedings of the ACM International Conference on Interactive Tabletops and Surfaces. ACM, Pages 85-92, 2009.

[5] Dakopoulos, D., Bourbakis, N., "Towards a 2D tactile vocabulary for navigation of blind and visually impaired.", Proceedings of the 2009 IEEE international conference on Systems, Man and Cybernetics, Pages: 45-51, ISSN: , 1062-922X, 2009.

[6] Nicolau, H., Guerreiro, J., Guerreiro, T., Carriço, L., "UbiBraille: Designing and Evaluating a Vibrotactile Braille-Reading Device", Proceedings of the 15th International ACM SIGACCESS Conference on Computers and Accessibility, Article No. 23. ACM New York, USA 2013.

[7] Rotard, M., Knödler, S., Ertl, T., "A Tactile Web Browser for the Visually Disabled". In Proceedings of the sixteenth ACM Conference on Hypertext and Hypermedia. ACM, New York, NY, USA, pages 15-22, 2005.

[8] Tixier, M., Lenay, C., Le-Bihan, G., Gapenne, O., Aubert, D., "Designing Interactive Content with Blind Users for a Perceptual Supplementation System", TEI 2013, 2013, in Proceedings of the 7th International Conference on Tangible, Embedded and Embodied Interaction, Pages 229-236, Barcelona, Spain, 2013.

[9] Kuber, R., Yu, W., McAllister, G., "Towards developing assistive haptic feedback for visually impaired Internet users." Proceedings of the SIGCHI Conference on Human Factors in Computing Systems. ACM, Pages 1525-1534, 2007.

[10] Wall, S., Brewster, S., "Feeling What You Hear: Tactile Feedback for Navigation of Audio Graphs". In Proceedings of the the premier international conference for human-computer interaction. Montreal, Canada, pp. 1123-1132, 2006.

Breaking Barriers with Assistive Macros

André Rodrigues
LaSIGE, Faculdade de Ciências,
Universidade de Lisboa
Campo Grande, C6 Piso3, 1749-016
Lisboa, Portugal
afrodrigues@fc.ul.pt

ABSTRACT

People with disabilities rely on assistive technology (AT) software to interact with their mobile device. The overall functionality of AT depends on a set of requirements that are not always fulfilled by application developers, often resulting in cumbersome and slow interactions, or even render content inaccessible. To address these issues we present *Assistive Macros,* an accessibility service developed to enable users to perform a sequence of commands with a single selection. Macros can be created manually by the user or automatically by detecting repeated sequences of interactions. In this paper, we report a preliminary case study with our prototype involving a motor impaired user and his caregivers

Categories and Subject Descriptors

H.5.m. Information interfaces and presentation (e.g., HCI): Miscellaneous; K4.2 [Computers and Society]: Social Issues – Assistive technologies for persons with disabilities.

General Terms

Performance, Design, Human Factors

Keywords

Mobile; Multi-impairment; Assistive Technologies; Macros

1. INTRODUCTION

Since the inclusion of accessibility software in modern touchscreen smartphones, such as screen readers (e.g. *Talkback*[1], *VoiceOver*[2]) and switch access (e.g. *Switch Control*[2], *Switch Access*[1]), they have gained popularity amongst people with visual and motor impairments. Smartphones have become a tool for independence and inclusion. To interact with this technology users often rely on alternative interaction methods that are provided by the accessibility software. Motor impaired users may rely on switches to navigate the interface and select options. In severe cases, navigation is accomplished relying on automatic scanning of the interface elements. Sequential navigation of elements can be extremely time consuming when performing a multiple step operation, even when using row-column or block scanning techniques. This is further exacerbated when interfaces have less relevant information scanned first. Previous research tried to tackle this issue with adaptive solutions that reordered interface items. However, this approach showed to be ineffective due to an increase in cognitive load [1].

Motor impaired users can face an insurmountable barrier when applications have options that can only be reached through a specific gestural interaction with no alternative selection method (e.g. app drawers). Since the underlying accessibility service to enable Switch Access also supports Screen Readers, blind and visually impaired (BVI) users can experience similar barriers and challenges when using mobile touchscreen devices.

To address the problems of time consuming navigation and inaccessible content, we developed *Assistive Macros*, an accessibility service that allows the creation of macros giving users the ability to perform a multiple step interaction with a single tap. *Assistive Macros* enables time-consuming or inaccessible interaction sequences to be recorded by the Person with Disability (PwD) or friend / family member. Once a macro has been captured, it can be accessed directly from the device's homescreen or from within the application; for which it provides functionality. Assistive Macros builds on the concepts presented in SWAT [3], a framework that enabled system-wide scanning navigation, leveraging its system-wide capabilities in the creation and reproduction of macros. *Macrodroid*[3] and *Tasker*[4] enable users to create macros based on a set of triggers and perform a restricted subset of device actions. However, these tools rely on developers integrating APIs and software hooks into their apps. Unlike the aforementioned tools, *Assistive Macros* requires no additional integration, and detects common interactions to suggest macros and enable richer macros that cross app boundaries and record actions in every application.

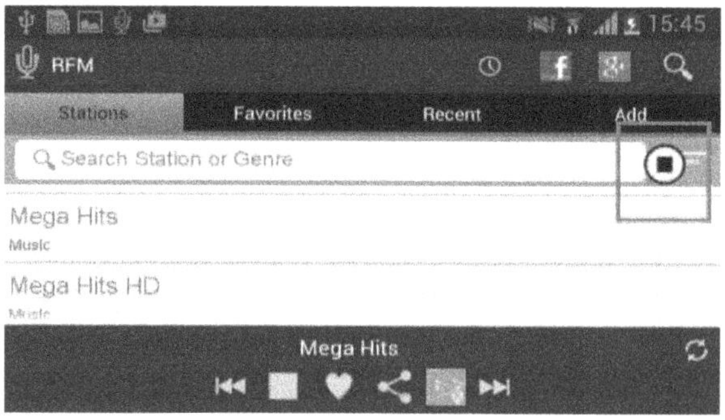

Figure 1- Overlay present over the interface to stop the macro manual recording.

[1]http://www.google.com/accessibility/
[2] https://www.apple.com/accessibility/ios/

[3]http://www.macrodroid.com/
[4] http://tasker.dinglisch.net/

ASSETS '15, October 26-28, 2015, Lisbon, Portugal
ACM 978-1-4503-3400-6/15/10.
http://dx.doi.org/10.1145/2700648.2811322

2. ASSISTIVE MACROS

Assistive Macros is an accessibility service designed for Android that can be used with any application, and in conjunction with other accessibility services (e.g. Switch Access, Explore by Touch). Users are able to manually record macros, consisting in a sequence of actions for future reproduction. Moreover, *Assistive Macros* continuously monitors users' interactions to identify repetitive sequences and suggest the generation of new macros.

2.1 Manual Macro Creation

The manual macro creation can record two types of actions, description- or gesture-based. In description-based actions the system stores the selected interactive element's description and its position in the interface hierarchical tree; it relies on the unequivocal description of elements to perform a selection, which enables Assistive Macros to adapt to dynamic interfaces (e.g. select item XPTO in a list). Gesture-based recording requires a higher level of permissions than typical android applications/services. When recording a gesture action, the raw touches are collected, which includes their position and timestamps. Thus gesture-based macros can enable complex gestural interactions, from taps to multi-touch gestures, with possibly otherwise inaccessible interfaces. There is no limit to the amount of actions *Assistive Macros* can chain. Description- and gesture-based actions can be combined within the same macro.

Users, caregivers, and friends can record a macro using *Assistive Macros* bundled app. The recording process starts from the homescreen, where to record, users simply perform the desired chain of actions and press 'stop' to finish (Figure 1). Afterwards they name the macro and a shortcut is created in the homescreen.

2.2 Automatic Macro Generation

When enabled, *Assistive Macros* captures all interactive elements selection sequences that are performed by the user. There are two types of sequences: *session* and *app*. S*ession* sequence begins when the screen is turned on and ends when it goes off. From these, we generate *app* sequences. *App* sequences are created from splitting *session* sequences when the user enters an application. With both types, we apply the Rabin-Karp [2] string-matching algorithm to identify repeated sequences. When a sequence is repeated beyond a configurable threshold, the user receives a pop-up asking if they would like to create a macro for that sequence of actions. *Session* sequences detect common multi-step actions that start from the homescreen and might contain interactions with more than one app, while *App* sequences are restricted to a single app.

2.3 Macro Reproduction

The stored macros possess a sequence of descriptions and/or gestures to be performed during their execution. The reproduction of gestures actions is straightforward - the service injects the same touches with the recorded time intervals in between. When reproducing description actions, *Assistive Macros* maintains an updated list of all interactive items of the screen. When an action is to be performed *Assistive Macros* checks the available items; if the target item is found, it is selected. Macros have two selection modes: Icon-based and Overlay-based. Icon-based reproduction is executed from the homescreen where macros appear as shortcuts. Overlay-based reproduction is triggered when an app is launched and has macros associated.

3. CASE STUDY

We conducted a preliminary study with John, a multi-impaired smartphone user (motor-, visually-, and speech-impaired), currently able to operate a single-button switch. Handling the radio application on his device was a daily struggle and at times impossible; John had to scan eleven options and make four selections, in the best case scenario, to reach the play/stop button of his favorite station. Any mistake could easily double the time taken since one of the interfaces is a list of all stations. Furthermore, the play/stop buttons had no description making it impossible for John to know their location in the scanning sequence. With *Assistive Macros* early version, John's parents, after a five minute explanation, were able to record macros that allowed him to play and stop his favorite channel through a selection of a macro in the home screen. At the end, his mother showed enthusiasm with the possibility of creating personalized macros to help her son live a more independent life.

4. CONCLUSIONS

Manual macro creation allows users and caregivers to have an active role in improving the device accessibility by creating shortcuts that not only convert long interaction sequences in a single selection but also enable users to overcome inaccessible applications. Automatic macro creation allows them to incrementally improve their interaction efficiency by leveraging their routine behaviors. Gesture-based steps allow PwD to perform gestures they would not be able to do otherwise in order to manipulate the interface (e.g. open app drawers).

In the future, we will enrich our data with contextual information. A macro that is adequate in the morning might not be at night. If we are able to detect patterns and give users the opportunity to create context-specific macros we will be able to provide the right macro at the right time further decreasing navigation times. Furthermore, with *Assistive Macros,* we aim to explore the opportunities of crowd-sourcing generated macros for applications to provide immediate support to users upon their first interaction with the application. When an app is installed, users can take advantage of crowd-generated macros, which address some of its inherent accessibility problems. Finally we intend to conduct a user study involving more participants to evaluate additional features of *Assistive Macros,* including the automatic macro generation, and measure its effect on device usability and accessibility.

5. REFERENCES

[1] Horstmann Koester, H. & Levine, S. (1994). Learning and performance of able-bodied individuals using scanning systems with and without word prediction. Assistive Technology, 6, 42—53.

[2] Karp, Richard M.; Rabin, Michael O. (March 1987). "Efficient randomized pattern-matching algorithms". IBM Journal of Research and Development 31 (2): 249–260.

[3] Rodrigues, A., Guerreiro, T. SWAT: Mobile System-Wide Assistive technologies. Proc. of BCS HCI (2014)

Making Connections: Modular 3D Printing for Designing Assistive Attachments to Prosthetic Devices

Megan Hofmann
Colorado State University, Fort Collins
Department of Computer Science
Carnegie Mellon, Pittsburgh
Human Computer Interaction Institute
mkh@rams.colostate.edu

ABSTRACT

In this abstract, we present a modular design methodology for prototyping and 3D printing affordable, highly customized, assistive technology. This methodology creates 3D printed attachments for prosthetic limbs that perform a diverse group of tasks. We demonstrate the methodology with two case studies where two participants with upper limb amputations help design devices to play the cello and use a hand-cycle.

Categories and Subject Descriptors

K.4.2 [Computers and Society]: Social Issues – assistive technologies for persons with disabilities.

Keywords

Assistive technology; disability; modularity; personal-scale fabrication; prosthetic; rapid prototyping; 3D printing.

1. INTRODUCTION

3D printing is a valuable resource for engineering affordable, highly customized, assistive technology and prosthetic devices [1, 5, 7]. However, it is difficult and time consuming to iteratively design complex devices. In this abstract, we present a modular prototyping methodology to design and modify assistive devices for prosthetic users.

The process uses three modular components: the prosthetic, the assistive device, and the attachment interface connecting them. Breaking a design into these components makes it easier for a designer to iteratively create multiple attachments for different tasks and test a variety of configurations. The final device is printed as two parts: a prosthetic and an attachable assistive device.

2. RELATED WORK

Highly customized assistive devices are expensive to engineer and produce, but are necessary to perform many tasks [4]. Recently, the popular media has reported on many successes of 3D printed prosthetics [3, 6]. For end users, online 3D modeling communities are a growing resource for assistive devices; however, impairments are unique to the individual and the original designs may not be appropriate for all users [2]. Our modular prototyping process modifies these open source designs to meet an end user's needs.

ASSETS '15, October 26-28, 2015, Lisbon, Portugal
ACM 978-2-4503-6/15/10.
http://dx.doi.org/10.1145/2700648.2811323

3. MODULAR PROTOTYPING

Our rapid prototyping process applies a modular design scheme to prototyping 3D printed prosthetic attachments. This design identifies three components of prosthetic attachments which can be tested separately and brought together to perform a task.

3.1 Components

3.1.1 *The Prosthetic*

A user and designer team, can build a 3D printed prosthetic or modify a professional prosthetic. When designing the prosthetic, it is important to consider factors such as the location of the amputation and the forces acting on the residual limb. A simple prosthetic wrist can be seen in Figure 1. A.

The modular prosthetic allows a user to adjust it as their body changes. As a separate component, it can be changed without adapting the assistive attachments a user and designer have created. This also allows the team to modify a prosthetic to optimize tasks, including altering the prosthetic to balance out the weight of heavier attachments or make use of mechanical motions for performing a repetitive task. These mechanics allow a user to translate their range of motion into the motions required to perform an assisted task.

3.1.2 *Assistive Device*

An assistive device can be any model that will support a user in performing a task, often replacing the functionality of a hand (e.g. supportive grips for utensils and tools). In many cases, the devices do not need to be explicitly for a person with a disability, but rather are tools that make performing a task easier for anyone. A variety of these devices are available online. In a case study described below, we modified a violin bow holder sourced from Thingiverse shown in Figure 1. D.

Unfortunately, these devices are rarely designed to be attached to a prosthetic. To utilize this resource, our prototyping process connects these devices to the user through their prosthetic. Because the methodology is modular, a user and designer would not need to redesign the prosthetic to interact with the device. The style or size of a prosthetic would be irrelevant; although, the assistive device would need to be remodeled and reoriented to optimize printing and interacting with an attachment interface. Furthermore, adapting the assistive devices does not require that changes be made to the other components, saving time. Also, since the assistive device is prosthetic agnostic, a designer could make their model available online as a resource for other prosthetic users.

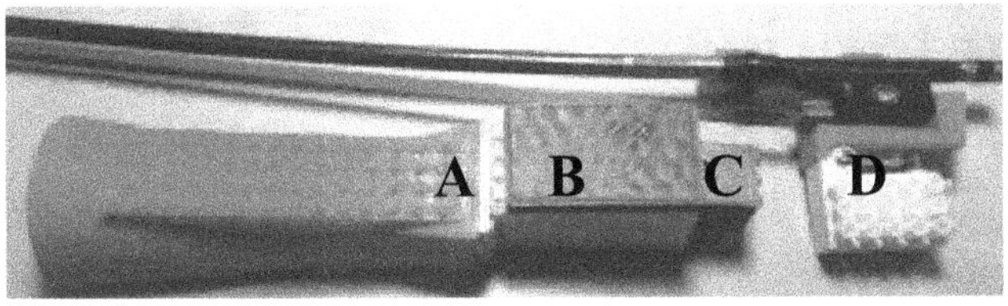

Figure 1. Demonstration of components of cello bow prosthetic in testing phase

3.1.3 *Attachment Interface*

Connecting these separate assistive devices requires an attachment interface that allows the user to attach to a variety of devices without reprinting their prosthetic. This interface maintains the modularity of the design process and allows the users to customize their prosthetic to perform different tasks.

The interface can be broken into two parts, a *lock* integrated with the attachment and a *key* attached to the assistive device. This locking mechanism is customized to utilize the user's range of motion (e.g. wrist rotation, elbow movement, etc.). One example of a lock and key can be seen in Figure 1.B and 1.C, respectively.

3.2 Designing a System Using Components

With these three components, a user and designer can collaborate to build a prosthetic attachment. They can iteratively test a variety of attachment interfaces in different positions on the prosthetic by means of a *testing interface*. Our testing interface uses 3D printed Lego studs to interlock the different components in a variety of positions in order to find a comfortable fit. These separate pieces can also be saved for creating future designs, speeding up the design and testing of new devices. Furthermore, if a user's prosthetic needs to be changed to accommodate growth, the prosthetic can be modified without adjusting old attachments.

Once a good fit has been found, the design can be printed without the testing interface. The design will come in two parts: the prosthetic with the key to the attachment interface, and an assistive device with the lock. The user can now attach themselves to the device, perform the assisted task, and detach. Then they can attach to another device or use a generalized prosthetic such as a hook or passive hand.

4. DEMONSTRATIONS

To test this prototyping process, we met with participants with upper limb amputations over a series of interviews and testing sessions.

4.1 Case 1: Playing the Cello

Our first participant was a 9 year old boy with a congenital amputation below the elbow on his right arm. For most tasks, he prefers not to use a prosthetic, but has no other way to hold the bow when playing the cello. Additionally, he is outgrowing his prosthetic, which was not designed specifically for the cello and thus lacks the control he would like.

We first acquired the designs for an adaptive violin bow holder from Thingiverse, and then attached Lego-like studs to the flat portion of the device that would connect at the wrist. We made modifications to the original holder to accommodate the different instrument. We also adapted a gauntlet design with Lego-like studs to the top of the forearm and end of the wrist (Figure 1).

This method made it easy to test a variety of attachment interfaces and positions without multiple prosthetics and bow holding attachments. It also allowed us to print a few prosthetic gauntlets in different sizes without redesigning the bow holder. Furthermore, it was simple to design the separate components and test a variety of configurations in rapid succession, since only one testing session with the testing interface was required.

4.2 Case 2: Attaching to a Hand-Cycle

Our next participant is 27 and has a congenital amputation below the elbow on her left arm. For recreation, she uses a hand-cycle, but cannot easily connect her arm to the left handle. This leaves most of the work of cycling to her dominant arm, causing strain. We are currently working with her to connect her preferred attachment interface to the hand-cycle. This would lock her in to the cycle similar to locking bike pedals.

This is an interesting case because the assistive device is a hand-cycle—a complex machine that cannot be 3D printed. However, our process is still effective. In this case, we designed an attachment interface for her prosthetic that uses Velcro as opposed to Lego-like studs to test positioning on the hand-cycle. Because the system is modular, we can adapt the existing hand-cycle to her prosthetic instead of engineering an expensive, custom machine.

5. CONCLUSIONS AND FUTURE WORK

In this abstract, we outlined a modular prototyping methodology for designing 3D printed attachments to prosthetic devices. The process produces highly customized and affordable designs that can be used with a variety of prosthetics.

In future work, we will design solutions for a more diverse set of users, tasks, and impairments. We also hope to create automation tools to generate assistive devices using this methodology. This is made simpler by the focus on modularity.

6. REFRENCES

[1] Buehler, E. et al. 2014. ABC and 3D: Opportunities and Obstacles to 3D Printing in Special Education Environments. *Proceedings of the 16th International ACM SIGACCESS Conference on Computers & Accessibility* (New York, NY, USA, 2014), 107–114.

[2] Buehler, E. et al. 2015. Sharing is Caring: Assistive Technology Designs on Thingiverse. *Proceedings of the 33rd Annual ACM Conference on Human Factors in Computing Systems* (New York, NY, USA, 2015), 525–534.

[3] Chao, V. 2014. The Boy With the Lego Hand. *The Atlantic.*

[4] Dawe, M. 2006. Desperately Seeking Simplicity: How Young Adults with Cognitive Disabilities and Their Families Adopt Assistive Technologies. *Proceedings of the SIGCHI Conference on Human Factors in Computing Systems* (New York, NY, USA, 2006), 1143–1152.

[5] Herbert, N. et al. 2005. A preliminary investigation into the development of 3-D printing of prosthetic sockets. *Journal of Rehabilitation Research and Development*. 42, 2 (Mar. 2005), 141–6.

[6] Polakoff, L. 2015. Boy gets real "bionic arm" with Iron Man Robert Downey Jr. thrown in. *The Washington Post.*

[7] Zuniga, J. et al. 2015. Cyborg beast: a low-cost 3d-printed prosthetic hand for children with upper-limb differences. *BMC research notes*. 8, 1 (2015), 10.

Sensory Substitution Training for Users Who Are Blind with Dynamic Stimuli, Games and Virtual Environments

Shachar Maidenbaum
ELSC & IMRIC, Hebrew university of Jerusalem, Israel
Shachar.maidenbaum@mail.huji.ac.il

ABSTRACT

Sensory Substitution Devices (SSDs) offer people who are blind access to visual information via other senses. One of the main bottlenecks to widespread adoption of sensory substitution is the difficulty of learning to use these devices – both mastering the device and learning to properly interpret visual information. We have recently upgraded the training offered in our lab to congenitally blind EyeMusic users from a static training paradigm to an interactive dynamic one in an attempt to address both challenges mentioned above. This offered us a unique opportunity to explore the effect of this change on both the users and on their sighted personal instructors. We explored users' ability to play simple interactive games and learn visual principles, and explored the feelings and opinions of both the users and instructors during the shift. We found that all users were able to successfully complete these tasks utilizing visual principles such as depth-size, reported a high level of enjoyment and satisfaction for them, viewed these sessions as more effective and highlighted their feelings of a higher sense of independence and control. The instructors were enthusiastic as well, mirrored the users' answers and especially highlighted the flexibility advantage.

Categories and Subject Descriptors

H.1.2 User/Machine Systems; H.5.2 User Interfaces: Auditory (non-speech) feedback;

General Terms

Performance, Experimentation, Human Factors, Standardization

Keywords

Sensory Substitution; training; visual rehabilitation; gamification; Universal access; blind; Auditory Interfaces;

1. Introduction

Imagine a simple game in which a player, target and obstacle are displayed on your screen. Bringing the player to the target without touching the obstacle is typically not a difficult task – as long as you can see. Without vision, identifying the objects and relative spatial layout and tracking their positions as you move is nearly impossible. Even using standard accessibility tools, such as screen readers, would not improve the situation by much – you may be able to "tab" between the objects, if the programmer pre-programmed it, but spatial layout and movement are not typically supported.

Sensory Substitution Devices (SSDs) offer us a tool for transforming visual information into other senses and offering it to people who are blind [1-4,6]. SSDs such as EyeMusic can capture the entire scene and sonify it, enabling users to perceive the visual information in their environment and perform tasks such as object recognition or navigation. Importantly, by sonifying the on-screen information they can do so without need for in-game pre-programming, and can utilize skills from other tasks for dealing with new ones such as the game detailed above.

However, despite recent advances which boost SSD availability and practicality beyond past failures, SSDs are still only in very limited use (For a review exploring these reasons and new mitigating factors in depth see [3]). One of the main causes for this is the bottleneck formed by the long and arduous training required. SSDs are notoriously difficult to learn and require long repetitive simple tasks to master, especially when starting out, leading to user frustration and abandonment of the technology. Furthermore, even once mastered users who are congenitally blind report difficulty in processing the visual information they are offered, such as being confused by occlusion, change of shape and size from different angles and distances etc.

One potential approach is using more dynamic gamified tasks [3,6], recently showing success in many other similar training situations [5,7]. In this work I explore the use of dynamic stimuli and games as a training paradigm for SSDs, specifically as a training paradigm for EyeMusic. We test the ability of a pool of 7 participants who are congenitally totally blind and who had previously trained with EyeMusic via static lessons to perform these dynamic tasks and explore their opinion of the different training sessions via behavioral challenges, surveys & interviews at several time-points. We wanted to explore if they could indeed perform these tasks successfully, how enjoyable and effective they feel it is, and in general gather their thoughts regarding such training games. We also addressed the same survey and interview to their instructors to explore the shift from their perspective.

2. The dynamic training & games

There were three types of additions to the training program (fig 1). All were controlled via keyboard (Arrow, Enter & Space keys).

The first was using dynamic stimuli instead of static ones. Specifically, instead of using many files of different shapes in different colors and locations, we used dynamic objects that could be manipulated by the user or instructor via the keyboard. Beyond saving the tedious work of stimuli creation, it enabled more interesting ad-hoc tasks and enabled sensorimotor perception. This was not a game, but rather a training tool building upon the importance of closing the sensory-motor loop during perception

The second were simple 2D games focused on deepening users' control of EyeMusic, with emphasis on parsing the visual scene for shapes, colors & locations.

The third type was virtual environments experienced from a 1st person perspective. Completing tasks in these environments requires the ability to understand the changes in the visual scene

ASSETS '15, October 26-28, 2015, Lisbon, Portugal
ACM 978-1-4503-3400-6/15/10.
http://dx.doi.org/10.1145/2700648.2811324

caused by user and vantage point movement and different dedicated tasks were focused on different visual principles.

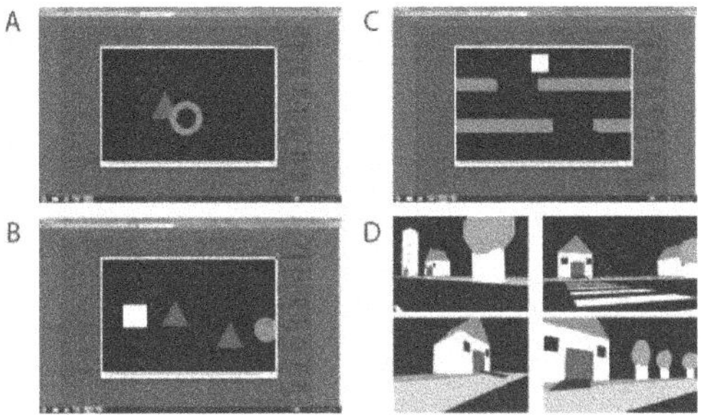

Figure 1 – Game screenshots: (A) Dynamic objects users could manipulate (move, rotate, change shape and color etc.). (B) Navigate to target – Bring the player (white square) to the target (red circle) while avoiding the obstacles (blue triangles). (C) Maze – Bring the player (white square) to the screen's other end while avoiding contact with the red flaming walls. (D) Screenshots from one of the virtual environments

2.1 EyeMusic

EyeMusic is a visual-to-auditory SSD conveying whole scene visual information including shape, location and color (fig 2). It is described in detail in [1] and was previously used for various tasks (e.g. [3] among many others). It is also freely available on iTunes and Google Play. Importantly, EyeMusic can capture the on-screen image and offer the user the visual information from a game without the need for any hardware beyond standard audio output (speakers/headphone). While here we used EyeMusic, it is only one of many auditory-to-visual SSDs currently available, such as The vOICe [4]. We do not claim here any advantages and indeed suggest our results can be generalized for to them as well.

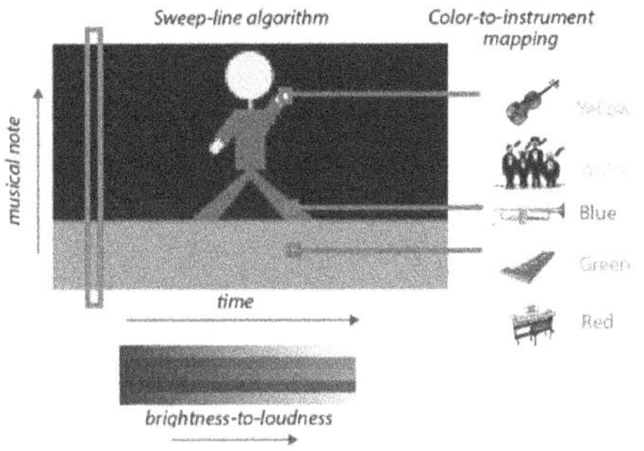

Figure 2. EyeMusic transformation. Left-to-right Sweep-line codes X-value to time, brightness as loudness, Y-Value coded as musical notes and color as different musical instruments.

3. Initial results - performance

All users were able to complete all tasks successfully, and both by self-report and by instructor report did so generally at ease.

The instructors reported frequent returning to the dynamic object trainer for short focused sessions ("I can have a lesson planned and then he has a lot of difficulty with some side point. So I can just stop and focus on that"." I9) and subconscious learning by the users ("when playing she could get around concepts she didn't get when I tried to teach directly. Especially angles and space, but also colors. She just got it by playing without noticing" I8).

4. Initial results - usability

All but one user recommended restructuring their training around the interactive dynamic additions, though both participants and instructors recommended using both types of training.

The interview and survey revealed that participants found the dynamic additions to be more enjoyable, less tiring and more efficient than the static training sessions. Nearly all participants reported that the main advantages of the dynamic session were in their increased feelings of control and independence ("In the dynamic sessions I can work by myself and make new shapes, the shapes that I want." P1, "The big advantage is the feedback I can interpret myself" P7) and enjoyment ("well, you know, the static is kind of boring. Not a lot of variance. The games are more challenging, more creative." P2. "It's just plain more fun." P3).

Instructors' replies mirrored those of the participants (verified by 2-tailed unpaired t-tests, corrected for multiple comparisons). They highlighted higher user engagement and independence ("It makes the training nicer for my participants; they become more active and engaged when they can move the shape themselves". I3 "the main difference between the two types of sessions is how involved, how much agency, the participant has.")

5. Conclusion & Future work

We found that that all participants were able to complete these tasks, utilize visual principles, reported a high level of enjoyment, satisfaction & preference for it and that they viewed these sessions as more effective. The participants highlighted an increased feeling of independence and control. Instructors were enthusiastic as well and highlighted its advantages in terms of flexibility.

This research is only a start in the direction of using structured interactive SSD training and is still far from a final training program. The next main steps are integrating more complex games, optimizing training based on the logged behavioral data from these sessions, comparatively exploring the effects of different games, and exploring generalization across different devices and visual rehabilitation approaches. Beyond training, another interesting aspect is the increase in accessibility of games in general via SSD. While the games presented here are relatively simple, participants saw the potential for future steps and made many suggestions for future games, with recurring requests for games that would enable practicing for the real world such as simulated environments of real-world locations.

6. REFERENCES

[1] Abboud, S., et al., EyeMusic: Introducing a "visual" colorful experience for the blind using auditory sensory substitution. Restorative neurology and neuroscience, 2014.

[2] Bach-y-Rita, P., Brain mechanisms in sensory substitution. 1972: academic Press.

[3] Maidenbaum, S., S. Abboud, and A. Amedi, Sensory substitution: Closing the gap between basic research and widespread practical visual rehabilitation. NBR, 2013.

[4] Meijer, P.B.L., An experimental system for auditory image representations. Biomedical Engineering, IEEE Transactions on, 1992. 39(2): p. 112-121.

[5] Rego, P., P.M. Moreira, and L.P. Reis. Serious games for rehabilitation: A survey and a classification towards a taxonomy. IEEE CISTI, 2010.

[6] Reynolds, Z. and B. Glenney, When Sensory Substitution Devices Strike Back: An Interactive Training Paradigm. Philosophy Study, 2012: p. 432.

[7] Waddington, J., et al., Participatory design of therapeutic video games for young people with neurological vision impairment. CHI 2015.

SlidePacer – Improving Class Pace for Deaf and Hard-of-Hearing Students

Alessandra Brandao
B. Thomas Golisano College of Computing and Information Sciences
Rochester Institute of Technology
Rochester, NY, USA
ard6573@rit.edu

ABSTRACT
Following multimedia lectures in mainstream classrooms in university education is challenging for deaf and hard-of-hearing (DHH) students even when they are provided accommodations to best address their individual needs. Due to multiple visual sources of information (teacher, slides, interpreter), these students struggle to divide their attention among several simultaneous sources of input, which may result in their missing important parts of the lecture content; as a result, DHH students' access to information can be limited in comparison to that of their hearing peers. This paper introduces SlidePacer, a tool aimed at improving coordination between the instructor's speech, the sign language interpretation of the lecture and the slide projection change. The goal of SlidePacer is to prevent DHH students' loss of information by promoting an adequate pace of the lecture, which can contribute to their learning and academic achievements.

Categories and Subject Descriptors
H.5.m [**Information Interfaces and Presentation**]: Miscellaneous. K4.2 [**Computers and Society**]: Social Issues – *Assistive technologies for persons with disabilities*.

Keywords
Deaf and Hard of Hearing; Learning; Pace; Lecture; Interpreter; Multimedia; Visual Sources; Presentation.

1. INTRODUCTION
The number of deaf and hard-of-hearing (DHH) college students has increased in the United States since the Individuals with Disabilities Education Act (Public Law 101-476) was announced in 1990 [7]. Classroom accommodations can provide DHH students the opportunity to follow the lectures, with access services consisting of sign language interpreters, captions, and/or note taking depending on a student's needs. Despite the availability of these services, DHH students still struggle to achieve an academic performance equal to that of their hearing peers [6]. One potential source of contribution to this struggle is that DHH must divide their attention between different sources of information in the classrooms (teacher, slides, blackboard, captions or interpreter). The students' switching of attention from one source of information to another may result in the loss of important content. As students move their eyes from one visual input to another, they arrive at the content (lecture, slides, captions, and interpreters) at different points, thus not getting a complete input message from any of the sources.

Not all instructors who use slides for their presentations are aware of the challenges DHH students face in mainstream classrooms, let alone of what could be done to help these students to better follow their lectures. The present work introduces SlidePacer as an assistive tool for those teachers that use PowerPoint slides in classes that have interpreters. As sign language interpreters must, of necessity, lag somewhat behind the lecturer, it is not uncommon for the interpreter and the slides to get out of sync. This has obvious potential for confusing deaf students and also means that the students will be unable to fully process the slides and/or interpreter if trying to visually process both at the same time. The goal of SlidePacer is to keep the pace of slide presentation in sync with that of the sign language interpreting so that DHH students will have time to process both forms of input.

In this paper, the SlidePacer software is introduced and a formative evaluation is presented. Future work, based on this evaluation, is outlined.

1.1 Related work
Previous research focused on assistive technologies for DHH students to manage multiple visual sources by integrating multiple views in a single screen or directing their attention to changes [2, 3, 4, 5]. However, students still have to integrate multiple visual sources of information, which overloads working memory and impacts their learning [1].

1.2 SlidePacer
SlidePacer has two parts: a) a PowerPoint add-in to be used by the instructor, and b) an Android application to be used by the interpreter. The instructor's computer and the interpreter's smartphone are connected by Bluetooth.

SlidePacer is designed so that throughout a lecture the instructor indicates the end of his or her presentation about each slide. This endpoint is indicated by the instructor pressing to advance to the next slide. The PowerPoint add-in communicates with the Android app, to signal to the interpreter that the presentation for the current slide is completed. The Android application has one screen with a big circular button that turns red (indicating to the interpreter that the instructor wants to change the slide and now is waiting for the interpretation to be finished).

When interpretation is finished, the interpreter taps the red button in the app and the student is given a few seconds to look at the next slide that will be projected only on the projection panel (not on the teacher's computer). Following this, the new slide will be

ASSETS '15, October 26-28, 2015, Lisbon, Portugal
ACM 978-1-4503-3400-6/15/10.
http://dx.doi.org/10.1145/2700648.2811325

visible on the teacher's screen as well, so he/she can continue speaking. The button on the Android app remains grey during slide transition, when the instructor is speaking, and during interpretation.

The SlidePacer workflow can be seen in Figure 1 that shows, from left to right: 1) Instructor changes the slide (but the slide in his computer will not be changed yet); 2) this change in 1 immediately makes the App with interpreter sign a red button; 3) interpreter finishes interpretation and taps the red button; the button turns grey waiting for the next cycle of change; 4) new content is shown on the projection panel for all students in the classroom so they can see the new slide for a set few seconds; 5) after these seconds, the slide in instructor screen is also changed; instructor starts speaking again, and instructor and students are in the same slide.

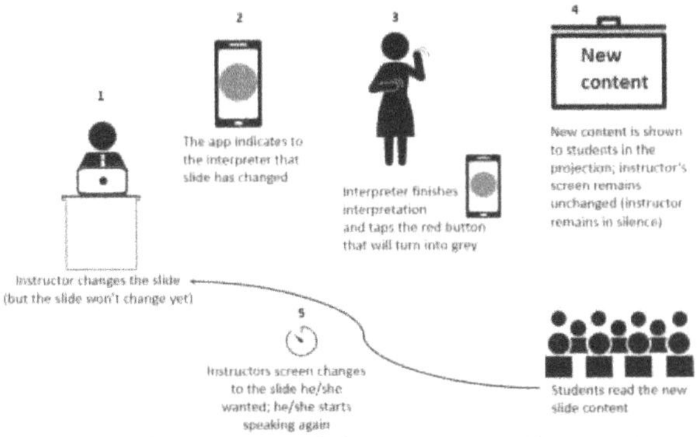

Figure 1 - SlidePacer - System workflow

2. EVALUATION

Prior to an experimental study, SlidePacer was informally shown (in separate sessions) to two instructors and three interpreters at the Rochester Institute of Technology (RIT):

2.1 Interpreters' feedback

During the session with the interpreters, the SlidePacer was shown in a mock-lecture setting with no students. All of them mentioned that adapting the pace in classrooms would definitely benefit DHH students. In addition, they agreed that SlidePacer could be advantageous to hearing students as well, since slides are sometimes dense or full of information. Considering the use of the app, the interpreters mentioned that their activity in classroom should be as unobtrusive as possible, and that the button in the app interface could be a source of distraction for the students. Therefore, investigations regarding the implementation of tactile SlidePacer feedback in a smart watch are currently underway.

2.2 Teachers' feedback

The two instructors that were presented in the instructor's session had prior experience in teaching both hearing and DHH students in their classes. However, these instructors have different class formats: one consistently uses PowerPoint and the other uses few slides since his classes are mostly based on group discussions. Both teachers agreed that SlidePacer might be beneficial to DHH students, but at the same time they mentioned that forcing a change of pace might interfere with the rhythm of the lecture and, hence, the instructors' flow of thoughts. One of the instructors, who has American Sign Language (ASL) skills, commented that he already tries to wait for the interpretation to finish before he changes slides since he knows the DHH students might lose information if he continues without them have finished watching the interpretation.

3. FUTURE WORK

This paper has presented the SlidePacer system, its workflow and the involved two groups of stakeholders that would interact with the system: teachers and interpreters. These stakeholders were generally positive of the goals, although did suggest some changes. We will use these changes to iteratively design and again evaluate SlidePacer with these stakeholders. In these future evaluations we aim i) to identify instructors' needs to be taken into account to better address their challenges when dealing with SlidePacer, and ii) to identify which improvements should be made to SlidePacer in order to render the interpreters' activity in classroom as unobtrusive as possible.

The ultimate test of the success of this SlidePacer, however, will be whether it improves learning for DHH students using sign language interpreters in a mainstream university environment. To this end, assuming supportive evaluations by instructors and interpreters, we will carry out an experimental study to measure lecture comprehension in classrooms with and without SlidePacer, considering participation of both hearing and DHH students. To be successful, SlidePacer will need to be easily accepted and used by both lecturer and interpreters, improve lecture comprehension for DHH students, and cause no decrements in learning for hearing students. Future work will tackle each of these issues.

4. ACKNOWLEDGMENTS

The author of this present paper would like to thank Dr. Vicki Hanson and Dr. Hugo Nicolau for their orientation and encouragement, and Shreya Tadas for her support. This study is sponsored by a start-up grant given to Dr. Hanson from RIT for the Center for Accessibility and Inclusion Research (CAIR). The author is also supported by CNPq (Conselho Nacional de Desenvolvimento Científico e Tecnológico – Brazil).

5. REFERENCES

[1] Ayres, P. and Sweller, J. 2005. The split-attention principle in multimedia learning. *The Cambridge handbook of multimedia learning*.

[2] Cavender, A.C. et al. 2009. ClassInFocus : Enabling Improved Visual Attention Strategies for Deaf and Hard of Hearing Students. (2009), 67–74.

[3] Kushalnagar, R.S. et al. 2010. Multiple View Perspectives: Improving Inclusiveness and Video Compression in Mainstream Classroom Recordings. *Proceedings of the 12th international ACM SIGACCESS conference on Computers and accessibility ASSETS 10*. (2010), 123–130.

[4] Kushalnagar, R.S. and Kushalnagar, P. 2014. Live and Collaborative Gaze Review for Deaf and Hard of Hearing Students. *International Conference on Computers Helping People*. (2014), 72–80.

[5] Lasecki, W.S. et al. 2014. Helping Students Keep Up with Real-Time Captions by Pausing and Highlighting. (2014).

[6] Marschark, M. et al. 2006. Classroom Interpreting and Visual Information Processing in Mainstream Education for Deaf Students: Live or Memorex? 42, 4 (2006), 727–761.

[7] Statistics, N.C. for E. 1999. *Integrated post-secondary education data system, Fall enrollment data file, Fall 1997*.

Sequential Gestural Passcodes on Google Glass

Abdullah Ali
University of Maryland Baltimore County
aal6@umbc.edu

ABSTRACT

This paper details an authentication mechanism aimed to aid individuals with visual impairments in accessing online accounts on desktop computers, and decrease the security threat of observers, or shoulder surfer, by providing an alternative to entering typical alphanumeric passwords on keyboards. The mechanism uses a head-mounted wearable device, Google Glass, because it provides feedback directly to the wearer obscuring it from observers, and it's easy-to-locate and interact with gesture pad, which accepts input from the user. The mechanism is in preparation to enter the testing phase with individuals of the targeted demographic.

Categories and Subject Descriptors

D.4.6 [**Security and Protection**]: Security and Protection – *Access Controls, Authentication, and Verification*

General Terms

Human Factors, Authentication

Keywords

Authentication, Visual Impairments, Wearable Computing, Gesture Interaction, Security

1. INTRODUCTION

Self-authentication through the use of a username and password combination is regularly needed to access online accounts such as emails, banking, or shopping. This process requires a user to memorize alphanumeric passwords, which can be stressful. People with visual impairments face added difficulties when entering alphanumeric passwords because of issues surrounding the use of screen readers while filling out log-in forms [1].

Many computer users, not only individuals with visual impairments, are under security threats when accessing online accounts. Such threats include shoulder surfing, the act of observers viewing password entry to gain unauthorized access to a target's online account. In addition to security threats, strong alphanumeric passwords that are hard to guess by others are also hard to memorize for the users themselves.

We developed this mechanism in aims to provide an assertive tool to aid individuals with visual impairments in the process of accessing online accounts, such as emails, on desktop computers without the fear of shoulder surfers. For this mechanism we used Google Glass because its form factor allows for the ability to provide complete personal feedback obscured from onlookers such as audio played directly into the user's ear via Google Glass's earpiece. Our mechanism uses the same wearable device to work with multiple computers, which creates an opportunity for a universal authentication method for multiple online accounts that can be used with multiple desktop computers.

ASSETS '15, October 26-28, 2015, Lisbon, Portugal
ACM 978-1-4503-3400-6/15/10.
http://dx.doi.org/10.1145/2700648.2811326

2. RELATED WORK

In order to address authentication difficulties, researchers have developed alternative authentication methods. Kuber et al. used tactile authentication for individuals with vision impairments [1] to improved security against shoulder surfers, but their system requires the use of a mouse which was problematic with individuals with visual impairments. A different alternative for traditional alphanumeric passwords was developed by Wobbrock, who used sequence passcodes to authenticate users by using a single binary sensor that accepts a sequence of taps and using it as a passcode [5].

Google Glass is a versatile device with many sensors, input, and output methods; it has been used as an assistive device in past research. For example, Kiryong Ha et al. used Google Glass to aid individuals with cognitive decline by using Google Glass's camera to capture a video feed, analyze it, and provide in-Glass feedback such as face and object recognition [2]. In a similar manner, Anam et al. used Google Glass to help individuals with visual impairments interpret non-verbal cues during face-to-face conversation by capitalizing on the in-ear auditory feedback [3].

Google Glass has also been used for authentication purposes. Bailey et al. used Google Glass while proposing a shift away from traditional passwords suggesting that Google Glass is immune to shoulder surfers [4]. They used Google Glass as an augmented reality device and relied heavily on the screen as an output method, which is not accessible to individuals with visual impairments.

3. PROTOTYPE DESIGN

Our prototype provides a universal authentication mechanism for multiple online accounts. It can be accessed easily on a wearable device, and can be used with multiple computer systems. Our prototype has three components: 1) A Google Glass application 2) A web server 3) A browser extension. Google Glass's multi-touch pad is used to capture a sequence of directional gestures, and then store and use that sequence to authenticate the user. The web server handles communication between the Google Glass application and the browser extension. It also stores passwords of the user's online account. The browser extension detects password fields on login pages and fills them with the user's passwords.

3.1 Interactions in our Glass Application

Our Google Glass application can be launched in one of two ways. Either, by navigating through the applications available on the device selecting it using the touchpad on the side of the device, or it can be launched using voice command. Once a user launches the application, they are presented with two options: 1) Swipe forward to set passcode 2) Swipe back to authenticate. The options are displayed on Glass's heads-up display and are played as an audio recording directly into the user's ear through Google Glass's earpiece. During the set-up process the user is asked to enter directional gestures, or swipes. These can be forward, back,

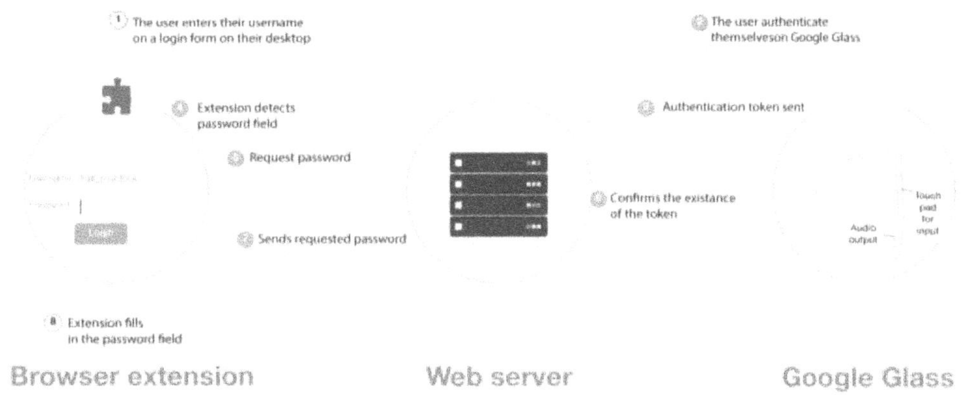

Figure 1. A diagram showing the flow of interactions in the mechanism

up, or down in any sequence or combination. The sequence in which these gestures are performed will be stored as a passcode,which these gestures are performed will be stored as a passcode, Using directional gestures identical to the gestures used for navigating the menus of Google Glass is done in an attempt of increasing the ambiguity of the authentication process making it harder for observers to steal the passcodes. Once the user is done creating their passcode, it is stored locally on the device for later use. The authentication process is accessed from the main menu by swiping back. The user is promoted via audio feedback to enter the sequence of gestures to authenticate themselves. Based on their entry they are either promoted to try again, or are presented with a message informing them of the successful authentication. A successful authentication sends a message to the web server part of the system to create a one-time-use token of authentication.

3.2 Web Server

The web server part of the system holds a list of account URLs and passwords. It also listens for messages coming from the Google Glass application informing it to create a one-time-use token of authentication. The server listens to messages coming from the web browser extension asking to retrieve a specific password from the list of URLs and passwords stored on the server. The retrieval of the password is only possible if an authentication token exists. Upon the retrieval of the password the token is promptly destroyed.

3.3 Web Browser Extension

The extension allows the user to add URLs of sites and the passwords of their accounts on those sites to be saved on the web server .The browser extension is able to detect when a password input field is currently active on a web page. Once the field is detected, the extension asynchronously checks the web server for the existence of a one-time-use token. If a token exists, the extension requests the password paired to the URL of the current page to be sent. Once the password is received from the web server, the extension fills the password field promoting the web server to destroy the token.

4. ONGOING WORK

Further development of the system is underway for improved stability and resolving bug issues. The next phase of the project is to start evaluating the system with a number of individuals with visual impairments over a period of time, possibly weeks, to test the viability of such a system for daily use. This is proposed to be done by distributing Google Glass to participants and asking them to use it for authenticating themselves on both their home and their work, or school computers. Participants will provide usability feedback on regular basis by filling out an online form, possibly once a week, and they will go through an introductory and exit interviews.

5. REFERENCES

1. Ravi Kuber and Shiva Sharma. 2010. Toward tactile authentication for blind users. In Proceedings of the 12th international ACM SIGACCESS conference on Computers and accessibility (ASSETS '10). ACM, New York, NY, USA, 289-290.
2. Kiryong Ha, Zhuo Chen, Wenlu Hu, Wolfgang Richter, Padmanabhan Pillai, and Mahadev Satyanarayanan. 2014. Towards wearable cognitive assistance. In Proceedings of the 12th annual international conference on Mobile systems, applications, and services (MobiSys '14). ACM, New York, NY, USA, 68-81.
3. Asm Iftekhar Anam, Shahinur Alam, and Mohammed Yeasin. 2014. Expression: a dyadic conversation aid using Google Glass for people with visual impairments. In Proceedings of the 2014 ACM International Joint Conference on Pervasive and Ubiquitous Computing: Adjunct Publication (UbiComp '14 Adjunct). ACM, New York, NY, USA, 211-214.
4. Yadav, Dhruv Kumar, Beatrice Ionascu, Sai Vamsi Krishna Ongole, Aditi Roy, and Nasir Memon. "Design and Analysis of Shoulder Surfing Resistant PIN based Authentication Mechanisms on Google Glass."
5. Jacob Otto Wobbrock. 2009. TapSongs: tapping rhythm-based passwords on a single binary sensor. In Proceedings of the 22nd annual ACM symposium on User interface software and technology (UIST '09). ACM, New York, NY, USA, 93-96.

Talkabel: A Labeling Method for 3D Printed Models

Lei Shi
Jacobs Technion-Cornell Institute
Cornell Tech
New York, NY
ls776@cornell.edu

ABSTRACT
Three-dimensional printed models are important learning tools for blind people. Unlike tactile graphics, there is no standard accessible way to label these models. We present *Talkabel*, a labeling method that enables blind people to access information in a model by simply tapping tactile markers that can be added almost anywhere on the model. We use a mobile phone that is propped on an attached scaffold to detect and classify the user's taps and then speak the appropriate label. We evaluated the feasibility of Talkabel with four 3D printed models, and our results showed that Talkabel could be implemented quickly and maintained a high accuracy with different models. We conclude with future work.

Categories and Subject Descriptors
H.5.2 [**Information Interfaces and Presentation**]: User Interfaces - Input devices and strategies.

Keywords
Labels, acoustic sensing, 3D models, visual impairments

1. INTRODUCTION
Three-dimensional models are important alternative tools to visual graphics for blind people. Visualizations are widely used in education to enhance learning and are commonly made accessible to blind people using tactile graphics and 3D models. 3D models are especially useful in presenting complex information like the structure of molecules and the scale of the Solar System [2]. Recent, modern consumer-grade 3D printing technology has begun to empower teachers, friends, and makers to create custom 3D models to enhance accessibility [3,4].

While 3D printed models can improve accessibility in education, there is no standard way to make accessible labels for models. Without labels, blind people can only perceive information through the shape and texture of a model; they must rely on someone's help or additional tools. Textual information for commercial 3D models (such as globes) is presented with standard visual labels that are inaccessible to blind people and difficult to make with consumer-grade 3D printers. Prior work on tactile graphics has explored several accessible labeling methods, but they have major limitations when applied to 3D printed models. In tactile graphics, labels are commonly represented in Braille, which is bulky and can only be read by less than forty percent of the functionally blind population in the United States [6]. Besides Braille, Baker *et al.* [1] presented a method where label information was presented in QR codes on a tactile graphic. However, both techniques would be difficult to implement directly on 3D printed models with complex spatial structures. Kolitsky presented a labeling method for 3D printed models that involved integrating additional electronics like sensors and circuits, which can speak labels when touched [5]. However, this largely increases the cost of the models. We believe that labels should be easy to make, easy to access, and cost-efficient.

ASSETS '15, October 26-28, 2015, Lisbon, Portugal
ACM 978-1-4503-3400-6/15/10.
http://dx.doi.org/10.1145/2700648.2811327

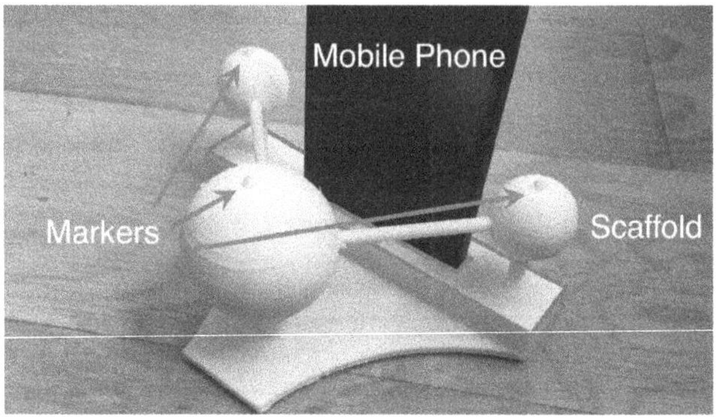

Figure 1. A model with Talkabel labels. It has three markers (red) showing label locations and a scaffold (blue) supporting a mobile phone that speaks the labels when they are tapped.

To address these criteria, we designed *Talkabel*, a labeling method that allows blind people to access label information by directly touching 3D printed models. Talkabel involves a mobile phone application and simple auxiliary components like markers and a scaffold (Figure 1). To access label information, a user places her phone in the scaffold and taps the markers on the model. The mobile phone application captures the acoustic signals produced by the tap with its microphone and classifies the signal to determine which marker was tapped. The phone then speaks the corresponding label information. To add label information to a model, a maker adds the auxiliary components to a 3D model and uses the application to record label information for each marker while tapping it.

In this paper, we describe (1) the design of the auxiliary components, and (2) the Talkabel detection and classification algorithm, which determines which marker the user taps with acoustic signals. We conducted a preliminary evaluation of the algorithm with four 3D printed models. Our results showed that our labeling method could achieve high performance after minimal training, and was reliable for different models.

2. AUXILIARY COMPONENTS
The auxiliary components consist of markers and a scaffold (Figure 1). A marker is a little tactile semi-sphere that represents a

label and indicates where users should tap while the scaffold stabilizes the mobile phone in a fixed position. A layperson can easily add these components to an existing model by adding our templates in any 3D modeling software, and printing them out along with the model.

3. ALGORITHM

Talkabel's algorithm comprises of two phases: (1) detecting a tap and (2) classifying the detected tap as one of the model's markers. The tap detection phase processes the data stream captured by a microphone and outputs the segment of the stream that corresponds to a tap. After this, the classification phase classifies the tap signal and outputs which marker was tapped.

The system uses the moving average of the acoustic signals' energy to detect a tap in the data stream. To do this, the algorithm calculates the Root Mean Square (RMS) (which represents the energy of the signal) over a moving window of data points in the stream. The algorithm then compares the RMS to a threshold (TH). If the value of the RMS is greater than TH for 0.002s, the algorithm regards these points as the start of a tap and sends the following 0.1s of data to the classifier.

We used the nearest neighbor classifier, which classifies signals based on the closest training example in the feature space. The classifier uses the components of the amplitude spectrum density (ASD) [7] of the tap signal as classification features. The ASD represents the energy distribution of the signal over different frequencies, and is calculated using a Fast Fourier Transform (FFT). Our preliminary results showed that including high-frequency ASD components had a negative effect on classification accuracy, so we only include components in a frequency range of 0 to 4800 Hz.

4. FEASIBILITY EVALUATION

The first step towards developing Talkabel was to test its feasibility of the marker classification algorithm and explore how factors like the number of training samples and the layout of models influence its performance.

4.1 Procedure

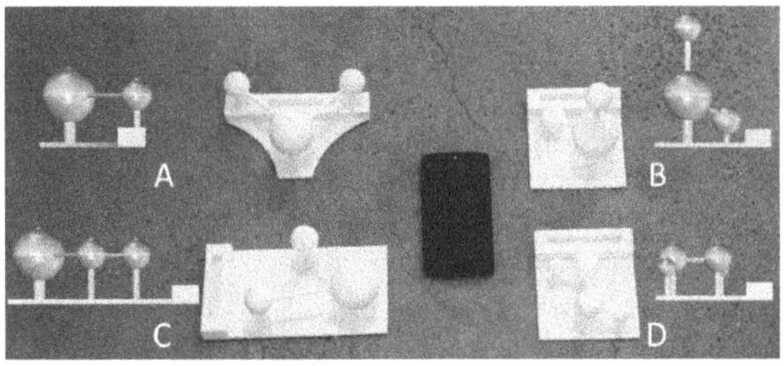

Figure 2. Four 3D printed models with a Nexus 5. The right views of the models are marked in grey.

We printed four versions of a molecule model (Figure 2). We chose a model with spheres because they are common in 3D models (*e.g.,* chemical and astronomical models). Each model has a unique layout: the three spheres in Model A are approximately equidistant to the center of the scaffold where the microphone will be placed; the spheres in Model C have different distances from the microphones; two spheres in Model B share one support pillar; and Model D has four small spheres.

We placed each model on a wooden table in an open-plan office environment and recorded the acoustic signals while tapping on the markers of the model. We used the bottom microphone of a Nexus 5 and recorded audio at a 48 kHz sampling rate. For each model, we recorded a total of 50 samples.

We performed offline classification with different numbers of training samples per marker. We evaluated classification accuracy with cross-validation.

4.2 Results and Analysis

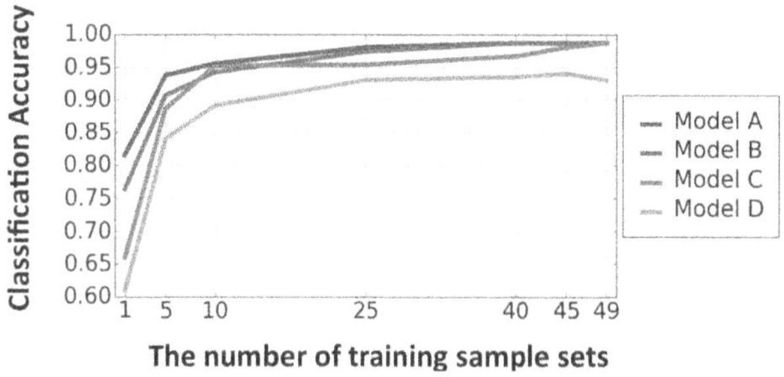

Figure 3. Offline cross-validation results

We plotted our results in Figure 3. For all models, Talkabel achieved a classification accuracy of over 83 percent with only 5 training samples per marker. A stable performance of 93 percent was reached with 25 training samples per marker. These results indicated that the method is promising because (1) the labels can potentially be accessed with high accuracy, and (2) model markers can potentially add labels fairly quickly. Talkabel performed similarly on Model A, Model B, and Model C, which also showed that our labeling method was reliable with different marker layouts. The classification accuracy of model D was slightly lower than the other models. This is likely due to the model's additional marker, but also to the smaller distances between the markers.

5. FUTURE WORK

We will improve the performance of Talkabel by modifying the structure of the scaffold to improve the quality of the acoustic signal. To continue developing Talkabel, we will design and evaluate a smartphone application that will enable markers to create labeled models and allow blind people to access the labels in those models.

6. REFERENCES

[1] Baker, C. M. *et al.* Tactile graphics with a voice: Using QR codes to access text in tactile graphics. *ASSETS'14.*

[2] Beck-Winchatz, B. *et al.* Using asteroid scale models in space science education for blind and visually impaired students. Astronomy Education Review (2003).

[3] Buehler, E. *et al.* Sharing is Caring: Assistive Technology Designs on Thingiverse. *CHI'15.*

[4] Buehler, E. *et al.* ABC and 3D: opportunities and obstacles to 3D printing in special education environments. *ASSETS'14.*

[5] Instructables, Making Tactile 3D Prints Talk. http://www.instructables.com/id/Making-Tactile-3D-Prints-Talk/, Accessed on June 25th, 2015

[6] The Braille Literacy Crisis in America: Facing the Truth, Reversing the Trend, Empowering the Blind. A Report to the Nation by the National Federation of the Blind (2009).

[7] Wang, J. *et al.* Ubiquitous keyboard for small mobile devices: harnessing multipath fading for fine-grained keystroke localization. *MobiSys'14.*

Haptic Gloves Prototype for Audio-Tactile Web Browsing

Andrii Soviak
Department of Computer Science, Stony Brook University, Stony Brook, USA
asoviak@cs.stonybrook.edu

ABSTRACT

Blind people rely on screen readers to interact with the Web. Since screen readers narrate the digital content serially, blind users can only form a one-dimensional mental model of the web page and, hence, cannot enjoy the benefits inherently offered by the 2-D layout; e.g., understanding the spatial relations between objects in a webpage or their locations on the screen helps navigate webpages. Haptic interfaces could provide blind people with a tactile "feel" for the 2-D layout and help them navigate web pages more efficiently. *Haptic Displays,* capable of high resolution tactile feedback, could render any webpage in a tactile form enabling blind people to exploit the aforementioned spatial relations and focus screen reading on specific parts of the webpage. In this paper, I report on the preliminary work toward the development of FeelX – a haptic gloves system that will enable tactile web browsing. FeelX will be used alongside regular screen readers, and will provide blind screen-reader users with the ability explore web pages by touch and audio.

Categories and Subject Descriptors

H.5.2 [**Information interfaces and presentation**]: User Interfaces - *ergonomics, interaction styles, haptic I/O, prototyping*

General Terms

Design, Performance, Experimentation, Human Factors

Keywords

Tactile interface; haptic glove; screen reader; blindness; wearable

1. INTRODUCTION

The Web has permeated many aspects of our lives and has become essential for connecting with others, obtaining information, shopping, banking, participating in civic activities, making travel arrangements, applying for college or employment, etc. While we all benefit from these online services, their utility is even greater for blind people who once required human assistance with most of these simple activities, and who can now use assistive technology to do them independently on the Web [9].

Unfortunately, while becoming more interactive and functional, web pages have also evolved from simple text files into web applications with sophisticated layouts. Due to the complexity of web applications and limitations of the assistive technology, blind people often struggle with web browsing and spend an excessive amount of time while doing simple tasks online [2].

Haptic Displays, capable of high-resolution tactile feedback, could render any webpage in tactile form. When augmented with screen readers, such displays could facilitate a more efficient navigation of webpages by exploiting the spatial information and focusing screen reading on specific regions of interest. Thus haptic feedback has the potential of significantly improving productivity and usability of non-visual web browsing.

ASSETS'15, October 26–28, 2015, Lisbon, Portugal.
ACM 978-1-4503-3400-6/15/10.
DOI: http://dx.doi.org/10.1145/2700648.2811329

2. RELATED WORK

There exist a number of **haptic display** prototypes: displays with electro-vibration feedback [1, 7] that can give a feeling of varying friction to a *single moving* finger; surfaces with temperature-sensitive hydrogel [6], which are slow and have no input interface or even a real screen; soft flexible displays with magnetorheological fluid actuated by an array of electromagnets to create different tactile sensations, but with low resolution [3], and others. An interested approach was proposed by Tactus Technology, which developed Phorm [8], a transparent tactile case for iPad that uses microfluids to raise the surface of the case and make a tactile keyboard dynamically appear within seconds.

A few haptic displays have been created specifically for accessibility purposes. A handscope device [4] translates numbers, such as five-star rating in websites, into simple height changes of its haptic pole; while it is good for rendering numerical values, the feedback is, unfortunately, one-dimensional. Although a number of haptic devices have been proposed, none could really render web pages with high resolution and low latency.

Perhaps the most relevant haptic technology is the pin-matrix devices [10] that can raise mechanical pins to form a tactile picture (but no touch input), but they are small, have very limited resolution (e.g., 120x60 BrailleDis9000), and are very expensive.

Hence, I propose to develop *FeelX*, a haptic gloves system which will enable tactile web browsing on any flat surface such as the desk or table. The FeelX system will be much cheaper than pin-matrix displays because they it will have fewer components, and it will also help overcome the size limitation since a larger work area will allow for bigger tactile objects and more spacing between them. The gloves will be used alongside regular screen readers with audio feedback, but the gloves will provide users with more ways to interact with web pages, explore web pages faster, and find and process web-based information efficiently.

A variety of **haptic glove** designs have been proposed in research literature, however, the majority of haptic gloves focus on virtual reality scenarios and give users the feeling of resistance and touch, when they grab virtual objects. Simple gloves have been proposed for accessibility, e.g., [5] describes a glove, which could enable navigation along the plot displayed on the touch screen. A pager motor is placed on the tip of each finger and the motors are used to indicate the direction in which the hand should move. The setup only provides a single tactile dot per finger. Alas, none of the existing gloves can be used in the proposed Project.

3. PRELIMINARY RESULTS

FeelX, whose architecture is presented in Figure 1, is composed of several components the Camera, Finger Tracker, Controller, Haptic Gloves, and Interface Manager. The Manager interacts with standard screen readers and web browsers via a browser Plug-In. The Camera, set up over the table, sends a live video feed of the gloves to the Finger Tracker, which uses a standard computer vision algorithm to resolve the $(X,Y)_i$ coordinates for each finger *i*, and sends the coordinates to the Interface Manager.

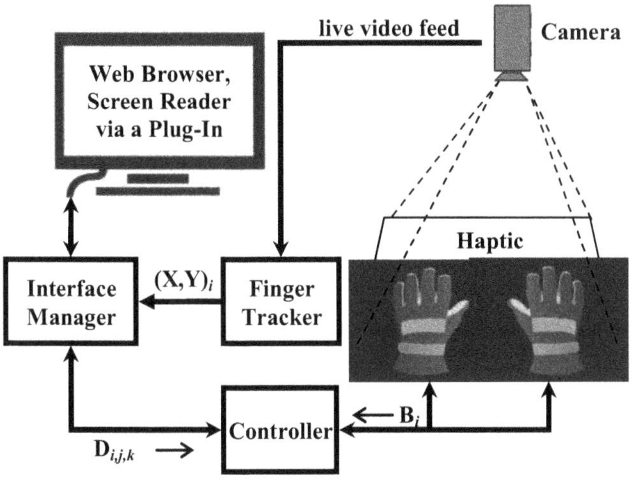

Figure 1 – The Architecture of FeelX

Via a browser Plug-In, the Interface Manager obtains geometric layout and content of web pages and maps the $(X,Y)_i$ finger coordinates to the browser screen coordinates. As needed, the Interface Manager, again via the Plug-In, triggers the Screen Reader to narrate specific content. The Interface Manager outputs haptic instructions that are sent via the Controller to the haptic gloves in the form of $D_{i,j,k}$, where (j,k) are the row and column of a tactile "dot" rendered on finger *i*. Each finger in the glove (other than the thumb) is equipped with haptic hardware unit capable of rendering a tactile matrix of size *j* by *k* on the finger. Each finger will also have a pressure sensor (button) that will send a signal B_i for finger *i* to the Interface Manager if the button is activated.

To enable the user to "feel" web content, I use Braille cells that render a 2x4 tactile grid to each finger with tactile "dots" spaced 2.5mm apart. The tactile matrix touches the pad of the Distal Phalanx, which is the most sensitive part of a human finger. Via the Controller, that is supplied with the Braille cells, I can activating different combinations of tactile dots, the gloves could render both Braille characters and simple shapes, such as lines and boxes which works great for navigating websites, most of which are typically styled into rectangular sections.

Finger tracking is required to identify the positions of fingers. Finger tracking is a well-studied field offering many approaches to identifying finger positions. In [11], a glove is outfitted with two infrared light-emitting diodes (LEDs) which are tracked by a camera. One light is placed on the tip of the pointing finger, and the other – on the top of the hand, enabling to recognize only simple gestures. In developing the glove, I also used infrared LEDs; however, to keep track of and distinguish between fingers as well as their pointing directions, I have placed a LED on the tip of each finger and in the middle of the finger. I used an off-the-shelf OpenCV computer vision library to identify finger positions captured by a regular web cam, which I converted into an infrared camera simply by removing the infrared filter.

4. CONCLUSION

The proposed gloves will help blind people quickly explore web-based information via touch, focus on what they need to read, and thus they will have the potential of reducing the cognitive load associated with web browsing. In contrast to pin matrix displays, the gloves will use few fewer Braille cells and thus will be significantly cheaper and more portable, while at the same time enabling a much larger tactile area limited only by the camera view angle and the area on the table the user can reach.

From the research perspective, the gloves will enable me as well as other researchers to conduct user studies to experiment with haptic feedback, different ways of representing content in tactile form, observe tactile behaviors of blind users, etc. From the practical perspective, haptic gloves have the potential of making the Web much more accessible for blind people, thus enabling them to participate fully in our Internet-based society.

5. REFERENCES

[1] Bau, O., I. Poupyrev, A. Israr, and C. Harrison, *TeslaTouch: electrovibration for touch surfaces*, in *Proceedings of the 23nd annual ACM symposium on User interface software and technology*. 2010, ACM: New York, New York, USA. p. 283-292.

[2] Borodin, Y., J.P. Bigham, G. Dausch, and I.V. Ramakrishnan, *More than meets the eye: a survey of screen-reader browsing strategies*, in *Proceedings of the 2010 International Cross Disciplinary Conference on Web Accessibility (W4A)*. 2010, ACM: Raleigh, North Carolina. p. 1-10.

[3] Jansen, Y., T. Karrer, and J. Borchers, *MudPad: tactile feedback and haptic texture overlay for touch surfaces*, in *ACM International Conference on Interactive Tabletops and Surfaces*. 2010, ACM: Saarbrücken, Germany. p. 11-14.

[4] Kim, D.-j. and Y.-k. Lim. *Handscope: enabling blind people to experience statistical graphics on websites through haptics*. in *Proceedings of the SIGCHI Conference on Human Factors in Computing Systems*. 2011: ACM.

[5] Manshad, M.S. and A.S. Manshad, *Multimodal vision glove for touchscreens*, in *Proceedings of the 10th international ACM SIGACCESS conference on Computers and accessibility*. 2008, ACM: Halifax, Nova Scotia, Canada. p. 251-252.

[6] Richter, A. and G. Paschew, *Optoelectrothermic Control of Highly Integrated Polymer-Based MEMS Applied in an Artificial Skin*. Advanced Materials, 2009. **21**(9): p. 979-983.

[7] Senseg. *Senseg's Tixel Technology*. 2011; Available from: http://senseg.com/technology/senseg-technology.

[8] TactusTechnology. *Phorm Case for iPad*. 2015; Available from: http://www.getphorm.com/.

[9] Thatcher, J., M. Burks, C. Heilmann, S. Henry, A. Kirkpatrick, P. Lauke, B. Lawson, B. Regan, R. Rutter, M. Urban, and C. Waddell, *Understanding Web Accessibility*. 2006, Apress. p. 1-51.

[10] Völkel, T., G. Weber, and U. Baumann, *Tactile Graphics Revised: The Novel BrailleDis 9000 Pin-Matrix Device with Multitouch Input Computers Helping People with Special Needs*, K. Miesenberger, et al., Editors. 2008, Springer Berlin / Heidelberg. p. 835-842.

[11] Williams, R.C. *Finger tracking and gesture interfacing using the Nintendo® wiimote*. in *Proceedings of the 48th Annual Southeast Regional Conference*. 2010: ACM.

Exploring New Paradigms for Accessible 3D Printed Graphs

Michele Hu
Macaulay Honors College
City University of New York
New York, NY
michele.hu@macaulay.cuny.edu

ABSTRACT

We explore new paradigms of representing bar graphs with 3D printing technology. Our goal is to make graphs more accessible to blind people. We co-designed with one blind participant and two teachers for the visually impaired (TVI) to refine our paradigms and created prototypes of bar graphs of varying levels of complexity with each paradigm. The paradigms we developed include: embossed graphs that are similar to traditional tactile graphics, freestanding graphs with guidelines connecting bars to the y-axis, and freestanding graphs with tick marks on each bar. We developed prototypes of a bar graph displaying one dataset, and a bar graph displaying two datasets.

Categories and Subject Descriptors

H.5.2 [**Information Interfaces and Presentation**]: **User Interfaces** – input devices and strategies. K.4.2 [Computer and Society]: Social Issues - Assistive technologies for persons with disabilities.

Keywords

Blind; accessibility; tactile graphics; 3D printing

1. INTRODUCTION

Tactile graphics are important accessibility tools for blind people, especially in STEM fields, where students need access to different visualizations to understand certain concepts. For many years, tactile graphics were created using swell paper, embossers, and thermoform to create raised lines and textures on a flat surface [3]. Recently, 3D printers have emerged as a promising alternative to create accessible tactile graphics.

Several research efforts have led us to believe that 3D models of visualizations may be more effective at conveying information to blind people than currently used tactile graphics. Jansen *et al.* [2] compared physical visualizations to on-screen images of 3D bar graphs. In a study with 16 participants, they found that people perceived more data from the physical visualizations than the on-screen images. More recently, researchers have developed physically dynamic bar charts that allow sighted users to manipulate data points to create different 3D bar graphs [6]. Both efforts involved visualizations designed for sighted people that were not necessarily accessible. Brown and Hurst [1] created accessible 3D printed tactile models of line graphs for blind people by using raised lines of different heights. While Brown and Hurst used raised lines similar to traditional tactile graphics, Kalia *et al.* found that people explored cutout shapes more globally, allowing them to better acquire graphical information from the cutouts as opposed to their embossed models [4]. Perhaps raised line representations of visualizations are not the most effective approach to representing accessible visualizations.

ASSETS '15, October 26-28, 2015, Lisbon, Portugal
ACM 978-1-4503-3400-6/15/10.
http://dx.doi.org/10.1145/2700648.2811330

In our research, we explore different paradigms for representing accessible bar graphs using 3D printing technology. We focus on bar graphs because they are a common type of visualization, and explore paradigms for representing three types of bar graphs: graphs with a single color, and graphs with multiple colors. We explored different ways of presenting the y-axis, creating and using textures, and adding labels. We co-designed the bar graph paradigms with two teachers for the visually impaired (TVI's) and one blind professional. In this paper, we describe our design process and the latest models, which we plan to evaluate with blind students in the future.

2. FORMATIVE WORK AND PARADIGMS

Prior work on 3D printed graphs [1] focused on line graphs, so we wanted to explore other kinds of graphs as well. According to the New York State P-12 Common Core Learning Standards for Mathematics [5] bar graphs and line graphs were the most common types of graphs. We thus decided to focus our work on bar graphs. Looking through dozens of Common Core worksheets, we concluded that questions about bar graphs typically involved determining (1) trends and (2) the y-value of certain bars. To enable blind people to better perceive the trend in a graph, we decided to explore freestanding graphs. Meanwhile, to improve access to y-values, we developed several paradigms and prototyped versions of a simple bar chart.

1. *Embossed:* 3D printed embossed tactile graph that represents the traditional method blind use to read graphs, making it a good standard to compare the other paradigms to.
2. *Freestanding with braille labels on top*: Braille index on the top of each bar to represent its y-value. As common in tactile graphics, the braille index maps to a table of braille labels.
3. *Freestanding with guidelines:* Guidelines run from the top of each bar to their respective values on the y-axis. The guidelines resemble gridlines in tactile graphics, which help users connect the top of the bar to the y-axis.
4. *Freestanding with tick marks:* Tick marks projected onto the bars, allowing users to determine bar values by directly touching each bar and enabling easier comparison among the bars.

3. CO-DESIGN PROCESS

3.1 Procedure

We co-designed the paradigms with two female sighted teachers for the visually impaired (TVI's), who we'll call Catherine and Amy, and one female blind professional, who we'll call Louise.

One of the TVIs had 4 years of experience and the other had 30 years, both teaching in the Vancouver school district.

We conducted two videoconferences with Catherine and Amy, where we showed them our initial prototypes. We asked about their experience and process of creating tactile graphs and what challenges they faced. We discussed properties of graphs that they emphasized when teaching students how to read paper-based tactile graphs and possible ways of conveying those properties with different 3D paradigms.

We met with the Louise in person and showed her the early prototypes of the graphs. The blind professional is an assistive technology coordinator and instructor. We asked her about her experience with tactile graphs and 3D models, her impression of the prototypes, and design ideas for creating new or improving the existing paradigms.

3.2 Findings

We summarized the feedback and suggestions from our co-designers below.

Exploring more complex graphs. Our co-designers were concerned that the bar graph we chose to model was too simple, and that an embossed version would present the information just as well. They suggested exploring the paradigms with examples of more complex graphs, especially those that are difficult to transform into tactile graphs with an embosser, like bar graphs with multiple colors.

Incorporating textures. The co-designers emphasized the use of texture because it is the most valuable property to a student when distinguishing among different datasets. Catherine and Amy suggested using textures made of dots and lines, which they claimed were the easiest for blind students to distinguish.

Requiring standard graph interpretation skills. Louise felt strongly that blind students should use and develop interpretative skills when interacting with the graphs. Placing the y-value of a bar on top of the bar would not enable students to develop these skills. However, she supported the "braille label on top" if it were used as additional assistance for students who were just learning how to interpret graphs.

Using tick marks on bars. Our co-designers all agreed that tick marks on the bars of a graph could make interpreting the graph easier. They thought it would be convenient to access the y-value of a bar by only touching the bar itself. When we handed Louise the prototype for this paradigm, she understood the concept immediately, suggesting it was easy to learn and interpret.

4. REVISED PARADIGMS & PROTOTYPES

Based on the co-designers' suggestions, we removed Paradigm 2 ("braille label on top") and explored ways of representing more complex graphs with the other three paradigms. We explored three kinds of graphs in increasing level of complexity: bar graphs with a single dataset (like our original prototype), bar graphs with two datasets (typically represented visually with bars of different colors), and bar graphs with a 2D array of bars. We describe how we present each type of bar graph with each paradigm.

1. *Embossed*: We created embossed models of single (figure 1a) and double (figure 1b) bar graphs, using raised lines for bar outlines, gridlines, and axes, and line and dot textures for different datasets.
2. *Freestanding with guidelines:* Freestanding graphs of a single (figure 2a) and double (figure 2b) bar graph with guidelines running from the top of the bar to their respective y-value on the y-axis. Line and dot textures were placed on the backs of the bars in the double bar graph to represent different datasets.
3. *Freestanding with tick marks:* Freestanding graphs of single (figure 3a) and double (figure 3b) bar graphs with tick marks projected onto the front of each of the bars. Double bar graphs had line and dot textures placed on the backs of the bars to differentiate between datasets.

Figure 1: (a) embossed version of a single bar graph and (b) embossed version of a double bar graph

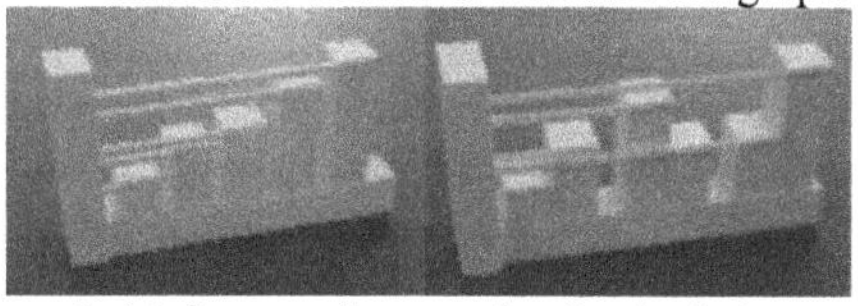

Figure 2: (a) freestanding graph of a single bar graph with guidelines and (b) freestanding graph of a double bar graph with guidelines.

Figure 3: (a) freestanding graph of a single bar graph with tick marks (texture not visible) and (b) freestanding graph of a double bar graph with tick marks (tick marks not visible).

5. CONCLUSION & FUTURE WORK

We explored several novel paradigms for representing bar graphs in an accessible format with 3D printing technology. Through a process of co-design with two TVIs and one blind professional, we created prototypes of bar graphs in each of three paradigms. In the future, we will conduct a study with blind people to evaluate their ability to access information from models with different paradigms and complexities. We want to incorporate the most effective paradigms into a movable bar that allows a blind person to independently create a graph using their own data points.

REFERENCES

1. Brown, C., & Hurst, A. (2012). VizTouch: automatically generated tactile visualizations of coordinate spaces. *Proc. TEI '12*. ACM.
2. Jansen, Y., *et al.* (2013). *Evaluating the efficiency of physical visualizations*. *Proc. CHI'13*. ACM.
3. Ladner, R. E., *et al.* (2005). *Automating tactile graphics translation*. *Proc. ASSETS'05*. ACM.
4. Kalia, A., Hopkins, R., Jin, D., *et al.* (2014). Perception of Tactile Graphics: Embossings Versus Cutouts. *Multisensory research*, *27*(2), 111-125.
5. National Governors Association Center for Best Practices & Council of Chief State School Officers. (2010). *Common Core State Standards for Mathematics*. Washington, DC.
6. Taher, F., Hardy, J., Karnik, A., Weichel, C., Jansen, Y., Hornbæk, K., & Alexander, J. (2015, April). Exploring interactions with physically dynamic bar charts. *Proc. CHI'15*. ACM.

The Effects of Automatic Speech Recognition Quality on Human Transcription Latency

Yashesh Gaur
Carnegie Mellon University
5000 Forbes Avenue
Pittsburgh PA 15213
yashesh@cs.cmu.edu

ABSTRACT

Converting speech to text quickly is the fundamental task for making aural content accessible to deaf and hard of hearing. Despite high cost, this is done by human captionists, as automatic speech recognition (ASR) does not give satisfactory performance in real world settings. Offering ASR output to captionists as a starting point seems more facile and economical, yet the effectiveness of this approach is clearly dependent on the quality of ASR because fixing inaccurate ASR output may take longer than producing the transcriptions without ASR support. In this paper, we empirically study how the time required by captionists to produce transcriptions from partially correct ASR output varies based on the accuracy of the ASR output. Our studies with 160 participants recruited on Amazon's Mechanical Turk indicate that starting with the ASR output is worse unless it is sufficiently accurate (Word Error Rate (WER) is under 30%).

Categories and Subject Descriptors

K.4.2 [**Computers and Society**]: Social Issues—*Assistive technologies for persons with disabilities*

1. INTRODUCTION

A lot of multimedia is being produced that needs to be accompanied with transcription for it to be accesible. This task is currently manual and expensive since it may require 3-4 times as long as the original audio. Decades of research on ASR has resulted in systems that can handle a variety of audio content with surprising accuracy but such automated systems alone cannot provide accurate transcriptions in all settings. Thus, human computation has become a popular approach for generating captions[1, 2]. This paper explores how mixing these two sources of captions can be traded off by studying the effect of error rates on workers' ability to edit partially correct ASR captions. Generation of captions from scratch can often be done with minimal cognizant processing of the content or meaning of the speech itself. On the other hand, editing content generated by ASR system requires less typing but requires more cognitive activities involved in undestanding text relative to speech. We designed a between-subjects design study to measure the task latency change that results from asking workers to edit real ASR generated text with increasing WER, and compared this to the cost of generating captions for the same audio segments from scratch.

ASSETS'15, October 26–28, 2015, Lisbon, Portugal.
ACM 978-1-4503-3400-6/15/10.
DOI: http://dx.doi.org/10.1145/2700648.2811331 .

2. RELATED WORK

To generate captions even in settings where ASR cannot perform reliably, recent work has leveraged human compuation to provide high quality transcription. Research in this area has sought to improve the efficiency, accuracy, and scope of these crowd-powered methods. For instance, Liem *et al.* [1] used an iterative, "dual pathway" approach to generate and evaulate worker input based on the input of others. Scribe [2] enables a group of non-expert typists to provide realtime captions with less than a five second latency, where years of training would have been required in the past. Others have looked at how crowds can be used to correct the output of ASR directly [5].

3. EXPERIMENTS

3.1 Apparatus

We designed a web based captioning interface (Figure 1) that included an audio player and a text box in which participants could type their transcriptions.Participants were provided shortcut keys to play, pause or return 5 seconds in the audio. Participants were asked to only use the keyboard, which was both more efficient and also allowed us to more tightly control the study because observed time did not include mouse movements used to control the audio. The interface also logged mouse clicks, key events, and text box clear events with associated time stamp for each participant.

3.2 Data Set and Preparation

For this study, we used TEDLIUM dataset [4] and Kaldi speech recognition toolkit [3]. ASR transcripts of varying quality were generated by changing the beam-width parameter in the speech decoder. 16 one minute long clips were selected randomly from the TEDLIUM test set. We decoded these 16 clips 9 times, with different "beam width" parameter, resulting in real ASR transcripts with WERs ranging from 15% to 55% at intervals of nearly 5%.

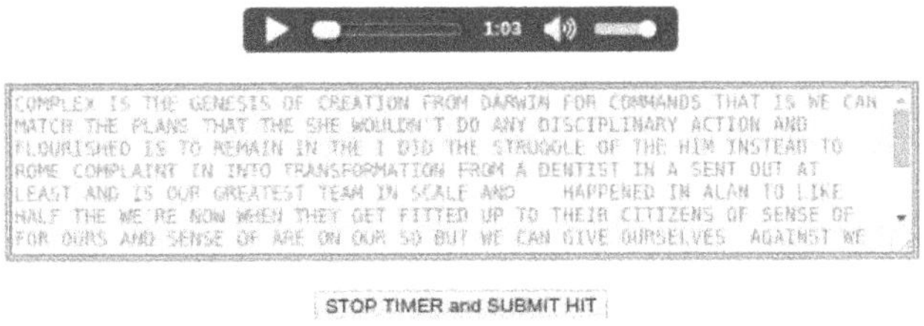

Figure 1: The transcription interface used in our study. Participants were previously informed of the shortcut keys that they could use to control the audio playback.

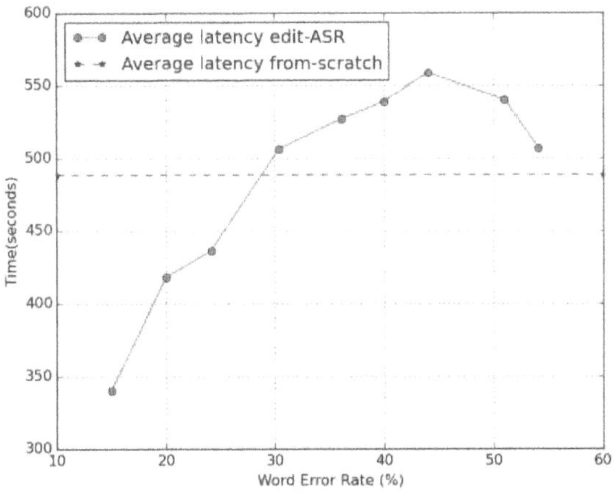

Figure 2: WER vs. latency

3.3 Study Procedures

Our between-subjects study included 10 separate groups recruited from Amazon's Mechanical Turk, each having 16 distinct workers. Each person in the group transcribed different but one of the 16 clips. The first group was asked to transcribe the clips without any ASR support (condition 1), while the remaining 9 groups were asked to edit the ASR output of varying accuracy (condition 2). The participants were asked to read the instructions and were allowed to begin the experiment when they were ready. In condition 1, the participants started with an empty text box while in condition 2, the ASR output was available in the text box all at once, as soon as the experiment had started. To ensure quality and discourage spammers, worker's response was accepted only if it had a WER less than 10% as compared to the dataset's ground truth. A qualifying WER threshold of 0% was not chosen to allow for minor errors by the workers. Threshold of 10% WER was decided based on our initial trials of the study which indicated that threshold values lesser than 10% resulted in too many worker submissions being rejected while with greater threshold values, risk of accepting low quality transcriptions was foreseen.

4. RESULTS AND DISCUSSION

Figure 2 shows the results from our experiments. We see that by the time ASR transcripts pass 30% WER, workers are faster just typing the content from the scratch. We note that after 50% WER mark, the average latency actually begins to decrease relative to the maximum seen at approximately 45% WER. The logs showed that for higher WERs, the workers simply deleted huge portions of texts and prefered to write from scratch. Looking at the number of occurences of workers removing more than 25% of the transcript in a given time step, we observed that for WERs under 30%, just 7.12% of workers cleared a large portion of text. For WERs under 50%, this ratio increases to 12.28%. For WERs of over 50% (where the latencies begin to decrease from their maximum), we see that 42.52% of workers clear the text they were given. This very large jump may explain why workers are less slowed down by increased error rates as the overwhelming number of errors in a given transcript becomes more evident up front.

5. CONCLUSION

In this paper, we explored the effect of ASR quality on its utility as a starting point for human transcription. Our results match our expectations that ASR is most useful as a starting point for transcription when it is fairly accurate (specifically, WER under 30%). Computational approaches may be used to decide when ASR input should be provided to workers to allow them to most effectively accomplish a captioning task. Being able to trade off between human and machine ability, and how one affects the other, is a key aspect of effective hybrid intelligence systems, and can greatly benefit human-powered access technology.

6. ACKNOWLEDGMENTS

This work was supported by National Science Foundation-Award IIS-1218209.

7. REFERENCES

[1] Y. C. Beatrice Liem, Haoqi Zhang. An iterative dual pathway structure for speech-to-text transcription. In *Proceedings of the 3rd Workshop on Human Computation (HCOMP '11)*, HCOMP '11, 2011.

[2] W. Lasecki, C. Miller, A. Sadilek, A. Abumoussa, D. Borrello, R. Kushalnagar, and J. Bigham. Real-time captioning by groups of non-experts. In *Proceedings of the 25th Annual ACM Symposium on User Interface Software and Technology*, UIST '12, pages 23–34, New York, NY, USA, 2012. ACM.

[3] D. Povey, A. Ghoshal, G. Boulianne, L. Burget, O. Glembek, N. Goel, M. Hannemann, P. Motlíček, Y. Qian, P. Schwarz, et al. The kaldi speech recognition toolkit. 2011.

[4] A. Rousseau, P. Deléglise, and Y. Estève. Ted-lium: an automatic speech recognition dedicated corpus. In *LREC*, pages 125–129, 2012.

[5] M. Wald. Crowdsourcing correction of speech recognition captioning errors. 2011.

Web Search Credibility Assessment for Individuals who are Blind

Ali Abdolrahmani, Ravi Kuber and William Easley
UMBC
aliab1@umbc.edu

ABSTRACT
While screen reading technologies offer considerable promise to individuals who are blind by providing an accessible overview of web-based content, difficulties can be faced determining the credibility of sites and their respective contents. This can impact the user's behavior, particularly if sensitive information needs to be entered (e.g. into a web-based form). In this paper, we describe an exploratory study examining the criteria which blind screen reader users utilize to assess credibility. More specifically, we have focused on the common task of web searching and exploring search results. Findings from the study have suggested that mismatches between the title of the search results and their respective snippets, along with the richness and accessibility of the content when search results are selected, can lead to users determining whether sites are indeed credible.

Categories and Subject Descriptors
K.4.2 [Assistive technologies for persons with disabilities]

General Terms
Design, Human Factors

Keywords
Blind, Credibility, Screen reader, Trust, Web content, Web search

1. INTRODUCTION
The benefits of the Web are numerous. However, the presence and sometimes, prominence of incorrect and misleading content on the Web can have serious consequences [5]. Examples may include the consequences of divulging sensitive information via an online form, or trusting content about treating a medical condition after reading about it on a medical site. Visual cues, such as the 'look and feel' of content, are often used to determine credibility of a site. However, for individuals who are blind, the process is more complex. Screen readers are used to provide a representation of web-based content in auditory or tactile format. However, these tools are known to be restrictive in nature [1], presenting information sequentially, and inadequately handling graphical content. If the web page has been poorly coded or content is unclear, the browsing process will be negatively impacted.

In this paper, a study is described examining the ways in which individuals who are blind determine credibility of sites and their respective content when using a screen reader. More specifically, we have focused on web search tasks, as these are commonly undertaken by both blind and sighted users. Findings can help to inform web designers interested in heightening levels of credibility among a more diverse audience.

ASSETS '15, October 26-28, 2015, Lisbon, Portugal
ACM 978-1-4503-3400-6/15/10.
http://dx.doi.org/10.1145/2700648.2811349

2. RELATED WORK
According to Fogg [2], the concept of credibility is made up of two dimensions: trustworthiness and expertise. If a web site conveys both qualities, it would be considered credible. The researcher suggests that users may be influenced by their first impressions of inspecting a site, and whether it is professional in its design (termed: *surface credibility*). Trust may also be established over time, influenced by the site's ease of use and its ability to provide credible information consistently (termed: *earned credibility*). Schwarz and Morris [5] developed visualizations to augment search results and web pages in order to help users to more accurately judge the credibility of online content. Findings from the study highlighted the potential of data aggregation and simple interventions to help people make more informed decisions as they search for information online.

While research examining issues associated with web credibility has been valuable, there has been limited work examining the needs of individuals with diverse abilities (e.g. individuals who are blind), to determine whether their needs differ from a mainstream audience. Information seeking behavior is known to vary between blind and sighted users [4]. As it can be challenging to access visual cues through a screen reader, the process of establishing credibility can be complex. In the study described in this paper, we aim to explore the criteria that are used by individuals who are blind to make credibility judgments.

3. EXPLORATORY STUDY
Four congenitally blind participants (two females, aged 20 – 32) were recruited for the study. All were experienced JAWS screen reader users, and used Google search engine as their preferred web search tool.

Two tasks were selected for the study: (1) conducting two searches based on a set of pre-defined search terms; (2) browsing five pairs of web pages exploring a set of pre-defined topics, including health and current affairs. During this process, participants were asked to 'think-aloud', walking through the process of searching the Web using the browser and screen reader of their choosing, and describing how levels of credibility could be established.

For the first task, participants were asked to identify answers to a particular question (e.g. "Who invented the screen reader?") and to undertake more open-ended searching (e.g. "What can you find out about the link between diabetes and blindness?). For the second task, each pair of pages referred to a similar topic (e.g. Ebola symptoms and treatment, energy saving tips for winter). However, each page differed in terms of the quality and volume of content and structural layout. Participants were instructed not to spend any longer than five minutes on each task. Comments made by participants, along with screen reader commands which were executed, were noted during the study. Data was then coded and analyzed.

4. RESULTS AND DISCUSSION

4.1 Browsing Strategy

Similarities between browsing styles were evident among participants. Techniques included 'skimming' through each of the search results, using the Control + Down Arrow shortcut to gain an overview. As search results were outputted, participants would listen out for keywords related to their search, in the hope that there would be information matching their query. This process required concentration. Three participants also used the 'h command' to navigate through a list of headings, with the same aim.

4.2 Credibility of Search Results

- **Verifying results are related to the intended search** - After identifying appropriate headings using the 'h command' described in 4.1, three participants checked the source URL associated with the search result, followed by the snippet. The snippet was used to verify that the search result heading was consistent with the search query keywords.
- **Putting faith in the ranking of search results** – Participants were generally trusting that search results are presented in an order of relevance to the term entered. P4 described browsing through the first sets of search results, as he felt the latter results would be less relevant to his original query and be time-consuming to read. If the results were irrelevant to his needs, he would access the 'Did You Mean' option, as this could help with the process if a spelling mistake had been made in the original search.
- **Mismatches** – When searching on a particular topic, participants identified mismatches between the search results and the respective text snippet. This resulted in time re-reading both items using a screen reader, and then double-checking the search box to ensure that they had searched on the correct terms. P3 pointed out that he would select the search result link to open the associated page, and check if the content on the page would match with the search result. Confusion would ensue if the back button was selected, as it would be difficult for him to find his previous location in the page of search results.

4.3 Credibility of Web Sites

- **Domain Name** - Familiarity with the organization whose site was being accessed, was the main criterion to determine the credibility of a site. If the information being sought (query) corresponded to the type of site where they would expect to read about this type of information, it would be easier for them to trust the content. For example, reading about Ebola symptoms on a well known medical web site (e.g. WebMD), or 2016 US election candidates in a respected venue (e.g. New York Times).
- **Domain Type** - All four participants found governmental and reputable organizations more credible compared to blogs, forums or pages that were opinion-based. As a result, domain types such as '.gov' would be considered to have greater levels of credibility, compared with '.biz'. However, participants highlighted that while they were aware that sighted users could glance at a URL to double-check the domain type being accessed, this would be a more time-consuming process to perform using a screen reader.
- **Accessibility of content** –All four participants appeared to associate levels of credibility with site accessibility. For example, sites containing images without alt text or headings formatted without the appropriate tags, were thought to be hastily designed. If time could not be spent improving accessibility of the site, it was possible that time was not spent verifying the accuracy of textual content on the site. As a result, these were considered to have lower levels of credibility compared with other more accessible sites.
- **Presence of extraneous content** –All four participants assessed pages with less irrelevant content as of a more credible source. Sites with adverts and other pop-ups were considered less credible, and skipped where at all possible.
- **Richness of content** - Other factors which influenced participants included (1) the *style of writing* (i.e. whether casual or professional), (2) *authors of the content* (in the case of news stories), (3) whether or not the content was *reviewed by an domain expert* (e.g. P3 found that the article about the Ebola symptoms in WebMD was reviewed by a medical doctor), and (4) presence of other *relevant article links*. *Experience of accessing web sites over time* had enabled participants to make judgment calls on whether sites were credible. For example, all four expected a web site examining a scientific topic, to be written professionally, which in turn informed credibility.

5. FUTURE WORK

We aim to expand the study, recruiting a larger sample of both blind and sighted web users. The aim would be to determine the ways in which credibility perception and assessment varies between both groups. Similar to [3]. we aim to specifically examine the ways in which the structural layout of information can impact blind users, as the visual layout of content on an interface is known to impact sighted users [2,5]. Insights from such a study can provide guidance to developers interested in heightening web credibility among a wider range of users.

6. ACKNOWLEDGMENTS

The authors would like to thank Jenna Tart for her assistance with this research.

7. REFERENCES

[1] Chandrashekar, S., 2010. *Is Hearing Believing? Perception of Online Information Credibility by Screen Reader Users who are Blind or Visually Impaired.* Doctoral thesis, University of Toronto, Canada.

[2] Fogg, B.J. 2003. *Persuasive Technology: Using Computers to Change What We Think and Do*. Morgan Kaufmann.

[3] Leuthold, S., Bargas-Avila, J.A., and Opwis, K., 2008. Beyond web content accessibility guidelines: Design of enhanced text user interfaces for blind internet users. *Int J Hum Comput Stud* 66, 4, 257-270.

[4] Sahib, N.G., Tombros, A. and Stockman, T., 2012. A comparative analysis of the information-seeking behavior of visually impaired and sighted searchers. *J Assoc Inf Sci Technol*, 63, 2 (Feb. 2012), 377–391.

[5] Schwarz, J. and Morris, M., 2011. Augmenting web pages and search results to support credibility assessment. In *Proceedings of the SIGCHI Conference on Human Factors in Computing Systems*, ACM, New York, NY, 1245–1254.

A Voting System for AAC Symbol Acceptance

E.A. Draffan, Mike Wald, Nawar Halabi
University of Southampton
Southampton, SO17 1BJ, UK
+44 (0)23 8059 7246
ead@ecs.soton.ac.uk

Amatullah Kadous
Amal Idris
Speech Therapy Dept., Hamad Medical Corporation (Qatar)

Nadine Zeinoun,
David Banes, Dana Lawand
MADA
Qatar

ABSTRACT
This paper aims to illustrate how an innovative voting system has been developed to allow AAC users, their therapists, carers and families show their degree of acceptance for newly developed symbols and their referents. The approach, taking a participatory model of research, occurs via an online symbol management system using a set of criteria that provide instant feedback to the developers and the project team. Scores and comments regarding the symbols are collated and where a majority vote has occurred, symbols are added to the Arabic Symbol Dictionary with lexical entries in both Arabic and English.

Categories and Subject Descriptors
H.5.2 [User Interfaces]: Graphical User Interfaces; K.4.2 [Social Issues]: Assistive Technologies for Persons with Disabilities

General Terms
Design, Human Factors

Keywords
Augmentative and Alternative Communication (AAC), language, voting, symbol acceptance, Arabic, dictionary

1. INTRODUCTION
The voting system for symbol acceptance presented in this paper has become part of a participatory approach adopted for the development of an Arabic Symbol Dictionary for Augmentative and Alternative Communication (AAC) users. The contents of the dictionary are intended to support not only communication skills but also literacy skills, general signage and language learning. Crowdsourcing methods have been used in the past to 'create fictional but plausible AAC communications' [1] but never to engage AAC users, their families, carers and therapists in evaluating the design of the visual representation of a symbol in relation to its referent in a bilingual and diglossia situation.

2. BACKGROUND
The development of an Arabic Symbol Dictionary was felt to be essential for the support of those working in the field of AAC with Arabic speaking families, who at present are mainly supported by English speaking therapists and specialist teachers using westernized symbols. There is also a limited public availability of Modern Standard Arabic lexicons or colloquial Arabic phrases for communication for AAC use. AAC centers tend to develop their own libraries of symbols which provide perfect personalization for individual users, but do not offer options for symbols to be shared across networks or for their use by others in the area.

Huer [2] points out that "communication across cultures reveal that nonsymbolic as well as symbolic forms of communication are culturally dependent" and that "participants' cultural/linguistic experiences may be significant elements to consider when selecting graphic symbols and when teaching consumers to represent meaning through them." [3]

3. METHODOLOGY
An online forum of AAC users, their therapists, carers and families was set up and discussions held about the best way to encourage participation in choices for newly developed symbols and an Arabic core vocabulary to complement the often used PCS Symbols from Mayer-Johnson. An overarching Symbol Management system was developed to host lexical entries and culturally adapted symbols along with definitions, various categories and a filtering system. A symbol rating system was added with four voting criteria each with a 1-5 Likert scale; participants logged in to cast their votes and make comments. Individual symbol scores and comments were made available via the Symbol Management System and Microsoft Excel was used to aggregate the data.

3.1 Development of the Symbol Management System
The online Symbol Management system was developed using the Nodejs framework, written in JavaScript using an open source, cross-platform framework for building network applications. On top of Node, the Expressjs plugin was used which turns Node into a Model-View-Controller (MVC) framework (Figure 1) for web development. The database used was Mongo dB, which is also open source and can easily be interfaced from Node.

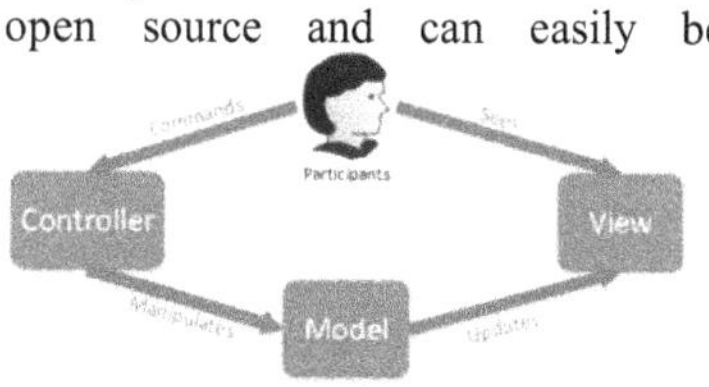

Figure 1. MVC Diagram (Model-View-Controller

3.2 Symbol voting
At the outset participants were made aware of the differences between the newly developed Arabic culturally sensitive symbols

ASSETS '15, October 26-28, 2015, Lisbon, Portugal
ACM 978-1-4503-3400-6/15/10.
http://dx.doi.org/10.1145/2700648.2811374

with which they were presented, in comparison to the symbols in daily use. Examples of differences came in the Arabic dress, food types, places, religion, use of a right hand for actions and arrows for past and future in opposite directions to English. There was an initial trial voting session that used PCS, ARASAAC and the new symbols on one page as a comparison. This proved to be too complex and further discussions with the offer of alternative activities and some rapid prototyping [4] resulted in a final much simplified voting system. This had a simple 'flashcard' interface with a large version of a single symbol plus increased sized fonts for lexical entries in MSA, Qatari and English above the voting criteria. The four criteria on which participants voted using the check boxes with a scale of 1-5 (where 5 was completely acceptable) were:

1. Feelings about the symbol as a whole
2. Represents the word or phrase
3. Color contrast
4. Cultural sensitivity

Plus the addition of any comments to help improve the symbol followed by large submit, previous or next buttons (Figure 2) so that voters could choose to retrace their steps to change votes (the final vote being the only one recorded). The whole system was also translated into Arabic via localization files. Each symbol was offered as one web page and could be activated via touch screen, mouse, keyboard or switch access.

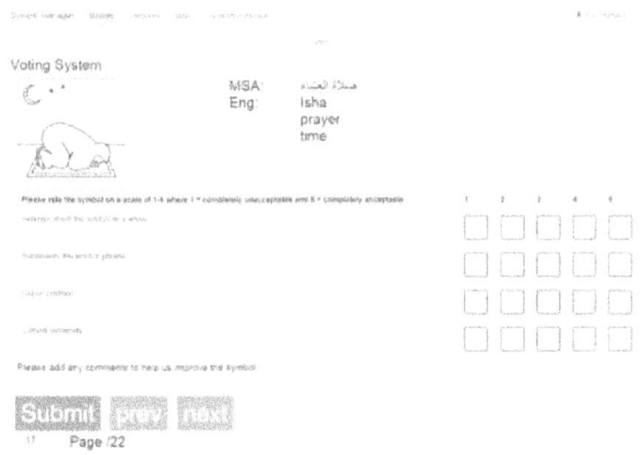

Figure 2. Voting system showing a black and white symbol for a prayer time with the criteria on a scale of 1-5 where five is completely acceptable.

Two young AAC users (who had cerebral palsy) aged 8 and 14 were also introduced to 21 adapted symbols using the same interface described above but via Grid 2 as their preferred AAC software. Rather than checkboxes they were presented with thumbs up, halfway and down to represent a simplified rating of 1-3 or with two intermediary thumb positions for a rating of 1-5. More AAC users and their families have only recently joined the project.

3.3 Results of individual symbol voting.

The first batch of symbols to be adapted had 63 participants logging into the Symbol Manager resulting in 2341 votes for 65 symbols. The votes collected for the four different criteria, as illustrated in Table 1, showed that all mean ratings were significantly greater than a rating of 3.5 denoting general acceptance of the initial batch of symbols. Comments also showed most preferred colored symbols and wanted gender illustrated for verbs rather than stick characters and liked different clothing styles for example it was deemed *"less distracting", "I like both, but prefer* option 1 for *Qatar" (voted for just Qatari dress) "one uncovered", "make one of them dressed in Abaya", "Make one of the girls wear abaya and one of the males wear a thowb"*

Table 1. One Sample T test for Difference of Mean Ratings from 3.5

Criteria	Number of voters	Mean rating	2 tail P Value for difference from 3.5
1	63	3.94	<0.0001
2	63	3.90	<0.0001
3	63	4.07	<0.0001
4	63	4.10	<0.0001

Where the average scoring for an individual symbol was lower than 3.5 out of 5, it was redrawn, taking into account any comments and resubmitted to a following batch of symbols for another vote.

4. CONCLUSION

The voting system produced speedy results and has encouraged participants to complete batches of up to 60 symbols within 40 minute sessions. The AAC users have had the support of a parent or teacher during their sessions and used eye gaze equipment to access their computers. It took longer for them to complete their 21 symbols and the results were collected on paper and kept separate from the general voting system. Stripping out interface complexities and providing good feedback with speedy results has been essential to ensure voter uptake remains high. The team learnt much from the process with comments such as: "It is amazing to see how one symbol can mean so many different things to so many people and such small details can be offensive to one ethnicity and small changes can be made to please another." Finally it is felt that this participatory methodology could be used for a wide range of projects where consensus needs to be achieved quickly with participants from different cultures, countries, abilities and skills.

5. ACKNOWLEDGMENTS

This research was made possible by the NPRP award [NPRP 6 - 1046 - 2 - 427] from the Qatar National Research Fund (a member of The Qatar Foundation) and thanks must go to all those participants in Doha and ARASAAC for allowing their symbols to be used in this project. The statements made herein are solely the responsibility of the authors.

6. REFERENCES

[1] Vertanen, K. & Kristensson, P.O. (2011) The Imagination of Crowds: Conversational AAC Language Modeling using crowdsourcing and large data sets. Computational Linguistics, pp.700–711.

[2] Huer, M. B. (1997). Culturally inclusive assessments for children using augmentative and alternative communication (AAC). Journal of Children's Communication Development, 19 (1), 23–34.

[3] Huer, M. B. (2000). Examining perceptions of graphic symbols across cultures: Preliminary study of the impact of culture/ethnicity. Augmentative and Alternative Communication 16 (3): 180–185.

[4] Kane, S. et al. (2012) What We Talk About: Designing a Context-Aware Communication Tool for People with Aphasia. ASSETS '12, ACM Press (2012), 49-56

A Direct TEX-to-Braille Transcribing Method

Andreas Papasalouros
Department of Mathematics
University of the Aegean
832 00 Karlovassi, Greece
andpapas@aegean.gr

Antonis Tsolomitis
Department of Mathematics
University of the Aegean
832 00 Karlovassi, Greece
atsol@aegean.gr

ABSTRACT

The TEX/LATEX typesetting system is the most widespread system for creating documents in Mathematics and Science. However, no reliable tool exists to this day for automatically transcribing documents from the above formats into Braille code. Thus, blind students who study related fields do not have access to the bulk of studying materials available in LATEX format. We develop a tool, named `latex2nemeth`, for transcribing directly LATEX documents to Nemeth Braille, thus facilitating the access of students with blindness to Science.

Categories and Subject Descriptors

I.7.2 [**Document and Text Processing**]: Document Preparation—*Format and Notation*; K.4.2 [**Computers and Society**]: Social Issues—*Assistive technologies for persons with disabilities*

General Terms

Human Factors, Languages

Keywords

LATEX, Braille, Nemeth, Mathematics

1. INTRODUCTION

The Nemeth Code, published in 1972 [8], describes rules for unambiguously encoding mathematical expressions using six-dot Braille symbols thus supporting the printing of mathematical/ technical documents in a form readable by blind persons. It defines the structure of complex mathematical expressions and contains an extensive list of symbols.

A number of tools exist for translating mathematical expressions from various formats into Braille/Nemeth form. However, although TEX/LaTeX is the most widespread system for creating documents in Mathematics and Science, to the best of our knowledge, no system exists for the reliable translation from TEX/LATEX to Braille and Nemeth.

The `liblouis` project [6] translates MathML to Braille. But the output is highly dependent on the quality of the MathML input. We have found that translators from LATEX to MathML (such as `tex4ht` [4]) although they produce valid MathML for, say, Mozilla products, they do not produce the MathML that `liblouis` expects, and very often the output is unreadable by blind students.

Commercial products also exist, but they only support a part of LATEX and, being closed source systems, their extension is not possible by third party contributors. More than that, it is not well documented which parts of LATEX they do support. As a consequence a user can not prepare his/her manuscript in such a way as to get guaranteed results. As a prominent example, Duxbury [1] can reliably translate LATEX files into Nemeth code only if the latter files are created with the proprietary Scientific WorkPlace editor [7], which is a serious constraint, since very few authors of mathematic books and notes use this particular editor.

In this paper we propose a direct method for transcribing Mathematics documents from TEX/LATEX and its derivatives to Braille. A software tool, named `latex2nemeth`, has been developed for the automatic transcription from TEX/LATEX documents directly to Braille. Given that the Mathematics symbol set of TEX is extensive, a number of its symbols are not supported by the Nemeth code. Thus, we also propose some new extensions to the Nemeth code so as to encode non-supported TEX symbols in Braille by using the Nemeth code extension mechanism. Our software supports an extensive number of mathematical symbols and aims at printed representations of technical/scientific documents, although it can be easily extended to support audio output as well, e.g. in the form of MathSpeak [3].

2. NEMETH EXTENSIONS AND TOOL IMPLEMENTATION

In its current version, our tool supports more than 800 mathematical LATEX symbols. These symbols are either already included in the Nemeth code or they are proposed by using extension rules also suggested by Nemeth. Furthermore, `latex2nemeth` supports all standard LATEX mathematical structures such as fractions, exponents, indices, roots, operators, arrays, etc., as well as their Nemeth representation.

For example, `\hookrightarrow` ($\hookrightarrow$), used to denote subspaces in Analysis, can be composed as ⠫ ⠈⠿⠒⠒⠕. Nemeth, in order to be able to use only 64 six-dot braille symbols to represent as many language/math symbols as possible, reserves some of the six-dot symbols to be used for special purposes. In the previous example, the symbol ⠫ is reserved to mean the beginning of the description of a symbol or picture. And although the symbols that follow ⠫ in the above, may have their own meaning (for example ⠕ is the letter "o"), when they are read after the ⠫ symbol their meaning changes until the required symbol gets composed and the reader reads a space. So in ⠫ ⠈⠿⠒⠒⠕ the symbol ⠿ is an ar-

ASSETS'15, October 26–28, 2015, Lisbon, Portugal.
ACM 978-1-4503-3400-6/15/10.
DOI: http://dx.doi.org/10.1145/2700648.2811376.

row head in symbol mode (after ⠫) but we only keep its upper part prefixing it by a ⠈ before it. Then the standard symbol of an arrow follows, thus to create the required symbol $\hookrightarrow$. We have followed this technique in order to be able to compose most of the common symbols.

However, it does not seem possible at this moment to support all the common symbols. In `http://myria.math.aegean.gr/labs/dt/braille/symbols-in-braille.pdf` the list of supported mathematical symbols and structures can be accessed.

The program, named `latex2nemeth`, runs as a command-line tool and takes as input a LaTeX source file as well as an auxiliary LaTeX file, that is produced after successfully running LaTeX on the input LaTeX sources. The auxiliary file contains information about numbering of certain elements in the document, such as equations, theorems, sections, etc. The input can be a single file or the main file in a multi-file LaTeX source configuration, all encoded in UTF-8. The program produces as output a set of Braille/Nemeth text files, with Braille six-dot characters encoded in UTF-16 or, alternatively, in PEF format [9], in order to be readily available for embossing in specialized printers.

The transcriber is based on a parser for the LaTeX language. The language of TeX/LaTeX has two distinct modes: text and mathematics. The parser recognizes the most common LaTeX commands and environments in text mode, supports both English and Greek characters and also covers most structures and mathematical symbols. The program is developed in the Java programming language using the JavaCC compiler generation tool [2] for the construction of the parser. The generation process is quite simple:

Text is parsed, each paragraph at a time, and appropriate Braille output is produced. In mathematical mode all expressions are parsed, thus creating appropriate abstract syntactical trees of mathematical expressions, which are independent of the source language of TeX/LaTeX. The above process implements the front-end of the mathematical parser, while the back-end is a Braille/Nemeth code generator, which complies with [8]. The object-oriented design of the program allows the easy implementation of different back-ends for other mathematics representation forms for the blind, such as MathSpeak [3].

3. EVALUATION AND CASE STUDY

As preliminary evaluation of the tool presented in this paper, we have generated Braille/Nemeth code by using `latex2nemeth` as well as two other tools mentioned above, Duxbury and `liblouis`. For the comparison we have chosen a document from AMSMath LaTeX samples [5]. From the whole document, which is rather extended, we chose pages 8 and 13 as representative of the kind of mathematics expressions encountered in university mathematics texts at both undergraduate and postgraduate level, containing various mathematical characters and symbols, environments and structures, references, indices and subindices, text-in-math structures, etc. Since our aim is to evaluate the production of mathematical expressions generated by `latex2nemeth`, we only transcribed the mathematics content of the original LaTeX sample, removing the textual content. The evaluation engaged a University Mathematics professor with deep knowledge of both the Braille system and LaTeX and an expert in Mathematics Education for visually impaired students.

The `latex2nemeth` software clearly outperformed the other two tools in terms of the errors in Braille Nemeth document generation. Both evaluators reported that each of the other tools generated at least 50 errors in the two pages, while `latex2nemeth` had almost absolute precision in translation (only a problem in the translation of dot character, due to its ambiguous meaning in mathematical documents). This result is expected, given the inherent limitations of the other tools in TeX translation, as discussed in the introduction.

We also conducted a case study which involved the transcription of a whole book from LaTeX to Braille/Nemeth format and the study of this book by a blind student of Mathematics in a Greek University. The book, entitled "Real Analysis" by A. Anoussis, V. Felouzis, and A. Tsolomitis, was written in Greek as a textbook on Mathematical Analysis. The book is available in Braille format at `http://myria.math.aegean.gr/labs/dt/braille/books/real.zip`. We have also transcribed other books and notes and we are in the process of creating a repository for Mathematics texts in Braille Nemeth form. The student has recently finished a course on Mathematical Analysis using the particular textbook. We have presented to the student a set of questions that form a structured interview in order to *assess her satisfaction* from the book. The questions involved understandability, difficulty, correctness and the overall quality of the generated Braille text.

In her answers, the student reported that the text produced by `latex2nemeth` is understandable and that she has not identified any mistakes in the mathematical part. Among others, she also reported that "... now I am at the same level with the other students. I feel that I am equal to the others while before I felt inferior ... My hands are untied because before I wrote some four hundred pages during a semester so that I feared that I would develop tendonitis."

Overall, the case study and the interview revealed that the book converted into Braille is appropriate for a blind mathematics student.

4. CONCLUSION

In this paper a new software for generating Braille/Nemeth code for blind persons from LaTeX source documents is presented. This software is found to reliably generate mathematical documents for blind persons.

We are currently in the process of an extensive evaluation of the perceived Information Quality (IQ) of the content generated by the proposed method and the comparison of IQ with content generated by existing tools. We are also in the process of designing an interactive environment for mathematics, based on refreshable Braille displays, in order to allow blind students to be engaged in dynamic mathematical activities.

5. REFERENCES

[1] Duxbury. `http://www.duxburysystems.com/`.

[2] The JavaCC compiler compiler. `https://javacc.java.net/`.

[3] MathSpeak™ initiative. `http://www.gh-mathspeak.com/`.

[4] The Tex4ht project. `https://www.tug.org/tex4ht/`.

[5] AMS. Sample paper for the `amsmath` package. `http://mirrors.ctan.org/macros/latex/required/amslatex/math/testmath.pdf`.

[6] C. Egli. *Liblouis – A universal solution for Braille transcription services*. Deutsche Zentralbibliothek für Blinde zu Leipzig (ZDB), Leipzig, 2011.

[7] Mackichan. Scientific WorkPlace. https://www.mackichan.com/.

[8] A. Nemeth. *The Nemeth Braille Code for Mathematics and Science Notation: 1972 revision*. American Printing House for the Blind, 1972.

[9] PEF. The portable embosser format. `http://pef-format.org/`.

Spoken Language, Conversational Assistive Systems for People with Cognitive Impairments? – Yes, If.

Ramin Yaghoubzadeh
CITEC, Bielefeld University
33501 Bielefeld, Germany
ryaghoubzadeh@uni-bielefeld.de

Stefan Kopp
CITEC, Bielefeld University
33501 Bielefeld, Germany
skopp@techfak.uni-bielefeld.de

ABSTRACT

We analyzed autonomous conversational spoken interaction as a modality for assistive systems in initial groups of older adults and people with cognitive impairments; we had previously explored this in a WOz setup. Solving a simple task in the domain of week planning, subjects readily interacted with the system. Performance was generally good, but dependent on successful adherence to a specific terse conversational style. Enforcing these patterns in a socially acceptable way during conversation is the next goal for the system.

Categories and Subject Descriptors

K.4.2 [**Computers and Society**]: Social Issues – assistive technologies for persons with disabilities

Keywords

Spoken interaction, cognitive impairment, daily assistant

1. INTRODUCTION

Both older adults and people with cognitive impairments can experience a higher quality of life when leading a self-determined lifestyle in their own home environment, but both groups may require assistance in some of the daily tasks that this entails. There are technological solutions for some areas, such as activity planning, home automation, facilitation of communication, or motivation for exercise [2]. Most of those solutions rely on textual information or the processing of task hierarchies and abstract visual symbols, which need to be acquired and can exclude a subset of the potential user groups.

In fact, many people are accustomed to requesting support using conversation with care personnel. This, together with the considerable advances of speech recognition in recent years, to a degree that acoustic models can cope with mildly dysarthric articulation better than ever before, opens the way for speech-controlled interfaces for wider user groups.

ASSETS '15, October 26–28, 2015, Lisbon, Portugal
ACM 978-1-4503-3400-6/15/10.
http://dx.doi.org/10.1145/2700648.281137.

Yet, current spoken interfaces generally either take the approach of navigating a constrained task graph step by step (such as the iconic pizza ordering systems), or of gathering all the information provided spontaneously and providing a contiguous chunk representing the most likely interpretation, after some processing (such as dictation systems or the systems familiar from modern phones). While the former provide low information density that can be suitable for people with cognitive impairments, they usually offer no leeway at all to escape the (often implicit) rigid patterns. Conversely, the latter approach accepts more unconstrained input, but does not guarantee appropriate information density. We study whether conversational approaches can combine the benefits of both, to a degree enabling their use by cognitively impaired people: the ability to offer a basic task structure to follow, to realize continous incremental interpretation of less constrained input, and to provide sufficiently transparent feedback, clarification requests or repairs.

2. STUDIES

2.1 Exploratory studies

In previous work, we explored the paradigm of a spoken conversational interaction with an embodied agent with both senior citizens and people with cognitive impairments (approx. ICD-10 F70), using a Wizard-of-Oz (covertly human-controlled) system in a week planning domain [3]. We found that the paradigm was very well received by the users and that they were generally willing and able to solve the given task of entering fictional appointments into a graphical calendar. We systematically introduced errors in the system replies, and employed two different sets of presentation and confirmation strategies to elucidate the limits for successful interaction, i.e. detection and repair of those errors. We found that the minimal information density (one piece of information per utterance, plus confirmation) was the most robust approach especially for the cognitively impaired users (86% repair rate as opposed to 50%) but was not rated less favorably than a more compact approach. In a control group of adults from a university environment, there were no differences between conditions since all errors were detected.

2.2 Conception of conversational system

The insights from the WOz experiments and subsequent conversational analyses led to the development of the flexdiam dialogue manager [4] that aims to fulfill all requirements for task-related conversational interfaces that are suitable also for people with cognitive impairments. The system

Figure 1: Setup and older participant (anonymized).

is able to yield at any time to the users' initiative, is aware of and able to cope with ambiguities resulting from misarticulation or users contradicting themselves, supports coping strategies to resolve repeated miscommunications and all basic forms of repairs employed in the task domains. Moreover, it supports introspection into the task structure, i.e. the system knows and can recapitulate where it is in the common task. Concurrent input and output includes speech but may extend to other modalities (currently, control of an embodied agent, a graphical display, and touch input).

2.3 Studies with autonomous system

In ongoing work, we run studies with this autonomous system. So far, we have recorded six senior participants (n=6, ages 78–87) [4] without noticeable cognitive impairments, and four people with cognitive impairments (n=4), insufficient for robust statistics but sufficient for valuable qualitative insights. We will extend the studies to another group of older adults and a different group of cognitively impaired people (n=12) who participated in the earlier experiments.

The system setup consisted of a speech recognizer (a locally running version of a leading brand), speech synthesis (CereVoice [1]), the dialogue system, and a screen with the agent and a graphical calendar (see Fig. 1). In the experiment, as in the earlier WOz experiment, participants solved the task of entering made-up appointments into a calendar using natural speech. They were provided with a sheet with iconic and textual representations of possible topics, to which they needed not adhere, but which were treated preferentially during speech recognition. Prior to the experiment proper, we conducted a short speech recognizer training session (<2 minutes of material), which completed successfully even for mildly dysarthric speakers. Participants were instructed to stay focused on the task, and that the agent would be able to only handle this topic. Interaction was split into two parts of up to three and at least five expected entries, respectively. Between phases, we scheduled an intervention where we could instruct users further if they could not communicate successfully with the system in the first phase. Instructions given here were related to refraining from paraverbal feedback ('u-huh'), between which the speech recognizer could not discern, and from verbose elaborations when asked for a specific bit of information.

All participants engaged readily in conversation with the system. In general, they were able to enter their fictional appointments [4]. Sometimes, concessions were made as to the wording of the entry. For one participant from each group, the system did not provide a pleasant and effective interaction. This was a direct result of the verbose interaction styles some participants employed; the interventions in the break between phases only made them change it for a short time before reverting to their previous style. The system in this iteration was configured to always yield the initiative to the human interlocutor.

3. DISCUSSION AND CONCLUSION

Conversational spoken interaction worked well unless the amount of information provided by the users overwhelmed the speech recognition and NLU modules. Always yielding the floor to the user only worked well for people that did not exhibit such behavior. Since explanatory interventions had no lasting effect, clearly a better solution would be to control the conversational structure in place. Naive strategies for this (such as simple heuristics over phrase lengths plus hard interruptions by barge-ins) would be efficacious, but would also violate the principles of cooperative and polite interlocutors and hence most likely harm long-term acceptance. Here, the employment of an embodied agent provides means of more subtle control of the pace, e.g. using gaze or gestural output, resorting to barge-ins only as a last resort. The design and selection of these strategies are the next areas of research carried out in a follow-up project, enabling a wider audience for conversational interfaces.

In summary, the results from the initial evaluations lend support to our assumption that spoken interaction can be a feasible interaction modality in assistive systems for persons with light to moderate cognitive impairment, using current speech recognition technology, and that the interactive, conversational approach is a suitable mechanism to prevent and repair miscommunications. Current work is focusing on socially acceptable conversational strategies for the system to control the flow of conversation to subtly increase adherence to structures the system can cope with.

4. ACKNOWLEDGMENTS

This research was partially supported by the German Federal Ministry of Education and Research (BMBF), and the Deutsche Forschungsgemeinschaft (DFG) in the Center of Excellence 'Cognitive Interaction Technology' (CITEC).

5. REFERENCES

[1] M. P. Aylett and C. J. Pidcock. *The CereVoice Characterful Speech Synthesiser SDK*. 2007.

[2] T. W. Bickmore, R. A. Silliman, K. Nelson, D. M. Cheng, M. Winter, L. Henault, and M. K. Paasche-Orlow. A randomized controlled trial of an automated exercise coach for older adults. *J American Geriatrics Society*, 61(10):1676–1683, 2013.

[3] R. Yaghoubzadeh, M. Kramer, K. Pitsch, and S. Kopp. Virtual agents as daily assistants for elderly or cognitively impaired people. In R. Aylett, B. Krenn, C. Pelachaud, and H. Shimodaira, editors, *IVA 2013*, volume 8108 of *LNAI*, pages 79–91. Springer, 2013.

[4] R. Yaghoubzadeh, K. Pitsch, and S. Kopp. Adaptive grounding and dialogue management for autonomous conversational assistants for elderly users. In W.-P. Brinkman, J. Broekens, and D. Heylen, editors, *Proc. 15th Int Conf on Intelligent Virtual Agents, IVA 2015*, volume 9238 of *LNAI*, pages 28–38. Springer, 2015.

Correction of the Fundamental Voice Frequency Using Tactile and Visual Feedback

Rodrigo Leone Alves
Department of Computing
Federal Institute of
Rio Grande do Norte – IFRN
+55 83988447385
rodrigo.leone@ifrn.edu.br

Carlos M. G. S. Lima
Department of Industrial Electronics
University of Minho – UMinho
+ 351 929256584
clima@dei.uminho.pt

Raimundo C. S. Freire
Department of Electrical Engineering
Federal University of Campina
Grande – UFCG
+55 996599440
rcsfreire@dee.edu.br

ABSTRACT
People who are deaf or hard of hearing require correction of the fundamental frequency that usually is achieved by help of a phonodiologist. The work of the phonodiologist can be however strongly reduced by using appropriate devices that can help the patient to train the voice positioning. This paper reports the development of such a system based on FPGA's technology that providing tactile and visual feedback. Contrary to the feedback from the phonodiologist that is usually relative, the feedback provided by a device can be provided in absolute terms. This feature can improve the learning process that however needs the initial learning provided by the phonodiologist.

Categories and Subject Descriptors
K.4.2 [**Computers and Society**]: Social Issues - *Assistive technologies for persons with disabilities*

General Terms
Reliability, Experimentation, Human Factors and Verification

Keywords
Deafness; speech, Assistive technology; tactile stimulation; visual stimulation

1. INTRODUCTION
Tact is being explored as a substitute the other senses, such as sight and hearing a long time. However, due to the development of electronic circuits and psychophysical studies only in the early twentieth century that there was a greater increase in research in this area [1]. The application of tactile stimuli as a means of transmitting acoustic information for people with hearing impairments was investigated by [2] that surveyed the use of vibration as a means of information transfer. From then, it has seen many haptic devices that assist the hearing impaired [3] [4].

Deafness causes changes in vocal quality, the level of awareness of the listeners [5]. Such a disorder in speech is noticeable when the corresponding acoustic signal is observed. Therefore, they can be monitored and treated by techniques based on acoustic analysis of voice signal. In that review of signs of voices hearing impaired, various methods have been studied and employees. Due to the fact that the fundamental frequency levels in the hearing impaired are generally changed, this is the first point of challenge when it is spoken in improving the voice quality of these individuals, since the auditory monitoring of these is modified. Thus, some techniques are based on measures of the fundamental frequency (frequency of vibration of the vocal folds), as jitter (disturbances in frequency) and Shimmer (disturbances in amplitude) [6] [7].

This paper proposes a device for the detection and measurement of the fundamental frequency of the voice using a real-time system based on FPGA (Field-Programmable Gate Array), for further feedback through tactile and visual stimulus. The goal is to develop a portable device to help people with hearing loss achieve real-time fundamental frequency of correct voice.

With respect to correction of the fundamental frequency of the voice through visual and tactile stimulation, this proposal aims to build new knowledge in broad areas such as reconfigurable computing combined with Assistive Technology.

2. METHODOLOGY
The development was done using the Quartus II Web Edition 13.0 consisting of a programming environment, which can be used in all phases of the design FPGA's, since it performs the steps synthesis, placement, and routing logic design to be synthesized. Incremental compilation, which is a configuration of the process of transforming the source program into an object program that serves to preserve the results of blocks that have not changed during the project was used. This tool allows the description of the code validation synthesis netlist generating (converted cells are to be set), mapping and routing as well as generating the bitstream, which constitutes the processing step of the conceptual model of a digital circuit ready for is released into the FPGA. The project was set in the Development Kit kit Mercurio® IV, the ALTERA manufacturer, this one comprises a EP4CE30F23C7 Cyclone IV FPGA Family And this has 30,000 logic elements and an input clock of 50 MHz.

For pitch extraction step was done using algorithms used in previous works. At this stage the relevant parameters are calculated for the proper processing, such as LPC, cepstral coefficients, the fundamental frequency and the storage of reference data. Such algorithms required for processing were developed in VHDL. To consolidate the verification of the functionality of the device volunteers were used. The samples collected from the voice signals in individuals with hearing impairments and hearing, by performing a comparative study.

ASSETS '15, October 26-28, 2015, Lisbon, Portugal.
ACM 978-1-4503-3400-6/15/10.
http://dx.doi.org/10.1145/2700648.2811378

3. RESULTS

After two months of testing, the sentences pronounced by the patients were recorded. Because it is a subjective assessment of voice quality improvement of the results were compared with the same sentences recorded before any use of visual and tactile feedback system.

Twenty volunteers have rated the sentences pronounced before and after the test and made a quantitative assessment of improved voice quality, according to the rating scale of Table 1. The results of the evaluators are shown in Figure 1.

Table 1. Quality Improvement of Quantitative Evaluation Vocal

Comparison of the pronunciation before and after test sections	*Rating scale*
No Change	0
Little change	1
Good Change	2
Much Change	3

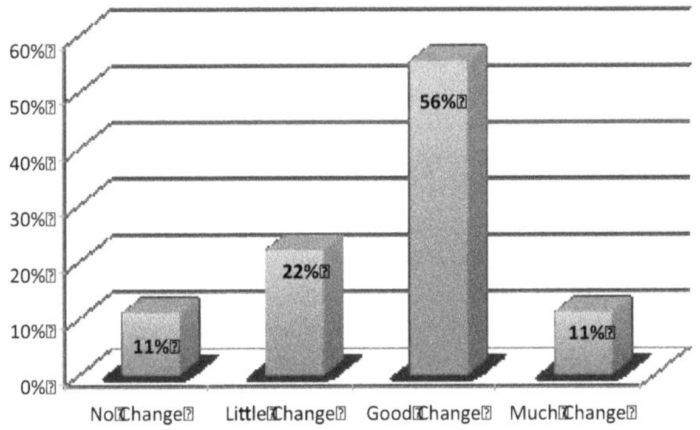

Figure 1. Voice quality assessment after use of the system

4. CONCLUSIONS

From the results, the following conclusions can be drawn: (1) In the majority of cases there was a change in the perception of voice quality; (2) In the case where there was no perceptible change the individual had profound pre-lingual deafness. This specific case needs more investigation to be concluded about the possibility of improvement with the use of the frequency correction system; (3) The tactile feedback together with the visual feedback provides the user more quickly reaches the target frequency; (4) The proposed system can be used as a portable device for real-time correction of the fundamental frequency of the voice in the deaf; (5) Experiments will be conducted in hearing people who work with the voice and need to maintain a certain frequency of voice, such as radio and TV journalists.

5. ACKNOWLEDGEMENTS

The authors thank all who contributed to the work. In particular the authors wish to thank the University of Minho and Federal Institute of Rio Grande do Norte - IFRN.

6. REFERENCES

[1] Geldard, F. A., Some neglected possibilities of communication. Science, 131:1583–1588, 1960.

[2] Gault, R.H. Progress in Experiments on Tactual Interpretations of Oral Speech. Journal of Abnormality Society Psychological. V19, 1924.

[3] Bernstein, L. E., The Evaluation of Tactile Aids (chapter 8), in Tactile Aids for The Hearing Impaired, Ians Summer (ed), Whurr Publishers, London, 1992.

[4] Weisenberger, J.M. Communication of the Acoustic Environment via Tactile Stimuli (chapter 4), in Tactile Aids for The Hearing Impaired, Ians Summer (ed), Whurr Publishers, London, 1992.

[5] Godino-Llorente, J. I.; Gomes-Vilda, P.; Blanco-Velasco, M. Dimensionality reduction of a pathological voice quality assessment system based on gaussian mixture models and short-term cepstral parameters. IEEE Transactions on Biomedical Engineering, vol. 53(10), pp. 1943–1953, 2006.

[6] Araujo, A. M. L. Jogos Computacionais fonoarticulatórios para Crianças com Deficiência Auditiva. Doctoral Thesis. Campinas: Universidade Estadual de Campinas; 2000.

[7] Lejska M. Voice field measurements: a new method of examination: the influence of hearing on the human voice. J Voice 2004;18 (2):209-15.

[8] Ramos S. Análise prosódica da fala do deficiente auditivo: parâmetros de duração e freqüência fundamental. Master Dissertation. São Paulo: Pontifícia Universidade Católica de São Paulo; 2000.

[9] Lopes, D. C. J.; Oliveira, I. B.; Avaliação da voz e fala de surdos após a aplicação de um procedimento terapêutico computadorizado. Distúrbios da Comunicação, 20(2): 183-192, São Paulo, agosto, 2008.

[10] Barbacena, I.L., Melhoria Da Qualidade Da Voz De Deficientes Auditivos Utilizando-se Correção Da Frequência Fundamental. Doctoral Thesis – UFCG, 2010

[11] Alves, R. L., Estudo sobre percepção Tátil Utilizando Dispositivos de Baixo Custo Para a Melhoria da Acessibilidade do Deficiente Visual. Dissertação de Mestrado, Universidade Federal de Campina Grande. Masters Dissertation – UFCG, 2007.

[12] Barros, A. T., Investigações sobre Estimulação Tátil Aplicada ao Ensino/aprendizagem da fala. Doctoral Thesis – UFCG, 2004.

TinyBlackBox: Supporting Mobile In-The-Wild Studies

Kyle Montague[1], André Rodrigues[2], Hugo Nicolau[3], Tiago Guerreiro[2]
[1]University of Dundee, [2]LaSIGE, Faculdade de Ciências da Universidade de Lisboa,
[3]Rochester Institute of Technology
kmontague@dundee.ac.uk, afrodrigues@fc.ul.pt, hmnics@rit.edu, tjvg@di.fc.ul.pt

ABSTRACT
Most work investigating mobile HCI is carried out within controlled laboratory settings; these spaces are not representative of the real-world environments for which the technology will predominantly be used. The result of which can produce a skewed or inaccurate understanding of interaction behaviors and users' abilities. While mobile in-the-wild studies provide more realistic representations of technology usage, there are additional challenges to conducting data collection outside of the lab. In this paper we discuss these challenges and present TinyBlackBox, a standalone data collection framework to support mobile in-the-wild studies with today's smartphone and tablet devices.

Categories and Subject Descriptors
H.5.2 [**User Interfaces**] Evaluation/Methodology, User- Centered Design; D.2.2 [**Design Tools and Techniques**]: Miscellaneous

Keywords
Mobile Computing, In-the-wild, User-Centered Design, Data Collection, Toolkit

1. INTRODUCTION
Mainstream success of smartphones and tablet devices has resulted in new forms of computer interactions - whereby the location and environment play a key role in the overall user experience. The mobile nature of these devices means that users are no longer confined to the traditional chair and desk setting, but are free to move around and interact on the go. This design space offers a vast number of opportunities for location-aware and context-specific interactions that were previously not possible. With more and more computer interactions shifting into the mobile design space, there is an urgency to understand what effect the environment has on the user experience and interaction effectiveness – thus, the need for user studies outside of the lab.

In recent years, there have been a growing number of HCI works that have explored in-the-wild or in-situ interactions with mobile technologies [1-4]. While these works report on the positive benefits from gathering real-world evidence and usage behaviors, they equally discuss the additional challenges and complexities that go with conducting HCI research outside the controlled laboratory environment, particularly capturing sufficient details and context to frame the device interaction. Having experienced these challenges firsthand in mobile accessibility research, we recognized the need for software solutions to better support the data gathering from mobile in-the-wild studies. To this end, we present TinyBlackBox (TBB), an open-source system-wide data collection solution for Android mobile devices. TBB is capable of capturing any and all sensor measurements from the device, low-level touchscreen interactions with the corresponding application interface elements. Data is captured locally on the device, then using opportunistic synchronization with Google cloud services, it can be aggregated with data from all other study participants. In addition to these collection mechanisms, TBB provides an API to extend the log files and capture study specific information. Finally, to aid the analysis of the log data, we developed a playback tool - allowing device interactions to be replayed within the context of the screen that they were recorded in (Figure 1).

ASSETS '15, October 26-28, 2015, Lisbon, Portugal
ACM 978-1-4503-3400-6/15/10.
http://dx.doi.org/10.1145/2700648.2811379

In this paper, we discuss the trends and challenges of mobile in-the-wild studies, highlighting the strengths and weaknesses of the current approaches. Moreover, we describe TinyBlackBox, the proposed no-code solution to mobile in-the-wild data collection.

2. MOBILE INTERACTIONS
Previous works have stressed the importance of studying technology use in the real-world, particularly when exploring accessibility challenges [1,3,4]. However, the research methods and data collection techniques can impose significant constraints on various aspects of the study, including: scale, sampling windows, validity of the data and the realism of the interactions. Froehlich *et al* [2], categorized current approaches of mobile data collection into *direct observations, in-situ self-reports* and *automatic logging*. *Direct observations*, require researchers to shadow the participants while they interact with the device, as used in [4]. Unfortunately, it does not scale well, and restricts data collection opportunities to conventional time intervals and acceptable observation locations. With that said, this approach allows the collection of real-world interactions, providing researchers with detailed context for the nature of the interactions. *In-situ self-reports,* such as diaries, can also be used to obtain insights into the real-world nature of technology usage. While the approach scales to support larger sample sizes and enables greater freedoms on data sampling windows, it does require a large amount of participation and effort from the users. Furthermore, diary entries are rarely recorded in the moment, often resulting in a loss of precision and context surrounding the events – without which it is challenging to attribute interaction behaviors to particular device or set of environmental factors. *Automatic logging* of the device sensors can be used to perceive environmental factors e.g. ambient light and noise levels. Similarly, logging the device interactions can provide precise details of usage behaviors and times, for example, application launch patterns. However, while the researchers were able to capture the natural app usage patterns of mobile devices, due to technical limitations, they were not able to record the low-level touchscreen inputs or access details surrounding the application interfaces themselves. In contrast, through instrumentation of experimental applications, it is possible to obtain low-level interactions as they are passed to the interface [3], but data collection is limited to interactions with the experimental

applications only. Moreover, *automatic logging* of device interactions does not provide an accurate measure of the user's intent, and additional steps are required [3].

While none of the current data collection approaches contribute a complete solution, they do provide a set complimentary strengths and weaknesses. Based on these existing collection methods, we developed a set of requirements for the TinyBlackBox framework.

3. TINYBLACKBOX

TinyBlackBox (TBB), is a standalone Accessibility Service, built for the Android 4.0+ OS. Once installed and activated, TBB will continuously run in the background of the OS, capturing the user's device interactions system-wide. TBB scrapes application data, including page layouts and interface elements – these are represented in a DOM tree structure, revealing information about the nesting of interface elements. TBB also records all of the interface interactions e.g. clicks and swipes made within applications. In addition to recognizing interface clicks, TBB provides overwritten touchscreen drivers. This enables TBB to receive the sub-gesture touch *begin*, *move* and *end* interactions, as typically recorded for touch modeling, and gesture analysis [3]. We ensure the security of user data by encrypting the log files locally on the device before they are transmitted using HTTPS protocols. TBB supports parameterized levels of data encryption i.e. *encrypt all text*, *only user generated* content such as personal SMS and emails, or *encrypt nothing*. We believe it is vital that the user is not only aware of what data is being recorded, but also entirely in control, as such; in future versions we plan to include application specific encryption rules. We have integrated TBB with Google Cloud storage to aggregate log data from multiple participants while the study is live. TBB will attempt to synchronize with the cloud storage when the device has an active WiFi connection, at least 40% battery remaining and the device is inactive or charging. Prior to uploading log files, they are compressed for network performance and to minimize cloud storage costs. In addition to transmitting users' log files, TBB periodically pings the cloud storage servers with a status report. We use this to verify that TBB is functioning correctly and that the participants are using the devices regularly – reducing the need to conduct field assessments of the devices and software.

While we present TBB as a standalone data collection service, we recognize that there is often the need for study specific information to be gathered. To support this need, we have also developed a small library that can be embedded into 3rd Party applications and services, providing APIs to facilitate communication with the standalone TBB service - enabling additional data to be captured along side the existing TBB data. Using this approach, we created an external logger, BlackBoxBuddy, to capture contextual information such as the user's location (from Google location services which leverages GPS, WiFi and Cell towers) when interacting with the device.

Finally, we have developed a suite of analysis tools to support data extraction, visualization and playback. Since TBB captures the device interactions into individual text files, we have created scripts to rebuild the logs into a local MySQL database. In this form it is possible to extract high-level statistics, such as application usage behaviors. To assist the deeper inspection of individual device sessions, we created TBB Player, an interactive web-based playback tool (Figure 1). TBB Player, renders a wireframe of the screen content that was visible to the user, and replays their touchscreen interactions in real-time. Researchers can pause and rewind interactions for further inspection. This tool is particularly useful for investigating gesture interactions that are context-specific, as each step of the device interaction is captured.

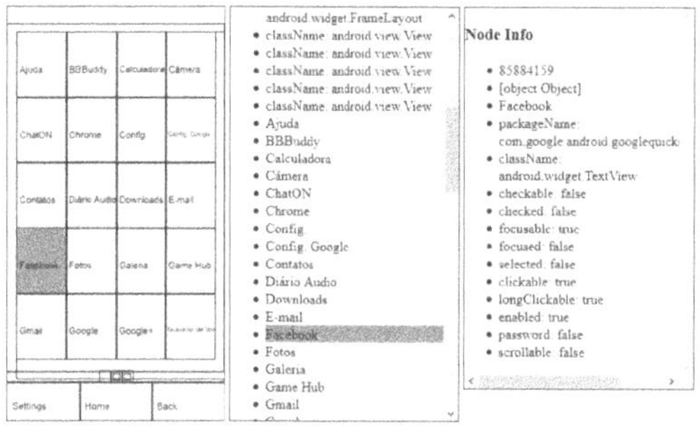

Figure 1. TBB Player - App drawer with interface element details

4. CONCLUSIONS AND FUTURE WORK

There is a demand for mobile HCI evaluations in-the-wild, particularly when investigating the interactions of populations with highly variable abilities and diverse needs. In this paper, we have explored the challenges of conducting mobile in-the-wild user studies, highlighting the strengths and weaknesses of current approaches to gathering data. In support of this demand and to address these weaknesses, we present TinyBlackBox, our standalone mobile data collection solution with analysis and interaction playback tools. We have successfully conducted a four-month user study with novice blind users, exploring their adoption experiences [6] and text-entry performances [5] using TBB. TBB supported a deeper comprehension of the interactions and habits faced by the users in their daily usage, and a detailed analysis of their finer-grained interactions with the onscreen keyboard and text-entry behaviors. TBB is open source, for the source code and documentation please see: http://goo.gl/VQTrJt

5. ACKNOWLEDGEMENTS

We thank all participants from Fundação Raquel e Martin Sain in Lisbon. This work was partially supported by: RIT's Center for Accessibility and Inclusion Research, RCUK (EP/G066019/1), and FCT (SFRH/BD/103935/2014, UID/CEC/00408/2013).

6. REFERENCES

[1] Anthony, L., Kim, Y., and Findlater, L. Analyzing user-generated youtube videos to understand touchscreen use by people with motor impairments. *In Proceedings of* CHI '13.

[2] Froehlich, J.E., Chen, M.Y., Consolvo, S., Harrison, B., and Landay, J.A. MyExperience: a system for in situ tracing and capturing of user feedback on mobile phones. *In Proceedings of* MobileHCI '07.

[3] Montague, K., Nicolau, H., and Hanson, V.L. *Motor-impaired touchscreen interactions in the wild. In Proceedings of* ASSETS '14.

[4] Naftali, M. and Findlater, L. Accessibility in context: understanding the truly mobile experience of smartphone users with motor impairments. *Proceedings of* ASSETS'14.

[5] Nicolau, H., Montague, K., Rodrigues, A., Guerreiro, T., and Hanson, V.L. Typing Performance of Blind Users: An Analysis of Touch Behaviors, Learning Effect, and In-Situ Usage. *In Proceedings of ASSETS '15.*

[6] Rodrigues, A., Montague, K., Nicolau, H., and Guerreiro, T. Getting Smartphones to TalkBack: Understanding the Smartphone Adoption Process of Blind Users. *In Proceedings of ASSETS '15.*

APLUS: A 3D Corpus of French Sign Language

Annelies Braffort
LIMSI-CNRS
Campus d'Orsay, bât 508
F-91405 Orsay cx, France
+33 1 69 85 80 68
annelies.braffort@limsi.fr

Mohamed Benchiheub
LIMSI-CNRS and CIAMS-UPSud
Campus d'Orsay, bât 508
F-91405 Orsay cx, France
+33 1 69 85 80 66
mohamed-el-fatah.benchiheub@u-psud.fr

Bastien Berret
CIAMS-UPSud
Campus d'Orsay, bât 335
F-91405 Orsay cx, France
+33 1 69 15 78 82
bastien.berret@u-psud.fr

ABSTRACT
In this paper, we present APlus, a corpus of French Sign Language that includes motion capture, video and eye-tracker data. We first explain the motivation for the creation of this resource; secondly we describe the preparation work to design the best setup regarding our constraints and aims, and then, the content of the corpus at this moment of the project.

Categories and Subject Descriptors
K.4.2 [**Computers and Society**]: Social issues – *assistive technologies for persons with disabilities.*

Keywords
French Sign Language, Motion Capture, Animation, Annotation, Movement Analysis.

1. MOTIVATION
French Sign Language (LSF) is a natural language used as primary means of communication in Deaf community in France. A majority of Deaf people have a low French reading level. Thus, software dedicated to LSF can improve Deaf people's access to teaching, information, and services. Research on SL processing is still in its infancy [2].

One of the promising applications is based on the generation of LSF content by means of a virtual signer (an animated 3D character). This approach allows producing SL discourses in an anonymous and modular way. At this moment, real applications such as Sign Smith Studio[1] or WebSourd[2] are using hand-made or predefined animations, using software or techniques such as motion capture or rotoscoping. This guarantees high quality of the generated discourse, but at high costs, and with little modularity. Methods based on more automatic processes, such as animation generation from symbolic descriptions, can be performed at low costs, but a lot remains to be done to obtain understandable animations [4].

[1] http://www.vcom3d.com/

[2] http://www.3dsigner.fr/

ASSETS '15, October 26-28, 2015, Lisbon, Portugal.
ACM 978-1-4503-3400-6/15/10.
http://dx.doi.org/10.1145/2700648.2811380

LSF, as many other SL, is a less-described language, and first of all, resources are needed to acquire more knowledge and allow for more accurate models to be designed, whatever scientific discipline is concerned. To date, there is a critical lack of resources for LSF, especially corpora containing 3D movement data recorded from human signers. If some mocap corpora are now available for researchers [3, 5, 6], this is not the case for LSF: they are not available or do not meet the requirements for multidisciplinary research as we envision it [1, 8].

We have therefore begun a multi-year project to collect, annotate and analyze a motion-capture corpus of LSF. The whole corpus (videos, mocap data and annotations) will be made available for the scientific community as this work progresses. This paper focuses on our efforts to construct this corpus, called APlus.

2. DESIGN OF THE SETUP
Since recently, we have access to a studio equipped with an optical system for motion capture that is generally used for human motor control research at the university. Optical systems utilize data captured from sensors to triangulate the 3D position of a subject between two or more cameras calibrated to provide overlapping projections. The subject wears a black suit where markers coated with a reflective material to reflect light generated near the cameras lens. These markers are located near each joint to identify the motion by the positions or angles between the markers. A reference frame with markers attached at known positions is used to calibrate the cameras and obtain their positions and the lens distortion of each camera is measured. If two calibrated cameras see a marker, its instantaneous three-dimensional location can be recovered. Thus, these systems produce data with 3 degrees of freedom for each marker, and rotational information of the limbs must be inferred from the relative orientation of three or more markers; for instance shoulder, elbow and wrist markers may be used to calculate the elbow joint angle in a stick body model. More generally, the 3D orientation of the forearm relative to any reference frame can be computed for an articulated rigid body model. Due to the possible occlusion between the various parts of the body, and because the markers are not identified and may appear identical (marker swapping), a post-processing is needed to clean up the data.

Our studio is equipped with 10 OptiTrack cameras (S250e), which has sufficient resolution for our purpose. It allows managing a correct amount of markers with various sizes, attached to the body but also to the face, where miniaturized markers are needed. Given the resolution of the cameras, we have designed a setup with 40 markers of various sizes allowing to track the motion of the limbs but also some important movements occurring on the face (eyebrow, eye lead, cheeks and mouth). However, this doesn't allow for accurate tracking of all the fingers. Only coarse information is given on finger movements.

The very first step of this work was to design the best setup for the camera and marker locations. For that we have conducted evaluations such that we can record sufficient details of the human performance for our various needs: animation replay with virtual signer, 3D data analysis, and linguistic annotation. A LSF signer is involved at this stage of the project to evaluate the quality of our setup, as a graphist expert in 3D animation. He has strong skills to evaluate the quality of the data for further use for animation replay, but also the completion of the data.

We have included in our tests the use of a Tobii eye tracker. This is a device that incorporates illumination, sensors and processing to track eye movements and gaze point. This device allows recording gaze direction. The data consist of a video where red dots show eye gaze location in the plan of the video. Our experiments show that these data can be useful to analyze the relationships between gaze and hand activity in signing, but has a drawback: when used, these glasses hide the eyebrows, which movements are also important in signing.

3. CONTENT

Several LSF native signers are involved in the project. They have various socio-linguistic profiles and signing styles, in order to have some insights on the inter-signer variability.

In order to provide various data for a number of studies in several scientific disciplines, we have defined four different tasks in order to cover various phenomena on both movement and linguistic aspects. All are of monologue type because our equipment doesn't allow to record dialog situations.

Task 1 is more specifically dedicated to the study of linear movements on the main three axes. The elicitation material consists of a set of 25 pictures showing many objects with peculiar geometrical properties (e.g. horizontal or vertical arrangements etc.). For the subject, the task consists of successively describing the images.

Task 2 is an explanation. The subject is asked to explain to a Deaf moderator the procedures taking place at the airport as if the other has never traveled by plane before. Pictures displaying different aspects as checking in, boarding, and baggage claim are shown in chronological order. This task is identical to one of the tasks designed for the multilingual Dicta-Sign corpus [7], in order to make comparison possible.

Task 3 is a narration: the retelling of a movie, "The Artist". The DVD has been sent to the subjects before the recording session. A high amount of sign language characteristic features (e.g. role shifts, non-manual movements) can be expected from this task.

Task 4 is also a narration. This consists of telling a famous event known by the French people, which have been often treated by the journalistic media. Here, a different level of language is expected.

4. PROGRESS STATE

So far, the first task has been recorded and four SLF signers were involved in the data set. The three other tasks of the APLUS corpus will be recorded in the following months.

The annotation is completed. It has been performed using a software that allows to visualize both video and mocap data, with the aim to begin multidisciplinary studies on a set of phenomena.

Various studies are in progress, on hand movements, eye gaze events, and linguistic structures that are used in SL to show the size and the shape of entities.

5. ACKNOWLEDGMENT

This research is supported in part by the French National Science Research Center (CNRS), by the HuMaIn Award Program.

6. REFERENCES

[1] Awad, Charly, Nicolas Courty, Kyle Duarte, Thibaut Le Naour, and Sylvie Gibet (2009). A combined semantic and motion capture database for real-time sign language synthesis. 9th Int Conf on Intelligent Virtual Agents (IVA'09), Amsterdam, volume 5773 of LNAI, 432-438.

[2] Braffort, A. and Filhol, M. Constraint-based Sign Language Processing, In Blache, P., Christiansen, H., Dahl, V., Duchier, D. and Villadsen, J. (Eds.), "Constraints and Language", Cambridge Scholar Publishing, 2014, 191-217.

[3] Jantunen T.; Burger,B.; De Weerdt,D.; Seilola,I. & Wainio,T. (2012). Experiences from collecting motion capture data on continuous signing. In Proc. of the 5th Workshop on the Representation and Processing of Sign Languages: Interactions Between Corpus and Lexicon, LREC conf, Istanbul, Turkey, 75-82.

[4] Kipp M., Héloir A., Nguyen Q. (2011). Sign Language Avatars: Animation and Comprehensibility. H. Högni Vilhjálmsson, S. Kopp, S. Marsella, K.R. Thórisson, 11th Int. Conf. Intelligent Virtual Agents,, IVA 2011, Reykjavik, Iceland, LNCS 6895, Springer, 113-126.

[5] Lu P. and Huenerfauth M. (2010). Collecting a Motion-capture Corpus of American Sign Language for Data-driven Generation Research. Workshop on Speech and Language Processing for Assistive Technologies (NAACL HLT SLPAT'10), 89-97, Stroudsburg, USA.

[6] Malaia, E., Borneman, J. and Wilbur. R.B. (2008). Analysis of ASL Motion Capture Data towards Identification of Verb Type. Semantics in Text Processing (STEP 2008), 1:155-64. Research in Computational Semantics. College Pub.

[7] Matthes, S., Hanke, T., Storz, J., Efthimiou, E., Dimiou, N., Karioris, P., Braffort, A., Choisier, A., Pelhate, J., Safar, E. (2010). Elicitation Tasks and Materials designed for Dicta-Sign's Multi-lingual Corpus. 4th Workshop on Representation and Processing of Sign Languages: Corpora and Sign Language Technologies/LREC conf, 158-163.

[8] Parisot, A.-M., Rinfret J., Villeneuve S. & Voghel A. (2010). Construire et déconstruire l'espace dans une langue des signes: démonstration d'un protocole d'enregistrement simultané des mouvements des membres supérieurs et du globe oculaire. In Proc. of Traitement automatique des langues des signes (TALS 2010), TALN conf, Montréal

Supporting Everyday Activities for Persons with Visual Impairments Through Computer Vision-Augmented Touch

Leah Findlater[1], Lee Stearns[2], Ruofei Du[2], Uran Oh[2], David Ross[3], Rama Chellappa[4], Jon E. Froehlich[2]

[1]College of Information Studies, [2]Dept. of Computer Science, [4]Dept. of Electrical and Computer Engineering
University of Maryland, College Park, MD 20742

[3]Atlanta VA R&D Center of Excellence in Vision and Neurocognitive Rehabilitation (CVNR)
1670 Clairmont Road, Decatur, GA 30033

ABSTRACT
The *HandSight* project investigates how wearable micro-cameras can be used to augment a blind or visually impaired user's sense of touch with computer vision. Our goal is to support an array of activities of daily living by sensing and feeding back non-tactile information (*e.g.*, color, printed text, patterns) about an object as it is touched. In this poster paper, we provide an overview of the project, our current proof-of-concept prototype, and a summary of findings from finger-based text reading studies. As this is an early-stage project, we also enumerate current open questions.

Categories and Subject Descriptors
K.4.2 [**Computer and Society**]: Social Issues – Assistive technologies for persons with disabilities

Keywords
Blind; visually impaired; wearable computing; computer vision; vision-augmented touch

1. INTRODUCTION
The majority of work on computer vision to support blind and visually impaired users has focused on at-a-distance information tasks such as navigation (*e.g.*, [1]) and spatial perception (*e.g.*, [3]). Instead, the *HandSight* project explores how computer vision can support proximal information accessed through touch. By sensing and feeding back non-tactile information about the physical world *as it is touched*, our goal is to support an array of activities of daily living (ADLs). This solution could, for example, allow the user to touch and read a printed page via real-time OCR and speech synthesis, touch a piece of clothing to hear suggestions for coordinating items, or pick up a bell pepper and recognize that it is red or green. Since touch is a highly attuned means of acquiring information for people with visual impairments (*e.g.*, [2]), we hypothesize that collocating sensing with the user's touch will enable new and intuitive assistive applications.

HandSight is part of a small but growing body of work on augmenting touch with wearable cameras and computer vision algorithms. Perhaps the most well-known system is *Orcam*, a recently introduced commercial head-mounted camera system designed to recognize objects and read printed text. While live demonstrations have been impressive[1], there is no academic work examining Orcam's effectiveness. This head-mounted camera approach could potentially complement HandSight's finger-mounted sensing. More closely related to HandSight are *Magic Finger* [8] and *FingerReader* [4,5]. Magic Finger uses a finger-mounted camera with the goal of "enabling any surface to act as a touch screen," although the focus is not for people with visual impairments—most problematically, the device covers the fingertip, thus interfering with tactile sensation [8]. FingerReader, in contrast, is a custom finger-mounted device with vibration motors designed to allow visually impaired wearers to read printed text by direct line-by-line scanning with the finger [4,5]. While promising, user evaluation of FingerReader to date has been limited to small qualitative studies (3-4 participants).

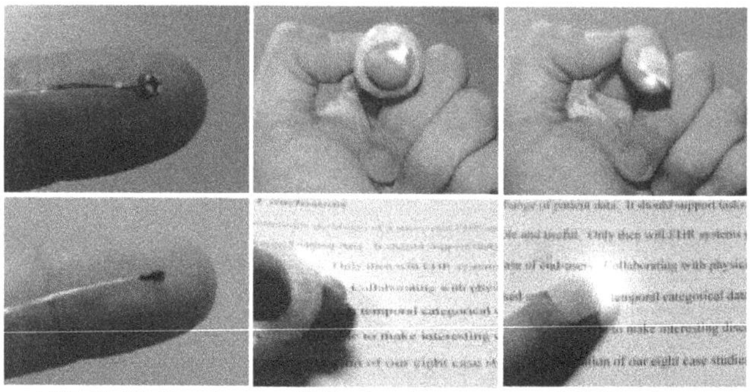

(a) NanEye2C with and without 4 LEDs. (b) Ring form factor (c) Nail form factor

Figure 1: HandSight uses a 1×1mm² AWAIBA NanEye 2C camera developed for minimally invasive surgeries (endoscopies) that can capture 250×250px images at 44fps. Early form factors also shown.

This poster paper provides an overview of HandSight's hardware and software, as well as a summary of findings from our initial area of exploration—reading printed text. Because this work is at an early stage, we also cover open questions and challenges that will need to be addressed as we expand to other application areas.

2. CURRENT PROTOTYPE
Our envisioned system consists of tiny CMOS cameras (1×1mm²) and micro-haptic actuators mounted on one or more fingers, computer vision and machine learning algorithms to support fingertip-based sensing, and a smartwatch for processing, power, and speech output. Figure 1 shows early form factors that we have been exploring, including mounting the camera on a ring or unobtrusively under an acrylic fingernail. Our overarching design goals are that HandSight should: (1) Support touch-based rather than at-a-distance interaction; (2) not hinder normal tactile function, such as covering the fingertip; (3) be easy-to-learn/use (an issue with many sensory aids) through speech and simple haptic feedback; (4) be always-available to allow for seamless transitions to/from real-world tasks; (5) be comfortable & robust to everyday stresses such as water and impact.

The current proof-of-concept prototype consists of a laptop running custom software, external speakers, a finger-mounted camera, and a custom haptic device. The camera is a self-illuminated Awaiba NanEye 2C CMOS camera with an LED ring (~40 fps, 250x250 pixels, 2.4mm diameter; Figure 1a), embedded in an adjustable ring and positioned above the finger. Because our initial application area is reading, this camera position is designed

ASSETS '15, October 26-28, 2015, Lisbon, Portugal
ACM 978-1-4503-3400-6/15/10.
http://dx.doi.org/10.1145/2700648.2811381

[1] OrCam TED@NYC. YouTube Video: http://youtu.be/_3XVsCsscyw?t=4m53

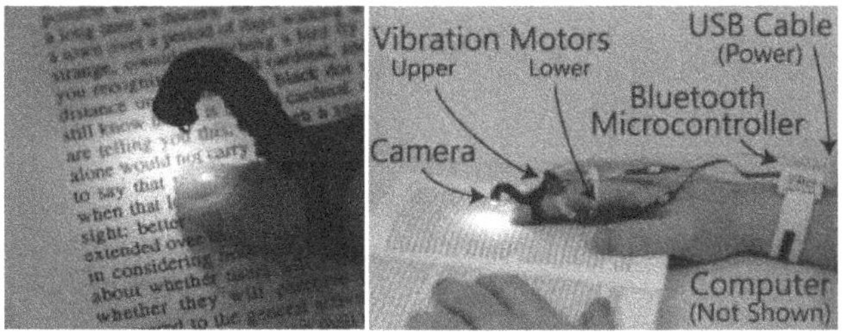

(a) Finger-mounted camera **(b) Current prototype**

Figure 2: Early design for our proof-of-concept prototype with the camera placed for reading printed text. Future designs may be made much smaller, for both the camera mount and the haptic feedback.

to offer a reasonably large field of view for optical character recognition (OCR) on a printed page. Two disc vibration motors (8mm diameter, 3.4mm thick), controlled by an Arduino Pro Micro, provide haptic feedback. The motors are attached to the user's right index finger with separate Velcro rings (Figure 2b), one on top of the finger on the intermediate phalange and one below the finger on the proximal phalange.

3. INITIAL APPLICATION: READING

We have initially explored HandSight to read printed text. Compared to handheld text scanners such as mobile phone applications, a finger-based approach has the potential to mitigate camera framing issues, enable a blind reader to better understand the spatial layout of a document, and provide better control over reading pace. However, such an approach also needs to guide the reader in physically navigating a document and tracing along lines of text. While previous work has proposed audio and haptic directional finger guidance for this purpose, user studies have been limited to 3 or 4 participants [4,5,7]. The most recent of these studies underscores the need for further investigation: all 3 participants found it difficult to read text with FingerReader [5]. This provokes the question: *why*? Are finger-based cameras a viable accessibility solution for reading printed text or simply too challenging to use given issues of accurate text capture and recognition as well as finger guidance?

To further investigate the feasibility of finger-based reading, we conducted two lab studies [6]. The first study included 20 blind participants and compared audio and haptic directional finger guidance during reading tasks. Users traced their finger left to right along each line of text and the system generated text-to-speech output. In this study, we isolated the user experience from the wearable prototype's OCR performance by displaying documents on an iPad (the touchscreen provided accurate sensing of the finger location). Audio guidance played a continuous tone when the user's finger strayed off the current line, with a low pitch indicating the need for downward movement and high pitch indicating upward. For haptic guidance, the lower motor (proximal phalange) vibrated to indicate downward movement and the upper motor indicated the opposite. Participants used both types of guidance in counterbalanced order to read plain text documents and magazine-style documents (with pictures).

The two types of guidance resulted in relatively similar line tracing performance, with speeds ranging from 106–120 WPM across all conditions. Audio, however, may offer an accuracy advantage—with the magazine document participants strayed farther from the line with haptic than with audio (M=15px *vs.* 11 px away from the middle of the line; $Z_{19}=-2.374$, $p=.018$, $r=.54$).

Preference was almost evenly split (11 of 20 participants preferred haptic guidance), reflecting contradictions found in previous research [4,5,7]. Open-ended comments also highlighted the tradeoffs of the two types of guidance. Some participants felt that audio interfered with the speech output: *"You could focus on the audio of the text, and not be listening for other sounds"* (P8), or *"I missed a couple words because I was being distracted by the [audio]"* (P16). Those who preferred the audio reported that haptic guidance required more effort and could lead to desensitization. Finally, while several participants appreciated the direct access to layout information provided with HandSight's exploration mode, important concerns arose overall about ease of use and the amount of concentration required.

In the second study, 4 blind participants used a proof-of-concept wearable prototype (Figure 2b) and KNFB Reader iOS, a state-of-the-art OCR application, to complete reading tasks. The findings highlighted the strengths and weaknesses of the two approaches. HandSight offered additional layout information and more immediate access to text content without the need to worry about framing the complete document within the camera's field of view. But, once the document was successfully scanned, KNFB Reader offered a faster and smoother reading experience, and was preferred by all participants. Further work is needed to assess the impacts of the tradeoffs on document comprehension.

4. DISCUSSION AND OPEN QUESTIONS

The goal of the HandSight project is to support an array of activities of daily living by sensing and feeding back non-tactile information (*e.g.*, color, printed text, visual patterns) about an object as it is touched. We plan to explore several application areas beyond reading; however, many open questions remain. While a finger-based camera is always available and may mitigate camera-framing issues that can occur with mobile devices (*e.g.*, smartphones), wearables introduce practical issues of robustness and social acceptability. Future prototypes will be smaller and less obtrusive, leveraging our tiny camera form factor. We are also studying how to incorporate smartwatches more effectively, such as offloading haptic feedback to the band of the watch. Still, whether blind users are interested in wearing a finger-mounted device for accessibility is an open question.

5. ACKNOWLEDGEMENTS

This work was supported by the Office of the Assistant Secretary of Defense for Health Affairs under Award W81XWH-14-1-0617.

6. REFERENCES

[1] Dakopoulos, D. and Bourbakis, N.G. Wearable Obstacle Avoidance Electronic Travel Aids for Blind: A Survey. *IEEE SMC, Part C (Applications and Reviews) 40*, 1 (2010), 25–35.

[2] Goldreich, D. and Kanics, I.M. Tactile Acuity is Enhanced in Blindness. *J. Neurosci. 23*, 8 (2003), 3439–3445.

[3] Khambadkar, V., Folmer, E. GIST: A Gestural Interface for Remote Nonvisual Spatial Perception. *Proc. ACM UIST'13*, (2013), 301–310.

[4] Shilkrot, R., Huber, J., Liu, C., Maes, P., and Chandima, N.S. FingerReader: a wearable device to support text reading on the go. *CHI '14 Extended Abstracts*, (2014), 2359–2364.

[5] Shilkrot, R., Huber, J., Wong, M.E., Maes, P., and Nanayakkara, S. FingerReader: a wearable device to explore printed text on the go. *Proc. ACM CHI'15*, (2015), 2363–2372.

[6] Stearns, L., Du, R., Oh, U., et al. Evaluating Haptic and Auditory Directional Guidance to Assist Blind Persons in Reading Printed Text Using Finger-Mounted Cameras. *In submission*.

[7] Stearns, L., Du, R., et al. The design and preliminary evaluation of a finger-mounted camera and feedback system to enable reading of printed text for the blind. *ACVR'14 Workshop at ECCV'14*, (2014).

[8] Yang, X.-D., Grossman, T., Wigdor, D., and Fitzmaurice, G. Magic finger: always-available input through finger instrumentation. Proc. ACM UIST '12, (2012), 147–156.

A Haptic Device to Support the Use of a Glucose Monitor by Individuals Who are Blind or Visually Impaired

Matthew Standard
Virginia Commonwealth University
401 West Main Street
Richmond, Virginia 23284
001-804-828-7839
standardms@vcu.edu

Jacob Park
Aesculap, Inc.
3773 Corporate Parkway
Center Valley, PA 18034
001-800-258-1946
parkje4@vcu.edu

Dianne T.V. Pawluk
Virginia Commonwealth University
401 West Main Street
Richmond, Virginia 23284
001-804-828-9491
dtpawluk@vcu.edu

ABSTRACT
We present a simple and affordable device developed in order to address difficulties that diabetics who are blind or visually impaired encounter when attempting to independently operate a glucometer.

Categories and Subject Descriptors
K.4.2 [**Computing Milieux**]: Computers and Society – Assistive technologies for persons with disabilities.

General Terms
Performance, Design, Experimentation, Human Factors

Keywords
Haptics; Assistive Technology

1. INTRODUCTION
Diabetes is the seventh leading cause of death in the United States and may actually be underreported as a cause of death [1]. Daily monitoring of glucose levels is essential for diabetic management and health. Both Type I and Type II diabetics are at risk of developing eye problems, such as glaucoma, cataracts and diabetic retinopathy, leading to visual impairment or blindness. Diabetic retinopathy is a leading cause of blindness in American adults [2]. Between 40 to 45 percent of Americans diagnosed with diabetes have some stage of diabetic retinopathy. This affects both eyes and can get worse with time, although it can be slowed with better blood sugar management. Managing one's blood sugar can also avoid problems that can lead to serious complications such as foot or leg amputations, stroke, kidney disease, heart disease and so on [1].

Affordable glucose monitors have been developed for at home monitoring, some of which provide auditory read-out for individuals who are blind or vision impaired (BVI). However, our research group was approached by two professionals working with individuals who are BVI in regard to problems with current glucometers. One was a nurse practitioner who found that her BVI patients had difficulty putting their blood on the test strip properly and without contamination. Failure involves the need for further finger pricks and test strips. Further finger pricks are undesirable, especially with those individuals who need to test their blood glucose 5 times a day. Additional test strips have to be paid out of pocket (as opposed to by insurance). Alternately, some people will skip the measurement, which is not good for their health.

ASSETS'15, October 26–28, 2015, Lisbon, Portugal.
ACM 978-1-4503-3400-6/15/10.
DOI: http://dx.doi.org/10.1145/2700648.2811382

For individuals who are deaf-blind, auditory read-outs still do not provide them with access to the glucose measurement. Lack of independent access to their glucose readings is the sole reason that several individuals who are deaf-blind have had to give up their independence and move to an assistive living home.

There are currently no existing alternatives to solve these two problems on the market. The Sof-Tact glucometer (Abbot Laboratories, no longer produced) and the Gio (Erick Forman and Sara Krugman, concept paper) both remove the need to align the finger with a test strip by providing a mechanism in the device to align the pricked point with the test strip. However, both devices only use a visual readout. In addition, the Gio only provides access to prick the tips of the fingers; this is problematic as most individuals who are BVI do not like pricking the pads of the fingers used to read Braille or interact tactually with their environment.

2. DESIGN
2.1 Design Requirements
One of the key concerns in developing a device(s) to solve these problems is that many potential users live below the poverty line and so cost is an important issue. We decided to develop very low cost add-ons for existing glucometers rather than provide a stand-alone glucometer itself. Ease of use was also a key concern as many people in the target population are elderly and unfamiliar with technology.

The difficulties in taking reliable blood glucose reading are correct alignment of the finger with the test strip and avoiding contamination. The test strip must be placed perpendicular to the pricked finger at the spot of the bleeding for correct absorption. The blood also needs to avoid being smeared on the finger to avoid contamination. In addition, potential users strongly desired that prick locations be obtainable from other spots than the pad of the fingertip and from multiple fingers.

There are three key issues in providing reading access to individuals who are deaf-blind. First, neither visual nor auditory feedback can be used. Second, most people who are visually impaired do not know Braille. Third, it must be easy to interpret correctly. Another complication is that approximately half of all people with diabetes have some sort of nerve damage, resulting in, for example, loss of feeling in the fingertips and toes [1].

2.2 Alignment Guide

The alignment guide is an add on device for existing glucometers made of plastic printed using a 3-D printer in one piece which allows the design to be easily altered to accommodate different models of glucometers to be placed in the main recess (A).

The design in Figure 1 is suited for the Prodigy Voice glucometer as recommended by clinicians and their patients as it relays testing information via audio. The test strip projects from the glucometer and lays in the outlined area in (B). The user inserts a finger into the opening of the cylindrical section (C) from either side until they feel a suitable lancing site protrude through the window at (D). Any part of the 10 fingers can be used as a blood test site (i.e., sites are not restricted to the distal pad). The tip of a commercially available lancing device is positioned at (D) which has a border around it to assist in the coordination of the lancing task. Once the site has been lanced, the user simply rotates their finger by following the haptic cues on the inside of the cylindrical section (Figure 1, insert) until they feel the test strip (a quarter turn).

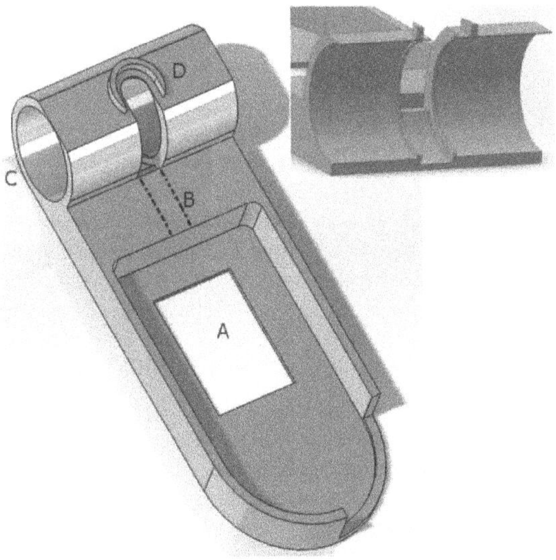

Figure 1: CAD model of the device. Insert: Ridges on the inside of the cylinder act as haptic cues to maintain alignment when rotating to the test strip.

2.3 Tactile Reading Access for the Deaf-Blind

While diabetics who are blind or visually impaired have at least talking glucometers as assistive technology, deaf-blind diabetics have no such resource. The deaf-blind must rely on solely the tactile channel for information. Tactile actuators are common in most mobile devices and smart phones which are becoming increasingly common and equitable to own. Many individuals who are BVI do own a smartphone. In order to keep the cost of an add-on low we have developed a low-cost method for individuals who are deaf-blind to obtain their glucose reading.

This new add on is a shelf-system which has the Alignment Guide placed on the lower shelf and a smartphone, with the camera side pointing downwards, on the upper shelf (Figure 2). The principle of the device is that the Smartphone uses Optical Character Recognition API tools to obtain the numeric readout of the measurement. The upper left hand corner of the upper-shelf contains a large dot (indicating the corner at which the ready signal will be made). Each of the three remaining corners of the upper-shelf are marked with thick raised letters for I (first digit), II (second digit) and III (third digit).

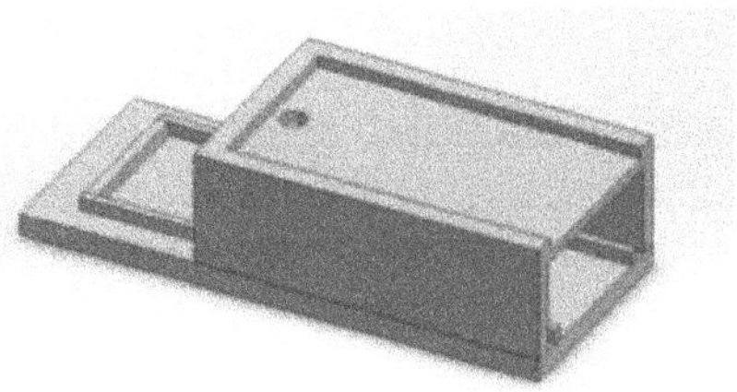

Figure 2: Shelf-system for Tactile Reading Access

The user places their finger or palm in the upper left hand corner (where the raised dot is located on the shelf) of the shelf/smartphone (which can be aligned through the shelf ridges) until they feel a vibration indicating the measurement is ready to be read. They then can proceed to any of the three other corners to tactually read the digits. The user taps the corner of the smartphone to indicate they are ready to read that particular digit. For number 0, there is no vibration. For numbers 1-4, short pulses in the amount of the digit are given. For numbers 5-9, a long pulse to indicate 5, followed by 1-4 short pulses for digits 6-9 are given. When a user breaks contact with the screen the vibrating readout for that digit is stopped.

3. TESTING

User testing is currently underway for the Alignment Guide after which it will be tested in combination with Tactile Read Access. The user testing of the Alignment Guide is in the process of recruiting 24 participants who are BVI who have diabetes. We compare a 16 day period without the use of our device to a 16 day period with the use of our device in a longitudinal study. We measure the number of test strips used per test, the number of finger pricks performed per test and a Likert scale measurement of stress, anger and frustration during testing. Preliminary feedback from our initial participants has been positive: participants have commented that it feels easier to take their blood glucose measurements with the Alignment Guide.

4. DISCUSSION

This paper proposes two low cost add-ons to current glucometer guides to provide access to individuals who are BVI and who are deaf-blind. Testing is currently under way to validate the effectiveness of their use and to determine any needed design improvements. We are also looking for a company to produce these devices through injection molding, which, once the mold is made, will only cost pennies to make. An alternate possibility (although somewhat more costly) would be to adapt the model used by "Enabling the Future", which is a global network of volunteers with 3-D printers that are willing to print out prosthetic parts and assembly them for those in need of a low-cost hand prosthesis.

5. ACKNOWLEDGMENTS

Supported by NSF IIS Grants 1218310 and 0712936.

6. REFERENCES

[1] American Diabetes Association accessed online at www.diabetes.org June, 2015.

[2] NEI Facts About Diabetic Eye Disease accessed online at hhttps://nei.nih.gov/health/diabetic/retinopathy June, 2015

Exploring Interface Design for Independent Navigation by People with Visual Impairments

Erin Brady[1], Daisuke Sato[2], Chengxiong Ruan[1], Hironobu Takagi[2], Chieko Asakawa[1,2]
[1] Carnegie Mellon University, [2] IBM Tokyo
{elbrady, cruan, chiekoa}@andrew.cmu.edu; {dsato, takagih}@jp.ibm.com

ABSTRACT
Most user studies of navigation applications for people with visual impairments have been limited by existing localization technologies, and appropriate instruction types and information needs have been determined through interviews. Using Wizard-of-Oz navigation interfaces, we explored how people with visual impairments respond to different instruction intervals, precision, output modalities, and landmark use during *in situ* navigation tasks. We present the results of an experimental study with nine people with visual impairments, and provide direction and open questions for future work on adaptive navigation interfaces.

Categories and Subject Descriptors
K.4.2 [**Social Issues**]: Assistive technologies for persons with disabilities.

Keywords
Non-visual navigation, interface design, visual impairment.

1. INTRODUCTION
People with visual impairments have unique navigation strategies, spatial understanding, and information needs. Prior work has examined navigation systems for people with visual impairments [5]; however, most studies focus on the effectiveness of a single system, and do not provide interface alternatives for users to choose amongst. Other work has explored the information that people with visual impairments desire while navigating independently [1, 4]; but these studies relied on interview data instead of exploring different navigation interfaces in practice.

To bridge the gaps between these related works, we performed experimental evaluations of navigation interfaces with nine users with visual impairments. We used Wizard-of-Oz design, where a human *wizard* triggered navigation commands by hand (instead of via automation) as the user reached specific landmarks or needed to make path adjustments. The Wizard-of-Oz design allowed us to test multiple interfaces in practice in a low-cost, flexible way.

2. RELATED WORK
There are differences in how people with visual impairments and sighted people perceive and understand spatial information. People with visual impairments can learn spatial information via audio or tactile cues in the environment, but their spatial understanding is not complete [2], and route-based, turn-by-turn instructions are more useful for them, while overhead, birds-eye descriptions are more useful for sighted people [3].

ASSETS '15, October 26-28, 2015, Lisbon, Portugal
ACM 978-1-4503-3400-6/15/10.
http://dx.doi.org/10.1145/2700648.2811383

Both research and commercial tools have been built to provide navigational instructions for people with visual impairments. These tools often use localization techniques to direct the user to a target [5]. But studies of these navigation tools often focus on the efficacy and ease-of-use of a single tool, rather than comparing two or more interfaces to find the best way to present information.

Many features of navigation interface design have been explored through interviews with people with visual impairment, including how they choose navigation aids [4] and their information needs during navigation [1]. However, these interview studies explore participants' high-level reflections on navigation, rather than their immediate reactions of how well different interfaces would work in real scenarios. We collected *in situ* experimental observations to complement and contrast findings from these interview studies.

3. EXPERIMENTAL DESIGN
We created a total of 14 interface variants: 13 interfaces testing navigation components (walking in direct paths, turning, and walking without veering), and one landmark-based interface. We tested interfaces with a mixture of output modalities (speech, non-speech audio, haptic), information specificity and frequency, and location. These features were chosen with input from one of the authors, who is totally blind, and a local O&M instructor. The 14 interface variants are described in more detail in Table 1.

For each interface variant, the participant wore bone-conduction headphones which played navigation instructions (except for the haptic interface, where participants wore mobile phones in armbands which vibrated directionally). A researcher serving as the *wizard* walked behind participants as they navigated through a university campus, manually triggering each command as participants passed landmarks or needed to course-correct.

After each navigation task, we asked participants to rank the ease of using the interface on a 10-point Likert scale, in order to explicitly compare the interfaces and prompt discussion. Between each set of interface types and in a closing interview, we asked participants for reflections on the different interface features.

4. RESULTS
Nine participants with visual impairments were recruited through personal connections and local organizations to test these interface variants. We sought participants with a variety of ages (from 22 to 73, avg. 54), genders (four female), and levels of vision (four totally blind, three legally blind, and two low-vision). Two had confounding hearing impairments, and one had cerebral palsy. Average ease-of-use Likert scores are shown in Table 1.

Interval and Specificity of Feedback: There was no consensus among participants about the appropriate feedback intervals. Four participants wanted as many instructions as possible during direct path navigation, to get continuous feedback that they were on the right path; two others preferred as few as possible to avoid missing ambient noises that provide clues about their environment. Intervals mattered more as participants approached a waypoint or destination; five participants wanted fixed

ID	Navigation	Modality	Output Type	Interval/Specificity	Location	AVG	STD.
1	Direct Path	Speech	*"50 feet to door"*	Every 10 feet	Indoor (empty)	**8.17**	1.70
2	Direct Path	Speech	*"40 feet to door"*	Every 20 feet	Indoor (empty)	**8.17**	1.27
3	Direct Path	Speech	*"30 feet to door"*	Every 30 feet	Indoor (empty)	7.00	**2.06**
4	Direct Path	Speech	*"30 steps to door"*	Every 10 steps	Indoor (empty)	7.28	1.68
5	Direct Path	Speech	*"20 steps to door"*	Every 20 steps	Indoor (empty)	7.33	1.87
6	Direct Path	Sonification	Fast clicks	1 click / second	Indoor (empty)	7.00	1.98
7	Direct Path	Sonification	Slow clicks	1 click / 2 seconds	Indoor (empty)	6.83	1.71
8	Veering	Speech	*"Move slightly right"*	N/A	Indoor (trafficked)	**8.17**	2.09
9	Veering	Sonification	Clicks on left or right	N/A	Indoor (trafficked)	6.50	2.32
10	Veering	Haptic	Vibration on left or right	N/A	Indoor (trafficked)	7.39†	**2.75†**
11	Turning	Speech	*"Turn to 11-o'clock"*	Clockwise	Indoor (trafficked)	**7.11**	**2.26**
12	Turning	Speech	*"Turk left 15 degrees"*	Degrees of turn	Indoor (trafficked)	5.28	1.89
13	Turning	Speech	*"Turn slightly left"*	Verbal	Indoor (trafficked)	6.72	1.64
14	Landmarks	Speech	*"This corridor is a wide area. The floor will be carpeted when you get closer to the door."*	At each landmark, (e.g. doors, stairs, railings, changes in floor type)	Both indoor areas, stairwell, lobby, and an outdoor quad	N/A	N/A

Table 1. Interface designs with average ease-of-use scores. Highest average score of each navigation type is bolded.
† *Two scores not given for haptic veering.*

instructions 5 or 10 feet before each point of interest, regardless of their preferred frequency for other instructions.

Exact specificity was not necessarily useful for participants. For turns, eight participants preferred clockwise or verbal instructions over degree of the turns, which were exact but took too long to parse. For long paths, an exact distance may be needlessly precise:

If I'm far away from something and it told me to walk 1400 steps, I would have no concept of how far it wanted me to go. (P6)

Modality of Feedback: All participants preferred speech for path navigation, finding it more distinguishable, more informational, and less distracting than non-speech, though tradeoffs existed:

The plus is, you don't have to think, you just listen to the beeps. But the minus is, you can't get a picture in your mind how far you're going to have to go. (P1)

Only two participants preferred vibrational interfaces over sound-based interfaces for veering, and both had some level of hearing impairment, which may have influenced their preferences.

Landmarks: While participants found many of the landmarks useful, some participants had trouble hearing all the landmarks as they tried to follow complex instructions while simultaneously dealing with surrounding noise from construction equipment and passing groups of conversing students. Though the information was valuable, the actual number of instructions received at any point may have been overwhelming and hard to keep track of.

5. DISCUSSION

Interviews with the participants revealed a variety of other information needs and how they could be used for navigation.

Seven participants said exploratory information about their surroundings, such as announcing which cross-streets they were currently between or what shops they were passing, could be useful for navigating to a target and confirming that they was on the correct path. However, five mentioned it would also be useful to announce important indoor locations, such as elevators or bathrooms, which may not be part of their route but would make the path easier to complete independently without asking for help.

Five participants mentioned that different levels of instruction are needed in familiar and unfamiliar spaces, also noted in prior work [1]. But many stated that familiar spaces can become unfamiliar due to obstacles, pedestrians, or environmental changes (snow in winter, outdoor café tables blocking a sidewalk in summer). While applications can offer different instructions for familiar and unfamiliar spaces, the definition of *familiar* should remain flexible, accommodating sporadic obstacles and other changes.

While participants had different preferences among the interfaces, all desired more information than was currently available to them. Even when they disliked an interface design, they felt the information provided could be useful. While she did not like using the step-counting interface, P7 still ranked it a 4, saying:

It's a little bit of help, so I'm not going to say it's a 1. (P7)

6. CONCLUSION

Navigation interfaces for people with visual impairments must be designed with appropriate flexibility, adaptability, and feedback. In this poster, we present the results of a user study with nine participants, exploring 14 experimental navigation interfaces. Though no specific interface emerged as perfect for everyone, participants identified a number of suggestions and criticisms, which we plan to distill into design recommendations and explore in a follow-up study with an adaptive navigation interface.

7. REFERENCES

[1] Banovic, N. et al.. Uncovering Information Needs for Independent Spatial Learning for Users who are Visually Impaired. ASSETS 2013.

[2] Cattaneo, Z. et al.. Imagery and spatial processes in blindness and visual impairment. Neuroscience and Biobehavioral Reviews. 2008.

[3] Noordzij, M.L. et al.. The influence of visual experience on the ability to form spatial mental models based on route and survey descriptions. Cognition. 2006.

[4] Williams, M.A. et al.. "Pray Before You Step Out": Describing Personal and Situational Blind Navigation Behaviors. ASSETS 2013.

[5] Zhang, J. et al. Navigation Systems for Individuals with Visual Impairment: A Survey. iCREATe 2008.

MoviTouch: Mobile Movement Capability Configurations

Jan David Smeddinck, Jorge Hey, Nina Runge, Marc Herrlich
Digital Media Lab, TZI
University of Bremen, Germany
{smeddinck,jorge,nr,mh}@tzi.de

Christine Jacobsen, Jan Wolters
RehaMed Delmenhorst, Wolters / Eybe / Schröder-Wolters GbR
Germany
chrisjacobsen188@gmail.com

Rainer Malaka
Digital Media Lab, TZI
University of Bremen, Germany
malaka@tzi.de

ABSTRACT

Strong adaptability is a major requirement and challenge in the physiotherapeutic use of motion-based games for health. For adaptation tool development, tablets are a promising platform due to their similarity in affordance compared to traditional clipboards. In a comparative study, we examined three different input modalities on the tablet that allow for configuring joint angles: direct-touch, classic interface components (e.g. buttons and sliders), and a combination of both. While direct touch emerged as the least preferable modality, the results highlight the benefits of the combination of direct-touch and classic interface components as the most accessible modality for configuring joint angle ranges. Furthermore, the importance of configuring joint angles along three distinct axes and the interesting use-case of configuration tools as communication support emerged.

Categories and Subject Descriptors

K.8.0 [**Personal Computing**]: General – *games*, H.5.2 [**Information Interfaces**]: User Interfaces – *interaction styles.*

General Terms

Design, Experimentation, Human Factors.

Keywords

Physiotherapy, rehabilitation, mobile, direct-touch, configuration, motion-based, games for health, communication, older adults.

1. INTRODUCTION

Demographic change and trends towards sedentary behavior increase the number of people who require physiotherapy, rehabilitation, and prevention (PRP). Older adults make up the largest sub-group of people that receive PRP, however there is also a large number of more specific sub-groups that are of interest to the accessibility community. In PRP, the physical capabilities of the patients are the very core of the profession. Communication amongst therapists and the considerations of each individual therapist are formally structured by the vocabulary and therapeutic approaches that they gained during their education. Amongst other aspects, this involves range of motion assessments based on joint angles, verbal communication, and communication via assessment sheets and notes that are often carried on clipboards. Due to differences in schooling, there can be notable differences in approaches employed by therapists even in one and the same practice. Objective means to communicate patient capabilities could thus be of great help. Likewise, with the recent advent of motion-based games for health (MGH) targeting the support of PRP, matching the individual player (patient) capabilities and needs has emerged as the grand challenge [4, 7]. Automated adaptivity can help tackle this challenge, but manual adaptation input by therapists (e.g. to indicate inoperable limbs, or medically sound goals, etc.) is also required. Tools that enable an efficient structured configuration of movement capabilities have the potential to foster objective communication amongst therapists, between therapists and patients, and they can also serve as configuration interfaces for motion-based games for health.

Tablets are a promising platform for such tools, since the form factor and interaction style ties in well with the established workflows that use the clipboard as a core tool for carrying information. However, that means that keyboard and mouse are not readily available as input devices, being replaced by touch (and perhaps stylus) based input. We thus began explorations on the research question *"How can applications best accommodate the situated use of a tablet in a practical setting, whilst respecting the user (therapists') expectations and facilitating an efficient, comprehensive, and unambiguous configuration of movement capabilities?"*. We present a comparison of the reception of three alternative input modalities (cf. Figure 1). Our work contributes to MGH research, but also concerns a tool that has potential as a communication platform for therapists to keep track of the capabilities of patients in an objective and consistent manner.

2. STATE OF THE ART

MGH are now an established research field with a wide variety of use-cases and target groups [3, 7] and first systems are entering practical use. However, to facilitate proper accessibility, safety, and efficiency, MGH must meet the complex and ever changing capabilities and needs of each user as well as possible, and much more exactly than what is required from general exergames or games or entertainment. The adaptability and adaptivity have repeatedly been isolated as a grand challenge of MGH [4, 7]. While automation arguably plays an important role in meeting the complex dual-flow [6] mixture of matching challenge to abilities, manual settings will play an important role for the foreseeable future as well. Settings interfaces that integrate seamlessly with regular therapy procedures are thus needed. Movement capability configurations are an important recurrent element of such interfaces. Therapist communication depends on the individual schooling. There are notable regional and subjective differences stemming from an ever modernizing education, leading to considerable practical consequences (e.g. notably low inter-therapist agreement in quality of motion judgements [5]). Tools that foster an objective and formal communication can play an important role in improving PRP by supporting better exchange amongst therapists (for example when handing over a patient), but also in improving therapist to patient communication. Clipboards structure the contemporary workday life in therapy practices much like flight strips have for a long time structured the work of air traffic controllers. However, tablet-based systems are already beginning to enter and modernize that work setting [1]. Focusing

ASSETS '15, October 26-28, 2015, Lisbon, Portugal.
ACM 978-1-4503-3400-6/15/10.
http://dx.doi.org/10.1145/2700648.2811384

new settings interface developments on that platform is reasonable, however it means that the input modalities change compared to traditional MGH settings interfaces. For some use cases traditional windows, icons, menus, pointer (WIMP) elements can still work best, while other use-cases likely benefit from (direct-)touch interaction modalities.

3. PRE-STUDY & DEVELOPMENT

A pre-study informed the application development. It consisted of interviews with 3 physiotherapists, featuring observations and a think-aloud protocol that were captured while the therapists enacted practical configurations for two persona on an arts manikin (jointed doll). The picture was completed by camera recordings of the hands and a closing interview. Concerning the central question whether axes would be manipulated simultaneously or separately we found that all participants preferred isolated axes (which is apparently more simple conceptually and also more precise) and noted that they would appreciate a numerical display of joint angles. While they said that they would like to use a tablet app for MGH settings based on a virtual manikin, they also highlighted the potential use of such a tool to communicate with patients and other therapists. Figure 1 shows a combined view of the three interface prototypes that were created with a technology pipeline consisting of MakeHuman, Blender, and Unity, following the insights from the pre-study.

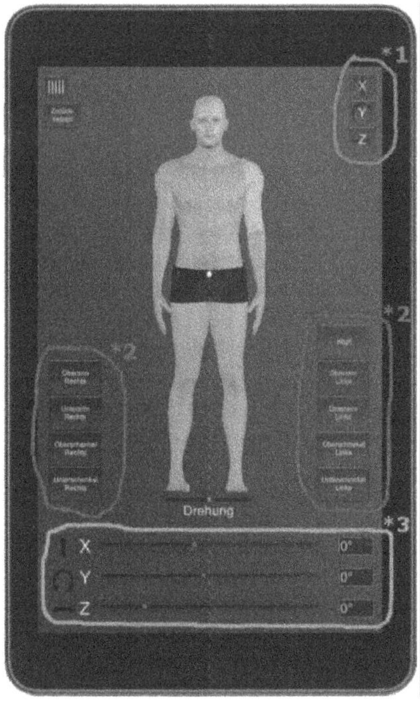

1. Direct-Touch (DT)
A direct manipulation approach: body parts are selected and dragged with direct-touch (1).

2. WIMP
Classic interface components: buttons for body part selection and sliders for angle manipulation (2,3).

3. Touch + WIMP (tWIMP)
A mixture using direct-touch for body part selection, yet sliders for angle manipulation (3).

The numbers in brackets indicate visible interface elements per modality.

Figure 1: Combined view of all three interface versions.

4. COMPARATIVE INTERFACE STUDY

To determine the preferred interface version, we performed a comparative study with six experts (therapists) between 25 and 54 years of age (M=37.7) following the same procedure and measures as the pre-study, but employing each of the interfaces (instead of a manikin) for configurations in a within-subjects design. In addition to the settings for a persona, the participants were asked to match two pre-rendered poses using each version of the interface. We also included a system usability score (SUS) [2] and follow-up interviews.

4.1 Results & Analysis

SUS results showed that the WIMP (M=71.5, SD=4.9) and the tWIMP (M=69.5, SD=12.5) versions received similar and good average SUS scores, while DT (M=48, SD=15.92) was clearly inferior. A single-coder video analysis for usability problems and participant remarks indicated that most notable events (30 instances hinting at conceptual problems such as a lack of an intuitive understanding of the direction of the manipulation) occurred with the DT interface, compared to the WIMP and tWIMP versions (17/11 instances). The interviews confirmed these findings with participants remarking that they *"find the touch version to be laborious"*, that *"the things sometimes simply don't move as expected"* and that the fingers or hand tend to obstruct the view. Participants found that they *"could make the most precise settings with the sliders"* and preferred touch for body part selection over buttons. Some said that they could imagine that the DT interface could be faster in practice and highlighted the importance of making settings swiftly. As in the pre-study, the experts highlighted the potential alternative use-cases in record keeping, therapist-therapist, and therapist-patient communication and all said that they could well imagine using such an interface for movement capability configurations: *"That was fun. I could really imagine working with something like this."*

5. DISCUSSION & CONCLUSION

In an explorative comparative study of three versions of a therapist interface for movement capability configurations on tablet devices, we observed a preference of a mixed model of direct-touch for body part activation with slider components for joint angle adjustments that avoid a view obstruction by the hands, while a direct-touch version has shown to be clearly inferior. Careful technical improvements might mitigate some of the observed weaknesses. We have also uncovered very promising secondary use-cases of such interfaces for a more graspable, structured, and unambiguous communication between therapists and between therapists and patients that add to the expected secondary use case of keeping objective patient records.

6. ACKNOWLEDGMENTS

We thank all members of the joint research project *Adaptify* (http://adaptify.de/), the participating experts of our study, and the supporting staff. This project was partially funded by the BMBF (Federal Ministry of Education and Research, Germany).

7. REFERENCES

[1] Boulos, M.N.K. et al. 2014. Mobile medical and health apps: state of the art, concerns, regulatory control and certification. *Online Jnl of Pub. Health Informatics*. 5, 3 (Feb. 2014), 229.

[2] Brooke, J. 1996. SUS: a "quick and dirty" usability scale. *Usability Evaluation in Industry*. P.W. Jordan et al., eds. Taylor & Francis. 189–194.

[3] Göbel, S. and Wiemeyer, J. eds. 2014. *Games for Training, Education, Health and Sports*. Springer Int. Publishing.

[4] Hocine, N. et al. 2014. Dynamic Difficulty Adaptation in Serious Games for Motor Rehabilitation. *Games for Training, Education, Health and Sports*. Springer. 115–128.

[5] Pomeroy, V.M. et al. 2003. Agreement between physiotherapists on quality of movement rated via videotape. *Clinical Rehabilitation*. 17, 3 (Jan. 2003), 264–272.

[6] Sinclair, J. et al. 2009. Exergame development using the dual flow model. *Proc. of the 6th Australasian Conf. on Interactive Entertainment* (NY, USA, 2009), 11:1–11:7.

[7] Smeddinck, J.D. et al. 2014. Anpassbare Computerspiele für Senioren. *Informatik-Spektrum*. 37, 6 (Dec. 2014), 575–579.

Feel the Web: Towards the Design of Haptic Screen Interfaces for Accessible Web Browsing

Andrii Soviak, Vikas Ashok, Yevgen Borodin, Yury Puzis, I.V. Ramakrishnan
Department of Computer Science, Stony Brook University, NY, USA
[asoviak,vganjiguntea,borodin,ypuzis,ram]@cs.stonybrook.edu

ABSTRACT

Web browsing with screen readers is tedious and frustrating, largely due to the inability of blind screen-reader users to get spatial information about the structure of web pages and utilize it for effective navigation. Haptic interfaces have the potential to provide blind users with a tactile "feel" for the 2-D layout of web pages and help them focus screen reading on specific parts of the webpage. In this preliminary work, we explore the utility of a simple haptic web-browsing interface – tactile overlays, and report on a preliminary user study with 10 blind participants who performed various web-browsing tasks with and without these overlays. We also analyzed the user-interaction behavior and explored the appropriate design choices and their tradeoffs in the space of haptic-interface design for accessible web browsing.

Categories and Subject Descriptors

H.5.2 [**Information interfaces and presentation**]: User Interfaces - *ergonomics, interaction styles, haptic I/O, prototyping*

General Terms

Design, Performance, Experimentation, Human Factors.

Keywords

Web Applications, Screen Reader, Web Accessibility, Haptic Interfaces, Tactile Feedback.

1. INTRODUCTION

Haptic interfaces (with tactile feedback) could provide blind people with a tactile "feel" for the 2-D layout of web pages. *Haptic Displays*, capable of high-resolution tactile feedback, could render any webpage in tactile form. The user would be able to simultaneously listen to and feel webpage sections, or the lines of text, or even individual controls such as links and buttons, while browsing the Web with a screen reader. Understanding webpage layout would also be substantially easier if the user could feel section borders. With haptic interfaces, the user would be able to explore webpages much faster than with audio alone, and would then decide what content is worth listening to.

Given the potential of haptic interfaces, it is important to understand how they could be used effectively for web browsing. Specifically, to make haptic-screen interfaces usable and desirable, it is crucial to determine the appropriate tactile-rendering approaches for the 2-D structure of a web page (or any application in general) so as to enable effective exploration and navigation of that page (or application). Also important is the understanding of the tactile behavior and strategies employed by blind users when exploring tactile content; this should inform the design of haptic interfaces and help define new gestures for effective and convenient haptic interaction. The focus of this paper is the identification of tactile browsing strategies and the empirical evaluation of possible haptic interface designs.

In the absence of a haptic display, we simulated it using embossed transparent plastic overlays attached to the iPad screen, alongside the VoiceOver [7] screen reader. A similar approach was used by the Talking Tactile Tablet [5], which enabled blind students to interact with graphical charts coupled with audio feedback.

We conducted a preliminary user study with 10 blind participants who performed various browsing tasks with and w/o tactile overlays. We analyzed user interaction behavior and identified the appropriate design choices. The study also showed the desirability of using haptic interfaces in web browsing by blind users.

ASSETS'15, October 26–28, 2015, Lisbon, Portugal.
ACM 978-1-4503-3400-6/15/10.
DOI: http://dx.doi.org/10.1145/2700648.2811385

2. USER STUDY

2.1 Recruitment

We recruited 10 blind VoiceOver users for a controlled laboratory study. The participants had to be familiar with web browsing using VoiceOver on iPad/iPhone. All participants self-reported to be frequent iOS users and proficient with VoiceOver screen reader. Gender representation was almost equal: 6 males and 4 females. Various adult age groups were represented: the average age of the participants was 37 years (median 33 years).

We grouped the participants mainly based on their level of expertise. Exactly half (5 out of 10) of the participants stated that they were comfortable or mildly comfortable with the iPad touch-screen device – we will refer to them as "Beginners", while the other half claimed that they were very comfortable or were experts with the iPad – we will refer to them as "Experts".

2.2 Conditions and Setup

In the experiment, we compared regular web browsing on touch screens (Condition A) with web browsing on a simulated haptic screen (Condition B). In both conditions, the iPad was placed on the desk right in front of the participants. In condition A, the participants used iPad with the standard VoiceOver screen-reader interface with the default text-to-speech settings. The iPad screen was overlaid with a clear plastic transparency affixed to the screen, so that the screen felt the same in both conditions. The iPad's responsiveness to gestures was not affected by the overlay; during the experiment, no inconsistencies were observed, and none of the participants complained about the overlay.

In condition B, the plastic overlay was embossed using a Braille printer/embosser to render web page layout in tactile form. The overlay enabled the participants to feel raised dotted lines encircling each semantically coherent section [3] (e.g., menu, article, news snippet, etc.) of the webpage. None of the embossed lines masked any page content.

2.3 Tasks

The participants were asked to perform specific browsing tasks on 3 pairs of typical online news web pages, where each page was from different websites, but each pair had similar layout and content density enabling us to use them for comparison. Each task involved subtasks that asked the user to find certain element(s) in some section, navigate back and forth between different sections, find the previously found elements again, find all elements that match a certain pattern, etc. Before the experiment, the participants were given an opportunity to practice with the tactile overlay in sample browsing tasks on a different set of webpages. Practicing with overlays helped the participants understand the layout of web pages without VoiceOver, as this screen reader does not speak when the screen is touched with multiple fingers, except for certain gestures. The participants could then use VoiceOver by employing regular swipe and rotor gestures or by listening to the content under their finger as they dragged it on the surface.

3. RESULTS

3.1 Objective Results

Overall, the participants were slightly faster in Condition B with Haptic Overlays (mean: 6.5 min per website) than in Condition A with VoiceOver alone (mean: 7 min per website). It is notable that the beginners, on average, completed tasks faster than the experts in both conditions. We believe this was a result of the experts attempting more sophisticated browsing strategies, and then falling back to simpler strategies that were used by beginners.

In Condition A, many users (mostly beginners) spent too much time navigating the web pages element-by-element using the standard left/right swipe gestures of VoiceOver. Also in Condition A, many participants got frustrated and impatient after a few swipes, and proceeded to swipe faster without properly listening to the narrated content, thereby "missing" the target elements they were looking for. This sometimes resulted in a loop where the participants went over the same content several times.

In Condition B, most participants saved time by refraining from using swipes, and looked for content by following along the embossed section boundaries. Whenever, these participants encountered an irrelevant section, they simply went to the next section, thereby saving time by avoiding listening to irrelevant content. Furthermore, whenever the participants found the section that they expected to contain the target, they restricted their search to that section by staying within the boundaries.

The standard SUS questionnaire [1] yielded the score of 65.50 for Condition A and 76.00 for Condition B. The general consensus [4] is that a score over 70 is considered to be usable. Although the difference was not statistically significant most participants identified Condition B as the more usable one.

3.2 Discussion on User Strategies

In Condition A, the participants failed to orient themselves in web pages. In this condition, we observed that almost all participants struggled to find the target elements specified by the tasks. For most tasks in Condition A, many participants placed their index finger in the top-left of the screen (hoping to start at the beginning of the page) and then went through the entire page by using the primitive VoiceOver right-swipe gesture.

In condition B, we did not restrict the participants from using the regular VoiceOver gestures while performing tasks with haptic overlays. As a result, we observed many interesting behavioral patterns on how the participants combined gestures and haptic feedback in exploring web pages and searching for content. In fact, one of the participants explicitly observed: "[tactile] lines help me come up with a meaningful navigation pattern."

Some of the experts cleverly used a combination of gestures, swipes, and tactile lines. For example, for a task requiring them to find an article link in the "Sports" section, they first used the tactile lines to find the sports section, and then used swipe gestures to find the target link within the Sports section. One of the participants noted: "The [tactile] lines give a parameter that I can use for not going too far." Another said: "Lines were helpful because they sectioned everything off."

The majority of the participants who liked the haptic overlays felt that they were useful for both data intensive web pages, such as front pages of news articles, and simple web pages with fewer sections, such as article pages. Overall, the results of this preliminary study suggest that haptics can increase the efficiency, usability, and desirability of tactile feedback while browsing.

3.3 Discussion on Haptic Interface Design

Based on our experience with the initial design of the overlays and the results of the user study, as well as considering the feedback from the users, we make the following suggestions for the design of haptic web-browsing interfaces:

1) The granularity of the interface (i.e. the extent of web-page partitioning) should be configurable. 2) Tactile feedback should be used for boundaries of densely packed sections with a lot of small-font content (i.e. content that can be easily missed while dragging a finger over the section content, as was also recommended in [6] and [2]). 3) Different tactile feedback is desired for different objects such as links, headings, etc. 4) We do not recommend using Braille labels within sections, because additional tactile feedback of the same type confuses users.

4. CONCLUSIONS AND FUTURE WORK

Overall, the user study has revealed that haptic feedback, even as simple as having tactile segments around webpage sections, was very useful in a variety of web browsing tasks. Overall, we have seen that, even with very little practice, the participants were able to complete tasks with haptic overlays considerably faster than without them; however, this result was not consistent across all the participants and was not statistically significant. Nevertheless, when it came to usability, the majority of the participants preferred browsing with haptic feedback to just VoiceOver.

5. REFERENCES

[1] Brooke, J., *SUS-A quick and dirty usability scale.* Usability evaluation in industry, 1996. **189**: p. 194.

[2] Feng, J.H. and H. Nicolau. *Accessibility and Computing.* in *A regular publication of the ACM Special Interest Group on Accessible Computing.* 2014.

[3] Islam, M.A., F. Ahmed, Y. Borodin, and I.V. Ramakrishnan, *Tightly coupling visual and linguistic features for enriching audio-based web browsing experience*, in *Proceedings of CIKM.* 2011, ACM: Glasgow, Scotland, UK. p. 2085-2088.

[4] Keith, R., *Eye Movements in Reading and Information Processing: 20 Years of Research.* Psychological Bulletin, 1998. **124**(3): p. 372-422.

[5] Landau, S. and L. Wells. *Merging tactile sensory input and audio data by means of the Talking Tactile Tablet.* in *EuroHaptics'03.* 2003.

[6] Sjöström, C., *Using haptics in computer interfaces for blind people*, in *CHI '01 Extended Abstracts on Human Factors in Computing Systems.* 2001, ACM: Seattle, WA. p. 245-246.

[7] VoiceOver, *Screen reader from Apple.* 2010.

Multimodal Application for the Perception of Spaces (MAPS)

Richard J. Adams
Barron Associates, Inc.
1410 Sachem Place, Suite 202
Charlottesville, Virginia 22901
001-434-973-1215
adams@barron-associates.com

Dianne T.V. Pawluk
Virginia Commonwealth University
401 West Main Street
Richmond, Virginia 23284
001-804-828-9491
dtpawluk@vcu.edu

Margaret A. Fields
Virginia Department for the Blind and Vision Impaired
397 Azalea Avenue
Richmond, Virginia 23227
001-804-371-3776
Margaret.Fields@dbvi.virginia.gov

Ryan Clingman
Virginia Commonwealth University
401 West Main Street
Richmond, Virginia 23284
001-804-828-7839
clingmanr@vcu.edu

ABSTRACT
MAPS (Multimodal Application for the Perception of Spaces) is a tablet App, with associated hardware, for providing on-the-go access to audio-tactile maps of unfamiliar indoor venues to individuals who are blind or visually impaired. Performance of the system was assessed using a survey knowledge task in which participants were exposed to three different cue combinations: audio only, audio with haptic cues provided by the tablet's built-in vibrational motor (built-in tactile), and audio with haptic feedback provided by special vibrating rings worn on two fingers (stereo-tactile). Of the three conditions, the combination of audio and built-in tactile feedback resulted in superior user performance in judging the relative direction to points of interest. Results indicate that the audio-tactile display improves survey knowledge both when used for a priori (pre-visit) map learning and on-the-go (within the environment) to provide just-in-time information.

Categories and Subject Descriptors
K.4.2 [**Computing Milieu**]: Social Issues – *Assistive technologies for persons with disabilities, Handicapped persons/special needs.*

Keywords
Wayfinding, orientation, spatial perception, tactile maps, visually impaired

1. INTRODUCTION
The challenge of acquiring familiarity with new environments remains one of the greatest obstacles to functional independence for individuals who are blind or visually impaired. Effective independence requires survey knowledge of areas in which daily activities outside of the home take place. This knowledge is best acquired by accessing a map that reveals the spatial layout and content of a venue. A few groups have considered providing audio-tactile maps for mobility purposes (e.g., [1],[2]) on tablet computers. Here we consider the use of audio feedback with different modes of tactile feedback on the resulting performance of the user in acquiring and demonstrating survey knowledge of unfamiliar interior spaces.

ASSETS '15, October 26-28, 2015, Lisbon, Portugal
ACM 978-1-4503-3400-6/15/10.
http://dx.doi.org/10.1145/2700648.2811386

2. SYSTEM DESIGN
The system developed includes an Android App that renders map content through audio (tonal and speech) feedback and tactile cues. Users exploring the touchscreen on the tablet computer receive feedback corresponding to the spatial feature immediately below each finger. These maps are graphically represented by a two-dimensional image (Figure 1) in which each color is keyed to unique audio and tactile content. When a finger passes over a feature, audio feedback (in the form of a tone, defined by frequency and amplitude) provides an indication of the underlying feature type. When the user lifts up a finger at a particular point, an audio clip is played with a short text narrative describing that map feature. Examples include hallways, walls, stairways, and exterior spaces; as well as special points of interest unique to each map (e.g., a door to a computer lab or a specific work of art in a museum). The audio feedback is rendered through the tablet's built-in speaker or via bone-conducting headphones.

Tactile feedback is provided alternatively through the built-in vibrator in the tablet (built-in tactile) or as stereo-tactile information rendered through a specially developed pair of "tactile finger buds." Built-in tactile feedback functions by vibrating the entire mobile device using the tablet's internal motor. In this condition, tactile cues are generated when a finger touch point traverses designated points of interest on the map. Stereo-tactile feedback results in independent vibrations directly at the pad of each of the user's fingers in the form of pulsed vibrations with different frequency, amplitude, and pulse characteristics (duration and inter-pulse delay). In the subsequent study feedback was provided to the index fingers on both hands. In this condition, tactile cues are generated both for points of interest as well as for other relevant map features. The tactile finger buds are a derivative of technology previously developed by Barron Associates under contract to NASA Glenn Research Center [2]. Each finger bud consists of a Linear Resonant Actuator (LRA) vibrational motor held within a specially fabricated flexible plastic ring worn on the user's finger. Driver electronics are housed in a small plastic enclosure that connects to the tablet via its micro-USB port. Figure 2 shows the tactile finger buds in use during map exploration with the Phase I prototype.

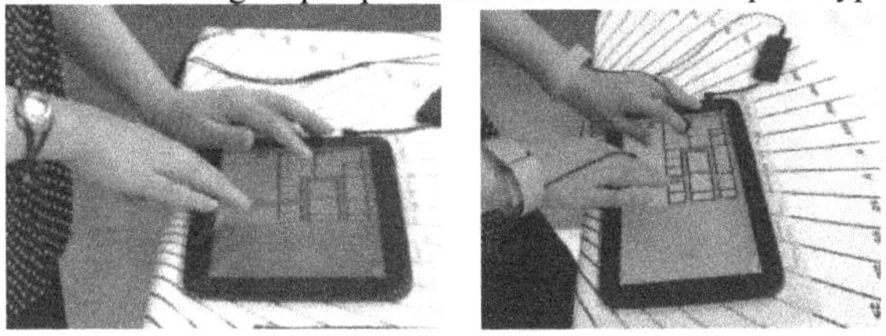

Figure 1. Prototype without tactile finger buds (left). Prototype with tactile finger buds (right).

3. EXPERIMENTAL ASSESSMENT

An experimental assessment was conducted to investigate the effectiveness of the different map displays in conveying spatial layout information on unfamiliar indoor spaces. Experiments were conducted in the Library and Resource Center (LRC) of the Virginia Department for the Blind and Vision Impaired (DBVI), Richmond, VA. Fourteen (14) individuals (age 29-69; 7 female) completed the study under the supervision of the Virginia Commonwealth University Institutional Review Board (IRB). All participants had a diagnosis of blindness (light perception only or total blindness) and were assessed to possess at least a basic level of O&M competency. Approximately half of the participants (6) became blind by age 2 and all but one of the participants read Braille. Subjects had no prior familiarity with the LRC.

During an initial familiarization period, participants completed a calibration routine designed to ensure audio and tactile "loudness" was optimized for each individual's perceptual threshold and preference. Participants subsequently completed a training exercise dubbed the "Survey Knowledge Game." In this training exercise, individuals explored a series of six different interior maps of buildings in the Richmond, VA area; two in each of the three different tactile feedback configurations. For each map, after an exploration period, participants were sequentially tasked to locate each of five points of interest on the display.

Success in utilization of the map display was then assessed through a survey knowledge task dubbed the "Judgment of Direction Activity (JDA)." Audio-tactile maps were created for each of three areas in the LRC of approximately equivalent size and complexity. Participants spent three minutes outside the chosen area of study in the LRC using the display to study a map of the chosen area (simulating pre-arrival map exploration) that included five unique points of interest. Individuals were then escorted by a test administrator to the actual location of one of these points of interest and asked to indicate the location of each of the remaining four. A special device was used to accurately assess pointing direction, comprising an eye-safe laser line generator, a battery pack, and the handle from a white cane (shown in 2). Participants were asked to align the handle with the direction of the target, resulting in projection of a red line of light to a compass rose. The magnitude of the difference between this user-identified direction and the true direction to each point of interest provided an absolute angular estimated error measurement (in degrees), used in subsequent analysis.

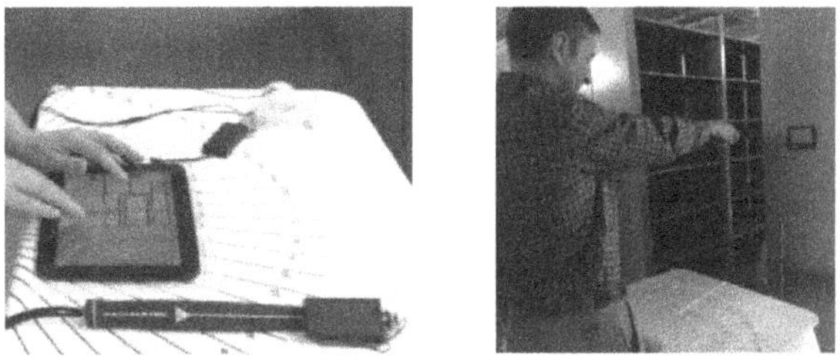

Figure 2. Pointing device and tablet lying on compass rose (left). Use of the pointing device during a measurement (right).

At each location, a second procedure was then executed to assess the potential for on-the-go usage of the map display (i.e. just-in-time map access in an unfamiliar environment). Participants were asked to use the map display to identify their current location and the location of one of the other points of interest, and then to immediately point at the point of interest; repeating this sequence for each of the four points. Each participant performed the JDA sequence three times, once in each of the three above-described tactile cue conditions, each time in a different area of the LRC. The combination of tactile condition, LRC area, and order of presentation was block randomized.

4. RESULTS

To quantify the benefit of map access vs. the absence of map access, actual JDA performance was compared to random guessing of target location. Monte Carlo simulation was employed to generate the predicted null distribution of angular estimation errors for uniform guessing over the angular range of 0 to 180 degrees (targets were not placed behind the subject). In all combinations of feedback and map access, the display provided a significant benefit in the form of improved judgment of direction. Overall, the best performance was observed in the built-in tactile condition, with a mean angular estimation error of 36.8 degrees with pre-arrival map access and 22.6 degrees for on-the-go access.

5. DISCUSSION

The provision of refreshable audio-tactile maps on tablets show promise in learning survey information about unfamiliar indoor spaces. In addition, access to on-the-go audio-tactile maps significantly improves performance, even when pre-exploration occurs ahead of time. Future analysis will provide more details and consideration of the effects that occurred.

6. ACKNOWLEDGMENTS

The authors wish to thank the Virginia Department for the Blind and Vision Impaired for support throughout the project. This work was funded by the National Institutes of Health, National Eye Institute; grant 1R43EY021978-01A1.

7. REFERENCES

[1] C. Goncu and K. Marriott, "GraVVITAS: Generic Multi-touch Presentation of Accessible Graphics," in Proceedings INTERACT, Lisbon, Portugal, 2011.

[2] N. Giudice, H. Palani, et al., "Learning Non-Visual Graphical Information Using a Touch-Based Vibro-Audio Interface," in Proceedings ACM Assets, Boulder, CO, 2012.

[3] R. Adams, A. Olowin, et al., "Glove-Enabled Computer Operations (GECO): Design and Testing of an Extra-Vehicular Activity Glove Adapted for Human-Computer Interface," in Proceedings of the AIAA International Conference on Environmental Systems, Vail, CO, 2013.

Opportunity: Inclusive Design for Interactive Simulations

Emily B. Moore
PhET Interactive Simulations
Department of Physics
University of Colorado Boulder
Boulder, CO, USA
Emily.Moore@colorado.edu

Clayton Lewis
Department of Computer Science
University of Colorado Boulder
Boulder, CO, USA
Clayton.Lewis@colorado.edu

ABSTRACT

Interactive simulations are becoming increasingly important in education, but these tools are not accessible to many learners. Here, we share some goals to guide the development of accessible simulations, and summarize early findings in development efforts. We also highlight challenges and opportunities where the unique expertise of the ASSETS community is needed. We hope to interest readers in participating in the growing community designing, developing, and researching accessible interactive simulations for learning.

Categories and Subject Descriptors
K.4.2 [**Social Issues**]: Assistive tech for persons with disabilities.

General Terms
Design, Human Factors

Keywords
interactive simulation; education; inclusive design

1. INTERACTIVE SIMULATIONS FOR LEARNING

Interactive science simulations can provide exploratory virtual environments to engage students in science practices and to support their learning [1]. Built with an underlying model that maps to physical phenomena, interactive simulations provide students with the opportunity to explore scenarios and conduct experiments not possible outside of a virtual environment [2]. Additionally, the use of simulations has added value by providing pedagogical support and feedback through interface design, and the ability to collect data on how students learn from the simulations. Interactive simulations provide an environment for students to engage in rapid experimentation and receive immediate feedback – all within a shareable representation, which can be used for group or class discussions. These affordances are provided without requiring specialized or hazardous equipment.

The use of interactive simulations for learning is increasing, with one suite of simulations – PhET simulations (http://phet.colorado.edu) – showing a rapid uptake in use since 2004 (see Figure 1) by teachers and students using the simulations as part of lecture presentations, in-class activities, labs, and homework [3]. As simulations become a mainstay in the classroom, this is an opportune time to address the challenge of making simulations more accessible to learners with disabilities.

Another reason this work is timely is that the educational simulations community is in transition, shifting from Java and Flash-based simulations to HTML5. This opens up new possibilities for interoperability, data collection, and widespread implementation of accessibility features. The complexity of interactive simulations coupled with an evolving HTML5 infrastructure has resulted in many challenges, but also opportunities for enhanced accessibility. A number of simulation development groups, accessible technology developers, assessment organizations, and researchers are working together to address these challenges. We describe goals for this work, and identify some preliminary progress, challenges, and opportunities. In doing so we are drawing on early experience in collaborative efforts to develop inclusive features for the PhET Interactive Simulations, the suite of free math and science simulations mentioned earlier. We hope this description may encourage other members of the ASSETS community to get involved.

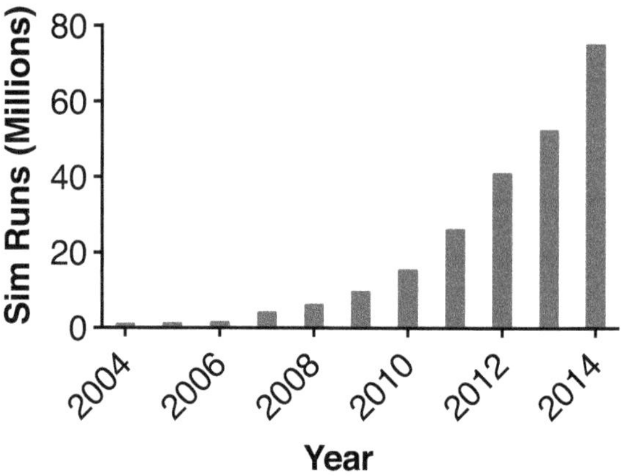

Figure 1. PhET simulation runs (online runs and downloads) from 2004-2014.

2. GOALS

Our collaborative efforts aim to address the following goals:

- *Create accessible simulations that support diverse students in engaging with interactive simulation tools for learning.* To do this, we are taking an inclusive approach with one-size-fits-one customizable simulations. This approach involves building flexible 'layers' of accessibility features into individual simulations, allowing for each simulation to be customized as needed on-the-fly – supporting classmates with different needs in working collaboratively.
- *Define and use consistent conventions for navigation and control.* Consistency will support easy transitions as learners move among different simulations.

ASSETS '15, October 26–28, 2015, Lisbon, Portugal.
ACM 978-1-4503-3400-6/15/10.
http://dx.doi.org/10.1145/2700648.2811387

- *Create a shareable code base with exemplars.* Make our progress as transparent and shareable as possible, to enable others to easily follow along – or join in. This approach can lower the cost for others to create accessible simulations, while also maximizing transfer among simulations for learners.
- *Develop simulations using commodity hardware, Web software, and without requiring software installation wherever possible.* The PhET project has attained wide adoption of their simulations by offering high-quality free resources that are easy to find, open, and use. Inclusion should be maximized, though we recognize that some inclusion challenges may not be fully addressed without additional resources (e.g., tactile displays).
- *Draw on, and where appropriate expand, the space of non-visual representations for scientific content, including interaction techniques not relying on vision and fine motor control.* Accessible interactive simulations provide a complex environment to experiment with 'layering' of accessibility features (e.g., simultaneously supporting intuitive non-visual and visual use). We anticipate insights gained from developing accessible simulations will reach into other areas of software development.

3. PROGRESS

Sonification: Our preliminary results suggest that audio representations can convey the strength and orientation of a dynamic electric field, information currently conveyed by a complex visual display in the *Radiating Charges* PhET simulation. We use Shepard tones [4] to represent orientation in such a way that the orientation of a continuously rotating or oscillating vector can be conveyed with no discontinuity (see http://claytonhalllewis.github.io/assetsNonViz/assetssonicfield.html.)

Keyboard Navigation: In collaboration with the Inclusive Design Centre in Ontario, Canada, we have successfully implemented keyboard navigation in the *Forces and Motion: Basics* PhET simulation [5]. We found in preliminary interviews that nested navigation can intuitively support efficient access to the many interactive elements in the simulation.

Auditory Descriptions: We have also successfully implemented auditory descriptions into the *Forces and Motion: Basics* PhET simulation [5]. We found it is useful to design keyboard navigation and auditory descriptions simultaneously, to ensure consistency across visual and non-visual navigation. We also aimed to develop auditory descriptions that emphasized key conceptual relationships in the simulation, rather than focusing on describing the visual representation. For example, on a screen where students use people pulling a rope to apply different amounts of force to either side of a cart, spatial references were included when foundational to the concept, e.g., "Attached to the *left* side of the cart…" – an important spatial cue for recognizing that forces can applied to the left and right sides of the cart, in opposing directions. The specific location of the non-pulling people in the simulation (below the cart) is not significant for understanding concepts or for navigation, so we used the description "Standing near this rope is a group of four people".

4. CHALLENGES AND OPPORTUNITIES

Control and Navigation: Sina Bahram (personal communication, 2015) has noted a trend toward spatial navigation using arrow keys to discover and activate invisible controls arranged spatially. We think this approach has promise in organizing the multiple complex controls required by many simulations. Work is needed to explore and realize this idea.

Browser and Screen Reader Compatibility: Browser differences and the specifics of screen reader interactions with browsers and interactive Web content are complex. High use from the uptake of interactive simulations and other dynamic browser-based applications like games, may help drive advancements in consistency in interoperability for browsers and screen readers.

An area where browser-based technologies can support our efforts is in developments like the Web Speech API. Use of this API could support learners who would benefit from the use of non-visual simulation features, but are not screen reader users.

Automatic Configuration: The Global Public Inclusive Infrastructure (GPII.net) offers a promising way for learners to specify their individual interface needs, in such a way that simulations can automatically configure themselves as needed.

Non-visual Presentation of Spatially Extended Behaviors: Many simulations require learners to notice and relate things that are happening simultaneously in different parts of the display. How can these relationships be conveyed non-visually?

Operation on Mobile Devices: Effective non-visual presentation of simulations may open the way to delivery of complex content on small screen devices, such as smartphones. This would increase access for learners, particularly in developing nations.

5. NEXT STEPS

Interactive simulations, even considering only the PhET simulations (~130 in total), use a large range of interaction and representation techniques. Increasing inclusiveness in this space can usefully employ the insights, skills, and effort of many people in the ASSETS community. We have created a Google Group (https://groups.google.com/forum/#!forum/inclusive-sims) as a virtual home for the accessible simulations community. Please join us online for resources, updates, and most importantly, collaborative conversations as we work towards more accessible interactive simulations for learning.

6. ACKNOWLEDGMENTS

Support for this work was provided by: The Hewlett Foundation; the FLOE project at OCAD University, Ontario, Canada; and the ATLAS Institute at the University of Colorado Boulder.

7. REFERENCES

[1] D'Angelo, C., Rutstein, D., Harrison, S., Bernard, R., Borokhovski, E., and Haertel, G. *Simulations for STEM Learning: Systematic Review and Meta-Analysis*. Menlo Park, CA: SRI International, 2014.

[2] Perkins, K.K., Loeblein, P.J., and Dessau, K.L. Sims for science: Powerful tools to support inquiry-based teaching. *Science Teacher 77*, 7 (2010), 46–51.

[3] Perkins, K. K., Moore, E. B., & Chasteen, S. V. 2015. Examining the Use of PhET Interactive Simulations in US College and High School Classrooms, in Proceedings of the 2014 Physics Education Research Conference (Minneapolis, MN, USA, July 2014) American Association of Physics Teachers, 207-210.

[4] Shepard, R.N. (1964). "Circularity in Judgements of Relative Pitch". *Journal of the Acoustical Society of America* **36** (12): 2346–53.

[5] PhET Interactive Simulations. 2015. Inclusive design feature prototypes. Retrieved June 22, 2015 from http://phet.colorado.edu/en/about/accessibility

Development of BCI based Softwares to Assist People with Mobility Limitations in the School Inclusion Process

Regina Heidrich, Marsal A. Branco, João B. Mossmann, Anderson Schuh, Emely Jensen
Universidade Feevale
ERS-239, 2755, Novo Hamburgo – RS, Brazil, 93525-075
+55 51 3586.8800
{rheidrich, marsal} @feevale.br {mossmann, anderschuh, emelyjensen} @gmail.com

ABSTRACT
Inclusive Education has been the agenda at all levels and modalities of the education system, which discusses how the school will face the diversity and teach students who have disabilities. According to the 2010 Census, in Brazil, people with physical disabilities account for almost 7% of the population. This project aims to design Digital Learning Constructs (DLC) as an inclusive education model implemented by use of Brain Computer Interface (BCI). Thus, it is intended to assist people with mobility limitations in the process of school inclusion. A DLC is any entity or device devised or built in a multidisciplinary way in the form of an educational game, helping players to build or redesign their knowledge. It has as features, dual nature, as an object of learning and also a game, working procedurally the contributions of each area without any subordination between them. Thus, via BCI, the user will not use mouse, but a specific low cost hardware, which will command the computer via brain waves. Future studies with the user will be conducted through a qualitative, quantitative and ergonomic design approach. The study subjects are people with motor and communication problems, of the municipal education network. The importance of studies linked to the autonomy of these subjects is due to the fact that many do not have freedom of movement, because of motor impairments. The aim of this project is to open paths for people with motor impairments and degenerative diseases, so they can use the computer in the classroom context.

Categories and Subject Descriptors
K.4.2 **[Computers and Education]**: Social Issues – *assistive technologies for persons with disabilities*.

General Terms
Design, Human Factors.

Keywords
Brain Computer Interface, Game, Cerebral Palsy, Inclusion.

1. INTRODUCTION
The school inclusion process has been widely discussed in all fields and it has been observed that behind the discourse of teachers not feeling prepared, lack of accessibility and training in digital inclusion area is still incipient. One solution is to partner with groups and research projects of universities that can collaborate in this process. The inclusion of people with cerebral palsy is not easy, as many have the cognitive preserved, but do not speak, walk, or both.

A Brain Computer Interface (BCI) allows a person to transfer commands to a computer directly. Instead of using a keyboard, mouse or other input device, the user of this interface simply sends commands through brain waves and, the computer responds to them. We intend to show here a learning objects solution developed with the use of BCI technology. The device used in this research is shown below (Figure 1). It is called Mindwave Mobile, by NeuroSky.

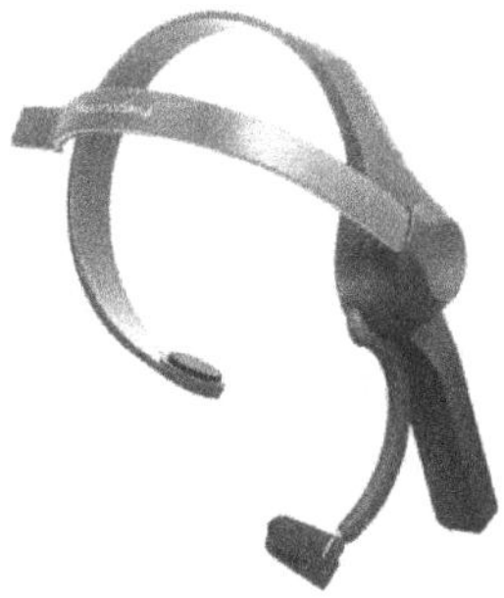

Figure 1. MindWave Mobile, by NeuroSky.

This device converts electrical brain waves and analogical processes in digital signals, to make measurements available to power the interface. Every interaction between neurons creates a tiny electric shock, measured by EEG (electroencephalograph) machines. By itself, these charges are impossible to measure outside the skull. However, a dominant mental state, driven by the activity of neurons, collectively created by hundreds of thousands of concurrent downloads, can be measured.

Different brain states are the result of different patterns of neural interaction. These wave patterns are characterized by different amplitudes and frequencies. Examples are brain waves between 12 and 30 Hz, beta waves, associated with concentration, while waves between 8 and 12 Hz, alpha waves, are associated with relaxation. Often, overshadowing brainwaves, the contraction of muscles is also associated with unique wave patterns called EMG (electromyogram). Isolating these EMG patterns is how some NeuroSky devices can detect the blink of the eye. Thus, Mindwave implements the algorithm that recognizes the blink of the eye. Thereby, it is capable of measuring the force with which the blink is performed, passing this information on integer values, which can vary from 1 to a slight blink, and 255 for a strong

ASSETS '15, October 26-28, 2015, Lisbon, Portugal.
ACM 978-1-4503-3400-6/15/10.
http://dx.doi.org/10.1145/2700648.2811388

blink. The games presented below make use of concentration and blink measurements as commands.

2. GAMES BEING DEVELOPED

Three games were developed. They are in phase of adjustments for further testing with people with cerebral palsy. The games are:

2.1 Neuronavegática

Neuronavegática is a knowledge test game, consisting of questions of school subjects like Portuguese and Mathematics. The user may choose through the blink of the eye, the subject and the level to the access of questions. The diver (the character), selects also with the blink of an eye, by the option of scanning on the screen, the correct answer to the question presented. The user has a time limit to select the correct answer, which allows the thinking on the matter, but also offers thrill to the challenge. A game screen example can be seen in Figure 2.

Figure 2. Neuronavegática gameplay example.

2.2 Questing Ruins

In Questing Ruins, the player takes the figure of an elder, who aims to get to the other side of town to disable a mechanism, and thus, to free his people from machines that brought destruction to his once thriving kingdom. To progress in the game, is used concentration and the eye blinking, allowing the player interact with objects in the scene. Below, a figure (Figure 3) with examples of these objects and the scenario.

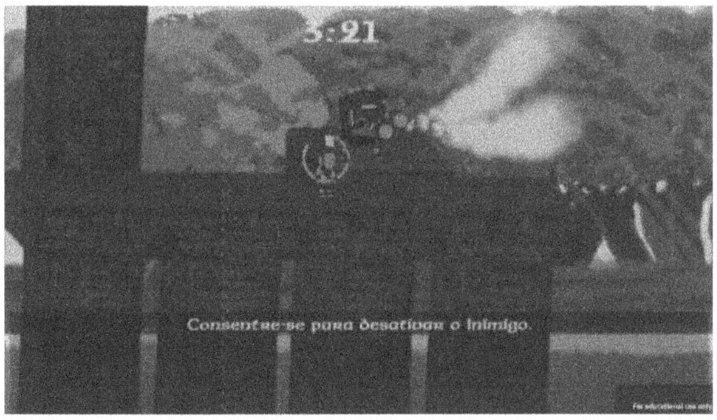

Figure 3. Questing Ruins concentration challenge example.

For example, when hitting an obstacle, the player must concentrate or control the intensity of the blink, so to overtake it. Along the way, the player encounters puzzles and only after beat them, the elder can continue walking. These puzzles consist of a disc that automatically rotates, having locks of different formats. When the player selects (by blinking) the correct lock and key, it gives continuity to the game. At the end of each stage, the player also find another puzzle, composed of pieces which must be rotated through concentration, in order to guide a water supply inlet to the outside of the frame, as can be seen in Figure 4.

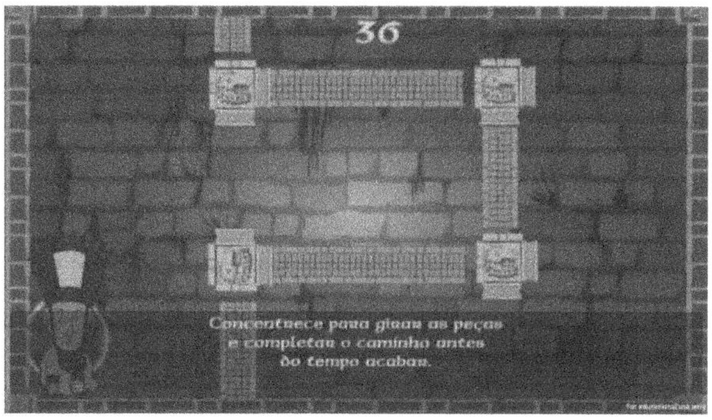

Figure 4. Final puzzle of the stage example.

2.3 Save the World

In Save the World, the player goes through everyday situations as to dispose the garbage in the proper recycle bin (Figure 5), cross the street safely, observe obstacles in the urban environment, among others. Each situation represents a new stage, and each next challenge needs higher levels of attention than the one before. The player competes with itself or with other users of the same computer, to beat previous scores and stay on top. Missing the response of an activity or not achieving the minimum attention level required, makes the character lose a "life". By losing three "lives", the player loses the challenge and have to start the game again. Although the level of required concentration increases as the phases advance, they reboot randomly at the start of each new game.

Figure 5. Save the World gameplay example.

3. ACKNOWLEDGMENTS

Special thanks to CNPq that finances this project through the Call No 84/2013 MCTI-SECIS/CNPq - Assistive Technology/B - Emerging Cores.

4. REFERENCES

[1] Secretaria de Direitos Humanos da Presidência da República. 2012. Cartilha do Censo 2010 - pessoas com deficiência: *http://www.pessoacomdeficiencia.gov.br/app/sites/default/files/publicacoes/cartilha-censo-2010-pessoas-com-deficienciareduzido.pdf*. Accessed: 2014-06-13.

The Impact of Stuttering; How Can a Mobile App Help?

Iva Demarin[1], Ljubica Leko[1], Maja Škrobo[1], Helena Germano[2], Patrícia Macedo[3], Rui Neves Madeira[3]
[1] Faculty of Education and Rehabilitation Sciences - University of Zagreb, Croatia
[2] Escola Superior de Saúde and [3]ESTSetúbal, Instituto Politécnico de Setúbal, Setúbal, Portugal
ivamaria_93@hotmail.com, {lleko91, maja.skrobo01}@gmail.com, helena.germano@ess.ips.pt, {patricia.macedo, rui.madeira}@estsetubal.ips.pt

ABSTRACT
The mobile application BroiStu was developed due to the need of having a better insight on the impact of stuttering on people who stutter's everyday life. This paper presents a study on this application, verifying which features of impact of stuttering found in scientific literature are included in the application and making a comparison with a similar application. Furthermore, it also summarises a user study conducted with a first panel of experts. New findings and obtained results are discussed.

Categories and Subject Descriptors
K.4.2 [**Computers and Society**]: Social Issues—*Assistive technologies for persons with disabilities*

General Terms
Experimentation, Design, Human Factors, Theory

Keywords
Mobile health; stuttering; speech and language therapy; self-care

1. INTRODUCTION
Stuttering is characterized by an abnormally high frequency and/or duration of stoppages in the forward flow of speech. It can be in the form of repetitions of sounds, syllables or one syllable words, prolongations of sounds or "blocks" of airflow or voicing in speech. These behaviours happen on an unconscious level and the person who stutters cannot control them [1]. People who stutter (PWS) do not have "just" problems in their speech. They can often develop negative attitudes related to speech, besides anxiety and depression which can be connected with feelings of insecurity and unpredictability of non-fluent speech [2].

There are many different approaches in stuttering therapy. All of them recognize the importance of understanding the impact that stuttering has on everyday communications and related emotions of PWS. The multidimensionality of this fluency disorder requires proper ways of data gathering during therapy. Due to the need of having a better insight on communication situations (CS), the mobile health (mHealth) application (app) BroiStu (Brothers in Stuttering), initially named iAmS, was developed [3].

ASSETS '15, October 26-28, 2015, Lisbon, Portugal.
ACM 978-1-4503-3400-6/15/10.
http://dx.doi.org/10.1145/2700648.2811389

2. BROTHERS IN STUTTERING
By using BroiStu, users can register their stuttering related situations (SS) (Fig.1a) to self-monitor their speech as a means of controlling stuttering in a daily basis [3]. Thus, they can see how they are evolving throughout therapy. The app provides reports and charts which help visualizing how SS evolve according to several features (e.g., mood, emotions felt (Fig.1b), relation between the context and the intensity of stuttering). BroiStu is just available in English and Portuguese languages, however it is prepared to easily integrate other languages.

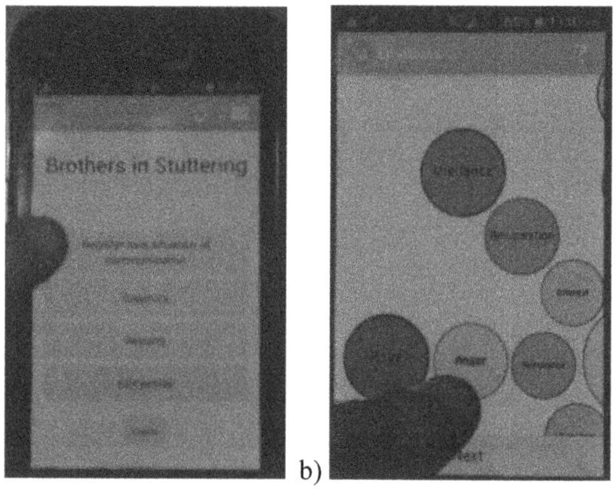

a) b)

Figure 1. BroiStu screens: a) menu with main functionalities; b) CAAT interface to select emotions felt in a SS [3].

After the release of the first prototype [3], four new modules have been integrated into BroiStu: **Personalisation** - the app automatically adapts itself according to demographic data (age and gender), interactions data (number of registered SS, exchanged messages), and contextual data (mood, emotions felt, etc.); **Exercises** - the user should follow different therapy techniques (e.g., pullout) that are presented; **Voice interaction** - used in the exercises (with speech to text); **Communications** - allows messages exchange between SLP (Speech-Language Pathologist) and PWS, and controls automatic notifications based on to the mood, etc.

3. HOW CAN BROISTU HELP?

3.1 BroiStu's Competitor
There are already some mobile apps [3] that are developed for addressing the stuttering issue. Most of them are more focused on the speech dysfluency and compensatory or avoidance behaviours of stuttering and the techniques for fluent speech and less focused on the impact that stuttering has on a person's everyday communications. The iOs app Fluency Tracker is the closest competitor of BroiStu since it is focused on similar features [3]. Table 1 presents a comparison between BroiStu and Fluency

Tracker, taking into account important features. The only feature not addressed by BroiStu is related to the avoidance behaviours.

Table 1. Comparing BroiStu (B) and Fluency Tracker (FT)

Features	B	FT
Avoidance behaviours	No	Yes
Feelings associated with speaking	Yes	Yes
Frequency of disfluency	Yes	Yes
Graph of changes in speaking behaviour	Yes	Yes
Graph of changes with context included	Yes	No
Module for SLP	Yes	No
Personalisation/adaptation	Yes	No
Repository server	Yes	No

3.2 BroiStu and the Impacts of Stuttering

The impacts of stuttering are in the spotlight of numerous studies [4-9], thus the review presented in Table 2 indicates that BroiStu still have to address a few more in order to improve its content.

Table 2. Impacts of stuttering and their inclusion in BroiStu

Impact of Stuttering	Included
Additional/compensatory movements [4]	No
Physiological reactions [4]	No
Feelings of effort and tension [4]	No
Fear of talking with someone [8]	Yes
Avoidance in communication situations [2]	Yes
Feelings of shame, helplessness and frustrations [8]	No
Feeling stupid and foolish [8]	No
Social anxiety [6]	No
Reduction of verbal input [4]	Yes
Avoiding eye contact [4]	Yes
Using circumlocutions, replacing words [4]	Yes
Acceptance of stuttering [9]	Yes
Feeling of embarrassment [7]	Yes
Avoidance of speaking situations [5]	Yes

3.3 User Study

The user tests were conducted with 7 participants (3 male and 4 female). 5 participants were SLP and 2 were PWS, very accustomed to having therapy. We made sure that each participant understood and got to use all functionalities of BroiStu. We asked them to rate several sentences using a 7-point Likert scale (1- "totally disagree" to 7- "totally agree"). It is noteworthy that: 6 participants considered the process of SS registration as being indeed user-friendly (Mean=5.4; SD=0.9), with the emotions screen generating more doubts with one participant rating it with 3 (Mean=5.1; SD=1.3); all participants thought BroiStu will be useful (Mean=6.3; SD=0.8) and 5 of them really want to use it (Mean=5.1; SD=1.1). A very interesting point is that all participants (3 rated 6; 4 rated 7) considered personalisation as an important feature for the success of BroiStu (Mean=6.6; SD=0.5).

4. HOW CAN BROISTU HELP MORE?

According to Tables 1 and 2, BroiStu still needs to address one feature and some impacts of stuttering. For instance, it is important to add features to deal with avoidance behaviours and the existence of compensatory movements, since they are characteristics of the stuttering pathology and it would be useful to monitor them. It would also be useful that BroiStu would provide a reminder when a PWS did not report new CS at the end of a day. Maybe s/he forgot to do it. Furthermore, it would be useful for users to have access to an "educational screen", which would detail what happens during stuttering. Finally, as many countries do not have mHealth apps which address the impact of stuttering on PWS's daily life, the deployment of the app in other languages, such as Croatian, will improve the usability of the app for users not fluent in English. It is important to have in mind that each language has its own specificities.

5. CONCLUSIONS

BroiStu is a novel m-Health app towards a better stuttering awareness in order to improve speech therapy. The purpose of this app is to extend the therapy to everyday life situations. This paper identifies which impacts of stuttering still need to be addressed. Mentioned disadvantages are guidelines for future work around this app. A thorough user study will be conducted during some weeks to assess the use of BroiStu with PWS in real situations.

6. REFERENCES

[1] Guitar, B. 2006. Introduction to Stuttering. In: *Stuttering – An integrated Approach to Its Nature and Treatment*, Philadelphia PA, R. R. Donnelley, 3-18.

[2] Sardelić, S. 2003. Etiologija mucanja – kratki prikaz. In: *Čimbur, P. Balada o mucanju*. Zagreb: Prosvjeta.

[3] Madeira, R.N., Macedo, P., Pita, P., Bonança, I., and Germano, H. 2013. Building on Mobile towards Better Stuttering Awareness to Improve Speech Therapy. In: *Proc. of MoMM '13*. ACM, 551-554.

[4] Bloodstein O., Ratner, B.N. 2008. Symptomatology. *A handbook on stuttering*. Delmar, Canada, 1-38.

[5] Conture, E.G., Curlee, R.F. 1999. Stuttering and Related Disorders of Fluency. (3rd ed.). New York: Thieme Medical Publisher, Inc.

[6] Craig, A., Blumgart, E., Tran, Y. 2009. The impact of stuttering on the quality of life in adults who stutter. *Journal of Fluency Disorders*, 34, 61-71.

[7] Gregory, H. H. 2003. Stuttering therapy. Rationale and Procedures. Boston: Pearson Education, Inc.

[8] Klompas, M., Ross, E., 2004. Life experiences of people who stutter, and the perceived impact of stuttering on quality of life: personal accounts of South African individuals. *Journal of Fluency Disorders*, 29, 275-305.

[9] Yaruss, J.S., Coleman, C.E., Quesal, R.W. 2012. Stuttering in School-Age Children: A Comprehensive Approach to Treatment. *Language, Speech and Hearing Services in School*, 43, 536-548.

Exploring the Potential of Wearables to Support Employment for People with Mild Cognitive Impairment

Victor Dibia
City University of Hong Kong
83 Tatchee Avenue, Kowloon, HK
dibia.victor@my.cityu.edu.hk

Shari Trewin, Maryam Ashoori, Thomas Erickson
IBM T.J. Watson Research Center
P.O. Box 704, Yorktown Hgts, NY 10598, USA
{trewin, maryam, snowfall }@us.ibm.com

ABSTRACT
We interviewed adults with mild cognitive impairment working in a sheltered workshop and three support professionals about competitive employment in the community, and what concerns or barriers they may have. While individuals were most concerned about managing their health, professionals also described personal safety and productivity challenges. Families' worries about the safety of their family members were reported to be a barrier to competitive employment. Using a smart watch as a technology probe, we identified three potential applications of wearable technology in tackling these challenges: health support, family support, and productivity support.

Categories and Subject Descriptors
K.4.2 [**Computers and Society**]: Social Issues - *Assistive technologies for persons with disabilities, Employment*

General Terms: Human Factors

Keywords
Wearables; user study; disability; cognitive impairment

1. INTRODUCTION
On leaving school, many young adults with developmental disabilities would prefer competitive employment in the community, rather than a place in a sheltered workshop environment. We report an initial exploration of ways in which wearable technology, specifically sensor-enabled wrist-worn devices, might help individuals with mild cognitive impairment achieve their employment goals.

1.1 Community-Based Employment
In 1999, the U.S. Supreme Court declared segregation of people with disabilities (when integrated community-based settings are an option), a form of discrimination under the Americans with Disabilities Act. Numerous government programs support community employment for people with disabilities, through training, assistive technology and job support. However, statistics suggest that progress has been slow. In 2014, 17.1% of people with a disability were employed, compared to 64.6% of those without a disability [8]. While the majority of adults with intellectual or developmental disabilities aspire to work in an integrated community setting [5], 76% are still served in sheltered workshops [5] , often working for less than minimum wage [1].

ASSETS '15, October 26-28, 2015, Lisbon, Portugal.
ACM 978-1-4503-3400-6/15/10
http://dx.doi.org/10.1145/2700648.2811390

1.2 Supported Employment Concerns
Prior studies have reported several barriers that make it difficult for individuals to thrive in community work environments. In their survey of 112 adults with developmental disabilities, Lemaire and Malik [3] identify inattention, interpersonal problems and behavior problems as frequent barriers to maintaining employment. Poor attendance, low work quality, and interpersonal issues were highlighted as causes of employment terminations. In the United States, job support programs and coaches are available to help individuals find and succeed in competitive employment. Coaches work with individuals in their workplace, helping them both to learn job requirements and to integrate socially. Coaches report using a range of strategies to help their clients manage challenges with memory, attention, psychomotor speed, and problem solving [4].

1.3 Wearables for Work
With the proliferation of consumer wearable devices (such as smartwatches), it has become both practical and financially feasible to harness them as assistive technologies in the workplace. Sensors on these devices such as heartrate, accelerometer, gyroscope, light, temperature, UV, ECG, and skin conductance sensors can be used to monitor health conditions, arousal, stress, physical activity, location, and other factors [6]. Wrist-worn wearables are good candidates for collecting individual data, as people are used to wearing wristwatches.. Smart watches have been used to deliver reminders to veterans with traumatic brain injury living independently in a smart home [2], and to monitor symptoms of Parkinson's Disease [7].

2. INTERVIEW
2.1 Participants
To understand barriers to competitive employment, and the role that wearable technology could play, we conducted interviews with two groups - six individuals with mild cognitive impairment currently working in a sheltered workshop, and three professionals. The individuals (three females and three males, age 38-50) had all been at the workshop doing packaging work for 10 to 20 years (in most cases since leaving school). All had mild cognitive impairment, with an IQ of 60 to 70, and were able to follow multi-step procedures. Two had prior experience of community employment. The group of three job support professionals (henceforth JSPs) included community and workshop job support coordinators, and a director of services at the same center.

2.2 Methodology

In 20-minute interviews with a JSP present, individuals were asked to share their experiences on their current and previous jobs (out in the community) and their concerns (if any) regarding working in the community. They were also shown a smartwatch (Microsoft Band) and asked how its features (heartrate monitor, step counter, calorie counter, skin temperature monitor, clock) might improve their work process or reduce work-related concerns. In separate interviews, JSPs shared their perspectives on the challenges faced by these individuals regarding employment integration and the value of wearables in such contexts.

2.3 Findings

2.3.1 Individual vs JSP Outlook

When asked about barriers and concerns with competitive employment, there were marked differences in the outlook of individuals and JSPs. Individuals were confident in their abilities to do the work itself, enthusiastic and only expressed health-related concerns. These included managing diabetes, the risk of a seizure, difficulty standing for long periods, risk of heart attack, and a need to avoid very hot or very cold environments.

"I would like to work as a volunteer in a nursing home [...] and meet new people. My concern about working in the community is regarding my health. I have a condition called pulmonary hypertension [...] I have to monitor my blood oxygen levels".

JSPs, on the other hand, showed more concern about the level of soft skills (social, communication) individuals possessed, distraction and memory challenges, and vulnerabilities of individuals. Their notion of vulnerabilities was nuanced in that they were concerned about the implicitly trusting nature of their clients as opposed to work related safety hazards they might face. They felt clients were susceptible to suggestions or soliciting from strangers or co-workers. They shared anecdotes such as a man who gave $20 of every paycheck to a 'friend' on the train, unbeknownst to his family. JSPs also emphasized that the worries and fears of family members could be a barrier to community-based work. Some families preferred their loved one to be in a sheltered environment, with caring professional staff support and onsite medical expertise. They cited examples where individuals in our interviews were prevented or deterred from accepting competitive work or traveling independently by their families.

2.3.2 Use Cases for Wearable Devices

With permission, wearables can collect data about individuals such as their health status, activity, and location. Although this data is sensitive, participants and JSPs both saw benefits in sharing their data in certain situations. One participant didn't want anybody to know his location except in emergency situations. Another was excited that the smartwatch could monitor her heart rate and said, "*Would be nice if my mom can see my heartrate's up*" (a good health signal for her). One participant expressed interest in having a quick and easy way to contact families and said, "*It would be good if I could press a button and talk with my family from the smartwatch*". The JSPs described situations where not knowing the location of the participant had caused worries for the family. The JSPs believed that parents might allow their adult children more independence if they could tell where they were, or easily prompt them to communicate their status.

3. DESIGNING AN ARTIFACT

Designing for Health Support: There is already much research examining wearables' potential for health support. Our data suggests that this type of application could be a key factor in improving work opportunities. An example is an application that detects unusually low/high heart rate, extreme stress, seizures, , and falls and performs an action accordingly (e.g. notifying co-workers and family about an unusual heart rate).

Designing for Family Support: The design objective here is to help ease worries faced by family members of individuals by sharing health/status data. An important design question is whether people would be willing to share such data, if it enabled them to have more independence. Such data sharing could be made more equitable if family members also shared their own data. A second design goal would be to ease vulnerability concerns. For example, tools to detect so-called 'stranger danger' and act to protect individuals or prompt them towards more careful decisions.

Designing for Productivity Support: Wearable devices could support productivity by helping individuals to stick to their work time schedules, tracking their hours automatically, or help with reading and spelling.

4. CONCLUSION

This initial investigation of challenges faced by people with mild cognitive impairment in work environments found that concerns of individuals were centered on health issues, while professionals observed a range of health, social and productivity barriers. Wearable devices like smartwatches could potentially address some of these barriers.

5. ACKNOWLEDGMENTS

Many thanks to our interviewees, and United Cerebral Palsy of Greater Suffolk, Inc.

6. REFERENCES

[1] Gottlieb, A., Myhill, W.N., and Blanck, P. Employment of People with Disabilities. *International Encyclopedia of Rehabilitation*, 2010. http://cirrie.buffalo.edu/encyclopedia/en/article/123/.

[2] Kearns, W., Jasiewicz, J.M., Fozard, J.L., Webster, P., Scott, S, Craighead, J., Bowen, M., and McCarthy, J.Temporo-spacial prompting for persons with cognitive impairment using smart wrist-worn interface. *Journal of Rehabilitation Research and Development 50*, 10 (2013), vii–xiv.

[3] Lemaire, G.S. and Mallik, K. Barriers to supported employment for persons With developmental disabilities. *Archives of Psychiatric Nursing 22*, 3 (2008), 147–155.

[4] McGurk, S.R. and Mueser, K.T. Strategies for coping with cognitive impairments of clients in supported employment. *Psychiatric Services (Washington, D.C.) 57*, 10 (2006), 1421–1429.

[5] Migliore, A., Manka, D., Grossi, T., and Rogan, P. Integrated employment or sheltered workshops: Preferences of adults with intellectual disabilities, their families, and staff. *Journal of Vocational Rehabilitation 26*, (2007), 5–19.

[6] Patel, S., Park, H., Bonato, P., Chan, L., and Rodgers, M.A. Review of wearable sensors and systems with application in rehabilitation. *Journal of NeuroEngineering and Rehabilitation 9*, 2012, 21.

[7] Sharma, V., Mankodiya, K., Torre, F., Zhang, A., Ryan, N., Ton, T., Gandhi, R. and Jain, S. SPARK: Personalized Parkinson disease interventions through Synergy between a smartphone and a smartwatch. *LNCS 8519*. (2014), 103-114.

[8] Statistics, U.S.B. of L. Persons with a disability: Labor Force Characteristics - 2014. 2015. http://www.bls.gov/news.release/pdf/disabl.pdf.

Predictive Link Following for Accessible Web Browsing

Jiri Roznovjak and John Magee
Department of Mathematics and Computer Science
Clark University, Worcester, MA, USA
{jroznovjak, jmagee}@clarku.edu

ABSTRACT

Users of mouse-replacement interfaces can have difficulty navigating web pages. Small links may be difficult to click, and cluttered pages can result in following an incorrect link. We propose a predictive link-following approach for web browsing that intercepts mouse click signals and instead follows links based on analysis of the user's mouse movement behavior. Our system can be integrated into web page scripting to provide accessibility without needing to install separate software. In a preliminary experiment, users were able to click particularly small targets more accurately with our system compared to traditional mouse clicks.

Categories and Subject Descriptors

H.5.2 [**Information Interfaces and Presentation**]: User Interfaces; K.4.2 [**Computer and Society**]: Social Issues—*assistive technologies for persons with disabilities*

General Terms

Human Factors

Keywords

Accessibility, Web Browsing, Mouse Replacement Interfaces, Camera Mouse, Target-Aware Pointing

1. INTRODUCTION

Point-and-click interfaces present users with the task of positioning a pointer over a user-interface element, and then performing a selection operation. Users with typical motion abilities using traditional interface devices such as mouse or touchpad have good results with this model. For web browsing, clicks are treated as a command to follow a link.

Users with low dexterity, involuntary movements, or tremors; or users of alternative interfaces such as accessible joysticks, trackballs, or computer-vision based interfaces can have difficulty with this interaction model. For example, it may be difficult for some people to stop the pointer motion over a link while they activate the click. This problem is especially evident in dwell-time selection interfaces [7]. Small links can be difficult to select, resulting in the user "missing" the link. Closely clustered links make the problem worse: users may unintentionally follow a nearby link.

ASSETS'15, October 26–28, 2015, Lisbon, Portugal.
ACM 978-1-4503-3400-6/15/10.
DOI: http://dx.doi.org/10.1145/2700648.2811391 .

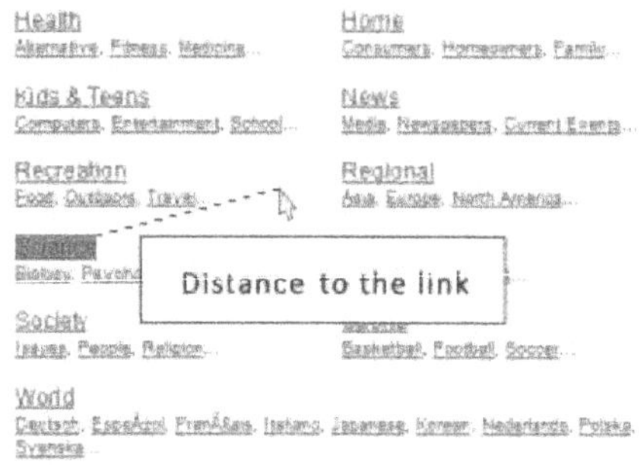

Figure 1: Mouse pointer distance to bounding box of all links. Selection normally requires clicking within the bounding box, our system can take into account near-misses.

Assistive pointing systems can be target-aware (e.g., [3]) or target-agnostic (e.g., [8]). Click actuation can be physical, manual, or inferred (e.g., [4, 7]). Mouse tracking techniques have been used for activity analysis [1, 9], psychological analysis [6], studying mental processes [5], and behavioral biometrics, among many others.

2. PREDICTIVE LINK FOLLOWING

We propose to analyze the mouse movement and clicks before instructing a web browser to follow a link. Our algorithm is implemented as a script that can be embedded in a webpage - so it can work with any general pointer interface and does not require any software installation. The system parameters allow it to be configured for different user's abilities and preferences. The proximity of a mouse movement, hovering, and clicking activities to every link on a web page contribute to its prediction score that is used in deciding if the link should be followed (see Fig 1). In this way, clicks are no longer *commands* to follow a link, instead becoming one of several pieces of evidence indicating a user's intention. A click that barely misses a link can still cause the link to be followed.

Each link a at time t has a prediction score $P_t(a)$:

$$P_t(a) = \tau * P_{t-1}(a) + \texttt{pointer}(a)$$

Where τ is a time decay factor, and $\texttt{pointer}(a)$ is a function related to the action of the mouse pointer in the current time instant:

$$\texttt{pointer}(a) = \begin{cases} \frac{1}{\texttt{dist}(a,\texttt{clickpoint})^\beta} * \gamma & \text{if clicked on the page} \\ \texttt{hoverScore} & \text{if hovered over link} \end{cases}$$

where β affects how much the distance from a link to the click increases the score, and γ weights the click score. `hoverScore` is a constant value added to a link's prediction score when the mouse hovers over the link. These parameters were found experimentally but will be learned in a future system.

At any time instant, if $P_t(a) > \texttt{threshold}$, the link a is followed and all scores reset to zero.

3. EXPERIMENTAL EVALUATION

We conducted a preliminary experiment to evaluate our prototype system.

3.1 Apparatus, Procedure, and Users

The Camera Mouse[1] [2], a computer-vision based mouse-replacement interface was used as the interaction modality for the experiment. The following settings were used: horizontal and vertical gain were *medium*, and dwell-clicking was selected with *normal* radius and *1.5 second* dwell-time.

The system was configured with Logitech C270 HD Webcam. The parameters chosen for our system were $\tau = 0.99$, $\gamma = 40$, $\beta = 2$, and `hoverScore` $= 0.4$. The `threshold` was 0.9.

Testing consisted of two conditions, performed in alternating order: normal dwell-time clicking and predictive clicking. Users are presented with a web page consisting of a section of links from the directory section of `myway.com`. This page is a representative of pages with dense groupings of small links. Users were asked to conduct ten trials as follows: control of the system is turned over to the user, the web page highlights a link in red (Fig. 1). When the user either successfully follows the link, unintentionally follows an incorrect link, or 5 seconds elapses, the trial ends and the system pauses for 1.5 seconds before starting the next trial. We recorded whether or not the user successfully followed the link.

A total of 7 participants were enrolled in the experiment. In this preliminary experiment, none of the participants identified as having any motion impairments. Overall, the experiment consisted of 7 users $\times$ 2 conditions $\times$ 10 links $=$ 140 total trials.

3.2 Results and Discussion

Out of 7 participants, 4 were more successful in selecting links using predictive clicking, 1 had equal results, and 2 were more successful using traditional dwell-time clicking. Overall, users were able to correctly select 46/70 links with our system versus 37/70 links with dwell-time clicking.

Qualitatively, users often successfully selected links with our system that would be missed with dwell-time clicking. Some unintentional selections occurred in both systems, especially when the users did not move the pointer in between trials, triggering an accidental click at the beginning of the next trial. Our system did a better job selecting links that the user intended, but did not provide much benefit in preventing unintentional links from being followed. This could be mitigated in a real system by restricting clicks as pages load, or in a future experiment by repositioning the mouse pointer.

[1]Available at: `http://www.cameramouse.org`

4. CONCLUSION

Development of our system is ongoing. We plan to learn parameters for a particular user's abilities. It is also possible to add other parameters beyond hovering and clicking. Our approach can be generalized beyond accessibility computing toward a system that can predict users' interaction with a web page. We will evaluate future iterations of the system with users with various motion abilities, involuntary motions, and alternative interfaces. We plan to include measurements of precision and completion time, perform statistical analysis, and normalize each trial by starting the pointer in a neutral position.

5. REFERENCES

[1] R. Atterer, M. Wnuk, and A. Schmidt. Knowing the user's every move: User activity tracking for website usability evaluation and implicit interaction. In *WWW '06*, pages 203–212. ACM, 2006.

[2] M. Betke, J. Gips, and P. Fleming. The Camera Mouse: Visual tracking of body features to provide computer access for people with severe disabilities. *IEEE Trans Neural Syst Rehabil Eng*, 10(1):1–10, Mar. 2002.

[3] M. Dixon, J. Fogarty, and J. Wobbrock. A general-purpose target-aware pointing enhancement using pixel-level analysis of graphical interfaces. In *CHI '12*, pages 3167–3176. ACM, 2012.

[4] T. Felzer and S. Rinderknecht. ClickerAID: A tool for efficient clicking using intentional muscle contractions. In *ASSETS '12*, pages 257–258. ACM, 2012.

[5] J. Freeman and N. Ambady. Mousetracker: Software for studying real-time mental processing using a computer mouse-tracking method. *Behavior Research Methods*, 42(1):226–241, 2010.

[6] E. Hehman, R. M. Stolier, and J. B. Freeman. Advanced mouse-tracking analytic techniques for enhancing psychological science. *Group Processes & Intergroup Relations*, 18(3):384–401, 2015.

[7] J. Magee, T. Felzer, and I. S. MacKenzie. Camera Mouse + ClickerAID: Dwell vs. Single-Muscle Click Actuation in Mouse-Replacement Interfaces. In *UAHCI/HCII 2015 , LNCS 9175*, pages 1–11. Springer, Aug. 2015. In press.

[8] J. J. Magee, S. Epstein, E. S. Missimer, C. Kwan, and M. Betke. Adaptive mouse-replacement interface control functions for users with disabilities. In *UAHCI/HCII 2011, LNCS 6766*, pages 332–341. Springer, July 2011.

[9] Y. Zhang, W. Chen, D. Wang, and Q. Yang. User-click modeling for understanding and predicting search-behavior. In *ACM KDD '11*, pages 1388–1396. ACM, 2011.

Appliance Displays: Accessibility Challenges and Proposed Solutions

Giovanni Fusco[1], Ender Tekin[1], Nicholas A. Giudice[2] and James M. Coughlan[1]

[1]The Smith-Kettlewell Eye Research Institute
2318 Fillmore St.
San Francisco, CA 94115 USA
{giofusco,ender,coughlan}@ski.org

[2]University of Maine
Dept. Spatial Information Science & Engineering
Orono, ME 04469 USA
nicholas.giudice@maine.edu

ABSTRACT

People who are blind or visually impaired face difficulties using a growing array of everyday appliances because they are equipped with inaccessible electronic displays. We report developments on our "Display Reader" smartphone app, which uses computer vision to help a user acquire a usable image of a display and have the contents read aloud, to address this problem. Drawing on feedback from past and new studies with visually impaired volunteer participants, as well as from blind accessibility experts, we have improved and simplified our user interface and have also added the ability to read seven-segment digit displays. Our system works fully automatically and in real time, and we compare it with general-purpose assistive apps such as Be My Eyes, which recruit remote sighted assistants (RSAs) to answer questions about video captured by the user. Our discussions and preliminary experiment highlight the advantages and disadvantages of fully automatic approaches compared with RSAs, and suggest possible hybrid approaches to investigate in the future.

Categories and Subject Descriptors

I.5.5 [**Pattern Recognition**]: Applications: Computer Vision

Keywords

Access; blindness; low vision

1. INTRODUCTION

People who are blind or visually impaired face severe difficulties using a growing array of everyday appliances because they are equipped with inaccessible electronic displays, often controlled with touch screens. Such appliances include microwave ovens, media players, digital blood pressure monitors, thermostats and vending machines. Current technology to make printed documents accessible to persons with visual impairments is not equipped to handle the challenges of reading text on electronic displays, which is significantly different in appearance from printed text, and is often obscured by glare, reflections or poor contrast.

There is a small but growing body of work on computer vision-based display readers. One influential early work is Clearspeech [4], in which special markers are affixed around the borders of a display to help the system localize and read the display characters in the image. More recent work focuses on detecting and reading display text without the use of markers [5], and [3] focuses on the use of computer vision and crowdsourcing to help visually impaired persons find and actuate appliance controls such as buttons. Our current "Display Reader" (DR) system builds on [2] and uses 3-4 markers around the display border in order to provide rapid and accurate feedback to help guide the user to find the display, but we aim to minimize or eliminate the need for markers in the future.

A key challenge in any camera-based system for blind or visually impaired users is that of aiming the camera properly to frame the target of interest [6]. We have designed the user interface (UI) for our system to provide explicit guidance to the user to help them capture the display of interest in the camera's field of view, and from a vantage point with minimal glare.

Systems that use remote sighted assistants (RSAs) to offer visual assistance, such as VizWiz [1], are becoming increasingly popular. However, a major drawback of using VizWiz for the purpose of interacting with appliances is that it typically takes about 30 sec. for the user to obtain feedback from a sighted operator on an image they have taken, and a frequent problem is that the image does not frame the object of interest properly. This latency is too slow to help the user obtain a usable picture of the appliance, which is typically an iterative process. Modern successors to VizWiz such as Be My Eyes (BME, see bemyeyes.org) provide a live video feed to a sighted operator, who can speak with the user and see whatever is captured by their camera. This approach offers real-time interaction between the user and operator and makes it possible for the operator to help the user acquire a usable picture of any desired target.

We describe recent developments to the DR system, including an improved UI and the ability of the system to automatically read seven-segment digits (which were chosen because they appear in many appliance displays and are non-standard fonts that are unreadable by many standard OCR systems, such as the KNFB Reader for iOS). We also report the start of a formative study that assesses the usability of DR and compares it with the use of BME to read displays, highlighting the advantages and disadvantages of fully automatic approaches compared with RSAs, and suggesting possible hybrid approaches to investigate in the future.

2. APPROACH

The current DR system consists of an Android smartphone, which is used to acquire images of the display of interest, running in conjunction with a laptop. (In the future we will port the software to the smartphone so that it runs as a self-contained app.) We affix 3-4 black-and-white fiducial paper markers (4 is an optimal number but space limitations may require the use of fewer markers) to each appliance, bordering the display of interest, to simplify and speed up our computer vision algorithms. We exploit the prior knowledge of the display encoded in a *display template*

ASSETS '15, October 26-28, 2015, Lisbon, Portugal
ACM 978-1-4503-3400-6/15/10.
http://dx.doi.org/10.1145/2700648.2811392

that we have constructed for each appliance [2]. Such display templates may be generated by a sighted friend or a crowdsourcing process in which sighted volunteers acquire images of appliances and manually annotate them, to be shared freely on the web, as in [3].

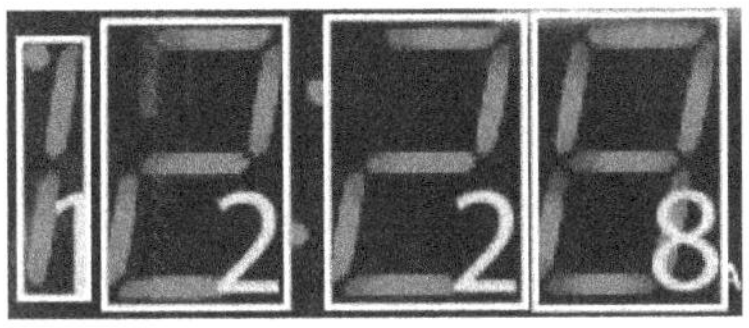

Figure 1. Sample LED display contains a string of digits, each of which is a standard seven-segment digit. For each digit, our algorithm estimates its bounding box (shown in white) and then reads it (results in yellow).

Based on past and new studies with blind and visually impaired volunteer participants and discussions with two blind accessibility experts (one of whom is a co-author on this paper), we improved upon our original UI [2]. Upon launch, the system sounds an ambient clock tone every few seconds to signal that the system is active but that no display is visible. The user is instructed to begin searching for the display using a strategy we call the "back-away" strategy: starting by holding the smartphone body flush with the surface of the display and then backing the smartphone away while keeping the body parallel to the display surface until audio feedback is heard. This strategy has proven effective with commercial apps such as the Digit-Eyes barcode scanner.[1]

The user's next goal is to move the smartphone camera to the *zone* (set of appropriate camera poses) that enables the display to be read, such that the display is roughly centered in the camera's field of view and the camera is far enough from the display to capture it in its entirety but still close enough to be well resolved. Any time the app detects one or more markers but determines that the camera is not in the designated zone, appropriate speech feedback ("up", "down", "left", "right", "closer", "back") is issued to help the user move the camera to enter the zone. For each video frame in which the camera is in the zone, the system estimates the amount of glare visible in the display region, and if the glare is acceptable then it interprets the display contents (see Fig. 1) and reads them aloud using text-to-speech. If the glare is above acceptable limits, then the system sounds another ambient tone every second to signal that the camera is in the zone but that a different vantage point is needed to find a view with less glare.

3. FORMATIVE STUDY

We conducted a formative study of the new version of DR with one volunteer participant who is completely blind. After a brief training session he was able to use the system to read three appliance displays (an LED clock, an LCD thermostat and an LED microwave). He read each display three times (for a total of 9 trials), with the correct reading obtained in all trials except for one erroneous reading caused by motion blur. The time it took to obtain a reading ranged from 7-48 sec. across all trials, with a median of 11 sec.

Next we asked the participant, who had previously installed BME on his own iPhone 6 but hadn't yet gotten it to work properly, to use his BME app to read the LED clock display with our guidance, which was successful. We then asked him to read the three appliance displays on his own using BME, but we found that he was unable to establish a connection more than once (despite a stable Wi-Fi connection). His first attempt to use BME on his own to read a display was partially successful; it took 64 sec. to get connected with a helper, who announced the reading 29 sec. later after providing verbal guidance to help him aim the camera. However, the helper made an interesting error, which was to read the display despite its left-most digit lying just outside of the camera's field of view. While BME is an extremely valuable app, even our limited experience with it in this study highlights the need for greater reliability and for some training on the part of the helpers in an RSA framework.

4. CONCLUSION

We have described recent developments on our DR project, which includes improvements to the UI, the addition of automatic digit recognition algorithms and the start of a formative study that assesses the usability of DR and compares it with the use of BME to read displays. While our new study is very preliminary, it highlights the relative advantages and disadvantages of fully automatic systems compared with RSAs, and reinforces the need for a hybrid approach (as in [3]) that combines elements of both technologies. In particular, the computer vision algorithms used in DR are effective for helping the user find a usable view of a display in much less time than might be required with RSAs such as BME, which requires a substantial amount of time to connect with a helper and frame a usable picture. However, it might be more effective to use an RSA to read the display contents rather relying on a computer vision algorithm, which could falter when confronted with unfamiliar display fonts and symbols.

5. ACKNOWLEDGMENTS

Giudice was supported by NSF grant CHS 1425337; the other authors acknowledge support from NIH, grant 2 R01 EY018890-05 and the National Institute on Disability, Independent Living and Rehabilitation Research, grant 90RE5008-01-00.

6. REFERENCES

[1] Brady, E., Morris, M.R., Zhong, Y., White, S.C. & Bigham, J.P. "Visual Challenges in the Everyday Lives of Blind People." Proc. ACM SIGCHI Conf. on Human Factors in Computing Systems (CHI 2013), Paris, France, 2013.

[2] Fusco, G., Tekin, E., Ladner, R. E., & Coughlan, J. M. (2014, October). "Using computer vision to access appliance displays." In Proc. 16th Int'l Conf. on Computers & Accessibility (ASSETS '14), pp. 281-282.

[3] Guo, A., Chen, X. A., & Bigham, J. P. (2015, April). "ApplianceReader: A Wearable, Crowdsourced, Vision-based System to Make Appliances Accessible." Proc. 33rd Annual ACM Conf. on Human Factors in Computing Systems (pp. 2043-2048). ACM.

[4] Morris, T., Blenkhorn, P., Crossey, L., Ngo, Q., Ross, M., Werner, D., Wong, C. "Clearspeech: a display reader for the visually handicapped." IEEE Trans. Neural Syst. Rehab. Eng. Dec 2006, 14(4), pp.492-500.

[5] Rasines, I., Iriondo, P. and Díez, I. "Real-Time Display Recognition System for Visually Impaired." Int'l Conf. on Computers Helping People with Special Needs (ICCHP '12). Linz, Austria, July 2012.

[6] Rasines, I., Iriondo, P. and Díez, I. "Real-Time Display Recognition System for Visually Impaired." Int'l Conf. on Computers Helping People with Special Needs (ICCHP '12). Linz, Austria, July 2012

[1] http://www.digit-eyes.com/cgi-bin/digiteyes.fcgi?action=scanningTips

People with Parkinson's Disease Using Computers

Maria Hartikainen
School of Information Sciences
University of Tampere, Finland
Kanslerinrinne 1, 33014 Tampere, Finland
lillimaria1@gmail.com

Saila Ovaska
School of Information Sciences
University of Tampere, Finland
Kanslerinrinne 1, 33014 Tampere, Finland
Saila.Ovaska@uta.fi

ABSTRACT
Parkinson's disease is a neurological, progressive disease that affects the ability of using computer input devices. We present findings from a small-scale qualitative study on how the Finnish participants with Parkinson's disease experience their everyday computer use, and describe the solutions they have applied in their difficulties.

Categories and Subject Descriptors
K.4.2. [**Computers and Society**]: Social Issues – *Assistive technologies for persons with disabilities;* H.5.2 [**Information Interfaces and Presentation**]: User Interfaces – *input devices and strategies*

General Terms
Human Factors

Keywords
Parkinson's disease, Motor disability, Home computer, Attitude

1. INTRODUCTION
Parkinson's disease (PD) is chronic, degenerative and progressive [3]. Due to variation in the symptoms and the sporadic nature of the disease, the symptoms vary from time to time and from one patient to another. The disease causes slowness and stiffness of movement, and tremor (rhythmic movement) often first in one arm (see, e.g., [3,4,7] for more detailed descriptions), which affect the abilities of using computer input devices.

People with Parkinson's disease, or PwP, have recently received attention as a user group whose life with computers could be made easier with proper technology, both by choice of input devices [1,4] or as monitoring tools [4,7]. Many HCI studies originally targeted at improvements in input technologies for motor impairments or dexterity problems (for instance, [6,8,9]), suggest adaptations or filters that could provide PwP with better solutions than the standard tabletop mouse and keyboard. However, many studies [1,3,4,7] still report that a key challenge is the lack of information of assistive technologies.

ASSETS '15, October 26-28, 2015, Lisbon, Portugal.
ACM 978-1-4503-3400-6/15/10.
http://dx.doi.org/10.1145/2700648.2811393

In a recent survey [2] targeted at people with Parkinson's disease, nearly 80 % of the respondents reported significant difficulties in their computer use. These findings have been extended in an observational test setup with participants [3] or in controlled experiments in the lab [8,9]. Some work has been conducted in designing for and with PwP [7], but we found in our literature review no studies conducted in their everyday environment.

2. STUDY
We wanted to understand how Finns diagnosed with PD use computers in their homes, what kind of devices they have, what input difficulties they have experienced and have they sought and received help in their computer use. The data collection was conducted by the first author as part of her MSc thesis project [5]. The call for participation was targeted at people with PD who experience problems using a computer, and it was posted in an online community forum for PD patients and their relatives.

Altogether 22 participants (15 female and 7 male; average age 60 years) took part in the study, 16 of them by email. The call for participation was set so that they can be interviewed on the phone if they find writing unpleasant. Three persons were interviewed on the phone. Three volunteers were interviewed in their own homes, where, in addition to asking them the same questions that were presented to all in the questionnaire, they were asked to demonstrate how they use their computers in some small tasks (using the web pages they access often, and writing an email to the researcher). These three sessions were videotaped.

3. FINDINGS
The findings are presented in the following subsections. All in all, they confirmed earlier findings, mainly that there is lack of information of what kind of assistive technologies would be available. Another, more surprising finding was in the attitudes of the respondents: often they expressed they should cope with ordinary devices, and adjust their own behavior to better match "standard" ways of how computers are used.

3.1 Laptops, Desktop Computers, and Tablets
Most of the respondents had a laptop computer (17 persons, 81%), either as their only computing device (11, 52%) or in addition to a desktop computer (2), or tablet device (2), or they had all three types of devices (2). If not a portable computer, they had desktop computers (3 persons) or a desktop computer and a tablet device (1 person).

All participants reported experiencing difficulties using their devices (reported in more detail in [5], in Finnish). Taking this into account, it was surprising to learn that a majority did not have or use any assistive technologies. One participant had a trackball, and one used a joystick and a physical key guard on top of the keyboard. This is in line with the Norwegian statistics [2] where less than a third of the respondents had tried out any special devices. One of the participants in our study had installed a filtering software tool (steadymouse.com).

3.2 Attitudes in Computer Use

One key finding in our study was that the people with PD are not searching for help in their difficulties of using the input devices. Only one in our group of 22 people had sought for external help to computer related difficulties. Though using the devices takes them much longer than for an able-bodied user, sometimes causing severe pain in their muscles, they try to cope with the standard way of operating the mouse and keyboard, and do not look for alternatives. In some occasions the same home computers were used by their relatives, too, and they did not want to draw attention to their own needs by requesting changes which might cause the device not to work for the others any more.

As an example, Figures 1 and 2 demonstrate one participant operating his home computer with the mouse in his left hand. The right hand was the dominant hand, but due to the tremor in the right hand caused by PD, the participant had switched to using the mouse with the other hand. The mouse, originally bought for the right hand, had not been adjusted for left-hand use.

Figure 1. Home computer setup for participant P3.

In Figure 2, the participant is using one finger of his left hand to type an email. The typing is error-prone and slow, and it soon gets tiring for the arm, too. He needs to hunt and peck each individual key when writing with his non-dominant hand. Had we not visited his home, these everyday challenges would not have surfaced.

Figure 2. Participant P3 using the keyboard with one finger.

4. DISCUSSION AND FUTURE WORK

The awareness of the needs of the people with Parkinson's disease is growing nationally, e.g., in Norway [1,2,3], Ireland [4], and the UK [7]. The population of patients is growing due to aging, and according to [7], also younger people are being diagnosed with the disease. Despite this, the special nature of the disease and its influence on interaction with computers are not well understood.

Our work is the first study about the situation in Finland, carried out as a non-funded academic thesis project. We learned that there is no online advice available in Finnish about recommendations of potentially helpful input devices or technologies in the difficulties caused by the disease. Making any recommendations is hard. Since the symptoms and state vary, the advice should take the conditions into account – one assistive solution or a standard setup will not fit all or suffice over time. Furthermore, advice for settings depend on the operating system versions. There often is no support for adjusting device settings, though in many cases simple changes in the mouse control panel would already help in removing extra clicks and removing the repeated key presses on the keyboard. Lastly, instructions for improving the ergonomics of the computer setup could sometimes be of assistance.

A lot remains to be done, both in the software and hardware fields and in the support that will be provided online for the people with Parkinson's disease.

5. REFERENCES

[1] Begnum, M. E. N. 2010. Improving computer interaction for people with Parkinson's disease. In *the Int. Conference on Universal Technologies Unitech2010.* Available at http://www.iu.hio.no/~frodes/unitech10/026-Begnum/

[2] Begnum, M. E.N. 2010. Challenges for Norwegian PC-users with Parkinson's disease – A survey. In *Proc. ICCHP 2010*, LNCS Vol. 6179, pp. 292-299. Springer. DOI = 10.1007/978-3-642-14097-6_47

[3] Begnum, M.E.N. and Begnum, K.M. 2012. On the usefulness of off-the-shelf computer peripherals for people with Parkinson's disease. *Univ Access Inf Soc* (2012) 11 (4): 347–357. DOI = 10.1007/s10209-011-0257-5

[4] Cunningham, L.M., Nugent, C.D., Finlay, D.D., Moore ,G., and Craig. D. 2009. A review of assistive technologies for people with Parkinson's disease. *Technology and Health Care* 17 (2009) 269–279. DOI = 10.3233/THC-2009-0547

[5] Hartikainen, M. 2015. People with Parkinson's disease using computers. MSc thesis, University of Tampere, Finland. http://urn.fi/URN:NBN:fi:uta-201506161735

[6] Keates, S. 2009. Motor impairments and universal access. In Stephanidis, S. (ed.), *The Universal Access Handbook*, 5-1 – 5-14. CRC Press.

[7] McNaney, R., et al. 2015. Designing for and with people with Parkinson's: A focus on exergaming. Proc. CHI'2015, 501-510. DOI = http://dx.doi.org/10.1145/2702123.2702292

[8] Trewin, S., and Pain, H. 1999. Keyboard and mouse errors due to motor disabilities. *Int. Journal of Human-Computer Studies*, 50(2), 109-144. DOI = 10.1006/ijhc.1998.0238.

[9] Trewin, S., and Pain, H. 1999. A model of keyboard configuration requirements. *Behaviour & Information Technology*, 18 (1), 27-35. DOI = 10.1145/274497.274530

Mobile Integrated Assistance to Empower People Coping with Parkinson's Disease

Carla Pereira
Escola Superior de Saúde
Instituto Politécnico de Setúbal
campus do IPS, Setúbal, Portugal
carla.pereira@ess.ips.pt

Patrícia Macedo
ESTSetúbal
Instituto Politécnico de Setúbal
campus do IPS, Setúbal, Portugal
patricia.macedo@estsetubal.ips.pt

Rui Neves Madeira
ESTSetúbal
Instituto Politécnico de Setúbal
campus do IPS, Setúbal, Portugal
rui.madeira@estsetubal.ips.pt

ABSTRACT
In this paper, we present the design of a mobile application to empower an integrated assistance to support users of the triad: "people with Parkinson's disease, their carers and healthcare professionals". Starting from a deep study of this triad's needs, a mobile application was designed to support not just the communication between the triad users, but also to help them finding relevant knowledge to support their clinical issues as well as allowing the supervision of patients` daily routine and the recommendation for daily exercises. This application aims to facilitate the access to knowledge and provide professional support for both people with Parkinson's disease and carers in their homes to improve the remote healthcare assistance.

Categories and Subject Descriptors
H.5 [**Information Interfaces and presentation**]: User Interfaces; K.4.2 [**Social Issues**]: Social Issues—*Assistive technologies for persons with disabilities*

General Terms
Experimentation, Design, Human Factors, Theory

Keywords
Parkinson's disease; mHealth; mobile computing; IBM Watson

1. INTRODUCTION
Mobile technology is transforming the way people communicate around the world, which has also impact in the health services provided. The concept of mobile health (mHealth) is changing how health care is delivered, with an increased support to the management of chronic diseases [1], such as Parkinson's disease (PD), which is the second most common neurodegenerative disease. It is estimated to affect more than 1 per 1 000 people in Europe and around 20 000 people in Portugal, changing both people with Parkinson's disease (PPD) and family's lives [2]. Most studies in this field have investigated the use of mobile applications (apps) to home-based monitoring and assessment of motor complications [3, 4]. Recently, apps have been developed mostly to recommend and give instructions about home exercises (e.g., Parkinson Home Exercises [5]). However, research findings about its effectiveness are scarce.

ASSETS '15, October 26-28, 2015, Lisbon, Portugal
ACM 978-1-4503-3400-6/15/10.
http://dx.doi.org/10.1145/2700648.2811394

Moreover, in the health services provided is important not only to involve the person (PPD), but also the carer/caregiver [6]. For both, it is important to understand the disease and its progression as a way to manage symptoms and find solutions for their daily challenges, as well as to maintain the communication with health professionals for an effective shared decision-making between the triad [7]. Additionally, nowadays, it is becoming very time consuming for healthcare professionals searching for credible information and maintaining updated about the best evidence available. The use of cognitive systems, such as IBM Watson can make processes more efficient and support an improvement of patients' outcomes [8]. According to literature and the study of the triad's needs, we proposed the development of an app that is based on the empowerment of this triad's users to help both PPD and carers to cope better with the Parkinson's disease.

2. PRELIMINARY USER STUDY
A survey was undertaken in order to explore the needs of each group of participants of the triad. A questionnaire was used to characterize the profiles of participants, based on mobile technology as well as on their knowledge needs and the functionalities they identified as helpful to have in the app. Thirty-six users from the Portuguese Parkinson Disease Association participated in the survey, including 11 PPD, 11 carers and 14 healthcare professionals (9 physiotherapists, 2 speech therapists, 2 psychologists and 1 neurologist).

Results highlighted the importance of developing a mobile application to support a remote healthcare assistance, with most of participants identifying it as "extremely relevant" (26/36). Moreover, all user groups reported difficulty finding trustworthy information about the Parkinson's disease. Even for some healthcare professionals (6/14), searching for reliable data to support clinical decisions was identified as a need, which emphasized the importance of incorporating Watson technology.

Moreover, participants rated several sentences using a 7-point Likert scale (1- "totally disagree" to 7- "totally agree"). It is noteworthy that all users reported the importance of finding easily answers about the PD (mean=6.3; SD=1.3), being able to write notes (mean=6.6; SD=0.8), having medication and exercise alerts (mean=6.4; SD=0.9) and communicating with healthcare professionals through the app (mean=6.5; SD=1.1).

3. MOBILE INTEGRATED ASSISTANCE

3.1 System Overview
The system, which we called Smoveen, consists of two main components (see Figure 1): the server, which contains a central database and manages all the requests from the diverse apps; and the client, which can be a mobile or web app. A first mobile app

prototype is being implemented in Java for the Android platform, taking into account the prospective market penetration. It is not required to be always connected to the Internet to use the app, but it will request connections periodically in order to do synchronizations with the server. It connects to the server to obtain and store the required data for all users. The Smoveen system connects to the IBM Watson platform's Q&A service.

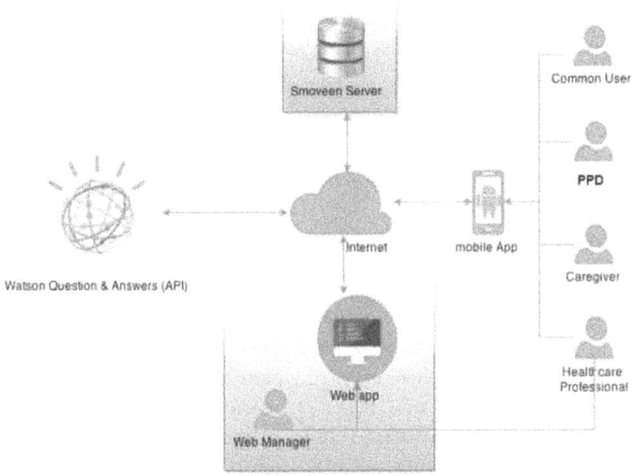

Figure 1. The system architecture.

3.2 Rationale and Design

Smoveen is aimed primarily to the aforementioned triad, although being available to the general public from GooglePlay store. We considered the existence of "common users", who can only consult the essential information and ask open questions related to PD (Figure 2 illustrates the use cases of the system).

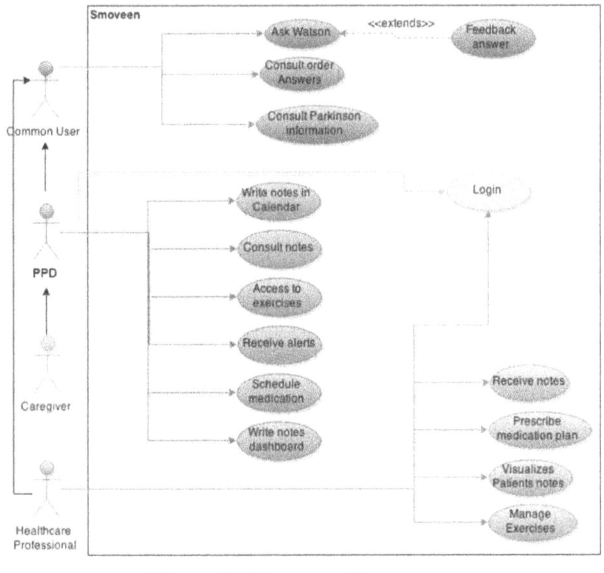

Figure 2. Diagram of use cases.

The latter corresponds to the use case "Ask Watson" and it is executed when the user is searching for credible information from the inside of Smoveen, in order to have an integrated perspective dealing with PD. Smoveen uses Watson's Q&A service, which interprets and answers user questions directly [8]. The service returns candidate responses with associated confidence levels and links to supporting evidence. The Smoveen app will treat these data accordingly before showing them to the user. The user will have an interface to classify the answers since this will help training the Watson's cognitive services. Moreover, right now, all user questions should be put to Watson in English. However, our system will have a Portuguese version and, in this case, we will have to implement an intermediate module for translations since some users are not used to the English language. The use cases related to the modules Exercises and Calendar on the app will be available only to the PPD and the carer (see Figure 3, 4th image). On the other hand, the web app will be available only to the healthcare professionals so they can manage their patients' information, and submit therapeutic exercises to the system.

Figure 3. Examples of screens design [from left to right]: logo (three heads representing the triad); login; menu with 2 options for common users; or 4 options for registered users.

4. FURTHER WORK

The preliminary study allowed us to gather initial feedback from potential end-users, which has validated our project's concept and "sketches". However, we will continue gathering feedback while developing the first prototype, assessing each one of its modules with the users. As part of this ongoing process, we are selecting a group of end-users from the preliminary study which should participate in all user tests.

5. REFERENCES

[1] Steinhubl, S., Muse, E., and Topol, E. 2013. Can Mobile Health Technologies transform health care? *The Journal of American Medical Association*, 310 (22), 2395-2396.

[2] European Commission. 2015. Neurodegenerative Disorders. *http://ec.europa.eu/health/major_chronic_diseases/diseases/brain_neurological*. Accessed 25th June 2015.

[3] Pan, D., Dhall, R., Lieberman, A., Petitti, D.B. 2015. A Mobile Cloud-Based Parkinson's Disease Assessment System for Home-Based Monitoring. *JMIR mHealth and uHhealth*, 3(1): e29.

[4] Patel, S., et al. 2009. Monitoring motor fluctuations in patients with Parkinson's disease using wearable sensors. *IEEE Trans. Inf. Technol. Biomed*, 13(6), 864–873.

[5] IAPRD.org. 2015. Parkinson Home Exercises app. *www.iaprd.org/publications.html*. Accessed 11th Aug 2015.

[6] Tod, A., McDonnell, A., et al. 2014. Putting people with Parkinson's in control: exploring the impact of quality social care. Project Report. Sheffield Hallam. University, Sheffield.

[7] McLaughlin, D., Hasson, F., Kernohan, W.G., Waldron, M., McLaughlin, M., Cochrane, B., Chambers, H. 2011. Living and coping with Parkinson's disease: Perceptions of informal carers. *Palliative Medicine*, 25(2), 177-182.

[8] IBM. 2015. IBM Watson. *www.ibm.com/smarterplanet/us/en/ibmwatson/what-is-watson.html*. Accessed 25th June 2015.

SECPT Framework – a Travelling Experience Based Framework for Visually Impaired People

Jing Guan
School of Design
The Hong Kong Polytechnic University
Kowloon, Hong Kong
Guanjing99@gmail.com

Clifford Sze-Tsan Choy
School of Design
The Hong Kong Polytechnic University
Kowloon, Hong Kong
mccliff@polyu.edu.hk

ABSTRACT
The right to fully participate into the community and enjoy the life is the same for people with or without a visual impairment. However, many existing research for assistive products or technology for visually impaired people are piecemeal, because there is no holistic and systemic research focus on the visually impaired people's travelling experience. We propose the SECPT Framework which based on the visually impaired people's travelling experience, can be a starting point of the design process for designers to encounter visually impaired people, and enable them to quick understanding the target group and determine their research area.

Categories and Subject Descriptors
H.1 [**Models and principles**]: User experience - *User-centered design*

Keywords
Visually impaired people, framework, travelling experience.

1. INTRODUCTION
According to De Potter (2006), going out to do some activities can improve visually impaired people's well-being, the perception of self-esteem and self-competence, and preserve them from handicap. A reasonable amount of work about assistive technology for visually impaired people's travelling has been researched, like tactile maps, obstacle sensors, interactive and multimodal maps on computers and smart phones etc. All of these products or design can enhance visually impaired people's travelling experience in some specific areas. However, it shows that many of them have their own limitations and problems, like some of them are not user-friendly for visually impaired people and the exploration area is limited (Ungar et al., 1997). Besides, we found that most of the previous designs are piecemeal in that they mainly focus on the orientation and mobility assistive technology. Few researchers studied how to help visually impaired people to determine the destination or how to recall the previous travelling process, which is also important to help visually impaired people enhance their travelling experience.

ASSETS'15, October 26-28, 2015, Lisbon, Portugal
ACM 978-1-4503-3400-6/15/10.
http://dx.doi.org/10.1145/2700648.2811395

One of the reasons caused by these problems is that it is difficult to develop new product for visually impaired people, and designers are not that experienced in interacting with them. However, to the best of our knowledge, there is no holistic and systemic research focus on the visually impaired people's travelling experience, which can be a starting point of the design process for designers to encounter visually impaired people, and enable them to quick understanding the target group and determine their research area. Therefore, there is a need for developing a framework, which is about allowing analysis visually impaired people's whole travelling experience and lets designers better understand limitations and concerns of visually impaired people, so that they can develop new products or services to support their everyday lives. In order to provide comprehensive and systemic travelling information of visually impaired people, there is a need for describing the framework based on their travelling experience, because analyzing the experience of users enables us to know what might make a particular product or design more pleasing or enjoyable to use (Wright, McCarthy & Meekison, 2005).

2. DESIGN OF THE FRAMEWORK
The comprehensive assistive technology (CAT) model from Hersh and Johnson (2010), is a tree-like structure model, the top level of which contains four branched including: context, person, activities and assistive technology. It is a good tool to be used for classification, synthesis and analysis of particular devices and support the development of new devices. However, the activity attribute in CAT model is not categorized in an efficient way. For example, the activity of shopping is classified into the daily living branch by the author, however, it is obvious that the process of shopping experience also involves mobility, communication or cognitive activities. Therefore, instead of categorizing by these functional activities, categorizing based on the experience of users will be more efficient and in a systematic. Based on the experience framework from Wright, McCarthy and Meekison (2005), there are six processes of sense making: anticipating, connecting, interpreting, reflecting, and appropriating. However, for the travelling experience of visually impaired people, it is also important to consider how to draw visually impaired people's attention and attract them to go outside, since it's much more difficult for them to gather travelling information from newspapers, magazines, or social media than sighted people. Besides, according to my previous study, considering the scenario of the travelling experience of visually impaired people is also important. Goal oriented travelling is the experience that visually impaired people can be planed ahead while goalless oriented travelling is much more difficult to plan since visually impaired people need to make sense of the current information from the

environment and make the navigation decision immediately. Therefore, we propose a framework to facilitate designer in designing interactive system for enhancing travelling experience of visually impaired people, which is the SECPT Framework (scenario, experience, context, person and technology framework).

3. THE COMPONENT OF SECPT FRAMEWORK

Specifically, travelling here can be defined as: moving outside of the place visually impaired people familiar with. And the framework can be represented as a tree-like structure framework, the top level of which contains five branched including: scenario, experience, context, person, and technology. The details of each attributes can be seen in the following figures (Figure 1).

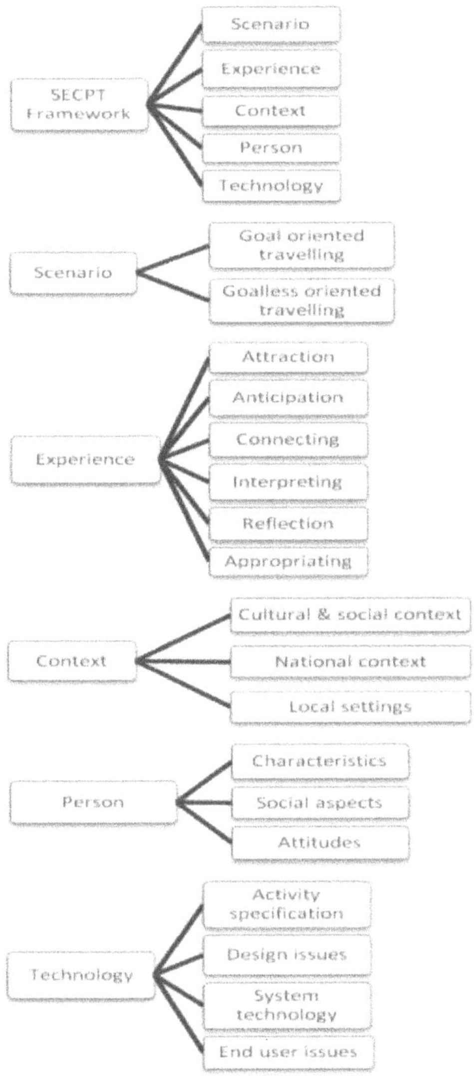

Figure 1. The component of SECPT Framework.

4. HOW TO USE IT

To be specific, the framework is proposed to guide the users with a different level of thinking. Firstly, the users are expected to consider the different scenarios of the travelling experience. Secondly, is the experience attribute, this attribute describes the process people use when making sense of experience in a systemic view, which encourages people to think technology as experience. The third attribute is the context attribute, since the assistive technology design is based on the users' existing context and does not require them to change it. Then turns to the person attribute since the people or people who are going to use a particular assistive technology are central to the success of the system. Last but not least is the technology attribute, which can be separated into four categories: activity specification, design issues, system technology issues, and end user issues.

5. CONCLUSION

Designers will face much more challenges when designing for these people comparing for sighted people. We try to provide insight into the travelling experience of people with visual impairment and introduce a framework for it. It is anticipated that the framework can provide a holistic and systemic view of their experience, which can be applied by members of a multidisciplinary team to understand visually impaired people's real needs and generate new and creative ways to develop proper assistive technology for them.

6. ACKNOWLEDGMENTS

The authors would like to thank The Hong Kong Polytechnic University for their support. This research was supported by the Research Grants Council for the Hong Kong PhD Scheme.

7. REFERENCES

[1] De Potter J. (2006). The contribution of sport and physical activity to the-well-being of visually impaired people. Science & sports. 21,249-250.

[2] Hersh, M., & Johnson, M. A. (2010). Assistive technology for visually impaired and blind people. Springer Science & Business Media.

[3] Packer, T. L., Small, J., & Darcy, S. (2008). Tourist experiences of individuals with vision impairment. Sustainable Tourism CRC.

[4] UNGAR, S., BLADES, M. & SPENCER, C. 1997. Teaching visually impaired children to make distance judgments from a tactile map. Journal of Visual Impairment and Blindness, 91, 163-174.

[5] Wright, P., McCarthy, J., & Meekison, L. (2005). Making sense of experience. In Funology (pp. 43-53). Springer Netherlands.

Depicting the Keypad Mouse Interface: Exploring Pointing Behaviors of Three Input Devices

J. Eduardo Pérez, Xabier Valencia, Myriam Arrue and Julio Abascal
EGOKITUZ: Laboratory of Human-Computer Interaction for Special Needs
University of the Basque Country UPV/EHU, School of Computer Science, Donostia-San Sebastian, Spain
[juaneduardo.perez, xabier.valencia, myriam.arrue, julio.abascal]@ehu.eus

ABSTRACT
Using standard keyboard for pointing and clicking interactions seems to be an affordable option for people who have difficulties handling a standard mouse due to a lack of dexterity or temporal disability conditions. The keypad mouse uses discrete input based on keystrokes to perform cursor movements. This distinctive feature along with others related to cursor motion behavior, make the keypad mouse a unique pointing interface when compared with alternatives. We have carried out a study with expert users of different pointing devices. Results of the study revealed significant differences in the performance values among participants in the three groups. Direction on aimed cursor movements proved to be a crucial factor to be taken into account for keyboard-only users. The findings presented in this paper have a broad application when it comes to designing effective predictive models as well as to proposing design guidelines, novel interaction techniques and adaptation techniques for this collective.

Categories and Subject Descriptors
H.5.2 [**Information interfaces and presentation**]: User interfaces – *input devices and strategies.* K.4.2 [**Computers and society**]: Social issues – *assistive technologies for persons with disabilities.*

General Terms
Experimentation, Human Factors, Performance.

Keywords
Pointing and clicking tasks, dexterity impairment, keypad mouse.

1. INTRODUCTION
Users with lack of dexterity in their upper-limbs tend to have a broader range of needs when choosing their preferred pointing device. Alternatives to the standard mouse for direct selection on graphical user interfaces (GUI) include trackballs, joysticks, head sensors and the use of the numeric keys on the keyboard [3].

Some people who have difficulties handling a mouse but are able to use a keyboard choose the keypad mouse alternative for pointing and clicking interactions. Current accessibility options of operating systems (e.g., MouseKeys for Windows) allow the use of the numeric keypad to perform these two fundamental actions by pressing the central '5' key for cursor clicking, and the surrounding number keys for moving the cursor in vertical, horizontal or diagonal directions.

ASSETS '15, October 26-28, 2015, Lisbon, Portugal
ACM 978-1-4503-3400-6/15/10.
http://dx.doi.org/10.1145/2700648.2811396

2. BACKGROUND
Many problems in HCI, as in other fields of knowledge, are explored through models. These are used to simplify a more complex phenomenon helping, in this way, to study the problem space.

2.1 Fitts' Law Model
Fitts' law was first applied to the study of input devices by Card et al. [2], and since then research in computer pointing is inseparable from this predictive model. The Fitts' law expression typically used nowadays is:

$$MT = a + b \log_2 (A/W + 1) \quad (1)$$

It predicts the movement time (*MT*, in seconds) required to reach a target of size W at a distance A in a rapid aimed movement. In Equation (1), the log_2 expression is referred as the index of difficulty (*ID*, in bits) of the task, and corresponds to a particular combination of A and W values. The intercept coefficient (*a*) and the slope (*b*) are constant values calculated via linear regression, determined through empirical tests. Finally the ratio $1/b$ is the Index of Performance (*IP*, in bits/s).

2.2 Keystroke-level Model
Unlike Fitts' law, the keyboard-level model (KLM) by Carl, Moran and Newel [1] was developed specially for analyzing human performance in interactive computing systems. The KLM predicts expert error-free task completion times, breaking down the corresponding task into a series of primitive operators. The model works with four motor-control operators (K = keystroking, P = pointing, H = homing, D = drawing), one mental operator (M = mental preparation) and one system response operator (R) counted only if the user has to wait. The total predicted time is the sum of the subtask times as shown in the following formulation:

$$T_{execute} = t_k + t_H + t_P + t_D + t_M + t_R \quad (2)$$

3. RESEARCH METHODOLOGY
The lack of data from genuine keyboard pointing users in the literature call for initial research within this issue. Next we describe a study to explore different pointing behaviors of 3 different pointing devices.

3.1 Participants
3 groups of users participated in the experiment with a total of 12 participants (7 females). Each group was made up of 4 subjects, and represented a different pointing device for performing cursor movements. The groups were: keyboard users group (KU, mean=49 years, SD=8), joystick users group (JU, mean=51 years, SD=17) and mouse users group (MU, mean=31 years, SD=2). All participants were experienced users with the pointing device used during experiment, as they regularly access desktop computers with that device. Participants in the KU and JU groups had motor

impairments in their upper-extremities, while subjects from the MU group were persons without disabilities.

3.2 Apparatus

The same equipment was utilized in all sessions: a Dell Precision M6700 laptop running Windows 7 Enterprise and an additional monitor (24 inches and 1920×1200 pixels resolution) to present stimuli to participants. The software test bed used during experimental sessions was an application designed for conducting and analyzing studies of human pointing performance [4].

3.3 Design

The study followed a mixed between- and within-subjects factorial design with repeated measures. The factors and levels were: pointing device (keyboard, joystick, mouse), Index of Difficulty (ID, 1.87 to 4.64 bits) based on different amplitudes (256, 512, 768 pixels) and widths (32, 64, 96 pixels), and approach angle (25 different). *Pointing Device* is a between-subjects factor, while *Amplitude*, *Width* and *Approach Angle* are within-subject factors. Each participant performed all 225 trials (3×3×25) in one session. The order of the conditions was randomized.

3.4 Procedure

Once participants were informed, they signed a consent form and information on demographics and expertise was collected through a brief pre-session interview. Prior to testing, the task was demonstrated to participants with a reduced sequence of warm-up trials. The exercise was a multidirectional "point-and-click" task with 25 circular targets arranged in a circular layout. The diameter of the layout circle and targets varied after each sequence of trials according to an amplitude and width condition defined for the experiment. Before starting, participants were reminded to attempt to reach the targets as quickly and accurately as possible. Duration of the session varied from around 5 minutes for the MU group, up to nearly an hour for the KU group.

4. PRELIMINARY RESULTS

Different values were considered in order to measure the performance of each group. The values studied were: movement time (MT) from starting point until clicking on the target, number of pauses (NP) within a pointing trajectory, and total duration of pauses (DP) within a pointing trajectory.

MT differs noticeably between the three user groups. Keyboard users needed more time (11233.33ms) than the joystick users (5007.38ms). Mouse users obtained the best values (854.31ms). A mean of 5.20 was calculated as NP for keyboard users. Joystick users obtained 2.44 as the mean NP and 0.60 was calculated for mouse users. The mean DP values for each user group was: 5230.66ms for KU, 480.49ms for JU and 59.46ms for MU. The Kruskal Wallis tests revealed significant effects for the device used on the 3 values: MT, NP and DP.

4.1 Approach Angle Influence

The obtained data led us to study the effect of approach angles (25 for each ID) on the 3 performance measures mentioned before.

4.1.1 Movement Time

Keyboard users obtained better MT values for those trials with approach angles close to the eight fixed trajectories ("multiple of 45º" vs. "not a Multiple of 45º"). The Friedman test revealed a significant effect of an approach angle in the MT values for KU group ($\chi^2(1)=77.88$ p=<0.001). A post-hoc test using the Wilcoxon Signed-rank test was used to calculate the effect size (r=0.31, p=<0.001). There was no significant effect for the other two groups: JU ($\chi^2(1)=0$ p=1) or MU ($\chi^2(1)=0.30$ p=0.586).

4.1.2 Number of Pauses

NP by keyboard users varies widely depending on the approach angles applied. Trials with angles close to the eight fixed trajectories obtained the lowest values of NP, indicating that these movements were easier to perform for KU. The Friedman test revealed that for KU there is a significant effect of an approach angle "Multiple of 45º" or "Not a Multiple of 45º" ($\chi^2(1)= 61.76$, p-value < 0.001). The effect size according to the Wilcoxon Signed-rank test was also calculated (r=0.30 p-value < 0.001). No significant effect was found for JU ($\chi^2(1)=0.05$, p=0.830) or MU groups ($\chi^2(1)= 0.19$, p-value = 0.661).

4.1.3 Pauses Duration

Similarly to the aforementioned MT and NP, the DP by keyboard users also achieved better values for those angles close to the eight fixed trajectories. The Friedman test revealed that there is a significant effect for the KU of an approach angle "Multiple of 45º" or "Not a Multiple of 45º" ($\chi^2(1)=72.96$, p-value < 0.001) with an effect size of (r=0.32 p=<0.001). No significance could be found for joystick users.

5. CONCLUSIONS

Results gathered in the user study revealed that approach angle of trials proved to have a significant effect on the performance values obtained for keyboard users group. In addition, the number of pauses and their duration proved to be an important component of the total movement time for these users. Based on these results, this user study revealed that an effective predictive model for keyboard-only users should consider the angle of the cursor movements to be performed. Besides, the time required in the pauses for adjusting and amending cursor trajectories should be also considered in such a model. Therefore, an effective predictive model should integrate two different components: the prediction of the movement time (without pauses) and the prediction of the total duration of pauses (time between keystroking).

6. ACKNOWLEDGEMENTS

Many thanks to the Elkartu association of people with physical disabilities and to the study participants.

This work was funded by the Ministry of Economy and Competitiveness of the Spanish Government and by the European Regional Development Fund - ERDF (eGovernAbility project, TIN2014-52665-C2-1-R). The EGOKITUZ Research Laboratory is supported by the Department of Education, Universities and Research of the Basque Government (Eusko Jaurlaritza/Gobierno Vasco) through Grant # IT-395-10.

7. REFERENCES

[1] Card, S. K., Moran, T. P., Newell, A. (1980). The keystroke-level model for user performance time with interactive systems. Communications of the ACM, 23, 396-410.

[2] Card, S.K., English, W.K. and Burr, B.J. (1978). Evaluation of mouse, rate-controlled isometric joystick, step keys, and text keys for text selection on a CRT. Ergonomics 21 (8), 601-613.

[3] Cook, A. M. and Polgar, J. M. (2015). Assistive Technologies: Principles and Practice, 4th Edition. *St. Louis: Elsevier.*

[4] Wobbrock, J. O., Harada, S., Cutrell, E., MacKenzie, I. S. FittsStudy, version 4.2.4 [software] http://depts.washington.edu/aimgroup/proj/fittsstudy/

A Model-Based Tool to Develop an Accessible Media Player

María González-García
LaBDA Group, Computer Science Department, Universidad Carlos III de Madrid, Spain
mgonza1@inf.uc3m.es

Lourdes Moreno
LaBDA Group, Computer Science Department, Universidad Carlos III de Madrid, Spain
lmoreno@inf.uc3m.es

Paloma Martínez
LaBDA Group, Computer Science Department, Universidad Carlos III de Madrid, Spain
pmf@inf.uc3m.es

ABSTRACT

Despite the myriad media content, there are users who cannot access it. Accessibility standards indicate that both the media content as the user agent that provides access to the media content must be accessible to everyone, with or without a disability. To address this issue, this work presents a Model-Based tool, which gives support to the development process of an accessible media player according to accessibility standards. Requirements and adaptation rules regarding the accessibility of a media player and video content are included in the tool design following a methodological approach. This authoring tool is a graphical editor which is aimed at being used by any professional without having a high level of expertise in accessibility.

Categories and Subject Descriptors

D.2.2 [**Software Engineering**]: Design Tools and Techniques. H.5.2 [**Information Interfaces and Presentation**]: User Interfaces – *interaction style, theory and methods, graphical user interface.*

General Terms

Design, Human Factors, Standardization, Languages

Keywords

Accessibility; media player; Model-Based Development

1. INTRODUCTION

The access to video content is not equal for all users. There are users, especially people with disabilities, who cannot access it due to the fact that a set of barriers both in the content and in the user agent (browser, media player, etc.) which delivers this content complicates it [1]. In the case of a media player and following standards, it is essential to provide alternatives (such as captions or audio description) to the video content and mechanism to access these alternatives (such as buttons to activate the alternatives). Therefore, both the content and the user agent should be accessible regarding accessibility standards.

Apart from the accessibility barriers, there is also a lack of methodological approaches that assist to develop accessible media players with quality and there are not authoring tools too. This lack of methodological approaches and technologies has motivated the line of research in which this work is framed.

ASSETS '15, October 26-28, 2015, Lisbon, Portugal.
ACM 978-1-4503-3400-6/15/10.
DOI: http://dx.doi.org/10.1145/2700648.2811397

2. FROM ACCESSIBILITY REQUIREMENTS TO A SUPPORT TOOL

In this section the process of developing a support tool from a requirements analysis to the final user interface is described. In order to generate the interface, a model-based approach according to the four levels of abstraction defined by the Cameleon reference framework[1] is used. In this case, these levels and their functionalities are: Task model which shows the interaction between a user and an accessible user agent, Abstract User Interface (AUI) which shows the structure of the interaction elements, Concrete User Interface (CUI) which concretizes an AUI for a given context of use, and Final User Interface (FUI) which is the operational user interface on a particular computing platform.

In this work a User Interface Description Language (UIDL) like UsiXML[2] and MARIA[3] are used. This approach allows the development of user interfaces at multiple levels of independence, independently of the interaction modality and of any computing platform of the FUI.

2.1 Accessibility requirement analysis

This first step in this developing process is to obtain a set of accessibility requirements taking into account a group of accessibility standards like Web Content Accessibility Guidelines (WCAG) 2.0, User Agent Accessibility Guidelines (UAAG) 2.0 and ISO 9241-171:2008 (Guidance on software accessibility) [2]. Among these requirements, two categories are distinguished:

- Native: Play/Pause, Stop, Resize, Mute and Volume.
- Additional: Rewind, Forward, Caption, AudioDescription, Size, Font, Color, LanguageCaption, LanguageAudio, Help and Find.

2.2 Task Model, AUI and CUI

This subsection briefly explains the three first levels of the methodological approach to design an accessible media player.

Accessibility requirements are included from the design phase. First of all, the accessibility requirements are transformed into tasks and relationships in the Task Model. For example, the Caption requirement is transformed into an interaction task called Caption. Apart from the task, some relationships between this task and the rest of the tasks are established [3].

The second level of abstraction is the AUI. Considering this level, presentation task sets (PTSs) which are the set of elements enabled at the same time are used to meet the semantic established

[1] Cameleon Reference framework: http://www.w3.org/2005/Incubator/model-based-ui/XGR-mbui-20100504/#crf
[2] UsiXML: http://www.usixml.org/
[3] MARIA: http://www.w3.org/wiki/images/3/36/MARIA.pdf

regarding the temporal binary relationships. For example, the Caption task can be enabled at the first moment (first task set).

After including the PTSs, the automatic transformation into AUI design primitives is done. The set of tasks are transformed into a set of Interactors (selection, edit, only output and control) which represents every type of user interaction object and Interactor Compositions (grouping, relation, composite description and repeater) which groups together design primitives that have a logical relationship [4] in the AUI model. In the case of the Caption task, this task is transformed into a control activator.

The first concrete level is the CUI. This level uses the design primitives which are dependent of platform and technology (and are the transformation of the AUI design primitives).

2.3 Authoring Support tool to create the FUI

For professionals without expertise in modeling shown in previous sections; a graphical editor to allow designing the FUI of an accessible media player is developed.

The CUI design primitives are constructors which are going to be used to design the media player in this authoring tool. Thanks to these constructors, the FUI, the last level, can be developed using objects which start from these constructors with implicit accessibility requirements following the standards previously mentioned (section 2.1).

In addition to the four-level architecture, this work has included adaptation rules (taking into consideration the access needs) [4]. The adaptation rules are provided through five profiles (default player, visual access, auditory access, simplified player and general player). These profiles have been integrated like design options in the support tool. Besides, this tool also follows the Authoring Tool Accessibility Guidelines (ATAG) due to the fact that it generates accessible content, in this case, a player, apart from other requirements such as being accessible via keyboard or screen reader. In addition to this, the tool assists the designer to fulfill and know what accessibility requirements are being considered through the contextual help.

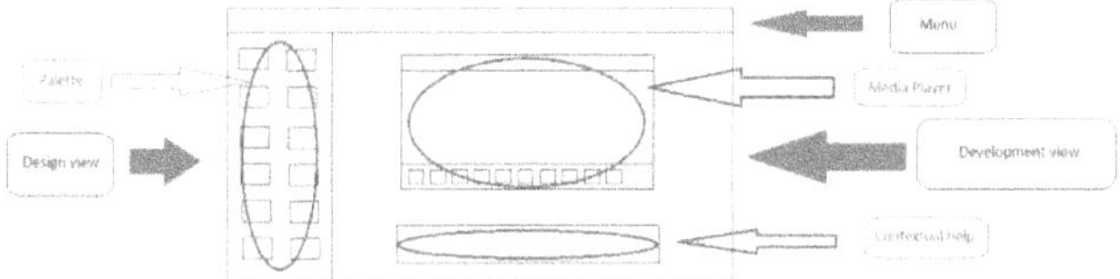

Figure 1 Components of the graphical editor´s interface

In general terms, the graphical editor's interface is composed of a palette of elements; a canvas in which a view of the final media player and a contextual help are presented and an upper menu (see Figure 1). It is classified as a WYSIWYG ("What You See Is What You Get") editor.

The current prototype has been implemented in Java technology, but this fact is being extended to Web technology, and it could be expanded to other platforms. Therefore, the culmination of the process is an executable version of the graphical editor (see Figure 2).

3. RELATED WORK

Some works that provide a Model-Based Graphical Editor are found. For example, Creissac and Alves present FlexiXML [5], a tool which supports the automatic generation of user interfaces through models expressed in UsiXML. And Miñon et al. present SPA4USXML, a graphical tool which assists the designer of ubiquitous services using UsiXML as well as others UIDL [6].

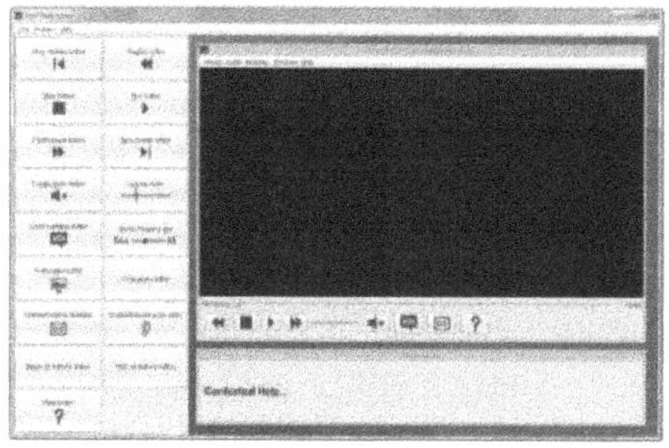

Figure 2 Screenshot of the graphical editor's final interface

4. CONCLUSIONS

As a result of a MBD process independently of the tool's user, this work presents a graphical editor which allows designing, running and exporting an accessible media player in different platforms in an easy way without being an expert in the area of accessibility. At the present, accessibility assessments of the final media player are being conducted.

5. ACKNOWLEDGMENTS

This work is supported by eGovernAbility-Access project (TIN2014-52665-C2-2-R)

6. REFERENCES

[1] Moreno, L., González, M., Martínez, P. and Iglesias, A. 2011. A Study of Accessibility Requirements for Media Players on the Web. 6th International Conference UAHCI 2011, Orlando, USA, July 9-14, 2011, pp.249-257

[2] González, M., Moreno, L. and Martínez, P. 2015. Approach design of an accessible media player. *International Journal UAIS,* Springer Vol 14, Is 1, 45-55

[3] González, M., Moreno, L. and Martínez, P. 2012. An approach to User Interface Design of an accessible user agent. DSAI'12. Procedia Computer Science, Vol 14, 254–262. DOI=http://dx.doi.org/10.1016/j.procs.2012.10.029.

[4] González, M., Moreno, L. and Martínez, P. 2014. Adaptation rules for Accessible Media Player Interface. *International Conference on Human Computer Interaction*. Tenerife, Spain. ACM, New York, NY, USA, Article 5. DOI= http://dx.doi.org/10.1145/2662253.2662258.

[5] Creissac Campos, J. and Alves Mendes, S. 2011. FlexiXML A portable user interface rendering engine for UsiXML. *UIDL'2011* - Interact' 2011 (Lisbon, Portugal) Workshop, (Eds.). 158-168. ISBN 978-2-9536757-1-9.

[6] Miñón, R., Moreno, L. and Abascal, J. 2013. A graphical tool to create user interface models for ubiquitous interaction satisfying accessibility requirements. *Universal Access in the Information Society*, Springer, Vol 12, Is 4, pp 427-439.

Video Analysis for Includification Requirements

Alexander Hofmann
University of Vienna
Faculty of Computer Science, Entertainment Computing Research Group
1090 Vienna
Vienna, Austria
a9130062@unet.univie.ac.at

Helmut Hlavacs
University of Vienna
Faculty of Computer Science, Entertainment Computing Research Group
1090 Vienna
Vienna, Austria
helmut.hlavacs@univie.ac.at

ABSTRACT

In extensive trials we asked participants with disabilities to play a set of computer games, demanding a variety of cognitive and physical skills. In particular we presented a Tetris variant we developed ourselves, which follows various includification guidelines. Participants were recorded on video in order to identify strengths and weaknesses in coping with the presented game challenges. In the videos we recorded the game screen, a frontal video of the participants showing emotional responses, and eye gaze. Post processing tasks are used to analyze and retrieve data from the videos. This helps to build up a video database for later analysis and answer questions raised after the recordings were taken.

Categories and Subject Descriptors

K.4.2 [**Computers and Society**]: Social Issues - Assisitive technologies for persons with disabilities; K.5.2 [**Information Interfaces and Presentation**]: User Interfaces - User-centered Design; K.8.0 [**Personal Computing**]: General - Games

General Terms

Computer Games, Includification, Accessibility, Video Analysis

1. INTRODUCTION

People with disabilities are usually not the target group for companies developing computer games, although according to [3] 23% of all gamers live with disabilities. Hence disabled gamers face various problems while playing computer games, problems that might easily be avoided if already taken into account during game development.

The project GETIN (Game and Entertainment Technology for Includification [1]) focuses on the research of new technologies [2] to not only make computer games accessible, but primarily develop strategies to actively help developers to enrich computer games with includification features. This might even go as far as adding software components using artificial intelligence to actively help gamers with disabilities to become competitive and thus improve their subjectively experienced self-efficacy.

This short paper describes requirements and methods to improve includification. In [4] Barlet & Spohn mention the need of new technology to make it possible that all gamers play the same games despite their disabilities. This is the purpose of GETIN.

ASSETS '15, October 26-28, 2015, Lisbon, Portugal.
ACM 978-1-4503-3400-6/15/10.
http://dx.doi.org/10.1145/2700648.2811398

2. PLAYING WITH DISABILITIES

To investigate the requirements for gamers with disabilities, our research group established a cooperation with a local caregiver, taking care of 29 clients with physical and intellectual disabilities. They receive special treatment by offering e.g. physical exercises. 18 of them agreed to participate in our investigations and this research project. Two students of our research group where responsible to set up a game computer to record trials for playing computer games on video, give instructions and supervise the trial.

2.1 Experimental Setup

Figure 1 shows a screenshot taken from a recording, showing participant Franz playing our own plain and detraction-preventive version of Tetris. On the left side the important part of the game scene is recorded, while on the right side at the bottom, the user is recorded showing emotions while playing. Above the keys on the keyboard used for steering the game are visible, a pressed key is rendered in light grey. The white circle in the game scene shows the current eye focus of the player, recorded with the Tobii EyeX [7] controller.

2.2 Recorded Parameters

To retrieve a broad range of biometric data of the game we first thought about using biometric sensors. However, the pure usage of such sensors might already introduce a measurement bias, e.g. with sensitive of phobic players. First, attaching the sensors might cause a major distraction, preventing players from focusing on the game. Another example is given by pulse meters, the basic hypothesis here being that the measured pulse frequency is a measure for general arousal or excitement. However, the act of attaching a pulse meter to a test participant alone is enough to raise the pulse frequency to an abnormally high level. Another problem is the need to synchronize biometric data to the recorded

Figure 1: Franz, playing our first plain Tetris game

videos. Biometric data thus must be annotated with appropriate timing data, but the same is true for recorded videos. We therefore decided to refrain from using biometric sensors, but instead use the recorded videos as sole sources for subsequent data analysis. The results thusly computable include reaction time being the time difference between the occurrence of two subsequent events (e.g. block spawn and first key pressed), pulse frequency [5], emotional expressions or an eye focus heatmap.

2.3 Video Recording

We made several recordings of the participants playing the described games. Screen recordings as shown in Figure 1 plus an additional camera from right or left behind the test person, showing the screen and the gamer, as shown in ??. We at first explained the game rules, then let them freely play for a while.

All the recordings are currently disclosed and off-limits to general public. Although all participants, involved care givers and parents agreed in an informed consent and also signed a media usage contract. Nevertheless we handle the recordings and images with respect and care, so decided to close them for academic evaluation and usage only.

2.3.1 Main Findings

The results of the evaluation of Tetris was quite astonishing. First it turned out that the Tetris rules are not self evident for players with intellectual disabilities. The gameplay is actually very difficult to understand, rotating the bricks is something the gamer has to figure out during the play, the speedup function (key down) was not mentioned to the participants at all. In the first trial the participants where often distracted by the various colors of the bricks. Therefore we developed another uni-colored Tetris version (just in blue) with Unity 3D and carried out more trials. Some participants had even more fun with building towers than sorting them in rows. Others had troubles with visuo-motor coordination, according to [6] being "a basic skill required for everyday activities involving movement, such as writing, dressing, walking, driving or playing sports. Playing video games also requires visuo-motoric coordination". Players often had to shift their eye gaze away from the screen down to the computer keyboard to be able to change keys from left/right and up for rotation. As a consequence they often subsequently missed the chance to react to game events in time. Essentially, for many of them, the game was simply too fast.

Furthermore, uncoordinated and superfluous key strokes often made it virtually impossible to rotate and position the blocks in a proper way. Sometimes, even if the bricks were positioned well at one time point, gamers accidentally hit a key and prevented the bricks from being positioned correctly when they finally arrived at the floor.

At other times, when a brick was already at the wall, some gamers continued hitting an arrow key again and again, although the brick could not change its position any further. Finally, some players wanted to move the blocks even after they had arrived at their final position on the floor, and did not understand why this was no more possible.

3. CONCLUSIONS

Within this paper we described a way to record trials in a way to build up a video repository for later analysis. Furthermore we describe practical trials carried out with several disabled participants at a Viennese care giver. Participants played several different computer games, include the well known Tetris game. By analyzing the game play using our video recordings, we found several ways of improving the includification factor of some games, most importantly of our own Tetris version.

4. ACKNOWLEDGMENTS

We appreciate all contributions by our students and especially the clients of our project partner who patiently played our Tetris prototype.

5. REFERENCES

[1] AbleGamers. Includification, 2015.

[2] A. Hofmann and H. Hlavacs. Gaming and entertainment technologies for includification. In *3rd IEEE VR International Workshop on Virtual and Augmented Assistive Technology (VAAT) 2015*. IEEE, 2015.

[3] T. M. Kevin Bierre, Michelle Hinn. Accessibility in games: Motivations and approaches. *IGDA Whitepapers*, 2004.

[4] P. A. Östblad, H. Engström, J. Brusk, P. Backlund, and U. Wilhelmsson. Inclusive game design audio interface in a graphical adventure game. pages 1–8. ACM Press, 2014.

[5] M.-Z. Poh, D. J. McDuff, and R. W. Picard. Non-contact, automated cardiac pulse measurements using video imaging and blind source separation. *Opt. Express*, 18(10):10762–10774, May 2010.

[6] I. Spence and J. Feng. Video games and spatial cognition. *Review of General Psychology*, 14(2):92–104, 2010.

[7] Tobii. Tobii eyex, http://www.tobii.com/en/eye-experience/, May 2015.

Accessible Mobile Biometrics for Elderly

Ramon Blanco-Gonzalo
University Carlos III of Madrid
Leganes, Spain. E-28911
rbgonzal@ing.uc3m.es

Raul Sanchez-Reillo
University Carlos III of Madrid
Leganes, Spain. E-28911
rsreillo@ing.uc3m.es

Loïc Martínez-Normand
Technical University of Madrid E-28040 Madrid, Spain
loic@fi.upm.es

Belen Fernandez-Saavedra
University Carlos III of Madrid
Leganes, Spain. E-28911
mbfernan@ing.uc3m.es

Judith Liu-Jimenez
University Carlos III of Madrid
Leganes, Spain. E-28911
jliu@ing.uc3m.es

ABSTRACT

Biometric recognition provides means to guarantee security in a wide range of services. Unfortunately, their usability is limited and they are not convenient for people with accessibility issues. To prevent the rejection of the technology, those systems should be improved by using a user-centric-design approach and by applying current accessibility standards. This work describes the design, development and evaluation of a mobile app for making payments in Points of Sale (PoS) using biometric recognition. The system has been tested by elderly persons. Our findings show accessibility issues and the most critical requirements to be covered. This is one of the first researches based on the European standard EN 301 549.

Categories and Subject Descriptors

J.2 [**Physical Sciences and Engineering**]: Engineering

General Terms

Performance, Design, Reliability, Experimentation, Security, Human Factors, Standardization, Verification

Keywords

Biometrics; mobile; accessibility; elderly

1. INTRODUCTION

The use of biometric recognition has been extended from early uses in forensics to nowadays, including access controls or mobile applications. The biometric growth has to do with its reliability when used in conjunction with other security solutions (e.g. PIN/passwords) and also with the final user's acceptance: biometric recognition does not require memorizing passwords or carrying tokens. Even when the reliability and acceptance of biometrics has been demonstrated, there is still work to be done in the usability of these systems. Now that biometrics is moving to mobile environments it is especially crucial to improve usability to guarantee a satisfactory user experience as well as to focus on accessibility issues. According to the state of the art on ICT products, there are several which provide features designed for those users who find the regular products cumbersome or impossible to use. For instance, several brand new smartphones incorporate accessible features (e.g. Talkback in Android) which allow people to use the technology fluently. Nevertheless, there are several common actions impossible to perform for those users like banking procedures. There exist solutions for making payments with smartphones such as Apple Pay, but it does not allow users to get money from an ATM and works only with fingerprints.

ASSETS '15, October 26-28, 2015, Lisbon, Portugal
ACM 978-1-4503-3400-6/15/10.
http://dx.doi.org/10.1145/2700648.2811332.

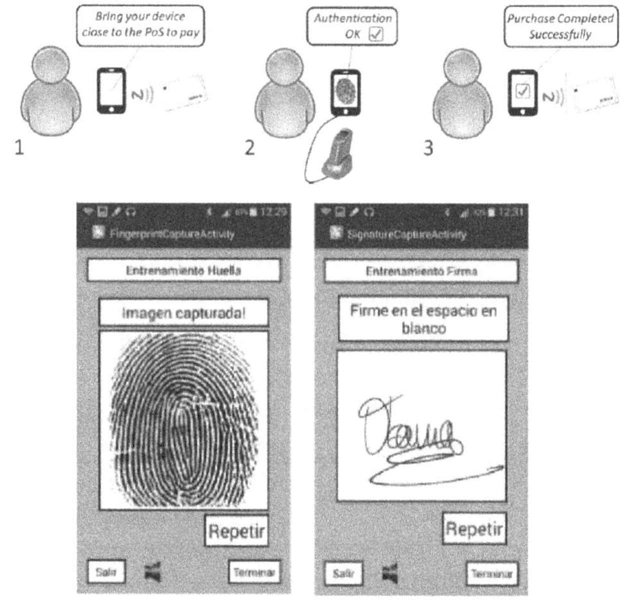

Figure 1. Example of app's use and enrolment interfaces (left: fingerprint / right: handwritten signature).

This work is intended to cover those kind of gaps being one of the first approaches to accessibility in biometrics [1]. It has been developed using a user-centred design approach, with the aim of adapting a biometric recognition solution to those users with accessibility issues, more specifically elderly persons. We have prepared a scenario for making fictitious payments in a PoS with a smartphone using biometric recognition and NFC to authenticate users. Users place the smartphone close to the PoS to pay (Figure 1-1) and then the authentication is made in the smartphone through fingerprint or signature recognition (Figure 1-2). Finally, users end the process placing the smartphone close to the PoS again (Figure 1-3). Also in Figure 1 an example of the app's interfaces is shown. The biometric recognition modalities considered as most suitable for mobile devices up to now are face, fingerprint, voice and signature. We have used two biometric systems that are considered less intrusive: fingerprint and signature recognition. By using two modalities we expect to increase the range of users who can properly use the app. For instance, users with Parkinson disease cannot generally use recognition properly, but they could probably use fingerprints. In the same way, users without fingerprints could sign. Once we had developed the system we made a checklist based accessibility evaluation (following EN 301 549 [2]) and a performance testing. Our main intention is to show how a common biometric recognition product fails when providing accessibility and how to fix these concerns with the application of the standards.

2. THE EVALUATION

The evaluation process was divided into 2 sessions and the evaluation roadmap is in Figure 2. An operator was always present to assist users and complete their personal data in case of problems. We have chosen elderly users because biometric recognition is mainly used to make procedures easy (guaranteeing security), so it could be highly useful for them who may find even more cumbersome to remember passwords or carry tokens.

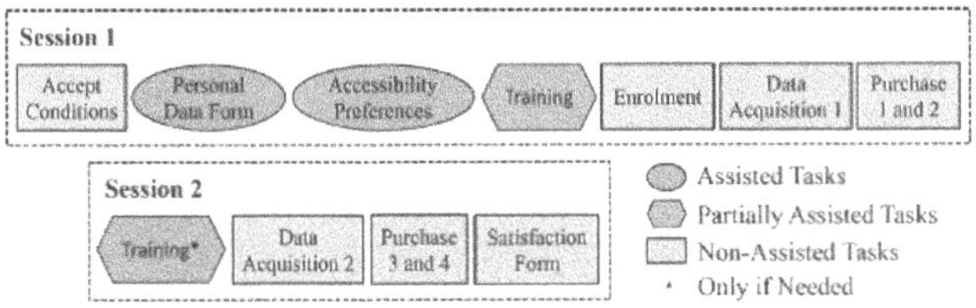

Figure 2. Evaluation Roadmap

3. PRELIMINARY RESULTS

The accessibility results show that most of the applicable requirements in clauses 5 (Generic requirements) and 8 (Hardware requirements) of the EN 301 549 have been satisfied by our system. The only non-satisfied requirements of those parts are the ones related to key repetition, because that functionality was not considered in the system. On the other hand, 15 of the 51 applicable clauses of chapter 11 (software) are not satisfied. This is mainly due to the developed prototype implementation did not use the platform accessibility services provided by Android. Then the application fails to satisfy several requirements under clause 11.3. In addition, some of the requirements in section 11.2, which are related to WCAG 2.0, are also not satisfied: provide enough colour contrast, enable text resizing, avoid images of text and provide programmatic access to the language of the user interface. There were 108 purchases in total, 66 with fingerprints and 42 with signatures. Only 13 purchases were unsuccessful (all of them with fingerprints). All the results are shown in Table 1, including Data Collections (DC) and Purchases (P) for both modalities. The differences in performance are noticeable between both modalities, being the signature more reliable than fingerprint in all cases.

4. DISCUSSION

The design of the app was made through general guidance on accessibility, but not the European standard EN 301 549. Even so, the results of the accessibility evaluation show a good coverage of the requirements of the EN. The biggest accessibility gap of the application lies in not using the accessibility services of the platform. That makes the app inaccessible for persons that require assistive technologies such as screen readers, screen magnifiers or alternative inputs. The performance results obtained are not in accordance with the current state of the art [3], where fingerprint is highly reliable and signature does not return as good results as in this experiment. The most plausible reasons of these results are: a) Elderly people are used to sign documents and not to place the fingerprint on biometric devices, then, the lack of practice can involve poor performance; b) fingerprints erode with time, especially in people who work with their hands. Then, for elderly, fingerprint recognition is not the most reliable biometric modality and bad performance should be expected; c) The initial inconveniences when signing on a mobile device with a stylus were overcome in the training phase. Thus, when users started the real evaluation they were already used to the device. There is not an improvement between session 1 and session 2, pointing that users did not learn how to deliver the biometric traits properly. This suggests that elderly people need more training sessions. Anyway, there is not too much room for improvements in fingerprint recognition as the removed fingerprints cannot be rebuilt. Regarding the purchases, it was an initial distrust from several users who felt unsure about making payments through a smartphone. This led to many users rejected to participate in the evaluation. There is a necessity of design interfaces to make users feel safer when making banking procedures.

Table 1. Performance results

Modality	DC1_EER	DC2_EER	P_unsuccessful
Fingerprin t	30,41%	35,84%	19,70%
Signature	1,85%	7,43%	0%

Our findings suggest that the accessibility concerns found do not involve a performance decrease, which is due to the poor quality of the fingerprints. Nevertheless, an improvement of the app interface would increase the usability for a wider percentage of people. This work shows that accessibility is more easily reached by following the standards. Otherwise common mistakes may drive to designs that are not properly usable. From a critical viewpoint, the accessibility requirements of the EN 301 549 do not analyse biometrics exhaustively (only clause 5.3 is directly related to biometrics and it only asks for alternative forms of biometric input). Biometric systems require a further study both in factors which influence on its accessibility as well as in a methodology to measure them. Thus, the development of a pure biometrics accessibility standard which integrates requirements and an evaluation methodology would be useful.

5. REFERENCES

[1] Sanchez-Reillo, R.; Sierra-Ramos, D.; Estrada-Casarrubios, R.; Amores- Duran, J.A., 'Strengths, weaknesses and recommendations in implementing biometrics in mobile devices,' ICCST, Rome, Italy, pp. 39- 44. Oct. 2014.

[2] CEN, CENELEC, ETSI. EN 301 549. v1.1.1. accessibility requirements suitable for public procurement of ICT products and services in Europe, Feb. 2014.

[3] Blanco-Gonzalo, R.; Sanchez-Reillo, R; Miguel-Hurtado, O.; Liu-Jimenez, L., 'Performance evaluation of handwritten signature recognition in mobile environments, ' IET Biometrics, vol. 3, no. 3, pp. 139- 146, Sep. 2014.

Can We Make Dynamic, Accessible and Fun One-Switch Video Games?

Sebastián Aced López
Politecnico di Torino
Corso Duca degli Abruzzi, 24
Turin, 10129 Italy
Tel.: +39 011 090 7191
E-mail:
sebastian.acedlopez@polito.it

Fulvio Corno
Politecnico di Torino
Corso Duca degli Abruzzi, 24
Turin, 10129 Italy
Tel.: +39 011 090 7053
E-mail:
fulvio.corno@polito.it

Luigi De Russis
Politecnico di Torino
Corso Duca degli Abruzzi, 24
Turin, 10129 Italy
Tel.: +39 011 090 7170
E-mail:
luigi.derussis@polito.it

ABSTRACT
This paper presents two one-switch games designed for children with severe motor disabilities, based on the GNomon framework. These mini games demonstrate that it is possible to make dynamic video games with time-dependent game mechanics and flexible layout configurations while being accessible and playable with a single switch. The games were designed in close collaboration with a team of speech therapists, physiotherapists, and psychologists from one of the Local Health Agencies in Turin, Italy. Moreover, the games have been already evaluated with a group of children with different motor impairments through a series of trials with encouraging results.

Categories and Subject Descriptors
K.4.2 [**Computers and Society**]: Social issues – *assistive technologies for persons with disabilities.* K.8 [**Personal Computing**]: Games

General Terms
Design, Human Factors

Keywords
Accessible games; One-switch interaction; Assistive technology; Children with disabilities; Single switch selection

1. INTRODUCTION
Video games differ from other type of games because of their interactiveness. They offer dynamic game mechanics, a wide variety of game genres and sophisticated interfaces that make them a unique entertaining experience to actively engage in. Moreover, video games not only entertain, but benefit players in cognitive, motivational, emotional and social aspects in ways never before afforded [1].

ASSETS '15, October 26-28, 2015, Lisbon, Portugal.
ACM 978-1-4503-3400-6/15/10.
http://dx.doi.org/10.1145/2700648.2811333

However, this is not always the case for many children with disabilities[1] because they do not have the sensorial, cognitive or motor skills for accessing off-the-shelf video games. In particular, children with motor disabilities often lack the ability to use standard input devices such as keyboard, mouse or game controllers, and thus they find *dynamic* video games completely unplayable.

The problem is that dynamic video games are fast-paced games that require rapid decision-making and timely responses from the player for successful interaction; conversely, one-switch interaction is typically based on *scanning*, a selection mechanism that is not intended for time-dependent tasks or rapid decision-making processes. As a result, one-switch users have access to static, time independent and barely interactive games. There is therefore a clear need for dynamic video games playable by children with severe motor disabilities that rely on the use of a single switch, as they want to play games similar to those played by their peers without disabilities, as found by Hernandez et al. in a year-long participatory study [3].

The objective of this study is to determine whether it is possible to develop dynamic, engaging and fun video games playable by children that rely on the use of single switches for accessing electronic devices.

2. GNOMON MINI GAMES
Two mini games, fully playable with just one switch, are presented in this demonstration: One Switch Ladybugs and One Switch Invaders (both games are freely downloadable from http://elite.polito.it/gnomon-games). These games are based on the GNomon framework, which is presented by Aced López et al. in [4] and further detailed in [5]. In a nutshell, GNomon enables the creation of accessible and dynamic one-switch video games, based on the NOMON interaction modality (described by Broderick and MacKay in [6]). In particular, GNomon allows creating game objects that can be selected without extra hardware (e.g. eye trackers) and without being arranged in any particular configuration.

[1] Although disability is a complex multidimensional experience that poses several challenges for measurement, UNICEF [2] estimates that the 5.1% and 0.7% of children (aged 0 to 14) worldwide live with "moderate to severe disabilities" and "severe disabilities", respectively.

2.1 One Switch Ladybugs

This simple game allows children to make one of four ladybugs jump. Each ladybug has a different color and gives a unique feedback (auditory and visual) when selected. The game does not have scores, constraints or penalties for poor performance as it is used to introduce the selection mechanism to the children. Figure 1 shows a screenshot of the game.

Figure 1: One Switch Ladybugs

2.2 One Switch Invaders

One Switch Invaders (depicted in Figure 2) is a dynamic game in which the players have to score as much points as possible by killing the multiple selectable game objects (i.e., aliens) that *move* down across the screen, before they touch the ground. One Switch Invaders cannot be implemented with current switch interfaces and selection methods, like scanning, as it is not possible to establish a scanning order without negatively affecting the game mechanics.

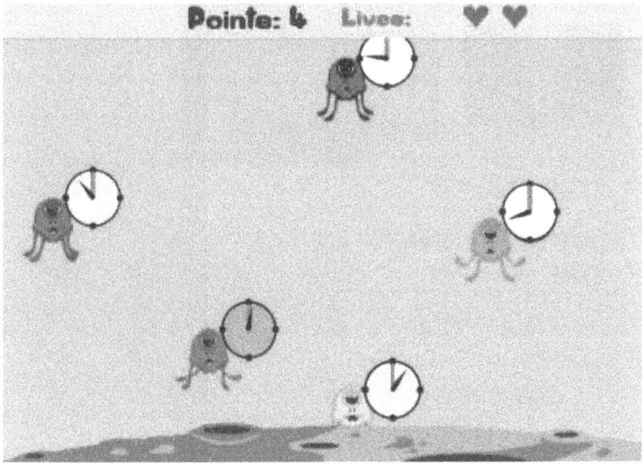

Figure 2: One Switch Invaders

3. EVALUATION

The playability of the mini games was evaluated in a two-session test by assessing their learnability, effectiveness, errors, satisfaction and memorability. The participants in the evaluation were eight children with severe motor disabilities assisted by one of the Local Health Agencies in Turin, Italy. An expert speech therapist (tester) held the sessions and two observers (one HCI researcher and another therapist from the Local Health Agency) carefully took notes. The tests were conducted in Italian at the Local Health Agency (a known environment for the children) with participants between 4 and 14 years old with severe motor disabilities, who already consistently use one-switch interfaces. Four participants had additional cognitive impairments, and two participants were non-verbal and communicated with the tester through alternative and augmentative communication (AAC) tables. A complete description of the materials and participants, as well as the full details of the first session of this study, is reported in [5].

The results were positive and indicate that GNomon-based interfaces are useful to make playable one-switch video games. The results about the playability of the two GNomon-based mini games were adequate and very promising. In particular, 7 out of 8 participants learned and were able to use the GNomon-based interface to play the games during the first session. Likewise, all the children recognized the interface in the second session and they remembered how to use it for selection. Moreover, all the participants who could play One Switch Invaders indicated that it was the funniest of the two mini games, and also that they had never played anything similar.

4. CONCLUSION AND FUTURE WORKS

This demo presents two GNomon-based mini games and the results of their evaluation. The results demonstrate that, in fact, we can make dynamic, engaging and fun video games playable by children that rely on the use of single switches for accessing electronic devices.

Future works will consist in studying the usability issues that emerged during the tests regarding the selection mechanism and to propose alternatives that are more suitable for interaction in game contexts.

REFERENCES

[1] Granic, I., Lobel, A. and Engels, R. C. M. E. 2014. "The benefits of playing video games." *American Psychologist*, vol. 69, no. 1, pp. 66–78.

[2] United Nations Children's Fund (UNICEF). 2013. *THE STATE OF THE WORLD'S CHILDREN 2013: Children with Disabilities*.

[3] Hernandez, Hamilton A. and Ye, Zi and Graham, T.C. Nicholas and Fehlings, Darcy and Switzer, Lauren. 2013. "Designing Action-based Exergames for Children with Cerebral Palsy." In *Proceedings of the SIGCHI Conference on Human Factors in Computing Systems,* ser. CHI '13. ACM, pp. 1261–1270.

[4] Aced López, S., Corno, F., and De Russis, L. 2015. "Gnomon: Enabling dynamic one-switch games for children with severe motor disabilities." In *Proceedings of the 33rd Annual ACM Conference Extended*, ser. CHI EA '15. New York, NY, USA: ACM, pp. 995–1000.

[5] Aced López, S., Corno, F., and De Russis, L. "Playable One-Switch Video Games for Children with Severe Motor Disabilities Based on GNomon." In *Proceedings of the 7th International Conference on Intelligent Technologies for Interactive Entertainment.* (in press).

[6] Broderick, T, and MacKay D. J. 2009. "Fast and flexible selection with a single switch." *PloS one,* vol. 4, no. 10.

ChatWoz: Chatting through a Wizard of Oz

Pedro Fialho
INESC-ID
Universidade de Évora
pedro.fialho@l2f.inesc-id.pt

Luísa Coheur
INESC-ID
Instituto Superior Técnico
Universidade de Lisboa
luisa.coheur@l2f.inesc-id.pt

ABSTRACT

Several cases of autistic children successfully interacting with virtual assistants such as Siri or Cortana have been recently reported. In this demo we describe CHATWOZ, an application that can be used as a Wizard of Oz, to collect real data for dialogue systems, but also to allow children to interact with their caregivers through it, as it is based on a virtual agent. CHATWOZ is composed of an interface controlled by the caregiver, which establishes what the agent will utter, in a synthesised voice. Several elements of the interface can be controlled, such as the agent's face emotions. In this paper we focus on the scenario of child-caregiver interaction and detail the features implemented in order to couple with it.

Categories and Subject Descriptors

K.3.1 [**Computer Uses in Education**]: Computer-assisted instruction (CAI); K.3.1 [**Computer Uses in Education**]: Computer-managed instruction (CMI); K.4.2 [**Social Issues**]: Assistive technologies for persons with disabilities

Keywords

Wizard of Oz, autistic children, interaction, emotion, speech

1. INTRODUCTION

A Wizard of Oz (WOZ) is the name given to the family of experiments in which a user interacts with a computer that is being controlled by an unseen human, being the user not aware of this fact. WOZ are important as they allow to understand what the specific (linguistic) needs of the application are [1]. In the literature we can found several studies regarding the building of WOZ applications (*e.g.* [2]), but also that show how WOZs have been used to collect data/improve different systems. For instance, the work from [4] focus on the type of data gathered by an WOZ (audio, video, etc.), while the study described in [3] shows how data collected by a WOZ can be used to learn dialogue strategies.

ASSETS'15, October 26–28, 2015, Lisbon, Portugal.
ACM 978-1-4503-3400-6/15/10.
DOI: http://dx.doi.org/10.1145/2700648.2811334 .

In the context of a project where we try to boost several capacities of autistic children, and being aware of recent reports of children enthusiastically interacting with virtual assistants[1], as well as studies, such as the one described in [5], we felt the need of developing a WOZ that would allow the child to interact with a caregiver through an avatar. In this paper we describe that system, the CHATWOZ.

2. GENERAL OVERVIEW

The design and deployment of CHATWOZ's front end is performed in Unity[2]. Several modules communicate by means of specific protocols, thus leveraging the capabilities of independent modules such as Text-to-Speech (TTS) (remote) or 3D rendering/animation. The main interface (Figure 1 – in Portuguese) is handled by one of the users (from now on, the caregiver), who will control what the agent will say.

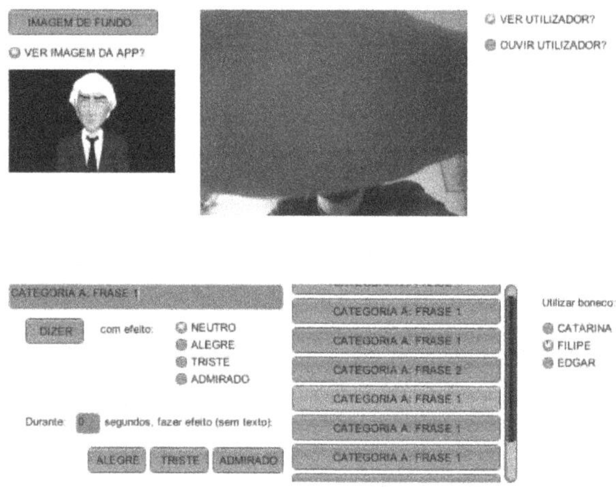

Figure 1: The main interface.

After choosing between predefined utterances or by entering a new sentence, the chosen text will be synthesised. The audio is played while the corresponding phonemes are mapped into visemes, represented as morph animations, being synchronized according to phoneme durations, provided by the speech synthesizer. An emotion can also be chosen

[1]See, for instance, http://www.nytimes.com/2014/10/19/fashion/how-apples-siri-became-one-autistic-boys-bff.html
[2]https://unity3d.com

to animate the agent's face, either when it is uttering the sentence, or when it is simply "listening". The second user (for now on, the child) will hear the agent saying the utterances provided by the caregiver, with the chosen emotion. Anything said by the child will reach the caregiver.

3. CHATWOZ MAIN FEATURES

The agent utterances and emotions are controlled by the caregiver. Concerning the agent utterances, the caregiver writes the sentences the agent will utter. However, if it is possible to know in advance which utterances the agent will be saying, it is possible to pre-record them (either by a human or by using a synthesiser). These utterances can also be clustered in categories. In the main interface, a menu with these utterances appears (keeping the categories organisation), which allows to ease/speed the process of choosing what the agent will say. Instead of writing, the caregiver only has to click on the appropriate utterance, which was already previously synthesized (or recorded by an human), which also speeds the process. Regarding the agent's emotions, the caregiver can choose between five different emotions regarding the agents's face when uttering a sentence. These are "neutro" ("neutral), "alegre" ("joyful"), "triste" ("sad") and "admired" ("surprised") (Figure 2). In what concerns the emotions expressed by the agent when it is listening to the child, these can be "alegre" ("joyful"), "triste" ("sad") and "admirado" ("surprised"). After expressing that emotion, the agent will go back to its neutral state.

Figure 2: The agent emotions

Also, several elements of ChatWoz can be customised, namely: a) The scenario, which can be changed, by simply uploading a new image; b) The audio and video regarding the child. The caregiver can decide, during the session, if he/she wants to hear/see the child or not. Obviously, activating these features can slow the interface (specially the video), which can be a problem with high latency connections; c) The child's interface, as the caregiver can also see it as displayed in the child's device screen; d) The agent. For the moment we can opt by Filipe, Catarina or Edgar (Figure 3). Agents can be changed during a session. One leaves and the other walks in.

Figure 3: Currently available agents (from left to right, Catarina, Filipe and Edgar)

4. DEMONSTRATING CHATWOZ

A person will act as the caregiver and a second person will act as the child. The first will have a laptop and will see ChatWoz's main interface; the latter will see the agent. They will "talk" through the avatar. The "caregiver" can choose what the agent will say, between a set of predefined sentences; he/she can also enter a new sentence. The "child" will simply hear and talk with the agent.

Besides deciding what the agent will say and which emotion it should have in its face, the caregiver can, in runtime: a) Change the agent ("Utilizar boneco" ("use agent") in the bottom right of the main interface); b) Change the back figure of the agent ("Imagem de fundo" ("back image"), in the top left corner of the main interface); c) Decide to have (or not) audio/video regarding the child actions ("Ver/Ouvir Utilizador" ("see/hear user) in the top right of the main interface).

We have made some preliminary tests and the only problem is to have the interface working with the video (and also with audios, although in a smaller scale), which can slow the interaction. We concluded that Unity is not suitable for video transmission.

5. CONCLUSIONS AND FUTURE WORK

We have described our WOZ, that we intend to use to make children interact with his/her caregiver through an avatar. We are currently trying to add some emotions to the TTS, by voice transfer, and also to fix latency issues related with audio/video transmission.

6. ACKNOWLEDGMENTS

This work was supported by Fundação para a Ciência e Tecnologia (FCT) with reference UID/CEC/50021/2013, and by projects CMUP-ERI/HCI/0051/2013 and H2020-ICT-21-2014/644187.

7. REFERENCES

[1] N. Dahlbäck, A. Jönsson, and L. Ahrenberg. Wizard of oz studies: Why and how. In *Proceedings of the 1st International Conference on Intelligent User Interfaces*, IUI '93, New York, NY, USA, 1993.

[2] S. R. Klemmer, A. K. Sinha, J. Chen, J. A. Landay, N. Aboobaker, and A. Wang. Suede: A wizard of oz prototyping tool for speech user interfaces. In *Proceedings of the 13th Annual ACM Symposium on User Interface Software and Technology*, pages 1–10, New York, NY, USA, 2000. ACM.

[3] V. Rieser and O. Lemon. Learning effective multimodal dialogue strategies from wizard-of-oz data : bootstrapping and evaluation. In *ACL-08: HLT : 46th annual meeting of the Association for Computational Linguistics: human language technologies*, 2008.

[4] P. Strauss, H. Hoffmann, W. Minker, H. Neumann, G. Palm, and S. S. et al. Wizard-of-oz data collection for perception and interaction in multi-user environments. In *International Conference on Language Resources and Evaluation (LREC)*, 2006.

[5] A. Tartaro and J. Cassell. Authorable Virtual Peers for Autism Spectrum Disorders. In *Proceedings of the Workshop on Language-Enabled Educational Technology at the 17th European Conference on Artificial Intelligence (ECAI06)*, Italy, 2006.

Eyes-free Exploration of Shapes with Invisible Puzzle

Andrea Gerino
Dept. of Computer Science
Università degli Studi di Milano
EveryWare Technologies
andrea.gerino@unimi.it

Lorenzo Picinali
School of Design Engineering
Imperial College London
l.picinali@imperial.ac.uk

Cristian Bernareggi
Dept. of Computer Science
Università degli Studi di Milano
EveryWare Technologies
cristian.bernareggi@unimi.it

Sergio Mascetti
Dept. of Computer Science
Università degli Studi di Milano
EveryWare Technologies
sergio.mascetti@unimi.it

ABSTRACT

Recent contributions proposed sonification techniques to allow people with visual impairment or blindness to extract information from images on touchscreen devices. In this contribution we introduce *Invisible Puzzle Game*, an application that is aimed at performing an instrumented remote evaluation of these sonification techniques. The aim is to reach a wide audience of both sighted and visually impaired users and to engage them, thanks to game elements, in playing over time, so that it is possible to evaluate how the performance of each sonification technique is affected by practice.

Categories and Subject Descriptors

H.5.2 [**INFORMATION INTERFACES AND PRESENTATION**]: User Interfaces—*Evaluation/methodology, Auditory (non-speech) feedback, User-centered design, Interaction styles*; K.4.2 [**COMPUTERS AND SOCIETY**]: Assistive technologies for persons with disabilities

Keywords

Accessibility; Visual impairment or blindness; Sonification; Games; Remote evaluation; Touchscreen devices

1. INTRODUCTION

Image exploration is an important task for people with visual impairment or blindness. It plays a fundamental role in many activities, like in the development of visuospatial skills and in education (e.g. while learning STEM subjects). Existing solutions to enable non-visual exploration of images are based on specialized hardware (like tactile drawings) or on software for traditional and mobile devices.

In a recent contribution we proposed 6 sonification modes specifically designed for touchscreen devices as well as an evaluation methodology based on an iPhone application, which in the following we call *Invisible Puzzle Prototype*, used to conduct an instrumented remote evaluation [4]. The application has been developed following user-centric design principles with feedback provided by many subjects, including 4 persons with visual impairment or blindness. Thanks to the proposed evaluation methodology we collected data from about 150 subjects, 18 of which are visually impaired or blind. While on one side this data yield interesting results, on the other side the number of representative users (i.e., people with visual impairment or blindness) is still limited and the impact of learning could be only measured in the relatively short test duration (about 15 minutes).

In this contribution we report our ongoing research devoted at extending *Invisible Puzzle Prototype* into a game (henceforth *Invisible Puzzle Game*) that is intended to be made publicly available. While the idea of developing a game targeted at people with visual impairment or blindness is not new in scientific literature (see [6] and [7]), our approach differs because we are using a game as a vehicle to test novel image sonification techniques. The aim is to reach a wide audience, in particular people with visual impairment or blindness, and engage them so that they are induced to play for a long time and in many sessions. During the game we collect anonymous usage data that can eventually be used to evaluate and compare the sonification techniques.

During the demo participants will be invited to conduct the formal test described in [4] and, most importantly, will have the opportunity to play with *Invisible Puzzle Game*.

2. INVISIBLE PUZZLE PROTOTYPE

Invisible Puzzle Prototype adopts 6 different sonification modes. In the first sonification mode, called "2-D", the user can freely explore the image along both dimensions, similarly to how people with visual impairment or blindness explore a drawing on swell paper. In 2-D, a pure tone sound is played whenever the user touches a white pixel in the image. The main limitation of 2-D is that it is time consuming [4].

In order to overcome this problem *Invisible Puzzle Prototype* implements 5 other sonification modes, referred as "1-D" modes, which restrict the user to explore the image along the vertical axis. 1-D modes simultaneously sonify all the pixels on the horizontal line (called "flush line") the user is touching and convey information about image fea-

ASSETS'15, October 26–28, 2015, Lisbon, Portugal.

ACM 978-1-4503-3400-6/15/10 ...$15.00.
DOI: http://dx.doi.org/10.1145/2700648.2811335.

tures trough spatialised sounds with varying pitch. The 5 sonification modes have different combinations of audio rendering techniques (that define which parts of each flush line is actually sonified) and sound generators.

Invisible Puzzle Prototype is designed to perform an instrumented remote evaluation of the sonification modes. Its main objective is to automate the testing procedure so that a large number of test subjects can be involved without the need of a supervisor. *Invisible Puzzle Prototype* presents a set of 'exploration tasks' during which the test subject is first invited to explore a hidden shape and then to recognize it in a set of four options. Video examples are available[1].

Invisible Puzzle Prototype introduces a single sonification mode to each test subject. The subject is trained with a short video (about 15 seconds) and with some learning tasks, in which the shape is visible and verbally described (for visually impaired users). Most importantly, following a gamification approach [3], exploration tasks are designed to gradually increase in difficulty and gradually introduce new elements (e.g., points, lines, polygons, etc...). This is in line with the "Flow theory" from Csikszentmihalyi [1].

Invisible Puzzle Prototype, as previously presented [4], implements 6 original sonification modes. During the demo two additional sonification modes, derived from existing solutions proposed in the literature [2, 8], will be available.

3. INVISIBLE PUZZLE GAME

Our objective is to collect a large amount of usage data from both representative users, i.e. people with visual impairment or blindness, and non representative ones, in order to further evaluate our sonification techniques. To reach this objective, we address two main challenges: firstly, to acquire a large number of players and, secondly, to encourage them to keep playing over time, thus providing historical data about the impact of learning. In order to answer these challenges, *Invisible Puzzle Game* presents two main differences with respect to *Invisible Puzzle Prototype* and introduces several game elements (see [5]).

One difference is that, while in *Invisible Puzzle Prototype* a single sonification mode is presented to each subject, in *Invisible Puzzle Game* players are first presented a single sonification mode and the others are gradually introduced as the player progress trough the game. When a new sonification is introduced, the game first forces the player to use it, hence ensuring that a minimum training is provided. Then, in selected exploration tasks, the player can select the preferred sonification mode among the available ones. This approach has two advantages. Firstly, new sonification modes are presented as rewards and help maintaining user's interest in playing while he/she master them. Secondly, the collected data will include performance measurements (e.g., time to complete an exploration task) for different sonification modes as well as the explicit player's choice on the preferred mode.

The organization of the game levels is another difference. In *Invisible Puzzle Prototype* each exploration task corresponds to a level. However we realized that players could easily cheat by totally avoiding the exploration phase and choosing a random answer. To tackle this problem in *Invisible Puzzle Game* each level comprises several exploration tasks: the level is cleared only if the user correctly completes a minimum number of them. With this solution it is much less likely to clear a level by providing random answers. Also, levels are organized into chapters, each one associated to a theme (e.g., chapter one has points as hidden shapes, while chapter two has lines).

The first group of game elements added to *Invisible Puzzle Game* belong to the "feedback" class (see [5]). In each cleared level we compute a performance indicator that considers the total time and the percentage of correct answers. This indicator is then associated to a measure (i.e, 0 to 3 golden stars) that provides an easy-to-read feedback and also stimulates the user to play the same level again. Also, a minimum number of stars must be obtained to proceed trough chapters. There are two reasons for this constraint. Firstly, it guarantees that players get acquainted with a sonification mode before proceeding to more challenging tasks. Secondly, players are challenged not only in clearing levels but also in achieving good performance.

A second group of game elements belong to the "reputations, ranks and levels" class. To define a form of reputation, players are granted achievements when some events occur during the game, like completing a chapter. This is meant to increase the involvement of the players in the game, as well as a tool to acquire new users: indeed each player is invited to share his/her achievement on social networks, thus making more people aware of the game and, possibly, turning them into players. Also, a global player ranking is defined, based on a number of factors, including the achievements, game progress and performance. This rank is published in an on-line scoreboard.

4. REFERENCES

[1] M. Csikszentmihalyi. *Flow*. Harper Perennial Modern Classics. HarperCollins, 2009.

[2] S. A. Dallas Jr and A. J. Erickson. Sound pattern generator, Mar. 29 1983. US Patent 4,378,569.

[3] S. Deterding, D. Dixon, R. Khaled, and L. Nacke. From game design elements to gamefulness: defining gamification. In *Proc. of the 15th Int. Academic MindTrek Conference: Envisioning Future Media Environments*. ACM, 2011.

[4] A. Gerino, L. Picinali, C. Bernareggi, N. Alabastro, and S. Mascetti. Towards large scale evaluation of novel sonification techniques for non visual shape exploration. In *Proc. of the 17th Int. conference on Computers & accessibility*. ACM, To appear.

[5] B. Reeves and J. L. Read. *Total engagement: How games and virtual worlds are changing the way people work and businesses compete*. Harvard Business Press, 2013.

[6] J. Sánchez, N. Baloian, T. Hassler, and U. Hoppe. Audiobattleship: Blind learners collaboration through sound. In *Extended Abstracts on Human Factors in Computing Systems*. ACM, 2003.

[7] T. Westin. Game accessibility case study: Terraformers–a real-time 3d graphic game. In *Proc. of the 5th Int. Conf. on Disability, Virtual Reality and Associated Technologies*, 2004.

[8] T. Yoshida, K. M. Kitani, H. Koike, S. Belongie, and K. Schlei. Edgesonic: image feature sonification for the visually impaired. In *Proc. of the 2nd Augmented Human Int. Conf.* ACM, 2011.

[1]`http://webmind.di.unimi.it/assetsip15/`

TactileMaps.net: A Web Interface for Generating Customized 3D-Printable Tactile Maps

Brandon Taylor
Carnegie Mellon University
5000 Forbes Ave
Pittsburgh, PA 15213
+1 412 268 2000
bttaylor@cs.cmu.edu

Anind Dey
Carnegie Mellon University
5000 Forbes Ave
Pittsburgh, PA 15213
+1 412 268 2000
anind@cs.cmu.edu

Dan Siewiorek
Carnegie Mellon University
5000 Forbes Ave
Pittsburgh, PA 15213
+1 412 268 2000
dps@cs.cmu.edu

Asim Smailagic
Carnegie Mellon University
5000 Forbes Ave
Pittsburgh, PA 15213
+1 412 268 2000
asim@cs.cmu.edu

ABSTRACT

Tactile maps are useful, but not commonly available, tools for providing visually impaired individuals with knowledge about their environment. We have developed a web tool to allow visually impaired users to specify locations and customize 3D map models for production with 3D printers. Our tool uses available online map data and encodes features such as roads and waterways into 3D-printable tactile features. We present a preliminary overview of our web interface and tactile map-generating software with a focus on the design choices that were informed by our pilot studies. We will also discuss additional findings from our focus group interviews and future plans for this work.

Categories and Subject Descriptors

H.5.2 [**Information Interfaces and Presentation**]: User Interfaces – *haptic I/O*; K.4.2 [**Computers and Society**]: Social Issues – *assistive technologies for persons with disabilities.*

General Terms

Design, Experimentation, Human Factors

Keywords

Tactile Map; Accessibility; 3D Printing

1. INTRODUCTION

Tactile maps are useful tools for providing visually impaired individuals with a practical knowledge of their environment [6]. Unfortunately, the costs associated with designing and manufacturing tactile maps have prevented their widespread adoption. Recently, the increased availability and reduced costs of 3D printers has made the fabrication of customized tactile maps a realistic possibility on a much larger scale. However, designing such maps still represents a significant barrier, especially to visually impaired individuals, as it generally requires the use of 3D modeling software. While automated tactile map generation has been proposed before [3,4], we are unaware of any publically available systems for fully generating customized maps for 3D printing at this time.

ASSETS '15, October 26-28, 2015, Lisbon, Portugal
ACM 978-1-4503-3400-6/15/10.
http://dx.doi.org/10.1145/2700648.2811336

In this work, we present an accessible web tool designed to allow visually impaired users to generate customized 3D map models for 3D printer fabrication. Our tool functions similarly to existing online mapping tools. Users can search for an address, mark the locations of nearby businesses, and select which geographic features to include. Our tool then invokes a server-hosted python script that generates a 3D model of the user-specified map.

The discussion of our work will be broken down into three sections. First will focus on the web interface of our tool. The second section will describe the tactile features generated by our 3D mapping software. Lastly, we will discuss our future plans for this project.

2. WEB INTERFACE

The primary goal of the web interface for our tool, shown in Figure 1, is allowing visually impaired users to generate customized maps without assistance. We've focused on keeping the design simple and clean and have followed the accessibility recommendations offered by AChecker [1].

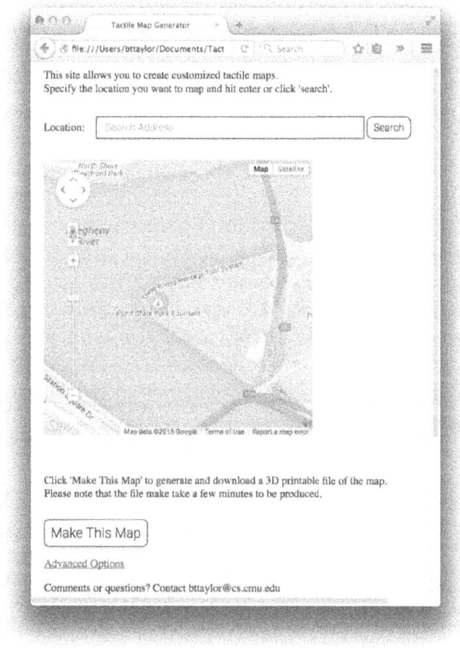

Figure 1. Screenshot of website interface.

This interface consists of a single textbox for typing a desired address. Upon clicking the search button, Google's Geocoding API [2] is called and the most likely returned location is selected. Clicking the 'Make This Map' button will then pass the geographic coordinates of the map to the map-generating script. This script will use default parameters to specify aspects such as the size of the map, the geographic area being mapped, the tactile representations of map features amongst other parameters.

Alternatively, the user may click the 'Advanced Options' link to manually set these parameters.

3. MAP FEATURES

Our 3D map generating software consists of python scripts that can be invoked using our web interface. The 3D map features are generated from OpenStreetMap data acquired using the OpenStreetMap API [5].

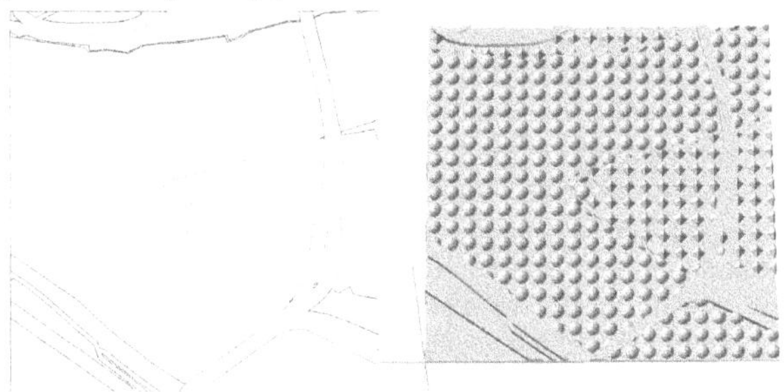

Figure 2. A map model of 'The Point' in Pittsburgh. On the left is a diagnostic image with different map feature boundaries represented by different colors. On the right is an image of the corresponding 3D file. Roadways are elevated, waterways represented by domes, and park areas are represented by pyramids.

Roads found within the geographic bounds are extruded up and assigned a thickness corresponding to the type of road specified by the 'highway' tag value. Smaller roads may also be disregarded when mapping larger geographic areas, in much the same way that interactive visual maps respond to zooming out.

Other map features, such as waterways, parks, building footprints, or topographical data can be assigned different tactile features that will then be extruded throughout the corresponding areas. Figure 2, for example, shows an area known as 'The Point' in Pittsburgh, PA, USA, where two rivers intersect. In this example the rivers are represented by small domes, park areas along the river are represented by pyramids, and the roads in the region appear as elevated lines. The flat area in the lower left corner is not designated as a 'road', 'waterway', or 'park' and is thus left as a lower surface.

The tactile features themselves have many parameters that can be adjusted (height, spacing, shape) programmatically and the additional features (such as braille labels) can be added as well. Ultimately, these different map features are stitched together into a .stl file.

4. DISCUSSION

Currently, we have many questions that we are exploring to improve our system. We have conducted a number of focus group interviews with a total of 10 visually impaired individuals. During the focus groups, we presented examples of printed maps and elicited feedback about our designs and potential use cases for our system. We have also published a version of our system online at www.tactilemaps.net. We are collecting usage statistics and soliciting feedback there as well. Some specific questions we are exploring are discussed below.

How to label map features? Our initial idea was that braille road labels could be extruded on the back of the map directly along the path of the roads on the front, much like how road labels overlay the roads on visual maps. However, in our focus groups, users tended to find the braille printed at odd angles to be confusing and suggested that using single-letter braille markers on the front, with a horizontally aligned legend on the back would be easier to use.

How to best scale the maps? We began our work with the goal of providing users with a preplanning tool for understanding the immediate geography around specific locations. We imagined use cases such as navigating between a bus stop and unfamiliar doctor's office; tasks that would take place within a few city blocks. In our pilot studies, however, users have expressed interest in a variety of goals ranging from understanding the geographic relationships between various neighborhoods in a city to discovering where exactly are the entrances to a building. How to build a tool that can accommodate these various goals at different scales without overly complicating the user interface is a difficult design trade-off.

What information density is best? Related to the question of scaling is a broader question of what density of information can be encoded into the map in an understandable way. Braille has specified physical dimensions, which places a limit on how many characters can be contained in an area. With 3D models, we have a great range of granularity in both horizontal and vertical dimensions, but using printer resolutions or even perceptual thresholds may result in overly dense and complicated maps. We hope to establish usability guidelines that can provide useful heuristics (i.e., the default settings of our software) for mapping different map features onto physical prints.

What else can be done? While the primary goal of our work is to provide a useful mapping tool for the visually impaired, the system we have built offers other interesting possibilities. In addition to representing topographical data along the z-axis, we are interested in the possibilities of incorporating other data sources (e.g., property values, pollution data) to automatically generate 3D map representations. We suspect that printing artifacts with differing data on the front and back faces offers an interesting method for drawing comparisons.

5. REFERENCES

[1] AChecker. 2011. Web Accessibility Checker. http://achecker.ca/checker/index.php.

[2] Google. 2015. Google Maps Geocoding API. https://developers.google.com/maps/documentation/geocoding/.

[3] Gotzelmann, T., Pavkovic, A. 2014. Towards Automatically Generated Tactile Detail Maps by 3D Printers for Blind Persons. In *Proc. Of ICCHP '14* (vol. Part II), Springer, 1-7.

[4] HaptoRender Team. 2009. HaptoRender. http://wiki.openstreetmap.org/wiki/HaptoRender.

[5] OpenStreetMap. 2013. OpenStreetMap API v0.6. http://wiki.openstreetmap.org/wiki/API_v0.6.

[6] Ungar, S., Blades, M. and Spencer, C. 2000. Can a Tactile Map Facilitate Learning of Related Information by Blind and Visually Impaired People? A Test of the Conjoint Retention Hypothesis. *Proc. Of Thinking with Diagrams.*

ARMStrokes: A Mobile App for Everyday Stroke Rehabilitation

Jin Guo, Ted Smith, David Messing, Ziying Tang, Sonia Lawson*, Jinjuan Heidi Feng
Department of Computer and Information Sciences
Towson University
Towson, MD21252, USA
{jgou2;tsmith60;ztang;jfeng}@towson.edu

*Dept. of Occupational Therapy & Occupational Science
Towson University
Towson, MD21252, USA
slawson@towson.edu

ABSTRACT

In this paper, we present a novel smartphone-based rehabilitation approach called ARMStrokes that provides real-time support for stroke survivors to complete rehabilitation exercises for upper extremity recovery. ARMStrokes allows stroke survivors to exercise through interactive games anytime and anywhere and receive instant feedback about the quality of their performance. Stroke survivors can also communicate with their therapists or physicians through the supporting web-based platform. Focus groups involving stroke survivors, caregivers, and therapists have been conducted to evaluate the system and the feedback is highly positive.

Categories and Subject Descriptors

H.5.m. Information interfaces and presentation: Miscellaneous

Keywords

Stroke; rehabilitation; smartphone-based game

1. INTRODUCTION

Stroke is a major contributor to adult disability in many countries. According to the Centers for Disease Control and Prevention (CDC), more than 795,000 people in the United States have a stroke each year [1]. Stroke often causes long-term disabilities that affect cognitive, physical, and speech functions. Intensive rehabilitation exercise is critical for stroke recovery during the early stage of a stroke. However, only 31 percent of stroke survivors actually complete the recommended exercises due to a variety of factors including lack of motivation [2]. Interactive games such as Wii or 3D games could serve as a tool that is not only motivating but also used to meet therapeutic goals in a more engaging way [e.g., 3]. Studies have shown that these types of game systems and haptic devices are effective in the rehabilitation process [4]. However, since the majority of stroke survivors are seniors, they may not have easy access to game systems or haptic devices when needed, or may not have the physical capability to use them due to poor postural control and standing balance, or they may not understand how to use these complicated new technologies. In contrast, smartphones can be easily carried to any place and do not require complicated installation or configuration processes. Although only 37% of people over 55 years old in the developed countries own a smartphone in 2013, the penetration rate was predicted to increase to 45 to 50% by the end of 2014 and exceed 80% by 2020 [5]. Therefore, it could be an easily accessible solution if smart phones were used as a rehabilitation platform. In this way, individuals can play rehabilitation games delivered through mobile phones while watching TV, relaxing in the park, or even waiting in line in a grocery store. In addition to the benefit of easy access, the mobile phone can also support timely communication between stroke survivors, therapists, and their caregivers, so that compliance to in-home exercise programs and progress can be monitored effectively.

ASSETS'15, October 26–28, 2015, Lisbon, Portugal.
ACM 978-1-4503-3400-6/15/10.
DOI: http://dx.doi.org/10.1145/2700648.2811337

Working closely with stroke survivors and therapists, we developed a novel smartphone-based rehabilitation approach called ARMStrokes. ARMStrokes is an interactive rehabilitation app that allows those with stroke to conduct rehabilitation exercises anytime and anywhere. Rather than using specialized sensors to track user movements, we focused on developing an approach on top of existing mainstream technology without the need for any additional hardware. Movements are detected through the built-in sensors of common smartphones. ARMStrokes can also be easily customized to fit each stroke survivor's specific functionalities in different recovery stages. The following section describes the design of ARMStrokes.

2. APPLICATION DESIGN

ARMStrokes is currently implemented in the iPhone environment. The app uses built-in sensors of an iPhone (accelerometer, gyroscope, and device orientation sensor) to capture users' movement speed and position information (e.g. pitch, roll and yaw value) during exercises.

2.1 Game Design

Because 66% of stroke survivors have a weak upper limb (arm and hand), we focus on improving upper extremity functions in the game design. Eight exercises for different muscles and joints of upper limbs were selected by the therapists, namely forearm rotation, elbow flexion, elbow raise to front, elbow raise to side, shoulder flexion, shoulder rotation, shoulder horizontal adduction, and shoulder abduction. Two games were developed using different metaphors: a monkey picking bananas (Figure 1(a)) and an astronaut exploring the space (Figure 1(b)). When a specific body movement is detected by the built-in sensors, the monkey or the astronaut rotates or jumps on the screen to reflect the movement detected.

(a) (b)

Figure 1. Screenshots of two games in ARMStrokes.

The app employs various methods to deliver feedback to users, including visual cues, audio cues, and haptic vibration. Stroke survivors can choose the type of feedback or feedback combinations that they prefer or that are prescribed by their therapists. They can also choose to disable the animation function to play the game with a static image on the screen.

2.2 Customized Rehabilitation

Stroke usually causes a wide range of disabilities that affect cognitive, physical and speech functions. Since each case is unique, one fixed rehabilitation approach will not be able to support a broad range of those recovering from stroke. Therefore, the app was designed to be easily customizable for the special needs of a specific person.

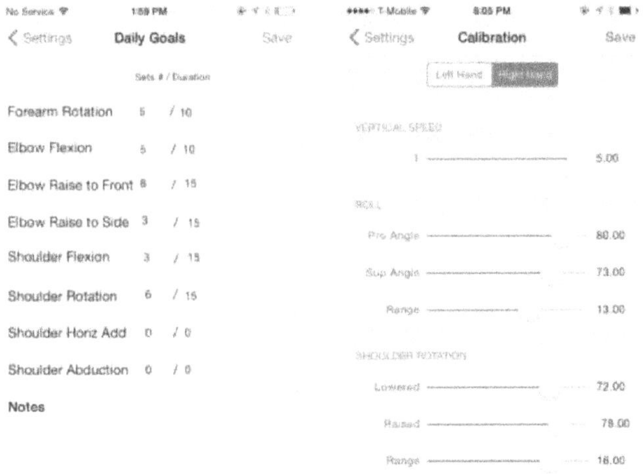

Figure 2. Daily goals and calibration settings

The goal of customized rehabilitation is achieved through two features: (1) rehabilitation plan; (2) functional calibration. During a patient's first visit, a therapist first conducts a thorough assessment of the patient's functional capabilities such as muscle strength, active and passive range of motion in shoulder and elbow flexion. The functional data allows the therapist to determine which exercises are appropriate for the patient. Then the therapist develops a rehabilitation plan for the patient that specifies the type of exercises, the number of sets for each exercise per day, and the length of each set. The rehabilitation plan is entered into the app through the 'Daily goals' page (Fig. 2). A specific daily goal not only provides a quantitative evaluation standard but also establishes observable achievement markers that motivate the users. Next, the functional data is used to set the appropriate calibration so that the movement of a patient with very limited range of motion or very slow speed can still be effectively detected (Fig. 2). Calibration information can also be used to detect intentional or unintentional cheating when the patient uses the unaffected arm to complete the exercises. Both the rehabilitation plan and the calibration information need to be updated as the patient's functionality gradually recovers.

3. PRELIMINARY EVALUATION

Four focus groups involving twelve stroke survivors and their caregivers, 3 therapists, and 1 physician have been conducted to evaluate ARMStrokes. After a training session of approximately 10 minutes, users could navigate among pages independently and use the app to complete exercises. The user feedback is highly positive. All were enthusiastic about using ARMStrokes on a daily basis. Many stroke survivors commented that the daily rehabilitation exercises at home were quite boring and the app would definitely motivate them to complete more exercises. They also liked the instant feedback provided right after each exercise. Currently, we are collaborating with the University of Maryland Rehabilitation and Orthopaedic Institute to conduct a two month field study involving 50 out-patients to determine whether the app could make a positive impact in the stroke recovery process. Usage patterns and interaction strategies are also examined. Based on the movement capabilities of the user, customized solutions (e.g., straps, gloves) are used to assist the appropriate placement of the phone. We would like to demo ARMStrokes at ASSETS and collect feedback for design improvement.

4. ACKNOWLEDGMENTS

This work is supported by the Aetna Foundation (#13-06691), and the School of Emerging Technologies at Towson University.

5. REFERENCES

[1] Centers for Disease Control and Prevention. (2015) Stroke facts. Retrieved at: http://www.cdc.gov/stroke/facts.htm

[2] Shaughnessy, M., Resnick, B.M., and Macko, R.F. (2006) Testing a model of post-stroke exercise behavior. *Rehabilitation Nursing*. 31(1), 15-21.

[3] Kaminer, C., LeBras, K., McCall, J. et al. (2014) An immersive physical therapy game for stroke survivors. *Proceedings of ASSETS 2014*. 299-300.

[4] Kam, N., Struzik, J., Jarus, T., & Rand, D. (2012) Is the Nintendo Wii suitable for stroke rehabilitation? A pilot feasibility and usability study. *The Israeli Journal of Occupational Therapy*, 21(1), 3- 25.

[5] Deloitt. The smartphone generation gap: over 55? There is no app for that. (2014) Retrieved at https://www2.deloitte.com/content/dam/Deloitte/global/Documents/Technology-Media-Telecommunications/gx-tmt-2014prediction-smartphone.pdf

READ: A (research) Platform for Evaluating Non-Visual Access Methods to Digital Documents

Laurent Sorin
University of Toulouse
UPS & UT2J; IRIT
118 route de Narbonne
31062 Toulouse
(+33)5.61.55.77.02
sorin@irit.fr

Julie Lemarié
University of Toulouse
UT2J; CLLE
5 allées Antonio Machado
31100 Toulouse
(+33)5.61.50.35.41
lemarie@univ-tlse2.fr

Mustapha Mojahid
University of Toulouse;
UPS; IRIT
118 route de Narbonne
31062 Toulouse
(+33)5.61.55.63.18
mojahid@irit.fr

ABSTRACT
READ (which stands for **D**ocuments **A**rchitecture **RE**stitution, in French), is a software allowing *augmented* access of tagged documents content. It was originally developed for a project aiming at evaluating informational and functional equivalents to text visual formatting [8] and was very recently tested in a user study (results unpublished yet). The design flexibility of this platform allows an easy implementation of input and output modalities, as well as navigation functions. We wish to publish this application for noncommercial reuse in the short run; the main goal is here to easily allow researchers to evaluate non-visual access methods to documents, since current assistive technologies are known to raise multiple issues [7]. A live demonstration of READ will enable attendees to experience the implemented output modalities and navigation functions, as well as the platform configuration and extension potential.

Categories and Subject Descriptors
H.5.2 [**Information Interfaces and Presentation**]: Input devices and strategies, *Auditory (non-speech) feedback*, *Prototyping;* K.4.2 [**Computers and Society**]: Social Issues-Assistive technologies for persons with disabilities

General Terms
Design, Human Factors

Keywords
Digital accessibility; non-visual interactions; documents accessibility; research platform

1. INTRODUCTION
READ was initially developed inside the frame of a project aiming at finding new access methods to restore information and functions provided by text formatting during visual reading [8], in order to improve digital documents accessibility. The terms restoration and restitution used here refer to the possibility for visually-impaired users to access the same information and as efficiently as non-disabled users. Regarding documents accessibility, much research work remains to be done.

ASSETS '15, October 26-28, 2015, Lisbon, Portugal
ACM 978-1-4503-3400-6/15/10.
http://dx.doi.org/10.1145/2700648.2811338

Indeed, if we take the example of the screen readers as the main tool used by visually-impaired people to access digital content, even though they present overall an extensive list of functions, their use remains frustrating and poorly efficient [6], even when accessing content following accessibility guidelines [7].

Audio and tactile linearity inherent to those modalities are often mentioned as an important part of the overall problem. Several initiatives emerged to provide non-linear access to content, such as concurrent speech [5] or aural glancing of texts [4]. Multimodality is also pointed as a solution to improve content accessibility regarding the potential information overload raised by linear access to information [3]. This kind of approach is also applied for accessing complex content such as mathematics [1].

The evaluation of those paradigms implies developing dedicated tools or modifying existing open source screen-readers. For the latter option, since they need to handle interactions with the operating system, screen-reader have a complex architecture to build on; READ can provide a simpler alternative when the focus is on documents accessibility. What we propose with READ is a software to reuse as a base for those evaluations, requiring few to none developments depending on the project. It provides a controlled MS-Windows environment for documents non-visual access, with customizable inputs and outputs. READ will be published as soon as possible under the CC BY-NC-SA[1] license.

2. SYSTEM DESIGN
Our general aim was to develop a fully configurable system with a modular design, based on XML[2] configuration files and plugins.

-Technical Specifications: The system was developed in C#, as .NET provides a library to use installed synthetic voices following the SAPI[3] norm. Any computer with a Windows OS with the framework .NET 3.5 (or more recent) can run the application. Application configuration is defined in XML files; XML was an obvious choice for flexibility and interoperability.

-Global architecture: The application was developed using a "blocks and events" paradigm; the document is turned into blocks of information, each block including one or several event, which can be played sequentially or in parallel depending on the configuration.

---

[1] **C**reative **C**ommons Attribution (by) **N**on**C**ommercial **S**hare**A**like

[2] Extensible Markup Language

[3] Speech Application Programming Interface

Figure 1. Screenshot of the READ system

The system also uses "relationships" between blocks, specified in a separate XML file; relationships can be visual relationships or discourse relationships, such as one block being an illustration of another. Those relationships can be used to implement navigation functions, for instance.

Finally several "modes" of access can be defined, by writing different configurations files. This allows switching between modes during navigation.

-Configuration overview: the configuration files (one by defined mode) basically specify how to render each tag of the original XML document (e.g. when encountering a *<p>* in the document, play a sound); note any vocabulary can be used to tag the original document (e.g. HTML or custom tags) as long as this vocabulary matches the one in the configuration files.

Configuration files also allows defining several types of events (reading text with Text-To-Speech, playing sounds, etc.) using implemented output capabilities with specific configurations (e.g. reading text with a specific voice, at a specific rate or pitch, etc.).

-Implemented outputs modalities and functions: Currently, READ can use any SAPI voice to read text, which can contain SSML[4] tags to control its parameters. Sounds store in WAV files (e.g. auditory icons) can be played, and any output sound or voice can be spatialized, that is to say the sound is played as if it came from a certain location in space (see [2] for an example of spatialized sound use for accessibility). READ also provide a basic visualization of the events being played *(on Figure 1. the original document is on the left and current events on the right).*

Navigation functions to move between blocks, jump to a given block from its type or relationships, are also implemented. For data analysis purposes, every user and system action is logged into a text file.

-Implementing new extensions: If other input or output devices need to be implemented, the application provides a plugin mechanism to do so. One can then add C# plugins to define new types of events, which can be afterwards used in the configuration files. Plugins defining new navigation functions can also be added to the software. Writing a new plugin consists in writing a code file implementing the defined programming interfaces, and placing it in the right folder.

3. CONCLUSION

This platform could be used to implement and combine several input or output devices (e.g. haptic devices) for multi-modality or non-linear rendering of documents. The applications range from the evaluation of navigation performances to content comprehension and learning. We believe READ will be useful to address this type of research questions in the frame of documents non-visual access.

Regarding the limitations of this software, the XML configurations files, the relationships files and the documents have to be manually edited. This can be a rather time-consuming process depending on the document size, yet it seems acceptable for a research usage.

We recently used READ to evaluate different rendering and navigation methods for textual documents in an experiment with 60 blindfolded and 12 blind participants; their main task was to understand a 1500 words structured text[5]. Even though the scope of the experiment was different from the software evaluation in itself (rendering methods were evaluated), it is important to note that READ was stable and bug-free for every participant. Besides, the usability scores obtained with a *SUS*[6] questionnaire were on average around 90 (over 100) for the best methods, showing that READ can be used to implement usable interactions.

4. ACKONWLEDGEMENTS

This research was funded by the *PRES-Toulouse* and the *Région Midi-Pyrénées*.

5. REFERENCES

[1] Bates, E. and Fitzpatrick, D.Spoken mathematics using prosody, earcons and spearcons. *ICCHP 2010*, (2010), 407–414.

[2] Cofino, J., Barreto, A., Abyarjoo, F., and Ortega, F.R.Sonically-Enhanced Tabular Screen-Reading. *International Technology and Persons with Disabilities Conference*, (2014).

[3] El-glaly, Y.N. and Quek, F.Digital Reading Support for The Blind by Multimodal Interaction. *ICMI'14*, (2014), 439–446.

[4] Gadde, P. and Bolchini, D.From Screen Reading to Aural Glancing : Towards Instant Access to Key Page Sections. *ASSETS'14*, (2014), 67–74.

[5] Guerreiro, J. and Gonçalves, D.Text-to-Speeches : Evaluating the Perception of Concurrent Speech by Blind People. *ASSETS '14*, (2014), 169–176.

[6] Lazar, J., Allen, A., Kleinman, J., and Malarkey, C.What Frustrates Screen Reader Users on the Web: A Study of 100 Blind Users. *International Journal of Human-Computer Interaction 22*, 3 (2007), 247–269.

[7] Power, C., Freire, A., Petrie, H., and Swallow, D.Guidelines are only half of the story: accessibility problems encountered by blind users on the web. *SIGCHI Conference on Human Factors in Computing Systems*, ACM (2012), 433–442.

[8] Sorin, L., Mojahid, M., Aussenac-gilles, N., and Lemarié, J.Improving the accessibility of digital documents for blind users : contributions of the Textual Architecture Model. *HCI International 2013*, Springer-Verlag Berlin Heidelberg (2013), 423–431.

[4] Speech Synthesis Markup Language

[5] The results will be published soon; the aim was to evaluate different text formatting restitution methods

[6] Standard Usability Scale

Using Dynamic Audio Feedback to Support Peripersonal Reaching in Visually Impaired People

Graham Wilson & Stephen A. Brewster
Glasgow Interactive Systems Group, School of Computing Science, University of Glasgow, UK
{first.last}@glasgow.ac.uk

ABSTRACT

Blind children engage with their immediate environment much less than sighted children, particularly through self-initiated movement or exploration. Research has suggested that providing dynamic feedback about the environment and the child's actions within/against it may help to encourage reaching activity and support spatial cognitive learning. This paper presents an initial study suggesting the accuracy of peripersonal reaching can be improved by the use of dynamic sound from both the objects to reach for and the reaching hand itself (via a worn speaker) that changes based on the proximity of the hand to the object. The demonstration will let attendees try the interaction and feedback designs.

Categories and Subject Descriptors

K.4.2 [**Computers and Society**]: *Social Issues* - Assistive technologies for persons with disabilities

General Terms

Design, Human Factors.

Keywords

Sound perception; reaching; visual impairment.

1. INTRODUCTION

Children who are congenitally or early blind can be less engaged with objects in their immediate environment [5], due to a lack of awareness of the object locations and a slower development of object existence/permanence [8]. Providing a means with which the child could, of his/her own accord, learn of the existence of objects, and their own position relative to them, could encourage more self-initiated movement [5,8] and so improve or expedite spatial cognitive learning. A computer-based system that can control the playing of environmental sounds based on the child's activity could provide more engaging feedback to encourage the child to be "more active against the world" [8]. Environmental sound may also be a way to support the development and performance of accurate reaching in peripersonal (arms-reach) space. Little research has looked at peripersonal reaching accuracy in visually impaired people [3,6]. As environmental sounds can encourage reaching [5,9] and wrist-based sound can improve spatial movements [2], we are investigating whether the combination of environmental sounds and wrist-based sound can improve reaching in blind and visually impaired people. As a first step, we ran an initial study with blind and visually impaired young adults (aged 18 to 19) to determine which of several audio designs best supports accurate reaching. We measured reaching accuracy and subjective responses about the feedback designs, including preferences and whether the sounds created a connection between the hand and the object. The research aim was supported by a focus group with 5 blind and visually impaired young adults (aged 18-19) who said that using external sounds to encourage and support reaching behaviours would be of benefit to blind children.

ASSETS '15, October 26-28, 2015, Lisbon, Portugal
ACM 978-1-4503-3400-6/15/10.
http://dx.doi.org/10.1145/2700648.2811339

2. FEEDBACK DESIGNS

Three feedback designs were compared: 1) a dynamic Geiger counter [4], 2) dynamic increasing pitch (utilising perceptual *streaming* [1]) and 3) a constant (unchanging) design. The first two designs changed dynamically based on the proximity of the hand to the (target) object, while the constant design played continuously and remained the same regardless of proximity. We wanted to measure the effect of feedback emanating from the object alone, the wrist alone and both the object and wrist combined, and so each feedback design had two aspects: an *Individual*, single speaker design and a two-speaker *Coalescent* design. Based on perceptual streaming [1], the feedback designs changed in a way that, at a distance, the hand and object may be perceived as separate, but as proximity increases, they may be perceived as a single source, increasing the association of hand to object. All the sound designs used synthetic "pluck" tones (similar to a guitar string) generated in Audacity. These sounds have an onset of 0ms and rapid decay to increase localisation accuracy [7].

2.1 Geiger Counter

In this design, a pluck tone of pitch C^5 (523.25Hz) was played with increasing temporal frequency as the hand approached the object. The sound was produced by either the object or wrist during the *Individual* speaker design, depending on the condition. The inter-tone delay decreased from 900ms at 50cm distance to 100ms (10Hz) at 7.5cm distance, decreasing 100ms for every 5cm advance (Table 1). The two-speaker *Coalescent* design was similar, but the pluck tones alternated between playing on the object and the wrist and both tones played when touching the object. To increase the perceptual distinction, the object used the C^5 tone and the wrist played a G^4 (392Hz) tone.

Table 1: The mapping of Geiger inter-tone delay (ITD) and Pitch to the distance of the hand to the target object.

Distance (cm)	**50**	**45**	**40**	**35**	**30**	**25**	**20**	**15**	**7.5**
ITD (ms)	900	800	700	600	500	400	300	200	100
Pitch Note	C^4	C^4	D^4	E^4	F^4	G^4	A^4	B^4	C^5

2.2 Increasing Pitch

Rapid notes close in pitch are grouped into a single perceptual stream, while notes distant in pitch are perceived as two separate streams [1]. Therefore, the *Individual* design played the 8 tones in a C major scale that increased in pitch from C^4 (261.63) up to C^5 (523.25Hz) as proximity increased (Table 1), at a temporal frequency of 10Hz. A discrete mapping was chosen over a continuous function to provide perceptually clear changes and to provide potentially more pleasant feedback (harmonious musical steps and feedback that was not continuously changing). For the *Coalescent* design, both the object and wrist speakers played tones at the same 10Hz rate, but played alternately, resulting in a frequency of 20Hz. In this case the object always played the highest C^5 tone and the wrist tone increased based on proximity as in the *Individual* design, so that the tones matched when touching the target.

2.3 Constant Design

The constant audio design was a continually playing repetition of the target object sound: the C^5 pluck tone repeated at a constant 5Hz. It either played from the target object, the wrist or both the object and the wrist. When both the object and wrist played, the tones were alternated at 10Hz, like the Geiger counter.

3. INITIAL EXPERIMENT

The setup consisted of 7 small speakers (weight 50g) connected to a Windows 8.1 PC via USB soundcards and a Microsoft Kinect v2 depth camera, which tracked the position of the participant's hand and the speakers to be reached for. Six of the speakers (KitSound Mini Buddy "Magic 8 Ball") were used as the target objects and positioned as shown in Figure 1. An "Owl" variant of the same model was used for the wrist speaker, attached by a rubber strap.

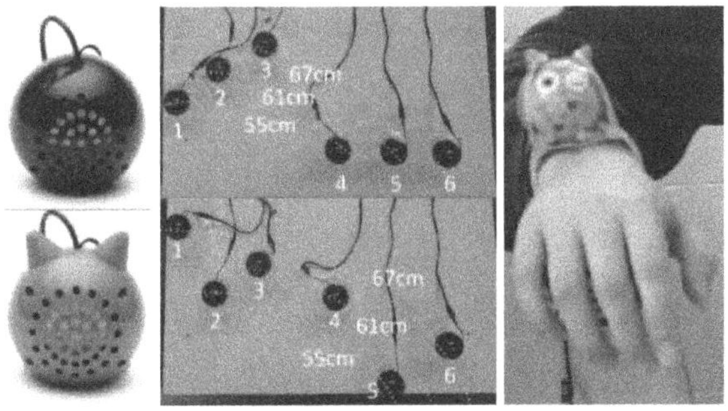

Figure 1: Left: Speakers used in experiment. Middle: Target speaker layouts 1 (top) and 2. Right: speaker worn on wrist.

The experiment had a 3 (Feedback Design) x 3 (Object, Wrist, Both Speakers) within-subjects design, plus a Control condition where only the initial target sound was played (silence thereafter). The 10 conditions were completed over 60 minutes in a random order and the speaker layout (Figure 1) was alternated between conditions to reduce learning effects. In a condition, each object speaker was the "target" to be reached for 3 times in a random order, following 6 practice trials. At the start of each trial the "target" object was indicated by five C^5 pluck tones played at 5Hz. The participant then reached for the target with the right hand. To "select" a speaker, the participant placed the palm of their right hand on top and pressed a keyboard key with the left hand.

Table 2: Mean reaching error (wrong speaker) and time.

	Wrist	Object	Both	Geiger	Pitch	Constant	Control
Error (%)	21.3	17.2	14.6	12.4	13.1	27.7	32.2
Time (ms)	3643	3372	3723	4049	3203	3478	2655

3.1 Initial Results

The results indicated a benefit of using dynamic feedback, compared to constant or no feedback. Objective measurements of reaching (Table 2) suggested that dynamic sounds led to significantly more accurate reaching, and sounds from reachable objects were more likely to help fast reaching than sounds from the wrist or from both the object and wrist together. When asked which of the audio designs they preferred, one participant had no preference, one preferred the Geiger counter, but three preferred the Pitch design. None preferred the Constant design. When asked why, the participant that preferred the Geiger counter said it was because he thought the changes in sound based on proximity were more "intuitive" than the changes in pitch, as people who are not musical may struggle to make use of the pitch changes. He, and another, also believed dynamic changes were "necessary" to help reaching accuracy, as the Constant design was unhelpful. In contrast, one of the participants who preferred the Pitch design believed it to be the more intuitive design, while the others preferred Pitch because the changes were more obvious, easier to distinguish and so more helpful. All designs were "pleasant" (> 4), with the Dynamic designs being slightly more so than the Constant.

Table 3: Mean Likert responses for the three Feedback Design questions. 1 = "Strongly Disagree", 7 = "Strongly Agree".

Question	Geiger	Pitch	Constant
"The sounds created a connection between the hand and the object"	6.2	6.2	4.4
"The combination of the hand and object speakers was beneficial"	3.6	3.4	3.0
"The sound was pleasant"	5.6	5.4	4.6

Table 3 shows the average responses for three questions asked about each *Feedback Design*. Both of the Dynamic designs produced a connection between the hand and the object, much more than the Constant design. This may help young children create an internal connection between his/her movements and the environment, potentially increasing the sense of agency and willingness to engage with nearby objects. Providing sounds from both the wrist and object did not really provide any benefit over one speaker alone, and two participants expressed that having sounds coming only from the wrist made reaching more difficult than having it from the object or from both.

4. ACKNOWLEDGEMENTS

Thank you to Jeremy Perrott and RNC students for their help.

5. REFERENCES

[1] Bregman, A. *Auditory Scene Analysis.* The MIT Press, Cambridge, MA.

[2] Cappagli, G., Baud-bovy, G., Cocchi, E., and Gori, M. Audio and proprioceptive space perception in sighted and visually impaired children. *Proceedings of IMRF 2014.*

[3] Macé, M., Dramas, F., and Jouffrais, C. Reaching to sound accuracy in the peri-personal space of blind and sighted humans. *Proceedings of ICCHP 2012*, pp 636–643.

[4] McGookin, D., Brewster, S., and Priego, P. Audio bubbles: Employing non-speech audio to support tourist wayfinding. *Proceedings of HAID 2009*, pp 41–50.

[5] Millar, S. *Understanding and Representing Space: Theory and Evidence from Studies with Blind and Sighted Children.* Oxford Press, Oxford.

[6] Parseihian, G., Jouffrais, C., and Katz, B. Reaching nearby sources: comparison between real and virtual sound and visual targets. *Frontiers in Neuroscience 8*, Sept. 2014, Article 269.

[7] Rakerd, B. and Hartmann, W. Localization of Sound in Rooms, III: Onset and Duration Effects. *Journal of the Acoustical Society of America 80*, 6, pp 1695–1706.

[8] Ross, S. and Tobin, M. Object Permanence, Reaching, and Locomotion in Infants Who Are Blind. *Journal of Visual Impairment & Blindness 91*, pp 25–32.

[9] Wishart, J., Bower, T., and Dunkeld, J. Reaching in the dark. *Perception 7*, pp 507–512.

An Enhanced Electrolarynx with Automatic Fundamental Frequency Control based on Statistical Prediction

Kou Tanaka, Tomoki Toda, Graham Neubig, Sakriani Sakti and Satoshi Nakamura
Graduate School of Information Science, Nara Institute of Science and Technology
8916-5 Takayama-cho, Ikoma, Nara, Japan
{ko-t, tomoki, neubig, ssakti, s-nakamura}@is.naist.jp

ABSTRACT

An electrolarynx is a type of speaking aid device which is able to mechanically generate excitation sounds to help laryngectomees produce electrolaryngeal (EL) speech. Although EL speech is quite intelligible, its naturalness suffers from monotonous fundamental frequency patterns of the mechanical excitation sounds. To make it possible to generate more natural excitation sounds, we have proposed a method to automatically control the fundamental frequency of the sounds generated by the electrolarynx based on a statistical prediction model, which predicts the fundamental frequency patterns from the produced EL speech in real-time. In this paper, we develop a prototype system by implementing the proposed control method in an actual, physical electrolarynx and evaluate its performance.

Categories and Subject Descriptors

K.4.2 [**Computers and Society**]: Social Issues - Assistive technologies for persons with disabilities

Keywords

electrolaryngeal speech, automatic fundamental frequency control

1. INTRODUCTION

Electrolaryngeal (EL) speech is one of the major speaking methods used by laryngectomees who are people who have had their larynx usually due to laryngeal cancer. EL speech is produced using an electrolarynx, which is typically held against the neck to mechanically generate artificial excitation signals. The generated excitation signals are conducted into the speaker's oral cavity, and are articulated to produce EL speech. EL speech is relatively intelligible but its naturalness is very low owing to unnatural fundamental frequency (F_0) patterns of the mechanically generated excitation signals. Consequently, quality of life of laryngectomees is significantly degraded.

ASSETS'15, October 26–28, 2015, Lisbon, Portugal.
ACM 978-1-4503-3400-6/15/10.
DOI: http://dx.doi.org/10.1145/2700648.2811340.

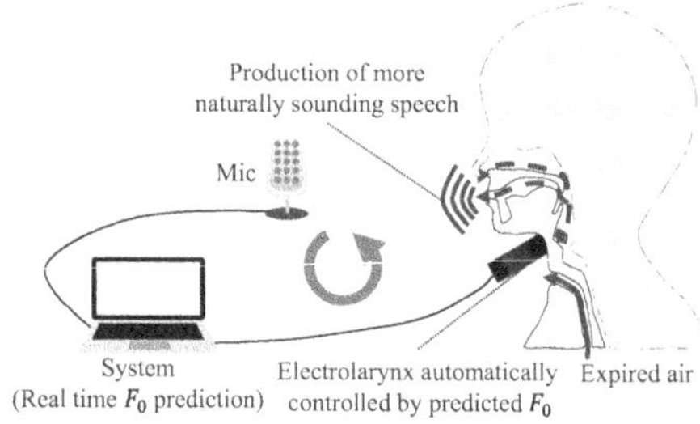

Figure 1: Proposed system to directly control electrolarynx using real-time statistical F_0 prediction.

To generate more natural F_0 patterns, we have proposed a method to control F_0 based on the statistical F_0 prediction [1]. In our proposed system based on this method, F_0 patterns are predicted from the produced EL speech signals as shown in Fig. 1. Relatively natural F_0 patterns can be predicted using statistics extracted in advance from parallel data consisting of utterance pairs of EL speech and natural speech. Therefore, this system allows laryngectomees to directly produce more natural EL speech in the same manner as in the traditional speaking method using the conventional electrolarynx. Our preliminary experimental results through simulation [1] have demonstrated that the proposed method yields significant improvements in naturalness while causing no degradation in listenability and intelligibility compared to the original EL speech.

In this paper, we develop a prototype system by implementing our proposed F_0 control method in an actual, physical electrolarynx and evaluate its performance. The experimental results demonstrate that the prototype system generates more natural excitation sounds, as in the simulation.

2. METHODOLOGY

Direct Control of Excitation Signals of Electrolarynx based on Statistical F_0 Prediction: Our proposed system allows a laryngectomee to produce EL speech with predicted F_0 patterns using two processes: prediction and articulation [1]. In the prediction process, the F_0 value is predicted frame by frame using the real-time voice conversion algorithm [2] from EL speech produced by the laryngectomee. This process causes a constant processing delay of 50 ms to make it possible to predict relatively natural F_0 patterns varying corresponding to linguistic contents. In the articulation process, the laryngectomee produces the EL speech by articulating the excitation sounds generated

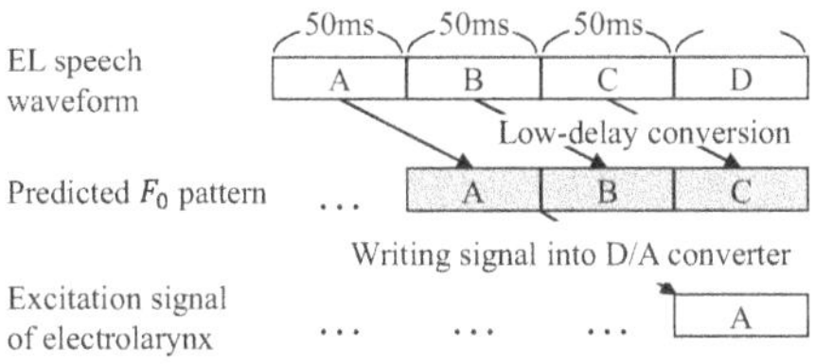

Figure 2: Latency caused by each process

from the electrolarynx based on the predicted F_0 values. These two processes are simultaneously and continuously performed. Consequently, EL speech with the predicted F_0 patterns can be directly produced by the laryngectomee but it always suffers from misalignment between the articulated sounds and F_0 patterns caused by the processing delay of 50 ms. The results of our previous evaluation through simulation have demonstrated that the impact of this misalignment on perception is small [1].

Development of Prototype System: A prototype system based on our proposed technique has been developed using a laptop and a digital/analog (D/A) converter shown in Table 1. As shown in Fig. 1, EL speech produced from mouth of a laryngectomee is detected with a standard close-talk microphone. The EL speech signal is recorded on a laptop and F_0 patterns of normal speech are predicted on the fly by using the real-time statistical F_0 prediction. The predicted F_0 values are linearly converted to voltage values to control the F_0 values of the excitation signal generated by an electrolarynx. Then, an electric signal corresponding to the determined voltage values is generated with the D/A converter connected from the laptop to the electrolarynx. The electrolarynx changes the F_0 values of the excitation signal according to the input electric signal generated from the D/A converter. As shown in Fig. 2, additional latency is caused by the D/A converter in the prototype system. It takes around 50 ms to write the digital signal on the D/A converter. Moreover, the digital signal to be written needs to be determined before starting writing. Consequently, the D/A part always causes 100 ms latency. In total, 150 ms latency is caused in the prototype system. Note that this latency in the D/A part may be addressed by the development of a special device for the electrolarynx.

3. EVALUATION AND RESULTS

We conducted an objective evaluation for evaluating prediction accuracy of F_0 patterns generated by the developed prototype compared to that confirmed in the simulation process [1]. The source speech was EL speech uttered by one non-disabled male speaker, and the target speech was normal speech uttered by a professional female speaker. Each speaker uttered about 50 sentences in the ATR phonetically

Table 1: Electronic devices on the prototype system

Electrolarynx	Yourtone
Microphone	Crown CM-311A
CPU of the laptop	Intel(R) Core(TM) i5-4200U
D/A converter	AIO-160802AY-USB

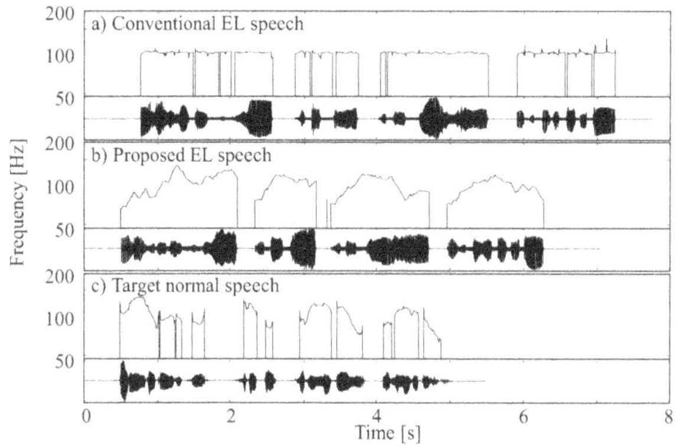

Figure 3: Example of waveforms and F_0 patterns of EL speech signals generated by conventional and proposed systems and those of target natural speech.

balanced sentence set [3]. We conducted a 5-fold cross validation test in which 40 utterance pairs were used for training of a statistical F_0 prediction model, and the remaining 10 utterance pairs were used for evaluation. Sampling frequency was set to 16 kHz.

Experimental results: The F_0 correlation coefficient between the prototype system and the simulation process is 0.91. This result shows that F_0 patterns predicted by the prototype system strongly correlate to those by the simulation process, which have already been confirmed to be effective for improving naturalness of EL speech [1]. An example of EL speech signals and their F_0 patterns are shown in Fig. 3. We can see that the prototype system makes it possible to produce EL speech with more naturally varying F_0 patterns compared to the conventional EL speech.

4. CONCLUSIONS

In this paper, we have developed a prototype system by implementing our proposed F_0 control method of an electrolarynx based on the statistical F_0 prediction technique and evaluate its performance. The experimental results have demonstrated that the prototype system enables a speaker to produce more naturally sounding electrolaryngeal speech.

5. ACKNOWLEDGMENTS

This work was supported in part of JSPS KAKENHI Grant Numbers: 26280060 and the authors would like to thank Mr. Y. Sugai of Densei Communication Inc., Japan, for advise to control an electrolarynx.

6. REFERENCES

[1] K. Tanaka, T. Toda, G. Neubig, S. Sakti, and S. Nakamura, "Direct F_0 control of an electrolarynx based on statistical excitation feature prediction and its evaluation through simulation," in *Proc. INTERSPEECH*, Sep 2014.

[2] T. Toda, T. Muramatsu, and H. Banno, "Implementation of computationally efficient real-time voice conversion." in *Proc. INTERSPEECH*, Sep 2012.

[3] M. Abe, Y. Sagisaka, T. Umeda, and H. Kuwabara, "Speech database," ATR Technical Report, TR-I-0166, Sep 1990.

Nonvisual Access to an Interactive Electric Field Simulation: Work in Progress

Clayton Lewis and Derek Riemer
Department of Computer Science
University of Colorado
Boulder CO USA
clayton.lewis@colorado.edu, derek.riemer@colorado.edu

ABSTRACT
We describe progress in creating an inclusive version of an interactive simulation that presents the dynamic electric field produced by a moving charge, using an audio presentation. The results illustrate opportunities and challenges in making this simulation usable for blind users.

Categories and Subject Descriptors
H.5.2 **[User Interfaces]** Auditory (non-speech) feedback; K.4.2 **[Social Issues]**: Assistive tech for persons with disabilities.

General Terms
Design, Human Factors

Keywords
Accessibility; inclusive design; interactive simulation

1. INTERACTIVE SIMULATIONS AND LEARNERS WHO CANNOT SEE.
Interactive simulations are becoming relatively easy to create, and are popular aids to education. For example, the PhET Project (http://phet.colorado.edu) offers more than 130 simulations (sims) that are widely used in primary, secondary, and university science courses. These sims are downloaded more than 75 million times a year. Attractively, most of these sims can be run in a standard browser with no software installation.

Unfortunately, these sims are useless for learners who cannot see. Not only is the behavior of the sims presented visually, in the form of pictorial animations, but also the control of the sims requires the use of a mouse in a way that is impossible if one cannot see the mouse cursor.

Distinguished blind computer scientist T.V. Raman has suggested that the visual system can be thought of as a means of querying a spatial database, that is, the visible world. If one has another means of asking the questions and getting the answers, one does not need the visual system (personal communication, 2009). This broad principle suggests an approach to making any communication, however exclusively visual it might seem to be, workable for blind users. One must ask what information the communication provides visually, and devise nonvisual ways of requesting this information and receiving the results.

ASSETS '15, October 26-28, 2015, Lisbon, Portugal.
ACM 978-1-4503-3400 6/15/10.
http://dx.doi.org/10.1145/2700648.2811341

2. A CHALLENGING, BUT PROMISING, EXAMPLE: RADIATING CHARGE
We have chosen one of the PhET sims, Radiating Charge, as a test bed for this approach. This sim produces animated graphics showing the lines of force representing the electric field produced by a moving charge (https://phet.colorado.edu/en/simulation/radiating-charge). The sim allows the user to observe how changes in the field propagate outward from the charge as the charge accelerates. The resulting patterns of lines of force are complex, and visually striking. For example, when the charge moves around a circular orbit, spiral patterns of disturbance emanate from the orbit and move outward in all directions. We have created a wholly nonvisual representation that can convey much, though not all, of the information available from the original, visual sim (http://claytonhalllewis.github.io/assetsNonViz/assetssonicfield.html).

2.1 An acoustical representation can convey the amplitude and orientation of a field at a point, over time.
The sim calculates a vector representing the electric field at a given point and at a given time. The length of this vector represents the strength of the field, and its direction the orientation of the field. We have represented both aspects of the field, strength and orientation, in a sound; as the field changes, this sound changes. The strength of the field is represented in a natural way by loudness. As the field gets stronger, the associated sound is louder.

2.1.1 Pitch can encode orientation.
A second readily perceptible quantitative aspect of a sound is its pitch, making this a natural candidate for representing the orientation of the field. We have chosen to assign a low tone to the direction of the positive X axis, with higher pitches as the field makes a larger angle with the X axis.

While this coding of representation is simple and easy to interpret, it does have a disadvantage. Frequently the field produced in the sim oscillates, and when its oscillation passes through the positive X-axis the pitch jumps between its lowest pitch (at angle 0 degrees) and its highest pitch, at just less than 360 degrees, giving the false impression of discontinuous change.

2.1.2 *Shepard tones can provide a continuous representation for change in orientation.*

To deal with this issue we use an alternate encoding using Shepard tones [1], a sequence of tones that give the paradoxical impression that each tone is higher than the previous, yet with the first tone sounding higher than the last. By playing the tones in one order an impression of steadily rising pitch can be sustained indefinitely; the reverse sequence gives an impression of steadily falling pitch. Using this representation, oscillations, and even multiple full rotations, never produce discontinuous jumps in pitch.

2.2 Probe position can be controlled by a mouse, nonvisually, using pointer locking.

When using the original, visual sim, the user can observe the field in different parts of space simply by looking at different places. We provide similar functionality by providing a probe under user control,that picks out the point in space for which the field characteristics will be presented. By moving the probe away from the center, for example, the user can discern that the field gets weaker; by moving the probe to points at different directions from the center they can discern how the orientation of the field changes in different parts of the space.

The obvious means of moving the probe would be the mouse, but how can that be made to work for someone who cannot see the mouse pointer? If (for example) arrow keys are used instead, it becomes more difficult to move the probe away from the center in a desired direction, or to move the probe in any other smooth way.

We have addressed this need by using a relatively new API (http://www.w3.org/TR/pointerlock/) that allows the sim to detect relative motion of a pointing device with no constraint based on the cursor location. We can position the probe under program control (something not possible with the mouse cursor), and move it in a direction and extent indicated using the pointing device.

2.3 The nonvisual sim supports much, but not all, of the functionality of the visual sim.

The nonvisual sim allows the user to control voicing mode (as just described), probe position and probe position feedback, the orientation encoding, and four patterns of movement of the charge: stationary, horizontal or vertical oscillation, and circular motion.

While the number of commands is not very large, it is large enough that a hierarchical arrangement will help users find and use them. Following a suggestion from Sina Bahram, based on observations of the TWBlue twitter client (http://twblue.es), we have adopted a spatial (but invisible) layout of commands, with a horizontal row of tabs, each containing one or more commands or options arranged vertically. The user can navigate among the commands, using the arrow keys, and use the space bar to select an option or execute a command. Bahram has suggested that use of such a spatial arrangement can be a helpful convention, potentially applicable to a wide range of applications.

2.3.1 *It may be possible to support manual movement of the charge.*

The original visual sim has a number of additional capabilities, such as control of the amplitude of the movement of the charge, which we believe can be incorporated in the nonvisual sim easily. A more challenging offering is the ability to drag the charge using the mouse. Using the mouse to move the charge would preclude our use of the mouse to move the probe, something a sighted user accomplishes visually. We intend to explore how well the effects of moving the charge by hand can be judged by listening to the field at a fixed probe position.

3. PERCEPTION OF SPATIAL PATTERNS OF BEHAVIOR WILL REQUIRE NEW APPROACHES.

While it appears that the audio representations we have created effectively convey the electric field at the location of the probe, there are other impressions available from the visual sim that the probe technique does not provide. Generally, a visual display conveys to sighted users a sense of what is happening simultaneously in different parts of the field. For example, as mentioned earlier, the visual sim presents a spiral pattern of disturbances. It would be impossible to reconstruct that pattern using the probe technique, as there is no way to make observations in more than one place simultaneously using the probe.

It may be possible to convey these extended dynamic patterns to blind users using a tactile display, which could be sensed in more than one place at once using hands or fingers. We have not prioritized this approach, however, as we want to learn what can be accomplished using only a standard browser and commodity hardware, in keeping with the minimal requirements of the PhET sims.

Common laptop computers can produce stereo sound, with no special equipment other than a headset. We plan to explore whether this approach can allow the output from more than one probe to be differentiated.

4. CONCLUSION: PROGRESS IN REPRESENTATION AND INCLUSION

Progress in inclusive design brings advances for all users, whatever their needs. Consider how learners can tell when the electric field is oscillating. In the lines of force representation, one has to do close reasoning, because the sparseness of the lines of force means that there is only occasionally a line shown passing through a given point. In the audio sim, especially when the Shepard tone encoding used for orientation, the oscillation is clear. We believe that work of the kind we present here has promise in expanding our repertoire of useful representations for many kinds of information, as well as making the content of interactive simulations more widely available.

5. ACKNOWLEDGMENTS

We are grateful to the ATLAS Institute (University of Colorado) for support for this work. We thank Sina Bahram, Bill Casson, Michael Dubson, Hunter Ewen, Noah Finkelstein, Owen Lewis Emily Moore, Stephen Pollock, and Michael Theodore for valuable suggestions and discussions.

6. REFERENCE

[1] Shepard , R.N.(1964). "Circularity in Judgements of Relative Pitch". *Journal of the Acoustical Society of America* **36** (12): 2346–53.

Balance Assessment in Fall-Prevention Oriented Exergames

Miguel Brito, João Jacob, Rui Nóbrega
Departamento de Engenharia Informática
Faculdade de Engenharia da Universidade do Porto
Porto, Portugal
{ei10104,joao.jacob,ruinobrega}@fe.up.pt

António Santos
Fraunhofer AICOS
Rua Alfredo Allen 455, 4200-135
Porto, Portugal
antonio.santos@fraunhofer.pt

ABSTRACT

To assess the success of fall-prevention oriented exergames two digital games were developed taking advantage of the Wii Balance Board (WBB) capabilities. The objective was to evaluate the exergames' potential to address elderly adults' declining motivation to exercise regularly despite the benefits related to fall-prevention. The system uses the WBB to keep track of the player's center of pressure and computes important balance assessment measures related to it to eventually provide a mean to monitor their patients. The presented demo will feature the two exergames.

Categories and Subject Descriptors

H.5.m. [**Applied computing**]: Health informatics; Computer games; H.5.m. [**Human-centered computing**]: Interaction device

Keywords

Fall-Prevention; Human-Computer Interaction; Natural User Interfaces; Exergames

1. INTRODUCTION

As age degrades biological elements that control the body, falls become more frequent and more severe [5]. Exercise is known to improve balance and strengthen the body which decreases fall risk and also mitigates fall consequences [1]. However, motivating seniors to do healthy exercises is difficult [5]. Recent affordable motion sensing devices permitted the development of digital games that require exercise to be played, i. e., exergames. These digital games are proven to be more motivating for regular physical activity practice than traditional exercise methods [7]. The Nintendo Wii Balance Board (WBB) measures the user's Center Of Pressure (COP) which computation has been proven to be useful in helping the therapists diagnose patients' balance [2]. In this demo, we present two WBB based exergames that ally game development techniques with fall-prevention exercises that record balance data for further evaluation.

ASSETS'15, October 26–28, 2015, Lisbon, Portugal.
ACM 978-1-4503-3400-6/15/10.
DOI: http://dx.doi.org/10.1145/2700648.2811342

2. RELATED WORK

Leading senior adults to exercise has been studied for more than a decade. Otago Exercise Programme [1] and Fitness and Mobility Exercise (FAME) [4] are two exercise sets developed and proved to decrease fall risk, which were used to identify potential exercises for our exergames. Balance evaluation can be done by tracking the COP with force plates while the patient is standing [3]. These force plates are expensive and impracticable to use in small clinics, thus subjective metrics based on exercise performance are used such as the Berg Balance Scale (BBS) and the Brunel Balance Assessment (BBA) [6]. Nevertheless, Clark et al. compared COP measured with the WBB and commercial force plates and suggested that the first can be used to assess balance in clinics [2]. Another quantitative measure is the Tandem Stance Test (TST) [6], where the time the patient can hold a heel toe standing stance is measured. This stance is used in Otago and FAME, thus can be used in exergames for both balance improvement and assessment.

3. EXERGAMES

Two digital games were developed under a framework that communicates with several devices. The WBB serves as a game controller and as balance assessment instrument. The following subsections describe the two digital games and automatic balance assessment.

3.1 Scooter Chase

In Scooter Chase, the player rides a scooter with the goal of catching a cat. The system uses a WBB, rotated 90° from its normal position, to simulate a scooter's base and a smartphone to simulate the handlebar. To move the character, the player must perform a heel-to-toe stance on the WBB. This exercise was chosen as it is part of Otago [1] and FAME [4] programs as well as part of multiple balance assessment scales such as BBS and TST [6]. Figure 1 shows the seniors feet while performing a heel toe stance in order to move the character and the game's interface. A balance assessment is given automatically in the end of the game based on the maximum time the player could maintain the tandem pose and accordingly to the TST.

3.2 Segway Stroll

Segway Stroll places the player traveling in the city with a Segway. To earn points, the player has to pass through

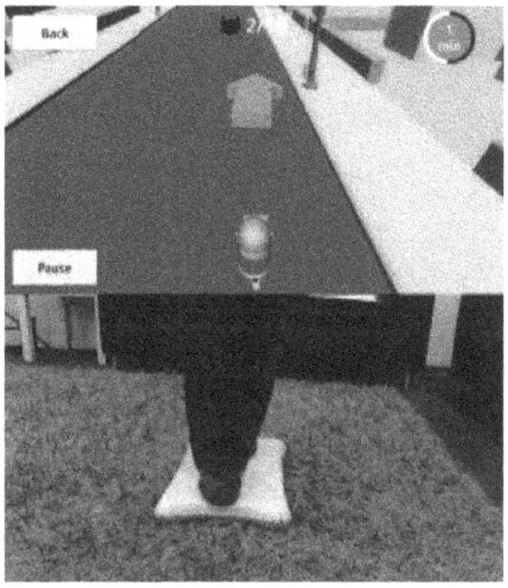

Figure 1: Scooter Chase interface and feet position when performing a heel toe stance.

checkpoints under a time limit. This game is played with the WBB alone. To accelerate, the player must perform a forward reach exercise and to break, toe raises. To turn, the player has to exert more pressure on one side of the WBB. These exercises are contained in the FAME program [4] and forward reach is used in BBA [6]. In addition, obstacles such as traffic lights forces the player to stand enabling measuring the player's COP while standing. Figure 2 shows a senior performing a forward reach while playing this game.

3.3 COP Analysis

While playing, the system can measure metrics based on COP readings. In Scooter Chase, while the player is performing a heel-to-toe stance, the system records the COP coordinates. The coordinates can be used to generate charts of the COP path, amplitude and a frequency map. At the same time of the recording, the system computes the COP mean velocity, total oscillation and the time the player maintains the pose. In the end, a balance score is given using the maximum time the player could maintain the pose based on the TST, i. e. low from 0 to 9 seconds, medium from 10 to 29 seconds and high if higher than 30 [6].

The same measures are applied on Segway Stroll when the player is standing. The COP's path, amplitude and frequency maps charts could be used by therapists to assess the player's balance [3]. A COP's path chart can be seen in figure 3.

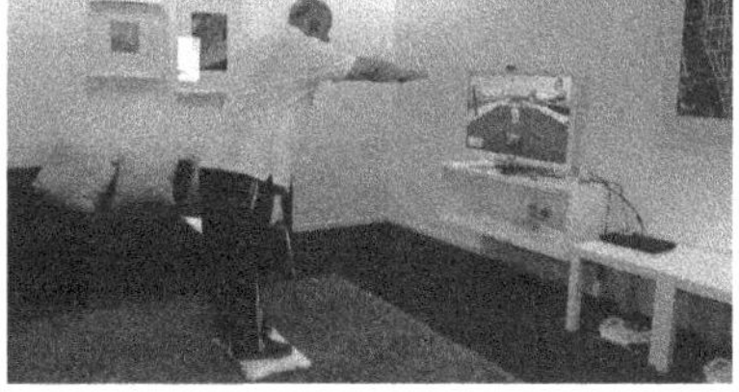

Figure 2: Senior performing a forward reach while playing Segway Stroll.

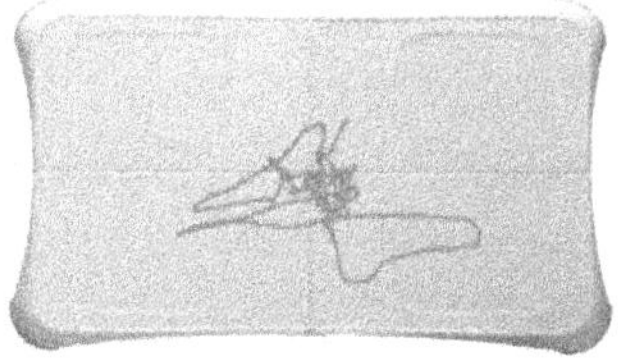

Figure 3: COP's path recorded while a senior played Segway Stroll.

4. CONCLUSIONS

Seventeen senior volunteers, with ages from 64 to 80 years old, were given the opportunity to interact with the developed games. Although they did not fully understand the games' mechanics and logic at their first attempt, they stated they had enjoyed playing them, would like to repeat it regularly and the experience motivated them to exercise. The games are now being tested with a larger population in order to assess the improvements in the balance of the elderly.

5. ACKNOWLEDGMENTS

The authors would like to thank the collaboration of MIEIC and DEI at Faculty of Engineering of University of Porto (FEUP) together with Fraunhofer AICOS through the project "Fall Competence Center" NORTE07-0124-FEDER-000041.

6. REFERENCES

[1] A. J. Campbell and M. C. Robertson. Otago Exercise Programme to Prevent Falls in Older Adults, 2003.

[2] R. a. Clark, A. L. Bryant, Y. Pua, P. McCrory, K. Bennell, and M. Hunt. Validity and reliability of the Nintendo Wii Balance Board for assessment of standing balance. *Gait and Posture*, 31:307–310, 2010. http://dx.doi.org/10.1016/j.gaitpost.2009.11.012.

[3] M. Duarte and S. M. S. F. Freitas. Revisão sobre Posturografia Baseada em Plataforma de Força para Avaliação do Equilíbrio. *Revista Brasileira de Fisioterapia*, 14(3):183–192, 2010. http://dx.doi.org/10.1590/s1413-35552010000300003.

[4] J. Eng, A. Dawson, and M. Pang. Fitness and Mobility Exercise Program: A community-based Group Exercise Program for People Living with Stroke, 2006.

[5] E. Mitty and S. Flores. *Geriatric Nursing*. http://dx.doi.org/10.1016/j.gerinurse.2007.10.005.

[6] K. M. Sibley, M. K. Beauchamp, K. Van Ooteghem, S. E. Straus, and S. B. Jaglal. Using the systems framework for postural control to analyze the components of balance evaluated in standardized balance measures: a scoping review. *Archives of physical medicine and rehabilitation*, 96(1):122–132.e29, Jan. 2015. http://dx.doi.org/10.1016/j.apmr.2014.06.021.

[7] S. Uzor and L. Baillie. Investigating the long-term use of exergames in the home with elderly fallers. *Proc. of CHI '14*, pages 2813–2822, 2014. http://dx.doi.org/10.1145/2556288.2557160.

ASL CLeaR: STEM Education Tools for Deaf Students

Jeanne Reis[1], Erin T. Solovey[2], Jon Henner[3], Kathleen Johnson[1], Robert Hoffmeister[1]

[1]Boston University (BU) Boston, MA 02215

[2]Drexel University Philadelphia, PA 19104

[3]College of the Holy Cross Worcester, MA 01610

jeanned@bu.edu, erin.solovey@drexel.edu, {jhenner, kjohnson, rhoff}@bu.edu

ABSTRACT

In this paper, we introduce the American Sign Language STEM Concept Learning Resource (ASL CLeaR), an educational application demo. The ASL CLeaR addresses a need for quality ASL STEM resources by featuring expertly presented STEM content in ASL, and employing an ASL-based search function and a visuocentric search interface. This paper discusses the main objectives of the ASL CLeaR, describes the components of the application, and suggests future work that could lead to improved educational outcomes for deaf and hard of hearing students in STEM topics.

Categories and Subject Descriptors

K.4.2 [**Computers and Society**]: Assistive technologies for persons with disabilities

General Terms

Design, Human Factors.

Keywords

American Sign Language, ASL, STEM education, deaf.

1. INTRODUCTION

All deaf and hard of hearing children are potential American Sign Language (ASL) and English print bilinguals, if immersed in complete and fully accessible language from early ages [6]. However, deaf children face a formidable array of linguistic challenges, beginning with *delayed first language input* [7] due to limited exposure to sign language. Lack of early accessible language leaves a high percentage of deaf children lagging non-deaf peers in educational outcomes, and is shown to pose serious issues for STEM learning [9,10], and proficiency with written English. Exacerbating the challenges of educating a population with language delays, many STEM concepts do not have an agreed upon ASL sign. Deaf students often learn different signs for the same STEM concept from one classroom to the next. Imagine a fourth grade teacher using a different term for "*Photosynthesis*" than the third grade teacher, without discussing the change in vocabulary. In addition, signs generated on the fly are often grammatically incorrect, resulting in learning materials that are not easily comprehensible, conceptually accurate, or engaging in ASL.

2. ASL CLeaR

The ASL STEM Concept Learning Resource (ASL CLeaR) is a free online resource intended to serve as both an educational tool and a language documentation and standardization effort. ASL CLeaR creates a mechanism for broadly sharing a collection of fluent, accurate and engaging ASL STEM lectures and a complete ASL dictionary of terms. It provides an avenue for curricula and language coordination among deaf students, parents, education professionals, and within the deaf community nationwide. It features both ASL-only as well as English navigation and search, provides context in ASL, is vetted by native (L1) ASL STEM domain experts, and uses human signers. The ASL CLeaR is also unique in its exploration of deaf geographies in web design, Universal Design and visually motivated signed language principles [1]. Three main components of ASL CLeaR are described below.

ASSETS '15, October 26-28, 2015, Lisbon, Portugal

ACM 978-1-4503-3400-6/15/10.

http://dx.doi.org/10.1145/2700648.2811343

Site	English Navigation & Search	ASL Navigation & Search	Context in ASL	Domain Expert Vetted	Native ASL Team	Human Signers	Free
ASL CLeaR	X	X	X	X	X	X	X
ASL STEM Forum	X			Some terms	Some terms	X	X
RIT ASL	X			Some terms	Some terms	X	X
Deaf TEC	X					X	X
DEAF STEM	X			Some terms		X	X
Signing App	X						
Signing Math & Science	X						
Embe Outreach	X					X	

Table 1. Comparison of online ASL STEM applications[1]

2.1 Topic Labs

In ***topic labs***, Deaf L1 ASL STEM and education experts lead all content development efforts and generate materials that adhere to curriculum guidelines, model effective, engaging and standardized STEM instruction in ASL, and are designed to improve content and vocabulary learning among deaf students [2]. The expertise of the team ensures that we avoid the linguistic and conceptual issues so commonly found in signed content online. Topic lab materials have been used to build the ASL CLeaR video collection and the ASL STEM dictionary. All ASL STEM terms, whether newly coined or widely accepted, are internally evaluated by the ASL CLeaR team for grammaticality and conceptual accuracy. Terms that meet criteria are first introduced and defined in the instructional context of an ASL STEM micro-lecture. Next, ASL dictionary entries for approved terms are composed and filmed by the content team. Entries include a stand-alone sign, an ASL definition and, in specified cases, an example. Each STEM sign is tagged with ASL linguistic meta-data in the Coding Tool (not depicted) to make the sign searchable via ASL features. At this point, a complete ASL entry has been created. To enable English print searches and bilingual search results, each ASL term is associated with its closest English translation and an English print definition, then tagged with English print metadata.

2.2 Vocabulary Evaluation Tool

To increase the likelihood of broad acceptance of ASL STEM terms, materials are first evaluated by L1 ASL STEM domain experts nationwide. To facilitate scaled evaluation, an online application has been developed, the ASL CLeaR ***Vocabulary Evaluation Tool*** (VET). The VET design filters content to give raters access only to material that aligns with their expertise. VET navigation is entirely ASL-based (Figure 1a), establishing the correct monolingual ASL frame for evaluations and preventing reliance

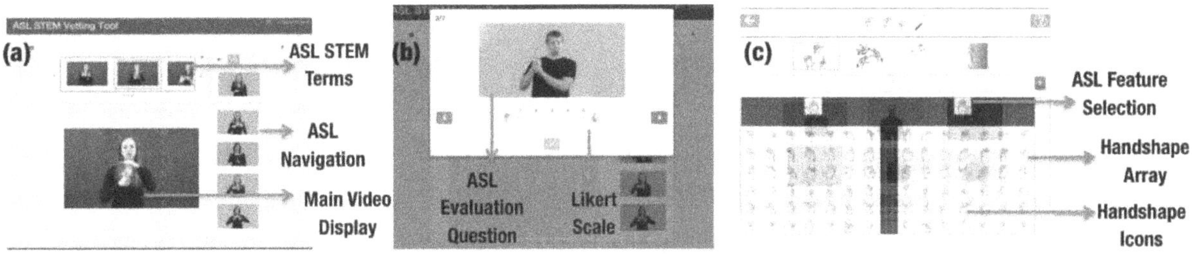

Figure 1. Components of ASL CLeaR with ASL based user interfaces: (a) Vocabulary Evaluation Tool, (b) Evaluation Screen and (c) Search Function: Handshape Screen

on English labels to ascertain meaning of ASL terms. The VET steers evaluators through a sequential protocol that repeats until all terms from a unit are evaluated: 1) view one complete micro-lecture, 2) view one ASL term from that lecture, 3) view ASL definition for that term, 4) view ASL example if provided, 5) respond to 7 ASL evaluation questions about the term by selecting from 5-part Likert scale or yes/no options (Figure 1b). In a small pilot (n=5), 16 of 20 terms scored at or above benchmark (M=4), suggesting potential for broad acceptance.

2.3 ASL CLeaR Search Function & Interface

The ASL ***search function and interface*** makes this a unique database that offers ASL search functionality via graphical representation of the string of visual building blocks that make up ASL signs, much like alphabetic print graphically represents the string of sounds that makes up a spoken word. ASL searches of tagged terms are conducted by selecting icons in three ASL feature arrays (Figure 1c). Clicking on any icon will bring up a results screen displaying all signs that contain the select feature, a design that provides instantaneous results and interactive training through use. Search results are presented in alignment with the principles of visual language. Freeze frames depict ASL STEM terms in recognizable form and hover play allows users to quickly scan, reject, and select terms from the results page. ASL CLeaR also provides STEM words in at least 3 ASL contexts to prevent the denotation and connotation confusion of single English word labeling. For example, a sign defined only with English word *table* could refer to an item of furniture, a chart, or a level (e.g. *water table*). Many users do not have the foundation to rely on contextual knowledge to bridge the information gaps, particularly early language deprived deaf children [8].

3. RELATED WORK

Seven U.S. online resources attempt to respond to the challenges faced by deaf students learning STEM (Table 1)[1]. While five sites attempt to resolve denotation confusion by associating signed terms with English definitions, this does not address connotation, provide ASL context, or constitute a monolingual ASL dictionary entry. Existing resources do not answer questions often asked by deaf students and educators relating to ASL connotation and correct usage of STEM signs in instructional contexts. DeafTEC offers signed definitions of STEM terms, but these do not consistently adhere to ASL grammatical rules; rather English syntax is imposed on borrowed ASL lexicon. Another proof of concept provides ASL-based search; however, the corpus of signs it uses have not been vetted by native signing Deaf STEM experts [3].

4. CONCLUSION

The ASL CLeaR provides complete, accurate, academically rigorous and standardized bilingual access to STEM material presented in instructional contexts by Deaf STEM experts, which will facilitate deeper understanding of academic content [4,5]. For K-12 deaf children, parents, and educators, the ASL CLeaR offers a rare opportunity to build understanding from the most basic STEM content to the most complex. The ASL CLeaR models consistent use of a single ASL term to represent a single concept such as *photosynthesis* in varying contexts. Deaf children deserve resources that build solid foundations in core STEM content and vocabulary, contribute to fundamental understandings of how the world works, foster logical, analogical and inference-making skills, open the door to post-secondary education, and lead to satisfying careers in STEM fields.

5. REFERENCES

[1] Bauman, D. 1997. Toward a poetics of vision, space, and the body: Sign language and literary theory. In Lennard Davis, ed. *The Disability Studies Reader*. New York, New York, USA: Routledge, 216–331.

[2] Beck, I., McKeown, M., & Kucan, L. (2013). *Bringing words to life: Robust vocabulary instruction*. Guilford Press.

[3] Bragg. D., Rector, K., & Ladner, R. A user-powered American Sign Language Dictionary in There's Just Something About Hands, CSCW. (2015). ACM, 1837-1848

[4] Cummins, J. 2006. The relationship between American Sign Language proficiency and English academic development: A review of the research. Workshop on Challenges, Opportunities, and Choices in Educating Minority Group Students.

[5] Hoffmeister, R.J., and Caldwell-Harris, C.L. 2014. Acquiring English as a second language via print: the task for deaf children. *Cognition* 132, 2, 229–42.

[6] Humphries, T., et al. 2014. Ensuring language acquisition for deaf children: What linguists can do. *Language*. 90, 2, 31–52.

[7] Mayberry, R. 1993. First-language acquisition after childhood differs from second-language acquisition: the case of American Sign Language. *J Speech Hear Res*. 36, 6, 1258–70.

[8] Novogrodsky, R., Fish, S., Hoffmeister, R. 2014. The Acquisition of Synonyms in American Sign Language (ASL): Toward a Further Understanding of the Components of ASL Vocabulary Knowledge. *Sign Lang Stud* 14, 2, 225–49.

[9] Pagliaro, C.M., Kritzer, K.L. 2013. The math gap: A description of the mathematics performance of preschool-aged deaf/hard-of-hearing children. *J. Deaf Stud. Deaf Educ.* 18 (2013), 139–160.

[10] Traxler, C.B. 2000. The Stanford Achievement Test, 9th Edition: National Norming and Performance Standards for Deaf and Hard-of-Hearing Students. *J. Deaf Stud. Deaf Educ.* 5, 4 (January 2000), 337–48.

[1] ASL STEM Forum: aslstem.cs.washington.edu,
RIT ASL: www.rit.edu/ntid/dictionary
DeafTEC: www.deaftec.org/stem-asl-video-dictionary
Deaf STEM: www.shodor.org/deafstemterms/
Signing App: signingapp.com
Signing Math & Science: signsci.terc.edu/,
Embe Outreach: www.needsoutreach.org/

EnTable: Rewriting Web Data Sets as Accessible Tables

Steven Gardiner
Carnegie Mellon University
sgardine@cs.cmu.edu

Anthony Tomasic
Carnegie Mellon University
tomasic@cs.cmu.edu

John Zimmerman
Carnegie Mellon University
johnz@cs.cmu.edu

Computer Science, Carnegie Mellon University; 5000 Forbes Ave; Pittsburgh PA 15213; USA

ABSTRACT

Today, many data-driven web pages present information in a way that is difficult for blind and low vision users to navigate and to understand. EnTable addresses this challenge. It re-writes confusing and complicated template-based data sets as accessible tables. EnTable allows blind and low vision users to submit requests for pages they wish to access. The system then employs sighted informants to markup the desired page with semantic information, allowing the page to be re-written using straightforward `<table/>` tags. Screen reader users who browse the web using the EnTable browser extension can report data sets that are confusing, and utilize data sets re-written with the `<table/>` tag based on their own requests or on the requests of other users.

Categories and Subject Descriptors

H.5.4 [**Information Interfaces and Presentation**]: Hypertext/Hypermedia—*transcoding, data sets*; K.4.2 [**Computers and Society**]: Social Issues—*assistive technologies*

General Terms

Web Accessibility

Keywords

web accessibility, data sets, transcoding, crowd-sourcing

1. INTRODUCTION

Most data-driven web pages communicate semantic information visually. Web sites employ complex CSS and javascript in order to provide aesthetically compelling pages that are easy to parse visually. In order to communicate these pages to blind users, screen readers face the daunting task of reverse-engineering the web designer's intention and rendering it as a stream of spoken text. In general, understanding web pages is beyond the capability of computers, and so screen readers address some important special cases where the intended semantics are roughly aligned with the structure. For example, screen readers provide sophisticated mechanisms for navigating and understanding web data that makes straightforward use of the `<table/>` tag. Many web pages that present data, however, do not use the simple `<table/>` layout [2].

ASSETS '15, October 26-28, 2015 Lisbon, Portugal
ACM 978-1-4503-3400-6/15/10
`http://dx.doi.org/10.1145/2700648.2811344`.

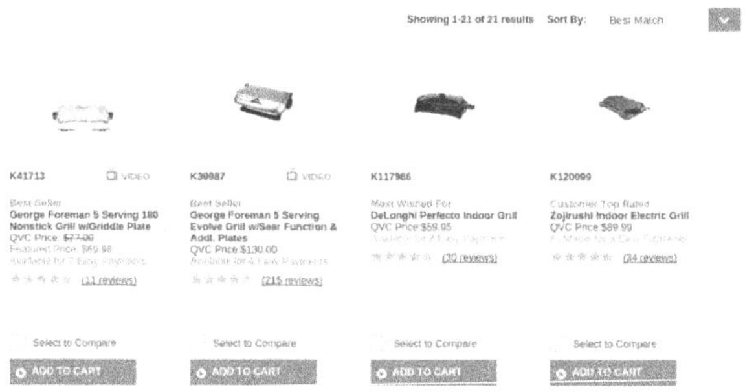

Figure 1: A web page presenting a data set as presented by the web author, using a grid layout

Figure 2: The same data set as in Figure 1 using a straightforward `<table/>` tag layout, which is easier to understand and navigate using a screen reader

Figure 1 shows the first row of data relating to a set of products, laid out as a grid of boxes. The grid layout makes it easy for sighted users to visually compare the products on the page. When accessed with a screen reader, however, the grid layout is disorienting and difficult to navigate. For example, there is no way to scan across the prices of the different products. Figure 2 presents the same information using a `<table/>` layout. The layout is a straightforward use of the `<table/>` tag in the sense that each row contains information about one product and each column contains exactly one attribute about that product. The table layout is substantially easier to access and understand using a screen reader. Users can move the cursor quickly and logically around the table. For example, they can scan down the column of prices to quickly compare several products or to screen out items outside their price range. Screen reader users can move within the logical structure of the table, skipping over the intervening content without devoting attention to it. EnTable effects this transformation by rewriting complex template layouts as simple tables. This transformation cannot be accomplished automatically by current technology [1], so EnTable employs the eyes of sighted users.

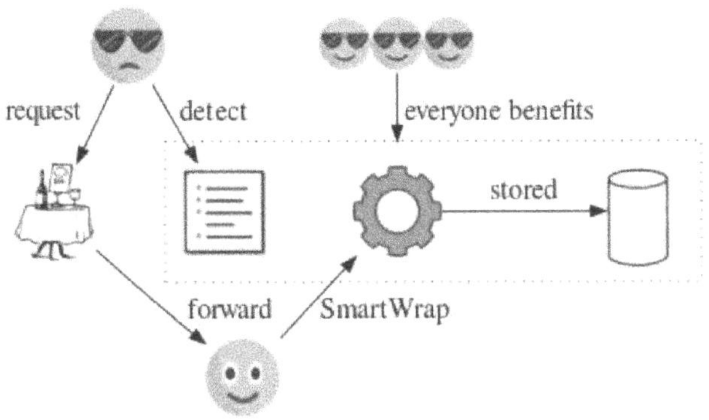

Figure 3: When an EnTable user detects a page with a confusing template, they submit a request to EnTable. EnTable forwards the request to a sighted crowdworker, who uses the SmartWrap interface (See Figure 4) to mark up the template as a table. The table description is stored in a repository, allowing all subsequent visitors to access this page as a table. (table drawing credit: Erik Blegvad)

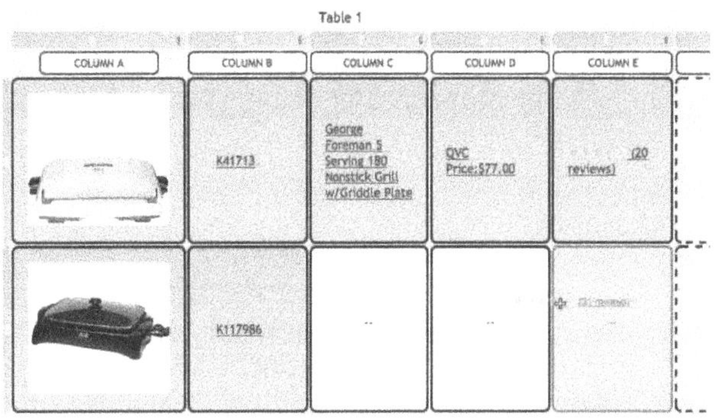

Figure 4: The SmartWrap interface. Sighted users drag-and-drop the information from the first two rows of the data set into a table. Based on the two example rows, SmartWrap extrapolates the pattern and presents the complete table for the user's approval. The extrapolated patterns are stored in the repository, so they can be used on different pages from the same website.

2. ARCHITECTURE

Sighted users are able to take advantage of the semantic information designers implicitly build in the visual layout of pages. Unfortunately, neither computers nor blind users can easily extract the meaning of these layouts. Since algorithmic extraction of data sets from HTML is beyond the current state of the art [1], we turn to the processing power of people. In common with crowdsourcing projects like Social Accessibility [3], EnTable employs a crowd of sighted users to re-write web pages to be more useful for screen reader users. Figure 3 depicts the workflow of the EnTable system.

Figure 3 illustrates the three main components of this socio-technical system. EnTable users make requests for specific pages to be added and view rewritten web pages using a proxied environment provided by a browser extension. EnTable stores page descriptions in a central server-side repository. Sighted crowdworkers contribute table descriptions using the SmartWrap browser extension. Our previous work [2] describes the SmartWrap extension and demonstrates that a large population of crowdworkers can effectively and inexpensively provide table descriptions of pages that use complex templates for layouts. One major challenge in the SmartWrap work is that table descriptions are small programs, equivalent to nested sets of XPath or CSS selectors, and most crowdworkers are not programmers. The SmartWrap interface, shown in Figure 4 works with nonprogrammers, by leveraging users' familiarity with spreadsheets. SmartWrap extrapolates the required selectors based on example elements provided by the user as the contents of the first two rows of a spreadsheet.

The reported version of the EnTable extension supplies two novel functions. First, it allows screen reader users to submit requests for specific pages. Sighted crowdworkers then use SmartWrap to generate table descriptions of these pages [2]. Second, upon subsequent visits to the requested page, EnTable users can access the page as a table.

3. CONCLUSIONS AND FUTURE WORK

EnTable provides an end-to-end system allowing screen reader users to report problematic data sets and view data sets that have been improved by sighted workers. For small demonstration purposes, the demonstrator can supply semantic information for all reported pages. In a full-scale deployment, however, it is obviously infeasible for a small team to handle all requests. Previous work suggests [2,3] that a substantial number of sighted users are willing to provide voluntary labor to benefit blind users. Whether sufficient numbers of screen reader problem reporters and sighted workers will participate to sustain the approach is an empirical question that the system allows us to study.

The implementation of the EnTable system also enables the study of several additional issues which we intend to address in future work. First is the question of how much benefit the rewriting of data sets in the more semantic form of a `<table/>` offers to screen reader users. But the difficult part of the EnTable system is the acquisition of semantic information from sighted workers, after which the rewriting with a `<table/>` tag is just a matter of formatting the information into an more usable relational form. The implementation of EnTable provides a platform for comparing various rewritten forms (or combinations of user selectable views of the data set), allowing screen reader users to provide feedback on which alternatives work best in practice.

4. ACKNOWLEDGEMENTS

This research and development has been funded by grants (H133E080019 and H133A130057) from the United States Department of Education through the National Institute on Disability and Rehabilitation Research and a grant (DTRT12-G-UTC11) from the US Department of Transportation. We also thank Jeff Bigham for his helpful comments.

5. REFERENCES

[1] Balakrishnan, S., Halevy, A.Y., Harb, B., et al. Applying WebTables in practice. *Conference on Innovative Data Systems Research*, (2015).

[2] Gardiner, S., Tomasic, A., and Zimmerman, J. SmartWrap: Seeing datasets with the crowd's eyes. *W4A*, (2015), 3:1–3:10.

[3] Sato, D., Kobayashi, M., Takagi, H., and Asakawa, C. Social Accessibility: The challenge of improving web accessibility through collaboration. *W4A*, (2010), 28:1–28:2.

A Game to Target the Spelling of German Children with Dyslexia

Maria Rauschenberger[1,2]
Silke Fuechsel[1]
[1]University of Applied Sciences Emden/Leer
[2]OFFIS, Institute for Information Technology
Oldenburg, Germany
rauschenberger.maria,sfuechsel
@student.fh-oow.de

Luz Rello
Clara Bayarri
Azuki Gòrriz
Cookie Cloud
Barcelona, Spain
luz,clara,azuki@cookie-cloud.com

ABSTRACT

Playing error-based exercises presented in a computer game was found to significantly improve the spelling skills of children with dyslexia in Spanish. Since there are no similar error-based exercises for German, we adapted the method to German and created 2,500 new word exercises. Since dyslexia manifestations are language dependent, the replication of the method required (i) collecting new texts written by German children with dyslexia; (ii) the annotation and the linguistic analysis of the errors; and (iii) the creation of exercises as well as their integration in the tool.

Keywords

Dyslexia; Serious Game; Spelling; Written Errors; German.

Categories and Subject Descriptors

K.4.2 [**Computers and Society**]: Social Issues—*Assistive technologies for persons with disabilities*; K.3 [**Computers in Education**]: Computer Uses in Education—*Computer-assisted instruction.*

1. INTRODUCTION

Motivation. In Germany, between 5 and 12% of students have dyslexia, a neurological learning disability which impairs a person's ability to read and write. Also in Germany, only 25% of the poor spellers achieve average spelling performance during primary school [7]. In a longitudinal study Esser *et al.* [1], showed that children who were diagnosed with dyslexia at the age of 8 achieved lower school performance and higher rates of unemployment than a control group (measured afterwards at the age of 25). Later, Schulte-Körne *et al.* [8] showed that it takes longer for a child with dyslexia to achieve school grades that are comparable to the others, even if they have an above-average socio-economic status and are given effective treatment.

ASSETS'15, October 26–28, 2015, Lisbon, Portugal.
ACM 978-1-4503-3400-6/15/10.
DOI: http://dx.doi.org/10.1145/2700648.2811345.

Background Research. To support the spelling of children with dyslexia in Spanish, Rello *et al.* [6] designed a method to create exercises based on the linguistic analysis of the errors made by children with dyslexia. It is called an error-based method because it uses written errors as a starting point since (1) dyslexic writing errors are related to the types of difficulties that they have [10]; and (2) readers with dyslexia cannot consciously see errors in words [3]. The exercises were integrated in an iOS game, *Dyseggxia (Piruletras)* [5], which was subsequently evaluated in a school. Over eight weeks, the authors carried out a within-subject experiment with 48 children from 6 to 11 years old. The children who played *DysEggxia* for four weeks in a row had significantly fewer writing errors in the tests than those playing *Word Search* –the control condition– for the same time [6].

Solution. In this demo we present the German extension of that tool and explain the adaptation of the method to create word exercises for children with dyslexia. It is worth noting that despite the universal neuro-cognitive basis of dyslexia, dyslexia manifestations are variable depending on the degree of consistency and regularity of the language orthography. German has a semi opaque language, that is, the relationships between letters and sounds are not as regular as in other transparent languages as Spanish [9]. In addition, it also has more complex syllabic structure [9]. Hence, the adaptation of the method from Spanish was not straightforward, raising a number of challenges. To the best of our knowledge, this is the first approach to create German error-based exercises for people with dyslexia.

2. RELATED WORK

Specifically for German we found *Lernserver*[1], a tool to diagnose and provide support exercises. The tool was evaluated in 2008 with the *Landesinstitut für Schule*, where 78.2% of the students ($N = 3{,}798$) improved their writing by using this tool [2]. *Klex 11*[2] is a tool to practice vocabulary in German adapted to a certain school degree. The exercises of *Klex* are not error-based since only the correct words are presented. We could not find literature on how *Klex* was developed and how the exercises have been created. Similarly, *CESAR schreiben 2.0*[3] is a strategy and educational game, which includes listening, spelling and vocabulary exercises.

[1]`http://www.lernserver.de/home.html`
[2]`http://www.legasthenie-software.de`
[3]`http://www.ces-verlag.de/deutsch/Schreiben2_0/schreiben2_produktinfo.php5`

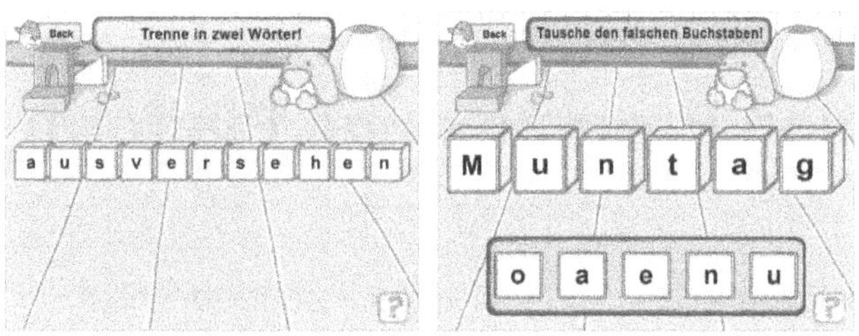

Figure 1: Screenshots for two types of exercises: *cut into words* **(left) and** *change a letter* **(right).**

To the best of our knowledge, there is no tool to support the spelling performance of children with dyslexia for German based on written errors that they make.

3. GERMAN ADAPTATIONS

Below, we explain the steps to replicate the method and describe the specificities added for German.

Texts Collection. The first step was the collection of dyslexic errors. We collected 47 texts (homework exercises, dictations and school essays) written by students with ages ranging from 8 to 17 years old. A total of 32 texts were written by children who have been diagnosed with dyslexia. The remaining 15 texts correspond to students with a high spelling error rate that were identified by their teachers. The students attended either primary school, comprehensive school (*Gesamtschule*), high school (*Gymnasium*) or a special school (*Förderschule*).

Error Annotation. We manually extracted the errors and annotated them with phonetic and visual features [4]. These features were specific to the German writing system and phonetics. For instance, German has letters and symbols, that do not exist in Spanish or English, *e.i.* ß, ä, ë, ö and ü. In addition to that, the handwriting systems broadly used in schools (*Lateinische Ausgangsschrift*) presents different letter forms, so the visual analysis of the letters was language specific.

Linguistic Analysis. Third, we analysed the errors linguistically. These analyses had to be specifically performed for German specific syllabic structure and semi opaque orthography, for instance, the group of letter <sch> are pronounced as only on phone [ʃ]. This resulted in different error categories as well as different linguistic criteria.

Creating the Exercises. We created exercises taking into account the previous linguistic analyses. As a result we had 8 types of exercise: (a) *add a letter*; (b) *remove a letter*, (c) *change a letter* (see Figure 1, right), (d) *choose the correct word ending*, (e) *cut into words* (see Figure 1, left), (f) *order the letters or syllables*, (g) *capital letter*, and (h) *wrong capital letter*. The last two exercises are specific to German where nouns are always written with capital letters, and missing capitalization is a frequent misspelling. Also, *cut into words* exercises included words and morphemes specific to German such as the *trennbare verben*, that is, verbs is that are preceded by prefixes.

Difficulty Levels: Thre are five difficulty levels: *Initial*, *Easy*, *Medium*, *Hard*, and *Expert*. Higher levels included less frequent words, longer words, and words with a more complex morphology. The criteria to define the levels were adapted to German. For instance, all levels presented longer words and morphology played a stronger role because German has a more complex morphology and longer words.

4. CONCLUSIONS AND FUTURE WORK

Using the adaptation of the method described above, we manually created 2,500 German exercises. The exercises were integrated into the iOS app *Dyseggxia (Piruletras)*.[4]

For future work we plan to carry out a longitudinal evaluation of this tool in a German school. Moreover, we will be able to compare how error-based games are more or less effective for certain types of languages.

Acknowledgements

We deeply thank Jörg Thomaschewski for making the connections between teams so this collaboration was possible. We also thank Miguel Ballesteros for his help creating the German dictionaries; Jörg Thomaschewski and Hendrik Witzel for helping with the phonetic error annotation; and Erin Brady for her helpful comments reviewing the text.

5. REFERENCES

[1] G. Esser, A. Wyschkon, and M. Schmidt. Was wird aus achtjährigen mit einer lese- und rechtschreibstörung? ergebnisse im alter von 25 jahren. *Zeitschrift für Klinische Psychologie und Psychotherapie*, 4:235–242, 2002.

[2] L. Flug. Projekt-evaluation bremen: Erprobungsphase des lernservers an bremischen schulen, 11.2007.

[3] L. Rello. *DysWebxia. A Text Accessibility Model for People with Dyslexia.* PhD thesis, Universitat Pompeu Fabra, 2014.

[4] L. Rello, R. Baeza-Yates, and J. Llisterri. DysList: An annotated resource of dyslexic errors. In *Proc. LREC'14*, pages 1289–1296, Reykjavik, Iceland, 2014.

[5] L. Rello, C. Bayarri, and A. Gorriz. What is wrong with this word? Dyseggxia: a game for children with dyslexia (demo). In *Proc. ASSETS '12*, pages 219–220, Boulder, USA, October 2012. ACM Press.

[6] L. Rello, C. Bayarri, Y. Otal, and P. Pielot. A computer-based method to improve the spelling of children with dyslexia using errors. In *Proc. ASSETS'14*, Rochester, USA, October 2014.

[7] H. Remschmidt and S. V. Aster. *Kinder- und Jugendpsychiatrie. Eine praktische Einführung: 177 Tabellen.* Thieme, Stuttgart [u.a.], 2005.

[8] G. Schulte-Körne, W. Deimel, and Jungermann, M. and Remschmidt, H. Nachuntersuchung einer stichprobe von lese-rechtschreibgestörten kindern im erwachsenenalter. *Zeitschrift für Kinder und Jugendpsychiatrie und Psychotherapie*, 31(4):267–276, 2003.

[9] P. H. K. Seymour, M. Aro, and J. M. Erskine. Foundation literacy acquisition in European orthographies. *British Journal of Psychology*, 94(2):143–174, 2003.

[10] C. Sterling, M. Farmer, B. Riddick, S. Morgan, and C. Matthews. Adult dyslexic writing. *Dyslexia*, 4(1):1–15, 1998.

[4]https://itunes.apple.com/us/app/dyseggxia/id534986729?l=ca&ls=1&mt=8

The Implementation of a Vocabulary and Grammar for an Open-Source Speech-Recognition Programming Platform

Jean K. Rodríguez-Cartagena
UPR Río Piedras
San Juan, PR
jeank02@hotmail.com

Andrea Claudio-Palacios
University High School
San Juan, PR
apclaudio1211@gmail.com

Natalia Pacheco-Tallaj
University High School
San Juan, PR
nataliamariapt@gmail.com

Valerie Santiago-González
UPR Río Piedras
San Juan, PR
vsg126@gmail.com

Patricia Ordonez-Franco, PhD
UPR Río Piedras
San Juan, PR
patricia.ordonez@upr.edu

ABSTRACT

Speech recognition software technology provides people with limited hand mobility or visual impairments the opportunity to work with computers through an alternative approach. However, when it comes to programming, voice recognition systems leave much to be desired. To tackle this problem, we have developed a generic vocabulary and grammar to help a user to program by voice in any C-based language. With the purpose of validating the aforementioned vocabulary and grammar, receiving feedback from the programming community and determining future features for enhancement, we administered a survey and distributed it among faculty members and advanced computer science and engineering students. Our objective is to create an assistive technology tool that will serve the community with limited hand mobility or visual impairments yet will be accepted and embraced as the spoken programming language and model of choice for implementation.

Categories and Subject Descriptors

H.5.2 [**Information Interfaces and Presentation**]: User Interfaces| *Input devices and strategies, Voice I/O*; K.4.2 [Computers and society]: Social Issues| assistive technologies for persons with disabilities

Keywords

Programming; voice recognition; Simon; open source

1. INTRODUCTION

Every programming language contains its own vocabulary and grammar to function. To write code, programmers need to follow guidelines, also known as syntax rules. Nonetheless, every programmer has a personal way of referring to code when saying it out loud. This variety creates ambiguity for speech-recognition software (SRS) as a result of its lack of structure. Since coding requires intensive typing and therefore the use of repetitive finger movements, many programmers suffer from carpal tunnel syndrome (a condition that causes numbness and tingling in the fingers and hands) or other repetitive motion disorders. With the purpose of creating clearness and an unambiguous vocabulary for an accurate dictation, we proposed the use of gerunds as keywords to differentiate voice commands. It was determined that gerunds provide certainty to the spoken programming platform because they are more phonetically distinguishable by speech-recognition software.

ASSETS'15, October 26–28, 2015, Lisbon, Portugal.
ACM 978-1-4503-3400-6/15/10.
DOI: http://dx.doi.org/10.1145/2700648.2811346

2. RELATED WORK

Voice-recognition technology is used by professionals for the purpose of improving personal efficiency levels; others use it for enhancing the lives of people with disabilities [2]. For the former, programmers have been developing methods to write code using voice commands instead of the keyboard typing. For example, in Pycon 2013, Tavis Rudd, a professional programmer, explained how he writes code by dictating instead of using the keyboard. He used Dragon Naturally Speaking and a Python speech extension, and stated that it was more efficient than with the traditional way of typing on the keyboard [5]. His video, "Using Python to Code by Voice" emphasized programming through a speech-driven platform is a "highly effective tool that could benefit all programmers" [5]. He implemented a grammar which used short sounds and mundane words as the input, but this grammar would represent struggle for people who are not programmers and need or want to learn to code initially by voice. Nevertheless, it precipitates the development of a vocabulary and grammar which is feasible for users to learn through a universal design.

With this objective, a Java program was created to develop a verbal system to use while programming, where Java developers should use Spoken Java to create programs. Spoken Java is a language system designed to speak Java naturally, based on Andrew Begel's Research Paper "An Assessment of a Speech-Based Programming Environment". As a result, it was concluded that the programmers had little trouble learning Spoken Java [4].

For these contributions to be available to the public and make programming universally accessible, we selected an open-source, voice-recognition software named Simon for this platform [6].

3. METHODOLOGY

After analyzing a Perl script that contained all the elements of the desired generic C-based programming language, the authors developed a vocabulary and grammar for a generic spoken programming language. This language was refined through the gathering of the feedback obtained from the programming community through a detailed survey that was developed. The survey's questions portrayed an array of commands on the programming control flow structures. (See Table 1)

The programming community consisted of random senior students and faculty members of the Computer Science and Computer Engineering Departments at the Polytechnic University of Puerto Rico and the University of Puerto Rico Río Piedras. Thirty-three (33) responses were received during the months of November and December of 2014.

Each question contained the purpose of the question, describing the **intended C++ action in black and bold**, the **proposed voice command in bold, Arial, and red**, the ***corresponding C++ code***, as a consequence of the voice command, ***in italics, bold, and black*** (this is the output produced by the voice-recognition software in an editor), and ***variables and literals presented in bold, italics, and green***. The survey contained ten (10) questions in all.

4. RESULTS

The final stage of the project consisted of performing a quantitative and qualitative analysis of the results obtained from the survey to determine the final vocabulary and grammar below.

Table 1: Selected elements of the generic open-source, spoken programming language of the Kavita Project [7]

Programming Structure	Voice Commands
First statement: defining a variable	defining integer variable *int ;* total *int total;*
Second statement: printing a string	printing literal *cout << " ";* hello world *cout << "hello world ";*
Third statement: printing a variable	printing variable *cout << ;* total *cout << total;*

The remaining programming structures not listed in Table 1 were 4) printing the result of an equation, 5) storing user input, 6) creating an expression using variables and modulus operator, 7) creating a relational expression, 8) creating an expression using logical operators, 9) creating a for loop structure, and 10) creating an if /else structure. Due to page limitations, more of examples could not be included in the abstract, but may be found at the project website [7].

5. FUTURE WORK

This work is the beginning of the creation of a generic spoken programming language for C-based programming languages. Currently, we have a working implementation of the language in Java. The next step is to evaluate the project with its intended audience, users with limited mobility in their hands. Afterwards we will begin to incorporate more C-based languages into the platform.

6. CONCLUSION

The final proposed vocabulary and grammar represents the first phase of a larger initiative, the Kavita Project [7], whose aim is to develop an open-source, generic, spoken programming language platform whose interface is so natural it will be attractive to all programmers. However, our primary intention is to make programming accessible to more people.

7. ACKNOWLEDGMENTS

The researchers would like to convey their gratitude to Dr. Blanca Tallaj for helping to distribute the survey in the Polytechnic University of Puerto Rico and to Xiomara Figueroa Fontánez, Rafael Esparra, Gustavo Gratacós, José Montero Felix, and Jessica Pagán for their role in the development of this project and their assistance in the process.

8. REFERENCES

[1] Pacheco-Tallaj, Natalia M., and Claudio-Palacios, Andrea P. "Development of a Vocabulary and Grammar for an Open-Source Speech-driven Programming Platform to Assist People with Limited Hand Mobility". Research report submitted to Keyla Soto, UHS Science Professor.

[2] Stodden, Robert A., and Kelly D. Roberts. "The Use Of Voice Recognition Software As A Compensatory Strategy For Postsecondary Education Students Receiving Services Under The Category Of Learning Disabled." Journal Of Vocational Rehabilitation 22.1 (2005): 49-64. Academic Search Complete. Web. 1 Mar. 2015.

[3] Begel, A., Graham, S.L. "An Assessment of a Speech-Based Programming Environment," Visual Languages and Human-Centric Computing, 2006. VL/HCC 2006, pp.116,120, 4-8 Sept. 2006.

[4] Rudd, T "Using Python to Code by Voice". Pycon US 2013. Retrieved April 25, 2015 from http://pyvideo.org/video/1735/using-python-to-code-by-voice

[5] Figueroa, X., Ordóñez, P. "Improving Programming Interfaces for People with Limited Mobility Using Voice Recognition", Assets 2014.

[6] Simon Listens. http://www.simon-listens.org/ Last accessed: 2015-08-24.

[7] The Kavita Project – 2014. http://www.thekavitaproject.org/. Last accessed: 2015-08-24.

Author Index

Abascal, Julio 413
Abdolrahmani, Ali 369
Acartürk, Cengiz 341
Aced López, Sebastián 421
Adams, Richard J. 393
Ahmetovic, Dragan 251
Alabastro, Nicolò 13
Albar, Lula 303
Ali, Abdullah 307, 359
Ali, Shareef S. 223
Alkhanifer, Abdulrhman A. 305
Alves, Rodrigo Leone 377
Anderson, Richard 259
Anjos, Marcelo 321
Armstrong, Mike 215, 347
Arrue, Myriam 413
Asakawa, Chieko 387
Ashok, Vikas 391
Ashoori, Maryam 401
Avila, Mauro 327
Azenkot, Shiri 239
Ballesteros, Miguel 39
Banes, David 371
Bayarri, Clara 445
Begel, Andrew 173
Behm, Gary W. 223
Benchiheub, Mohamed 381
Bernareggi, Cristian 13, 425
Berret, Bastien 381
Beust, Pierre 349
Bigham, Jeffrey P. 39, 307
Blanco-Gonzalo, Ramon 419
Bornschein, Jens 117
Borodin, Yevgen 391
Bradford, Glenn 333
Brady, Erin 387
Braffort, Annelies 381
Brajnik, Giorgio 319
Branco, Marsal A. 397
Brandao, Alessandra 357
Branham, Stacy M. 163
Brewster, Stephen 339, 433
Brito, Miguel 439
Britto Mattos, Andrea 343
Brück, Rainer 301
Buehler, Erin 281
Candeias, Sara 341
Carrington, Patrick ....
Chang, Kevin 193
Chang, Yao-Jen 313, 317
Chang, Yao-Sheng 313, 317
Chellappa, Rama 383
Cheng, Jinghui 291, 333
Choy, Clifford Sze-Tsan 411
Cibrian, Franceli 315
Claudio-Palacios, Andrea 447
Clingman, Ryan 393
Coheur, Luísa 345, 423
Comrie, Niara 281
Condado, Paulo A. 33
Consel, Charles 77
Corno, Fulvio 421
Correia, Walter 321
Coughlan, James M. 251, 405
Crabb, Michael 215, 347
Cullen, Breda 339
Cutrell, Edward 259
Dahman, Maria 333
De Russis, Luigi 421
Dell, Nicola 259
Demarin, Iva 399
Dey, Anind 427
Dias, Gaël 349
Dias, Miguel Sales 341
Dibia, Victor 401
Draffan, E. A. 371
Du, Ruofei 383
Dunlop, Mark D. 323
Dupuy, Lucile 77
Easley, William 281, 369
Ebling, Sarah 147
Eguchi Yairi, Ikuko 335
Erazo, Mario 309
Erickson, Thomas 401
Evans, Jonathan 339
Fabbro, Sara 319
Felzer, Torsten 303
Feng, Jinjuan Heidi 429
Fernandez-Saavedra, Belen 419
Fialho, Pedro 423
Fields, Margaret A. 393
Filho, Anderson 321
Findlater, Leah 383
Florentin, Fabiana 321
Frauenberger, Christopher 89
Freire, Raimundo C. S. 377
Freitas, João Dinis 341
Friedman, Batya 203
Froehlich, Jon E. 383
Fuechsel, Silke 445
Funk, Markus 185, 327
Fusco, Giovanni 97, 405
Gale, Elaine 139
Gardiner, Steven 443
Gaur, Yashesh 367
Gerino, Andrea 13, 425
Germano, Helena 399
Giudice, Nicholas A. 405
Gonçalves, Daniel 3
Goncu, Cagatay 311
González-García, María 415
Gorriz, Azuki 445
Gouveia, Tatiana 321
Guan, Jing 411
Guerreiro, João 3
Guerreiro, Tiago 23, 59, 273, 379
Gulliksen, Jan 69
Guo, Jin 429
Halabi, Nawar 371
Hamilton, Harley 331
Hanson, Vicki L. 273
Hariharan, Dhananjai 139
Hartikainen, Maria 407
Heidrich, Regina 397
Henner, Jon 441
Henze, Niels 327

Herrlich, Marc 389
Hey, Jorge 389
Hlavacs, Helmut 417
Hoffmeister, Robert 441
Hofmann, Alexander 417
Hofmann, Megan 353
Hörz, Thomas 337
Hsu, Chia-Lo 127
Hu, Michele 365
Huenerfauth, Matt 139, 147
Hughes, Chris J. 215
Hurst, Amy 193, 281
Idris, Amal 371
Imperatore, Gennaro 323
Iwasawa, Yusuke 335
Jacob, João 439
Jacobsen, Christine 389
Jamieson, Matthew 339
Jensen, Emely 397
Johansson, Stefan 69
Johnson, Kathleen 441
Jones, Michael D. 331
Jones, Rhianne 215, 347
Jordon, Darrell 337
Kacorri, Hernisa 147
Kadous, Amatullah 371
Kane, Shaun K. 163
Kang, Ya-Shu 313, 317
Kao, Chia Chun 317
Kelstone, Aaron W. 223
Kientz, Julie A. 203
Kobayashi, Iwao 325
Kölz, Manuel 337
Kopp, Stefan 375
Kuber, Ravi 303, 369
Kurtz, Peter 337
Kushalnagar, Raja S. 223
Ladner, Richard E. 203
Laiola Guimarães, Rodrigo 343
Lantz, Ann 69
Lawand, Dana 371
Lawson, Sonia 429
Leko, Ljubica 399
Lemarié, Julie 431
Lewis, Clayton 395, 437
Lima, Carlos M. G. S. 377
Liu, Hung-Huan 313, 317
Liu-Jimenez, Judith 419
Lobo, Fernando G. 33
Ludi, Stephanie 305
Lundh, Maud Veronica 329
Macedo, Patrícia 399, 409
Madeira, Rui Neves 399, 409
Magee, John 403
Maidenbaum, Shachar 355
Malaka, Rainer 389
Manduchi, Roberto 251
Marques, Diogo 59
Marriott, Kim 311
Martínez, Paloma 415
Martínez-Normand, Löic 419
Mascetti, Sergio 13, 251, 425
Mason, Lee 155
Matsuo, Yutaka 335
Maurel, Fabrice 349
Mayer, Sven 185
McDonald, Samantha 281
McGee-Lennon, Marilyn 339
Mei, Chao 155
Mendonça, Vânia 345
Mentis, Helena 193
Messing, David 429
Mielke, Matthias 301
Milne, Lauren 203
Mitkov, Ruslan 49
Mojahid, Mustapha 431
Montague, Kyle 23, 273, 379
Moore, Emily B. 395
Morash, Valerie S. 97
Moreno, Lourdes 415
Morris, Meredith Ringel 173
Mossmann, João B. 397
Nagamine, Koya 335
Nakamura, Satoshi 435
Nemoto, Nami 325
Neubig, Graham 435
Nicolau, Hugo 23, 273, 379
Nóbrega, Rui 439
Nunokawa, Hiroshi 325
Ogasawara, Naohiro 325
Oh, Uran 383
Ordonez-Franco, Patricia 447
Ortega, Deysi 315
Ovaska, Saila 407
Pacheco-Tallaj, Natalia 447
Papasalouros, Andreas 373
Park, Jacob 385
Patel, Kasmira 147
Pawluk, Dianne T. V. 385, 393
Penha, Marcelo 321
Penly, Brian 139
Pereira, Carla 409
Pérez, J. Eduardo 413
Petmecky, James 331
Picinali, Lorenzo 13, 425
Pighin, Chiara 319
Prescher, Denise 117
Putnam, Cynthia 291, 333
Puzis, Yury 391
Quarles, John 155
Ramakrishnan, I.V. 391
Rauschenberger, Maria 445
Rector, Kyle 203
Reis, Jeanne 441
Rello, Luz 39, 307, 445
Riemer, Derek 437
Rodrigues, André 23, 273, 351, 379
Rodríguez-Cartagena, Jean K. 447
Rose, Emma 333
Ross, David 383
Routoure, Jean-Marc 349
Roznovjak, Jiri 403
Ruan, Chengxiong 387
Runge, Nina 389
Rusch, Doris C. 291
Safi, Waseem 349
Sakti, Sakriani 435
Sanchez-Reillo, Raul 419
Sandnes, Frode Eika 329
Santiago-González, Valerie 447
Santos, Andre L. M. 321
Santos, António 439
Sardinha, Alberto 345
Sato, Daisuke 387

Sato, Kiwamu 325
Saulynas, Sidas 303
Sauzéon, Hélène 77
Schmidt, Albrecht 185
Schuh, Anderson 397
Schull, Jon 1
Shi, Lei 361
Shiver, Brent N. 231
Siebra, Clauirton 321
Siewiorek, Dan 427
Silva, Fabio Q. B. 321
Silva, Samuel 341
Škrobo, Maja 399
Smailagic, Asim 427
Smeddinck, Jan David 389
Smith, Ted 429
Solovey, Erin T. 441
Sorin, Laurent 431
Sousa, Luís 341
Soviak, Andrii 363, 391
Standard, Matthew 385
Stangl, Abigale 127
Stearns, Lee 383
Szpiro, Sarit 239
Takagi, Hironobu 387
Tanaka, Kou 435
Tang, Ziying 429
Taylor, Brandon 427
Teixeira, António 341
Tekin, Ender 405
Temnikova, Irina 49
Tentori, Monica 315
Toda, Tomoki 435
Tomasic, Anthony 443
Treviranus, Jutta 107
Trewin, Shari 59, 401
Tsolomitis, Antonis 373
Valencia, Xabier 413
Vashistha, Aditya 259
Vieira, Diogo 341
Wald, Mike 371
Wang, Cheng-Chieh 317
Watanabe, Kaito 325
Weber, Gerhard 117
Wiedermann, Ben 173
Willard, Mackenzie 139, 147
Wilson, Graham 433
Wolfe, Rosalee 231
Wolters, Jan 389
Yaghoubzadeh, Ramin 375
Yaneva, Victoria 49
Yeh, Tom 127
Zeinoun, Nadine 371
Zhao, Yuhang 239
Zimmerman, John 443
Zimmermann, Gottfried 309
Zou, Hong 107

www.ingramcontent.com/pod-product-compliance
Ingram Content Group UK Ltd.
Pitfield, Milton Keynes, MK11 3LW, UK
UKHW051414290926
15471UKWH00009B/1592

9 781450 341004